BICENTENNIAL
1807
WILEY
2007
BICENTENNIAL

THE WILEY BICENTENNIAL—KNOWLEDGE FOR GENERATIONS

*E*ach generation has its unique needs and aspirations. When Charles Wiley first opened his small printing shop in lower Manhattan in 1807, it was a generation of boundless potential searching for an identity. And we were there, helping to define a new American literary tradition. Over half a century later, in the midst of the Second Industrial Revolution, it was a generation focused on building the future. Once again, we were there, supplying the critical scientific, technical, and engineering knowledge that helped frame the world. Throughout the 20th Century, and into the new millennium, nations began to reach out beyond their own borders and a new international community was born. Wiley was there, expanding its operations around the world to enable a global exchange of ideas, opinions, and know-how.

For 200 years, Wiley has been an integral part of each generation's journey, enabling the flow of information and understanding necessary to meet their needs and fulfill their aspirations. Today, bold new technologies are changing the way we live and learn. Wiley will be there, providing you the must-have knowledge you need to imagine new worlds, new possibilities, and new opportunities.

Generations come and go, but you can always count on Wiley to provide you the knowledge you need, when and where you need it!

WILLIAM J. PESCE
PRESIDENT AND CHIEF EXECUTIVE OFFICER

PETER BOOTH WILEY
CHAIRMAN OF THE BOARD

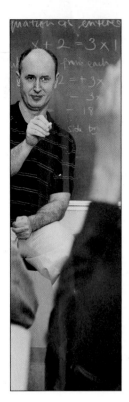

TO THE INSTRUCTOR

WileyPLUS is built around the activities you perform

Prepare & Present

Create outstanding class presentations using a wealth of resources, such as PowerPoint™ slides, image galleries, interactive simulations, and more. Plus you can easily upload any materials you have created into your course, and combine them with the resources Wiley provides you with.

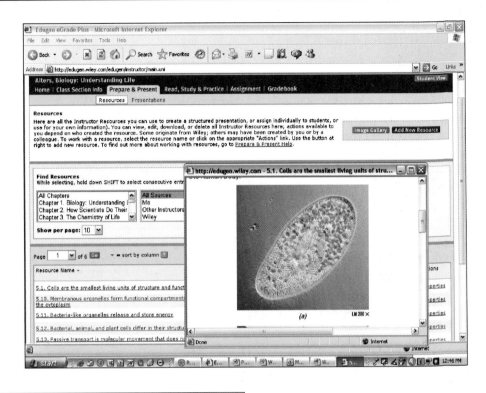

Create Assignments

Automate the assigning and grading of homework or quizzes by using the provided question banks, or by writing your own. Student results will be automatically graded and recorded in your gradebook. *WileyPLUS* also links homework problems to relevant sections of the online text, hints, or solutions—context-sensitive help where students need it most!

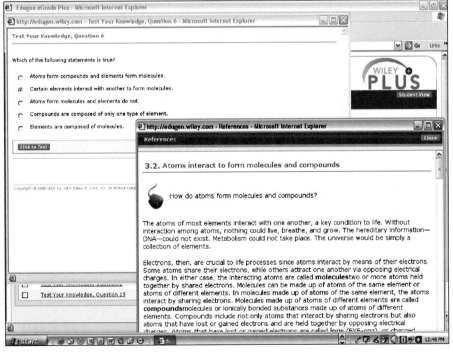

* Based on a spring 2005 survey of 972 student users of *WileyPLUS*

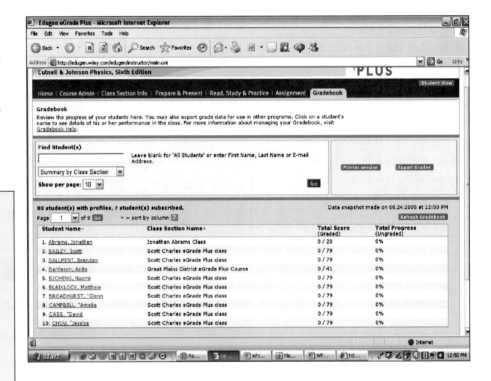

TO THE STUDENT

You have the potential to make a difference!

Will you be the first person to land on Mars? Will you invent a car that runs on water? But, first and foremost, will you get through this course?

WileyPLUS is a powerful online system packed with features to help you make the most of your potential, and get the best grade you can!

With Wiley**PLUS** you get:

A complete online version of your text and other study resources

Study more effectively and get instant feedback when you practice on your own. Resources like self-assessment quizzes, tutorials, and animations bring the subject matter to life, and help you master the material.

Problem-solving help, instant grading, and feedback on your homework and quizzes

You can keep all of your assigned work in one location, making it easy for you to stay on task. Plus, many homework problems contain direct links to the relevant portion of your text to help you deal with problem-solving obstacles at the moment they come up.

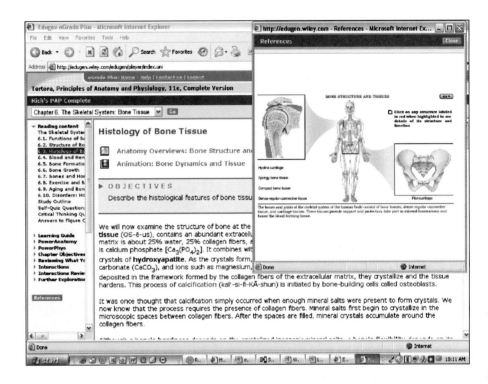

The ability to track your progress and grades throughout the term.

A personal gradebook allows you to monitor your results from past assignments at any time. You'll always know exactly where you stand.

If your instructor uses *WileyPLUS*, you will receive a URL for your class. If not, your instructor can get more information about *WileyPLUS* by visiting www.wiley.com/college/wileyplus

"It has been a great help, and I believe it has helped me to achieve a better grade."
Michael Morris, *Columbia Basin College*

69% of students surveyed said it helped them get a better grade.*

Operations Management
An Integrated Approach
Third Edition

R. Dan Reid

Nada R. Sanders

BICENTENNIAL
BICENTENNIAL
1807
WILEY
2007
BICENTENNIAL
BICENTENNIAL

John Wiley & Sons, Inc.

EXECUTIVE EDITOR	Beth Golub
ASSISTANT EDITOR	Jen Devine
DEVELOPMENT EDITOR	Johnna Barto
SENIOR PRODUCTION EDITOR	Patricia McFadden
MARKETING MANAGER	Jillian Rice
CREATIVE DIRECTOR	Harry Nolan
SENIOR DESIGNER	Kevin Murphy
SENIOR ILLUSTRATION EDITOR	Anna Melhorn
SENIOR PHOTO EDITOR	Hilary Newman
SENIOR EDITORIAL ASSISTANT	Maria Guarascio
SENIOR MEDIA EDITOR	Allison Morris
PRODUCTION MANAGEMENT SERVICES	Jeanine Furino/GGS Book Services
COVER PHOTO	© Ilene MacDonald/Alamy
INTERIOR AND COVER DESIGN	Michael Jung

This book was set in 10/12 Time Roman by GGS Book Services, and printed and bound by Quebecor/Versailles. The cover was printed by Phoenix Color.

This book is printed on acid free paper. ∞

To order books or for customer service, please call 1-800-CALL WILEY (225-5945).

ISBN 978-0-470-28351-6

Printed in the United States of America

10 9 8 7 6 5 4 3 2

Preface

Today, companies are competing in a very different environment than they were only a few years ago. Rapid economic changes such as global competition, e-business, the Internet, and advances in technology have required businesses to adapt their standard practices. Operations management is the critical function through which companies can succeed in this competitive landscape.

Operations management concepts are not confined to one department. Rather they are far-reaching, affecting every functional aspect of the organization. Whether studying accounting, finance, human resources, information technology, management, marketing, or purchasing, students need to understand the critical impact operations management has on any business.

We each have more than 20 years of teaching experience and understand the challenges inherent in teaching and taking the introductory OM course. The vast majority of students taking this course are not majoring in operations management. Rather, classes are typically composed of students from various business disciplines or students who are undecided about their major and have little knowledge of operations management. The challenge is not only to teach the foundation of the field, but also to help students understand the impact operations has on the business as a whole, and the close relationship or operations management with other business functions.

We were motivated to write this book to help students understand operations management and to make it easier for faculty to teach the introductory operations management course. We continue to have three major goals for this book.

GOALS OF THE BOOK

1. Provide a Solid Foundation of Operations Management

Our book provides a solid foundation of OM concepts and techniques, but also covers the latest on emerging topics such as e-business and supply chain management, enterprise resource planning (ERP), and information technology. We give equal time to strategic and tactical decisions and provide coverage of both service and manufacturing organizations. We look closely at some of the unique challenges faced by service operations.

2. Provide an Integrated Approach to Operations Management

While several excellent textbooks provide appropriate foundation coverage, we believe that few provide sufficient motivation for students. We are aware that a major teaching challenge in OM is that students aren't motivated to study OM because they don't understand its relevance to their majors. We think the course textbook can greatly support the professor in this area; therefore, a chief goal of this book is to integrate coverage of why and how OM is integral to all organizations. Interfunctional coordination and decision making have become the norm in today's business environment. Throughout each chapter we discuss information flow between business functions and the role of each function in the organization. On the opening page of each chapter we ask the reader "What's in OM for Me?" and the chapter ends with a section called "OM Across the Organization" to review the answers to that question.

The text also illustrates the linkages and integration between the various OM topics. Our end-of-chapter feature entitled "Within OM: How It All Fits Together" describes how the chapter topic is related to other OM decisions. It addresses the issue that OM topics are linked and interdependent, not independent of one another.

As supply chain management (SCM) has taken on an increasingly important role, we have added an end-of-chapter section titled "Supply Chain Link" which explains the relationships between the specific chapter topic covered and supply chain management.

3. Help Students to Understand the Concepts

This course remains challenging for students to take and professors to teach. Students often have no prior exposure to operations concepts and little real business experience. Students have a broad spectrum of quantitative sophistication and often find the math in the course extremely challenging. Therefore, a chief goal of the text and supplement package is to help students with these concepts. We begin each chapter with an example from everyday life, often a consumer or personal example, to help students intuitively understand what the chapter will be about. Then we explain each concept clearly and carefully, with *enough* depth for non-majors.

The new edition is focused on helping students by offering problem-solving hints and tips as part of the solution to most examples and solved problems throughout the entire text. Two unique supplements support student comprehension. A "Quantitative Survival Guide" available as an optional supplement packaged with the text provides "help with the math" for all chapters. WileyPLUS (available on line via a password packaged with all new books) provides plenty of homework practice, feedback for students, an e-book, and much more. In addition, algorithmic homework problems have been designed for each chapter in order to provide unlimited practice opportunity.

ORGANIZATION AND CONTENT OF THE BOOK

We have arranged the topics in the book in progressive order from strategic to tactical. Early in the book we cover operations topics that require a strategic perspective and a cultural change within the organization, such as supply chain management, total quality management, and just-in-time systems. Progressively we move to more tactical issues, such as work management, inventory management, and scheduling concerns. We recognize that most faculty will select the chapters relevant to their needs. To make it easier to students and faculty, each chapter can stand alone. Any specific knowledge needed for a chapter is summarized at the beginning of each chapter, with specific topic and page references for easy review.

Balanced Coverage of Quantitative and Qualitative Topics

We have tried to find a balance between the quantitative and qualitative treatment and coverage of OM topics. To meet students' needs, this text presents the application of OM concepts through the extensive use of practical and relevant business examples. We eliminated from the printed book coverage of topics less frequently covered at the introductory level. However, complete supplementary chapters on spreadsheet modeling, optimization, simulation, and waiting line models are available on the book's website (www.wiley.com/college/reid).

Integrated Technology Perspective

E-commerce and the Internet are transforming the business environment, and we integrate these concepts in every chapter. We discuss a range of topics from enterprise resource planning (ERP) and electronic data interchange (EDI) to quality issues of buying goods on-line.

Changes to this Edition

We have made a number of changes to this edition in order to make the text as current, user friendly, and relevant as possible. We have updated all the chapters in order to incorporate the latest available information, increase the emphasis on service operations, increase emphasis on e-business and information technology, update business examples, expand the number of problems and cases, and increase the number of problem-solving hints. As in the previous editions, we continue to emphasize interfunctional coordination and decision making, and have added a number of new features.

Before You Begin. In order to help students when solving quantitative problems we have added a feature called *Before You Begin*, placed immediately prior to the solution of most in-chapter example problems and end-of-chapter solved problems. Emphasizing our focus on strong pedagogy, this feature provides problem solving tips and hints that the student should consider before proceeding to solve the problem.

Supply Chain Link. To emphasize the increasingly important role of supply chain management, we have added a new end-of-chapter section titled *Supply Chain Link*. The purpose of this feature is to clearly explain the relationship between the specific chapter topic and supply chain management, highlighting our interfunctional focus.

Problem-Solving. While our goal is to provide balanced coverage of quantitative and qualitative topics, the new edition further emphasizes and integrates problem-solving to help students experience the course more successfully. We provide algorithmic homework problems for every chapter of the text (via WileyPlus) for unlimited practice opportunities, include problem-solving help in the book ('Before You Begin') and online via WileyPlus, and provide step-by-step solved problems in the book and online. We also provide 'help with math' as needed via WileyPlus. We believe that these changes to the new edition greatly enhance student learning.

FEATURES OF THE BOOK

We have developed our pedagogical features to implement and reinforce the goals discussed previously and address the many challenges in this course.

Pedagogy that Provides an Integrated Approach

To maintain a competitive position in the marketplace, a company must have a long-range plan. This plan needs to include the company's long-term goals, an understanding of the marketplace, and a way to differentiate the company from its competitors. All other decisions must support this long-range plan. Otherwise, each person in the company would pursue goals that he or she considered important, and the company would quickly fall apart.

The functioning of a football team on the field is similar to the functioning of a business and provides a good example of the importance of a plan or vision. Before the plays are made, the team prepares a game strategy. Each player on the team must perform a particular role to support this strategy. The strategy is a "game plan"

©AP/Wide World Photos

Chapter Opening Vignettes and Within OM: How It All Fits Together

To help students intuitively understand the topic, each chapter begins with a description of a personal problem that can be solved using the concepts discussed in the chapter. Our objective is to attract the attention of the student by starting with a personal example to which they can relate. We demonstrate that OM is not just about operating a plant or a business, but that it is relevant in everything that we do. An end-of-chapter section titled *Within OM: How It All Fits Together* describes how the chapter topic is related to other OM decisions. It emphasizes the point that OM decisions are not made independent of one another, but that they are linked together and are dependent on one another.

Links to Practice

LINKS TO PRACTICE

FedEx Corporation
www.federalexpress.com

©AP/Wide World Photos.

FedEx is an example of a company that competes based on time. The company's claim is to "absolutely, positively" deliver packages on time. To support this strategy, the operation function had to be designed to promote speed. Bar code technology is used to speed up processing and handling, and the company uses its own fleet of airplanes. FedEx relies on a very flexible part-time workforce, such as college students who are willing to work a few hours at night. FedEx can call on this part-time workforce at a moment's notice, providing the company with a great deal of flexibility. This allows FedEx to cover workforce requirements during peak periods without having to schedule full-time workers.

Other OM texts have many boxes and sidebars, which make it difficult for students to understand what they need to know. Furthermore, the many examples frequently interrupt the flow of the text and make a chapter difficult to read and assimilate. We recognize the importance of including "real world" examples, but believe they should be integrated into the stream of the text instead of interrupting the text. Therefore, we have developed embedded boxes titled *Links to Practice* which provide brief examples from actual companies in every chapter. Embedded by both content and design into the general text discussion, each provides a concise and relevant example without interrupting the flow of the text.

Current textbooks typically do not use business examples to which students can relate. The typical examples provided are from large corporations such as General Motors, IBM, or Xerox. Primarily using these types of examples creates the impression for students that this is a field that is either beyond their reach or irrelevant to their needs. We have found that students understand the concepts better when these concepts are also presented in a context that is smaller in scale. The examples chosen range from large multinational organizations to small local businesses.

OM Across the Organization and Cross Functional Icons

Unique to this book is an end-of-chapter summary titled *OM Across the Organization* that highlights the relationship between OM and key business functions, such as accounting, finance, human resources, information technology, management, marketing, and purchasing. This section is designed to help students

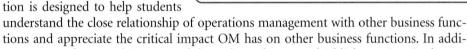

OM ACROSS THE ORGANIZATION

Now that we know the role of the operations management function and the decisions that operations managers make, let's look at the relationship between operations and other business functions. As mentioned previously, most businesses are supported by three main functions: operations, marketing, and finance. Although these functions involve different activities, they must interact to achieve the goals of the organization. They must also follow the strategic direction developed at the top level of the organization. Figure 1-8 shows the flow of information from the top to each business function, as well as the flow between functions.

Many of the decisions made by operations managers are dependent on information from the other functions. At the same time, other functions cannot be carried out properly without information from operations. Figure 1-9 shows these relationships.

MKT **Marketing** is not fully capable of meeting customer needs if marketing managers do not understand what operations can produce, what due dates it can and cannot meet, and what types of customization operations can deliver. The marketing department can

understand the close relationship of operations management with other business functions and appreciate the critical impact OM has on other business functions. In addition, a cross-functional icon is used throughout the text to highlight sections in the text where the relationships between OM and other key business functions are discussed.

Cases

Each chapter ends with three cases that reinforce the issues and topics discussed in the chapter. The first two cases are within the text, while the third is an online case. The cases can provide the basis for group discussion or can be assigned as individual exercises for students. Many cases conclude with a list of questions for students to answer.

In addition, each chapter offers a unique interactive learning exercise titled *Internet Challenge* where students are provided with a short case and given specific Internet assignments.

Interactive Online

This Web-based case features an Internet site for a simulated hospital which has hired the Kaizen Consulting Company to help solve operations problems. Students are "hired" as interns by Kaizen and given assignments that require them to use information provided at the book Web site to develop solutions for the hospital. These exercises offer students hands-on ex-

INTERACTIVE CASE **Virtual Company** www.wiley.com/college/reid

On-line Case: Operations Strategy at Valley Memorial Hospital

Assignment: *Getting Acquainted with Valley Memorial Hospital* With a few more weeks before you join Kaizen and start working for its client Valley Memorial Hospital, it is essential for you to get some broad insights into the company and its operations. Bob Reilly has given you a few preliminary research projects to work on in order to familiarize yourself with VMH and the healthcare industry. This assignment will enable you to enhance your knowledge of the material in Chapter 2 while continuing to prepare you for a successful internship.

To access the Web site:

- Go to **www.wiley.com/college/reid**
- Click **Student Companion Site**
- Click **Virtual Company**
- Click **Kaizen Consulting, Inc.**
- Click **Consulting Assignments**
- Click **Getting Acquainted with Valley Memorial Hospital**

perience in the areas of supply chain management, statistical quality control, forecasting, just-in-time, aggregate planning, scheduling, and project management, and help tie all the topics of the book together.

Pedagogy to Help Students Master the Course

Learning Objectives At the beginning of each chapter, students are provided with a short statement of what they need to either know or review from previous chapters, referring students to specific topic and page information. This enables students to review previous material necessary to understand the topic being covered.

LEARNING OBJECTIVES

After completing this chapter you should be able to:

1 Define operations management.
2 Explain the role of operations management in business.
3 Describe decisions that operations managers make.
4 Describe the differences between service and manufacturing operations.
5 Identify major historical developments in operations management.

Before You Go On

By now you should have a clear understanding of how an operations strategy is developed and its role in helping the organization decide which competitive priorities to focus on. There are four categories of competitive priorities: *cost, quality, time,* and *flexibility*. A company must make trade-offs in deciding which priorities to focus on. The operations strategy and the competitive priorities dictate the design and plan for the operations function, which includes the structure and infrastructure of the operation. This is a dynamic process, and as the environment changes, the organization must be prepared to change accordingly. Operations strategy plays a key role in an organization's ability to compete. In the next section we discuss a way to measure a company's competitive capability.

Before You Go On Sections strategically placed within every chapter summarize key material the student should know before continuing. Often the material in chapters can be overwhelming. We felt that breaking up the chapter with a brief summary of key material is highly beneficial in aiding learning and comprehension.

Key Terms and Definitions Key terms and concepts are highlighted in boldface when they are first explained in the text, are defined in the margin next to their discussion in the text, and are listed at the end of the chapter with page references.

Before You Begin Most example problems within the chapters, and end-of-chapter solved problems, have an added feature called *Before You Begin.* The feature provides the student with problem solving tips and hints they need to consider before solving the problem. The purpose is to help students with their problem solving ability.

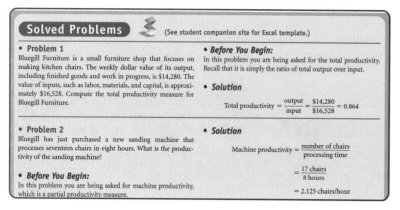

Solved Problems (See student companion site for Excel template.)

• **Problem 1**

Bluegill Furniture is a small furniture shop that focuses on making kitchen chairs. The weekly dollar value of its output, including finished goods and work in progress, is $14,280. The value of inputs, such as labor, materials, and capital, is approximately $16,528. Compute the total productivity measure for Bluegill Furniture.

• *Before You Begin:*

In this problem you are being asked for the total productivity. Recall that it is simply the ratio of total output over input.

• **Solution**

$$\text{Total productivity} = \frac{\text{output}}{\text{input}} = \frac{\$14,280}{\$16,528} = 0.864$$

• **Problem 2**

Bluegill has just purchased a new sanding machine that processes seventeen chairs in eight hours. What is the productivity of the sanding machine?

• *Before You Begin:*

In this problem you are being asked for machine productivity, which is a partial productivity measure.

• **Solution**

$$\text{Machine productivity} = \frac{\text{number of chairs}}{\text{processing time}}$$

$$= \frac{17 \text{ chairs}}{8 \text{ hours}}$$

$$= 2.125 \text{ chairs/hour}$$

Solved Problems Numerous solved problems are provided, complete with step-by-step explanations to ensure students understand the process and why the problem is solved in a particular way. Where appropriate we provide a series of steps for problem solving and offer *Problem Solving Tips.*

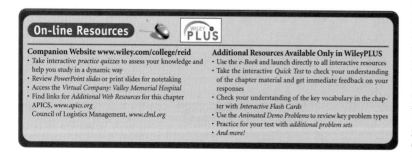

On-line Resources WILEY PLUS

Companion Website www.wiley.com/college/reid	Additional Resources Available Only in WileyPLUS
· Take interactive *practice quizzes* to assess your knowledge and help you study in a dynamic way	· Use the *e-Book* and launch directly to all interactive resources
· Review *PowerPoint slides* or print slides for notetaking	· Take the interactive *Quick Test* to check your understanding of the chapter material and get immediate feedback on your responses
· Access the *Virtual Company: Valley Memorial Hospital*	
· Find links for *Additional Web Resources* for this chapter APICS, www.apics.org	· Check your understanding of the key vocabulary in the chapter with *Interactive Flash Cards*
Council of Logistics Management, www.clml.org	· Use the *Animated Demo Problems* to review key problem types
	· Practice for your test with *additional problem sets*
	· And more!

On-line Resources Using the Text and the Web Site We have created a number of interactive learning activities for students, which will help them learn the material in a dynamic and interesting way. At the end of each chapter, there is a list of activities available on the Web site. Students can work on these activities on their own, and instructors have the flexibility to assign material for individual or group study. The activities include the Online Case, interactive simulations, interactive spreadsheets, company tours, *Internet Challenge,* and additional Web resources.

INSTRUCTIONAL SUPPORT PACKAGE

Our supporting material has been designed to make learning OM easier for students and teaching OM easier for faculty.

Instructor Resources

1. The Instructor's Resource Website A comprehensive resource guide designed to assist professors in preparing lectures and assignments, including:

- **Instructor's Manual:** Includes a suggested course outline, teaching tips and strategies, war stories, answers to all end-of-chapter material, brief description of the additional resources referenced in the Interactive Learning box, additional in-class exercises, and tips on integrating the theory of constraints.
- **Solutions Manual:** A complete set of detailed solutions is provided for all problems.
- **Video Guide:** A guide to help instructors use the NBR videos includes a brief description of each video clip, additional discussion questions, and suggested answers to all of the discussion questions.
- **Test Bank:** A comprehensive Test Bank comprised of approximately 1700 questions that consist of multiple choice, true-false, essay questions, and open-ended problems for each chapter. The Test Bank is also available in a computerized version that allows instructors to customize their exams.
- **Lecture Slides in Microsoft® PowerPoint:** PowerPoint Slides are available for use in class. Full-color slides highlight key figures from the text as well as many additional lecture outlines, concepts, and diagrams. Together, these provide a versatile opportunity to add high-quality visual support to lectures.

2. WileyPLUS In addition to the rich content provided on the Instructor's Resource page, we offer a premium version of the Web site that allows instructors to create their own teaching and learning environment. This premium Web site powered by Wiley's Edugen technology platform provides many additional tools and resources for both students and instructors.

- Course administration tools help instructors manage their courses and additional sections of that course.
- A "Prepare and Present" tool contains all of the Wiley-provided resources, such as PowerPoint slides and Instructor's Manual content, making your preparation time more efficient. You may easily adapt, customize, and add to Wiley content to meet the needs of your course.
- An "Assignment" area is one of the most powerful features of Wiley's premium Web sites. This area of the Web site allows professors to assign homework and quizzes comprised of new content and end-of-chapter exercises. An Instructor's Gradebook will keep track of student progress and allow instructor's to analyze individual and overall class results to determine student progress and level of understanding.
- Newly-created clicker questions written by Morgan Henrie of the University of Alaska, for use in the P-9 classroom.

3. Operations Management Video Series The comprehensive Video package offers video selections that tie directly to the theme of operations management and bring to life many of the examples used in the text.

4. Business Extra Select (www.wiley.com/college/bxs)

Business Extra Select enables you to add copyright-cleared articles, cases, and readings from such leading business resources as INSEAD, Ivey, Harvard Business School Cases, *Fortune, The Economist, The Wall Street Journal*, and more. You can create your own custom CoursePack, combining these resources with content from Wiley's business textbooks, your own content such as lecture notes, and any other third-party content. Or you can use a ready-made CoursePack for Reid and Sanders' *Operations Management, Second Edition*.

Student Resources

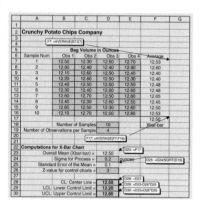

1. Student Resource Website. The online student resources contain the following resources:

- **Supplemental Chapters:** The supplement chapters include Supplement A: Spreadsheet Modeling: An Introduction; Supplement B: Introduction to Optimization; Supplement C: Introduction to Simulation; Supplement D: Waiting Line Models.

- **Excel Spreadsheets:** Templates are provided so that students can model and solve problems presented in the textbook. A spreadsheet icon appears next to those examples and problems in the textbook that have an accompanying Excel template available on the student website. Step-by-step directions are provided. Directions prompt students as they work through each spreadsheet. Expected outcomes and questions are also given.

2. Quantitative Survival Guide. (0-471-67877-5) This provides chapter-by-chapter review of the math necessary to understand and solve the problems in each chapter and includes extra practice problems.

For Students and Instructors: Operations Management Web Site www.wiley.com/college/reid

An extensive Web site has been developed in support of *Operations Management*. The site is available at www.wiley.com/college/reid, and offers a range of information for instructors and students. The Web site includes the following resources:

- **Virtual Company Case:** (described above)
- **Company Tours:** Web links to the plant tours of various companies are provided, along with a brief description of the tour and discussion questions for students to consider after viewing the tour.
- **Web Links:** Direct links to related Web sites are provided.

WileyPLUS This premium version of our student Web site provides a wealth of support materials that will help students develop their conceptual understanding of class materials. On the premium site, students will find the following resources:

- In the "Study and Practice" section, the full multimedia version of the book is available to students. This multimedia text will allow students to review content as they are completing assignments.

- An "Assignment" area helps students stay "on task" by providing homework assignments in one location. Many of these homework problems have a link to the relevant sections of the multimedia book, providing context-sensitive help that allows them to conquer problem-solving obstacles.
- A Personal Gradebook for each student that will allow students to view their results from the past assignment at any time.

ACKNOWLEDGMENTS

The development of this third edition of *Operations Management* benefited greatly from the comments and suggestions of colleagues who teach operations management courses. We would like to acknowledge the contributions made by the following individuals:

Dennis Agboh
Morgan State University

Karen Eboch
Bowling Green State University

Greg Graman
Michigan Tech University

GG Hegde
University of Pittsburgh

Seung-Lae Kim
Drexel University

John Kros
East Carolina University

Anita Lee-Post
University of Kentucky

David Little
High Point University

Robert Vokurka
Texas A&M University

John Wang
Montclair State University

Reviewers of the second edition include:

Ajay Aggarwal, *Millsaps College*; Nezih Altay, *University of Richmond*; Suad Alway, *Chicago State University*; Robert Amundsen, *New York Institute of Technology*; Gordon Bagot, *California State University, Los Angeles*; Cliff Barber, *California Polytechnic State University, San Luis Obispo*; Hooshang Beheshti, *Radford University*; Prashanth Bharadwaj, *Indiana University of Pennsylvania*; Joe Biggs, *California Polytechnic State University*; Debra Bishop, *Drake University*; Vincent Calluzzo, *Iona College*; James Campbell, *University of Missouri–St. Louis*; Kevin Caskey, *SUNY New Paltz*; Sohail Chaudhry, *Villanova University*; Chin-Sheng Chen, *Florida International University*; Kathy Dhanda, *University of Portland*; Barb Downey, *University of Missouri-Columbia*; Joe Felan, *University of Arkansas at Little Rock*; Wade Ferguson, *Western Kentucky University*; Teresa Friel, *Butler University*; Daniel Heiser, *DePaul University*; Lewis Hofmann, *The College of New Jersey*; Lisa Houts, *California State University, Fullerton*; Tony Inman, *Louisiana Tech University*; Richard Insinga, *SUNY Oneonta*; Tim Ireland, *Oklahoma State University*; Mehdi Kaighobadi, *Florida Atlantic University*; Hale Kaynak, *The University of Texas-Pan American*; William Coty Keller, *St. Josephs College*; Robert Kenmore, *Keller Graduate School of Management*; Jennifer Kohn, *Montclair State University*; Dennis Krumwiede, *Idaho State University*; Kevin Lewis, *University of Wyoming*; Ardeshir Lohrasbi, *University of Illinois at Springfield*; Chris McDermott, *Rensselaer Polytechnic Institute*; John Miller, *Mercer University*; Ajay Mishra, *SUNY Binghamton*; Ken Murphy, *Florida International University*; Abraham Nahm, *University of Wisconsin-Eau Claire*; Len Nass, *New Jersey City University*; Joao Neves, *The College of New Jersey*; Susan Norman, *Northern Arizona University*; Muhammad Obeidat, *Southern Polytechnic State University*; Barbara Osyk, *The University of Akron*; Taeho Park, *San Jose State University*; Eddy Patuwo, *Kent State University*; Carl Poch, *Northern Illinois University*; Leonard Presby, *William Paterson University*; Will Price, *University of the Pacific*; Randy Rosenberger, *Juniata College*; George Schneller, *Baruch College-CUNY*; Kaushik Sengupta, *Hofstra University*; LW Schell, *Nicholls States University*; William Sherrard,

San Diego State University; Samia Siha, *Kennesaw State University*; Susan Slotnick, *Cleveland State University*; Ramesh Soni, *Indiana University of Pennsylvania*; Ted Stafford, *University of Alabama in Huntsville*; Peter Sutanto, *Prairie View A&M University*; Fataneh Taghaboni-Dutta, *University of Michigan-Flint*; Nabil Tamimi, *University of Scranton*; John Visich, *Bryant College*; Tom Wilder, *California State University, Chico*; Peter Zhang, *Georgia State University*; Faye X. Zhu, *Rowan University*.

The first edition was reviewed by:

David Alexander, *Angelo State University*; Stephen L. Allen, *Truman State University*; Jerry Allison, *University of Central Oklahoma*; Suad Alwan, *Chicago State University*; Tony Arreola-Risa, *Texas A&M University*; Gordon F. Bagot, *California State University–Los Angeles*; Brent Bandy, *University of Wisconsin—Oshkosh*; Joseph R. Biggs, *California Polytechnic State University at San Luis Obispo*; Jean-Marie Bourjolly, *Concordia University*; Ken Boyer, *DePaul University*; Karen L. Brown, *Southwest Missouri State University*; Linda D. Brown, *Middle Tennessee State University*; James F. Campbell, *University of Missouri–St. Louis*; Cem Canel, *University of North Carolina at Wilmington*; Chin-Sheng Chen, *Florida International University*; Louis Chin, *Bentley College*; Sidhartha R. Das, *George Mason University*; Greg Dobson, *University of Rochester*; Ceasar Douglas, *Grand Valley State University*; Shad Dowlatshahi, *University of Missouri–Kansas City*; L. Paul Dreyfus, *Athens State University*; Lisa Ferguson, *Hofstra University*; Mark Gershon, *Temple University*; William Giauque, *Brigham Young University*; Greg Graman, *Wright State University*; Jatinder N.D. Gupta, *Ball State University*; Peter Haug, *Western Washington University*; Daniel Heiser, *DePaul University*; Ted Helmer, *F. Theodore Helmer and Associates, Inc.*; Lew Hofmann, *The College of New Jersey*; Lisa Houts, *California State University–Fresno*; Tim C. Ireland, *Oklahoma State University*; Peter T. Ittig, *University of Massachusetts–Boston*; Jayanth Jayaram, *University of Oregon*; Robert E. Johnson, *University of Connecticut*; Mehdi Kaighobadi, *Florida Atlantic University*; Yunus Kathawala, *Eastern Illinois University*; Basheer Khumawala, *University of Houston*; Thomas A. Kratzer, *Malone College*; Ashok Kumar, *Grand Valley State University*; Cynthia Lawless, *Baylor University*; Raymond P. Lutz, *University of Texas at Dallas*; Satish Mehra, *University of Memphis*; Brad C. Meyer, *Drake University*; Abdel-Aziz M. Mohamed, *California State University–Northridge*; Charles L. Munson, *Washington State University*; Kenneth E. Murphy, *Florida International University*; Jay Nathan, *St. Johns University*; Harvey N. Nye, *University of Central Oklahoma*; Susan E. Pariseau, *Merrimack College*; Carl J. Poch, *Northern Illinois University*; Claudia H. Pragman, *Minnesota State University*; Willard Price, *University of the Pacific*; Feraidoon Raafat, *San Diego State University*; William D. Raffield, *University of St. Thomas*; Ranga Ramasesh, *Texas Christian University*; Paul H. Randolph, *Texas Tech University*; Robert M. Saltzman, *San Francisco State University*; George O. Schneller IV, *Baruch College—City University of New York*; A. Kimbrough Sherman, *Loyola College in Maryland*; William R. Sherrard, *San Diego State University*; Chwen Sheu, *Kansas State University*; Sue Perrott Siferd, *Arizona State University*; Samia M. Siha, *Kennesaw State University*; Natalie Simpson, *State University of New York–Buffalo*; Barbara Smith; *Niagara College*; Victor E. Sower, *Sam Houston State University*; Linda L. Stanley, *Our Lady of the Lake University*; Donna H. Stewart, *University of Wisconsin–Stout*; Manouchehr Tabatabaei, *University of Tampa*; Nabil Tamimi, *University of Scranton*; Larry Taube, *University of North Carolina–Greensboro*; Giri K. Tayi, *State University of New York at Albany*; Charles J. Teplitz, *University of San Diego*; Timothy L. Urban, *The University of Tulsa*; Michael L. Vineyard, *Memphis State University*; John Visich, *University of Houston*; Robert Vokurka, *Texas A&M University*; George Walker, *Sam Houston State University*; John Wang, *Montclair State University*; Theresa Wells, *University of Wisconsin–Eau Claire*; T.J. Wharton, *Oakland University*; Barbara Withers, *University of San Diego*; Steven A. Yourstone, *University of New Mexico*.

SPECIAL THANKS

We would also like to personally thank and acknowledge the work of our supplements authors who worked diligently to create a variety of support materials for both instructors and students: Roger Grinde, University of New Hampshire, wrote the supplements on spreadsheet modeling, optimization, simulation, and waiting line models. Peter Royce, University of New Hampshire, prepared the Solutions Manual; Kevin Caskey, SUNY New Paltz, prepared the Instructor's Manual and Video Guide; George Brower authored the Test Bank, Web Quizzes, Pre/Post Lecture Quizzes, and PowerPoints. The Virtual Company Consulting Case is based on cases developed by Ted Helmer, Theodore Helmer and Associates, Inc., and Jon Ozmun, Northern Arizona University.

We would also like to express our appreciation to Mark Sullivan, AIA, NCARB, of Mark Sullivan Architects and Susan O'Hara, RN, MPH, of O'Hara HealthCare Consultants who generously contributed a simulation showing the before and after designs of an ambulatory surgery unit. A working example of the Extend simulation they used to optimize the design of the renovated facility is available on the student CD. For more information on their work, please visit www.marksullivanarchitects.com or www.oharahealthcare.com.

We would like to offer special acknowledgment to the publishing team at Wiley for their creativity, talent, and hard work. Their great personalities and team spirit have made working on the book a pleasure. Special thanks go to Beth Lang Golub, Acquisitions Editor, Johnna Barto, Development Editor, Jillian Rice, Marketing Manager, and Trish McFadden, Production Editor, for all their effort. We could not have done it without you.

Other Wiley staff who contributed to the text and media are: Jen Devine, Associate Editor; Allison Morris, New Media Editor; Kevin Murphy, Senior Designer; Anna Melhorn, Illustration Editor; Hilary Newman, Photo Editor; Maria Guarascio, Editorial Assistant; and Elyse Ryder, Photo Researcher. We would also like to thank David Krahl of Imagine That, Inc. for developing the Extend simulations.

About the Authors

R. Dan Reid is Associate Professor of Operations Management at the Whittemore School of Business and Economics at the University of New Hampshire. He holds a Ph.D. in Operations Management from The Ohio State University, an M.B.A. from Angelo State University, and a B.A. in Business Management from the University of Maryland. During the past twenty years, he has taught at The Ohio State University, Ohio University, Bowling Green State University, Otterbein College, and the University of New Hampshire.

Dr. Reid's research publications have appeared in numerous journals such as the *Production and Inventory Management Journal, Mid-American Journal of Business, Cornell Hotel and Restaurant Administration Quarterly, Hospitality Research and Education Journal, Target,* and the *OM Review.* His research interests include manufacturing planning and control systems, quality in services, purchasing, and supply chain management. He has worked for, or consulted with, organizations in the telecommunications, consumer electronics, defense, hospitality, and capital equipment industries. Dr. Reid has served as Program Chair and President of the Northeast Region of the Decision Sciences Institute (NEDSI) and as Associate Program Chair and Proceedings Editor of the First International DSI Conference, and held numerous positions within DSI. He has been the Program Chair and Chair of the Operations Management Division of the Academy of Management. Dr. Reid has also served as President of the Granite State Chapter of the American Production and Inventory Control Society. He has been a board member of the Operations Management Association and the Manchester Manufacturing Management Center. Dr. Reid is a past Editor of the *OM Review.*

Dr. Reid has designed and taught courses for undergraduates, graduates, and executives on topics such as resource management, manufacturing management, introduction to operations management, purchasing management, and manufacturing planning and control systems. In 2002 Dr. Reid received a University of New Hampshire Excellence in Teaching Award.

Nada R. Sanders is Professor of Operations Management at the Raj Soin College of Business at Wright State University. She holds a Ph.D. in Operations Management from The Ohio State University, an M.B.A. from The Ohio State University, and a B.S. degree in Mechanical Engineering from Franklin University. She has taught for more than twenty years at a variety of academic institutions including The Ohio State University, Capital University, and Wright State University, in addition to lecturing to various industry groups. She has designed and taught classes for undergraduates, graduates, and executives on topics such as operations management, operations strategy, forecasting, and supply chain management. She has received a number of teaching awards including the College of Business Outstanding Teacher Award.

Dr. Sanders has extensive research experience and has published in numerous journals such as *Decisions Sciences, Journal of Operations Management, Sloan Management Review, Omega, Interfaces, Journal of Behavioral Decision Making, Journal of Applied Business Research,* and *Production & Inventory Management Journal.* She has authored chapters in books and encyclopedias such as the *Forecasting Principles Handbook* (Kluwer Academic Publishers), *Encyclopedia of Production and Manufacturing Management* (Kluwer Academic Publishers) and the *Encyclopedia of Electrical and Electronics Engineering* (John Wiley & Sons). Dr. Sanders has served as Vice President of Decision Sciences Institute (DSI), President of the Midwest Decision Sciences Institute, and has held numerous other positions within the Institute. In addition to DSI, Dr. Sanders is active in the Production Operations Management Society (POMS), APICS, INFORMS, Council of Supply Chain Management Professions (CSCMP), and the International Institute of Forecasters (IIF). She has served on review boards and/or as a reviewer for numerous journals including *Decision Sciences, Journal of Business Logistics, Production Operations Management, International Journal of Production Research, Omega,* and others. In addition, Dr. Sanders has worked and/or consulted for companies in the telecommunications, pharmaceutical, steel, automotive, warehousing, retail, and publishing industries, and is frequently called upon to serve as an expert witness.

Contents

CHAPTER 5 TOTAL QUALITY MANAGEMENT 136

CHAPTER 6 STATISTICAL QUALITY CONTROL 171

CHAPTER 7 JUST-IN-TIME AND LEAN SYSTEMS 219

CHAPTER 11 WORK SYSTEM DESIGN 379

CHAPTER 12 INDEPENDENT DEMAND INVENTORY MANAGEMENT 416

CHAPTER 13
AGGREGATE PLANNING 468

CHAPTER 14
RESOURCE PLANNING 521

CHAPTER 15
SCHEDULING 557

CHAPTER 16
PROJECT MANAGEMENT 593

Available on-line only, at www.wiley.com/college/reid:

SUPPLEMENT D WAITING LINE MODELS D1

CHAPTER 1

Introduction to Operations Management

LEARNING OBJECTIVES

After completing this chapter you should be able to:

1. Define operations management.
2. Explain the role of operations management in business.
3. Describe decisions that operations managers make.
4. Describe the differences between service and manufacturing operations.
5. Identify major historical developments in operations management.
6. Identify current trends in operations management.
7. Describe the flow of information between operations management and other business functions.

CHAPTER OUTLINE

WHAT'S IN OM FOR ME?

 ACC

 FIN

 MKT

 OM

 HRM

 MIS

Big Cheese Photo/SUPERSTOCK

Many of you reading this book may think that you don't know what operations management (OM) is or that it is not something you are interested in. However, after reading this chapter you will realize that you already know quite a bit about operations management. You may even be working in an operations management capacity and have used certain operations management techniques. You will also realize that operations management is probably the most critical business function today. If you want to be on the frontier of business competition, you want to be in operations management.

Today companies are competing in a very different environment than they were only a few years ago. To survive, they must focus on quality, time-based competition, efficiency, international perspectives, and customer relationships. Global competition, e-business, the Internet, and advances in technology require flexibility and responsiveness. This new focus has placed operations management in the business limelight, because it is the function through which companies can achieve this type of competitiveness.

Consider some of today's most successful companies, such as Wal-Mart, Southwest Airlines, General Electric, Starbucks, Toyota, FedEx, and Procter & Gamble. These companies have achieved world-class status in large part due to a strong focus on operations management. In this book you will learn specific tools and techniques of operations management that have helped these, and other companies, achieve their success.

The purpose of this book is to help prepare you to be successful in this new business environment. Operations management will give you an understanding of how to help your organization gain a competitive advantage in the marketplace. Regardless of whether your area of expertise is marketing, finance, MIS, or operations, the techniques and concepts in this book will help you in your business career. The material will teach you how your company can offer goods and services cheaper, better, and faster. You will also learn that operations management concepts are far-reaching, affecting every aspect of the organization and even everyday life.

WHAT IS OPERATIONS MANAGEMENT?

Every business is managed through three major functions: finance, marketing, and operations management. Figure 1-1 illustrates this by showing that the vice presidents of each of these functions report directly to the president or CEO of the company. Other business functions—such as accounting, purchasing, human resources, and engineering—support these three major functions. Finance is the function responsible

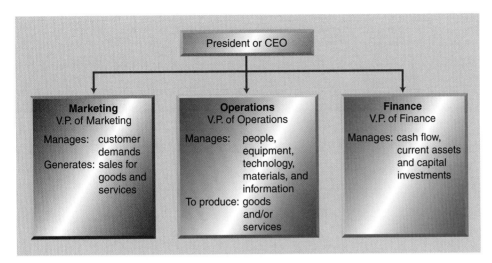

FIGURE 1-1

Organizational chart showing the three major business functions

for managing cash flow, current assets, and capital investments. Marketing is responsible for sales, generating customer demand, and understanding customer wants and needs. Most of us have some idea of what finance and marketing are about, but what does operations management do?

Operations management (**OM**) is the business function that plans, organizes, coordinates, and controls the resources needed to produce a company's goods and services. Operations management is a *management* function. It involves managing people, equipment, technology, information, and many other resources. Operations management is the central core function of every company. This is true whether the company is large or small, provides a physical good or a service, is for-profit or not-for-profit. Every company has an operations management function. Actually, all the other organizational functions are there primarily to support the operations function. Without operations, there would be no goods or services to sell. Consider a retailer such as The Gap, which sells casual apparel. The marketing function provides promotions for the merchandise, and the finance function provides the needed capital. It is the operations function, however, that plans and coordinates all the resources needed to design, produce, and deliver the merchandise to the various retail locations. Without operations, there would be no goods or services to sell to customers.

The **role of operations management** is to transform a company's inputs into the finished goods or services. Inputs include human resources (such as workers and managers), facilities and processes (such as buildings and equipment), as well as materials, technology, and information. Outputs are the goods and services a company produces. Figure 1-2 shows this *transformation process*. At a factory the transformation is the physical change of raw materials into products, such as transforming leather and rubber into sneakers, denim into jeans, or plastic into toys. At an airline it is the efficient movement of passengers and their luggage from one location to another. At a hospital it is organizing resources such as doctors, medical procedures, and medications to transform sick people into healthy ones.

Operations management is responsible for orchestrating all the resources needed to produce the final product. This includes designing the product; deciding what resources are needed; arranging schedules, equipment, and facilities; managing inventory; controlling quality; designing the jobs to make the product; and designing work methods. Basically, operations management is responsible for all aspects of the process of transforming inputs into outputs. Customer feedback and performance

▶ **Operations management**
The business function responsible for planning, coordinating, and controlling the resources needed to produce a company's goods and services.

▶ **Role of operations management**
To transform organizational inputs into outputs

FIGURE 1-2

The transformation
process

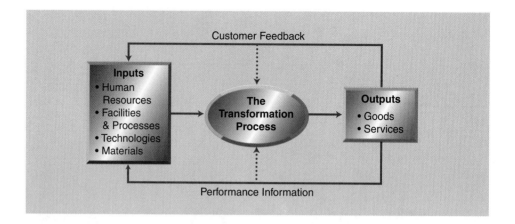

information are used to continually adjust the inputs, the transformation process, and characteristics of the outputs. As shown in Figure 1-2, this transformation process is dynamic in order to adapt to changes in the environment.

Proper management of the operations function has led to success for many companies. For example, in 1994 Dell Computer Corporation was a second-rate computer maker that managed its operations similarly to others in the industry. Then Dell implemented a new business model that completely changed the role of its operations function. Dell developed new and innovative ways of managing the operations function that have become one of today's best practices. These changes enabled Dell to provide rapid product delivery of customized products to customers at a lower cost. Today Dell customized computers can be en route to the customer within 36 hours, at a price 10–15 percent lower than industry standard. Dell's model is one many have tried to emulate and is the key to its being an industry leader.

Just as proper management of operations can lead to company success, improper management of operations can lead to failure. This is illustrated by Kozmo.com, a Web-based home delivery company founded in 1997. Kozmo's mission was to deliver products to customers—everything from the latest video to ice cream—in less than an hour. Kozmo was technology enabled and rapidly became a huge success. However, the initial success gave rise to overly fast expansion. The company found it difficult to manage the operations needed in order to deliver the promises made on its Web site. The consequences were too much inventory, poor deliveries, and losses in profits. The company rapidly tried to change its operations, but it was too late. It had to cease operations in April 2001.

LINKS TO PRACTICE

The E-tailers
www.Amazon.com
www.Barnesandnoble.
com

Jennifer Bladow/
Getty Images, Inc.

The Web-based age has created a highly competitive world of on-line shopping that poses special challenges for operations management. The Web can be used for on-line purchasing of everything from CDs, books, and groceries to prescription medications and automobiles. The Internet has given consumers flexibility; it has also created one of the biggest challenges for companies: delivering exactly what the customer ordered at the time promised. As we saw with the example of Kozmo.com, making promises on a Web site is one thing; delivering on those promises is yet another. Ensuring that orders are delivered from "mouse to house" is the job of operations and is much more complicated than it might seem. In the 1990s many dot-com companies discovered just how difficult this is. They were not able to generate a profit and went out of business. To ensure meeting promises, companies must forecast what customers want and maintain adequate inventories of goods, manage distribution centers and warehouses, operate fleets of trucks, and schedule deliveries while keeping costs low and customers satisfied. Many companies like Amazon.com manage almost all aspects of their operation. Other companies hire outside firms for certain functions, such as outsourcing the management of inventories and deliveries to UPS. Competition among e-tailers has become intense as customers demand increasingly shorter delivery times and highly customized products. Same-day service has become common in metropolitan areas. For example, Barnesandnoble.com provides same-day delivery in Manhattan, Los Angeles, and San Francisco. Understanding and managing the operations function of an on-line business has become essential in order to remain competitive.

For operations management to be successful, it must add value during the transformation process. We use the term **value added** to describe the net increase between the final value of a product and the value of all the inputs. The greater the value added, the more productive a business is. An obvious way to add value is to reduce the cost of activities in the transformation process. Activities that do not add value are considered a waste; these include certain jobs, equipment, and processes. In addition to value added, operations must be efficient. **Efficiency** means being able to perform activities well, and at the lowest possible cost. An important role of operations is to analyze all activities, eliminate those that do not add value, and restructure processes and jobs to achieve greater efficiency. Because today's business environment is more competitive than ever, the role of operations management has become the focal point of efforts to increase competitiveness by improving value added and efficiency.

▶ **Value added**
The net increase created during the transformation of inputs into final outputs.

▶ **Efficiency**
Performing activities at the lowest possible cost.

DIFFERENCES BETWEEN MANUFACTURING AND SERVICE ORGANIZATIONS

Organizations can be divided into two broad categories: **manufacturing organizations** and **service organizations**, each posing unique challenges for the operations function. There are two primary distinctions between these categories. First, manufacturing organizations produce physical, tangible goods that can be stored in inventory before they are needed. By contrast, service organizations produce intangible products that cannot be produced ahead of time. Second, in manufacturing organizations most customers have no direct contact with the operation. Customer contact occurs through distributors and retailers. For example, a customer buying a car at a car dealership never comes into contact with the automobile factory. However, in service organizations the customers are typically present during the creation of the service. Hospitals, colleges, theaters, and barber shops are examples of service organizations in which the customer is present during the creation of the service.

The differences between manufacturing and service organizations are not as clearcut as they might appear, and there is much overlap between them. Most manufacturers provide services as part of their business, and many service firms manufacture physical goods that they deliver to their customers or consume during service delivery. For example, a manufacturer of furniture may also provide shipment of goods and assembly of furniture. A barber shop may sell its own line of hair care products.

▶ **Manufacturing organizations**
Organizations that primarily produce a tangible product and typically have low customer contact.

▶ **Service organizations**
Organizations that primarily produce an intangible product, such as ideas, assistance, or information, and typically have high customer contact.

FIGURE 1-3

Characteristics of
manufacturing and
service organizations

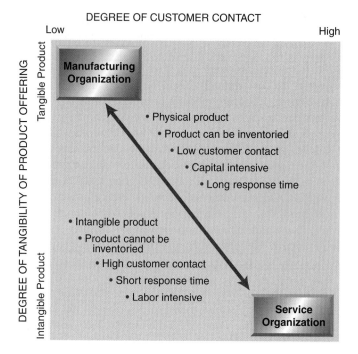

You might not know that General Motors' greatest return on capital does not come
from selling cars, but rather from postsales parts and service. Figure 1-3 shows the
differences between manufacturing and services, focusing on the dimensions of
product tangibility and the degree of customer contact. It shows the extremes of pure
manufacturing and pure service, as well as the overlap between them.

Even in pure service companies some segments of the operation may have low customer contact while others have high customer contact. The former can be thought of
as "back room" or "behind the scenes" segments. Think of a fast-food operation such
as Wendy's, for which customer service and customer contact are important parts of
the business. However, the kitchen segment of Wendy's operation has no direct customer contact and can be managed like a manufacturing operation. Similarly, a hospital is a high-contact service operation, but the patient is not present in certain
segments, such as the lab where specimen analysis is done.

In addition to pure manufacturing and pure service, there are companies that have
some characteristics of each type of organization. It is difficult to tell whether these
companies are actually manufacturing or service organizations. Think of a post office,
an automated warehouse, or a mail-order catalog business. They have low customer
contact and are capital intensive, yet they provide a service. We call these companies
quasi-manufacturing organizations.

Lee Snider/
The Image Works

The U.S. Postal Service is an example of a quasi-
manufacturing type of company. It provides a service: speedy, reliable delivery of letters, documents,
and packages. Its output is intangible and cannot be
stored in inventory. Yet most operations management decisions made at the Postal Service are similar to those that occur in manufacturing. Customer
contact is low, and at any one time there is a large

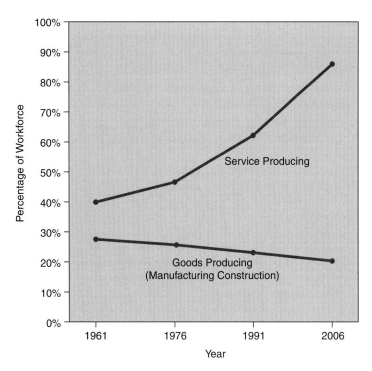

FIGURE 1-4

U.S. employment by economic sector

Source: *U.S. Department of Commerce*

amount of inventory. The Postal Service is capital intensive, having its own facilities and fleet of trucks and relying on scanners to sort packages and track customer orders. Scheduling enough workers at peak processing times is a major concern, as is planning delivery schedules. Note that although the output of the U.S. Postal Service is a service, inputs include labor, technology, and equipment. The responsibility of OM is to manage the conversion of these inputs into the desired outputs. Proper management of the OM function is critical to the success of the U.S. Postal Service.

It is important to understand how to manage both service and manufacturing operations. However, managing service operations is of especially high importance. The reason is that the service sector constitutes a dominant segment of our economy. Since the 1960s, the percentage of jobs in the service-producing industries of the U.S. economy has increased from less than 50 to 80 percent of total nonfarm jobs. The remaining 20 percent are in the manufacturing and goods-producing industries. Figure 1-4 illustrates this large growth of the service sector.

OPERATIONS MANAGEMENT DECISIONS

In this section we look at some of the specific decisions that operations managers have to make. The best way to do this is to think about decisions we would need to make if we started our own company—say, a company called Gourmet Wafers that produces praline–pecan cookies from an old family recipe. Think about the decisions that would have to be made to go from the initial idea to actual production of the product: that is operations management. Table 1-1 breaks these down into the generic decisions that would be appropriate for almost any good or service, the specific decisions required for our example, and the formal terms for these decisions that are used in operations management.

TABLE 1-1

Operations Management Decisions for Gourmet Wafers

General Decisions To Be Made	Decisions Specific for Cookie Production	Operations Management Term
What are the unique features of the business that will make it competitive?	The business offers freshly baked cookies "homemade" style, in a fast-food format.	Operations strategy
What are the unique features of the product?	The unique feature of the cookies is that they are loaded with extra-large and crunchy pecans and are fresh and moist.	Product design
What are the unique features of the process that give the product its unique characteristics?	A special convection oven is used to make the cookies in order to keep them fresh and moist. The dough is allowed to rise longer than usual to make the cookies extra light.	Process selection
What sources of supply should we use to ensure regular and timely receipt of the exact materials we need? How do we manage these sources of supply?	The key ingredients, pecans and syrup, will be purchased from only one supplier located in South Carolina because it offers the best products. A relationship is worked out in which the supplier sends the ingredients on the exact schedule that they are needed.	Supply chain management
How will managers ensure the quality of the product, measure quality, and identify quality problems?	A quality check is made at each stage of cookie production. The dough is checked for texture; the pecans are checked for size and freshness; the syrup is checked for consistency.	Quality management
What is the expected demand for the product?	Expected sales for each day of the week have been determined; for example, it is expected that more cookies will be sold during the weekday and most during the lunch hour. Expected cookie sales for each month and for the year have also been determined.	Forecasting
Where will the facility be located?	After looking at locations of customers and location costs, it is decided that the facility will be located in a shopping mall.	Location analysis
How large should the facility be?	The business needs to be able to produce 200 cookies per hour, or up to 2000 cookies per day.	Capacity planning
How should the facility be laid out? Where should the kitchen and ovens be located? Should there be seating for customers?	Decisions are made about where the kitchen will be located and how the working area will be arranged for maximum efficiency. The business is competing on the basis of *speed* and *quality*; therefore, the facility should be arranged to promote these features. There will be a small seating area for customers and a large counter and display case for buying.	Facility layout
What jobs will be needed in the facility, who should do what task, and how will their performance be measured?	Two people will be needed in the kitchen during busy periods and one during slow periods. Their job duties are determined. One person will be needed for order taking at all times.	Job design and work measurement
How will the inventory of raw materials be monitored? When will orders be placed and how much will be kept in stock?	A different policy is developed for common ingredients, such as flour and sugar. These ingredients will be ordered every two weeks for a two-week supply. A special purchasing arrangement is worked out with the supplier of specialty ingredients.	Inventory management
Who will work on what schedule?	Two people will work the counter in split shifts. One kitchen employee will work a full shift, with a second employee working part-time.	Scheduling

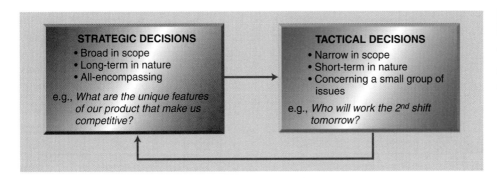

FIGURE 1-5

The relationship between strategic and tactical decisions

Note in the Gourmet Wafers example that the first decisions made were very broad in scope (e.g., the unique features of our product). We needed to do this before we could focus on more specific decisions (e.g., worker schedules). Although our example is simple, this decision-making process is followed by every company, including IBM, General Motors, Land's End, and your local floral shop. Also note in our example that before we can think about specific day-to-day decisions, we need to make decisions for the whole company that are long-term in nature. Long-term decisions that set the direction for the entire organization are called **strategic decisions**. They are broad in scope and set the tone for other, more specific decisions. They address questions such as: What are the unique features of our product? What market do we plan to compete in? What do we believe will be the demand for our product?

Short-term decisions that focus on specific departments and tasks are called **tactical decisions**. Tactical decisions focus on more specific day-to-day issues, such as the quantities and timing of specific resources. Strategic decisions are made first and determine the direction of tactical decisions, which are made more frequently and routinely. Therefore, we have to start with strategic decisions and then move on to tactical decisions. This relationship is shown in Figure 1-5. Tactical decisions must be aligned with strategic decisions, because they are the key to the company's effectiveness in the long run. Tactical decisions provide feedback to strategic decisions, which can be modified accordingly.

You can see in the example of Gourmet Wafers how important OM decisions are. They are critical to all types of companies, large and small. In large companies these decisions are more complex because of the size and scope of the organization. Large companies typically produce a greater variety of products, have multiple location sites, and often use domestic and international suppliers. Managing OM decisions and coordinating efforts can be a complicated task, and the OM function is critical to the company's success.

▶ **Strategic decisions**
Decisions that set the direction for the entire company; they are broad in scope and long-term in nature.

▶ **Tactical decisions**
Decisions that are specific and short-term in nature and are bound by strategic decisions.

We can illustrate this point by looking at operations management decisions made by Texas Instruments (TI) in order to position itself for global collaboration with customers, distributors, and suppliers. TI realized its business was growing exponentially, with more than 120,000 monthly orders received and processed electronically. The coordination effort encompassed 56 factories, including subcontractors, and the management of over 45,000 products. To succeed, the company needed to develop a system to generate better forecasts, coordinate manufacturing of products, manage orders, and track deliveries. Managing and coordinating global operations management functions was considered paramount to the company's success.

LINKS TO PRACTICE

Texas Instruments Incorporated
www.ti.com

TI adopted a comprehensive software package called enterprise resource planning (ERP) that integrates information throughout the organization, manages forecasts, and coordinates factory operations. Designing and implementing the ERP system at TI required an understanding of all the strategic and tactical operations decisions; otherwise, it would not be effective. The system has proven to be a success and a major achievement, enabling TI to consistently manage factory operations across the globe.

▶ PLAN OF THIS BOOK

The purpose here is to provide concepts and techniques that give you the ability to efficiently plan, order, and control the resources needed to produce a company's goods and services. The topics progress from strategic to tactical, similar to the order of decisions used in the Gourmet Wafers example. Figure 1-6 shows the plan of the book. We begin with broad, overarching issues such as product design and process selection. Also early on we cover operations topics that require a strategic perspective and a cultural change within the organization, such as supply chain management, total quality management, and just-in-time systems. We progress to more tactical issues, such as work measurement, inventory management, and scheduling concerns.

We have designed the chapters to provide relevant operations management concepts and techniques that are important to business professionals regardless of their field of study. Throughout the chapters we show how the tools and concepts discussed relate to other functions in the organization and that operations management concepts are far-reaching, affecting every aspect of the organization.

Before You Go On

You should understand that operations management (OM) is the business function responsible for planning, coordinating, and controlling the resources needed to produce a company's goods and services. OM is directly responsible for managing the transformation of a company's inputs (e.g., materials, technology, and information) into finished products and services. OM requires a wide range of strategic and tactical decisions. Strategic decisions are long-range and very broad in scope (e.g., unique features of the company's product and process). They determine the direction of tactical decisions, which are more short-term and narrow in scope (e.g., policy for ordering raw materials). All organizations can be separated into manufacturing and service operations, which differ based on product tangibility and degree of customer contact. Service and manufacturing organizations have very different operational requirements.

FIGURE 1-6

Plan of the book

Type of Decision	Operations Management Topic	Chapter
Strategic		
↑	Operations Strategy	Ch. 2
	Product Design and Process Selection	Ch. 3
	Supply Chain Management	Ch. 4
	Total Quality Management	Ch. 5 and 6
	Just-in-Time and Lean Systems	Ch. 7
	Forecasting	Ch. 8
	Capacity Planning and Location Analysis	Ch. 9
	Facility Layout	Ch. 10
	Work System Design	Ch. 11
↓	Inventory and Resource Planning	Ch. 12, 13, and 14
Tactical	Scheduling Issues	Ch. 15 and 16

HISTORICAL DEVELOPMENT

Why OM?

Business did not always recognize the importance of operations management. In fact, following World War II the marketing and finance functions were predominant in American corporations. The United States had just emerged from the war as the undisputed global manufacturing leader due in large part to efficient operations. At the same time, Japan and Europe were in ruins, their businesses and factories destroyed. U.S. companies had these markets to themselves, and so the post-World War II period of the 1950s and 1960s represented the golden era for U.S. business. The primary opportunities were in the areas of marketing, to develop the large potential markets for new products, and in finance, to support the growth. Since there were no significant competitors, the operations function became of secondary importance, because companies could sell what they produced. Even the distinguished economist John Kenneth Galbraith observed, "The production problem has been solved."

Then in the 1970s and 1980s, things changed. American companies experienced large declines in productivity growth, and international competition began to be a challenge in many markets. In some markets such as the auto industry, American corporations were being pushed out. It appeared that U.S. firms had become lax due to the lack of competition in the 1950s and 1960s. They had forgotten about improving their methods and processes. In the meantime, foreign firms were rebuilding their facilities and designing new production methods. By the time foreign firms had recovered, many U.S. firms found themselves unable to compete. To regain their competitiveness, companies turned to operations management, a function they had overlooked and almost forgotten about.

The new focus on operations and competitiveness has been responsible for the recovery of many corporations, and U.S. businesses experienced a resurgence in the 1980s and 1990s. Operations became the core function of organizational competitiveness. Although U.S. firms have rebounded, they are fully aware of continued global competition. Companies have learned that to achieve long-run success they must place much importance on their operations.

Historical Milestones

When we think of what operations management does—namely, managing the transformation of inputs into goods and services—we can see that as a function it is as old as time. Think of any great organizational effort, such as organizing the first Olympic games, building the Great Wall of China, or erecting the Egyptian pyramids, and you will see operations management at work. Operations management did not emerge as a formal field of study, however, until the late 1950s and early 1960s, when scholars began to recognize that all production systems face a common set of problems and to stress the systems approach to viewing operations processes.

Many events helped shape operations management. We will describe some of the most significant of these historical milestones and explain their influence on the development of operations management. Later we will look at some current trends in operations management. These historical milestones and current trends are summarized in Table 1-2.

TABLE 1-2

Historical Development of Operations Management

Concept	Time	Explanation
Industrial Revolution	Late 1700s	Brought in innovations that changed production by using machine power instead of human power.
Scientific management	Early 1900s	Brought the concepts of analysis and measurement of the technical aspects of work design and development of moving assembly lines and mass production.
Human relations movement	1930s to 1960s	Focused on understanding human elements of job design, such as worker motivation and job satisfaction.
Management science	1940s to 1960s	Focused on the development of quantitative techniques to solve operations problems.
Computer age	1960s	Enabled processing of large amounts of data and allowed widespread use of quantitative procedures.
Environmental issues	1970s	Considered waste reduction, the need for recycling, and product reuse.
Just-in-time systems (JIT)	1980s	Designed to achieve high-volume production with minimal inventories.
Total quality management (TQM)	1980s	Sought to eliminate causes of production defects.
Reengineering	1980s	Required redesigning a company's processes in order to provide greater efficiency and cost reduction.
Global competition	1980s	Designed operations to compete in the global market.
Flexibility	1990s	Offered customization on a mass scale.
Time-based competition	1990s	Based on time, such as speed of delivery.
Supply chain management	1990s	Focused on reducing the overall cost of the system that manages the flow of materials and information from suppliers to final customers.
Electronic commerce	2000s	Uses the Internet and World Wide Web for conducting business activity.
Outsourcing and flattening of the world	2000s	Convergence of technology has enabled outsourcing of virtually any job imaginable from anywhere around the globe, therefore "flattening" the world.

The Industrial Revolution

▶ **Industrial Revolution**
An industry movement that changed production by substituting machine power for labor power.

The **Industrial Revolution** had a significant impact on the way goods are produced today. Before this time, products were made by hand by skilled craftspeople in their shops or homes. Each product was unique, painstakingly made by one person. The Industrial Revolution changed all that. It started in the 1770s with the development of a number of inventions that relied on machine power instead of human power. The most important of these was the steam engine, which was invented by James Watt in 1764. The steam engine provided a new source of power that was used to replace human labor in textile mills, machine-making plants, and other facilities. The concept

Courtesy Library of Congress

Steamboat and railroad forging during the Industrial Revolution

Terry Vine/Stone/Getty Images, Inc.

Today's modern work environment

of the factory was emerging. In addition, the steam engine led to advances in transportation, such as railroads, that allowed for a wider distribution of goods.

About the same time, the concept of *division of labor* was introduced. First described by Adam Smith in 1776 in *The Wealth of Nations*, this concept would become one of the important ideas behind the development of the assembly line. Division of labor means that the production of a good is broken down into a series of small, elemental tasks, each of which is performed by a different worker. The repetition of the task allows the worker to become highly specialized in that task. Division of labor allowed higher volumes to be produced, which, coupled with the advances in transportation of steam-powered boats and railroads, opened up distant markets.

A few years later, in 1790, Eli Whitney introduced the concept of *interchangeable parts*. Prior to that time, every part used in a production process was unique. Interchangeable parts are standardized so that every item in a batch of items fits equally. This concept meant that we could move from one-at-a-time production to volume production, for example, in the manufacture of watches, clocks, and similar items.

Scientific Management

Scientific management was an approach to management promoted by Frederick W. Taylor at the turn of the twentieth century. Taylor was an engineer with an eye for efficiency. Through scientific management he sought to increase worker productivity and organizational output. His concept had two key features. First, it assumed that workers are motivated only by money and are limited only by their physical ability. Taylor believed that worker productivity is governed by scientific laws and that it is up to management to discover these laws through measurement, analysis, and observation. Workers are to be paid in direct proportion to how much they produce. The second feature of this approach was the separation of the planning and doing functions in a company, which meant the separation of management and labor. Management is responsible for designing productive systems and determining acceptable worker output. Workers have no input into this process—they are permitted only to work.

Many people did not like the scientific management approach, especially workers, who thought that management used these methods to unfairly increase output without paying them accordingly. Still, many companies adopted the scientific management approach. Today many view scientific management as a major influence in the

▶ **Scientific management**
An approach to management that focused on improving output by redesigning jobs and determining acceptable levels of worker output.

field of operations management. For example, *piece-rate incentives*, in which workers are paid in direct proportion to their output, came out of this movement. Also, Taylor introduced a widely used method of work measurement, *stopwatch time studies*. In stopwatch time studies, observations are made and recorded of a worker performing a task over many cycles. This information is then used to set a time standard for performing the particular task. This method is still used today to set a time standard for short, repetitive tasks.

The scientific management approach was popularized by Henry Ford, who used the techniques in his factories. Combining technology with scientific management, Ford introduced the *moving assembly line* to produce Ford cars. Ford also combined scientific management with the division of labor and interchangeable parts to develop the concept of *mass production*. These concepts and innovations helped him increase production and efficiency at his factories.

The Human Relations Movement

▶ **Hawthorne studies**
The studies responsible for creating the human relations movement, which focused on giving more consideration to workers' needs.

The scientific management movement and its philosophy dominated in the early twentieth century. However, this changed with the publication of the results of the **Hawthorne studies**. The purpose of the Hawthorne studies, conducted at a Western Electric plant in Hawthorne, Illinois, in the 1930s, was to study the effects of environmental changes, such as changes in lighting and room temperature, on the productivity of assembly-line workers. The findings from the study were unexpected: the productivity of the workers continued to increase regardless of the environmental changes made. Elton Mayo, a sociologist from Harvard, concluded that the workers were actually motivated by the attention they were given. The idea of workers responding to the attention they are given came to be known as the *Hawthorne effect*.

▶ **Human relations movement**
A philosophy based on the recognition that factors other than money can contribute to worker productivity.

The study of these findings by many sociologists and psychologists led to the **human relations movement**, an entirely new philosophy based on the recognition that factors other than money can contribute to worker productivity. The impact of this new philosophy on the development of operations management has been tremendous. Its influence can be seen in the implementation of a number of concepts that motivate workers by making their jobs more interesting and meaningful. For example, the Hawthorne studies showed that scientific management had made jobs too repetitive and boring. *Job enlargement* is an approach in which workers are given a larger portion of the total task to do. Another approach to giving more meaning to jobs is *job enrichment*, in which workers are given a greater role in planning.

Recent studies have shown that environmental factors in the workplace, such as adequate lighting and ventilation, can have a major impact on productivity. However, this does not contradict the principle that attention from management is a positive factor in motivation.

Management Science

▶ **Management science**
A field of study that focuses on the development of quantitative techniques to solve operations problems.

While some were focusing on the technical aspects of job design and others on the human aspects of operations management, a third approach, called **management science**, was developing that would make its own unique contribution. Management science focused on developing quantitative techniques for solving operations problems. The first mathematical model for inventory management was developed by F. W. Harris in 1913. Shortly thereafter, statistical sampling theory and quality control procedures were developed.

World War II created an even greater need for the ability to quantitatively solve complex problems of logistics control, for weapons system design and deployment of missiles. Consequently, the techniques of management science grew more robust during the war and continued to develop after the war was over. Many quantitative tools emerged to solve problems in forecasting, inventory control, project management, and other areas. A mathematically oriented field, management science provides operations management with tools to assist in decision making. A popular example of such a tool is linear programming.

The Computer Age

In the 1970s the use of computers in business became widespread. With computers, many of the quantitative models developed by management science could be employed on a larger scale. Data processing became easier, with important effects in areas such as forecasting, scheduling, and inventory management. A particularly important computerized system, material requirements planning (MRP), was developed for inventory control and scheduling. Material requirements planning was able to process huge amounts of data in order to compute inventory requirements and develop schedules for the production of thousands of items, processing that was impossible before the age of computers. Today the exponential growth in computing capability continues to impact operations management.

Just-in-Time

Just-in-time (**JIT**) is a major operations management philosophy, developed in Japan in the 1980s, that is designed to achieve high-volume production using minimal amounts of inventory. This is achieved through coordination of the flow of materials so that the right parts arrive at the right place in the right quantity; hence the term *just-in-time*. However, JIT is much more than the coordinated movement of goods. It is an all-inclusive organizational philosophy that employs teams of workers to achieve continuous improvement in processes and organizational efficiency by eliminating all organizational waste. Although JIT was first used in manufacturing, it has been implemented in the service sector, for example, in the food service industry. JIT has had a profound impact on the way companies manage their operations. It is credited with helping turn many companies around and is used by companies such as Honda, Toyota, and General Motors. JIT promises to continue to transform businesses in the future.

> ▶ **Just-in-time** (**JIT**)
> A philosophy designed to achieve high-volume production through elimination of waste and continuous improvement.

Total Quality Management

As customers demand ever higher quality in their products and services, companies have been forced to focus on improving quality in order to remain competitive. **Total quality management** (**TQM**) is a philosophy—promulgated by "quality gurus" such as W. Edwards Deming—that aggressively seeks to improve product quality by eliminating causes of product defects and making quality an all-encompassing organizational philosophy. With TQM, everyone in the company is responsible for quality. Practiced by some companies in the 1980s, TQM became pervasive in the 1990s and is an area of operations management that no competitive company has been able to ignore. Its importance is demonstrated by the number of companies achieving ISO 9000

> ▶ **Total quality management** (**TQM**)
> Philosophy that seeks to improve quality by eliminating causes of product defects and by making quality the responsibility of everyone in the organization.

certification. ISO 9000 is a set of quality standards developed for global manufacturers by the International Organization for Standardization (ISO) to control trade into the then-emerging European Economic Community (EEC). Today ISO 9000 is a global set of standards, with many companies requiring their suppliers to meet the standards as a condition for obtaining contracts.

Business Process Reengineering

▶ **Reengineering**
Redesigning a company's processes to make them more efficient.

Business process **reengineering** means redesigning a company's processes to increase efficiency, improve quality, and reduce costs. In many companies things are done in a certain way that has been passed down over the years. Often managers say, "Well, we've always done it this way." Reengineering requires asking why things are done in a certain way, questioning assumptions, and then redesigning the processes. Operations management is a key player in a company's reengineering efforts.

Flexibility

▶ **Flexibility**
An organizational strategy in which the company attempts to offer a greater variety of product choices to its customers.

▶ **Mass customization**
The ability of a firm to highly customize its goods and services at high volumes.

Traditionally, companies competed by either mass-producing a standardized product or offering customized products in small volumes. One of the current competitive challenges for companies is the need to offer to customers a greater variety of product choices of a traditionally standardized product. This is the challenge of **flexibility**. For example, Procter and Gamble offers 13 different product designs in the Pampers line of diapers. Although diapers are a standardized product, the product designs are customized to the different needs of customers, such as the age, sex, and stage of development of the child using the diaper.

One example of flexibility is **mass customization**, which is the ability of a firm to produce highly customized goods and services and to do it at the high volumes of mass production. Mass customization requires designing flexible operations and using delayed product differentiation, also called postponement. This means keeping the product in generic form as long as possible and postponing completion of the product until specific customer preferences are known.

Time-Based Competition

▶ **Time-based competition**
An organizational strategy focusing on efforts to develop new products and deliver them to customers *faster* than competitors.

One of the most important trends within companies today is **time-based competition**—developing new products and services faster than the competition, reaching the market first, and meeting customer orders most quickly. For example, two companies may produce the same product, but if one is able to deliver it to the customer in two days and the other in five days, the first company will make the sale and win over the customers. Time-based competition requires specifically designing the operations function for speed.

Supply Chain Management

▶ **Supply chain management (SCM)**
Management of the flow of materials from suppliers to customers in order to reduce overall cost and increase responsiveness to customers.

Supply chain management (**SCM**) involves managing the flow of materials and information from suppliers and buyers of raw materials all the way to the final customer. The network of entities that is involved in producing and delivering a finished product to the final customer is called a supply chain. The objective is to have everyone in the chain work together to reduce overall cost and improve quality and service delivery. Supply chain management requires a team approach, with functions such as marketing, purchasing, operations, and engineering all working together. This approach has been shown to result in more satisfied customers, meaning that everyone in the chain profits. SCM has become possible with the development of information technology (IT) tools that enable collaborative planning and scheduling. The technologies allow synchronized supply chain execution and design collaboration, which enables companies to respond better and faster to changing market needs. Numerous companies, including Dell Computer, Wal-Mart, and Toyota, have achieved world-class status by effectively managing their supply chains.

Global Marketplace

Today businesses must think in terms of a **global marketplace** in order to compete effectively. This includes the way they view their customers, competitors, and suppliers. Key issues are meeting customer needs and getting the right product to markets as diverse as the Far East, Europe, or Africa. Operations management is responsible for most of these decisions. OM decides whether to tailor products to different customer needs, where to locate facilities, how to manage suppliers, and how to meet local government standards. Also, global competition has forced companies to reach higher levels of excellence in the products and services they offer. Regional trading agreements, such as the North American Free Trade Agreement (NAFTA), the European Union (EU), and the global General Agreement on Tariffs and Trade (GATT), guarantee continued competition on the international level.

▶ **Global marketplace**
A trend in business focusing on customers, suppliers, and competitors from a global perspective.

Environmental Issues

There is increasing emphasis on the need to reduce waste, recycle, and reuse products and parts. Society has placed great pressure on business to focus on air and water quality, waste disposal, global warming, and other **environmental issues**. Operations management plays a key role in redesigning processes and products in order to meet and exceed environmental quality standards. The importance of this issue is demonstrated by a set of standards termed ISO 14000. Developed by the International Organization for Standardization (ISO), these standards provide guidelines and a certification program documenting a company's environmentally responsible actions.

▶ **Environmental issues**
A trend in business to consciously reduce waste, recycle, and reuse products and parts.

Electronic Commerce

Electronic commerce (e-commerce) is the use of the Internet for conducting business activities, such as communication, business transactions, and data transfer. The Internet, developed from a government network called ARPANET created in 1969 by the U.S. Defense Department, has become an essential business medium since the late 1990s, enabling efficient communication between manufacturers, suppliers, distributors, and customers. It has allowed companies to reach more customers at a speed infinitely faster than ever before. It also has significantly cut costs, as it provides direct links between entities.

The electronic commerce that occurs between businesses, known as **B2B** (**business-to-business**) commerce, makes up the highest percentage of transactions. The most common B2B exchanges occur between companies and their suppliers, such as General Electric's Trading Process Network. A more familiar type of e-commerce occurs between businesses and their customers, known as **B2C** exchange, as engaged in by online retailers such as Amazon.com. E-commerce also occurs between customers, known as **C2C** exchange, as on consumer auction sites such as eBay. E-commerce is creating virtual marketplaces that continue to change the way business functions.

▶ **Business to business (B2B)**
Electronic commerce between businesses.

▶ **Business to customers (B2C)**
Electronic commerce between businesses and their customers.

▶ **Customer to customer (C2C)**
Electronic commerce between customers.

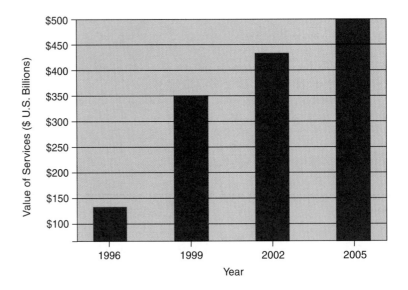

FIGURE 1-7

U.S. market for outsourcing services 1996–2000

Outsourcing and Flattening of the World

Outsourcing is when companies obtain goods or services from an outside provider. This can range from outsourcing of one aspect of the operation, such as shipping, to outsourcing an entire part of the manufacturing process. The practice has rapidly grown in recent years, as you can see in Figure 1-7. It has helped companies be more efficient by focusing on what they do best. Outsourcing has been touted as the enabling factor that helps companies achieve the needed speed and flexibility to be competitive. Management guru Tom Peters has been quoted as saying, "Do what you do best and outsource the rest."

The convergence of technologies at the turn of this century has taken the concept of outsourcing to a new level. Massive investments in technology, such as worldwide broadband connectivity, the increasing availability and lower cost of computers, and the development of software such as e-mail, search engines, and other software, allow individuals to work together in real time from anywhere in the world. This has enabled countries like India, China, and many others to become part of the global supply chain for goods and services and has created a "flattening" of the world. Such "flattening," or leveling of the playing field, has enabled workers anywhere in the world to compete globally for intellectual work. The result has been the outsourcing of virtually any job imaginable. Manufacturers have outsourced software development and product design to engineers in India; accounting firms have outsourced tax preparation to India; even some hospitals have outsourced the reading of CAT scans to doctors in India and Australia. The "flattening" of the world has created a whole new level of global competition that is more intense than ever before.

TODAY'S OM ENVIRONMENT

▶ **Lean systems**
A concept that takes a total system approach to creating efficient operations.

Today's OM environment is very different from what it was just a few years ago. Customers demand better quality, greater speed, and lower costs. In order to succeed, companies have to be masters of the basics of operations management. To achieve this, many companies are implementing a concept called **lean systems**. Lean systems take a total system approach to creating an efficient operation and pull together best practice concepts, including just-in-time (JIT), total quality management (TQM), continuous improvement, resource planning, and supply chain management (SCM). The need for efficiency has also led many companies to implement large information systems called **enterprise resource planning** (**ERP**). ERP systems are large, sophisticated software programs for identifying and planning the enterprise-wide resources needed to coordinate all activities involved in producing and delivering products to customers.

Applying best practices to operations management is not enough to give a company a competitive advantage. The reason is that in today's information age best practices are quickly passed to competitors. To gain an advantage over their competitors, companies are continually looking for ways to better respond to customers. This requires them to have a deep knowledge of their customers and to be able to anticipate their demands. The development of **customer relationship management** (**CRM**) has made it possible for companies to have this detailed knowledge. CRM encompasses software solutions that enable the firm to collect customer-specific data, information that can help the firm identify profiles of its most loyal customers and provide customer-specific solutions. Also, CRM software can be integrated with ERP software to connect customer requirements to the entire resource network of the company.

Another characteristic of today's OM environment is the increased use of **cross-functional decision making**, which requires coordinated interaction and decision making among the different business functions of the organization. Until recently, employees of a company made decisions in isolated departments, called "functional silos." Today many companies bring together experts from different departments into cross-functional teams to solve company problems. Employees from each function must interact and coordinate their decisions, which require employees to understand the roles of other business functions and the goals of the business as a whole, in addition to their own expertise.

▶ **Enterprise resource planning (ERP)**
Large, sophisticated software systems used for identifying and planning the enterprise-wide resources needed to coordinate all activities involved in producing and delivering products.

▶ **Customer relationship management (CRM)**
Software solutions that enable the firm to collect customer-specific data.

▶ **Cross-functional decision making**
The coordinated interaction and decision making that occur among the different functions of the organization.

OPERATIONS MANAGEMENT IN PRACTICE

Of all the business functions, operations is the most diverse in terms of the tasks performed. If you consider all the issues involved in managing a transformation process, you can see that operations managers are never bored. Who are operations managers and what do they do?

The head of the operations function in a company usually holds the title of vice president of operations, vice president of manufacturing, V.P., or director of supply chain operations and generally reports directly to the president or chief operating officer. Below the vice president level are midlevel managers: manufacturing manager, operations manager, quality control manager, plant manager, and others. Below these managers are a variety of positions, such as quality specialist, production analyst, inventory analyst, and production supervisor. These people perform a variety of functions: analyzing production problems, developing forecasts, making plans for new products, measuring quality, monitoring inventory, and developing employee schedules. Thus, there are many job opportunities in operations management at all levels of the company. In addition, operations jobs tend to offer high salaries, interesting work, and excellent opportunities for advancement. Many corporate CEOs today have come through the ranks of operations. For example, the current president and CEO of Wal-Mart, H. Lee Scott, comes from a background in operations and logistics. Also from the operations background are the current CEO of Home Depot, Bob Nardelli, and the CEO of Lowe's, Robert Tillman.

As you can see, all business functions need information from operations management in order to perform their tasks. At the same time, operations managers are highly dependent on input from other areas. This process of information sharing is dynamic, requiring that managers work in teams and understand each other's roles.

WITHIN OM: HOW IT ALL FITS TOGETHER

Just as OM decisions are linked with those of other business functions, decisions *within* the OM function need to be linked together. We learned that OM is responsible for a wide range of strategic and tactical decisions. These decisions directly impact each other and need to be carefully linked together, following the company's strategic direction. In the Gourmet Wafers example we observed that decisions on product design are directly tied to process selection (Chapter 3). The reason is that the process of a company needs to be capable of producing the desired product (Chapter 6). Similarly, the forecast of expected demand (Chapter 8) directly impacts functions such as capacity planning (Chapter 9), inventory management (Chapter 12), and scheduling (Chapter 15). These are just a few examples of linkages within the OM function.

Throughout this book we will study different OM functions and will learn how each impacts the other. You will realize that OM decisions are not made in isolation. Rather, each decision is intertwined with other business functions and other OM decisions.

OM ACROSS THE ORGANIZATION

Now that we know the role of the operations management function and the decisions that operations managers make, let's look at the relationship between operations and other business functions. As mentioned previously, most businesses are supported by three main functions: operations, marketing, and finance. Although these functions involve different activities, they must interact to achieve the goals of the organization. They must also follow the strategic direction developed at the top level of the organization. Figure 1-8 shows the flow of information from the top to each business function, as well as the flow between functions.

Many of the decisions made by operations managers are dependent on information from the other functions. At the same time, other functions cannot be carried out properly without information from operations. Figure 1-9 shows these relationships.

Marketing is not fully capable of meeting customer needs if marketing managers do not understand what operations can produce, what due dates it can and cannot meet, and what types of customization operations can deliver. The marketing department can

FIGURE 1-8

Organizational chart showing flow of information

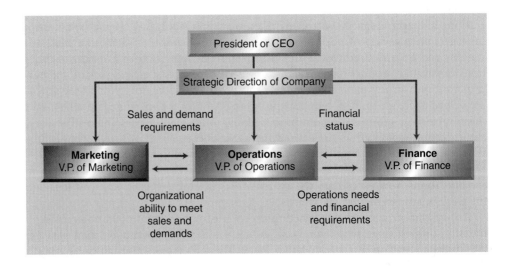

FIGURE 1-9

Information flow between operations and other business functions

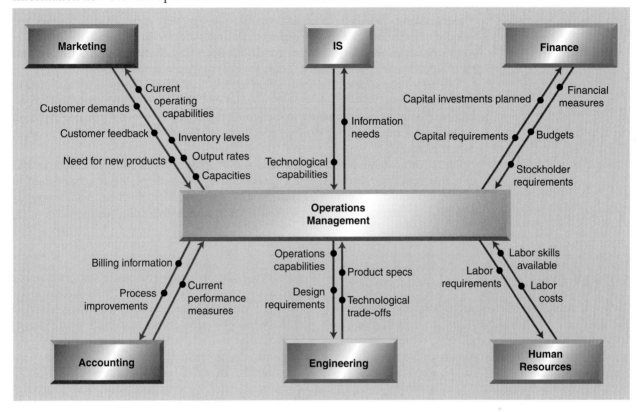

develop an exciting marketing campaign, but if operations cannot produce the desired product, sales will not be made. In turn, operations managers need information about customer wants and expectations. It is up to them to design products with characteristics that customers find desirable, and they cannot do this without regular coordination with the marketing department.

Finance   cannot realistically judge the need for capital investments, make-or-buy decisions, plant expansions, or relocation if finance managers do not understand operations concepts and needs. On the other hand, operations managers cannot make large financial expenditures without understanding financial constraints and methods of evaluating financial investments. It is essential for these two functions to work together and understand each other's constraints.

Information systems (IS)   is a function that enables information to flow throughout the organization and allows OM to operate effectively. OM is highly dependent on information such as forecasts of demand, quality levels being achieved, inventory levels, supplier deliveries, and worker schedules. IS must understand the needs of OM in order to design an adequate information system. Usually, IS and OM work together to design an information network. This close relationship needs to be ongoing. IS must be capable of accommodating the needs of OM as they change in response to market demands. At the same time, it is up to IS to bring the latest capabilities in information technology to the organization to enhance the functioning of OM.

Human resource managers must understand job requirements and worker skills if they are to hire the right people for available jobs. To manage employees effectively, operations managers need to understand job market trends, hiring and layoff costs, and training costs.

Accounting needs to consider inventory management, capacity information, and labor standards in order to develop accurate cost data. In turn, operations managers must communicate billing information and process improvements to accounting, and they depend heavily on accounting data for cost management decisions.

Engineering and other disciplines that are not in the business field are also tied to operations. Operations management provides engineering with the operations capabilities and design requirements, and engineering, in turn, provides valuable input on technological trade-offs and product specifications. These are essential for the product design process.

The coordinated interaction and decision making between all these functions and OM are needed for success in today's competitive environment. It is also important to extend this coordination to organizations that make up a supply chain, such as suppliers, manufacturers, and retailers. This is discussed in the following box.

SUPPLY CHAIN LINK

Today's companies understand that successfully managing their own OM functions is not enough to maintain leadership in a highly competitive marketplace. The reason is that every company is dependent on other members of the supply chain to successfully deliver the right product to the final customer in a timely and cost-effective manner. For example, a company is dependent on its suppliers for the delivery of raw materials and components in time to meet production needs. If these materials are delivered late or are of insufficient quality, production will be delayed. Similarly, a company depends on its distributors and retailers for the delivery of the product to the final customer. If these are not delivered on time, are damaged in the transportation process, or are poorly displayed at the retail location, sales will suffer. Also, if the OM function of other members of the supply chain is not managed properly, excess costs will result, which will be passed down to other members of the supply chain in the form of higher prices. Therefore, each company in the supply chain must successfully manage its OM function. Also, the companies that comprise a supply chain need to coordinate and link their OM functions so that the entire chain is operating in a seamless and efficient manner. Just consider the fact that most of the components Dell uses are warehoused within a fifteen-minute radius of its assembly plant and Dell is in constant communication with its suppliers. Dell considers this essential to its ability to produce and deliver components quickly.

Chapter Highlights

1 Operations management is the business function that is responsible for managing and coordinating the resources needed to produce a company's products and services. Without operations management there would be no products or services to sell.

2 The role of operations management is to transform organizational inputs—human resources, facilities, materials, technology, and information—into a company's finished goods or services.

3 Operations management is responsible for a wide range of decisions, ranging from strategic decisions, such as

designing the unique features of a product and process, to tactical decisions, such as planning worker schedules.

4 Organizations can be divided into manufacturing and service operations, which differ in the tangibility of the product and the degree of customer contact. Manufacturing and service operations have very different operational requirements.

5 A number of historical milestones have shaped operations management into what it is today. Some of the more significant of these are the Industrial Revolution, scientific management, the human relations movement, management science, and the computer age.

6 OM is a highly important function in today's dynamic business environment. Among the trends that have had a significant impact on business are just-in-time, total quality management, reengineering, flexibility, time-based competition, supply chain management, a global marketplace, and environmental issues.

7 Operations managers need to work closely with all other business functions in a team format. Marketing needs to provide information about customer expectations. Finance needs to provide information about budget constraints. In turn, OM must communicate its needs and capabilities to the other functions.

Key Terms

operations management (OM) 3
role of operations management 3
value added 5
efficiency 5
manufacturing organizations 5
service organizations 5
strategic decisions 9
tactical decisions 9
Industrial Revolution 12
scientific management 13

Hawthorne studies 14
human relations movement 14
management science 14
just-in-time (JIT) 15
total quality management (TQM) 15
reengineering 16
flexibility 16
mass customization 16
time-based competition 16
supply chain management (SCM) 16

global marketplace 17
environmental issues 17
business to business (B2B) 17
business to customers (B2C) 17
customer to customer (C2C) 17
lean systems 18
enterprise resource planning (ERP) 19
customer relationship management
  (CRM) 19
cross-functional decision making 19

Discussion Questions

1. Define the term *operations management.*

2. Explain the decisions operations managers make and give three examples.

3. Describe the transformation process of a business. Give three examples. What constitutes the transformation process at an advertising agency, a bank, and a TV station?

4. What are the three major business functions, and how are they related to one another? Give specific examples.

5. What are the differences between strategic and tactical decisions, and how are they related to each other?

6. Find an article that relates to operations management in either the *Wall Street Journal, Fortune,* or *Business Week.* Come to class prepared to share with others what you learned in the article.

7. Examine the list of *Fortune* magazine's top 100 companies. Do most of these companies have anything in common? Are there industries that are most represented?

8. Identify the two major differences between service and manufacturing organizations. Find an example of a service and manufacturing company and compare them.

9. What are the three historical milestones in operations management? How have they influenced management?

10. Identify three current trends in operations management and describe them. How do you think they will change the future of OM?

11. Define the terms *total quality management, just-in-time,* and *reengineering.* What do these terms have in common?

12. Describe today's OM environment. How different is it from that of a few years ago? Identify specific features you think characterize today's OM environment.

13. Describe the impact of e-commerce on operations management. Identify the challenges posed by e-commerce on operations management.

14. Find a company you are familiar with and explain how it uses its operations management function. Identify what the company is doing correctly. Do you have any suggestions for improvement?

CASE: Hightone Electronics, Inc.

George Gonzales, operations director of Hightone Electronics, Inc., sat quietly at the conference table overlooking the lobby of the corporate headquarters office in Palo Alto, California. He reflected on the board meeting that had just adjourned and the challenge that lay ahead for him. The board had just announced their decision to start an Internet-based division of HEI. Web-based purchasing in the electronics industry had been growing rapidly. The board felt that HEI needed to offer on-line purchasing to their customers in order to maintain its competitive position. The board looked to George to outline the key operations management decisions that needed to be addressed in creating a successful Internet-based business. The next board meeting was just a week away. He had his work cut out for him.

Hightone Electronics, Inc. was founded in Palo Alto, California over fifty years ago. Originally, the company provided radio components to small repair shops. Products were offered for sale through a catalogue that was mailed to prospective customers every four months. The company built its reputation on high quality and service. As time passed, HEI began supplying more than just radio parts, adding items such as fuses, transformers, computers, and electrical testing equipment. The expansion of the product line had been coupled with an increase in the number and type of customers the company served. Although the traditional repair shops still remained a part of the company's market, technical schools, universities, and well-known corporations in the Silicon Valley were added to the list of customers.

Today HEI operates the Palo Alto facility with the same dedication to supplying quality products through catalogue sales that it had when it was first founded. Customer service remains the top priority. HEI stocks and sells over 22,000 different items. Most customers receive their orders within 48 hours, and all components are warranted for a full year.

Expanding HEI to include Web-based purchasing seems to be a natural extension of catalogue sales that the company already does successfully. George Gonzales agrees that the company has no choice but to move in this competitive direction. However, George does not agree with the opinion of the board that this would be "business as usual." He believes that there are many operations decisions that need to be identified and addressed. As he stated in the meeting, "Having a slick Web site is one thing, but making sure the right product is delivered to the right location is another. Operations is the key to making this happen." His challenge for the next board meeting was to identify the key operations decision and persuade the board that these issues needed serious consideration.

Case Questions

1. Explain why operations management is critical to the success of a business. Why would developing an Internet-based business require different operations consideration for HEI? Is George Gonzales correct in his assessment that this would not be "business as usual"?

2. Recall that HEI wishes to continue its reputation of high quality and service. Identify key operations management decisions that need to be considered. How different will these decisions be for the Internet business?

CASE: Creature Care Animal Clinic (A)

It has been three years since Dr. Julia Barr opened Creature Care Animal Clinic, a suburban veterinary clinic. Dr. Barr thought that by now she would be enjoying having her own practice. She had spent many years in college and worked to save money in order to start a business. Instead, she felt overwhelmed with business problems that were facing the clinic. She thought to herself: "I don't produce anything. I just provide a service doing something I enjoy. How can this be so complicated?"

Company Background

Dr. Barr opened Creature Care Animal Clinic as a veterinary clinic specializing in the care of dogs and cats. The clinic was set to operate Monday through Friday during regular business hours, with half days on Saturday and extended hours on Wednesday evening. Dr. Barr hired another full-time veterinarian, Dr. Gene Yen, a staff of three nurses, an office manager, and an office assistant. Both doctors were to work during the week and rotate the shift for Wednesday evenings and Saturdays. A similar schedule was set up for the nurses. The office manager worked during regular business hours, and the assistant worked on Wednesday evenings and Saturdays. Dr. Barr set up this schedule based on a clinic she had observed as a resident and thought it sounded reasonable.

Since the clinic was small, Dr. Barr did not have a formal system of inventory management. All physicians and nurses were allowed to place purchase orders based on need. Initially this system worked well, but after a few months problems started developing. Frequently, there was excess inventory of certain items and in many cases there were multiple brands of the same product. Sometimes medications passed their expiration dates and had to be thrown away. At the same time, the clinic often unexpectedly ran out of stock of certain supplies and rush orders had to be placed. On one occasion they ran so low on bandages that the assistant had to be sent to the local drug store.

Dr. Barr continued to rotate with Dr. Yen for coverage on Saturdays and Wednesday evenings. However, demand was increasing so rapidly on Saturdays that one doctor was not enough to provide needed coverage. Also, the Friday afternoon schedule was usually so packed that the staff frequently had to stay late in the evening. At the same time, there was little demand on Wednesday evenings and Dr. Barr found herself working on paperwork on those evenings, while the nurse and office assistant performed menial office tasks.

Case Questions

1. Identify the operations management problems that Dr. Barr is having at the clinic.

2. The schedule Dr. Barr set up worked well at the clinic where she was a resident. What are some of the reasons why it might not be working here?

3. Identify some of the reasons why the clinic is having inventory problems.

4. What should Dr. Barr have done differently to avoid some of the problems she is currently experiencing?

5. What suggestions would you make to Dr. Barr now?

INTERACTIVE CASE Virtual Company www.wiley.com/ college/reid

On-line Case: Valley Memorial Hospital

Assignment: *Welcome to Kaizen Consulting* Bob Reilly, head of Kaizen Consulting, Inc. just called you to let you know that you have just been accepted as an intern for his company. Kaizen handles many different clients, but you will primarily be working with one of their healthcare clients, *Valley Memorial Hospital.* Your internship will start in a few weeks. Bob has advised you to get thoroughly familiar with the company and its operations before you start working on the specific tasks that will be assigned to you. This assignment will enable you to enhance your knowledge of the material in Chapter 1 while preparing you for a successful internship.

To access the Web site:

- Go to **www.wiley.com/college/reid**
- Click **Student Companion Site**
- Click **Virtual Company**
- Click **Kaizen Consulting, Inc.**
- Click **Consulting Assignments**
- Click **Welcome to Kaizen Consulting**

INTERNET CHALLENGE Demonstrating Your Knowledge of OM

Visit the Web sites of at least one service and one manufacturing company. For each company, identify at least five characteristic OM decisions and show your results in a table. Which decisions are strategic and which are tactical? How do these decisions differ between the two companies? Here are some Web sites to consider.

Select service company Web sites:

    www.ritzcarlton.com (Ritz-Carlton Hotel)

    www.sprint.com (Sprint Corporation)

    www.yellowcorp.com (Yellow Corporation)

    www.kmart.com (Kmart Corporation)

    www.yahoo.com (Yahoo!)

Select manufacturing company Web sites:

    www.saturn.com (Saturn Corporation)

    www.alcoa.com (Alcoa Inc.)

    www.milliken.com (Milliken & Company)

    www.Intel.com (Intel Corporation)

    www.ge.com (General Electric Company)

On-line Resources

Companion Website www.wiley.com/college/reid

- Take interactive *practice quizzes* to assess your knowledge and help you study in a dynamic way
- Review *PowerPoint slides* or print slides for notetaking
- Access the *Virtual Company: Valley Memorial Hospital*
- Find links for *Additional Web Resources* for this chapter APICS, *www.apics.org* Council of Logistics Management, *www.clml.org*

Additional Resources Available Only in WileyPLUS

- Use the *e-Book* and launch directly to all interactive resources
- Take the interactive *Quick Test* to check your understanding of the chapter material and get immediate feedback on your responses
- Check your understanding of the key vocabulary in the chapter with *Interactive Flash Cards*
- Use the *Animated Demo Problems* to review key problem types
- Practice for your test with *additional problem sets*
- *And more!*

Selected Bibliography

Beach, R., A.P. Muhlemann, D.H.R. Price, A. Paterson, and J.A. Sharp. "Manufacturing Operations and Strategic Flexibility: Survey and Cases," *International Journal of Operations and Production Management*, 20, 1, 2000, 7–30.

Carter, P.J., R.M. Monczka, and J. Mossconi. "Looking at the Future of Supply Management," *Supply Chain Management Review*, December 2005, 27–29.

Chase. R.B., F.B. Jacob, and N.J. Aquilano. *Operations Management for a Competitive Advantage*, Eleventh Edition. New York: Irwin McGraw-Hill, 2006.

Dennis, Michael J., and Ajit Kambil. "Service Management: Building Profits After the Sale," *Supply Chain Management Review*, January–February, 2003, 42–48.

Dischinger, J., D.J. Closs, E. McCulloch, C. Speier, W. Grenoble, and D. Marshall. "The Emerging Supply Chain Management Profession," *Supply Chain Management Review*, January–February 2006, 62–68.

Friedman, T.L. *The World is Flat*, New York: Farrar Straus and Giroux, 2005.

Fugate, B.S., and J.T. Mentzer. "Dell's Suply Chain DNA," *Supply Chain Management Review*, 2004, 20–24.

Galbraith, J.K. *The Affluent Society*. Boston: Houghton Mifflin, 1958.

Klassen, R.D., and D.C. Whybark. "Environmental Management in Operations: The Selection of Environmental Technologies," *Decision Sciences*, 30, 3, 1999, 601–631.

Skinner, W. *Manufacturing in the Corporate Strategy*. New York: John Wiley & Sons, 1978.

Skinner, W. "Manufacturing Strategy on the 'S' Curve," *Production and Operations Management*, Spring 1996, 3–14.

Wu, John C. "Anatomy of a Dot-Com," *Supply Chain Management Review*, November–December, 2001, 42–51.

CHAPTER 2

Operations Strategy and Competitiveness

Before studying this chapter you should know or, if necessary, review

1. The role of the OM function in organizations, Chapter 1, pp. 3–4.
2. Differences between strategic and tactical decisions, Chapter 1, 7–9.

LEARNING OBJECTIVES

After studying this chapter you should be able to

1. Define the role of business strategy.
2. Explain how a business strategy is developed.
3. Explain the role of operations strategy in the organization.
4. Explain the relationship between business strategy and operations strategy.
5. Describe how an operations strategy is developed.
6. Identify competitive priorities of the operations function.
7. Explain the strategic role of technology.
8. Define productivity and identify productivity measures.
9. Compute productivity measures.

CHAPTER OUTLINE

WHAT'S IN OM FOR ME?

ACC	FIN	MKT	OM	HRM	MIS

©AP/Wide World Photos

To maintain a competitive position in the marketplace, a company must have a long-range plan. This plan needs to include the company's long-term goals, an understanding of the marketplace, and a way to differentiate the company from its competitors. All other decisions must support this long-range plan. Otherwise, each person in the company would pursue goals that he or she considered important, and the company would quickly fall apart.

The functioning of a football team on the field is similar to the functioning of a business and provides a good example of the importance of a plan or vision. Before the plays are made, the team prepares a game strategy. Each player on the team must perform a particular role to support this strategy. The strategy is a "game plan" designed so that the team can win. Imagine what would occur if individual players decided to do plays that they thought were appropriate. Certainly the team's chance of winning would not be very high. A successful football team is a unified group of players using their individual skills in support of a winning strategy. The same is true of a business.

The long-range plan of a business, designed to provide and sustain shareholder value, is called the **business strategy**. For a company to succeed, the business strategy must be supported by each of the individual business functions, such as operations, finance, and marketing. **Operations strategy** is a long-range plan for the operations function that specifies the design and use of resources to support the business strategy. Just as the players on a football team support the team's strategy, the role of everyone in the company is to do his or her job in a way that supports the business strategy.

Let's look at two companies operating in the same industry, but with very different business strategies. The first is Southwest Airlines, which has a strategy to compete on cost. Southwest offers low-cost services aimed at price-sensitive customers. To support this strategy, every aspect of Southwest's operation is focused on cutting costs out of the system. Later in this chapter we will look at specific operations decisions that Southwest has made to achieve this. The second company is Singapore Airlines, which has a strategy to compete on service. To support this strategy the airline offers free drinks, complimentary headsets, meals prepared by gourmet chefs, comfortable cabins, and even the biggest bed in business class, called the "spacebed." Both airlines began as regional carriers, and each has grown to be a highly successful major airline. Although they are in the same industry, their operations decisions are different because of their different business strategies.

▶ **Business strategy**
A long-range plan for a business.

▶ **Operations strategy**
A long-range plan for the operations function that specifies the design and use of resources to support the business strategy.

In today's highly competitive, Internet-based, and global marketplace, it is important for companies to have a clear plan for achieving their goals. In this chapter we discuss the role of operations strategy, its relationship to the business strategy, and ways in which the operations function can best support the business strategy. We conclude with a discussion of productivity, one measure of a company's competitiveness.

THE ROLE OF OPERATIONS STRATEGY

The role of operations strategy is to provide a plan for the operations function so that it can make the best use of its resources. Operations strategy specifies the policies and plans for using the organization's resources to support its long-term competitive strategy. Figure 2-1 shows this relationship.

Remember that the operations function is responsible for managing the resources needed to produce the company's goods and services. Operations strategy is the plan that specifies the design and use of resources to support the business strategy. This includes the location, size, and type of facilities available; worker skills and talents required; use of technology, special processes needed, special equipment; and quality control methods. The operations strategy must be aligned with the company's business strategy and enable the company to achieve its long-term plan. For example, the business strategy of FedEx, the world's largest provider of expedited delivery services, is to compete on time and dependability of deliveries. The operations strategy of FedEx developed a plan for resources to support its business strategy. To provide speed of delivery, FedEx acquired its own fleet of airplanes. To provide dependability of deliveries, FedEx invested in a sophisticated bar code technology to track all packages.

The Importance of Operations Strategy

Operations strategy did not come to the forefront until the 1970s. Up to that time, U.S. companies emphasized mass production of standard product designs. There were no serious international competitors, and U.S. companies could pretty much sell anything

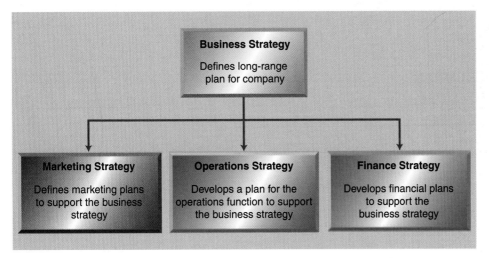

FIGURE 2-1

Relationship between the business strategy and the functional strategies

they produced. However, that changed in the 1970s and 1980s. Japanese companies began offering products of superior quality at lower cost, and U.S. companies lost market share to their Japanese counterparts. In an attempt to survive, many U.S. companies copied Japanese approaches. Unfortunately, merely copying these approaches often proved unsuccessful; it took time to really understand the Japanese approaches. It became clear that Japanese companies were more competitive because of their operations strategy; that is, all their resources were specifically designed to directly support the company's overall strategic plan.

Harvard Business School professor Michael Porter says that companies often do not understand the differences between *operational efficiency* and *strategy*. Operational efficiency is performing operations tasks well, even better than competitors. Strategy, on the other hand, is a plan for competing in the marketplace. An analogy might be that of running a race efficiently, but the wrong race. Strategy is defining in what race you will win. Operational efficiency and strategy must be aligned; otherwise, you may be *very efficiently performing the wrong task*. The role of operations strategy is to make sure that all the tasks performed by the operations function are the *right tasks*. Consider a software company that recently invested millions of dollars in developing software with features not provided by competitors, only to discover that these were features customers did not particularly want.

Now that we know the meaning of *business strategy* and *operations strategy* and their importance, let's look at how a company would go about developing a business strategy. Then we will see how an operations strategy would be developed to support the company's business strategy.

▶ DEVELOPING A BUSINESS STRATEGY

A company's business strategy is developed after its managers have considered many factors and have made some strategic decisions. These include developing an understanding of what business the company is in (the company's *mission*), analyzing and developing an understanding of the market (*environmental scanning*), and identifying the company's strengths (*core competencies*). These three factors are critical to the development of the company's long-range plan, or business strategy. In this section we describe each of these elements in detail and show how they are combined to formulate the business strategy.

Mission

▶ **Mission**
A statement defining *what* business an organization is in, *who* its customers are, and *how* its core beliefs shape its business.

Every organization, from IBM to the Boy Scouts, has a mission. The **mission** is a statement that answers three overriding questions:

- *What* business will the company be in ("selling personal computers," "operating an Italian restaurant")?
- *Who* will the customers be, and what are the expected customer attributes ("homeowners," "college graduates")?
- *How* will the company's basic beliefs define the business ("gives the highest customer service," "stresses family values")?

Following is a list of some well-known companies and parts of their mission statements:

Dell Computer Corporation: "to be the most successful computer company in the world"

Delta Air Lines: "worldwide airlines choice"

IBM: "translate advanced technologies into values for our customers as the world's largest information service company"

Lowe's: "helping customers build, improve and enjoy their homes"

Ryder: "offers a wide array of logistics services, such as distribution management, domestically and globally"

The mission defines the company. In order to develop a long-term plan for a business, you must first know exactly what business you are in, what customers you are serving, and what your company's values are. If a company does not have a well-defined mission, it may pursue business opportunities about which it has no real knowledge or that are in conflict with its current pursuits, or it may miss opportunities altogether.

For example, Dell Computer Corporation has become a leader in the computer industry in part by following its mission. If it did not follow its mission, Dell might decide to pursue other opportunities, such as producing mobile telephones similar to those manufactured by Motorola and Nokia. Although there is a huge market for mobile telephones, it is not consistent with Dell's mission of focusing on computers.

Environmental Scanning

A second factor to consider is the external environment of the business. This includes trends in the market, in the economic and political environment, and in society. These trends must be analyzed to determine business opportunities and threats. **Environmental scanning** is the process of monitoring the external environment. To remain competitive, companies have to continuously monitor their environment and be prepared to change their business strategy, or long-range plan, in light of environmental changes.

► **Environmental scanning**
Monitoring the external environment for changes and trends to determine business opportunities and threats.

What Does Environmental Scanning Tell Us? Environmental scanning allows a company to identify *opportunities* and *threats*. For example, through environmental scanning we could see gaps in what customers need and what competitors are doing to meet those needs. A study of these gaps could reveal an opportunity for our company, and we could design a plan to take advantage of it. On the other hand, our company may currently be a leader in its industry, but environmental scanning could reveal competitors that are meeting customer needs better—for example, by offering a wider array of services. In this case, environmental scanning would reveal a threat and we would have to change our strategy so as not to be left behind. Just because a company is an industry leader today does not mean it will continue to be a leader in the future. In the 1970s Sears, Roebuck and Company was a retail leader, but it fell behind the pack in the 1990s.

What Are Trends in the Environment? The external business environment is always changing. To stay ahead of the competition, a company must constantly look out for trends or changing patterns in the environment, such as *marketplace trends*. These might include changes in customer wants and expectations and ways in which competitors are meeting those expectations. For example, in the computer industry customers are demanding speed of delivery, high quality, and low price. Dell has become a leader in the industry because of its speed of delivery and low price. Other computer giants, such as Compaq, have had to redesign their business and operations strategies to compete with Dell. Otherwise, they would be left behind. It is through environmental scanning that companies like Compaq can see trends in the market, analyze the competition, and recognize what they need to do to remain competitive.

There are many other types of trends in the marketplace. For example, we are seeing changes in the use of technology, such as point-of-sale scanners, automation, computer-assisted processing, electronic purchasing, and electronic order tracking. One rapidly growing trend is e-commerce. For retailers like The Gap, Eddie Bauer, Fruit of the Loom, Inc., Barnes & Noble, and others, e-commerce has become a significant part of their business. Victoria's Secret has even used the Internet to conduct a fashion show in order to boost sales. Some companies began using e-commerce early in its development. Others, like Sears, Roebuck, waited and then found themselves working hard to catch up to the competition.

In addition to market trends, environmental scanning looks at economic, political, and social trends that can affect the business. *Economic trends* include recession, inflation, interest rates, and general economic conditions. Suppose that a company is considering obtaining a loan in order to purchase a new facility. Environmental scanning could show that interest rates are particularly favorable and that this may be a good time to go ahead with the purchase.

Political trends include changes in the political climate—local, national, and international—that could affect a company. For example, the creation of the European Union has had a significant impact on strategic planning for such global companies as IBM, Hewlett-Packard, and PepsiCo. Similarly, changes in trade relations with China have opened opportunities that were not available earlier. There has been a change in how companies view their environment, a shift from a national to a global perspective. Companies seek customers and suppliers all over the globe. Many have changed their strategies in order to take advantage of global opportunities, such as forming partnerships with international firms, called *strategic alliances*. For example,

Pepsi seeks customers and suppliers all over the globe.

©AP/Wide Photos

companies like Motorola and Xerox want to take advantage of opportunities in China and are developing strategic alliances to help them break into that market.

Finally, *social trends* are changes in society that can have an impact on a business. An example is the awareness of the dangers of smoking, which has made smoking less socially acceptable. This trend has had a huge impact on the tobacco industry. In order to survive, many of these companies have changed their strategy to focus on customers overseas, where smoking is still socially acceptable, or have diversified into other product lines.

Core Competencies

The third factor that helps define a business strategy is an understanding of the company's strengths. These are called **core competencies**. In order to formulate a long-term plan, the company's managers must know the competencies of their organization. Core competencies could include special skills of workers, such as expertise in providing customized services or knowledge of information technology. Another example might be flexible facilities that can handle the production of a wide array of products. To be successful, a company must compete in markets where its core competencies will have value. Table 2-1 shows a list of some core competencies that companies may have.

Highly successful firms develop a business strategy that takes advantage of their core competencies or strengths. To see why it is important to use core competencies, think of a student developing plans for a successful professional career. Let's say that this student is particularly good at mathematics but not as good in verbal communication and persuasion. Taking advantage of core competencies would mean developing a career strategy in which the student's strengths could provide an advantage, such as engineering or computer science. On the other hand, pursuing a career in marketing would place the student at a disadvantage because of a relative lack of skills in persuasion.

Increased global competition has driven many companies to clearly identify their core competencies and outsource those activities considered noncore. Recall from

▶ **Core competencies**
The unique strengths of a business.

1. **Workforce**	Highly trained Responsive in meeting customer needs Flexible in performing a variety of tasks Strong technical capability Creative in product design
2. **Facilities**	Flexible in producing a variety of products Technologically advanced An efficient distribution system
3. **Market Understanding**	Skilled in understanding customer wants and predicting market trends
4. **Financial Know-how**	Skilled in attracting and raising capital
5. **Technology**	Use of latest production technology Use of information technology Quality control techniques

TABLE 2-1

Organizational Core Competencies

FIGURE 2-2

Three inputs in
developing a business
strategy

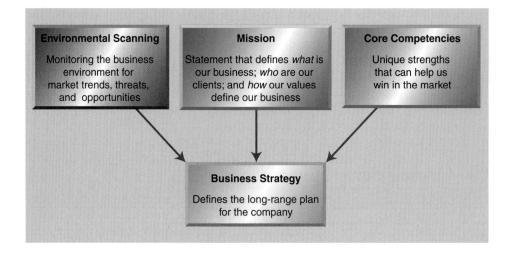

Chapter 1 that outsourcing is obtaining goods or services from an outside provider. By outsourcing noncore activities, a company can focus on its core competencies. For example, Meijer, a grocery and general merchandise retailer, outsources the transportation of all its merchandise to a company called Total Logistics Control (TLC). TLC is responsible for all deliveries, route scheduling, and all activities involved in maintaining a fleet of trucks, allowing Meijer to focus on its core competencies.

Putting It Together

Figure 2-2 shows how the mission, environmental scanning, and core competencies help in the formulation of the business strategy. This is an ongoing process that is constantly allowed to change. As environmental scanning reveals changes in the external environment, the company may need to change its business strategy to remain competitive while taking advantage of its core competencies and staying within its mission.

LINKS TO PRACTICE

**Dell Computer
Corporation**
www.dell.com

Let's look at how Dell Computer Corporation combined its mission, environmental scanning, and core competencies to develop a highly successful business strategy. Dell's mission is to "be the most successful computer company in the world at delivering the best customer experience in markets we serve. In doing so, Dell will meet customer expectations of: highest quality, leading technology, competitive pricing, individual and company accountability, best-in-class service and support, flexible customization capability, superior corporate citizenship, and financial stability." The mission defined what business Dell is in: highest quality, leading technology, computer company. It also defined Dell's customers: focus on markets served. Finally, it defined how Dell would do this: through competitive pricing, best-in-class service and support, and flexible customization capability. You can see how this mission defines Dell as a company.

An environmental scan revealed that competing computer manufacturers, such as IBM and Compaq, used intermediate resellers to sell computers. This led to higher inventory, higher costs, and slower responsiveness to customer wants. Michael Dell's idea was to sell directly to the customer and be able to put together exactly the system the customer wanted within a short time. Dell defined its core competencies as flexible manufacturing and the latest technological offering. Together, the mission, environmental scan, and core competencies were used to develop a competitive business strategy that provides customized computer solutions to customers within 36 hours at a highly competitive price.

Dell's business strategy was to take advantage of an opportunity in the market. However, to implement this strategy, the company needed to develop an operations strategy that arranged all the resources in ways that would support the business strategy. Operations strategy designs a plan for resources in order to take the business strategy from concept to reality. In the next section we look at how an operations strategy is developed.

Before You Go On

Make sure that you understand the role of the *business strategy* in defining a company's long-term plan. Without a business strategy the company would have no overriding plan. Such a plan acts like a compass, pointing the company in the right direction. To be effective, a long-range plan must be supported by each of the business functions. The *operations strategy* looks at the business strategy and develops a long-range plan specifically for the operations function. In the next section we will see how the operations strategy is developed.

DEVELOPING AN OPERATIONS STRATEGY

Once a business strategy has been developed, an operations strategy must be formulated. This will provide a plan for the design and management of the operations function in ways that support the business strategy. The operations strategy relates the business strategy to the operations function. The operations strategy focuses on specific capabilities of the operation that give the company a competitive edge. These capabilities are called **competitive priorities**. By excelling in one of these capabilities, a company can become a winner in its market. These competitive priorities and their relationship to the design of the operations function are shown in Figure 2-3. Each part of this figure is discussed next.

▶ **Competitive priorities**
Capabilities that the operations function can develop in order to give a company a competitive advantage in its market.

Competitive Priorities

Operations managers must work closely with marketing in order to understand the competitive situation in the company's market before they can determine which competitive priorities are important. There are four broad categories of competitive priorities:

1. Cost Competing based on **cost** means offering a product at a low price relative to the prices of competing products. The need for this type of competition emerges from the business strategy. The role of the operations strategy is to develop a plan for the use of resources to support this type of competition. Note that a low-cost strategy can result in a higher profit margin, even at a competitive price. Also, low cost does not imply low quality. Let's look at some specific characteristics of the operations function we might find in a company competing on cost.

▶ **Cost**
A competitive priority focusing on low cost.

FIGURE 2-3

Operations strategy and the design of the operations function

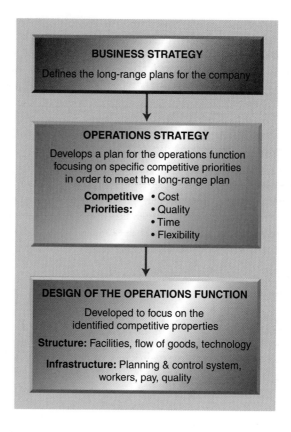

To develop this competitive priority, the operations function must focus primarily on cutting costs in the system, such as costs of labor, materials, and facilities. Companies that compete based on cost study their operations system carefully to eliminate all waste. They might offer extra training to employees to maximize their productivity and minimize scrap. Also, they might invest in automation in order to increase productivity. Generally, companies that compete based on cost offer a narrow range of products and product features, allow for little customization, and have an operations process that is designed to be as efficient as possible.

LINKS TO PRACTICE

Southwest Airlines Company
www.southwest.com

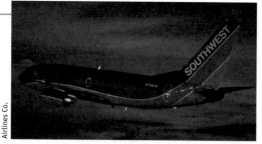

Courtesy Southwest Airlines Co.

A company that successfully competes on cost is Southwest Airlines. Southwest's entire operations function is designed to support this strategy. Facilities are streamlined: only one type of aircraft is used, and flight routes are generally short. This serves to minimize costs of scheduling crew changes, maintenance, inventories of parts, and many administrative costs. Unnecessary costs are completely eliminated: there are no meals, printed boarding passes, or seat assignments. Employees are trained to perform many functions and use a team approach to maximize customer service. Because of this strategy, Southwest has been a model for the airline industry for a number of years.

2. Quality Many companies claim that **quality** is their top priority, and many customers say that they look for quality in the products they buy. Yet quality has a subjective meaning; it depends on who is defining it. For example, to one person quality could mean that the product lasts a long time, such as with a Volvo, a car known for its longevity. To another person quality might mean high performance, such as a BMW. When companies focus on quality as a competitive priority, they are focusing on the dimensions of quality that are considered important by their customers.

Quality as a competitive priority has two dimensions. The first is *high-performance design*. This means that the operations function will be designed to focus on aspects of quality such as superior features, close tolerances, high durability, and excellent customer service. The second dimension is *goods and services consistency*, which measures how often the goods or services meet the exact design specifications. A strong example of product consistency is McDonald's, where we know we can get the same product every time at any location. Companies that compete on quality must deliver not only high-performance design but goods and services consistency as well.

A company that competes on this dimension needs to implement quality in every area of the organization. One of the first aspects that needs to be addressed is *product design quality*, which involves making sure the product meets the requirements of the customer. A second aspect is *process quality*, which deals with designing a process to produce error-free products. This includes focusing on equipment, workers, materials, and every other aspect of the operation to make sure it works the way it is supposed to. Companies that compete based on quality have to address both of these issues: the product must be designed to meet customer needs, and the process must produce the product exactly as it is designed.

To see why product and process quality are both important, let's say that your favorite fast-food restaurant has designed a new sandwich called the "Big Yuck." The restaurant could design a process that produces a perfect "Big Yuck" every single time. But if customers find the "Big Yuck" unappealing, they will not buy it. The same would be true if the restaurant designed a sandwich called the "Super Delicious" to meet the desires of its customers. Even if the "Super Delicious" were exactly what the customers wanted, if the process did not produce the sandwich the way it was designed, often making it soggy and cold instead, customers would not buy it. Remember that the product needs to be designed to meet customer wants and needs, and the process needs to be designed to produce the exact product that was intended, consistently without error.

3. Time **Time** or speed is one of the most important competitive priorities today. Companies in all industries are competing to deliver high-quality products in as short a time as possible. Companies like FedEx, LensCrafters, United Parcel Service (UPS), and Dell compete based on time. Today's customers don't want to wait, and companies that can meet their need for fast service are becoming leaders in their industries.

Making time a competitive priority means competing based on all time-related issues, such as *rapid delivery* and *on-time delivery*. Rapid delivery refers to how quickly an order is received; on-time delivery refers to how often deliveries are made on time. Another time-competitive priority is development speed, which is the time needed to take an idea to the marketplace. This is especially critical in technology and computer software fields. When time is a competitive priority, the job of the operations function is to critically analyze the system and combine or eliminate processes in order to save time. Often companies use technology to speed up processes, rely on a flexible workforce to meet peak demand periods, and eliminate unnecessary steps in the production process.

▶ **Quality**
A competitive priority focusing on the quality of goods and services.

▶ **Time**
A competitive priority focusing on speed and on-time delivery.

LINKS TO PRACTICE

FedEx Corporation
www.federalexpress.com

©AP/Wide World Photos.

FedEx is an example of a company that competes based on time. The company's claim is to "absolutely, positively" deliver packages on time. To support this strategy, the operation function had to be designed to promote speed. Bar code technology is used to speed up processing and handling, and the company uses its own fleet of airplanes. FedEx relies on a very flexible part-time workforce, such as college students who are willing to work a few hours at night. FedEx can call on this part-time workforce at a moment's notice, providing the company with a great deal of flexibility. This allows FedEx to cover workforce requirements during peak periods without having to schedule full-time workers.

4. Flexibility As a company's environment changes rapidly, including customer needs and expectations, the ability to readily accommodate these changes can be a winning strategy. This is **flexibility**. There are two dimensions of flexibility. One is the ability to offer a wide variety of goods or services and customize them to the unique needs of clients. This is called *product flexibility*. A flexible system can quickly add new products that may be important to customers or easily drop a product that is not doing well. Another aspect of flexibility is the ability to rapidly increase or decrease the amount produced in order to accommodate changes in the demand. This is called *volume flexibility*.

▶ **Flexibility**
A competitive priority focusing on offering a wide variety of goods or services.

You can see the meaning of flexibility when you compare ordering a suit from a custom tailor to buying it off the rack at a retailer. Another example would be going to a fine restaurant and asking to have a meal made just for you, versus going to a fast-food restaurant and being limited to items on the menu. The custom tailor and the fine restaurant are examples of companies that are flexible and will accommodate customer wishes. Another example of flexibility is Empire West Inc., a company that makes a variety of products out of plastics, depending on what customers want. Empire West makes everything from plastic trays to body guards for cars.

Companies that compete based on flexibility often cannot compete based on speed, because it generally requires more time to produce a customized product. Also, flexible companies typically do not compete based on cost, because it may take more resources to customize the product. However, flexible companies often offer greater customer service and can meet unique customer requirements. To carry out this strategy, flexible companies tend to have more general-purpose equipment that can be used to make many different kinds of products. Also, workers in flexible companies tend to have higher skill levels and can often perform many different tasks in order to meet customer needs.

The Need for Trade-Offs

You may be wondering why the operations function needs to give special focus to some priorities but not all. Aren't all the priorities important? As more resources are dedicated toward one priority, fewer resources are left for others. The operations function must place emphasis on those priorities that directly support the business strategy. Therefore, it needs to make **trade-offs** between the different priorities. For example, consider a company that competes on using the highest-quality component parts in its products. Due to the high quality of parts, the company may not be able to offer the final product at the lowest price. In this case, the company has made a trade-off between quality and price. Similarly, a company that competes on making each product individually based on customer specifications will likely not be able to compete on speed. Here, the trade-off has been made between flexibility and speed.

> ▶ **Trade-off**
> The need to focus more on one competitive priority than on others.

It is important to know that every business must achieve a basic level of each of the priorities, even though its primary focus is only on some. For example, even though a company is not competing on low price, it still cannot offer its products at such a high price that customers would not want to pay for them. Similarly, even though a company is not competing on time, it still has to produce its product within a reasonable amount of time; otherwise, customers will not be willing to wait for it.

One way that large facilities with multiple products can address the issue of trade-offs is using the concept of plant-within-a-plant (PWP), introduced by well-known Harvard professor Wickham Skinner. The PWP concept suggests that different areas of a facility be dedicated to different products with different competitive priorities. These areas should be physically separated from one another and should even have their own separate workforce. As the term suggests, there are multiple plants within one plant, allowing a company to produce different products that compete on different priorities. For example, hospitals use PWP to achieve specialization or focus in a particular area, such as the cardiac unit, oncology, radiology, surgery, or pharmacy. Similarly, department stores use PWP to isolate departments, such as the Sears auto service department versus its optometry center.

Order Winners and Qualifiers

To help a company decide which competitive priorities to focus on, it is important to distinguish between *order winners* and *order qualifiers*, which are concepts developed by Terry Hill, a professor at Oxford University. **Order qualifiers** are those competitive priorities that a company has to meet if it wants to do business in a particular market. **Order winners**, on the other hand, are the competitive priorities that help a company win orders in the market. Consider a simple restaurant that makes and delivers pizzas. Order qualifiers might be low price (say, less than $10.00) and quick delivery (say, under 15 minutes), because this is a standard that has been set by competing pizza restaurants. The order winners may be "fresh ingredients" and "home-made taste." These characteristics may differentiate the restaurant from all the other pizza restaurants. However, regardless of how good the pizza, the restaurant will not succeed if it does not meet the minimum standard for order qualifiers. Knowing the order winners and order qualifiers in a particular market is critical to focusing on the right competitive priorities.

> ▶ **Order qualifiers**
> Competitive priorities that must be met for a company to qualify as a competitor in the marketplace.
>
> ▶ **Order winners**
> Competitive priorities that win orders in the marketplace.

It is important to understand that order winners and order qualifiers change over time. Often when one company in a market is successfully competing using a particular order winner, other companies follow suit over time. The result is that the order winner becomes an industry standard, or an order qualifier. To compete successfully, companies then have to change their order winners to differentiate themselves. An excellent example of this occurred in the auto industry. Prior to the 1970s, the order-winning criterion in the American auto industry was price. Then the Japanese automobile manufacturers entered the market competing on quality at a reasonable price. The result was that quality became the new order winner and price became an order qualifier, or an expectation. Then by the 1980s American manufacturers were able to raise their level of quality to be competitive with the Japanese. Quality then became an order qualifier, as everyone had the same quality standard.

Translating Competitive Priorities into Production Requirements

Operations strategy makes the needs of the business strategy specific to the operations function by focusing on the right competitive priorities. Once the competitive priorities have been identified, a plan is developed to support those priorities. The operations strategy will specify the design and use of the organization's resources; that is, it will set forth specific operations requirements. These can be broken down into two categories.

▶ **Structure**
Operations decisions related to the design of the production process, such as facilities, technology, and the flow of goods and services through the facility.

▶ **Infrastructure**
Operations decisions related to the planning and control systems of the operation, such as organization of operations, the skills and pay of workers, and quality measures.

1. **Structure**—Operations decisions related to the design of the production process, such as characteristics of facilities used, selection of appropriate technology, and the flow of goods and services through the facility.
2. **Infrastructure**—Operations decisions related to the planning and control systems of the operation, such as the organization of the operations function, the skills and pay of workers, and quality control approaches.

Together, the structure and infrastructure of the production process determine the nature of the company's operations function.

The structure and infrastructure of the production process must be aligned to enable the company to pursue its long-term plan. Suppose we determined that *time* or *speed* of delivery is the order winner in the marketplace and the competitive priority we need to focus on. We would then design the production process to promote speedy product delivery. This might mean having a system that does not necessarily produce the product at the absolutely lowest cost, possibly because we need costlier or extra equipment to help us focus on speed. The important thing is that every aspect of production of a product or delivery of a service needs to focus on supporting the competitive priority. However, we cannot neglect the other competitive priorities. A certain level of order qualifiers must be achieved just to remain in the market. The issue is not one of focusing on one priority to the exclusion of the others. Rather, it is a matter of degree.

Let's return to the example of Dell Computer Corporation. Earlier we explained how Dell used its mission, environmental scanning, and core competencies to develop its business strategy. But to make this business plan a reality, the company needed to develop an operations strategy to create its structure and infrastructure. The focus was on customer service, cost, and speed. Dell set up a system in which customers could order computers directly from the company, without going through an intermediary, such as a retailer. An operations system was designed so that ordering of components and assembly of computers did not occur until an order was actually placed. This kept costs low because Dell did not have computers sitting in inventory. A warehousing system was designed so that when components were needed, suppliers would deliver them to the plant within fifteen minutes; in contrast, competitors like IBM and Compaq must wait hours or even days to receive needed components. To further increase speed, Dell set up a shipping arrangement with United Parcel Service (UPS). With this structure and infrastructure, Dell was able to implement its business plan.

Before You Go On

By now you should have a clear understanding of how an operations strategy is developed and its role in helping the organization decide which competitive priorities to focus on. There are four categories of competitive priorities: *cost, quality, time,* and *flexibility.* A company must make trade-offs in deciding which priorities to focus on. The operations strategy and the competitive priorities dictate the design and plan for the operations function, which includes the structure and infrastructure of the operation. This is a dynamic process, and as the environment changes, the organization must be prepared to change accordingly. Operations strategy plays a key role in an organization's ability to compete. In the next section we discuss a way to measure a company's competitive capability.

STRATEGIC ROLE OF TECHNOLOGY

Over the last decade we have seen an unprecedented growth in technological capability. Technology has enabled companies to share real-time information across the globe, to improve the speed and quality of their processes, and to design products in innovative ways. Companies can use technology to help them gain an advantage over their competitors. For this reason technology has become a critical factor for companies in achieving a competitive advantage. In fact, studies have shown that companies that invest in new technologies tend to improve their financial position over those that do not. However, the technologies a company acquires should not be decided on randomly, such as following the latest fad or industry trend. Rather, the selected technology needs to support the organization's competitive priorities, as we learned in the example of FedEx. Also, technology needs to be selected to enhance the company's core competencies and add to its competitive advantage.

Research in Motion Limited.
All Rights Reserved.

Types of Technologies

There are three primary types of technologies. They are differentiated based upon their application, but all three areas of technology are important to operations managers. The first type is *product technology*, which is any new technology developed by a firm. An example of this would include Teflon®, the material used in no-stick fry pans. Teflon became an emerging technology in the 1970s and is currently used in numerous applications. Other examples include CDs and flat-screened monitors. Product technology is important as companies must regularly update their processes to produce the latest types of products.

A second type of technology is *process technology*. It is the technology used to improve the process of creating goods and services. Examples of this would include computer-aided design (CAD) and computer-aided manufacturing (CAM). These are technologies that use computers to assist engineers in the way they design and manufacture products. Process technologies are important to companies, as they enable tasks to be accomplished more efficiently. We will learn more about these technologies in Chapter 3.

The last type of technology is *information technology*, which enables communication, processing, and storage of information. Information technology has grown rapidly over recent years and has had a profound impact on business. Just consider the changes that have occurred due to the Internet. The Internet has enabled electronic commerce and the creation of the virtual marketplace and has linked customers and buyers. Another example of information technology is enterprise resource planning (ERP), which functions via large software programs used for planning and coordinating all resources throughout the entire enterprise. ERP systems have enabled companies to reduce costs and improve responsiveness but are highly expensive to purchase and implement. Consequently, as with any technology, investment in ERP needs to be a strategic decision.

Technology as a Tool for Competitive Advantage

Technology can be acquired to improve processes and maintain up-to-date standards. Technology can also be used to gain a competitive advantage. For example, by acquiring technology a company can improve quality, reduce costs, and improve product delivery. This can provide an advantage over the competition and help gain market share. However, investing in technology can be costly and entails risks, such as overestimating the benefits of the technology or incurring the risk of obsolescence due to rapid new inventions.

Technology should be acquired to support the company's chosen competitive priorities, not just to follow the latest market fad. Also, technology may require the company to rethink its strategy. For example, when the Internet became available it was generally assumed that it would replace traditional ways of doing business. This has not turned out to be the case. In fact, for many companies the Internet has enhanced traditional methods. Physical activities such as shipping, warehousing, transportation, and even physical contact must still be performed. For example, pharmacy chains such as Walgreens and CVS have found that although customers place orders over the Internet, they prefer to pick them up in person. Similarly, the airlines have discovered that an easy-to-use Web site can increase airline bookings. However, successful use of a technology such as the Internet requires companies to develop strategies that integrate the technology. As you can see, acquiring technology is an important strategic decision for companies. Operations managers must consider many factors when making a purchase decision.

PRODUCTIVITY

Sound business strategy and supporting operations strategy make an organization more competitive in the marketplace. But how does a company measure its competitiveness? One of the most common ways is by measuring productivity. In this section we will look at how to measure the productivity of each of a company's resources as well as the entire organization.

Measuring Productivity

▶ **Productivity**
A measure of how efficiently an organization converts inputs into outputs.

Recall that operations management is responsible for managing the transformation of many inputs into outputs, such as goods or services. A measure of how efficiently inputs are being converted into outputs is called **productivity**. Productivity measures how well resources are used. It is computed as a ratio of outputs (goods and services) to inputs (e.g., labor and materials). The more efficiently a company uses its resources, the more productive it is:

$$\text{Productivity} = \frac{\text{output}}{\text{input}} \qquad (2\text{-}1)$$

This equation can be used to measure the productivity of one worker or many, as well as the productivity of a machine, a department, the whole firm, or even a nation. The possibilities are shown in Table 2-2.

TABLE 2-2

Productivity Measures

Total Productivity Measure	$\dfrac{\text{Output produced}}{\text{All inputs used}}$
Partial Productivity Measure	$\dfrac{\text{Output}}{\text{Labor}}$ or $\dfrac{\text{Output}}{\text{Machines}}$ or
	$\dfrac{\text{Output}}{\text{Materials}}$ or $\dfrac{\text{Output}}{\text{Capital}}$
Multifactor Productivity Measure	$\dfrac{\text{Output}}{\text{Labor + machines}}$ or
	$\dfrac{\text{Output}}{\text{Labor + materials}}$ or
	$\dfrac{\text{Output}}{\text{Labor + capital + energy}}$

When we compute productivity for all inputs combined, such as labor, machines, and capital, we are measuring **total productivity**. For example, let's say that the weekly dollar value of a company's output, such as finished goods and work in progress, is $10,200 and that the value of its inputs, such as labor, materials, and capital, is $8600. The company's total weekly productivity would be computed as follows:

▶ **Total productivity**
Productivity computed as a ratio of output to all organizational inputs.

$$\text{Total productivity} = \frac{\text{output}}{\text{input}} = \frac{\$10,200}{\$8600} = 1.186$$

Often it is much more useful to measure the productivity of one input variable at a time in order to identify how efficiently each is being used. When we compute productivity as the ratio of output relative to a single input, we obtain a measure of **partial productivity**, also called single-factor productivity. Following are two examples of the calculation of partial productivity:

▶ **Partial productivity**
Productivity computed as a ratio of output to only one input (e.g., labor, materials, machines).

1. A bakery oven produces 346 pastries in four hours. What is its productivity?

$$\text{Machine productivity} = \text{number of pastries/oven time}$$

$$= \frac{346 \text{ pastries}}{4 \text{ hours}} = 86.5 \text{ pastries/hour}$$

2. Two workers paint tables in a furniture shop. If the workers paint 22 tables in 8 hours, what is their productivity?

$$\text{Labor productivity} = \frac{22 \text{ tables}}{2 \text{ workers} \times 8 \text{ hours}} = 1.375 \text{ tables/hour}$$

Examples of select partial productivity measures are shown in Table 2-3.

Sometimes we need to compute productivity as the ratio of output relative to a group of inputs, such as labor and materials. This is a measure of **multifactor productivity**. For example, let's say that output is worth $382 and labor and materials costs are $168 and $98, respectively. A multifactor productivity measure of our use of labor and materials would be

▶ **Multifactor productivity**
Productivity computed as a ratio of output to several, but not all, inputs.

$$\text{Multifactor productivity} = \frac{\text{output}}{\text{labor + materials}}$$

$$= \frac{\$382}{\$168 + \$98} = 1.436$$

EXAMPLE 2.1

Computing Productivity

Long Beach Bank employs three loan officers, each working eight hours per day. Each officer processes an average of five loans per day. The bank's payroll cost for the officers is $820 per day and there is a daily overhead expense of $500. The bank has just purchased new computer software that should enable each officer to process eight loans per day, although the overhead expense will increase to $550. Evaluate the change in labor and multifactor productivity before and after implementation of the new computer software.

- **Before You Begin:** When solving productivity problems, make sure that the value of outputs and inputs is computed over the same time period, such as day, week, month, or year. Also, when evaluating a *change* in productivity, compute the productivity before and after the expected change and calculate the percentage difference.

- **Solution:**

$$\text{Labor productivity (old)} = \frac{3 \text{ officers} \times 5 \text{ loans/day}}{24 \text{ labor-hours}} = \frac{15 \text{ loans/day}}{24 \text{ labor-hours}}$$

$$= 0.625 \text{ loans per labor-hour}$$

$$\text{Labor productivity (new)} = \frac{3 \text{ officers} \times 8 \text{ loans/day}}{24 \text{ labor-hours}} = \frac{24 \text{ loans/day}}{24 \text{ labor-hours}}$$

$$= 1.00 \text{ loan per labor-hour}$$

$$\text{Multifactor productivity (old)} = \frac{15 \text{ loans/day}}{\$820/\text{day} + \$500/\text{day}} = 0.0113 \text{ loans/dollar}$$

$$\text{Multifactor productivity (new)} = \frac{24 \text{ loans/day}}{\$820/\text{day} + \$550/\text{day}} = 0.0175 \text{ loans/dollar}$$

The change in labor productivity is from 0.625 to 1.00 loans per labor-hour. This results in an increase of 1.00/0.625 = 1.6, or an increase of 60 percent. The change in multifactor productivity is from 0.0113 to 0.0175 loans per dollar. This results in an increase of 0.0175/0.0113 = 1.55, or an increase of 55 percent.

TABLE 2-3

Examples of Partial Productivity Measures

Business Type	Productivity Measure
Restaurant	$\dfrac{\text{Customers served}}{\text{Labor-hour}}$ or $\dfrac{\text{Customers served}}{\text{Square foot}}$
Hospital	$\dfrac{\text{Patients}}{\text{hospital bed}}$ or $\dfrac{\text{Patients}}{\text{Nurse-hour}}$
Amusement park	$\dfrac{\text{Visitors}}{\text{Square foot}}$ or $\dfrac{\text{Visitors}}{\text{Attraction}}$
Cattle ranch	$\dfrac{\text{Cattle}}{\text{Pound of feed}}$ or $\dfrac{\text{Cattle}}{\text{Acre of land}}$
Garment manufacturer	$\dfrac{\text{Sweaters}}{\text{Pound of yarn}}$ or $\dfrac{\text{Sweaters}}{\text{Machine-hour}}$

Interpreting Productivity Measures

To interpret the meaning of a productivity measure, it must be compared with a similar productivity measure. For example, if one worker at a pizza shop produces 17 pizzas in two hours, the productivity of that worker is 8.5 pizzas per hour. This number by itself does not tell us very much. However, if we compare it to the productivity of two other workers, one who produces 7.2 pizzas per hour and another 6.8 pizzas per hour, it is much more meaningful. We can see that the first worker is much more productive than the other two workers. But how do we know whether the productivity of all three workers is reasonable? What we need is a standard. In Chapter 11 we will discuss ways to set standards and how those standards can help in evaluating the performance of our workers.

It is also helpful to measure and compare productivity over time. Let's say that we want to measure the total productivity of our three pizza makers (our "labor") and we compute a labor productivity measure of 7.5 pizzas per hour. This number does not tell us much about the workers' performance. However, if we compare weekly productivity measures over time, perhaps over the last four weeks, we get much more information:

Week	1	2	3	4
Productivity (pizzas/labor hour)	5.4	6.8	7.1	7.5

Now we see that the workers' productivity is improving over time. In fact, productivity changed from 5.4 to 7.5 pizzas per labor-hour, resulting in an increase of 7.5/5.4 = 1.39, or an increase of 39 percent. But what if we find out that our main competitor, a pizzeria down the street, has a productivity of 9.5 pizzas per labor-hour? This productivity rate is 26.7 percent (9.5/7.5 = 1.267) higher than our productivity in week 4. Suddenly we know that even though our productivity is going up, it should be higher. We may have to analyze our processes and increase our productivity in order to be competitive. By comparing our productivity over time and against similar operations, we have a much better sense of how high our productivity really is.

When evaluating productivity and setting standards for performance, we also need to consider our strategy for competing in the marketplace—namely, our competitive priorities. A company that competes based on speed would probably measure productivity in units produced over time. However, a company that competes based on cost might measure productivity in terms of costs of inputs such as labor, materials, and overhead. The important thing is that our productivity measure provides information on how we are doing relative to the competitive priority that is most important to us.

Productivity and Competitiveness

Productivity is essentially a scorecard of how efficiently resources are used and a measure of competitiveness. Productivity is measured on many levels and is of interest to a wide range of people. As we showed in earlier examples, productivity can be measured for individuals, departments, or organizations. It can track performance over time and help managers identify problems. Similarly, productivity can be measured for an entire industry and even a country.

The economic success of a nation and the quality of life of its citizens are related to its competitiveness in the global marketplace. Increases in productivity are directly related to increases in a nation's standard of living. That is why business and government leaders continuously monitor the productivity at the national level and by industry sectors.

Productivity in the United States had been increasing for over 100 years. Then in the 1970s and 1980s productivity dropped, even lagging behind that of other industrial nations. Fortunately, productivity rebounded in the mid- and late 1990s. Today, companies understand the importance of competitiveness, and productivity in the United States continues to improve. Changes in U.S. productivity can be seen in Figure 2-4.

FIGURE 2-4

Percentage change in
U.S. business sector
productivity (output
per hour)

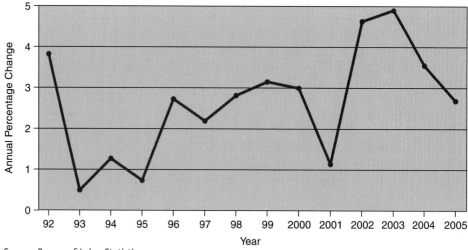

Source: *Bureau of Labor Statistics*

Productivity and the Service Sector

Service sector companies have a unique challenge when trying to measure productivity. The reason is that traditional productivity measures tend to focus on tangible outcomes, as seen with goods-producing activities. Services primarily produce intangible products, such as ideas and information, making it difficult to evaluate quality. Consequently, accurately measuring productivity improvements can be difficult. A good example of the difficulty in using traditional productivity measures in the service sector is the emergency room. Here inputs are the medical staff, yet outputs may not exist if no one needed treatment on that shift. In that case, using traditional measures, productivity would be zero! The real issue in this type of environment is the level of readiness, and the challenge is to adequately measure it.

As we discussed previously, employment in the service sector of the U.S. economy has grown rapidly over the past thirty years. Unfortunately, productivity gains in this sector have been much lower than those of manufacturing. It is hoped that advancements in information technology will help standardize services and accelerate productivity in this sector.

OPERATIONS STRATEGY WITHIN OM: HOW IT ALL FITS TOGETHER

We have learned that the strategic decisions of a firm drive its tactical decisions. Operations strategy decisions are critical in this process as they serve as a linkage between the business strategy and all the other operations decisions. Recall that operations strategy provides a plan for the OM function that supports the business strategy. In turn, decisions regarding operations strategy directly impact decisions on organizational structure and infrastructure of the company. This includes selection of the facilities (Chapter 10), type of process (Chapter 8), choice of technology (Chapter 3), quality control decisions (Chapters 5 and 6), skills and pay of workers (Chapter 11), and numerous other decisions. As in the example of Southwest Airlines, an operations strategy that focuses on cost competition would translate into specific operations decisions that eliminate all frills from the system.

In subsequent chapters of this book, we will study specific decisions that pertain to organizational structure and infrastructure. We will see that these decisions are governed by the firm's operations strategy. We will also learn how these specific decisions impact each other.

OPERATIONS STRATEGY ACROSS THE ORGANIZATION

The business strategy defines the long-range plan for the entire company and guides the actions of each of the company's business functions. Those functions, in turn, develop plans to support the business strategy. However, in defining their individual strategies, it is important for the functions to work together and understand each other's needs.

Marketing identifies target markets, studies competition, and communicates with customers. In developing its own strategy, marketing needs to fully understand the capabilities of the operations function, the types of resources being used, and the way those resources are utilized. Otherwise, marketing's strategy could entail making promises that operations cannot deliver. In turn, marketing needs to communicate to operations all its observed and anticipated market changes.

Finance develops financial plans to support the business strategy. However, since it is the operations function that manages all the organization's resources, the financial plans in effect support operations activities. Before it can develop its own strategy, finance needs to communicate with operations in order to understand the financial requirements of planned resources. In turn, operations managers cannot fully develop a strategy until they have a clear understanding of financial capabilities.

The strategies of all the business functions need to support each other in achieving the goals set by the business strategy and are best developed through a team approach.

SUPPLY CHAIN LINK

The operations strategy of a firm directly impacts decisions on its structure and infrastructure, including its supply chain. This includes the design of the supply chain, such as its length, and the relationships the firm has with its supply chain partners. Together, the operations strategy and the firm's supply chain must support the business strategy of the firm. This can be illustrated by the competitive priorities of the firm, which directly impact the type of supply chain a company has in place. For example, a company that competes on cost must have a highly efficient supply chain with high integration of the OM function between supply chain partners. The reason is that the supply chain plays a critical role in keeping both production and delivery costs down. Therefore, a firm competing on cost might structure its supply chain so that the least-expensive suppliers are used rather than those with the highest-quality supplies.

In contrast, a company that competes on quality will likely have a different supply chain. Competing on quality means that a company's products and services are known for their premium nature, such as product consistency and reliability. Many aspects of the supply chain are altered when companies compete on quality versus another competitive priority, such as cost. The company will likely source its components from suppliers known for quality who have implemented total quality management throughout their production process. The concept of quality will also be embedded in other aspects of the supply chain, such as transportation, delivery, and packaging.

An excellent example of aligning operations strategy with the supply chain is illustrated by Wal-Mart. Sam Walton, Wal-Mart's founder, was a strategic visionary who developed the low-cost retail strategy that is supported by its supply chain. Wal-Mart's supply chain is designed to not buy from distributors but directly from manufacturers in order to lower costs and offer a broad range of merchandise. In fact, Wal-Mart has had a legendary partnership with Procter & Gamble, where replenishment of inventories is done automatically. These supply chain actions were designed to help Wal-Mart meet its overall competitive strategy, which is to provide its customers with a wide product offering at a low price. This has helped Wal-Mart become the world's largest retailer.

Chapter Highlights

1 A business strategy is a long-range plan and vision for a business. Each of the individual business functions needs to support the business strategy.

2 An organization develops its business strategy by doing environmental scanning and considering its mission and its core competencies.

3 The role of operations strategy is to provide a long-range plan for the use of the company's resources in producing the company's primary goods and services.

4 The role of business strategy is to serve as an overall guide for the development of the organization's operations strategy.

5 The operations strategy focuses on developing specific capabilities called competitive priorities. In designing its operation, an organization is governed by the operations strategy and the specific competitive priorities it has chosen to develop.

6 There are four categories of competitive priorities: cost, quality, time, and flexibility.

7 Technology can be used by companies to gain a competitive advantage and should be acquired to support the company's chosen competitive priorities.

8 Productivity is a measure that indicates how efficiently an organization is using its resources.

9 Productivity is computed as the ratio of organizational outputs divided by inputs.

Key Terms

business strategy 28
operations strategy 28
mission 30
environmental scanning 31
core competencies 33
competitive priorities 35
cost 35

quality 37
time 37
flexibility 38
trade-off 39
order qualifiers 39
order winners 39
structure 40

infrastructure 40
productivity 42
total productivity 43
partial productivity 43
multifactor productivity 43

Formula Review

$$\text{Productivity} = \frac{\text{output}}{\text{input}}$$

Solved Problems (See student companion site for Excel template.)

• Problem 1

Bluegill Furniture is a small furniture shop that focuses on making kitchen chairs. The weekly dollar value of its output, including finished goods and work in progress, is $14,280. The value of inputs, such as labor, materials, and capital, is approximately $16,528. Compute the total productivity measure for Bluegill Furniture.

• Before You Begin:

In this problem you are being asked for the total productivity. Recall that it is simply the ratio of total output over input.

• Solution

$$\text{Total productivity} = \frac{\text{output}}{\text{input}} = \frac{\$14,280}{\$16,528} = 0.864$$

• Problem 2

Bluegill has just purchased a new sanding machine that processes seventeen chairs in eight hours. What is the productivity of the sanding machine?

• Before You Begin:

In this problem you are being asked for machine productivity, which is a partial productivity measure.

• Solution

$$\text{Machine productivity} = \frac{\text{number of chairs}}{\text{processing time}}$$

$$= \frac{17 \text{ chairs}}{8 \text{ hours}}$$

$$= 2.125 \text{ chairs/hour}$$

• Problem 3

Bluegill has hired two new workers to paint chairs. They have painted ten chairs in four hours. What is their labor productivity?

• Before You Begin:

Remember that you should compute the labor productivity of both workers combined.

• Solution

$$\text{Labor productivity} = \frac{10 \text{ chairs}}{2 \text{ workers} \times 4 \text{ hours}}$$

$$= 1.25 \text{ chairs/hour}$$

• Problem 4

On average, Bluegill produces thirty-five chairs per day. Labor costs average $480, material costs are typically $200, and overhead cost is $250. If Bluegill sells the chairs to a retailer for $70 each, determine the multifactor productivity.

• Before You Begin:

When computing multifactor productivity remember to compute the total value of the inputs before taking the ratio.

• Solution

$$\frac{\text{Multifactor}}{\text{productivity}} = \frac{\text{value of output}}{\text{labor costs} + \text{material cost} + \text{overhead}}$$

$$= \frac{35 \text{ chairs} \times \$70/\text{chair}}{\$480 + \$200 + \$250}$$

$$= \frac{\$2450}{\$930}$$

$$= \$2.63 \text{ of sales per dollar}$$

• Problem 5

Last week employees at Bluegill produced forty-six chairs after working a total of 200 hours. Of the forty-six chairs produced, twelve were damaged due to a problem with the new sanding machine. The damaged chairs can be discounted and sold for $25 each. The undamaged chairs are sold to a department store retail chain for $70 each. What was the labor productivity ratio for last week? If labor productivity was $15 in sales per hour the previous week, what was the change in labor productivity?

• Before You Begin:

To compute productivity you must include the total value of the output. Notice that in this problem there are different quantities of products that have different values (damaged and good chairs). You must compute the value of each type of chair and add them together to obtain the total value before taking the ratio.

• Solution

$$\text{Value to output} = (12 \text{ damaged chairs} \times \$25/\text{damaged chair})$$
$$+ (34 \text{ good chairs} \times \$70/\text{good chair})$$

$$= \$2680$$

Labor hours of input = 200 hours

$$\text{Labor productivity} = \frac{\text{value of output}}{\text{labor hours of input}}$$

$$\text{Labor productivity} = \frac{\$2680}{200 \text{ hours}}$$

$$= \$13.40 \text{ in sales per hour}$$

The change in labor productivity was from $15 to $13.40 in sales per hour, or a reduction of 10.67 percent.

Discussion Questions

1. Explain the importance of a business strategy.

2. Explain the role of operations strategy in a business.

3. Describe how a business strategy is developed.

4. Describe how an operations strategy is formulated from the business strategy.

5. Explain what is meant by the term *competitive priority* and describe the four categories of competitive priorities discussed in the chapter.

6. Find an example of a company that makes quality its competitive priority. Find another company that makes flexibility its competitive priority. Find another company that makes flexibility its competitive priority. Compare these strategies.

7. What is meant by the terms *order qualifiers* and *order winners?* Explain why they are important.

8. Describe the three types of technologies. Explain the strategic role of technology.

9. Describe the meaning of productivity. Why is it important?

10. Explain the three types of productivity measures.

Problems

1. Two workers have the job of placing plastic labels on packages before the packages are shipped out. The first worker can place 1000 labels in thirty minutes. The second worker can place 850 labels in twenty minutes. Which worker is more productive?

2. Last week a painter painted three houses in five days. This week she painted two houses in four days. In which week was the painter more productive?

3. One type of bread-making machine can make six loaves of bread in five hours. A new model of the machine can make four loaves in two hours. Which model is more productive?

4. A company that makes kitchen chairs wants to compare productivity at two of its facilities. At facility #1, six workers produced 240 chairs. At facility #2, four workers produced 210 chairs during the same time period. Which facility was more productive?

5. A painter is considering using a new high-tech paint roller. Yesterday he was able to paint three walls in forty-five minutes using his old method. Today he painted two walls of the same size in twenty minutes. Is the painter more productive using the new paint roller?

6. Aztec Furnishings makes hand-crafted furniture for sale in its retail stores. The furniture maker has recently installed a new assembly process, including a new sander and polisher. With this new system, production has increased to ninety pieces of furniture per day from the previous sixty pieces of furniture per day. The number of defective items produced has dropped from 10 pieces per day to 1 per day. The production facility operates strictly eight hours per day. Evaluate the change in productivity for Aztec using the new assembly process.

7. Howard Plastics produces plastic containers for use in the food packaging industry. Last year its average monthly production included 20,000 containers produced using one shift five days a week with an eight-hour-a-day operation. Of the items produced 15 percent were deemed defective. Recently, Howard Plastics has implemented new production methods and a new quality improvement program. Its monthly production has increased to 25,000 containers with 9 percent defective.

(a) Compute productivity ratios for the old and new production system.

(b) Compare the changes in productivity between the two production systems.

8. Med-Tech labs is a facility that provides medical tests and evaluations for patients, ranging from analyzing blood samples to performing magnetic resonance imaging (MRI). Average cost to patients is $60 per patient. Labor costs average $15 per patient, materials costs are $20 per patient, and overhead costs are averaged at $20 per patient.

(a) What is the *multifactor* productivity ratio for Med-Tech? What does your finding mean?

(b) If the average lab worker spends three hours for each patient, what is the *labor* productivity ratio?

9. Handy-Maid Cleaning Service operates five crews with three workers per crew. Different crews clean a different number of homes per week and spend a differing amount of hours. All the homes cleaned are about the same size. The manager of Handy-Maid is trying to evaluate the productivity of each of the crews. The following data have been collected over the past week.

Work Crew	Hours	Homes Cleaned
Anna, Sue, and Tim	35	10
Jim, Jose, and Andy	45	15
Dan, Wendy, and Carry	56	18
Rosie, Chandra, and Seth	30	10
Sherry, Vicky, and Roger	42	18

Assuming the quality of cleaning was consistent between crews, which crew was most productive?

CASE: Prime Bank of Massachusetts

Prime Bank of Massachusetts was started in 1964 with James Rogers as CEO, who is now chairman of the board. Prime Bank had been growing steadily since its beginning and has developed a loyal customer following. Today there are forty-five bank locations throughout Massachusetts, with corporate headquarters in Newbury, Massachusetts. The bank offers a wide array of banking services to commercial and noncommercial customers.

Prime Bank has considered itself to be a conservative, yet innovative, organization. Its locations are open Monday–Friday 9–4 and Saturday 9–12. Most of the facilities are located adjacent to well-established shopping centers, with multiple ATM machines and at least three drive-through windows. However, Prime Bank's growth has brought on certain problems. Having the right amount of tellers available in the bank as well as in the drive-through window has been a challenge. Some commercial customers had recently expressed frustration due to long waiting time. Also, the parking lot has often become crowded during peak periods.

While Prime Bank was going through a growth period, the general banking industry had been experiencing tougher competition. Competitors were increasingly offering lower interest rates on loans and higher yields on savings accounts and certificates of deposit. Also, Prime Bank was experiencing growing pains, and something needed to be done soon or it would begin losing customers to competition.

The board, headed by James Rogers, decided to develop a more aggressive strategy for Prime Bank. While many of its competitors were competing on *cost*, the board decided that Prime Bank should focus on *customer service* in order to differentiate itself from the competition. The bank had already begun moving in that direction by offering a twenty-four-hour customer service department to answer customers' banking questions. Yet, there were difficulties with this effort, such as poor staffing and not enough telephone lines. James Rogers wanted Prime Bank to aggressively solve all customer service issues, such as staffing, layout, and facilities. He also wanted greater creativity in adding improvements in customer service, such as on-line banking, and special services for large customers. He believed that improving most aspects of the bank's operation would give Prime Bank a competitive advantage.

The board presented their new strategy to Victoria Chen, vice president of operations. Victoria had recently been promoted to the V.P. level and understood the importance of operations management. She was asked to identify all changes that should be made in the operation function that would support this new strategy and present them at the next board meeting. Victoria had been hoping for an opportunity to prove herself since she began with the bank. This was her chance.

Case Questions

1. Why is the operations function important in implementing the strategy of an organization? Explain why the changes put in place by Victoria Chen and her team could either hurt or help the bank.

2. Develop a list of changes for the operations function that should be considered by the bank. Begin by identifying operations management decisions that would be involved in operating a bank, for example, layout of facility, staff, drive-through service. Then identify ways that they can be improved at Prime Bank in order to support the strategy focused on customer service.

3. Think of the improvements identified in answering question 2. How different would these improvements be if the bank had a strategy of cutting cost rather than supporting customer service?

CASE: Boseman Oil and Petroleum (BOP)

Boseman Oil and Petroleum (BOP) is one of many oil companies operating offshore petroleum platforms in the Gulf of Mexico. The company identifies offshore sites for exploration drilling and constructs drilling platforms. Once exploration activities are successful, the platforms are converted to a production platform to extract crude oil and natural gas. BOP operates multiple platforms and an onshore facility that serves as the primary interface between the platforms. Boats with specialized crews provide logistics services between the platforms and the onshore facility. The boats deliver fuel, water, equipment, and other needed supplies multiple times a day to the platforms. Accurate and timely delivery of materials is absolutely necessary for successful platform operations.

BOP had traditionally focused on exploration and production activities, paying little attention to operating costs. However, operating costs had been increasing rapidly. A particularly significant cost was the operating of boats and crews needed to provide logistics services between platforms and the onshore facility. The boats are highly specialized, with built-in storage tanks and unique cargo space designs. The boat crews are specially trained, and operating the boats and crews is highly expensive. Although BOP is dependent on the boat deliveries, it does not use the boats at full capacity and they are often idle.

Jeff Kessinger, director of offshore operations for BOP, is now faced with the decision of how to reduce operating costs. One option is to outsource the logistics service to a company specializing in providing offshore logistics services. Logistics-Offshore Inc. is such a company, owning and maintaining its own fleet of boats and crews. Logistics-Offshore could be hired to perform this function. BOP could sell its boats and focus on oil exploration. Jeff is aware that outsourcing is an important strategic decision and there is much to consider. He is not sure where to begin.

Case Questions

1. Identify the potential strategic advantages and disadvantages for BOP in outsourcing the boat logistics service to Logistics-Offshore. Explain the strategic implications of each.

2. Identify the type of information Jeff Kessinger needs to gather and evaluate in order to make his decision.

INTERACTIVE CASE   Virtual Company

www.wiley.com/college/reid

On-line Case: Operations Strategy at Valley Memorial Hospital

Assignment: *Getting Acquainted with Valley Memorial Hospital*
With a few more weeks before you join Kaizen and start working for its client Valley Memorial Hospital, it is essential for you to get some broad insights into the company and its operations. Bob Reilly has given you a few preliminary research projects to work on in order to familiarize yourself with VMH and the healthcare industry. This assignment will enable you to enhance your knowledge of the material in Chapter 2 while continuing to prepare you for a successful internship.

To access the Web site:

- Go to **www.wiley.com/college/reid**
- Click **Student Companion Site**
- Click **Virtual Company**
- Click **Kaizen Consulting, Inc.**
- Click **Consulting Assignments**
- Click **Getting Acquainted with Valley Memorial Hospital**

INTERNET CHALLENGE   Understanding Strategic Differences

Select two companies in the same industry, either in service or manufacturing. You can select industries such as fast-food, banking, healthcare, computer manufacturing, or auto manufacturing. Use the Internet to visit the selected companies' Web sites and collect the following information: their mission statement, target market, and specifics of their product and service offerings. Explain the differences between the companies' business strategies and target markets. How do their product and service offerings differ relative to their target markets and their overall strategies? Finally, how does their operations function support their business strategies? Try to explain how operations utilizes specific organizational resources to support the business strategy.

Web sites to consider:

www.lhcargo.com (Lufthansa Cargo)
www.ualcargo.com (United Airlines, United Cargo)

On-line Resources

Companion Website www.wiley.com/college/reid
• Take interactive *practice quizzes* to assess your knowledge and help you study in a dynamic way
• Review *PowerPoint slides* or print slides for notetaking
• Access the *Virtual Company: Valley Memorial Hospital*

• Find links to *Company Tours* for this chapter
  The Boeing Company
  Sensenich Propeller Manufacturing Company
• Find links for *Additional Web Resources* for this chapter
  The Association for Manufacturing Excellence, *www.ame.org*

Selected Bibliography

Ahlstrom, P., and R. Westbrook. "Implications of Mass Customization for OM: An Exploratory Survey," *International Journal of Operations and Production Management*, 19, 3, 1999, 262–274.

Fine, Charles H. *Clock Speed, Winning Industry Control in the Age of Temporary Advantage.* New York: Perseus Books, 1998.

Gordon, Benjamin H. "The Changing Face of Third Party Logistics," *Supply Chain Management Review,* March/April, 2003, 50–57.

Grover, V., and M.K. Malhotra. "A Framework for Examining the Interface Between Operations and Information Systems: Implications for Research in the New Millennium," *Decision Sciences,* 30, 4, 1999, 901–919.

Hayes, Robert H., and Steven C. Wheelwright. *Restoring Our Competitive Edge: Competing through Manufacturing.* New York: John Wiley & Sons, 1984.

Hayes, Robert H., Gary Pisano, D. Upton, and S.C. Wheelwright. *Operations Strategy and Technology: Pursuing the Competitive Edge.* New York: John Wiley & Sons, 2005.

Hill, Terry. *Manufacturing Strategy Text and Cases.* New York: McGraw-Hill, 2000.

Kendall, Ken E. "The Significance of Information Systems Research on Emerging Technologies," *Decision Sciences,* 28, 4, 1997, 775–792.

Peters, T.J. *In Search of Excellence: Lessons from America's Best Run Companies.* New York: Warner Books, 1984.

Porter, Michael E. "What Is Strategy?" *Harvard Business Review* 74 (November–December 1996), 61–78.

Robert, Michel. *Strategy Pure and Simple II.* New York: McGraw-Hill, 1998.

Rondeau, P.J., M.S. Vonderembse, and T.S. Raghunathan. "Exploring Work System Practices for Time-Based Manufacturers: Their Impact on Competitive Capabilities," *Journal of Operations Management,* 18, 2000, 509–529.

Spring, M., and J.F. Dalrymple. "Product Customization and Manufacturing Strategy," *International Journal of Operations and Production Management,* 20, 2000, 4, 441–467.

Vickery, S., C. Droge, and R. Germain. "The Relationship between Product Customization and Organizational Culture," *Journal of Operations Management,* 17, 1999, 277–301.

Vokurka, R.J., and S.W. O'Leary-Kelly. "A Review of Empirical Research on Manufacturing Flexibility," *Journal of Operations Management,* 18, 2000, 485–501.

Ward, P.T., and R. Duray. "Manufacturing Strategy in Context: Environment, Competitive Strategy, and Manufacturing Strategy," *Journal of Operations Management,* 18, 2000, 123–138.

CHAPTER 3

Product Design and Process Selection

Before studying this chapter you should know or, if necessary, review

1. Differences between manufacturing and service organizations, Chapter 1, pp. 5–7.
2. Differences between strategic and tactical decisions, Chapter 1, pp. 7–9.
3. Competitive priorities, Chapter 2, pp. 35–38.

LEARNING OBJECTIVES

After completing this chapter you should be able to

1 Define product design and explain its strategic impact on the organization.

2 Describe the steps used to develop a product design.

3 Use break-even analysis as a tool in deciding between alternative products.

4 Identify different types of processes and explain their characteristics.

5 Understand how to use a process flowchart.

6 Understand how to use process performance metrics.

7 Understand current technological advancements and how they impact process and product design.

8 Understand issues of designing service operations.

CHAPTER OUTLINE

WHAT'S IN OM FOR ME?

 ACC   **FIN**   **MKT**   **OM**   **HRM**   **MIS**

Burke/Triolo Productions/Foodpix/Jupiter Images Corp.

Have you ever been with a group of friends and decided to order pizzas? One person wants pizza from Pizza Hut because he likes the taste of stuffed-crust pizza made with cheese in the crust. Someone else wants Donatos pizza because she likes the unique crispy-thin crust. A third wants pizza from Spagio's because of the wood-grilled oven taste. Even a simple product like a pizza can have different features unique to its producer. Different customers have different tastes, preferences, and product needs. The variety of product designs on the market appeal to the preferences of a particular customer group. Also, the different product designs have different processing requirements. This is what product design and process selection are all about.

We can all relate to the product design of a pizza just from everyday life. Now consider the complexities involved in designing more sophisticated products. For example, Palm, Inc. (www.palm.com) is a leading provider of handheld computers whose slogan is "different people, different needs, different handhelds." The company designs different products with differing capabilities, such as personal information management, wireless Internet access, and games, intended for different types of customers. The company also has to decide on the best process to produce the different types of handhelds.

The challenge of product design can also be illustrated by an example from the Alza Corporation. Alza is a leader in designing new ways that pharmaceutical drugs can be administered to different types of patients. One of their product designs is an under-the-skin implant for pharmaceutical drugs that previously could only be administered by injection. The product design had to include time release of the drug, as well as the best material and shape for the implant. In addition to the product design, a process had to be designed to produce the unique product.

These examples illustrate that a product design that meets customer needs, although challenging, can have a large impact on a company's success. In fact, product design is so important that leading-edge companies routinely invest in product designs well into the future. For example, DaimlerChrysler has been conducting research to design intelligent technologies for its vehicles that would have pedestrian and street sign recognition systems. This type of innovative product design can give a company a significant competitive advantage.

In this chapter we will learn about *product design*, which is the process of deciding on the unique characteristics and features of the company's product. We will also learn about *process selection*, which is the development of the process necessary to produce the designed product. Product design and process selection decisions are typically made together. A company can have a highly innovative design for its product, but if it has not determined how to make the product in a cost-effective way, the product will stay a design forever.

Product design and process selection affect product quality, product cost, and customer satisfaction. If the product is not well designed or if the manufacturing process is not true to the product design, the quality of the product may suffer. Further, the product has to be manufactured using materials, equipment, and labor skills that are efficient and affordable; otherwise, its cost will be too high for the market. We call this the product's **manufacturability**—the ease with which the product can be made. Finally, if a product is to achieve customer satisfaction, it must have the combined characteristics of good design, competitive pricing, and the ability to fill a market need. This is true whether the product is pizzas or cars.

▶ **Manufacturability**
The ease with which a product can be made.

PRODUCT DESIGN

Most of us might think that the design of a product is not that interesting. After all, it probably involves materials, measurements, dimensions, and blueprints. When we think of design we usually think of car design or computer design and envision engineers working on diagrams. However, product design is much more than that. Product design brings together marketing analysts, art directors, sales forecasters, engineers, finance experts, and other members of a company to think and plan strategically. It is exciting and creative, and it can spell success or disaster for a company.

Product design is the process of defining all the features and characteristics of just about anything you can think of, from Starbuck's cafe latte or Jimmy Dean's sausage to GM's Saturn or HP's DeskJet printer. Product design also includes the design of services, such as those provided by Salazar's Beauty Salon, La Petite Academy Day Care Center, or FedEx. Consumers respond to a product's appearance, color, texture, and performance. All of its features, summed up, are the product's design. Someone came up with the idea of what this product will look like, taste like, or feel like so that it will appeal to you. This is the purpose of product design. **Product design** defines a product's characteristics, such as its appearance, the materials it is made of, its dimensions and tolerances, and its performance standards.

▶ **Product design**
The process of defining all of the product's characteristics.

Design of Services versus Goods

The design elements discussed are typical of industries such as manufacturing and retail in which the product is tangible. For service industries, where the product is intangible, the design elements are equally important, but they have an added dimension.

Service design is unique in that both the service and the entire *service concept* are being designed. As with a tangible product, the service concept is based on meeting customer needs. The service design, however, adds the aesthetic and psychological benefits of the product. These are the service elements of the operation, such as promptness and friendliness. They also include the ambiance, image, and "feel-good" elements of the service. Consider the differences in service design of a company like Canyon Ranch, which provides a pampering retreat for health-conscious

©AP/Wide World Photos

Product design of cell phones combines portability, features and aesthetics.

▶ **Service design**
The process of establishing all the characteristics of the service, including physical, sensual, and psychological benefits.

but overworked professionals, versus Gold's Gym, which caters to young athletes. As with a tangible product, the preference for a service is based on its product design. **Service design** defines the characteristics of a service, such as its physical elements, and the aesthetic and psychological benefits it provides.

THE PRODUCT DESIGN PROCESS

Certain steps are common to the development of most product designs: idea generation, product screening, preliminary design and testing, and final design. These steps are shown in Figure 3-1. Notice that the arrows show a circular process. Product designs are never finished, but are always updated with new ideas. Let's look at these steps in more detail.

Idea Development

All product designs begin with an idea. The idea might come from a product manager who spends time with customers and has a sense of what customers want, from an engineer with a flare for inventions, or from anyone else in the company. To remain competitive, companies must be innovative and bring out new products regularly. In some industries, the cycle of new product development is predictable. We see this in the auto industry, where new car models come out every year, or the retail industry, where new fashion is designed for every season.

In other industries, new product releases are less predictable but just as important. The Body Shop, retailer of plant-based skin care products, periodically comes up with new ideas for its product lines. The timing often has to do with the market for a product and whether sales are declining or continuing to grow.

Ideas from Customers, Competitors, and Suppliers The first source of ideas is customers, the driving force in the design of goods and services. Marketing is a vital link between customers and product design. Market researchers collect customer

FIGURE 3-1

Steps in the product design process

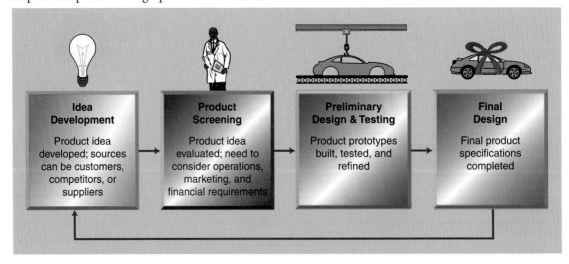

information by studying customer buying patterns and using tools such as customer surveys and focus groups. Management may love an idea, but if market analysis shows that customers do not like it, the idea is not viable. Analyzing customer preferences is an ongoing process; customer preferences next year may be quite different from what they are today. For this reason, the related process of forecasting future consumer preferences is important, though difficult.

Competitors are another source of ideas. A company learns by observing its competitors' products and their success rate. This includes looking at product design, pricing strategy, and other aspects of the operation. Studying the practices of companies considered "best-in-class" and comparing the performance of one's own company against theirs is called **benchmarking**. We can benchmark against a company in a completely different line of business and still learn from some aspect of that company's operation. For example, Lands' End is well known for its successful catalog business, and companies considering catalog sales often benchmark against Lands' End. Similarly, American Express is a company known for its success at resolving complaints, and it, too, is used for benchmarking.

▶ **Benchmarking**
The process of studying the practices of companies considered "best-in-class" and comparing your company's performance against theirs.

The importance of benchmarking can be seen by IBM's efforts to improve its distribution system. In 1997, IBM found its distribution costs increasing while customers were expecting decreasing times from factory to delivery. It appeared that IBM's supply chain practices were not keeping up with those of its competitors. To evaluate and solve this problem, IBM hired Mercer Management Consultants, who performed a large benchmarking study. IBM's practices were compared to those of market leaders in the personal computer (PC) industry, as well as to the best logistics practices outside the technology area. The objective was to evaluate IBM's current performance, that of companies considered best-in-class, and identify the gaps. Through the study, IBM discovered which specific costs exceeded industry benchmarks and which parts of the cycle time were excessively long. It also uncovered ways to simplify and reorganize its processes to gain efficiency. Based on findings from the benchmarking effort, IBM made changes in its operations. The results were reduced costs, improved delivery, and improved relationships with suppliers. IBM found benchmarking so beneficial that it plans to perform similar types of studies on an ongoing basis in the future.

China Photos/Getty Images, Inc.

LINKS TO PRACTICE

IBM Corporation
www.ibm.com

Reverse Engineering Another way of using competitors' ideas is to buy a competitor's new product and study its design features. Using a process called **reverse engineering**, a company's engineers carefully disassemble the product and analyze its parts and features. Ford Motor Company used this approach to design its Taurus model. Ford engineers disassembled and studied many other car models, such as BMW and Toyota, and adapted and combined their best features. Product design ideas are also generated by a company's R & D (research and development) department, whose role is to develop product and process innovation.

Suppliers are another source of product design ideas. To remain competitive, more companies are developing partnering relationships with their suppliers to jointly satisfy the end customer. For example, DaimlerChrysler chooses its suppliers well before

▶ **Reverse engineering**
The process of disassembling a product to analyze its design features.

▶ **Early supplier involvement (ESI)**
Involving suppliers in the early stages of product design.

parts are designed. Suppliers participate in a program called **early supplier involvement (ESI)**, which involves them in the early stages of product design.

Product Screening

After a product idea has been developed, it is evaluated to determine its likelihood of success. This is called *product screening*. The company's product screening team evaluates the product design idea according to the needs of the major business functions. In their evaluation executives from each function area may explore issues such as the following:

- **Operations** What are the production needs of the proposed new product, and how do they match our existing resources? Will we need new facilities and equipment? Do we have the labor skills to make the product? Can the material for production be readily obtained?

- **Marketing** What is the potential size of the market for the proposed new product? How much effort will be needed to develop a market for the product, and what is the long-term product potential?

- **Finance** The production of a new product is a financial investment like any other. What is the proposed new product's financial potential, cost, and return on investment?

Unfortunately, there is no magic formula for deciding whether or not to pursue a particular product idea. Managerial skill and experience, however, are key. Companies generate new product ideas all the time, whether for a new brand of cereal or a new design for a car door. Approximately 80 percent of ideas do not make it past the screening stage. Management analyzes operations, marketing, and financial factors and then makes the final decision. Fortunately, we have decision-making tools to help us evaluate new product ideas. A popular one is break-even analysis, which we look at next.

▶ **Break-even analysis**
A technique used to compute the amount of goods a company would need to sell to cover its costs.

Break-Even Analysis: A Tool for Product Screening **Break-even analysis** is a technique that can be useful when evaluating a new product. It computes the quantity of goods a company needs to sell just to cover its costs, or break even, called the "break-even" point. When evaluating an idea for a new product, it is helpful to compute its break-even quantity. An assessment can then be made as to how difficult or easy it will be to cover costs and make a profit. A product with a break-even quantity that is hard to attain might not be a good product choice to pursue. Next we look at how to compute the break-even quantity.

▶ **Fixed costs**
Costs a company incurs regardless of how much it produces.

▶ **Variable costs**
Costs that vary directly with the amount of units produced.

The total cost of producing a product or service is the sum of its fixed and variable costs. A company incurs **fixed costs** regardless of how much it produces. Fixed costs include overhead, taxes, and insurance. For example, a company must pay for overhead even if it produces nothing. **Variable costs**, on the other hand, are costs that vary directly with the amount of units produced and include items such as direct materials and labor. Together, fixed and variable costs add up to total cost:

$$\text{Total cost} = F + (VC)Q$$

where F = fixed cost
VC = variable cost per unit
Q = number of units sold

Figure 3-2 shows a graphical representation of these costs as well as the break-even quantity. Fixed cost is represented by a horizontal line as this cost is the same regardless of how much is produced. Adding variable cost to fixed cost creates *total cost*, represented by the diagonal line above fixed cost. When $Q = 0$, total cost is only equal to fixed cost. As Q increases, total cost increases through the variable cost component. The blue diagonal in the figure is revenue, the amount of money brought in from sales:

$$\text{Revenue } (SP)Q$$

where SP = selling price per unit

When $Q = 0$, revenue is zero. As sales increase, so does revenue. Remember, however, that to cover all costs we have to sell the break-even amount. This is the quantity Q_{BE}, where revenue equals total cost. If we sell below the break-even point, we incur a loss, since costs exceed revenue. To make a profit, we have to sell above the break-even point. Since revenue equals total cost at the break-even point, we can use the previous equations to compute the value of the break-even quantity:

$$\text{Total cost} = \text{total revenue}$$

$$F + (VC)Q = (SP)Q$$

Solving for Q, we get the following equation:

$$Q_{BE} = \frac{F}{SP - VC}$$

Note that we could also find the break-even point by drawing the graph and finding where the total cost and revenue lines cross.

Break-even analysis is useful for more than just deciding between different products. It can be used to make other decisions, such as evaluating different processes or deciding whether the company should make or buy a product.

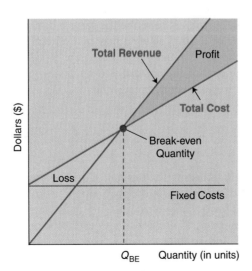

FIGURE 3-2

Graphical approach to break-even analysis

EXAMPLE 3.1

Computing the Break-Even Quantity

Fred Boulder, owner of Sports Feet Manufacturing, is considering whether to produce a new line of footwear. Fred has considered the processing needs for the new product as well as the market potential. He has also estimated that the variable cost for each product manufactured and sold is $9 and the fixed cost per year is $52,000.

(a) If Fred offers the footwear at a selling price of $25, how many pairs must he sell to break even?
(b) If Fred sells 4000 pairs at the $25 price, what will be the contribution to profit?

• **Solution:**
(a) To compute the break-even quantity:

$$Q = \frac{F}{SP - VC}$$

$$= \frac{\$52,000}{\$25 - \$9} = 3250 \text{ pairs}$$

The break-even quantity is 3250 pairs. This is how much Fred would have to sell to cover costs.

(b) To compute the contribution to profit with sales of 4000 pairs, we can go back to the relationship between cost and revenue:

$$\text{Profit} = \text{total revenue} - \text{total cost}$$

$$= (SP)Q - [F + (VC)Q]$$

$$\text{Profit} = \$25(4000) - [\$52,000 + \$9(4000)]$$

$$= \$12,000$$

The contribution to profit is $12,000 if Fred can sell 4000 pairs from his new line of footwear.

Preliminary Design and Testing

Once a product idea has passed the screening stage, it is time to begin preliminary design and testing. At this stage design engineers translate general performance specifications into technical specifications. Prototypes are built and tested. Changes are made based on test results, and the process of revising, rebuilding a prototype, and testing continues. For service companies this may entail testing the offering on a small scale and working with customers to refine the service offering. Fast-food restaurants are known for this type of testing, where a new menu item may be tested in only one particular geographic area. Product refinement can be time-consuming, and there may be a desire on the part of the company to hurry through this phase to rush the product to market. However, rushing creates the risk that all the "bugs" have not been worked out, which can prove very costly.

Final Design

Following extensive design testing the product moves to the final design stage. This is where final product specifications are drawn up. The final specifications are then translated into specific processing instructions to manufacture the product, which include selecting equipment, outlining jobs that need to be performed, identifying specific materials needed and suppliers that will be used, and all the other aspects of organizing the process of product production.

DFM Guidelines	TABLE 3-1
1. Minimize parts.	Guidelines for DFM
2. Design parts for different products.	
3. Use modular design.	
4. Avoid tools.	
5. Simplify operations.	

FACTORS IMPACTING PRODUCT DESIGN

Here are some additional factors that need to be considered during the product design stage.

Design for Manufacture

When we think of product design we generally first think of how to please the customer. However, we also need to consider how easy or difficult it is to manufacture the product. Otherwise, we might have a great idea that is difficult or too costly to manufacture. **Design for manufacture** (**DFM**) is a series of guidelines that we should follow to produce a product easily and profitably. DFM guidelines focus on two issues:

▶ **Design for manufacture (DFM)**
A series of guidelines to follow in order to produce a product easily and profitably.

1. *Design simplification* means reducing the number of parts and features of the product whenever possible. A simpler product is easier to make, costs less, and gives higher quality.
2. *Design standardization* refers to the use of common and interchangeable parts. By using interchangeable parts, we can make a greater variety of products with less inventory and significantly lower cost and provide greater flexibility. Table 3-1 shows guidelines for DFM.

An example of the benefits of applying these rules is seen in Figure 3-3. We can see the progression in the design of a toolbox using the DFM approach. All of the pictures

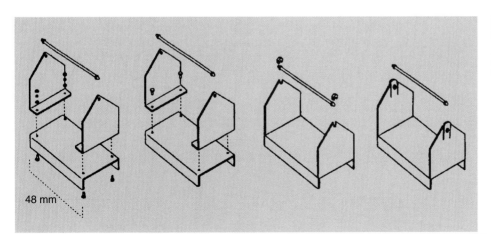

FIGURE 3-3

Progressive design of a toolbox using DFM

48 mm

show a toolbox. However, the first design shown requires twenty parts. Through simplification and use of modular design, the number of parts required has been reduced to two. It would certainly be much easier to make the product with two parts versus twenty parts. This means fewer chances for error, better quality, and lower costs due to shorter assembly time.

Product Life Cycle

▶ **Product life cycle**
A series of stages that products pass through in their lifetime, characterized by changing product demands over time.

Another factor in product design is the stage of the life cycle of the product. Most products go through a series of stages of changing product demand called the **product life cycle**. There are typically four stages of the product life cycle: introduction, growth, maturity, and decline. These are shown in Figure 3-4.

Products in the introductory stage are not well defined and neither is their market. Often all the "bugs" have not been worked out and customers are uncertain about the product. In the growth stage, the product takes hold and both product and market continue to be refined. The third stage is that of maturity, where demand levels off and there are usually no design changes: the product is predictable at this stage and so is its market. Many products, such as toothpaste, can stay in this stage for many years. Finally, there is a decline in demand, because of new technology, better product design, or market saturation.

The first two stages of the life cycle can collectively be called the early stages because the product is still being improved and refined and the market is still in the process of being developed. The last two stages of the life cycle can be referred to as the later stages because here the product and market are both well defined.

Understanding the stages of the product life cycle is important for product design purposes, such as knowing at which stage to focus on design changes. Also, when considering a new product, the expected length of the life cycle is critical in order to estimate future profitability relative to the initial investment. The product life cycle can be quite short for certain products, as seen in the computer industry. For other products it can be extremely long, as in the aircraft industry. A few products, such as paper, pencils, nails, milk, sugar, and flour, do not go through a life cycle. However, almost all products do, and some may spend a long time in one stage.

FIGURE 3-4

Stages of the product life cycle

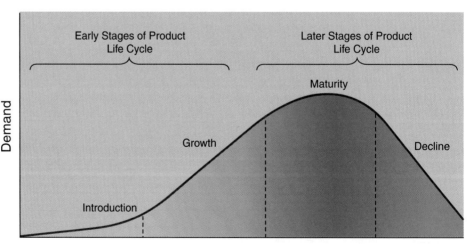

Concurrent Engineering

Concurrent engineering is an approach that brings many people together in the early phase of product design in order to simultaneously design the product and the process. This type of approach has been found to achieve a smooth transition from the design stage to actual production in a shorter amount of development time with improved quality results.

The old approach to product and process design was to first have the designers of the idea come up with the exact product characteristics. Once their design was complete they would pass it on to operations, who would then design the production process needed to produce the product. This was called the "over-the-wall" approach, because the designers would throw their design "over-the-wall" to operations, who then had to decide how to produce the product.

There are many problems with the old approach. First, it is very inefficient and costly. For example, there may be certain aspects of the product that are not critical for product success but are costly or difficult to manufacture, such as a dye color that is difficult to achieve. Since manufacturing does not understand which features are not critical, it may develop an unnecessarily costly production process with costs passed down to the customers. Because the designers do not know the cost of the added feature, they may not have the opportunity to change their design or may do so much later in the process, incurring additional costs. Concurrent engineering allows everyone to work together so these problems do not occur. Figure 3-5 shows the difference between the "over-the-wall" approach and concurrent engineering.

▶ **Concurrent engineering**
An approach that brings together multifunction teams in the early phase of product design in order to simultaneously design the product and the process.

FIGURE 3-5

The first illustration shows sequential design with walls between functional areas. The second illustration shows concurrent design with walls broken down.

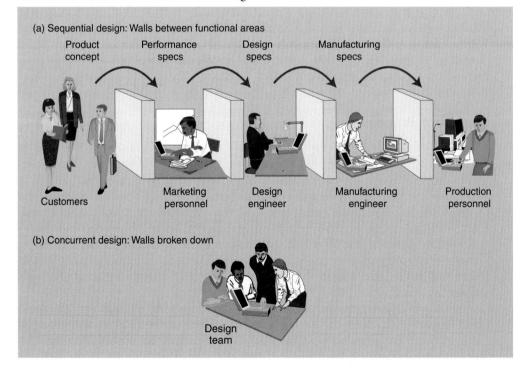

A second problem is that the "over-the-wall" approach takes a longer amount of time than when product and process design are performed concurrently. As you can see in Figure 3-5, when product and process design are done together, much of the work is done in parallel rather than in sequence. In today's markets, new product introductions are expected to occur faster than ever. Companies do not have the luxury of enough time to follow a sequential approach and then work the "bugs" out. They may eventually get a great product, but by then the market may not be there!

The third problem is that the old approach does not create a team atmosphere, which is important in today's work environment. Rather, it creates an atmosphere where each function views its role separately in a type of "us versus them" mentality. With the old approach, when the designers were finished with the designs, they considered their job done. If there were problems, each group blamed the other. With concurrent engineering, the team is responsible for designing and getting the product to market. Team members continue working together to resolve problems with the product and improve the process.

Remanufacturing

▶ **Remanufacturing**
The concept of using components of old products in the production of new ones.

Remanufacturing is a concept that has been gaining increasing importance as our society becomes more environmentally conscious and focuses on recycling and eliminating waste. **Remanufacturing** uses components of old products in the production of new ones. In addition to the environmental benefits, there are significant cost benefits because remanufactured products can be half the price of their new counterparts. Remanufacturing has been quite popular in the production of computers, televisions, and automobiles.

PROCESS SELECTION

So far we have discussed issues involved in product design. Though product design is important for a company, it cannot be considered separately from the selection of the process. In this section we will look at issues involved in process design. Then we will show how product design and process selection issues are linked together.

Types of Processes

When you look at different types of companies, ranging from a small coffee shop to IBM, it may seem like there are hundreds of different types of processes. Some locations are small, like your local Starbuck's, and some are very large, like a Ford Motor Company plant. Some produce standardized "off-the-shelf" products, like Pepperidge Farm's frozen chocolate cake, and some work with customers to customize their product, like cakes made to order by a gourmet bakery. Though there seem to be large differences between the processes of companies, many have certain processing characteristics in common. In this section we will divide these processes into groups with similar characteristics, allowing us to understand problems inherent with each type of process.

All processes can be grouped into two broad categories: intermittent operations and repetitive operations. These two categories differ in almost every way. Once we understand these differences, we can easily identify organizations based on the category of process they use.

Felicia Martinez/PhotoEdit

Designing a custom-made cake is an example of an intermittent operation.

John Zoiner/Getty Images/Getty Images, Inc.

An assembly line is an example of a repetitive operation.

Intermittent Operations **Intermittent operations** are used to produce a variety of products with different processing requirements in lower volumes. Examples are an auto body shop, a tool and die shop, or a healthcare facility. Because different products have different processing needs, there is no standard route that all products take through the facility. Instead, resources are grouped by function and the product is routed to each resource as needed. Think about a healthcare facility. Each patient, "the product," is routed to different departments as needed. One patient may need to get an X-ray, go to the lab for blood work, and then go to the examining room. Another patient may need to go to the examining room and then to physical therapy.

To be able to produce products with different processing requirements, intermittent operations tend to be labor intensive rather than capital intensive. Workers need to be able to perform different tasks, depending on the processing needs of the products produced. Often we see skilled and semiskilled workers in this environment, with a fair amount of worker discretion in performing their jobs. Workers need to be flexible and able to perform different tasks as needed for the different products. Equipment in this type of environment is more general-purpose to satisfy different processing requirements. Automation tends to be less common, because automation is typically product-specific. Given that many products are being produced with different processing requirements, it is usually not cost efficient to invest in automation for only one product type. Finally, the volume of goods produced is directly tied to the number of customer orders.

Repetitive Operations **Repetitive operations** are used to produce one or a few standardized products in high volume. Examples are a typical assembly line, cafeteria, or automatic car wash. Resources are organized in a line flow to efficiently accommodate production of the product. Note that in this environment it is possible to arrange resources in a line because there is only one type of product. This is directly the opposite of what we find with intermittent operations.

To efficiently produce a large volume of one type of product, these operations tend to be capital intensive rather than labor intensive. An example is "mass-production" operations, which usually have much invested in their facilities and equipment to provide a high degree of product consistency. Often these facilities rely on automation and technology to improve efficiency and increase output rather than on labor skill.

▶ **Intermittent operations**
Processes used to produce a variety of products with different processing requirements in lower volumes.

▶ **Repetitive operations**
Processes used to produce one or a few standardized products in high volume.

TABLE 3-2

Differences between
Intermittent and
Repetitive Operations

Decision	Intermittent Operations	Repetitive Operations
Product variety	Great	Small
Degree of standardization	Low	High
Organization of resources	Grouped by function	Line flow to accommodate processing needs
Path of products through facility	In a varied pattern, depending on product needs	Line flow
Factor driving production	Customer orders	Forecast of future demands
Critical resource	Labor-intensive operation (worker skills important)	Capital-intensive operation (equipment automation, technology important)
Type of equipment	General-purpose	Specialized
Degree of automation	Low	High
Throughput time	Longer	Shorter
Work-in-process inventory	More	Less

The volume produced is usually based on a forecast of future demands rather than on direct customer orders.

The most common differences between intermittent and repetitive operations relate to two dimensions: (1) the amount of product volume produced, and (2) the degree of product standardization. Product volume can range from making a unique product one at a time to producing a large number of products at the same time. Product standardization refers to a lack of variety in a particular product. Examples of standardized products are white undershirts, calculators, toasters, and television sets. The type of operation used, including equipment and labor, is quite different if a company produces one product at a time to customer specifications instead of mass production of one standardized product. Specific differences between intermittent and repetitive operations are shown in Table 3-2.

The Continuum of Process Types Dividing processes into two fundamental categories of operations is helpful in our understanding of their general characteristics. To be more detailed, we can further divide each category according to product volume and degree of product standardization, as follows. Intermittent operations can be divided into *project processes* and *batch processes*. Repetitive operations can be divided into *line processes* and *continuous processes*. Figure 3-6 shows a continuum of process types. Next we look at what makes these processes different from each other.

- **Project processes** are used to make one-of-a-kind products exactly to customer specifications. These processes are used when there is high customization and low product volume, because each product is different. Examples can be seen in construction, shipbuilding, medical procedures, creation of artwork, custom tailoring, and interior design. With project processes the customer is usually involved in deciding on the design of the product. The artistic baker you hired to bake a wedding cake to your specifications uses a project process.

▶ **Project process**
A type of process used to make a one-at-a-time product exactly to customer specifications.

- **Batch processes** are used to produce small quantities of products in groups or batches based on customer orders or product specifications. They are also known as job shops. The volumes of each product produced are still small and there can still be a high degree of customization. Examples can be seen in bakeries, education, and printing shops. The classes you are taking at the university use a batch process.

▶ **Batch process**
A type of process used to produce a small quantity of products in groups or batches based on customer orders or specifications.

- **Line processes** are designed to produce a large volume of a standardized product for mass production. They are also known as flow shops, flow lines, or assembly lines. With line processes the product that is produced is made in high volume with little or no customization. Think of a typical assembly line that produces everything from cars, computers, television sets, shoes, candy bars, even food items.

▶ **Line process**
A type of process used to produce a large volume of a standardized product.

- **Continuous processes** operate continually to produce a very high volume of a fully standardized product. Examples include oil refineries, water treatment plants, and certain paint facilities. The products produced by continuous processes are usually in continual rather than discrete units, such as liquid or gas. They usually have a single input and a limited number of outputs. Also, these facilities are usually highly capital intensive and automated.

▶ **Continuous process**
A type of process that operates continually to produce a high volume of a fully standardized product.

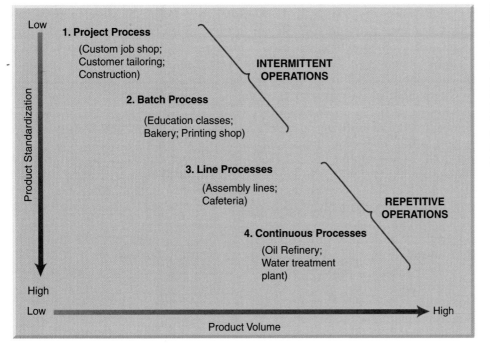

FIGURE 3-6

Types of processes based on product volume and product standardization
Source: Adapted from Robert H. Hayes and Steven C. Wheelwright, "Link Manufacturing Process and Product Life Cycles," *Harvard Business Review*, January–February, 1979, 133–140.

Note that both project and batch processes have low product volumes and offer customization. The difference is in the volume and degree of customization. Project processes are more extreme cases of intermittent operations compared to batch processes. Also, note that both line and continuous processes primarily produce large volumes of standardized products. Again, the difference is in the volume and degree of standardization. Continuous processes are more extreme cases of high volume and product standardization than are line processes.

Figure 3-6 positions these four process types along the diagonal to show the best process strategies relative to product volume and product customization. Companies whose process strategies do not fall along this diagonal may not have made the best process decisions. Bear in mind, however, that not all companies fit into only one of these categories: a company may use both batch and project processing to good advantage. For example, a bakery that produces breads, cakes, and pastries in batches may also bake and decorate cakes to order.

DESIGNING PROCESSES

▶ **Process flow analysis**
A technique used for evaluating a process in terms of the sequence of steps from inputs to outputs with the goal of improving its design.

▶ **Process flowchart**
A chart showing the sequence of steps in producing the product or service.

Now that we know about different types of processes, let's look at a technique that can help with process design.

Process flow analysis is a technique used for evaluating a process in terms of the sequence of steps from inputs to outputs with the goal of improving its design. One of the most important tools in process flow analysis is a process flowchart. A **process flowchart** is used for viewing the sequence of steps involved in producing the product and the flow of the product through the process. It is useful for seeing the totality of the operation and for identifying potential problem areas.

There is no exact format for designing a flowchart. It can be very simple or highly detailed. The typical symbols used are arrows to represent flows, triangles to represent decision points, inverted triangles to represent storage of goods, and rectangles as tasks. Let's begin by looking at some elements used in developing a flowchart, as shown in Figure 3-7. Shown first, in Figure 3-7(a), are flows between stages in a simple multistage process, which is a process with multiple activities ("stages"). You can see that the arrows indicate a simple flow of materials between the different stages.

Often, multiple stages have storage areas or "buffers" between them for placement of either partially completed (work-in-process) or fully completed (finished goods) inventory, shown in Figure 3-7(b). This enables the two stages to operate independently of each other. Otherwise, the first stage would have to produce a product at the same exact rate as the second stage. For example, let's say that the first stage of a multistage process produces one product in forty seconds and the second stage in sixty seconds. That means that for every unit produced the first stage would have to stop and wait twenty seconds for the second stage to finish its work. Because the capacity of the second stage is holding up the speed of the process, it is called a **bottleneck**. Now let's see what happens if the first stage takes sixty seconds to produce a product and the second stage forty seconds. In this case the first stage becomes the bottleneck, and the second stage has to wait twenty seconds to receive a product. Obviously, the best is for both stages to produce at the same rate, though this is often not possible. Inventory is then placed between the stages to even out differences in production capacity.

▶ **Bottleneck**
Longest task in the process.

Often stages in the production process can be performed in parallel, as shown in Figure 3-7(c) and (d). The two stages can produce different products (c) or the same

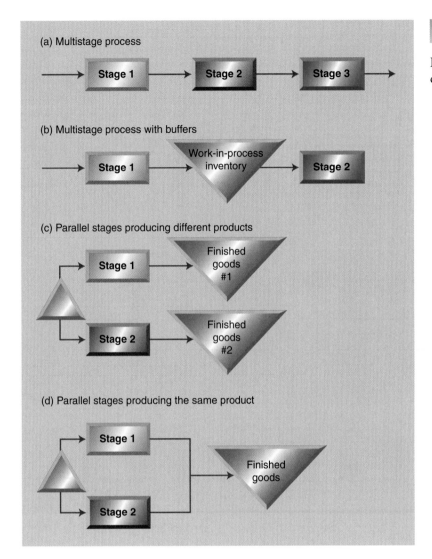

FIGURE 3-7

Elements of flowchart development

product (d). Notice that in the latter case this would mean that the capacity of the stage performed in parallel has effectively been doubled.

Now let's look at an illustration of a flowchart using Antonio's Pizzeria as an example. Let's say that Antonio produces three different styles of pizzas to satisfy different types of customers. First are cheese pizzas made with standard ingredients and a standard crust. They are the most popular items and Antonio makes them ahead of time to ensure that they are always available upon demand. This is called a **make-to-stock strategy**. Second are pizzas that use a standard crust prepared ahead of time but are assembled based on specific customer requests. This is called an **assemble-to-order strategy**. Lastly are pizzas made to order based on specific customer requirements, allowing choices of different types of crusts and toppings. This is called a **make-to-order strategy**. We will look at these product strategies more closely later in this chapter. For now, let's look at the flowcharts for the three processes in Figure 3-8. Notice that although the flowcharts are similar, they show customer interaction at different points in the process.

▶ **Make-to-stock strategy**
Produces standard products and services for immediate sale or delivery.

▶ **Assemble-to-order strategy**
Produces standard components that can be combined to customer specifications.

▶ **Make-to-order strategy**
Produces products to customer specifications after an order has been received.

FIGURE 3-8

Flowcharts for different product strategies at Antonio's Pizzeria

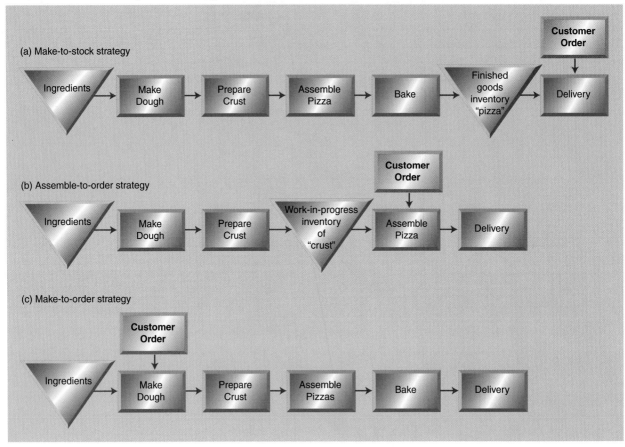

Process flowcharts can also be used to map the flow of the customer through the process and to identify potential problem areas. Figure 3-9 shows a flowchart for Antonio's Pizzeria that includes the steps involved in placing and processing a customer order. The points in the process for potential problems are indicated. Management can then monitor these problem areas. The chart could be even more detailed, including information such as frequency of errors or approximate time to complete a task. As you can see, process flowcharts are very useful tools when designing and evaluating processes.

PROCESS PERFORMANCE METRICS

▶ **Process performance metrics**
Measurements of different process characteristics that tell how a process is performing.

An important way of ensuring that a process is functioning properly is to regularly measure its performance. **Process performance metrics** are measurements of different process characteristics that tell us how a process is performing. Just as accountants and finance managers use financial metrics, operations managers use process performance metrics to determine how a process is performing and how it is changing over time. There are many process performance metrics that focus on different aspects of the process. In this section we will look at some common metrics used by operations managers. These are summarized in Table 3-3 (see page 72).

FIGURE 3-9

Process flowchart of customer flow at Antonio's Pizzeria

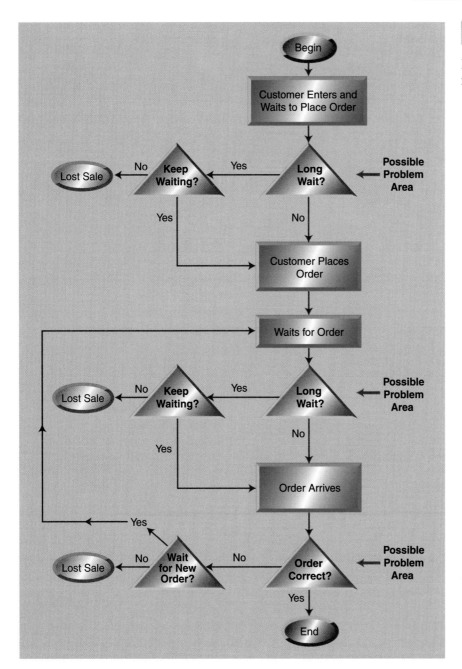

A basic process performance metric is **throughput time**, which is the average amount of time it takes a product to move through the system. This includes the time someone is working on the product as well as the waiting time. A lower throughput time means that more products can move through the system. One goal of process improvement is to reduce throughput time. For example, think about the time spent at your last doctor's appointment. The total amount of time you spent at the facility, regardless of whether you were waiting, talking with the physician, or having lab work performed, is throughput time.

Quite possibly much of the time at your last doctor's appointment was spent waiting. An important metric that measures how much wasted time exists in a process is

▶ **Throughput time**
Average amount of time it takes a product to move through the system.

	Measure	Definition
TABLE 3-3 Process Performance Metrics	1. Throughput time	Average amount of time product takes to move through the system
	2. Process velocity $= \dfrac{\text{throughput time}}{\text{value-added time}}$	A measure of wasted time in the system
	3. Productivity $= \dfrac{\text{output}}{\text{input}}$	A measure of how well a company uses its resources
	4. Utilization $= \dfrac{\text{time a resource used}}{\text{time a resource available}}$	The proportion of time a resource is actually used
	5. Efficiency $= \dfrac{\text{actual output}}{\text{standard output}}$	Measures performance relative to a standard

▶ **Process velocity**
Ratio of throughput time to value-added time.

process velocity. Process velocity is computed as a ratio of throughput time to value-added time:

$$\text{Process velocity} = \frac{\text{throughput time}}{\text{value-added time}}$$

where value-added time is the time spent actually working on the product. Notice that the closer this ratio is to 1.00, the lower the amount of time the product spends on non-value-adding activities (e.g., waiting). Again recall your last doctor's appointment. What was the value-added time? What was the throughput time? Can you estimate the process velocity?

▶ **Productivity**
Ratio of outputs over inputs.

Another important metric is **productivity**, which is the ratio of outputs over inputs. Productivity measures how well a company converts its inputs to outputs. Productivity was discussed in detail in Chapter 2, so we will not repeat its computation here. Also important is **utilization**, which is the ratio of the time a resource is actually used versus the time it is available for use. Unlike productivity, which tends to focus on financial measures (e.g., dollars of output), utilization measures the actual time that a resource (e.g., equipment or labor) is being used. Last, **efficiency** is a metric that measures actual output relative to some standard of output. It tells us whether we are performing at, above, or below standard.

▶ **Utilization**
Ratio of time a resource is used to time it is available for use.

▶ **Efficiency**
Ratio of actual output to standard output.

EXAMPLE 3.2

Measuring Process Performance

Frantz Title Company is analyzing its operation in an effort to improve performance. The following data have been collected:

It takes an average of four hours to process and close a title, with value-added time estimated at thirty minutes per title.

Each title officer is on payroll for eight hours per day, though working six hours per day on average, accounting for lunches and breaks. Industry standard for labor utilization is 80 percent.

The company closes on eight titles per day, with an industry standard of ten titles per day for a comparable facility.

Determine process velocity, labor utilization, and efficiency for the company. Can you draw any conclusions?

- **Before You Begin:** When computing process performance metrics, be careful to make sure you use consistent units in the numerator and denominator of the equation you are using.

- **Solution:**

$$\text{Process Velocity} = \frac{\text{throughput time}}{\text{value-added time}} = \frac{4 \text{ hours/title}}{\frac{1}{2} \text{ hour/title}} = 8$$

$$\text{Labor utilization} = \frac{6 \text{ hours/day}}{8 \text{ hours/day}} = .75 \text{ or } 75\%$$

$$\text{Efficiency} = \frac{8 \text{ titles/day}}{10 \text{ titles/day}} = .80 \text{ or } 80\%$$

A process velocity of 8 indicates that the amount of time spent on non-value-added activities is 8 times that of value-added activities. Also, labor utilization and efficiency are both below standard.

Before You Go On

Make sure that you understand the key issues in product design. Be familiar with the different stages of the product life cycle. Recall that products in the early stages of the life cycle are still being refined based on the needs of the market. This includes product characteristics and features. At this stage the market for the product has not yet been fully developed and product volumes have not reached their peak. By contrast, products in the later stages of their life cycle have well-developed characteristics and demand volumes for them are fairly stable.

Review the different types of processes and their characteristics. Recall that intermittent processes are designed to produce products with different processing requirements in smaller volumes. Repetitive operations, on the other hand, are designed for one or a few types of products produced in high volumes.

Next we discuss how product design and process selection decisions are interrelated.

LINKING PRODUCT DESIGN AND PROCESS SELECTION

Decisions concerning product design and process selection are directly linked and cannot be made independently of one another. The type of product a company produces defines the type of operation needed. The type of operation needed, in turn, defines many other aspects of the organization. This includes how a company competes in the marketplace (competitive priorities), the type or equipment and its arrangement in the facility, the type of organizational structure, and future types of products that can be produced by the facility. Table 3-4 summarizes some key decisions and

Decision	Intermittent Operations	Repetitive Operations
Product design	Early stage of product life cycle	Later stage of product life cycle
Competitive priorities	Delivery, flexibility, and quality	Cost and quality
Facility layout	Resources grouped by function	Resources arranged in a line
Product strategy	Make-to-order/assemble-to-order	Make-to-stock
Vertical integration	Low	High

TABLE 3-4

Differences in Key Organizational Decisions for Different Types of Operations how they differ for intermittent and repetitive types of operations. Next we look at each of these decision areas.

Product Design Decisions

Intermittent and repetitive operations typically focus on producing products in different stages of the product life cycle. Intermittent operations focus on products in the early stage of the life cycle because facilities are general-purpose and can be adapted to the needs of the product. Because products in the early stage of the life cycle are still being refined, intermittent operations are ideally suited to them. Also, demand volumes for these products are still uncertain, and intermittent operations are designed to focus on producing lower volumes of products with differing characteristics.

Once a product reaches the later stages of the life cycle, both its product features and its demand volume are predictable. As volumes are typically larger at this stage, a facility that is dedicated to producing a large volume of one type of product is best from both efficiency and cost perspectives. This is what a repetitive operation provides. Recall that repetitive operations are capital intensive, with much automation dedicated to the efficient production of one type of product. It would not be a good decision to invest such a large amount of resources for a product that is uncertain relative to its features or market. However, once a product is well defined with a sizable market, repetitive types of operations are a better business alternative. This is why repetitive operations tend to focus on products in the later stages of their life cycle.

The product focus of both types of operations has significant implications for a company's future product choices. Once a company has an intermittent operation in place, designed to produce a variety of products in low volumes, it is a poor strategic decision to pursue production of a highly standardized product in the same facility. The same holds true for attempting to produce a newly introduced product in a repetitive operation.

The differences between the two types of operations are great, including the way they are managed. Not understanding their differences is a mistake often made by companies. A company may be very successful at managing a repetitive operation that produces a standardized product. Management may then see an opportunity involving products in the early stage of the life cycle. Not understanding the differences in the operational requirements, management may decide to produce this new product by applying their "know-how." The results can prove disastrous.

LINKS TO PRACTICE

The Babcock & Wilcox Company
www.babcock.com

Michael Rosenfeld/ Stone/Getty Images

The problems that can arise when a company does not understand the differences between intermittent and repetitive operations are illustrated by the experience of The Babcock & Wilcox Company in the late 1960s. B & W was very successful at producing fossil-fuel boilers, a standardized product made via repetitive operation. Then the company decided to pursue production of nuclear pressure vessels, a new product in the early stages of its life cycle that required an intermittent operation. B & W saw the nuclear pressure vessels as a wave of the future. Because they were successful at producing boilers, they believed they could apply those same skills to production of the new product. They began managing the production of nuclear pressure vessels—an intermittent operation—as if it were a repetitive operation. They focused primarily on cost rather than delivery, did not give enough time for product refinement, and did not invest in labor skills necessary for a new product. Consequently, the venture failed and the company almost went out of business. It was saved by its success in the production of boilers, to which it was able to return.

Competitive Priorities

The decision of how a company will compete in the marketplace—its competitive priorities—is largely affected by the type of operation it has in place. Intermittent operations are typically less competitive on cost than repetitive operations. The reason is that repetitive operations mass-produce a large volume of one product. The cost of the product is spread over a large volume, allowing the company to offer that product at a comparatively lower price.

Think about the cost difference you would incur if you decided to buy a business suit "off the rack" from your local department store (produced by a repetitive operation) versus having it custom made by a tailor (an intermittent operation). Certainly a custom-made suit would cost considerably more. The same product produced by a repetitive operation typically costs less than one made by an intermittent operation. However, intermittent operations have their own advantages. Having a custom-made suit allows you to choose precisely what you want in style, color, texture, and fit. Also, if you were not satisfied, you could easily return it for adjustments and alterations. Intermittent operations compete more on flexibility and delivery compared to continuous operations.

Today all organizations understand the importance of quality. However, the elements of quality that a company focuses on may be different depending on the type of operation used. Repetitive operations provide greater consistency among products. The first and last products made in the day are almost identical. Intermittent operations, on the other hand, offer greater variety of features and workmanship not available with mass production.

It is important that companies understand the competitive priorities best suited for the type of process that they use. It would not be a good strategic decision for an intermittent operation to try to compete primarily on cost, as it would not be very successful. Similarly, the primary competitive priority for a repetitive operation should not be variety of features, because this would take away from the efficiency of the process design.

Facility Layout

Facility layout, covered in Chapter 10, is concerned with the arrangement of resources in a facility to enhance the production process. If resources are not arranged properly, a company will have inefficiency and waste. The type of process a company uses directly affects the facility layout and the inherent problems encountered.

Intermittent operations resources are grouped based on similar processes or functions. There is no one typical product that is produced; rather, a large variety of items are produced in low volumes, each with its own unique processing needs. Since no one product justifies the dedication of an entire facility, resources are grouped based on their function. Products are then moved from resource to resource, based on their processing needs. The challenge with intermittent operations is to arrange the location of resources to maximize efficiency and minimize waste of movement. If the intermittent operation has not been designed properly, many products will be moved long distances. This type of movement adds nothing to the value of the product and contributes to waste. Any two work centers that have much movement between them should be placed close to one another. However, this often means that another work center will have to be moved out of the way. This can make the problem fairly challenging.

Intermittent operations are less efficient and have longer production times due to the nature of the layout. Material handling costs tend to be high and resource scheduling is a challenge. Intermittent operations are common in practice. Examples include a doctor's office or a hospital. Departments are grouped based on their function, with examining rooms in one area, lab in another, and X-rays in a third. Patients are moved from one department to another based on their needs. Another example is a bakery that makes custom cakes and pastries. The work centers are set up to perform different functions, such as making different types of dough, different types of fillings, and different types of icing and decorations. The product is routed to different workstations depending on the product requirements. Some cakes have the filling in the center (e.g., Boston cream pie), others only on top (e.g., sheet cake), and some have no filling at all (e.g., pound cake).

Repetitive operations have resources arranged in sequence to allow for efficient production of a standardized product. Since only one product or a few highly similar products are being produced, all resources are arranged to efficiently meet production needs. Examples are seen on an assembly line, in a cafeteria, or even a car wash. Numerous products, from breakfast cereals to computers, are made using repetitive operations.

Though repetitive operations have faster processing rates, lower material handling costs, and greater efficiency than intermittent operations, they also have their shortcomings. Resources are highly specialized and the operation is inflexible relative to the market. This type of operation cannot respond rapidly to changes in market needs for the products or to changes in demand volume. The challenge is to arrange workstations in sequence and designate the jobs that will be performed by each to produce the product in the most efficient way possible. Figure 3-10 illustrates the differences in facility layout between intermittent and repetitive operations.

FIGURE 3-10

Facility layouts for intermittent versus repetitive operations

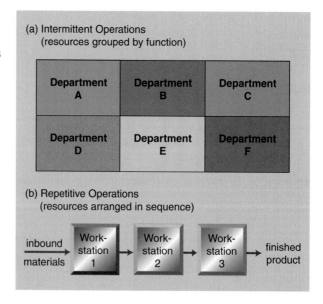

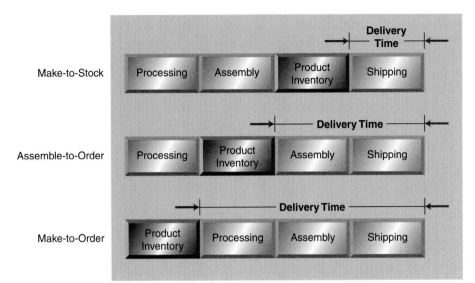

FIGURE 3-11

Product and service strategy options

Product and Service Strategy

The type of operation a company has in place is directly related to its product and service strategy. As we learned earlier in this chapter in the example of Antonio's Pizzeria, product and service strategies can be classified as make-to-stock, assemble-to-order, and make-to-order. These strategies differ by the length of their delivery lead time, which is the amount of time from when the order is received to when the product is delivered. These strategies also differ by the degree of product customization. Figure 3-11 illustrates these differences.

Make-to-stock is a strategy that produces finished products for immediate sale or delivery, in anticipation of demand. Companies using this strategy produce a standardized product in larger volumes. Typically, this strategy is seen in repetitive operations. Delivery lead time is the shortest, but the customer has no involvement in product design. Examples include off-the-shelf retail apparel, soft drinks, standard automotive parts, or airline flights. A hamburger patty at a fast-food restaurant such as McDonald's or Burger King is made-to-stock as is a taco at Taco Bell. As a customer you gain speed of delivery but lose the ability to customize the product.

Assemble-to-order strategy, also known as build-to-order, produces standard components that can be combined to customer specifications. Delivery time is longer than in the make-to-stock strategy but allows for some customization. Examples include computer systems, prefabricated furniture with choices of fabric colors, or vacation packages with standard options.

Make-to-order is a strategy used to produce products to customer specifications after an order has been received. The delivery time is longest, and product volumes are low. Examples are custom-made clothing, custom-built homes, and customized professional services. Ordering a hamburger to your liking in a sit-down restaurant is another example of this strategy. This strategy is best for an intermittent operation.

Degree of Vertical Integration

The larger the number of processes performed by a company in the chain from raw materials to product delivery, the higher the vertical integration. Vertical integration is a strategic decision that should support the future growth direction of the company.

Vertical integration is a good strategic option when there are high volumes of a small variety of input materials, as is the case with repetitive operations. The reason is that the high volume and narrow variety of input material allows task specialization and cost justification. An example is Dole Food Company, which owns and controls most of its canned pineapple production from pineapple farms to the processing plant. The company has chosen to be vertically integrated so as to have greater control of costs and product quality.

It is typically not a good strategic decision to vertically integrate into specialized processes that provide inputs in small volumes. This would be the case for intermittent operations. For example, let's consider a bakery that makes a variety of different types of cakes and pies. Maybe the bakery purchases different fillings from different sources, such as apple pie filling from one company, chocolate filling from another, and cream filling from a third. If the company were to purchase production of the apple filling, it would not gain much strategically because it still relies on other suppliers. In this case, outsourcing may be a better choice. However, if the bakery shifted its production to making only apple pies, then the vertical integration might be a good choice.

In summary, vertical integration is typically a better strategic decision for repetitive operations. For intermittent operations it is generally a poor strategic choice.

TECHNOLOGY DECISIONS

Advancements in technology have had the greatest impact on process design decisions. Technological advances have enabled companies to produce products faster, with better quality, at a lower cost. Many processes that were not imaginable only a few years ago have been made possible through technology. In this section we look at some of the greatest impacts technology has had on process design.

Information Technology

▶ **Information technology (IT)**
Technology that enables storage, processing, and communication of information within and between firms.

Information technology (**IT**) is technology that enables storage, processing, and communication of information within and between firms. It is also used to organize information to help managers with decision making. One type of information technology we are all familiar with is the *Internet*, which has had the greatest impact on the way companies conduct business. The Internet has linked trading partners—customers, buyers, and suppliers—and has created electronic commerce and the virtual marketplace.

▶ **Enterprise resource planning (ERP)**
Large software programs used for planning and coordinating all resources throughout the entire enterprise.

Enterprise software is another powerful information technology, such as **enterprise resource planning** (**ERP**). These are large software programs used for planning and coordinating all resources throughout the entire enterprise. They allow data sharing and communication within and outside of the firm, enabling collaborative decision making. We will learn more about ERP in Chapter 14.

Other examples of IT include *wireless communication technologies*. We are all familiar with cellular phones and pagers in our own lives. These technologies can also significantly improve business operations. For example, wireless homing devices and wearable computers are being used in warehouses to quickly guide workers to locations of goods. Wireless technologies enhanced by satellite transmission can rapidly transmit information from one source to another. For example, Wal-Mart uses company-owned satellites to automatically transmit point-of-sale data to computers at replenishment warehouses.

Global positioning systems (**GPS**) comprise another type of wireless technology that uses satellite transmission to communicate exact locations. GPS was originally developed by the Department of Defense in 1978 in order to help coordinate U.S. military operations. Today GPS has numerous business and individual applications. Large trucking companies use GPS technology to identify the exact locations of their vehicles. Farmers use GPS while riding on tractors to identify their exact location and apply the proper mix of nutrients to the correct plot of land. GPS capability is also available for personal use in handheld computers, such as the Palm Garmin iQue, that can identify the person's location and plot a route to a destination.

Alamy Images

GPS has even found its use in advertising. For example, Nielsen Media Research, the firm known for rating television shows, is using GPS to test billboard advertising. The company has recruited a sample of adults with known demographic characteristics and is using GPS to monitor their minute-by-minute movements. This information will then be used to determine the best placement for particular billboard advertisements targeted to the particular demographic group.

Radio frequency identification (**RFID**) is another wireless technology that promises to dramatically change business operations. RFID uses memory chips equipped with tiny radio antennas that can be attached to objects to transmit streams of data about the object. For example, RFID can be used to identify any product movement, reveal a missing product's location, or have a shipment of products "announce" their arrival. Empty store shelves can signal that it is time for replenishment using RFID, or low inventories can signal the vendor that it is time to ship more products. RFID can also be used in the service environment, enabling innovative applications in locating and tracking people and assets. In fact, RFID has the potential to become the backbone of an infrastructure that can identify and track billions of individual objects all over the world, in real time.

A big adopter of RFID is Wal-Mart, which is investing heavily in RFID tags for its warehouses. Wal-Mart went live with RFID in January 2005 after pilot testing them at distribution centers in Dallas. The company has already seen a return on its investment. For example, out-of-stock items that are RFID tagged are replenished three times faster than before. The company is also experimenting with adding sensor tags to perishable items. This way, for example, it can track how long a crate of bananas has been in transit and how fresh it is.

Automation

An important decision in designing processes is whether the firm should automate, to what degree, and the type of automation that should be used. **Automation** is the use of machinery able to perform work without human operators and can involve a single machine or an entire factory. Although there are tremendous advantages to automation,

▶ **Global positioning systems (GPS)**
A type of wireless technology that uses satellite transmission to communicate exact locations.

LINKS TO PRACTICE

Using GPS Technology in Product Advertising

▶ **Radio frequency identification (RFID)**
A wireless technology that uses memory chips equipped with radio antennas attached to objects used to transmit streams of data.

▶ **Automation**
Using machinery to perform work without human operators.

there are also disadvantages. Companies need to consider these carefully before making the final decision.

Automation has the advantage of product consistency and ability to efficiently produce large volumes of product. With automated equipment, the last part made in the day will be exactly like the first one made. Because automation brings consistency, quality tends to be higher and easier to monitor. Production can flow uninterrupted throughout the day, without breaks for lunch, and there is no fatigue factor.

However, automation does have its disadvantages. First, automation is typically very costly. These costs can be justified only by a high volume of production. Second, automation is typically not flexible in accommodating product and process changes. Therefore, automation would probably not be good for products in the early stages of their life cycle or for products with short life cycles. Automation needs to be viewed as another capital investment decision: financial payback is critical. For all these reasons automation is typically less present in intermittent than in repetitive operations.

Automated Material Handling   In the past, the primary method of moving products was the conveyor in the form of belts or chains. Today's material handling devices can read bar codes that tell them which location to go to and which are capable of moving in many directions. One such device is an *automated guided vehicle* (*AGV*), a small battery-driven truck that moves materials from one location to the other. The AGV is not operated by a human and takes its directions from either an on-board or central computer. Even AGVs have become more sophisticated over time. The older models followed a cable that was installed under the floor. The newer models follow optical paths and can go anywhere there is aisle space, even avoiding piles of inventory in their way. One of the biggest advantages of AGVs is that they can pretty much go anywhere, as compared to traditional conveyor belts. Managers can use them to move materials wherever they are needed.

Another type of automated material handling includes *automated storage and retrieval systems* (*AS/RSs*), which are basically automated warehouses. AS/RSs use AGVs to move material and also computer-control led racks and storage bins. The storage bins can typically rotate like a carousel, so that the desired storage bin is available for either storage or retrieval. All this is controlled by a computer that keeps track of the exact location and quantity of each item and controls how much will be stored or retrieved in a particular area. AS/RSs can have great advantages over traditional warehouses. Though they are much more costly to operate, they are also much more efficient and accurate.

Jeff Greenberg/The Image Works
Handheld scanner reading a barcode.

► **Flexible manufacturing system (FMS)**
A type of automated system that combines the flexibility of intermittent operations with the efficiency of continuous operations.

Flexible Manufacturing Systems (FMS)   A **flexible manufacturing system** (**FMS**) is a type of automation system that combines the flexibility of intermittent operations with the efficiency of repetitive operations. As you can see by the definition, this is a *system* of automated machines, not just a single machine. An FMS consists of groups of computer-controlled machines and/or robots, automated handling devices for moving, loading, and unloading, and a computer-control center.

Based on the instructions from the computer-control center, parts and materials are automatically moved to appropriate machines or robots. The machines perform their tasks and then the parts are moved to the next set of machines, where the parts automatically are loaded and unloaded. The routes taken by each product are determined with the goal of maximizing the efficiency of the operation. Also, the FMS "knows" when one machine is down due to maintenance or if there is a backlog of work on a machine, and it will automatically route the materials to an available machine.

Flexible manufacturing systems are still fairly limited in the variety of products that they handle. Usually they can only produce similar products from the same family. For this reason, and because of their high cost, flexible manufacturing systems are not very widespread. A decision to use an FMS needs to be long-term and strategic, requiring a sizable financial outlay.

Robotics A robot in manufacturing is usually nothing more than a mechanical arm with a power supply and a computer-control mechanism that controls the movements of the arm. The arm can be used for many tasks, such as painting, welding, assembly, and loading and unloading of machines. Robots are excellent for physically dangerous jobs such as working with radioactive or toxic materials. Also, robots can work twenty-four hours a day to produce a highly consistent product.

Robots vary in their degree of sophistication. Some robots are fairly simple and follow a repetitive set of instructions. Other robots follow complex instructions, and some can be programmed to recognize objects and even make simple decisions. One type of automation similar to simple robotics is the **numerically controlled** (**NC**) **machine**. NC machines are controlled by a computer and can do a variety of tasks such as drilling, boring, or turning parts of different sizes and shapes. Factories of the future will most likely be composed of a number of robots and NC machines working together.

Michael Rosenfeld/Stone/ Getty Images

Production line robot placing windshield on car

▶ **Numerically controlled (NC) machine**
A machine controlled by a computer that can perform a variety of tasks.

The use of robots has not been very widespread in U.S. firms. However, this is an area that can provide a competitive advantage for a company. Cost justification should not only consider reduction in labor costs but also the increased flexibility of operation and improvement in quality. The cost of robots can vary greatly and depends on the robots' size and capabilities. Generally, it is best for a company to consider purchasing multiple robots or forms of automation to spread the costs of maintenance and software support. Also, the decision to purchase automation such as robotics needs to be a long-term strategic one that considers the totality of the production process. Otherwise, the company may have one robot working twenty-four hours a day and piling up inventory while it waits for the other processes to catch up.

Robots can be used to improve operations of almost any business—even literal "operations." Recently, robots have been used to perform certain medical surgeries. For example, at New York University doctors use minimally invasive robotic surgery to repair human heart valves. To perform the surgery, doctors use a robot arm to cut a six-centimeter incision between

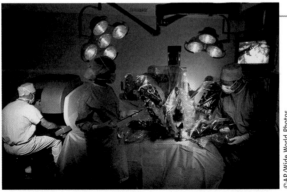

©AP/Wide World Photos

LINKS TO PRACTICE

Performing Robotic Surgery

the ribs and to place an endoscope that allows the surgeons to see what they are doing. The robot arm is controlled through a complex robotic surgical system. The doctors, seated at a workstation, manipulate conventional surgical instruments while the robotic surgical system mirrors these movements on an ultra-fine scale. The advantage of robots is that they can perform delicately fine, small, motor movements, have consistent finger dexterity, and require only tiny incisions. The prediction is that robots will become involved in performing many surgeries, such as eye surgery, neurosurgery, and cosmetic surgery.

e-Manufacturing

Today's Web-based environment has created numerous opportunities for business collaboration. This includes collaboration in product and process design, where customers, buyers, and designers can share information and jointly make decisions in real time. Let's look at some of the computer systems that can aid e-manufacturing.

▶ **Computer-aided design (CAD)**
A system that uses computer graphics to design new products.

Computer-Aided Design (CAD)   Computer-aided design (CAD) is a system that uses computer graphics to design new products. Gone are the days of drafting designs by hand. Today's powerful desktop computers combined with graphics software allow the designer to create drawings on the computer screen and then manipulate them geometrically to be viewed from any angle. With CAD the designer can rotate the object, split it to view the inside, and magnify certain sections for closer view.

CAD can also perform other functions. Engineering design calculations can be performed to test the reactions of the design to stress and to evaluate strength of materials. This is called *computer-aided engineering* (*CAE*). For example, the designer can test how different dimensions, tolerances, and materials respond to different conditions such as rough handling or high temperatures. The designer can use the computer to compare alternative designs and determine the best design for a given set of conditions. The designer can also perform cost analysis on the design, evaluating the advantages of different types of materials.

Another advantage of CAD is that it can be linked to manufacturing. We have already discussed the importance of linking product design to process selection. Through CAD this integration is made easy. *Computer-aided manufacturing* (*CAM*) is the process of controlling manufacturing through computers. Since the product designs are stored in the computer database, the equipment and tools needed can easily be simulated to match up with the processing needs. Efficiencies of various machine choices and different process alternatives can be computed.

Geoff Tompkinson/Science Photo Library/Photo Researchers

Using computer technology in molecular modeling of proteins

CAD can dramatically increase the speed and flexibility of the design process. Designs can be made on the computer screen and printed out when desired. Electronic versions can be shared by many members of the organization for their input. Also, electronic versions can be archived and compared to future versions. The designer can catalogue features based on their characteristics—a very valuable feature. As future product designs are being considered, the designer can quickly retrieve certain features from past designs and test them for inclusion in the design being currently developed. Also, by using *collaborative product commerce* (*CPC*) *software*, sharing designs with suppliers is possible.

▶ **Computer-integrated manufacturing (CIM)**
A term used to describe the integration of product design, process planning, and manufacturing using an integrated computer system.

Computer-Integrated Manufacturing   Computer-integrated manufacturing (CIM) is a term used to describe the integration of product design, process planning, and manufacturing using an integrated computer system. Computer-integrated manufacturing systems vary greatly in their complexity. Simple systems might integrate computer-aided design (CAD) with some numerically controlled machines (NC machines). A complex system, on the other hand, might integrate purchasing, scheduling, inventory control, and distribution, in addition to the other areas of product design.

The key element of CIM is the integration of different parts of the operation process to achieve greater responsiveness and flexibility. The purpose of CIM is to improve how quickly the company can respond to customer needs in terms of product design and availability, as well as quality and productivity, and to improve overall efficiency.

DESIGNING SERVICES

Most of the issues discussed in this chapter are as applicable to service organizations as they are to manufacturing. However, there are issues unique to services that pose special challenges for service design.

Most of us think we know what is needed to run a good service organization. After all, we encounter services almost every day, at banks, fast-food restaurants, doctor's offices, barber shops, grocery stores, and even the university. We have all experienced poor service quality and would gladly offer advice as to how we think it could be better. However, there are some very important features of services you may not have thought about. Let's see what they are.

How Are Services Different from Manufacturing?

In Chapter 1 we learned about two basic features that make service organizations different from manufacturing. These are the intangibility of the product produced and the high degree of customer contact. Next we briefly review these and see how they impact service design.

Intangible Product Service organizations produce an intangible product, which cannot be touched or seen. It cannot be stored in inventory for later use or traded in for another model. The service produced is *experienced* by the customer. The design of the service needs to specify exactly what the customer is supposed to experience. For example, it may be relaxation, comfort, and pampering, such as offered by Canyon Ranch Spa. It may be efficiency and speed, such as offered by FedEx. Defining the customer experience is part of the service design. It requires identifying precisely what the customer is going to feel and think and consequently how he or she is going to behave. This is not always as easy as it might seem.

The experience of the customer is directly related to customer expectations. For services to be successful, the customer experience needs to meet or even exceed these expectations. However, customer expectations can greatly vary depending on the type of customer and customer demographic, including customer age, gender, background, and knowledge. The expectation is developed through product marketing to a particular market segment. It is highly important in designing the service to identify the target market the service is geared to and to create the correct expectation.

High Degree of Customer Contact Service organizations typically have a high degree of customer contact. The customer is often present while the service is being delivered, such as at a theater, restaurant, or bank. Also, the contact between the customer and service provider is often the service itself, such as what you experience at a doctor's office. For a service to be successful, this contact needs to be a positive experience for the customer, and this depends greatly on the service provider.

Unfortunately, since services often have multiple service providers, there can be great variation in the type of service delivered. We have all had experiences where the service of one organization varied greatly depending on the skills of the service provider. This could be a hairdresser at a hair salon, a food server at a restaurant, or a teller at a bank. We have all heard people say something similar to "I often have dinner at Aussie Steak Grill and I insist that Jenny be my server." Similarly, someone might say, "I go to Olentangy Family Physicians, but I won't see Dr. Jekyl because he is rude and unfriendly." For a service to be successful, the service experience must be consistent at all times. This requires close quality management to ensure high consistency and reliability. Many of the procedures used in manufacturing to ensure high quality, such as standardization and simplification, are used in services as well. Fast-food restaurants such as McDonald's and Wendy's are known for their consistency. The same is true of hotel chains such as Holiday Inn and Embassy Suites.

To ensure that the service contact is a positive experience for the customer, employees of the service need to have training that encompasses a great array of skills that include courtesy, friendliness, and overall disposition. The service company also needs to structure the proper incentive system to motivate employees.

How Are Services Classified?

We can classify service organizations based on similar characteristics in order to understand them better. A common way to classify services is based on the degree of customer contact. This is illustrated in Figure 3-12.

Services with low customer contact are called "quasi-manufacturing." These firms have a high degree of service standardization, have higher sales volumes, and are typically less labor intensive. These firms have almost no face-to-face contact with customers and are in many ways similar to manufacturing operations. Examples include warehouses, distribution centers, environmental testing laboratories, and back-office operations.

Services with high customer contact are called "pure services." These firms have high face-to-face contact and are highly labor intensive. There is low product standardization, as each customer has unique requirements, and sales volumes tend to be low. Pure

FIGURE 3-12

Classification of service operations

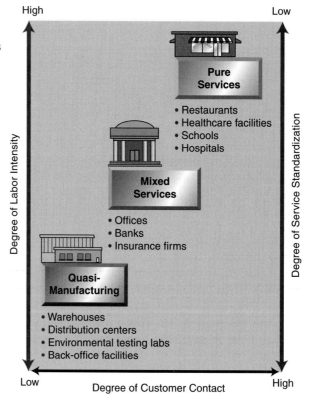

service firms have an environment of lowest system efficiency compared to other service firms. The reason is that the service is typically customized. As each customer has unique requirements, there is less predictability in managing the operating environment. Examples include hospitals, restaurants, barber shops, and beauty salons.

Services that combine elements of both of these extremes are called "mixed services." Some parts of their operation have face-to-face customer contact, though others do not. They include offices, banks, and insurance firms.

It is important to understand that companies with different levels of customer contact need to be managed differently. These differences also apply to high-contact and low-contact areas of firms. For example, companies should specifically hire people-oriented workers for high-contact areas, whereas technical skills are more important in low-contact areas. Also, noncontact activities should be partitioned from the customer to avoid disruptions in the flow of work. Noncontact areas can be managed borrowing tools from manufacturing, whereas high-contact areas need to focus on accommodating the customer.

The Service Package

The really successful service organizations do not happen spontaneously. They are carefully thought out and planned, down to every employee action. To design a successful service, we must first start with a service concept or idea, which needs to be very comprehensive. We have learned that when purchasing a service, customers actually buy a **service package** or service bundle. The service package is a grouping of features that are purchased together as part of the service. There are three elements of the service package: (1) the physical goods, (2) the sensual benefits, and (3) the psychological benefits. The physical goods of the service are the tangible aspects of the service that we receive, or are in contact with, during service delivery. In a fine-dining restaurant the physical goods are the food consumed, as well as facilities such as comfortable tables and chairs, tablecloths, and fine china. The sensual benefits are the sights, smell, and sounds of the experience—all the items we experience through our senses. Finally, the psychological benefits include the status, comfort, and well-being provided by the experience.

▶ **Service package**
A grouping of physical, sensual, and psychological benefits that are purchased together as part of the service.

It is highly important that the design of the service specifically identify every aspect of the service package. When designing the service, we should not focus only on the tangible aspects; it is often the sensual and psychological benefits that are the deciding factors in the success of the service. The service package needs to be designed to precisely meet the expectations of the target customer group.

Once the service package is identified, it can then be translated into a design using a process that is not too different from the one used in manufacturing. Details of the service, such as quality standards and employee training, can later be defined in keeping with the service concept. The service providers—the individuals who come in direct contact with the customers—must be trained and motivated to precisely understand and satisfy customer expectations.

Imagine going to a fast-food restaurant and having the server take his time asking you how you want your hamburger cooked and precisely what condiments you would like to accompany it, then waiting a long time to receive your food. Similarly, imagine going to an expensive hair salon and having the staff rush you through the process. In both cases, you as the customer would not be satisfied because the service delivery did not meet your expectations. Next time you might choose to go somewhere else. These examples illustrate what happens when there is a mismatch between the service concept and the service delivery.

Differing Service Designs

There is no one model of successful service design. The design selected should support the company's service concept and provide the features of the service package that the target customers want. Different service designs have proved successful in different environments. In this section we look at three very different service designs that have worked well for the companies that adopted them.

Substitute Technology for People Substituting technology for people is an approach to service design that was advocated some years ago by Theodore Levitt.[1] Levitt argued that one way to reduce the uncertainty of service delivery is to use technology to develop a production-line approach to services. One of the most successful companies to use this approach is McDonald's. Technology has been substituted wherever possible to provide product consistency and take the guesswork away from employees. Some examples of the use of technology include the following:

- Buzzers and lights are used to signal cooking time for frying perfect french fries.
- The size of the french fryer is designed to produce the correct amount of fries.
- The french fry scoop is the perfect size to fill an order.
- "Raw materials" are received in usable form (e.g., hamburger patties are premade; pickles and tomatoes are presliced; french fries are precut).
- There are 49 steps for producing perfect french fries.
- Steps for producing the perfect hamburger are detailed and specific.
- Products have different-colored wrappings for easy identification.

In addition to the use of technology in the production of the product, there is consistency in facilities and a painstaking focus on cleanliness. For example, the production process at McDonald's is not left to the discretion of the workers. Rather, their job is to follow the technology and preset processes.

Today we are all accustomed to the product consistency, speed of delivery, and predictability that are a feature of most fast-food restaurants. However, this concept was very new in the early 1970s. It is this approach to services that has enabled McDonald's to establish its global reputation.

Substituting technology for people is an approach we have seen over the years in many service industries. For example, almost all gas stations have reduced the number of cashiers and attendants with the advent of credit cards at self-serve pumps. Also, many hospitals are using technology to monitor patient heart rate and blood pressure without relying exclusively on nurses. As technologies develop in different service industries, we will continue to see an ever-increasing reliance on its use and an increase in the elimination of workers.

Get the Customer Involved A different approach to service design was proposed by C. H. Lovelock and R. F. Young.[2] Their idea was to take advantage of the customer's presence during the delivery of the service and have him or her become an active participant. This is different from traditional service designs where the customer passively

---

[1]Theodore Levitt, "Production Line Approach to Services," *Harvard Business Review*, 50, 5 (September–October 1972), 41–52.

[2]C.H. Lovelock and R.F. Young. "Look to Customers to Increase Productivity," *Harvard Business Review*, 57, 2, 168–178.

waits for service employees to deliver the service. Lovelock and Young proposed that since the customers are already there, "get them involved."

We have all seen a large increase in the self-serve areas of many service firms. Traditional salad bars have led to self-serve food buffets of every type. Many fast-food restaurants no longer fill customer drink orders, but have the customers serve themselves. Grocery stores allow customers to select and package baked goods on their own. Many hotels provide in-room coffee makers and prepackaged coffee, allowing customers to make coffee at their convenience.

Bruce Ayres/Stone/Getty Images

This type of approach has a number of advantages. First, it takes a large burden away from the service provider. The delivery of the service is made faster, and costs are reduced due to lowered staffing requirements. Second, this approach empowers customers and gives them a greater sense of control in terms of getting what they want, which provides a great deal of customer convenience and increases satisfaction. However, since different types of customers have different preferences, many facilities are finding that it is best to offer full-service and self-service options. For example, many breakfast bars still allow a request for eggs cooked and served to order, and most gas stations still offer some full-service pumps.

High Customer Attention Approach A third approach to service design is providing a high level of customer attention. This is in direct contrast to the first two approaches. The first approach discussed automates the service and makes it more like manufacturing. The second approach requires greater participation and responsibility from the customer. The third approach is different from the first two in that it does not standardize the service and does not get the customer involved. Rather, it is based on customizing the service to the needs unique to each customer and having the customer be the passive and pampered recipient of the service. This approach relies on developing a personal relationship with each customer and giving the customer precisely what he or she wants.

There are a number of examples of this type of approach. Nordstrom, Inc. department stores is recognized in the retail industry for its attention to customer service. Salespeople typically know their customers by name and keep a record of their preferences. Returns are handled without question, and the customer is always right. Another example of this is a midwestern grocer called Dorothy Lane Market. Dorothy Lane prides itself on its ability to provide unique cuts of specialty meats precisely to customer order. As at Nordstrom, a list is kept of primary customers and their preferences. Customers are notified of special purchases, such as unique wines, specialty chocolates, and special cuts of meat.

Whereas the first two approaches to service design result in lowered service costs, this third approach is geared toward customers who are prepared to pay a higher amount for the services they receive. As you can see, different approaches are meant to serve different types of customers. The design chosen needs to support the specific service concept of the company.

PRODUCT DESIGN AND PROCESS SELECTION WITHIN OM: HOW IT ALL FITS TOGETHER

Product design decisions are strategic in nature. The features and characteristics of a product need to support the overall strategic direction of the company. In turn, product design decisions directly dictate the type of process selected. They determine the types of facilities that will be needed to produce the product, types of machines, worker skills, degree of automation, and other decisions. Most companies continually design new products. The design of these new products has to take into account the type of processes the company has, otherwise facilities may not be available to produce the new product design. Therefore, product design and process selection decisions are directly tied to each other.

Product design and process selection decisions are further linked to all other areas of operations management. They are linked to decisions such as the level of capacity needed (Chapter 9), degree of quality (Chapters 5 and 6), layout (Chapter 10), and location of facilities (Chapter 9), types of workers (Chapter 11), and many others. As we go through this book we will see how product design and process selection specifically impact other operations decisions.

PRODUCT DESIGN AND PROCESS SELECTION ACROSS THE ORGANIZATION

The strategic and financial impact of product design and process selection mandates that operations work closely with other organizational functions to make these decisions. Operations is an integral part of these decisions because it understands issues of production, ease of fabrication, productivity, and quality. Now let's see how the other organizational functions are involved with product design and process selection.

Marketing is impacted by product design issues because they determine the types of products that will be produced and affect marketing's ability to sell them. Marketing's input is critical at this stage because marketing is the function that interfaces with customers and understands the types of product characteristics customers want. It is marketing that can provide operations with information on customer preferences, competition, and future trends.

Process selection decisions impact marketing as well. They typically require large capital outlays, and once made, they are typically difficult to change and are in place for a long time. Process decisions affect the types of future products that the company can produce. Because of this, marketing needs to be closely involved in ensuring that the process can meet market demands for many years to come.

Finance plays an integral role in product design and process selection issues because these decisions require large financial outlays. Finance needs to be a part of these decisions to evaluate the financial impact on the company. Process selection decisions should be viewed as any other financial investment, with risks and rewards. Finance must ensure that the trade-off between the risks and rewards is acceptable. Also, it is up to finance to provide the capital needed for this investment and to balance that against future capital requirements.

Information systems needs to be part of the process selection decisions. Operations decisions, such as forecasting, purchasing, scheduling, and inventory control, differ based on the type of operation the company has. Information systems will be quite different for intermittent versus continuous operations. Therefore, the information system has to be developed to match the needs of the production process being planned.

Human resources provides important input to process selection decisions because it is the function directly responsible for hiring employees. If special labor skills are needed in the process of production, human resources needs to be able to provide information on the available labor pool. The two types of operations discussed, intermittent and continuous, typically require very different labor skills. Intermittent operations usually require higher-skilled labor than continuous operations. Human resources needs to understand the specific skills that are needed.

Purchasing works closely with suppliers to get the needed parts and raw materials at a favorable price. It is aware of product and material availability, scarcity, and price. Often certain materials or components can use less expensive substitutes if they are designed properly. For this reason it is important to have purchasing involved in product design issues from the very beginning.

Engineering needs to be an integral part of the product design and process selection decisions because this is the function that understands product measurement, tolerances, strength of materials, and specific equipment needs. There can be many product design ideas, but it is up to engineering to evaluate their manufacturability.

As you can see, product design and process selection issues involve many functions and affect the entire organization. For this reason, product design and process selection decisions need to be made using a team effort, with all these functions working closely together to come up with a product plan that is best for the company.

SUPPLY CHAIN LINK

In today's competitive environment companies typically have a very short window of opportunity to enter the market with a new product design. Most companies are aware that they must get to the market early with an innovative product before their competitors. This requires the support of the entire supply chain, where suppliers must be involved in the product design process. We have already learned about the time-saving advantages of concurrent engineering and early supplier involvement. These require a carefully integrated supply chain that allows collaboration and simultaneous product design between suppliers and manufacturers.

Another important supply chain link relates to the technology decisions the firm makes. As companies acquire new technologies, they must consider how these technologies will be aligned with the technologies used by their supply chain partners. When an entire supply chain uses technologies that are compatible, great strides can be made in the efficiency of production and movement of goods. Consider that Wal-Mart has mandated that its top 300 suppliers must put RFID tags on all their shipping crates and pallets and expects this number to reach 600 by January 2007. Although RFID tags are expensive, this move has already incurred huge savings by increasing efficiency, better tracking of products, and a reduction in inventory.

Chapter Highlights

1 Product design is the process of deciding on the unique characteristics and features of a company's product. Process selection, on the other hand, is the development of the process necessary to produce the product being designed. Product design is a big strategic decision for a company, because the design of the product defines who the company's customers will be, as well as the company's image, its competition, and its overall future growth.

2 Steps in product design include idea generation, product screening, preliminary design and testing, and final design. A useful tool at the product-screening stage is break-even analysis.

3 Break-even analysis is a technique used to compute the amount of goods that have to be sold just to cover costs.

4 Production processes can be divided into two broad categories: intermittent and repetitive operations. Intermittent operations are used when products with different characteristics are being produced in smaller volumes. These types of operations tend to organize their resources by grouping similar processes together and having the products routed through the facility based on their needs. Repetitive operations are used when one or a few similar products are produced in high volume. These operations arrange resources in sequence to allow for an efficient buildup of the product. Both intermittent and repetitive operations have their advantages and disadvantages. Intermittent operations provide great flexibility but have high material handling costs and challenge scheduling resources. Repetitive operations are highly efficient but inflexible.

5 Product design and process selection decisions are linked. The type of operation a company has in place is defined by the product the company produces. The type of operation then affects other organizational decisions, such as competitive priorities, facility layout, and degree of vertical integration.

6 A process flowchart is used for viewing the flow of the processes involved in producing the product. It is a very useful tool for seeing the totality of the operation and for identifying potential problem areas. There is no exact format for designing the chart. The flowchart can be very simple or very detailed.

7 Different types of technologies can significantly enhance product and process design. These include automation, automated material handling devices, computer-aided design (CAD), numerically controlled (NC) equipment, flexible manufacturing systems (FMS), and computer-integrated manufacturing (CIM).

8 Designing services have more complexities than manufacturing, because services produce an intangible product and typically have a high degree of customer contact. Different service designs include substituting technology for people, getting the customer involved, and paying great attention to the customer.

Key Terms

manufacturability 55
product design 55
service design 56
benchmarking 57
reverse engineering 57
early supplier involvement (ESI) 58
break-even analysis 58
fixed costs 58
variable costs 58
design for manufacture (DFM) 61
product life cycle 62
concurrent engineering 63
remanufacturing 64
intermittent operations 65
repetitive operations 65

project process 67
batch process 67
line process 67
continuous process 67
process flow analysis 68
process flowchart 68
bottleneck 68
make-to-stock strategy 69
assemble-to-order strategy 69
make-to-order strategy 69
process performance metrics 70
throughput time 71
process velocity 72
productivity 72
utilization 72

efficiency 72
information technology (IT) 78
enterprise resource planning (ERP) 78
global positioning systems (GPS) 79
radio frequency identification (RFID) 79
automation 79
flexible manufacturing system (FMS) 80
numerically controlled (NC) machine 81
computer-aided design (CAD) 82
computer-integrated manufacturing (CIM) 82
service package 85

Formula Review

1. Total cost = fixed cost + variable cost

2. Revenue = $(SP)Q$

3. $F + (VC)Q = (SP)Q$

4. $Q_{BE} = \dfrac{F}{SP - VC}$

5. Process velocity = $\dfrac{\text{throughput time}}{\text{value-added time}}$

6. Utilization = $\dfrac{\text{time a resource used}}{\text{time a resource available}}$

7. Efficiency = $\dfrac{\text{actual output}}{\text{standard output}}$

Solved Problems

(See student companion site for Excel template.)

• Problem 1

Joe Jenkins, owner of Jenkins Manufacturing, is considering whether to produce a new product. He has considered the operations requirements for the product as well as the market potential. Joe estimates the fixed costs per year to be $40,000 and variable costs for each unit produced to be $50.

(a) If Joe sells the product at a price of $70, how many units of product does he have to sell in order to break even? Use both the algebraic and graphical approaches.

(b) If Joe sells 3000 units at the product price of $70, what will be his contribution to profit?

• Before You Begin:

To solve this problem you must first use the break-even formula. Then to compute the contribution to profit, recall that profit is computed as

$$\text{Profit} = \text{total revenue} - \text{total cost}$$

• Solution:

(a) To compute the break-even quantity, we follow the equation and substitute the appropriate numerical values:

$$Q = \frac{F}{SP - VC} = \frac{\$40,000}{\$70 - \$50} = 2000 \text{ units}$$

The break-even quantity is 2000 units. This is how much Joe would have to sell in order to cover costs.

Graphically, we can obtain the same result. This is shown in the figure.

(b) To compute the contribution to profit with sales of 3000 units:

$$\text{Profit} = \text{total revenue} - \text{total cost}$$
$$= (SP)Q - [F + (VC)Q]$$

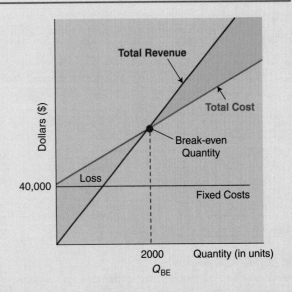

Now we can substitute numerical values:

$$\text{Profit} = \$70(3000) - [\$40,000 + \$50(3000)]$$
$$= \$20,000$$

The contribution to profit is $20,000 if Joe can sell 3000 units of product.

• Problem 2

Joe Jenkins, owner of Jenkins Manufacturing, has decided to produce the new product discussed in Problem 1. The product can be produced with the current equipment in place. However, Joe is considering the purchase of new equipment that would produce the product more efficiently. Joe's fixed cost would be raised to $60,000 per year, but the variable cost would be reduced to $25 per unit. Joe still plans to sell the product at $70 per unit.

Should Joe produce the new product with the new or current equipment described in Problem 1? Specify the volume of demand for which you would choose each process.

• Solution

As we mentioned in the chapter, break-even analysis can also be used to evaluate different processes. Here we show how this can be done. To decide which process to use, we first need to compute the point of indifference between the two processes. The point of indifference is where the cost of the two processes is equal. If we label the current equipment A and the new equipment B, the point of indifference occurs when the costs for each process are equal. This is shown as

$$\text{Total cost}_{\text{Equipment A}} = \text{total cost}_{\text{Equipment B}}$$

Again, total cost is the sum of fixed and variable costs:

$$\$40,000 + \$50\,Q = \$60,000 + \$25\,Q$$
$$\$25\,Q = 20,000$$
$$Q = 800 \text{ units produced}$$

$Q = 800$ units is the point of indifference, that is, the point where the cost of either equipment is the same. If demand is expected to be less than 800 units, equipment A should be used given that it has a lower fixed cost. If demand is expected to be greater than 800 units, equipment B should be used given that it has a lower variable cost. This is shown graphically.

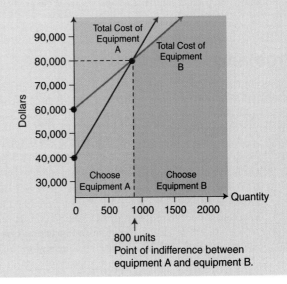

800 units
Point of indifference between
equipment A and equipment B.

• Problem 3

Zelle's Dry Cleaners has collected the following data for its processing of dress shirts:

It takes an average of $3\frac{1}{2}$ hours to dry clean and press a dress shirt, with value-added time estimated at 110 minutes per shirt.

Workers are paid for a 7-hour workday and work $5\frac{1}{2}$ hours per day on average, accounting for breaks and lunch; labor utilization is 75 percent in the industry.

The dry cleaner completes twenty-five shirts per day, with an industry standard of twenty-eight shirts per day for a comparable facility.

Determine process velocity, labor utilization, and efficiency for the company.

• Before You Begin:

When solving this problem, remember to keep the units of measure consistent in the numerator and denominator of each equation.

• Solution

$$\text{Process velocity} = \frac{\text{throughput time}}{\text{value-added time}}$$

$$= \frac{210 \text{ minutes/shirt}}{110 \text{ minutes/shirt}} = 1.90$$

$$\text{Labor utilization} = \frac{5\frac{1}{2} \text{ hours/day}}{7 \text{ hours/day}} = .786 \text{ or } 78.6\%$$

$$\text{Efficiency} = \frac{25 \text{ shirts/day}}{28 \text{ shifts/day}} = .89 \text{ or } 89\%$$

Process velocity shows room for process improvement, as throughput time is almost twice that of value-added time. Labor utilization is just above the industry standard, though overall efficiency is below.

Discussion Questions

1. Define product design and explain its relationship to business strategy.
2. What are the differences between product and service design?
3. Explain the meanings of *benchmarking* and *reverse engineering*.
4. Explain the meaning of *design for manufacture (DFM)* and give some examples.
5. Describe the stages of the product life cycle. What are demand characteristics at each stage?
6. Explain the term *concurrent engineering*. Why is it important?
7. Identify the two general types of operations. What are their characteristics?

8. What is meant by the term *vertical integration?* What types of companies are more likely to become vertically integrated?
9. What is a process flowchart and what is it used for?
10. Give some examples of automation. How has automation changed the production process?
11. Discuss the benefits of computer-aided design (CAD).
12. What is meant by the term *service package?*
13. Name three service companies and describe their service package.
14. Give examples of services that have a good match between customer expectations and service delivery. Give examples of services that do not have a good match.

Problems

1. See-Clear Optics is considering producing a new line of eyewear. After considering the costs of raw materials and the cost of some new equipment, the company estimates fixed costs to be $40,000 with a variable cost of $45 per unit produced.
   (a) If the selling price of each new product is set at $100, how many units need to be produced and sold to break even? Use both the graphical and algebraic approaches.
   (b) If the selling price of the product is set at $80 per unit, See-Clear expects to sell 2000 units. What would be the total contribution to profit from this product at this price?
   (c) See-Clear estimates that if it offers the product at the original target price of $100 per unit, the company will sell about 1500 units. Will the pricing strategy of $100 per unit or $80 per unit yield a higher contribution to profit?

2. Med-First is a medical facility that offers outpatient medical services. The facility is considering offering an additional service, mammography screening tests, on-site. The facility estimates the annual fixed cost of the equipment and skills necessary for the service to be $120,000. Variable costs for each patient processed are estimated at $35 per patient. If the clinic plans to charge $55 for each screening test, how many patients must it process a year in order to break even?

3. Tasty Ice Cream is a year-round take-out ice cream restaurant that is considering offering an additional product, hot chocolate. Considering the additional machine it would need plus cups and ingredients, it estimates fixed costs to be $200 per year and the variable cost to be $0.20. If it charges $1.00 for each hot chocolate, how many hot chocolates does it need to sell in order to break even?

4. Slick Pads is a company that manufactures laptop notebook computers. The company is considering adding its own line of computer printers as well. It has considered the implications from the marketing and financial perspectives and estimates fixed costs to be $500,000. Variable costs are estimated at $200 per unit produced and sold.

(a) If the company plans to offer the new printers at a price of $350, how many printers does it have to sell to break even?

(b) Describe the types of operations considerations that the company needs to consider before making the final decision.

5. Perfect Furniture is a manufacturer of kitchen tables and chairs. The company is currently deciding between two new methods for making kitchen tables. The first process is estimated to have a fixed cost of $80,000 and a variable cost of $75 per unit. The second process is estimated to have a fixed cost of $100,000 and a variable cost of $60 per unit.

(a) Graphically plot the total costs for both methods. Identify which ranges of product volume are best for each method.

(b) If the company produces 500 tables a year, which method provides a lower total cost?

6. Harrison Hotels is considering adding a spa to its current facility in order to improve its list of amenities. Operating the spa would require a fixed cost of $25,000 a year. Variable cost is estimated at $35 per customer. The hotel wants to break even if 12,000 customers use the spa facility. What should be the price of the spa services?

7. Kaizer Plastics produces a variety of plastic items for packaging and distribution. One item, container #145, has had a low contribution to profits. Last year, 20,000 units of container #145 were produced and sold. The selling price of the container was $20 per unit, with a variable cost of $18 per unit and a fixed cost of $70,000 per year.

(a) What is the break-even quantity for this product? Use both graphic and algebraic methods to get your answer.

(b) The company is currently considering ways to improve profitability by either stimulating sales volumes or reducing variable costs. Management believes that sales can be increased by 35 percent of their current level or that variable cost can be reduced to 90 percent of their current level. Assuming all other costs equal, identify which alternative would lead to a higher profit contribution.

8. George Fine, owner of Fine Manufacturing, is considering the introduction of a new product line. George has considered factors such as costs of raw materials, new equipment, and requirements of a new production process. He estimates that the variable costs of each unit produced would be $8 and fixed costs would be $70,000.

(a) If the selling price is set at $20 each, how many units have to be produced and sold for Fine Manufacturing to break even? Use both graphical and algebraic approaches.

(b) If the selling price of the product is set at $18 per unit, Fine Manufacturing expects to sell 15,000 units. What would be the total contribution to profit from this product at this price?

(c) Fine Manufacturing estimates that if it offers the product at the original target price of $20 per unit, the company will sell about 12,000 units. Which pricing strategy—$18 per unit or $20 per unit—will yield a higher contribution to profit?

(d) Identify additional factors that George Fine should consider in deciding whether to produce and sell the new product.

9. Handy-Maid Cleaning Service is considering offering an additional line of services to include professional office cleaning. Annual fixed costs for this additional service are estimated to be $9000. Variable costs are estimated at $50 per unit of service. If the price of the new service is set at $80 per unit of service, how many units of service are needed for Handy-Maid to break even?

10. Easy-Tech Software Corporation is evaluating the production of a new software product to compete with the popular word processing software currently available. Annual fixed costs of producing the item are estimated at $150,000, and the variable cost is $10 per unit. The current selling price of the item is $35 per unit, and the annual sales volume is estimated at 50,000 units.

(a) Easy-Tech is considering adding new equipment that would improve software quality. The negative aspect of this new equipment would be an increase in both fixed and variable costs. Annual fixed costs would increase by $50,000 and variable costs by $3. However, marketing expects the better-quality product to increase demand to 70,000 units. Should Easy-Tech purchase this new equipment and keep the price of their product the same? Explain your reasoning.

(b) Another option being considered by Easy-Tech is the increase in the selling price to $40 per unit to offset the additional equipment costs. However, this increase would result in a decrease in demand to 40,000 units. Should Easy-Tech increase its selling price if it purchases the new equipment? Explain your reasoning.

11. Zodiac Furniture is considering the production of a new line of metal office chairs. The chairs can be produced in-house using either process A or process B. The chairs can also be purchased from an outside supplier. Specify the levels of demand for each processing alternative given the costs in the table.

	Fixed Cost	Variable Cost
Process A	$20,000	$30
Process B	$30,000	$15
Outside Supplier	$0	$50

12. Mop and Broom Manufacturing is evaluating whether to produce a new type of mop. The company is considering the operations requirements for the mop as well as the market potential. Estimates of fixed costs per year are $40,000 and the variable cost for each mop produced is $20.

(a) If the company sells the product at a price of $25, how many units of product have to be sold in order to break even? Use both the algebraic and graphical approaches.

(b) If the company sells 10,000 mops at the product price of $25, what will be the contribution to profit?

13. Mop and Broom Manufacturing, from Problem 12, has decided to produce a new type of mop. The mop can be made with the current equipment in place. However, the company is considering the purchase of new equipment that would produce

the mop more efficiently. The fixed cost would be raised to $50,000 per year, but the variable cost would be reduced to $15 per unit. The company still plans to sell the mops at $25 per unit. Should Mop and Broom produce the mop with the new or current equipment described in Problem 12? Specify the volume of demand for which you would choose each process.

14. Jacob's Baby Food Company must go through the following steps to make mashed carrots: (1) unload carrots from truck; (2) inspect carrots; (3) weigh carrots; (4) move to storage; (5) wait until needed; (6) move to washer; (7) boil in water; (8) mash carrots; (9) inspect. Draw a process flow diagram for these steps.

15. Draw a process flow diagram of your last doctor's office visit. Identify bottlenecks. Did any activities occur in parallel?

16. Oakwood Outpatient Clinic is analyzing its operation in an effort to improve performance. The clinic estimates that a pa-

tient spends on average $3\frac{1}{2}$ hours at the facility. The amount of time the patient is in contact with staff (i.e., physicians, nurses, office staff, lab technicians) is estimated at forty minutes. On average the facility sees forty-two patients per day. Their standard has been forty patients per day. Determine process velocity and efficiency for the clinic.

17. Oakwood Outpatient Clinic rents a magnetic resonance imaging (MRI) machine for thirty hours a month for use on its patients. Last month the machine was used twenty-eight hours out of the month. What was machine utilization?

18. Mop and Broom Manufacturing estimates that it takes $4\frac{1}{2}$ hours for each broom to be produced, from raw materials to final product. An evaluation of the process reveals that the amount of time spent working on the product is 3 hours. Determine process velocity.

CASE: Biddy's Bakery (BB)

Biddy's Bakery was founded by Elizabeth McDoogle in 1984. Nicknamed "Biddy," Elizabeth started the home-style bakery in Cincinnati, Ohio as an alternative to commercially available baked goods. The mission of Biddy's Bakery was to produce a variety of baked goods with old-fashioned style and taste. The goods produced included a variety of pies and cakes and were sold to the general public and local restaurants.

The operation was initially started as a hobby by Elizabeth and a group of her friends. Many of the recipes they used had been passed down for generations in their families. The small production and sales facility was housed in a mixed commercial and residential area on the first floor of "Biddy's" home. Elizabeth ("Biddy") and three of her friends worked in the facility from 6 AM to 2 PM making and selling the pies. The operation was arranged as a job shop with workstations set up to perform a variety of tasks as needed. Most of the customers placed advanced orders and Biddy's Bakery took pride in accepting special requests. The bakery's specialty was the McDoogle pie, a rich chocolate confection in a cookie crust.

Meeting Capacity Needs
Initially sales were slow and there were periods when the business operated at a loss. However, after a few years Biddy's Bakery began to attract a loyal customer following. Sales continued to grow slowly but steadily. In 1994 a first floor storage area was expanded to accommodate the growing business. However, Biddy's Baker quickly outgrew its current capacity. In May of 2000 Elizabeth decided to purchase the adjacent building and move the entire operation into the much larger facility. The new facility had considerably more capacity than needed, but the expectation was that business would continue to grow. Unfortunately, by the end of 2000 Elizabeth found that her sales expectations had not been met and she was paying for a facility with unused space.

Getting Management Advice
Elizabeth knew that her operations methods, though traditional, were sound. A few years ago she had called upon a team of busi-

ness students from a local university for advice as part of their course project. They had offered some suggestions but were most impressed with the efficient manner with which she ran her operation. Recalling this experience, she decided to contact the same university for another team of business students to help her with her predicament.

After considerable analysis the team of business students came up with their plan: Biddy's Bakery should primarily focus on production of the McDoogle pie in large volumes, with major sales to go to a local grocery store. The team of business students discussed this option with a local grocery store chain that was pleased with the prospect. Under the agreement Biddy's Bakery would focus its production on the McDoogle pie, which would be delivered in set quantities to one store location twice a week. The volume of pies required would use up all of the current excess capacity and take away most of the capacity from production of other pies.

Elizabeth was confused. The alternative being offered would solve her capacity problems, but it seemed that the business would be completely different, though she did not understand how or why. For the first time in managing her business she did not know what to do.

Case Questions
1. Explain the challenge faced by Elizabeth in meeting her capacity needs. What should she have considered before moving into the larger facility?

2. What is wrong with the proposal made by the team of business students? Why?

3. What type of operation does Biddy's Bakery currently have in place? What type of operation is needed to meet the proposal made by the team of business students? Explain the differences between these two operations.

4. Elizabeth senses that the business would be different if she accepts the proposal but does not know how and why. Explain how it would be different.

5. What would you advise Elizabeth?

CASE: Creature Care Animal Clinic (B)

Company Background

Creature Care Animal Clinic is a suburban veterinary clinic specializing in the medical care of dogs and cats. Dr. Julia Barr opened the clinic three years ago, hiring another full-time veterinarian, a staff of three nurses, an office manager, and an office assistant. The clinic operates Monday through Friday during regular business hours, with half days on Saturdays and extended hours on Wednesday evenings. Both doctors work during the week and take turns covering Wednesday evenings and Saturdays.

Dr. Barr opened the clinic with the intent of providing outpatient animal care. Overnight services are provided for surgical patients only. No other specialized services are offered. The facility for the clinic was designed for this type of service, with a spacious waiting and reception area. The examining and surgical rooms are in the rear, just large enough to accommodate their initial purpose.

As time has passed, however, the number of patients requesting specialized services has increased. Initially the requests were few, so Dr. Barr tried to accommodate them. As one of the nurses was also trained in grooming services, she began to alternate between her regular duties and pet grooming. Pet grooming was performed in the rear of the reception area, as it was spacious and there was no other room for this job. At first this was not a problem. However, as the number of pets being groomed increased, the flow of work began to be interrupted. Customers waiting with their pets would comment to the groomer in the rear, who had difficulty focusing on the work. The receptionist was also distracted, as were the animals.

The number of customers requesting grooming services was growing rapidly. Customers wanted to drop off their pets for a "package" of examining, grooming, and even minor surgical procedures requiring overnight stays. The space for grooming and overnight services was rapidly taking over room for other tasks. Also, most of the staff was not trained in providing the type of service customers were now requiring.

The Dilemma

Dr. Barr sat at her desk wondering how to handle the operations dilemma she was faced with. She started her business as a medical clinic but found that she was no longer sure what business she was in. She didn't understand why it was so complicated given that she was only providing a service. She was not sure what to do.

Case Questions

1. Identify the operations management problems that Dr. Barr is having at the clinic.

2. How would you define the "service bundle" currently being offered? How is this different from the initial purpose of the clinic?

3. Identify the high-contact and low-contact segments of the operation. How should each be managed?

4. What should Dr. Barr have done differently to avoid the problems she is currently experiencing? What should Dr. Barr do now?

INTERACTIVE CASE ▶ Virtual Company

 www.wiley.com/college/reid

On-line Case: Product Design and Process Selection at Valley Memorial Hospital

Assignment: *Service Package and Processes at Valley Memorial Hospital* With just a couple of weeks left before you start working at Kaizen for its client Valley Memorial Hospital, it is essential for you to get some specific insights into the company's operations. This assignment will enable you to enhance your knowledge of the material in Chapter 3 while continuing to prepare you for a successful internship. Bob Reilly suggests you learn more about the service package at VMH.

To access the Web site:

- Go to **www.wiley.com/college/reid**
- Click **Student Companion Site**
- Click **Virtual Company**
- Click **Kaizen Consulting, Inc.**
- Click **Consulting Assignments**
- Click **Service Package and Processes at Valley Memorial Hospital**

INTERNET CHALLENGE   Country Comfort Furniture

You have just taken a position with Country Comfort Furniture, a furniture manufacturer known for its custom-designed country furniture. The primary focus of the company has been on kitchen and dining room furniture in the upper portion of the high-price range. Due to competitive pressures and changes in the market, Country Comfort is now considering production of prefabricated kitchen and dining room furniture in the medium-price range.

You have been asked to help Country Comfort evaluate the new product design it is considering. Perform an Internet search to identify at least two major competitors that Country Comfort would have if it chooses to pursue the new product line. Next, identify key product design features of each competitor's products, their target market, and price range. Based on your search, what are your recommendations to Country Comfort on product design and current competition?

On-line Resources

Companion Website www.wiley.com/college/reid
• Take interactive *practice quizzes* to assess your knowledge and help you study in a dynamic way
• Review *PowerPoint slides* or print slides for notetaking
• Download *Excel Templates* to use for problem solving

• Access the *Virtual Company: Valley Memorial Hospital*
• Find links to *Company Tours* for this chapter
  Ercol Furniture Ltd.
• Find links for *Additional Web Resources* for this chapter
  Institute for Supply Chain Management, *www.ism.ws*

Selected Bibliography

Boyer, K.K. "Evolutionary Patterns of Flexible Automation and Performance: A Longitudinal Study," *Management Science*, 45, 6, 1999, 824–842.

Dennis, M.J., and A. Kambil. "Service Management: Building Profits after the Sale," *Supply Chain Management Review*, January–February, 2003, 42–49.

D'Souza, D.E., and F.P. Williams. "Toward a Taxonomy of Manufacturing Flexibility Dimensions," *Journal of Operations Management*, 18, 2000, 577–593.

Fitzsimmons, J.A., and M.J. Fitzsimmons. *Service Management: Operations, Strategy, and Information Technology*, Fifth Edition. New York: Irwin McGraw-Hill, 2005.

Flynn, B.B., R.G. Schroeder, and E.J. Flynn. "WCM: An Investigation of Hayes and Wheelwright's Foundation," *Journal of Operations Management*, 17, 1999, 249–269.

Hayes, R.H., and S.C. Wheelwright. *Restoring Our Competitive Edge: Competing Through Manufacturing*. New York: Wiley, 1984.

Hayes, R.H., and S.C. Wheelwright. "Link Manufacturing Process and Product Life Cycles," *Harvard Business Review*, 57, January–February, 1979, 133–140.

Hayes, R.H., G. Pisano, D. Upton, and S.C. Wheelwright. *Operations Strategy and Technology: Pursuing the Competitive Edge*. New York: John Wiley & Sons, 2005.

Hill, Terry. *Manufacturing Strategy: Text and Cases*. Third Edition. New York: McGraw-Hill, 2000.

Klassen, R.D., and D.C. Whybark. "Environmental Management in Operations: The Selection of Environmental Technologies," *Decision Sciences*, 30, 3, 1999, 601–631.

Pannirselvam, G.P., L.A. Ferguso, R.C. Ash, and S.P. Sifered. "Operations Management Research: An Update for the 1990's," *Journal of Operations Management*, 18, 1999, 95–112.

Rondeau, P.J., M.A. Vonderembse, and T.S. Raghunathan. "Exploring Work System Practices for Time-Base Manufacturers: Their Impact on Competitive Capabilities," *Journal of Operations Management*, 18, 2000, 509–529.

Ward, P.C., T.K. McCreery, L.P. Ritzman, and D. Sharma. "Competitive Priorities in Operations Management," *Decision Science*, 29, 4, 1998, 1035–1046.

Supply Chain Management

Before studying this chapter you should know or, if necessary, review

1. The implications of competitive priorities, Chapter 2, pages 35–38.
2. Product design considerations, Chapter 3, pages 56–64.
3. Process selection considerations, Chapter 3, pages 64–68.

LEARNING OBJECTIVES

After studying this chapter, you should be able to

1. Describe the structure of supply chains.
2. Describe the bullwhip effect.
3. Describe issues affecting supply chain management.
4. Describe B2B and B2C electronic commerce.
5. Describe global issues in supply chain management.
6. Describe the role of purchasing in supply chain management.
7. Describe ethics in supplier management.
8. Describe sourcing issues.
9. Describe strategic purchasing partnerships.
10. Describe supply chain distribution.
11. Describe integrated supply chain management.
12. Describe supply chain performance measures.
13. Describe trends in supply chain management.

CHAPTER OUTLINE

WHAT'S IN **OM** FOR ME?

 ACC   **FIN**   **MKT**   **OM**   **HRM**   **MIS**

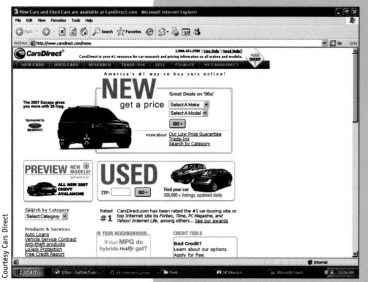

Buying a product used to mean browsing through mail-order catalogs or getting dressed, leaving home, and shopping at stores or malls until you found what you wanted. Today, most of us can go on-line anytime during the day, seven days a week, and buy just about anything over the Internet. You can shop while sitting at your computer and never need to leave home. You can order food from a supermarket or a restaurant on-line or buy clothing and household goods. You can buy books, videos, CDs, or more expensive products like diamonds and cars, or even book your vacation—the Internet has revolutionized the way we do business by allowing us access to numerous suppliers around the world.

The Internet also has allowed companies to change the way they find the materials and supplies that are needed for their operations. Business-to-business (B2B) transactions are conducted between companies and their suppliers, distributors, and customers. Even though direct sales to the general public are more familiar, B2B transactions make up the majority of Internet transactions.

One of the most publicized examples is Covisint, a global business-to-business automotive supplier exchange site, begun in 2000 as an initiative by the U.S. automakers Ford Motor Company, General Motors, DaimlerChrysler, Nissan/Renault, and PSA Peugeot Citroën. Covisint became the largest industry-sponsored net marketplace. In February 2006, Covisint reported that it had 266,000 users, representing 30,000 different companies, located in 96 different countries. Covisint is the electronic marketplace for the auto industry, providing on-line purchasing services and promoting supply chain collaboration between major direct suppliers and automakers.

▶ WHAT IS A SUPPLY CHAIN?

▶ **Supply chain**
A network of all the activities involved in delivering a finished product to the customer.

A **supply chain** is the network of activities that delivers a finished product or service to the customer. These include sourcing raw materials and parts, manufacturing and assembling the products, warehousing, order entry and tracking, distribution through the channels, and delivery to the customer. An organization's supply chain is facilitated by an information system that allows relevant information such as sales data, sales forecasts, and promotions to be shared among members of the supply chain. Figure 4-1 shows a basic supply chain structure.

At the beginning of the chain are the external suppliers who supply and transport raw materials and components to the manufacturers. Manufacturers transform these materials into finished products that are shipped either to the manufacturer's own distribution centers or to wholesalers. Next, the product is shipped to retailers who sell the product to the customer. Goods flow from the beginning of the chain through the

FIGURE 4-1

Basic supply chain

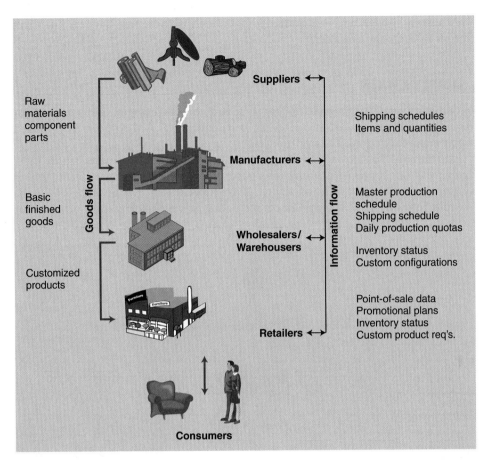

manufacturing process to the customer. Relevant information flows back and forth among members of the supply chain.

Supply chain management is the vital business function that coordinates and manages all the activities of the supply chain linking suppliers, transporters, internal departments, third-party companies, and information systems. Supply chain management entails

▶ **Supply chain management** Coordinates and manages all the activities of the supply chain.

- Coordinating the movement of goods through the supply chain from suppliers to manufacturers to distributors to the final customers
- Sharing relevant information such as sales forecasts, sales data, and promotional campaigns among members of the chain

A prime example of operations management (OM), supply chain management provides the company with a sustainable, competitive advantage, such as quick response time, low cost, state-of-the-art quality design, or operational flexibility.

Dell Computer Corporation is a good example of a company using its supply chain to achieve a sustainable competitive advantage. Quick delivery of customized computers at prices 10–15 percent lower than the industry standard is Dell's competitive advantage. A customized Dell computer can be en route to the customer within thirty-six hours. This quick response allows Dell to reduce its inventory level to approximately thirteen days of supply compared to Compaq's twenty-five days of supply. Dell achieves this in part through its warehousing plan. Most of the components Dell uses are warehoused within fifteen minutes travel time to an assembly plant. Dell does not order components at its Austin, Texas, facility; instead, suppliers restock warehouses as needed, and Dell is billed for items only after they are shipped. The result is better value for the customer.

COMPONENTS OF A SUPPLY CHAIN

A company's supply chain structure has three components: external suppliers, internal functions of the company, and external distributors. Figure 4-2 shows a simplified supply chain for packaged dairy products.

External suppliers include the dairy farmer, cardboard container manufacturer, label company, plastic container manufacturer, paper mill, chemical processing plant, lumber company, and chemical extraction plant. Internal functions include the processing of the raw milk into consumer dairy products and packaging and labeling dairy products for

FIGURE 4-2

Dairy products supply chain

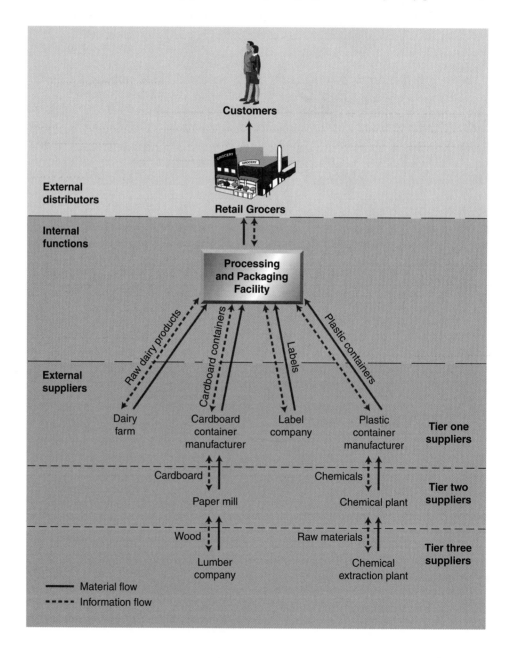

distribution to retail grocery outlets. The external distributors transport finished products from the manufacturer to retail grocers, where the products are sold to the customer. The supply chain includes every activity from collecting the raw milk, producing the consumer dairy products, packaging the dairy products, distributing the packaged dairy products to retail grocers, to selling the finished dairy products to the customer.

Let's look at each component of the supply chain in detail.

External Suppliers

Dairy products manufacturing involves several companies, as shown in Figure 4-2. The dairy products are packaged either in cardboard or plastic containers made by **tier one suppliers**. Note that any supplier that provides materials directly to the processing facility is designated as a tier one supplier (in this case, the dairy farm, the cardboard container manufacturer, the label company, and the plastic container manufacturer).

The paper mill and the chemical processing plant are **tier two suppliers** because they directly supply tier one suppliers but do not directly supply the packaging operation. The lumber company that provides wood to the paper mill is a **tier three supplier**, as is the chemical extraction plant that supplies raw materials to the chemical processing plant.

Companies put substantial effort into developing the external supplier portion of the supply chain because the cost of materials might represent 50–60 percent or even more of the cost of goods sold. A company is typically involved in a number of supply chains and often in different roles. In the supply chain for the plastics container manufacturer shown in Figure 4-2, for example, the chemical plant is now a tier one supplier and the chemical extraction facility is a tier two supplier. Even though the plastics container manufacturer was a tier one supplier to the milk processing facility, the plastic container manufacturer still has its own unique supply chain. Now consider the supply chain for a retail grocer: the tier one suppliers are providers of packaged consumer products, and the grocer has no external distributors because the customers buy directly from the store. As you can see, supply chains come in all shapes and sizes.

Remember that tier one suppliers (the cardboard container manufacturer, dairy farm, label company, and plastics container manufacturer in Figure 4-2) directly supply the consumer product manufacturer (packaged dairy products), whereas tier two suppliers (paper mill and chemical processing plant) directly supply tier one suppliers. To summarize: supply chains are a series of linked suppliers and customers in which each customer is a supplier to another part of the chain until the product is delivered to the final customer.

▶ **Tier one supplier**
Supplies materials or services directly to the processing facility.

▶ **Tier two supplier**
Directly supplies materials or services to a tier one supplier in the supply chain.

▶ **Tier three supplier**
Directly supplies materials or services to a tier two supplier in the supply chain.

Internal Functions

Internal functions in, for example, a dairy products supply chain are as follows:

- Processing, which converts raw milk into dairy products and packages these products for distribution to retail grocery outlets;
- Purchasing, which selects appropriate suppliers, ensures that suppliers perform up to expectations, administers contracts, and develops and maintains good supplier relationships;
- Production planning and control, which schedules the processing of raw milk into dairy products;
- Quality assurance, which oversees the quality of the dairy products;
- Shipping, which selects external carriers and/or a private fleet to transport the product from the manufacturing facility to its destination.

▶ **Logistics**
Activities involved in obtaining, producing, and distributing materials and products in the proper place and in proper quantities.

▶ **Traffic management**
Responsible for arranging the method of shipment for both incoming and outgoing products or materials.

▶ **Distribution management**
Responsible for movement of material from the manufacturer to the customer.

External Distributors

External distributors transport finished products to the appropriate locations for eventual sale to customers. Logistics managers are responsible for managing the movement of products between locations. **Logistics** includes *traffic management* and *distribution management*. **Traffic management** is the selection and monitoring of external carriers (trucking companies, airlines, railroads, shipping companies, and couriers) or internal fleets of carriers. **Distribution management** is the packaging, storing, and handling of products at receiving docks, warehouses, and retail outlets.

Next, we will look at a common challenge to supply chain managers called the bullwhip effect.

THE BULLWHIP EFFECT

▶ **Bullwhip effect**
Inaccurate or distorted demand information created in the supply chain.

Sharing product demand information between members of a supply chain is critical. However, inaccurate or distorted information can travel through the chain like a bullwhip uncoiling. The **bullwhip effect**, as this is called, causes erratic replenishment orders placed on different levels in the supply chain that have no apparent link to final product demand. The results are excessive inventory investment, poor customer service levels, ineffective transportation use, misused manufacturing capacity, and lost revenues. We will discuss the causes of the bullwhip effect, and how they send inaccurate or distorted information down the supply chain. First, however, let's look at the traditional supply chain, shown in Figure 4-3, and follow the product demand information flow from the final seller back to the manufacturer of the product:

1. The final seller periodically places replenishment orders with the next level of the supply chain, which could be a local distributor. The timing and order quantity—for example, monthly orders in varying amounts—are determined by the final seller. The timing and quantity can be fixed or variable.

FIGURE 4-3

Traditional supply chain information flow

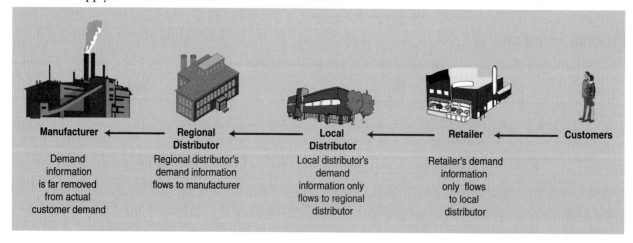

Manufacturer	Regional Distributor	Local Distributor	Retailer	Customers
Demand information is far removed from actual customer demand	Regional distributor's demand information flows to manufacturer	Local distributor's demand information only flows to regional distributor	Retailer's demand information only flows to local distributor	

2. The local distributor has many customers (final sellers) placing replenishment orders. Each final seller uses it own product demand estimates and quantity rules. Based on these replenishment orders, the local distributor places replenishment orders with its supplier, which could be a regional distribution center (RDC).

3. As before, the customers (the local distributors) determine the timing and quantity of orders placed with the RDC. Each RDC periodically places orders based on demand at the RDC by ordering from the manufacturer of the finished good.

4. In turn, the manufacturer develops plans and schedules production orders based on orders from the RDCs. The manufacturer does not know what the demand is for the finished good by the final customer but knows only what the RDCs order.

The greater the number of levels in the supply chain, the further away the manufacturer is from final customer demand. Since suppliers in the chain do not know what customer demand is or when a replenishment order might arrive, suppliers stockpile inventory.

Causes of the Bullwhip Effect

The causes of the bullwhip effect are demand forecast updating, order batching, price fluctuation, and rationing and gaming. Let's look at each of these causes.

Each member in the supply chain, beginning with the retailers, does *demand forecast updating* with every inventory review. Based on actual demand, the retailers update their demand forecast. The retailers review their current inventory level and, based on their inventory policies, determine whether a replenishment order is needed. The wholesalers repeat the process. Note that the demand is from the retailers' inventory replenishments and may not reflect actual customer demand at the retail level. The wholesalers update their demand forecast and place appropriate replenishment orders with the distribution centers. The distributors repeat the process, updating their demand forecasts based on demand from the wholesalers. The distributors review their inventory levels and place the appropriate orders with the manufacturer. These orders are determined by the inventory policies at the distributors. Orders placed with the manufacturer end up replenishing each level in the supply chain rather than being directly linked to end-customer demand.

A company does *order batching* when, instead of placing replenishment orders right after each unit is sold, it waits some period of time, sums up the number of units sold, and then places the order. This changes constant product demand to lumpy demand— a situation where certain levels in the supply chain experience periods of no demand. Order batching policies amplify variability in order timing and size.

Price fluctuations cause companies to buy products before they need them. Price fluctuations follow special promotions like price discounts, quantity discounts, coupons, and rebates. Each of these price fluctuations affects the replenishment orders placed in the supply system. When prices are lower, members of the supply chain tend to buy in larger quantities. When prices increase, order quantities decrease. Price fluctuations create more demand variability within the supply chain.

Rationing and shortage gaming result when demand exceeds supply and products are rationed to members of the supply chain. Knowing that the manufacturer will ration items, customers within the supply chain often exaggerate their needs. For example, if you know the company is supplying only 50 percent of the order quantity, you double the order size. If you really need 100 pieces, you order 200 so you are sure to get what you need. Such game-playing distorts true demand information in the system.

Counteracting the Bullwhip Effect

Here are four ways of counteracting the bullwhip effect:

1. Change the way suppliers forecast product demand by making this information from the final-seller level available to all levels of the supply chain. This allows all levels to use the same product demand information when making replenishment decisions. Companies can do this by collecting point-of-sale (POS) information, a function available on most cash registers.

2. Eliminate order batching. Companies typically use large order batches because of the relatively high cost of placing an order. Supply chain partners can reduce ordering costs by using electronic data interchange (EDI) to transmit information. Lower ordering costs eliminate the need for batch orders.

3. Stabilize prices. Manufacturers can eliminate incentives for retail forward buying by creating a uniform wholesale pricing policy. In the grocery industry, for example, major manufacturers use an everyday low-price policy or a value-pricing strategy to discourage forward buying.

4. Eliminate gaming. Instead of filling an order based on a set percentage, manufacturers can allocate products in proportion to past sales records. Customers then have no incentive to order a larger quantity to get the quantity they need.

ISSUES AFFECTING SUPPLY CHAIN MANAGEMENT

Information Technology

Information technology enablers for supply chain management include the Internet, the Web, EDI (electronic data interchange), intranets and extranets, bar code scanners, and point-of-sales demand information. We begin by looking at the use of the Internet and the Web as a way of doing business.

E-Commerce

▶ **E-commerce**
Using the Internet and Web to transact business.

E-commerce and e-business are defined as the use of the Internet and the Web to transact business. E-business refers to transactions and processes within an organization, such as a company's on-line inventory control system, that support supply chain management. E-commerce includes B2B (business-to-business) and B2C (business-to-consumer) transactions. Let's take a closer look B2B e-commerce.

Business-to-Business (B2B) E-Commerce

▶ **Business-to-business e-commerce (B2B)**
Businesses selling to other businesses.

In **business-to-business e-commerce**, companies sell to other businesses. B2B is the largest segment of e-commerce. By 2006, much of the $16 trillion B2B trade in the United States will be done on the Internet. Before the Internet, B2B was relatively inefficient. It took time and resources to search for products, to arrange for purchasing and payment, to arrange for shipping, and then to receive the items. By automating at least part of the procurement process, significant dollars are saved by organizations.

As an example, General Electric hoped to save $10 billion in 2003 by using such B2B methods. Let's look at how B2B commerce has developed.

The Evolution of B2B Commerce

B2B commerce began in the 1970s with **automated order entry systems** that used telephone models to send digital orders to suppliers. One company, Baxter Healthcare Corporation, placed telephone modems in a customer's purchasing department to automate reordering supplies from Baxter's computerized inventory database. This technology changed in the 1980s to personal computers and in the 1990s to Internet workstations that access on-line catalogs. Automated order entry systems are seller-side solutions. They are owned by the supplier and only offer the supplier's product line. The primary benefits to the customers are reduced inventory replenishment costs and supplier-paid system costs.

▶ **Automated order entry system**
A method using telephone models to send digital orders to suppliers.

In the late 1970s, **electronic data interchange (EDI)** emerged. EDI is a form of computer-to-computer communication standardized for sharing business documents such as invoices, purchase orders, shipping bills, product stocking numbers, etc. Most large firms have EDI systems and most inventory groups have industry standards for defining the documents to be communicated. EDI systems are buyer-side solutions: they are designed to reduce the procurement costs for the buyer. EDI systems generally serve a specific industry.

▶ **Electronic data interchange (EDI)**
A form of computer-to-computer communications that enables sharing business documents.

In the mid-1990s, **electronic storefronts** emerged. Electronic showplaces are on-line catalogs of products made available to the general public by a single supplier. These storefronts evolved from the automated order entry systems. They are far less expensive than their predecessors because (1) they use the Internet as the communication medium, and (2) the storefronts tend to carry products that serve a number of different industries.

▶ **Electronic storefronts**
On-line catalogs of products made available to the general public by a single supplier.

Net marketplaces emerged in the late 1990s. Net marketplaces bring hundreds or thousands of suppliers (each with electronic catalogs) and significant numbers of purchasing firms into a single Internet-based environment to conduct trade. Covisint is an example of a successful net marketplace. Net marketplaces price goods with fixed catalog prices or dynamic pricing (negotiation, auction, and bid-ask exchange models). Net marketplaces generate revenue through transaction fees, subscription fees, service fees, software licensing fees, advertising and marketing, and sales of data and information.

▶ **Net marketplaces**
Suppliers and buyers conduct trade in a single Internet-based environment.

Private industrial networks are Internet-based communication environments that extend beyond procurement. For example, private industrial networks allow buyers and suppliers to share product design and development, inventory, production scheduling, and work as partners.

The Benefits of B2B E-Commerce

The potential benefits from Internet-based B2B commerce include:

- Lower procurement administrative costs,
- Low-cost access to global suppliers,
- Lower inventory investment due to price transparency and reduced response times,
- Better product quality because of increased cooperation between buyers and sellers, especially during the product design and development.

Business-to-Consumer (B2C) E-Commerce

▶ **Business-to-consumer e-commerce (B2C)**
On-line businesses sell to individual consumers.

▶ **Advertising revenue model**
Provides users with information on services and products and provides an opportunity for suppliers to advertise.

▶ **Subscription revenue model**
A Web site that charges a subscription fee for access to its contents and services.

▶ **Transaction fee model**
A company receives a fee for executing a transaction.

▶ **Sales revenue model**
A means of selling goods, information, or services directly to customers.

▶ **Affiliate revenue model**
Companies receive a referral fee for directing business to an affiliate.

▶ **Intranets**
Networks that are internal to an organization.

▶ **Extranets**
Intranets that are linked to the Internet so that suppliers and customers can be included in the system.

In **business-to-consumer e-commerce**, on-line businesses try to reach individual consumers. Let's examine the different models that on-line businesses use to generate revenue. In the **advertising revenue model**, a Web site offers its users information on services and products, and provides an opportunity for providers to advertise. The company receives fees for the advertising. Yahoo.com derives its primary revenue from selling advertising such as banner ads.

In the **subscription revenue model**, a Web site that offers content and services charges a subscription fee for access to the site. One example is Consumer Reports Online (www.consumerreports.org), which provides access to its content only to subscribers at a rate of $3.95 per month. Companies using this model must offer content perceived to be of high value that is not readily available elsewhere on the Internet for free.

In the **transaction fee model**, a company receives a fee for executing a transaction. For example, Orbitz (www.orbitz.com) charges a small fee to the consumer when an airline reservation is made. Another example, E*Trade Financial Corporation, an on-line stockbroker (www.etrade.com), receives a transaction fee each time it executes a stock transaction.

In the **sales revenue model**, companies sell goods, information, or services directly to customers. Amazon.com, primarily a book and music seller, Travelocity.com, an airline and hotel reservations provider, and DoubleClick Inc. (www.doubleclick.net), a company that gathers information about on-line users and sells it to other companies, all use the sales revenue model.

In the **affiliate revenue model**, companies receive a referral fee for directing business to an "affiliate" or receive some percentage of the revenue resulting from a referred sale. For example, MyPoints.com receives money for connecting companies with potential customers by offering special deals. When members take advantage of the deal, they earn points that can later be redeemed for goods.

In addition to the Internet, companies use other technology to help manage supply chains. For example, **intranets** are networks internal to an organization. Intranets allow a company to network groups of internal computers together to form more effective information systems. Typically, members of the organization communicate internally on the intranet. Organizations can link intranet systems of the Internet to form **extranets**. The extranet can be expanded to include both a company's suppliers and customers. Typically, real-time inventory status is available on the extranet as well as production schedules. Extranets allow suppliers and customers to "see" within the organization. The primary difference between the Internet, intranets, and extranets is who has access to the system. The Internet is wide open, the intranet is open to members of an organization, and the extranet is open to members of the organization as well as to suppliers and customers.

Consumer Expectations and Competition Resulting from E-Commerce

On-line retailing, or business-to-consumer e-commerce, has shifted the power from the suppliers to the consumers. This shift in power has occurred because the Internet greatly reduced search and transaction costs for the consumer. It was estimated as early as April, 2001, that some 100 million people and over 80 percent of all individuals with Internet access had purchased something (either a product or a service) on-line. In addition, millions more customers researched products on-line and subsequently bought those items off-line. The capability to quickly search, evaluate, compare, and purchase products gives the consumer considerable power. Examples of successful B2C businesses are Amazon.com, eBay, BMG Music Service, Barnes&Noble.com, Columbia House, Half.com, and JCPenney. E-tailers have penetrated significantly the following markets: computer hardware and software, books, travel, music and videos, collectibles and antiques, and event tickets.

Since customers have access to so many suppliers, it is important for suppliers to differentiate themselves by providing customers with excellent value. Dell Computer Corporation, Gateway, Inc., L.L.Bean, Inc., Lands' End, Inc., Amazon.com, UPS, and FedEx are good examples of companies that put a premium on values such as preferred customer service, short lead times, and/or quality guarantees. Dell differentiates itself with short lead times. The company does this by warehousing most of the components used to assemble its computers within fifteen minutes of the assembly facility and building customized computers in an assemble-to-order strategy.

Consider how Lands' End uses technology in its business. Lands' End went on-line in 1995. The company sold only $160 worth of gear the first month. Today, Lands' End is one of the nation's largest apparel retailers on-line. The company has a live chat room that allows customers to ask questions about merchandise. It also offers a "shopping with a friend" service that allows a customer, his or her friend or friends, and a customer service

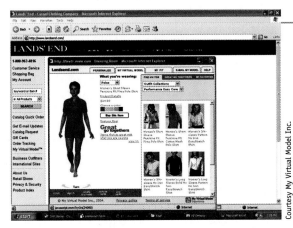

Courtesy My Virtual Model Inc.

LINKS TO PRACTICE

Lands' End, Inc.
www.landsend.com

representative to be linked together. Lands' End's "virtual model" highlights how far technology has advanced. A few strokes on the keyboard and the shopper is able to produce an on-screen model with his or her body measurements. Even though this virtual model is not perfect, over 1 million shoppers have built their own models at the Lands' End site.

An additional issue here is how companies handle the return of unwanted merchandise and provide for product exchanges or refunds. The Boston Consulting Group (BCG) reported that the "absence of a good return mechanism" was the second-highest reason shoppers cited for not shopping on the Web. There are methods for handling returns. An on-line company often first requires authorization to return an item, then the customer must pack up the item, pay to ship it back to the company, insure the item, and then wait for a credit to be made. Once the item is returned, the original seller must unpack the item, inspect the item, check the paperwork, and try to resell the item. Typically, neither the buyer nor seller is happy with the process.

Another approach allows the customer to drop the returned items at collection stations (sometimes the physical stores of the company, for example, Staples, Inc., Sears, OfficeMax, Inc., etc.). The returned items can then be sold from the receiving store or picked up in bulk and returned to the distribution point. Another approach is to completely outsource returns. FedEx and UPS provide such services.

In addition to buying products on-line, consumers also buy on-line services. Finance, insurance, real estate services, business services, and health services are the largest on-line service industries. Business services include consulting, advertising and marketing, and information processing.

Service organizations are categorized either as those that do transaction brokering or those that provide a "hands-on" service. An example of transaction brokering is a company providing financial services that has stockbrokers acting as intermediaries between buyers and sellers of stock. An example of a "hands-on" service is a legal service that interacts directly with the consumer to create a legal document. In general, most service organizations are knowledge- and information-intense. To provide value to consumers, these service companies must process considerable information (legal services or medical services) and employ a highly educated and skilled workforce (lawyers and doctors).

Globalization

As globalization increases, supply chains often cover greater geographical distances, face more uncertainty, and can be less efficient. Consider some recent events. In the commodities industry, prices for steel, oil, copper, cement, and coal began rising at double-digit rates in 2004. Because of this, buyers looked globally for better prices. After purchasing these items offshore, companies were challenged with moving the commodities over longer distances. This increase in volume resulted in a transportation capacity crunch and caused higher transportation rates. These rates rose even higher due to much higher oil prices. When supply chains are less efficient, inventory levels can rise. The U.S. Commerce Department reported the level of inventory in November 2004 was 1.24. This means that it took approximately $1.24 of inventory to support every dollar of sales.

Another recent event is the increased trade volume being shipped from Asia to the United States. Ocean carriers predict that volume to the United States will continue double-digit increases annually. Most of these inbound goods are shipped from Asia through U.S. West Coast ports. The higher trade level is causing port congestion in California and Washington state. In an attempt to ease congestion, in 2004, ocean carriers introduced larger ships to use on the transpacific routes. It was hoped that these larger ships would add needed capacity and reduce operating costs. Unfortunately, due to the size of the larger ships, only a few U.S. ports are capable of handling them. They take longer to unload and reload, thus tying up the port five to seven days instead of the normal two to three days. The longer time at the port reduces port terminal efficiency. In the past, importers have been allowed more free time (the time cargo may occupy assigned space free of storage charges) for containers at U.S. port terminals. Container free time basically provided a cheap form of portable warehousing for importers. Container free time is now being reduced, and ports have increased fees in an effort to turn equipment around faster.

Another issue is border security. Since September 11, 2001, the U.S. Bureau of Customs and Border Protection (CBP) has implemented new requirements. Essentially, these programs result in additional processing time. The CBP has also increased inspections at ports of suspicious cargo, creating additional port delays.

As supply chains expand globally, they share some common logistical characteristics. For example, with ocean shipping, goods tend to arrive at a warehouse in very large quantities. Because of bulk arrivals, greater break-bulk activity is required.

Break-bulk entails sorting the bulk shipments into smaller customer shipments. These global supply chains typically have higher inventory levels. Managing global supply chains will be challenging in the near future.

Government Regulation and E-Commerce

The issue of government regulation of the Internet is still unresolved. Although early Internet users claimed the Internet could not be controlled given its decentralized design and its ability to cross borders, it is clear that the Internet can be controlled. In China, Malaysia, and Singapore, access to the Internet is controlled from government-owned centralized routers. This allows these countries to block access to U.S. or European Web sites. Search engines operating in these countries self-censor their Asian content by using only government-approved news sources. In other countries, freedom of expression has limited restrictions on the Internet. In order for leading Internet company Google to access China's fast-growing market, it agreed to censor its search services. E-mail, chat room, and blogging services will also not be available because of concerns the government could demand users' personal information. Google indicated that it would notify users when access had been restricted on certain search terms.

Another issue of concern is taxation. The question is how, and if, remote sales should be taxed. Think of the advantage gained by e-tailers over local merchants when no taxes are charged to the consumer. In addition to sales taxes, the issue of customs and tariffs must be addressed. Taxation remains a very complicated issue for Internet sales.

Copyright infringement is also an issue. The U.S. copyright law protects original forms of expression such as writing (books, periodicals), art, drawings, photographs, music, motion pictures, performances, and computer programs from being copied by others for a minimum of 50 years. One exception to the U.S. copyright law is the doctrine of fair use. This doctrine allows teachers and writers to use materials without permission under certain circumstances. In response to copyright issues, the U.S. government enacted the Digital Millennium Copyright Act (DMCA) of 1998. The DMCA declares it illegal to make, distribute, or use devices that circumvent technology-based protections of copyrighted materials and attaches stiff fines and prison sentences for violations.

Another issue concerns public safety and welfare. In the United States, e-commerce issues of safety and welfare center around the protection of children, strong anti-pornography sentiments, strong antigambling sentiments, and protecting public health by restricting sales of drugs and cigarettes. It is clear that many issues concerning government regulation of the Internet are yet to be determined.

The Environmental Implications of E-Commerce

Recycling, sustainable eco-efficiency, and waste minimization affect supply chain management. A company that is a global provider must understand the shipping restrictions (packaging, customs, etc.) in countries around the world. According to the European Union's packaging requirements, for instance, cardboard boxes must be removed from consumption sites and recycled, so U.S. automobile parts producers ship parts in reusable containers rather than disposable containers. Reusable packaging products are used to move, store, and distribute product within a single operation or an entire supply chain. Plastic reusable packaging, one form of reusables, can be used to package raw materials to finished goods. It can be used within reverse logistics to return empty containers or pallets for reuse or replenishment. Products include hand-held containers, pallets, bulk containers, protective interiors, and custom-designed and engineered packaging. Supply chains need to focus on the final disposition of products and packaging and develop processes to successfully recycle materials. A company also must have efficient methods for shipping a large number of small, individual orders globally.

Geographically Dispersed Members

Since a global supply chain has members located around the world, the actual distances between the physical locations of the members are typically larger. Larger distances between physical locations can mean longer replenishment transit times. In addition, companies can experience replenishment delays when items are detained clearing customs. Incomplete documentation can further delay shipments.

By definition, longer replenishment lead times mean that the company has a higher investment in pipeline inventory (see Chapter 12). A higher degree of uncertainty with regard to actual delivery times means that manufacturers need to carry additional safety stock (Chapter 12) to assure continuous operations. Scheduling uncertainty and longer delivery times increase the inventory that is necessarily held in the supply chain and contribute to the bullwhip effect. The volatility of demand in the supply chain leads to stockouts, poorer customer service, and higher administrative costs.

Forecasting Accuracy

Greater distances between members and longer delivery times complicate supply chain forecasting (Chapter 8). Global supply chains also have members operating in different cultural environments, using different languages, and observing different operating practices, all of which can cause communication problems and create inaccurate or distorted demand information. Since actual customer-demand forecasting is likely to be poorer, additional safety stock is needed to meet customer service objectives.

Exchange Rates

Members in a global supply chain must be aware of fluctuating currency exchange rates and the impact such changes can have on input costs (materials and labor), sales prices, and sales volume. A firm can develop a global supply chain to take advantage of weaker currencies by establishing links with suppliers in a variety of countries. That way, when the firm needs materials or outsources work, it can take advantage of currency fluctuations to decrease its costs.

Infrastructure Issues

Global supply chains with members in developing countries can face substantial infrastructure issues (such as inadequate transportation networks, limited telecommunication capabilities, uncertain power continuity, low worker skill, poor supply availability and quality, etc.). Each of these issues increases uncertainty in supply and demand for the supply chain, which results in higher costs and poorer service.

Inadequate transportation networks increase distribution lead times. Roads may be inadequate to transport heavy loads (necessitating the creation of smaller loads), rail travel may not be available or very limited in terms of frequency (once or twice a week), air service may be limited in frequency (one or two flights per day or less), and ocean shipping may be limited by the capabilities of the port. It is not unusual for an item to change hands four to eight times before reaching the final customer.

Poor telephone service can restrict the timely availability of supply and demand information. Because of this, a more extensive information system to keep track of items is often required. An unstable power supply can significantly affect the output of a supplier, both in terms of when the product can be produced and the effect on product quality caused by unstable power.

A lack of specific worker skills can limit the technology a firm uses. For example, numerically controlled (NC) machines use more easily trained machine setters and programmers rather than more highly skilled machinists. The increased use of NC machines in South America is a result of an inadequate number of skilled machinists.

A lack of available local materials and competent suppliers can force a firm to redesign its process, or even its product, to minimize or eliminate the use of scarce materials. Imported raw materials may be difficult to obtain due to import restrictions. In some cases, no local suppliers are available. A case in point is McDonald's. When McDonald's started operations in Russia, it had considerable problems developing high-quality Russian suppliers. McDonald's used a vertically integrated strategy, developing its own plant and distribution facility for processing meat patties, producing french fries, preparing dairy products, and baking buns and apple pies. Initially, McDonald's even grew its own potatoes.

Product Proliferation

Global competition forces firms to supply highly customized products and services to multiple national markets. Usually, a firm manufactures a basic product that is adaptable to many markets. The basic product contains most of the features and components of the finished product along with some market-specific add-on components. For example, computer products have country-specific power supplies to accommodate local voltage, frequency, and plug types. In addition, keyboards and manuals must match the local language. Such minor variations create a large number of unique finished-product configurations to be managed. Product proliferation further complicates accurate demand forecasting.

Before You Go On

You need to understand the structure of a supply chain, the bullwhip effect, and the issues affecting supply chains. A supply chain structure has external suppliers, internal functions of the firm, and external distributors. Information technology enables supply chain management. E-commerce provides an effective means for communications between an organization and its suppliers and customers. Demand data provided through point of sales data (POS) helps counteract the bullwhip effect and reduces distorted demand information throughout the supply chain. As supply chains globalize, many additional issues such as greater geographical distances between members, increased inventory in the pipeline, poorer forecasting accuracy, fluctuating exchange rates, governmental and environmental regulations, inadequate infrastructures, and product proliferation must be addressed.

SOURCING ISSUES

Which products or services are provided in-house by the manufacturer and which are provided to the manufacturer by other members of the supply chain? **Vertical integration** is a measure of how much of the supply chain is owned or operated by the manufacturer. Products or services provided by the manufacturer are **insourced**. Products or services not provided by the manufacturer are **outsourced**. Outsourcing means that the manufacturer pays suppliers or third-party companies for their products or services, a practice that is on the rise. A recent survey reported that 35 percent of more than 1000 large companies have increased their outsourcing. Another survey of large companies reported that 86 percent outsourced at least some materials or services. The activity most frequently outsourced was manufacturing.

Backward integration is a company's acquisition or control of sources of raw materials and component parts: the company acquires, controls, or owns the sources that were previously external suppliers in the supply chain. **Forward integration** is a company's acquisition or control of its channels of distribution—what used to be the external distributors in the supply chain.

A company bases its level of vertical integration on its objectives. The greater the vertical integration, the lower is the level of outsourcing. Conversely, the higher the level of outsourcing, the lower is the level of vertical integration. Some factors favor vertical integration. For example, companies needing a high volume of a product or service can sometimes achieve economies of scale by providing the product or service in-house. Companies with special skills may find that it is cheaper to provide certain products or services in-house. Other factors encourage outsourcing. For example, companies with low volumes generally find it cheaper to outsource a product or service rather than provide it in-house. Sometimes a company can get a better-quality product or service from a supplier than it can provide itself.

Now let's look at the financial calculations behind insourcing and outsourcing decisions.

▶ **Vertical integration**
A measure of how much of the supply chain is actually owned or operated by the manufacturing company.

▶ **Insource**
Processes or activities that are completed in-house.

▶ **Outsource**
Processes or activities that are completed by suppliers.

▶ **Backward integration**
Owning or controlling sources of raw materials and components.

▶ **Forward integration**
Owning or controlling the channels of distribution.

Insourcing versus Outsourcing Decisions

It may be easy to calculate the costs of insourcing versus outsourcing and make the right financial decision. But such decisions involve more than financial calculations. Is a particular product or service critical to your company's success? Is the product or service one of your company's core competencies? Is it something your company must do to survive? If the answer is yes to any of these questions, your company will provide the product or service in-house. If the product or service is not one of its core competencies, the company needs to decide whether it should make or buy the product or service. Other considerations are, for example, whether the products or services provided in-house are identical to those outsourced. Is product quality in-house comparable to product quality in the marketplace? Is product functionality comparable, or does one product have an advantage in terms of quality or functionality? Finally, does the company have the capital needed for any up-front costs to provide the product or service in-house?

Now let's look at how a company might make the financial calculations. To make a financial calculation, we look at the total costs involved in either producing the entire quantity in-house or buying the entire quantity from a supplier. The total cost of buying the item is any fixed annual cost associated with buying the product plus a variable cost for each item bought during the year, or

$$TC_{Buy} = FC_{Buy} + (VC_{Buy} \times Q)$$

where TC_{Buy} = total annual costs of buying the item from a supplier
FC_{Buy} = fixed annual costs associated with buying the item from the supplier
VC_{Buy} = variable costs per unit associated with buying the item from the supplier
Q = quantity of units bought

Similarly, we calculate the total cost of making the item in-house as

$$TC_{Make} = FC_{Make} + (VC_{Make} \times Q)$$

where TC_{Make} = total annual costs of making the item in-house
FC_{Make} = fixed annual costs associated with making the item in-house
VC_{Make} = variable costs per unit associated with making the item in-house
Q = quantity of units made in-house

The first step in solving the make-or-buy decision is to determine at what quantity the total costs of the two alternatives are equal. To do this, we set the total annual cost of buying equal to the total annual cost of making:

$$FC_{Buy} + (VC_{Buy} \times Q) = FC_{Make} + (VC_{Make} \times Q)$$

Solving this tells us the *indifference point*—that is, how many units we must buy or produce when the total costs are equal. If we need this exact amount, we would be indifferent to whether we bought the item or produced it in-house. If we need less than this quantity, we choose the alternative with the lower fixed cost and the higher variable cost. If we need more than this quantity, we choose the alternative with the lower variable costs.

Let's look at a numerical example. Remember that when the quantity needed exceeds the indifference point, use the alternative with the lower variable cost. If the usage quantity is below the indifference point, then choose the alternative with the lower fixed cost.

THE ROLE OF PURCHASING

A company's purchasing department plays an important role in supply chain management decisions. Purchasing is typically responsible for selecting suppliers, negotiating and administering long-term contracts, monitoring supplier performance, placing orders to suppliers, developing a responsive supplier base, and maintaining good supplier relations. Since material costs may represent at least 50–60 percent of the cost of goods sold, purchasing significantly affects profitability. Moreover, changes in product cost structure, with materials comprising the bulk of the cost of goods sold, have elevated the role of purchasing in many organizations.

Outsourcing requires decisions about which supplier to contract with for products or services. These decisions in turn depend on the criticality and frequency of the product or service, and they determine the relationship the company forms with the supplier. For example, if the purchase is one-time only, the company does not need to develop a relationship with the supplier. However, if the company wants a reliable supplier for a critical product or service, it needs to develop a long-term relationship with the supplier.

EXAMPLE 4.1

**MS Bagel Shop:
A Make-or-Buy
Decision**

Two recent college graduates, Mary and Sue, have decided to open a bagel shop. Their first decision is whether they should make the bagels on-site or buy the bagels from a local bakery. They do some checking and learn the following:

- If they buy from the local bakery, they will need new airtight containers in which to store the bagels delivered from the bakery. The fixed cost for buying and maintaining these containers is $1000 annually.
- The bakery has agreed to sell the bagels to Mary and Sue for $0.40 each.
- If they make the bagels in-house, they will need a small kitchen with a fixed cost of $15,000 annually and a variable cost per bagel of $0.15.
- They believe they will sell 60,000 bagels in the first year of operation.

(a) Should Mary and Sue make or buy the bagels?
(b) If Mary and Sue are uncertain as to the demand for bagels next year, what is the indifference point between making or buying the bagels.

- **Before You Begin:** To make their decision when demand is known, Mary and Sue need to calculate the total cost of making or buying 60,000 bagels. Determine the relevant data for these calculations. To find the total annual cost of buying 60,000 bagels, you need both the annual fixed costs ($1000) and the variable cost per bagel ($0.40). To calculate the total annual cost of making the 60,000 bagels, you need the annual fixed costs ($15,000) and the variable cost per bagel ($0.15).

- **Solution:**
  (a) The total cost for buying 60,000 bagels is $25,000. That is $1000 in annual fixed cost plus 60,000 bagels multiplied by the $0.04 unit variable cost. The total cost for making 60,000 bagels is $24,000. That is $15,000 in annual fixed costs plus the 60,000 bagels multiplied by the $0.15 unit variable cost.
  (b) If Mary and Sue don't know the demand for bagels. They can find the indifference point by setting the total annual costs of each option equal to the other, as shown below. Although in this problem we are comparing the options of making or buying, we could just as easily compare two different suppliers or two different internal processes.
      Set the total annual costs equal to each other using the formula.

$$FC_{Buy} + (VC_{Buy} \times Q) = FC_{Make} + (VC_{Make} \times Q)$$

  or

$$\$1000 + (\$0.40 \times Q) = \$15,000 + (\$0.15 \times Q)$$

Solving for Q, we have $(\$0.25Q) = \$14,000$, or $Q = 56,000$ bagels. Since the costs are equal at 56,000 bagels and Mary and Sue expect to use 60,000 bagels, they should make the bagels in-house rather than buy them from the local bakery. By making the bagels, the cost for each additional bagel above 56,000 is $0.15 instead of the $0.40 they would pay the local bakery for each bagel.

Ethics in Supply Management

A constant concern within purchasing departments is the issue of ethics in managing suppliers. Sales representatives from suppliers often offer buyers free lunches, free tickets to sporting or entertainment events, free weekend getaways or valuable gifts. While suppliers may view these merely as promotional activities, at some point buyers need to consider how much is too much. Because buyers are in a position to influence or determine which supplier is awarded business, buyers must make certain that they avoid any appearance of unethical behavior or a conflict of interest.

Loyalty to Your Organization / Justice to Those with Whom You Deal / Faith in Your Profession

From these principles are derived the ISM (Institute for Supply Management) global standards of supply management conduct.

1. Avoid the intent and appearance of unethical or compromising practice in relationships, actions, and communications.
2. Demonstrate loyalty to the employer by diligently following the lawful instructions of the employer, using reasonable care and granted authority.
3. Avoid any personal business or professional activity that would create a conflict between personal interests and the interests of the employer.
4. Avoid soliciting or accepting money, loans, credits, or preferential discounts, and the acceptance of gifts, entertainment, favors, or services from present or potential suppliers that might influence, or appear to influence, supply management decisions.
5. Handle confidential or proprietary information with due care and proper consideration of ethical and legal ramifications and government regulations.
6. Promote positive supplier relationships through courtesy and impartiality.
7. Avoid improper reciprocal agreements.
8. Know and obey the letter and the spirit of laws applicable to supply management.
9. Encourage support for small, disadvantaged, and minority-owned businesses.
10. Acquire and maintain professional competence.
11. Conduct supply management activities in accordance with national and international laws, customs and practices, your organization's policies, and these ethical principles and standards of conduct.
12. Enhance the stature of the supply management profession.

TABLE 4-1

ISM Principles and Standards of Ethical Supply Management Conduct

Reprinted with permission from the publisher, the Institute for Supply Management™, *Principles and Standards of Ethical Supply Management Conduct*, approved January 2002.

Many companies have specific policies outlining what constitutes an acceptable gift or promotion. In some companies, buyers are not allowed to accept anything from a supplier, not even a pen. In other companies, there are dollar limits on what may be accepted. To guide purchasing employees, the Institute for Supply Management (ISM) has approved a set of principles and standards, which are shown in Table 4-1.

Developing Supplier Relationships

A strong supplier base is essential to the success of many organizations. Choosing a supplier is like choosing where to shop for something you want to buy. The first thing you decide is which merchants have the product or service you want. Adequate quality for the product or service is usually a prerequisite for even considering a merchant. What else is important to you when choosing a merchant? Availability, perhaps size and color for clothing, freshness and appearance for produce, and physical proximity so you can see the product or try it on. Quick response time, such as overnight shipping or rapid alterations; price, of course; ease of doing business; reputation; and warranty or service agreements are all considerations.

What is important to you as an individual when choosing a merchant is also important for your company when choosing a supplier. In general, we want merchants or suppliers who give us good value. Several studies report that the top three criteria for selecting suppliers are price, quality, and on-time delivery. Even more important, however, is that the choice of suppliers be consistent with a company's mission. For example, if your company is competing on the basis of quick response time, your suppliers must offer minimal lead times and be able to respond quickly.

How Many Suppliers?

Once your company has chosen its suppliers, the next question is: Should you give a single supplier all your business for a particular product or service? Or should you use multiple suppliers? Table 4-2 lists arguments in favor of a single supplier and multiple suppliers.

For some operations, like make-to-order products, it is easier to deal with a single supplier. This is especially true for scheduling deliveries, resolving problems, minimizing the cost of dies or tools, developing computer links, and so forth. In addition, using a single supplier can improve the quality of your finished product by ensuring the consistency of the input materials.

TABLE 4-2

Arguments in Favor of One Supplier and of Multiple Suppliers

Pros of One Supplier	Pros of Multiple Suppliers
• The supplier may be the exclusive owner of essential patents and/or processes and thus be the only possible source.	• Competition among suppliers may provide better service and price.
• By using one supplier, quantity discounts may be achieved.	• Probability of assured supply is better. Multiple suppliers spreads the risks.
• The supplier will be more responsive if it has all of your business for the item.	• Eliminates a supplier's dependence on the purchaser.
• Contractual agreements may prohibit the splitting of an order.	• Provides a greater flexibility of volume.
• The supplier is so outstanding that no other supplier is a serious contender.	• No single supplier may have sufficient capacity.
• Single sourcing is a prerequisite for partnering.	• Allows for testing of new suppliers without jeopardizing the flow of materials.
• The order is too small to split between suppliers.	• Government regulations may require multiple sources.
• When the purchase involves a die, tool, mold, or expensive setup, the cost of duplicating may be prohibitive.	
• Deliveries can be scheduled more easily.	
• Supports just-in-time manufacturing and EDI.	
• Allows for better supplier relations.	
• The just-in-time philosophy can be better utilized.	

On the other hand, multiple suppliers reduce the risk of a disrupted supply—that is, if one supplier suffers a disaster, other suppliers can pick up the slack. Further, multiple suppliers can more easily support changing quantity requirements. For example, if you need a larger quantity than a single supplier can supply, the order can be split among multiple suppliers. This is referred to as flexibility of volume. Finally, government regulations may require the use of multiple suppliers for some projects.

The answer to how many suppliers depends on your supply chain structure. If your company wants to integrate its supply chain, then partnering or using a single supplier makes sense. For example, the trend in industry is toward a smaller supply base. A benchmarking study of twenty-four industries done by the Center for Advanced Purchasing Studies in 1994 reported a 6.5 percent average decrease in the number of active suppliers.

Developing Partnerships

One compelling argument in support of using single suppliers is that it is often a prerequisite for developing a partnering relationship. **Partnering** with a supplier requires a commitment from both the company and the supplier. The goal is to establish an ongoing relationship in which both parties benefit from the arrangement—what is called a "win-win situation."

The two kinds of partnerships are *basic* and *expanded*. A basic partnership is built on mutual respect, honesty, trust, open and frequent communications, and a shared understanding of each partner's role in helping the supply chain achieve its objectives. Expanded partnerships are reserved for a few key suppliers. These are long-term relationships built on mutual strategic goals. Expanded partners must be committed to helping each other succeed. They must place a high priority on maintaining the relationship and on sharing information, risks, opportunities, and technologies.

▶ **Partnering**
A process of developing a long-term relationship with a supplier based on mutual trust, shared vision, shared information, and shared risks.

The Timken Company produces high-quality, antifriction, tapered roller bearings and specialty alloy steels for global consumption. In 1987, Timken started a coordinated sourcing strategy aimed at improving the value of purchased products and reducing the supplier base. A cross-functional team at Timken initiated the process.

At a supplier conference, Timken executives explained to prospective suppliers the company's concept of total value. Timken defines total value as quality, delivery, price, and responsiveness. Timken chose Wayne Steel Company, a steel service center, as its provider of strip steel. Wayne Steel has cutting-edge equipment and is known for its response to customers' quality and service requirements. In addition, Wayne is a leader in close-tolerance, just-in-time programs. Because of this, Wayne can ship small quantities quickly to its customers—a major competitive advantage. Timken and Wayne struggled for three years to establish the partnership. This partnership enabled Timken to save $1 million because of a fixed-price clause during the first year of the contract and another $350,000 annually through reduction in freight and slitting costs. Wayne was able to reduce Timken's lead time from three months to five days for cut-to-length flats and forty-eight hours for coils. Wayne delivered exact requirements (no minimum quantity requirements) to Timken. This eliminated the need for 7500 square feet of warehouse

Courtesy Timken

LINKS TO PRACTICE

The Timken Company
www.timken.com

MKT

space. Inventory turns went from four to forty and inventory investment was reduced by $1.5 million. Wayne's use of better material improved the yield rate at Timken by 4 percent.

For Wayne Steel, the benefits of the partnership were also obvious. With long-term commitments, Wayne was able to invest in the equipment and systems needed to differentiate itself from other steel service centers. Long-term relationships also support Wayne Steel's business philosophy. Wayne has a no-layoff policy because achieving its corporate objectives requires loyal and committed personnel. Long-term relationships also ensure a continuous level of business. This stability allows Wayne to invest in its workforce.

The Timken–Wayne partnership illustrates the need for both partners to benefit if the partnership is to survive.

Critical Factors in Successful Partnering

Impact, intimacy, and vision are critical factors in successful partnering. Impact means attaining levels of productivity and competitiveness that are not possible through normal supplier relationships. Intimacy means the working relationship between partners. Vision means the mission or objectives of the partnership. Let's look at each of these factors.

Impact comes through mutual change. The supplier and the customer must be willing to make changes. Studies suggest that the three sources of impact are reduction of duplication and waste, leveraging core competence, and creating new opportunities.

Duplication can involve any activity done by both the supplier and the customer. For example, suppliers count items before shipping, and customers count the same items after receipt. What value is added by having both parties count the same items?

Waste reduction means eliminating any activity that does not add value. For example, moving items into and out of storage adds no value. It makes sense to have items delivered to and stored where they are used.

Michael Newman/PhotoEdit

Duplication can also be eliminated in paperwork and administration. Sweetheart, a manufacturer of paper drinking cups, faced price-cutting demands from a major customer. Sweetheart was told prices needed to be reduced 10 percent or the customer would use a different supplier. To meet this challenge, Sweetheart partnered with paperboard producer Georgia-Pacific. A shared electronic data interface reduced paperwork and administration and cut expensive inventory. Joint planning optimized production plans, giving Sweetheart a more consistent product from Georgia-Pacific at a better price. Sweetheart can satisfy its high-volume customers, and Georgia-Pacific benefits through more business.

Leveraging core competence is about sharing knowledge. Different companies have different strengths or competencies. Instead of making the supplier or the customer reinvent the wheel, all partners can benefit from shared expertise. Following is an example.

Hillenbrand Industries, a manufacturer of hospital room equipment products, has six geographically dispersed manufacturing facilities. The company uses its own

400-truck fleet and both domestic and international carriers. Hillenbrand decided to partner with UPS to improve the cost, quality, and responsiveness of Hillenbrand's overall logistics. For UPS, fleet management is a core competence; for Hillenbrand, fleet management is an expensive, noncore requirement. Hillenbrand does not want to incur the expense of building a world-class core competence in fleet management. By partnering with UPS, Hillenbrand can leverage and benefit from its partner's expertise. Hillenbrand was able to create $1.5 million in cost improvements during the first year of the partnership. UPS revenues with Hillenbrand have grown by almost $2 million. Both the supplier and the customer have benefited.

Creating new opportunities means partners working together to produce something that neither could have achieved alone. Let's look at an example involving a tier one supplier to an automobile manufacturer.

This supplier used to make daily truckload deliveries of a major subassembly to the auto assembly plant approximately 1200 miles away. Every day, four trucks left the supplier filled with subassemblies, and every day four of the supplier's empty trucks left the auto assembly plant. The supplier was wasting significant transport capacity, with empty trucks returning to its facility. To remedy the problem, the supplier worked with the automobile manufacturer to develop a new truck trailer that carried subassemblies to the automaker and also hauled new autos back to a major metropolitan area. Thus, the auto manufacturer could send new cars to market and eliminate wasted transport capacity. Because the supplier transported the cars to market in an enclosed truck, protected from weather and road hazards, the cars arrived customer-ready. By using the empty trucks to haul the new autos to this market, the supplier eliminated the wasted transport capacity, provided a valuable service to the auto manufacturer, and generated cost savings for both partners. The partnership created a win-win situation that neither could have created alone.

Intimacy comes from the working relationship between partners. Because partners share confidential information, trust between them is critical. Intimacy means eliminating surprises: sharing daily information with partners prevents surprises. For example, a tier one supplier to the automotive industry needs to know how many autos are produced daily, any planned changes in production rates, and the current number of days of finished goods inventory. This information shows the supplier near-term demand and facilitates better customer service to the auto producer.

Supermarkets use bar-code scanners for obtaining point-of-sale information.

Monika Graff/The Image Works

TABLE 4-3	• Have a long-term orientation
	• Are strategic in nature
Characteristics of Partnership Relations	• Share information
	• Share risks and opportunities
	• Share a common vision
	• Share short- and long-term plans
	• Are driven by end-customer expectations

Intimacy is a result of sharing information. This information includes sales data collected at the point of sale; order change notices such as additional orders or cancellations; global inventory management, both quantity and location; and global sourcing opportunities so that supply chain members can improve purchase leveraging and component standardization.

The benefits of information sharing can be significant. When Osram GmbH bought GTE's Sylvania lighting division, it initiated a supply chain integration program. Within six months, fill rates were at 95 percent and climbing; individual stock keeping unit (SKU) forecast accuracy had improved by 16 percent; obsolete inventory was down 10 percent; and the company had saved more than $300,000 on transportation costs.

Vision is the mission or objective of the partnership. The partners must articulate and share their vision. This shared vision provides the structure for the partnership and the role each partner plays in achieving success for the supply chain.

Successful partnering needs a substantial commitment by both partners. Many companies try to reduce the number of their suppliers and develop a smaller, highly focused supplier base. The emphasis is on finding viable suppliers and developing long-term partner relationships. Table 4-3 summarizes the different aspects of partner relationships.

Benefits of Partnering

▶ **Early supplier involvement (ESI)**
Involvement of critical suppliers in new product design.

Early supplier involvement (ESI) is a natural result of partnering relationships and is one way to create impact. Critical suppliers become part of a cross-functional, new-product design team. These suppliers provide technical expertise in the initial phases of product design. Early involvement by suppliers often shortens new-product development time, improves competitiveness, and reduces costs. One example of early supplier involvement is Whirlpool Corporation's partnership with Eaton, a supplier of gas valves and regulators. Whirlpool used Eaton's design expertise to bring a new gas range to market several months sooner than it could have using Whirlpool's in-house design skills.

SUPPLY CHAIN DISTRIBUTION

The Role of Warehouses

Warehouses include plant, regional, and local warehouses. They can be owned or operated by the supplier or wholesaler, or they can be public warehouses. A further classification is general warehouse or distribution warehouse.

A **general warehouse** is used for storing goods for long periods with minimal handling. A **distribution warehouse** is used for moving and mixing goods. Within the supply chain, warehouses have three roles: transportation consolidation, product mixing or blending, and service. The business of a general warehouse is storage. The business of a distribution warehouse is movement and handling; therefore, the size of the facility is less important than its throughput. At a distribution warehouse, goods are received in large-volume lots and broken down into small individual orders.

▶ **General warehouse**
Used for long-term storage.

▶ **Distribution warehouse**
Used for short-term storage, consolidation, and product mixing.

A good example of the importance of distribution warehousing in support of e-commerce is Fingerhut's warehouse in St. Cloud, Minnesota. Employees rush through the warehouse on forklifts and cargo haulers filling orders for on-line retailers. Every item is encoded to speed packing. Red lasers scan each package as it rushes down the conveyor, verifying the actual package weight against expected package

Courtesy Fingerhut

LINKS TO PRACTICE

Fingerhut Direct Marketing, Inc.
www.fingerhut.com

weight. Packages that do not match are pushed aside for further inspection. The crew at this warehouse can process as many as 30,000 items per hour.

Transportation Consolidation occurs when warehouses consolidate less-than-truckload (LTL) quantities into truckload (TL) quantities. This consolidation can be both in supplier shipments to the manufacturer and in finished goods shipped to distant warehouses. The goal is to use TL shipments for as much of the distance as possible because TL shipments are cheaper than LTL shipments.

For inbound supplier shipments, a manufacturer can have small LTL deliveries from several suppliers consolidated at a convenient warehouse and then shipped to the manufacturer in TL shipments. For outbound shipments, the manufacturer can send TL deliveries to distant warehouses that break down the shipment for LTL delivery to local markets. Transportation consolidation is usually done to reduce transportation costs.

Product Mixing is a value-added service for customers. With product mixing, the customer places an order to the warehouse for a variety of products. The warehouse groups the items together and ships the mixture of items directly to the customer. Without product mixing, the customer would have to place individual orders for each item and pay shipping for each item. Instead, product mixing enables quicker customer service and reduces transportation costs.

Services offered by the warehouses can improve customer service by moving goods closer to the customer and thus reducing replenishment time. For example, a tier one automotive supplier can use a warehouse located near an automotive assembly plant to store instrument panels. The producer requires the supplier to provide these instrument panels in VIN (vehicle identification number) order sequence within an hour. That means the warehouse must load and deliver the parts in the correct sequence to match the production as it occurs on the line, that is, right color, right style, right identification number, and so on.

Warehouses can also be used to finish custom products. For example, when manufacturers use **postponement** in their product design process, almost-finished products

▶ **Postponement**
A strategy that shifts production differentiation closer to the consumer by postponing final configuration.

are delivered to the warehouse. When actual customer orders are received, the warehouse finishes the product according to the specifications of the customer. For example, in the furniture industry products can be left unstained until the customer order is received. The stain is then applied and the customer receives a custom product in minimal time. In the electronic industry, a unit may need to have the appropriate power supply and cord attached based on the location of the customer. Using the warehouse in this manner allows a manufacturer to maintain flexibility with almost-finished products and also to quickly provide a custom product for the customer.

Crossdocking

▶ **Crossdocking**
Eliminates the storage and order-picking functions of a distribution warehouse.

Crossdocking eliminates the storage and order-picking functions of a distribution warehouse while still performing its receiving and shipping functions. Trucks arrive at a crossdock with goods to be sorted, consolidated with other products, and loaded onto outbound trucks. Those trucks may be headed to a manufacturer, a retailer, or another crossdock. Shipments are transferred directly from inbound trailers to outbound trailers without any storage in between. Shipments should spend less than twenty-four hours in a crossdock.

What is the big difference between crossdocking and traditional distribution warehousing? In a traditional setting, the warehouse holds stock until a customer places an order, then the item is picked, packed, and shipped. The customer typically is not known before the items arrive at the warehouse. With crossdocking, the customer is known before the items arrive at the warehouse and there is no reason to move the items into storage.

Crossdocking has two major advantages. First, the retailer reduces inventory holding costs by replacing inventory with information and coordination. Second, crossdocking can consolidate shipments to achieve truckload quantities and significantly reduce a company's inbound transportation costs.

▶ **Manufacturing crossdocking**
The receiving and consolidating of inbound supplies and materials to support just-in-time manufacturing.

▶ **Distributor crossdocking**
The receiving and consolidating of inbound products from different vendors into a multi-SKU pallet.

▶ **Transportation crossdocking**
Consolidation of LTL shipments to gain economies of scale.

▶ **Retail crossdocking**
Sorting product from multiple vendors onto outbound trucks headed for specific stores.

Types of Crossdocking **Manufacturing crossdocking** is the receiving and consolidating of inbound supplies to support just-in-time manufacturing. In this case, the warehouse might be near the manufacturing facility and used to prep subassemblies or consolidate kits of parts. **Distributor crossdocking** is the receiving and consolidating of inbound products from different vendors into a multistock-keeping unit pallet that is delivered once the last product is received. **Transportation crossdocking** is the consolidating of shipments from LTL and small-package industries to gain economies of scale. **Retail crossdocking** is sorting product from multiple vendors onto outbound trucks headed for specific retail stores.

LINKS TO PRACTICE

FedEx Freight
www.fedexfreight.
fedex.com

David J. Sams/Stone/
Getty Images, Inc.

Home Depot, Inc., Wal-Mart, Costco Wholesale Corporation, and FedEx Freight are examples of companies using crossdocking. At FedEx Freight, pickup and delivery drivers are busy during the day picking up freight that must be delivered that night and making deliveries. Each evening, drivers return to the crossdock. Freight is unloaded, sorted, and placed onto outbound trucks.

The trucks travel through the night to their destinations, where the freight is unloaded and sorted onto local delivery trucks. FedEx Freight has achieved economies of scale that allow cost-effective transportation to areas with relatively little freight traffic.

Radio Frequency Identification Technology (RFID)

RFID is an automated data collection technology. It uses radio frequency waves to transfer data between a reader and an RFID tag. The information is transmitted automatically so no one needs to unpack or scan individual bar-code labels, yet it provides accurate data transmittal.

▶ **Radio frequency identification (RFID)** Unpowered microchips are used to wirelessly transmit encoded information through antennae.

The RFID tags contain encoded information that identifies items at the case, pallet, or container level. Rolls-Royce now uses RFID technology to track components used in military transport and combat aircraft and helicopters. In states with toll highways, RFID technology is used to collect tolls automatically. As a car with an RFID tag slowly passes through a collection lane, the RFID reader records the relevant vehicle data and the appropriate toll charge is processed.

In a survey concerning RFID implementation, nearly half of consumer goods makers, a third of food and beverage makers, and a quarter of textile and apparel manufacturers indicated that they were implementing RFID technology because of a mandate from Wal-Mart. The survey further indicated that 59 percent of companies in the automotive industry would deploy RFID technology during the coming year. Worldwide, RFID is forecasted to surpass $2.5 billion by 2010. There is some potential controversy regarding personal privacy in some possible future uses of RFID technology.

Third-Party Service Providers

The ease of developing an electronic storefront has allowed the discovery of suppliers from around the world. A good example is the success of artisans in Kenya, who by marketing over the Internet increased annual export earnings to $2 million from only $10,000. While smaller companies have benefited from these electronic storefronts, they often are not prepared to handle the logistics aspect. Many of these B2C companies outsource the delivery and return of products to companies such as FedEx and UPS. This works especially well when the consumer is paying for delivery.

A good example is Bike World, a company known for its high-quality bicycles, expert advice, and personalized service. After beginning Internet operations in 1996, Bike World found itself overwhelmed processing orders, manually shipping packages, and responding to customer inquiries regarding order status. Because of this, Bike World outsourced its order fulfillment to FedEx. FedEx offered reasonably priced delivery that exceeded customers' expectations.

Even larger companies often outsource their logistics. Consider when over 5400 CVS stores unveiled Gillette's Fusion, a new shaving product, all on the same day. Eight to ten weeks of planning was needed for this one-day event. The product was shipped to five of the CVS distribution centers. At the distribution centers, CVS coordinated pick-and-pack activities and readied the product for shipping to the stores. CVS used expedited shipping through a third-party logistics provider, delivering razors to all stores by noon that day. It was the first chain to have the new product available, providing it with increased market share.

INTEGRATED SUPPLY CHAIN MANAGEMENT

Implementing integrated supply chain management needs considerable effort on the part of the initiating company. This strategic change often is a result of external pressures on the company, such as global competitors, industry consolidation, the switch to e-commerce, or major technological changes within the industry.

A company's first step in improving performance is to analyze the supply chain. Typically, a small cross-functional team leads the effort and may reveal that some functional areas are performing at suboptimal levels.

Most companies start by integrating internal functions because they are under the company's direct control. These functions include production planning and control, and purchasing and distribution. The focus is on improving system performance through shared information by using a common database and compatible computer software.

The next step is to integrate external suppliers through partner relationships, first by establishing the characteristics of a desired partner and then by evaluating potential partners. Table 4-4 shows possible objectives for the manufacturer and the supplier.

A company evaluating potential partners looks at the following aspects of the potential partner's business:

- History, sales volume, product lines, market share, number of employees, major customers, and major suppliers;
- Current management team in terms of past performance, stability, and strategic vision;
- Labor force in terms of skill, experience, commitment to quality, and relations with the supplier;
- Internal cost structure, process and technology capabilities, financial stability, information system compatibility, supplier sourcing strategies, and long-term relationship potential.

The company reduces the selection pool to a few potential partners, identifies a single partner, and commits to the partnership. At this point, both parties agree on how to measure the performance of the partnership. The partners set time frames for the frequency and methods of performance assessment and decide how problems will be resolved. When they reach agreement on these issues, the partners develop supply chain operating procedures and put the partnership into motion.

TABLE 4-4	Manufacturer's Goals	Supplier's Goals
Possible Supply Chain Objectives	• Reduce costs	• Increase sales volume
	• Reduce duplication of effort	• Increase customer loyalty
	• Improve quality	• Reduce costs
	• Reduce lead time	• Improve demand data
	• Implement cost reduction program	• Improve profitability
	• Involve suppliers earlier	• Reduce inventory
	• Reduce time to market	
	• Reduce inventory	

SUPPLY CHAIN PERFORMANCE MEASUREMENT

When measuring performance, a company can use traditional financial measures such as return on investment (ROI), profitability, market share, and revenue growth, as well as additional measures, such as customer service levels, and traditional inventory performance measures, such as inventory turns; weeks of supply; and inventory obsolescence (all discussed in Chapter 12). In addition, it is important to measure different supply chain activities so that members understand how their performance directly affects the supply chain. Companies use supply chain management to respond to pressures from customers for better-quality products or services, quicker response time, lower costs, and better value. It is important for companies to measure activities that add these values.

Since customers demand better-quality products or services, the company needs ways to measure improvements. The company can measure product quality by warranty costs, products returned, and cost reductions allowed because of product defects. In Chapters 5 and 6, you will learn about different aspects of quality and methods for measuring product quality. These quality measures could easily track product and service quality improvement in a supply chain.

In Chapter 15, you will learn about scheduling performance measures that could be used to evaluate the company's response time as well as to evaluate how well the company is using its capacity. Excess capacity may enable much quicker response times, but the company must assess the cost of low capacity utilization.

Purchasing can also track transaction costs to determine if the supply chain linkage has reduced these costs. The company can also track transportation costs to see if efficiencies have occurred.

The company needs to determine what customer satisfaction means to its customers. Does it mean filling the entire order? Does it mean how quickly it can respond to customer requests? Or is it more important to have the product always arrive on time? Answering these questions identifies the activities that support the supply chain's objectives. These are the activities that must be measured.

In a study of U.S.–Mexican maquiladora operations, performance measurements were measured in the order of cycle-time reduction (response time), routing and scheduling (on-time delivery, response time, and capacity utilization), and outbound cross-border transportation. The bottom line is that companies must measure performance of the supply chain and the measurements must support behavior that is consistent with the supply chain objectives.

The Supply Chain Operations Reference (SCOR) model is an effort to standardize measurement of supply chain performance. The SCOR model examines four different operational perspectives: reliability, flexibility, expenses, and assets/utilization. From a reliability perspective, the supply chain is measured on on-time delivery, order fulfillment lead time, and fill rate (the fraction of demand met from stock). In terms of flexibility, supply chain response time and production flexibility are measured. For expenses, supply chain management cost, warranty cost as a percentage of revenue, and value added per employee are examined. In terms of assets/utilization, total inventory days of supply, cash-to-cash cycle time, and net asset turns can be measured.

TRENDS IN SUPPLY CHAIN MANAGEMENT

The past few years have seen increased use of electronic marketplaces that bring thousands of suppliers together with thousands of buyers. The objectives of these net marketplaces are to have suppliers compete on price, to encourage automated low-cost transactions, and to reduce the price of industrial supplies.

▶ **E-distributors**
Independently owned net marketplaces having catalogs representing thousands of suppliers and designed for spot purchases.

▶ **E-purchasing**
Companies that connect on-line MRO suppliers to businesses who pay fees to join the market, usually for long-term contractual purchasing.

▶ **Value chain management (VCM)**
Automation of a firm's purchasing or selling processes.

▶ **Exchanges**
A marketplace that focuses on spot requirements of large firms in a single industry.

▶ **Industry consortia**
Industry-owned markets that enable buyers to purchase direct inputs from a limited set of invited suppliers.

▶ **Supply chain velocity**
The speed at which product moves through a pipeline from the manufacturer to the customer.

E-distributors are the most common form of net marketplace. E-distributors provide electronic catalogs representing the products of thousands of suppliers. E-distributors are independently owned intermediaries that provide a single source for customers to make spot purchases. About 40 percent of a company's items are purchased on a spot basis. E-distributors typically have fixed prices, but do offer quantity discounts to large customers (see Chapter 12). The primary benefits of e-distribution to the manufacturing company are lower product search costs, lower transaction costs, a wide selection of suppliers, rapid product delivery, and low prices.

E-purchasing companies connect on-line suppliers offering maintenance, repair parts, and operating supplies (MRO) to businesses who pay fees to join the market. E-procurement companies are typically used for long-term contractual purchasing and offer value chain management services to both buyers and sellers. **Value chain management (VCM)** automates a firm's purchasing or selling processes. VCM automates purchase orders, requisitions, product sourcing, invoicing, and payment. For suppliers, VCM automates order status, order tracking, invoicing, shipping, and order corrections.

On-line **exchanges** connect hundreds of suppliers to unlimited buyers. Exchanges create a marketplace focusing on spot requirements of large firms in a single industry, such as the automotive industry or electronics industry. Examples of exchanges include ProcureSteel.com (a market for steel products), e-Greenbiz.com (spot market for nursery supplies), and Smarterwork.com (professional services from web design to legal advice).

The last type of net marketplace is an industry consortium. **Industry consortia** are industry-owned markets that enable buyers to purchase direct inputs from a limited set of invited participants. The objective of an industry consortium is the unification of supply chains within entire industries through a common network and computing platform. Examples of industry consortia include Covisint.com (automotive industry), Avendra.com (hospitality industry), and ForestExpress.com (paper and forest products). It is clear that net marketplaces will be a dominant factor in effective supply chain management now and in the future. Technology continues to bring suppliers, buyers, and distributors closer together so that supply chains can be managed effectively.

As supply chains cover greater distances, they experience greater uncertainty and generally are less efficient. It is likely that **supply chain velocity** in these global chains will decrease. Practitioners have identified the following characteristics associated with lower-velocity supply chains: lumpy supply/demand (goods tend to arrive at the warehouse in large quantities and sometimes without notice), more break-bulk activity because of the larger quantities, more slow long-distance moves as companies source offshore, and higher inventory levels in the pipeline due to longer transit times. These lower-velocity supply chains raise additional questions, such as distribution center location, or a better understanding of the economics of break-bulk and more emphasis on pipeline design.

Some believe that a more strategic and integrated approach is needed to move supply chain operations to the next level. They argue that a new model of supply chain excellence will combine world-class supply chain management, process leadership in lean manufacturing disciplines, and "on-demand" technology, information technology that is paid for as it is used, not on a per-license basis. The name of this approach is the *dynamic on-demand supply chain*.

As you can see, a number of issues still remain for supply chain managers. The only clear trend is that information technology will be a primary enabler of successful supply chain management.

SUPPLY CHAIN MANAGEMENT WITHIN OM: HOW IT ALL FITS TOGETHER

Supply chain management (SCM) is directly linked to many OM activities. The degree of supply chain management is a strategic decision for the organization (Chapter 2) and determines the level of vertical integration in the organization. SCM is concerned with external suppliers, internal operations, and external distributors.

Effective SCM requires supplier partnerships. Using the ISM Principles and Standards of Ethical Supply Management Conduct, purchasing develops partnerships with suppliers to assure a continuous supply of materials at a reasonable cost. Purchasing also works with suppliers to improve communications, to develop flexibility in meeting changes of demand, to improve quality of materials, and to assure on-time delivery. This assured, continuous supply of materials allows the production planners to effectively schedule jobs (Chapter 14) and to use equipment and personnel efficiently.

SCM also provides for streamlined communications between suppliers and the company, thus reducing purchasing lead time. As we will learn when studying inventory management in Chapter 12, reduced lead time results in lower inventory levels. The improved communications within the supply chain improve demand forecasting accuracy. This reduces demand uncertainty, allowing lower safety stock investment while still maintaining customer service levels. Improved demand forecast accuracy also contributes to the development of better staffing plans (Chapter 13), which can lead to lower personnel costs, lower inventory costs, and improved customer service.

SCM affects product and process design (Chapter 3) by specifying which items are done in-house and which items are outsourced. Good supply chain management provides timely, accurate information that is critical to successful operations management.

SCM ACROSS THE ORGANIZATION

Supply chain management changes the way companies do business. Consider how supply chain management affects different functional areas within the organization.

Accounting shares some of the benefits and responsibilities of supply chain management. As inventory levels decrease, customer service levels increase. Accounting is exposed to the risks of information sharing and involved in developing long-term partnerships. With information sharing comes the need for increased confidentiality and trust.

Marketing benefits by improved customer service levels achieved by POS data collection. A shared database provides marketing with current demand trends and eliminates demand filtering between levels of the supply chain. POS data also facilitates quicker customer response time.

Information systems are critical for supply chain management. Information systems provide the means for collecting relevant demand data, developing a common database, and providing a means for transmitting order information. Information systems enable information sharing through POS data, EDI, RFID, the Internet, intranets, and extranets.

Purchasing has an important role in supply chain management. Purchasing is responsible for sourcing materials and developing a strong global supplier base through long-term partnering agreements.

Operations uses timely demand information to more effectively plan production schedules and use manufacturing capacity. Operations responds more quickly to changing customer demand data thus providing improved customer service levels.

Who is responsible for supply chain management within an organization? In a manufacturing company, it is often the materials manager, since he or she is more familiar with external suppliers, internal functions, and external distributors. The person who does supply chain management must see the "big picture" so that local priorities do not overshadow global priorities. In a service organization, the operations or office manager may be responsible for supply chain management.

THE SUPPLY CHAIN LINK

This chapter provides the framework for understanding supply chain management. Supply chains consist of external suppliers, internal processes, and external distributors. Internal processes (purchasing, processing, production planning and control, quality assurance, and shipping) are integrated first since the manufacturer has direct control over these activities. Integrating external suppliers into the supply chain begins with sourcing decisions and subsequent strategic partnership development by the purchasing function.

Electronic net marketplaces facilitate sourcing by bringing together thousands of suppliers and buyers to a common site. Distributors are usually the last segment of the chain to be integrated. Warehouses can be used for consolidation, product mixing, or finalizing products. Crossdocking can reduce transit time as well as reduce handling of goods. RFID helps track materials as they flow through the supply chain. POS demand data is provided to all members of the supply chain to reduce uncertainty and to assure that all members of the supply chain work with common data.

Chapter Highlights

1 Every organization is part of a supply chain, either as a customer or as a supplier. Supply chains include all the processes needed to make a finished product, from the extraction of raw materials through to the sale to the end user. Supply chain management is the integration and coordination of all these activities.

2 The bullwhip effect distorts product demand information passed between levels of the supply chain. The more levels that exist, the more distortion that is possible. Variability results from updating demand estimates at each level, order batching, price fluctuations, and rationing.

3 Many issues affect supply chain management. The Internet, the Web, EDI, intranets, extranets, bar-code scanners, and POS data are supply chain management enablers. Technology advancements facilitate information sharing among supply chain members. Intranets and extranets improve communication flow within organizations and supply chains. Through the use of electronic net marketplaces, the Internet greatly reduces the cost of researching suppliers. Customer expectations are high as they demand better service, better product quality, quicker response times, reasonable prices, and an easy way to return merchandise.

4 B2B and B2C electronic commerce enable supply chain management. Net marketplaces bring together thousands of suppliers and customers, allowing for efficient sourcing and lower transaction costs.

5 Global supply chains increase geographical distances between members, causing greater uncertainty in delivery times. Increased uncertainty often results in additional inventory investment. Forecasting accuracy tends to be poorer too. Fluctuating exchange rates, inadequate transportation networks, limited telecommunication capabilities, uncertain power continuity, low skill levels of workers, and poor local supply availability all complicate global supply chains.

6 Purchasing has a major role in supply chain management. Purchasing is involved in sourcing decisions and developing strategic long-term partnerships. Purchasing develops and maintains a supplier base capable of assuring material availability, timely delivery performance, high-quality products, and reasonable prices.

7 Ethics in supply management is an ongoing concern. Since buyers are in a position to influence or award business, it is imperative that buyers avoid any appearance of unethical behavior or conflict of interest. The Institute for Supply Management has established a set of principles and standards to guide buyers.

8 Companies make insourcing and outsourcing decisions. These make-or-buy decisions are based on financial and strategic criteria. Companies typically do not outsource activities that are part of their core competencies.

9 Partnerships require sharing information, risks, technologies, and opportunities. Impact, intimacy, and vision are critical to successful partnering. Impact means attaining higher levels of productivity and competitiveness that are not possible through normal supplier relationships. Intimacy requires trust as companies share confidential information. Vision means having common objectives.

10 Supply chain distribution requires effective warehousing operations. The warehouses provide transportation consolidation, product mixing, and service. Warehouses consolidate (LTL) quantities into (TL) quantities. Product mixing adds value for the customer because the warehouse groups the items and ships them directly to the customer. Warehouses can improve customer service by placing goods closer to the customer to reduce response time. Crossdocking is an effective method for reducing transportation costs. RFID is gaining use as a means of accurately tracking shipments. Much of the distribution function has been outsourced to third-party logistics providers.

11 Integrated supply chain management usually begins with the manufacturer integrating internal processes first. Then, the company tries to integrate the external suppliers. The last step is integrating the external distributors.

12 A company needs to evaluate the performance of its supply chain. Regular performance metrics (ROI, profitability, market share, customer service levels, etc.) and other measures that reflect the objectives of the supply chain are used. In addition, the company can use the Supply Chain Operations Reference (SCOR) model to standardize its supply chain performance.

13 The emergence of net marketplaces has significantly affected supply chain management. As supply chains become longer, it is likely that supply chain velocity will decrease. It is possible that a more strategic and integrated approach is needed to advance supply chain management to the next level. Such an approach will combine world-class supply chain management, process leadership in lean manufacturing techniques, and "on-demand" information technology.

Key Terms

supply chain 98
supply chain management 99
tier one supplier 101
tier two supplier 101
tier three supplier 101
logistics 102
traffic management 102
distribution management 102
bullwhip effect 102
e-commerce 104
business-to-business e-commerce
  (B2B) 104
automated order entry system 105
electronic data interchange (EDI) 105
electronic storefronts 105
net marketplaces 105

business-to-consumer e-commerce
  (B2C) 106
advertising revenue model 106
subscription revenue model 106
transaction fee model 106
sales revenue model 106
affiliate revenue model 106
intranets 106
extranets 106
vertical integration 112
insource 112
outsource 112
backward integration 112
forward integration 112
partnering 117
early supplier involvement (ESI) 120

general warehouse 121
distribution warehouse 121
postponement 121
crossdocking 122
manufacturing crossdocking 122
distributor crossdocking 122
transportation crossdocking 122
retail crossdocking 122
radio frequency identification
  (RFID) 123
e-distributors 126
e-purchasing 126
value chain mamagent 126
exchanges 126
industry consortia 126
supply chain velocity 126

Formula Review

For insourcing or outsourcing:

$$FC_{Buy} + (VC_{Buy} \times Q) = FC_{Make} + (VC_{Make} \times Q)$$

Solved Problems

• Problem 1

Jack Smith, owner of Jack's Auto Sales, is deciding whether his company should process its own auto loan applications or out-source the process to Loans Etc. If Jack processes the auto loan applications internally, he faces an annual fixed cost of $2500 for membership fees, allowing him access to the TopNotch credit company, and a variable cost of $25 each time he processes a loan application. Loans Etc. will process the loans for $35 per application but Jack must lease equipment from Loans Etc. at a fixed annual cost of $1000. Jack estimates processing 125 loan applications per year. What do you think Jack should do?

(a) Should Jack process the loans internally or outsource the loans if demand is expected to be 125 loan applications?

(b) Is Jack indifferent to internal processing and outsourcing at one level of loan applications?

• Before You Begin:

To make his decision when demand is known, Jack needs to calculate the total cost of processing the auto loans in-house and compare it to the total cost of outsourcing the loan processing. You need to identify the relevant costs. If Jack processes the loans internally, he has an annual fixed cost of $2500 plus a per loan variable cost of $25. If the loan processing is outsourced, Jack has a fixed annual cost of $1000 and a per loan variable cost of $35.

• Solution

(a) The total cost for processing 125 loan applications internally is $5625. That is $2500 in annual fixed costs plus 125

loan applications multiplied by the $25 per application variable cost. The total cost for outsourcing the applications is $5375. That is $1000 in annual fixed costs plus 125 loan applications multiplied by the $35 per application variable cost. At 125 loan applications, it is cheaper for Jack to outsource the loan application processing.

(b) When demand is not known, set the total costs of each alternative equal to each other, or $1000 + ($35 * Q) = $2500 + ($25 * Q). Solving for Q, we have 10Q = $1500, or Q = 150 loan applications. Since the costs are equal at 150 loan applications and Jack expects to need 125 applications processed, he is better off outsourcing the loan applications to Loans Etc.

• Problem 2

Big State University (BSU) is considering whether or not it should outsource its housekeeping service. Currently, BSU employs 400 housekeepers at an average annual wage of $23,000 plus another 39 percent for fringe benefits. Annual fixed costs associated with housekeeping are $1,278,800.

Eric's Efficient Cleaners (EEC) will provide similar housekeeping for a fixed annual cost of $7,500,000 plus a variable cost of $20,000 per housekeeper required. Because Eric uses state-of-the-art equipment and well-trained employees, his company would need only 80 percent of the current BSU housekeeper staff (or 320 housekeepers).

(a) Calculate the annual cost of BSU using its current housekeeping staff.
(b) Calculate the annual cost if BSU lets EEC do the housekeeping.
(c) Find the indifference point for the two alternatives.

• Before You Begin:

Identify the relevant costs. You need to know the cost to BSU for using its own housekeeping staff. The average annual salary per housekeeper is $23,000 plus fringe benefits (39 percent of the average annual salary). The annual fixed cost associated with housekeeping is $1,278,800. If housekeeping is outsourced, BSU doesn't need to pay fringe benefits. EEC will provide similar service for a fixed annual cost of $7,500,000 plus a

variable cost of $20,000 per housekeeper. Remember that he only needs 320 housekeepers for the job.

• Solution

(a) If BSU does its housekeeping with its current staff, the cost is $14,066,800

Cost per housekeeper ($23,000 + 39% fringe benefits)
= $31,970

Cost for 400 housekeepers (400 × $31,970) =	$12,788,800
Annual fixed costs =	1,278,000
Total annual costs	$14,066,800

(b) If BSU has EEC do the housekeeping, the cost is $13,900,000.

Cost for 320 housekeepers (320 × $20,000) =	$ 6,400,000
Annual fixed costs =	7,500,000
Total annual costs	$13,900,000

(c) The indifference point is found by setting the two cost functions equal to each other. Since EEC only needs 80% as many employees as BSU, we need to adjust the cost functions.

$$\$1,278,800 + \$31,970(Q) = \$7,500,000 + (0.8Q)(\$20,000)$$

Q = 389.55, or 390 employees. Therefore, if the school needs fewer than 390 in-house housekeepers, it should do the housekeeping rather than outsource it. If BSU needs more than 390 housekeepers, it should outsource with EEC.

Discussion Questions

1. Discuss the different types of e-commerce.
2. Explain the different revenue models used in e-commerce.
3. Give two examples from the Internet for each of the different revenue models used in e-commerce.
4. Describe the evolution of business-to-business (B2B) e-commerce.
5. For the next item you buy, determine its supply chain.

6. How do supply chains for service organizations differ from supply chains for manufacturing organizations?
7. How can companies satisfy increasing customer expectations?
8. Describe the additional factors that affect global supply chains.
9. Think of your last major purchase. What criteria did you use to select the supplier?

10. Explain the concept of partnering, including advantages and disadvantages.

11. Explain the benefits of using a single supplier as opposed to multiple suppliers.

12. Describe the kinds of information that are necessary in a supply chain.

13. Describe the role of warehouses in a supply chain.

14. Describe radio frequency identification (RFID) and how it could be used by an organization.

15. Describe the current trends in e-commerce and how they affect supply chain management.

Problems

1. Gabriela Manufacturing must decide whether to insource or outsource a new toxic-free miracle carpet cleaner that works with its Miracle Carpet Cleaning Machine. If it decides to insource the product, the process would incur $300,000 of annual fixed costs and $1.50 per unit of variable costs. If it is outsourced, a supplier has offered to make it for an annual fixed cost of $120,000 and a variable cost of $2.25 per unit in variable costs.

(a) Given these two alternatives, determine the indifference point (where total costs are equal).

(b) If the expected demand for the new miracle cleaner is 300,000 units, what would you recommend that Gabriela Manufacturing do?

2. Gabriela Manufacturing was able to find a new supplier that would provide the item for $1.80 per unit with an annual fixed cost of $200,000. Should Gabriela Manufacturing insource or outsource the item?

3. Downhill Boards (DB), a producer of snow boards, is evaluating a new process for applying the finish to its snow boards. Durable Finish Company (DFC) has offered to apply the finish for $170,000 in fixed costs and a unit variable cost of $0.65. Downhill Boards currently incurs a fixed annual cost of $125,000 and has a variable cost of $0.90 per unit. Annual demand for the snow boards is 160,000.

(a) Calculate the annual cost of the current process used at Downhill Boards.

(b) Calculate the annual cost if Durable Finish Company applies the finish.

(c) Find the indifference point for these two alternatives.

(d) How much of a change in demand is needed to justify outsourcing the process?

4. Fast Finish, Inc. (FFI) has made a technological breakthrough in snow board finish application. FFI will apply the finish for $0.23 per unit in variable costs plus a fixed annual cost of $230,000. Use the cost and demand information given in Problem 3 for Downhill Boards to evaluate this proposal.

(a) What will it cost Downhill Boards to outsource the finishing process?

(b) At what demand level does it make sense economically to outsource the finishing process?

(c) What additional factors should be considered when making this outsourcing decision?

5. Henri of Henri's French Cuisine (HFC), a chain of 12 restaurants, is trying to decide if it makes sense to outsource the purchasing function. Currently, Henri employs two buyers at an annual fixed cost of $85,000. Henri estimates that the variable cost of each purchase order placed is $15. Value-Buy (VB), a group of purchasing specialists, will perform the purchasing function for a fixed annual fee of $100,000 plus $5 for each purchase order placed. Last year, HFC placed 1450 purchase orders.

(a) What was the cost last year to HFC when doing the purchasing in-house?

(b) What would the cost have been last year had HFC used Value-Buy?

(c) What is the indifference point for the two alternatives?

(d) If HFC estimates it will place 1600 purchase orders next year, should it use VB?

(e) What additional factors should be considered by HFC?

6. Cal's Carpentry is considering outsourcing its accounts receivable function. Currently, Cal employs two full-time clerks and one part-time clerk to manage accounts receivables. Each full-time clerk has an annual salary of $36,000 plus fringe benefits costing 30 percent of their salary. The part-time clerk makes $18,000 per year but has no fringe benefits. Total salary plus fringe cost is $111,600. Cal estimates that each account receivable incurs a $10 variable cost. The Small Business Accounts Receivables Group (SBARG) specializes in handling accounts receivable for small- to medium-size companies. Doris Roberts from SBARG has offered to do the account receivables for Cal's Carpentry at a fixed cost of $75,000 per year plus $30 per account receivable. Next year, Cal expects to have 2000 accounts receivables.

(a) Calculate the cost for Cal's Carpentry to continue doing accounts receivable in-house.

(b) Calculate the cost for Cal's Carpentry to use SBARG to handle the accounts receivable.

(c) If the fixed annual cost offered by SBARG is nonnegotiable but it is willing to negotiate the variable cost, what variable cost from SBARG would make Cal indifferent to the two options?

(d) What other alternatives might Cal consider in terms of his current staffing for accounts receivable?

(e) What additional criteria should be considered by Cal before outsourcing the accounts receivable?

CASE: Electronic Pocket Calendars Supply Chain Management Game

In this supply chain game, retailers sell electronic pocket calendars to their customers and place replenishment orders to their wholesaler. The wholesaler sells the pocket calendars to the retailers and orders the calendars from a distributor. The distributor sells the pocket calendars to the wholesalers and orders calendars directly from the factory. The distribution system is shown in the figure. For each period the game is played, participants must follow the same sequence:

1. Receive any shipments into inventory.
2. Ship calendars to satisfy both new customer demand and any back orders, as long as sufficient product is available.
3. Determine the ending inventory (a negative value indicates backorders exist).
4. Determine the inventory position (ending inventory plus any quantity already ordered).
5. Place replenishment orders.

For this game, inventory holding costs will be $10 per case per week and back order costs will be $15 per case per week.

Each person must keep track of his or her own costs. The weekly demand at the retailers will be provided by your professor. Once the demand is known by the retailers, the retailers place the appropriate replenishment orders with the wholesalers. The wholesalers update their inventory records and place the necessary orders with the distributor. At this point, the distributor updates its inventory records and places the appropriate replenishment order with the factory. Lead time throughout the supply chain is two weeks. For example, once the factory releases an order to be manufactured, it is two weeks before it is available or when the distributor orders pocket calendars from the factory, it is two weeks before they arrive.

A number of participants are needed in this game (see the figure). One person manages the factory (1). There are three distribution centers, each needing a manager (3). Each distribution center supplies two different wholesalers (6), and each wholesaler supplies two unique retailers (12). In some cases, a location may have co-managers to speed up the transactions. The accompanying table provides information regarding each location in the supply chain.

For each period of the game, retailers follow these procedures:

1. The retailer accepts into stock any orders due to arrive during the current period. The beginning inventory plus the arriving order determine how much inventory the location has available to satisfy demand during that period.
2. Next, your professor provides each retailer with actual demand data for that period. The demand is given to the retailer on a paper order form. The data are not shown to other members of the supply chain but are treated as confidential information.
3. Retailers fill orders as long as sufficient inventory (calculated in Step 1) is available.
4. Retailers calculate their ending inventory level. If sufficient inventory is available, ending inventory is beginning inven-

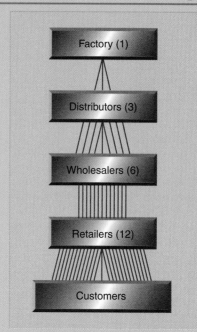

Electronic pocket calendar supply chain

tory minus that period's actual demand. If there is not sufficient inventory, then back orders occur. When a back order occurs, your ending inventory value is negative. For example, if you only have 30 units available and demand is 32 units, your inventory balance is −2 units.

5. Retailers calculate their inventory position. Inventory position is the ending inventory plus any quantity already ordered that has not yet arrived. For example, if your ending inventory is −2 but you have placed an order for 90 additional cases, your inventory position is 88 cases (−2 + 90).

6. If the retailer's inventory position is at or below its re-order point, the retailer places an order with its wholesaler. Retailers A11 and A12 order from wholesaler A1, retailers A21 and A22 order from wholesaler A2, and so on. These orders are made in writing and delivered to the appropriate wholesaler. No other communication is permitted.

For the wholesalers, the procedure each period is the following:

1. The wholesaler accepts into stock any orders due to arrive during the current period. The beginning inventory plus the arriving order determine how much inventory the location has available to satisfy demand during that period.
2. Next, the wholesalers look at the replenishment orders from the retailers for that period. These data are not shown to other members of the supply chain but are treated as confidential information.
3. Wholesalers fill orders as long as sufficient inventory (calculated in Step 1) is available.
4. Wholesalers calculate their ending inventory level. If sufficient inventory is available, ending inventory is beginning inven-

Individual Location Information

	Replenishment Order Quantity (cases)	Reorder Point (cases)	Beginning Inventory (cases)	Average Weekly Demand (cases)
Factory	350	190	277	175
Distributor A	120	125	185	60
Distributor B	180	190	280	90
Distributor C	100	52	77	25
Wholesaler A1	90	95	140	45
Wholesaler A2	60	31	46	15
Wholesaler B1	105	110	163	52.5
Wholesaler B2	75	80	118	37.5
Wholesaler C1	60	31	46	15
Wholesaler C2	40	21	31	10
Retailer A11	60	62	92	30
Retailer A12	30	31	46	15
Retailer A21	45	24	35	11.25
Retailer A22	15	8	13	3.75
Retailer B11	75	78	116	37.5
Retailer B12	60	31	46	15
Retailer B21	40	42	62	20
Retailer B22	35	37	55	17.5
Retailer C11	40	21	31	10
Retailer C12	20	11	16	5
Retailer C21	20	12	18	5.5
Retailer C22	20	10	15	4.5

tory minus that period's actual demand. If there is not sufficient inventory then back orders occur. When a back order occurs, your ending inventory value is negative.

5. Wholesalers calculate their inventory position. Inventory position is the ending inventory plus any quantity already ordered that has not yet arrived.

6. If the wholesaler's inventory position is at or below its reorder point, the wholesaler places an order with its distributor. Wholesalers A1 and A2 order from distributor A, wholesalers B1 and B2 order from distributor B, and so on. These orders are in writing and delivered to the appropriate distributor. No other communication is permitted.

For the distributors, the procedure followed each period is the following:

1. The distributor accepts into stock any orders due to arrive during the current period. The beginning inventory plus the arriving order determine how much inventory the location has available to satisfy demand during that period.

2. Next, the distributor looks at the replenishment orders from its wholesalers for that period. These data are not shown to other members of the supply chain but are treated as confidential information.

3. Distributors fill orders as long as sufficient inventory (calculated in Step 1) is available.

4. Distributors calculate their ending inventory level. If sufficient inventory is available, ending inventory is beginning inventory minus that period's actual demand. If there is not sufficient inventory then back orders occur.

5. Distributors calculate their inventory position. Inventory position is the ending inventory plus any quantity already ordered that has not yet arrived.

6. If the distributor's inventory position is at or below its reorder point, the distributor places an order with the factory. These orders are in writing and delivered to the appropriate distributor. No other communication is permitted.

The factory follows these procedures each period:

1. The factory accepts into stock any manufacturing orders completed for the current period. The beginning inventory plus the arriving order determine how much inventory the location has available to satisfy demand during that period.

2. Next, the factory looks at the replenishment orders from the distributors for that period.

3. The factory fills orders as long as sufficient inventory (calculated in Step 1) is available.

4. The factory calculates its ending inventory level. If sufficient inventory is available, ending inventory is beginning inventory minus that period's actual demand. If there is not sufficient inventory then back orders occur. When a back order occurs, your ending inventory value is negative.

5. The factory calculates its inventory position. Inventory position is the ending inventory plus any quantity already ordered that has not yet arrived.

6. If the factory's inventory position is at or below its reorder point, the factory releases an order to manufacturing.

Procedures for all locations include the following:

1. At the end of each period, record the amount of actual inventory you have left, the actual number of back orders, the cost of holding the inventory, the cost of the back orders, and the total cost.

2. Update your total statistics, that is, keep a running total of the cases of inventory, the number of back orders, and the cumulative holding costs, cumulative back order costs, and total costs.

End of Game Discussion Questions

1. How well does the distribution system seem to work? Talk about it in terms of customer service, costs, effective use of inventory, and information flows.

2. Given the amount of inventory in the system, why did back orders occur?

3. In this distribution chain, what happened to customer demand data?

4. How should customer demand data be communicated through the system?

5. What would you recommend be done differently?

CASE: ## Supply Chain Management at Durham International Manufacturing Company (DIMCO)

Lucille Jenkins, the CEO for the Durham International Manufacturing Company (DIMCO), believes that the company can significantly increase its operating profit by implementing supply chain management. DIMCO manufactures a variety of consumer electronic products, from hair dryers to humidifiers to massagers for the world market.

Lucille believes that DIMCO has already integrated its internal processes and is ready to proceed with external integration. However, she is uncertain as to which direction to take. Should the company work on integrating the suppliers or the distributors first? Currently, DIMCO uses approximately 1350 different components and/or raw materials in manufacturing its product line. Those components and raw materials are purchased from approximately 375 different suppliers around the world. In terms of distribution, DIMCO currently sends its finished products to a central warehouse that supplies ten regional distribution centers (RDC); six are domestic and four are located outside of the United States. Each RDC, supplies an average of twelve local distributors that each supply an average of thirty-five retailers.

Lucille is looking for some advice.

1. Briefly describe DIMCO's supply chain.

2. What are the advantages that DIMCO can gain by implementing supply chain management?

3. What would you recommend DIMCO attempt next? Should it work on integrating the suppliers or the distributors first? Or should it work on both simultaneously?

4. What are your recommendations with regard to the external suppliers?

5 What are your recommendations with regard to the external distributors?

INTERACTIVE CASE ### Virtual Company www.wiley.com/college/reid

On-line Case: Supply Chain Management at Valley Memorial Hospital

Bob Reilly, head of Kaizen, just called you to say that he was impressed with your progress in familiarizing yourself with the operations at VMH—both the strategic details pertaining to its mission and competitive priorities and the specific details concerning its products and processes. He tells you that with all the buzz about supply chain management (SCM) that you hear these days, VMH is actively interested in exploring how SCM concepts and techniques could be adopted in their operations. Maintaining an adequate and timely supply of a variety of laboratory equipment, surgical instruments, and supplies is critical to VMH. Meg Willoughby, the head of materials management at VMH, has a couple of specific assignments that you will work on later. For now, Meg has suggested that you prepare a concise research report for top management addressing SCM issues relevant to VMH. She has also put together a few specific questions for you to address. This assignment will enable you to enhance your knowledge of the material covered in Chapter 4.

To access the Web site:

- Go to **www.wiley.com/college/reid**
- Click **Student Companion Site**
- Click **Virtual Company**
- Click **Kaizen Consulting, Inc.**
- Click **Consulting Assignments**
- Click **Supply Chain Management at Valley Memorial Hospital**

INTERNET CHALLENGE Global Shopping

Since the Internet provides access to products around the world, your challenge involves some global shopping. This year you have been given a budget of $10,000 to furnish and decorate your off-campus apartment. You have chosen a global theme. Your job is to find items from as many different parts of the world as you can to use in your apartment. You can spend up to $10,000 but you cannot exceed your budget. Do not forget that shipping must be included in your budget. You can choose more than a single item from any country.

(a) Visit the Internet to find products for your apartment. You need to furnish a one-bedroom apartment. You do not need to worry about major appliances (computer, television, stereo, oven, refrigerator, dishwasher, etc.) but you do need everything else. Since you plan to host a major party in your new apartment, everything you buy must be delivered within six weeks.

(b) Provide a list of all of the items you would buy, the cost of each item, and the total money spent. Organize your list by the room the item is intended for. Be sure to identify the country of origin for each item. Have fun shopping!

On-line Resources

Companion Website www.wiley.com/college/reid
- Take interactive *practice quizzes* to assess your knowledge and help you study in a dynamic way
- Review *PowerPoint slides* or print slides for notetaking
- Access the *Virtual Company: Valley Memorial Hospital*
- Find links to *Company Tours* for this chapter
  Broad Run Cheese House, Curtains & Lace
  BMW Manufacturing Corporation
  Toyota Motor Corporation

- Find links for *Additional Web Resources* for this chapter
  Nummi (New United Motor Manufacturing, Inc.),
  www.nummi.org
  IBM, *www.ibm.com/us*
  Institute for Supply Management, *www.ISM.ws*
  www.manufacturingiscool.com

Selected Bibliography

Bovet, David, and Yossi Sheffi. "The Brave New World of Supply Chain Management," *Supply Chain Management Review*, Spring 1998, 14.

Gue, Kevin R. "Crossdocking: Just-In-Time for Distribution." Thesis. Naval Postgraduate School, Monterey, Calif., May 2000.

Harrington, Lisa, Sandor Boyson, and Thomas Corsi. "Choreographing the New Supply Chain," *Inbound Transportation*, January 2003.

Hotchkiss, D'Anne. "Long-Term Strategy Is Key to Financial Return," *Logistics Management*, August 30, 2005.

LaLonde, Bud. "Crunch Time in the Supply Chain—Huge Domestic and Global Developments Could Radically Change the Way We Think about Supply Chain Management," *Supply Chain Management Review*, March 1, 2005.

LaLonde, Bud. "As the World Goes Global, Supply Chain Velocity Will Actually Decrease in Many Instances. The Key Is How You Respond," *Supply Chain Management Review*, January 1, 2006.

Laudon, Kenneth C., and Carol Guercio Traver. *E-Commerce: Business, Technology, Society.* Reading, Mass.: Addison-Wesley, 2002.

Lawrence, F. Barry, Daniel F. Jennings, and Brian E. Reynolds. *eDistribution.* Cincinnati, Ohio: South-Western, a division of Thomson Learning, 2003.

Lee, Hau L., V. Padmanabban, and Seungjin Whang. "The Bullwhip Effect in Supply Chains," *Sloan Management Review*, Spring 1997, 93–102.

Norek, Christopher D., and Monica Isabell. "The Infrastructure Squeeze on Global Supply Chains," *Supply Chain Management Review*, October 1, 2005.

O'Neill, Jeff. "CVS Rolls Out Gillette's Fusion before Super Bowl," *Modern Materials Handling*, February 1, 2006.

Schlegel, Gregory L., and Richard C. Smith, "The Next Stage of Supply Chain Excellence," *Supply Chain Management Review*, March 1, 2006.

Smith, Jim. "The Right Supply Chain Stuff—Speed and Flexibility Can Mean the Difference for Maximum Efficiency," *Industrial Distribution*, February 1, 2005.

Turban, Efraim, Ephraim McLean, and James Wetherbe. *Information Technology for Management*, Fourth Edition. New York: John Wiley & Sons, 2004.

"Worldwide RFID Spending to Reach 2.5bn in 2010 Report." *Logistics Management*, February 15, 2006.

CHAPTER 5

Total Quality Management

Before studying this chapter you should know or, if necessary, review

1. Trends in total quality management (TQM), Chapter 1, page 15.
2. Quality as a competitive priority, Chapter 2, page 37.

WHAT'S IN OM FOR ME?

 ACC
 FIN
 MKT
 OM
 HRM
 MIS

Dana White/PhotoEdit

Everyone has had experiences of poor quality when dealing with business organizations. These experiences might involve an airline that has lost a passenger's luggage, a dry cleaner that has left clothes wrinkled or stained, poor course offerings and scheduling at your college, a purchased product that is damaged or broken, or a pizza delivery service that is often late or delivers the wrong order. The experience of poor quality is exacerbated when employees of the company either are not empowered to correct quality inadequacies or do not seem willing to do so. We have all encountered service employees who do not seem to care. The consequences of such an attitude are lost customers and opportunities for competitors to take advantage of the market need.

Successful companies understand the powerful impact customer-defined quality can have on business. For this reason, many competitive firms continually increase their quality standards. For example, both the Ford Motor Company and the Honda Motor Company have recently announced that they are making customer satisfaction their number-one priority. The slow economy of 2003 impacted sales in the auto industry. Both firms believe that the way to rebound is through improvements in quality, and each has outlined specific changes to their operations. Ford is focusing on tightening already strict standards in their production process and implementing a quality program called Six-Sigma. Honda, on the other hand, is focused on improving customer-driven product design. Although both firms have been leaders in implementing high quality standards, they believe that customer satisfaction is still what matters most.

In this chapter you will learn that making quality a priority means putting customer needs first. It means meeting and exceeding customer expectations by involving everyone in the organization through an integrated effort. **Total quality management (TQM)** is an integrated organizational effort designed to improve quality at every level. In this chapter you will learn about the philosophy of TQM, its impact on organizations, and its impact on your life. You will learn that TQM is about meeting quality expectations as defined by the customer; this is called **customer-defined quality**. However, defining quality is not as easy as it may seem, because different people have different ideas of what constitutes high quality. Let's begin by looking at different ways in which quality can be defined.

▶ **Total quality management (TQM)**
An integrated effort designed to improve quality performance at every level of the organization.

▶ **Customer-defined quality**
The meaning of quality as defined by the customer.

DEFINING QUALITY

The definition of quality depends on the point of view of the people defining it. Most consumers have a difficult time defining quality, but they know it when they see it. For example, although you probably have an opinion as to which manufacturer of athletic shoes provides the highest quality, it would probably be difficult for you to define your quality standard in precise terms. Also, your friends may have different opinions regarding which athletic shoes are of highest quality. The difficulty in defining quality exists regardless of product, and this is true for both manufacturing and service organizations. Think about how difficult it may be to define quality for products such as airline services, child day-care facilities, college classes, or even OM textbooks. Further complicating the issue is that the meaning of quality has changed over time.

Today, there is no single, universal definition of quality. Some people view quality as "performance to standards." Others view it as "meeting the customer's needs" or "satisfying the customer." Let's look at some of the more common definitions of quality.

▶ **Conformance to specifications**
How well a product or service meets the targets and tolerances determined by its designers.

• **Conformance to specifications** measures how well the product or service meets the targets and tolerances determined by its designers. For example, the dimensions of a machine part may be specified by its design engineers as 3 ± .05 inches. This would mean that the target dimension is 3 inches but the dimensions can vary between 2.95 and 3.05 inches. Similarly, the wait for hotel room service may be specified as 20 minutes, but there may be an acceptable delay of an additional 10 minutes. Also, consider the amount of light delivered by a 60-watt light bulb. If the bulb delivers 50 watts, it does not conform to specifications. As these examples illustrate, conformance to specification is directly measurable, though it may not be directly related to the consumer's idea of quality.

▶ **Fitness for use**
A definition of quality that evaluates how well the product performs for its intended use.

• **Fitness for use** focuses on how well the product performs its intended function or use. For example, a Mercedes-Benz and a Jeep Cherokee both meet a fitness for use definition if one considers transportation as the intended function. However, if the definition becomes more specific and assumes that the intended use is for transportation on mountain roads and carrying fishing gear, the Jeep Cherokee has a greater fitness for use. You can also see that fitness for use is a user-based definition in that it is intended to meet the needs of a specific user group.

▶ **Value for price paid**
Quality defined in terms of product or service usefulness for the price paid.

• **Value for price paid** is a definition of quality that consumers often use for product or service usefulness. This is the only definition that combines economics with consumer criteria; it assumes that the definition of quality is price sensitive. For example, suppose that you wish to sign up for a personal finance seminar and discover that the same class is being taught at two different colleges at significantly different tuition rates. If you take the less expensive seminar, you will feel that you have received greater value for the price.

▶ **Support services**
Quality defined in terms of the support provided after the product or service is purchased.

• **Support services** provided are often how the quality of a product or service is judged. Quality does not apply only to the product or service itself; it also applies to the people, processes, and organizational environment associated with it. For example, the quality of a university is judged not only by the quality of staff and course offerings but also by the efficiency and accuracy of processing paperwork.

- **Psychological criteria** is a subjective definition that focuses on the judgmental evaluation of what constitutes product or service quality. Different factors contribute to the evaluation, such as the atmosphere of the environment or the perceived prestige of the product. For example, a hospital patient may receive average healthcare, but a very friendly staff may leave the impression of high quality. Similarly, we commonly associate certain products with excellence because of their reputation; Rolex watches and Mercedes-Benz automobiles are examples.

▶ **Psychological criteria**
A way of defining quality that focuses on judgmental evaluations of what constitutes product or service excellence.

Differences between Manufacturing and Service Organizations

Defining quality in manufacturing organizations is often different than it is for service organizations. Manufacturing organizations produce a tangible product that can be seen, touched, and directly measured. Examples include cars, CD players, clothes, computers, and food items. Therefore, quality definitions in manufacturing usually focus on tangible product features.

The most common quality definition in manufacturing is *conformance*, which is the degree to which a product characteristic meets preset standards. Other common definitions of quality in manufacturing include *performance*, such as acceleration of a vehicle; *reliability*, meaning that the product will function as expected without failure; *features*, the extras that are included beyond the basic characteristics; *durability*, the expected operational life of the product; and *serviceability*, how readily a product can be repaired. The relative importance of these definitions is based on the preferences of each individual customer. It is easy to see how different customers can have different definitions in mind when they speak of high product quality.

In contrast to manufacturing, service organizations produce a product that is intangible. Usually, the complete product cannot be seen or touched. Rather, it is experienced. Examples include delivery of healthcare, the experience of staying at a vacation resort, and learning at a university. The intangible nature of the product makes defining quality difficult. Also, since a service is experienced, perceptions can be highly subjective. In addition to tangible factors, quality of services is often defined by perceptual factors. These include responsiveness to customer needs, *courtesy* and *friendliness* of staff, *promptness* in resolving complaints, and *atmosphere*. Other definitions of quality in services include *time*, the amount of time a customer has to wait for the service; and *consistency*, the degree to which the service is the same each time. For these reasons, defining quality in services can be especially challenging. Dimensions of quality for manufacturing versus service organizations are shown in Table 5-1.

Manufacturing Organizations	Service Organizations
Conformance to specifications	Intangible factors
Performance	Consistency
Reliability	Responsiveness to customer needs
Features	Courtesy/friendliness
Durability	Timeliness/promptness
Serviceability	Atmosphere

TABLE 5-1

Dimensions of Quality for Manufacturing versus Service Organizations

General Electric Company
www.ge.com
Motorola, Inc.
www.motorola.com

PhotoDisc, Inc./ Getty Images

Today's customers demand and expect high quality. Companies that do not make quality a priority risk long-run survival. World-class organizations such as General Electric and Motorola attribute their success to having one of the best quality management programs in the world. These companies were some of the first to implement a quality program called, Six Sigma, where the level of defects is reduced to approximately 3.4 parts per million. To achieve this, everyone in the company is trained in quality. For example, individuals highly trained in quality improvement principles and techniques receive a designation called "Black Belt." The full-time job of Black Belts is to identify and solve quality problems. In fact, Motorola was one of the first companies to win the prestigious Malcolm Baldrige National Quality Award in 1988 due to its high focus on quality. Both GE and Motorola have had a primary goal of achieving total customer satisfaction. To this end, the efforts of these organizations have included eliminating almost all defects from products, processes, and transactions. Both companies consider quality to be the critical factor that has resulted in significant increases in sales and market share, as well as cost savings in the range of millions of dollars.

COST OF QUALITY

The reason quality has gained such prominence is that organizations have gained an understanding of the high cost of poor quality. Quality affects all aspects of the organization and has dramatic cost implications. The most obvious consequence occurs when poor quality creates dissatisfied customers and eventually leads to loss of business. However, quality has many other costs, which can be divided into two categories. The first category consists of costs necessary for achieving high quality, which are called *quality control costs*. These are of two types: *prevention costs* and *appraisal costs*. The second category consists of the cost consequences of poor quality, which are called *quality failure costs*. These include *external failure costs* and *internal failure costs*. These costs of quality are shown in Figure 5-1. The first two costs are incurred in the hope of preventing the second two.

Prevention costs are all costs incurred in the process of preventing poor quality from occurring. They include quality planning costs, such as the costs of developing and implementing a quality plan. Also included are the costs of product and process design, from collecting customer information to designing processes that achieve conformance to specifications. Employee training in quality measurement is included as part of this cost, as well as the costs of maintaining records of information and data related to quality.

Appraisal costs are incurred in the process of uncovering defects. They include the cost of quality inspections, product testing, and performing audits to make sure that quality standards are being met. Also included in this category are the costs of worker time spent measuring quality and the cost of equipment used for quality appraisal.

Internal failure costs are associated with discovering poor product quality before the product reaches the customer site. One type of internal failure cost is *rework*, which is the cost of correcting the defective item. Sometimes the item is so defective that it cannot be corrected and must be thrown away. This is called *scrap*, and its costs include

► **Prevention costs**
Costs incurred in the process of preventing poor quality from occurring.

► **Appraisal costs**
Costs incurred in the process of uncovering defects.

► **Internal failure costs**
Costs associated with discovering poor product quality before the product reaches the customer.

FIGURE 5-1

Costs of quality

Prevention costs.	Costs of preparing and implementing a quality plan.
Appraisal costs.	Costs of testing, evaluating, and inspecting quality.
Internal failure costs.	Costs of scrap, rework, and material losses.
External failure costs.	Costs of failure at customer site, including returns, repairs, and recalls.

all the material, labor, and machine cost spent in producing the defective product. Other types of internal failure costs include the cost of machine downtime due to failures in the process and the costs of discounting defective items for salvage value.

External failure costs are associated with quality problems that occur at the customer site. These costs can be particularly damaging because customer faith and loyalty can be difficult to regain. They include everything from customer complaints, product returns, and repairs to warranty claims, recalls, and even litigation costs resulting from product liability issues. A final component of this cost is lost sales and lost customers. For example, manufacturers of lunch meats and hot dogs whose products have been recalled due to bacterial contamination have had to struggle to regain consumer confidence. Other examples include auto manufacturers whose products have been recalled due to major malfunctions such as problematic braking systems and airlines that have experienced a crash with many fatalities. External failure can sometimes put a company out of business almost overnight.

▶ **External failure costs**
Costs associated with quality problems that occur at the customer site.

Companies that consider quality important invest heavily in prevention and appraisal costs in order to prevent internal and external failure costs. The earlier defects are found, the less costly they are to correct. For example, detecting and correcting defects during product design and product production is considerably less expensive than when the defects are found at the customer site. This is shown in Figure 5-2.

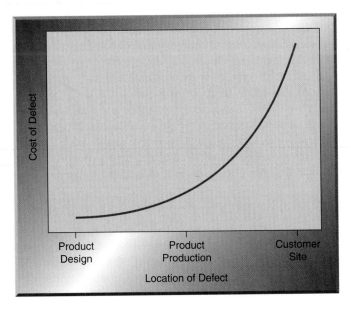

FIGURE 5-2

Cost of defects

External failure costs tend to be particularly high for service organizations. The reason is that with a service the customer spends much time in the service delivery system, and there are fewer opportunities to correct defects than there are in manufacturing. Examples of external failure in services include overbooking airline flights, long delays in airline service, and lost luggage.

THE EVOLUTION OF TOTAL QUALITY MANAGEMENT (TQM)

The concept of quality has existed for many years, though its meaning has changed and evolved over time. In the early twentieth century, quality management meant inspecting products to ensure that they met specifications. In the 1940s, during World War II, quality became more statistical in nature. Statistical sampling techniques were used to evaluate quality, and quality control charts were used to monitor the production process. In the 1960s, with the help of so-called "quality gurus," the concept took on a broader meaning. Quality began to be viewed as something that encompassed the entire organization, not only the production process. Since all functions were responsible for product quality and all shared the costs of poor quality, quality was seen as a concept that affected the entire organization.

The meaning of quality for businesses changed dramatically in the late 1970s. Before then quality was still viewed as something that needed to be inspected and corrected. However, in the 1970s and 1980s, many U.S. industries lost market share to foreign competition. In the auto industry, manufacturers such as Toyota and Honda became major players. In the consumer goods market, companies such as Toshiba and Sony led the way. These foreign competitors were producing lower-priced products with considerably higher quality.

To survive, companies had to make major changes in their quality programs. Many hired consultants and instituted quality training programs for their employees. A new concept of quality was emerging. One result was that quality began to have a strategic meaning. Today, successful companies understand that quality provides a competitive advantage. They put the customer first and define quality as meeting or exceeding customer expectations.

Since the 1970s, competition based on quality has grown in importance and has generated tremendous interest, concern, and enthusiasm. Companies in every line of business are focusing on improving quality in order to be more competitive. In many industries quality excellence has become a standard for doing business. Companies that do not meet this standard simply will not survive. As you will see later in the chapter, the importance of quality is demonstrated by national quality awards and quality certifications that are coveted by businesses.

The term used for today's new concept of quality is *total quality management* or *TQM*. Figure 5-3 presents a time line of the old and new concepts of quality. You can see that the old concept is *reactive*, designed to correct quality problems after they occur. The new concept is *proactive*, designed to build quality into the product and process design. Next, we look at the individuals who have shaped our understanding of quality.

Quality Gurus

To fully understand the TQM movement, we need to look at the philosophies of notable individuals who have shaped the evolution of TQM. Their philosophies and teachings have contributed to our knowledge and understanding of quality today. Table 5-2 summarizes their individual contributions.

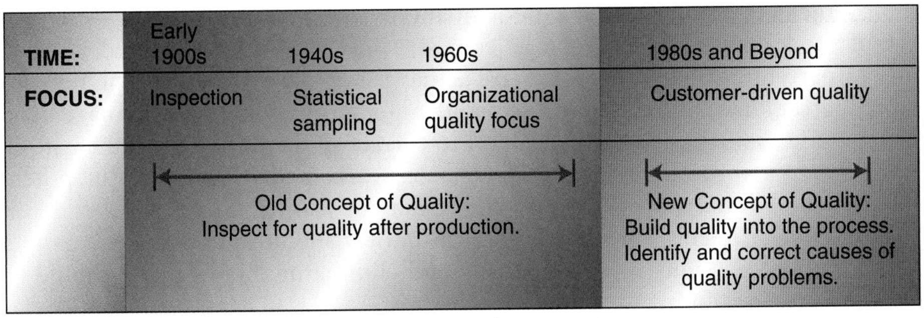

FIGURE 5-3

Time line showing the differences between old and new concepts of quality

Walter A. Shewhart Walter A. Shewhart was a statistician at Bell Labs during the 1920s and 1930s. Shewhart studied randomness and recognized that variability existed in all manufacturing processes. He developed quality control charts that are used to identify whether the variability in the process is random or due to an assignable cause, such as poor workers or miscalibrated machinery. He stressed that eliminating variability improves quality. His work created the foundation for today's statistical process control, and he is often referred to as the "grandfather of quality control."

W. Edwards Deming W. Edwards Deming is often referred to as the "father of quality control." He was a statistics professor at New York University in the 1940s. After World War II, he assisted many Japanese companies in improving quality. The Japanese regarded him so highly that in 1951 they established the *Deming Prize*, an annual award given to firms that demonstrate outstanding quality. It was almost 30 years before American businesses began adopting Deming's philosophy.

A number of elements of Deming's philosophy depart from traditional notions of quality. The first is the role management should play in a company's quality

Quality Guru	Main Contribution
Walter A. Shewhart	–Contributed to understanding of process variability. –Developed concept of statistical control charts.
W. Edwards Deming	–Stressed management's responsibility for quality. –Developed "14 Points" to guide companies in quality improvement.
Joseph M. Juran	–Defined quality as "fitness for use." –Developed concept of cost of quality.
Armand V. Feigenbaum	–Introduced concept of total quality control.
Philip B. Crosby	–Coined phrase "quality is free." –Introduced concept of zero defects.
Kaoru Ishikawa	–Developed cause-and-effect diagrams. –Identified concept of "internal customer."
Genichi Taguchi	–Focused on product design quality. –Developed Taguchi loss function.

TABLE 5-2

Quality Gurus and Their Contributions

improvement effort. Historically, poor quality was blamed on workers—on their lack of productivity, laziness, or carelessness. However, Deming pointed out that only 15 percent of quality problems are actually due to worker error. The remaining 85 percent are caused by processes and systems, including poor management. Deming said that it is up to management to correct system problems and create an environment that promotes quality and enables workers to achieve their full potential. He believed that managers should drive out any fear employees have of identifying quality problems and that numerical quotas should be eliminated. Proper methods should be taught, and detecting and eliminating poor quality should be everyone's responsibility.

Deming outlined his philosophy on quality in his famous "14 Points." These points are principles that help guide companies in achieving quality improvement. The principles are founded on the idea that upper management must develop a commitment to quality and provide a system to support this commitment that involves all employees and suppliers. Deming stressed that quality improvements cannot happen without organizational change that comes from upper management.

Joseph M. Juran After W. Edwards Deming, Dr. **Joseph M. Juran** is considered to have had the greatest impact on quality management. Juran originally worked in the quality program at Western Electric, a former equipment division of AT&T. He became better known in 1951 after the publication of his book *Quality Control Handbook*. In 1954, he went to Japan to work with manufacturers and teach classes on quality. Though his philosophy is similar to Deming's, there are some differences. Whereas Deming stressed the need for an organizational "transformation," Juran believed that implementing quality initiatives should not require such a dramatic change and that quality management should be embedded in the organization.

One of Juran's significant contributions was his focus on the definition of quality and the cost of quality. Juran is credited with defining quality as fitness for use rather than simply conformance to specifications. As we have learned in this chapter, defining quality as fitness for use takes into account customer intentions for use of the product, instead of focusing only on technical specifications. Juran is also credited with developing the concept of cost of quality, which allows us to measure quality in dollar terms rather than on the basis of subjective evaluations.

Juran is well known for originating the idea of the quality trilogy: quality planning, quality control, and quality improvement. The first part of the trilogy, *quality planning*, is necessary so that companies identify their customers, product requirements, and overriding business goals. Processes should be set up to ensure that the quality standards can be met. The second part of the trilogy, *quality control*, stresses the regular use of statistical control methods to ensure that quality standards are met and to identify variations from the standards. The third part of the quality trilogy is *quality improvement*. According to Juran, quality improvements should not be just breakthroughs, but continuous as well. Together with Deming, Juran stressed that to implement continuous improvement, workers need to have training in proper methods on a regular basis.

Armand V. Feigenbaum Another quality leader is **Armand V. Feigenbaum**, who introduced the concept of total quality control. In his 1961 book *Total Quality Control*, he outlined his quality principles in 40 steps. Feigenbaum took a total system approach to quality. He promoted the idea of a work environment where quality developments are integrated throughout the entire organization, where management and employees have a total commitment to improve quality, and where people learn from each other's successes. This philosophy was adapted by the Japanese and termed "company-wide quality control."

Philip B. Crosby **Philip B. Crosby** is another recognized guru of TQM. He worked in the area of quality for many years, first at Martin Marietta and then, in the 1970s, as the vice president for quality at ITT. He developed the phrase "Do it right the first time" and the notion of *zero defects*, arguing that no amount of defects should be considered acceptable. He scorned the idea that a small number of defects is a normal part of the operating process because systems and workers are imperfect. Instead, he stressed the idea of prevention.

To promote his concepts, Crosby wrote a book titled *Quality Is Free*, which was published in 1979. He became famous for coining the phrase "quality is free" and for pointing out the many costs of quality, which include not only the costs of wasted labor, equipment time, scrap, rework, and lost sales but also organizational costs that are hard to quantify. Crosby stressed that efforts to improve quality more than pay for themselves because these costs are prevented. Therefore, quality is free. Like Deming and Juran, Crosby stressed the role of management in the quality improvement effort and the use of statistical control tools in measuring and monitoring quality.

Kaoru Ishikawa **Kaoru Ishikawa** is best known for the development of quality tools called cause-and-effect diagrams, also called fishbone or Ishikawa diagrams. These diagrams are used for quality problem solving, and we will look at them in detail later in the chapter. He was the first quality guru to emphasize the importance of the "internal customer," the next person in the production process. He was also one of the first to stress the importance of total company quality control, rather than just focusing on products and services.

Dr. Ishikawa believed that everyone in the company needed to be united with a shared vision and a common goal. He stressed that quality initiatives should be pursued at every level of the organization and that all employees should be involved. Dr. Ishikawa was a proponent of implementation of *quality circles*, which are small teams of employees who volunteer to solve quality problems.

Genichi Taguchi Dr. **Genichi Taguchi** is a Japanese quality expert known for his work in the area of product design. He estimates that as much as 80 percent of all defective items are caused by poor product design. Taguchi stresses that companies should focus their quality efforts on the design stage, as it is much cheaper and easier to make changes during the product design stage than later during the production process.

Taguchi is known for applying a concept called *design of experiment* to product design. This method is an engineering approach based on developing **robust design**, a design that results in products that can perform over a wide range of conditions. The idea is that it is easier to design a product that can perform over a wide range of environmental conditions than it is to control the environmental conditions.

Taguchi has also had a large impact on today's view of the costs of quality. He pointed out that the traditional view of costs of conformance to specifications is

▶ **Robust design**
A design that results in a product that can perform over a wide range of conditions.

FIGURE 5-4

Traditional view of the cost of nonconformance

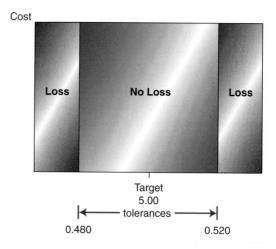

incorrect and proposed a different way to look at these costs. Let's briefly look at Dr. Taguchi's view of quality costs.

Recall that conformance to specification specifies a target value for the product with specified tolerances, say 5.00 ± 0.20. According to the traditional view of conformance to specifications, losses in terms of cost occur if the product dimensions fall outside of the specified limits. This is shown in Figure 5-4. However, Dr. Taguchi noted that from the customer's view there is little difference whether a product falls just outside or just inside the control limits. He pointed out that there is a much greater difference in the quality of the product between making the target and being near the control limit. He also stated that the smaller the variation around the target, the better the quality. Based on this, he proposed the following: as conformance values move away from the target, loss increases as a quadratic function. The **Taguchi loss function** is shown in Figure 5-5. According to the function, smaller differences from the target result in smaller costs: the larger the differences, the larger the cost. The Taguchi loss function has had a significant impact on changing views of quality cost.

▶ **Taguchi loss function**
Costs of quality increase as a quadratic function as conformance values move away from the target.

FIGURE 5-5

Taguchi view of the cost of nonconformance—the Taguchi loss function

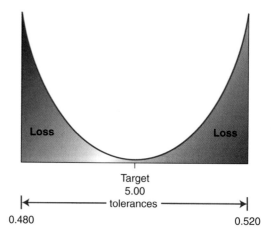

THE PHILOSOPHY OF TQM

What characterizes TQM is the focus on identifying root causes of quality problems and correcting them at the source, as opposed to inspecting the product after it has been made. Not only does TQM encompass the entire organization but it stresses that quality is customer driven. TQM attempts to embed quality in every aspect of the organization. It is concerned with the technical aspects of quality as well as the involvement of people in quality, such as customers, company employees, and suppliers. Here we look at the specific concepts that make up the philosophy of TQM. These concepts and their main ideas are summarized in Table 5-3.

Customer Focus

The first, and overriding, feature of TQM is the company's focus on its customers. Quality is defined as meeting or exceeding customer expectations. The goal is to first identify and then meet customer needs. TQM recognizes that a perfectly produced product has little value if it is not what the customer wants. Therefore, we can say that quality is *customer driven*. However, it is not always easy to determine what the customer wants, because tastes and preferences change. Also, customer expectations often vary from one customer to the next. For example, in the auto industry trends change relatively quickly, from small cars to sports utility vehicles and back to small cars. The same is true in the retail industry, where styles and fashion are short-lived. Companies need to continually gather information by means of focus groups, market surveys, and customer interviews in order to stay in tune with what customers want. They must always remember that they would not be in business if it were not for their customers.

Continuous Improvement

Another concept of the TQM philosophy is the focus on **continuous improvement**. Traditional systems operated on the assumption that once a company achieved a certain level of quality, it was successful and needed to make no further improvements.

▶ **Continuous improvement (kaizen)**
A philosophy of never-ending improvement.

Concept	Main Idea
Customer focus	Goal is to identify and meet customer needs.
Continuous improvement	A philosophy of never-ending improvement.
Employee empowerment	Employees are expected to seek out, identify, and correct quality problems.
Use of quality tools	Ongoing employee training in the use of quality tools.
Product design	Products need to be designed to meet customer expectations.
Process management	Quality should be built into the process; sources of quality problems should be identified and corrected.
Managing supplier quality	Quality concepts must extend to a company's suppliers.

TABLE 5-3

Concepts of the TQM Philosophy

We tend to think of improvement in terms of plateaus that are to be achieved, such as passing a certification test or reducing the number of defects to a certain level. Traditionally, for American managers change involves large magnitudes, such as major organizational restructuring. The Japanese, on the other hand, believe that the best and most lasting changes come from gradual improvements. To use an analogy, they believe that it is better to take frequent small doses of medicine than to take one large dose. Continuous improvement, called **kaizen** by the Japanese, requires that the company continually strive to be better through learning and problem solving. Because we can never achieve perfection, we must always evaluate our performance and take measures to improve it.

Now let's look at two approaches that can help companies with continuous improvement: the plan–do–study–act (PDSA) cycle and benchmarking.

▶ **Kaizen**
A Japanese term that describes the notion of a company continually striving to be better through learning and problem solving.

▶ **Plan–do–study–act (PDSA) cycle**
A diagram that describes the activities that need to be performed to incorporate continuous improvement into the operation.

The Plan–Do–Study–Act Cycle The **plan–do–study–act (PDSA) cycle** describes the activities a company needs to perform in order to incorporate continuous improvement in its operation. This cycle, shown in Figure 5-6, is also referred to as the Shewhart cycle or the Deming wheel. The circular nature of this cycle shows that continuous improvement is a never-ending process. Let's look at the specific steps in the cycle.

- **Plan** The first step in the PDSA cycle is to *plan*. Managers must evaluate the current process and make plans based on any problems they find. They need to document all current procedures, collect data, and identify problems. This information should then be studied and used to develop a plan for improvement as well as specific measures to evaluate performance.

- **Do** The next step in the cycle is implementing the plan (*do*). During the implementation process managers should document all changes made and collect data for evaluation.

- **Study** The third step is to *study* the data collected in the previous phase. The data are evaluated to see whether the plan is achieving the goals established in the *plan* phase.

- **Act** The last phase of the cycle is to *act* on the basis of the results of the first three phases. The best way to accomplish this is to communicate the results to other members of the company and then implement the new procedure if it has been successful. Note that this is a cycle; the next step is to plan again. After we have acted, we need to continue evaluating the process, planning, and repeating the cycle again.

FIGURE 5-6

The plan–do–study–act cycle

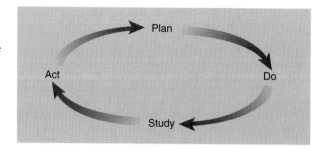

Benchmarking Another way companies implement continuous improvement is by studying business practices of companies considered "best in class." This is called **benchmarking**. The ability to learn and study how others do things is an important part of continuous improvement. The benchmark company does not have to be in the same business as long as it excels at something that the company doing the study wishes to emulate. For example, many companies have used Lands' End to benchmark catalog distribution and order filling because Lands' End is considered a leader in this area. Similarly, many companies have used American Express to benchmark conflict resolution.

▶ **Benchmarking**
Studying the business practices of other companies for purposes of comparison.

Employee Empowerment

Part of the TQM philosophy is to empower all employees to seek out quality problems and correct them. Under the old concept of quality, employees were afraid to identify problems for fear that they would be reprimanded. Often, poor quality was passed on to someone else in order to make it "someone else's problem." The new concept of quality, TQM, provides incentives for employees to identify quality problems. Employees are rewarded for uncovering quality problems, not punished.

In TQM, the role of employees is very different from what it was in traditional systems. Workers are empowered to make decisions relative to quality in the production process. They are considered a vital element of the effort to achieve high quality. Their contributions are highly valued, and their suggestions are implemented. In order to perform this function, employees are given continual and extensive training in quality measurement tools.

To further stress the role of employees in quality, TQM differentiates between *external* and *internal customers*. *External customers* are those that purchase the company's goods and services. *Internal customers* are employees of the organization who receive goods or services from others in the company. For example, the packaging department of an organization is an internal customer of the assembly department. Just as a defective item would not be passed to an external customer, a defective item should not be passed to an internal customer.

Team Approach TQM stresses that quality is an organizational effort. To facilitate the solving of quality problems, it places great emphasis on teamwork. The use of teams is based on the old adage that "two heads are better than one." Using techniques such as brainstorming, discussion, and quality control tools, teams work regularly to correct problems. The contributions of teams are considered vital to the success of the company. For this reason, companies set aside time in the workday for team meetings.

Teams vary in their degree of structure and formality, and different types of teams solve different types of problems. One of the most common types of teams is the **quality circle**, a team of volunteer production employees and their supervisors whose purpose is to solve quality problems. The circle is usually composed of eight to ten members, and decisions are made through group consensus. The teams usually meet weekly during work hours in a place designated for this purpose. They follow a preset process for analyzing and solving quality problems. Open discussion is promoted, and criticism is not allowed. Although the functioning of quality circles is friendly and casual, it is serious business. Quality circles are not mere "gab sessions." Rather, they do important work for the company and have been very successful in many firms.

▶ **Quality circle**
A team of volunteer production employees and their supervisors who meet regularly to solve quality problems.

LINKS TO PRACTICE

The Walt Disney Company
www.disney.com

Andrew Ross/AFP/Getty Images, Inc.

The importance of exceptional quality is demonstrated by The Walt Disney Company in the operation of its theme parks. The focus of the parks is customer satisfaction. This is accomplished through meticulous attention to every detail, with particular focus on the role of employees in service delivery. Employees are viewed as the most important organizational resource, and great care is taken in employee hiring and training. All employees are called "cast members," regardless of whether they are janitors or performers. They are extensively trained in customer service, communication, and quality awareness. Continual monitoring of quality is considered important, and employees meet regularly in teams to evaluate their effectiveness. All employees are shown how the quality of their individual jobs contributes to the success of the park.

Use of Quality Tools

You can see that TQM places a great deal of responsibility on all workers. If employees are to identify and correct quality problems, they need proper training. They need to understand how to assess quality by using a variety of quality control tools, how to interpret findings, and how to correct problems. In this section we look at seven different quality tools, often called the seven tools of quality control (Figure 5-7). They are easy to understand, yet extremely useful in identifying and analyzing quality problems. Sometimes workers use only one tool at a time, but often a combination of tools is most helpful.

▶ **Cause-and-effect diagram**
A chart that identifies potential causes of particular quality problems.

Cause-and-Effect Diagrams **Cause-and-effect diagrams** identify potential causes of particular quality problems. They are often called fishbone diagrams because they look like the bones of a fish (Figure 5-8). The "head" of the fish is the quality problem, such as damaged zippers on a garment or broken valves on a tire. The diagram is drawn so that the "spine" of the fish connects the "head" to the possible cause of the problem. These causes could be related to the machines, workers, measurement, suppliers, materials, and many other aspects of the production process. Each of these possible causes can then have smaller "bones" addressing specific issues that relate to each cause. For example, a problem with machines could be due to a need for adjustment, old equipment, or tooling problems. Similarly, a problem with workers could be related to lack of training, poor supervision, or fatigue.

Cause-and-effect diagrams are problem-solving tools commonly used by quality control teams. Specific causes of problems can be explored through brainstorming. The development of a cause-and-effect diagram requires the team to think through all the possible causes of poor quality.

▶ **Flowchart**
A schematic of the sequence of steps involved in an operation or process.

Flowcharts A **flowchart** is a schematic diagram of the sequence of steps involved in an operation or process. It provides a visual tool that is easy to use and understand. By seeing the steps involved in an operation or process, everyone develops a clear picture of how the operation works and where problems could arise.

1. Cause-and-Effect Diagram

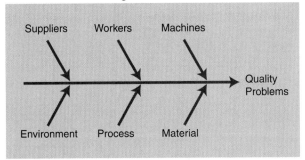

2. Flowchart

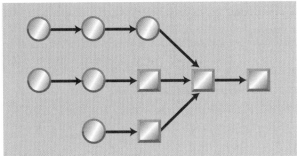

3. Checklist

Defect Type	No. of Defects	Total
Broken zipper	✓✓✓	3
Ripped material	✓✓✓✓✓✓✓	7
Missing buttons	✓✓✓	3
Faded color	✓✓	2

4. Control Chart

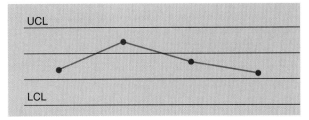

5. Scatter Diagram

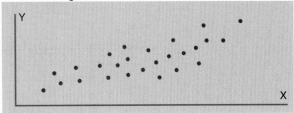

6. Pareto Chart

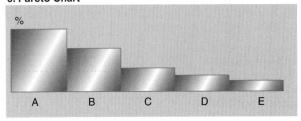

7. Histogram

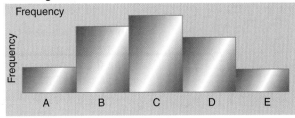

FIGURE 5-7

The seven tools of quality control

Checklists A **checklist** is a list of common defects and the number of observed occurrences of these defects. It is a simple yet effective fact-finding tool that allows the worker to collect specific information regarding the defects observed. The checklist in Figure 5-7 shows four defects and the number of times they have been observed. It is clear that the biggest problem is ripped material. This means that the plant needs to focus on this specific problem—for example, by going to the source of supply or seeing whether the material rips during a particular production process. A checklist can also be used to focus on other dimensions, such as location or time. For example, if a defect is being observed frequently, a checklist can be developed that measures the number of occurrences per shift, per machine, or per operator. In this fashion we can isolate the location of the particular defect and then focus on correcting the problem.

▶ **Checklist**
A list of common defects and the number of observed occurrences of these defects.

FIGURE 5-8

A general cause-and-effect (fishbone) diagram

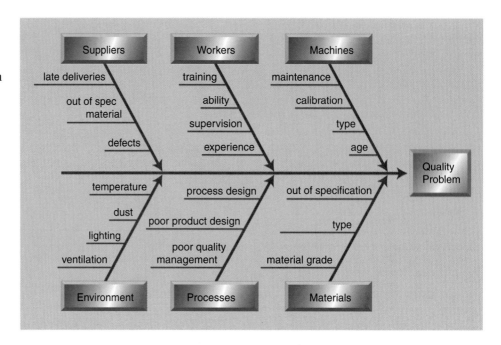

▶ **Control charts**
Charts used to evaluate whether a process is operating within set expectations.

Control Charts **Control charts** are a very important quality control tool. We will study the use of control charts at great length in the next chapter. These charts are used to evaluate whether a process is operating within expectations relative to some measured value such as weight, width, or volume. For example, we could measure the weight of a sack of flour, the width of a tire, or the volume of a bottle of soft drink. When the production process is operating within expectations, we say that it is "in control."

To evaluate whether or not a process is in control, we regularly measure the variable of interest and plot it on a control chart. The chart has a line down the center representing the average value of the variable we are measuring. Above and below the center line are two lines, called the upper control limit (UCL) and the lower control limit (LCL). As long as the observed values fall within the upper and lower control limits, the process is in control and there is no problem with quality. When a measured observation falls outside of these limits, there is a problem.

▶ **Scatter diagrams**
Graphs that show how two variables are related to each other.

Scatter Diagrams **Scatter diagrams** are graphs that show how two variables are related to one another. They are particularly useful in detecting the amount of correlation, or the degree of linear relationship, between two variables. For example, increased production speed and number of defects could be correlated positively; as production speed increases, so does the number of defects. Two variables could also be correlated negatively, so that an increase in one of the variables is associated with a decrease in the other. For example, increased worker training might be associated with a decrease in the number of defects observed.

The greater the degree of correlation, the more linear are the observations in the scatter diagram. On the other hand, the more scattered the observations in the diagram, the less correlation exists between the variables. Of course, other types of relationships can also be observed on a scatter diagram, such as an inverted ∪. This may be the case when one is observing the relationship between two variables such as oven temperature and number of defects, since temperatures below and above the ideal could lead to defects.

Pareto Analysis **Pareto analysis** is a technique used to identify quality problems based on their degree of importance. The logic behind Pareto analysis is that only a few quality problems are important, whereas many others are not critical. The technique was named after Vilfredo Pareto, a nineteenth-century Italian economist who determined that only a small percentage of people controlled most of the wealth. This concept has often been called the 80–20 rule and has been extended to many areas. In quality management the logic behind Pareto's principle is that most quality problems are a result of only a few causes. The trick is to identify these causes.

> ► **Pareto analysis**
> A technique used to identify quality problems based on their degree of importance.

One way to use Pareto analysis is to develop a chart that ranks the causes of poor quality in decreasing order based on the percentage of defects each has caused. For example, a tally can be made of the number of defects that result from different causes, such as operator error, defective parts, or inaccurate machine calibrations. Percentages of defects can be computed from the tally and placed in a chart like those shown in Figure 5-7. We generally tend to find that a few causes account for most of the defects.

Histograms A **histogram** is a chart that shows the frequency distribution of observed values of a variable. We can see from the plot what type of distribution a particular variable displays, such as whether it has a normal distribution and whether the distribution is symmetrical.

> ► **Histogram**
> A chart that shows the frequency distribution of observed values of a variable.

In the food service industry the use of quality control tools is important in identifying quality problems. Grocery store chains, such as Kroger and Meijer, must record and monitor the quality of incoming produce, such as tomatoes and lettuce. Quality tools can be used to evaluate the acceptability of product quality and to monitor product quality from individual suppliers. They can also be used to evaluate causes of quality problems, such as long transit time or poor refrigeration. Similarly, restaurants use quality control tools to evaluate and monitor the quality of delivered goods, such as meats, produce, or baked goods.

©AP/Wide World Photos

> **LINKS TO PRACTICE**
>
> **The Kroger Company**
> www.kroger.com
>
> **Meijer Stores Limited Partnership**
> www.meijer.com

Product Design

Quality Function Deployment A critical aspect of building quality into a product is to ensure that the product design meets customer expectations. This typically is not as easy as it seems. Customers often speak in everyday language. For example, a product can be described as "attractive," "strong," or "safe." However, these terms can have very different meaning to different customers. What one person considers to be strong, another may not. To produce a product that customers want, we need to translate customers' everyday language into specific technical requirements. However, this can often be difficult. A useful tool for translating the voice of the customer into specific technical requirements is **quality function deployment (QFD)**. Quality function deployment is also useful in enhancing communication between different functions, such as marketing, operations, and engineering.

> ► **Quality function deployment (QFD)**
> A tool used to translate the preferences of the customer into specific technical requirements.

QFD enables us to view the relationships among the variables involved in the design of a product, such as technical versus customer requirements. This can help us analyze the big picture—for example, by running tests to see how changes in certain technical requirements of the product affect customer requirements. An example is an automobile manufacturer evaluating how changes in materials affect customer safety requirements. This type of analysis can be very beneficial in developing a product design that meets customer needs, yet does not create unnecessary technical requirements for production.

QFD begins by identifying important customer requirements, which typically come from the marketing department. These requirements are numerically scored based on their importance, and scores are translated into specific product characteristics. Evaluations are then made of how the product compares with its main competitors relative to the identified characteristics. Finally, specific goals are set to address the identified problems. The resulting matrix looks like a picture of a house and is often called the *house of quality*.

We will consider the example of manufacturing a backpack to show how we would use QFD. We will start with a relationship matrix that ties customer requirements to product characteristics, shown in Figure 5-9.

- **Customer Requirements**   Remember that our goal is to make a product that the customer wants. Therefore, the first thing we need to do is survey our customers to find out specifically what they would be looking for in a product—in this case, a backpack for students. To find out precisely what features students

FIGURE 5-9

Relationship matrix

Customer Requirements	Relative Importance	No. of Zippers & Compartments	Weight of Backpack	Strength of Backpack	Grade of Dye Color	Cost of Materials	Competitive Evaluation
Durable	25	✓	✓	⊘	✓	⊘	1 2 B3 A4 US5
Lightweight	20	Ⓧ	Ⓧ	X		✓	1 A2 US/B3 4 5
Roomy	25	✓	X				1 2 US/A3 B4 5
Looks Nice	20	✓			⊘	✓	1 US2 B3 A4 5
Low Cost	10	X	X	X	X	Ⓧ	1 US2 B3 A4 5
TOTAL	100						

Product Characteristics

Relationship
⊘ Strong Positive
✓ Positive
X Negative
Ⓧ Strong Negative

US = Our Backpack
A = Competitor A
B = Competitor B

would like in a backpack, the marketing department might send representatives to talk to students on campus, conduct telephone interviews, and maybe conduct focus groups. Let's say that students have identified five desirable features: the backpack should be durable, lightweight and roomy, look nice, and not cost very much (Figure 5-10). The importance customers attach to each of these requirements is also determined and shown in Figure 5-10. This part of the figure looks like the chimney of the "house." You can see that durability and roominess are given the greatest importance.

- **Competitive Evaluation** On the far right of our relationship matrix is an evaluation of how our product compares to those of competitors. In this example there are two competitors, A and B. The evaluation scale is from 1 to 5—the higher the rating, the better. The important thing here is to identify which customer requirements we should pursue and how we fare relative to our competitors. For example, you can see that our product excels in durability relative to competitors, yet it does not look as nice. This means that we could gain a competitive advantage by focusing our design efforts on a more appealing product.

- **Product Characteristics** Specific product characteristics are on top of the relationship matrix. These are technical measures. In our example they include the number of zippers and compartments, the weight of the backpack, strength of the backpack, grade of the dye color, and the cost of materials.

- **The Relationship Matrix** The strength of the relationship between customer requirements and product characteristics is shown in the relationship matrix. For example, you can see that the number of zippers and compartments is negatively related to the weight of the backpack. A negative relationship means that as we increase the desirability of one variable, we decrease the desirability of the other. At the same time, roominess is positively related to the number of zippers and compartments, as is appearance. A positive relationship means that an increase in desirability of one variable is related to an increase in the desirability of another. This type of information is very important in coordinating the product design.

- **The Trade-off Matrix** You can see how the relationship matrix is beginning to look like a house. Figure 5-10 shows the complete house of quality. The next step in our building process is to put the "roof" on the house. This is done through a trade-off matrix, which shows how each product characteristic is related to the others and thus allows us to see what trade-offs we need to make. For example, the number of zippers is negatively related to the weight of the backpack.

- **Setting Targets** The last step in constructing the house of quality is to evaluate competitors' products relative to the specific product characteristics and to set targets for our own product. The bottom row of the house is the *output* of quality function deployment. These are specific, measurable product characteristics that have been formulated from general customer requirements.

The house of quality has been very useful. You can see how it translates everyday terms like "lightweight," "roominess," and "nice looking" into specific product characteristics that can be used in manufacturing the product. Note also how the house of quality can help in the communication between marketing, operations, and design engineering.

FIGURE 5-10

House of quality

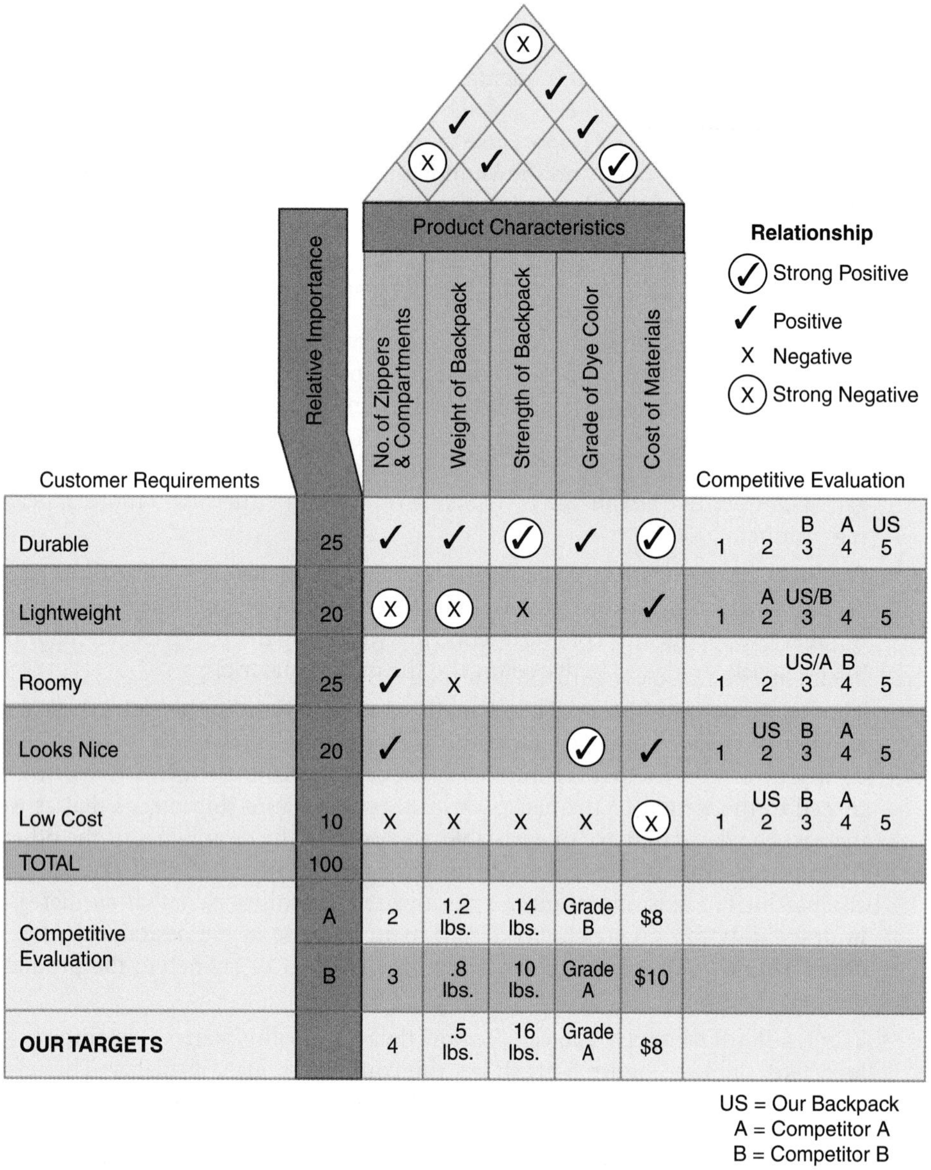

Customer Requirements	Relative Importance	No. of Zippers & Compartments	Weight of Backpack	Strength of Backpack	Grade of Dye Color	Cost of Materials	Competitive Evaluation
Durable	25	✓	✓	✓ (strong)	✓	✓ (strong)	1 2 B·3 A·4 US·5
Lightweight	20	X (strong)	X (strong)	X		✓	1 A·2 US/B·3 4 5
Roomy	25	✓	X				1 2 US/A·3 B·4 5
Looks Nice	20	✓			✓ (strong)	✓	1 US·2 B·3 A·4 5
Low Cost	10	X	X	X	X	X (strong)	1 US·2 B·3 A·4 5
TOTAL	100						
Competitive Evaluation — A	A	2	1.2 lbs.	14 lbs.	Grade B	$8	
Competitive Evaluation — B	B	3	.8 lbs.	10 lbs.	Grade A	$10	
OUR TARGETS		4	.5 lbs.	16 lbs.	Grade A	$8	

Relationship
✓ (circled) Strong Positive
✓ Positive
X Negative
X (circled) Strong Negative

US = Our Backpack
A = Competitor A
B = Competitor B

Reliability An important dimension of product design is that the product functions as expected. This is called **reliability**, the probability that a product, service, or part will perform as intended for a specified period of time under normal conditions. We are all familiar with product reliability in the form of product warranties. We also know that no product is guaranteed with 100 percent certainty to function properly. However, companies know that high reliability is an important part of customer-oriented quality and try to build this into their product design.

Reliability is a probability, a likelihood, or a chance. For example, a product with a 90 percent reliability has a 90 percent chance of functioning as intended. Another way to look at it is that the probability the product will fail is $1 - .90 = .10$, or 10 percent. This also means that 1 out of 10 products will not function as expected.

The reliability of a product is a direct function of the reliability of its component parts. If all the parts in a product must work for the product to function, then the reli-

▶ **Reliability**
The probability that a product, service, or part will perform as intended.

ability of the system is computed as the *product* of the reliabilities of the individual components:

$$R_s = (R_1)(R_2)(R_3) \dots (R_n)$$

where R_s = reliability of the product or system
$R_{1\dots n}$ = reliability of components 1 through n

Assume that a product has two parts, both of which must work for the product to function. Part 1 has a reliability of 80 percent and part 2 has a reliability of 90 percent. Compute the reliability of the product.

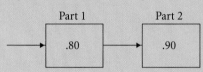

• **Before You Begin:** Remember that the reliability of the system is simply the product of the individual reliabilities.

• **Solution:**
The reliability of the product is

$$R = (0.80)(0.90) = 0.72$$

Notice in the example that the reliability of the "system" is lower than that of individual components. The reason is that all the components in a series, as in the example, must function for the product to work. If only one component doesn't work, the entire product doesn't work. The more components a product has, the lower its reliability. For example, a system with five components in series, each with a reliability of .90, has a reliability of only $(.90)(.90)(.90)(.90)(.90) = (.90)^5 = .59$.

The failure of certain products can be very critical. One way to increase product reliability is to build *redundancy* into the product design in the form of backup parts. Consider the blackout during the summer of 2003, when most of the northeastern part of the United States was out of power for days. Critical facilities, such as hospitals, immediately switched to backup power generators that are available when the main systems fail. Consider other critical systems, such as the navigation system of an aircraft, systems that operate nuclear power plants, the space shuttle, or even the braking system of your car. What gives these systems such high reliability is the redundancy built into the product design that serves to increase reliability.

Redundancy is built into the system by placing components in parallel so that when one component fails the other component takes over. In this case, the reliability of the system is computed by adding the reliability of the first component to the reliability of the second (backup) component, multiplied by the probability of needing the backup. The equation is as follows:

$$R_s = \begin{bmatrix} \text{Reliability} \\ \text{of } 1^{st} \\ \text{Component} \end{bmatrix} + \left\{ \begin{bmatrix} \text{Reliability} \\ \text{of } 2^{nd} \\ \text{Component} \end{bmatrix} \times \begin{bmatrix} \text{Probability} \\ \text{of needing} \\ 2^{nd} \text{ Component} \end{bmatrix} \right\}$$

Notice that if the reliability of the first component is .90, the probability of needing a second component is equal to the first component failing, which is $(1 - .90) = .10$. Now let's look at an example.

EXAMPLE 5.2

**Computing
Product
Reliability with
Redundancy**

Two power generators provide electricity to a facility's main and backup generator. The main generator has a reliability of .95 and the backup a reliability of .90. What is the reliability of the system?

- **Before You Begin:** Notice in this problem that redundancy has been added to the system in the form of a backup component. Remember to draw the backup in parallel to the original component and compute the total reliability accordingly.

- **Solution:**
  The system can be represented in the following way

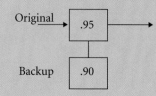

The reliability of the system is

$$R_s = .95 + [(.90) \times (1 - .95)] = .995$$

Process Management

> ▶ **Quality at the source**
> The belief that it is best to uncover the source of quality problems and eliminate it.

According to TQM, a quality product comes from a quality process. This means that quality should be built into the process. **Quality at the source** is the belief that it is far better to uncover the source of quality problems and correct it than to discard defective items after production. If the source of the problem is not corrected, the problem will continue. For example, if you are baking cookies you might find that some of the cookies are burned. Simply throwing away the burned cookies will not correct the problem. You will continue to have burned cookies and will lose money when you throw them away. It will be far more effective to see where the problem is and correct it. For example, the temperature setting may be too high; the pan may be curved, placing some cookies closer to the heating element; or the oven may not be distributing heat evenly.

Quality at the source exemplifies the difference between the old and new concepts of quality. The old concept focused on inspecting goods after they were produced or after a particular stage of production. If an inspection revealed defects, the defective products were either discarded or sent back for reworking. All this cost the company money, and these costs were passed on to the customer. The new concept of quality focuses on identifying quality problems at the source and correcting them.

In Chapter 6 we will learn how to monitor process quality using quality tools, such as control charts.

Managing Supplier Quality

TQM extends the concept of quality to a company's suppliers. Traditionally, companies tended to have numerous suppliers who engaged in competitive price bidding. When materials arrived, they were inspected for quality. TQM views this practice as contributing to poor quality and wasted time and cost. The philosophy of TQM extends the concept of quality to suppliers and ensures that they engage in the same quality practices. If suppliers meet preset quality standards, materials do not have to be inspected upon arrival. Today, many companies have a representative residing at their supplier's location, thereby involving the supplier in every stage from product design to final production.

Before You Go On

Today's concept of quality, called total quality management (TQM), focuses on building quality into the process, as opposed to simply inspecting for poor quality after production. TQM is customer driven and encompasses the entire company. Before you go on, you should know the four categories of quality costs. These are *prevention and appraisal costs*, which are costs that are incurred to prevent poor quality, and *internal and external failure costs*, which are costs that the company hopes to prevent. You should understand the evolution of TQM and the notable individuals who have shaped our knowledge of quality. Last, you should know the seven concepts of the TQM philosophy: *customer focus, continuous improvement, employee empowerment, use of quality tools, product design, process management, and managing supplier quality.*

QUALITY AWARDS AND STANDARDS

The Malcolm Baldrige National Quality Award (MBNQA)

The **Malcolm Baldrige National Quality Award** was established in 1987 when Congress passed the Malcolm Baldrige National Quality Improvement Act. The award is named after the former Secretary of Commerce, Malcolm Baldrige, and is intended to reward and stimulate quality initiatives. It is designed to recognize companies that establish and demonstrate high-quality standards and is given to no more than two companies in each of three categories: manufacturing, service, and small business. Past winners include Motorola Corporation, Xerox, FedEx, 3M, IBM, and the Ritz-Carlton.

To compete for the Baldrige Award, companies must submit a lengthy application, which is followed by an initial screening. Companies that pass this screening move to the next step, in which they undergo a rigorous evaluation process conducted by certified Baldrige examiners. The examiners conduct site visits and examine numerous company documents. They base their evaluation on seven categories, which are shown in Figure 5-11. Let's look at each category in more detail.

The first category is *leadership*. Examiners consider commitment by top management, their effort to create an organizational climate devoted to quality, and their active involvement in promoting quality. They also consider the firm's orientation toward meeting customer needs and desires, as well as those of the community and society as a whole.

▶ **Malcolm Baldrige National Quality Award**
An award given annually to companies that demonstrate quality excellence and establish best-practice standards in industry.

FIGURE 5-11

Malcolm Baldrige National Quality Award criteria

Categories	Points
1 Leadership	120
2 Strategic Planning	85
3 Customer and Market Focus	85
4 Information and Analysis	90
5 Human Resource Focus	85
6 Process Management	85
7 Business Results	450
TOTAL POINTS	**1000**

Alexander Rusche/dpa/Landov LLC

The Ritz-Carlton is one of the past winners of the Malcolm Baldrige National Quality Award.

The second category is *strategic planning*. The examiners look for a strategic plan that has high-quality goals and specific methods for implementation. The next category, *customer and market focus*, addresses how the company collects market and customer information. Successful companies should use a variety of tools toward this end, such as market surveys and focus groups. The company then needs to demonstrate how it acts on this information.

The fourth category is *information and analysis*. Examiners evaluate how the company obtains data and how it acts on the information. The company needs to demonstrate how the information is shared within the company as well as with other parties, such as suppliers and customers.

The fifth and sixth categories deal with management of human resources and management of processes, respectively. These two categories together address the issues of people and process. *Human resource focus* addresses issues of employee involvement. This entails continuous improvement programs, employee training, and functioning of teams. Employee involvement is considered a critical element of quality. Similarly, *process management* involves documentation of processes, use of tools for quality improvement, such as statistical process control, and the degree of process integration within the organization.

The last Baldrige category receives the highest points and deals with *business results*. Numerous measures of performance are considered, from percentage of defective items to financial and marketing measures. Companies need to demonstrate progressive improvement in these measures over time, not just a one-time improvement.

The Baldrige criteria have evolved from simple award criteria to a general framework for quality evaluation. Many companies use these criteria to evaluate their own performance and set quality targets even if they are not planning to formally compete for the award.

The Deming Prize

▶ **Deming Prize**
A Japanese award given to companies to recognize efforts in quality improvement.

The **Deming Prize** is a Japanese award given to companies to recognize their efforts in quality improvement. The award is named after W. Edwards Deming, who visited Japan after World War II upon the request of Japanese industrial leaders and engineers. While there, he gave a series of lectures on quality. The Japanese considered him such an important quality guru that they named the quality award after him.

The award has been given by the Union of Japanese Scientists and Engineers (JUSE) since 1951. Competition for the Deming Prize was opened to foreign companies in 1984. In 1989, Florida Power & Light was the first U.S. company to receive the award.

ISO 9000 Standards

▶ **ISO 9000**
A set of international quality standards and a certification demonstrating that companies have met all the standards specified.

Increases in international trade during the 1980s led to the development of universal standards of quality. Universal standards were seen as necessary in order for companies to be able to objectively document their quality practices around the world. Then in 1987 the International Organization for Standardization (ISO) published its first set of standards for quality management, called **ISO 9000**. The purpose of the International Organization for Standardization (ISO) is to establish agreement on international quality standards. It currently has members from 91 countries, including the United States. It created ISO 9000 to develop and promote international quality standards. ISO 9000 consists of a set of standards and a certification process for companies. ISO 9000 certification demonstrates that companies have met the standards. The standards are applicable to all types of companies and have gained global acceptance.

In many industries ISO certification has become a requirement for doing business. Also, ISO 9000 standards have been adopted by the European Community as a standard for companies doing business in Europe.

In December 2000 the first major changes to ISO 9000 were made, introducing the following three new standards:

- ISO 9000:2000, *Quality Management Systems—Fundamentals and Standards:* Provides the terminology and definitions used in the standards. It is the starting point for understanding the system of standards.
- ISO 9001:2000, *Quality Management Systems—Requirements:* This is the standard for the certification of a firm's quality management system. It is used to demonstrate the conformity of quality management systems to meet customer requirements.
- ISO 9004:2000, *Quality Management Systems—Guidelines for Performance:* Provides guidelines for establishing a quality management system. It focuses not only on meeting customer requirements but also on improving performance.

These three standards are the most widely used and apply to the majority of companies. However, ten more published standards and guidelines exist as part of the ISO 9000 family of standards.

To receive ISO certification, a company must provide extensive documentation of its quality processes. This includes methods used to monitor quality, methods and frequency of worker training, job descriptions, inspection programs, and statistical process control tools used. High-quality documentation of all processes is critical. The company is then audited by an ISO 9000 registrar, who visits the facility to make sure the company has a well-documented quality management system and that the process meets the standards. If the registrar finds that all is in order, certification is received. Once a company is certified, it is registered in an ISO directory that lists certified companies. The entire process can take eighteen to twenty-four months and can cost anywhere from $10,000 to $30,000. Companies have to be recertified by ISO every three years.

One of the shortcomings of ISO certification is that it focuses only on the process used and conformance to specifications. In contrast to the Baldrige criteria, ISO certification does not address questions about the product itself and whether it meets customer and market requirements. Today there are over 40,000 companies that are ISO certified. In fact, certification has become a requirement for conducting business in many industries.

ISO 14000 Standards

The need for standardization of quality created an impetus for the development of other standards. In 1996, the International Standards Organization introduced standards for evaluating a company's environmental responsibility. These standards, termed **ISO 14000**, focus on three major areas:

- **Management systems** standards measure systems development and integration of environmental responsibility into the overall business.
- **Operations** standards include the measurement of consumption of natural resources and energy.
- **Environmental systems** standards measure emissions, effluents, and other waste systems.

With greater interest in green manufacturing and more awareness of environmental concerns, ISO 14000 may become an important set of standards for promoting environmental responsibility.

▶ **ISO 14000**
A set of international standards and a certification focusing on a company's environmental responsibility.

WHY TQM EFFORTS FAIL

In this chapter we have discussed the meaning of TQM and the great benefits that can be attained through its implementation. Yet there are still many companies that attempt a variety of quality improvement efforts and find that they have not achieved any or most of the expected outcomes. The most important factor in the success or failure of TQM efforts is the genuineness of the organization's commitment. Often, companies look at TQM as another business change that must be implemented due to market pressure without really changing the values of their organization. Recall that TQM is a complete philosophy that has to be embraced with true belief, not mere lip service. Looking at TQM as a short-term financial investment is a sure recipe for failure.

Another mistake is the view that the responsibility for quality and elimination of waste lies with employees other than top management. It is a "let the workers do it" mentality. A third common mistake is over- or underreliance on statistical process control (SPC) methods. SPC is not a substitute for continuous improvement, teamwork, and a change in the organization's belief system. However, SPC *is* a necessary tool for identifying quality problems. Some common causes for TQM failure are

- Lack of a genuine quality culture
- Lack of top management support and commitment
- Over- and underreliance on statistical process control (SPC) methods

Companies that have attained the benefits of TQM have created a quality culture. These companies have developed processes for identifying customer-defined quality. In addition, they have a systematic method for listening to their customers, collecting and analyzing data pertaining to customer problems, and making changes based on customer feedback. You can see that in these companies there is a systematic process for prioritizing customer needs that encompasses the entire organization.

TOTAL QUALITY MANAGEMENT (TQM) WITHIN OM: HOW IT ALL FITS TOGETHER

Implementing total quality management requires broad and sweeping changes throughout a company. It also affects all other decisions *within* operations management. The decision to implement total quality management concepts throughout the company is strategic in nature. It sets the direction for the firm and the level of commitment. For example, some companies may choose to directly compete on quality, whereas others may just want to be as good as the competition. It is operations strategy that then dictates how all other areas of operations management will support this commitment.

The decision to implement TQM affects areas such as product design (Chapter 3), which needs to incorporate customer-defined quality. Processes are then redesigned in order to produce products with higher quality standards. Job design (Chapter 11) is affected, as workers need to be trained in quality tools and become responsible for rooting out quality problems. Also, supply chain management (Chapter 4) is affected as the commitment to quality translates into partnering with suppliers. As you can see, virtually every aspect of the operations function must change to support the commitment to total quality management.

TOTAL QUALITY MANAGEMENT (TQM) ACROSS THE ORGANIZATION

As we have seen, total quality management impacts every aspect of the organization. Every person and every function is responsible for quality and is affected by poor quality. For example, recall that Motorola implemented its Six Sigma concept not only in the production process but also in the accounting, finance, and administrative areas. Similarly, ISO 9000 standards do not apply only to the production process—they apply equally to all departments of the company. A company cannot achieve high quality if its accounting is inaccurate or the marketing department is not working closely with customers. TQM requires the close cooperation of different functions in order to be successful. In this section we look at the involvement of these other functions in TQM.

Marketing plays a critical role in the TQM process by providing key inputs that make TQM a success. Recall that the goal of TQM is to satisfy customer needs by producing the exact product that customers want. Marketing's role is to understand the changing needs and wants of customers by working closely with them. This requires a solid identification of target markets and an understanding of whom the product is intended for. Sometimes, apparently small differences in product features can result in large differences in customer appeal. Marketing needs to accurately pass customer information along to operations, and operations needs to include marketing in any planned product changes.

Finance is another major participant in the TQM process because of the great cost consequences of poor quality. General definitions of quality need to be translated into specific dollar terms. This serves as a baseline for monitoring the financial impact of quality efforts and can be a great motivator. Recall the four costs of quality discussed earlier. The first two costs, prevention and appraisal, are preventive costs; they are intended to prevent internal and external failure costs. Not investing enough in preventive costs can result in failure costs, which can hurt the company. On the other hand, investing too much in preventive costs may not yield added benefits. Financial analysis of these costs is critical. You can see that finance plays a large role in evaluating and monitoring the financial impact of managing the quality process. This includes costs related to preventing and eliminating defects, training employees, reviewing new products, and all other quality efforts.

Accounting is important in the TQM process because of the need for exact costing. TQM efforts cannot be accurately monitored and their financial contribution assessed if the company does not have accurate costing methods.

Engineering efforts are critical in TQM because of the need to properly translate customer requirements into specific engineering terms. Recall the process we followed in developing quality function deployment (QFD). It was not easy to translate a customer requirement such as "a good-looking backpack" into specific terms such as materials, weight, color grade, size, and number of zippers. We depend on engineering to use general customer requirements in developing technical specifications, identifying specific parts and materials needed, and identifying equipment that should be used.

Purchasing is another important part of the TQM process. Whereas marketing is busy identifying what the customers want and engineering is busy translating that information into technical specifications, purchasing is responsible for acquiring the materials needed to make the product. Purchasing must locate sources of supply, ensure that the parts and materials needed are of sufficiently high quality, and negotiate a purchase price that meets the company's budget as identified by finance.

Human resources   is critical to the effort to hire employees with the skills necessary to work in a TQM environment. That environment includes a high degree of teamwork, cooperation, dedication, and customer commitment. Human resources is also faced with challenges relating to reward and incentive systems. In TQM, rewards and incentives are different from those found in traditional environments that focus on rewarding individuals rather than teams.

Information systems (IS)   is highly important in TQM because of the increased need for information accessible to teams throughout the organization. IS should work closely with a company's TQM development program in order to understand exactly the type of information system best suited for the firm, including the form of the data, the summary statistics available, and the frequency of updating.

THE SUPPLY CHAIN LINK

The ultimate goal of TQM is to produce and deliver a good or service that provides value to the final customer. This can only be achieved if the concepts of TQM are adopted by all members of the supply chain. The reason is that the supply chain is a system of organizations that are linked together and that are dependent on each other's performance. If just one member of the chain produces poor quality, the entire chain will suffer, as the defective product will be passed down the chain until the defect is finally discovered. This will result in higher cost for all chain members and possibly the loss of customers. That is why one of the main ideas of TQM is to extend quality concepts to a company's suppliers. In the chapter we discussed the differences between the external and internal customer, stressing that no one in the company should pass a defective item on to the internal customer. Just as all the internal functions of an organization are dependent upon one another, so are the members of a supply chain. For this reason, the concepts of TQM must be extended to everyone in the chain.

Chapter Highlights

1 Total quality management (TQM) is different from the old concept of quality because its focus is on serving customers, identifying the causes of quality problems, and building quality into the production process.

2 There are four categories of quality costs. The first two are prevention and appraisal costs, which are incurred by a company in attempting to improve quality. The last two costs are internal and external failure costs, which are the costs of quality failures that the company wishes to prevent.

3 The seven most notable individuals who shaped today's concept of quality are Walter A. Shewhart, W. Edwards Deming, Joseph M. Juran, Armand V. Feigenbaum, Philip B. Crosby, Kaoru Ishikawa, and Genichi Taguchi.

4 Seven features of TQM combine to create the TQM philosophy: customer focus, continuous improvement, employee empowerment, use of quality tools, product design, process management, and managing supplier quality.

5 Quality function deployment (QFD) is a tool used to translate customer needs into specific engineering requirements. Seven problem-solving tools are used in managing quality. Often called the seven tools of quality control, they are cause-and-effect diagrams, flowcharts, checklists, scatter diagrams, Pareto analysis, control charts, and histograms.

6 Reliability is the probability that the product will function as expected. The reliability of a product is computed as the product of the reliabilities of the individual components.

7 The Malcolm Baldrige Award is given to companies to recognize excellence in quality management. Companies are evaluated in seven areas, including quality leadership and performance results. These criteria have become a standard for many companies that seek to improve quality. ISO 9000 is a certification based on a set of quality standards established by the International Organization for Standardization. Its goal is to ensure that quality is built into production processes. ISO 9000 focuses mainly on quality of conformance.

W. Edwards Deming

Catherine Karnow/ Corbis Images

Philip B. Crosby

Courtesy Philip Crosby Associates

Joseph M. Juran

Courtesy Juran Institute

Key Terms

Formula Review

1. Reliability of parts in series:

$$R_s = (R_1)(R_2) \ldots (R_n)$$

2. Reliability of parts with redundancy (in parallel):

$$R_s = \begin{bmatrix} \text{Reliability} \\ \text{of } 1^{st} \\ \text{Component} \end{bmatrix} + \left\{ \begin{bmatrix} \text{Reliability} \\ \text{of } 2^{nd} \\ \text{Component} \end{bmatrix} \times \begin{bmatrix} \text{Probability} \\ \text{of needing} \\ 2^{nd} \text{ Component} \end{bmatrix} \right\}$$

Solved Problems

• Problem 1

An office security system at Delco, Inc. has two component parts, both of which must work for the system to function. Part 1 has a reliability of 80 percent, and part 2 has a reliability of 98 percent. Compute the reliability of the system.

• Before You Begin:

Before you begin solving reliability problems, it is best to first draw a diagram of the components. Remember that the system of components is drawn in series, except when there is redundancy built into the system through a backup component. In that case, the backup component is drawn in parallel. Always read the problem carefully to determine whether redundancy is built into the system.

• Solution

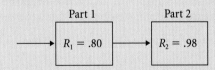

The reliability of the system is

$$R_s = R_1 \times R_2$$
$$R_s = (.80)(.98) = .784$$

• Problem 2

Delco, Inc., from Problem 1, is not happy with the reliability of its security system and has decided to improve it. The company will add a backup component to part 1 of its security system. The backup component will also have a reliability of .80. What is the reliability of the improved security system?

• Before You Begin:

Notice that in this problem there is redundancy in the form of a backup component for part 1. This means that when drawing the diagram you should place the two components for part 1 in parallel. Proceed by computing the reliability for part 1 and then the entire system.

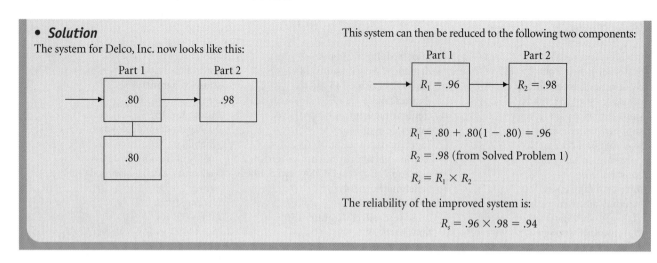

• **Solution**

The system for Delco, Inc. now looks like this:

Part 1 .80, Part 2 .98, .80

This system can then be reduced to the following two components:

Part 1 $R_1 = .96$, Part 2 $R_2 = .98$

$R_1 = .80 + .80(1 - .80) = .96$

$R_2 = .98$ (from Solved Problem 1)

$R_s = R_1 \times R_2$

The reliability of the improved system is:

$$R_s = .96 \times .98 = .94$$

Discussion Questions

1. Define quality for the following products: a university, an exercise facility, spaghetti sauce, and toothpaste. Compare your definitions with those of others in your class.

2. Describe the TQM philosophy and identify its major characteristics.

3. Explain how TQM is different from the traditional notions of quality. Also, explain the differences between traditional organizations and those that have implemented TQM.

4. Find three local companies that you believe exhibit high quality. Next, find three national or international companies that are recognized for their quality achievements.

5. Describe the four dimensions of quality. Which do you think is most important?

6. Describe each of the four costs of quality: prevention, appraisal, internal failure, and external failure. Next, describe how each type of cost would change (increase, decrease, or remain the same) if we designed a higher-quality product that was easier to manufacture.

7. Think again about the four costs of quality. Describe how each would change if we hired more inspectors without changing any other aspects of quality.

8. Explain the meaning of the plan–do–act–study cycle. Why is it described as a cycle?

9. Describe the use of quality function deployment (QFD). Can you find examples in which the voice of the customer was not translated properly into technical requirements?

10. Describe the seven tools of quality control. Are some more important than others? Would you use these tools separately or together? Give some examples of tools that could be used together.

11. What is the Malcolm Baldrige National Quality Award? Why is this award important, and what companies have received it in the past?

12. What are ISO 9000 standards? Who were they set by and why? Can you describe other certifications based on the ISO 9000 certification?

13. Who are the seven "gurus" of quality? Name at least one contribution made by at least three of them.

Problems

1. A CD player has five components that all must function for the player to work. The average reliability of each component is .90. What is the reliability of the CD player?

2. A jet engine has ten components in series. The average reliability of each component is .998. What is the reliability of the engine?

3. An office copier has four main components in a series with the following reliabilities: .89, .95, .90, and .90. Determine the reliability of the copier.

4. An engine system consists of three main components in a series, all having the same reliability. Determine the level of reliability required for each of the components if the engine is to have a reliability of .998.

5. A bank loan processing system has three components with individual reliabilities as shown:

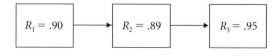

$R_1 = .90$, $R_2 = .89$, $R_3 = .95$

What is the reliability of the bank loan processing system?

6. What would be the reliability of the bank system above if each of the three components had a backup with a reliability of .80? How would the total reliability be different?

7. An LCD projector in an office has a main light bulb with a reliability of .90 and a backup bulb, the reliability of which is .80. The system looks as follows:

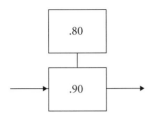

What is the reliability of the system?

8. A University Web server has five main components each with the same reliability. All five components must work for the server to function as intended. If the University wants to have a 95 percent reliability, what must be the reliability of each of each of the components?

9. BioTech Research Center is working to develop a new vaccine for the West Nile Virus. The project is so important that the firm has created three teams of experts to work on the project from different perspectives. Team 1 has a 90 percent chance of success, team 2 an 85 percent chance of success, and team 3 a 70 percent chance. What is the probability that BioTech will develop the vaccine?

10. The following system of components has been proposed for a new product. Determine the reliability of the system.

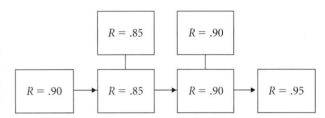

CASE: Gold Coast Advertising (GCA)

George Stein sat in his large office overlooking Chicago's Michigan Avenue. As CEO of Gold Coast Advertising he seemed to always be confronted with one problem or another. Today was no exception. George had just come out of a long meeting with Jim Gerard, head of the board for the small advertising agency. Jim was concerned about a growing problem with lowered sales expectations and a decreasing customer base. Jim warned George that something had to be done quickly or Jim would have to go to the board for action. George acknowledged that sales were down but attributed this to general economic conditions. He assured Jim that the problems would be addressed immediately.

As George pondered his next course of action, he admitted to himself that the customer base of GCA was slowly decreasing. The agency did not quite understand the reason for this decrease. Many regular customers were not coming back and the rate of new customers seemed to be slowly declining. GCA's competitors seemed to be doing well. George did not understand the problem.

What Do Customers Want?

GCA was a Chicago-based advertising agency that developed campaigns and promotions for small- and medium-sized firms.

Its expertise was in the retail area, but it worked with a wide range of firms from the food service industry to the medical field. GCA competed on price and speed of product development. Advertising in the retail area was competitive and price had always been important. Also, since retail fashions change rapidly, speed in advertising development was thought to be critical.

George reminded himself that price and speed had always been what customers wanted. Now he felt confused that he really didn't know his customers. This was just another crisis that would pass, he told himself. But he needed to deal with it immediately.

Case Questions

1. What is wrong with how Gold Coast Advertising measures its quality? Explain why Gold Coast should ask its customers about how they define quality.

2. Offer suggestions to George Stein on ways of identifying quality dimensions GCA's customers consider important.

3. Develop a short questionnaire to be filled out by GCA's customers that evaluates how customers define quality.

CASE: Delta Plastics, Inc. (A)

Company Background

Delta Plastics, Inc. specialized in the design and manufacture of plastic containers, primarily for kitchen and household use. Its products were sold through merchandise retailers and were recognized for high quality. Delta also had an active R&D group that was continuously working to develop new plastic materials and new product designs. Delta was a recognized industry leader

and was aggressively looking to increase brand recognition and market share.

Delta's R&D group had recently developed a new plastic material that tolerates rapid changes in temperature, from heating to deep cooling. This material could be used to make containers for kitchen use that could immediately be moved from the oven to the refrigerator. Unlike glass containers with this capability, the plastic containers would not break or chip. Delta's marketing group was eager to promote sales of containers made with the new material. Marketing believed the new material could revolutionize the industry, so it pushed for rapid production, arguing that the sooner the new products were available to customers, the sooner the company could corner the market.

The Decision

The decision whether to initiate production or continue with material testing was made during a heated meeting on April 28. Isabelle Harrison, director of R&D, stated that more product testing was needed in order to fine-tune the characteristics of the new material. Although there was no question regarding product safety, she wanted to refine the material to make sure that no unexpected defects occurred during production. Jose De Costa, director of manufacturing, supported this position, stating that the new material may be susceptible to cracking. However, George Chadwick, director of marketing, countered that millions of dollars had already been spent on design and testing.

He argued that production needed to be as rapid as possible before a competitor came out with a similar design. At one point George looked at Isabelle and asked: "Are you certain that the product is safe?" She replied that it was. "Then" he said, "conducting more testing is unnecessary."

The final decision came from Jonathan Fine, Delta's CEO. He agreed with George. "If product safety is guaranteed, small problems in production should not be a big deal. Let's initiate production as soon as possible."

The Problem

On June 15, exactly one month after production began, Jose De Costa sat at his desk looking at the latest production quality report. The report showed weekly defects for products made with the new material (dubbed by marketing as "super plastic") versus the standard material. Jose knew he needed to conduct a better analysis of the data to see whether there were indeed differences in defects between the two materials. Jose was nervous. Even if there were differences in quality, he was not sure what actions to take.

Quality Report
I Standard Material

Defect Type	Week 1 M	T	W	Th	F	Week 2 M	T	W	Th	F
1. Uneven edges	1	2	2	3	2	3	1	1	2	0
2. Cracks	2	3	2	3	0	3	2	2	1	3
3. Scratches	3	1	2	3	4	2	1	0	2	3
4. Air bubbles	4	2	2	3	4	4	3	2	4	3
5. Thickness variation	1	0	4	0	2	0	1	1	2	0

Defect Type	Week 3 M	T	W	Th	F	Week 4 M	T	W	Th	F
1. Uneven edges	2	2	1	3	2	3	1	1	2	2
2. Cracks	3	2	2	0	2	1	2	2	3	3
3. Scratches	3	1	0	1	3	3	1	0	1	3
4. Air bubbles	3	1	2	2	4	2	3	2	4	1
5. Thickness variation	1	1	3	0	2	2	1	1	2	0

II Super Plastic (New Material)

Defect Type	Week 1 M	T	W	Th	F	Week 2 M	T	W	Th	F
1. Uneven edges	2	2	3	2	0	3	1	1	2	3
2. Cracks	6	6	4	3	7	4	4	4	3	3
3. Scratches	0	1	0	1	0	0	1	0	2	2
4. Air bubbles	2	0	2	1	3	4	3	2	4	3
5. Thickness variation	1	0	2	1	2	0	1	2	2	0

Defect Type	Week 3 M	T	W	Th	F	Week 4 M	T	W	Th	F
1. Uneven edges	1	2	2	2	3	3	2	1	2	0
2. Cracks	4	6	4	4	3	5	7	6	3	7
3. Scratches	0	1	2	1	0	1	1	0	2	3
4. Air bubbles	4	5	5	5	3	6	5	4	6	5
5. Thickness variation	1	0	4	0	1	0	1	1	2	0

Case Questions

1. Identify the different costs of quality described in the case. Explain the trade-offs between the costs of quality that Delta made in its decision. Was George Chadwick correct that conducting more tests was unnecessary?

2. Use one of the quality tools described in the chapter to analyze the defects in the case. How do the quality dimensions differ between the two materials? Are there more defects associated with the super plastic versus the standard material?

3. Given your findings, what should Jose do?

INTERACTIVE CASE Virtual Company www.wiley.com/college/reid

On-line Case: Total Quality Management at Valley Memorial Hospital

Assignment: *Total Quality Management* For this assignment, you'll be working with Jane Starr of Valley Memorial Hospital's Risk Management Department. You know the assignment has something to do with quality, but you're wondering how quality applies to healthcare. At the hospital, you find Jane Starr's office. She greets you and says, "Let me tell you a bit about what you'll be doing for us. We've been working on quality measures for several years, and now we have to focus on quality even more. The Joint Commission for Accreditation of Healthcare Organizations is currently looking hard at quality when it visits hospitals and decides whether to accredit them. We need your help in

bringing ideas together on how to measure quality in a service organization."

To access the Web site:

- Go to **www.wiley.com/college/reid**
- Click **Student Companion Site**
- Click **Virtual Company**
- Click **Kaizen Consulting, Inc**
- Click **Consulting Assignments**
- Click **Total Quality Management at Valley Memorial Hospital**

INTERNET CHALLENGE Snyder Bakeries

You have recently taken a position with Snyder Bakeries, a producer of a variety of different types of baked goods that are packaged and sold directly to grocery chains. Snyder Bakeries has been in business since 1978. It is a small company with 95 employees, earning roughly $2.5 million annually. Competition in the baked goods market has been increasing steadily, and Snyder Bakeries is being forced to look at its operations. In addition, turnover and dissatisfaction among Snyder employees have been high. Mr. Lowell Snyder, President of Snyder Bakeries, is looking to you for help in redesigning the company's quality program. He would like you to focus on helping Snyder

Bakeries develop a team approach among its employees as part of the implementing principles of total quality management.

To help Mr. Snyder, use the Internet as a source of information. Perform an Internet search to to identify at least two companies that Snyder Bakeries can use as a benchmark for developing a team approach among employees. Explain how each of these competitors uses teams, how the teams are developed, how incentives are provided, and how employees are motivated. Also identify the benefits these companies have gained from using the team approach. Finally, outline a plan for Mr. Snyder based on the information you have gathered.

On-line Resources

Companion Website www.wiley.com/college/reid

- Take interactive *practice quizzes* to assess your knowledge and help you study in a dynamic way
- Review *PowerPoint slides* or print slides for notetaking
- Access the *Virtual Company: Valley Memorial Hospital*

- Find links to *Company Tours* for this chapter
  Stickley, Inc., _www.Stickley.com_
- Find links for *Additional Web Resources* for this chapter
  American Society for Quality Control, _www.asqc.org_
  National Institute of Standards and Technology (NIST) quality program—Baldrige Award
  www.quality.nist.gov

Additional Resources Available Only in WileyPLUS
- Use the *e-Book* and launch directly to all interactive resources
- Take the interactive *Quick Test* to check your understanding of the chapter material and get immediate feedback on your responses.
- Check your understanding of the key vocabulary in the chapter with *Interactive Flash Cards*
- Use the *Animated Demo Problems* to review key problem types.
- Practice for your tests with *additional problem sets*
- *And more!*

Selected Bibliography

Clark, Bill, John Chang, and Marcus Chao. "Helping Suppliers to Focus on Quality," *Supply Chain Management Review*, Jan.–Feb. 2006, 54–61.

Crosby, Philip B. *Quality Is Free.* New York: New American Library, 1979.

Crosby, Philip. *Quality Without Tears: The Art of Hassle-Free Management.* New York: McGraw-Hill, 1984.

Deming, W. Edwards. *Out of Crisis.* Cambridge, Mass.: MIT Center for Advanced Engineering Study, 1986.

Evans, James R., and William M. Lindsay. *The Management and Control of Quality.* Fourth Edition. Cincinnati: South-Western, 1999.

Garvin, David A. "Competing on the Eight Dimensions of Quality," *Harvard Business Review*, Nov.–Dec., 1987, 101–10.

Garvin, David A. *Managing Quality.* New York: Free Press, 1988.

Goetsch, David L., and Stanley Davis. *Implementing Total Quality.* Upper Saddle River, N.J.: Prentice-Hall, 1995.

Hall, Robert. *Attaining Manufacturing Excellence.* Burr Ridge, Ill.: Dow-Jones Irwin, 1987.

Juran, Joseph M. "The Quality Trilogy," *Quality Progress* 10, 8, 1986, 19–24.

Juran, Joseph M. *Quality Control Handbook.* Fourth Edition. New York: McGraw-Hill, 1988.

Juran, Joseph M. *Juran on Planning for Quality.* New York: Free Press, 1988.

Kitazawa, S., and J. Sarkis. "The Relationship Between ISO 14001 and Continuous Source Reduction Programs," *International Journal of Operations and Production Management*, 20, 2, 2000, 225–248.

Medori, D., and D. Steeple. "A Framework for Auditing and Enhancing Performance Measurement Systems," *International Journal of Operations and Production Management*, 20, 5, 2000, 520–533.

Rosenberg, Jarrett. "Five Myths about Customer Satisfaction," *Quality Progress* 29, 12, December 1996, 57–60.

Zimmerman, R.E., L. Steinmann, and V. Schueler. "Designing Customer Surveys that Work," *Quality Progress*, October 1996, 22–28.

CHAPTER 6

Statistical Quality Control

Before studying this chapter you should know or, if necessary, review

1. Quality as a competitive priority, Chapter 2, page 37.
2. Total quality management (TQM) concepts, Chapter 5, pages 142–164.

LEARNING OBJECTIVES

After studying this chapter you should be able to

1. Describe categories of statistical quality control (SQC).
2. Explain the use of descriptive statistics in measuring quality characteristics.
3. Identify and describe causes of variation.
4. Describe the use of control charts.
5. Identify the differences between x-bar, R-, p-, and c-charts.
6. Explain the meaning of process capability and the process capability index.
7. Explain the concept Six Sigma.
8. Explain the process of acceptance sampling and describe the use of operating characteristic (OC) curves.
9. Describe the challenges inherent in measuring quality in service organizations.

CHAPTER OUTLINE

WHAT'S IN OM FOR ME?

ACC

FIN

MKT

OM

HRM

MIS

Mary Kate Denny/PhotoEdit

We have all had the experience of purchasing a product only to discover that it is defective in some way or does not function the way it was designed to. This could be a new backpack with a broken zipper or an "out of the box" malfunctioning computer printer. Many of us have struggled to assemble a product the manufacturer has indicated would need only "minor" assembly, only to find that a piece of the product is missing or defective. As consumers, we expect the products we purchase to function as intended. However, producers of products know that it is not always possible to inspect every product and every aspect of the production process at all times. The challenge is to design ways to maximize the ability to monitor the quality of products being produced and eliminate defects.

One way to ensure a quality product is to build quality into the process. Consider Steinway & Sons, the maker of premier pianos used in concert halls all over the world. Steinway has been making pianos since the 1880s. Since that time, the company's manufacturing process has not changed significantly. It takes the company nine months to a year to produce a piano by fashioning some 12,000 hand-crafted parts, carefully measuring and monitoring every part of the process. Although many of Steinway's competitors have moved to mass production, where pianos can be assembled in twenty days, Steinway has maintained a strategy of quality defined by skill and craftsmanship. Steinway's production process is focused on meticulous process precision and extremely high product consistency. This has contributed to making its name synonymous with top quality.

WHAT IS STATISTICAL QUALITY CONTROL?

MKT

In Chapter 5 we learned that total quality management (TQM) addresses organizational quality from managerial and philosophical viewpoints. TQM focuses on customer-driven quality standards, managerial leadership, continuous improvement, quality built into product and process design, identifying quality problems at the source, and making quality everyone's responsibility. However, talking about solving quality problems is not enough. We need specific tools that can help us make the right quality decisions. These tools come from the field of statistics and are used to help identify quality problems in the production process as well as in the product itself. Statistical quality control is the subject of this chapter.

Statistical quality control (SQC) is the term used to describe the set of statistical tools used by quality professionals. Statistical quality control can be divided into three broad categories:

1. **Descriptive statistics** are used to describe quality characteristics and relationships. Included are statistics such as the mean, standard deviation, the range, and a measure of the distribution of data.

▶ **Statistical quality control (SQC)**
The general category of statistical tools used to evaluate organizational quality.

▶ **Descriptive statistics**
Statistics used to describe quality characteristics and relationships.

2. **Statistical process control (SPC)** involves inspecting a random sample of the output from a process and deciding whether the process is producing products with characteristics that fall within a predetermined range. SPC answers the question of whether the process is functioning properly or not.

3. **Acceptance sampling** is the process of randomly inspecting a sample of goods and deciding whether to accept the entire lot based on the results. Acceptance sampling determines whether a batch of goods should be accepted or rejected.

The tools in each of these categories provide different types of information for use in analyzing quality. Descriptive statistics are used to describe certain quality characteristics, such as the central tendency and variability of observed data. Although descriptions of certain characteristics are helpful, they are not enough to help us evaluate whether there is a problem with quality. Acceptance sampling can help us do this. It helps us decide whether desirable quality has been achieved for a batch of products and whether to accept or reject the items produced. Although this information is helpful in making the quality acceptance decision *after* the product has been produced, it does not help us identify and catch a quality problem *during* the production process. For this we need tools in the statistical process control (SPC) category.

All three of these statistical quality control categories are helpful in measuring and evaluating the quality of products or services. However, statistical process control (SPC) tools are used most frequently because they identify quality problems during the production process. For this reason, we will devote most of the chapter to this category of tools. The quality control tools we will be learning about do not only measure the value of a quality characteristic; they also help us identify a *change* or variation in some quality characteristic of the product or process. We will first see what types of variation we can observe when measuring quality. Then we will be able to identify the specific tools to use for measuring this variation.

▶ **Statistical process control (SPC)**
A statistical tool that involves inspecting a random sample of the output from a process and deciding whether the process is producing products with characteristics that fall within a predetermined range.

▶ **Acceptance sampling**
The process of randomly inspecting a sample of goods and deciding whether to accept the entire lot based on the results.

Variation in the production process leads to quality defects and lack of product consistency. The Intel Corporation, the world's largest and most profitable manufacturer of microprocessors, understands this. Therefore, Intel has implemented a program it calls "copy-exactly" at all its manufacturing facilities. The idea is that regardless of whether the chips are made in Arizona, New Mexico, Ireland, or any of its other plants, they are made in exactly the same way. This means using the same equipment, the same exact materials, and performing the same tasks in the exact same order. The level of detail to which the "copy-exactly" concept goes is meticulous. For example, when a chipmaking machine was found to be a few feet longer at one facility than another, Intel made them match. When water quality was found to be different at one facility, Intel instituted a purification system to eliminate any differences. Even when a worker was found polishing equipment in one direction, he was asked to do it in the approved circular pattern. Why such attention to exactness of detail? The reason is to minimize all variation. Now let's look at the different types of variation that exist.

©AP/Wide World Photos

LINKS TO PRACTICE

Intel Corporation
www.intel.com

SOURCES OF VARIATION: COMMON AND ASSIGNABLE CAUSES

► **Common causes of variation**
Random causes that cannot be identified.

If you look at bottles of a soft drink in a grocery store, you will notice that no two bottles are filled to exactly the same level. Some are filled slightly higher and some slightly lower. Similarly, if you look at blueberry muffins in a bakery, you will notice that some are slightly larger than others and some have more blueberries than others. These types of differences are completely normal. No two products are exactly alike because of slight differences in materials, workers, machines, tools, and other factors. These are called **common, or random, causes of variation**. Common causes of variation are based on random causes that we cannot identify. These types of variation are unavoidable and are due to slight differences in processing.

An important task in quality control is to find out the range of natural random variation in a process. For example, if the average bottle of a soft drink called Cocoa Fizz contains 16 ounces of liquid, we may determine that the amount of natural variation is between 15.8 and 16.2 ounces. If this were the case, we would monitor the production process to make sure that the amount stays within this range. If production goes out of this range—bottles are found to contain on average 15.6 ounces—this would lead us to believe that there is a problem with the process because the variation is greater than the natural random variation.

► **Assignable causes of variation**
Causes that can be identified and eliminated.

The second type of variation that can be observed involves those where the causes can be precisely identified and eliminated. These are called **assignable causes of variation**. Examples of this type of variation are poor quality in raw materials, an employee who needs more training, or a machine in need of repair. In each of these examples, the problem can be identified and corrected. If the variation is allowed to persist, it will continue to create a problem in the quality of the product. In the example of the soft drink bottling operation, bottles filled with 15.6 ounces of liquid would signal a problem. The machine may need to be readjusted, an assignable cause of variation. We can assign the variation to a particular cause (machine needs to be readjusted) and we can correct the problem (readjust the machine).

DESCRIPTIVE STATISTICS

Descriptive statistics can be helpful in describing certain characteristics of a product and a process. The most important descriptive statistics are measures of central tendency such as the mean, measures of variability such as the standard deviation and range, and measures of the distribution of data. We first review these descriptive statistics and then see how we use them to measure changes in product and process characteristics.

The Mean

► **Mean (average)**
A statistic that measures the central tendency of a set of data.

In the soft-drink bottling example, we stated that the average bottle is filled with 16 ounces of liquid. The arithmetic average, or the **mean**, is a statistic that measures the central tendency of a set of data. Knowing the central point of a set of data is highly important. Just think how important that number is when you receive test scores!

To compute the mean, we simply sum all the observations and divide by the total number of observations. The equation for computing the mean is

$$\bar{x} = \frac{\sum_{i=1}^{n} x_i}{n}$$

where $\bar{x}$ = the mean
x_i = observation $i, i = 1, \ldots, n$
n = number of observations

The Range and Standard Deviation

In the bottling example, we also stated that the amount of natural variation in the bottling process is between 15.8 and 16.2 ounces. This information provides us with the amount of variability of the data. It tells us how spread out the data is around the mean. There are two measures that can be used to determine the amount of variation in the data. The first measure is the **range**, which is the difference between the largest and smallest observations. In our example, the range for natural variation is 0.4 ounces.

Another measure of variation is the **standard deviation**. The equation for computing the standard deviation is

$$\sigma = \sqrt{\frac{\sum\limits_{i=1}^{n}(x_i - \bar{x})^2}{n-1}}$$

where σ = standard deviation of a sample
$\bar{x}$ = the mean
x_i = observation $i, i = 1, \ldots, n$
n = the number of observations in the sample

Small values of the range and standard deviation mean that the observations are closely clustered around the mean. Large values of the range and standard deviation mean that the observations are spread out around the mean. Figure 6-1 illustrates the differences between a small and a large standard deviation for our bottling operation. You can see that the figure shows two distributions, both with a mean of 16 ounces. However, in the first distribution the standard deviation is large and the data are spread out far around the mean. In the second distribution the standard deviation is small and the data are clustered close to the mean.

Distribution of Data

A third descriptive statistic used to measure quality characteristics is the shape of the distribution of the observed data. When a distribution is symmetric, there are the same number of observations below and above the mean. This is what we commonly find when only normal variation is present in the data. When a disproportionate number of observations are either above or below the mean, we say that the data have a *skewed distribution*. Figure 6-2 shows symmetric and skewed distributions for the bottling operation.

► **Range**
The difference between the largest and smallest observations in a set of data.

► **Standard deviation**
A statistic that measures the amount of data dispersion around the mean.

STATISTICAL PROCESS CONTROL METHODS

Statistical process control methods employ descriptive statistics to monitor the quality of the product and process. As we have learned so far, there are common and assignable causes of variation in the production of every product. Using statistical process control, we want to determine the amount of variation that is common or normal. Then we monitor the production process to make sure production stays within this

FIGURE 6-1

Normal distributions with varying standard deviations

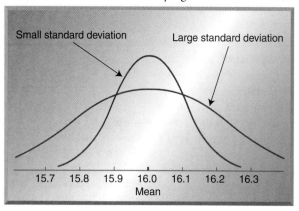

FIGURE 6-2

Differences between symmetric and skewed distributions

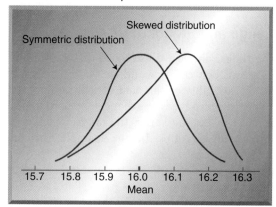

normal range. That is, we want to make sure the process is in a *state of control*. The most commonly used tool for monitoring the production process is a control chart. Different types of control charts are used to monitor different aspects of the production process. In this section we will learn how to develop and use control charts.

Developing Control Charts

▶ **Control chart**
A graph that shows whether a sample of data falls within the common or normal range of variation.

▶ **Out of control**
The situation in which a plot of data falls outside preset control limits.

A **control chart** (also called process chart or quality control chart) is a graph that shows whether a sample of data falls within the common or normal range of variation. A control chart has upper and lower control limits that separate common from assignable causes of variation. The common range of variation is defined by the use of control chart limits. We say that a process is **out of control** when a plot of data reveals that one or more samples fall outside the control limits.

Figure 6-3 shows a control chart for the Cocoa Fizz bottling operation. The *x* axis represents samples (#1, #2, #3, etc.) taken from the process over time. The *y* axis represents the quality characteristic that is being monitored (ounces of liquid). The center line (CL) of the control chart is the mean, or average, of the quality characteristic that is being measured. In Figure 6-3 the mean is 16 ounces. The upper control limit (UCL) is the maximum acceptable variation from the mean for a process that is in a state of control. Similarly, the lower control limit (LCL) is the minimum acceptable variation from the mean for a process that is in a state of control. In our example, the upper

FIGURE 6-3

Quality control chart for Cocoa Fizz

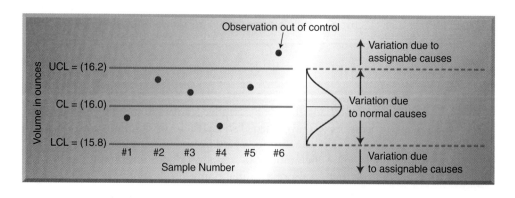

and lower control limits are 16.2 and 15.8 ounces, respectively. You can see that if a sample of observations falls outside the control limits, we need to look for assignable causes.

The upper and lower control limits on a control chart are usually set at ± 3 standard deviations from the mean. If we assume that the data exhibit a normal distribution, these control limits will capture 99.74 percent of the normal variation. Control limits can be set at ± 2 standard deviations from the mean. In that case, control limits would capture 95.44 percent of the values. Figure 6-4 shows the percentage of values that fall within a particular range of standard deviation.

Looking at Figure 6-4, we can conclude that observations falling outside the set range represent assignable causes of variation. However, there is a small probability that a value that falls outside the limits is still due to normal variation. This is called Type I error, with the error being the chance of concluding that there are assignable causes of variation when only normal variation exists. Another name for this is alpha (α) risk, where alpha refers to the sum of the probabilities in both tails of the distribution that falls outside the confidence limits. The chance of this happening is given by the percentage or probability represented by the shaded areas of Figure 6-5. For limits of ± 3 standard deviations from the mean, the probability of a Type I error is 0.26 percent (100% − 99.74%), whereas for limits of ± 2 standard deviations it is 4.56 percent (100% − 95.44%).

Types of Control Charts

Control charts are one of the most commonly used tools in statistical process control. They can be used to measure any characteristic of a product, such as the weight of a cereal box, the number of chocolates in a box, or the volume of bottled water. The different characteristics that can be measured by control charts can be divided into two groups: **variables** and **attributes**. A *control chart for variables* is used to monitor characteristics that can be measured and have a continuum of values, such as height, weight, or volume. A soft-drink bottling operation is an example of a variable measure, since the amount of liquid in the bottles can be measured and can take on a number of different values. Other examples are the weight of a bag of sugar, the temperature of a baking oven, or the diameter of plastic tubing.

▶ **Variable**
A product characteristic that can be measured and has a continuum of values (e.g., height, weight, or volume).

▶ **Attribute**
A product characteristic that has a discrete value and can be counted.

FIGURE 6-4

Chance of Type I error for $\pm 3\sigma$ (sigma-standard deviations)

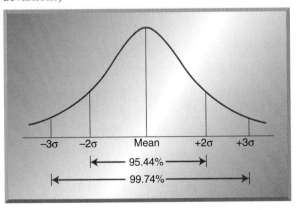

FIGURE 6-5

Percentage of values captured by different ranges of standard deviation

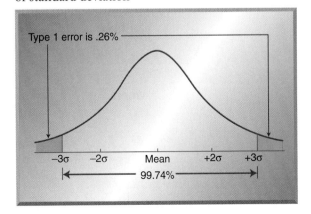

A *control chart for attributes*, on the other hand, is used to monitor characteristics that have discrete values and can be counted. Often they can be evaluated with a simple yes-or-no decision. Examples include color, taste, or smell. The monitoring of attributes usually takes less time than for variables because a variable needs to be measured (e.g., the bottle of soft drink contains 15.9 ounces of liquid). An attribute requires only a single decision, such as yes or no, good or bad, acceptable or unacceptable (e.g., the apple is good or rotten, the meat is good or stale, the shoes have a defect or do not have a defect, the light bulb works or it does not work) or counting the number of defects (e.g., the number of broken cookies in the box, the number of dents in the car, the number of barnacles on the bottom of a boat).

Statistical process control is used to monitor many different types of variables and attributes. In the next two sections we look at how to develop control charts for variables and control charts for attributes.

CONTROL CHARTS FOR VARIABLES

Control charts for variables monitor characteristics that can be measured and have a continuous scale, such as height, weight, volume, or width. When an item is inspected, the variable being monitored is measured and recorded. For example, if we were producing candles, height might be an important variable, so we could take samples of candles and measure their heights. Two of the most commonly used control charts for variables monitor both the central tendency of the data (the mean) and the variability of the data (either the standard deviation or the range). Note that each chart monitors a different type of information. When observed values go outside the control limits, the process is assumed not to be in control. Production is stopped, and employees attempt to identify the cause of the problem and correct it. Next we look at how these charts are developed.

Mean (x-Bar) Charts

▶ **x-bar chart**
A control chart used to monitor changes in the mean value of a process.

A mean control chart is often referred to as an **x-bar chart**. It is used to monitor changes in the mean of a process. To construct a mean chart, we first need to construct the center line of the chart. To do this we take multiple samples and compute their means. Usually these samples are small, with about four or five observations. Each sample has its own mean, $\bar{x}$. The center line of the chart is then computed as the mean of all k sample means, where k is the number of samples:

$$\bar{\bar{x}} = \frac{\bar{x}_1 + \bar{x}_2 + \cdots + \bar{x}_k}{k}$$

To construct the upper and lower control limits of the chart, we use the following formulas:

$$\text{Upper control limit (UCL)} = \bar{\bar{x}} + z\sigma_{\bar{x}}$$

$$\text{Lower control limit (LCL)} = \bar{\bar{x}} - z\sigma_{\bar{x}}$$

where $\bar{\bar{x}}$ = the average of the sample means
   z = standard normal variable (2 for 95.44% confidence, 3 for 99.74% confidence)
   $\sigma_{\bar{x}}$ = standard deviation of the distribution of sample means, computed as $\sigma/\sqrt{n}$
   σ = population (process) standard deviation
   n = sample size (number of observations per sample)

Example 6.1 shows the construction of a mean (x-bar) chart.

A quality control inspector at the Cocoa Fizz soft drink company has taken twenty-five samples with four observations each of the volume of bottles filled. The data and the computed means are shown in the table. If the standard deviation of the bottling operation is 0.14 ounces, use this information to develop control limits of 3 standard deviations for the bottling operation.

EXAMPLE 6.1

Constructing a Mean (x-Bar) Chart

Sample Number	Observations (bottle volume in ounces)				Average $\bar{x}$	Range R
	1	2	3	4		
1	15.85	16.02	15.83	15.93	15.91	0.19
2	16.12	16.00	15.85	16.01	15.99	0.27
3	16.00	15.91	15.94	15.83	15.92	0.17
4	16.20	15.85	15.74	15.93	15.93	0.46
5	15.74	15.86	16.21	16.10	15.98	0.47
6	15.94	16.01	16.14	16.03	16.03	0.20
7	15.75	16.21	16.01	15.86	15.96	0.46
8	15.82	15.94	16.02	15.94	15.93	0.20
9	16.04	15.98	15.83	15.98	15.96	0.21
10	15.64	15.86	15.94	15.89	15.83	0.30
11	16.11	16.00	16.01	15.82	15.99	0.29
12	15.72	15.85	16.12	16.15	15.96	0.43
13	15.85	15.76	15.74	15.98	15.83	0.24
14	15.73	15.84	15.96	16.10	15.91	0.37
15	16.20	16.01	16.10	15.89	16.05	0.31
16	16.12	16.08	15.83	15.94	15.99	0.29
17	16.01	15.93	15.81	15.68	15.86	0.33
18	15.78	16.04	16.11	16.12	16.01	0.34
19	15.84	15.92	16.05	16.12	15.98	0.28
20	15.92	16.09	16.12	15.93	16.02	0.20
21	16.11	16.02	16.00	15.88	16.00	0.23
22	15.98	15.82	15.89	15.89	15.90	0.16
23	16.05	15.73	15.73	15.93	15.86	0.32
24	16.01	16.01	15.89	15.86	15.94	0.15
25	16.08	15.78	15.92	15.98	15.94	0.30
Total					398.75	7.17

• **Before You Begin:** Before developing control limits and constructing the chart, calculate the mean of all twenty-five samples. This will be the center line of the control data. Then compute the upper and lower control limits. To complete the control chart, notice that you actually plot sample means, *not* individual samples.

• **Solution:**
The center line of the control data is the average of the samples:

$$\bar{\bar{x}} = \frac{398.75}{25}$$

$$\bar{\bar{x}} = 15.95$$

The control limits are

$$\text{UCL} = \bar{\bar{x}} + z\sigma_{\bar{x}} = 15.95 + 3\left(\frac{0.14}{\sqrt{4}}\right) = 16.16$$

$$\text{LCL} = \bar{\bar{x}} - z\sigma_{\bar{x}} = 15.95 - 3\left(\frac{0.14}{\sqrt{4}}\right) = 15.74$$

The resulting control chart is

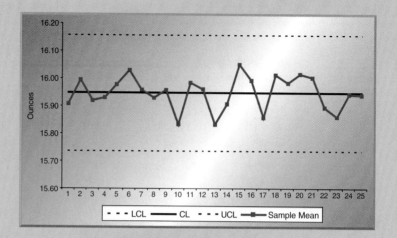

This can also be computed using a spreadsheet, as shown here.

	A	B	C	D	E	F	G
1							
2	**x-Bar Chart: Cocoa Fizz**						
3							
4			F7: =AVERAGE(B7:E7)		G7: =MAX(B7:E7)-MIN(B7:E7)		
5			**Bottle Volume in Ounces**				
6	Sample Num	Obs 1	Obs 2	Obs 3	Obs 4	Average	Range
7	1	15.85	16.02	15.83	15.93	15.91	0.19
8	2	16.12	16.00	15.85	16.01	16.00	0.27
9	3	16.00	15.91	15.94	15.83	15.92	0.17
10	4	16.20	15.85	15.74	15.93	15.93	0.46
11	5	15.74	15.86	16.21	16.10	15.98	0.47
12	6	15.94	16.01	16.14	16.03	16.03	0.20
13	7	15.75	16.21	16.01	15.86	15.96	0.46
14	8	15.82	15.94	16.02	15.94	15.93	0.20
15	9	16.04	15.98	15.83	15.98	15.96	0.21
16	10	15.64	15.86	15.94	15.89	15.83	0.30
17	11	16.11	16.00	16.01	15.82	15.99	0.29
18	12	15.72	15.85	16.12	16.15	15.96	0.43
19	13	15.85	15.76	15.74	15.98	15.83	0.24
20	14	15.73	15.84	15.96	16.10	15.91	0.37
21	15	16.20	16.01	16.10	15.89	16.05	0.31
22	16	16.12	16.08	15.83	15.94	15.99	0.29
23	17	16.01	15.93	15.81	15.68	15.86	0.33
24	18	15.78	16.04	16.11	16.12	16.01	0.34
25	19	15.84	15.92	16.05	16.12	15.98	0.28
26	20	15.92	16.09	16.12	15.93	16.02	0.20
27	21	16.11	16.02	16.00	15.88	16.00	0.23
28	22	15.98	15.82	15.89	15.89	15.90	0.16
29	23	16.05	15.73	15.73	15.93	15.86	0.32
30	24	16.01	16.01	15.89	15.86	15.94	0.15
31	25	16.08	15.78	15.92	15.98	15.94	0.30
32						15.95	0.29
33		Number of Samples		25		Xbar-bar	R-bar
34	Number of Observations per Sample		4				
35				F32: =AVERAGE(F7:F31)		G32: =AVERAGE(G7:G31)	
36							

	A	B	C	D	E	F	G
39	**Computations for X-Bar Chart**				D40: =F32		
40		Overall Mean (Xbar-bar) =		15.95			
41		Sigma for Process =		0.14	ounces	D42: =D41/SQRT(D34)	
42		Standard Error of the Mean =		0.07			
43		Z-value for control charts =		3			
44					D45: =D40		
45		CL: Center Line =		**15.95**	D46: =D40-D43*D42		
46		LCL: Lower Control Limit =		**15.74**	D47: =D40+D43*D42		
47		UCL: Upper Control Limit =		**16.16**			

Another way to construct the control limits is to use the sample range as an estimate of the variability of the process. Remember that the range is simply the difference between the largest and smallest values in the sample. The spread of the range can tell us about the variability of the data. In this case, control limits would be constructed as follows:

$$\text{Upper control limit (UCL)} = \bar{\bar{x}} + A_2\bar{R}$$

$$\text{Lower control limit (LCL)} = \bar{\bar{x}} - A_2\bar{R}$$

where $\bar{\bar{x}}$ = average of the sample means
$\bar{R}$ = average range of the samples
A_2 = factor obtained from Table 6-1.

Notice that A_2 is a factor that includes 3 standard deviations of ranges and is dependent on the sample size being considered.

EXAMPLE 6.2

Constructing a Mean (x-Bar) Chart from the Sample Range

A quality control inspector at Cocoa Fizz is using the data from Example 6.1 to develop control limits. If the average range ($\bar{R}$) for the twenty-five samples is 0.29 ounces (computed as $\frac{7.17}{25}$) and the average mean ($\bar{\bar{x}}$) of the observations is 15.95 ounces, develop 3-sigma control limits for the bottling operation.

- **Before You Begin:** To compute control limits from the sample range, remember that you need to look up the value of factor A_2 from Table 6-1.

- **Solution:**

$$\bar{\bar{x}} = 15.95 \text{ ounces} \qquad \bar{R} = 0.29$$

The value of A_2 is obtained from Table 6-1. For $n = 4$, $A_2 = 0.73$. This leads to the following limits:

$$\text{The center of the control chart} = \text{CL} = 15.95 \text{ ounces}$$

$$\text{UCL} = \bar{\bar{x}} + A_2\bar{R} = 15.95 + (0.73)(0.29) = 16.16$$

$$\text{LCL} = \bar{\bar{x}} - A_2\bar{R} = 15.95 - (0.73)(0.29) = 15.74$$

TABLE 6-1

Factors for three-sigma control limits of $\bar{x}$- and R-charts

Source: Factors adapted from the *ASTM Manual on Quality Control of Materials.*

Sample Size n	Factor for $\bar{x}$-Chart	Factors for R-Chart	
	A_2	D_3	D_4
2	1.88	0	3.27
3	1.02	0	2.57
4	0.73	0	2.28
5	0.58	0	2.11
6	0.48	0	2.00
7	0.42	0.08	1.92
8	0.37	0.14	1.86
9	0.34	0.18	1.82
10	0.31	0.22	1.78
11	0.29	0.26	1.74
12	0.27	0.28	1.72
13	0.25	0.31	1.69
14	0.24	0.33	1.67
15	0.22	0.35	1.65
16	0.21	0.36	1.64
17	0.20	0.38	1.62
18	0.19	0.39	1.61
19	0.19	0.40	1.60
20	0.18	0.41	1.59
21	0.17	0.43	1.58
22	0.17	0.43	1.57
23	0.16	0.44	1.56
24	0.16	0.45	1.55
25	0.15	0.46	1.54

Range (R) Charts

▶ **Range (R) chart**
A control chart that monitors changes in the dispersion or variability of a process.

Range (R) charts are another type of control chart for variables. Whereas x-bar charts measure a shift in the central tendency of the process, range charts monitor the dispersion or variability of the process. The method for developing and using R-charts is the same as that for x-bar charts. The center line of the control chart is the average range, and the upper and lower control limits are computed as follows:

$$CD = \bar{R}$$
$$UCL = D_4\bar{R}$$
$$LCL = D_3\bar{R}$$

where values for D_4 and D_3 are obtained from Table 6-1.

EXAMPLE 6.3

Constructing a Range (R) Chart

The quality control inspector at Cocoa Fizz would like to develop a range (R) chart in order to monitor volume dispersion in the bottling process. Use the data from Example 6.1 to develop control limits for the sample range.

- **Before You Begin:** To develop control limits for the sample range, first compute the average range of all twenty-five samples. Then use Table 6-1 to develop upper and lower control limits. To complete the control chart, you plot the sample ranges.

- **Solution:**
From the data in Example 6.1 you can see that the average sample range is

$$\bar{R} = \frac{7.17}{25}$$

$$\bar{R} = 0.29$$

$$n = 4$$

From Table 6-1 for $n = 4$:

$$D_4 = 2.28$$

$$D_3 = 0$$

$$\text{UCL} = D_4\bar{R} = 2.28(0.29) = 0.6612$$

$$\text{LCL} = D_3\bar{R} = 0(0.29) = 0$$

The resulting control chart is

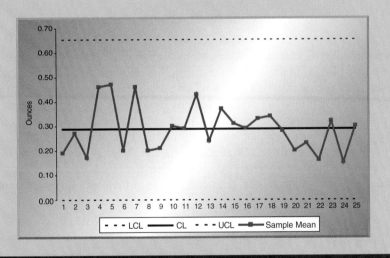

Using Mean and Range Charts Together

You can see that mean and range charts are used to monitor different variables. The mean or x-bar chart measures the central tendency of the process, whereas the range chart measures the dispersion or variance of the process. Since both variables are important, it makes sense to monitor a process using both mean and range charts. It is possible to have a shift in the mean of the product but not a change in the dispersion.

FIGURE 6-6

Process shifts captured by
$\bar{x}$-charts and R-charts

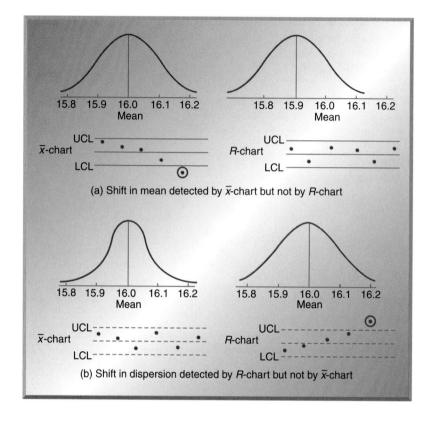

(a) Shift in mean detected by $\bar{x}$-chart but not by R-chart

(b) Shift in dispersion detected by R-chart but not by $\bar{x}$-chart

For example, at the Cocoa Fizz bottling plant the machine setting can shift so that the average bottle filled contains not 16.0 ounces, but 15.9 ounces of liquid. The dispersion could be the same, and this shift would be detected by an x-bar chart but not by a range chart. This is shown in part (a) of Figure 6-6. On the other hand, there could be a shift in the dispersion of the product without a change in the mean. Cocoa Fizz may still be producing bottles with an average fill of 16.0 ounces. However, the dispersion of the product may have increased, as shown in part (b) of Figure 6-6. This condition would be detected by a range chart but not by an x-bar chart. Because a shift in either the mean or the range means that the process is out of control, it is important to use both charts to monitor the process.

CONTROL CHARTS FOR ATTRIBUTES

Control charts for attributes are used for quality characteristics that are counted rather than measured. Attributes are discrete in nature and entail simple yes-or-no decisions, for example, the number of nonfunctioning light bulbs, the proportion of broken eggs in a carton, the number of rotten apples, the number of scratches on a tile, or the number of complaints received. Two of the most common types of control charts for attributes are p-charts and c-charts.

P-charts are used to measure the proportion of items in a sample that are defective. Examples are the proportion of broken cookies in a batch and the proportion of cars produced with a misaligned fender. P-charts are appropriate when both the number of defectives measured and the size of the total sample can be counted. A proportion can then be computed and used as the statistic of measurement.

C-charts count the actual number of defects. For example, we can count the number of complaints from customers in a month, the number of bacteria in a petri dish, or the number of barnacles on the bottom of a boat. However, we *cannot* compute the proportion of complaints from customers, the proportion of bacteria in a petri dish, or the proportion of barnacles on the bottom of a boat. To summarize:

P-charts: Used when observations are placed in *either of two* groups.

Examples:

- Defective or not defective
- Good or bad
- Broken or not broken

C-charts: Used when defects can be *counted* per unit of measure.

Examples:

- *Number of* dents *per* item
- *Number of* complaints *per* unit of time (e.g., hour, month, year)
- *Number of* tears *per* unit of area (e.g., square foot, square meter)

Problem-Solving Tip   The primary difference between using a *p*-chart and a *c*-chart is as follows. A *p*-chart is used when both the total sample size and the number of defects can be computed. A *c*-chart is used when we can compute *only* the number of defects but cannot compute the proportion that is defective.

P-Charts

P-charts are used to measure the proportion that is defective in a sample. The computation of the center line as well as the upper and lower control limits is similar to the computation for the other kinds of control charts. The center line is computed as the average proportion defective in the population, $\bar{p}$. This is obtained by taking a number of sample observations at random and computing the average value of p across all samples.

▶ *p*-chart
A control chart that monitors the *proportion* of defects in a sample.

To construct the upper and lower control limits for a *p*-chart, we use the following formulas:

$$UCL = \bar{p} + z\sigma_p$$

$$LCL = \bar{p} - z\sigma_p$$

where z = standard normal variable
$\bar{p}$ = the sample proportion defective
σ_p = the standard deviation of the average proportion defective

As with the other charts, z is selected to be either 2 or 3 standard deviations, depending on the amount of data we wish to capture in our control limits. Usually, however, the deviations are set at 3.

The sample standard deviation is computed as follows:

$$\sigma_p = \sqrt{\frac{\bar{p}(1 - \bar{p})}{n}}$$

where n is the sample size.

EXAMPLE 6.4

Constructing a p-Chart

A production manager at a tire manufacturing plant has inspected the number of defective tires in twenty random samples with twenty observations each. Following are the number of defective tires found in each sample:

Sample Number	Number of Defective Tires	Number of Observations Sampled	Fraction Defective
1	3	20	0.15
2	2	20	0.10
3	1	20	0.05
4	2	20	0.10
5	1	20	0.05
6	3	20	0.15
7	3	20	0.15
8	2	20	0.10
9	1	20	0.05
10	2	20	0.10
11	3	20	0.15
12	2	20	0.10
13	2	20	0.10
14	1	20	0.05
15	1	20	0.05
16	2	20	0.10
17	4	20	0.20
18	3	20	0.15
19	1	20	0.05
20	1	20	0.05
Total	40	400	

Construct a 3-sigma control chart ($z = 3$) with this information.

- **Before You Begin:** To solve this problem, you should use a p-chart because both the total sample size and the number of defects are provided.

- **Solution:**
The center line of the chart is

$$CL = \bar{p} = \frac{\text{total number of defective tires}}{\text{total number of observations}} = \frac{40}{400} = 0.10$$

$$\sigma_p = \sqrt{\frac{\bar{p}(1 - \bar{p})}{n}} = \sqrt{\frac{(0.10)(0.90)}{20}} = 0.067$$

$$UCL = \bar{p} + z(\sigma_p) = 0.10 + 3(0.067) = 0.301$$

$$LCL = \bar{p} - z(\sigma_p) = 0.10 - 3(0.067) = -0.101 \longrightarrow 0$$

In this example the lower control limit is negative, which sometimes occurs because the computation is an approximation of the binomial distribution. When this occurs, the LCL is rounded up to zero because we cannot have a negative control limit.

The resulting control chart is as follows:

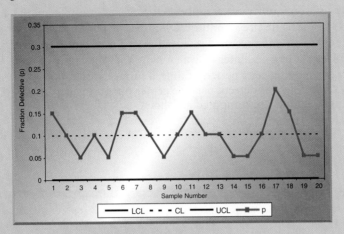

This can also be computed using a spreadsheet, as shown here.

	A	B	C	D
1				
2	**Constructing a p-Chart**			
3				
4	Size of Each Sample		20	
5	Number Samples		20	
6				
7	**Sample #**	**# Defective Tires**	**Fraction Defective**	C8: =B8/C$4
8	1	3	0.15	
9	2	2	0.10	
10	3	1	0.05	
11	4	2	0.10	
12	5	1	0.05	
13	6	3	0.15	
14	7	3	0.15	
15	8	2	0.10	
16	9	1	0.05	
17	10	2	0.10	
18	11	3	0.15	
19	12	2	0.10	
20	13	2	0.10	
21	14	1	0.05	
22	15	1	0.05	
23	16	2	0.10	
24	17	4	0.20	
25	18	3	0.15	
26	19	1	0.05	
27	20	1	0.05	

	A	B	C	D	E	F
29	**Computations for p-Chart**					
30		p bar =	0.100	C30: =SUM(B8:B27)/(C4*C5)		
31		Sigma_p =	0.067	C31: =SQRT((C30*1-C30))/C4)		
32	Z-value for control charts =		3			
33						
34	CL: Center Line =		**0.100**	C34: =C30		
35	LCL: Lower Control Limit =		**0.000**	C35: =MAX(C$30-C$32*C$31,0)		
36	UCL: Upper Control Limit =		**0.301**	C36: =C$30+C$32*C$31		

C-Charts

▶ *c*-chart
A control chart used to monitor the *number* of defects per unit.

C-charts are used to monitor the number of defects per unit. Examples are the number of returned meals in a restaurant, the number of trucks that exceed their weight limit in a month, the number of discolorations on a square foot of carpet, and the number of bacteria in a milliliter of water. Note that the types of units of measurement we are considering are a period of time, a surface area, or a volume of liquid.

The average number of defects, $\bar{c}$, is the center line of the control chart. The upper and lower control limits are computed as follows:

$$\text{UCL} = \bar{c} + z\sqrt{\bar{c}}$$

$$\text{LCL} = \bar{c} - z\sqrt{\bar{c}}$$

EXAMPLE 6.5

Computing a c-Chart

The number of weekly customer complaints are monitored at a large hotel using a *c*-chart. Complaints have been recorded over the past twenty weeks. Develop 3-sigma control limits using the following data:

Week	1	2	3	4	5	6	7	8	9	10	11	12	13	14	15	16	17	18	19	20	Total
No. of Complaints	3	2	3	1	3	3	2	1	3	1	3	4	2	1	1	1	3	2	2	3	**44**

• **Before You Begin:** To solve this problem, you should use a *c*-chart because only the number of defects (complaints) is provided and you cannot compute the proportion defective.

• **Solution:**
The average number of complaints per week is $\frac{44}{20} = 2.2$. Therefore, $\bar{c} = 2.2$.

$$\text{UCL} = \bar{c} + z\sqrt{\bar{c}} = 2.2 + 3\sqrt{2.2} = 6.65$$

$$\text{LCL} = \bar{c} - z\sqrt{\bar{c}} = 2.2 - 3\sqrt{2.2} = -2.25 \longrightarrow 0$$

As in the previous example, the LCL is negative and should be rounded up to zero. Following is the control chart for this example:

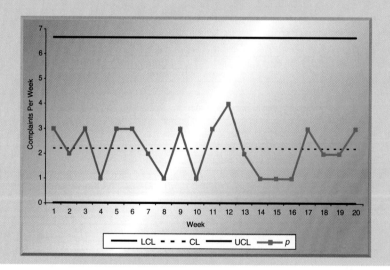

This can also be computed using a spreadsheet, as shown here.

	A	B
1		
2	**Computing a c-Chart**	
3		
4	**Week**	**Number of Complaints**
5	1	3
6	2	2
7	3	3
8	4	1
9	5	3
10	6	3
11	7	2
12	8	1
13	9	3
14	10	1
15	11	3
16	12	4
17	13	2
18	14	1
19	15	1
20	16	1
21	17	3
22	18	2
23	19	2
24	20	3

	A	B	C	D	E	F	G
26	**Computations for a c-Chart**			C27: =AVERAGE(B5:B24)			
27		c bar =	2.2				
28		Z-value for control charts =	3	C30: =SQRT(C27)			
29							
30		Sigma_c =	1.4832397	C32: =C27			
31				C33: =MAX(C$27-C$28*C$28,0)			
32		CL: Center Line =	**2.20**	C34: =C$27+C$28*C$30			
33		LCL: Lower Control Limit =	**0.00**				
34		UCL: Upper Control Limit =	**6.65**				

Before You Go On

We have discussed several types of statistical quality control (SQC) techniques. One category of SQC techniques consists of descriptive statistics such as the mean, range, and standard deviation. These tools are used to describe quality characteristics and relationships. Another category of SQC techniques consists of statistical process control (SPC) methods that are used to monitor changes in the production process. To understand SPC methods you must understand the differences between common and assignable causes of variation. Common causes of variation are random causes that cannot be identified. A certain amount of common or normal variation occurs in every process due to differences in materials, workers, machines, and other factors. Assignable causes of variation, on the other hand, are variations that can be identified and eliminated. An important part of statistical process control (SPC) is monitoring the production process to make sure that the only variations in the process are those due to common or normal causes. Under these conditions, we say that a production process is in a *state of control*.

You should also understand the different types of quality control charts that are used to monitor the production process: *x*-bar charts, *R* (range) charts, *p*-charts, and *c*-charts.

PROCESS CAPABILITY

▶ **Process capability**
The ability of a production process to meet or exceed preset specifications.

▶ **Product specifications**
Preset ranges of acceptable quality characteristics.

So far, we have discussed ways of monitoring the production process to ensure that it is in a *state of control* and that there are no assignable causes of variation. A critical aspect of statistical quality control is evaluating the ability of a production process to meet or exceed preset specifications. This is called **process capability**. To understand exactly what this means, let's look more closely at the term *specification*. **Product specifications**, often called *tolerances*, are preset ranges of acceptable quality characteristics, such as product dimensions. For a product to be considered acceptable, its characteristics must fall within this preset range. Otherwise, the product is not acceptable. Product specifications, or tolerance limits, are usually established by design engineers or product design specialists.

For example, the specifications for the width of a machine part may be specified as 15 inches ± 0.3. This means that the width of the part should be 15 inches, though it is acceptable if it falls within the limits of 14.7 inches and 15.3 inches. Similarly, for Cocoa Fizz, the average bottle fill may be 16 ounces with tolerances of ± 0.2 ounces. Although the bottles should be filled with 16 ounces of liquid, the amount can be as low as 15.8 or as high as 16.2 ounces.

Specifications for a product are preset on the basis of how the product is going to be used or what customer expectations are. As we have learned, any production process has a certain amount of natural variation associated with it. To be capable of producing an acceptable product, the process variation cannot exceed the preset specifications. Process capability thus involves evaluating process variability relative to preset product specifications in order to determine whether the process is capable of producing an acceptable product. In this section we will learn how to measure process capability.

Measuring Process Capability

Simply setting up control charts to monitor whether a process is in control does not guarantee process capability. To produce an acceptable product, the process must be *capable* and *in control* before production begins. Let's look at three examples of process variation relative to design specifications for the Cocoa Fizz soft-drink company. Let's say that the specification for the acceptable volume of liquid is preset at 16 ounces ± 0.2 ounces, which is 15.8 and 16.2 ounces. In part (a) of Figure 6-7 the process produces 99.74 percent (3 sigma) of the product with volumes between 15.8 and 16.2 ounces. You can see that the process variability closely matches the preset specifications. Almost all the output falls within the preset specification range.

In part (b) of Figure 6-7, however, the process produces 99.74 percent (3 sigma) of the product with volumes between 15.7 and 16.3 ounces. The process variability is outside the preset specifications, and a large percentage of the product will fall outside the specified limits. This means that the process is *not capable* of producing the product within the preset specifications.

Part (c) of Figure 6-7 shows that the production process produces 99.74 percent (3 sigma) of the product with volumes between 15.9 and 16.1 ounces. In this case, the process variability is within specifications and the process exceeds the minimum capability.

Process capability is measured by the **process capability index**, C_p, which is computed as the ratio of the specification width to the width of the process variability:

▶ **Process capability index**
An index used to measure process capability.

$$C_p = \frac{\text{specification width}}{\text{process width}} = \frac{\text{USL} - \text{LSL}}{6\sigma}$$

where the specification width is the difference between the upper specification limit (USL) and the lower specification limit (LSL) of the process. The process width is computed as 6 standard deviations (6σ) of the process being monitored. The reason

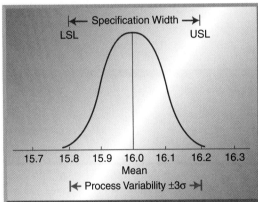

(a) Process variability meets specification width

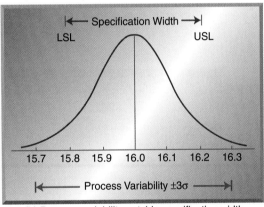

(b) Process variability outside specification width

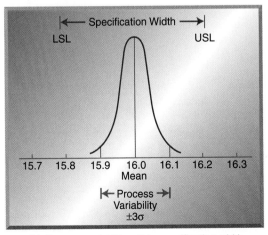

(c) Process variability within specification width

FIGURE 6-7

Relationship between process variability and specification width we use 6σ is that most of the process measurement (99.74 percent) falls within ± 3 standard deviations, which is a total of 6 standard deviations.

There are three possible ranges of values for C_p that also help us interpret its value:

$C_p = 1$: A value of C_p equal to 1 means that the process variability just meets specifications, as in Figure 6-7(a). We would then say that the process is minimally capable.

$C_p \leq 1$: A value of C_p below 1 means that the process variability is outside the range of specification, as in Figure 6-7(b). This means that the process is not capable of producing within specification and must be improved.

$C_p \geq 1$: A value of C_p above 1 means that the process variability is tighter than specifications and the process exceeds minimal capability, as in Figure 6-7(c).

A C_p value of 1 means that 99.74 percent of the products produced will fall within the specification limits. This also means that 0.26 percent (100% − 99.74%) of the products will not be acceptable. Although this percentage sounds very small, when we think of it in terms of parts per million (ppm), we can see that it can still result in a lot of defects. The number 0.26 percent corresponds to 2600 parts per million (ppm) defective ($0.0026 \times 1,000,000$). That number can seem very high if we think of it in terms of 2600 wrong prescriptions out of a million, or 2600 incorrect medical procedures out of a million, or even 2600 malfunctioning aircraft out of a million. You can see that this number of defects is still high. The way to reduce the ppm defective is to increase process capability.

EXAMPLE 6.6

Computing the C_p Value at Cocoa Fizz

Three bottling machines at Cocoa Fizz are being evaluated for their capability:

Bottling Machine	Standard Deviation
A	0.05
B	0.1
C	0.2

If specifications are set between 15.8 and 16.2 ounces, determine which of the machines are capable of producing within specifications.

• **Before You Begin:** To solve this problem, you need to compute the process capability index, C_p, for each machine. The machine with a C_p value at or above 1 is capable of producing within specifications.

• **Solution:**
To determine the capability of each machine, we need to divide the specification width (USL − LSL = 16.2 − 15.8 = .4) by 6σ for each machine:

Bottling Machine	σ	USL − LSL	6σ	$C_p = \dfrac{USL - LSL}{6\sigma}$
A	0.05	0.4	0.3	1.33
B	0.1	0.4	0.6	0.67
C	0.2	0.4	1.2	0.33

Looking at the C_p values, only machine A is capable of filling bottles within specifications because it is the only machine that has a C_p value at or above 1.

C_p is valuable in measuring process capability. However, it has one shortcoming: it assumes that process variability is centered on the specification range. Unfortunately, this is not always the case. Figure 6-8 shows data from the Cocoa Fizz example. In the figure the specification limits are set between 15.8 and 16.2 ounces, with a mean of 16.0 ounces. However, the process variation is not centered; it has a mean of 15.9 ounces. Because of this, a certain proportion of products will fall outside the specification range.

The problem illustrated in Figure 6-8 is not uncommon, and it can lead to mistakes in the computation of the C_p measure. Because of this, another measure for process capability is used more frequently:

$$C_{pk} = \min\left(\frac{\text{USL} - \mu}{3\sigma}, \frac{\mu - \text{LSL}}{3\sigma}\right)$$

where μ = the mean of the process
   σ = the standard deviation of the process

This measure of process capability helps us address a possible lack of centering of the process over the specification range. To use this measure, the process capability of each half of the normal distribution is computed and the minimum of the two is used.

Looking at Figure 6-8, we can see that the computed C_p is 1:

Process mean: $\mu = 15.9$

Process standard deviation $\sigma = 0.067$

LSL $= 15.8$

USL $= 16.2$

$C_p = \dfrac{0.4}{6(0.067)} = 1$

The C_p value of 1.00 leads us to conclude that the process is capable. However, from the graph you can see that the process is *not* centered on the specification range and is producing out-of-spec products. Using only the C_p measure would lead to an incorrect

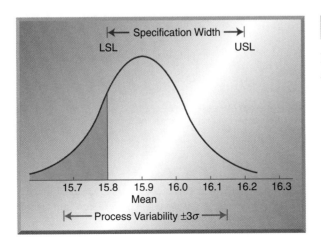

FIGURE 6-8

Process variability not centered across specification width

conclusion in this case. Computing C_{pk} gives us a different answer and leads us to a different conclusion:

$$C_{pk} = \min\left(\frac{USL - \mu}{3\sigma}, \frac{\mu - LSL}{3\sigma}\right)$$

$$C_{pk} = \min\left(\frac{16.2 - 15.9}{3(.1)}, \frac{15.9 - 15.8}{3(.1)}\right)$$

$$C_{pk} = \min(1.00, 0.33)$$

$$C_{pk} = \frac{0.1}{0.3} = 0.33$$

The computed C_{pk} value is less than 1, revealing that the process is not capable.

EXAMPLE 6.7

Computing the C_{pk} Value

Compute the C_{pk} measure of process capability for the following machine and interpret the findings. What value would you have obtained with the C_p measure?

$$\text{Machine data: USL} = 110$$
$$\text{LSL} = 50$$
$$\text{Process } \sigma = 10$$
$$\text{Process } \mu = 60$$

- **Before You Begin:** To solve this problem, you should compute both the C_{pk} and C_p measures and compare the findings. Remember that each measure needs to be at or above 1 for the process to be considered capable.

- **Solution:**
Compute the C_{pk} measure of process capability:

$$C_{pk} = \min\left(\frac{USL - \mu}{3\sigma}, \frac{\mu - LSL}{3\sigma}\right)$$

$$= \min\left(\frac{110 - 60}{3(10)}, \frac{60 - 50}{3(10)}\right)$$

$$= \min(1.67, 0.33)$$

$$= 0.33$$

This means that the process is not capable.
The C_p measure of process capability gives us the following measure:

$$C_p = \frac{60}{6(10)} = 1$$

leading us to believe that the process is capable. The reason for the difference in the measures is that the process is not centered on the specification range, as shown in Figure 6-9.

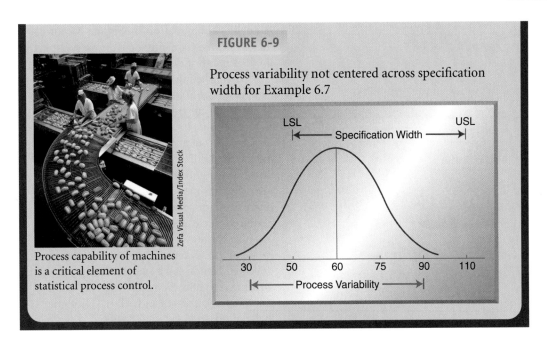

FIGURE 6-9

Process variability not centered across specification width for Example 6.7

Process capability of machines is a critical element of statistical process control.

SIX SIGMA QUALITY

The term **Six Sigma®** was coined by the Motorola Corporation in the 1980s to describe the high level of quality the company was striving to achieve. Sigma (σ) stands for the number of standard deviations of the process. Recall that ± 3 sigma (σ) means that 2600 ppm are defective. The level of defects associated with Six Sigma is approximately 3.4 ppm. Figure 6-10 shows a process distribution with quality levels of ± 3 sigma (σ) and ± 6 sigma (σ). You can see the difference in the number of defects produced.

▶ **Six Sigma quality**
A high level of quality associated with approximately 3.4 defective parts per million.

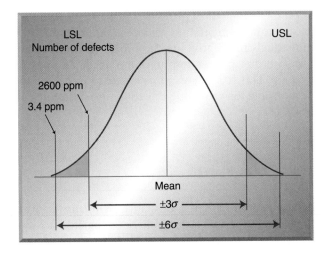

FIGURE 6-10

PPM defective for $\pm 3\sigma$ versus $\pm 6\sigma$ quality (*not to scale*)

Courtesy Motorola

To achieve the goal of Six Sigma, Motorola has instituted a quality focus in every aspect of its organization. Before a product is designed, marketing ensures that product characteristics are exactly what customers want. Operations ensures that exact product characteristics can be achieved through product design, the manufacturing process, and the materials used. The Six Sigma concept is an integral part of other functions as well. It is used in the finance and accounting departments to reduce costing errors and the time required to close the books at the end of the month. Numerous other companies, such as General Electric and Texas Instruments, have followed Motorola's leadership and have also instituted the Six Sigma concept. In fact, the Six Sigma quality standard has become a benchmark in many industries.

There are two aspects to implementing the Six Sigma concept. The first is the use of technical tools to identify and eliminate causes of quality problems. These technical tools include the statistical quality control tools discussed in this chapter and also the problem-solving tools discussed in Chapter 5, such as cause-and-effect diagrams, flow charts, and Pareto analysis. In Six Sigma programs, the use of these technical tools is integrated throughout the entire organizational system.

The second aspect of Six Sigma implementation is people involvement. In Six Sigma, all employees have the training to use technical tools and are responsible for rooting out quality problems. Employees are given martial arts titles that reflect their skills in the Six Sigma process. *Black belts* and *master black belts* are individuals who have extensive training in the use of technical tools and are responsible for carrying out the implementation of Six Sigma. They are experienced individuals who oversee the measuring, analyzing, process controlling, and improving. They achieve this by acting as coaches, team leaders, and facilitators of the process of continuous improvement. *Green belts* are individuals who have sufficient training in technical tools to serve on teams or on small, individual projects.

Successful Six Sigma implementation requires commitment from top company leaders. These individuals must promote the process, eliminate barriers to implementation, and ensure that proper resources are available. A key individual is a *champion* of Six Sigma. This is a person who comes from the top ranks of the organization and is responsible for providing direction and overseeing all aspects of the process.

► ACCEPTANCE SAMPLING

Acceptance sampling, the third branch of statistical quality control, refers to the process of randomly inspecting a certain number of items from a lot or batch in order to decide whether to accept or reject the entire batch. What makes acceptance sampling different from statistical process control is that acceptance sampling is performed either *before* or *after* the process, rather than during the process. Acceptance sampling *before* the process involves sampling materials received from a supplier, such as randomly inspecting crates of fruit that will be used in a restaurant, boxes of glass dishes that will be sold in a department store, or metal castings that will be used in a machine shop. Sampling *after* the process involves sampling finished items that are to be shipped either to a customer or to a distribution center. Examples include randomly testing a certain number of computers from a batch to make sure they meet operational requirements and randomly inspecting snow boards to make sure that they are not defective.

You may be wondering why we would inspect only some items in the lot and not the entire lot. Acceptance sampling is used when inspecting every item is not physically possible or would be overly expensive or when inspecting a large number of items would lead to errors due to worker fatigue. This last concern is especially important when a large number of items are processed in a short period of time. Another example of when acceptance sampling would be used is in destructive testing, such as testing eggs for salmonella or crash-testing vehicles. Obviously, in these cases it would not be helpful to test every item! However, 100 percent inspection does make sense if the cost of inspecting an item is less than the cost of passing on a defective item.

As you will see in this section, the goal of acceptance sampling is to determine the criteria for acceptance or rejection based on the size of the lot, the size of the sample, and the level of confidence we wish to attain. Acceptance sampling can be used in both attribute and variable measures, though it is most commonly used for attributes. In this section we will look at the different types of sampling plans and at ways to evaluate how well sampling plans discriminate between good and bad lots.

Sampling involves randomly inspecting items from a lot.

Sampling Plans

A **sampling plan** is a plan for acceptance sampling that precisely specifies the parameters of the sampling process and the acceptance/rejection criteria. The variables to be specified include the size of the lot (N), the size of the sample inspected from the lot (n), the number of defects above which a lot is rejected (c), and the number of samples that will be taken.

There are different types of sampling plans. Some call for *single sampling*, in which a random sample is drawn from every lot. Each item in the sample is examined and is labeled as either "good" or "bad." Depending on the number of defects or "bad" items found, the entire lot is either accepted or rejected. For example, a lot size of 50 cookies is evaluated for acceptance by randomly inspecting 10 cookies from the lot. The cookies may be inspected to make sure they are not broken or burned. If 4 or more of the 10 cookies inspected are bad, the entire lot is rejected. In this example, the lot size is $N = 50$, the sample size is $n = 10$, and the maximum number of defects at which a lot is accepted is $c = 4$. These parameters define the acceptance sampling plan.

Another type of acceptance sampling is called *double sampling*. This provides an opportunity to sample the lot a second time if the results of the first sample are inconclusive. In double sampling we first sample a lot of goods according to preset criteria for definite acceptance or rejection. However, if the results fall in the middle range,

▶ **Sampling plan**
A plan for acceptance sampling that precisely specifies the parameters of the sampling process and the acceptance/rejection criteria.

they are considered inconclusive and a second sample is taken. For example, a water treatment plant may sample the quality of the water ten times in random intervals throughout the day. Criteria may be set for acceptable or unacceptable water quality, such as 0.05 percent chlorine and 0.1 percent chlorine. However, a sample of water containing between .05 percent and 0.1 percent chlorine is inconclusive and calls for a second sample of water.

In addition to single- and double-sampling plans, there are *multiple-sampling plans*. Multiple sampling plans are similar to double-sampling plans except that criteria are set for more than two samples. The decision as to which sampling plan to select has a great deal to do with the cost involved in sampling, the time consumed by sampling, and the cost of passing on a defective item. In general, if the cost of collecting a sample is relatively high, single sampling is preferred. An extreme example is collecting a biopsy from a hospital patient. Because the actual cost of getting the sample is high, we want to get a large sample and sample only once. The opposite is true when the cost of collecting the sample is low but the actual cost of testing is high. This may be the case at a water treatment plant, where collecting the water is inexpensive but the chemical analysis is costly. In this section we focus primarily on single-sampling plans.

Operating Characteristic (OC) Curves

▶ **Operating characteristic (OC) curve**
A graph that shows the probability or chance of accepting a lot given various proportions of defects in the lot.

As we have seen, different sampling plans have different capabilities for discriminating between good and bad lots. At one extreme is 100 percent inspection, which has perfect discriminating power. However, as the size of the sample inspected decreases, so does the chance of accepting a defective lot. We can show the discriminating power of a sampling plan on a graph by means of an **operating characteristic (OC) curve**. This curve shows the probability or chance of accepting a lot given various proportions of defects in the lot.

Figure 6-11 shows a typical OC curve. The *x* axis shows the percentage of items that are defective in a lot. This is called "lot quality." The *y* axis shows the probability or chance of accepting a lot. You can see that if we use 100 percent inspection, we are certain of accepting only lots with zero defects. However, as the proportion of defects in the lot increases, our chance of accepting the lot decreases. For example, we have a 90 percent probability of accepting a lot with 5 percent defects and an 80 percent probability of accepting a lot with 8 percent defects.

▶ **Acceptable quality level (AQL)**
The small percentage of defects that consumers are willing to accept.

▶ **Lot tolerance percent defective (LTPD)**
The upper limit of the percentage of defective items consumers are willing to tolerate.

Regardless of which sampling plan we have selected, the plan is not perfect. That is, there is still a chance of accepting lots that are "bad" and rejecting "good" lots. The steeper the OC curve, the better our sampling plan is for discriminating between "good" and "bad." Figure 6-12 shows three different OC curves, A, B, and C. Curve A is the most discriminating and curve C the least. You can see that the steeper the slope of the curve, the more discriminating is the sampling plan. When 100 percent inspection is not possible, there is a certain amount of risk for consumers in accepting defective lots and a certain amount of risk for producers in rejecting good lots.

There is a small percentage of defects that consumers are willing to accept. This is called the **acceptable quality level (AQL)** and is generally in the order of 1–2 percent. However, sometimes the percentage of defects that passes through is higher than the AQL. Consumers will usually tolerate a few more defects, but at some point the number of defects reaches a threshold level beyond which consumers will not tolerate them. This threshold level is called the **lot tolerance percent defective (LTPD)**. The

FIGURE 6-11

Example of an operating characteristic (OC) curve

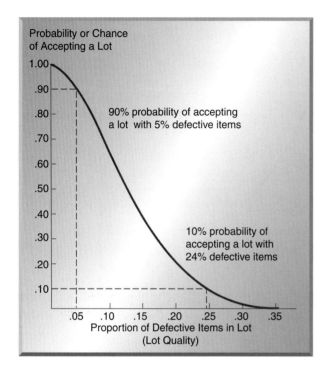

FIGURE 6-12

OC curves with different steepness levels and different levels of discrimination

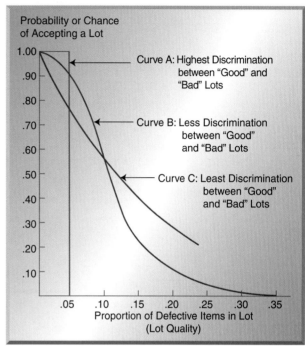

LTPD is the upper limit of the percentage of defective items consumers are willing to tolerate.

Consumer's risk is the chance or probability that a lot will be accepted that contains a greater number of defects than the LTPD limit. This is the probability of making a Type II error—that is, accepting a lot that is truly "bad." Consumer's risk or Type II error is generally denoted by beta (β). The relationships among AQL, LTPD, and β are shown in Figure 6-13. **Producer's risk** is the chance or probability that a lot containing an acceptable quality level will be rejected. This is the probability of making a Type I error—that is, rejecting a lot that is "good." It is generally denoted by alpha (α). Producer's risk is also shown in Figure 6-13.

We can determine from an OC curve what the consumer's and producer's risks are. However, these values should not be left to chance. Rather, sampling plans are usually designed to meet specific levels of consumer's and producer's risk. For example, one common combination is to have a consumer's risk (β) of 10 percent and a producer's risk (α) of 5 percent, though many other combinations are possible.

▶ **Consumer's risk**
The chance of accepting a lot that contains a greater number of defects than the LTPD limit.

▶ **Producer's risk**
The chance that a lot containing an acceptable quality level will be rejected.

Developing OC Curves

An OC curve graphically depicts the discriminating power of a sampling plan. To draw an OC curve, we typically use a cumulative binomial distribution to obtain

FIGURE 6-13

An OC curve showing producer's risk (α) and consumer's risk (β)

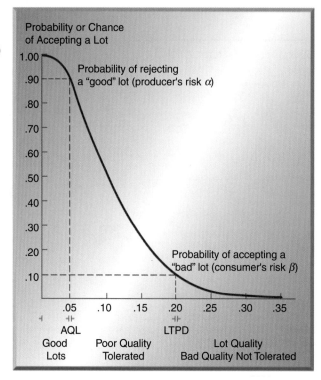

probabilities of accepting a lot given varying levels of lot defects.[1] The cumulative binomial table is found in Appendix C, and a small part is reproduced in Table 6-2. The top of the table shows values of p, which represents the proportion of defective items in a lot (5 percent, 10 percent, 20 percent, etc.). The left-hand column shows values of n, which represents the sample size being considered, and x represents the cumulative number of defects found. Let's use an example to illustrate how to develop an OC curve for a specific sampling plan using the information from Table 6-2.

TABLE 6-2

Partial Cumulative Binomial Probability Table

		\multicolumn{10}{c}{**Proportion of Items Defective (p)**}
		.05	**.10**	**.15**	**.20**	**.25**	**.30**	**.35**	**.40**	**.45**	**.50**
n	x										
5	0	.7738	.5905	.4437	.3277	.2373	.1681	.1160	.0778	.0503	.0313
	1	.9974	.9185	.8352	.7373	.6328	.5282	.4284	.3370	.2562	.1875
	2	.9988	.9914	.9734	.9421	.8965	.8369	.7648	.6826	.5931	.5000

[1]For $n \geq 20$ and $p \leq .05$, a Poisson distribution is generally used.

EXAMPLE 6.8

Constructing an OC Curve

Let's say that we want to develop an OC curve for a sampling plan in which a sample of $n = 5$ items is drawn from lots of $N = 1000$ items. The accept/reject criteria are set up in such a way that we accept a lot if *no more than* one defect ($c = 1$) is found.

• **Solution:**

Let's look at the partial binomial distribution in Table 6-2. Since our criteria require us to sample $n = 5$, we will go to the row where n equals 5 in the left-hand column. The " x " column tells us the cumulative number of defects found at which we reject the lot. Since we are not allowing more than one defect, we look for an x value that corresponds to 1. The row corresponding to $n = 5$ and $x = 1$ tells us our chance or probability of accepting lots with various proportions of defects using this sampling plan. For example, with this sampling plan we have a 99.74 percent chance of accepting a lot with 5 percent defects. If we move down the row, we can see that we have a 91.85 percent chance of accepting a lot with 10 percent defects, a 83.52 percent chance of accepting a lot with 15 percent defects, and a 73.73 percent chance of accepting a lot with 20 percent defects. Using these values and those remaining in the row, we can construct an OC chart for $n = 5$ and $c = 1$. This is shown in Figure 6-14.

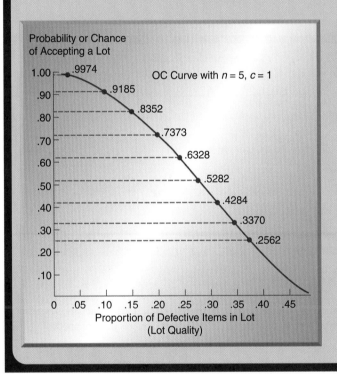

FIGURE 6-14

OC curve with $n = 5$ and $c = 1$

Average Outgoing Quality

As we observed with the OC curves, the higher the quality of the lot, the higher the chance that it will be accepted. Conversely, the lower the quality of the lot, the greater the chance that it will be rejected. Given that some lots are accepted and some rejected, it is useful to compute the **average outgoing quality (AOQ)** of lots to get a sense of the overall outgoing quality of the product. Assuming that all lots have the

▶ **Average outgoing quality (AOQ)**
The expected proportion of defective items that will be passed to the customer under the sampling plan.

same proportion of defective items, the average outgoing quality can be computed as follows:

$$AOQ = (P_{ac})p\left(\frac{N - n}{N}\right)$$

where P_{ac} = probability of accepting a given lot
   p = proportion of defective items in a lot
   N = the size of the lot
   n = the sample size chosen for inspection

Usually, we assume the fraction in the previous equation to equal 1 and simplify the equation to the following form:

$$AOQ = (P_{ac})$$

We can then use the information from Figure 6-14 to construct an AOQ curve for different levels of probabilities of acceptance and different proportions of defects in a lot. As we will see, an AOQ curve is similar to an OC curve.

EXAMPLE 6.9

Constructing an AOQ Curve

Let's go back to our initial example, in which we sampled 5 items ($n = 5$) from a lot of 1000 ($N = 1000$) with an acceptance range of no more than $1(c = 1)$ defect. Here we will construct an AOQ curve for this sampling plan and interpret its meaning.

• **Solution:**
For the parameters $N = 1000$, $n = 5$, and $c = 1$, we can read the probabilities of P_{ac} from Figure 6-14. Then we can compute the value of AOQ as $AOQ = (P_{ac})p$.

p	.05	.10	.15	.20	.25	.30	.35	.40	.45	.50
P_{ac}	.9974	.9185	.8352	.7373	.6328	.5282	.4284	.3370	.2562	.1875
AOQ	.0499	.0919	.1253	.1475	.1582	.1585	.1499	.1348	.1153	.0938

Figure 6–15 shows a graphical representation of the AOQ values. The AOQ varies, depending on the proportion of defective items in the lot. The largest value of AOQ, called the average outgoing quality limit (AOQL), is around 15.85 percent. You can see from Figure 6-15 that the average outgoing quality will be high for lots that are either very good or very bad. For lots that have close to 30 percent of defective items, the AOQ is the highest. Managers can use this information to compute the worst possible value of their average outgoing quality given the proportion of defective items (p). Then this information can be used to develop a sampling plan with appropriate levels of discrimination.

FIGURE 6-15

The AOQ for $n = 5$ and $c = 1$

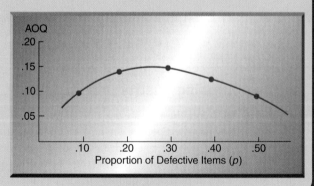

IMPLICATIONS FOR MANAGERS

In this chapter we have learned about a variety of different statistical quality control (SQC) tools that help managers make decisions about product and process quality. However, to use these tools properly managers must make a number of decisions. In this section we discuss some of the most important decisions that must be made when implementing SPC.

How Much and How Often to Inspect

Consider Product Cost and Product Volume As you know, 100 percent inspection is rarely possible. The question then becomes one of how often to inspect in order to minimize the chances of passing on defects and still keep inspection costs manageable. This decision should be related to the *product cost* and *product volume* of what is being produced. At one extreme are high-volume, low-cost items, such as paper, pencils, nuts and bolts, for which the cost of 100 percent inspection would not be justified. Also, with such a large volume, 100 percent inspection would not be possible because worker fatigue sets in and defects are often passed on. At the other extreme are low-volume, high-cost items, such as parts that will go into a space shuttle or be used in a medical procedure, that require 100 percent inspection.

Most items fall somewhere between the two extremes just described. For these items, frequency of inspection should be designed to consider the trade-off between the cost of inspection and the cost of passing on a defective item. Historically, inspections were set up to minimize these two costs. Today, it is believed that defects of any type should not be tolerated and that eliminating them helps reduce organizational costs. Still, the inspection process should be set up to consider issues of product cost and volume. For example, one company will probably have different frequencies of inspection for different products.

Consider Process Stability Another issue to consider when deciding how much to inspect is the stability of the process. Stable processes that do not change frequently do not need to be inspected often. On the other hand, processes that are unstable and change often should be inspected frequently. For example, if it has been observed that a particular type of drilling machine in a machine shop often goes out of tolerance, that machine should be inspected frequently. Obviously, such decisions cannot be made without historical data on process stability.

Consider Lot Size The size of the lot or batch being produced is another factor to consider in determining the amount of inspection. A company that produces a small number of large lots will have a smaller number of inspections than a company that produces a large number of small lots. The reason is that every lot should have some inspection, and when lots are large, there are fewer lots to inspect.

Where to Inspect

Since we cannot inspect every aspect of a process all the time, another important decision is where to inspect. Some areas are less critical than others. Following are some points that are typically considered most important for inspection.

Inbound Materials   Materials that are coming into a facility from a supplier or distribution center should be inspected before they enter the production process. It is important to check the quality of materials before labor is added to it. For example, it would be wasteful for a seafood restaurant not to inspect the quality of incoming lobsters only to later discover that its lobster bisque is bad. Another reason for checking inbound materials is to check the quality of sources of supply. Consistently poor quality in materials from a particular supplier indicates a problem that needs to be addressed.

Finished Products   Products that have been completed and are ready for shipment to customers should also be inspected. This is the last point at which the product is in the production facility. The quality of the product represents the company's overall quality. The final quality level is what will be experienced by the customer, and an inspection at this point is necessary to ensure high quality in such aspects as fitness for use, packaging, and presentation.

Prior to Costly Processing   During the production process it makes sense to check quality before performing a costly process on the product. If quality is poor at that point and the product will ultimately be discarded, adding a costly process will simply lead to waste. For example, in the production of leather armchairs in a furniture factory, chair frames should be inspected for cracks before the leather covering is added. Otherwise, if the frame is defective, the cost of the leather upholstery and workmanship may be wasted.

Which Tools to Use

In addition to where and how much to inspect, managers must decide which tools to use in the process of inspection. As we have seen, tools such as control charts are best used at various points in the production process. Acceptance sampling is best used for inbound and outbound materials. It is also the easiest method to use for attribute measures, whereas control charts are easier to use for variable measures. Surveys of industry practices show that most companies use control charts, especially x-bar and R-charts, because they require less data collection than p-charts.

STATISTICAL QUALITY CONTROL IN SERVICES

Statistical quality control (SQC) tools have been widely used in manufacturing organizations for quite some time. Manufacturers such as Motorola, General Electric, Toyota, and others have shown leadership in SQC for many years. Unfortunately, service organizations have lagged behind manufacturing firms in their use of SQC. The primary reason is that statistical quality control requires measurement, and it is difficult to measure the quality of a service. Remember that services often provide an intangible product and that perceptions of quality are often highly subjective. For example, the quality of a service is often judged by such factors as friendliness and courtesy of the staff and promptness in resolving complaints.

A way to measure the quality of services is to devise quantifiable measurements of the important dimensions of a particular service. For example, the number of complaints received per month, the number of telephone rings after which a response is received, or customer waiting time can be quantified. These types of measurements are not subjective or subject to interpretation. Rather, they can be measured and recorded. As in manufacturing, acceptable control limits should be developed and the variable in question should be measured periodically.

Another issue that complicates quality control in service organizations is that the service is often consumed during the production process. The customer is often present during service delivery, and there is little time to improve quality. The workforce that interfaces with customers is part of the service delivery. The way to manage this issue is to provide a high level of workforce training and to empower workers to make decisions that will satisfy customers.

Tim Boyle/
Getty Images,
Inc.

LINKS TO PRACTICE

The Ritz-Carlton Hotel Company, L.L.C.
www.ritzcarlton.com

Nordstrom, Inc.
www.nordstrom.com

One service organization that has demonstrated quality leadership is The Ritz-Carlton Hotel Company. This luxury hotel chain caters to travelers who seek high levels of customer service. The goal of the chain is to be recognized for outstanding service quality. To this end, computer records are kept of regular clients' preferences. To keep customers happy, employees are empowered to spend up to $2,000 on the spot to correct any customer complaint. Consequently, The Ritz-Carlton has received a number of quality awards, including winning the Malcolm Baldrige National Quality Award twice. It is the only company in the service category to do so.

Another leader in service quality that uses the strategy of high levels of employee training and empowerment is Nordstrom Department Stores. Outstanding customer service is the goal of this department store chain. Its organizational chart places the customer at the head of the organization. Records are kept of regular clients' preferences, and employees are empowered to make decisions on the spot to satisfy customer wants. The customer is considered to always be right.

©AP/Wide World Photos

LINKS TO PRACTICE

Marriott International, Inc.
www.marriott.com

Service organizations must also use statistical tools to measure their processes and monitor performance. For example, the Marriott is known for regularly collecting data in the form of guest surveys. The company randomly surveys as many as a million guests each year. The collected data is stored in a large database and continually examined for patterns, such as trends and changes in customer preferences. Statistical techniques are used to analyze the data and provide important information, such as identifying areas that have the highest impact on performance and those areas that need improvement. This information allows Marriott to provide a superior level of customer service, anticipate customer demands, and allocate resources to service features most important to customers.

STATISTICAL QUALITY CONTROL (SQC) WITHIN OM: HOW IT ALL FITS TOGETHER

The decision to increase the level of quality and reduce the number of product defects requires support from every function within operations management. Two areas of operations management that are particularly affected are product and process design (Chapter 3). Process design needs to be modified to incorporate customer-defined quality and simplification of design. Processes need to be continuously monitored and changed to build quality into the process and reduce variation. Other areas that are affected are job design (Chapter 11), as the role of employees is expanded to become responsible for monitoring quality levels and to use statistical quality control tools. Supply chain management and inventory control (Chapter 12) are also affected as quality standard requirements from suppliers are increased and change are made on the materials used. All areas of operations management are involved when increasing the quality standard of a firm.

STATISTICAL QUALITY CONTROL (SQC) ACROSS THE ORGANIZATION

It is easy to see how operations managers can use the tools of SQC to monitor product and process quality. However, you may not readily see how these statistical techniques affect other functions of the organization. In fact, SQC tools require input from other functions, influence their success, and are actually used in designing and evaluating their tasks.

Marketing plays a critical role in setting up product and service quality standards. It is up to marketing to provide information on current and future quality standards required by customers and those being offered by competitors. Operations managers can incorporate this information into product and process design. Consultation with marketing managers is essential to ensure that quality standards are being met. At the same time, meeting quality standards is essential to the marketing department, since sales of products are dependent on the standards being met.

Finance is an integral part of the statistical quality control process because it is responsible for placing financial values on SQC efforts. For example, the finance department evaluates the dollar costs of defects, measures financial improvements that result from tightening of quality standards, and is actively involved in approving investments in quality improvement efforts.

Human resources becomes even more important with the implementation of TQM and SQC methods, as the role of workers changes. To understand and utilize SQC tools, workers need ongoing training and the ability to work in teams, take pride in their work, and assume higher levels of responsibility. The human resources department is responsible for hiring workers with the right skills and setting proper compensation levels.

Information systems is a function that makes much of the information needed for SQC accessible to all who need it. Information systems managers need to work closely with other functions during the implementation of SQC so that they understand exactly what types of information are needed and in what form. As we have seen, SQC tools are dependent on information, and it is up to information systems managers to make that information available. As a company develops ways of using TQM and SQC tools, information systems managers must be part of this ongoing evolution to ensure that the company's information needs are being met.

All functions need to work closely together in the implementation of statistical process control. Everyone benefits from this collaborative relationship: operations is able to produce the right product efficiently; marketing has the exact product customers are looking for; and finance can boast of an improved financial picture for the organization.

SQC also affects various organizational functions through its direct application in evaluating quality performance in all areas of the organization. SQC tools are not used only to monitor the production process and ensure that the product being produced is within specifications. As we have seen in the Motorola Six Sigma example, these tools can be used to monitor both quality levels and defects in accounting procedures, financial record keeping, sales and marketing, office administration, and other functions. Having high quality standards in operations does not guarantee high quality in the organization as a whole. The same stringent standards and quality evaluation procedures should be used in setting standards and evaluating the performance of all organizational functions.

THE SUPPLY CHAIN LINK

The theme of this chapter has been measuring variation of key quality characteristics of the product or process in order to ensure a high level of quality. We learned that variation in the production process leads to quality defects and contributes to product inconsistency. We also learned how leading companies, such as Intel, make minimizing product variation a priority. For this reason, Intel has implemented the "copy-exactly" program, where the production process must be the same at every facility. This concept of minimizing product variation also has to extend to other members of the supply chain, who are responsible for supplying component parts or delivering the product to the final customer. A product is only as good as the quality of its component parts. Just as variation between production facilities contributes to product inconsistency, so does variation between suppliers, retailers, or distributors. To minimize product variation, precise standards of quality control must be implemented and SQC tools used by others in the supply chain. These standards must be consistent across the supply chain. To help achieve this, many companies today are using ISO 9000 and ISO 14000 certification as part of the supplier selection process. This helps to determine process capability up front and avoid long-term acceptance sampling needs. These standards are especially important in today's environment, where companies find sources of supply all around the globe and need a way to ensure supplier quality. Otherwise, the consequences will be unreliable product quality.

Chapter Highlights

1 Statistical quality control (SQC) refers to statistical tools that can be used by quality professionals. Statistical quality control can be divided into three broad categories: descriptive statistics, acceptance sampling, and statistical process control (SPC).

2 Descriptive statistics are used to describe quality characteristics, such as the mean, range, and variance. Acceptance sampling is the process of randomly inspecting a sample of goods and deciding whether to accept or reject the entire lot. Statistical process control (SPC) involves inspecting a random sample of output from a process and deciding whether the process is producing products with characteristics that fall within preset specifications.

3 There are two causes of variation in the quality of a product or process: common causes and assignable causes. Common causes of variation are random causes that we cannot identify. Assignable causes of variation are those that can be identified and eliminated.

4 A control chart is a graph used in statistical process control that shows whether a sample of data falls within the normal range of variation. A control chart has upper and lower control limits that separate common from assignable causes of variation. Control charts for variables monitor characteristics that can be measured and have a continuum of values, such as height, weight, or volume. Control charts for attributes are used to monitor characteristics that have discrete values and can be counted.

5   Control charts for variables include *x*-bar charts and *R*-charts. *X*-bar charts monitor the mean or average value of a product characteristic. *R*-charts monitor the range or dispersion of the values of a product characteristic. Control charts for attributes include *p*-charts and *c*-charts. *P*-charts are used to monitor the proportion of defects in a sample. *C*-charts are used to monitor the actual number of defects in a sample.

6   Process capability is the ability of the production process to meet or exceed preset specifications. It is measured by the process capability index, C_p, which is computed as the ratio of the specification width to the width of the process variability.

7   The term *Six Sigma* indicates a level of quality in which the number of defects is no more than 3.4 parts per million.

8   The goal of acceptance sampling is to determine criteria for acceptance or rejection based on lot size, sample size, and the desired level of confidence. Operating characteristic (OC) curves are graphs that show the discriminating power of a sampling plan.

9   It is more difficult to measure quality in services than in manufacturing. The key is to devise quantifiable measurements for important service dimensions.

Key Terms

statistical quality control (SQC) 172
descriptive statistics 172
statistical process control (SPC) 173
acceptance sampling 173
common causes of variation 174
assignable causes of variation 174
mean (average) 174
range 175
standard deviation 175
control chart 176

out of control 176
variable 177
attribute 177
x-bar chart 178
range (*R*) chart 182
p-chart 185
c-chart 188
process capability 190
product specifications 190
process capability index 191

Six Sigma quality 195
sampling plan 197
operating characteristic (OC) curve 198
acceptable quality level (AQL) 198
lot tolerance percent defective (LTPD) 198
consumer's risk 199
producer's risk 199
average outgoing quality (AOQ) 201

Formula Review

1. Mean: $\bar{x} = \dfrac{\sum_{i=1}^{n} x_i}{n}$

2. Standard deviation: $\sigma = \sqrt{\dfrac{\sum_{i=1}^{n}(x_i - \bar{x})^2}{n-1}}$

3. Control limits for *x*-bar charts: Upper control limit
    $(\text{UCL}) = \bar{\bar{x}} + z\sigma_{\bar{x}}$

    Lower control limit
    $(\text{LCL}) = \bar{\bar{x}} - z\sigma_{\bar{x}}$

    $\sigma_{\bar{x}} = \dfrac{\sigma}{\sqrt{n}}$

4. Control limits for *x*-bar charts using sample range as an estimate of variability:

    Upper control limit
    $(\text{UCL}) = \bar{\bar{x}} + A_2\bar{R}$

    Lower control limit
    $(\text{LCL}) = \bar{\bar{x}} - A_2\bar{R}$

5. Control limits for *R*-charts: $\text{UCL} = D_4\bar{R}$
    $\text{LCL} = D_3\bar{R}$

6. Control limits for *p*-charts: $\text{UCL} = \bar{p} + z(\sigma_p)$
    $\text{LCL} = \bar{p} - z(\sigma_p)$

7. Control limits for *c*-charts: $\text{UCL} = \bar{c} + z\sqrt{\bar{c}}$
    $\text{LCL} = \bar{c} + z\sqrt{\bar{c}}$

8. Measures for process capability:

    $$C_p = \frac{\text{specification width}}{\text{process width}} = \frac{\text{USL} - \text{LSL}}{6\sigma}$$

    $$C_{pk} = \min\left(\frac{\text{USL} - \mu}{3\sigma}, \frac{\mu - \text{LSL}}{3\sigma}\right)$$

9. Average outgoing quality: $\text{AOQ} = (P_{ac})p$

• Problem 1

A quality control inspector at the Crunchy Potato Chip Company has taken ten samples with four observations each of the volume of bags filled. The data and the computed means are shown in the following table:

Sample of Potato Chip Bag Volume in Ounces

Sample Number	Observations			
	1	2	3	4
1	12.5	12.3	12.6	12.7
2	12.8	12.4	12.4	12.8
3	12.1	12.6	12.5	12.4
4	12.2	12.6	12.5	12.3
5	12.4	12.5	12.5	12.5
6	12.3	12.4	12.6	12.6
7	12.6	12.7	12.5	12.8
8	12.4	12.3	12.6	12.5
9	12.6	12.5	12.3	12.6
10	12.1	12.7	12.5	12.8
Mean $\bar{x}$	12.4	12.5	12.5	12.6

If the standard deviation of the bagging operation is 0.2 ounces, use the information in the table to develop control limits of 3 standard deviations for the bagging operation.

• Before You Begin:

To compute the control limits, you must first calculate the mean of the four samples and then use the UCL and LCL formulas.

• Solution

The center line of the control data is the average of the samples:

$$\bar{\bar{x}} = \frac{12.4 + 12.5 + 12.5 + 12.6}{4} = 12.5 \text{ ounces}$$

The control limits are:

$$\text{UCL} = \bar{\bar{x}} + z\sigma_{\bar{x}} = 12.5 + 3\left(\frac{0.2}{\sqrt{4}}\right) = 12.80$$

$$\text{LCL} = \bar{\bar{x}} - z\sigma_{\bar{x}} = 12.5 - 3\left(\frac{0.2}{\sqrt{4}}\right) = 12.20$$

Following is the associated control chart:

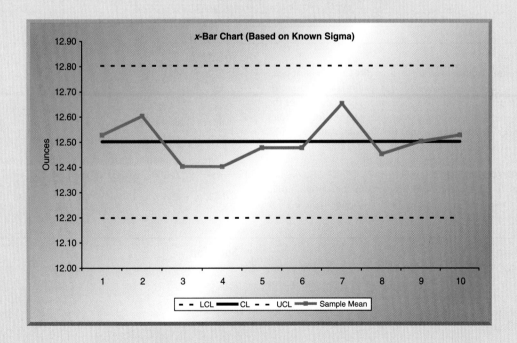

The problem can also be solved using a spreadsheet.

	A	B	C	D	E	F	G
1							
2	**Crunchy Potato Chips Company**						
3							
4		F7: =AVERAGE(B7:E7)					
5			Bag Volume in Ounces				
6	Sample Num	Obs 1	Obs 2	Obs 3	Obs 4	Average	
7	1	12.50	12.30	12.60	12.70	12.53	
8	2	12.80	12.40	12.40	12.80	12.60	
9	3	12.10	12.60	12.50	12.40	12.40	
10	4	12.20	12.60	12.50	12.30	12.40	
11	5	12.40	12.50	12.50	12.50	12.48	
12	6	12.30	12.40	12.60	12.60	12.48	
13	7	12.60	12.70	12.50	12.80	12.65	
14	8	12.40	12.30	12.60	12.50	12.45	
15	9	12.60	12.50	12.30	12.60	12.50	
16	10	12.10	12.70	12.50	12.80	12.53	
17						12.50	
18			Number of Samples	10		Xbar-bar	
19	Number of Observations per Sample			4			
20			F17: =AVERAGE(F7:F16)				
21							
22	**Computations for X-Bar Chart**				D23: =F17		
23		Overall Mean (Xbar-bar) =		12.50			
24		Sigma for Process =		0.2	ounces	D25: =D24/SQRT(D19)	
25		Standard Error of the Mean =		0.1			
26		Z-value for control charts =		3			
27					D28: =D23		
28		CL: Center Line =		12.50	D29: =D23-D26*D25		
29		LCL: Lower Control Limit =		12.20	D30: =D23+D26*D25		
30		UCL: Upper Control Limit =		12.80			

• Problem 2

Use of the sample range to estimate variability can also be applied to the Crunchy Potato Chip operation. A quality control inspector has taken four samples with five observations each, measuring the volume of chips per bag. If the average range for the four samples is 0.2 ounces and the average mean of the observations is 12.5 ounces, develop 3-sigma control limits for the bottling operation.

• Before You Begin:

Recall that to compute control limits from the sample range you need to look up the value of factor A_2 from Table 6-1 for the appropriate value of n. In this problem $n = 5$.

• Solution

$$\bar{\bar{x}} = 12.5 \text{ ounces}$$
$$\bar{R} = 0.2$$

The value of A_2 is obtained from Table 6-1. For $n = 5$, $A_2 = 0.58$. This leads to the following limits:

The center of the control chart is CL = 12.5 ounces
$$\text{UCL} = \bar{\bar{x}} + A_2\bar{R} = 12.5 + (0.58)(0.2) = 12.62$$
$$\text{LCL} = \bar{\bar{x}} - A_2\bar{R} = 12.5 - (0.58)(0.2) = 12.38$$

• Problem 3

Ten samples with five observations each have been taken from the Crunchy Potato Chip Company plant in order to test for volume dispersion in the bagging process. The average sample range was found to be 0.3 ounces. Develop control limits for the sample range.

• Before You Begin:

To compute the control limits for the sample range, remember to look up the values for D_4 and D_3 from Table 6-1 for the appropriate value of n. In this problem $n = 5$.

• Solution

$$\bar{R} = 0.3 \text{ ounces}$$
$$n = 5$$

From Table 6-1 for $n = 5$:
$$D_4 = 2.11$$
$$D_3 = 0$$

Therefore,
$$\text{UCL} = D_4\bar{R} = 2.11(0.3) = 0.633$$
$$\text{LCL} = D_3\bar{R} = 0(0.3) = 0$$

• Problem 4

A production manager at a light bulb plant has inspected the number of defective light bulbs in ten random samples with thirty observations each. Following are the numbers of defective light bulbs found:

Sample	Number Defective	Number of Observations in Sample
1	1	30
2	3	30
3	3	30
4	1	30
5	0	30
6	5	30
7	1	30
8	1	30
9	1	30
10	1	30
Total	17	300

Construct a 3-sigma control chart ($z = 3$) with this information.

• Before You Begin:

To solve this problem, you should use a *p*-chart because both the total sample size and the number of defects are provided.

• Solution

The center line of the chart is:

$$CL = \bar{p} = \frac{\text{number defective}}{\text{number of observations}} = \frac{17}{300} = 0.057$$

$$\sigma_p = \sqrt{\frac{\bar{p}(1 - \bar{p})}{n}} = \sqrt{\frac{(0.057)(0.943)}{30}} = 0.042$$

$$UCL = \bar{p} + z(\sigma_p) = 0.057 + 3(0.042) = 0.183$$

$$LCL = \bar{p} - z(\sigma_p) = 0.057 - 3(0.042) = -0.069 \longrightarrow 0$$

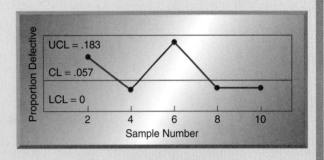

This is also solved using a spreadsheet.

	A	B	C	D	E	F	G
1							
2	**p-Chart for Light Bulb Quality**						
3							
4		Sample Size	30				
5		Number Samples	10				
6							
7	**Sample #**	**# Defectives**	**p**	C8: =B8/C$4			
8	1	1	0.03333333				
9	2	3	0.1				
10	3	3	0.1				
11	4	1	0.03333333				
12	5	0	0				
13	6	5	0.16666667				
14	7	1	0.03333333				
15	8	1	0.03333333				
16	9	1	0.03333333				
17	10	1	0.03333333				
18				C19: =SUM(B8:B17)/(C4*C5)			
19		p bar =	0.05666667	C20: =SQRT((C19*(1-C19))/C4)			
20		Sigma_p =	0.04221199				
21	Z-value for control charts =		3				
22				C23: =C19			
23		CL: Center Line =	**0.05666667**	C24: =MAX(C$19-C$21*C$20,0)			
24		LCL: Lower Control Limit =	**0**	C25: =C$19+C$21*C$20			
25		UCL: Upper Control Limit =	**0.18330263**				

• Problem 5

Kinder Land Child Care uses a c-chart to monitor the number of customer complaints per week. Complaints have been recorded over the past twenty weeks. Develop a control chart with 3-sigma control limits using the following data:

Week	Number of Complaints	Week	Number of Complaints
1	0	11	4
2	3	12	3
3	4	13	1
4	1	14	1
5	0	15	1
6	0	16	0
7	3	17	2
8	1	18	1
9	1	19	2
10	0	20	2
		Total	30

• Before You Begin

Notice that in this problem only the number of defects (complaints) has been collected over time. This means that you cannot compute the proportion that is defective and therefore you should use a c-chart.

• Solution

The average weekly number of complaints is $\frac{30}{20} = 1.5$. Therefore,

$$\text{UCL} = \bar{c} + z\sqrt{\bar{c}} = 1.5 + 3\sqrt{1.5} = 5.17$$

$$\text{LCL} = \bar{c} - z\sqrt{\bar{c}} = 1.5 - 3\sqrt{1.5} = -2.17 \longrightarrow 0$$

The resulting control chart is shown below.

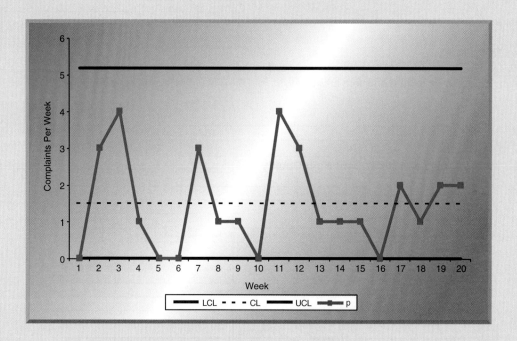

• Problem 6

Three bagging machines at the Crunchy Potato Chip Company are being evaluated for their capability. The following data are recorded:

Bagging Machine	Standard Deviation
A	0.2
B	0.3
C	0.05

If specifications are set between 12.35 and 12.65 ounces, determine which of the machines are capable of producing within specification.

• Before You Begin:

To solve this problem, you need to compute the process capability index, C_p, for each of the three bagging machines. The machine that has a $C_p \geq 1$ is capable of producing within specification.

• Solution

To determine the capability of each machine, we need to divide the specification width (USL − LSL = 12.65 − 12.35 = 0.3) by 6σ for each machine:

Bagging Machine	σ	USL − LSL	6σ	$C_p = \dfrac{USL - LSL}{6\sigma}$
A	0.2	0.3	1.2	0.25
B	0.3	0.3	1.8	0.17
C	0.05	0.3	0.3	1.00

Looking at the C_p values, only machine C is capable of bagging the potato chips within specifications because it is the only machine that has a C_p value at or above 1.

• Problem 7

Compute the C_{pk} measure of process capability for the following machine and interpret the findings. What value would you have obtained with the C_p measure?

Machine data: USL = 80

LSL = 50

Process $\sigma = 5$

Process $\mu = 60$

• Before You Begin:

In this problem you should compute both the C_p and C_{pk} measures following the formulas from the text. For each measure, a numerical value at or above 1 indicates that the process is capable.

• Solution

To compute the C_{pk} measure of process capability:

$$C_{pk} = \min\left(\frac{USL - \mu}{3\sigma}, \frac{\mu - LSL}{3\sigma}\right)$$

$$= \min\left(\frac{80 - 60}{3(5)}, \frac{60 - 50}{3(5)}\right)$$

$$= \min(1.33, 0.67)$$

$$= 0.67$$

This means that the process is not capable. The C_p measure of process capability gives us the following measure:

$$C_p = \frac{30}{6(5)} = 1.0$$

which leads us to believe that the process is capable.

Discussion Questions

1. Explain the three categories of statistical quality control (SQC). How are they different, what different information do they provide, and how can they be used together?

2. Describe three recent situations in which you were directly affected by poor product or service quality.

3. Discuss the key differences between common and assignable causes of variation. Give examples.

4. Describe a quality control chart and how it can be used. What are upper and lower control limits? What does it mean if an observation falls outside the control limits?

5. Explain the differences between x-bar and R-charts. How can they be used together and why would it be important to use them together?

6. Explain the use of p-charts and c-charts. When would you use one rather than the other? Give examples of measurements for both p-charts and c-charts.

7. Explain what is meant by process capability. Why is it important? What does it tell us? How can it be measured?

8. Describe the process of acceptance sampling. What types of sampling plans are there? What is acceptance sampling used for?

9. Describe the concept of Six Sigma quality. Why is such a high quality level important?

Problems

1. A quality control manager at a manufacturing facility has taken four samples with four observations each of the diameter of a part.
   (a) Compute the mean of each sample.
   (b) Compute an estimate of the mean and standard deviation of the sampling distribution.
   (c) Develop control limits for 3 standard deviations of the product diameter.

Samples of Part Diameter in Inches

1	2	3	4
5.8	6.2	6.1	6.0
5.9	6.0	5.9	5.9
6.0	5.9	6.0	5.9
6.1	5.9	5.8	6.1

2. A quality control inspector at the Beautiful Shampoo Company has taken three samples with four observations each of the volume of shampoo bottles filled. The data collected by the inspector and the computed means are shown here:

Samples of Shampoo Bottle Volume in Ounces

Observation	1	2	3
1	19.7	19.7	19.7
2	20.6	20.2	18.7
3	18.9	18.9	21.6
4	20.8	20.7	20.0
Mean	20.0	19.875	20.0

If the standard deviation of the shampoo bottle-filling operation is 0.2 ounces, use the information in the table to develop control limits of 3 standard deviations for the operation.

3. A quality control inspector has taken four samples with five observations each at the Beautiful Shampoo Company, measuring the volume of shampoo per bottle. If the average range for the four samples is 0.4 ounces and the average mean of the observations is 19.8 ounces, develop 3-sigma control limits for the bottling operation.

4. A production manager at Ultra Clean Dishwashing company is monitoring the quality of the company's production process. There has been concern relative to the quality of the operation to accurately fill the 16 ounces of dishwashing liquid. The product is designed for a fill level of 16.00 ± 0.30. The company collected the following sample data on the production process:

	Observations			
Sample	1	2	3	4
1	16.40	16.11	15.90	15.78
2	15.97	16.10	16.20	15.81
3	15.91	16.00	16.04	15.92
4	16.20	16.21	15.93	15.95
5	15.87	16.21	16.34	16.43
6	15.43	15.49	15.55	15.92
7	16.43	16.21	15.99	16.00
8	15.50	15.92	l6.12	16.02
9	16.13	16.21	16.05	16.01
10	15.68	16.43	16.20	15.97

(a) Are the process mean and range in statistical control?
(b) Do you think this process is capable of meeting the design standard?

5. Ten samples with five observations each have been taken from the Beautiful Shampoo Company plant in order to test for volume dispersion in the shampoo bottle-filling process. The average sample range was found to be 0.3 ounces. Develop control limits for the sample range.

6. The Awake Coffee Company produces gourmet instant coffee. The company wants to be sure that the average fill of coffee containers is 12.0 ounces. To make sure the process is in control, a worker periodically selects at random a box of six containers of coffee and measures their weight. When the process is in control, the range of the weight of coffee samples averages 0.6 ounces.
(a) Develop an R-chart and an $\bar{x}$-chart for this process.
(b) The measurements of weight from the last five samples taken of the six containers follow:

Sample	$\bar{x}$	R
1	12.1	0.7
2	11.8	0.4
3	12.3	0.6
4	11.5	0.4
5	11.6	0.9

Is the process in control? Explain your answer.

7. A production manager at a Contour Manufacturing plant has inspected the number of defective plastic molds in five random samples of twenty observations each. Following are the number of defective molds found in each sample:

Sample	Number of Defects	Number of Observations in Sample
1	1	20
2	2	20
3	2	20
4	1	20
5	0	20
Total	6	100

Construct a 3-sigma control chart ($z = 3$) with this information.

8. A tire manufacturer has been concerned about the number of defective tires found recently. In order to evaluate the true magnitude of the problem, a production manager selected ten random samples of twenty units each for inspection. The number of defective tires found in each sample are as follows:
(a) Develop a p-chart with a $z = 3$.
(b) Suppose that the next four samples selected had 6, 3, 3, and 4 defects. What conclusion can you make?

Sample	Number Defective
1	1
2	3
3	2
4	1
5	4
6	1
7	2
8	0
9	3
10	1

9. U-learn University uses a c-chart to monitor student complaints per week. Complaints have been recorded over the past ten weeks. Develop 3-sigma control limits using the following data:

Week	Number of Complaints
1	0
2	3
3	1
4	1
5	0
6	0
7	3
8	1
9	1
10	2

10. University Hospital has been concerned with the number of errors found in its billing statements to patients. An audit of 100 bills per week over the past twelve weeks revealed the following number of errors:

Week	Number of Errors
1	4
2	5
3	6
4	6
5	3
6	2
7	6
8	7
9	3
10	4
11	3
12	4

(a) Develop control charts with $z = 3$.
(b) Is the process in control?

11. Three ice-cream packing machines at the Creamy Treat Company are being evaluated for their capability. The following data are recorded:

Packing Machine	Standard Deviation
A	0.2
B	0.3
C	0.05

If specifications are set between 15.8 and 16.2 ounces, determine which of the machines are capable of producing within specifications.

12. Compute the C_{pk} measure of process capability for the following machine and interpret the findings. What value would you have obtained with the C_p measure?

$$\text{Machine data: USL} = 100$$
$$\text{LSL} = 70$$
$$\text{Process } \sigma = 5$$
$$\text{Process } \mu = 80$$

13. Develop an OC curve for a sampling plan in which a sample of $n = 5$ items is drawn from lots of $N = 1000$ items. The accept/reject criteria are set up in such a way that we accept a lot if no more than one defect ($c = 1$) is found.

14. Quality Style manufactures self-assembling furniture. To reduce the cost of returned orders, the manager of its quality control department inspects the final packages each day using randomly selected samples. The defects include wrong parts, missing connection parts, parts with apparent painting problems, and parts with rough surfaces. The average defect rate is three per day.
(a) Which type of control chart should be used? Construct a control chart with 3-sigma control limits.
(b) Today the manager discovered nine defects. What does this mean?

15. Develop an OC curve for a sampling plan in which a sample of $n = 10$ items is drawn from lots of $N = 1000$. The accept/reject criteria are set up in such a way that we accept a lot if no more than one defect ($c = 1$) is found.

16. The Fresh Pie Company purchases apples from a local farm to be used in preparing the filling for its apple pies. Sometimes the apples are fresh and ripe. Other times they can be spoiled or not ripe enough. The company has decided that it needs an acceptance sampling plan for the purchased apples. Fresh Pie has decided that the acceptable quality level is 2 defective apples per 100, and the lot tolerance proportion defective is 5 percent. Producer's risk should be no more than 5 percent and consumer's risk 10 percent or less.
(a) Develop a plan that satisfies the above requirements.
(b) Determine the AOQL for your plan, assuming that the lot size is 1000 apples.

17. A computer manufacturer purchases microchips from a world-class supplier. The buyer has a lot tolerance proportion defective of 10 parts in 5000, with a consumer's risk of 15 percent. If the computer manufacturer decides to sample 2000 of the microchips received in each shipment, what acceptance number, c, would they want?

18. Joshua Simms has recently been placed in charge of purchasing at the Med-Tech Labs, a medical testing laboratory. His job is to purchase testing equipment and supplies. Med-Tech currently has a contract with a reputable supplier in the industry. Joshua's job is to design an appropriate acceptance sampling plan for Med-Tech. The contract with the supplier states that the acceptable quality level is 1 percent defective. Also, the lot tolerance proportion defective is 4 percent, the producer's risk is 5 percent, and the consumer's risk is 10 percent.

(a) Develop an acceptance sampling plan for Joshua that meets the stated criteria.

(b) Draw the OC curve for the plan you developed.

(c) What is the AOQL of your plan, assuming a lot size of 1000?

19. Breeze Toothpaste Company makes tubes of toothpaste. The product is produced and then pumped into tubes and capped. The production manager is concerned whether the filling process for the tubes of toothpaste is in statistical control. The process should be centered on 6 ounces per tube. Six samples of five tubes were taken and each tube was weighed. The weights are:

	Ounces of Toothpaste per Tube				
Sample	**1**	**2**	**3**	**4**	**5**
1	5.78	6.34	6.24	5.23	6.12
2	5.89	5.87	6.12	6.21	5.99
3	6.22	5.78	5.76	6.02	6.10
4	6.02	5.56	6.21	6.23	6.00
5	5.77	5.76	5.87	5.78	6.03
6	6.00	5.89	6.02	5.98	5.78

(a) Develop a control chart for the mean and range for the available toothpaste data.

(b) Plot the observations on the control chart and comment on your findings.

20. Breeze Toothpaste Company has been having a problem with some of the tubes of toothpaste leaking. The tubes are packed in containers with 100 tubes each. Ten containers of toothpaste have been sampled. The following number of toothpaste tubes were found to have leaks:

Sample	Number of Leaky Tubes	Sample	Number of Leaky Tubes
1	4	6	6
2	8	7	10
3	12	8	9
4	11	9	5
5	12	10	8
		Total	85

Develop a *p*-chart with 3-sigma control limits and evaluate whether the process is in statistical control.

21. The Crunchy Potato Chip Company packages potato chips in a process designed for 10.0 ounces of chips with an upper specification limit of 10.5 ounces and a lower specification limit of 9.5 ounces. The packaging process results in bags with an average net weight of 9.8 ounces and a standard deviation of 0.12 ounces. The company wants to determine if the process is capable of meeting design specifications.

22. The Crunchy Potato Chip Company sells chips in boxes with a net weight of 30 ounces per box (850 grams). Each box contains ten individual 3-ounce packets of chips. Product design specifications call for the packet-filling process average to be set at 86.0 grams so that the average net weight per box will be 860 grams. Specification width is set for the box to weigh 850 ± 12 grams. The standard deviation of the packet-filling process is 8.0 grams per box. The target process capability ratio is 1.33. The production manager has just learned that the packet-filling process average weight has dropped down to 85.0 grams. Is the packaging process capable? Is an adjustment needed?

CASE: Scharadin Hotels

Scharadin Hotels is a national hotel chain started in 1957 by Milo Scharadin. What started as one upscale hotel in New York City turned into a highly reputable national hotel chain. Today, Scharadin Hotels serves over 100 locations and is recognized for its customer service and quality. Scharadin hotels are typically located in large metropolitan areas close to convention centers and centers of commerce. They cater to both business and nonbusiness customers and offer a wide array of services. Maintaining high customer service has been considered a priority for the hotel chain.

A Problem with Quality

The Scharadin Hotel in San Antonio, Texas, had recently been experiencing a large number of guest complaints due to billing errors. The complaints seem to center around guests disputing charges on their final hotel bill. Guest complaints ranged from extra charges, such as meals or services that were not purchased, to confusion for not being charged at all. Most hotel guests use express checkout on their day of departure. With express checkout, the hotel bill is left under the guest's door in the early morning hours and, if all is in order, does not require any additional action on the guest's part. Express checkout is a welcome service by busy travelers who are free to depart the hotel at their convenience. However, the increased number of billing errors began creating unnecessary delays and frustration for the guests who unexpectedly needed to settle their bill with the front desk. The hotel staff often had to calm frustrated guests who were rushing to the airport and were aggravated that they were getting charged for items they had not purchased.

Identifying the Source of the Problem

Larraine Scharadin, Milo Scharadin's niece, had recently been appointed to run the San Antonio hotel. A recent business school graduate, Larraine had grown up in the hotel business. She was poised and confident and understood the importance of high quality for the hotel. When she became aware of the billing problem, she immediately called a staff meeting to uncover the source of the problem.

During the staff meeting discussion quickly turned to problems with the new computer system and software that had been put in place. Tim Coleman, head of MIS, defended the system, stating that it was sound and the problems were exaggerated. Tim claimed that a few hotel guests made an issue of a few random problems. Scott Schultz, head of operations, was not so sure. Scott said that he noticed that the number of complaints seems to have significantly increased since the new system was installed. He said that he had asked his team to perform an audit of fifty random bills per day over the past thirty days. Scott showed the following numbers to Larraine, Tim, and the other staff members.

Day	Number of Incorrect Bills	Day	Number of Incorrect Bills	Day	Number of Incorrect Bills
1	2	11	1	21	3
2	2	12	2	22	3
3	1	13	3	23	3
4	2	14	3	24	4
5	2	15	2	25	5
6	3	16	3	26	5
7	2	17	2	27	6
8	2	18	2	28	5
9	1	19	1	29	5
10	2	20	3	30	5

Everyone looked at the data that had been presented. Then Tim exclaimed, "Notice that the number of errors increases in the last third of the month. The computer system had been in place for the entire month so that can't be the problem. Scott, it is probably the new employees you have on staff that are not entering the data properly." Scott quickly retaliated, "The employees are trained properly! Everyone knows the problem is the computer system!"

The argument between Tim and Scott become heated, and Larraine decided to step in. She said, "Scott, I think it is best if you perform some statistical analysis of that data and send us your findings. You know that we want a high quality standard. We can't be Motorola with Six Sigma quality, but let's try for 3 sigma. Would you develop some control charts with the data and let us know if you think the process is in control?"

Case Questions

1. Set up 3-sigma control limits with the given data.
2. Is the process in control? Why?
3. Based on your analysis, do you think the problem is the new computer system or something else?
4. What advice would you give to Larraine based on the information that you have?

CASE: Delta Plastics, Inc. (B)

Jose De Costa, director of manufacturing at Delta Plastics, sat at his desk looking at the latest production quality report, showing the number and type of product defects per week (see the quality report in Delta Plastics, Inc. Case A, Chapter 5). He was faced with the task of evaluating production quality for products made with two different materials. One of the materials was new and called "super plastic" due to its ability to sustain large temperature changes. The other material was the standard plastic that had been successfully used by Delta for many years.

The company had started producing products with the new "super plastic" material only a month earlier. Jose suspected that the new material could result in more defects during the production process than the standard material they had been using.

Jose was opposed to starting production until R&D had fully completed testing and refining the new material. However, the CEO of Delta ordered production despite objections from manufacturing and R&D. Jose carefully looked at the report in front of him and prepared to analyze the results.

Case Questions

1. Prepare a 3-sigma control chart for both production processes, using the new and standard material (use the quality report in Delta Plastics, Inc. Case A, Chapter 5). Are both processes in control? What can you conclude?
2. Are both materials equally subject to the defects?
3. Given your findings, what advice would you give Jose?

INTERACTIVE CASE   Virtual Company

www.wiley.com/college/reid

On-line Case: Statistical Quality Control at Valley Memorial Hospital

Assignment: *Statistical Quality Control*   This assignment involves controlling nursing hours at Valley Memorial Hospital. Lee Jordan, director of the hospital's Medical/Surgical Nursing Unit, has already told you that VMH employs more than 500 nurses, with an annual nursing budget of $5,000,000. "We're trying for a 5 percent reduction in nursing FTEs—full-time equivalents," he says. "I've been personally recording the nursing hours per patient per day for over three months in Med/Surg. I would like you to look at the numbers and see if you can tell me how to meet our goals."

To access the Web site:

Go to **www.wiley.com/college/reid**
Click **Student Companion Site**
Click **Virtual Company**
Click **Kaizen Consulting, Inc.**
Click **Consulting Assignments**
Click **Statistical Quality Control**

INTERNET CHALLENGE Safe-Air

To gain business experience, you have volunteered to work at Safe-Air, a nonprofit agency that monitors airline safety records and customer service. Your first assignment is to compare three airlines based on their on-time arrivals and departures. Your manager has asked you to get your information from the Internet. Select any three airlines. For an entire week check the daily arrival and departure schedules of the three airlines from your city or closest airport. Remember that it is important to compare the arrivals and departures from the same location and during the same time period to account for factors such as the weather. Record the data that you collect for each airline. Then decide which types of statistical quality control tools you are going to use to evaluate the airlines' performances. Based on your findings, draw a conclusion regarding the on-time arrivals and departures of each of the airlines. Which is best and which is worst? Are there large differences in performance among the airlines? Also describe the statistical quality control tolls you have decided to use to monitor performance. If you have chosen to use more than one tool, are you finding the tools equally useful or is one better at capturing differences in performance? Finally, based on what you have learned so far, how would you perform this analysis differently in the future?

On-line Resources

Companion Website www.wiley.com/college/reid
- Take interactive *practice quizzes* to assess your knowledge and help you study in a dynamic way
- Review *PowerPoint slides* or print slides for notetaking
- Download *Excel Templates* to use for problem solving
- Access the *Virtual Company: Valley Memorial Hospital*
- Find links to *Company Tours* for this chapter
  The Peanut Roaster
  Welded Tubes, Inc.
- Find links for *Additional Web Resources* for this chapter
  American Society for Quality Control, _www.asqc.org_
  Australian Quality Council, _www.aqc.org.au_

Additional Resources Available Only in WileyPLUS
- Use the *e-Book* and launch directly to all interactive resources
- Take the interactive *Quick Test* to check your understanding of the chapter material and get immediate feedback on your responses.
- Check your understanding of the key vocabulary in the chapter with *Interactive Flash Cards*
- Use the *Animated Demo Problems* to review key problem types.
- Practice for your tests with *additional problem sets*
- *And more!*

Selected Bibliography

Brue, G. *Six Sigma for Managers*. New York: McGraw-Hill, 2002.

Duncan, A.J. *Quality Control and Industrial Statistics*. Fifth Edition. Homewood, Ill.: Irwin, 1986.

Evans, James R., and William M. Lindsay. *The Management and Control of Quality*, Fourth Edition. Cincinnati: South-Western, 1999.

Feigenbaum, A.V. *Total Quality Control*. New York: McGraw-Hill, 1991.

Grant, E.L., and R.S. Leavenworth. *Statistical Quality Control*. Sixth Edition. New York: McGraw-Hill, 1998.

Hoyer, R.W., and C.E. Wayne. "A Graphical Exploration of SPC, Part 1." *Quality Progress*, 29, 5, May 1996, 65–73.

Juran, J.M., and F.M. Gryna. *Quality Planning and Analysis*, Second Edition. New York: McGraw-Hill, 1980.

Spector, Robert E. "How Constraint Management Enhances Lean and Six Sigma," *Supply Chain Management Review* Jan.–Feb. 2006, 42–47.

Wadsworth, H.M., K.S. Stephens, and A.B. Godfrey. *Modern Methods for Quality Control and Improvement*. New York: Wiley, 1986.

CHAPTER 7

Just-in-Time and Lean Systems

Before studying this chapter you should know or, if necessary, review

1. JIT as a trend in OM, Chapter 1, page 15.
2. Time as a competitive priority, Chapter 2, page 37.
3. Total quality management concepts, Chapter 5, pages 142–164.

LEARNING OBJECTIVES

After studying this chapter you should be able to

1 Explain the core beliefs of the just-in-time (JIT) philosophy.

2 Describe the meaning of waste in JIT.

3 Explain the differences between "push" and "pull" production systems.

4 Explain the key elements of JIT manufacturing.

5 Explain the elements of total quality management (TQM) and their role in JIT.

6 Describe the role of people in JIT and why respect for people is so important.

7 Understand the impact of JIT on service and manufacturing organizations.

8 Understand the impact of JIT on all functional areas of the company.

CHAPTER OUTLINE

WHAT'S IN OM FOR ME?

 ACC   **FIN**   **MKT**   **OM**   **HRM**   **MIS**

How many times have you looked frantically for a school paper or notebook, only to find it much later in the most unexpected place? Have you ever wasted time looking for a personal item—say, a particular shirt or shoes or maybe a bill you needed to pay—and wondered how much easier life would be if everything was in its place? Have you ever purchased extra amounts of an item, maybe paper towels or laundry detergent, and then found that they were taking up space and getting in the way? Wouldn't life be much simpler if you could somehow receive the items that you need exactly when you need them, without having to keep extra quantities in storage?

We have all experienced these situations. They illustrate the problem of waste: wasted time looking for things we misplaced, wasted space and cost of keeping extra items, and wasted energy because of frustration of not finding things when we need them. These are the types of problems that just-in-time systems (JIT) seek to eliminate.

Waste has a large negative impact on the functioning of a business, resulting in high cost and lost customers. To eliminate these problems, many companies have turned to JIT. In fact, today the entire auto industry uses JIT as a standard of operations. DaimlerChrysler's plants use JIT principles to keep low levels of inventories of raw materials and parts. Saturn relies on JIT principles to keep a uniform flow of parts from its suppliers. BMW is using JIT principles to create an easy vehicle-ordering system for customers and a flexible operation that can rapidly respond to customer demands. However, JIT principles are not just used in manufacturing. They are equally applicable in services and are seen in companies such as McDonald's, Wendy's, Pizza Hut, and FedEx.

▶ **Just-in-time (JIT) philosophy**
Getting the right quantity of goods at the right place at the right time.

▶ **Waste**
Anything that does not add value.

▶ **A broad view of JIT**
A philosophy that encompasses the entire organization.

The **just-in-time (JIT) philosophy** in the simplest form means getting the right quantity of goods at the right place and at the right time. The goods arrive just-in-time, which is where the term *JIT* comes from. Although many people think that JIT is an inventory reduction program or another type of manufacturing process, it is far more than that. JIT is an all-encompassing philosophy that is founded on the concept of eliminating waste. The word *waste* might make you think of garbage, or paper, or inventory. But JIT considers **waste** anything that does not add value—*anything*.

The **broad view of JIT** is now often termed *lean production* or *lean systems*. Its implementation has contributed to the success of many organizations and is used by companies worldwide. The benefits that can be attained through JIT are so impressive that JIT has become a standard of operations in many industries, including the auto and computer industries. However, JIT is applicable to service organizations as well as to manufacturing and can even be used in your everyday life. JIT is not about any one factor, such as quality or inventory or efficiency. It is an entirely different way of looking at things. As we will see, JIT is a philosophy that overrides all aspects of the organization, from administrative issues to manufacturing, worker management, supplier management, and even housekeeping. It has contributed to the success of companies like Toyota (called the Toyota Production System or "TPS"), Honda (called "the Honda Way"), and General Motors, and it can even contribute to success in your own life.

THE PHILOSOPHY OF JIT

The philosophy of JIT originated in Japan. After World War II, the Japanese set themselves the goal of strengthening their industrial base, which included full employment and a healthy trade balance. Just-in-time (JIT) developed out of the nation's need to survive after the devastation caused by the war. Although many authors say that the origins of JIT can be traced back to the early 1900s, no one can argue that the philosophy gained worldwide prominence in the 1970s. It was developed at the Toyota Motor Company, and the person most often credited with its development is Taiichi Ohno, a vice president of the company. JIT helped propel Toyota into a leadership position in the areas of quality and delivery. Since then, JIT has been widely adopted in all types of industries and has been credited with impressive benefits, including significant reductions in operating costs, improved quality, and increased customer responsiveness. Companies such as Honda, General Motors, GE, Ford, Boeing, Hewlett-Packard, and IBM are among those that have made JIT part of their operations.

The central belief of the JIT philosophy is *elimination of waste*, but there are other beliefs that help define JIT philosophy. These include a broad view of operations, simplicity, continuous improvement, visibility, and flexibility. Next we look more closely at each of these beliefs.

▶ **Defining beliefs of JIT**
Broad view of operations, simplicity, continuous improvement, visibility, and flexibility.

Boeing production line

Tom & Pat Leeson/Photo Researchers

Eliminate Waste

▶ **Types of waste**
Material, energy, time, and space.

The underlying premise of JIT is that all waste must be eliminated. Many think that the roots of the philosophy can be traced to the Japanese environment, which lacks space and natural resources. Because of this, the Japanese have been forced to learn to use all their resources very efficiently, and waste of any kind is not tolerated. In JIT *waste* is anything that does not add value. **Types of waste** can include material, such as excess inventory to protect against uncertain deliveries by suppliers or poor quality. Waste can be equipment that is used as a backup because regular equipment is not maintained properly. Other types of waste include time, energy, space, or human activity that does not contribute to the value of the product or service being produced.

The concept of waste addresses every aspect of the organization and has a far-reaching impact. For example, waste can be found in the production process itself, and JIT requires perfect synchronization in order to eliminate waiting and excess stock. Waste is also found in improper layout that necessitates the transportation of goods from one part of the facility to another. JIT requires a streamlined layout design so that resources are in close proximity to one another and material handling is kept to a minimum. Also, JIT requires compact layouts and increased visibility so that everyone can see what everyone else is doing. Waste can also take the form of poor quality, because scrap and rework cost money and add no value. Total quality management (TQM) programs thus are an integral part of JIT. Waste is also found in unnecessary motion, and JIT requires studying processes to eliminate unnecessary steps.

A Broad View of Operations

▶ **Broad view of the organization**
Tasks and procedures are important only if they meet the company's overall goals.

Part of the philosophy of JIT is that everyone in the organization should have a **broad view of the organization** and work toward the same goal, which is serving the customer. In traditional organizations, it is very easy for employees to focus exclusively on their own jobs and have a narrow view of the organization that includes only their assigned tasks. Companies whose employees have a narrow view become production-oriented, forgetting that individual tasks and procedures are important only if they meet the overall goals of the company. One example is an employee who will not help a customer with a problem, saying, "It's not my job." This might occur at a grocery store when a customer asks for the location of an item from an employee who is "only responsible for stocking shelves." A broad view of operations involves understanding that all employees are ultimately responsible for serving the customer.

Simplicity

▶ **Simplicity**
The simpler a solution, the better it is.

JIT is built on **simplicity**—the simpler the better. JIT encourages employees to think about problems and come up with simple solutions. Although this may seem easy and crude, it is actually quite difficult. It is often tempting to solve an organizational problem using a complex and perhaps expensive method. It is far more difficult to think of a simple solution that goes directly to the root of the problem. The value of simple solutions is demonstrated by a company whose delivery truck was lodged in a passageway because it was too high to pass through. Many costly and complex solutions were being considered, such as getting a smaller truck or expanding the height of the doorway. After a bit of thought, an employee came up with a simple solution: reduce the air in the tires to bring down the height of the truck. The solution worked.

Continuous Improvement

A major aspect of the JIT philosophy is an emphasis on quality. **Continuous improvement**, called **kaizen** by the Japanese, in every aspect of the operation is a cornerstone of this philosophy. Continuous improvement applies to everything from reducing costs to improving quality to eliminating waste.

To understand the full impact of continuous improvement, try answering this question: When has JIT been implemented fully? The answer: Never. The reason is that an organization is never perfect and can always be improved in some way.

A number of companies are utilizing a powerful JIT approach called the "kaizen blitz." This is an improvement tool that utilizes cross-functional teams to plan and deliver improvements to specific processes during two- or three-day marathon sessions. This process allows a small group of people to concentrate on a bite-size chunk of the problem for a short period of time. Companies find that a kaizen blitz can quickly deliver dramatic and low-cost improvements to processes.

▶ **Continuous improvement (kaizen)**
A philosophy of never-ending improvement.

Visibility

Part of the JIT philosophy is to make all waste **visible**. Waste can be eliminated only when it is seen and identified. Also, if we see waste we can come up with simple solutions to eliminate it. When waste is hidden we forget about it, which creates problems.

Think about the closets in your home. Because the closet doors are closed, we often forget the clutter and junk we have inside. Now imagine that the closet doors were open and the inside was visible to us and everyone else. Certainly it would remind us that we need to eliminate the clutter.

JIT facilities are open and clean, with plenty of floor space. There is no clutter, and everyone can see what everyone else is doing. No one can hide extra inventory in a corner of his or her office or take a short nap in the afternoon. Also, part of the JIT philosophy is that a cluttered environment creates confusion and disrespect toward the workplace. By contrast, a clean and orderly environment creates calm and clear thoughts. Just because space is available, it should not automatically be filled. Visibility allows us to readily see waste. We can then eliminate it.

▶ **Visibility**
Problems must be visible to be identified and solved.

Flexibility

JIT was based on the need for survival, and survival means being **flexible** in order to adapt to changes in the environment. A company can be flexible in many ways. First, flexibility can mean being able to make changes in the volume of a product produced. JIT accomplishes this by keeping the costs of facilities, equipment, and operations at such a low level that breaking even typically is not a problem.

A second way in which a company can be flexible is by being able to produce a wide variety of products. Although this is difficult to achieve, JIT systems are designed with the ability to produce different product models with different features through a manufacturing process that can easily switch from one product type to another by flexible workers who can perform many different tasks. Part of the JIT philosophy is to design operations that are highly efficient but flexible in order to accommodate changing customer demands.

▶ **Flexibility**
A company can quickly adapt to the changing needs of its customers.

ELEMENTS OF JIT

► **JIT system**
The three elements are just-in-time manufacturing, total quality management, and respect for people.

Now that you understand the core beliefs that define the philosophy of JIT, let's look at the major elements that make up a **JIT system**. Three basic elements work together to complete a JIT system: *just-in-time manufacturing, total quality management*, and *respect for people*. These are shown in Figure 7-1 as overlapping circles. Often, it is assumed that JIT refers only to just-in-time manufacturing. However, this is only one element of JIT. Each of the three elements is dependent on the others to create a true JIT system.

Just-in-Time Manufacturing

► **Just-in-time manufacturing**
The element of JIT that focuses on the production system to achieve value-added manufacturing.

JIT is a philosophy based on elimination of waste. Another way to view JIT is to think of it as a philosophy of *value-added manufacturing*. By focusing on value-added processes, JIT is able to achieve high-volume production of high-quality, low-cost products while meeting precise customer needs. **Just-in-time manufacturing** is the element of JIT that focuses directly on the production system to make this possible. Many aspects of JIT manufacturing combine to provide a performance advantage. Later in the chapter we will look at some aspects of JIT manufacturing in more detail. First, let's take an overall view.

The manufacturing process in JIT starts with the final assembly schedule, often called the *master production schedule*, which is a statement of which products and quantities will be made in specific time periods. The master production schedule is usually fixed for a few months into the future to allow all work centers and suppliers to plan their schedules. For the current month, the schedule is "leveled," or developed so that the same amount of each product is produced in the same order every day. Note that with this arrangement there is repetition in the schedule from day to day, which places a constant demand on suppliers and work centers. Also, some quantity of every item is produced every day in accordance with what is needed. This is very different from traditional operations, which typically produce a large quantity of one product on one day. Since this quantity is usually more than what is immediately needed, the goods are stored in inventory. On a second day a large quantity of another product is produced, and it, too, is stored in inventory, resulting in high inventory costs.

JIT relies on a coordination system that withdraws parts from a previous work center and moves them to the next. The system typically relies on cards, called *kanban*, to *pull* the needed products through the production system. For this reason, JIT is often

FIGURE 7-1

The three elements of JIT

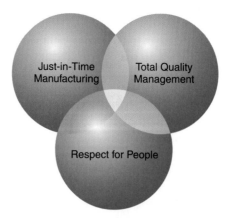

referred to as a *pull system.* The kanban specifies what is needed. There is no excess production because the only products and quantities produced are those specified by the kanban. Traditional manufacturing systems, in contrast, are *push* systems: they push products through the production system by producing an amount that has been set by a forecast of future demand. This type of production results in a higher level of inventory, which is stored for future consumption. Later in the chapter we will look in detail at how the kanban system works.

The reason traditional systems produce large quantities of one type of product before switching to production of another is high **setup cost.** This is the cost incurred when equipment is set up for a new production run. Setup includes activities such as recalibrating and cleaning equipment, changing blades, and readjusting equipment settings. Because setup costs are high in traditional systems, the objective is to produce as many units of a product as possible before having to incur the setup cost again. Of course, that means incurring a high inventory cost because of the extra goods that are kept in storage. JIT systems have been very efficient at reducing setup costs, which is a key to the success of JIT manufacturing. Setup times have been reduced from hours to mere seconds, and the goal is to reduce them to zero. Low setup times mean that small lot sizes of products can be produced as needed and that production lead times will be shorter. The ultimate goal of JIT is to produce products in a lot size of 1.

A major aspect of JIT manufacturing is its view of inventory. JIT manufacturing views inventory as a waste that needs to be eliminated. According to JIT, inventory is carried to cover up a wide variety of problems, such as poor quality, slow delivery, inefficiency, lack of coordination, and demand uncertainty. Inventory costs money and provides no value. Inventory also hurts the organization in another way: it does not allow us to see problems. According to JIT, by eliminating inventory we can clearly identify problems and work to eliminate them. An analogy that is often used to describe JIT's view of inventory is that of a stream, as shown in Figure 7-2. The rocks in the stream represent problems. When the water in the stream covers the rocks we cannot see what they are. By reducing the amount of water in the stream (by reducing inventory), we can finally identify the problems. However, identifying the problems is not enough—we have to solve them.

▶ **Setup cost**
Cost incurred when setting up equipment for a production run.

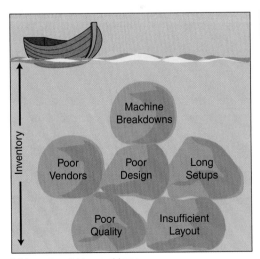

(a) Inventory hides problems

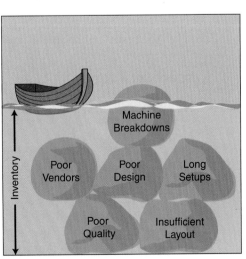

(b) Reducing inventory exposes problems

FIGURE 7-2

Inventory hides problems

In sum, JIT manufacturing is an efficiently coordinated production system that makes it possible to deliver the right quantities of products to the place they are needed just in time.

Total Quality Management (TQM)

► **Total quality management (TQM)**
An integrated effort designed to improve quality performance at every level of the organization.

The second major element of JIT is **total quality management** (**TQM**), which is integrated into all functions and levels of the organization. The foundation of JIT is to produce the exact product that the customer wants. Quality is defined by the customer, and an effort is made by the whole company to meet the customer's expectations.

Quality is an integral part of the organization; it permeates every activity and function. The benefits of JIT cannot occur if the company is not working toward eliminating scrap and rework. Traditional quality control systems use the concept of *acceptable quality level (AQL)* to indicate the acceptable number of defective parts. In JIT there is no such measure—no level of defects other than zero is acceptable.

Poor quality is considered a waste in JIT. Quality defects lead to scrap, rework, servicing returned parts, and customer dissatisfaction. Quality defects cost money and can lead to lost customers. In JIT the entire organization is responsible for quality. Rather than hide poor quality or blame it on others, it is everyone's goal to uncover and correct quality problems.

► **Quality at the source**
Uncovering the root cause of a quality problem.

The concept of **quality at the source** is part of JIT. The objective is not only to identify a quality problem but to uncover its root cause. Simply identifying and removing a defective product does not solve the problem. If the cause of the problem is not identified, the problem will keep repeating itself. For example, a quality control check in a bakery might reveal that pies are overcooked and burned. Quality at the source tells us to identify the cause of the problem, such as an incorrect temperature setting or too long a baking time. Simply removing the burned pies does not eliminate the cause of the problem; overcooking will continue to occur.

The concept of continuous improvement is embedded in quality, which means that the company must continuously and actively work to improve. In JIT continuous improvement governs everything, from reducing the number of defects to lowering setup costs and lot sizes. For example, when implementing a JIT program we cannot expect to eliminate inventories immediately. Continuous improvement tells us that we must do it gradually, slowly identifying and solving problems and then reducing inventory appropriately. However, continuous improvement goes beyond JIT manufacturing. It includes improvement of worker skills, supplier quality and relationships, and even the performance of management.

Respect for People

► **Respect for people**
An element of JIT that considers human resources as an essential part of the JIT philosophy.

The third element of JIT is **respect for people**. Often, the study of JIT focuses exclusively on JIT manufacturing. However, the involvement of workers is central to the JIT philosophy. None of the improvements developed by JIT could be possible without respect for people. JIT requires total organizational reform and participation by everyone in the company. Everyone is equally important and equally involved. In a JIT system all functions of the company must work together to meet customer needs. Managers are not isolated in an administrative wing but spend time on the production floor.

Employees in JIT organizations are expected to be active participants in meeting customer needs, from developing improvements in the production process to making sure quality standards are met at every level. JIT also relies on workers to perform multiple tasks and to work in teams, including management, labor, staff, and even suppliers.

JIT considers people to be a company's most precious resource. The JIT philosophy believes in treating all employees with respect, providing job security, and offering significant rewards for well-performed tasks. Respect for people extends to suppliers. JIT believes in developing long-term relationships with suppliers in a partnership format.

The Saturn Corporation provides an excellent example of the success that can be achieved by respecting and empowering people. Saturn is a highly successful division of General Motors Corporation, producing and marketing vehicles in the small-car market segment. Saturn has been recognized for its quality and productivity. It has also become a model for successful use of self-managed teams.

Joe Polimeni/UPI/Landov LLC

LINKS TO PRACTICE

Saturn Corporation
www.saturn.com

Self-managed teams are groups of workers that have no supervisors, inspectors, time clocks, or union stewards. Each team is responsible for every aspect of its business, such as productivity, quality, cost, production, and people. The crux of self-managed teams is respect for employees and their ability to be in charge of their own work. At Saturn, people are empowered to make decisions and everyone is involved in the decision-making process. Workers are motivated through a system that directly rewards them for achieving their goals. Saturn views its workforce as a long-term asset, providing ongoing training and encouraging a sense of security and organizational belonging. Saturn demonstrates the success that can be attained when an organization respects its people.

Before You Go On

You should know that JIT is an all-encompassing philosophy that affects every level and function of the organization. The beliefs that make up the JIT philosophy include the following: (1) *elimination of waste*, (2) *a broad view of operations*, (3) *simplicity*, (4) *continuous improvement*, (5) *visibility*, and (6) *flexibility*. The philosophy of JIT is founded on these beliefs, and they govern all aspects of the organization. These beliefs are embodied in three specific elements: (1) JIT manufacturing, (2) total quality management, and (3) respect for people. In the next section we look at specific features of each of these elements.

JUST-IN-TIME MANUFACTURING

The Pull System

Traditional manufacturing operations are push-type systems. They are based on the assumption that it is better to anticipate future production requirements and plan for them. Traditional systems produce goods in advance in order to have products in place when demand occurs. Products are pushed through the system and are stored in anticipation of demand, which often results in overproduction because anticipated demand may not materialize. Also, there are costs associated with having inventories of products sitting in storage and waiting for consumption.

As noted earlier, JIT uses a **pull system** rather than a push system to move products through the facility. Communication in JIT starts either with the last workstation in the production line or with the customer and works backward through the system. Each station requests the precise amount of products that is needed from the previous workstation. If products are not requested, they are not produced. In this manner, no excess inventory is generated.

To see the difference between a push and a pull system, suppose that you have decided to have a backyard cookout for your friends. You have invited twenty people and are anticipating that each one will eat at least one hamburger and one hot dog. When your friends arrive, you decide to cook all the meat as quickly as you can process it on your grill, given your anticipation of demand for food. Your goal is to make it available for your guests. At the end of the party, however, you find that you are left with some hamburgers and quite a few hot dogs. Some people didn't want both a hamburger and a hot dog, some people didn't like one or the other, and some were vegetarian and didn't want either one. As a result, after the party you are left with some cold, dried-out meat. This is the problem with a push system that produces large quantities in anticipation of demand that may or may not materialize.

Another way you could handle the cookout would be to grill a smaller quantity of meat—say, three hamburgers and three hot dogs, an amount that will fit on a serving tray. When the serving tray becomes empty you could fill it with the meat on the grill, again enough to fill the tray. When the meat that was on the grill is removed, you can put fresh meat on the grill, again in a small quantity. No additional meat is placed on the grill until the cooked meat on the grill is removed. In this example, consumption of the food is pulling the meat through the system in small quantities. By "producing" the food in this manner you will not end up with large amounts of "inventory" at the end of the cookout.

Kanban Production

You can see that for the pull system to work there must be good communication between the work centers. This communication is made possible by the use of a device called a **kanban card**; *kanban* means "signal" or "card" in Japanese. Most often a kanban card has such information on it as the product name, the part number, and the quantity that needs to be produced. The kanban is attached to a container. When workers need products from a preceding workstation, they pass the kanban and the empty container to that station. The kanban authorizes the worker at the preceding station to produce the amount of goods specified on the kanban. In effect, the kanban is a production authorization record. In our cookout example, the tray size served the purpose of the container. Now imagine that you had a card attached to the tray that specified three hamburgers and three hot dogs and that you could not produce any more or less than that amount. This procedure is similar to the way a kanban card works.

To make the system work smoothly and control the movement of empty and full containers, there are actually two types of kanban cards: **production cards** that authorize production and **withdrawal cards** that authorize withdrawal of materials. Figure 7-3 shows a diagram of how a pull system with two kanban cards works.

▶ **Pull system**
JIT is based on a "pull" system rather than a "push" system.

▶ **Kanban card**
A card that specifies the exact quantity of product that needs to be produced.

▶ **Production card**
A kanban card that authorizes production of material.

Withdrawal card
A kanban card that authorizes withdrawal of material.

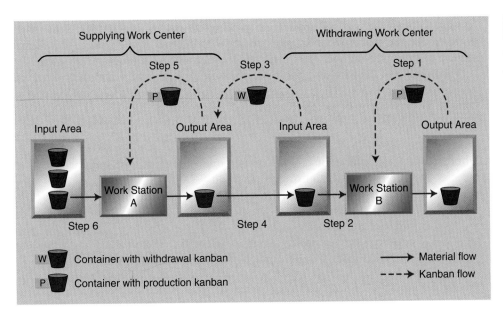

FIGURE 7-3

The pull system with two kanban cards

Let's look at the steps involved in this process.

Step 1.   The worker at workstation B received an empty container to which a production kanban is attached. This means that the worker must produce enough of the requested material to fill the empty container.

Step 2.   To fill the requirement of the production kanban, the worker at workstation B takes a full container of material from its input area.

Step 3.   To replenish the material just taken, the worker at workstation B generates a request for more input from workstation A by sending a withdrawal kanban to the output area of process A.

Step 4.   Notice that workstation A already has some parts available in its output area. The worker at workstation A attaches the withdrawal kanban to the full container and sends it immediately to workstation B.

Step 5.   The worker at workstation B takes the production kanban that was originally attached to the full container and places it on an empty container, generating production at workstation A.

Step 6.   The worker at workstation A removes a container of materials from its input area. The same sequence of steps is then repeated between all the workstations.

When this process is used, the amount produced at any one time is the amount in one container. Production cannot take place unless a container is empty and a production card has authorized production. A full container cannot be withdrawn unless a withdrawal kanban authorizes it. It is the kanban cards that coordinate the pull production system. Without kanbans, the withdrawal and production of materials cannot take place. Another advantage of the kanban is that it is *visual*. Kanban cards and containers are all placed in clearly visible areas for everyone to see.

There are as many kanban cards in the system as there are containers. If there are too many kanbans in the production system, there may be too much production and too much inventory. On the other hand, if there are not enough kanbans, the system may not be producing quickly enough. Sometimes the production manager may decide to add to or subtract from the number of kanbans to bring the system into balance. Remember, however, that the goal is to continually improve the efficiency of the system. This means striving to reduce the number of kanbans and the amount of inventory in the system.

The number of kanbans and, therefore, the number of containers in the system is a very important decision. The formula to compute the number of kanbans needed to control the production of a particular product is as follows:

$$N = \frac{DT + S}{C}$$

where N = total number of kanbans or containers (one card per container)
D = demand rate at a using workstation
T = the time it takes to receive an order from the previous workstation (also called the lead time)
C = size of container
S = safety stock to protect against variability or uncertainty in the system (usually given as a percentage of demand during lead time)

Problem-Solving Tip The demand (D) and lead time (T) have to be in the same time units.

You can see from this equation that the number of containers needed at a workstation is dependent on four things: the demand rate, the size of the container, the lead time, and the safety stock level. To control the amount of inventory, the size of containers used is typically much smaller than the demand. For example, the containers generally do not hold more than 10 percent of the daily demand. The number of kanbans in the system can be reduced as efficiency improves. Let's look at an example to see how this would work.

EXAMPLE 7.1

Computing the Number of Kanbans

Jordan Tucker works for a production facility that makes aspirin. His job is to fill the bottles of aspirin, and he is expected to process 200 bottles of aspirin an hour. The facility where Jordan works uses a kanban production system in which each container holds 25 bottles. It takes thirty minutes for Jordan to receive the bottles he needs from the previous workstation. The factory sets safety stock at 10 percent of demand during lead time. How many kanbans are needed for the filling process?

• **Solution:**

D = 200 bottles per hour

T = 30 minutes = $\frac{1}{2}$ hour

C = 25 bottles per container

$S = 0.10 \left(200 \times \frac{1}{2} \right) = 10$ bottles

$N = \frac{DT + S}{C}$

$$= \frac{(200 \text{ bottles/hour})\left(\frac{1}{2} \text{ hour}\right) + 10}{25 \text{ bottles}} = 4.4 \text{ kanbans and containers}$$

The number of containers can be rounded up or down. Notice that rounding down to four containers would force us to make improvements in the operation. Rounding up to five would provide additional slack.

Variations of Kanban Production

In many facilities the *kanban* system has been modified so that actual cards do not exist but some other type of signal is used to pull the goods through. This may be as simple as an empty place on the floor that identifies where the material should be stored. This is called a *kanban square* and is shown in Figure 7-4. An empty square indicates that it is time for the supplying operation to produce more goods. A full square indicates that no parts are needed.

Another type of signal might be some type of flag, as shown in Figure 7-5, that is used to indicate it is time to produce the next container of goods. This is called a *signal kanban* and is often used when inventory between workstations is necessary. When the inventory level is reduced to the point of reaching the signal, the signal is removed and placed on an order post, indicating that it is time for production.

The system of kanbans can also be used to coordinate delivery of goods by suppliers. These are called *supplier kanbans*. The suppliers bring the filled containers to the point of usage in the factory and at the same time pick up an empty container with a kanban to be filled later. Since a manufacturer may have multiple suppliers, "mailboxes" can be set up at the factory for each supplier. The suppliers can check their "mailboxes" to pick up their orders. Kanbans are usually made of plastic or metal, but there are also bar-coded kanbans and electronic kanbans that further ease communication with suppliers.

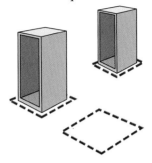

A kanban square

Small Lot Sizes and Quick Setups

A principal way of eliminating inventory and excess processing while increasing flexibility is through **small-lot production**, which means that the amount of products produced at any one time is small—say, 10 versus 1000. This allows the manufacturer to produce many lots of different types of products. It also shortens the *manufacturing lead time*, the actual time it takes to produce a product, since it takes less time to produce 10 units than to produce 1000. Shorter lead time means that customers receive

▶ **Small-lot production**
The ability to produce small quantities of products.

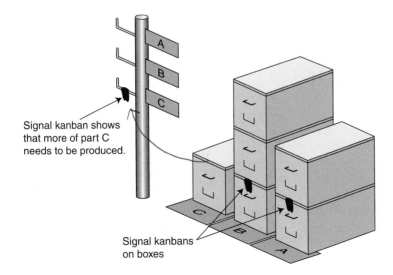

Signal kanban shows that more of part C needs to be produced.

Signal kanbans on boxes

FIGURE 7-5

A signal kanban

the specific products they want faster. The ultimate goal of JIT is to be able to economically produce one item at a time as the customer wants it.

Small-lot production gives a company a tremendous amount of flexibility and allows it to respond to customer demands more quickly. However, to be able to achieve small-lot production, companies have to reduce setup time. Recall that setup time is the time it takes to set up equipment for a production run. This includes cleaning and recalibrating equipment, changing blades and other tools, and all other activities necessary to switch production from one product to another.

To see the impact of setup time, let's pretend that we are a producer of ice cream and that we make two different flavors—chocolate and vanilla—on the same production line. The system works by first producing a certain amount of chocolate ice cream. The equipment is then cleaned and the machines are reset for the proper ingredients (this is setup time) in order to switch production to vanilla ice cream. A traditional manufacturing approach would be to produce as much chocolate ice cream as possible, since everything is already set up for this product. Then we would set up the machines for production of vanilla ice cream and make as much of it as possible before we have to clean the equipment again. The problem with this approach is that we end up producing extra amounts of ice cream. The extra ice cream is inventory. It costs money and requires storage space, and some of it will probably go to waste.

A more effective approach would be to lower the time it takes to change from production of one flavor of ice cream to another. Then we can produce only what we need and no more. We would not have the cost of extra inventory. This approach would also allow us to respond quickly to changes in demand. For example, if a customer needed extra chocolate ice cream, producing it would not be a problem. This has been the approach used by JIT. Many large manufacturers, such as General Motors, have been able to reduce setup times from many hours to only a few minutes, which has resulted in tremendous flexibility.

To produce economically in small-lot sizes, JIT has found ways to reduce setup times. The goal is to achieve *single setups*, or setup times in single digits of minutes. There are a number of ways to achieve these low setup times. One approach is to separate setup into two components: *internal setups* and *external setups*. **Internal setups** require the machine to be stopped for the setup to be performed. **External setups** can be performed while the machine is still running. Almost all setups in traditional manufacturing systems are internal. With JIT, much of the setup process has been converted to external setups. This requires engineering ingenuity and cleverly designed fixtures and tools. In a number of companies, the workers even practice the setup process and try to increase their speed.

Uniform Plant Loading

Demand for a product can show sudden increases or decreases, which can mean disruptive changes in production schedules. These demand changes are typically magnified throughout the production line and the supply chain. They contribute to inefficiency and create waste. The JIT philosophy is to eliminate the problem by making adjustments as small as possible and setting a production plan that is frozen for the month. This is called **uniform plant loading** or "leveling" the production schedule. The term *leveling* comes from the fact that the schedule is uniform or constant throughout the planning horizon.

To meet demand and keep inventories low, a "level" schedule is developed so that the same mix of products is made every day in small quantities. This is in contrast to

▶ **Internal setup**
Requires the machine to be stopped in order to be performed.

▶ **External setup**
Can be performed while the machine is still running.

▶ **Uniform plant loading**
A constant production plan for a facility with a given planning horizon.

traditional systems, which produce large quantities of one product on one day and of another product on the next day, causing large buildups of inventory. Table 7-1 shows how a level production system works in contrast to a traditional production system. In the table, a company produces five products: A, B, C, D, and E. The weekly production requirements for all products are met with both types of system. However, with the JIT system there is day-to-day repetition in the schedule, which prevents the company from having to carry large amounts of inventory and places predictable demands on all work centers and suppliers.

Flexible Resources

A key element of JIT is having flexible resources in order to meet customer demands and produce small lots. One aspect of flexibility is relying on general-purpose equipment capable of performing a number of different functions. For example, a general-purpose drilling machine may be able to drill holes in an engine block and also perform some milling and threading operations. This is very different from having specialized equipment that can perform only one task. General-purpose equipment provides flexibility of operations and eliminates waste of space, movement from one machine to another, and setup of other machines. You can see how this concept works in your own life. Isn't it easier to have one machine that is a printer, copier, and fax machine all in one, rather than have three different machines? With the press of a button you can print a copy and then fax it, rather than walk from one machine to the other, setting up each machine, not to mention solving the space requirements of three machines.

Another element of flexibility is the use of **multifunction workers** who can perform more than one job—an essential aspect of JIT. To meet changing production requirements, workers in JIT are trained to operate and set up different machines. This provides flexibility in the schedule because workers can be moved around as needed. Also, workers in JIT are responsible for performing simple maintenance on their machines

▶ **Multifunction workers**
Capable of performing more than one job.

Weekly Production Requirements by Product					
A:	10 units/week				
B:	20 units/week				
C:	5 units/week				
D:	5 units/week				
E:	10 units/week				
Monday	**Tuesday**	**Wednesday**	**Thursday**	**Friday**	
A A A A A	B B B B B	B B B B B	D D D D D	E E E E E	
A A A A A	B B B B B	B B B B B	C C C C C	E E E E E	
Monday	**Tuesday**	**Wednesday**	**Thursday**	**Friday**	
A A B B B	A A B B B	A A B B B	A A B B B	A A B B B	
C D E E	C D E E	C D E E	C D E E	C D E E	
Time					

TABLE 7-1

Contrasting Level versus Traditional Production

Traditional Production Plan

JIT Production with Level Scheduling

and are trained to perform quality control procedures. As we will see later in the chapter, workers in JIT have considerable responsibility and perform many duties. Their many abilities give a tremendous amount of flexibility to JIT.

The flexibilities of workers and machines combine to produce great advantages. Note that the operating time of a machine is usually different from that of a worker because there is a period of time while the machine is running and the worker has nothing to do. A multifunction worker can operate more than one machine at a time.

Facility Layout

Proper arrangement and layout of work centers and equipment is critical to JIT manufacturing, a topic that is covered in detail Chapter 10. Physical proximity and easy access contribute to the efficiency of the production process. Streamlined production is an important part of JIT; it relies heavily on assembly lines, dedicated to the production of a family of products.

▶ **Cell manufacturing**
Placement of dissimilar machines and equipment together to produce a family of products with similar processing requirements.

JIT also relies on **cell manufacturing**, the placement of dissimilar machines and equipment together in order to produce a family of products with similar processing requirements. These machines create a small assembly line, and their grouping is usually called a cell. The machines in one grouping can be those needed to manufacture a set of parts belonging to the same family of products. The equipment in a work cell is usually arranged in a U shape, with the worker placed in the center of the U. This arrangement has a number of advantages. First, the use of cells provides production efficiency with the flexibility to produce a variety of different products. Second, the U shape allows workers to have easy reach and flexibility. No special material handling is needed because everything is within reach. Finally, worker satisfaction is higher because of the ability to perform a variety of tasks.

Each cell produces similar items, so setup times within cells are low and lot sizes and inventories can be kept small. Figure 7-6 compares traditional production with cell manufacturing.

Robert Llewellyn/Alamy Images

Companies such as Whirlpool, Xerox, Target Stores, and Saturn of General Motors have adopted JIT as a way of doing business. To achieve their goals, these companies need just-in-time deliveries. For this they use Ryder Integrated Logistics, a global and domestic provider of transportation and distribution management services that offers just-in-time pickup and delivery of goods from suppliers. Ryder ensures that materials flow smoothly into assembly or manufacturing plants with properly sequenced deliveries. It uses a dedicated fleet of vehicles, onboard computers, and satellite/cellular communications as well as a sophisticated distribution system that enables it to support multiple suppliers. Also, to reduce cycle time, Ryder uses bar-code technology, EDI, and special software to enable the consolidation and distribution of goods in and out of facilities. All this adds up to an organization dedicated to meeting the challenge of JIT.

(a) Traditional layout

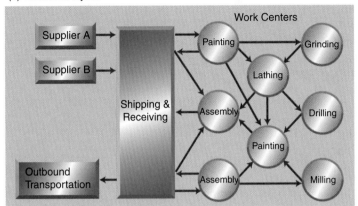

FIGURE 7-6

Traditional versus cell manufacturing

(b) JIT with cell manufacturing

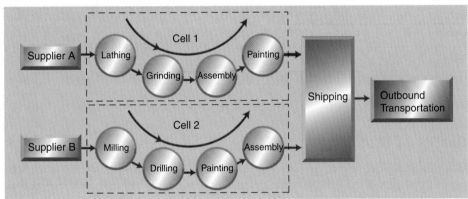

TOTAL QUALITY MANAGEMENT

Quality is a difficult term to define because it means different things to different people. A narrow viewpoint, typically used by traditional manufacturers, is to define quality as meeting specified target quality standards. This would mean producing a product within specified tolerances set by engineers and not exceeding the specified acceptable defect rate. However, today's definition of quality takes a much broader view: quality is defined as meeting or exceeding customer expectations.

As customer needs and standards drive the production system, the company must define quality as it is seen by users of the product. The customer's definition of quality then must be interpreted by engineers and production managers. This process is not always easy; customers are not always sure what they want or may not be able to articulate their needs effectively. However, once quality has been defined in measurable terms, it needs to be monitored on an ongoing basis. Targets for improvement need to be set and systematic methods for improvement developed. These methods include continual training of workers so they can identify and correct quality problems. Together, this process outlines a strategy for quality improvement in JIT, as shown in Table 7-2. Note that the steps in Table 7-2 show an ongoing, dynamic process. Customers' quality definitions must be monitored continuously as customers' expectations and needs change over time.

TABLE 7-2 Strategy for Quality Improvement	Step 1: Define quality as seen by the customer. Step 2: Translate customer needs into measurable terms. Step 3: Measure quality on an ongoing basis. Step 4: Set improvement targets and deadlines. Step 5: Develop a systematic method for improvement.

Product versus Process

The costs of poor quality can be quite high when one includes product redesign, rework, scrap, servicing returned products, or even losing customers. All this represents waste. Phil Crosby, a leading quality "guru," pointed out that "quality is free." It is poor quality that is costly. For these reasons, JIT does not tolerate poor quality.

In JIT the quality of the product is distinguished from the quality of the process used to produce the product. The idea is that a faulty product is a result of a faulty process. We may be able to repair a faulty product, but if we do not correct the process, we are not addressing the root cause of the problem and will continue to produce faulty products. Quality in JIT is centered on building quality into the process. A production process that is well within the set quality control limits should not produce a defective product.

Quality at the Source

The notion of *quality at the source* means that the root cause of quality problems needs to be identified. This could be a problem with the design, suppliers, the process, or any other area. We know that it is much easier and less costly to build quality into a process than to try to correct problems after they occur.

Quality problems can come from many sources. Some examples of sources of quality problems are the following:

Product design. In the design process, customer needs may be misunderstood and not incorporated into the product design.

Process design. Management and equipment problems may stem from the design of the production process. Operator error actually contributes to only about 15 percent of quality problems.

Suppliers. Quality problems caused by suppliers include low-quality materials and are often due to misunderstandings between manufacturer and supplier.

▶ **Jidoka**
Authority given to workers to stop the production line if a quality problem is detected.

Monitoring quality is the responsibility of everyone in the organization. Workers are given the authority to stop the production line if quality problems are encountered; this is called **jidoka**. To perform jidoka, each worker can use a switch above his or her workstation to turn on a call light or stop production. A green light means that production is flowing normally; a yellow light is a signal for help; and a red light means that the line is stopped. When a red light goes on, all personnel rush to the troubled spot to determine what the problem is. In JIT environments, stopping the line is not only allowed but expected. At JIT facilities, if a certain amount of time has passed without a line stoppage, personnel become concerned that quality problems are passing undetected.

You can see that workers have much responsibility in a JIT system. Analyzing production problems is considered a serious business and is performed as part of the regular workday, not in one's spare time. For this reason, JIT systems usually operate with seven hours of production and one hour of problem solving and working with teams. Called *undercapacity scheduling*, it is necessary in order to leave ample time for problem-solving activities.

To help workers identify quality problems, JIT relies on visual signals. One such signal is kanban control. Others include color coding, bulletin boards, lights, process control charts, and other visual displays. For example, color-coding tools and bins helps workers know which tools belong in which bins. Color-coding different sections of the work area helps workers identify stocking points and different processing sections. Material handling routes are clearly marked in different colors. Instructional photographs located near equipment provide visual explanations of machine usage. Another type of visual signal is **poka-yoke**. The term means "foolproof" and refers to a device or mechanism that prevents defects from occurring. The device could be a clamp that can be placed only in a certain way or a lid that can be turned in only one direction.

> ▶ **Poka-yoke**
> Foolproof devices or mechanisms that prevent defects from occurring.

Preventive Maintenance

An important aspect of quality management in JIT is preventive maintenance. Not only do machines rarely break down at convenient times but breakdowns are costly in terms of lost production, unmet deadlines, disruption of work schedules, and unhappy customers—all considered wastes in JIT. To avoid unexpected machine stoppages, a company invests in *preventive maintenance*, which is regular inspections and maintenance designed to keep machines operational. Although preventive maintenance is costly, the costs are significantly smaller than the cost of an unexpected machine breakdown. You know from your own experience how important preventive maintenance is, such as taking your car for a tune-up and oil change or going to the dentist for regular cleaning and checkups. Neither is fun and both are costly, but we do these things because we know that the alternatives could be much costlier.

According to JIT, workers should perform routine preventive maintenance activities, including cleaning, lubricating, recalibrating, and making other adjustments to equipment. These duties are viewed as part of the worker's job. JIT also places a great deal of importance on care of equipment and in training workers to operate and maintain machines properly. Included are designing products so they can be easily produced on current machines that can be easily operated and maintained.

Work Environment

Another important element of quality management is the overall work environment. Order and simplicity are considered highly important. According to JIT, an orderly environment creates a calm, clear mind, whereas a disorganized environment creates disorganized thoughts. Also, an orderly environment encourages respect for the workplace. It is much easier to hide waste in a cluttered room. When there is plenty of empty space and everything is in its place, it is easy to see if something is out of order. When entering a JIT facility the first thing one notices is that it is very clean and orderly, with ample space and no clutter. Keeping the facility clean is the workers' responsibility. Every worker is responsible for cleaning equipment and tools after using them and putting them back in their place. Everyone is responsible, so no one can blame anyone else if something is misplaced. All this creates a positive work environment, which is considered essential to the quality of work life and contributes to employee satisfaction.

RESPECT FOR PEOPLE

Respect for people is considered central to the JIT philosophy. Of all the issues discussed in this chapter, none departs more from traditional systems than the role of employees in a firm. According to JIT, *genuine* and *meaningful respect for employees* must exist for a company to get the best from its workers. Employees perform a great many functions in JIT, and for true JIT to exist they must be genuinely respected and appreciated. Their inputs must be valued, and they must feel secure. The key words here are *genuine* and *meaningful*. Achieving this state is sometimes difficult in environments with a history of adversarial relationships, particularly between labor and management. Managers cannot mandate genuine and meaningful respect. They cannot send out a memo on a Friday saying, "On Monday there will be genuine and meaningful respect for people!" This is something that requires a complete change in organizational culture. Often it takes much effort and time.

JIT organizations rely on all employees to work together, including management and labor. The organizational hierarchy is generally flatter in JIT than in traditional organizations, and organizational layers are not strictly defined. Great responsibility and autonomy is given to ordinary workers. All levels of employees often work in teams, and in many JIT organizations all dress the same way regardless of level, which helps break down traditional barriers and makes it easier for people to work together. In this section we look at some specific issues that relate to respect for people in JIT.

The Role of Production Employees

In traditional systems, production employees often perform their jobs in an automatic fashion. In JIT, the role of production employees is just the opposite: workers are actively engaged in pursuing the goals of the company. JIT relies on *cross-functional worker skills*, meaning the ability of workers to perform many different tasks on many different machines. Part of workers' duties is to be actively engaged in improving the production process, monitoring quality, and correcting quality problems. Continuous improvement relies heavily on the knowledge and skills of the workers closest to the operation. They are the ones best suited to make improvements in their jobs.

Production workers are required to continually check and monitor the quality of the production process. This includes inspecting their own work as well as the materials received from previous operations. This is necessary in order to detect quality problems before a defective part can proceed to additional processing. For this system to succeed, workers need to have a very different attitude toward poor quality than in traditional systems. In JIT, discovering quality problems is a goal, not something that should be covered up or blamed on someone else. As we have learned, quality at the source means that all employees are responsible for getting to the root cause of quality problems.

Another part of a worker's responsibility is recording data, such as the number of setups completed, the number of units produced, the number of defects and scrap, quality process control data, equipment malfunctions, and hours worked. It is up to the worker to understand how to use the data. One way to motivate workers is to use visible displays of data, such as performance measures, on a flip chart or chalk board near each workstation. Information such as quality problems or stoppages can be recorded on the chart for everyone to see.

However, merely recording data is not enough. Record keeping and posting results also serve to remind workers that they need to act on the information. The real task of production employees is to search for causes of problems in quality and production. Time needs to be set aside at the end of a shift for data analysis. Once data have been analyzed, problem-solving activities usually take place, using the team approach in group meetings. When workers become used to their new level of responsibility and respect, they develop the initiative to solve many problems on their own. The key in problem solving is to give workers the authority and incentive to solve problems rather than view problem solving as someone else's responsibility.

Participation by all employees is vital to the success of JIT. For this reason, JIT uses a style of management called **bottom-round management,** which means consensus management by committees or teams. When a decision needs to be made, it is discussed at all levels, starting at the bottom, so that everyone in the company contributes to the decision. This decision-making process is very slow, but it achieves consensus among all involved. In JIT, top management is usually concerned with strategic issues and leaves other decisions to employees.

▶ **Bottom-round management**
Consensus management by committees or teams.

Because everyone needs to work together, teams are an integral part of JIT. One of the most popular types of team is the **quality circle.** Quality circles are groups of about five to twelve employees who volunteer to solve quality problems in their area. Although participation is usually voluntary, the meetings take place during regular work hours. Quality circles usually meet weekly and attempt to develop solutions to problems and share them with management. Usually these work groups are led by a supervisor or a production employee and are made up of employees from the particular areas involved.

▶ **Quality circles**
Small teams of employees that volunteer to solve quality problems.

You can see that in JIT the role of production employees is very different from their role in traditional organizations. Employees have much more responsibility and autonomy. Table 7-3 summarizes some of the key elements of the role of production employees in JIT.

Lifetime Employment

Japanese companies have traditionally provided lifetime employment for most of their permanent employees. Employees must feel secure if they are to work in teams, feel free to say what they think, and act on their ideas. Today, lifetime employment covers a relatively small percentage of the total workforce. Even though

• Workers have cross-functional skills.
• Workers are actively engaged in solving production and quality problems.
• Workers are empowered to make production and quality decisions.
• Quality is everyone's responsibility.
• Workers are responsible for recording and visually displaying performance data.
• Workers work in teams to solve problems.
• Decisions are made through bottom-round management.
• Workers are responsible for preventive maintenance.

TABLE 7-3

Role of Production Employees in JIT

lifetime employment is rarely possible, a company must do certain things to reduce employee insecurity and encourage trust and openness. One answer is to commit to a policy of making no layoffs as a result of productivity improvements. This helps alleviate fears that productivity improvements made by employees will result in job loss.

Most JIT facilities have company unions that work to build cooperative relationships between management and labor. It is understood that if the company performs well, the workers will share in the rewards through bonuses. This policy encourages workers to work harder.

The Role of Management

A team of employees working to solve a problem

Just as the role of production employees is different under JIT, so is the role of management. Actually, it can often be difficult for management to truly accept the new role of production employees as being responsible for duties that traditionally were performed exclusively by management. However, in successful JIT environments managers realize that all employees are on the same team and that a higher level of worker responsibility means more success for the firm as a whole.

The role of management is to create the cultural change necessary for JIT to succeed. This is one of the most difficult tasks of JIT. It involves creating an organizational culture that provides an atmosphere of close cooperation and mutual trust. Remember that JIT relies on ordinary workers to independently solve production problems and take on many tasks. To be able to do this, employees must be problem solvers and be empowered to take action based on their ideas. Workers must feel secure in their jobs and know that they will not be reprimanded or lose their jobs for being proactive. They must also feel comfortable enough to discuss their ideas openly. It is up to management to develop an incentive system for employees that rewards this type of behavior.

In the JIT environment, the role of managers becomes more of a supporting function. Managers are seen as facilitators and coaches rather than "bosses." Their job is to help develop the capabilities of employees, to teach, make corrections, help individuals develop their skills, and serve as motivators. They assist with teamwork and problem solving. Managers are also responsible for providing motivation and necessary recognition to employees. Their job also includes sharing information such as profitability and performance results, as well as making sure ample time is scheduled for all the activities employees must perform. Remember that the additional activities, such as quality control charting, maintenance, and working in teams, are not done during "free time" but during regular work hours. The role of management, summarized in Table 7-4, is highly important for JIT to succeed.

TABLE 7-4	
Role of Management in JIT	• Be responsible for creating a JIT culture. • Serve as coaches and facilitators, not "bosses." • Develop an incentive system that rewards workers for their efforts. • Develop employee skills necessary to function in a JIT environment. • Ensure that workers receive multifunctional training. • Facilitate teamwork.

Supplier Relationships

JIT's respect for people also extends to suppliers. With JIT, a company respects suppliers and focuses on building long-term supplier relationships. The traditional approach of competitive bidding and buying parts from the cheapest supplier runs counter to the JIT philosophy. JIT companies understand that they are in a partnership with their suppliers, who are viewed as the *external factory*. The number of suppliers is typically much smaller than in traditional systems, and the goal is to shift to **single-source suppliers** that provide an entire family of parts for one manufacturer.

▶ **Single-source suppliers**
Suppliers that supply an entire family of parts for one manufacturer.

The benefits of a long-term relationship with a small number of suppliers are many. Together the supplier and manufacturer focus on improving process quality controls. There are fewer contacts by buyers, and there is a focused effort on developing a personal relationship. There is also greater accountability for quality, delivery, or service problems. Having few suppliers makes it easier to develop stable and repetitive delivery schedules and eliminate paperwork.

With a long-term relationship, a supplier can act as a service provider rather than a one-time seller. Part of such a relationship is cost and information sharing. The manufacturer shares information about forecasts and production schedules, allowing the supplier to "see" what is going to be ordered. The supplier, in turn, shares cost information and cost-cutting efforts with the manufacturer. Both parties help each other and together reap the benefits. Also, long-term relationships provide greater incentive for continuous quality improvement. Finally, with a long-term relationship suppliers are better able to plan capacity and production mix requirements, resulting in lower costs.

To provide JIT service to manufacturers, suppliers often locate near their customers. Good examples are the Nissan and Saturn plants in the Tennessee Valley, as well as the Honda plant in Marysville, Ohio. These plants are surrounded by their suppliers. If close proximity is not possible, many suppliers have small warehouses near the manufacturing plant, which can be used for housing frequently delivered items. Because JIT suppliers are extensions of the manufacturing facility, the "pull system" concept applies to them as well. JIT suppliers use standardized containers and make deliveries according to a preset schedule. As companies advance in JIT, they expect progressively shorter delivery cycles from their suppliers and will often fine them for not meeting the schedule. Often, a few suppliers will join together to help each other make small deliveries.

Many suppliers have become JIT certified, which means that they have received one or more designations that indicate they meet certain high quality standards. Once a supplier has been certified, fewer quality checks are needed since quality standards are built into the certification process. A certified JIT supplier with a long-term agreement also has the advantage of receiving payment at regular intervals rather than on delivery of goods. Paperwork is eliminated, and electronic linkages can be set up between manufacturer and supplier. These result in direct savings for both the supplier and the manufacturer. For example, suppliers to Otis Elevator of North America provide over 40 percent of the total material or component requirements directly to the production line. Replenishment is triggered by a visual kanban system and by a direct link from the Otis receiving dock to the supplier's computer system.

As you can see, supplier relationships in JIT are another fundamental departure from traditional systems. Companies have learned much from JIT, and the new way of

TABLE 7-5

Key Elements of JIT Supplier Relationships

- Suppliers viewed as external factory.
- Use of single-source suppliers.
- Long-term supplier relationships developed.
- Suppliers locate near customer.
- Stable delivery schedules.
- Cost and information sharing.

dealing with suppliers is the wave of the future, even for firms that do not fully implement JIT. Table 7-5 shows some of the key aspects of JIT supplier relationships.

BENEFITS OF JIT

TABLE 7-6

Benefits of JIT

- Reduction in inventory
- Improved quality
- Reduced space requirements
- Shorter lead times
- Lower production costs
- Increased productivity
- Increased machine utilization
- Greater flexibility

The benefits of JIT are very impressive. For this reason, many companies rush to adopt JIT without realizing all that is involved. Many of these companies do not reap the benefits because they do not take the time to implement the culture necessary for JIT to succeed. A recent study of JIT benefits has found that over a five-year period companies using JIT have experienced an 80–90 percent reduction in inventory investment, an 80–90 percent reduction in lead time, a 75 percent reduction in rework and setup, a 50 percent reduction in space requirements, and a 50 percent reduction in material handling equipment.

The first implementation of JIT took place at the Toyota Motor Company in Japan in the early 1970s. Thus, much of what we have learned about JIT comes from Toyota's experience. Since then, hundreds of companies have successfully implemented JIT, including General Motors, Ford, General Electric, IBM, 3M, Nissan/Renault, Saturn, and many others. Even for companies that do not achieve the dramatic benefits of a full JIT implementation, JIT provides many benefits. Table 7-6 lists key benefits of JIT.

One of the greatest benefits of JIT is that it has changed the attitude of many firms toward eliminating waste, improving responsiveness, and competing based on time. Time-based competition is one of the primary ways in which companies operate today, and JIT is what makes it possible. Even companies that have not implemented JIT have had to make some changes in order to compete in a world that has left behind many traditional ways of doing business.

LINKS TO PRACTICE

Alcoa Inc.
www.alcoa.com

Michael L. Abramson/
Getty Images, Inc.

The large benefits JIT can bring to a company are demonstrated by the success achieved by Alcoa, a leader in the aluminum industry. Alcoa's accomplishment included reducing inventories by more than a quarter of a billion dollars in 1999 while increasing sales by almost $1 billion. This was a direct benefit of implementing Toyota's JIT system just a year earlier. In 1998, Alcoa found itself ill-prepared to meet customer needs. It was piling up inventory, yet not providing what the customer wanted. Alcoa turned to a full JIT "pull" manufacturing system. Benefits quickly began to appear at facilities all over the country. For example, an extrusion plant in Mississippi lost money in 1998 but within a year was capable of delivering customer orders in two days.

IMPLEMENTING JIT

We have seen that JIT affects every aspect of the organization. Therefore, the implementation of a true JIT system requires a complete cultural change for the organization. To implement JIT successfully, a company does not need sophisticated systems. What is needed are the correct attitude, employee involvement, and continuous improvement. A change of such profound magnitude needs to be driven by top management. JIT implementation cannot succeed if it is done only by middle or lower management.

Implementation needs to start with a shared vision of where the company is and where it wants to go. This vision needs to consider everyone who has a stake in the company, including customers, employees, suppliers, stockholders, and even the community in which the company is located.

Once the vision has been developed, it is up to top management to create the right atmosphere. Managers need to involve workers in a meaningful way and not merely give lip service to the concept. Part of the change in atmosphere should consist of breaking down the barriers between departments and instilling "we" thinking in place of an "us-versus-them" attitude. Reward systems should be put in place to reward ideas and team cooperation.

A "champion" for JIT implementation must be designated, whether it is a plant manager, the CEO, or a steering committee. The purpose is to have a person or group oversee all the steps necessary in implementing such a large change. This person or group will be responsible for reviewing progress, addressing any problems that may develop, making sure ample resources are available, and ensuring that a proper reward system is in place. Another job of the JIT champion is sharing results with everyone in the company. Such information is not shared with production workers in traditional systems. However, in JIT sharing of this type of information with everyone in the company is considered a key to success and is done frequently and regularly. Financial information cannot be kept secret if everyone is to work together and share in the benefits.

In making specific changes in JIT manufacturing, some changes need to be implemented before others. Not all things can or should be changed at once. Following is a sequence of steps that should be followed in the implementation process:

1. **Make quality improvements.** Usually it is best to start the implementation process by improving quality. The reason is that quality is pervasive and all the JIT objectives are dependent on quality improvement.

2. **Reorganize workplace.** Reorganizing the workplace is the next step. This means proper facility layout, cleaning and organizing the work environment, designating storage spaces for everything, and removing clutter.

3. **Reduce setup times.** The next step is to focus on reducing setup times, which will involve manufacturing and industrial engineering. It will require analysis of current setup procedures, elimination of unneeded steps, and streamlining of motions. Workers will need to be trained in the proper setup procedures.

4. **Reduce lot sizes and lead times.** Once setup times have been reduced, the focus is on reducing lot sizes and lead times. This in turn will reduce the inventory between workstations and free up space. The empty space will contribute to visibility.

5. **Implement layout changes.** The next step is to arrange equipment and workstations in close proximity to one another and to form work cells.

6. **Switch to pull production.** After the preceding changes have been implemented, it is time to switch to pull production. Changing from a push system to a pull system, including worker training, needs to be planned very carefully.

However, the change needs to be made at once because a production facility cannot use a push and a pull system at the same time.

7. **Develop relationship with suppliers.** Changes in relationships with suppliers should be among the last steps implemented. Demands for smaller and more frequent deliveries should be instituted gradually.

By now you should understand that JIT is made up of many ideas that define its philosophy. Because of that, implementation of JIT is complicated. Most companies are so eager to receive the benefits of JIT that they jump in and begin making changes without thinking them through. Often, company executives will learn that for JIT implementation to succeed inventory needs to be eliminated, so they begin ordering reductions in inventory. This unplanned approach can have disastrous effects. Inventory is there to cover up problems. Unless the problems are solved first, simply reducing inventory can completely halt production.

Finally, when it comes to implementation, remember that the concept of continuous improvement is an integral part of JIT. This means that the implementation process will not start and end in definite time periods. Rather, it will be a gradual process. Reductions in inventory have to be preceded by improvements in quality, changes in layout, reductions in setup times, and worker training. As improvements are made, inventory can be reduced. As new problems become visible, they must be solved before further reductions in inventory are made. This is an ongoing, gradual process. Implementation is never complete, because improving performance is a never-ending task.

JIT IN SERVICES

People who think of JIT as applying only to manufacturing may not see how JIT could be applicable to service organizations. However, we have seen in this chapter that JIT is an all-encompassing philosophy that includes eliminating waste, improving quality, continuous improvement, increased responsiveness to customers, and increased speed of delivery. That philosophy is equally applicable to any organization, service or manufacturing.

Following are examples of JIT concepts seen in service firms.

Improved Quality

Service quality is often measured by intangible factors such as timeliness, service consistency, and courtesy. Building quality into the process of service delivery and implementing concepts such as quality at the source can significantly improve service quality dimensions. For example, McDonald's has become famous by building quality into the process and standardizing the service delivery system. Regardless of location, McDonald's customers receive the same product and service consistency.

Uniform Facility Loading

The challenge for service operations is synchronizing their production with demand. Many service firms have developed unique ways to level customer demand in order to provide better service responsiveness. For example, hotels and restaurants use reservation systems. Differential pricing systems can also be used to even out demand, such as an airlines requiring a Saturday night stay for lower fares or the post office charging more for next-day delivery.

Use of Multifunction Workers

The use of multifunction workers in service organizations helps improve quality and customer responsiveness. An example of this is seen in department stores, where workers make sales, clean sales areas, and arrange displays.

Reductions in Cycle Time

Competition based on speed is common in services, as can be seen in such companies as McDonald's, Wendy's, FedEx, and LensCrafters. These companies have used JIT concepts to reduce their cycle time and, consequently, increase their speed. One strategy is to eliminate unnecessary activities. For example, any processing step that does not add value is eliminated. Processing steps that add some value are reanalyzed and reengineered to improve their efficiency and reduce processing time.

Minimizing Setup Times and Parallel Processing

The concept of setup time minimization and parallel processing can be seen in cleaning companies. Merry Maids is a cleaning company that uses teams of workers to clean homes. Each member of the team is designated to carry out a specific category of cleaning tasks. For example, one worker may be responsible for all the dusting, another for all the bathrooms, and another for the vacuuming. This minimizes setup time, and parallel processing reduces the cycle time.

Workplace Organization

Improved housekeeping has become a priority for many service organizations, particularly since the customer is present during part of the production process. Service companies like Disney and McDonald's pride themselves on the cleanliness of their facilities.

JIT AND LEAN SYSTEMS WITHIN OM: HOW IT ALL FITS TOGETHER

As you have seen, JIT is about eliminating waste of every kind in order to be more efficient. As JIT is an overriding philosophy, it affects all other operations decisions. For example, JIT is directly linked to quality improvements within the operation (Chapters 5 and 6), partnering with suppliers as in supply chain management (Chapter 4), and changing job designs (Chapter 11) of production employees and management. JIT decisions also impact facility layout (Chapter 10) since they require rearrangements of the flow of materials, changes in the production process (Chapter 3) to a pull system with small lot sizes and uniform facility loading, and changes in inventory levels (Chapter 12). Virtually all operations decisions are linked to the implementation of JIT and lean systems.

JIT AND LEAN SYSTEMS ACROSS THE ORGANIZATION

Implementing a philosophy such as JIT will inevitably have consequences for every aspect of the organization. The entire organization is affected by JIT, primarily because organizational barriers are eliminated. Functions that have not had much communication with each other in the past must now work together. Included are functions such as marketing, manufacturing, and engineering, which in traditional systems have separate agendas but now need to work together to achieve the goals of the organization as a whole. Let's see how some of these functions are affected.

Accounting is strongly affected by JIT. Traditional accounting systems generally allocate overhead on the basis of direct labor hours. The problem with this method is that it does not accurately describe the actual use of overhead by different jobs. For example, jobs that are labor intensive in nature may be assigned a disproportionately high share of overhead. These numbers may lead management to make inappropriate decisions. JIT relies on *activity-based costing* to allocate overhead. In activity-based costing, specific costs are identified and then assigned to various types of activities, such as inspection, movement of goods, and machine processing. Overhead costs are then assigned to jobs depending on how many activities a particular job takes up.

Marketing plays a large role in JIT, as the interface with customers becomes more important. JIT focuses on customer-driven quality, not quality as defined by the producer. Marketing managers must understand customer needs and ensure that this information is passed on to operations managers for proper design, production, and delivery of the product or service.

Finance is responsible for approving and evaluating financial investments. Switching to a JIT system proves financially beneficial in the long run but generally requires an investment in resources. Included are hiring consultants, training workers, purchasing or modifying equipment, more record keeping, and rearrangement of facilities. Finance must evaluate these investments and measure their performance, which requires an understanding of JIT.

Engineering plays a major role in JIT. As we have seen in this chapter, reduction of setup time is critical to the success of JIT. It is up to engineering to design machines so as to reduce setup time and to design poka-yoke, or foolproof devices, that prevent defects from occurring. Engineering is largely responsible for designing the mechanisms that enable JIT to function as desired. Without engineering, true JIT could not exist.

Information systems (IS) create the network of information necessary for JIT to function. JIT is based on the assumption that information about quality, inventory levels, order status, and product returns is available to everyone in the organization. This type of information needs to be readily available and up-to-date. Otherwise, a JIT system would come to a halt. Communication with suppliers is another prerequisite of JIT that requires a high-level information system. JIT cannot function without the ongoing involvement of IS. In turn, IS needs to understand JIT functioning and information requirements.

THE SUPPLY CHAIN LINK

The concept of JIT naturally extends itself to the entire supply chain. The philosophy of JIT teaches us that waste anywhere in the system hinders efficiency, doesn't provide value to the customer, and ultimately increases cost. Every organization is just one element of an entire supply chain system. As such, waste anywhere in the supply chain is ultimately passed down to other members of the chain and the final customer. Also recall that JIT views a company's suppliers as the external factory, focuses on building long-term relationships with suppliers, and promotes sharing data along the supply chain. In fact, a company's pull system cannot work properly unless its suppliers are also using it. Otherwise, the JIT system of the company would not be able to function properly, as there would be no guarantee of stable deliver-

ies. Therefore, the principles of JIT need to be adopted by all members of a supply chain in order to have a full impact. This is often referred to as a lean supply chain.

Dell provides a good example of the impact JIT can have when it is implemented along the supply chain. The company has a build-to-order model that produces computers only when there is actual customer demand. Dell has implemented a JIT system throughout its supply chain and shares demand information with its suppliers. As a result, Dell is able to introduce new technologies in its computers much quicker than competitors because they are seamlessly available in the supply chain. Dell also works closely with its suppliers to reduce inventories, align processes, and eliminate waste across the supply chain. The result has been high responsiveness at a competitive price.

Chapter Highlights

1 JIT is a philosophy that was developed by the Toyota Motor Company in the mid-1970s. It has since become the standard of operation for many industries. It focuses on simplicity, eliminating waste, taking a broad view of operations, visibility, and flexibility. Three key elements of this philosophy are JIT manufacturing, total quality management, and respect for people.

2 JIT views waste as anything that does not add value, such as unnecessary space, energy, time, or motion.

3 Traditional manufacturing systems use "push" production, whereas JIT uses "pull" production. Push systems anticipate future demand and produce in advance in order to have products in place when demand occurs. This system usually results in excess inventory. Pull systems work backwards. The last workstation in the production line (or the customer) requests the precise amounts of materials required.

4 JIT manufacturing is a coordinated production system that enables the right quantities of parts to arrive when they are needed precisely where they are needed. Key elements of JIT manufacturing are the pull system and kanban production, small lot sizes and quick setups, uniform plant loading, flexible resources, and streamlined layout.

5 Total quality management (TQM) creates an organizational culture that defines quality as seen by the customer. The concepts of continuous improvement and quality at the source are integral to allowing for continual growth and the goal of identifying the causes of quality problems.

6 JIT considers people to be the organization's most important resource. All employees are highly valued members of the organization. Workers are empowered to make decisions and are rewarded for their efforts. Team efforts make possible cross-functional and multilayer coordination.

7 JIT is equally applicable in service organizations, particularly with the push toward time-based competition and the need to cut costs.

8 JIT success is dependent on interfunctional coordination and effort. Marketing must work closely with customers to define customer-driven quality. IS must design a powerful information system. Engineering must develop equipment with low setup time and design jobs with foolproof devices. Finance must monitor financial improvements with realistic expectations. Accounting must develop appropriate costing mechanisms.

Key Terms

just-in-time (JIT) philosophy 220
waste 220
a broad view of JIT 220
defining beliefs of JIT 221
types of waste 222
broad view of the organization 222
simplicity 222
continuous improvement (kaizen) 223
visibility 223
flexibility 223
JIT system 224

just-in-time manufacturing 224
setup cost 225
total quality management (TQM) 226
quality at the source 226
respect for people 226
pull system 228
kanban card 228
production card 228
withdrawal card 228
small-lot production 231
internal setup 232

external setup 232
uniform plant loading 232
multifunction workers 233
cell manufacturing 234
jidoka 236
poka-yoke 237
bottom-round management 239
quality circles 239
single-source suppliers 241

Formula Review

Determining the number of kanbans:

$$N = \frac{DT + S}{C}$$

Solved Problem

• Problem 1

Suzie Sizewick works for a manufacturer of ballpoint pens, which come in packages of five pens each. Her job is to fill the packages with pens, and she is expected to process 100 packages an hour. The facility where Suzie works uses a kanban production system in which each container holds ten pen packages. It takes fifteen minutes to receive the packages she needs from the previous workstation. The facility uses a safety stock of 12 percent. How many kanbans are needed for the filling process?

- **Before You Begin:**
Remember to always check your units and make sure that demand (D) and lead time (T) are over the same time period.

Step 1

$$N = \frac{DT + S}{C}$$

- **Solution**

$D = 100$ packages per hour

$T = 15$ minutes $= \frac{1}{4}$ hour

$C = 10$ packages per container

$S = 0.12\left(100 \times \frac{1}{4}\right) = 3$ packages

Step 2

$$N = \frac{(100 \text{ packages/hour})(\frac{1}{4} \text{ hour}) + 3}{10 \text{ packages}}$$

$$= 2.8 \text{ kanbans and containers}$$

Discussion Questions

1. Describe the core beliefs of the JIT philosophy.
2. Identify the three major elements of JIT.
3. Explain how JIT manufacturing works and its key elements.
4. Find an example of successful JIT manufacturing.
5. Explain the importance of total quality management in JIT.
6. Find an example of successful TQM implementation.
7. Explain the importance of respect for people in JIT.
8. Find an example of a company that has high respect for people.
9. Describe the JIT implementation process. Why should some things be changed before others?
10. Find examples of JIT in services. Which aspects of JIT are easiest to apply in services?
11. Explain how you could use JIT to make your life more efficient.

Problems

1. Jason Carter works for a producer of soaps that come in packages of six each. His job is to fill the packages with soap, and he is expected to process thirty packages an hour. The facility where Jason works uses a kanban production system in which each container holds five packages of soap. It takes twenty minutes to receive the packages he needs from the previous workstation. How many kanbans are needed for the filling process?

2. A manufacturer of thermostats uses a kanban system to control the flow of materials. The packaging center processes ten thermostats an hour and receives completed thermostats every thirty minutes. Containers hold five thermostats each.
   (a) How many kanbans are needed for the packaging center?
   (b) If management decides to keep two thermostats as safety stock, how many kanbans will be needed?

3. A production cell at Canderberry Candle facility operates five hours per day and uses a pull method to supply wicks to the assembly line. The wicks are used at a rate of 300 per day. Each container holds 20 wicks and usually waits twenty minutes in the production cell. Management wants a safety stock of 10 percent. How many containers should be used at the Canderberry Candle facility for purposes of pull production?

4. Carlos Gonzales is production manager at an assembly plant that manufactures cordless telephones. The company is planning to install a pull system. The process is being planned to have a usage rate of fifty pieces per hour. Each container is designed to hold ten pieces. It takes an average of thirty minutes to complete a cycle.
   (a) How many containers will be needed?
   (b) How will the number of needed containers change as the system improves?

5. A dye cell at the Acme Clothing Factory uses 500 pounds of dye each day. The dye is moved in vats at a rate of approximately one per hour. Each vat holds 10 pounds of dye. Management has set safety stock at 10 percent. The facility operates eight hours per day. How many vats should be used?

6. Anna works on an assembly line where it takes her thirty minutes to produce twenty units of a product needed to fill a container. It takes her an additional five minutes to transport the container to Josh, who works at the next station. The company uses a safety stock of 20 percent. The current assembly line uses five kanbans between Anna's and Josh's stations. Compute the demand for the product.

7. Robert produces 300 units of a product per hour and 30 units are needed to fill a container. It takes fifteen minutes to receive the materials needed from the previous workstation. The company currently uses a safely stock of 10 percent. Determine

the number of kanbans needed between Robert's station and the previous process.

8. Consider the information from Problem 7. Determine how the number of kanbans and the inventory level will be affected if the time required for Robert to receive the material increases to thirty minutes.

9. Consider the information from Problem 7. Determine how the number of kanbans and the inventory level will be affected if:
   (a) The container size is decreased to 15 units.
   (b) The container size is increased to 40 units.
   (c) The safety stock is increased to 20 percent.

CASE: Katz Carpeting

Josh Wallace, president of Katz Carpeting, had much on his mind. The end-of-year performance numbers for the carpet manufacturer were below expectations. Inventories of carpets were high, yet they had frequently been out of stock of items customers wanted. It seemed that the plant was producing a lot of what they already had, yet not enough of what was needed. Quality was also becoming a problem, with customers frequently returning carpeting for rips or incorrect dye color. It seemed to Josh that operations was not doing its job. Something had to be done.

Background

Katz Carpeting is a manufacturer of high-end commercial and residential carpeting. Katz produces two product lines of carpeting. The first line, a group of standardized products called "standards," is sold through catalogs and samples available at retail sites. The second line is "specials," carpet products made to customer specifications of color and pattern. Currently, the volume of business is approximately evenly divided between standards and specials.

At Katz, standards and specials are made using a line operation and sharing the same facilities (see Figure 7-7). Production

of standards is made in a predictable and easily timed manner. The process begins with making the dye in large vats and dying the yarn. The yarn is then rolled, bonded, and added to a backing. The product is then cut and sent to shipping.

Production of specials is not as simple. The dying and weaving processes of specials are considerably more difficult due to the time necessary to ensure the dyes are correct. Colors of standards are well established. However, colors of specials require an initial trial dying before full dying can begin. Also, patterns are frequently requested in special orders, and each pattern is typically unique. Because of the customized nature of producing specials, the time required for production is much longer, as is the cost involved.

At Katz, the marketing department is responsible for generating forecasts, taking orders, and establishing due dates. This information is passed on to operations on a weekly basis, and a production schedule is made. Information on special "rush" orders is passed on daily and requests are frequent. Operations tries to meet all the orders and produce extra inventories of standards to be prepared for unexpected demand.

FIGURE 7-7

Production process at Katz Carpeting

(a) Production of standard
Setup time: 15 minutes

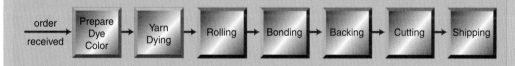

(b) Production of specials
Setup time: $2\frac{1}{2}$ hours

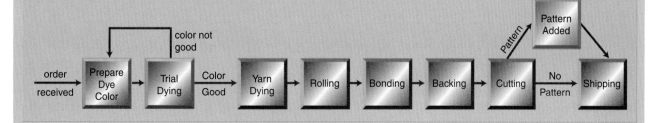

Considering JIT

Josh Wallace called a meeting with Evelyn Jones, newly hired head of operations. He explained the problems Katz was facing. Evelyn agreed that there were problems with inventory and customer service but noted that these were just symptoms of a problem. "One big problem is the setup and changeover time between the two product lines," she explained. "The changeover from one standard product to another is approximately 15 minutes, enough time for the new dye color to be loaded onto the machine. However, the changeover from one standard product to a special can be as much as hours. As both products are made on the same line, production of the specials holds up production of the standards. Also, operations frequently stops planned production to meet special rush orders."

Evelyn then explained that the facility needed to move toward just-in-time production. "Yes, I have heard of that. That is a manufacturing process based on zero inventory," said Josh. "I have even heard that workers are paid to sit around and discuss quality problems. Well, not here. Here they need to get rid of that inventory!"

Under the circumstances, Evelyn suggested that a consultant be brought in to guide Katz through the process of switching to JIT production. Josh reluctantly agreed.

Case Questions

1. What suggestions do you have for implementing JIT at Katz? Should specials and standards be produced on the same line? (*Hint:* Do they require the same type of operation?)

2. If production of standards and specials is separated, how different will JIT implementation be for production of the different products? Explain what would be needed in JIT implementation for both products.

3. What suggestions do you have for improving the way the production schedule is currently made?

4. How would you characterize Josh's view of JIT? What challenges do you think a consultant will face in implementing JIT at Katz? If you were a consultant, how would you approach these problems?

CASE: Dixon Audio Systems

Dixon Audio Systems had developed a reputation as a leading producer of speakers, audio systems, and car stereos. Dixon accomplished this through creating strict organizational quality standards and demanding these same standards of its suppliers. Meeting quality standards was critical, particularly of plastic component parts. These parts were sourced from a number of vendors and required considerable experience and skill to make. However, as Dixon's quality standards increased, the number of defective components returned to vendors increased too. This was increasingly holding up production and costing the company in excess inventory and unmet orders.

Dixon's director of purchasing proposed a new approach to dealing with the vendor quality problem. She proposed that they develop a new arrangement with their top vendor of plastic components, D&S Plastics. Under the relationship, D&S Plastics would become Dixon's JIT supplier. The arrangement would require D&S to station a full-time representative at Dixon's headquarters. The representative would be paid by D&S but would work as a plastics buyer for Dixon, placing orders to D&S. The representative would also monitor material requirements on plastic components that D&S supplied to Dixon and become in-

volved in manufacturing planning at Dixon. The plan would provide the D&S representative full access to Dixon's facilities, personnel, and computer systems. D&S Plastics would be a sole supplier to Dixon and was guaranteed business, provided it maintained the quality and delivery requirements. Dixon was assured a reliable supply of plastic component parts.

The proposed arrangement would completely change the way in which the two companies worked together and had a number of risks. Dixon's managers worried that the company would lose control of its procurement process. Although Dixon was one of D&S's biggest accounts, D&S worried that it would lose control of its operations. Many factors had to be considered before embarking on this type of arrangement.

Case Questions

1. Identify the pros and cons of a JIT relationship from a supplier's point of view.

2. Identify the pros and cons of a JIT relationship from a buyer's point of view.

3. What factors should Dixon and D&S consider before making a decision on this relationship?

INTERACTIVE CASE   Virtual Company   www.wiley.com/college/reid

On-line Case: JIT and Lean Systems at Valley Memorial Hospital

Assignment: *Just-in-Time at VMH*   Bob Reilly just called to congratulate you on your report on supply chain management.

It was very well received by the managers at VMH. Meg Willoughby, head of materials management at VMH, was especially impressed with your ideas on partnering with suppliers and purchasing supplies and equipment. She has now suggested that you prepare a concise research report for top management addressing just-in-time (JIT) issues relevant to VMH. Managers at VMH have heard a great deal about JIT, but many wonder how JIT concepts could be applied at VMH. They have put together a few specific questions for you to address in your report. This assignment will enable you to enhance your knowledge of the material in Chapter 7.

To access the Web site:
- Go to **www.wiley.com/college/reid**
- Click **Student Companion Site**
- Click **Virtual Company**
- Click **Kaizen Consulting, Inc.**
- Click **Consulting Assignments**
- Click **Just-in-Time at Valley Memorial Hospital**

INTERNET CHALLENGE   Truck-Fleet Inc.

Truck-Fleet Inc., is a small company that offers domestic logistics services such as distribution management and transportation management. Truck-Fleet owns a small fleet of trucks and offers movement, tracking, and handling of inventory for clients. Although Truck-Fleet is relatively small, with revenues of $500 million annually, it is growing rapidly as companies place greater emphasis on fast transportation. Truck-Fleet utilizes technology such as bar coding to facilitate consolidation and distribution of products. Its strength lies in its dedicated employees, such as drivers with excellent driving and safety records and a good management staff.

Truck-Fleet needs to become a JIT service provider to remain competitive. You have just been hired to help direct its growth. Use the Internet to identify Truck-Fleet's main competitors and their capabilities. Identifying specific companies that offer just-in-time pickup and delivery against which Truck-Fleet can benchmark. Then, identify the characteristics of main competitors that enable them to provide just-in-time services. Finally, establish specific guidelines for Truck-Fleet to follow in becoming a JIT service provider. Problem-Solving Tip: One potential competitor is Ryder (www.ryder.com).

On-line Resources

Companion Website www.wiley.com/college/reid
- Take interactive *practice quizzes* to assess your knowledge and help you study in a dynamic way
- Review *PowerPoint slides* or print slides for notetaking
- Access the *Virtual Company: Valley Memorial Hospital*
- Find links to *Company Tours* for this chapter
  Toyota Motor Corporation

- Find links for *Additional Web Resources* for this chapter
  The Association for Manufacturing Excellence, *www.ame.org*
  APICS—The Educational Society for Resource Management, *www.apics.org*

Selected Bibliography

Garg, D., O.N. Kaul, and S.G. Deshmukh. "JIT Implementation: A Case Study," *Production and Inventory Management Journal,* Third Quarter, 1998, 26–31.

Hall, R.W. *Attaining Manufacturing Excellence.* Burr Ridge, Ill.: Irwin Professional Publishing, 1987.

Hanna, M.D., W.R. Newman, and P. Johnson. "Linking Operational and Environmental Improvement Through Employee Involvement," *International Journal of Operations and Production Management,* 20, 2, 2000, 148–165.

Koste, L.L., and M.K. Malhotra. "Trade-offs Among the Elements of Flexibility: A Comparison From the Automotive Industry," *Omega,* 28, 2000, 693–710.

Monden, Yasuchiro. *The Toyota Management System: Linking the Seven Key Functional Areas.* Cambridge, Mass.: Productivity Press, 1993.

Ohno, T. *Toyota Production System: Beyond Large-Scale Production.* Cambridge, Mass.: Productivity Press, 1988. (Original Japanese version published 1978.)

Pun, K., and K.H. Wong. "Implementing JIT/MRP in a PCB Manufacturer," *Production and Inventory Management Journal,* First Quarter, 1998, 10–16.

Shingo, Shigeo. *Modern Approaches to Manufacturing Improvement.* Cambridge, Mass.: Productivity Press, 1990.

Vergin, R.C. "An Examination of Inventory Turnover in the Fortune 500 Industrial Companies," *Production and Inventory Management Journal,* First Quarter, 1998, 51–56.

Vitasek, K., K.B. Manrodt, and J. Abbott. "What Makes a Lean Supply Chain?" *Supply Chain Management Review,* Oct. 2005, 39–45.

Womack, J.P., D.T. Jones, and D. Roos. *The Machine That Changed the World.* New York: Macmillan, 1990.

Forecasting

Before studying this chapter you should know or, if necessary, review

The role of forecasting in operations management decisions, Chapter 1, page 0.

LEARNING OBJECTIVES

After studying this chapter you should be able to

1 Identify principles of forecasting.
2 Explain the steps involved in the forecasting process.
3 Identify types of forecasting methods and their characteristics.
4 Describe time series models and causal models.
5 Generate forecasts for data with different patterns, such as level, trend, and seasonality and cycles.
6 Describe causal modeling using linear regression.
7 Compute forecast accuracy.
8 Explain the factors that should be considered when selecting a forecasting model.

CHAPTER OUTLINE

WHAT'S IN OM FOR ME?

ACC

FIN

MKT

OM

HRM

MIS

ave you ever gone to a restaurant and been told that they are sold out of their "specials," or gone to the university bookstore and found that the texts for your course are on backorder? Have you ever had a party at your home only to realize that you don't have enough food for everyone invited? Just like getting caught unprepared in the rain, these situations show the consequences of poor forecasting. Planning for any event requires a forecast of the future. Whether in business or in our own lives, we make forecasts of future events. Based on those forecasts we make plans and take action.

Forecasting is one of the most important business functions because all other business decisions are based on a forecast of the future. Decisions such as which markets to pursue, which products to produce, how much inventory to carry, and how many people to hire all require a forecast. Poor forecasting results in incorrect business decisions and leaves the company unprepared to meet future demands. The consequences can be very costly in terms of lost sales and can even force a company out of business.

Patti McConville/The Image Bank/Getty Images

Forecasts are so important that companies are investing billions of dollars in technologies that can help them better plan for the future. For example, the ice cream giant Ben & Jerry's has invested in business intelligence software that tracks the life of each pint of ice cream, from ingredients to sale. Each pint is stamped with a tracking number that is stored in an Oracle database. Then the company uses the information to track trends, problems, and new business opportunities. They can track such things as seeing if the ice cream flavor Chocolate Chip Cookie Dough is gaining on Cherry Garcia for the top sales spot, product sales by location, and rates of change. This information is then used to more accurately forecast product sales. Numerous other companies, such as Procter & Gamble, General Electric, Lands' End, Sears, and Red Robin Gourmet Burgers, are investing in the same type of software in order to improve forecast accuracy.

In this chapter you will learn about forecasting, the different types of forecasting methods available, and how to select and use the proper techniques. You will also learn about the latest available software that can help managers analyze and process data to generate forecasts.

▶ **Forecasting**
Predicting future events.

PRINCIPLES OF FORECASTING

There are many types of forecasting models. They differ in their degree of complexity, the amount of data they use, and the way they generate the forecast. However, some features are common to all forecasting models. They include the following:

1. *Forecasts are rarely perfect.* Forecasting the future involves uncertainty. Therefore, it is almost impossible to make a perfect prediction. Forecasters know that

they have to live with a certain amount of error, which is the difference between what is forecast and what actually happens. The goal of forecasting is to generate good forecasts *on the average* over time and to keep forecast errors as low as possible.

2. *Forecasts are more accurate for groups or families of items rather than for individual items.* When items are grouped together, their individual high and low values can cancel each other out. The data for a group of items can be stable even when individual items in the group are very unstable. Consequently, one can obtain a higher degree of accuracy when forecasting for a group of items rather than for individual items. For example, you cannot expect the same degree of accuracy if you are forecasting sales of long-sleeved hunter green polo shirts that you can expect when forecasting sales of all polo shirts.

3. *Forecasts are more accurate for shorter than longer time horizons.* The shorter the time horizon of the forecast, the lower the degree of uncertainty. Data do not change very much in the short run. As the time horizon increases, however, there is a much greater likelihood that changes in established patterns and relationships will occur. Because of that, forecasters cannot expect the same degree of forecast accuracy for a long-range forecast as for a short-range forecast. For example, it is much harder to predict sales of a product two years from now than to predict sales two weeks from now.

STEPS IN THE FORECASTING PROCESS

Regardless of what forecasting method is used, there are some basic steps that should be followed when making a forecast:

1. *Decide what to forecast.* Remember that forecasts are made in order to plan for the future. To do so, we have to decide what forecasts are actually needed. This is not as simple as it sounds. For example, do we need to forecast sales or demand? These are two different things, and sales do not necessarily equal the total amount of demand for the product. Both pieces of information are usually valuable.

   An important part of this decision is the level of detail required for the forecast (e.g., by product or product group), the units of the forecast (e.g., product units, boxes, or dollars), and the time horizon (e.g., monthly or quarterly).

2. *Evaluate and analyze appropriate data.* This step involves identifying what data are needed and what data are available. This will have a big impact on the selection of a forecasting model. For example, if you are predicting sales for a new product, you may not have historical sales information, which would limit your use of forecasting models that require quantitative data.

   We will also see in this chapter that different types of patterns can be observed in the data. It is important to identify these patterns in order to select the correct forecasting model. For example, if a company was experiencing a high increase in product sales for the past year, it would be important to identify this growth in order to forecast correctly.

3. *Select and test the forecasting model.* Once the data have been evaluated, the next step is to select an appropriate forecasting model. As we will see, there are many models to choose from. Usually we consider factors like *cost* and *ease of use* in selecting a model. Another very important factor is *accuracy*. A common proce-

dure is to narrow the choices to two or three different models and then test them on historical data to see which one is most accurate.

4. *Generate the forecast.* Once we have selected a model we use it to generate the forecast. But we are not finished, as you will see in the next step.

5. *Monitor forecast accuracy.* Forecasting is an ongoing process. After we have made a forecast, we should record what actually happened. We can then use that information to monitor our forecast accuracy. This process should be carried out continuously, because environments and conditions often change. What was a good forecasting model in the past might not provide good results for the future. We have to constantly be prepared to revise our forecasting model as our data changes.

The rapid growth of information technology (IT) has created a forecasting challenge for manufacturers of industry components such as microchips and semiconductors. Companies like Intel have had difficulty in forecasting demand for information technology used in internal applications. Forecasts are critical in order to plan production and have enough product to meet demand.

©AP/Wide World Photos

LINKS TO PRACTICE

Intel Corporation
www.intel.com

However, overforecasting means having too much of an expensive product that will quickly become obsolete. The exponential growth in requirements and a short product life cycle have added much uncertainty to the forecasting process. Intel has had to consider many factors when generating its forecasts, such as key technology trends that are driving the information revolution and future directions in the use of IT.

TYPES OF FORECASTING METHODS

Forecasting methods can be classified into two groups: *qualitative* and *quantitative*. Table 8-1 shows these two categories and their characteristics.

Qualitative forecasting methods, often called judgmental methods, are methods in which the forecast is made subjectively by the forecaster. They are educated guesses by

▶ **Qualitative forecasting methods**
Forecast is made subjectively by the forecaster.

TABLE 8-1

Types of Forecasting Methods

	Qualitative Methods	Quantitative Methods
1. Characteristics	Based on human judgment, opinions; subjective and nonmathematical.	Based on mathematics; quantitative in nature.
2. Strengths	Can incorporate latest changes in the environment and "inside information."	Consistent and objective; able to consider much information and data at one time.
3. Weaknesses	Can bias the forecast and reduce forecast accuracy.	Often quantifiable data are not available. Only as good as the data on which they are based.

forecasters or experts based on intuition, knowledge, and experience. When you decide, based on your intuition, that a particular team is going to win a baseball game, you are making a qualitative forecast. Because qualitative methods are made by people, they are often biased. These biases can be related to personal motivation ("They are going to set my budget based on my forecast, so I'd better predict high."), mood ("I feel lucky today!"), or conviction ("That pitcher can strike anybody out!").

▶ **Quantitative forecasting methods**
Forecast is based on mathematical modeling.

Quantitative forecasting methods, on the other hand, are based on mathematical modeling. Because they are mathematical, these methods are consistent. The same model will generate the exact same forecast from the same set of data every time. These methods are also objective. They do not suffer from the biases found in qualitative forecasting. Finally, these methods can consider a lot of information at one time. Because people have limited information-processing abilities and can easily experience information overload, they cannot compete with mathematically generated forecasts in this area.

Both qualitative and quantitative forecasting methods have strengths and weaknesses. Although quantitative methods are objective and consistent, they require data in quantifiable form in order to generate a forecast. Often, we do not have such data, for example, if we are making a strategic forecast or if we are forecasting sales of a new product. Also, quantitative methods are only as good as the data on which they are based. Qualitative methods, on the other hand, have the advantage of being able to incorporate last-minute "inside information" in the forecast, such as an advertising campaign by a competitor, a snowstorm delaying a shipment, or a heat wave increasing sales of ice cream. Each method has its place, and a good forecaster learns to rely on both.

LINKS TO PRACTICE

Improving Sales Forecasting

Reuters New Media Inc./
Corbis Images

Inaccurate forecasts can cost companies billions of dollars in missed sales or excess inventory. One factor that can significantly impact sales is the weather. In the past, there was little companies could do to plan for weather problems. However, new businesses have sprung up to help companies use weather data to predict consumer behavior and manage weather risk. It could be as simple as predicting a hot summer, a cold winter, or an early spring. This type of information can help companies move the right inventories to areas where consumers will be more likely to buy them.

Planalytics Inc. is a company that helps businesses use weather data to make their business plans. Its clients include Gillette's Duracell® Batteries, Home Depot, and Wal-Mart. In one example, Planalytics helped Duracell move a large number of batteries to areas expecting to be hit by hurricanes during the hurricane season. Although using weather data does not replace traditional forecasting methods, it is one additional tool that can help companies improve their forecasting and planning.

Qualitative Methods

There are many types of qualitative forecasting methods, some informal and some structured. Regardless of how structured the process is, however, remember that these models are based on subjective opinion and are not mathematical in nature. Some common qualitative methods are shown in Table 8-2 and are described in this section.

Type	Characteristics	Strengths	Weaknesses
Executive opinion	A group of managers meet and come up with a forecast.	Good for strategic or new-product forecasting.	One person's opinion can dominate the forecast.
Market research	Uses surveys and interviews to identify customer preferences.	Good determinant of customer preferences.	It can be difficult to develop a good questionnaire.
Delphi method	Seeks to develop a consensus among a group of experts.	Excellent for forecasting long-term product demand, technological changes, and scientific advances.	Time-consuming to develop.

TABLE 8-2

Qualitative Forecasting Methods

Executive Opinion **Executive opinion** is a forecasting method in which a group of managers meet and collectively develop a forecast. This method is often used for strategic forecasting or forecasting the success of a new product or service. Sometimes it can be used to change an existing forecast to account for unusual events, such as an unusual business cycle or unexpected competition.

Although managers can bring good insights to the forecast, this method has a number of disadvantages. Often the opinion of one person can dominate the forecast if that person has more power than the other members of the group or is very domineering. Think about times when you were part of a group for a course or for your job. Chances are that you experienced situations in which one person's views dominated.

▶ **Executive opinion**
Forecasting method in which a group of managers collectively develop a forecast.

Market Research **Market research** is an approach that uses surveys and interviews to determine customer likes, dislikes, and preferences and to identify new product ideas. Usually, the company hires an outside marketing firm to conduct a market research study. There is a good chance that you were a participant in such a study if someone called you and asked about your product preferences.

Market research can be a good determinant of customer preferences. However, it has a number of shortcomings. One of the most common has to do with how the survey questions are designed. For example, a market research firm may call and ask you to identify which of the following is your favorite hobby: gardening, working on cars, cooking, or playing sports. But maybe none of these is your favorite because you prefer playing the piano or fishing, and these options are not included. This question is poorly designed because it forces you to pick a category that you really don't fit in, which can lead to misinterpretation of the survey results.

▶ **Market research**
Approach to forecasting that relies on surveys and interviews to determine customer preferences.

The Delphi Method The **Delphi method** is a forecasting method in which the objective is to reach a consensus among a group of experts while maintaining their anonymity. The researcher puts together a panel of experts in the chosen field. These experts do not have to be in the same facility or even in the same country. They do not know who the other panelists are. The process involves sending questionnaires to the panelists, then summarizing the findings and sending them an updated questionnaire incorporating the findings. This process continues until a consensus is reached.

The idea behind the Delphi method is that a panel of experts in a particular field might not agree on certain things, but what they do agree on will probably happen.

▶ **Delphi method**
Approach to forecasting in which a forecast is the product of a consensus among a group of experts.

Dennis MacDonald/PhotoEdit

Market research being conducted in a shopping mall.

Jean Louis Batt/Taxi/Getty Images, Inc.

Computers have made the use of quantitative models much easier.

The researcher's job is to identify what the experts agree on and use that as the forecast. This method has the advantage of not allowing anyone to dominate the consensus, and it has been shown to work very well. Although it takes a large amount of time, it has been shown to be an excellent method for forecasting long-range product demand, technological change, and scientific advances in medicine. For example, if you wished to predict the timing for an AIDS vaccine or a cure for cancer, you would probably use this technique.

Quantitative Methods

Quantitative methods are different from qualitative ones because they are based on mathematics. Quantitative methods can also be divided into two categories: *time series models* and *causal models*. Although both are mathematical, the two categories differ in their assumptions and in the manner in which a forecast is generated. In this section we will study some common quantitative models, which are summarized in Table 8-3.

Time series models assume that all the information needed to generate a forecast is contained in the *time series* of data. A **time series** is a series of observations taken at regular intervals over a specified period of time. For example, if you were forecasting quarterly corporate sales and had collected five years of quarterly sales data, you would have a time series. Time series analysis assumes that we can generate a forecast based on patterns in the data. As a forecaster, you would look for patterns such as trend, seasonality, and cycle and use that information to generate a forecast.

Causal models, sometimes called associative models, use a very different logic to generate a forecast. They assume that the variable we wish to forecast is somehow related to other variables in the environment. The forecaster's job is to discover how these variables are related in mathematical terms and use that information to forecast

▶ **Time series models**
Based on the assumption that a forecast can be generated from the information contained in a time series of data.

▶ **Time series**
A series of observations taken over time.

▶ **Causal models**
Based on the assumption that the variable being forecast is related to other variables in the environment.

the future. For example, we might decide that sales are related to advertising dollars and GNP. From historical data we would build a model that explains the relationship of these variables and use it to forecast corporate sales.

Time series models are generally easier to use than causal models. Causal models can be very complex, especially if they consider relationships among many variables. However, time series models can often be just as accurate and have the advantage of simplicity. They are easy to use and can generate a forecast more quickly than causal models, which require model building. Each of these models is used for forcasting in operations management and will be described in the next section.

TABLE 8-3

Quantitative Forecasting Models

Type	Description	Strengths	Weaknesses
Time Series Models			
Naïve	Uses last period's actual value as a forecast.	Simple and easy to use.	Only good if data change little from period to period.
Simple Mean	Uses an average of past data as a forecast.	Good for level pattern.	Requires carrying a lot of data.
Simple Moving Average	A forecasting method in which only n of the most recent observations are averaged.	Only good for level pattern.	Important to select the proper moving average.
Weighted Moving Average	A forecasting method where n of the most recent observations are averaged and past observations may have different weights.	Good for level pattern; allows placing different weights on past demands.	Selection of weights requires good judgment.
Exponential Smoothing	A weighted average procedure with weights declining exponentially as data become older.	Provides excellent forecast results for short- to medium-length forecasts.	Choice of alpha is critical.
Trend-Adjusted Exponential Smoothing	An exponential smoothing model with separate equations for forecasting the level and trend.	Provides good results for trend data.	Should only be used for data with trend.
Linear Trend Line	Technique uses the least squares method to fit a straight line to past data over time.	Easy to use and understand.	Data should display a clear trend over time.
Seasonal Indexes	Computes the percentage amount by which data for each season are above or below the mean.	Simple and logical procedure for computing seasonality.	Make sure seasonality is actually present.
Causal (Associative) Models			
Linear Regression	Uses the least-squares method to model a linear relationship between two variables.	Easy to understand; provides good forecast accuracy.	Make sure a linear relationship is present.
Multiple Regression	Similar to linear regression, but models the relationship of multiple variables with the variable being forecast.	A powerful tool in forecasting when multiple variables are being considered.	Significantly increases data and computational requirements.

TIME SERIES MODELS

Remember that time series analysis assumes that all the information needed to generate a forecast is contained in the time series of the data. The forecaster looks for patterns in the data and tries to obtain a forecast by projecting that pattern into the future. The easiest way to identify patterns is to plot the data and examine the resulting graphs. If we did that, what could we observe? There are four basic patterns, which are shown in Figure 8-1. Any of these patterns, or a combination of them, can be present in a time series of data:

▶ **Level or horizontal pattern**
Pattern in which data values fluctuate around a constant mean.

1. *Level or horizontal.* A **level or horizontal pattern** exists when data values fluctuate around a constant mean. This is the simplest pattern and the easiest to predict. An example is sales of a product that do not increase or decrease over time. This type of pattern is common for products in the mature stage of their life cycle, in which demand is steady and predictable.

▶ **Trend**
Pattern in which data exhibit increasing or decreasing values over time.

2. *Trend.* When data exhibit an increasing or decreasing pattern over time, we say that they exhibit a **trend**. The trend can be upward or downward. The simplest type of trend is a straight line, or linear trend.

▶ **Seasonality**
Any pattern that regularly repeats itself and is constant in length.

3. *Seasonality.* A seasonal pattern is any pattern that regularly repeats itself and is of a constant length. Such **seasonality** exists when the variable we are trying to forecast is influenced by seasonal factors such as the quarter or month of the year or day of

FIGURE 8-1

Types of data patterns

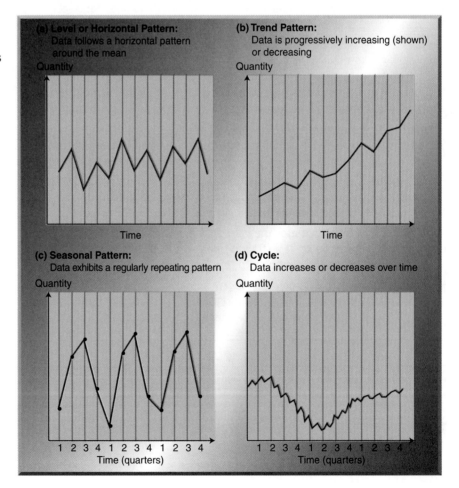

the week. Examples are a retail operation with high sales during November and December or a restaurant with peak sales on Fridays and Saturdays.

4. *Cycles.* Patterns that are created by economic fluctuations such as those associated with the business cycle are called **cycles**. These could be recessions, inflation, or even the life cycle of a product. The major distinction between a seasonal pattern and a cyclical pattern is that a cyclical pattern varies in length and magnitude and therefore is much more difficult to forecast than other patterns.

▶ **Cycles**
Data patterns created by economic fluctuations.

Random variation is unexplained variation that cannot be predicted. So if we look at any time series, we can see that it is composed of the following:

▶ **Random variation**
Unexplained variation that cannot be predicted.

$$\text{Data} = \underbrace{\text{level} + \text{trend} + \text{seasonality} + \text{cycles}} + \text{random variation}$$

$$\text{Data} = \qquad\qquad \text{pattern} \qquad\qquad + \text{random variation}$$

The first four components of the data are part of a pattern that we try to forecast. Random variation cannot be predicted. Some data have a lot of random variation and some have little. The more random variation a data set has, the harder it is to forecast accurately. As we will see, many forecasting models try to eliminate as much of the random variation as possible.

Forecasting Level or Horizontal Pattern

The simplest pattern is the level or horizontal pattern. In this section we look at some forecasting models that can be used to forecast the level of a time series.

The Naïve Method The **naïve method** is one of the simplest forecasting models. It assumes that the next period's forecast is equal to the current period's actual. For example, if your sales were 500 units in January, the naïve method would forecast 500 units for February. It is assumed that there is little change from period to period. Mathematically, we could put this in the following form:

▶ **Naïve method**
Forecasting method that assumes next period's forecast is equal to the current period's actual value.

$$F_{t+1} = A_t$$

where F_{t+1} = forecast for next period, $t + 1$
A_t = actual value for current period, t
t = current time period

A restaurant is forecasting sales of chicken dinners for the month of April. Total sales of chicken dinners for March were 320. If management uses the naïve method to forecast, what is their forecast of chicken dinners for the month of April?

EXAMPLE 8.1

Forecasting with the Naïve Method

• **Before You Begin:** Remember that with the naïve method the forecast for next period (April) is equal to the current period's actual value, which is 320 dinners for the month of March.

• **Solution:**
Our equation is

$$F_{t+1} = A_t$$

Adding the appropriate time period:

$$F_{\text{April}} = A_{\text{March}}$$
$$F_{\text{April}} = 320 \text{ dinners}$$

The naïve method can be modified to take trend into account. If we see that our trend is increasing by 10 percent and the current period's sales are 100 units, a naïve method with trend would give us current period's sales plus 10 percent, which is a forecast of 110 units for the next period. The naïve method can also be used for seasonal data. For example, suppose that we have monthly seasonality and know that sales for last January were 230 units. Using the naïve method, we would forecast sales of 230 units for next January.

One advantage of the naïve method is that it is very simple. It works well when there is little variation from one period to the next. Most of the time we use this method to evaluate the forecast performance of other, more complicated forecasting models. Because the naïve method is simple and effortless, we expect the forecasting model that we are using to perform better than naïve.

▶ **Simple mean or average**
The average of a set of data.

Simple Mean or Average   One of the simplest averaging models is the **simple mean or average**. Here the forecast is made by simply taking an average of all data:

$$F_{t+1} = \frac{\Sigma A_t}{n} = \frac{A_t + A_{t-1} + \cdots + A_{t-n}}{n}$$

where F_{t+1} = forecast of demand for next period, $t + 1$
A_t = actual value for current period, t
n = number of periods or data points to be averaged

EXAMPLE 8.2

Forecasting with the Mean

New Tools Corporation is forecasting sales for its classic product, Handy-Wrench. Handy-Wrench sales have been steady, and the company uses a simple mean to forecast. Weekly sales over the past five weeks are available. Use the mean to make a forecast for week 6.

Time Period (in weeks)	Actual Sales	Forecast
1	51	
2	53	
3	48	
4	52	
5	50	
6	—	50.8

• **Before You Begin:** Remember that using the mean requires the averaging of all the available data.

• **Solution:**
The basic equation for the mean is

$$F_{t+1} = \frac{\Sigma A_t}{n}$$

$$F_6 = \frac{51 + 53 + 48 + 52 + 50}{5}$$

$$F_6 = 50.8$$

This model is only good for a level data pattern. As the average becomes based on a larger and larger data set, the random variation and the forecasts become more stable. One of the advantages of this model is that only two historical pieces of information need to be carried: the mean itself and the number of observations the mean was based on.

Simple Moving Average The **simple moving average (SMA)** is similar to the simple average except that we are not taking an average of all the data, but are including only n of the most recent periods in the average. As new data become available, the oldest are dropped; the number of observations used to compute the average is kept constant. In this manner, the simple moving average "moves" through time. Like the simple mean, this model is good only for forecasting level data. The formula is as follows:

▶ **Simple moving average (SMA)**
A forecasting method in which only n of the most recent observations are averaged.

$$F_{t+1} = \frac{\Sigma A_t}{n} = \frac{A_t + A_{t-1} + \cdots + A_{t-n}}{n}$$

where F_{t+1} = forecast of demand for the next period, $t + 1$
A_t = actual value for current period, t
n = number of periods or data points used in the moving average

The formula for the moving average is the same as that for the simple average, except that we use only a small portion of the data to compute the average. For example, if we used a moving average of $n = 3$, we would be averaging only the latest three periods. If we were using a moving average of $n = 5$, we would be averaging only the latest five periods.

Sales forecasts for a product are made using a three-period moving average. Given the following sales figures for January, February, and March, make a forecast for April.

Month	Actual Sales
January	200
February	300
March	200

EXAMPLE 8.3

Forecasting with the Simple Moving Average (Three-Period MA)

• **Before You Begin:** Remember that to use a three-period moving average, you have to compute the average of the latest three observations. As new data become available, you drop off the oldest data, always averaging the latest three observations.

• **Solution:**
To find the forecast for April we take an average of the last three observations:

$$F_{t+1} = \frac{\Sigma A_t}{n}$$

$$F_{April} = \frac{A_{January} + A_{February} + A_{March}}{3} = \frac{200 + 300 + 200}{3} = 233.3$$

If the actual sales for April turn out to be 300, let's make a forecast for May. Using a three-period moving average, we take an average of the latest three observations. Since we are now able to include actual sales for April, we drop the sales for January:

$$F_{May} = \frac{A_{February} + A_{March} + A_{April}}{3} = \frac{300 + 200 + 300}{3} = 266.9$$

Similarly, if the actual sales for May turn out to be 400, we can make a forecast for June:

$$F_{June} = \frac{A_{March} + A_{April} + A_{May}}{3} = \frac{200 + 300 + 400}{3} = 300.0$$

Then, if the actual sales for June turn out to be 500, the forecast for July is computed as

$$F_{July} = \frac{A_{April} + A_{May} + A_{June}}{3} = \frac{300 + 400 + 500}{3} = 400.0$$

The other forecasts follow in a similar fashion. If actual sales for July and August turn out to be 600 and 650, respectively, then the respective forecasts for August and September are

$$F_{August} = \frac{A_{May} + A_{June} + A_{July}}{3} = \frac{400 + 500 + 600}{3} = 500.0$$

$$F_{September} = \frac{A_{June} + A_{July} + A_{August}}{3} = \frac{500 + 600 + 650}{3} = 583.3$$

Here is a summary of the forecasts we have made and the actual sales values:

Month	Actual Sales	Forecast Three-Period Moving Average
January	200	—
February	300	—
March	200	—
April	300	233.3
May	400	266.9
June	500	300.0
July	600	400.0
August	650	500.0
September	—	583.3

Just like the mean, the moving average is good only for a level pattern. You can see this in Example 8.3. The data shown in the example are level in the first four periods. However, after the fourth period the data begin to show a trend. You can see that the forecasts made with the moving average also begin to show an upward trend. Do you see a problem with the forecasts?

The problem is that the forecasts are trailing behind the actual data. We say that they are "lagging" the data. This is what happens when you apply a model that is good only for a level pattern to data that have a trend. You will not obtain a good forecast.

EXAMPLE 8.4

Forecasts with the Simple Moving Average (Five-Period MA)

Using data from Example 8.3, make forecasts for the months of June, July, August, and September using a five-period moving average.

• **Before You Begin:** In this problem we are going to compute the average of the last five available observations. As we move through time and new data become available, we will drop the oldest data and add the most recent, always averaging the latest five observations.

• **Solution:**
Notice that we are now going to average the last five available observations. Using a five-period moving average, the forecasts for June, July, August, and September are computed as follows:

$$F_{June} = \frac{A_{January} + A_{February} + A_{March} + A_{April} + A_{May}}{5} = \frac{200 + 300 + 200 + 300 + 400}{5}$$

$$F_{June} = 280$$

$$F_{July} = \frac{A_{February} + A_{March} + A_{April} + A_{May} + A_{June}}{5} = \frac{300 + 200 + 300 + 400 + 500}{5}$$

$$F_{July} = 340$$

$$F_{August} = \frac{A_{March} + A_{April} + A_{May} + A_{June} + A_{July}}{5} = \frac{200 + 300 + 400 + 500 + 600}{5}$$

$$F_{August} = 400$$

$$F_{September} = \frac{A_{April} + A_{May} + A_{June} + A_{July} + A_{August}}{5} = \frac{300 + 400 + 500 + 600 + 650}{5}$$

$$F_{September} = 490$$

Following is a summary of the forecasts and the actual sales values:

Month	Actual Sales	Forecast Five-Period Moving Average
January	200	
February	300	
March	200	
April	300	
May	400	
June	500	280
July	600	340
August	650	400
September	—	490

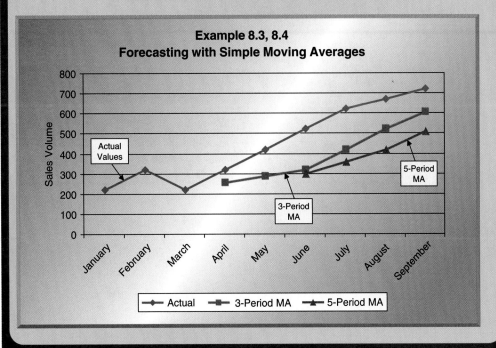

Example 8.3, 8.4
Forecasting with Simple Moving Averages

Comparing the three-period and five-period moving average forecasts, we can see that the three-period moving average forecasts are more responsive to the period-to-period changes in the actual data—they follow the data more closely. The reason is that the smaller the number of observations in the moving average, the more *responsive* the forecast is to changes in demand. However, the forecast is also more subject to the random changes in the data. If the data contain a lot of randomness, high responsiveness could lead to greater errors. On the other hand, the larger the number of observations in the moving average, the less responsive the forecast is to changes in the demand, but also to the randomness. These forecasts are more *stable*. One is not better than the other. Selection of the number of observations in the moving average should be based on the characteristics of the data.

Weighted Moving Average   In the simple moving average each observation is weighted equally. For example, in a three-period moving average each observation is weighted one-third. In a five-period moving average each observation is weighted one-fifth. Sometimes a manager wants to use a moving average but gives higher or lower weights to some observations based on knowledge of the industry. This is called a **weighted moving average**. In a weighted moving average, each observation can be weighted differently provided that all the weights add up to 1.

▶ **Weighted moving average**
A forecasting method in which *n* of the most recent observations are averaged and past observations may be weighted differently.

$$F_{t+1} = \Sigma C_t A_t = C_1 A_1 + C_2 A_2 + \cdots + C_t A_t$$

where F_{t+1} = next period's forecast
C_t = weight placed on the actual value in period t
A_t = actual value in period t

EXAMPLE 8.5

Forecasting with a Weighted Moving Average

A manager at Fit Well department store wants to forecast sales of swimsuits for August using a three-period weighted moving average. Sales for May, June, and July are as follows:

Month	Actual Sales	Forecast
May	400	
June	500	
July	600	

The manager has decided to weight May (.25), June (.25), and July (.50).

• **Before You Begin:** Remember that to compute a weighted moving average you need to multiply each observation by its corresponding weight. These values are then summed in order to get a weighted average.

• **Solution:**
The forecast for August is computed as follows:

$$F_{t+1} = \Sigma C_t A_t$$

$$F_{August} = (.25)A_{May} + (.25)A_{June} + (.50)A_{July}$$

$$= (.25)400 + (.25)500 + (.50)600$$

$$= 525$$

Exponential Smoothing The **exponential smoothing model** is a forecasting model that uses a sophisticated weighted average procedure to obtain a forecast. Even though it is sophisticated in the way it works, it is easy to use and understand. To make a forecast for the next time period, you need three pieces of information:

▶ **Exponential smoothing model**
Uses a sophisticated weight average procedure to generate a forecast.

1. The current period's forecast,
2. The current period's actual value
3. The value of a smoothing coefficient, α, which varies between 0 and 1.

The equation for the forecast is quite simple:

Next period's forecast = α (current period's actual) + $(1 - \alpha)$ (current period's forecast)

In mathematical terms:

$$F_{t+1} = \alpha A_t + (1 - \alpha)F_t$$

where F_{t+1} = forecast of demand for next period, $t + 1$
A_t = actual value for current period, t
F_t = forecast for current period, t
α = smoothing coefficient

Exponential smoothing models are the most frequently used forecasting techniques and are available on almost all computerized forecasting software. These models are widely used, particularly in operations management. They have been shown to produce accurate forecasts under many conditions, yet are relatively easy to use and understand.

The Hot Tamale Mexican restaurant uses exponential smoothing to forecast monthly usage of tabasco sauce. Its forecast for September was 200 bottles, whereas actual usage in September was 300 bottles. If the restaurant's managers use an α of 0.70, what is their forecast for October?

EXAMPLE 8.6

Forecasting with Exponential Smoothing

• **Before You Begin:** In this problem you are to use the exponential smoothing equation to get a forecast. You have been given the three pieces of information you need: the current period's forecast (200 bottles), the current period's actual value (300 bottles), and the value for the smoothing coefficient α, 0.70.

• **Solution:**
The general equation for exponential smoothing is

$$F_{t+1} = \alpha A_t + (1 - \alpha)F_t$$

$$F_{\text{October}} = \alpha A_{\text{September}} + (1 - \alpha)F_{\text{September}}$$

$$= (0.70)(300) + (0.30)200$$

$$= 270 \text{ bottles}$$

Selecting α Note that depending on which value you select for α, you can place more weight on either the current period's actual or the current period's forecast. In this manner the forecast can either depend more heavily on what happened most recently or on the current period's forecast. Values of α that are low—say, 0.1 or 0.2—generate forecasts that are very stable because the model does not place much weight on the current period's actual demand. Values of α that are high, such as 0.7 or 0.8, place a lot of weight on the current period's actual demand and can be influenced by random variations in the data. Thus, how α is selected is very important in getting a good forecast.

Starting the Forecasting Process with Exponential Smoothing One thing you may notice with exponential smoothing is that you need the current period's actual and current period's forecast to make a forecast for the next period. However, what if you are just starting the forecasting process and do not have a value for the current period's forecast? There are many ways to handle this, but the most common is to use the naïve method to generate an initial forecast. Another option is to average the last few periods—say, the last three or four—just to get a starting point.

EXAMPLE 8.7

Comparing Forecasts with Different Values of α

To illustrate the differences between different values of α, let's consider two series of forecasts for a data set. One set of forecasts was developed using exponential smoothing with $\alpha = 0.10$, another with an $\alpha = 0.60$.

| | | Exponential Smoothing Forecasts | |
Time Period (t)	Actual Demand	$\alpha = 0.10$	$\alpha = 0.60$
1	50	—	—
2	46	50	50
3	52	49.60	47.60
4	51	49.84	50.24
5	48	49.96	50.70
6	45	49.77	49.08
7	52	49.29	46.63
8	46	49.56	49.85
9	51	49.20	47.54
10	48	49.38	49.62

• **Before You Begin:** When using the exponential smoothing equation, always make sure you have the three pieces of information needed: the current period's forecast, the current period's actual value, and a value for the smoothing coefficient, α. This problem illustrates how you can begin the exponential smoothing process when you do not have initial forecast values.

• **Solution:**
Notice that we used the naïve method to derive initial values of forecasts for period 2. Then to obtain forecasts for period 3, we used the exponential smoothing equation with different values of α. For an $\alpha = 0.10$, the forecast for period 3 is computed as

$$F_3 = (0.10)(46) + (0.90)(50) = 49.6$$

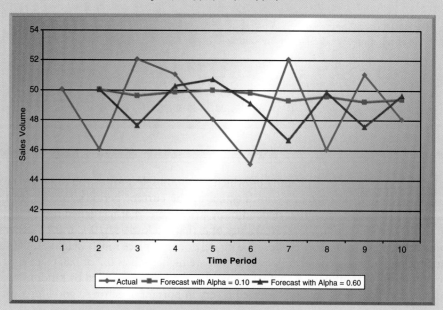

For an $\alpha = 0.60$, the forecast for period 3 is computed as:

$$F_3 = (0.60)(46) + (0.40)(50) = 47.6$$

The remaining forecasts are computed in the same manner. We can see from the graph that the forecasts with a lower value of α (0.10) have less variation than those with the higher value of α (0.60), indicating that they are more stable.

Before You Go On

We have discussed the principles of forecasting, how to forecast, and different types of qualitative and quantitative forecasting models. We have also learned about different types of patterns present in the data. You should understand that to obtain a good forecast the forecasting model should be matched to the patterns in the available data. Our example of the moving average shows what happens when the data show a trend but the model selected is useful only for forecasting a level pattern.

All the quantitative models discussed so far are meant only for level data patterns. In the next section we turn to quantitative models that can be used for other data patterns, such as trend and seasonality. However, remember that the models already discussed are the foundation of forecasting.

Forecasting Trend

There are many ways to forecast trend patterns in data. Most of the models used for forecasting trend are the same models used to forecast the level patterns, with an additional feature added to compensate for the lagging that would otherwise occur. Here we will look at two of the most common trend models.

Trend-Adjusted Exponential Smoothing Trend-adjusted exponential smoothing uses three equations. The first smooths out the level of the series, the second smooths out the trend, and the third generates a forecast by adding up the findings from the first two equations. Because we are using a second exponential smoothing equation to compute trend, we have two smoothing coefficients. In addition to α, which is used to smooth out the level of the series, we have a second coefficient, β, which is used to smooth out the trend of the series. Like α, β can theoretically vary between 0 and 1, though we tend to keep the value conservatively low, around 0.1 or 0.2.

▶ **Trend-adjusted exponential smoothing** Exponential smoothing model that is suited to data that exhibit a trend.

Three steps must be followed to generate a forecast with trend:

Step 1 Smoothing the Level of the Series

$$S_t = \alpha A_t + (1 - \alpha)(S_{t-1} + T_{t-1})$$

Step 2 Smoothing the Trend

$$T_t = \beta(S_t - S_{t-1}) + (1 - \beta)T_{t-1}$$

Step 3 Forecast Including Trend

$$FIT_{t+1} = S_t + T_t$$

where FIT_{t+1} = forecast including trend for next period, $t + 1$
S_t = exponentially smoothed average of the time series in period t
T_t = exponentially smoothed trend of the time series in period t
α = smoothing coefficient of the level
β = smoothing coefficient of the trend

Note that the last step simply adds up the findings from the first two steps. Next we will look at an example of how this works.

EXAMPLE 8.8

Forecasting with Trend-Adjusted Exponential Smoothing

Green Grow is a lawn care company that uses exponential smoothing with trend to forecast monthly usage of its lawn care products. At the end of July the company wishes to forecast sales for August. The trend through June has been 15 additional gallons of product sold per month. Average sales have been 57 gallons per month. The demand for July was 62 gallons. The company uses $\alpha = 0.20$ and $\beta = 0.10$. Make a forecast including trend for the month of August.

• **Before You Begin:** When solving this type of problem always begin by identifying the information that is given in the problem.

The information we have is

$$S_{June} = 57 \text{ gallons/month}$$

$$T_{June} = 15 \text{ gallons/month}$$

$$A_{July} = 62 \text{ gallons}$$

$$\alpha = 0.20$$

$$\beta = 0.10$$

Next, use the three equations needed to generate a forecast including trend. For each equation we will substitute the appropriate values.

• **Solution:**

Step 1   Smoothing the level of the Series

$$S_t = \alpha A_t + (1 - \alpha)(S_{t-1} + T_{t-1})$$

$$S_{July} = \alpha A_{July} + (1 - \alpha)(S_{June} + T_{June})$$

$$= (0.20)(62) + (0.80)(57 + 15)$$

$$= 70$$

Step 2   Smoothing the Trend

$$T_t = \beta(S_t - S_{t-1}) + (1 - \beta)T_{t-1}$$

$$T_{July} = \beta(S_{July} - S_{June}) + (1 - \beta)T_{June}$$

$$= (0.1)(70 - 57) + (0.90)15$$

$$= 14.8$$

Step 3   Forecast Including Trend

$$FIT_{t+1} = S_t + T_t$$

$$FIT_{August} = S_{July} + T_{July}$$

$$= 70 + 14.8$$

$$84.8 \text{ gallons}$$

Linear Trend Line   Linear trend line is a time series technique that computes a forecast with trend by drawing a straight line through a set of data. This approach is a version of the linear regression technique, covered later in this chapter, and is useful for computing a forecast when data display a clear trend over time. The method is simple, easy to use, and easy to understand.

A linear trend line uses the following equation to generate a forecast:

$$Y = a + bX$$

where Y = forecast for period X
X = the number of time periods from $X = 0$
a = value of Y at $X = 0$ (Y intercept)
b = slope of the line

The coefficients a and b are computed using the least-squares method, which minimizes the sum of the squared errors. Developing the equations for a and b can be complicated, so we will only provide the equations needed for computation. The steps for computing the forecast using a linear trend line are as follows:

Step 1 Compute parameter b:

$$b = \frac{\Sigma XY - n\overline{X}\,\overline{Y}}{\Sigma X^2 - n\overline{X}^2}$$

Step 2 Compute parameter a:

$$a = \overline{Y} - b\overline{X}$$

Step 3 Generate the linear trend line:

$$Y = a + bX$$

Step 4 Generate a forecast (Y) for the appropriate value of time (X)

A manufacturer has plotted product sales over the past four weeks. Use a linear trend line to generate a forecast for week 5.

EXAMPLE 8.9

Forecasting with a Linear Trend Line

• **Before You Begin:** Remember to follow the four steps given in the text for generating a forecast using a linear trend line.

• **Solution:**

	Weeks	Sales		
	X	Y	X^2	XY
	1	2,300	1	2,300
	2	2,400	4	4,800
	3	2,300	9	6,900
	4	2,500	16	10,000
Totals	**10**	**9,500**	**30**	**24,000**

$$\overline{Y} = 2375 \qquad \overline{X} = 2.5$$

Step 1 Compute parameter b:

$$b = \frac{\Sigma XY - n\overline{X}\,\overline{Y}}{\Sigma X^2 - n\overline{X}^2} = \frac{24,000 - 4(2.5)(2375)}{30 - 4(2.5)^2} = \frac{250}{5} = 50$$

Step 2 Compute parameter a:

$$a = \overline{Y} - b\overline{X} = 2375 - (50)(2.5) = 2250$$

Step 3   Compute the linear trend line:

$$Y = a + bX$$

$$= 2250 + 50X$$

Step 4   For the fifth week, the value of sales would be

$$Y = 2250 + 50(5) = 2500$$

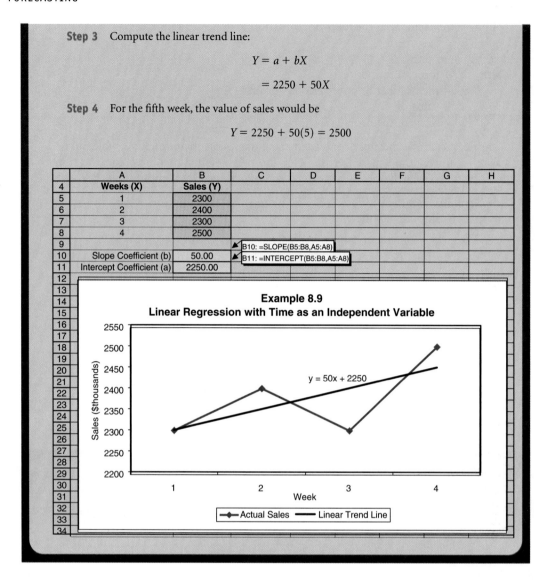

	A	B	C	D	E	F	G	H
4	**Weeks (X)**	**Sales (Y)**						
5	1	2300						
6	2	2400						
7	3	2300						
8	4	2500						
9								
10	Slope Coefficient (b)	50.00						
11	Intercept Coefficient (a)	2250.00						

B10: =SLOPE(B5:B8,A5:A8)
B11: =INTERCEPT(B5:B8,A5:A8)

Example 8.9
Linear Regression with Time as an Independent Variable

y = 50x + 2250

Sales ($thousands)

Week

Actual Sales   Linear Trend Line

Forecasting Seasonality

Recall that any regularly repeating pattern is a seasonal pattern. We are all familiar with quarterly and monthly seasonal patterns. Whether your university is on a quarter or semester plan, you can see that enrollment varies between quarters or semesters in a fairly predictable way. For example, enrollment is usually much higher in the fall than in the summer. Other examples of seasonality include sales of turkeys before Thanksgiving or ham before Easter, sales of greeting cards, hotel registrations, and sales of gardening tools.

The amount of seasonality is the extent to which actual values deviate from the average or mean of the data. Here we will consider only *multiplicative seasonality,* in which the seasonality is expressed as a percentage of the average. The percentage by which the value for each season is above or below the mean is a **seasonal index**. For example, if enrollment for the fall semester at your university is 1.30 of the mean, the fall enrollment is 30 percent above the average. Similarly, if enrollment for the summer semester is .70 of the mean, then summer enrollment is 70 percent of the average.

▶ **Seasonal index**
Percentage amount by which data for each season are above or below the mean.

Here we will show only the procedure for computing quarterly seasonality that lasts a year, though the same procedure can be used for any other type of seasonality. The procedure consists of the following steps:

Step 1 **Calculate the Average Demand for Each Quarter or "Season."** This is done by dividing the total annual demand by 4 (the number of seasons per year).

Step 2 **Compute a Seasonal Index for Every Season of Every Year for Which You Have Data.** This is done by *dividing* the actual demand for each season by the average demand per season (computed in Step 1).

Step 3 **Calculate the Average Seasonal Index for Each Season.** For each season, compute the average seasonal index by adding up the seasonal index values for that season and dividing by the number of years.

Step 4 **Calculate the Average Demand per Season for Next Year.** This could be done by using any of the methods used to compute annual demand. Then we would divide that by the number of seasons to determine the average demand per season for next year.

Step 5 **Multiply Next Year's Average Seasonal Demand by Each Seasonal Index.** This will produce a forecast for each season of next year.

U-R-Smart University wants to develop forecasts for next year's quarterly enrollment. It has collected quarterly enrollments for the past two years. It has also forecasted total annual enrollment for next year to be 90,000 students. What is the forecast for each quarter of next year?

EXAMPLE 8.10

Forecasting Seasonality

Enrollment (in thousands)

Quarter	Year 1	Year 2
Fall	24	26
Winter	23	22
Spring	19	19
Summer	14	17
Total	**80**	**84**

● **Before You Begin:** You can see that the data exhibit a seasonal pattern, with each quarter representing a "season." To compute the forecast for each quarter of next year, follow the five steps given in the text on forecasting with seasonality.

● **Solution:**

Step 1 **Calculate the Average Demand for Each Quarter or "Season."** We do this by dividing the total annual demand for each year by 4:

$$\text{Year 1: } 80/4 = 20$$

$$\text{Year 2: } 84/4 = 21$$

Step 2 **Compute a Seasonal Index for Every Season of Every Year for Which You Have Data.** To do this we divide the actual demand for each season by the average demand per season.

Enrollment (in thousands)

Quarter	Year 1	Year 2
Fall	24/20 = 1.20	26/21 = 1.238
Winter	23/20 = 1.15	22/21 = 1.048
Spring	19/20 = 0.95	19/21 = 0.905
Summer	14/20 = 0.70	17/21 = 0.810

Step 3   Calculate the Average Seasonal Index for Each Season. You can see that the seasonal indexes vary from year to year for the same season. The simplest way to handle this is to compute an average index, as follows:

Quarter	Average Seasonal Index
Fall	$(1.2 + 1.238)/2 = 1.219$
Winter	$(1.15 + 1.048)/2 = 1.099$
Spring	$(0.95 + 0.905)/2 = 0.928$
Summer	$(0.70 + 0.810)/2 = 0.755$

Step 4   Calculate the Average Demand per Season for Next Year. We are told that the university forecast annual enrollment for the next year to be 90,000 students. The average demand per season, or quarter, is

$$90,000/4 = 22,500$$

Step 5   Multiply Next Year's Average Seasonal Demand by Each Seasonal Index. This last step will give us the forecast for each quarter of next year:

Quarter	Forecast (Students)
Fall	$22,500(1.219) = 27,428$
Winter	$22,500(1.099) = 24,728$
Spring	$22,500(0.928) = 20,880$
Summer	$22,500(0.755) = 16,988$

This can also be computed using a spreadsheet, as shown below. Notice slight differences in final numbers due to rounding.

	A	B	C	D	E	F
4		**Enrollment (thousands)**				
5	**Quarter**	**Year 1**	**Year 2**			
6	Fall	24	26			
7	Winter	23	22			
8	Spring	19	19			
9	Summer	14	17	C10: =SUM(C6:C9)		
10	Total Demand	80	84	C11: =C10/4		
11	Average Demand per Quarter	20	21			
12					B16: =B6/B$11 (copied down)	
13	**Calculate Seasonal Indices**					
14		**Individual**				
15	**Quarter**	**Year 1**	**Year 2**	**Average**	C16: =C6/C$11 (copied down)	
16	Fall	1.200	1.238	1.219		
17	Winter	1.150	1.048	1.099	D16: =(B16+C16)/2 (copied down)	
18	Spring	0.950	0.905	0.927		
19	Summer	0.700	0.810	0.755		
20						
21	**Calculate Forecast for Next Year**					
22	Estimated annual enrollment	90000				
23	Average per Quarter	22500	B23: =B22/4			
24						
25	Expected Quarterly Enrollment, Based on Historical Seasonal Indices					
26	**Quarter**	**Forecast**				
27	Fall	27429	B27: =B$23*D16 (copied down)			
28	Winter	24723				
29	Spring	20866				
30	Summer	16982				

Forecasting demand at ski resorts such as Snowshoe, Holiday Valley, and Seven Springs can be very challenging because data are highly seasonal. Multiple seasonal factors need to be considered, including the month of the year, day of the week, and holidays and long weekends, in addition to considering the weather forecast. Historical data are used to develop the indexes for these seasons. In addition, the ski industry has been experiencing an upward trend over the past years, particularly with the growth of snowboarding. A simple way to make forecasts in this industry is to forecast the trend and then make adjustments based on developed seasonal indexes.

LINKS TO PRACTICE

The Ski Industry Forecast

Marc Muench/Corbis Images

CAUSAL MODELS

Recall that causal, or associative, models assume that the variable we are trying to forecast is somehow related to other variables in the environment. The forecasting challenge is to discover the relationships between the variable of interest and these other variables. These relationships, which can be very complex, take the form of a mathematical model, which is used to forecast future values of the variable of interest. Some of the best-known causal models are regression models. In this section we look at linear and multiple regression and how they are used in forecasting.

Linear Regression

In **linear regression** the variable being forecast, called the dependent variable, is related to some other variable, called the independent variable, in a linear (or straight line) way. Figure 8-2 shows how a linear regression line relates to the data. You can see

► **Linear regression**
Procedure that models a straight-line relationship between two variables.

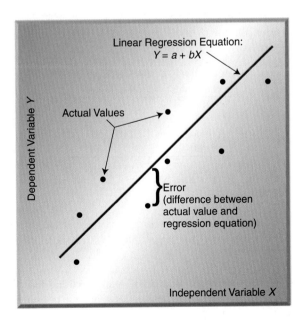

FIGURE 8-2

Linear regression line fit to historical data

that the dependent variable is linearly related to the independent variable. The relationship between two variables is the equation of a straight line:

$$Y = a + bX$$

where Y = dependent variable
X = independent variable
a = Y intercept of the line
b = slope of the line

There are many straight lines that could be drawn through the data. Linear regression selects parameters a and b, which define a straight line that minimizes the sum of the squared errors, or deviations from the line. This is called the *least-squares straight line*. Developing the values for a and b can be complicated, so we simply give their computation here. You can assume that computing a and b in this way will produce a straight line through the data that minimizes the sum of the squared errors. The steps in computing the linear regression equation are as follows:

Step 1   Compute parameter b:

$$b = \frac{\Sigma XY - n\overline{X}\,\overline{Y}}{\Sigma X^2 - n\overline{X}^2}$$

where $\overline{Y}$ = average of the Y values
$\overline{X}$ = average of the X values
n = number of data points

We compute parameter b first because that calculation is needed to compute parameter a.

Step 2   Compute parameter a:

$$a = \overline{Y} - b\overline{X}$$

Step 3   Substitute these values to obtain the linear regression equation:

$$Y = a + bX$$

Step 4   To make a forecast for the dependent variable (Y), substitute the appropriate value for the independent variable (X).

EXAMPLE 8.11

Forecasting with Linear Regression

A maker of personalized golf shirts has been tracking the relationship between sales and advertising dollars over the past four years. The results are as follows:

Sales Dollars (in thousands)	Advertising Dollars (in thousands)
130	32
151	52
150	50
158	55

Use linear regression to find out what sales would be if the company invested $53,000 in advertising for next year.

• **Before You Begin:** When using linear regression, always identify the independent and dependent variables. Remember that the dependent variable is the one you are trying to forecast.

• **Solution:**
In this example sales are the *dependent variable* (Y) and advertising dollars are the *independent variable* (X). We assume that there is a relationship between these two variables. To compute the linear regression equation, we set up the following table of information:

Y	X	XY	X²	Y²
130	32	4160	2304	16,900
151	52	7852	2704	22,801
150	50	7500	2500	22,500
158	55	8690	3025	24,964
Total	**589**	**189**	**28,202**	**9,253**	**87,165**

$$\overline{X} = 47.25 \qquad \overline{Y} = 147.25$$

Now let's follow the steps necessary for computing a linear regression equation:

Step 1 Compute parameter b:

$$b = \frac{\Sigma XY - n\overline{X}\overline{Y}}{\Sigma X^2 - n\overline{X}^2} = \frac{28,202 - 4(47.25)(147.25)}{9,253 - 4(47.25)^2} = \frac{371.75}{322.75} = 1.15$$

Step 2 Compute parameter a:

$$a = \overline{Y} - b\overline{X} = 147.25 - (1.15)(47.25) = 92.83$$

Step 3 Compute the linear regression equation:

$$Y = a + bX$$
$$= 92.8^3 + 1.15X$$

Step 4 Now that we have the equation, we can compute the value of Y for any value of X. To compute the value of sales when advertising dollars are $53,000, we can substitute that number for X:

$$Y = 92.8^3 + 1.15(53) = \$153.87 \text{ (in thousands)}$$

This can also be computed using a spreadsheet, as shown here.

	A	B	C	D	E	F	G	H
4	**Year**	**Advertising Dollars (thousands)**	**Sales (thousands)**					
5	1	32	130					
6	2	52	151					
7	3	50	150					
8	4	55	158	C9: =AVERAGE(C5:C8)				
9	Average	47.25	147.25					
10				C11: =SLOPE(C5:C8,B5:B8)				
11	Slope Coefficient (b)		1.15	C12: =INTERCEPT(C5:C8,B5:B8)				
12	Intercept Coefficient (a)		92.83					

Example 8.11
Sales (thousands) vs Advertising (thousands)

y = 1.15x + 92.83

Correlation Coefficient

► **Correlation coefficient**
Statistic that measures the direction and strength of the linear relationship between two variables.

When performing linear regression, it is helpful to compute the **correlation coefficient**, which measures the direction and strength of the linear relationship between the independent and dependent variables. The correlation coefficient is computed using the following equation:

$$r = \frac{n(\Sigma XY) - (\Sigma X)(\Sigma Y)}{\sqrt{[n(\Sigma X^2) - (\Sigma X)^2]} \cdot \sqrt{[n(\Sigma Y^2) - (\Sigma Y)^2]}}$$

Although the equation seems complicated, it is easy to compute and the values of r can be easily interpreted. Values of r range between -1 and $+1$ and have the following meanings:

   $r = +1$: There is a perfect positive linear relationship between the two variables. For every 1-unit increase in the independent variable, there is a 1-unit increase in the dependent variable.

   $r = -1$: There is a perfect negative linear relationship between the two variables. Just because the relationship is negative does not mean that there is no relationship. It is still a linear relationship except that it is negative; the two variables move in opposite directions. A unit increase in the independent variable is accompanied by a unit decrease in the dependent variable.

   $r = 0$: There is no linear relationship between the variables.

Obviously, the closer the value of r is to 1.00 or -1.00, the stronger is the linear relationship between the two variables. If we square the correlation coefficient, r^2, we can determine how well the independent variable explains changes in the dependent variable. This statistic shows how well the regression line "fits" the data. The higher the r, the better. A high r^2—say, .80 or higher—would indicate that the independent variable can be used effectively as a predictor of the dependent variable.

EXAMPLE 8.12

Computing the Correlation Coefficient

Using the information from Example 8.11, compute the correlation coefficient and evaluate the strength of the linear relationship between sales and advertising dollars.

• **Before You Begin:** To solve this problem, compute the correlation coefficient using the formula from the text. Remember that the closer the computed value is to 1, the stronger the relationship between the two variables.

• **Solution:**
Given our information, we can compute the correlation coefficient as follows:

$$r = \frac{n(\Sigma XY) - (\Sigma X)(\Sigma Y)}{\sqrt{[n(\Sigma X^2) - (\Sigma X)^2]} \cdot \sqrt{[n(\Sigma Y^2) - (\Sigma Y)^2]}}$$

$$= \frac{4(28,202) - (189)(589)}{\sqrt{[4(9,253) - (189)^2]} \cdot \sqrt{[4(87,165) - (589)^2]}} = .992$$

The computed correlation coefficient is close to 1, which means that there is a strong positive linear relationship between the two variables. Also, if we compute r^2 we get .984, which means that 98.4 percent of the variability in sales is explained by advertising dollars.

Multiple Regression

Multiple regression is an extension of linear regression. However, unlike in linear regression where the dependent variable is related to one independent variable, multiple regression develops a relationship between a dependent variable and multiple independent variables. The general formula for multiple regression is as follows:

$$Y = B_0 + B_1X_1 + B_2X_2 + \cdots + B_KX_K$$

where Y = dependent variable
  B_0 = the Y intercept
  $B_1 \ldots B_K$ = coefficients that represent the influence of the independent variables on the dependent variable
  $X_1 \ldots X_K$ = independent variables

For example, the dependent variable might be sales and the independent variables might be number of sales representatives, number of store locations, area population, and per capita income.

Multiple regression is a powerful tool for forecasting and should be used when multiple factors influence the variable that is being forecast. However, multiple regression does significantly increase data and computational requirements needed for forecasting. Fortunately, most standard statistical software programs have multiple regression capabilities.

MEASURING FORECAST ACCURACY

One of the basic principles of forecasting is that forecasts are rarely perfect. However, how does a manager know how much a forecast can be off the mark and still be reasonable? One of the most important criteria for choosing a forecasting model is its accuracy. Also, data can change over time, and a model that once provided good results may no longer be adequate. The model's accuracy can be assessed only if forecast performance is measured over time. For all these reasons it is important to track model performance over time, which involves monitoring forecast errors.

Forecast Accuracy Measures

Forecast error is the difference between the forecast and actual value for a given period, or

$$E_t = A_t - F_t$$

where E_t = forecast error for period t
  A_t = actual value for period t
  F_t = forecast for period t

However, error for one time period does not tell us very much. We need to measure forecast accuracy over time. Two of the most commonly used error measures are the **mean absolute deviation (MAD)** and the **mean squared error (MSE)**. *MAD* is the average of the sum of the absolute errors:

$$MAD \frac{\Sigma|\text{actual} - \text{forecast}|}{n}$$

MSE is the average of the squared error:

$$MSE = \frac{\Sigma(\text{actual} - \text{forecast})^2}{n}$$

▶ **Forecast error**
Difference between forecast and actual value for a given period.

▶ **Mean absolute deviation (MAD)**
Measure of forecast error that computes error as the average of the sum of the absolute errors.

▶ **Mean squared error (MSE)**
Measure of forecast error that computes error as the average of the squared error.

One of the advantages of *MAD* is that it is based on absolute values. Consequently, the errors of opposite signs do not cancel each other out when they are added. We sum the errors regardless of sign and obtain a measure of the average error. If we are comparing different forecasting methods, we can then select the method with the lowest *MAD*.

MSE has an additional advantage: due to the squaring of the error term, large errors tend to be magnified. Consequently, *MSE* places a higher penalty on large errors. This can be a useful error measure in environments in which large errors are particularly destructive. For example, a blood bank forecasts the demand for blood. Because forecasts are rarely perfect, there will be errors. However, in this environment a large error could be very damaging. Using *MSE* as an error measure would highlight any large errors in the blood bank's forecast. As with *MAD*, when comparing the forecast performance of different methods we would select the method with the lowest *MSE*.

To evaluate forecast performance, you need to use only one forecast error measure. However, a good forecaster learns to rely on multiple methods to evaluate forecast performance. Example 8.13 illustrates the use of *MAD* and *MSE*.

EXAMPLE 8.13

Measuring Forecast Accuracy

Standard Parts Corporation is comparing the accuracy of two methods that it has used to forecast sales of its popular valve. Forecasts using method A and method B are shown against the actual values for January through May. Which method provided better forecast accuracy?

• **Before You Begin:** In this problem you are to compare the forecast accuracy of two forecasting methods. Since a good forecaster relies on multiple error measures, compute both the *MAD* and *MSE* using the formulas given in the text. The method that gives the lowest *MAD* and *MSE* provides the better accuracy.

• **Solution:**

Month	Actual Sales	Method A Forecast	Method A Error	Method A Error	Method A Error^2	Method B Forecast	Method B Error	Method B Error	Method B Error^2
January	30	28	2	2	4	30	0	0	0
February	26	25	1	1	1	28	−2	2	4
March	32	32	0	0	0	36	−4	4	16
April	29	30	−1	1	1	30	−1	1	1
May	31	30	1	1	1	28	3	3	9
Total			**3**	**5**	**7**		**−4**	**10**	**30**

Accuracy for method A:

$$MAD = \frac{\Sigma |\text{actual} - \text{forecast}|}{n} = \frac{5}{5} = 1$$

$$MSE = \frac{\Sigma (\text{actual} - \text{forecast})^2}{n} = \frac{7}{5} = 1.4$$

Accuracy for method B:

$$MAD = \frac{\Sigma |\text{actual} - \text{forecast}|}{n} = \frac{10}{5} = 2$$

$$MSE = \frac{\Sigma (\text{actual} - \text{forecast})^2}{n} = \frac{30}{5} = 6$$

Of the two methods, method A produced a lower *MAD* and a lower *MSE*, which means that it provides better forecast accuracy. Note that the magnitude of difference in values is greater for

MSE than for *MAD*. Recall that *MSE* magnifies large errors through the squaring process. For the month of March, method B had a magnitude of error that was much larger than for other periods, causing *MSE* to be high. This can also be computed using a spreadsheet, as shown next.

	A	B	C	D	E	F	G	H	I	J
4					Method A			Method B		
5	Month	Actual Sales	Forecast	Error	Absolute Error	Error²	Forecast	Error	Absolute Error	Error²
6	January	30	28	2	2	4	30	0	0	0
7	February	26	25	1	1	1	28	-2	2	4
8	March	32	32	0	0	0	36	-4	4	16
9	April	29	30	-1	1	1	30	-1	1	1
10	May	31	30	1	1	1	28	3	3	9
11	Totals			3	5	7		-4	10	30
12										
13				MAD =	1.0			MAD =	2.0	
14				MSE =	1.4			MSE =	6.0	
23										
24	Key Formulas (similar formulas for method B)									
25	D6	=$B6-C6 (copied down)								
26	E6	=ABS(D6) (copied down)								
27	F6	=D6^2 (copied down)								
28	E13	=AVERAGE(E6:E10)								
29	E14	=AVERAGE(F6:F10)								

Tracking Signal

When there is a difference between forecast and actual values, one problem is to identify whether the difference is caused by random variation or is due to a *bias* in the forecast. **Forecast bias** is a persistent tendency for a forecast to be over or under the actual value of the data. We cannot do anything about random variation, but bias can be corrected.

One way to control for forecast bias is to use a *tracking signal*. A **tracking signal** is a tool used to monitor the quality of the forecast. It is computed as the ratio of the algebraic sum of the forecast errors divided by *MAD*:

$$\text{Tracking signal} = \frac{\text{algebraic sum of forecast errors}}{MAD}$$

or

$$\text{Tracking signal} = \frac{\Sigma(\text{actual} - \text{forecast})}{MAD}$$

As the forecast errors are summed over time, they can indicate whether there is a bias in the forecast. To monitor forecast accuracy, the values of the tracking signal are compared against predetermined limits. These limits are usually based on judgment and experience and can range from ±3 to ±8. In this chapter we will use the limits of ±4, which compare to limits of 3 standard deviations. If errors fall outside these limits, the forecast should be reviewed.

▶ **Forecast bias**
A persistent tendency for a forecast to be over or under the actual value of the data.

▶ **Tracking signal**
Tool used to monitor the quality of a forecast.

EXAMPLE 8.14

Developing a Tracking Signal

A company uses a tracking signal with limits of ±4 to decide whether a forecast should be reviewed. Compute the tracking signal given the following historical information and decide when the forecast should be reviewed. The *MAD* for this item was computed as 2.

Weeks	Actual	Forecast	Deviation	Cumulative Deviation	Tracking Signal
				4	2
1	8	10			
2	11	10			
3	12	10			
4	14	10			

- **Before You Begin:** In this problem you have to compute the tracking signal for weeks 1 through 4 and determine if it exceeds the set limit of ±4. Remember that the tracking signal is the sum of the forecast errors (the cumulative deviation) divided by the *MAD*. In this problem *MAD* has been computed as 2. You need to compute the cumulative deviation for each period and divide by the *MAD*.

- **Solution:**

Weeks	Actual	Forecast	Cumulative Deviation	Tracking Deviation	Signal
				4	2
1	8	10	−2	2	1
2	11	10	1	3	1.5
3	12	10	2	5	2.5
4	14	10	4	9	4.5

The forecast should be reviewed in week 4 because the tracking signal has exceeded +4.

SELECTING THE RIGHT FORECASTING MODEL

A number of factors influence the selection of a forecasting model. They include the following:

1. *Amount and type of available data.* Quantitative forecasting models require certain types of data. If there are not enough data in quantifiable form, it may be necessary to use a qualitative forecasting model. Also, different quantitative models require different amounts of data. Exponential smoothing requires a small amount of historical data, whereas linear regression requires considerably more. The amount and type of data available play a large role in the type of model that can be considered.

2. *Degree of accuracy required.* The type of model selected is related to the degree of accuracy required. Some situations require only rough forecast estimates, whereas others require precise accuracy. Often, the greater the degree of accuracy required, the higher is the cost of the forecasting process. This is because increasing accuracy means increasing the costs of collecting and processing data, as well as the cost of the computer software required. A simpler and less

costly forecasting model may be better overall than one that is very sophisticated but expensive.

3. *Length of forecast horizon.* Some forecasting models are better suited to short forecast horizons, whereas others are better for long horizons. It is very important to select the correct model for the forecast horizon being used. For example, a manufacturer that wishes to forecast sales of a product for the next three months will use a very different forecasting model than an electric utility that wishes to forecast demand for electricity over the next twenty-five years.

4. *Data patterns present.* It is very important to identify the patterns in the data and select the appropriate model. For example, lagging can occur when a forecasting model meant for a level pattern is applied to data with a trend.

FORECASTING SOFTWARE

Today much commercial forecasting is performed using computer software. Many software packages that can be used for forecasting. Some can handle thousands of variables and manipulate huge databases. Others specialize in one forecasting model. Consequently, it may be difficult to select the right forecasting software. Most forecasting software packages fall into one of three categories: (1) spreadsheets, (2) statistics packages, and (3) specialty forecasting packages. In this section we look at the differences among these categories. Then we present some guidelines for selecting a software package for forecasting.

Spreadsheets

Spreadsheets, such as Microsoft Excel®, Quattro Pro®, and Lotus 1-2-3®, are prevalent in business, and most people are familiar with at least one of them. These packages provide basic forecast capability, such as simple exponential smoothing and regression. Also, simple forecasting programs can be written very quickly for most spreadsheet programs. However, the disadvantage of using spreadsheets for forecasting is that they do not have the capability for statistical analysis of forecast data. As we have seen, proper forecasting requires much data analysis. This involves analyzing the data for patterns, studying relationships among variables, monitoring forecast errors, and evaluating the performance of different forecasting models. Unfortunately, spreadsheets do not offer this capability as readily as packages designed specifically for forecasting.

Statistical Packages

Statistical software includes packages designed primarily for statistical analysis, such as SPSS, SAS, NCSS, and Minitab. Almost all of these packages also offer forecasting capabilities, as well as extensive data analysis capability. There are large differences among statistical packages, particularly between those versions for mainframe versus those for microcomputers. Overall, these packages offer large capability and a variety of options. However, their many features can be overwhelming for someone interested only in forecasting. Statistical software packages are best for a user who seeks many statistical and graphical capabilities in addition to forecasting features.

Specialty Forecasting Packages

Specialized forecasting software is specifically intended for forecasting use. These packages often provide an extensive range of forecasting capability, though they may not offer large statistical analysis capability. Popular packages include Forecast Master, Forecast Pro, SIBYL/Runner, Autobox, and SCA. Some of these packages offer a wide range of forecasting models, whereas others specialize in a particular model category. Forecasters who need extensive statistical analysis capability may need to use a statistical package in addition to the forecasting package.

Guidelines for Selecting Forecasting Software

There are many forecasting software packages to choose from, and the process can be overwhelming. Following are some guidelines for selecting the right package:[1]

1. *Does the package have the facilities you want?* The first question to ask is whether the forecasting methods you are considering using are available in the package. Other issues to consider are the software's graphics capabilities, data management, and reporting facilities. You need to consider how important these are given the purpose of the forecasts you will be generating.

2. *What platform is the package available for?* You obviously need to make sure that the software is available for the platform you are using. Also, it may be necessary to consider the availability for multiple platforms, depending on who will use the software and whether there will be transferring of files.

3. *How easy is the package to learn and use?* Some packages offer many capabilities but may be hard to use. Generally, the more comprehensive the array of capabilities, the more difficult the package is to use. Make sure that you can master the software. Also check the ease of importing and exporting data.

4. *Is it possible to implement new methods?* Often forecasters prefer to modify existing methods to fit their particular needs. Many forecasting packages allow the addition of new models or the modification of existing ones through a programming language.

5. *Do you require interactive or repetitive forecasting?* In many operations management situations we need to make forecasts for hundreds of items on a regular basis, such as monthly or quarterly. For these situations it is very useful to have a "batch" forecasting capability. This is not necessary, however, for forecasts that are generated interactively with the forecaster.

6. *Do you have very large data sets?* Almost all packages have a limit on how many variables and how many observations can be processed. Sometimes very powerful forecasting packages can handle only relatively small data sets. Make sure the package you purchase is capable of processing the data you need.

7. *Is there any local support?* Make sure there is ample documentation and good technical support, and check for any other local support that may be available. Remember that all packages can encounter glitches. A number of forecasting vendors offer seminars, and there are often courses that can be taken for the more popular methods, such as SAS and SPSS.

---

[1]S. Makridakis, S. Wheelwright, and R. Hyndman, *Forecasting Methods and Applications*, 3rd ed. (New York: John Wiley, 1998).

8. *Does the package give the right answers?* Most people assume that a computer package will generate correct results. However, this is not always the case. There are small differences in output between different packages due to differences in the algorithms used for computing. Some differences can result from actual errors in the programs, especially when large data sets are used. One recommendation is to compare output from the software against published results or against output from another package.

Another factor to consider is the *cost of the package* relative to the importance of its use. Some packages are very expensive and comprehensive, while others are less expensive. Evaluate the use of the forecasts generated and their importance in the managerial situation before purchasing a highly expensive package. Finally, you need to consider *compatibility with existing software*, especially for other operations management applications such as scheduling and inventory control. The output from forecasting usually feeds into these systems, so you need to make sure these systems can communicate with one another.

FOCUS FORECASTING

Focus forecasting is a forecasting approach that has gained some popularity in business. It was developed by Bernie Smith,[2] who argues that statistical methods do not work well for forecasting. He believes simple rules that have worked well in the past are best used to forecast the future. The idea behind focus forecasting is to test these rules on past data and evaluate how they perform. New rules can be added at any time, and old ones that have not performed well can be eliminated.

Focus forecasting uses a computer simulation program that evaluates the forecast performance of a number of rules on past data. The program keeps track of the rules and evaluates how well they perform. Following are some examples of rules:

1. We will sell over the next three months what we sold over the last three months.

2. What we sold in a three-month period last year, we will sell in the same three-month period this year.

3. We will sell over the next three months 5 percent of what we sold over the last three months.

4. We will sell over the next three months 15 percent of what we sold over the same three-month period last year.

You can see that these rules use commonsense concepts. In focus forecasting, managers can come up with any new rules that they believe reflect accurate forecasts in their business and then test their value on historical data.

Smith claims to have achieved great success with focus forecasting. He states that he has compared its accuracy to that of conventional methods, such as exponential smoothing, and that focus forecasting consistently provides superior results.

COMBINING FORECASTS

One approach to forecasting that has been shown to result in improved forecast accuracy is to combine forecasts from two or more different forecasting methods. Studies have shown that combining forecasts can lead to forecast accuracy that is better than

[2]Bernard T. Smith, *Focus Forecasting: Computer Techniques for Inventory Control* (Boston: CBI, 1984).

that of the individual forecasts. The forecasting methods that are combined should be different and can even be based on different information or data.

One of the simplest ways to combine is to use a simple average of the individual forecasts. Even though there are more sophisticated ways of combining, a simple average has been shown to be very effective in improving forecast accuracy.

Ralph Wetmore/Stone/
Getty Images

The idea of relying on different types of forecasting methods and combining their results to get a final forecast has even been used by weather forecasters. Weather forecasting can be challenging, and many factors need to be considered, such as long-range trends and current weather fronts. Weather forecasters have been able to improve their forecast accuracy by combining the results of forecasts made at different time intervals. For example, a weather forecast for the upcoming weekend may be formulated by *combining* computer-generated forecasts made on the preceding Monday, Tuesday, and Wednesday. This method is called "ensemble forecasting" and has proven to be very successful.

COLLABORATIVE PLANNING, FORECASTING, AND REPLENISHMENT (CPFR)

Collaborative Planning, Forecasting, and Replenishment (CPFR) is a collaborative process between two trading partners that establishes formal guidelines for joint forecasting and planning. The premise behind CPFR is that companies can be more successful if they join forces to bring value to their customers, share risks of the marketplace, and improve their performances.

In previous chapters we learned about the benefits that can be attained by sharing information with suppliers and developing long-term relationships. CPFR is a formal way of achieving this. By implementing CPFR, trading partners jointly set forecasts, plan production, replenish inventories, and evaluate their success in the marketplace. The most complete form of CPFR utilizes a nine-step process:

1. *Establish collaborative relationships.* Buyers and sellers formally establish their relationship, including expectations and performance measures. This is usually reevaluated annually.

2. *Create a joint business plan.* Buyers and sellers develop a joint business plan.

3. *Create a sales forecast.* Sales forecasts are generated based on available data. This is usually done monthly or weekly.

4. *Identify exceptions for sales forecasts.* Items that are exceptions to the sales forecast are identified.

5. *Resolve/collaborate on exceptions to sales forecasts.* Buyers and sellers jointly investigate exceptions by analyzing shared data.

6. *Create order forecast.* An order forecast is generated that supports the shared sales forecast and joint business plan.

7. *Identify exceptions for order forecast.* Buyers and sellers jointly identify which items are exceptions to the order forecast.

8. *Resolve/collaborate on exceptions to order forecast.* Exceptions are identified and resolved by analyzing shared data.

9. *Generate order.* Usually performed weekly or daily.

Most of the outlined steps are performed on a weekly or monthly basis, and the agreement between parties is evaluated annually. You can see that a large amount of time is spent jointly identifying and reconciling exceptions, with the focus on supporting the jointly set business plan. Also, note that CPFR is an iterative process. That means that it is done over and over again.

CPFR has contributed to the success of many companies, including Wal-Mart, Target, Black & Decker, and Ace Hardware. The German-based manufacturer of household cleaners and home care products, Henkel KgaA, was able to significantly improve sales forecasts and reduce error rates in just six months by implementing CPFR.

FORECASTING WITHIN OM: HOW IT ALL FITS TOGETHER

Forecasts impact not only other business functions but all other operations decisions. Operations managers make many forecasts, such as the expected demand for a company's products. These forecasts are then used to determine product designs that are expected to sell (Chapter 2), the quantity of product to produce (Chapters 5 and 6), and the amount of supplies and materials that are needed (Chapter 12). Also, a company uses forecasts to determine future space requirements (Chapter 10), capacity and location needs (Chapter 9), and the amount of labor needed (Chapter 11). Forecasts drive strategic operations decisions, such as choice of competitive priorities, changes in processes, and large technology purchases (Chapter 3). Forecast decisions also serve as the basis for tactical planning, such as developing worker schedules (Chapter 11). Virtually all operations management decisions are based on a forecast of the future.

FORECASTING ACROSS THE ORGANIZATION

Forecasting is an excellent example of an activity that is critical to the management of all functional areas within a company. In business organizations, forecasts are made in virtually every function and at every organizational level. Budgets are set, resources allocated, and schedules made based on forecasts. Without a forecast of the future, a company would not be able to make any plans, including day-to-day and long-range plans. In this section we look at how forecasting affects some of the other functions of an organization.

Marketing relies heavily on forecasting tools to generate forecasts of demand and future sales. However, the marketing department also needs to forecast sizes of markets, new competition, future trends, and changes in consumer preferences. Most of the forecasting methods discussed in this chapter are used by marketing. Marketing often works in conjunction with operations to assess future demands.

Finance uses the tools of forecasting to predict stock prices, financial performance, capital investment needs, and investment portfolio returns. The accuracy of demand forecasts, in turn, affects the ability of finance to plan future cash flow and financial needs.

Information systems play an important role in the forecasting process. Today's forecasting requires sharing of information and databases not only within a business but also between business entities. Often companies share their forecasts or demand information with their suppliers. These capabilities would not be possible without an up-to-date information system.

Human resources relies on forecasting to determine future hiring requirements. In addition, forecasts are made of the job market, labor skill availability, future wages and compensation, hiring and layoff costs, and training costs. In order to recruit proper talent, it is necessary to forecast labor needs and availability.

Economics relies on forecasting to predict the duration of business cycles, economic turning points, and general economic conditions that affect business. Whenever a plan of action is required, that plan is based on some anticipation of the future—a forecast. Whether in business, industry, government, or in other fields such as medicine, engineering, and science, proper planning for the future starts with a good forecast.

THE SUPPLY CHAIN LINK

All entities of a supply chain are working to fulfill final customer demands. The forecast of demand is critical, as it affects all the plans made by each company in the supply chain. When entities of the supply chain make their forecasts independent of one another, they each have their own separate forecast of demand. The consequences of this are a mismatch between supply and demand because each company is working to fulfill a different level of demand. Consider that Dell starts its planning process with a forecast of future demand to determine the amount of components it needs to order. At the same time, Intel, who supplies Dell with microprocessors, needs to determine its production and inventory schedules. If Dell and Intel made their forecasts separately, their forecasts would be different and Intel would not be able to supply the exact amounts Dell needs. In contrast, when there is collaboration between suppliers and manufacturers in generating the forecast, all entities are responding to the same level of demand. A good example of this is the implementation of collaborative planning, forecasting, and replenishment (CPFR), which we discussed earlier in the chapter.

Chapter Highlights

1 Three basic principles of forecasting are: forecasts are rarely perfect; forecasts are more accurate for groups or families of items rather than for individual items; and forecasts are more accurate for shorter than longer time horizons.

2 The forecasting process involves five steps: decide what to forecast; evaluate and analyze appropriate data; select and test a forecasting model; generate the forecast; and monitor forecast accuracy.

3 Forecasting methods can be classified into two groups: *qualitative* and *quantitative*. Qualitative forecasting methods generate a forecast based on the subjective opinion of the forecaster. Some examples of qualitative methods include *executive opinion, market research*, and the *Delphi method*. Quantitative forecasting methods are based on mathematical modeling. They can be divided into two categories: *time series models* and *causal models*.

4 Time series models are based on the assumption that all the information needed for forecasting is contained in the time series of data. Causal models assume that the variable being forecast is related to other variables in the environment.

5 There are four basic patterns of data: *level* or *horizontal, trend, seasonality*, and *cycles*. In addition, data usually contain *random variation*. Some forecasting models that can be used to forecast the level of a time series are *naïve, simple mean, simple moving average, weighted moving average*, and *exponential smoothing*. Separate models are used to forecast trend, such as *trend-adjusted exponential smoothing*. Forecasting seasonality requires a procedure in which we compute a *seasonal index*, the percentage by which each season is above or below the mean.

6 A simple causal model is linear regression, in which a straight-line relationship is modeled between the variable we are forecasting and another variable in the environment. The correlation coefficient is used to measure the strength of the linear relationship between these two variables.

7 Three useful measures of forecast accuracy are mean absolute deviation (*MAD*), mean square error (*MSE*), and a tracking signal.

8 There are four factors to consider when selecting a forecasting model: the amount and type of data available, the degree of accuracy required, the length of forecast horizon, and patterns present in the data.

Key Terms

forecasting 253
qualitative forecasting methods 255
quantitative forecasting methods 256
executive opinion 257
market research 257
Delphi method 257
time series models 258
time series 258
causal models 258
level or horizontal pattern 260

trend 260
seasonality 260
cycles 261
random variation 261
naïve method 261
simple mean or average 262
simple moving average (SMA) 263
weighted moving average 266
exponential smoothing model 267
trend-adjusted exponential smoothing 269

seasonal index 272
linear regression 275
correlation coefficient 278
forecast error 279
mean absolute deviation (*MAD*) 279
mean squared error (*MSE*) 279
forecast bias 281
tracking signal 281

Formula Review

Name	Formula
1. Naïve	$F_{t+1} = A_t$
2. Simple mean	$F_{t+1} = \dfrac{\Sigma A_t}{n}$
3. Moving average	$F_{t+1} = \dfrac{\Sigma A_t}{n}$
4. Weighted moving average	$F_{t+1} = \Sigma C_t A_t$
5. Exponential smoothing	$F_{t+1} = \alpha A_t + (1 - \alpha)F_t$
6. Trend-adjusted exponential smoothing	**Step 1:** Smoothing the level of the series: $S_t = \alpha A_t + (1 - \alpha)(S_{t-1} + T_{t-1})$ **Step 2:** Smoothing the trend: $T_t = \beta(S_t - S_{t-1}) + (1 - \beta)T_{t-1}$ **Step 3:** Forecast including trend: $FIT_{t+1} = S_t + T_t$
7. Seasonality	**Step 1:** Calculate the average demand for each season. **Step 2:** Compute a seasonal index for every season of every year you have data.
8. Linear trend line/linear regression	**Step 1:** Compute parameter *b*: $b = \dfrac{\Sigma XY - n\overline{XY}}{\Sigma X^2 - n\overline{X}^2}$ **Step 2:** Compute parameter *a*: $a = \overline{Y} - b\overline{X}$ **Step 3:** Obtain equation: $Y = a + bX$

Name	Formula
9. Correlation coefficient	$r = \dfrac{n(\Sigma XY) - (\Sigma X) - (\Sigma Y)}{\sqrt{[n(\Sigma X^2) - (\Sigma X)^2]} \cdot \sqrt{[n(\Sigma Y^2) - (\Sigma Y)^2]}}$
10. Forecast error	$E_t = A_t - F_t$
11. Mean absolute deviation	$MAD = \dfrac{\Sigma |\text{actual} - \text{forecast}|}{n}$
12. Mean squared error	$MSE = \dfrac{\Sigma(\text{actual} - \text{forecast})^2}{n}$
13. Tracking signal	$\text{Tracking signal} = \dfrac{\Sigma(\text{actual} - \text{forecast})}{MAD}$

Solved Problems (See student companion site for Excel template.)

• Problem 1

Given the following data, calculate forecasts for months 4, 5, 6, and 7 using a three-month moving average and an exponential smoothing forecast with an alpha of 0.3. Assume a forecast of 61 for month 3:

Month	Actual Sales	Forecast 3-Month Moving Average	Forecast Exponential Smoothing
1	56		
2	76		
3	58		
4	67		
5	75		
6	76		
7			

• Before You Begin:

To use a three-period moving average, remember that you always have to compute the average of the latest three observations. As new data become available, drop off the oldest data. For the exponential smoothing part of this problem, before you begin make sure that you have the three pieces of information you need: the current period's forecast (61 for month 3), the current period's actual value (58), and a value for the smoothing coefficient ($\alpha = 0.3$).

• Solution

Month	Actual Sales	Forecast 3-Month Moving Average	Forecast Exponential Smoothing
1	56		
2	76		
3	58		
4	67	63.33	60.1
5	75	67.00	62.17
6	76	66.66	66.02
7		72.66	69.01

To compute the moving average forecasts:

$$F_{t+1} = \frac{\Sigma A_t}{n}$$

$$F_4 = \frac{A_1 + A_2 + A_3}{3} = \frac{56 + 76 + 58}{3} = 63.33$$

$$F_5 = \frac{A_2 + A_3 + A_4}{3} = \frac{76 + 58 + 67}{3} = 67.00$$

$$F_6 = \frac{A_3 + A_4 + A_5}{3} = \frac{58 + 67 + 75}{3} = 66.66$$

$$F_7 = \frac{A_4 + A_5 + A_6}{3} = \frac{67 + 75 + 76}{3} = 72.66$$

To compute the exponential smoothing forecasts:

$$F_{t+1} = \alpha A_t + (1 - \alpha)F_t$$

$$F_4 = \alpha A_3 + (1 - \alpha)F_3$$

$$F_4 = (0.30)(58) + (0.70)61 = 60.1$$

$$F_5 = (0.30)(67) + (0.70)60.1 = 62.17$$

$$F_6 = (0.30)(75) + (0.70)62.17 = 66.02$$

$$F_7 = (0.30)(76) + (0.70)66.02 = 69.01$$

This can also be computed using a spreadsheet, as shown here.

	A	B	C	D	E	F	G	H	I
4			alpha =	0.30					
5									
6			**Forecasts**						
7	**Month**	**Actual Sales**	**3-month Moving Avg**	**Exponential Smoothing**	C11: =AVERAGE(B8:B10) (copied down)				
8	1	56							
9	2	76			D11: =D$4*B10+(1-D$4)*D10 (copied down)				
10	3	58	61	61					
11	4	67	63.33	60.10					
12	5	75	67.00	62.17					
13	6	76	66.67	66.02					
14	7		72.67	69.01					

Solved Problem 8.1
Moving Average and Exponential Smoothing Forecasts

• Problem 2

True Beauty is a cosmetics company that uses exponential smoothing with trend to forecast monthly sales of its special face cream. At the end of November, the company wants to forecast sales for December. The trend through October has been ten additional boxes sold per month. Average sales have been sixty boxes per month. The demand for November was sixty-eight boxes. The company uses $\alpha = 0.20$ and $\beta = 0.10$. Make a forecast including trend for the month of December.

• Before You Begin:

Before you begin solving this type of problem, first identify the information given in the problem.

The information we have is:

$$S_{Oct} = 60 \text{ boxes/month}$$
$$T_{Oct} = 10 \text{ boxes/month}$$
$$A_{Nov} = 68 \text{ boxes}$$
$$\alpha = 0.20$$
$$\beta = 0.10$$

Now we can follow the three steps in the chapter for trend-adjusted exponential smoothing.

• Solution

We need to use three equations to generate a forecast including trend. For each equation we substitute the appropriate values:

Step 1 Smoothing the level of the series:

$$S_t = \alpha A_t + (1 - \alpha)(S_{t-1} + T_{t-1})$$

$$S_{Nov} = \alpha A_{Nov} + (1 - \alpha)(S_{Oct} + T_{Oct})$$

$$= (0.20) + (0.80)(60 + 10)$$

$$= 69.6$$

Step 2 Smoothing the trend:

$$T_t = \beta(S_t - S_{t-1}) + (1 - \beta)T_{t-1}$$

$$T_{Nov} = \beta(S_{Nov} + S_{Oct}) + (1 - \beta)T_{Oct}$$

$$= (0.1)(68) + (69 - 60) + (0.90)10$$

$$= 9.9$$

Step 3 Forecast including trend:

$$FIT_{t+1} = S_t + T_t$$

$$FIT_{Dec} = S_{Nov} + T_{Nov}$$

$$= 69 + 9.9$$

$$= 78.9 \text{ boxes}$$

• Problem 3

A gardener wants to develop a forecast for next year's quarterly sales of cactus trees. He has collected quarterly sales for the past two years and expects total sales for next year to be 500 cactus trees. The data clearly exhibit seasonality. How much can he expect to sell during each quarter of next year accounting for seasonality?

Cactus Trees Sold

Season	Year 1	Year 2
Fall	100	110
Winter	82	95
Spring	180	173
Summer	110	110
Total	**472**	**488**

• Before You Begin:

To solve this problem, follow the five steps given in the chapter for forecasting seasonality.

• Solution

We follow the steps used in developing seasonal indexes:

Step 1 Calculate the average demand for each season:

$$\text{Year 1: } 472/4 = 118$$

$$\text{Year 2: } 488/4 = 122$$

Step 2 Compute a seasonal index for every season of every year for which there is data.

Cactus Trees Sold

Season	Year 1	Year 2
Fall	100/118 = .847	110/122 = .902
Winter	82/118 = .695	95/122 = .778
Spring	180/118 = 1.53	173/122 = 1.42
Summer	110/118 = .932	110/122 = .902

Step 3 Calculate the average seasonal index for each season.

Season	Average Seasonal Index
Fall	(.847 + .902)/2 = .875
Winter	(.695 + .778)/2 = .737
Spring	(1.53 + 1.42/2 = 1.48
Summer	(.932 + .902)/2 = .917

Step 4 Calculate the average demand per season for next year.

We are told that the sales forecast for next year is 500 cactus trees. The average demand per season, or quarter, is

$$500/4 = 125$$

Step 5 Multiply next year's average seasonal demand by each seasonal index.

Season	Forecast (Cactus Trees)
Fall	125(.875) = 109.4
Winter	125(.737) = 92.13
Spring	125(1.48) = 185.0
Summer	125(.917) = 114.4

• Problem 4

A sneaker manufacturer has plotted sales of its most popular brand of sneakers over the past four months. Use a linear trend line to compute sales of sneakers for month 5.

• Before You Begin:

To solve this problem, follow the four steps given in the chapter for finding a linear trend line.

• Solution

Month X	Sales Y	X^2	XY
1	100	1	100
2	120	4	240
3	118	9	354
4	125	16	500
Total 10	**463**	**30**	**1194**

$$\overline{Y} = 115.75 \qquad \overline{X} = 2.5$$

Step 1 Compute parameter b:

$$b = \frac{(\Sigma XY) - n\overline{XY}}{\Sigma X^2 - n\overline{X}^2}$$

$$= \frac{1194 - 4(2.5)(115.75)}{30 - 4(2.5)^2} = \frac{36.5}{5} = 7.3$$

Step 2 Compute parameter a:

$$a = \overline{Y} - b\overline{X} = 115.75 - (7.3)(2.5) = 97.5$$

Step 3 Compute the linear trend line.

$$Y = a + bX$$
$$Y = 97.5 + 7.3X$$

Step 4 For the fifth month, the value of sales would be

$$Y = 97.5 + 7.3(5) = 134 \text{ sneakers}$$

• Problem 5

A retailer of household appliances has collected data on the relationship between the company's sales and disposable household income. For the presented data:
(a) Obtain a linear regression equation for the data;
(b) Compute a correlation coefficient and determine the strength of the linear relationship;
(c) Use the linear regression equation to develop a forecast of sales if disposable household income is 37,800.

• Before You Begin:

To solve this problem follow the four steps given in the chapter for generating a forecast using linear regression. Make sure to clearly identify the independent and dependent variables. As you proceed, remember that you first compute parameter b, then parameter a, then develop the regression equation, and finally generate the forecast.

• Solution

Sales (in 000s of $) Y	Disposable Household Income (in 000s of $) X	XY	X^2	Y^2
29.8	16.8	500.6	282.2	888.0
35.9	18.4	660.6	338.6	1,228.8
38.8	20.4	791.5	416.2	1,505.4
43.6	22.9	998.4	524.4	1,900.9
46.8	25.7	1,202.8	660.5	2,190.2
49.5	27.3	1,351.4	745.3	2,450.3
52.3	32.1	1,678.8	1,030.4	2,735.3
55.2	35.2	1,943.0	1,239.0	3,047.0
57.2	36.3	2,076.4	1,317.7	3,271.8
58.6	38.2	2,238.5	1,459.2	3,433.9
Total 467.7	273.3	13,442.0	8,013.5	22,711.6

$$\overline{X} = 27.3 \qquad \overline{Y} = 46.8$$

(a) **Step 1** Compute parameter b:

$$b = \frac{(\Sigma XY) - n\overline{XY}}{\Sigma X^2 - n\overline{X}^2} = \frac{13,442.0 - (10)(27.3)(46.8)}{8,013.5 - (10)(27.3)^2}$$

$$= 1.19$$

Step 2 Computer parameter a:

$$a = \overline{Y} - b\overline{X} = 46.8 - (1.19)(27.3) = 14.31$$

Step 3 Compute the linear regression line:

$$Y = a + bX$$
$$Y = 14.31 + 1.19X$$

(b) Computing the correlation coefficient:

$$r = \frac{n(\Sigma XY) - (\Sigma X)(\Sigma Y)}{\sqrt{n(\Sigma X^2) - (\Sigma X)^2} \cdot \sqrt{n(\Sigma Y^2) - (\Sigma Y)^2}}$$

$$r = \frac{10(13,442) - (273.3)(467.7)}{\sqrt{10(8,013.5) - (273.3)^2} \cdot \sqrt{10(22,711.6) - 467.7^2}}$$

$$r = .977$$

The correlation coefficient is close to 1.00, indicating a strong positive linear relationship.

(c) $Y = 14.31 + 1.19(37.8) = 59.29$

This means that if disposable household income is $37,800, the company's sales are expected to be $59,290.

• Problem 6

A company is comparing the accuracy of two different forecasting methods. Use *MAD* to compare the accuracies of these methods for the past five weeks of sales. Which method provides greater forecast accuracy?

• Before You Begin:

Remember that MAD is the average of the sum of the absolute errors and that a *lower* MAD indicates better forecast accuracy.

• Solution

Week	Actual Sales	Method A Forecast	Method A Error	Method A |Error|	Method B Forecast	Method B Error	Method B |Error|
1	25	30	−5	5	30	−5	5
2	18	20	−2	2	16	2	2
3	26	23	3	3	25	1	1
4	28	29	−1	1	30	−2	2
5	30	25	5	5	28	2	2
Total			**0**	**16**		**−2**	**12**

Accuracy for method A:

$$MAD = \frac{\Sigma|actual - forecast|}{n} = \frac{16}{5} = 3.2$$

Accuracy for method B:

$$MAD = \frac{\Sigma|actual - forecast|}{n} = \frac{12}{5} = 2.4$$

Of the two methods, method B produced a lower *MAD*, which means that it provides greater forecast accuracy. Note, however, that the sum of the errors was actually 0 for method A, which shows how this error measure can be misleading.

Discussion Questions

1. Give three examples showing why a business needs to forecast.

2. Give three examples from your life in which you may forecast the future.

3. Describe the steps involved in forecasting.

4. Identify the key differences between qualitative and quantitative forecasting methods. Which is better in your opinion and why?

5. What are the main types of data patterns? Give examples of each type.

6. Describe the different assumptions of time series and causal models.

7. What are the differences among models that forecast the level, trend, and seasonality?

8. Explain why it is important to monitor forecast errors.

9. Explain some of the factors to be considered in selecting a forecasting model.

Problems

1. Sales for a product for the past three months have been 200, 350, and 287. Use a three-month moving average to calculate a forecast for the fourth month. If the actual demand for month 4 turns out to be 300, calculate the forecast for month 5.

2. Lauren's Beauty Boutique has experienced the following weekly sales:

Week	Sales
1	432
2	396
3	415
4	458
5	460

Forecast sales for week 6 using the naïve method, a simple average, and a three-period moving average.

3. Hospitality Hotels forecasts monthly labor needs.

(a) Given the following monthly labor figures, make a forecast for June using a three-period moving average and a five-period moving average.

Month	Actual Values
January	32
February	41
March	38
April	39
May	43

(b) What would be the forecast for June using the naïve method?

(c) If the actual labor figure for June turns out to be 41, what would be the forecast for July using each of these models?

(d) Compare the accuracy of these models using the mean absolute deviation (*MAD*).

(e) Compare the accuracy of these models using the mean squared error (*MSE*).

4. The following data are monthly sales of jeans at a local department store. The buyer would like to forecast sales of jeans for the next month, July.

(a) Forecast sales of jeans for March through June using the naïve method, a two-period moving average, and exponential smoothing with an $\alpha = 0.2$. (*Hint:* Use naïve to start the exponential smoothing process.)

(b) Compare the forecasts using *MAD* and decide which is best.

(c) Using your method of choice, make a forecast for the month of July.

Month	Sales
January	45
February	30
March	40
April	50
May	55
June	47

5. The manager of a small health clinic would like to use exponential smoothing to forecast demand for laboratory services in the facility. However, she is not sure whether to use a high or low value of α. To make her decision, she would like to compare the forecast accuracy of a high and low α on historical data. She has decided to use an $\alpha = 0.7$ for the high value and $\alpha = 0.1$ for the low value. Given the following historical data, which do you think would be better to use?

Week	Demand (lab requirements)
1	330
2	350
3	320
4	370
5	368
6	343

6. The manager of the health clinic in Problem 5 would also like to use exponential smoothing to forecast demand for emergency services in the facility. As in Problem 5, she is not sure whether to use a high or low value of α. To make her decision, she would like to compare the forecast accuracy of a high and low α on historical data. Again, she has decided to use an $\alpha = 0.7$ for the high value and $\alpha = 0.1$ for the low value.

(a) Given the following historical data, which value of α do you think would be better to use?

(b) Is your answer the same as in Problem 5? Why or why not?

Week	Demand (in patients serviced)
1	430
2	289
3	367
4	470
5	468
6	365

7. The following historical data have been collected representing sales of a product. Compare forecasts using a three-period moving average, exponential smoothing with a $\alpha = 0.2$, and linear regression. Using *MAD* and *MSE*, which forecasting model is best? Are your results the same using the two error measures?

Week	Demand
1	20
2	31
3	36
4	38
5	42
6	40

8. A manufacturer of printed circuit boards uses exponential smoothing with trend to forecast monthly demand of its product. At the end of December, the company wishes to forecast sales for January. The estimate of trend through November has been 200 additional boards sold per month. Average sales have been around 1000 units per month. The demand for December was 1100 units. The company uses $\alpha = 0.20$ and $\beta = 0.10$. Make a forecast including trend for the month of January.

9. Demand at Nature Trails Ski Resort has a seasonal pattern. Demand is highest during the winter, as this is the peak ski season. However, there is some ski demand in the spring and even fall months. The summer months can also be busy as visitors often come for summer vacation to go hiking on the mountain trails. The owner of Nature Trails would like to make a forecast for each season of the next year. Total annual demand has been estimated at 4000 visitors. Given the last two years of historical data, what is the forecast for each season of the next year?

	Visitors	
Season	Year 1	Year 2
Fall	200	230
Winter	1400	1600
Spring	520	580
Summer	720	831

10. Rosa's Italian restaurant wants to develop forecasts of daily demand for the next week. The restaurant is closed on Mondays and experiences a seasonal pattern for the other six

days of the week. Mario, the manager, has collected information on the number of customers served each day for the past two weeks. If Mario expects total demand for next week to be around 350, what is the forecast for each day of next week?

Day	Number of Customers	
	Week 1	Week 2
Tuesday	52	48
Wednesday	36	32
Thursday	35	30
Friday	89	97
Saturday	98	99
Sunday	65	69

11. The president of a company was interested in determining whether there is a correlation between sales made by different sales teams and hours spent on employee training. These figures are shown.

Sales (in thousands)	Training Hours
25	10
40	12
36	12
50	15
11	6

(a) Compute the correlation coefficient for the data. What is your interpretation of this value?
(b) Using the data, what would you expect sales to be if training was increased to eighteen hours?

12. The number of students enrolled at Spring Valley Elementary has been steadily increasing over the past five years. The school board would like to forecast enrollment for years 6 and 7 in order to better plan capacity. Use a linear trend line to forecast enrollment for years 6 and 7.

Year	Enrollment
1	220
2	245
3	256
4	289
5	310

13. Happy Lodge Ski Resorts tries to forecast monthly attendance. The management has noticed a direct relationship between the average monthly temperature and attendance.
(a) Given five months of average monthly temperatures and corresponding monthly attendance, compute a linear regression equation of the relationship between the two. If next month's average temperature is forecast to be 45 degrees, use your linear regression equation to develop a forecast.

Month	Average Temperature	Resort Attendance (in thousands)
1	24	43
2	41	31
3	32	39
4	30	38
5	38	35

(b) Compute a correlation coefficient for the data and determine the strength of the linear relationship between average temperature and attendance. How good a predictor is temperature for attendance?

14. Small Wonder, an amusement park, experiences seasonal attendance. It has collected two years of quarterly attendance data and made a forecast of annual attendance for the coming year. Compute the seasonal indexes for the four quarters and generate quarterly forecasts for the coming year, assuming annual attendance for the coming year to be 1525.

Quarter	Park Attendance (in thousands)	
	Year 1	Year 2
Fall	352	391
Winter	156	212
Spring	489	518
Summer	314	352

15. Burger Lover Restaurant forecasts weekly sales of cheeseburgers. Based on historical observations over the past five weeks, make a forecast for the next period using the following methods: simple average, three-period moving average, and exponential smoothing with $\alpha = 0.3$, given a forecast of 328 cheeseburgers for the first week.

Week	Cheeseburger Sales
1	354
2	345
3	367
4	322
5	356

If actual sales for week 6 turn out to be 368, compare the three forecasts using *MAD*. Which method performed best?

16. A company uses exponential smoothing with trend to forecast monthly sales of its product, which show a trend pattern. At the end of week 5, the company wants to forecast sales for week 6. The trend through week 4 has been twenty additional cases sold per week. Average sales have been eighty-five cases per week. The demand for week 5 was ninety cases. The company uses $\alpha = 0.20$ and $\beta = 0.10$. Make a forecast including trend for week 6.

17. The number of patients coming to the Healthy Start maternity clinic has been increasing steadily over the past eight

months. Given the following data, use a linear trend line to forecast attendance for months 9 and 10.

Month	Clinic Attendance (in thousands)
1	3.4
2	3.9
3	4.5
4	5.0
5	5.8
6	5.9
7	6.5
8	6.7

18. Given the following data, use exponential smoothing with $\alpha = 0.2$ and $\alpha = 0.5$ to generate forecasts for periods 2 through 6. Use *MAD* and *MSE* to decide which of the two models produced a better forecast.

Period	Actual	Forecast
1	15	17
2	18	
3	14	
4	16	
5	13	
6	16	

19. Pumpkin Pies Galore is trying to forecast sales of pies for the month of December. Demand for pies in September, October, and November has been 230, 304, and 415, respectively. Edith, the company's owner, uses a three-period weighted moving average to forecast sales. Based on her experience, she chooses to weight September as 0.1, October as 0.3, and November as 0.6.
(a) What would Edith's forecast for December be?
(b) What would her forecast be using the naïve method?
(c) If actual sales for December turned out to be 420 pies, which method was better (use *MAD*)?

20. A company has used three different methods to forecast sales for the past five months. Use *MAD* and *MSE* to evaluate the performance of the three methods.
(a) Which forecasting method performed best? Do *MAD* and *MSE* give the same results?

Period	Actual	Method A	Method B	Method C
1	10	10	9	8
2	8	11	10	11
3	12	12	8	10
4	11	13	12	11
5	12	14	11	12

(b) Which of these is actually the naïve method?

21. Two different forecasting models were used to forecast sales of a popular soda on a college campus. Actual demand and the two sets of forecasts are shown. Use *MAD* to explain which method provided a better forecast.

Period	Actual Demand	Forecast 1	Forecast 2
1	90	78	87
2	87	85	88
3	92	84	90
4	95	92	97
5	98	100	102
6	98	102	101

22. A producer of picture frames uses a tracking signal with limits of ±4 to decide whether a forecast should be reviewed. Given historical information for the past four weeks, compute the tracking signal and decide whether the forecast should be reviewed. The *MAD* for this item was computed as 2.

Weeks	Actual Sales	Forecast	Deviation	Cumulative Deviation	Tracking Signal
				6	3
1	12	11			
2	14	13			
3	14	14			
4	16	14			

23. Mop and Broom Manufacturing has tracked the number of units sold of their most popular mop over the past twenty-four months. This is shown.

Month	Sales	Month	Sales	Month	Sales
1	239	9	310	17	369
2	248	10	335	18	378
3	256	11	348	19	367
4	260	12	353	20	383
5	271	13	355	21	394
6	280	14	368	22	393
7	295	15	379	23	405
8	305	16	358	24	412

(a) Develop a linear trend line for the data.
(b) Compute a correlation coefficient for the data and evaluate the strength of the linear relationship.
(c) Using the linear trend line equation, develop a forecast for the next period, month 25.

24. Given the sales data from Problem 23, generate forecasts for months 7–24 using a six-period and a three-period moving average. Use *MAD* to compare the forecasts. Which forecast is more stable? Which is more responsive and why?

25. The following data were collected on the study of the relationship between a company's retail sales and advertising dollars:

Retail Sales ($)	Advertising ($)
29,789	16,893
35,434	18,398
38,732	20,376
43,585	22,982
46,821	25,732
49,283	27,281
52,271	32,182
55,289	35,298
57,298	36,281
58,293	38,178

(a) Obtain a linear regression line for the data.
(b) Compute a correlation coefficient and determine the strength of the linear relationship.
(c) Using the linear regression equation, develop a forecast of retail sales for advertising dollars of $40,000.

CASE: Bram-Wear

Lenny Bram, owner and manager of Bram-Wear, was analyzing performance data for the men's clothing retailer. He was concerned that inventories were high for certain clothing items, meaning that the company would potentially incur losses due to the need for significant markdowns. At the same time, it had run out of stock for other items early in the season. Some customers appeared frustrated by not finding the items they were looking for and needed to go elsewhere. Lenny knew that the problem, though not yet serious, needed to be addressed immediately.

Background

Bram-Wear was a retailer that sold clothing catering to young, urban, professional men. It primarily carried upscale, casual attire, as well as a small quantity of outerwear and footwear. Its success did not come from carrying a large product variety, but from a very focused style with an abundance of sizes and colors.

Bram-Wear had extremely good financial performance over the past five years. Lenny had attributed the company's success to a group of excellent buyers. The buyers seemed able to accurately target the style preferences of their customers and correctly forecast product quantities. One challenge was keeping up with customer buying patterns and trends.

The Data

To determine the source of the problem, Lenny had requested forecast and sales data by product category. Looking at the sheets of data, it appeared that the problem was not with the specific styles or items carried in stock; rather, the problem appeared to be with the quantities ordered by the buyers. Specifically, the problem centered on two items: an athletic shoe called Urban Run and the five-pocket cargo jeans.

Urban Run was a popular athletic shoe that had been carried by Bram-Wear for the past four years. Quarterly data for the past four years are shown in the table. The company seemed to always be out of stock of this athletic shoe. The model used by buyers to forecast sales for this item had been seasonal exponential smoothing. Looking at the data, Lenny wondered if this was the best method to use. It seemed to work well in the beginning, but now he was not so sure.

The data for the five-pocket cargo jean seemed also to point to a forecasting problem. When the product was introduced last year, it was expected to have a large upward trend. The buyers believed the trend would continue and used an exponential smoothing model with trend to forecast sales. However, they seemed to have too much inventory of this product. As with the Urban Run athletic shoe, Lenny wondered if the right forecasting model was being applied to the data. It seemed he would have to dig out his old operations management text to solve this problem.

Demand for Urban Run Athletic Shoe

Quarter	Year 1 Demand	Year 2 Demand	Year 3 Demand	Year 4 Demand
I	10	14	20	30
II	29	31	26	31
III	26	29	28	33
IV	15	18	30	35

Demand for 5-Pocket Cargo Jeans

Month	Year 1 Demand	Year 2 Demand
January	36	98
February	42	101
March	56	97
April	75	99
May	85	100
June	94	95
July	101	107
August	108	104
September	105	98
October	114	104
November	111	100
December	110	102

Case Questions

1. Is seasonal exponential smoothing the best model for forecasting Urban Run athletic wear? Why?

2. Explain what has happened to the data for Urban Run. What are the consequences of continuing to use seasonal exponential smoothing? What model would you use? Generate a forecast for the four quarters of the fourth year using your model. Determine your forecast error and the inventory consequences.

3. Is exponential smoothing with trend the best model for forecasting five-pocket cargo jeans? Why?

4. What method would you use to forecast monthly cargo jean demand for the second year given the previous year's monthly demand? Explain why you selected your approach. Generate the forecasts for each month of the second year with your method. Determine your forecast error and the inventory consequences.

CASE: The Emergency Room (ER) at Northwest General (A)

Jenn Kostich is the new department director for emergency services at Northwest General Hospital. One of her responsibilities is to ensure proper staffing in the emergency room (ER) by scheduling nurses to appropriate shifts. This has historically been a problem for the ER. The former director did not base nurse schedules on forecasts, but used the same fixed schedule week after week.

Jenn had recently received her degree in operations management. She knew that schedules needed to be based on forecasts of demand. She needed to start by analyzing historical data in order to determine the best forecasting method to use. Jenn's assistant provided her with information on patient arrivals in the ER by hour and day of the week for the previous month, October. October was considered a typical month for the ER, and Jenn thought it was a good starting point. Jenn reviewed the information (shown in the chart) that she had requested and wondered where to begin.

Hourly Patient Arrivals in the ER

Day of Week	W	T	F	S	S	M	T	W	T	F	S	S	M	T	W	T	F	S	S	M	T	W	T	F	S	S	M	T	W	T	F
Day of Month	1	2	3	4	5	6	7	8	9	10	11	12	13	14	15	16	17	18	19	20	21	22	23	24	25	26	27	28	29	30	31
Time (hr)																															
01	1	1	2	1	1	0	1	1	0	2	2	2	0	1	0	1	2	1	0	0	1	0	1	0	1	0	1	0	0	0	0
02	0	1	2	1	1	0	0	0	0	3	1	2	0	1	2	1	2	1	2	0	1	3	1	2	1	0	0	1	1	1	0
03	4	2	1	3	1	1	0	3	3	0	0	1	1	0	2	3	0	2	0	1	0	1	0	2	3	2	0	1	2	1	2
04	2	4	3	3	3	1	1	3	4	0	3	3	1	1	3	3	0	3	3	2	3	2	1	0	3	3	0	2	3	1	2
05	0	2	1	3	3	1	1	1	3	3	3	3	1	1	3	2	4	3	4	0	2	3	1	4	2	4	2	3	3	1	4
06	1	2	2	3	2	0	1	1	1	4	3	2	1	0	0	2	2	2	3	1	2	1	3	1	0	1	0	1	1	0	0
07	1	0	0	0	2	3	2	0	1	2	1	3	2	3	2	1	1	0	1	1	1	2	0	0	0	1	1	1	2	2	1
08	1	1	1	2	2	2	1	1	3	1	0	2	3	1	3	0	0	4	1	4	0	2	2	2	2	3	1	0	2	1	2
09	2	2	1	1	2	1	1	3	4	1	2	2	1	2	3	2	1	0	3	0	1	3	1	2	4	3	1	1	4	3	2
10	3	2	4	3	5	0	1	3	3	4	3	1	1	0	4	2	5	4	4	1	1	4	0	3	4	4	4	2	3	0	3
11	2	4	5	6	4	2	3	2	3	5	5	4	1	2	1	3	4	6	5	2	3	2	3	5	2	4	0	4	3	2	4
12	3	3	4	5	5	1	4	2	2	3	6	3	0	3	2	4	4	6	4	0	4	2	2	5	4	5	2	3	2	3	5
13	5	6	4	3	5	4	3	4	2	4	4	6	3	4	3	5	5	2	6	4	5	3	4	4	5	6	4	3	2	4	5
14	5	4	6	4	6	4	4	5	4	4	4	4	4	3	5	4	5	4	6	3	3	5	5	5	6	6	3	4	5	3	5
15	4	4	5	5	5	3	4	5	3	2	6	5	3	5	5	4	6	5	4	3	4	5	3	6	6	4	3	5	5	5	6
16	2	3	5	4	5	3	3	3	2	4	4	5	3	2	3	4	5	4	5	3	3	3	3	0	0	1	2	2	0	2	2
17	0	1	4	4	5	3	2	0	2	5	4	4	3	3	2	0	5	4	5	3	2	3	2	2	1	1	3	1	1	3	0
18	2	3	2	2	2	2	1	3	1	4	3	2	3	2	1	3	0	2	3	2	3	0	2	3	2	3	2	0	2	3	3
19	1	2	2	0	0	0	1	2	4	1	2	2	1	1	1	2	2	0	1	1	1	1	0	5	4	5	2	3	3	1	5
20	3	1	2	0	0	1	1	1	3	3	3	1	1	0	2	1	3	1	1	2	0	2	1	5	4	5	1	3	3	0	5
21	4	5	4	5	3	3	1	5	1	4	0	2	2	2	5	4	3	4	0	0	1	5	2	2	4	0	2	0	3	4	1
22	3	2	4	6	5	2	0	4	0	3	5	5	2	3	3	3	6	6	5	2	0	3	4	3	4	5	3	0	5	3	3
23	4	1	5	6	5	3	3	3	3	5	4	4	2	4	2	2	6	6	6	3	2	3	6	6	6	5	0	1	3	2	6
24	4	0	3	4	3	3	3	3	3	2	5	6	4	0	2	0	2	4	5	3	0	1	0	6	6	6	3	2	1	0	6

Case Questions

1. What is your opinion of the level at which the data is being collected? What are some of the advantages of collecting data at this level?

2. Aggregate the original data for October as you see appropriate (e.g., sum up by day of week, time of day, week of the month, etc.). This will give you a new data set to work with. Analyze your data for patterns. Can you find any?

3. Use at least two different forecasting models on the new data set you developed in question 2 by aggregating the original data. Compare their forecast performance and provide an evaluation.

INTERACTIVE CASE   Virtual Company   www.wiley.com/college/reid

On-line Case: Forecasting at Valley Memorial Hospital

Assignment: *Forecasting*   Today, your assignment has taken you out to City Central Airfield. You'll be meeting with Jean Burger, director of the Valley Memorial Helicopter Service (VMHS), the air transportation arm of the medical center. She's asked you to meet her at the VMHS hangar. As you drive up, she comes out to greet you. "We have a forecasting problem for you. For the past five years or so, we've had three helicopters. As they age, they need more maintenance, which means more downtime and more missed flights. We probably need to add another helicopter or, at a minimum, replace the oldest one—or maybe even both."

To access the Web site:

• Go to **www.wiley.com/college/reid**
• Click **Student Companion Site**
• Click **Virtual Company**
• Click **Kaizen Consulting, Inc.**
• Click **Consulting Assignments**
• Click **Forecasting**

INTERNET CHALLENGE   On-line Data Access

You have been hired by a government agency to collect and analyze economic data and generate economic forecasts. Since you do not have much experience in this area, your manager, Ms. Hernandez, has decided to give you a chance to practice your skills. Ms. Hernandez believes that it would be a good idea for you to use the Internet to collect and monitor a sample of economic data. She has given you a list of Web sites to access. Your first assignment is to collect a sample of local, national, or international economic data from one of these sites. Next, try to analyze the data you have collected and identify any patterns. Then, using one of the techniques discussed in the chapter, generate a forecast for the future. Finally, as new data are posted, evaluate your performance using the error measures discussed in the chapter. How did you do, and what have you learned about the data you collected?

Web sites:

1. Census Bureau—provides economic and demographic information from the U.S. economy (http://www.census.gov/)

2. Penn World Tables—provides international economic data (http://www.hbs.edu/units/bgie/internet/penn.html)

3. Regional Economic Information System—provides regional, state, and local data (http://www.ciesin.org/datasets/reis/reis-home.html)

4. Resources for Economists on the Internet—provides business and economic data (http://www.rfe.org)

On-line Resources

Companion Website www.wiley.com/college/reid
- Take interactive *practice quizzes* to assess your knowledge and help you study in a dynamic way
- Review *PowerPoint slides* or print slides for notetaking
- Download *Excel Templates* to use for problem solving
- Access the *Virtual Company: Valley Memorial Hospital*
- Find links to *Company Tours* for this chapter
  Artesyn Communication Products, LLC
  Ercol Furniture
- Find links for *Additional Web Resources* for this chapter
  Forecasting Principles, *www.forecastingprinciples.org*
  Institute of Business Forecasters, *www.ibf.org*
  International Institute of Forecasting, *www.ms.ic.ac.uk/iif/index.htm*

Selected Bibliography

Andraski, J.C., and J. Haedicke. "CPFR: Time for the Breakthrough?" *Supply Chain Management Review*, May–June, 2003, 54–60.

Armstrong, J. Scott. "Evaluating and Selecting Forecasting Methods." In J. Scott Armstrong (ed.), *Principles of Forecasting: A Handbook for Researchers and Practitioners*. Norwell, Mass.: Kluwer Academic Publishers, 2001.

Armstrong, J. Scott. *Long-Range Forecasting from Crystal Ball to Computer*. Second Edition. New York: John Wiley & Sons, 1985.

Cattani, K., and W. Hauseman. "Why Are Forecast Updates Often Disappointing?" *Manufacturing & Service Operations Management*, 2, 2, spring 2000, 119–127.

Clements, M.P., and D.F. Hendry. *Forecasting Economic Time Series*. Cambridge, England: Cambridge University Press, 1998.

Fischer, I., and N. Harvey. "Combining Forecasts: What Information Do Judges Need to Outperform the Simple Average?" *International Journal of Forecasting*, 15, 3, 1999, 227–246.

Lawrence, M., and M. O'Connor. "Sales Forecasting Updates: How Good Are They in Practice?" *International Journal of Forecasting*, 16, 3, 2000, 369–383.

Makridakis, S., S. Wheelwright, and R. Hyndman. *Forecasting Methods and Applications*, Third Edition. New York: John Wiley & Sons, 1998.

McCullough, B.D. "Is It Safe to Assume That Software Is Accurate?" *International Journal of Forecasting*, 16, 3, 2000, 349–358.

Pearson, R. "Increasing the Credibility of Your Forecasts: 7 Suggestions," FORESIGHT, 3, February, 2006, 27–32.

Smith, B. *Focus Forecasting: Computer Techniques for Inventory Control*. Boston: CBI, 1984.

CHAPTER 9

Capacity Planning and Facility Location

Before studying this chapter you should know or, if necessary, review

1. Globalization, Chapter 1, page 17.
2. Differences between strategic and tactical decisions, Chapter 1, page 9.
3. Break-even analysis, Chapter 3, pages 58–59.
4. Qualitative forecasting methods, Chapter 8, pages 256–258.

LEARNING OBJECTIVES

After studying this chapter you should be able to

1. Define capacity planning.
2. Define location analysis.
3. Describe the relationship between capacity planning and location and their importance to the organization.
4. Explain the steps involved in capacity planning and location analysis.
5. Describe the decision support tools used in capacity planning.
6. Identify key factors in location analysis.
7. Describe the decision support tools used in location analysis.

CHAPTER OUTLINE

WHAT'S IN OM FOR ME?

 ACC

 FIN

 MKT

 OM

 HRM

 MIS

Have you ever signed up for a course at your college or university only to find out that it is closed? Have you ever attended a class that was held in a remote location and found that the room was overcrowded? Most of us have had these experiences as students. These examples illustrate problems of poor capacity planning and location—problems that can greatly affect the success of a business. Students have been known to drop out of a course that is uncomfortable to sit in, difficult to get to, or even to leave a program in which courses are frequently closed. Similarly, businesses can lose customers by not being able to produce enough goods or by being in an inconvenient location.

©AP/Wide World Photos

Matching the capacity of a business with customer demand can be a challenge. Having too much capacity is just as problematic as not having enough capacity. The first leads to excess cost from having idle facilities, workers, and equipment. The second leads to lost sales as the company cannot satisfy customer demands.

After the terrorist attacks of September 11, 2001, many firms in the hospitality industry found themselves with excess capacity. This included such businesses as hotels, airlines, cruise ships, and amusement parks. Many of these companies, such as the Marriott Corporation, Walt Disney Company, and Carnival Cruises, offered promotional incentives to increase customer demand. Similarly, after the SARS epidemic in 2003 many international airlines offered large discounts on fares as they found themselves with excess capacity in the form of idle aircraft.

Capacity planning and location analysis are actually two separate decisions. Capacity planning deals with the maximum output rate that a facility can have, determined by the size of facilities and equipment. Location analysis, on the other hand, deals with the best location for a facility. You can probably see why these two decisions are usually made simultaneously. When a company decides to open a new facility, it must also decide on both the size of the facility and its location. The size of the facility may also be affected by the location.

In this chapter we will learn about both capacity planning and location analysis. We will see how companies make both kinds of decisions. We will also see how both of these issues can affect not only the success of a company but your everyday life as well.

CAPACITY PLANNING

▶ **Capacity**
The maximum output rate that can be achieved by a facility.

Capacity can be defined as the maximum output rate that can be achieved by a facility. The facility may be an entire organization, a division, or only one machine. Planning for capacity in a company is usually performed at two levels, each corresponding to either strategic or tactical decisions, as discussed in Chapter 1. The first level of capacity decisions is strategic and long-term in nature. This is where a company decides what investments in new facilities and equipment it should make. Because these decisions are strategic in nature, the company will have to live with them for a long time. Also, they require large capital expenditures and will have a great impact on the company's ability to conduct business. The second level of capacity decisions is more tactical in nature, focusing on short-term issues that include planning of workforce, inventories, and day-to-day use of machines. In this chapter we focus on the long-term, strategic capacity decisions. Short-term capacity decisions are discussed in Chapter 14.

Why Is Capacity Planning Important?

▶ **Capacity planning**
The process of establishing the output rate that can be achieved by a facility.

Capacity planning is the process of establishing the output rate that can be achieved by a facility. If a company does not plan its capacity correctly, it may find that it either does not have enough output capability to meet customer demands or has too much capacity sitting idle. In our university example, that would mean either not being able to offer enough courses to accommodate all students or, on the other hand, having too few students in the classrooms. Both cases are costly to the university. Another example is a bakery. Not having enough capacity would mean not being able to produce enough baked goods to meet sales. The bakery would often run out of stock, and customers might start going somewhere else. Also, the bakery would not be able to take advantage of the true demand available. On the other hand, if there is too much capacity, the bakery would incur the cost of an unnecessarily large facility that is not being used, as well as much higher operating costs than necessary.

LINKS TO PRACTICE

Capacity Planning in the ER

A hospital emergency room (ER) exemplifies the challenges of capacity planning. The problems of over- or undercapacity we just discussed also occur in the ER, only with potentially dire consequences. A number of factors contribute to the capacity of the ER. One is the number of beds and the amount of space available. If there are not enough beds, patients may have to wait long periods of time to be examined. Too many empty beds, on the other hand, result in wasted space.

Another factor affecting the ER's capacity is the number of nurses and doctors scheduled to work on a shift. If not enough staff is available, patients may not have anyone to treat them. The consequences of not having enough capacity can be grave. However, scheduling more staff than needed results in excess capacity in the form of highly paid professionals not having anything to do.

Capacity planning problems are notorious in the ER, partly due to high fluctuations in demand and the high costs of insufficient capacity. In fact, the American College of Emergency Physicians estimates that 62 percent of U.S. emergency rooms are at or above capacity. Particularly troubling are long patient waiting times that average over 47 minutes before a doctor is seen, but can be as long as many hours. Many ERs are looking at ways to address this problem. One alternative being implemented is to immediately screen patients and identify those with minor ailments. These patients are then put into a "fast-track" category to be quickly treated and released. This technique serves to free up capacity for those patients that need it.

Planning for capacity is important if a company wants to grow and take full advantage of demand. At the same time, capacity decisions are complicated because they require long-term commitments of expensive resources, such as large facilities. Once these commitments have been made, it is costly to change them. Think about a business that purchases a larger facility in anticipation of an increase in demand, only to find that the demand increase does not occur. It is then left with a huge expense, no return on its investment, and the need to decide how to use a partially empty facility. Recall from Chapter 8 that forecasting future demands entails a great deal of uncertainty and risk; this makes long-term facility purchases inherently risky.

Another issue that complicates capacity planning is the fact that capacity is usually purchased in "chunks" rather than in smooth increments. Facilities, such as buildings and equipment, are acquired in large sizes, and it is virtually impossible to achieve an exact match between current needs and needs based on future demand. You can see this in the classroom example. If a university anticipates a large demand for a particular course, it may offer multiple sections. Each additional section adds capacity in chunks equal to one class size. If one class can hold a maximum of 45 students, opening up another class means adding capacity for up to an additional 45 students. The university must consider its forecast of the additional demand for the course. If the forecast for additional demand is only 4 additional students, the university will probably not open up another section. The reason is that the cost for each section takes the form of chunks that include the room, the instructor, and utilities. This cost is the same whether 1 student or 45 students attend.

Because of the uncertainty of future demand, the overriding capacity planning decision becomes one of whether to purchase a larger facility in anticipation of greater demand or to expand in slightly smaller but less efficient increments. Each strategy has its advantages and disadvantages. Think about a young married couple who want to purchase a home. They can purchase a very small home that would be more affordable, knowing that if they have children they eventually will need to face the disruption and cost of moving. On the other hand, if they purchase a larger home now they will be better prepared for the future but will be paying for additional space that they currently do not need.

Measuring Capacity

Although our definition of capacity seems simple, there is no one way to measure it. Different people have different interpretations of what capacity means, and the units of measurement are often very different. Table 9-1 shows some examples of how capacity might be measured by different organizations.

TABLE 9-1

Examples of Different
Capacity Measures

Type of Business	Input Measures of Capacity	Output Measures of Capacity
Car manufacturer	Labor hours	Cars per shift
Hospital	Available beds per month	Number of patients per month
Pizza parlor	Worker hours per day	Number of pizzas per day
Ice cream manufacturer	Operational hours per day	Gallons of ice cream per day
Retail store	Floor space in square feet	Revenues per day

Note that each business can measure capacity in different ways and that capacity can be measured using either inputs or outputs. Output measures, such as the number of cars per shift, are easier to understand. However, they do not work well when a company produces many different kinds of products. For example, if we operate a bakery that bakes only pumpkin pies, then a measure such as pies per day would work well. However, if we made many different kinds of pies and varied the combination from one day to the next, then simply using pies per day as our measure would not work as well, especially if some pies took longer to make than others. Suppose that pecan pies take twice as long to make as pumpkin pies. If one day we made twenty pumpkin pies and the next day we made ten pecan pies, using *pies per day* as our measure would make it seem as if our capacity was underutilized on the second day, even though it was equally utilized on both days. When a company produces many different kinds of products, input measures work better.

When discussing the capacity of a facility, we need two types of information. The first is the *amount of available capacity*, which will help us understand how much capacity our facility has. The second is *effectiveness of capacity use*, which will tell us how effectively we are using our available capacity. Next we look at how to quantify and interpret this information.

Measuring Available Capacity   Let's return to our bakery example for a moment. Suppose that on the average we can make twenty pies per day. However, if we are really pushed, such as during holidays, maybe we can make thirty pies per day. Which of these is our true capacity? We can make thirty pies per day at a maximum, but we cannot keep up that pace for long. Saying that thirty per day is our capacity would be misleading. On the other hand, saying that twenty pies per day is our capacity does not reflect the fact that we can, if necessary, push our production to thirty pies.

E. Dygas/Taxi/Getty Images, Inc.

Overcrowding is a sign of insufficient capacity.

▶ **Design capacity**
The maximum output rate that can be achieved by a facility under ideal conditions.

Through this example you can see that different measures of capacity are useful because they provide different kinds of information. Following are two of the most common measures of capacity:

Design capacity is the maximum output rate that can be achieved by a facility under ideal conditions. In our example, this is thirty pies per day. Design capacity can be sustained only for a relatively short period of time. A company achieves this output rate by using many temporary measures, such as overtime, overstaffing, using equipment to the maximum, and subcontracting.

Effective capacity is the maximum output rate that can be sustained under normal conditions. These conditions include realistic work schedules and breaks, regular staff levels, scheduled machine maintenance, and none of the temporary measures that are used to achieve design capacity. Note that effective capacity is usually lower than design capacity. In our example, effective capacity is twenty pies per day.

► **Effective capacity**
The maximum output rate that can be sustained under normal conditions.

Measuring Effectiveness of Capacity Use Regardless of how much capacity we have, we also need to measure how well we are utilizing it. **Capacity utilization** simply tells us how much of our capacity we are actually using. Certainly there would be a big difference if we were using 50 percent of our capacity, meaning our facilities, space, labor and equipment, rather than 90 percent. Capacity utilization can simply be computed as the ratio of actual output over capacity:

► **Capacity utilization**
Percentage measure of how well available capacity is being used.

$$\text{Utilization} = \frac{\text{actual output rate}}{\text{capacity}}\,(100\%)$$

However, since we have two capacity measures, we can measure utilization relative to either design or effective capacity:

$$\text{Utilization}_{\text{effective}} = \frac{\text{actual output}}{\text{effective capacity}}\,(100\%)$$

$$\text{Utilization}_{\text{design}} = \frac{\text{actual output}}{\text{design capacity}}\,(100\%)$$

In the bakery example, we have established that design capacity is thirty pies per day and effective capacity is twenty pies per day. Currently the bakery is producing twenty-seven pies per day. What is the bakery's capacity utilization relative to both design and effective capacity?

EXAMPLE 9.1

Computing Capacity Utilization

- **Before You Begin:** To compute capacity utilization, you need to calculate the ratio of actual output (twenty-seven pies per day) over capacity. The difference between the two capacity measures is that one uses effective capacity (twenty pies per day) and the other uses design capacity (thirty pies per day).

- **Solution:**

$$\text{Utilization}_{\text{effective}} = \frac{\text{actual output}}{\text{effective capacity}}\,(100\%) = \frac{27}{20}\,(100\%) = 135\%$$

$$\text{Utilization}_{\text{design}} = \frac{\text{actual output}}{\text{design capacity}}\,(100\%) = \frac{27}{30}\,(100\%) = 90\%$$

The utilization rates show that the bakery's current output is only slightly below its design capacity and output is considerably higher than its effective capacity. The bakery can probably operate at this level for only a short time.

Capacity Considerations

We have seen that changing capacity is not as simple as acquiring the right amount of capacity to exactly match our needs. The reason is that capacity is purchased in discrete chunks. Also, capacity decisions are long term and strategic in nature. Acquiring anticipated capacity ahead of time can save cost and disruption in the long run. Later, when demand increases, output can be increased without incurring additional fixed cost. Extra capacity can also serve to intimidate and preempt competitors from entering the market. Important implications of capacity that a company needs to consider when changing its capacity are discussed in this section.

▶ **Best operating level**
The volume of output that results in the lowest average unit cost.

Economies of Scale Every production facility has a volume of output that results in the lowest average unit cost. This is called the facility's **best operating level**. Figure 9-1 illustrates how the average unit cost of output is affected by the volume produced. You can see that as the number of units produced is increased, the average cost per unit drops. The reason is that when a large amount of goods is produced, the costs of production are spread over that large volume. These costs include the fixed costs of buildings and facilities, the costs of materials, and processing costs. The more units are produced, the larger the number of units over which costs can be spread—that is, the greater the **economies of scale**. The concept of economies of scale is very well known. It basically states that the average cost of a unit produced is reduced when the amount of output is increased.

▶ **Economies of scale**
A condition in which the average cost of a unit produced is reduced as the amount of output is increased.

You use the concept of economies of scale in your daily life, whether you are aware of it or not. Suppose you decide to make cookies in your kitchen. Think about the cost per cookie if you make only five cookies. There would be a great deal of effort—getting the ingredients, mixing the dough, shaping the cookies—all for only five cookies. If you had everything set up, making five additional cookies would not cost much more. Perhaps making even ten more cookies would cost only slightly more because you had already set up all the materials. This lower cost is due to economies of scale.

Diseconomies of Scale What if you continued to increase the number of cookies you chose to produce? For a while, making a few more cookies would not require much additional effort. However, after a certain point there would be so much material that the kitchen would become congested. You might have to get someone to help because there was more work than one person could handle. You might have to make cookies longer than expected, and the cleanup job might be much more difficult. You would be experiencing **diseconomies of scale**. Diseconomies of scale occur at a point beyond the best operating level, when the cost of each additional unit made increases. Diseconomies of scale are also illustrated in Figure 9-1.

▶ **Diseconomies of scale**
A condition in which the cost of each additional unit made increases.

Operating a facility close to its best operating level is clearly important because of the impact on costs. However, we have to keep in mind that different facility sizes have different best operating levels. In our cookie example, we can see that the number of

FIGURE 9-1

Different operating levels of a facility

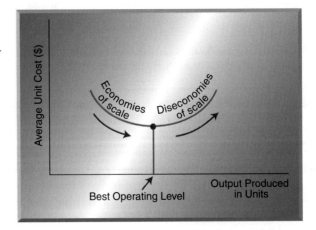

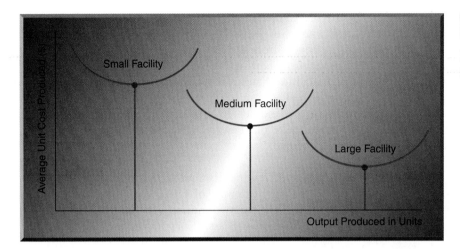

FIGURE 9-2

Best operating levels as functions of facility size

cookies comfortably produced by one person in a small kitchen would be much lower than the number produced by three friends in a large kitchen. Figure 9-2 shows how best operating level varies between facilities of different sizes.

You can see that each facility experiences both economies and diseconomies of scale. However, their best operating levels are different. This is a very important consideration when changing capacity levels. The capacity of a business can be changed by either expanding or reducing the amount of capacity. Although both decisions are important, expansion is typically a costlier and more critical event.

When expanding capacity, management has to choose between one of the following two alternatives:

Alternative 1: Purchase one large facility, requiring one large initial investment.
Alternative 2: Add capacity incrementally in smaller chunks as needed.

The first alternative means that we would have a large amount of excess capacity in the beginning and that our initial costs would be high. We would also run the risk that demand might not materialize and we would be left with unused overcapacity. On the other hand, this alternative allows us to be prepared for higher demand in the future. Our best operating level is much higher with this alternative, enabling us to operate more efficiently when meeting higher demand. Our costs would be lower in the long run, since one large construction project typically costs more than many smaller construction projects due to startup costs. Thus, alternative 1 provides greater rewards but is more risky. Alternative 2 is less risky but does not offer the same opportunities and flexibility. It is up to management to weigh the risks versus the rewards in selecting an alternative.

Focused Factories Facilities can respond more efficiently to demand if they are small, specialized, and focused on a narrow set of objectives; this concept is referred to as **focused factories.** We encountered this concept in Chapter 7 when we studied just-in-time (JIT) systems. Focused factories are only one of many factors that contribute to the success of JIT, but the concept is applicable to any facility.

▶ **Focused factories**
Facilities that are small, specialized, and focused on a narrow set of objectives.

The idea that large facilities are necessary for success because they bring economies of scale is rather dated. Today's facilities must succeed in a business environment that has short product and technology life cycles and in which flexibility is more important than ever before. Large facilities tend to be less flexible because they generally contain larger machines or process technology that is costly to change in order to make other goods and services. Many companies have realized that to be more agile they need to be focused. A smaller, specialized facility can be more efficient because it can focus on a smaller number of tasks and fewer goals.

Even a large facility can benefit from the concept of the focused factory by creating what is known as a *plant within a plant*, or PWP. A PWP is a large facility divided into smaller, more specialized facilities that have separate operations, competitive priorities, technology, and workforce. They can be physically separated with a wall or barrier and kept independent from one another. In this manner, unnecessary layers of bureaucracy are eliminated, and each "plant" is free to focus on its own objectives. PWP was discussed in detail in Chapter 3.

LINKS TO PRACTICE

Focus in the Retail Industry

Rob Kim/Landov LLC

Recent trends in the retail industry provide an excellent example of factory focus. In the 1980s, retail sales were dominated by large department stores such as Sears, JC Penney's, and Federated Department Stores. However, in the 1990s, gains in sales were made by specialty stores such as the Gap, The Limited, and Ann Taylor, while large department stores faltered. The reason is that consumer preferences change very rapidly, and each small specialty store can focus precisely on the needs of its customer group. Specialty stores are able to focus on a specific set of customers and respond to their unique needs. The Limited and the Gap are excellent examples of factory focus, with specialty stores such as Limited Too, Baby Gap, and Gap Kids.

Subcontractor Networks Another alternative to having a large production facility is to develop a large network of subcontractors and suppliers who perform a number of tasks. This is one of the fastest-growing trends today. Companies are realizing that to be successful in today's market, they need to focus on their core capabilities—for example, by hiring third parties or subcontractors to take over tasks that the company does not need to perform itself. Companies such as American Airlines and Procter & Gamble have hired outside firms to manage noncritical inventories. Also, many companies are contracting with suppliers to perform tasks that they used to perform themselves. A good example is in the area of quality management. Historically, companies performed quality checks on goods received from suppliers. Today, suppliers and manufacturers work together to achieve the same quality standards, and much of the quality checking of incoming materials is performed at the supplier's site. Another example can be seen in the auto industry, where manufacturers are placing more responsibility on suppliers to perform tasks such as design of packaging and transportation of goods. By placing more responsibility on subcontractors and suppliers, a manufacturer can focus on tasks that are critical to its success, such as product development and design.

MAKING CAPACITY PLANNING DECISIONS

The three-step procedure for making capacity planning decisions is as follows:

Step 1   Identify Capacity Requirements The first step is to identify the levels of capacity needed by the company now, as well as in the future. A company cannot decide whether to purchase a new facility without knowing exactly how much capacity it will need in the future. It also needs to identify the gap between available capacity and future requirements.

Step 2   Develop Capacity Alternatives Once capacity requirements have been identified, the company needs to develop a set of alternatives that would enable it to meet future capacity needs.

Step 3   Evaluate Capacity Alternatives The last step in the procedure is to evaluate the capacity alternatives and select the one alternative that will best meet the company's requirements.

Let's look at these steps in a little more detail.

Identify Capacity Requirements

Long-term capacity requirements are identified on the basis of forecasts of future demand. Certainly, companies look for long-term patterns such as trends when making forecasts. However, long-term patterns are not enough at this stage. Planning, building, and starting up a new facility can take well over five years. Much can happen during that time. When the facilities are operational, they are expected to be utilized for many years into the future. During this time frame numerous changes can occur in the economy, consumer base, competition, technology, and demographic factors, as well as in government regulation and political events.

Forecasting Capacity Capacity requirements are identified on the basis of forecasts of future demand. Forecasting at this level is performed using qualitative forecasting methods, some of which are discussed in Chapter 8. Qualitative forecasting methods, such as *executive opinion* and the *Delphi method*, use subjective opinions of experts. These experts may consider inputs from quantitative forecasting models that can numerically compute patterns such as trends. However, because so many variables can influence demand at this level, the experts use their judgment to validate the quantitative forecast or modify it based on their own knowledge.

One way to proceed with long-range demand forecasting at this stage is to first forecast overall market demand. For example, experts might forecast the total market for overnight delivery to be $30 billion in five years. Then the company can estimate its market share as a percentage of the total. For example, our market share may be 15 percent. From that we can compute an estimate of demand for our company in five years by multiplying the overall market demand with the percentage held by our company (0.15 × $30 billion = $4.5 billion). That forecast of demand can then be translated into specific facility requirements.

Capacity Cushions Companies often add **capacity cushions** to their regular capacity requirements. A capacity cushion is an amount of capacity added to the needed capacity in order to provide greater flexibility. Capacity cushions can be helpful if demand is greater than expected. Also, cushions can help the ability of a business to respond to customer needs for different products or different volumes. Finally, businesses that operate too close to their maximum capacity experience many costs due to diseconomies of scale and may also experience deteriorating quality.

▶ **Capacity cushion**
Additional capacity added to regular capacity requirements to provide greater flexibility.

Strategic Implications Finally, a company needs to consider how much capacity its competitors are likely to have. Capacity is a strategic decision, and the position of a company in the market relative to its competitors is very much determined by its capacity. At the same time, plans by all major competitors to increase capacity may signal the potential for overcapacity in the industry. Therefore, the decision as to how much capacity to add should be made carefully.

Large expansion alternatives often involve construction of new facilities.

Develop Capacity Alternatives

Once a company has identified its capacity requirements for the future, the next step is to develop alternative ways to modify its capacity. One alternative is to do nothing and reevaluate the situation in the future. With this alternative, the company would not be able to meet any demands that exceed current capacity levels. Choosing this alternative and the time to reevaluate the company's needs is a strategic decision. The other alternatives require deciding whether to purchase one large facility now or add capacity incrementally, as discussed earlier in the chapter.

Capacity Alternatives: 1. Do nothing
2. Expand large now
3. Expand small now, with option to add later

Evaluate Capacity Alternatives

There are a number of tools that we can use to evaluate our capacity alternatives. Recall that these tools are only decision-support aids. Ultimately, managers have to use many different inputs, as well as their judgment, in making the final decision. One of the most popular of these tools is the decision tree. In the next section we look more closely at how decision trees can be helpful to managers at this stage.

DECISION TREES

Decision trees are useful whenever we have to evaluate interdependent decisions that must be made in sequence and when there is uncertainty about events. For that reason, they are especially useful for evaluating capacity expansion alternatives given that future demand is uncertain. Remember that our main decision is whether to purchase a large facility or a small one with the possibility of expansion later. You can see that the decision to expand later is dependent on choosing a small facility now. Which alternative ends up being best will depend on whether demand turns out to be high or low. Unfortunately, we can only forecast future demand and have to incur some risks.

A **decision tree** is a diagram that models the alternatives being considered and the possible outcomes. Decision trees help by giving structure to a series of decisions and providing an objective way of evaluating alternatives. Decision trees contain the following information:

- *Decision points.* These are the points in time when decisions, such as whether or not to expand, are made. They are represented by squares, called "nodes."
- *Decision alternatives.* Buying a large facility and buying a small facility are two decision alternatives. They are represented by "branches" or arrows leaving a decision point.
- *Chance events.* These are events that could affect the value of a decision. For example, demand could be high or low. Each chance event has a probability or likelihood of occurring. For example, there may be a 60 percent chance of high demand and a 40 percent chance of low demand. Remember that the sum of the probabilities of all chances must add up to 100 percent. Chance events are "branches" or arrows leaving circular nodes.
- *Outcomes.* For each possible alternative an outcome is listed. In our example, that may be expected profit for each alternative (expand now or later) given each chance event (high demand or low demand).

These diagrams are called decision trees because the diagram of the decisions resembles a tree. Simple decision trees are not hard to understand. Next we look at an example to see how a decision tree might be used to solve a capacity alternative problem.

▶ **Decision tree**
Modeling tool used to evaluate independent decisions that must be made in sequence.

Anna, the owner of Anna's Greek Restaurant, has determined that she needs to expand her facility. The decision is whether to expand now with a large facility, incurring additional costs and taking the risk that demand will not materialize, or expand now on a smaller scale, knowing that she will have to consider expanding again in three years. She has estimated the following chances for demand:

- The likelihood of demand being high is .70.
- The likelihood of demand being low is .30.

She has also estimated profits for each alternative:

- Large expansion has an estimated profitability of either $300,000 or $50,000, depending on whether demand turns out to be high or low.
- Small expansion has a profitability of $80,000, assuming that demand is low.
- Small expansion with an occurrence of high demand would require considering whether to expand further. If she expands at that point, her profitability is expected to be $200,000. If she does not expand further, profitability is expected to be $150,000.

Next we develop a decision tree to solve Anna's problem.

- **Before You Begin:** Remember that before you begin a decision tree problem, you should first draw a decision tree diagram. Then add the given information to the diagram and proceed to evaluate it.

- **Solution:**
To solve this problem we first need to draw the decision tree. Table 9-2 shows steps in drawing a decision tree.

EXAMPLE 9.2

Using Decision Trees

TABLE 9-2	
Procedure for Drawing a Decision Tree	1. Draw a decision tree from left to right. Use squares to indicate decisions and circles to indicate chance events.
	2. Write the probability of each chance event in parentheses.
	3. Write out the outcome for each alternative in the right margin.

A decision tree is shown in Figure 9-3. We read the diagram from left to right, with node 1 representing the first decision point. The two alternatives at that decision point are presented as branches. They are labeled with the two alternatives, "Expand Small" and "Expand Large." Regardless of which alternative is followed, some chance events will take place. In our example the chance events are the occurrence of either high or low demand. The circular node represents the chance events, with the branches providing the label and the probability of the event. For example, the chance of high demand is .70 and the chance of low demand is .30.

If we start with a small expansion and high demand occurs, we will have to decide whether or not to expand further. This second decision point is represented by node 2. The dollar amounts at the end of each alternative are the estimated profits. Now that we have drawn the decision tree, let's see how we can solve it. The procedure for solving a decision tree is outlined in Table 9-3.

We drew the decision tree from left to right. To evaluate it, we work backward, from right to left, to determine the expected value. The **expected value (*EV*)** is a weighted average of the chance events, where each chance event is given a probability of occurrence. We start with the profitability of each alternative, working backward and selecting the most profitable alternative. For example, at node 2 we should decide to expand further, because the profits from that decision are higher ($200,000 versus $150,000). If we come to that point, that is the decision we should make. The expected value (*EV*)

▶ **Expected value (*EV*)**
A weighted average of chance events, where each chance event is given a probability of occurrence.

FIGURE 9-3	
Decision tree for Anna's restaurant	

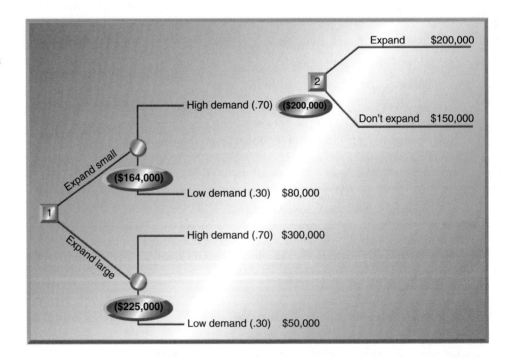

TABLE 9-3

Procedure for Solving
a Decision Tree

1. To solve a decision tree, work from right to left. At each circle representing chance events, compute the expected value (*EV*).

2. Write the *EV*s below each circle.

3. Select the alternative with the highest *EV*.

of profits at that point is written below node 2. This is the expected value if we decide on a small expansion and high demand occurs.

To compute the expected value (*EV*) of the small expansion, we evaluate it as a weighted average of estimated profits given the probability of occurrence of each chance event:

$$EV_{\text{small expansion}} = 0.30(\$80,000) + 0.70(\$200,000) = \$164,000$$

$$EV_{\text{large expansion}} = 0.30(\$50,000) + 0.70(\$300,000) = \$225,000$$

The large expansion gives the higher expected value. This means that Anna should pursue a large expansion now.

Before You Go On

Up to this point we have focused exclusively on capacity planning. By now you should understand that capacity is the maximum output rate of a facility. Capacity is defined in different ways, depending on the nature of the business. You should understand the basic trade-off made in choosing between capacity planning alternatives and the procedure used to evaluate alternatives. Finally, make sure you understand the relationship between capacity planning and location analysis. In the next section we discuss location analysis, which is another decision area for operations managers. Note, however, that location analysis is usually made in conjunction with capacity planning. Because the size of a facility is typically tied to its location, these decisions are made together. Make sure you understand the relationship between these decisions and their strategic implications for the firm.

LOCATION ANALYSIS

▶ **Location analysis**
Techniques for determining location decisions.

You might have heard the old real estate adage: the three most important factors in the value of a property are location, location, location. Have you ever left a service provider that you liked—say, a doctor, barber, or tailor—because they were in a location that was difficult to get to or too far away? Look at the business locations in your own neighborhood. We have all seen facilities in certain locations that have a high turnover of businesses and owners. The type of business and owners may be completely different, yet something about the location does not make it successful. Why do most fast-food restaurants locate near one another? In order to draw customers to one location. Why are the large automakers centered in Michigan? To draw suppliers to one area. Why do many medical facilities locate near hospitals? To be accessible to patients. Why do retail stores typically locate near each other? To attract a higher volume of customers.

These examples illustrate the strategic importance of location decisions. All other aspects of a business can be designed efficiently, but if the location is selected poorly, the business will have a harder time being successful. Different types of businesses emphasize different factors when making location decisions. Service organizations such as restaurants, movie theaters, and banks focus on locating near their customers. Manufacturing organizations seek to be close to sources of transportation, suppliers, and abundant resources such as labor. However, many other factors need to be considered.

What Is Facility Location?

Facility location is determining the best geographic location for a company's facility. Facility location decisions are particularly important for two reasons. First, they require long-term commitments in buildings and facilities, which means that mistakes can be difficult to correct. Second, these decisions require sizable financial investment and can have a large impact on operating costs and revenues. Poor location can result in high transportation costs, inadequate supplies of raw materials and labor, loss of competitive advantage, and financial loss. Businesses therefore have to think long and hard about where to locate a new facility.

In most cases, there is no one best location for a facility. Rather, there are a number of acceptable locations. One location may satisfy some factors whereas another location may be better for others. If a new location is being considered in order to provide more capacity, the company needs to consider options such as expanding the current facility if the current location is satisfactory. Another option might be to add a new facility but also keep the current one. As you can see, there is a lot to consider.

Factors Affecting Location Decisions

Many factors can affect location decisions, including proximity to customers, transportation, source of labor, community attitude, proximity to suppliers, and many other factors. The nature of the firm's business will determine which factors should dominate the location decision. As already mentioned, service and manufacturing firms will focus on different factors. Profit-making and nonprofit organizations will also focus on different factors. Profit-making firms tend to locate near the markets they serve, whereas nonprofit organizations generally focus on other criteria.

It is important to identify factors that have a critical impact on the company's strategic goals. For example, even though proximity to customers is typically a critical factor for service firms, if the firm provides an in-home service (say, carpet cleaning), this may not be a critical issue. Also, while profit-making firms might locate near the markets they serve, nonprofit firms might choose to be near their major benefactors. Managers should also eliminate factors that are satisfied by every location alternative. Next we look more closely at some factors that affect location decisions.

Proximity to Sources of Supply   Many firms need to locate close to sources of supply. The reasons for this can vary. In some cases, the firm has no choice, such as in farming, forestry, or mining operations, where proximity to natural resources is necessary. In other cases, the location may be determined by the perishable nature of goods, such as in preparing and processing perishable food items. Dole Pineapple has its pineapple farm and plant in Hawaii for both these purposes. Similarly, Tropicana has its processing plant in Florida, near the orange-growing orchards.

Another reason to locate close to sources of supply is to avoid high transportation costs—for example, if a firm's raw materials are much bulkier and costlier to move than the finished product. Transporting the finished product outbound is less costly than transporting the raw materials inbound, and the firm should locate closer to the source of supply. A paper mill is an example. Transporting lumber would be much more costly than transporting the paper produced.

©AP/Wide World Photos

The importance of location decisions can be seen in the case of Internet companies during the boom of the dot-coms. Locating in Silicon Valley or San Francisco had become a major priority in the 1990s, for close proximity to highly skilled talent. Dot-coms were seeking over four million square feet of space in San Francisco, where only one million square feet was available. Consequently, the cost of locating there, including rent and leasing requirements, had become increasingly expensive. Tenants were paying $60 per square foot, an increase from the $40 per square foot paid just six months earlier. Landlords had also become picky about their tenants, and some were making unusual demands. Many were requiring as much as two years rent in advance. Others were even asking for equity in the company.

Then came the fall of the dot-coms. Space became abundant as many companies went out of business, and the cost of space dropped. Other companies, in an effort to remain financially viable, sought less costly locations. Almost overnight the importance of locating in Silicon Valley diminished.

Proximity to Customers Locating near the market they serve is often critical for many organizations, particularly service firms. To capture their share of the business, service firms need to be accessible to their customers. For this reason, service firms typically locate in high-population areas that offer convenient access. Examples include retail stores, fast-food restaurants, gas stations, grocery stores, dry cleaners, and flower shops. Large retail firms often locate in a central area of the market they serve. Smaller service firms usually follow the larger retailers because of the large number of the customers they attract. The smaller firms can usually count on getting some of the business.

Other reasons for locating close to customers may include the perishable nature of the company's products or high costs of transportation to the customer site. Food items such as groceries and baked goods, fresh flowers, and medications are perishable and need to be offered close to the market. Also, items such as heavy metal sheets, pipes, and cement need to be produced close to the market because the costs of transporting these materials are high.

Proximity to Source of Labor Proximity to an ample supply of qualified labor is important in many businesses, especially those that are labor intensive. The company needs to consider the availability of a particular type of labor and whether special skills are required. Some companies, such as those looking for assembly-line workers, want to be near a supply of blue-collar labor. Other companies may be looking for computer or technical skills and should consider locating in areas with a concentration of those types of workers.

Other factors that should be considered are local wage rates, the presence of local unions, and attitudes of local workers. Work ethics and attitudes toward work can vary greatly in different parts of the country and between urban and rural workers. Attitudes toward factors such as absenteeism, tardiness, and turnover can greatly affect a company's productivity.

Community Considerations   The success of a company at a particular location can be affected by the extent to which it is accepted by the local community. Many communities welcome new businesses, viewing them as sources of tax revenues, opportunities for jobs, and as contributing to the overall well-being of the community. However, communities do not want businesses that bring pollution, noise, and traffic and that lower the quality of life. Extreme examples are a nuclear facility, a trash dump site, and an airport. Less extreme examples are companies like Wal-Mart, which often are not accepted by smaller communities, which may view such large merchants as a threat to their way of life and thus actively work to discourage them from locating there.

Site Considerations   Site considerations for a particular location include factors such as utility costs, taxes, zoning restrictions, soil conditions, and even climate. These factors are not too different from those one would consider when purchasing a home or a lot to build on. Just as most homeowners consider their purchase to be an investment, so does a business. Inspectors should be hired to perform a thorough evaluation of the grounds, such as checking for adequate drainage. Site-related factors can also limit access roads for trucks and make it difficult for customers to reach the site.

Quality-of-Life Issues   Another important factor in location decisions is the quality of life a particular location offers the company's employees. This factor can also become important in the future when the business is recruiting high-caliber employees. Quality of life includes factors such as climate, a desirable lifestyle, good schools, and a low crime rate. Certainly quality of life would not be considered the most critical factor in selecting a location. However, when other factors do not differ much from one location to another, quality of life can be the decisive factor.

Other Considerations   In addition to the factors discussed so far, there are others that companies need to consider. They include room for customer parking, visibility, customer and transportation access, as well as room for expansion. Room for expansion may be particularly important if the company has decided to expand now and possibly expand further at a later date. Other factors include construction costs, insurance, local competition, local traffic and road congestion, and local ordinances.

Globalization

▶ **Globalization**
The process of locating facilities around the world.

In addition to considering the specific factors affecting site location in the United States, companies need to consider how they will be affected by a major trend in business today: globalization. **Globalization** is the process of locating facilities around the world. Over the past decade it has become not only a trend but a matter-of-fact way of conducting business. Technology such as faxes, e-mails, video conferencing, and overnight delivery have made distance less relevant than ever before. Markets and competition are increasingly global. To compete effectively based on cost, many companies have had to expand their operations to include global sources of supply. Factors other than mere distance have become critical in selecting a geographic location.

Deciding to expand an operation globally is not a simple decision. There are many things to consider, and the problems must be weighed along with the benefits. In this section we look at both advantages and disadvantages of global operations. We also look at some additional implications of global operations that managers need to consider.

Advantages of Globalization There are many reasons why companies choose to expand their operations globally. The main one, however, is to take advantage of foreign markets. The demand for imported goods has grown tremendously and these markets offer a new arena for competition. Also, locating production facilities in foreign countries reduces the stigma associated with buying imports. This concept works not only for U.S. companies abroad but for foreign companies in the United States as well. For example, Japanese automobile manufacturers have located in the United States and employed American workers, which has gone a long way toward eliminating negative attitudes about buying Japanese cars. Being in the United States has also reduced their exposure to currency variations between the dollar and yen.

Another advantage of global locations is reduction of trade barriers. By producing goods in the country where customers are located, a company can avoid import quotas. Trade barriers have also been reduced through the creation of trading blocs such as the European Union, and trade agreements such as NAFTA (North American Free Trade Agreement) and GATT (General Agreement on Tariffs and Trade). We discussed the contribution of these agreements to globalization in Chapter 1.

Cheap labor in countries such as Korea, Taiwan, and China has also attracted firms to locate there. Often it is cheaper to send raw materials to these countries for fabrication and assembly and then ship them elsewhere for final consumption than it is to keep the process in this country. The cost of labor can be so low that it more than offsets the additional transportation costs.

An area that has further encouraged globalization is the growth of just-in-time manufacturing, which encourages suppliers and manufacturers to be in close proximity to one another. Many suppliers have moved closer to the manufacturers they supply, and some manufacturers have moved closer to their suppliers.

Disadvantages of Globalization Although there are advantages to globalization, there are also a number of disadvantages that companies should consider. Political risks can be large, particularly in countries with unstable governments. For example, during a period of political unrest a company may have its technology confiscated. Foreign governments may also impose restrictions, tariffs on particular industries, and local ordinances that must be obeyed.

Using offshore suppliers might mean that a company may need to share some of its proprietary technology. Today's age of total quality management encourages the sharing of this type of information between manufacturers and suppliers to the advantage of both parties. A manufacturer may want to think carefully before sharing, however.

Another issue is whether to use local employee skills. Companies are often attracted to cheap foreign labor. However, the company might find that worker attitudes toward tardiness and absenteeism are different. Also, worker skills and productivity may be considerably lower, offsetting the benefits of lower wages.

The local infrastructure is another important issue. Many foreign countries do not have the developed infrastructure necessary for companies to operate in the manner that they do in their home country. Infrastructure includes everything from roads to utilities as well as other support services.

Issues to Consider in Locating Globally Firms are attracted to foreign locations in order to take advantage of foreign markets, cheaper suppliers or labor, and natural resources such as copper, aluminum, and timber. However, there are many issues to consider when locating globally. One such issue is the effect of a *different culture*. Each culture has a different set of values, norms, ethics, and standards. For example, in France it is considered polite to be slightly late for an appointment, and such lateness is quite customary. The British, on the other hand, consider punctuality highly important and tardiness very rude. You can see how misunderstandings can develop even through simple differences like this one.

Language barriers are another potential problem. Employees need to be able to communicate easily in their work environment. Engaging in discussions, following instructions, and understanding exactly what is being said can become difficult when employees speak different languages. Even when one language is translated into another, the translation may have lost very essential parts of the meaning, resulting in damaging misunderstanding.

Different laws and regulations—including everything from pollution regulations to labor laws—may require changes in business practices. Also, what is acceptable in one culture may be completely unacceptable or even illegal in another. For example, in some countries offering a bribe may be an acceptable part of doing business, whereas in others it may land a person in jail.

Although it is important to know the factors affecting facility location, it is not enough for making good location decisions. In the next section we look at specific tools that can help managers with facility location decisions.

MAKING LOCATION DECISIONS

Procedure for Making Location Decisions

As with capacity planning, managers need to follow a three-step procedure when making facility location decisions. These steps are as follows:

Step 1   Identify Dominant Location Factors. In this step managers identify the location factors that are dominant for the business. This requires managerial judgment and knowledge.

Step 2   Develop Location Alternatives. Once managers know what factors are dominant, they can identify location alternatives that satisfy the selected factors.

Step 3   Evaluate Location Alternatives. After a set of location alternatives have been identified, managers evaluate them and make a final selection. This is not easy, because one location may be preferred based on one set of factors, whereas another may be better based on a second set of factors.

Procedures for Evaluating Location Alternatives

There are a number of procedures that can help in evaluating location alternatives. These are decision-support tools that help structure the decision-making process. Some of them help with qualitative factors that are subjective, such as quality of life. Others help with quantitative factors that can be measured, such as distance. A manager may choose to use multiple procedures to evaluate alternatives and come up with a final decision. Remember that the location decision is one that a company will have to live with for a long time. It is highly important that managers make the right decision.

Factor Rating You have seen by now that many of the factors that managers need to consider when evaluating location alternatives are qualitative in nature. Their importance is also highly subjective, based on the opinion of who is evaluating them. An excellent procedure that can be used to give structure to this process is called factor rating. **Factor rating** can be used to evaluate multiple alternatives based on a number of selected factors. It is valuable because it helps decision makers structure their opinions relative to the factors identified as important. The following steps are used to develop a factor rating:

▶ **Factor rating**
A procedure that can be used to evaluate multiple alternative locations based on a number of selected factors.

Step 1 Identify dominant factors (e.g., proximity to market, access, competition, quality of life).

Step 2 Assign weights to factors reflecting the importance of each factor relative to the other factors. The sum of these weights must be 100.

Step 3 Select a scale by which to evaluate each location relative to each factor. A commonly used scale is a 5-point scale, with 1 being poor and 5 excellent.

Step 4 Evaluate each alternative relative to each factor, using the scale selected in Step 3. For example, if you chose to use a 5-point scale, a location that was excellent based on quality of life might get a 5 for that factor.

Step 5 For each factor and each location, multiply the weight of the factor by the score for that factor and sum the results for each alternative. This will give you a score for each alternative based on how you have rated the factors and how you have weighted each of the factors at each location.

Step 6 Select the alternative with the highest score.

Let's look at an example to see how this procedure is used.

Using Factor Rating   EXAMPLE 9.3

Antonio is evaluating three different locations for his new Italian restaurant. Costs are comparable at all three locations. He has identified seven factors that he considers important and has decided to use factor rating to evaluate his three location alternatives based on a 5-point scale, with 1 being poor and 5 excellent. Table 9-4 shows Antonio's factors, the weights he has assigned to each factor, as well as the factor score for each factor at each location.

Table 9-4   Factor Rating for Antonio's Italian Restaurant

| Factor | Factor Weight | Factor Score at Each Location | | | Weighted Score for Each Location (Factor Weight × Factor Score) | | |
		Location 1	Location 2	Location 3	Location 1	Location 2	Location 3
Appearance	20	5	3	2	100	60	40
Ease of expansion	10	4	4	2	40	40	20
Proximity to market	20	2	3	5	40	60	100
Customer parking	15	5	3	3	75	45	45
Access	15	5	2	3	75	30	45
Competition	10	2	4	5	20	40	50
Labor supply	10	3	3	4	30	30	40
Total	**100**				**380**	**305**	**340**

From Table 9-4 it is clear that Antonio considers facility appearance and proximity to market the two most important factors, because he has rated each of these with a 20. Other factors are slightly less important. Note that Antonio selected the factors first. Then he decided to weight them based on his perception of their importance. He then computed a factor score for each factor at each location. Looking at the factor scores he selected, it appears that location 1 is excellent based on appearance, parking, and access, but poor based on closeness to the market. Location 3 is just the opposite, being excellent based on closeness to the market but poor based on facility appearance. Location 2 appears to be somewhere in the middle. To evaluate which location alternative is best, Antonio needed to multiply the factor weight by the factor score for each factor at each location and then sum them. The best location alternative is that with the highest factor rating score. In Antonio's case, it is location 1. This problem can also be solved with a spreadsheet as shown:

	A	B	C	D	E	F	G
1							
2	**Factor Rating for Antonio's Italian Restaurant**						
3							
4		**Factor Scores (1-5 scale)**					
5	**Factor**	**Location 1**	**Location 2**	**Location 3**	**Factor Weight**		
6	Appearance	5	3	2	20		
7	Ease of expansion	4	4	2	10		
8	Proximity to market	2	3	5	20		
9	Customer parking	5	3	3	15		
10	Access	5	2	3	15		
11	Competition	2	4	5	10		
12	Labor supply	3	3	4	10		
13				Total	100	E13: =SUM(E6:E12)	
14							
15	**Compute Weighted Factor Scores and Overall Scores for Each Location**						
16		**Weighted Factor Scores**					
17	**Factor**	**Location 1**	**Location 2**	**Location 3**	B18: =B6*$E6 (copied to B18:D24)		
18	Appearance	100	60	40			
19	Ease of expansion	40	40	20			
20	Proximity to market	40	60	100			
21	Customer parking	75	45	45	B25: =SUM(B18:B24) (copied right)		
22	Access	75	30	45			
23	Competition	20	40	50			
24	Labor supply	30	30	40			
25	Totals	**380**	**305**	**340**			
26							
27	Best Total Score	**380**	B27: =MAX(B25:D25)				
28	Best Location	**Location 1**	B28: =INDEX(B17:D17,MATCH(B27,B25:D25,0))				

► **Load–distance model**
A procedure for evaluating location alternatives based on distance.

The Load–Distance Model The **load–distance model** is a procedure for evaluating location alternatives based on distance. The distance to be measured could be proximity to markets, proximity to suppliers or other resources, or proximity to any other facility that is considered important. The objective of the model is to select a location that minimizes the total amount of loads moved weighted by the distance traveled. What is a load? A load represents the goods moved in or out of a facility or the number of movements between facilities. For example, if 200 boxes of Kellogg's cereal are shipped between the local warehouse and a grocery store, that is the load between the warehouse and grocery store. The idea is to reduce the amount of distance between facilities that have a high load between them.

The model is shown in Table 9-5. Relative locations are compared by computing the load–distance, or *ld*, score for each location. The *ld* score for a particular location

ld score for a location $= \Sigma\, l_{ij}d_{ij}$ where l_{ij} = load between locations i and j d_{ij} = distance between locations i and j	**TABLE 9-5** The Load–Distance Model

is obtained by multiplying the load (denoted by l) for each location by the distance traveled (denoted by d) and then summing over all the locations. This score is a surrogate measure for movement of goods, material handling, or even communication. Our goal is to make the ld score as low as possible by reducing the distance the large loads have to travel.

Next we look at the steps in developing the load–distance model.

Step 1 Identify Distances. The first step is to identify the distances between location sites. It is certainly possible to use the actual mileage between locations. However, it is much quicker, and just as effective, to use simpler measures of distance. A frequently used measure of distance is **rectilinear distance**, the shortest distance between two points measured by using only north–south and east–west movements. To measure rectilinear distance, we place grid coordinates on a map and use them to measure the distance between two locations. Figure 9-4 presents an example of how the distance between locations A and B could be measured using rectilinear distance.

▶ **Rectilinear distance** The shortest distance between two points measured by using only north–south and east–west movements.

The rectilinear distance between two locations, A and B, is computed by summing the absolute differences between the x coordinates and the absolute differences between the y coordinates. The equation is as follows:

$$d_{AB} = |x_A - x_B| + |y_A - y_B|$$

In our example, the coordinates for location A are (30, 40). The coordinates for location B are (10, 15). Therefore, the rectilinear distance between these two points is

$$d_{AB} = |30 - 10| + |40 - 15| = 45 \text{ miles}$$

Step 2 Identify Loads. The next step is to identify the loads between different locations. The notation l_{ij} is used to indicate the load between locations i and j.

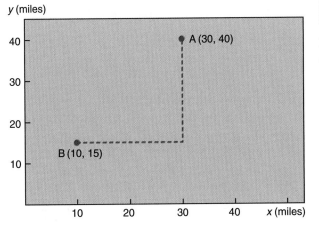

FIGURE 9-4

Rectilinear distance between points A and B

Step 3   Calculate the Load–Distance Score for Each Location. Next we calculate the load–distance score for each location by multiplying the load, l_{ij}, by the distance, d_{ij}. We then compute the sum of $l_{ij}d_{ij}$ to get the ld score. Finally, we then select the site with the lowest load–distance score.

Next we look at an example to see how to use the model.

EXAMPLE 9.4

Using the Load–Distance Model

Matrix Manufacturing Corporation is considering where to locate its warehouse in order to service its four stores located in four Ohio cities: Cleveland, Columbus, Cincinnati, and Dayton. Two possible sites for the warehouse are being considered. One is in Mansfield, Ohio, and the other is in Springfield, Ohio. Let's follow the steps of the load–distance model to select the best location for the warehouse.

• **Before You Begin:** To solve this problem, follow the three steps given in the text for selecting a location with the load–distance model.

• **Solution:**

Step 1   Identify Distances. The distances between the locations can be seen in Figure 9-5, which shows a map of the cities with grid coordinates. The coordinates allow us to compute the distances between the cities. To compute the specific distances, we use the rectilinear distance measure.

FIGURE 9-5

Location map for Matrix Manufacturing

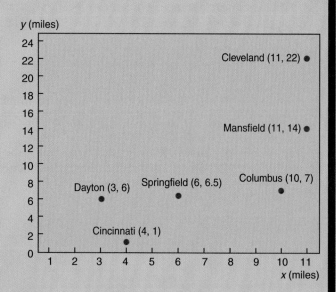

From Figure 9-5 we can compute the distances between the four cities and the Springfield site as follows:

City	Distance to Springfield
Cleveland	$\lvert 11 - 6\rvert + \lvert 22 - 6.5\rvert = 20.5$
Columbus	$\lvert 10 - 6\rvert + \lvert 7 - 6.5\rvert = 4.5$
Cincinnati	$\lvert 4 - 6\rvert + \lvert 1 - 6.5\rvert = 7.5$
Dayton	$\lvert 3 - 6\rvert + \lvert 6 - 6.5\rvert = 3.5$

Similarly, we can compute the distance between the four cities and the Mansfield site as follows:

City	Distance to Mansfield
Cleveland	$|11 - 11| + |22 - 14| = 8$
Columbus	$|10 - 11| + |7 - 14| = 8$
Cincinnati	$|4 - 11| + |1 - 14| = 20$
Dayton	$|3 - 11| + |6 - 14| = 16$

Step 2   Identify Loads. The next step is to identify the loads between the four cities and the warehouse. Remember that these loads will be the same regardless of where the warehouse is located. For this reason, we want to locate the warehouse at a place that will minimize the amount of distance large loads will have to travel.

City	Load between City and Warehouse
Cleveland	15
Columbus	10
Cincinnati	12
Dayton	4

Step 3   Calculate the Load–Distance Score for Each Location. The final step is to calculate the load–distance score for each location. The computation for Springfield is shown in Table 9-6.

Table 9-6   Computing the Load–Distance Score for Springfield

City	Load (l_{ij})	Distance (d_{ij})	$l_{ij}d_{ij}$
Cleveland	15	20.5	307.5
Columbus	10	4.5	45
Cincinnati	12	7.5	90
Dayton	4	3.5	14
Total		Load–Distance Score: (456.5)	

The load–distance score computed for Springfield does not tell us very much by itself. This number is useful only when comparing relative locations—that is, when we compare it to another load–distance score. The load–distance score for Mansfield is shown in Table 9-7.

Table 9-7   Computing the Load–Distance Score for Mansfield

City	Load (l_{ij})	Distance (d_{ij})	$l_{ij}d_{ij}$
Cleveland	15	8	120
Columbus	10	8	80
Cincinnati	12	20	240
Dayton	4	16	64
Total		Load–Distance Score: (504)	

The load–distance score for Mansfield is higher than the score for Springfield. Therefore, Matrix Manufacturing should locate its warehouse in Springfield. Note in the computation for the load–distance score for Mansfield that the load between the city and the warehouse did not change. What changed was the distance. Through the load–distance model we select a location that will minimize the distance large loads travel. This can also be computed using a spreadsheet, as shown.

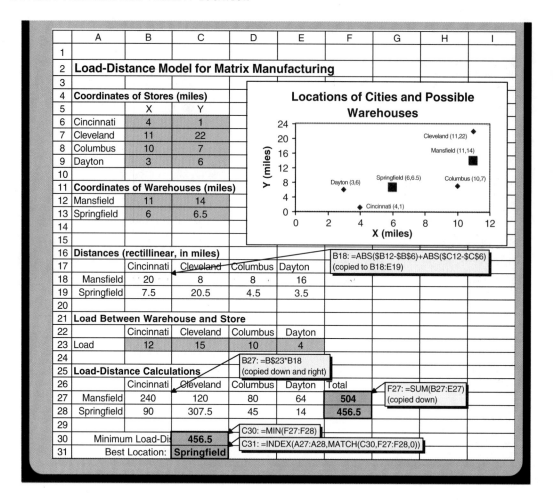

	A	B	C	D	E	F	G	H	I
1									
2	**Load-Distance Model for Matrix Manufacturing**								
3									
4	**Coordinates of Stores (miles)**								
5		X	Y						
6	Cincinnati	4	1						
7	Cleveland	11	22						
8	Columbus	10	7						
9	Dayton	3	6						
10									
11	**Coordinates of Warehouses (miles)**								
12	Mansfield	11	14						
13	Springfield	6	6.5						
14									
15									
16	**Distances (rectilinear, in miles)**					B18: =ABS($B12-$B$6)+ABS($C12-$C$6)			
17		Cincinnati	Cleveland	Columbus	Dayton	(copied to B18:E19)			
18	Mansfield	20	8	8	16				
19	Springfield	7.5	20.5	4.5	3.5				
20									
21	**Load Between Warehouse and Store**								
22		Cincinnati	Cleveland	Columbus	Dayton				
23	Load	12	15	10	4				
24					B27: =B$23*B18				
25	**Load-Distance Calculations**				(copied down and right)				
26		Cincinnati	Cleveland	Columbus	Dayton	Total	F27: =SUM(B27:E27)		
27	Mansfield	240	120	80	64	504	(copied down)		
28	Springfield	90	307.5	45	14	456.5			
29					C30: =MIN(F27:F28)				
30		Minimum Load-Dis	456.5		C31: =INDEX(A27:A28,MATCH(C30,F27:F28,0))				
31		Best Location:	Springfield						

The Center of Gravity Approach   When we used the load–distance model we compared only two location alternatives. The load–distance was lower for Springfield than for Mansfield. However, we can also use the model to find other locations that may give an even lower load–distance score than Springfield. An easy way to do this is to start by testing the location at the center of gravity of the target area. The X and Y coordinates that give us the center of gravity for a particular area are computed in the following way:

$$X_{\text{c.g.}} = \frac{\Sigma\, l_i x_i}{\Sigma\, l_i}$$

$$Y_{\text{c.g.}} = \frac{\Sigma\, l_i y_i}{\Sigma\, l_i}$$

c.g. = center of gravity

The X coordinate for the center of gravity is computed by taking the X coordinate for each point and multiplying it by its load. These are then summed and divided by the sum of the loads. The same procedure is used to compute the Y coordinate.

The location identified with the center of gravity puts a larger penalty on long distances. This can have practical value given that longer distances impose more costs on the organization. However, the location identified may not be a feasible site because of geographic restrictions. For example, the center of gravity might turn out to be in the middle of Lake Michigan. However, the center of gravity provides an excellent starting point. We can use it to test the load–distance score of other locations in the area.

Find the center of gravity for the Matrix Manufacturing problem.

EXAMPLE 9.5

Computing the Center of Gravity

• **Before You Begin:** To solve this problem, use the center of gravity equations. Remember that you need to find both the X and Y coordinates.

• **Solution:**

Location	Coordinates (X, Y)	Load (l_i)	$l_i x_i$	$l_i y_i$
Cleveland	$(11, 22)$	15	165	330
Columbus	$(10, 7)$	10	100	70
Cincinnati	$(4, 1)$	12	48	12
Dayton	$(3, 6)$	4	12	24
Total		**41**	**325**	**436**

Now we need to find the coordinates for the center of gravity:

$$X_{c.g.} = \frac{\Sigma\, l_i x_i}{\Sigma\, l_i} = \frac{325}{41} = 7.9$$

$$Y_{c.g.} = \frac{\Sigma\, l_i y_i}{\Sigma\, l_i} = \frac{436}{41} = 10.6$$

Break-Even Analysis Break-even analysis is a technique used to compute the amount of goods that must be sold just to cover costs. The break-even point is precisely the quantity of goods a company needs to sell to break even. Whatever is sold above that point will bring a profit. Below that point the company will incur a loss. We discussed break-even analysis in Chapter 3 as a technique for evaluating the success of different products. In this chapter we use break-even analysis to evaluate different location alternatives. Remember that break-even analysis works with costs, such as fixed and variable costs. It can be an excellent technique when the factors under consideration can be expressed in terms of costs. Let's briefly review the basic break-even equations:

▶ **Break-even analysis**
Technique used to compute the amount of goods that must be sold just to cover costs.

$$\text{Total cost} = F + cQ$$

$$\text{Total revenue} = pQ$$

where F = fixed cost
c = variable cost per unit
Q = number of units sold
p = price per unit

At the break-even point, total cost and total revenue are equal. We can use those equations to solve for Q, which is the break-even quantity:

$$Q = \frac{F}{p - c}$$

As we saw in Chapter 3, these quantities can be obtained graphically. Now let's look at the basic steps in using break-even analysis for location selection.

Step 1:   For Each Location, Determine Fixed and Variable Costs. Recall from Chapter 3 that fixed costs are incurred regardless of how many units are produced and include items such as overhead, taxes, and insurance. Variable costs are costs that vary directly with the number of units produced and include items such as materials and labor. Total cost is the sum of fixed and variable costs.

Step 2:   Plot the Total Costs for Each Location on One Graph. To plot any straight line we need two points. One point is Q = 0, which is the y intercept. Another point can be selected arbitrarily, but it is best to use the expected volume of sales in the future.

Step 3:   Identify Ranges of Output for Which Each Location Has the Lowest Total Cost.

Step 4:   Solve Algebraically for the Break-Even Points over the Identified Ranges. Select the location that gives the lowest cost for the range of output required by the new facility.

| EXAMPLE 9.6 | **Using Break-Even Analysis** |

Clean-Clothes Cleaners is a dry cleaning business that is considering four possible sites for its new operation. The annual fixed and variable costs for each site have been estimated as follows:

Location	Fixed Costs	Variable Costs
A	$350,000	$ 5/unit
B	$170,000	$25/unit
C	$100,000	$40/unit
D	$250,000	$20/unit

(a) Plot the total cost curves for each location on the same graph and identify the range of output for which each location provides the lowest total cost.

(b) If demand is expected to be 10,000 units per year, which is the best location?

• **Before You Begin:** To solve this problem, follow the four steps given in the text for using break-even analysis in location selection.

• **Solution:**

(a) Step 1 in the break-even procedure has already been completed; that is, we have identified the fixed and variable costs. The next step is to plot the total costs of each location on a graph. For each line that we have to plot, we need two points. The first point can be Q = 0. We can compute the second point using expected demand, which is Q = 10,000 units. For Q = 10,000 units we compute the following total costs for each location:

Location	Fixed Cost	Variable Cost	Total Cost
A	$350,000	$ 5 (10,000)	$400,000
B	$170,000	$25 (10,000)	$420,000
C	$100,000	$40 (10,000)	$500,000
D	$250,000	$20 (10,000)	$450,000

The plots of these graphs are shown in Figure 9-6. You can see that depending on the range of output, locations C, B, and A are best. Location D is never a best option.

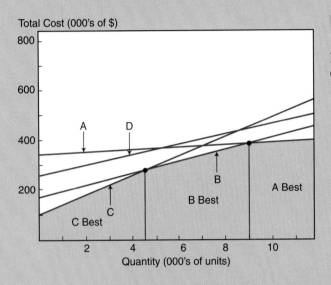

FIGURE 9-6

Break-even graph for Clean-Clothes Cleaners

(b) We can see the approximate ranges for each location in Figure 9-6. We can compute the exact ranges for each output location by finding the exact output level for which locations C and B are equal and for which locations B and A are equal. We can do this by computing the output levels at which the total cost equations for these locations are equal:

$$\text{Total cost equation for C} = \text{Total cost equation for B}$$

$$100,000 + \$40\ Q = 170,000 + \$25\ Q$$

$$Q = 4666.7 \text{ units}$$

Thus, the point between C and B is 4666.7, or roughly 4667 units.

$$\text{Total cost equation for B} = \text{Total cost equation for A}$$

$$170,000 + \$25\ Q = 350,000 + \$5\ Q$$

$$Q = 9000 \text{ units}$$

The breaking point between B and A is 9000 units, which means that location A would provide the lowest cost if we produce 9000 units or more. If we plan to meet a demand of 10,000 units, we should select location A. This problem can also be solved using a spreadsheet, as shown.

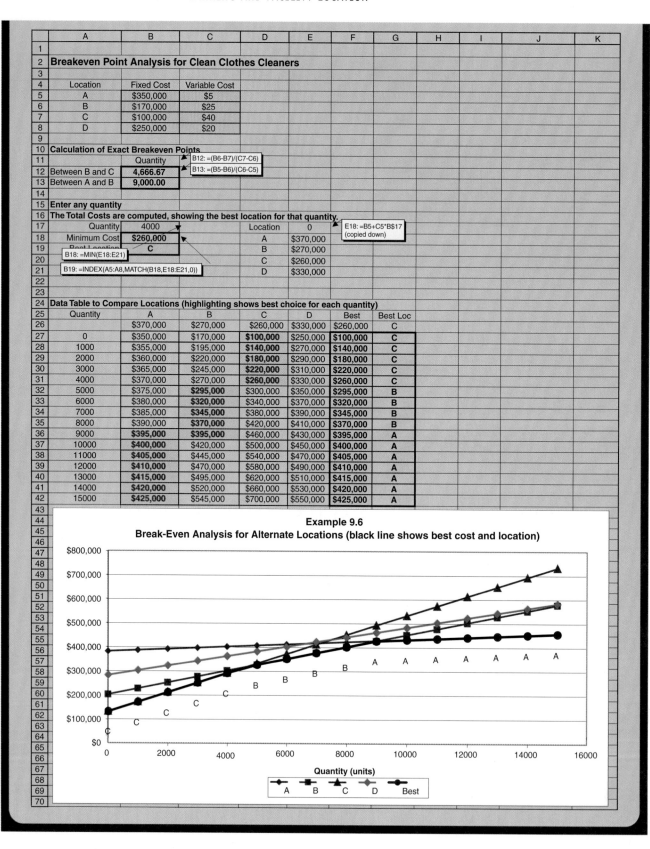

The Transportation Method The transportation method of linear programming is a useful technique for solving specific location problems; it is discussed in detail in the supplement for this text. The method relies on a specific algorithm to evaluate the cost impact of adding potential location sites to the network of existing facilities. For example, an existing network of facilities may consist of multiple sending and receiving sites. Our task might be to evaluate adding a new location site to this network, either a receiving site or a sending site. We might also wish to evaluate adding multiple new sites or completely redesigning the network. The transportation method can efficiently analyze all these situations and provide the lowest cost for each configuration considered.

CAPACITY PLANNING AND FACILITY LOCATION WITHIN OM

Decisions about capacity and location are highly dependent on forecasts of demand (Chapter 8). Forecasts determine the size of current and future capacity needs. Incorrect forecasts, where capacity is either over- or underestimated, can have a devastating affect on the capacity decision. Capacity is also affected by operations strategy (Chapter 2), as size of capacity is a key element of organizational structure. For example, the decision whether to expand now or later can be an important strategic choice. The former can preempt competition by enabling the company to be ready to meet demand. The latter can provide flexibility. Other operations decisions that are affected by capacity and location are issues of job design and labor skills (Chapter 11), choice on the mix of labor and technology, as well as choices on technology and automation (Chapter 3).

CAPACITY PLANNING AND FACILITY LOCATION ACROSS THE ORGANIZATION

By now it should be clear how capacity planning and location analysis affect operations management. However, these decisions are also important to many other functions in the company. In particular, finance and marketing have a great stake in capacity planning and location decisions.

Finance must be actively involved in the organization's capacity planning decisions. At the same time, operations managers need input from finance in order to finalize their capacity decisions. The reason should be clear. Capacity planning requires large financial expenditures. Building a large facility now would mean that funds would be tied up in excess capacity from which no financial return would be obtained for several years. At the same time, expanding capacity in increments could prove to be a greater financial drain due to poor planning. Location analysis, which is tied to the capacity planning decision, is basically a financial investment. Certain locations may be cheaper but may prove to be a poorer business investment. Finance needs to be an active participant in both the capacity planning and location analysis decisions.

Marketing is another function that is highly affected by capacity planning and location decisions. The amount of current and future capacity restricts the ability to meet demand. Building a large facility that enables the company to capture future demand and position itself in the marketplace could be advantageous from a marketing perspective. On the other hand, given future demands and competition this may not be a critical issue. Marketing is the function that has this information. Also, locating near customers can be critical for certain businesses, particularly service organizations. Marketing managers are in the best position to understand which location factors are most important to customers.

Capacity planning and location analysis are excellent examples of decisions that must be made by operations, finance, and marketing working together. As you can see, each of these functional areas has its domain of expertise and provides information that the others do not have. Together, they must arrive at capacity and location decisions that are best for the company in the long run.

THE SUPPLY CHAIN LINK

Think of a supply chain as a pipeline that supplies a certain level of customer demand. In order for the pipeline to satisfy this demand, the pipeline must flow smoothly without disruption. This can only happen if capacity is uniform throughout the entire supply chain and is matched between entities. For example, a manufacturer must make sure that the capacity of its suppliers is sufficient to meet its own capacity needs and that there is no gap in product delivery.

The link to supply chains also ties to the location decision. Many firms locate close to their source of supply or require their suppliers to locate in close proximity to them. Recall that Dell requires its suppliers to be located within a fifteen-minute radius of its production facility. Without close proximity and a match in capacity between supply chain entities, smooth flow throughout the supply chain would not be possible.

Chapter Highlights

1. Capacity planning is deciding on the maximum output rate of a facility.

2. Location analysis is deciding on the best location for a facility.

3. Capacity planning and location analysis decisions are often made simultaneously because the location of a facility is usually related to its capacity. When a business decides to expand, it usually also addresses the issue of where to locate. These decisions are very important because they require long-term investments in buildings and facilities, as well as a sizable financial outlay. Also, if capacity planning and location analysis are not done properly, a business will not be able to meet customer demands or may find that it is losing customers due to lack of proximity to the market.

4. In both capacity planning and location analysis, managers must follow a three-step process to make a good decision. The steps are assessing needs, developing alternatives, and evaluating alternatives.

5. To choose between capacity planning alternatives managers may use decision trees, which are a modeling tool for evaluating independent decisions that must be made in sequence.

6. Key factors in location analysis include proximity to customers, transportation, source of labor, community attitude, and proximity to supplies. Service and manufacturing firms focus on different factors. Profit-making and nonprofit organizations also focus on different factors.

7. Several tools can be used to facilitate location analysis. Factor rating is a tool that helps managers evaluate qualitative factors. The load–distance model and center of gravity approach evaluate the location decision based on distance. Break-even analysis is used to evaluate location decisions based on cost values. The transportation method is an excellent tool for evaluating the cost impact of adding sites to the network of current facilities.

Key Terms

capacity 304
capacity planning 304
design capacity 306
effective capacity 307
capacity utilization 307
best operating level 308

economies of scale 308
diseconomies of scale 308
focused factories 309
capacity cushion 311
decision tree 313
expected value (*EV*) 314

location analysis 315
globalization 318
factor rating 321
load–distance model 322
rectilinear distance 323
break-even analysis 327

Formula Review

1. $ld = \Sigma \, l_{ij}d_{ij}$

2. $\text{Utilization}_{\text{effective}} = \dfrac{\text{actual output}}{\text{effective capacity}} \, (100\%)$

3. $\text{Utilization}_{\text{design}} = \dfrac{\text{actual output}}{\text{design capacity}} \, (100\%)$

4. $X_{\text{c.g.}} = \dfrac{\Sigma \, l_i x_i}{\Sigma \, l_i}$

   $Y_{\text{c.g.}} = \dfrac{\Sigma \, l_i y_i}{\Sigma \, l_i}$

5. $Q = \dfrac{F}{p - c}$

Solved Problems

(See student companion site for Excel template.)

• Problem 1

A manufacturer of ballet shoes has determined that its production facility has a design capacity of 300 shoes per week. The effective capacity, however, is 230 shoes per week. What is the manufacturer's capacity utilization relative to both design and effective capacity if output is 200 shoes per week?

• Before You Begin:

Remember that utilization is computed as the ratio of actual output over capacity. The difference between the two capacity measures is that one uses effective capacity and the other design capacity.

• Solution

$$\text{Utilization}_{\text{effective}} = \frac{\text{actual output}}{\text{effective capacity}} \, (100\%)$$

$$= \frac{200}{230} \, (100\%) = 86.9\%$$

$$\text{Utilization}_{\text{design}} = \frac{\text{actual output}}{\text{design capacity}} \, (100\%)$$

$$= \frac{200}{300} \, (100\%) = 66.7\%$$

The utilization rates computed show that the facility's current output is comfortably below its design capacity. It is also slightly below effective utilization, which means that the manufacturer is not using capacity to its fullest extent.

• Problem 2

EKG Software Development Corporation has determined that it needs to expand its current capacity. The decision has come down to whether to expand now with a large facility, incurring additional costs and taking the risk that the demand will not materialize, or to undertake a small expansion, knowing that the decision will have to be reconsidered in five years. Management has estimated the following chances for demand:

- The likelihood of demand being high is .60.
- The likelihood of demand being low is .40.

Profits for each alternative have been estimated:

- Large expansion has an estimated profitability of either $1,000,000 or $600,000, depending on whether demand turns out to be high or low.
- Small expansion has a profitability of $500,000, assumming that demand is low.
- Small expansion with an occurrence of high demand would require considering whether to expand further. If the company expands at that point, the profitability is expected to be $700,000. If it does not expand further, the profitability is expected to be $500,000.

• Before You Begin:

Always begin a decision tree problem by drawing a decision tree diagram and adding the information that you are given. Then you can proceed to evaluate it.

• Solution

To solve this problem we need to draw the decision tree and evaluate it. A decision tree for this problem is shown in Figure 9-7. We read the diagram from left to right, with node 1 representing the first decision point: expanding with a large facility or expanding small. Following each decision are chance events, which are the occurrence of either high or low demand. The probabilities for each event are shown on each branch. Notice that decision point 2 is where we may have to make our second decision, but only if we expand small now and demand turns out to be high. Then in five years we would decide whether to expand further. The estimated profits are shown in the right margins. We can see that at node 2 we should decide to expand further because the profits from that decision are higher ($700,000 versus $500,000). The expected value (*EV*) of profits at that point is written below node 2. The dollar amounts at the end of each alternative are the estimated profits.

Now that we have drawn the decision tree, let's see how we can solve it. We do this by computing the expected value (EV) of the small and large expansions:

$$EV_{\text{small expansion}} = .60\ (\$700{,}000) + .40\ (\$500{,}000)$$
$$= \$620{,}000$$

$$EV_{\text{large expansion}} = .60\ (\$1{,}000{,}000) + .40\ (\$600{,}000)$$
$$= \$840{,}000$$

A large expansion now gives us a higher expected value.

FIGURE 9-7

Decision tree for EKG Corporation

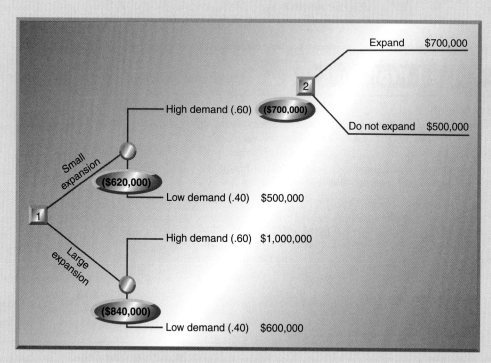

• Problem 3

As a recent business school graduate, you are considering two job opportunities that both require relocation. The two jobs are identical and have the same career potential. Therefore, your decision will be based on an evaluation of the two locations. You have decided to use factor rating to make your decision and have identified the most important factors. You have also placed a weight on each factor that reflects its importance and have developed a factor score for each location based on a 5-point scale. This information is shown in the table. Using the procedure for factor rating, complete the table.

• Before You Begin:

To solve this problem, for each location multiply the weight of the factor by the score for that factor and sum the results for each alternative. Then select the alternative with the highest score.

• Solution

The completed factor rating spreadsheet is shown on the next page.

		Factor Score at Each Location	
Factor	Factor Weight	Location 1	Location 2
Cost of living	10	5	2
Proximity to family	20	4	2
Climate	30	2	5
Transportation system	10	5	3
Quality of life	30	3	5

	A	B	C	D	E	F
1						
2	**Job Opportunity Location Analysis**					
3						
4		**Factor Scores (1-5 scale)**				
5	**Factor**	**Location 1**	**Location 2**	**Factor Weight**		
6	Cost of Living	5	2	10		
7	Proximity to family	4	2	20		
8	Climate	2	5	30		
9	Transportation System	5	3	10		
10	Quality of Life	3	5	30		
11			Total	100		D11: =SUM(D6:D10)
12						
13	**Compute Weighted Factor Scores and Overall Scores for Each Location**					
14		**Weighted Factor Scores**				B16: =B6*$D6 (copied to B16:C20)
15	**Factor**	**Location 1**	**Location 2**			
16	Cost of Living	50	20			B21: =SUM(B16:B20) (copy right)
17	Proximity to family	80	40			
18	Climate	60	150			
19	Transportation System	50	30			
20	Quality of Life	90	150			
21	Totals	**330**	**390**			
22						
23	Best Total Score	**390**				B23: =MAX(B21:C21)
24	Best Location	**Location 2**				B24: =INDEX(B15:C15,MATCH(B23,B21:C21,0))

Based on these results, you should move to location 2.

• Problem 4

Shoeless Joe is a specialty retailer that is deciding where to locate its new facility. The annual fixed and variable costs for each site under consideration have been estimated as follows:

Location	Fixed Costs	Variable Costs
A	$70,000	$1/unit
B	$34,000	$5/unit
C	$20,000	$8/unit
D	$50,000	$4/unit

If demand is expected to be 2000 units, which location is best?

• Solution

For $Q = 2000$, units we compute the following total costs for each location:

Location	Fixed Cost	Variable Cost	Total Cost
A	$70,000	$1 (2000)	$72,000
B	$34,000	$5 (2000)	$44,000
C	$20,000	$8 (2000)	$36,000
D	$50,000	$4 (2000)	$58,000

Shoeless Joe should locate at location C because it provides the lowest total cost for the expected demand of 2000 units.

• Before You Begin:

To solve this problem, you must first determine fixed and variable costs and add them to compute total cost. Then select the location with the lowest total cost.

Discussion Questions

1. Explain why capacity planning is important to a business.

2. Explain the differences between design capacity and effective capacity.

3. How is capacity utilization computed, and what does it tell us?

4. What are the steps in capacity planning?

5. What are decision trees, and how do they help us make better decisions?

6. Find and discuss business examples of overcapacity and undercapacity.

7. Explain the consequences of poor location decisions for a business.

8. Find examples of good and bad location decisions.

9. Describe three advantages and three disadvantages of globalization.

10. Describe the steps used to make location decisions.

11. Describe five factors that should be considered in the location decision.

12. Explain the differences among factor rating, the load–distance model, and break-even analysis. What criteria does each method use to make the location decision?

Problems

1. Joe's Tasty Burger has determined that its production facility has a design capacity of 400 hamburgers per day. The effective capacity, however, is 250 hamburgers per day. Lately Joe has noticed that output has been 300 hamburgers per day. Compute both design and effective capacity utilization measures. What can you conclude?

2. A manufacturer of printed circuit boards has a design capacity of 1000 boards per day. The effective capacity, however, is 700 boards per day. Recently, the production facility has been producing 950 boards per day. Compute the design and effective capacity utilization measures. What do they tell you?

3. Beth's Bakery can comfortably produce 60 brownies in one day. If Beth takes some unusual measures, such as hiring her two aunts to help in the kitchen and work overtime, she can produce up to 100 brownies in one day.

   (a) What are the design and effective capacities for Beth's Bakery?

   (b) If Beth is currently producing 64 brownies, compute the capacity utilization for both measures. What can you conclude?

4. The town barber shop can accommodate thirty-five customers per day. The manager has determined that if two additional barbers are hired, the shop can accommodate eighty customers per day. What are the design and effective capacities for the barber shop?

5. The design and effective capacities for a local paper manufacturer are 1000 and 600 pounds of paper per day, respectively. At present, the manufacturer is producing 500 pounds per day. Compute capacity utilization for both measures. What can you conclude?

6. The design and effective capacities for a local emergency facility are 300 and 260 patients per day, respectively. Currently the emergency room processes 250 patients per day. What can you conclude from these figures?

7. The Steiner-Wallace Corporation has determined that it needs to expand in order to accommodate growing demand for its laptop computers. The decision has come down to either expanding now with a large facility, incurring additional costs and taking the risk that the demand will not materialize, or expanding small, knowing that in three years management will need to reconsider the question.

Management has estimated the following chances for demand:

- The likelihood of demand being high is .60.
- The likelihood of demand being low is .40.

Profits for each alternative have been estimated as follows:

- Large expansion has an estimated profitability of either $100,000 or $60,000, depending on whether demand turns out to be high or low.
- Small expansion has a profitability of $50,000, assuming that demand is low.
- Small expansion with an occurrence of high demand would require considering whether to expand further. If the company expands at that point, the profitability is expected to be $70,000. If it does not expand further, the profitability is expected to be $45,000.

   (a) Draw a decision tree showing the decisions, chance events, and their probabilities, as well as the profitability of outcomes.

   (b) Solve the decision tree and decide what Steiner-Wallace should do.

8. The owners of Sweet-Tooth Bakery have determined that they need to expand their facility in order to meet their increased demand for baked goods. The decision is whether to expand now with a large facility or expand small with the possibility of having to expand again in five years.

The owners have estimated the following chances for demand:

- The likelihood of demand being high is .70
- The likelihood of demand being low is .30

Profits for each alternative have been estimated as follows:

- Large expansion has an estimated profitability of either $80,000 or $50,000, depending on whether demand turns out to be high or low.
- Small expansion has a profitability of $40,000, assuming demand is low.
- Small expansion with an occurrence of high demand would require considering whether to expand further. If the bakery expands at this point, the profitability is to be $50,000.

(a) Draw a decision tree showing the decisions, chance events, and their probabilities, as well as the profitability of outcomes.

(b) Solve the decision tree and decide what the bakery should do.

9. Demand has grown at Dairy May Farms, and it is considering expanding. One option is to expand by purchasing a very large farm that will be able to meet expected future demand. Another option is to expand the current facility by a small amount now and take a wait-and-see attitude, with the possibility of a larger expansion in two years.

Management has estimated the following chances for demand:

- The likelihood of demand being high is .70.
- The likelihood of demand being low is .30.

Profits for each alternative have been estimated as follows:

- Large expansion has an estimated profitability of either $40,000 or $20,000, depending on whether demand turns out to be high or low.
- Small expansion has a profitability of $15,000, assuming that demand is low.
- Small expansion with an occurrence of high demand would require considering whether to expand further. If the company expands at that point, the profitability is expected to be $35,000. If it does not expand further, the profitability is expected to be $12,000.

(a) Draw a decision tree diagram for Dairy May Farms.

(b) Solve the decision tree you developed. What should Dairy May Farms do?

10. Spectrum Hair Salon is considering expanding its business, as it is experiencing a large growth. The question is whether it should expand with a bigger facility than needed, hoping that demand will catch up, or with a small facility, knowing that it will need to reconsider expanding in three years.

The management at Spectrum has estimated the following chances for demand:

- The likelihood of demand being high is .70.
- The likelihood of demand being low is .30.

Estimated profits for each alternative are as follows:

- Large expansion has an estimated profitability of either $100,000 or $70,000, depending on whether demand turns out to be high or low.

- Small expansion has a profitability of $50,000, assuming that demand is low.
- Small expansion with an occurrence of high demand would require considering whether to expand further. If the business expands at this point, the profitability is expected to be $90,000. If it does not expand further, the profitability is expected to be $60,000.

Draw a decision tree and solve the problem. What should Spectrum do?

11. Jody of Jody's Custom Tailoring is considering expanding her growing business. The question is whether to expand with a bigger facility than she needs or with a small facility, knowing that she will have to reconsider expanding in three years.

Jody has estimated the following chances for demand:

- The likelihood of demand being high is .50.
- The likelihood of demand being low is .50.

She has also estimated profits for each alternative:

- Large expansion has an estimated profitability of either $200,000 or $100,000, depending on whether demand turns out to be high or low.
- Small expansion has a profitability of $80,000, assuming that demand is low.
- Small expansion with an occurrence of high demand would require considering whether to expand further. If the business expands at that point, the profitability is expected to be $120,000. If it does not expand further, the profitability is expected to be $70,000.

Draw a decision tree and solve it. What should Jody's Custom Tailoring do?

12. The owners of Speedy Logistics, a company that provides overnight delivery of documents, are considering where to locate their new facility in the Midwest. They have narrowed their search down to two locations and have decided to use factor rating to make their decision. They have listed the factors they consider important and assigned a factor score to each location based on a 5-point scale. The information is shown here. Using the procedure for factor rating, decide on the better location.

Factor	Factor Weight	Factor Score at Each Location	
		Location 1	Location 2
Proximity to airport	40	5	3
Proximity to road access	30	4	1
Proximity to labor source	10	3	5
Size of facility	20	2	4

13. Sue and Joe are a young married couple who are considering purchasing a new home. Their search has been reduced to two homes that they both like, at different locations. They have decided to use factor rating to help them make their decision. They have listed the factors they consider important and assigned a factor score to each location based on a 5-point scale. The information is shown here. Using the procedure for factor rating, complete the table and help Sue and Joe make their decision.

| Factor | Factor Weight | Factor Score at Each Location | |
		Location 1	Location 2
Proximity to work	10	5	2
Proximity to family	20	4	2
Size of home	30	2	5
Transportation system	10	5	3
Neighborhood	30	3	5

14. The Bakers Dozen Restaurant is considering opening a new location. It has considered many factors and identified the ones that are most important. Two locations are being evaluated based on these factors, using factor rating. Each location has been evaluated relative to the factors on a 5-point scale. These numbers are shown here. Use factor rating to help the restaurant decide on the better location.

| Factor | Factor Weight | Factor Score at Each Location | |
		Location 1	Location 2
Proximity to customers	30	5	2
Proximity to competition	10	4	2
Proximity to labor supply	30	2	5
Transportation system	20	5	3
Quality of life	10	3	5

15. Joe's Sports Supplies Corporation is considering where to locate its warehouse in order to service its four stores in four towns: A, B, C, and D. Two possible sites for the warehouse are being considered, one in Jasper and the other in Longboat. The following table shows the distances between two locations being considered and the four store locations. Also shown are the loads between the warehouse and the four stores. Use the load–distance model to determine whether the warehouse should be located in Jasper or in Longboat.

Town	Distance to Jasper	Distance to Longboat	Load between City and Warehouse
A	30	12	15
B	6	12	10
C	10.5	30	12
D	4.5	24	8

16. Given here are the coordinates for each of the four towns to be serviced by the warehouse in Problem 15. Use the information from Problem 15 and the center of gravity method to determine coordinates for the warehouse.

Town	Coordinates (X, Y)
A	(4, 18)
B	(12, 2)
C	(10, 8)
D	(8, 15)

17. Shoeless Joe is a specialty retailer that is deciding where to locate a new facility. The annual fixed and variable costs for each possible site have been estimated as follows:

Location	Fixed Costs	Variable Costs
A	$70,000	$1/unit
B	$34,000	$5/unit
C	$20,000	$8/unit
D	$50,000	$4/unit

If demand is expected to be 2000 units, which location is best?

18. The Quick Copy center for document copying is deciding where to locate a new facility. The annual fixed and variable costs for each site it is considering have been estimated as follows:

Location	Fixed Costs	Variable Costs
A	$85,000	$2/unit
B	$49,000	$7/unit
C	$35,000	$10/unit
D	$65,000	$6/unit

If demand is expected to be 3000 units, which location is best?

CASE: Data Tech Inc.

Data Tech Inc. is a small but growing company started by Jeff Styles. Data Tech is a business that transfers hard copies of documents, such as invoices, bills, or mailing lists, onto CDs. As more companies move to a paperless environment, placing data on CDs is the wave of the future. Jeff had started the company in his two-car garage three years earlier by purchasing the necessary software and signing two large corporations as his first customers. Now he was about to sign on two additional corporate customers. Suddenly what was a small garage operation was turning into a major business.

The Business

The operations function of Data Tech seems deceptively simple. Every day Data Tech receives packages of mail from corporate customers containing documents they want transferred to disk. Data Tech usually receives anywhere from 10,000 to 30,000 pieces of mail per day that need to be processed. The first step requires workers to unpack and sort the mail received. Next, workers scan each item through one of two scanning machines that transfer content to disc. An accuracy check is then made to ensure that information was transferred correctly. This stage is particularly important as many of the documents contain important private information. Finally, the discs and the documents are packaged and sent back to the customer, with Data Tech keeping a backup disc for its records.

The Need for Capacity and Relocation

Running a full-time business out of his two-car garage is a challenge for Jeff Styles. Jeff has spent a great deal of time ensuring that the operation of Data Tech runs smoothly without any bottlenecks. He has been successful, and his two original customers have just signed long-term contracts with him. In addition, he has acquired two additional customers. This means that Data Tech needs to move to a larger facility that could accommodate the larger size of the business.

Jeff has narrowed his search to three potential locations. He has identified the factors that were important to him and rated each location considering a number of criteria. Some factors are especially important, such as proximity to the postal service that delivers the daily packages. Another is closeness to the airport, as Jeff frequently travels to customer locations.

A factor that is particularly troubling for Jeff is the issue of capacity. Two of the locations he is considering are larger than he currently needs and offer excess growth capacity. The third location would meet current capacity needs but would not offer ample room for expansion. He doesn't know which is a better strategy. In his list of factor weights Jeff has made spaces for both capacity options, giving himself some time to think about the issues.

Factor	Factor Weight	Factor Score at Each Location		
		#1	#2	#3
Proximity to airport	20	3	4	4
Proximity to postal service	30	4	2	5
Facility with excess capacity	?	4	5	0
Facility with potential for expansion	?	0	1	5
Close to business community	10	5	4	4
Pleasant environment	10	3	4	4

The information that Jeff has compiled is shown in the table.

To Expand Large or Small

Jeff is not sure how to evaluate whether he should focus on moving into a larger facility now or moving into a smaller facility with potential for expansion. He has estimated the following chances for demand:

- The likelihood of demand being high is .70.
- The likelihood of demand being low is .30.

He also estimates profitability for each alternative:

- Moving into a large facility has a profitability of either $1,000,000 or $600,000, depending on whether demand turns out to be high or low.
- Moving into a small facility has a profitability of $500,000, assuming that demand is low.
- Moving into a small facility would require considering expanding if demand turned high. If Data Tech decided to expand at that point, profitability would be $800,000. If it did not expand further, the profitability would be $500,000.

Case Questions

1. Help Jeff decide whether he should give greater priority to a smaller facility with possibility for expansion or move into a larger facility immediately. Decide on which is the best alternative and choose weights for the two capacity factors based on your findings.

2. Once you have selected the factors for the two capacity alternatives, use factor rating to select a new location for Data Tech.

3. How would your factor analysis be different if you had selected a different capacity alternative?

CASE: The Emergency Room (ER) at Northwest General (B)

Jenn Kostich, director of emergency services at Northwest General Hospital, is faced with a decision on how to respond to a recent memo. Her response could affect the entire ER operation and she wants to make sure it is prepared correctly.

The Problem

Jenn has just learned that the board of Northwest General has approved plans for a large remodeling and expansion project. All department directors of the hospital have been asked to provide an assessment of their capacity needs, if they were requesting an increase in their departmental space. The directors were told to specify the amount of increase they required and provide justification for the request. They were also directed to base their requests on the average of their departments' demand requirements.

The ER desperately needs more space, and Jenn is easily able to provide the needed documentation. However, she is not sure whether it is reasonable to base capacity requirements for the ER on average demand.

Background

Northwest General is the only major hospital in the area between Seattle and Vancouver. Its ER is always busy, since it is the only hospital servicing the local population and visitors during the long tourist season.

The area has been stable in population growth over the past ten years. The area is also a significant tourist destination for campers, hikers, and nature lovers. During the tourist season—consisting of summer months (June, July, and August), winter holidays (December), and spring break (March and April)—the population swells by as much as 30 percent.

The ER has been able to meet demand adequately during the nontourist season. However, it does not have sufficient capacity to meet demand when tourists arrive. These peak periods, amounting to six out of twelve months, have been extremely difficult for the ER staff. The ER does not have enough space capacity for the large number of patients during these periods. Frequently, they have to resort to using hallways and closets for patient space. The staff feel that this is unacceptable, not to mention unsafe.

The capacity problems occur only during the busy tourist season. Computing the average of the capacity requirements does not reveal this problem, as the peak demands are averaged with the lower demands during the nontourist season.

Case Questions

1. Discuss the pros and cons of using average demand to assess capacity requirements. Is this a reasonable approach for the ER?

2. Make a recommendation for Jenn as to what she should do and the information that she should provide in her request.

INTERACTIVE CASE Virtual Company

www.wiley.com/college/reid

On-line Case: Capacity Planning at Valley Memorial Hospital

Assignment: *Capacity Analysis at Valley Memorial Hospital*
Bob Reilly just called to congratulate you on your excellent work on the various assignments at VMH. He now wants you to do some capacity analysis for Lee Jordan, director of the Medical/Surgical Nursing Unit. Lee has been concerned about the capacity of the beds in the maternity ward to meet the projected patient demand next year and wants some quick analysis done prior to exploring options for capacity expansion. The maternity ward currently has 80 beds and expects to admit about 9125 patients next year. On average, a patient stays for three days. Lee wants you to address a few specific questions. This as-

signment will enable you to enhance your knowledge of the material in this chapter.

To access the Web site:

- Go to **www.wiley.com/college/reid**
- Click **Student Companion Site**
- Click **Virtual Company**
- Click **Kaizen Consulting, Inc.**
- Click **Consulting Assignments**
- Click **Capacity Analysis at Valley Memorial Hospital**

INTERNET CHALLENGE   EDS Office Supplies, Inc.

EDS is a national distributor of office supplies that delivers goods to department and specialty stores. It is planning to build a large distribution center in your state and is analyzing different location sites. You have been assigned the task of selecting the major city in your state that you think should be the site of the new distribution center. Here are some facts to consider. At present EDS has no other distribution center in your state. The goal is to locate in a major city that has easy access to major roadways; this will enable EDS to reach other destinations in the state. Although your decision will be subjective, be prepared to justify it. Go to the Internet to find a map of your state. Analyze roadways, distances, and access to other locations. Then use the Internet to get other information, such as traffic patterns, populations, and other geographic factors. Decide on the best location for the EDS distribution center and explain your decision.

On-line Resources

Companion Website www.wiley.com/college/reid
- Take interactive *practice quizzes* to assess your knowledge and help you study in a dynamic way
- Review *PowerPoint slides* or print slides for notetaking
- Download *Excel Templates* to use for problem solving
- Access the *Virtual Company: Valley Memorial Hospital*
- Find links to *Company Tours* for this chapter
  Northeast Knitting Mills
  Coppley Apparel Group

- Find links for *Additional Web Resources* for this chapter
  The Association for Manufacturing Excellence, *www.ame.org*
  APICS—The Educational Society of Resource Management, *www.apics.org*

Selected Bibliography

Berry, W.L., and T. Hill. "Linking Systems to Strategy," *International Journal of Operations and Production Management*, 12, 10, 1992, 3–15.

Florida, R. "Lean and Green: The Move to Environmentally Conscious Manufacturing," *California Management Review*, 39, 1, 1996, 80–105.

Francis, R.L., J.A. White, and L. McGinniss. *Facility Layout and Location: An Analytical Approach*, Second Edition. Englewood Cliffs, N.J.: Prentice Hall, 1991.

Meijboom, B., and B. Vos. "International Manufacturing and Location Decisions: Balancing Configuration and Coordination Aspects," *International Journal of Operations and Production Management*, 17, 8, 1997, 790–805.

Pagell, M., and D.R. Krause. "A Multiple Method Study of Environmental Uncertainty and Manufacturing Flexibility," *Journal of Operations Management*, 17, 1999, 307–325.

Swink, M., and W.J. Hegarty. "Core Manufacturing Capabilities and Their Link to Product Differentiation," *International Journal of Operations and Production Management*, 18, 4, 1998, 374–396.

Upton, D.M. "Flexibility as Process Mobility: The Management of Plant Capabilites for Quick Response Manufacturing," *Journal of Operations Management*, 12, 1995, 205–224.

Ward, P.T., R. Duray, G.K. Leong, and C.C. Sum. "Business Environment, Operations Strategy and Performance: An Empirical Study of Singapore Manufacturers," *Journal of Operations Management*, 13, 2, 1995, 99–115.

Wysocki, Bernard, Jr. "Hospitals Cut ER Waits," *Wall Street Journal*, July 3, 2002.

Facility Layout

Before studying this chapter you should know or, if necessary, review

1. The Hawthorne studies and human relations movement, Chapter 1, page 14.
2. Types of operations and their characteristics, Chapter 3, pages 65–68.
3. The load–distance model for location planning, Chapter 9, pages 322–326.
4. Measuring rectilinear distance, Chapter 9, page 323.

LEARNING OBJECTIVES

After studying this chapter you should be able to

1. Define layout planning and explain its importance.
2. Identify and describe different types of layouts.
3. Compare process layouts and product layouts.
4. Describe the steps involved in designing a process layout.
5. Describe the steps involved in designing a product layout.
6. Explain the advantages of hybrid layouts.
7. Explain the meaning of group technology (cell) layouts.

CHAPTER OUTLINE

WHAT'S IN OM FOR ME?

ACC

FIN

MKT

OM

HRM

MIS

Michael Rosenfeld/Stone/Getty Images, Inc.

Wouldn't it be frustrating if every time you wanted to get a cup of coffee you had to go to one end of the kitchen to get a cup, then to another end to get the coffee, and then to a third end to get a spoon? What if when you wanted to study you had to go to one room to get your backpack, then to another room to get your books, and then to a third room to get your writing material? What if when you went to your college cafeteria for lunch you had to go to one area of the cafeteria for a tray, then to another area for the plates, and then to yet another area for the utensils? You would be experiencing wasted energy and time, as well as disorganization due to poor layout planning. As you can see from these examples, your experience would be frustrating. Now imagine the same kinds of problems in a company and you will appreciate the consequences of poor layout planning.

Proper layout planning cuts costs by eliminating unnecessary steps and increasing efficiency. However, a good layout plan can do much more for a company by improving worker attitude and creating a positive organizational climate. Consider the SAS Institute, a software company known for having its facilities arranged for comfort and enjoyment of their employees. The company has on-site child care facilities, a cafeteria with a pianist, a gym with swimming pool, horseback riding, and a health clinic. The facility layout was designed to be aesthetically pleasing to the employees. The consequences have been high productivity and a very low turnover. For this reason, SAS is regularly on *Fortune* magazine's list of top companies to work for.

In this chapter you will learn why layout planning is important. You will also learn about different types of layouts and how to design them so as to maximize efficiency.

WHAT IS LAYOUT PLANNING?

Layout planning is deciding on the best physical arrangement of all resources that consume space within a facility. These resources might include a desk, a work center, a cabinet, a person, an entire office, or even a department. Decisions about the arrangement of resources in a business are not made only when a new facility is being designed; they are made any time there is a change in the arrangement of resources, such as a new worker being added, a machine being moved, or a change in procedure being implemented. Also, layout planning is performed any time there is an expansion in the facility or a space reduction.

The arrangement of resources in a facility can significantly affect the productivity of a business. As you saw in the opening examples, a lot of wasted time, energy, and confusion can result from a poor layout. There are also other reasons why layout planning is important. In many work environments, such as office settings,

▶ **Layout planning**
Deciding on the best physical arrangement of all resources that consume space within a facility.

face-to-face interaction between workers is important. Proper layout planning can be critical in building good working relationships, increasing the flow of information, and improving communication. Similarly, in retail organizations layout can affect sales by promoting visibility of key items and contributing to customer satisfaction and convenience. As you can see, layout planning affects many areas of a business, and its importance should not be underestimated.

In Chapter 3 we learned about different types of operations based on degree of product standardization and volume of output. We learned that there are two broad categories of operations: intermittent and repetitive processing systems. **Intermittent processing systems** are seen in organizations that produce a large variety of different products, each in low volume. An example is a typical job shop. On the other hand, **repetitive processing systems** are used to produce a small variety of standardized products in high volume. An example is an assembly line. As we will see in this chapter, the nature of a company's operations is directly related to the type of layout it uses.

▶ **Intermittent processing systems**
Systems used to produce low volumes of many different products.

▶ **Repetitive processing systems**
Systems used to produce high volumes of a few standardized products.

TYPES OF LAYOUTS

There are four basic layout types: *process, product, hybrid,* and *fixed position.* In this section we look at the basic characteristics of each of these types. Then we examine the details of designing some of the main types.

Process Layouts

▶ **Process layouts**
Layouts that group resources based on similar processes or functions.

Process layouts are layouts that group resources based on similar processes or functions. This type of layout is seen in companies with intermittent processing systems. You would see a process layout in environments in which a large variety of items are produced in a low volume. Since many different items are produced, each with unique processing requirements, it is not possible to dedicate an entire facility to each item. It is more efficient to group resources based on their function. The products are then moved from one resource to another, based on their unique needs.

Process layouts arrange items by type as seen in this grocery store.

The challenge in process layouts is to arrange resources to maximize efficiency and minimize waste of movement. If the process layout has not been designed properly, many products will have to be moved long distances, often on a daily basis. This type of movement adds nothing to the value of the product and contributes to waste. Any pair of work centers that has a large number of goods moved between them should be placed in close proximity to each other. However, this often means that some other work center will have to be moved out of the way. The process layout problem thus can become quite complex, since we are not only looking at the relationship of two resources at one time but at all our resources simultaneously.

Process layouts are very common. A hospital is an example of process layout. Departments are grouped based on their function, such as cardiology, radiology, laboratory, oncology, and pediatrics. The patient, the product in this case, is moved between departments based on his or her individual needs. A university is another example. Colleges and departments are grouped based on their function. You, the student, move between departments based on the unique program you have chosen. Another example is a metalworking shop, where resources such as drills, welding, grinding, and painting are each grouped based on the function they perform. Other examples include a printing facility that prints books, magazines, and newspapers, or a bakery that makes many different baked goods.

A tool and die manufacturing plant is an example of a process layout.

HMS Images/The Image Bank/ Getty Images, Inc.

Recall that process layouts are designed to produce many different items, often to customer specifications. To achieve this goal they have certain unique characteristics:

1. *Resources used are general purpose.* The resources in a process layout need to be capable of producing many different products.
2. *Facilities are less capital intensive.* Process layouts have less automation, which is typically devoted to the production of one product.
3. *Facilities are more labor intensive.* Process layouts typically rely on higher-skilled workers who can perform different functions.
4. *Resources have greater flexibility.* Process layouts need to have the ability to easily add or delete products from their existing product line, depending on market demands.
5. *Processing rates are slower.* Process layouts produce many different products and there is greater movement between workstations. Consequently, it takes longer to produce a product.
6. *Material handling costs are higher.* It costs more to move goods from one process to another.
7. *Scheduling resources is more challenging.* Scheduling equipment and machines is particularly important in this environment. If it is not done properly, long waiting lines can form in front of some work centers while others remain idle.
8. *Space requirements are higher.* This type of layout needs more space due to higher inventory storage needs.

Improper design of process layouts can result in costly inefficiencies, such as high material handling costs. A good design can help bring order to an environment that might otherwise be very chaotic.

The importance of a good process layout is illustrated by Wal-Mart, a company that has revolutionized retailing. A great deal of thought and analysis went into designing the layout of the Wal-Mart facilities. Most Wal-Mart locations have the same layout to provide predictability and comfort to customers. As in most retail operations, the merchandise is grouped by category. For example, all shoes are grouped in one location, as are clothing items, stationery, and snack items. However, Wal-Mart layouts provide for maximum use of floor space. For example, the layouts are designed with multiple narrow aisles as opposed to a smaller number of wide aisles. The reason is to maximize customer exposure to merchandise. Also, Wal-Mart makes maximum use of height to store inventory and give product visibility to customers. These are some of the reasons Wal-Mart is the world's largest retailer today.

Product Layouts

▶ **Product layouts**
Layouts that arrange resources in sequence to allow for an efficient buildup of the product.

Product layouts are layouts that arrange resources in a straight-line fashion to promote efficient production. They are called product layouts because all resources are arranged to meet the production needs of the product. This type of layout is used by companies that have repetitive processing systems and produce one, or a few, standardized products in large volume.

Examples of product layouts are seen on assembly lines, in cafeterias, or even at a car wash. In product layouts the material moves continuously and uniformly through a series of workstations until the product is completed. The challenge in designing product layouts is to arrange workstations in sequence and designate the jobs that will be performed by each station in order to produce the product in the most efficient way possible. Operations managers must decide exactly what tasks will be performed by every workstation in the sequence. They need to consider the logical order in which jobs should be done. For example, at a car wash you cannot perform drying before you have performed washing. Managers also need to consider how fast production occurs and how many units can be processed through the system. The faster production occurs, the more units that can be processed through the system.

Remember that product layouts are designed to produce one type, or just a few types, of products in high volume. Product layouts have the following characteristics:

1. *Resources are specialized.* Product layouts use specialized resources designed to produce large quantities of a product.

2. *Facilities are capital intensive.* Product layouts make heavy use of automation, which is specifically designed to increase production.

3. *Processing rates are faster.* Processing rates are fast, as all resources are arranged in sequence for efficient production.

4. *Material handling costs are lower.* Due to the arrangement of work centers in close proximity to one another, material handling costs are significantly lower than for process layouts.

Product layouts arrange resources in a line fashion to promote efficiency. Here workers at See's Candies plant in San Francisco prepare 4-pound boxes of chocolates for Valentine's Day.

©AP/Wide World Photos

A cafeteria line is a good example of a product layout.

Michael Roenfeld/Stone/Getty Images, Inc.

5. *Space requirements for inventory storage are lower.* Product layouts have much faster processing rates and less need for inventory storage.

6. *Flexibility is low relative to the market.* Because all facilities and resources are specialized, product layouts are locked into producing one type of product. They cannot easily add or delete products from the existing product line.

The characteristic differences between process and product layouts are shown in Table 10-1.

Process Layouts	Product Layouts
Able to produce a large number of different products.	Able to produce a small number of products efficiently.
Resources used are general purpose.	Resources used are specialized.
Facilities are more labor intensive.	Facilities are more capital intensive.
Greater flexibility relative to the market.	Low flexibility relative to the market.
Slower processing rates.	Processing rates are faster.
High material handling costs.	Lower material handling costs.
Higher space requirements.	Lower space requirements.

TABLE 10-1

Characteristics of Process and Product Layouts

TOSHIFUMI KITAMURA/AFP/
Getty Images, Inc.

The importance of an efficient product layout can be seen at the Toyota Motor Corporation, the leader of just-in-time production. Toyota had pioneered the pull production system in the 1970s, which has been widely used in practice. The work centers are arranged in a line fashion and are in close proximity to one another, allowing easy transfer of work between stations. On the production line, a worker with any problem (e.g., a product defect or a malfunctioning machine) can pull a cord that summons a team leader to address the problem. The line has been designed so that workers can easily communicate their needs to one another. Upstream workers can respond to "pull" signals from workers downstream who require orders of goods. Also, the layout of the facility is designed so that workers can see each other, as visibility of the operation is considered highly important. Toyota's system is focused on eliminating waste from every aspect of the operation and is the factor that has contributed to Toyota's large success.

Hybrid Layouts

▶ **Hybrid layouts**
Layouts that combine characteristics of process and product layouts.

Hybrid layouts combine aspects of both process and product layouts. This is the case in facilities where part of the operation is performed using an intermittent processing system and another part is performed using a continuous processing system. For example, Winnebago, which makes mobile campers, manufactures both the vehicle itself as well as the curtains and bedspreads that go into the camper. The vehicles are produced on a typical assembly line, whereas the curtains and bedspreads are made in a fabrication shop that uses a process layout. Hybrid layouts are very common. Often, some elements of the operation call for the production of standardized parts, which can be produced more efficiently in a product layout, whereas other parts need to be made individually in a process layout.

▶ **Group technology
or cell layouts**
Hybrid layout that creates groups of products based on similar processing requirements.

Hybrid layouts are often created in an attempt to bring the efficiencies of a product layout to a process layout environment. To develop a hybrid layout, we can try to identify parts of the process layout operation that can be standardized and produce them in a product layout format. One example of this is called **group technology (GT) or cell layouts**. First, families of products that are similar in their processing characteristics and resource requirements are identified. Managers can then create **cells**, or small product layouts, that are dedicated to the production of these families of products. This approach brings greater efficiency to the process layout environment. Later in the chapter we will learn more about group technology.

Other examples of hybrid layouts can be seen in everyday life. For example, retail stores and grocery stores use hybrid layouts. In these environments, goods such as dairy items, meat, or produce are stored based on their function. From that standpoint these are process layouts. However, the layout is also designed to consider a path or sequence of purchases in a straight-line fashion, making it similar to a product layout. For example, pasta is stored immediately following spaghetti sauce.

Fixed-Position Layouts

A **fixed-position layout** is used when the product is large and cannot be moved due to its size. All the resources for producing the product—including equipment, labor, tools, and all other resources—have to be brought to the site where the product is located. Examples of fixed-position layouts include building construction, dam or bridge construction, shipbuilding, or large aircraft manufacture. The challenge with a fixed-position layout is scheduling different work crews and jobs and managing the project. Project management is discussed more fully in Chapter 16.

▶ **Fixed-position layout**
A layout in which the product cannot be moved due to its size and all the resources have to come to the production site.

DESIGNING PROCESS LAYOUTS

We have mentioned that the objective in designing process layouts is to place resources close together based on the need for proximity. This need could stem from the number of trips that are made between these resources or from other factors, such as sharing of information and communication.

There are three steps in designing process layouts:

Step 1 Gather information.
Step 2 Develop a block plan or schematic of the layout.
Step 3 Develop a detailed layout.

Next we look at how each of these steps is performed.

Step 1: Gather Information

The first step is to collect information that will be used to design an initial layout. Several kinds of information are needed.

Identify Space Needed The first piece of information to be collected is the amount of space needed for each of the organization's key resources. At this stage, managers generally focus on larger resources, such as departments and work centers. Operations managers must identify the space requirements of each department relative to their capacity needs, such as size of equipment and number of employees, as well as circulation room, such as aisles.

Recovery First Sports Medicine Clinic is an outpatient medical facility that provides a variety of medical services to patients suffering from sports injuries. The services include exams and X rays, physical therapy, and outpatient surgery. The departments housed in the medical facility and their exact space requirements in square feet are shown here:

Department	Area Needed (square feet)
A. Radiology	400
B. Laboratory	300
C. Lobby and waiting area	300
D. Examining rooms	800
E. Surgery and recovery	900
F. Physical therapy	1050
Total	**3750**

EXAMPLE 10.1

Recovery First Sports Medicine Clinic: Developing a Block Plan

FIGURE 10-1

Block plan for Recovery First

| A Radiology | B Laboratory | C Lobby & Waiting Area |
| D Examining Room | E Surgery & Recovery | F Physical Therapy |

75 × 50 feet

Identify Available Space The available space of a facility is best seen by using a **block plan**, a schematic that shows the placement of departments in a facility. Using a block plan, we can visualize the available space and evaluate whether we can meet space needs. The current block plan for Recovery First is shown in Figure 10-1. The facility is 75 feet long by 50 feet wide, meaning that there are 3750 square feet of available space. The available space meets our total space requirements, but we will have to allocate more space to some departments. The first step in designing a process layout is to determine the best location of departments relative to one another. The easiest way to do this is to divide the available space into equal sizes to determine the departments' relative location. Much later, in the detail design stage, we can give more or less space to individual departments based on need.

Identify Closeness Measures Recall that the main criterion in deciding the location of departments relative to one another is the importance of proximity between them. At this stage we need a measure of the importance of having any pair of departments in close proximity to one another. There are two simple tools that can be used for this purpose: a from–to matrix and a REL chart. Both provide measures of the importance of having any pair of resources, such as work centers or departments, close together. This information can be used to design a good layout.

A **from–to matrix** is a table that shows the number of trips or units of product moved between any pair of departments. Table 10-2 shows the from–to matrix for Recovery First, with daily trips made between each pair of departments. The number of trips between departments can be obtained in many ways; for example, from routing slips or order forms, by performing statistical sampling to determine frequencies, or by interviewing management. Note in Table 10-2 that all entries are above the diagonal of the matrix. Remember that we are interested in the total amount of movement

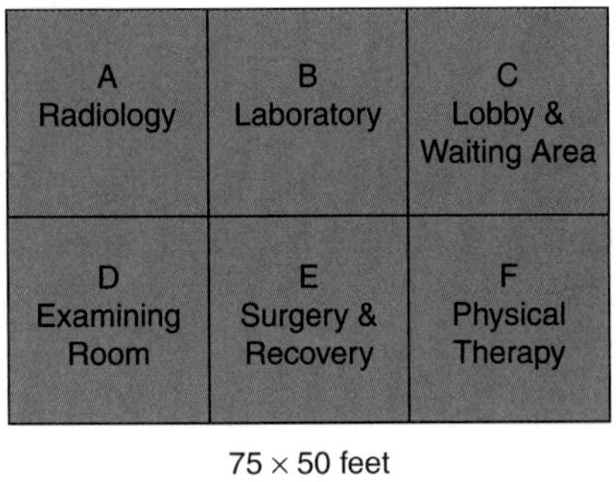

▶ **Block plan**
Schematic showing the placement of resources in a facility.

▶ **From–to matrix**
Table that gives the number of trips or units of product moved between any pair of departments.

TABLE 10-2

From–To Matrix for Recovery First

Department	A	B	C	D	E	F
A. Radiology	—	—	—	45	12	25
B. Laboratory		—	—	45	14	5
C. Lobby and waiting area			—	50	20	43
D. Examining rooms				—	—	12
E. Surgery and recovery						—
F. Physical therapy						—

between any two departments, regardless of direction. Therefore, the matrix has consolidated movements from both directions. For example, the total number of trips between departments A and D is 45. This could mean that 20 trips are being made from A to D and 25 trips from D to A. However, for our purpose here we are not concerned with the direction of the trips, but only with the *total number* of trips in order to measure the importance of having these departments close together.

Another tool that can be used to provide information about the importance of proximity is a REL chart, short for relationship chart. A **REL chart** is a tool that reflects opinions of managers with regard to the importance of having any two departments close together. It is a good tool to use when we need to consider the judgments of managers in deciding where to locate departments. This would be the case when other factors need to be considered in making a location decision, such as communication in an office setting, face-to-face contact, or customer access as in retail businesses. In these environments it is often impossible to obtain numerical values of product flow. Using a relationship chart to develop acceptable layouts is part of a classic layout technique called *systematic layout planning* (SLP). A REL chart can be used in much the same way as a from–to matrix.

A REL chart for Recovery First is shown in Table 10-3. The importance of having departments close together is calculated using a predetermined scale, which is shown with the table. Values in the chart can be obtained by interviewing management and staff.

Finally, in addition to considering closeness information, a company needs to take into account other information when making layout decisions. It is very common not to be able to move certain departments due to physical constraints. For example, Recovery First has decided not to move department C, the lobby and waiting area, because it is closest to the parking lot.

Now that we have collected all the needed information, let's move to the next step in designing a process layout.

▶ **REL chart**
Table that reflects opinions of managers with regard to the importance of having any two departments close together.

TABLE 10-3

REL Chart for Recovery First

Closeness Rating between Departments						
Department	**A**	**B**	**C**	**D**	**E**	**F**
A. Radiology	—	U	U	O	A(2)	O
B. Laboratory		—	U	O	I(3)	U
C. Lobby and waiting area			—	E(1)	X(4)	I(1)
D. Examining rooms				—	O	I(1)
E. Surgery and recovery						O
F. Physical therapy						—

Explanation of Rating Codes			
Rating	**Definition**	**Code**	**Meaning**
A	Absolutely necessary	1	Patient convenience
E	Especially important	2	Sharing of medical staff
I	Important	3	Access to equipment
O	Ordinary closeness	4	Patient privacy
U	Unimportant		
X	Undesirable		

Step 2: Develop a Block Plan

The next step in the layout planning process is to develop a new block plan or a better block plan than the one already in existence. A block plan can be developed either by trial and error or by choosing from a variety of decision-support tools. We will first use trial and error to develop a better block plan for Recovery First. When the layout problem is small in scope, trial and error can work well. However, when the layout problem is large, it may be necessary to rely on available software. Regardless of whether you choose to use software to make your layout decisions, it is important to understand the logic behind trial and error, because decision-support tools are based on heuristics that use logic similar to that used in trial and error. To understand how the decision-support tools work, you need to understand the trial-and-error process.

Using Trial and Error Recall that the goal is to develop a layout that places departments close together that have been identified as needing close proximity by either the from–to matrix or the REL chart. Recovery First has decided to develop a layout that minimizes the number of trips made in order to improve its efficiency. We will use information in the from–to matrix in Table 10-2 to identify critical pairings of departments.

Looking at the from–to matrix, we begin by identifying pairs of departments that need to be located close together. We look for pairs of departments with a high number of trips between them. From Table 10-2 we can identify the following pairs of departments:

Departments C and D, which have 50 trips between them
Departments A and D, which have 45 trips between them
Departments B and D, which have 45 trips between them
Departments C and F, which have 43 trips between them

These departments have a much higher number of trips between them compared to the other department pairs. However, note that this is an arbitrary decision, one that uses judgment. If the trips are close in numerical value, the operations manager can use information from the REL chart to decide on critical pairings of departments.

Based on these criteria, we can propose the block plan shown in Figure 10-2. This plan appears to meet set criteria, but how do we know whether it is indeed better than the current layout? We need a way to measure its effectiveness quantitatively. We can do this by using the **load–distance model** that was discussed in Chapter 9. The model is shown in Table 10-4. Recall that relative locations can be compared by computing the *ld* score, which is obtained by multiplying the load for each department by the distance traveled and then summing over all the departments. The resulting score is a surrogate measure for material handling, movement, or communication. Our goal is to make the *ld* score as low as possible by reducing the distance large loads have to travel.

▶ **Load–distance model**
Model used to compare the relative effectiveness of different layouts.

FIGURE 10-2

Proposed block plan for Recovery First

| A
Radiology | D
Examining rooms | C
Lobby & Waiting area |
| E
Surgery & recovery | B
Laboratory | F
Physical Therapy |

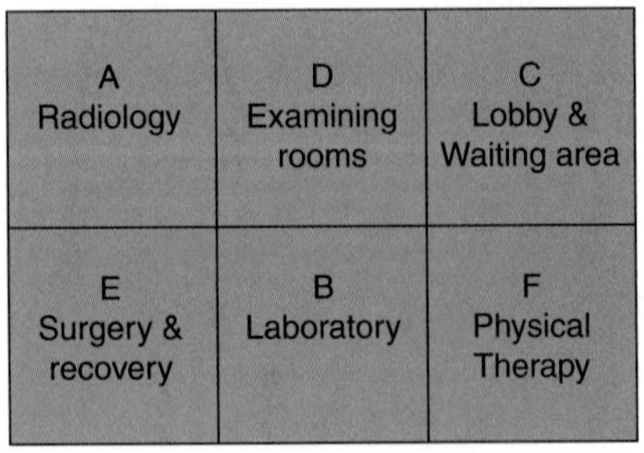

$$ld \text{ score for a layout} = \Sigma l_{ij}d_{ij}$$

where l_{ij} = load between departments i and j, obtained from either the from–to matrix or the REL chart

d_{ij} = distance between departments i and j, obtained from a block plan

TABLE 10-4

The Load–Distance Model

The load is the number obtained from the from–to matrix; it shows the number of trips between departments. But how do we determine the distance? We can obtain the distance from the block plan. Because the size of each block is the same, we do not need to measure the distance in feet. Rather, to keep it simple we can use one block as a measure of distance. To measure the distance between departments, we typically use *rectilinear distance*, which we studied in Chapter 9. Remember that the **rectilinear distance** between any two locations is the shortest distance using only north–south and east–west movements. Therefore, from our proposed block plan we can see that the distance between departments A and D is one block unit. Between A and C the distance is two block units, and between A and F it is three block units. Using this logic, let's compute the load–distance score for the current and proposed layouts and decide which layout is better.

▶ **Rectilinear distance**
The shortest distance between two locations using north–south and east–west movements.

Table 10-5 shows computations of *ld* scores for both the current and proposed layouts for Recovery First. We can see that the proposed layout is better than the current one, as it has a lower *ld* score. In fact, the proposed layout is an almost 30 percent improvement over the current layout. To get the actual distance in feet, we could have

TABLE 10-5

ld Score Computations for Current and Proposed Layouts for Recovery First

Departments	Number of Trips (obtained from from–to matrix) *l*	Current Layout		Proposed Layout	
		Distance (obtained from current block plan) *d*	Load–Distance Score *ld*	Distance (obtained from proposed block plan) *d*	Load–Distance Score *ld*
A and D	45	1	45	1	45
A and E	12	2	24	1	12
A and F	25	3	75	3	75
B and D	45	2	90	1	45
B and E	14	1	14	1	14
B and F	5	2	10	1	5
C and D	50	3	150	1	50
C and E	20	2	40	3	60
C and F	43	1	43	1	43
D and F	12	2	24	2	24
		Total	**515**		**373**

multiplied the distance in the figure by 25, as each block is 25 feet long. However, multiplying both sides by 25 would not change their relative relationship.

The solution to the layout problem for Recovery First can also be solved using a spreadsheet, as shown.

	A	B	C	D	E	F	G
1							
2	**Block Layout for Recovery First Clinic**						
3							
4	Existing Layout				Proposed Layout		
5	A	B	C		A	D	C
6	D	E	F		E	B	F
7							
8					Current Layout		Proposed Layout
9	Departments		Number of Trips	Distance	Load-Distance	Distance	Load-Distance
10	A	D	45	1	45	1	45
11	A	E	12	2	24	1	12
12	A	F	25	3	75	3	75
13	B	D	45	2	90	1	45
14	B	E	14	1	14	1	14
15	B	F	5	2	10	1	5
16	C	D	50	3	150	1	50
17	C	E	20	2	40	3	60
18	C	F	43	1	43	1	43
19	D	F	12	2	24	2	24
20				Total	**515**	Total	**373**
21							
22		E10: =$C10*D10 (copied down, similar formulas for G10:G19)			E20: =SUM(E10:E19) (similar formula for G20)		
23							
24							

Using Decision Support Tools Using trial and error to develop a layout plan can often lead to satisfactory results. If we continued with trial and error in our example, we could find a solution that lowered the *ld* score even further. However, when dealing with layout problems of a more realistic size, we need to use decision-support tools. The reason is that the layout problem is a combinatorial problem. For a block plan of six departments, there are actually 6! different solutions, or 720 possible solutions. You can imagine how many layout alternatives there would be for a facility with fifty different departments.

▶ **ALDEP and CRAFT**
Computer software packages for designing process layouts.

There are a number of computer software packages that can be used as decision-support tools in making the layout decision. Two of the most popular are **ALDEP** (automated layout design program) and **CRAFT** (computerized relative allocation of facilities technique). They are called decision-support tools because they use different heuristics to develop a solution. They do not give an optimal solution, and they consider only one criterion at a time in designing a layout. The best way to use these software packages is to consider the software solution as a starting point in developing a final layout.

ALDEP works from a REL chart. It constructs a layout within the boundaries of the facility by trying to link together departments that have either an A or an E rating in the REL chart. Remember that an A rating stands for absolutely necessary and an E rating for especially important. ALDEP uses this logic to link these departments together. The first department is selected randomly. To evaluate a layout, the computer program computes a score that is similar to the *ld* score we computed using trial and error. Depending on the starting point selected, many different layouts can be obtained.

CRAFT works differently from ALDEP. It is also a heuristic, but it uses a different logic to find a solution. CRAFT uses a from–to matrix and an existing layout as a starting point. It proceeds by making paired exchanges of departments that lead to a reduction of the *ld* score and continues in this manner until there are no more exchanges that can reduce the *ld* score. The solution with the lowest *ld* score is the final solution.

There are many other sophisticated computer software packages for layout planning that can be used to design office buildings, warehouses, and other large facilities. They are capable of designing layouts for multiple floors, and they can consider height for assigning storage locations, as in retail or warehousing. For example, SPACE-CRAFT is a modified version of CRAFT developed for designing multistory layouts. These software programs, including ALDEP and CRAFT, can work with a large number of departments of different sizes and shapes.

Step 3: Develop a Detailed Layout

The last step in designing a process layout is the development of a detailed layout design. At this stage the block plan is translated into a more realistic schematic. We begin to consider exact sizes and shapes of departments and work centers. We also focus on specific work elements, such as desks, cabinets, and machines, as well as aisles, stairways, and corridors. Operations managers can use a variety of tools in this final stage; they include drawings, three-dimensional models, and computer graphics software.

SPECIAL CASES OF PROCESS LAYOUT

A number of unique cases of process layout require special attention. In this section we look at two special cases: *warehouse layouts* and *office layouts*.

Warehouse Layouts

Warehouse layouts have the key characteristics of process layouts: products are stored based on their function, and there is movement of goods. The main difference is that movement within a warehouse is primarily between the loading/unloading dock and the areas where goods are stored. Typically, there is no movement between the storage areas themselves; the primary function of a warehouse is to provide storage space, so the only movement is inbound or outbound. Think about a warehouse that stores computer equipment and supplies. Printers might be stored in one area, keyboards in another, and ink cartridges in a third. Certainly there would be no movement between the keyboard storage area and the area where ink cartridges are stored. The movement would consist of bringing items either in or out of the warehouse.

Storage Areas of Equal Sizes The primary decision in designing warehouse layouts is to decide where to locate individual departments relative to the dock. Using the same logic we used for process layouts in general, the goal is to assign departments to locations in order to minimize the number of trips to the dock. As before, we need a from–to matrix that shows the number of trips. Since the movements are only between the departments and the dock, we simply locate the departments with the highest number of trips closest to the dock. Next, we locate the department with the second-highest number of trips in the next available space closest to the dock. We proceed in this manner until all the departments have been assigned. Example 10.2 illustrates a simple example.

In a warehouse distribution center, items are stored based on their function.

Charlie Westerman/Stone/Getty Images, Inc.

EXAMPLE 10.2

**Green Grocer
Makes Location
Assignments**

Green Grocer stores its dry goods in a nearby warehouse. The different categories of foods are stored in departments that each take up the same amount of space, shown in Figure 10-3. Given the available warehouse space and the number of trips made for each category of foods, Green Grocer needs to decide where to locate each department.

FIGURE 10-3

Warehouse storage areas for
Green Grocer

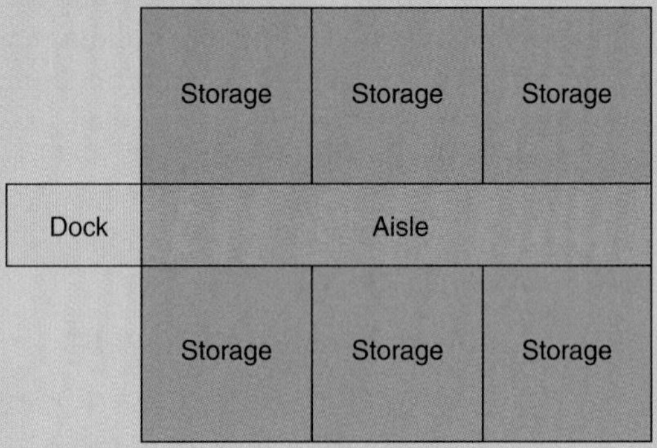

Department	Food Category	Trips to and from Dock
1	Canned goods	50
2	Cereals	63
3	Condiments	35
4	Diapers and baby products	55
5	Cookies and candies	48
6	Fruit and vegetable juices	60

• **Before You Begin:** Remember that when solving warehouse layouts the objective is to place the departments with the highest number of trips closest to the dock.

• **Solution:**
To assign departments to specific storage areas, we progressively assign departments with the highest number of trips closest to the dock. Department 2 is placed closest because it has the highest number of trips. Next comes department 6, and so forth. Using this logic we develop the block plan shown in Figure 10-4.

FIGURE 10-4

Block plan for Green Grocer
warehouse

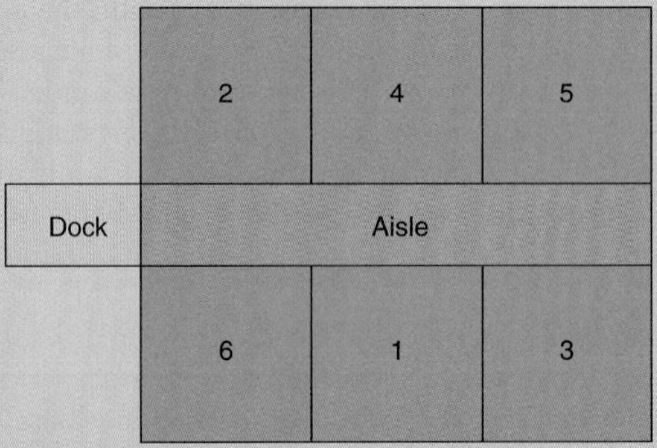

Storage Areas of Unequal Size In Example 10.2 all the departments required equal-sized storage areas. What would happen if the storage areas required were of different sizes? It is common for some departments to need more room than others based on the size of the product or volumes needed. Number of trips is not a good measure because it can be misleading. For example, if department A takes up four

SPECIAL CASES OF PROCESS LAYOUT • **357**

storage areas and makes twenty trips to the dock, it actually has fewer trips per area than department B, which takes up one storage area and makes fifteen trips. The reason is that when trips per area are considered, department A only has five trips whereas B has fifteen.

To make location assignments when departments take up storage areas of unequal size, we need to follow these steps:

Step 1 Take the ratio of the number of trips relative to the storage area required.

Step 2 Use the ratios from Step 1 to make assignments. Assign the department with the highest ratio closest to the dock. Next, assign the department with the second-highest ratio second closest to the dock. Continue in this manner until all departments have been assigned.

Example 10.3 is another example of how this would work.

EXAMPLE 10.3

Looking Good Clothes Assigns Storage Areas

Looking Good Clothes is a clothing retailer for teenagers and young adults. The company is in the process of assigning storage areas in its warehouse in order to minimize the number of trips made to retrieve items needed. Following are the departments that need to be located, the number of trips made per week for each department, and the area needed by each department:

Department	Trips to and from Dock	Area Needed
1. Backpacks	160	2
2. Hiking boots	150	3
3. Jeans	100	1
4. T-shirts	120	1
5. Bomber jackets	270	3

The warehouse block plan is shown in Figure 10-5.

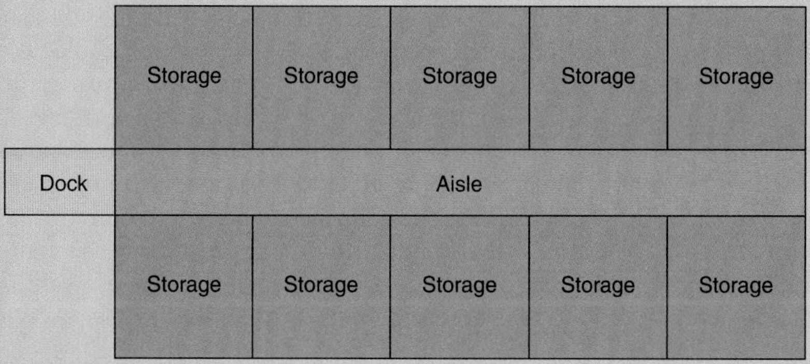

FIGURE 10-5

Warehouse storage areas for Looking Good Clothes

Storage	Storage	Storage	Storage	Storage

Dock	Aisle

Storage	Storage	Storage	Storage	Storage

• **Before You Begin:** To solve this problem, follow the two-step process given for making location assignments when storage areas are of unequal size.

• **Solution:**

Step 1: Take the ratio of trips to the number of areas taken up by the department.

Department	Trips to and from Dock	Area Needed	Ratio of Trips to Area Needed
1. Backpacks	160	2	80
2. Hiking boots	150	3	50
3. Jeans	100	1	100
4. T-shirts	120	1	120
5. Bomber jackets	270	3	90
Total Area		10	

Step 2:   Use the ratios from Step 1 to assign departments to storage areas. These are shown in the block plan in Figure 10-6.

FIGURE 10-6

Block plan for Looking Good Warehouse

3	5	5	1	2

Dock	Aisle

4	5	1	2	2

Office Layouts

Office layouts are another special case of process layouts. Merely looking at the number of trips between departments or the movement of goods is not sufficient to design a good office layout because human interaction and communication are the primary factors that need to be considered when designing office layouts. Recall from Chapter 1 that an important lesson learned from the Hawthorne studies in the 1930s was that workers respond greatly to their physical environment and have many psychological needs. This information, coupled with the fact that almost half of the workforce in the United States works in an office environment, makes office layouts very important.

Proximity versus Privacy   One of the key trade-offs that has to be made in an office layout is between proximity and privacy. The ability of workers to communicate and interact with one another is highly important in an office environment. As companies increasingly embrace team approaches, open office environments are valued because they provide visibility and allow workers to interact easily. Studies have shown

A properly designed office layout can significantly improve productivity.

Chuck Keeler/Stone/Getty Images, Inc.

that workers who are in close proximity to one another have greater understanding, tolerance, and trust for one another.

However, office layouts that enhance team interactions do not allow privacy. Often, employees need privacy to think and work quietly without being interrupted. Also, it may be difficult to have confidential conversations with coworkers and clients in an open office environment. When designing an office layout, these considerations must be addressed in order to enhance productivity.

Other Factors in Designing Office Environments One important consideration in designing any layout is flexibility. **Flexible layouts** remain desirable many years into the future or can be easily modified to meet changing demands. Traditional load-bearing walls provide privacy but do not provide flexibility. Partitions, on the other hand, are very flexible but do not offer privacy.

Companies are becoming more creative in meeting the needs of their employees, enhancing productivity, and designing flexible layouts. One option is to use what is commonly called *office landscaping*. This entails using plants, decor, and indoor landscaping to provide natural-looking partitions and sections that allow for privacy and flexibility and still have the feel of an open office environment. In addition, the natural look of office landscaping provides a pleasant working environment.

▶ **Flexible layouts**
Layouts that remain desirable many years into the future or can be easily modified to meet changing demand.

Before You Go On

We have described several different types of layouts. By now you should know how to design process layouts and understand the unique characteristics of warehouse and office layouts. We will now learn how to design product layouts. Since process and product layouts are very different, make sure you review these differences. Before proceeding further, also review the characteristics of product layouts.

DESIGNING PRODUCT LAYOUTS

Recall that product layouts arrange resources in sequence so the product can be made as efficiently as possible. This type of layout is used in repetitive processing systems that produce a large volume of one standardized product.

Product layouts are completely different from process layouts. In product layouts the material moves continuously and uniformly through a sequence of operations until the work is completed. The sequence of operations allows for the simultaneous performance of work. When designing product layouts, our objective is to decide on the sequence of tasks to be performed by each workstation. To accomplish this we need to consider the logical order of the tasks to be performed and the time required to perform each task. Also, we need to consider the speed of the production process, which will tell us how much time there is at each workstation to perform the assigned tasks. This entire process is called **line balancing**. Next we will go through the steps that must be followed in designing product layouts.

▶ **Line balancing**
The process of assigning tasks to workstations in a product layout in order to achieve a desired output and balance the workload among stations.

Step 1: Identify Tasks and Their Immediate Predecessors

The first step in designing product layouts is to identify the tasks or work elements that must be performed in order to produce the product. We also need to determine how long each task takes to perform and which tasks must be performed in sequence. The task or tasks that must be performed immediately before another task can be done is called the task's **immediate predecessor**. We use an example to illustrate this point.

▶ **Immediate predecessor**
A task that must be performed immediately before another task.

EXAMPLE 10.4

Vicki's Pizzeria and the Precedence Diagram

Vicki's Pizzeria is planning to make boxed take-out versions of its famous pepperoni, sausage, and mushroom pizza. The pizzas will be made on a small assembly line. Vicki has identified the tasks that need to be performed, the time required for each task, and each task's immediate predecessor. This information is shown here:

Work Element	Task Description	Immediate Predecessor	Task Time (in seconds)
A	Roll dough	None	50
B	Place on cardboard backing	A	5
C	Spread sauce	B	25
D	Sprinkle cheese	C	15
E	Add pepperoni	D	12
F	Add sausage	D	10
G	Add mushrooms	D	15
H	Shrinkwrap pizza	E, F, G	18
I	Pack in box	H	15
		Total task time	**165**

▶ **Precedence diagram**
A visual representation of the precedence relationships between tasks.

Often it is helpful to have a visual representation of the precedence relationships between the tasks that need to be performed. This is called a **precedence diagram**. Figure 10-7 illustrates the precedence diagram for assembling Vicki's pizzas. The diagram is read from left to right. The circles, or nodes, represent the tasks, and the arrows, or arcs, show the connections between them. Together, they show how the tasks are connected. To find a task's immediate predecessor, follow the arrows backward from your task. In the diagram you can see that the first task that must be performed is task A. After A has been completed, B should be done. Next comes task C and then D. After task D, however, we can do either E, F, or G. However, to be able to complete task H, we must have completed all the predecessors of H—namely, E, F, and G. Finally, after all the other tasks have been completed, task I can be performed.

FIGURE 10-7

Precedence diagram for Vicki's Pizzeria

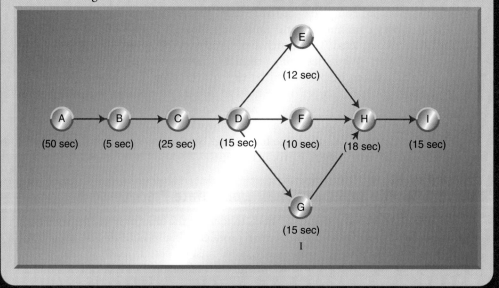

Step 2: Determine Output Rate

The next step is to determine how many units of product we wish to produce over a period of time, called the **output rate**. Then we can design a product layout that produces the desired number of units with as few work centers as possible and balance the workload at each workstation. In our example, Vicki has decided that she wishes to produce 60 pizzas per hour in order to meet her growing demand.

▶ **Output rate**
The number of units we wish to produce over a specific period of time.

Notice that the total task time to produce one pizza is 165 seconds. If Vicki wants to perform all nine work elements herself, her maximum output in one hour would be:

$$\text{Maximum output} = \frac{3600 \text{ seconds/hour}}{165 \text{ seconds/unit}} = 21.8 \text{ pizzas/hour}$$

If Vicki wants to produce 600 pizzas in an hour, she will have to divide the work among a number of people working simultaneously at workstations to achieve her desired output rate. Let's see what Vicki has to consider.

Step 3: Determine Cycle Time

Cycle time is the maximum amount of time each workstation has to complete its assigned tasks. Cycle time also tells us how frequently a product is completed. Recall that in product layouts work is being performed on many workstations that are arranged in sequence. At the beginning of the line, workers are carrying out the initial stages of putting the product together. At the end of the line, the last steps of production are being completed. If you were to stop the process at any one point in time, you would find products at all stages of production, from raw materials through work in process, as well as completed products.

▶ **Cycle time**
The maximum amount of time each workstation has to complete its assigned tasks.

Cycle time is directly related to the volume that can be produced. The faster the cycle time (the lower its numerical value), the greater the output. A cycle time of 50 seconds means that each workstation has 50 seconds to perform its assigned tasks and that one unit is completed every 50 seconds. By contrast, a cycle time of 100 seconds would give more time to each workstation. It also means that a product would be completed every 100 seconds. You can see that by producing a unit every 50 seconds we will produce more units at the end of the day, as opposed to producing a unit every 100 seconds. Therefore, cycle time is directly related to output.

$$\text{Output} = \frac{\text{available time}}{\text{cycle time}}$$

General Cycle Time Equation Cycle time can be computed from the preceding equation as follows:

$$\text{Cycle time} = C = \frac{\text{available time}}{\text{output}}$$

Computing Cycle Time When Output Is in Units per Hour Cycle time is generally computed in seconds per unit. Note that available time and output are measured over a period of time, such as per hour or per day. Remember that these need to be over the same time period for the computation to work. For example,

$$\text{Cycle time (seconds/unit)} = C = \frac{\text{available time (seconds/hour)}}{\text{output (units/hour)}}$$

Note that the "per hour" in the numerator cancels out the "per hour" in the denominator and the final measure is "seconds per unit."

Computing Cycle Time When Output Is in Units per Day The same type of computation would be performed if we were given the desired output in units per day:

$$\text{Cycle time (seconds/unit)} = C = \frac{\text{available time (seconds/day)}}{\text{output (units/day)}}$$

As before, the "per day" in the numerator cancels out the "per day" in the denominator and the final measure is "seconds per unit." The important thing is to use the same units in the denominator as in the numerator.

Now let's compute the cycle time for Vicki's assembly line. Vicki said that she wanted to produce 60 pizzas per hour as her desired output. We start with the general equation for cycle time. Then we substitute the specific numerical values and perform the computations:

$$\text{Cycle time (seconds/unit)} = C = \frac{\text{available time (seconds/hour)}}{\text{desired output (units/hour)}}$$

$$= \frac{60 \text{ minutes/hour} \times 60 \text{ seconds/minute}}{60 \text{ units/hour}}$$

$$= \frac{3600 \text{ seconds/hour}}{60 \text{ units/hour}}$$

$$= 60 \text{ seconds/unit}$$

Vicki needs to have a cycle time of 60 seconds per unit to produce 60 pizzas in an hour. This means that each workstation has 60 seconds to perform its task. Also, this means that one completed pizza will be finished every 60 seconds. After one hour, Vicki will have 60 pizzas.

Relationship between Minimum Cycle Time (Bottleneck) and Maximum Output What if Vicki changed her mind and wanted to produce more than 60 pizzas per hour? This would mean that her cycle time would have to be faster (its numerical value would be lower), and pizzas would be produced more frequently than every 60 seconds. Perhaps she could lower the cycle time to 55 seconds or even 50 seconds. But what is the lowest value for the cycle time possible?

Note that if Vicki lowered the cycle time below 50 seconds, there would not be enough time to do task A, which requires 50 seconds. Therefore, given the current task times, 50 seconds is the lowest cycle time Vicki's assembly line could have. Task A is the longest task and thus acts as a constraint. This is called the **bottleneck**. The bottleneck constrains the production process and determines the lowest or minimum cycle time.

▶ **Bottleneck task**
The longest task in a process.

Sometimes it is possible to reduce the bottleneck by splitting the task into smaller ones that can be done separately. For example, maybe our bottleneck task, which is rolling dough, can be divided into smaller tasks, such as placing dough on a floured board and rolling it out. However, there will always be a bottleneck. Once we eliminate one bottleneck, the next-longest task becomes the bottleneck.

The bottleneck is important because it provides the lowest limit on the cycle time. Cycle time is related to the amount of output; therefore, this minimum cycle time determines the maximum output that can be achieved given current tasks. The relationship can be derived as follows:

$$\text{Maximum output} = \frac{\text{available time}}{\text{minimum cycle time (bottleneck)}}$$

Using this equation, we can compute the maximum output Vicki can have on her assembly line given that task A (the bottleneck) takes 50 seconds:

$$\text{Maximum output} = \frac{3600 \text{ seconds/hour}}{50 \text{ seconds/unit}} = 72 \text{ units/hour, or 72 pizzas per hour}$$

The maximum that Vicki can produce on her assembly line is 72 pizzas per hour.

Maximum versus Minimum Cycle Time We learned that the *minimum cycle time* is equal to the bottleneck, or longest, task. In our example, the minimum cycle time was 50 units per second, resulting in an output of 72 pizzas per hour. This would require that the work be spread out over multiple workstations working simultaneously. The *maximum cycle time* is equal to the sum of the task times, or 165 seconds. As we saw earlier, this would result in the production of 21.8 pizzas per hour and would require that all tasks be performed at a single workstation.

The minimum and maximum cycle times are important because they establish the range of output for the production line. In our case, the range of output is between 21.8 and 72 pizzas per hour and is dependent on the cycle time. Vicki's desired output, 60 pizzas per hour, falls within this range.

Step 4: Compute the Theoretical Minimum Number of Stations

Before we decide to assign specific tasks to workstations, it is usually helpful to compute the theoretical minimum number of stations, or *TM*. The **theoretical minimum number of stations** is the number of workstations that would be needed if the line was 100 percent efficient. Rarely do we achieve 100 percent efficiency, and often we will have more stations than the theoretical minimum. However, computing this number gives us a baseline for the number of stations we should have. The computation for the theoretical minimum number of stations is as follows:

▶ **Theoretical minimum number of stations**
The number of workstations needed on a line to achieve 100% efficiency.

$$TM = \frac{\Sigma t}{C}$$

where Σt = sum of the task times needed to complete a unit
C = cycle time

For Vicki's assembly line, the theoretical minimum number of stations (*TM*) is

$$TM = \frac{165 \text{ seconds}}{60 \text{ seconds}} = 2.75, \text{ or 3 stations}$$

Theoretical minimum numbers of stations that end with a fraction are always rounded up because there can be no partial workstations. Notice that the theoretical minimum number of stations results in the production of daily requirements when no inefficiency exists.

Step 5: Assign Tasks to Workstations (Balance the Line)

Given the tasks we have to perform and their precedence relationships as well as the cycle time, we can now proceed to assign tasks to workstations. To do this, there are a number of rules that can be used at this stage. We will use the *longest task time rule*, which basically states that when selecting from a group of tasks we should pick the task that takes the longest time. However, in practice a number of other rules can be used. Following are the basic steps in this process:

TABLE 10-6

Assignments of Tasks to
Workstations for Vicki's
Pizzeria

Workstation	Eligible Task	Task Selected	Task Time	Idle Time
1	A	A	50	10
	B	B	5	5
2	C	C	25	35
	D	D	15	20
	E, F, G	G	15	5
3	E, F	E	12	48
	F	F	10	38
	H	H	18	20
	I	I	15	5

Cycle time = 60 seconds

Steps	Procedure for Assigning Tasks to Workstations
A	Start with the first station; make a list of eligible tasks to be performed, following precedence relationships.
B	Select from the eligible task list by picking the task that takes the longest time (*longest task time rule*). If only one task is eligible, we do not need to use the rule.
C	When the cycle time has been used up at one station or no tasks can be assigned to the remaining time, start a new station.

Let's see how these steps apply to Vicki's Pizzeria. A convenient method is to make a table with columns labeled "Workstation," "Eligible Task," "Task Selected," "Task Time," and "Idle Time." We can then fill in the table by following the steps we have outlined and keeping a cycle time of 60 seconds. This is shown in Table 10-6.

Step 6: Compute Efficiency, Idle Time, and Balance Delay

▶ **Efficiency**
The ratio of total productive time divided by total time, given as a percentage.

After tasks have been assigned to workstations, we should compute the efficiency of the arrangement. **Efficiency** is the ratio of total productive time divided by total time, given as a percentage:

$$\text{Efficiency (\%)} = \frac{\Sigma t}{NC}(100)$$

where Σt = sum of the task times
N = number of workstations
C = cycle time

Note that in this equation the numerator is the actual work time, whereas the denominator is the time allocated for performing tasks. To improve efficiency, we try to assign as much work to the lowest number of workstations needed to produce the volume of product desired while keeping the workloads balanced.

▶ **Balance delay**
The amount by which the line efficiency falls short of 100 percent.

Often it is helpful to compute the amount by which the efficiency of the line falls short of 100 percent. Called the **balance delay**, it is computed as follows:

$$\text{Balance delay (\%)} = 100 - \text{efficiency}$$

For Vicki's assembly line, we can compute the efficiency and balance delay:

$$\text{Efficiency (\%)} = \frac{165 \text{ seconds}}{3 \text{ stations} \times 60 \text{ seconds}} (100) = \frac{165}{180} = 91.66\%$$

$$\text{Balance delay (\%)} = 100 - 91.66 = 8.34\%$$

EXAMPLE 10.5

Computing Efficiency and Balance Delay

Other Considerations

In designing *process layouts* we went from a crude block plan to the design of a detailed layout. Similarly, there are many details of *product layout* design that need to be addressed in addition to the ones we have discussed.

Shape of the Line We know that product layouts arrange work centers in sequence to allow for efficient production. Even though this sequence is linear, the actual shape of the product layout usually is not one long, straight line. If it were, we would need an unusually long, straight building. Also, having a long, straight line may not be best from a productivity standpoint. Arranging the shape of the line so that workers can see and communicate with one another can improve productivity and worker satisfaction. The actual shape of the line can be an **S** shape, a **U** shape, an **O**, or an **L**. Much thought should go into the choice of an appropriate shape. For example, shapes such as **U** and **O** can store frequently used resources in the center, where they are accessible to everyone.

Paced versus Unpaced Lines Another issue to decide on is whether to have a paced or an unpaced line. On **paced lines** the product being worked on is physically attached to the line and automatically moved from one station to the next when cycle time elapses. The amount of time workers have to perform their tasks is identical to cycle time. Unpaced lines, on the other hand, allow the product to be physically removed from the line to be worked on. Workers can then vary the amount of time they spend working on the product. Storage areas for inventory are often placed between workstations, to be used when there is a delay in production at a station.

The work environment has a significant impact on worker satisfaction and productivity. Some studies have found that unpaced lines lead to greater productivity when they are coupled with a good incentive program. This situation provides more autonomy and freedom for workers. However, in some environments a paced line is the only option—for example, when the product is very large and cannot be moved. This would be the case when assembling large and heavy items such as a large refrigerator or an automobile.

Number of Product Models Produced Another consideration is whether to have a single-model or a mixed-model line. A **single-model line** is designed to produce only one version of a product. A **mixed-model line**, on the other hand, is designed to produce many versions. For example, a single line might produce only Jeep Wranglers, whereas a mixed-model line might produce two types of Jeeps, such as the Wrangler and the Cherokee. A mixed model is more flexible, but there may be more complications with regard to scheduling and changing production from one model to the other.

Manon Vatasyayana/Getty Images, Inc.

On paced lines the product being worked on automatically moves from one station to the next.

▶ **Paced line**
A system in which the product being worked on is physically attached to the line and automatically moved to the next station when the cycle time has elapsed.

▶ **Single-model line**
A line designed to produce only one version of a product.

▶ **Mixed-model line**
A line designed to produce many versions of a product.

Before You Go On

Both process and product layouts have their strengths and weaknesses. Process layouts are flexible and can produce many different kinds of products. Process layouts are less efficient than product layouts because material handling costs can create much inefficiency. Product layouts, on the other hand, are less flexible because all their resources are devoted to the production of one type of product. However, they are very efficient and create little waste. Make sure you understand these differences, because in the next section we will look at ways of combining some of the strengths of process and product layouts.

GROUP TECHNOLOGY (CELL) LAYOUTS

▶ **Group technology (GT)**
Brings the efficiencies of a product layout to a process layout.

Hybrid layouts combine characteristics of both process and product layouts. They are created whenever possible in order to combine the strengths of each type of layout. One of the most popular types of hybrid layouts is **group technology (GT)** or cell layouts. Group technology has the advantage of bringing the efficiencies of a product layout to a process layout environment.

If we look at a company that produces many different products, we may find that some products are similar to each other in the way they are made and the resources they require. For example, a company may produce 500 different products. However, if we analyze how each of the products is manufactured, we may be able to create groups of products—say, one group of 150, another group of 100, and so on—that are very similar in the way they are produced. To be efficient, we could place all the resources needed for each group in a separate area, called a *cell*. The production of a group, or family, of items would be done very efficiently because all the resources required would be in close proximity. This is the goal of group technology.

Group technology is the process of creating groupings of products based on similar processing requirements. For example, Figure 10-8 shows parts that all belong to the same family. These parts are all different, but they are very similar in the way they are made. Group technology essentially creates small product layouts dedicated to the production of a group of items. Figure 10-9 shows process flows before and after the use of GT cells. The first picture is a process layout with different product routes for the many products a company produces. The second picture shows the implementation of group technology in that environment. Cells have been created for each family, and there is a much more orderly flow through the facility.

FIGURE 10-8

Unorganized and organized parts

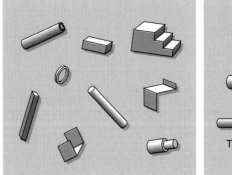

Unorganized parts

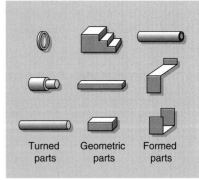

Turned parts   Geometric parts   Formed parts

Parts organized by families

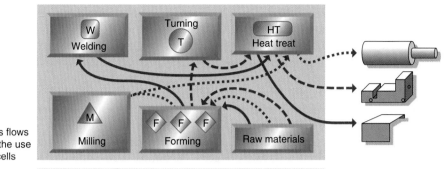

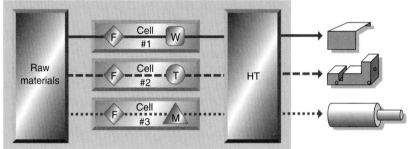

(a) Process flows before the use of GT cells

(b) Process flows after the use of GT cells

FIGURE 10-9

Process flows before and after the use of GT cells

FACILITY LAYOUT WITHIN OM: HOW IT ALL FITS TOGETHER

As you have learned in this chapter, layout decisions are directly related to issues of product design and process selection (Chapter 3). The company's process dictates the type of layout the company will have. In turn, facility layout decisions are linked with a number of other operations decisions. One such issue is that of job design, as process layouts tend to require greater worker skills than do product layouts (Chapter 11). Another issue is the degree of automation, as product layouts tend to be more capital intensive and use more automation compared to process layouts (Chapter 3). Layout decisions are also affected by implementation of just-in-time (JIT) systems, which dictate a line flow and the use of group technology (GT) cells (Chapter 7). As layout decisions specify the flow of goods through the facility, they impact all other aspects of operations management.

FACILITY LAYOUT ACROSS THE ORGANIZATION

We have seen in this chapter why layout planning is important for operations management. The production process could not run efficiently, and there would be much waste, if we did not design a proper layout for a facility. Layout planning is also important for other functions in the organization.

Marketing is highly affected by layout planning, particularly in environments where customers and clients come to the site. This is especially true in retail environments. The location and placement of goods in the facility, their visibility, and ease of access can greatly influence sales. In these types of environments the marketing of the product takes place, in part, through the layout of a facility. For example, attractive displays and product positioning in a grocery store can promote advertising and sales. Thus, it is very important for marketing to work with operations in designing the layout.

Human resources knows how the management of people can be affected by layout planning. Studies have shown that people who work and interact together on a regular basis have better working relationships. Managers need to give much thought to which groups of people need to work closely together and place them in close proximity to one another to facilitate teamwork and cooperation.

Finance is involved whenever large financial outlays and cost considerations are at stake. This is certainly true in layout planning. Redesign of layouts can be very costly, particularly if they are large scale, as when switching to an open office environment or a cell layout. Finance needs to measure the value of these investments and work with operations to create budgets. They must also understand the long-range implications of a good layout for the entire organization in order to evaluate them properly.

Everyone in the company is affected by the design of a facility's layout. Whatever organization you work at, you are somehow affected by its layout design, including the location of your office and department, the appearance of your office, and the degree of privacy you have. Also included are proximity to coworkers and other people you must interact with, whether you must travel long distances to get supplies or clerical assistance, and the aesthetics of the layout. Regardless of what business function you are in, the degree of satisfaction with your work environment is greatly dependent on the layout.

THE SUPPLY CHAIN LINK

Entities that make up a supply chain must be linked efficiently, with product flowing smoothly throughout the chain. This includes efficient shipments and deliveries between entities. Facility layout plays an important role in making sure this takes place. Arranging layouts for efficient delivery of materials to move directly to the production line is important. In locating the shipping and receiving docks consideration must be given to the layout of the production facility and the shape of the production line to enable smooth flow between inbound and outbound shipments and the production facility. Similarly, in the retail environment delivery of products must be done in a manner that enhances sales. For example, suppliers may deliver products on display-ready pallets to directly and efficiently move the product onto the retail flow, eliminating the need for unloading and stocking shelves. Arranging the facility layout to be linked to inbound and outbound shipments can greatly enhance the smooth flow of products throughout the supply chain.

Chapter Highlights

1 Layout planning is deciding on the best physical arrangement of all resources that consume space within a facility. Proper layout planning is highly important for the efficient running of a business. Otherwise, there can be much wasted time and energy, as well as confusion.

2 There are four basic types of layouts: *process, product, hybrid,* and *fixed position.* Process layouts group resources based on similar processes or functions, as in a hospital or a machine job shop. Product layouts arrange resources in straight-line fashion, as on an assembly line. Hybrid layouts combine elements of both process and product layouts in their operation. Finally, fixed-position layouts occur when the product is large and cannot be moved.

3 Process layouts provide much flexibility and allow for the production of many products with differing characteristics. Product layouts, on the other hand, provide great efficiency when producing one type of product.

4 The steps in designing a process layout are (1) gathering information about space needs, space availability, and closeness requirements of departments; (2) developing a block plan or schematic of the layout; and (3) developing a detailed layout.

5 The steps in designing a product layout are (1) identifying tasks that need to be performed and their immediate predecessors; (2) determining output rate; (3) determining cycle time; (4) computing the theoretical minimum number of stations; (5) assigning tasks to workstations; and (6) computing efficiency, idle time, and balance delay.

6 Hybrid layouts have advantages over other layout types because they combine elements of both process and product layouts to increase efficiency.

7 An example of hybrid layouts is group technology or cell layouts. Group technology is the process of creating groupings of products based on similar processing requirements. Cells are created for each grouping of products, resulting in a more orderly flow of products through the facility.

Key Terms

layout planning 343
intermittent processing systems 344
repetitive processing systems 344
process layouts 344
product layouts 346
hybrid layouts 348
group technology or cell layouts 348
fixed-position layout 349
block plan 350
from–to matrix 350

REL chart 351
load–distance model 352
rectilinear distance 353
ALDEP and CRAFT 354
flexible layouts 359
line balancing 359
immediate predecessor 359
precedence diagram 360
output rate 361
cycle time 361

bottleneck task 362
theoretical minimum number
 of stations 363
efficiency 364
balance delay 364
paced line 365
single-model line 365
mixed-model line 365
group technology (GT) 366

Formula Review

1. ld score $= \Sigma l_{ij} d_{ij}$

2. Cycle time $= C = \dfrac{\text{available time}}{\text{output}}$

3. Output $= \dfrac{\text{available time}}{\text{cycle time}}$

4. Maximum output $= \dfrac{\text{available time}}{\text{minimum cycle time (bottleneck)}}$

5. $TM = \dfrac{\Sigma t}{C}$

6. Efficiency (%) $= \dfrac{\Sigma t}{NC}(100)$

7. Balance delay (%) $= 100 -$ efficiency

Solved Problems   (See student companion site for Excel template.)

• Problem 1

Jeff-Co Industries is a metalworking shop that is redesigning its layout. The from–to matrix of the numbers of trips between departments is shown in Table 10-7.

Table 10-7 From–To Matrix for Jeff-Co Industries

Department	A	B	C	D	E	F
		Trips between Departments				
A	—	10	15	—	—	50
B		—	—	20	10	20
C			—	45	—	10
D				—	—	20
E					—	
F						—

The current layout is shown in Figure 10-10. Find an improved layout using trial and error. Which departments should you locate close together?

FIGURE 10-10

Current layout for Jeff-Co Industries

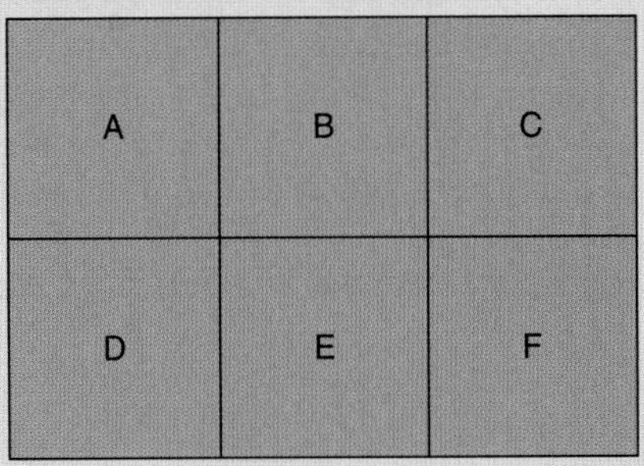

A	B	C
D	E	F

• Before You Begin:

To solve this problem, begin by identifying the departments with the highest number of trips between them from the from–to matrix in Table 10-7. Then redesign the initial layout by bringing the identified departments in close proximity to one another. Compute the *ld* scores for the initial and proposed layouts and compare.

• Solution

The following departments have the highest numbers of trips between them and should be located close together:

A and F, which have fifty trips between them
C and D, which have forty-five trips between them

Using this as our criterion we can construct the proposed layout shown in Figure 10-11.

We can now compute the *ld* scores for both the current and proposed layouts in order to make an evaluation. See Table 10-8 on the next page.

FIGURE 10-11

Proposed layout for Jeff-Co Industries

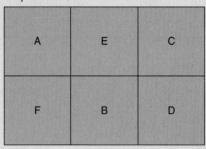

Based on the *ld* score, the proposed layout is an improvement of 43 percent over the current layout. This problem can also be solved using a spreadsheet. This is shown in the spreadsheet below.

	A	B	C	D	E	F	G
1							
2	**Block Layout for Jeff-Co Industries**						
3							
4	**Current Layout**				**Proposed Layout**		
5	A	B	C		A	E	C
6	D	E	F		F	B	D
7							
8				**Current Layout**		**Proposed Layout**	
9	**Departments**		**Number of Trips**	**Distance**	**Load-Distance**	**Distance**	**Load-Distance**
10	A	B	10	1	10	2	20
11	A	C	15	2	30	2	30
12	A	F	50	3	150	1	50
13	B	D	20	2	40	1	20
14	B	E	10	1	10	1	10
15	B	F	20	2	40	1	20
16	C	D	45	3	135	1	45
17	C	F	10	1	10	3	30
18	D	F	20	2	40	2	40
19				Total	**465**	Total	**265**
20		E10: =$C10*D10					
21		(copied down, similar			E19: =SUM(E10:E18)		
22		formulas for G10:G18)			(Similar formula for G19)		
23							

Table 10-8   *ld* Score Computations for Current and Proposed Layouts for Jeff-Co Industries

Departments	Number of Trips (obtained from from–to matrix) l	Current Layout Distance (obtained from current block plan) d	Load–Distance Score ld	Proposed Layout Distance (obtained from proposed block plan) d	Load–Distance Score ld
A and B	10	1	10	2	20
A and C	15	2	30	2	30
A and F	50	3	150	1	50
B and D	20	2	40	1	20
B and E	10	1	10	1	10
B and F	20	2	40	1	20
C and D	45	3	135	1	45
C and F	10	1	10	3	30
D and F	20	2	40	2	40
		Total	**465**		**265**

• Problem 2

Parachutes By Dave is a parachute production facility that assembles and packages parachutes. Table 10-9 shows the tasks required to perform the job, the times required by each task, and their immediate predecessors.

Table 10-9   Task Information for Parachutes By Dave

Work Element	Task Description	Immediate Predecessor	Task Time (sec)
A	Cast lines	None	45
B	Attach harness	A	15
C	Sew rings	A	27
D	Attach lines to chute	B	52
E	Perform safety check	C, D	7
F	Pack chute	E	18
		Total	**164 seconds**

If Dave wants to produce fifty parachutes per hour, compute the following:

(a) The appropriate cycle time
(b) The theoretical minimum number of stations
(c) Which tasks should be assigned to which workstations (using the longest task time rule)
(d) The efficiency and balance delay of your solution

• Before You Begin:

To solve this problem, use the steps given for designing product layouts. Notice that the sum of the task time is 164 seconds.

• Solution

(a) Cycle time $= C = \dfrac{\text{available time per hour}}{\text{output per hour}}$

$$= \dfrac{3600 \text{ seconds/hour}}{50 \text{ units/hour}} = 72 \text{ seconds/unit}$$

(b) Theoretical minimum number of stations:

$$TM = \dfrac{\Sigma t}{C} = \dfrac{164 \text{ seconds}}{72 \text{ seconds/unit}}$$

$$= 2.28 \text{ stations, or 3 stations}$$

(c) Assigning tasks to workstations with a cycle time of 72 seconds and using the longest task time rule, we obtain the following solution:

Workstation	Eligible Task	Task Selected	Task Time	Idle Time
1	A	A	45	27
	B, C	C	27	0
2	B	B	15	57
	D	D	52	5
3	E	E	7	65
	F	F	18	47

Cycle time $= 72$ seconds

(d)   Efficiency (%) $= \dfrac{\Sigma t}{N \times C}(100) = \dfrac{164}{3 \times 72}(100)$

$$= 75.93\%$$

Balance delay (%) $= 24.07\%$

Discussion Questions

1. Explain the importance of layout planning for a business. What are the consequences of a poor layout?

2. Explain the importance of layout planning for everyday life. How has poor layout planning affected your life?

3. Identify the four types of layouts and their characteristics.

4. Identify the steps in designing a process layout.

5. Find examples of a process layout in local businesses. Draw a picture of the locations of departments.

6. Identify the steps in designing a product layout.

7. Find examples of a product layout in local businesses. Draw a picture to show the workstations and the tasks performed.

8. Explain the concept of cycle time and how it affects output. Give an example.

9. Define group technology. Why is it important?

10. Give an example of a poor layout. Find a better solution for that layout problem.

Problems

1. Fresh Foods Grocery is considering redoing its facility layout. The from–to matrix showing daily customer trips between departments is shown in Table 10-10, and their current layout is shown in Figure 10-12. Fresh Foods is considering exchanging the locations of the dry groceries department (A) and the health and beauty aids department (F). Compute the *ld* score for Fresh Foods' current and proposed layouts. Which is better?

Table 10-10   From–To Matrix for Fresh Foods

| | Trips between Departments | | | | | |
Department	A	B	C	D	E	F
A. Dry groceries	—	15	45	25	10	50
B. Bread		—	30	16	25	25
C. Frozen foods			—	34	15	20
D. Meats				—	40	10
E. Vegetables						20
F. Health and beauty aids						—

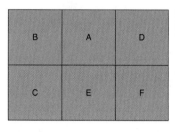

FIGURE 10-13

Current layout for Mason Machine Tools

Table 10-11   From–To Matrix for Mason Machine Tools

| | Trips between Departments | | | | | |
Department	A	B	C	D	E	F
A	—	5	20	5	—	8
B		—	—	30	10	10
C			—	20	15	5
D				—	—	—
E						17
F						—

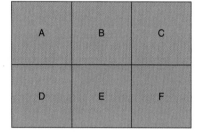

FIGURE 10-12

Current layout for Fresh Foods

2. Use trial and error to find a better layout for Fresh Foods Grocery in Problem 1. Compute the *ld* score and compare it to the *ld* scores computed for Fresh Foods' current and proposed layouts. Which is best?

3. Mason Machine Tools is reevaluating its facility layout. The current layout is shown in Figure 10-13 and the from–to matrix is in Table 10-11. Mason has to leave department C in its current location because relocation costs are too high. It is considering exchanging departments B and D. Evaluate the proposal by computing the *ld* score for both layouts.

4. Use trial and error to find a better layout for Mason Machine Tools in Problem 3. Compute the *ld* score and compare it to Mason's current and proposed layouts in Problem 3.

5. Gator Office Systems is comparing two layouts for the design of its office building. It has interviewed managers in order to develop the from–to matrix shown in Table 10-12. The two layouts considered are shown in Figure 10-14. Which layout do you think is better for Gator Office Systems, using the load–distance model?

Table 10-12   From–To Matrix for Gator Office Supplies

| | Trips between Departments | | | | | |
Department	A	B	C	D	E	F
A	—	30	—	34	50	25
B		—	—	55	10	10
C			—	—	15	5
D				—	—	—
E						30
F						—

Current layout

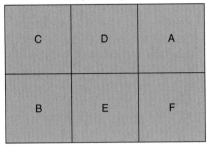

FIGURE 10-14

Current and proposed layouts for Gator Office Supplies

Proposed layout

FIGURE 10-15

Warehouse storage areas for T-Shirts Unlimited

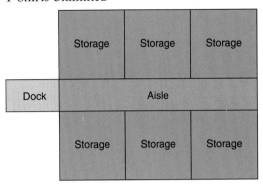

6. Use trial and error to develop a better layout for Gator Office Supplies. Which departments do you think need to be in close proximity to one another?

7. T-Shirts Unlimited is a retailer that sells every kind of T-shirt imaginable. The different types of T-shirts are stored in departments that all take up the same amount of space. Given the available warehouse space (Figure 10-15) and a from–to matrix showing the number of trips to and from each department (Table 10-13), help T-Shirts Unlimited decide where to store each type of T-shirt.

8. David's Sport Supplies is a store that sells sports equipment and gear for teenagers and young adults. David's is in the process of assigning the location of storage areas in its warehouse (Figure 10-16) to minimize the number of trips made to retrieve needed items. Given here in Table 10-14 are the departments that need to be located, the number of trips made per week for each department, and the area needed by each department.

Table 10-14   Department Information for David's Sport Supplies

Department	Trips to and from Dock	Area Needed
1. Baseball equipment	160	2
2. Football gear	100	1
3. Hockey equipment	150	3
4. Basketball equipment	120	1
5. Sports clothes	270	3

9. MMS Associates is a telecommunications service provider. The company is currently redesigning its main office to accommodate six newly hired salespeople. Some of the salespeople are expected to work in teams, so office assignments are very important. Table 10-15 presents the from–to matrix showing the expected

Table 10-13   From–To Matrix for T-Shirts Unlimited

Department	Category	Trips to and from Dock
1	Sports T-shirts	50
2	Men's T-shirts	63
3	Women's T-shirts	35
4	Children's T-shirts	55
5	Fashion T-shirts	48
6	Undershirts	60

FIGURE 10-16

Warehouse storage areas for David's Sport Supplies

frequency of contacts between members of the new sales staff. The block plan in Figure 10-17 shows the assigned office locations for the six sales members. Assume equal-sized offices and rectilinear distances. How would you evaluate the developed layout? What is the *ld* score for MMS Associates?

Table 10-15   Number of Contacts Between Sales Staff

Sales Person	A	B	C	D	E	F
A	—	6	12	18	1	1
B		—	4	19	3	0
C			—	5	0	0
D				—	7	19
E					—	0
F						—

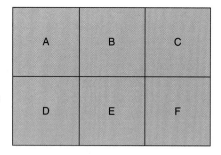

FIGURE 10-17

Assigned office locations for sales staff at MMS Associates

10. Michael Marc, the President of MMS Associates, is considering an alternative plan for the sales staff situation described in Problem 9. His alternative plan is shown in Figure 10-18. What is the *ld* score for this plan? How does it compare to the original plan considered in Problem 9?

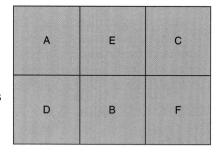

FIGURE 10-18

Alternative office locations for sales staff at MMS Associates

11. Use trial and error to find a better layout for MMS Associates. Which salespeople will be your priority to keep together?

12. A manufacturing company is designing an assembly line to produce its main product. The line should be able to produce sixty units per hour. The following data in Table 10-16 give the necessary information.

Table 10-16   Task Information for Problem 12

Task	Immediate Predecessor	Task Time (sec)
A	None	35
B	A	50
C	A	21
D	B	38
E	C	25
F	D, E	58
G	F	15

(a) Which task is the bottleneck?
(b) Draw a precedence diagram for the above information.
(c) Compute the cycle time with a desired output of sixty units per hour.

13. An assembly line must be designed to produce fifty packages per hour. The following data in Table 10-17 give the necessary information.

Table 10-17   Task Information for Problem 13

Task	Immediate Predecessor	Task Time (sec)
A	None	25
B	A	60
C	B	35
D	B	45
E	B	10
F	C, D, E	50

(a) Draw a precedence diagram.
(b) Compute the cycle time (in seconds) to achieve the desired output rate.
(c) What is the theoretical minimum number of stations?
(d) Which work element should be assigned to which workstation?
(e) What are the resulting efficiency and balance delay percentages?

14. An assembly line must be designed to produce forty containers per hour. The following data in Table 10-18 give the necessary information.

Table 10-18   Task Information for Problem 14

Task	Immediate Predecessor	Task Time (sec)
A	None	60
B	A	12
C	B	35
D	A	55
E	D	10
F	E	50
G	F, C	5

(a) Draw a precedence diagram.
(b) Compute the cycle time (in seconds) to achieve the desired output rate.
(c) What is the theoretical minimum number of stations?

(d) Which work element should be assigned to which work-station?

(e) What are the resulting efficiency and balance delay percentages?

15. The ABC Corporation is designing its new assembly line. The line will produce fifty units per hour. The tasks, their times, and their immediate predecessors are shown in Table 10-19.

Table 10-19   Task Information for ABC Corporation

Task	Immediate Predecessor	Task Time (sec)
A	None	55
B	A	30
C	A	22
D	B	35
E	B, C	50
F	C	15
G	F	5
H	G	10

(a) Which task is the bottleneck?

(b) Compute the cycle time with a desired output of fifty units per hour.

(c) Use a cycle time of 72 seconds/unit to assign tasks to workstations.

(d) Compute the theoretical minimum number of stations. Did you end up using more stations than the theoretical minimum?

(e) Compute the efficiency and balance delay of the line.

16. Kiko Teddy Bear is a manufacturer of stuffed teddy bears. Kiko would like to be able to produce 40 teddy bears per hour on its assembly line. Use the information provided in Table 10-20 to answer the following:

Table 10-20   Task Information for Kiko Teddy Bear

Work Element	Task Description	Immediate Predecessor	Task Time (sec)
A	Cut teddy bear pattern	None	90
B	Sew teddy bear cloth	A	75
C	Stuff teddy bear	B	50
D	Glue on eyes	C	20
E	Glue on nose	C	15
F	Sew on mouth	C	35
G	Attach manufacturer's label	B	15
H	Inspect and pack teddy bear	D, E, F, G	40

(a) Draw a precedence diagram.

(b) What is the cycle time?

(c) What is the theoretical minimum number of stations?

(d) Assign tasks to specific workstations using the cycle time you computed in part (b).

(e) What are the efficiency and balance delay of the line?

(f) Which task is the bottleneck?

(g) Compute the maximum output.

17. Use the longest task time rule to balance the assembly line described in Table 10-21; the line can produce thirty units per hour.

Table 10-21   Assembly Line Task Information

Work Element	Immediate Predecessor	Task Time (sec)
A	None	25
B	A	30
C	A	15
D	A	30
E	C, D	40
F	D	20
G	B	10
H	G	15
I	E, F, H	35
J	I	25
K	J	25

(a) What is the cycle time?

(b) What is the theoretical minimum number of stations?

(c) Which work elements are assigned to which workstations?

(d) What are the resulting efficiency and balance delay percentages?

18. A dress-making operation is being designed as an assembly line. Table 10-22 shows the tasks that need to be performed, their task times, and preceding tasks. If the goal is to produce thirty dresses per hour, answer the questions.

Table 10-22   Dress-Making Task Information

Work Element	Immediate Predecessor	Task Time (sec)
A. Cut dress body	None	30
B. Cut sleeves	None	40
C. Cut collar	None	20
D. Sew dress body	A	100
E. Sew sleeves to dress	B, D	25
F. Sew collar to dress	C, D	50
G. Hem dress	D, E, F	50
H. Package dress	G	90

(a) Compute the cycle time.

(b) Which task is the bottleneck?

(c) What is the maximum output for this line?

(d) Compute the theoretical minimum number of stations.

(e) Assign work elements to stations, using the longest task time rule.

(f) Compute the efficiency and balance delay of your assignment.

19. Table 10-23 shows the tasks required to assemble an aluminum storm door and the length of time needed to complete each task.

Table 10-23   Task Information for Problem 19

Task	Immediate Predecessor	Task Time (sec)
A	None	32
B	A	43
C	A	12
D	A	23
E	B, C, D	15
F	E	25
G	None	20
H	F, G	5

(a) Calculate the cycle time needed to produce 480 doors in an eight-hour work day.

(b) What is the minimum number of workstations that can be used on the line and still achieve the desired production rate? Balance the line and calculate its efficiency.

(c) What is the maximum output possible with these data? The minimum?

20. Use the data from Problem 19 to rebalance the line with a cycle time of 90 seconds. How does the number of workstations change? What happens to the output and the line's efficiency?

CASE: Sawhill Athletic Club (A)

Sawhill Athletic Club was an athletic facility in suburban Scottsdale, Arizona. It was designed to provide a wide range of athletic opportunities, including racquetball courts and exercise facilities. The facilities were modern and the staff focused on providing high customer service. To provide flexibility to its members, the club had a wide range of hours of operation. The members were primarily families and young professionals who lived in the area.

Membership at the club had been steady since it opened five years ago. To monitor the club's quality, members were often asked to fill out satisfaction surveys. Most members liked the club's attention to customer satisfaction, but many complained that the facilities did not have a good layout. They complained of having to walk long distances from one location to another, citing this as a significant inconvenience. Another complaint was that all the departments were separated with high walls, creating a "closed-in" feeling. A new athletic facility was going to be opening in the area in the near future. The owners of Sawhill thought that they had better listen to the requests of their customers in order to remain competitive.

Improving the Layout

Lauren Nicole was hired to manage Sawhill and to offer any recommendations for changing the layout of the facility. She was told to be creative and use her knowledge of facility layout

design. She was even provided with a diagram of the facility and averages of daily trips made by clients between each of the departments in the facility.

Lauren began looking at the information she received, shown in the table. She noticed that all the departments were of approximately equal size except the racquetball courts and exercise facilities. These were approximately twice the size of the other departments and could not be split. All the departments were eligible to be moved. She would take that into consideration as she decided to study the information and redesign the facility. Then she would think about which walls to lower between departments to create a more open environment. Decorating would come last.

Case Questions

1. Develop an *ld* score for the current layout. What problems can you identify with the current layout?

2. Use trial and error to come up with a better layout that lowers the *ld* score. Explain the departments you thought needed to be in close proximity to one another.

3. Imagine an athletic facility such as Sawhill. What strategies would you suggest for creating an open environment?

Layout of Sawhill Athletic Club

Lobby	Racquetball Courts	
Exercise and Weight Room E	Food Court	Pro Shop
	Showers/Locker Room G	Day Care Facility F

Department	Number of Trips between Departments						
	A	B	C	D	E	F	G
A. Lobby	—	15	34	32	14	54	76
B. Racquetball courts		—	2	2	34	0	72
C. Food court			—	26	0	47	3
D. Pro shop				—	9	1	4
E. Exercise & weight room					—	7	74
F. Child care facility						—	57
G. Showers & locker							—

CASE: Sawhill Athletic Club (B)

Sawhill Athletic Club, an athletic facility in Scottsdale, Arizona, was known for providing a high level of customer service to its members. Member complaints were taken seriously and immediately addressed. Lauren Nicole, the new manager of Sawhill, was now faced with having to resolve another service problem.

Sawhill provided a clean towel to each member upon entering the women's or men's locker room. However, the facility had been regularly running out of clean towels for some time. Over the past month, members have complained loudly that something had to be done because they were tired of waiting for clean towels.

Currently the facility had one industrial-size washing machine and one dryer, each with a capacity to hold twenty towels. The washing machine took twenty minutes to complete a load, and the dryer took sixty minutes. Following the drying process, the towels were folded and made available to members. The folding process took approximately one hour for sixty towels. The washing, drying, and folding of towels was done on an al-

most continual basis with at least one full-time person assigned to the area. The demand averaged sixty towels per hour. The process operated as follows:

WASHING → DRYING → FOLDING

"The solution is simple. We will purchase an additional washer and dryer. That will solve the problem." Lauren said confidently.

Case Questions

1. What is the reason Sawhill is regularly running out of towels?

2. What is the cycle time of the current washing-drying-folding process? What should the cycle time be in order to meet towel demand?

3. Will purchasing an additional washer and dryer solve the problem? How will the cycle time change with an additional washer and dryer? Suggest a solution to the problem.

INTERACTIVE CASE ▶ Virtual Company

www.wiley.com/college/reid

On-line Case: Facility Layout Design at Valley Memorial Hospital

Assignment: *Layout Design at Valley Memorial Hospital* Bob Reilly just called to tell you about a new assignment for you at VMH. Based on the projected growth in demand and the changing needs of the community VMH serves, the top management is considering setting up a larger and more modern out-patient clinic in a vacant lot adjacent to the main building. This new facility, housed in a building with 4000 square feet of usable floor space (100 ft. by 40 ft.) will serve walk-in and minor emergency patients. Carol Gardner, assistant to the chief administrator, has a preliminary block plan indicating the layout of the different departments, such as Lobby and Registration, Radiology, and Nurses' Station, that has been prepared by the emergency department staff. She wants you to analyze the preliminary layout

and also examine an alternate layout based on some changes that she thinks might be worth considering. Data on the traffic (i.e., number of trips) between the departments have also been compiled. This assignment will enable you to enhance your knowledge of the material in this chapter.

To access the Web site:

- Go to www.wiley.com/college/reid
- Click Student Companion Site
- Click **Virtual Company**
- Click **Kaizen Consulting, Inc.**
- Click **Consulting Assignments**
- Click **Layout Design at Valley Memorial Hospital**

INTERNET CHALLENGE ▶ DJ and Associates, Inc.

The law firm of DJ and Associates has just moved into a new facility. The spacious reception space has room for three receptionists and a client waiting area. The law firm has hired you to help with the layout of the reception area. It has given you a budget of

$15,000 and asked you to purchase furniture for the reception area that will fit into the layout, given certain constraints.

The reception area is 50 feet long by 20 feet wide. The client waiting area is 400 square feet, leaving 600 square feet for the three receptionists, their desks, chairs, file cabinets, and aisle room. The furniture for the client waiting area has been purchased. Your job is to purchase furniture for the receptionists. For each receptionist you are to purchase a desk with two chairs and two large file cabinets that will fit the constraints of the room and your budget. Since appearance is an important factor, the desks must be made of a high-grade wood. Also, there must be at least 5 feet of walking space between desks.

Use the Internet to carry out your assignment. Find Web sites for commercial office furniture sellers and browse sites for the specific furniture you need, checking dimensions and prices. Finally, come up with a plan of purchase and suggestions for a layout. It may be a good idea to read up on office layouts to get suggestions. The firm is considering hiring you for future work, so you want to develop a good plan that might include additional suggestions that were not asked for.

On-line Resources

Companion Website   www.wiley.com/college/reid
- Take interactive *practice quizzes* to assess your knowledge and help you study in a dynamic way
- Review *PowerPoint slides* or print slides for notetaking
- Download *Excel Templates* to use for problem solving
- Access the *Virtual Company: Valley Memorial Hospital*
- Find links to *Company Tours* for this chapter
    Thomson-Shore, Inc.
    Konica Corporation
- Find links for *Additional Web Resources* for this chapter
    Association for Manufacturing Excellence, *www.ame.org*
    APICS—The Educational Society for Resource Management, *www.apics.org*

Additional Resources Available Only in WileyPLUS
- Use the *e-Book* and launch directly to all interactive resources
- Take the interactive *Quick Test* to check your understanding of the chapter material and get immediate feedback on your responses.
- Check your understanding of the key vocabulary in the chapter with *Interactive Flash Cards*
- Use the *Animated Demo Problems* to review key problem types.
- Practice for your tests with *additional problem sets*
- *And more!*

Selected Bibliography

Binkley, C. "Sheraton Chain Gets a Makeover from Orange Shag to Pin Stripes," *The Wall Street Journal*, April 19, 2000.

Goldstein, L. "Whatever Space Works for You," *Fortune*, July 10, 2000, 269–270.

Lee, L. "Nordstrom Cleans Out Its Closets," *Business Week*, May 22, 2000, 105–108.

Muther, R., and K. McPherson. "Four Approaches to Computerized Layout Planning," *Industrial Engineering*, 2, 1970, 39–42.

Umble, M.M., and M.L. Srikanth. *Synchronous Manufacturing*. Cincinnati, Ohio: South-Western Publishing, 1990.

Upton, D.M., "What Really Makes Factories Flexible," *Harvard Business Review*, July–August 1995, 74–84.

Vokurka, R.J., S.W. O'Leary-Kelly, and B. Flores. "Approaches to Manufacturing: Use and Performance Implication," *Production and Inventory Management Journal*, Second Quarter, 1998, 42–48.

Work System Design

CHAPTER **11**

Before studying this chapter you should know or, if necessary, review

1. Competitive priorities, Chapter 2, pages 35–38.
2. Process selection, Chapter 3, pages 64–68.
3. Layout types, Chapter 10, pages 344–349.

LEARNING OBJECTIVES

After studying this chapter, you should be able to

1 Describe the elements of work system design and the objectives of each element.
2 Describe relevant job design issues.
3 Describe methods analysis.
4 Understand the importance of work measurement.
5 Describe how to do a time study.
6 Describe how to do work sampling.
7 Develop standard times.
8 Show how to use work standards.
9 Describe compensation plans.
10 Describe learning curves.

CHAPTER OUTLINE

WHAT'S IN OM FOR ME?

ACC

FIN

MKT

OM

HRM

MIS

Andy Sacks/Stone/Getty Images, Inc.

Have you ever been to a restaurant, a store, or any other place where one person seems to be doing several different jobs? For example, is that person the maitre d', the wine steward, the wait staff, the chef, and the dishwasher? And does that person have to switch jobs at a moment's notice?

Productive employees are employees who know what is expected of them and what to expect of themselves. They know what their role is in the company, and they understand the goals of their job.

Because of the seasonal nature of its business, UPS has spent considerable time designing jobs, making sure to clearly define expectations. This is critical for UPS since it uses more than 95,000 part-time seasonal employees during the period from Thanksgiving to Christmas. UPS part-time employees typically work 4–5 hours daily. The different jobs include driver helpers, package handlers and sorters, and extra delivery drivers. The sheer size of this increase in the workforce demands that each person know his or her role.

Designing a work system that supports a company's objectives is essential to the company's success. Let's look at how companies design their work systems.

DESIGNING A WORK SYSTEM

First, a company determines its objectives, and then it develops an operations strategy to achieve those objectives. Part of the operations strategy is designing a work system, which provides the structure for the productivity of the company. The work system includes job design, work measurement, and worker compensation. The company determines the purpose of each job, what the job consists of, and the cost of the employees to do the job. A job must add value and enable the company to achieve its objectives.

Suppose your company is an organization with an objective to operate a fancy, upscale restaurant. To achieve its objective, the restaurant must define a set of jobs, the tasks each job consists of, and a system for evaluating the employee's performance in the job. The set of jobs at your restaurant would include a chef, a trained kitchen staff, a professional wait staff, a maitre d', a wine steward, and so forth. The chef's tasks would include developing the food motif and menu, for example. The performance measurement would be based on revenue.

Job design ensures that each employee's duties and responsibilities are geared toward achieving the restaurant's mission. Methods analysis eliminates unnecessary tasks and improves the process for completing tasks. Work measurement is a process for evaluating employee performance and comparing alternative processes. Let's begin with job design.

Designing a Job

Job design specifies the work activities of an individual or group in support of an organization's objectives. You design a job by answering questions such as: What is your description of the job? What is the purpose of the job? Where is the job done? Who does the job? What background, training, or skills does an employee need to do the job? For example, if one of your company's objectives is to establish itself as a leader in customer service, jobs must be designed to encourage and reward good customer service practices. In addition, performance measurements for each job must validate the behavior that supports the company's objective. Let's look at three additional factors in job design: technical feasibility, economic feasibility, and behavioral feasibility.

▶ **Job design**
Specifies the contents of the job.

Technical Feasibility The **technical feasibility** of a job is the degree to which an individual or group of individuals is physically and mentally able to do the job. The more demanding the job, the smaller is the applicant pool for that job. Suppose your company requires the candidate for a job to be capable of lifting up to 250 pounds. Few people will qualify for the job. But if the company can reduce the lifting requirement to 50 pounds, many more people will qualify.

▶ **Technical feasibility**
The job must be physically and mentally doable.

Good job design eliminates unreasonable requirements and ensures that any constraining requirements are necessary to do the job. This in turn widens the applicant pool and gives your company a chance to hire the best candidates on the market.

Economic Feasibility The **economic feasibility** of a job is the degree to which the value a job adds and the cost of having the job done create profit for the company. If the job as it is designed costs more than the value it adds, then it is not economically feasible. Suppose your company can reduce a job's lifting requirement from a maximum 250 pounds to a maximum 50 pounds because the company can buy materials in smaller quantities and pack them in lighter boxes. If the materials are more expensive, however, the company has to weigh the higher material costs against the higher labor costs, choose the alternative that makes more sense economically, or even come up with a third alternative—for example, hire two workers to lift the heavy packages.

▶ **Economic feasibility**
Cost of the job should be less than the value it adds.

Behavioral Feasibility The **behavioral feasibility** of a job is the degree to which an employee derives intrinsic satisfaction from doing the job. The challenge is to design a job so the worker feels good about doing the job *and* adds value by doing it. This presents two problems. First, what motivates one worker may not motivate another worker. Second, someone has to do the boring jobs. One solution is to provide an enjoyable work environment. Employees at companies like The AES Corporation, The Men's Wearhouse, SAS, and Southwest Airlines stay with their companies because work is fun. In this case, fun means working in a place where people can use their talents and skills and work with others in an atmosphere of mutual respect.

▶ **Behavioral feasibility**
Degree to which the job is intrinsically satisfying to the employee.

In 2006, SAS was recognized for the ninth straight year as one of the top 100 companies to work for by *Fortune* magazine. Six times, SAS has been ranked in the top 10 companies. This year, SAS and 21 other companies earned membership in *Fortune's* Hall of Fame of the Best Companies to Work For. Each of the inductees has appeared in every list of the 100 Best since the ranking began in 1998.

Courtesy SAS Institute, Inc.

LINKS TO PRACTICE

SAS Institute Inc.
www.sas.com

How does the world's largest privately held software manufacturer earn a spot in the top 10 of *Fortune's* "100 Best Companies to Work for in America"? It does it by creating an infrastructure with little stress, treating employees as adults, and not having a lot of rules. SAS doesn't demand long hours from its employees; instead, it closes its facility at 6:00 PM. Employees are not allowed to work later. SAS wants employees to have time for a life outside of work. Full-time employees at SAS work a 35-hour week and have live piano music in the cafeteria, an on-site gym, a dance studio, childcare facilities, an on-site health clinic, and an indoor lap pool. The atmosphere at SAS is part of its corporate strategy—a strategy that seeks individuals who are not ego-driven and who want to be part of something of value. In 2006, SAS ranked number one in childcare and was listed as one of the companies with the best healthcare and work–life balance. SAS continues to place great importance on providing a supportive workplace environment for its employees.

A final concern in job design is whether or not the job can and should be automated. Let's discuss the pros and cons of machines versus people in job design.

Machines or People?

When a company considers the technical, economic, and behavioral feasibility of job design, a central question is: Should the job or some part of it be automated? Obviously, machines do some things better than people, whereas people do other things better than machines. For example, we use calculators to do arithmetic or when we need high levels of precision. We use a machine when a job might be dangerous. We also use machines to lift or move very heavy objects or very hot objects or to do simple, repetitive tasks. On the other hand, people are vastly superior to machines in a number of activities. Examples are personal interactions with others, creative thinking, judgments involving multiple variables, expressions of compassion or empathy, complex operations that may not follow linear logic, and teaching.

Using machines versus people is both a tangible economic decision in job design and a decision based on intangibles, such as customer acceptance. For example, automated voice messaging systems are the norm in offices today. But do these automated systems create a favorable impression on the customer? Is it worth the extra expense to provide a live receptionist so your customers can talk to a person rather than a machine? When your company makes a decision about machines versus people in job design, support of the company's objectives is the deciding factor.

If a job is designed for people rather than machines, the next question is how specialized an employee should be.

Level of Labor Specialization

▶ **Specialization**
The breadth of the job design.

The higher the level of **specialization**, the narrower is the employee's scope of expertise. The professions—medicine, law, academics—are highly specialized; however, some low-level assembly or service jobs are also specialized.

In the professions, worker satisfaction is one reason for specialization in a particular area of expertise. A doctor who specializes in heart disease, a lawyer who specializes in international law, or a professor who specializes in operations management may do

Specialization from Management's Perspective	
Advantages	**Disadvantages**
Readily available labor	Lack of flexibility
Minimal training needed	Worker dissatisfaction characterized by
Reasonable wage cost	• high absenteeism
High productivity	• high turnover rates
	• high scrap rates
	• grievances filed
Specialization from the Employee's Perspective	
Advantages	**Disadvantages**
Minimal credentials needed	Boredom
Minimal responsibilities	Little growth opportunity
Minimal mental effort needed	Little control over work
Reasonable wages	Little room for initiative
	Little intrinsic satisfaction

TABLE 11-1

The Advantages and Disadvantages of Specialization in Job Design

so because of intrinsic satisfaction in the job. Without question, other factors also influence people to enter into particular professional careers.

On the other hand, an assembly or service worker whose work is highly specialized often has a monotonous job. These individuals may have narrowly focused jobs because their skill levels are limited. Yet specialized assembly and service workers contribute to organizational objectives because they yield high productivity and low unit costs. Consider the assembly worker who inserts and tightens four bolts into each product as it passes by on the assembly line. The work is repetitive, but the worker quickly becomes very proficient. A file clerk who spends eight hours each day filing documents and the data-entry person keying in data eight hours each day also have highly specialized, narrowly focused jobs.

Table 11-1 highlights some of the advantages and disadvantages of using specialization in job design. The table shows that management benefits from specialization because the jobs are narrowly defined and easily learned, so less training is needed. Workers achieve high productivity and wage costs are reasonable. The table also shows that a disadvantage of specialization is worker dissatisfaction, resulting in high turnover and absenteeism, a high number of grievances filed, higher scrap rates, and sabotage.

From the worker's point of view, this type of job design minimizes the education and skills required, requires little mental effort, has minimal job responsibility, and provides reasonably good wages given the skill requirements. The major disadvantages of such job designs are worker boredom, little room for growth or advancement, little control over the work, and minimal self-fulfillment. In an effort to reduce workers' boredom, a number of behavioral approaches have been suggested. Discussion of these approaches follows.

Eliminating Employee Boredom

Companies that choose highly specialized job design have several options for reducing worker boredom, including job enlargement, job enrichment, and job rotation.

Job enlargement is the horizontal expansion of a job. The job designer adds other related tasks to the job so the worker produces a portion of the final product that he or she can recognize. For example, an assembly worker gets to do additional tasks that

▶ **Job enlargement**
A horizontal expansion of the job through increasing the scope of the work assigned.

complete a portion of the final product, which enables the worker to experience pride in the final product. The worker can then point to the final product and take pride in the portion that he or she was responsible for building. By reducing the level of specialization, however, job enlargement may result in some lost productivity compared to what was specified in the original job design.

One example of job enlargement concerns employees proofreading telephone directories. Rather than proofreading randomly assigned pages, a proofreader is responsible for specific letters in the alphabet. The proofreader can identify those portions of the directory that he or she proofread. Job enlargement is used to instill worker pride in the final product and give the employee some task variety.

▶ **Job enrichment**
A vertical expansion of the job through increased worker responsibility.

Job enrichment is the vertical expansion of a job. The job designer adds worker responsibility for work planning and/or inspection. This allows the worker some control over the workload in terms of scheduling—although not in terms of how much work to do—and instills a sense of pride in the worker. For example, workers know they must complete 100 model A's, 50 model B's, and 150 model C's in one week, but the sequence is up to them. They can do all of the C's first, then the B's followed by the A's, and so forth, as long as the work is finished in one week. Or, for example, workers do their own inspection before the part or product is passed to the next workstation. This procedure instills pride in the output and has the worker perform tasks usually done at a higher level in the organization.

▶ **Job rotation**
Workers shift to different jobs to increase understanding of the total process.

Job rotation exposes a worker to other jobs in the work system. Rotation allows workers to see how the output from their previous assignment is used later in the production or service process. Workers see more of the big picture and have a better overall understanding of the work system. In addition, they acquire more skills that may increase their value to the company. Job rotation provides more flexibility for the company, as its workers have upgraded skills.

Team Approaches to Job Design

Another option for job design is using teams rather than individuals for certain assignments. Problem-solving teams, special-purpose teams, and self-directed teams are three different kinds of employee teams.

▶ **Problem-solving teams**
Small groups of employees and supervisors trained in problem-solving techniques who meet to identify, analyze, and propose solutions to workplace problems.

Problem-solving teams are small groups of employees who meet to identify, analyze, and solve operational problems. Employees typically volunteer to participate in problem-solving teams, and team members are trained in problem-solving techniques and data collection. A team may meet once a week, during normal working hours, for one to two hours. After the team has completed its initial training, it concentrates on a particular operational problem. The team analyzes the problem, collects data, develops alternative solutions, and then presents a proposed solution to upper management. Management then decides whether or not to use the proposed solution.

The purpose of problem-solving teams is to use the employees' knowledge of operational procedures. Management cannot know as much about detailed operations as the employees who do the work daily. Problem-solving teams are useful for improving operations and as a way to improve communications between employees and management.

▶ **Special-purpose teams**
Highly focused, short-term teams addressing issues important to management and labor.

Special-purpose teams address issues of major significance to the company. They are often short-term, special task forces with a focused agenda. Members of special-purpose teams typically represent several functional areas for an overall view of the problem. For example, a university might use a special-purpose team to hire a new, high-level administrator. The team has a specific task and a limited time frame to do that task. Since the new administrator will have many constituencies, the team may consist of representatives from each college, the operating staff, the professional/administrative staff, trustees, alumni, and students. Including each constituency in the selection process ensures that their concerns are made known.

Self-directed or self-managed teams are designed to achieve a high level of employee involvement and an integrated team approach. Their purpose is to allow the people most knowledgeable about the process to control the workflow. This approach also allows employees to develop a sense of ownership and pride in their work.

▶ **Self-directed teams**
Integrated teams empowered to control portions of their process.

A good example of self-directed work teams is The Santa Cruz Operation, Inc. At The Santa Cruz Operation, the initial team consisted of twelve people, including five assemblers and a quality control person, for both the day and evening shifts. The team subsequently added two material handlers, a product specialist, and a master scheduler. The team was responsible for building sixty-five computer operating system products on

LINKS TO PRACTICE

The Santa Cruz Operation, Inc.
www.sco.com

a single assembly line. Before the self-managing teams, the company had a problem with product consistency. Each shift did things its own way and blamed the other shift for any problems. The self-directed team approach greatly improved communication between shifts and allowed workers to resolve product-consistency problems. The team reduced person-minutes per unit by 22.4 percent, decreased defects to 1.5 or fewer per 1000 units built, cross-trained its members, and documented the procedures for what needed to be done and how it should be done. Although most workers continue to perform on-site at the company's facilities, many employees now work in alternative workplaces.

The Alternative Workplace

The **alternative workplace** is a combination of nontraditional work practices, settings, and locations that supplements traditional offices. The alternative workplace moves the work to the worker rather than the worker to the work.

▶ **Alternative workplace**
Brings work to the worker rather than the worker to the workplace.

Companies have begun using alternative workplaces for the benefits they afford in terms of cost reduction, productivity, and flexibility. The cost reduction is achieved through eliminating offices people do not need, consolidating others, and thereby reducing overhead expenses. Alternative workplaces can improve productivity because employees tend to devote more time to customers and/or meaningful work activities and less time on unproductive office routines like socializing, making up work to look busy, and attending unnecessary meetings. A survey of alternative workplace employees at IBM revealed that 87 percent believe their personal productivity and job effectiveness had increased significantly. The alternative workplace offers the flexibility some employees need to balance work and family, which helps companies build and keep a valuable workforce.

The alternative workplace comes in several different varieties. It can be as simple as putting some workers on different shifts or travel schedules and letting those workers share desk and office space. Still another approach is the use of satellite offices to break up large, centralized facilities into a network of smaller workplaces that can be located closer to customers. Telecommuting—working electronically from wherever the worker chooses—is another alternative workplace idea and is typically done from home offices. Most companies use a combination of alternative workplaces customized to their individual company needs.

Disadvantages of alternative workplaces include increased logistics associated with workers in several locations as well as a lack of cohesiveness or shared focus among employees.

Courtesy Herman Miller, Inc.

More and more corporations are implementing the practice of alternative workspaces. AT&T, for example, provides flexible workstations so workers can rotate in and out as needed. At Cisco Systems, employees choose an available workstation as they arrive for the workday (a practice known as "hot desking"). Also, Sun Microsystems gives many of its designers the option to work at home. Companies such as KPMG Peat Marwick, Ernst & Young, and Andersen Consulting Accenture practice "hotelling," in which either hotel workspaces are furnished, equipped, and supported with typical office services or corporate workspaces are reserved by an employee via the company "concierge." In both instances, the space can be booked by the hour (also referred to as "motelling"), day, or week. Today, more than 30 million employees work in alternative workspaces.

METHODS ANALYSIS

▶ **Methods analysis**
Process concerned with the detailed process for doing a particular job.

Methods analysis is the study of how a job is done. Whereas job design shows the structure of the job and names the tasks within the structure, methods analysis details the tasks and how to do them.

Methods analysis is used by companies when developing new products or services and for improving the efficiency of methods currently in use. Suppose your restaurant has an accepted procedure for communicating a customer's dinner choices to the kitchen without errors. Methods analysis documents this accepted procedure, including specific notations that identify customer preferences. The result is a standard operating procedure your restaurant can use for training new employees and for evaluating the performance of existing employees.

Methods analysis consists of the following steps:

1. Identify the operation to be analyzed.
2. Gather all relevant information about the operation, including tools, materials, and procedures.
3. Talk with employees who use the operation or have used similar operations. They may have suggestions for improving it.
4. Chart the operation, whether you are analyzing an existing operation or a new operation.
5. Evaluate each step in the existing operation or proposed new operation. Does the step add value? Does it only add cost?
6. Revise the existing or new operation as needed.
7. Put the revised or new operation into effect, then follow up on the changes or new operation. Do your changes to the existing operation improve it? Does your new operation add to the company's overall operations?

Now let's look at an example of methods analysis for an established operation.

METHODS ANALYSIS • 387

Methods Analysis at FEAT Company   EXAMPLE 11.1

Companies typically try to identify operations that are labor intensive; are done often; are dangerous, tedious, or fatiguing; and/or are designated as problem operations. In this example, the FEAT Company, a producer of electronic consumer goods, uses a particular transformer (Figure 11-1) in several of its finished products. A transformer changes the current in the primary circuit to the current needed in the secondary circuit. You have the task of applying methods analysis to one of FEAT's problem operations.

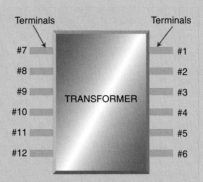

FIGURE 11-1

A 12-terminal transformer

You decide to concentrate your methods analysis on the transformer wiring operation because it has been a source of quality problems in the past. After talking with the current operators, you develop a flowchart of the operation, as shown in Figure 11-2. The flowchart shows that the operator has to solder six individual wires onto six individual terminals of the transformer (Figure 11-2).

FIGURE 11-2

Chart of the wiring activity

PROCESS FLOWCHART Job: Solder wires to transformer	Analyst: A. Maize		Page 1 of 1	
Details of method	Operation	Movement	Inspection	Delay	Storage
Transformer to work location	○		□	D	▽
Wire and solder iron to terminal #1			□	D	▽
Solder wire to terminal #1	●	⇒	□	D	▽
Solder iron to holder	○	⇒	□		▽
Wire and solder iron to terminal #2	○		□	D	▽
Solder wire to terminal #2	●	⇒	□	D	▽
Solder iron to holder	○	⇒	□		▽
Wire and solder iron to terminal #3	○		□	D	▽
Solder wire to terminal #3	●	⇒	□	D	▽
Solder iron to holder	○	⇒	□		▽
Wire and solder iron to terminal #4	○		□	D	▽
Solder wire to terminal #4	●	⇒	□	D	▽
Solder iron to holder	○	⇒	□		▽
Wire and solder iron to terminal #5	○		□	D	▽
Solder wire to terminal #5	●	⇒	□	D	▽
Solder iron to holder	○	⇒	□		▽
Wire and solder iron to terminal #6	○		□	D	▽
Solder wire to terminal #6	●	⇒	□	D	▽
Solder iron to holder	○	⇒	□		▽
Transformer to finished units	○	⇒	□	D	

The operator follows these steps to solder the wires onto the terminal.

1. Picks up the appropriate wire with the left hand and moves the wire to the terminal to be soldered.

2. Simultaneously picks up the solder iron in the right hand and moves it to the terminal to be soldered.

3. Solders the wire to the terminal and replaces the solder iron in its holder.

4. Solders terminal number 1, then solders terminals 2 through 6, going from right to left.

The layout of the operator's workstation is shown in Figure 11-3.

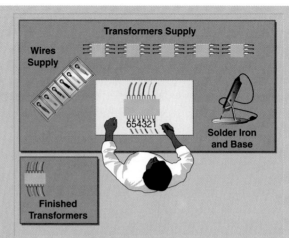

FIGURE 11-3

Wiring the transformer

The FEAT Company is concerned about this operation—significant rework is needed because of poor solder joints and the operation is not efficient. You analyze the operation and realize that attaching the wires from right to left is problematic for a right-handed operator. You also note that when soldering the next terminal, the operator places the soldering iron directly above the recently soldered joint. This slows down the process because the operator now has to be careful not to disturb that joint.

Following your methods analysis, you make this recommendation to the FEAT Company to improve the operation:

Reverse the order in which the wires are soldered to the terminals, beginning at terminal 6 and ending at terminal 1. Now the right-handed operator does not reach directly over the recently soldered joints and can improve both the quality and efficiency of the operation.

The final step in your methods analysis is to follow up to make sure that the new operation resolves the quality problems the FEAT Company was concerned about.

THE WORK ENVIRONMENT

So far we have discussed job design and methods analysis in detail. We also need to understand the effect of working conditions on worker productivity, product quality, and worker safety.

Temperature, relative humidity, ventilation, lighting, and noise level are all factors in work system design. People work well when the temperature is comfortable; typically, the more strenuous the work, the lower the temperature should be. Excess humidity is uncomfortable for most people and can be detrimental to some equipment. Too little humidity results in dry air and may create undesirable static charges. Exchanging or filtering the air can prevent the stale air caused by poor ventilation. Inadequate lighting can lead to production mistakes and/or physical discomfort such as headaches. Detailed work normally needs stronger light. Also, high noise levels can be distracting and can result in errors or accidents as well as impair hearing.

Concern for worker safety brought about the enactment in 1970 of the Occupational Safety and Health Act (OSHA), which created the Occupational Safety and Health Administration. The law was designed to ensure that all workers have healthy and safe working conditions. It mandates specific safety conditions that are inspected randomly by OSHA inspectors. Violations can result in warnings, fines, and/or court-imposed shutdowns. The law requires the company to ensure a safe working environment for its employees. Therefore, worker safety is the primary concern in work system design. Workplace accidents are usually the result of worker carelessness or workplace hazards. Carelessness is defined as unsafe acts, such as failing to use protective equipment, overriding safety controls, disregarding safety procedures, or improperly using tools and equipment. Workplace hazards include conditions such as unprotected equipment, poor lighting, and poor ventilation.

WORK MEASUREMENT

The third component in work system design, **work measurement**, is a way of determining how long it should take to do a job. Work measurement techniques are used to set a standard time for a specific job. The **standard time** is the time it should take a qualified operator, working at a sustainable pace and using the appropriate tools and process, to do the job. The standard time is the sustainable time it takes to do either a whole job or a portion or element of a job. In our restaurant example, the time needed to take the customer's order and communicate that information to the kitchen staff can be calculated as the standard time.

Why should a company set the standard time for a job? Companies use standard times for costing, evaluating, and planning.

▶ **Work measurement**
Determines how long it should take to do a job.

▶ **Standard time**
The length of time it should take a qualified worker using appropriate process and tools to complete a specific job, allowing time for personal fatigue, and unavoidable delays.

Costing

When costing a product, a company includes labor in the total cost estimate. Instead of timing the labor to build single units, companies typically use a standard labor cost. To do this, they multiply the standard labor time by a given hourly labor cost to determine the direct labor content of a product. For example, if a company invests three standard hours of labor in building a product and its labor cost is $22 per hour, then the standard labor content is $66 per unit. This does not mean each unit has exactly three hours of labor spent on it: some units will have slightly more labor content and others will have slightly less. Thus the company estimates that it should take three hours of labor to build that product. For pricing purposes, the company charges for three labor hours of content in each unit.

Standard times allow companies to evaluate new product proposals, the use of new materials and equipment, new processes or techniques for building a product, and individual operator proficiency. The standard time provides a benchmark for companies to use when evaluating other alternatives.

Let's return to the transformer operation in which six wires are soldered to the transformer. FEAT Company might consider buying transformers with individual wires already attached to each of the terminals, as shown in Figure 11-4. The transformer has wires attached to all twelve terminals so the operator has to remove the six extra wires.

EXAMPLE 11.2

An Alternative Material for FEAT Company

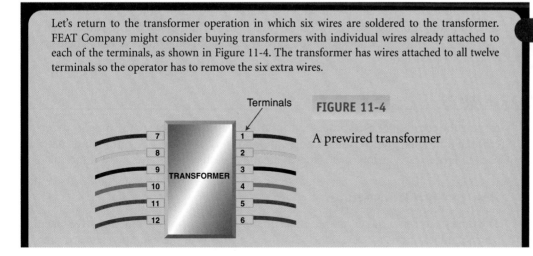

FIGURE 11-4

A prewired transformer

Suppose FEAT evaluates this change in material and process by determining the change in standard time and comparing that with the change in material costs. The result is a trade-off between reduced labor costs versus higher material costs. For example, what should FEAT do if the prewired transformer costs $0.40 more than the unwired transformer, but the standard time is reduced by forty-five seconds per unit and the hourly labor cost is $22?

- **Before You Begin:** For this problem we are comparing the increased cost for the transformer with the decreased labor cost. You need to determine the value of the labor saved on each transformer that is used. You do this by finding the hourly labor rate ($22.00) and multiplying by the forty-five seconds (or 0.0125 hour) saved per unit. Compare this labor savings with the additional cost of $0.40 per transformer.

- **Solution:**
  The value of the labor saved is $0.275 per transformer. The additional material cost is $0.40 per unit. If FEAT changes to the prewired transformer, it will cost an additional $0.125 per transformer ($0.40 − $0.275), the difference between the increased material cost and the reduced labor cost. If FEAT is concerned only with the economics, it should not change to prewired transformers. However, if FEAT can improve quality, this benefit must be factored in to the decision.

  We can do evaluations of this kind for any new idea. Moreover, we can use standard times to find out whether workers are producing at the expected level.

Performance

If the standard time shows that a worker should produce ninety-six units per eight-hour shift, a supervisor can then track the worker's performance and see whether that worker is matching the standard time. If a worker fails to match the standard time, the company should provide training to improve the worker's performance.

Planning

Standard times also help a company to plan. If you know how long it takes to do a job and how often that job is repeated, you can plan your workload from that job.

If an operation takes 0.30 standard hour of labor and you need 1000 of these operations to complete a job, then you need 300 standard hours to complete the job (0.30 hour times 1000 operations). This information allows you to make workload forecasts, plan the labor needed, and schedule work. If you know how long a job should take, you know how long your resources will be busy with that job before you can start the next job. With this knowledge you can schedule jobs and promise viable delivery dates to your customers.

SETTING STANDARD TIMES

Among the commonly used processes for setting standard times are the time study, elemental time data, predetermined time data, and work sampling. The time study dates back to Frederick Winslow Taylor in the late nineteenth century.

How to Do a Time Study

▶ **Time study**
A technique for developing a standard time based on actual observations of the operator.

The **time study** sets a standard time based on timed observations of one employee taken over a number of cycles. A cycle includes all the elements of the job. This standard time is applied to all workers doing the job. Table 11-2 shows the steps in a time study.

Step 1. Choose the job for the time study.

Step 2. Tell the worker whose job you will be studying.

Step 3. Break the job into easily recognizable units.

Step 4. Calculate the number of cycles you must observe.

Step 5. Time each element, record the times, and rate the worker's performance.

Step 6. Compute normal time.

Step 7. Compute the standard time.

TABLE 11-2

Procedure for a Time Study

Now let's look at these steps in detail.

Step 1. As an individual, you set standards for yourself based on the tasks that are typical of your workday. The same is true for your company: you base standard times on the routine, labor-intensive jobs rather than one-of-a-kind jobs. Use this criterion for choosing your time-study job in Step 1.

Step 2. It is also important to inform the employee in advance that you will be making a time study of the job. Be sensitive to how the employee will feel as you time performance.

Step 3. To break a job down into easily recognizable elements, think about making a hand-tossed pizza:

1. Find the right size ball of dough (this depends on the pizza size).
2. Flatten out the dough.
3. Spin and toss the dough until it is the size you want.
4. Put the pizza on the working area.
5. Add sauce.
6. Add cheese.
7. Add additional toppings.
8. Put the pizza in the oven and bake.

Each of these elements has a clear starting and ending point, and you cannot break it down any further.

Step 4. When making a time study, you need to know how many cycles, or how many times, you must observe the worker to ensure the results you want. The number of cycles is a function of the variability of observed times, the desired level of accuracy or precision, and the desired level of confidence for the estimated standard times. We often express the desired accuracy level as a percentage of the mean observed times. For example, we might want an accuracy level so that the standard time is within 10 percent of the true mean of the time it takes to do the job.

The formula for determining the number of observations needed is

$$n \geq \left[\left(\frac{z}{a} \right) \left(\frac{s}{\bar{x}} \right) \right]^2$$

where n = the number of observations of an element that are needed

z = the number of normal standard deviations needed for desired confidence

s = the standard deviation of the sample

a = the desired accuracy or precision

$\bar{x}$ = the mean of the sample observations

Hand-tossing dough

Michael Newman/PhotoEdit

TABLE 11-3	Desired Confidence (%)	z Value
Common z Values	90	1.65
	95	1.96
	95.5	2.00
	96	2.05
	97	2.17
	98	2.33
	99	2.58

To compute the number of observations needed, we begin by making a small number of observations so that we can determine the sample mean and standard deviation. We also need to know the appropriate value of z to use because it determines our confidence level. Common values of z are shown in Table 11-3. Calculating the number of observations needed will be demonstrated by Example 11.3.

EXAMPLE 11.3

Observing Pizza Preparation at Pat's Pizza Place

To determine the number of observations needed, we take some initial observations of the job being studied. In this case, let's observe how long it takes to prepare a large, hand-tossed pepperoni and cheese pizza.

We begin by taking ten observations of each of the seven elements. The elements, the standard deviation of the observed times for each element, and the mean observed time for each element are shown in Table 11-4. Determine the appropriate sample size if the standard time for any work element is to be within 5 percent of the true mean 95 percent of the time.

Table 11-4   Mean Observed Times

Work Unit	Standard Deviation (minutes)	Mean Observed Time (minutes)
1. Get appropriate ball of dough.	0.010	0.12
2. Flatten dough.	0.030	0.25
3. Spin and toss dough.	0.040	0.50
4. Place dough on work counter.	0.005	0.12
5. Pour sauce on formed dough.	0.035	0.30
6. Place grated cheese on top of sauce.	0.025	0.25
7. Place pepperoni on formed dough.	0.030	0.24

• **Before You Begin:** To solve this problem, use the formula shown in Step 4. The formula requires that you know the number of normal standard deviations needed for the desired confidence level (from Table 11-3 you can see that a 95 percent confidence level requires 1.96 normal standard deviations). You also need the desired accuracy or precision (5 percent, or .05 in this case). The sample standard deviation and the mean of the sample observations come from Table 11-4. After calculating the required number of observations for each element, we select the highest number of observations as the appropriate number for our time study.

• Solution:

The calculations are shown here. All noninteger solutions are rounded up.

$$\text{Work element 1: } n \geq \left[\left(\frac{1.96}{0.05}\right)\left(\frac{0.01}{0.12}\right)\right]^2 = 11 \text{ observations}$$

$$\text{Work element 2: } n \geq \left[\left(\frac{1.96}{0.05}\right)\left(\frac{0.03}{0.25}\right)\right]^2 = 23 \text{ observations}$$

$$\text{Work element 3: } n \geq \left[\left(\frac{1.96}{0.05}\right)\left(\frac{0.04}{0.50}\right)\right]^2 = 10 \text{ observations}$$

$$\text{Work element 4: } n \geq \left[\left(\frac{1.96}{0.05}\right)\left(\frac{0.005}{0.12}\right)\right]^2 = 3 \text{ observations}$$

$$\text{Work element 5: } n \geq \left[\left(\frac{1.96}{0.05}\right)\left(\frac{0.035}{0.30}\right)\right]^2 = 21 \text{ observations}$$

$$\text{Work element 6: } n \geq \left[\left(\frac{1.96}{0.05}\right)\left(\frac{0.025}{0.25}\right)\right]^2 = 16 \text{ observations}$$

$$\text{Work element 7: } n \geq \left[\left(\frac{1.96}{0.05}\right)\left(\frac{0.03}{0.24}\right)\right]^2 = 25 \text{ observations}$$

Work element 7 requires the most observations (25) to ensure the accuracy and confidence needed.

Step 5. From the calculations completed in Example 11.3, you know that 15 additional cycles must be observed (25 needed less 10 previously completed). Table 11.5 shows the revised **mean observed times**.

▶ **Mean observed time**
The average of the observation times for each of the work elements.

Table 11-5 Revised Mean Observed Times

Work Element	Mean Observed Time (minutes)
1	0.15
2	0.25
3	0.60
4	0.15
5	0.30
6	0.28
7	0.28

From the revised mean observed times for each work element, we can determine the normal time for the elements. The normal time is different from the observed times because we multiply it by a performance rating factor and the frequency of occurrence.

Performance Rating Factor This section deals with setting a normalized standard time based on observed times. The observed work pace may be average, above average, or below average. As the time study analyst, you must make a judgment about the work pace of the observed worker in terms of how far from the average it is. This is a factor of 1.0 called the **performance rating factor**. If a factor of 1.0 represents an average work pace, any performance rating below 1.0 is a below-average work pace. A performance rating of above 1.0 is an above-average work pace. Performance rating is an attempt to counterbalance any unusual patterns noted in the worker's performance. For any element in which the worker performs below average, the worker may need additional training to improve efficiency.

▶ **Performance rating factor**
A subjective estimate of a worker's pace relative to a normal work pace.

It is not uncommon for workers to work faster than normal when they are observed or, in some cases, to work more slowly than normal when they are observed. The performance rating is used to develop a standard that is fair to the worker and to the company.

Frequency of Occurrence One other factor to consider when calculating the time standard is the **frequency of occurrence** (*F*) for each work element. We expect most elements to be done every cycle, so they would have a frequency of occurrence equal to 1. However, some elements are not done each cycle, so we adjust the frequency accordingly. If an element is done every other cycle, it would have a frequency equal to 0.5, or, on average, half of it is done each cycle. If an element is done once every 5 cycles, *F* = 0.2. We calculate the frequency of occurrence by dividing 1 by the number of cycles between occurrences (1 divided by 10 cycles between occurrences means that *F* = 0.1).

► **Frequency of occurence**
How often the work element must be done each cycle.

Step 6.   We compute the **normal time** for each work element by multiplying the mean observed time by the performance rating factor by the frequency of occurrence [*NT* = (*OT*)(*PRF*)(*F*)]. The normal time calculations are shown in Table 11-6. Remember that the performance rating factor scores and the frequency of occurrence must be known for you to calculate the normal time. The normal time for preparing a large cheese and pepperoni pizza is 1.966 minutes. This normal time reflects how long it may take to produce a single large cheese and pepperoni pizza. However, it does not allow for personal time, fatigue, or unavoidable delays (*PFD*) during the typical workday. Therefore, we adjust the normal time with an **allowance factor**.

► **Normal time**
The mean observed time multiplied by the performance rating factor by the frequency of occurrence.

Allowance Factor Personal time, fatigue, and unavoidable delays affect how much an employee can produce during the day. There are two methods used to convert the job's normal time into the job's standard time. With the first method, the *PFD* allowance is based on individual jobs the worker does throughout the day. This is typically used when workers perform several different types of jobs, with some of the jobs more fatiguing than others and other jobs having longer unavoidable delays. In this case, the amount of output expected must take into account the actual jobs performed by the worker. The PFD allowance factor is computed as

► **Allowance factor**
The amount of time the analyst allows for personal time, fatigue, and unavoidable delays.

$$AF_{Job} = 1 + PFD$$

where *PFD* = percentage allowance adjustment based on the individual job. The other method is used when all of the different jobs an employee does are similar, having the same allowance factor. We compute this allowance factor as

$$AF_{\text{Time worked}} = \frac{1}{1 - PFD}$$

TABLE 11-6

Calculated Normal Times

Work Element	Mean Observed Time (minutes)	Performance Rating Factor	Frequency	Normal Time (minutes)
1	0.15	0.90	1	0.135
2	0.25	1.00	1	0.250
3	0.60	0.85	1	0.510
4	0.15	1.10	1	0.165
5	0.30	1.20	1	0.360
6	0.28	1.00	1	0.280
7	0.28	0.95	1	0.266
			Total	**1.966**

Let's look at a numerical comparison of the two methods for setting the allowance factor. If the allowance factors of $PFD = 0.15$, we compute allowance based on the job as

$$AF_{\text{Job}} = 1 + 0.15 = 1.15, \text{ or } 115\%$$

When computing the allowance based on time worked, the result is

$$AF_{\text{Time worked}} = \frac{1}{1 - 0.15} = 1.176, \text{ or } 117.6\%$$

Step 7. Now that we know how to calculate the allowance factor, let's continue with our pizza-making example and determine a standard time. The standard time equals the normal time multiplied by the allowance factor.

To determine the standard time, we multiply the normal time by the allowance factor. For the large, hand-tossed cheese and pepperoni pizza, we use an allowance factor of 15 percent based on time worked because all the hand-tossed pizza preparations should have a similar allowance.

EXAMPLE 11.4

Calculating Standard Time for a Hand-Tossed Cheese and Pepperoni Pizza

- **Before You Begin:** To compute the standard time for each element, you need to know the normal time (shown in Table 11-6) and the allowance factor (15 percent based on time worked). Multiply the normal time for the element by the allowance factor.

- **Solution:**
We calculate the standard time for each work element as follows.

$$ST = (NT)(AF)$$

where ST = standard time
NT = normal time
AF = allowance factor

Solving for work element 1 in our example, we have

$$ST_{\text{Element 1}} = (0.135)\left(\frac{1}{1 - 0.15}\right) = 0.159 \text{ minute}$$

The standard times for each element using a 15 percent allowance based on work time are shown in Table 11-7.

Table 11-7   Standard Times for Making Large Cheese and Pepperoni Pizza

Work Element	Normal Time (minutes)	Standard Time (minutes)
1. Get appropriate ball of dough.	0.135	0.159
2. Flatten dough.	0.250	0.294
3. Spin and toss dough.	0.510	0.600
4. Place dough on work counter.	0.165	0.194
5. Pour sauce on formed dough.	0.360	0.424
6. Place grated cheese on top of sauce.	0.280	0.329
7. Place pepperoni on top of cheese.	0.266	0.313
Total	1.966	2.313

The standard time for preparing a large, hand-tossed cheese and pepperoni pizza is 2.313 minutes. This means that during an eight-hour day, our worker should be able to prepare 207 (480 minutes per eight-hour shift, divided by the standard time of 2.313 minutes) large, hand-tossed cheese and pepperoni pizzas.

Before You Go On

Before you go on, let's make sure you understand how to do a time study. Remember, the first step is identifying the job you will study. Break the job into small, easily recognizable work elements, which allows you to analyze the different elements, look for ways to improve the existing operation, and identify areas where workers need additional training.

To determine the number of observations needed, you must consider the variability of observed times, the desired level of accuracy, and the desired level of confidence for the estimated standard time. Take some observations so you can determine the variability of the observed times. The degree of accuracy and level of confidence factors are managerial decisions.

After determining the number of observations needed, perform any necessary additional observations. Using the observed times, calculate the mean observed time for each work element. Calculate the normal time by multiplying the mean observed time by the performance rating factor and the frequency of occurrence for each work element. Adjust the normal time by multiplying it by the appropriate allowance factor.

Elemental Time Data

▶ **Elemental time data**
Establishes standards based on previously completed time studies, stored in an organization's database.

After your company performs and validates time studies, it stores those accepted time studies in an **elemental time database** for possible future use. Many jobs consist of the same work elements. For example, in many jobs the operator has to reach for materials, position an item, or insert and tighten something. Instead of recalculating the time it should take to do a particular work element, the time study analyst checks the database for a valid time study. If the company has already done a time study for that work element, the analyst uses it in the standard time for the job. When a time-study analyst uses standard elemental times, the procedure is as follows:

1. Identify the standard elements of the job.
2. Check the database for time studies done on these elements.
3. If no valid studies exist for this or a similar work element, do a time study for the new work element.
4. Adjust the database times if needed. Note that you can adjust database times if the work element is slightly different. Suppose the database has time studies on reaching 6 inches for a tool and reaching 12 inches for a tool, but for the job you are studying, the operator reaches 9 inches for the tool. Instead of developing a new time study, you can interpolate between the two values and derive a reasonable time for reaching 9 inches.
5. Add the element times to determine the normal time, then multiply by the allowance factor to determine the standard time.

The advantage of using standard elemental times is that you need fewer time studies. The results of each time study go into the database and are available for setting future standard times. Also, using standard elemental times eliminates the workplace disruptions caused by making time studies. The disadvantage is that using standard elements may discourage new process development and improvements.

Predetermined Time Data

Just as elemental time databases are useful for individual companies, predetermined time data are useful for the many companies that share similar work elements. **Predetermined time data** is a large database of valid work element times. One commonly used system is methods-time measurement (MTM), which was developed in the 1940s. The tables used in MTM deal with basic elemental motions and associated times. An example of an MTM table is shown in Table 11-8.

Let's take a closer look at Table 11-8. The first column shows how far the operator must move the object in inches. Columns A through E explain the activity. Column A applies when the operator has to reach for an object in a fixed location or an object in the operator's other hand. Column B applies when the operator has to reach for a single object in a location that may vary slightly from cycle to cycle. Columns C and D apply when the operator has to reach for an object jumbled with other objects in a group (search and select), when the operator has to reach for a very small object, or when the operator needs an accurate grasp. Column E applies when the operator has to reach for an indefinite location to position the hand for the next motion. The last two columns on the right-hand side (labeled A and B) represent the time measurement units (TMUs) if the hand is already in motion.

▶ **Predetermined time data**
Published database of elemental time data used for establishing standard times.

Distance Moved (inches)	Time (TMUs)				Hand in Motion		Cases and Descriptions	
	A	B	C or D	E	A	B		
3/4 or less	2.0	2.0	2.0	2.0	1.6	1.6	A	Reach to object in fixed location or to object in other hand or on which other hand rests
1	2.5	2.5	3.6	2.4	2.3	2.3		
2	4.0	4.0	5.9	3.8	3.5	2.7		
3	5.3	5.3	7.3	5.3	4.5	3.6		
4	6.1	6.4	8.4	6.8	4.9	4.3	B	Reach to single object in location, which may vary slightly from cycle to cycle
5	6.5	7.8	9.4	7.4	5.3	5.0		
6	7.0	8.6	10.1	8.0	5.7	5.7		
7	7.4	9.3	10.8	8.7	6.1	6.5		
8	7.9	10.1	11.5	9.3	6.5	7.2	C	Reach to object jumbled with other objects in a group so that search and select occur
9	8.3	10.8	12.2	9.9	6.9	7.9		
10	8.7	11.5	12.9	10.5	7.3	8.6		
12	9.6	12.9	14.2	11.8	8.1	10.1		
14	10.5	14.4	15.6	13.0	8.9	11.5	D	Reach to a very small object or where accurate grasp is required
16	11.4	15.8	17.0	14.2	9.7	12.9		
18	12.3	17.2	18.4	15.5	10.5	14.4		
20	13.1	18.6	19.8	16.7	11.3	15.8		
22	14.0	20.1	21.2	18.0	12.1	17.3	E	Reach to indefinite location to get hand in position for body balance or next motion or out of way
24	14.9	21.5	22.5	19.2	12.9	18.8		
26	15.8	22.9	23.9	20.4	13.7	20.2		
28	16.7	24.4	25.3	21.7	14.5	21.7		
30	17.5	25.8	26.7	22.9	15.3	23.2		

TABLE 11-8

MTM Reach Table
Source: Copyright by the MTM Association for Standards and Research. Reprinted with permission from the MTM Association, 1111 East Touhy Ave., Des Plaines, IL 60018.

When using predetermined time data, you split the job into basic elements (reach, grasp, move, engage, insert, turn, disengage), measure the distances involved (how far must the operator reach?), and rate the difficulty of the item (does the operator grasp a single piece of wire or one of many wires?). For each job, you find the time for the individual elements in the appropriate data table and sum the times to get the normal time for the job. You adjust the normal time by the *PFD* allowance factor to determine the standard time. Element times are typically in time measurement units (TMUs): there are 100,000 TMUs in one hour; one TMU equals 0.0006 minute.

To use predetermined time data, you must be skilled in the method of calculating a standard time and knowledgeable about the job being studied. You must understand how the job is done, the appropriate workplace layout, and the level of difficulty of different work elements. The advantages of using predetermined time data are that you do not have to rate individual operator performance, you do not disrupt the workplace to determine the standard time, and you can calculate standard times before the job even begins. The disadvantages are the skill level needed and the variability among analysts in assessing the level of difficulty of different work elements.

Work Sampling

▶ **Work sampling**
A technique for estimating the proportion of time a worker spends on a particular activity.

Work sampling is a method used for estimating the proportion of time that an employee or machine spends on different work activities. Work sampling does not provide a standard time for an activity, but instead provides an estimate of what portion of the day a worker uses for that activity. For example, a secretary may spend the day managing files, generating letters, taking phone calls, greeting visitors, and maintaining an appointment schedule. Work sampling does not specify how long it should take the secretary to generate a particular letter, but does say what proportion of the day is typically spent on generating letters. For a machine, the company may use work sampling to determine what proportion of the day the machine is used for rush jobs or is idle.

You do not time activities for work sampling. Instead, you make random observations and note the kind of activity. For example, you walk into the secretary's office and see that the secretary is composing, editing, and printing letters. You record your observations and use them to estimate the proportion of time the employee spends on different activities. Work sampling consists of the following procedures:

1. Identify the worker or machine to be sampled.

2. Define the activities to be observed.

3. Estimate the sample size based on the desired level of accuracy and confidence.

4. Develop the random observation schedule. Make your observations over a time period that is representative of normal work conditions.

5. Make your observations and record the data. Check to see whether the estimated sample size remains valid.

6. Estimate the proportion of time spent on the given activity.

In the following example, we use work sampling to estimate the proportion of time a secretary spends scheduling appointments. You can use work sampling to estimate the proportion of delays a worker experiences and also as input when calculating the *PFD* (personal, fatigue, and delay) allowance factor. For example, you can observe whether a worker is working or experiencing delays. After you make enough observations, you can estimate delay time and use it as part of the *PFD* allowance factor.

We use work sampling to estimate the proportion of time a secretary spends doing a given activity during a normal office day. The secretary's normal activities are managing files, generating letters, taking phone calls, greeting visitors, maintaining an appointment schedule, and being idle. We want to know how much of the secretary's time is used for scheduling appointments.

• **Before You Begin:** To use work sampling to estimate the proportion of time spent on a particular activity like scheduling appointments, you begin with an estimate of the time spent on the activity. When you have no initial estimate of the proportion, you do a preliminary sample size calculation setting the proportion equal to .50. You then take some initial observations, enough to represent a normal distribution (30) and determine the appropriate proportion to use in calculating the sample size actually needed.

• **Solution:**

Determine how many observations to make. Work sampling is designed to produce a value, $\hat{p}$, which estimates the true proportion, p, that a particular activity normally occurs, within some allowable error, e. To estimate the number of observations needed for a given level of error, we use the following formula.

$$n \geq \left(\frac{z}{e}\right)^2 \hat{p}(1 - \hat{p})$$

where n = the number of observations that are needed
  z = the number of normal standard deviations needed for desired confidence
  e = the allowable error level (given as a percentage)

Let's assume that we want to estimate with 97 percent confidence ($z = 2.17$), the proportion of time the secretary spends on scheduling appointments. We want the resulting estimate to be within 5 percent of the true value. To solve the equation, we need a sample estimate. When we do not know the sample estimate of $\hat{p}$, we calculate a preliminary estimate of the sample size by setting $\hat{p} = .50$. Since we do not have an estimate for the sample proportion, we compute the preliminary sample size for our work sampling example as follows:

$$n \geq \left(\frac{2.17}{0.05}\right)^2 .5(1 - .5) = 470.89 \text{ observations}$$

If we use a preliminary sample size, we verify that the sample size is correct after we make initial observations and compute the proportion sample. For example, we observed the secretary thirty times and he was scheduling appointments during six of those observations. The proportion sample is .2 (6 times arranging meetings/30 observations). The new estimate of the sample size is

$$n \geq \left(\frac{2.17}{0.05}\right)^2 .2(1 - .2) = 301.37 \text{ observations}$$

Whenever the value of n is not a whole number, we round up to the next whole number. In our example, we may need to check our sample size once more after completing more observations just to be sure that we are using the right sample size. After completing the 302 observations, we see that the secretary was scheduling appointments on 60 separate occasions, or 19.9 percent (60/302) of the time. We examine the other activities to estimate the proportion of time the secretary spends on each. The company can use these estimates to describe the job to prospective employees or in performance reviews for the current secretary.

LINKS TO PRACTICE

Pace Productivity
www.paceproductivity.com

Pace Productivity offers the TimeCorder for conducting work-sampling time studies. The device, developed in 1989 by Mark Ellwood, was completely redesigned and reintroduced in 2004. It allows employees to easily track time by pushing buttons associated with precoded activities, a system they can learn in a few seconds. The employee pushes a coded button and time begins recording on that activity, similar to a stopwatch. When a new button is pushed, time stops for the previous activity and starts for the new activity. A typical study takes six to eight weeks. The company identifies the objectives of the study, determines the activities for each job, and selects employees to participate. Participants use the TimeCorder for two weeks, the devices are returned to Pace Productivity, and the data are analyzed and a report provided to the company. The analysis focuses on opportunities for the company to improve productivity.

COMPENSATION

Worker compensation is the third part of work system design. Companies need to develop compensation systems that reinforce the behaviors needed to meet the company's objectives.

Compensation systems are typically based either on time spent working or on output generated. Time-based systems compensate the employee according to the number of hours worked during the pay period. Compensation is not linked to employee performance but to employee presence at the workplace. Output-based or incentive systems link employee pay to performance. Employees are paid based on their output and not on the number of hours they work.

Time-Based Systems

▶ **Time-based compensation systems**
Pay based on the number of hours worked.

Time-based compensation systems are normally used when measuring output per employee is not applicable—say, for managers, administrative support staff, and some direct laborers. Consider an employee working in your company's research and development group. This employee is doing creative work, which is not easily measured in terms of output. The advantage of the time-based system is its simplicity. For the company, wages are easily calculated. For the employees, the pay is steady and they know what they will get in their regular paycheck.

Output-Based Systems

▶ **Output-based (incentive) systems**
Pay based on the number of units completed.

Output-based (incentive) systems, or piece-rate systems, or commission systems can be linked to Frederick Taylor's theory that man is economically motivated. These systems reward workers for their output. The more the worker produces, the more the worker earns. The assumption is that some workers are motivated by money and produce more when pay is linked to performance.

These incentive systems can be designed to compensate either the individual or an entire group of employees. Individual incentive plans typically provide a base salary for the employee, plus a bonus for output achieved above the standard. For example, an employee has a base salary of $250 per week regardless of how much is produced. The standard for the employee is to produce fifty units per week. The employee earns $250 per week until the employee's output exceeds the standard fifty units per week. For every unit above fifty, the employee earns an additional $7. If the employee produces fifty-five units during the week, he or she earns $285 for that pay period—$250 base, plus a bonus of $35 (five extra units at $7 each). An employee producing sixty units per week would earn $320.

Successful individual incentive plans are linked to quality as well as to quantity. Encouraging a worker to produce low-quality units faster does not make good business sense. The incentive plan must be clear on how output is counted.

Group Incentive Plans

Group incentive plans are designed to reward employees when the company achieves certain performance objectives. Two methods are profit sharing and gain sharing. Profit sharing rewards employees when certain profitability levels are achieved by the company.

Profit Sharing One variation of profit sharing places half the profits in excess of the minimum return on investment into a bonus pool for employees. Individual bonuses can then be based on an employee's base pay, on the percentage of time during the past year the employee worked for the company, or on similar arrangements. For example, a company may give a bonus equal to 15 percent of an employee's base pay. If employee Heather Jones has a base salary of $34,000, her bonus would be $5100 ($34,000 times 0.15). This may seem like a substantial bonus, but if the company fails to meet its profitability levels, Heather's bonus is zero.

Gain Sharing Gain sharing emphasizes the costs of output rather than profit levels. With this plan, employees share the benefits of quality and productivity improvements made during the year. The pool of money for the bonuses comes from the cost items under the control of employees. The individual bonuses should represent an appropriate share of the gains.

A survey of the pay practices of *Fortune* 1000 firms between 1987 and 1993 reported that the percentage of companies using individual incentive plans for at least 20 percent of their employees increased from 38 percent to 50 percent. The same survey reported that the proportion of companies using profit sharing decreased from 45 percent to 43 percent. At the same time, companies reduced the proportion of retail salespeople paid solely on straight salary from 21 percent to 7 percent.

Incentive Plan Trends

Despite a trend toward using individual incentive systems, there are a number of disadvantages. Such systems have been shown to undermine teamwork and give employees a short-term focus. A study of twenty Social Security Administration offices showed that an individual merit pay system had no effect on worker performance. This finding tells us that individual incentive plans need significantly more data collection by management than time-based systems.

Some evidence suggests that group incentive systems suffer from the "free-rider" problem. The free-rider is the person who does not do his or her fair share but is still rewarded by the work of the group. Still, the extent of free-riding is modest, most likely because of group pressure. Overall, companies using group incentive systems tend to outperform companies that do not use such systems.

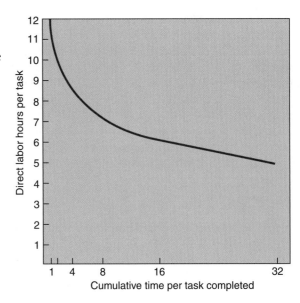

FIGURE 11-5

Learning curve

LEARNING CURVES

An important factor in calculating labor times is the learning effect. We all can recall a new task or job that took a long time to finish the first time we tried. However, each subsequent time we did the task, it took less time. This is the basis of learning curve theory. People learn from doing a task and get quicker each time they repeat that task. A learning curve is shown in Figure 11-5.

The major attributes of a learning curve are that it takes less time to complete the task each additional time it is done by the same employee, and the time savings decrease with each additional time that task is done by that employee. When the number of times the task is completed doubles, the decrease in time per task affects the rate of the learning curve. For example, if a learning curve has an 85 percent learning rate, the second time the task is done will take 85 percent of the time it took the first time the task was done. The fourth time the task is done will take 85 percent of the time it took the second time. The eighth time will take 85 percent of the time it took the fourth time, and so on. The formula for calculating the time the task should take is

$$T \times L^n = \text{time required for } n\text{th time the task is done}$$

where T = time needed to complete task the first time
L = learning curve rate
n = number of times the task is doubled

If the first time the task was done, the employee took twelve labor hours, and the learning rate is 85 percent, calculate how long the sixteenth time that task is done should take.

$$\text{Hours needed for 16th task} = 12 \times (.85)^4 = 6.26 \text{ hours}$$

The sixteenth time the task is done will be the fourth doubling of output—the second time, the fourth time, the eighth time, and finally the sixteenth time.

Understanding learning curves is important. The amount of labor needed to finish the same task or build the same product a number of times can be calculated, which allows a company to better estimate the labor cost. The company can also better schedule its workload since it knows how much labor is needed to complete the task a specific number of times. Calculating the learning rate also is a means for evaluating

An early use of the learning curve

"THERE IS A FAIRLY STEEP LEARNING CURVE. BUT ONCE YOU GET THE HANG OF IT YOU'LL WONDER HOW YOU EVER GOT ALONG WITHOUT BURNING EVERYTHING IN YOUR PATH."

©John Caldwell

productivity. The company can compare its learning rate with that of its competitors. The rate of learning is affected when there are changes in designs, personnel, or procedures. Changes mean that an employee must learn something new, which slows down the improvement rate.

An alternative method of calculating the time required to produce a specific unit is to use a table of learning curve coefficients, as shown in Table 11-9. This table allows you to calculate the time it should take to build the n th unit as well as to calculate the total production time required to build the entire production run when the nth unit is the last one completed.

EXAMPLE 11.6

Using the Table of Learning Curve Coefficients

You have been asked to develop a time estimate for an order of twenty-four conveyor bucket systems. Your best estimate is that the first system will take 120 hours of labor, and an 85 percent learning curve is expected.

(a) How many labor-hours should the twelfth conveyor bucket system require?
(b) How many labor-hours will the twenty-fourth conveyor bucket system require?
(c) How many total labor-hours will be needed to build all twenty-four systems?

• **Solution:**
(a) To determine how many hours the twelfth system requires, we use Table 11-9, the Learning Curve Coefficients table. Looking in the row for the twelfth unit and the column for an 85 percent learning curve, we find the coefficient is 0.558. We multiply the number of labor hours for the first unit by the coefficient: 120 hours × 0.558 = 66.96 hours.
(b) The coefficient for the twenty-fourth unit is 0.475, so the twenty-fourth unit should require 57 hours, or 120 hours × 0.475.
(c) The total time required to produce the twenty-four systems is calculated by finding the coefficient for total time in the row for the twenty-fourth unit and the column titled total time for the 85 percent learning curve. In this case, the coefficient is 14.331. Now multiply the hours for the first unit times the coefficient. Total labor required to build the twenty-four systems is 1719.72 hours, or 120 hours × 14.331.

TABLE 11-9

Learning Curve Coefficients

Unit Number	70% Unit Time	70% Total Time	75% Unit Time	75% Total Time	80% Unit Time	80% Total Time	85% Unit Time	85% Total Time	90% Unit Time	90% Total Time
1	1.000	1.000	1.000	1.000	1.000	1.000	1.000	1.000	1.000	1.000
2	.700	1.700	.750	1.750	.800	1.800	.850	1.850	.900	1.900
3	.568	2.268	.634	2.384	.702	2.502	.773	2.623	.846	2.746
4	.490	2.758	.562	2.946	.640	3.142	.723	3.345	.810	3.556
5	.437	3.195	.513	3.459	.596	3.738	.686	4.031	.783	4.339
6	.398	3.593	.475	3.934	.562	4.299	.657	4.688	.762	5.101
7	.367	3.960	.446	4.380	.534	4.834	.634	5.322	.744	5.845
8	.343	4.303	.422	4.802	.512	5.346	.614	5.936	.729	6.574
9	.323	4.626	.402	5.204	.493	5.839	.597	6.533	.716	7.290
10	.306	4.932	.385	5.589	.477	6.315	.583	7.116	.705	7.994
11	.291	5.223	.370	5.958	.462	6.777	.570	7.686	.695	8.689
12	.278	5.501	.357	6.315	.449	7.227	.558	8.244	.685	9.374
13	.267	5.769	.345	6.660	.438	7.665	.548	8.792	.677	10.052
14	.257	6.026	.334	6.994	.428	8.092	.539	9.331	.670	10.721
15	.248	6.274	.325	7.319	.418	8.511	.530	9.861	.663	11.384
16	.240	6.514	.316	7.635	.410	8.920	.522	10.383	.656	12.040
17	.233	6.747	.309	7.944	.402	9.322	.515	10.898	.650	12.690
18	.226	6.973	.301	8.245	.394	9.716	.508	11.405	.644	13.334
19	.220	7.192	.295	8.540	.388	10.104	.501	11.907	.639	13.974
20	.214	7.407	.288	8.828	.381	10.485	.495	12.402	.634	14.608
21	.209	7.615	.283	9.111	.375	10.860	.490	12.892	.630	15.237
22	.204	7.819	.277	9.388	.370	11.230	.484	13.376	.625	15.862
23	.199	8.018	.272	9.660	.364	11.594	.479	13.856	.621	16.483
24	.195	8.213	.267	9.928	.359	11.954	.475	14.331	.617	17.100
25	.191	8.404	.263	10.191	.355	12.309	.470	14.801	.613	17.713

WORK SYSTEM DESIGN WITHIN OM: HOW IT ALL FITS TOGETHER

Work system design includes job design, methods analysis, and work measurement. Manufacturing or industrial engineers often do these activities. Job design determines exactly how the product or service will be done and is linked directly to product and process design. Based on the type of product (standard or custom) and its proposed process (mass-producing or producing one at a time), a company determines the skills set needed by its employees as well as the necessary equipment.

Method analysis provides a means for evaluating different processes and materials, thus allowing a company to focus on continuous improvement. This ties in directly with a company's total quality management (TQM) focus.

Work measurement techniques allow a company to develop standards to use as a basis for evaluating the cost and effectiveness of different methods and materials for building a product or providing a service. These time standards provide a time estimate to use as a basis for establishing detailed work schedules and for determining long-term staffing levels. These time estimates can be used as a basis for making delivery or completion-time promises to customers. Standard times are used to develop lead-time estimates, which are inputs for the MRP (material requirement planning) system as well as the MPS (master production schedule) process.

Work system design provides the means for setting standards against which to compare new methods, new materials, and new designs, assures that employees know how to do their job, and provides the information needed by the company to calculate its costs.

WORK SYSTEM DESIGN ACROSS THE ORGANIZATION

Work system design affects functional areas throughout a company. Let's look at why individual functional areas are concerned with work system design.

Accounting calculates the cost of products manufactured or services provided. Labor can be a significant portion of the cost of goods sold, especially in the service industries. Accounting measures variances between planned product cost and actual product cost. Accounting also typically measures operational efficiency, which is based on work standards. Work system design is an important resource for accounting activities.

Marketing is concerned with work system design because it is the basis for determining lead time. Accurate work projections enable marketing to make viable promise dates to customers.

Information systems uses estimates of job duration and resources in the software for scheduling and tracking operations.

Purchasing handles requests for materials based on a schedule projected from the work system design. Accurate scheduling enables cost-effective materials and labor purchasing decisions. Standard time provides a benchmark for evaluation of new materials and processes.

Manufacturing responds to effective job design, process analysis, and work measurement with high levels of performance and on-time delivery of finished goods.

Human resources uses work sampling to establish and validate hiring criteria.

You can see that work system design involves all aspects of an organization and has an impact on how well the organization performs. In many manufacturing companies, job design and process analysis are both done by a manufacturing or industrial engineer. The engineer works with product blueprints and the workforce to develop job instructions. From these detailed job instructions, the company can develop time standards. Work measurement information is often provided by workers as they complete a job. Accounting may use this information to report the efficiency of manufacturing operations. In a service organization, an operations manager or operations analyst may do the job design and process analysis.

Work system design helps companies understand the total costs of making a product or providing a service. It allows companies to evaluate their product or service line and view the bottom line for each product or service.

THE SUPPLY CHAIN LINK

Work system design includes job design, methods analysis, work measurement, and compensation. Each of these is critical to successful supply chain management. Job design requires clearly specifying what has to be done, who has to do it, how it should be done, and how it should be measured. Every member of the supply chain needs to have their role similarly defined. Methods analysis is used to improve processes and eliminate non-value-adding activities. Such analysis can reduce duplicate efforts among supply chain members. Work measurement is used to develop standards for activities performed by members of the supply chain. Standards for picking and packing materials at warehouses or standards for unloading and loading at crossdocks are critical for coordinating material flow within the supply chain. Using standards to measure job performance is critical to improving supply chain success.

Chapter Highlights

1 Work system design involves job design, methods or process analysis, and work measurement. Job design specifies the work activities of an individual or group in support of organizational objectives.

2 Relevant job design issues include design feasibility, the choice of human or machine, the use of teams, and the location where the work is to be done. Technical feasibility is the degree to which an individual or group of individuals is physically and mentally able to do the job. Economic feasibility is the degree to which the value a job adds and the cost of having the job done are profitable for the company. Behavioral feasibility is the degree to which an employee derives intrinsic satisfaction from doing the job. Another job design issue concerns whether the job should be done by people or by machines. If a person does the job, you need to decide on the level of specialization. If jobs are extremely specialized, you will probably need a way to reduce boredom. Rather than individual job design, an organization can use team approaches. These include problem-solving teams, special-purpose teams, and self-directed teams. An additional consideration is the location where the work is done. Many employees may work in alternative workplaces in the future.

3 Methods or process analysis is concerned with how the employee does the job. Methods analysis can also be used to improve the efficiency of an operation.

4 Work measurement is used to determine standard times. A standard time is how long it should take a qualified operator, using the appropriate process, material, and equipment, and working at a sustainable pace, to do a particular job. Standard times are used for product costing, process and material evaluation, and for planning workloads and staffing. Standard times are usually based on time studies. Work sampling is used to estimate the proportion of time that should be spent on an activity.

5 To do a time study, you identify the job and break the job into work elements. Then you determine the number of observations needed and perform the observations.

6 Work sampling involves random observations of a worker. Each time you observe the worker, you note what activity the worker is doing. After numerous observations, you can project the expected proportion of time the worker should spend on different activities.

7 Standard times are developed with either time studies, elemental time data, or predetermined time data. You learned how to develop standard times using time studies. After conducting the time study, you compute the mean observed time for each work element. You compute the normal time for the work element by multiplying the mean observed time by the performance rating factor. You find the standard time for each work element by multiplying the normal time by the allowance factor.

8 Standards are used to compare alternative processes, evaluate new materials or components, and evaluate individual worker performance. Standards also allow you to determine when a job should be completed or how many units can be done in a period of time.

9 Worker compensation systems are either time-based or output-based. Time-based systems pay the employee for the number of hours worked. Output-based systems pay the employee for the number of units completed. Compensation schemes can be based on either individual or group performance.

10 Learning curves show the rate of learning that occurs when an employee repeats the same task. Using learning curves, you can estimate how long a particular task will take. It allows the company to schedule better and calculate costs more accurately.

Key Terms

job design 381
technical feasibility 381
economic feasibility 381
behavioral feasibility 381
specialization 382
job enlargement 383

Formula Review

1. Calculating the number of observations for an element in a time study

$$n \geq \left[\left(\frac{z}{a}\right)\left(\frac{s}{\bar{x}}\right) \right]^2$$

2. Calculating the allowance factor based on job time

$$AF_{\text{Job}} = 1 + PFD$$

3. Calculating the allowance factor based on time worked

$$AF_{\text{Time worked}} = \frac{1}{1 - PFD}$$

4. Calculating standard time

$$ST = (NT)(AF)$$

5. Calculating the number of observations for work sampling

$$n \geq \left(\frac{z}{e}\right)^2 \hat{p}(1 - \hat{p})$$

6. Calculating the time required for the nth time the task is done

$$T \times L^n$$

Solved Problems   (See student companion site for Excel template.)

• Problem 1

Frank's BBQ Delight restaurant sells barbecued chicken sandwiches. The owner wants to set a standard time for assembling each kind of sandwich he sells. You have been asked to set a standard time for the Super Chicken sandwich—8 ounces of barbecued chicken served on a bulkie roll.

(a) Determine the number of observations you need to make if the owner wants the standard time to be within 5 percent of the true value 90 percent of the time. Results from your first ten observations are shown here.

Work Element	Standard Deviation	Mean Observed Time
1. Get bulkie rolls (box of 12).	0.200	2.40
2. Prepare bulkie roll, move to prep area, open up roll.	0.005	0.08
3. Get barbecued chicken (4-lb. box).	0.550	4.00
4. Place 8 oz. chicken on roll.	0.015	0.25
5. Spread on special BBQ sauce.	0.010	0.10
6. Close bulkie roll, slice in half.	0.0125	0.10
7. Wrap sandwich, place in pickup area.	0.010	0.15

(b) Determine the normal time for each of the activities. Determine the standard time if the owner decides to use a 10 percent allowance factor based on the time of the job.

(c) If an employee works at the standard time, how many Super Chicken sandwiches can the employee prepare per hour?

(d) If the owner expects demand for the Super Chicken sandwich to be 100 per hour, how many employees should be assigned to preparing the Super Chicken sandwiches?

• Before You Begin:

To determine the number of observations needed for an element in a time study, use the formula: $n \geq [(z/a)(s/\bar{x})^2]$. The owner has the desired confidence and accuracy. The standard deviation and the mean observed time for each element is provided for you in Section a.

• Solution a

With $z = 1.65$ and $e = 0.05$, determine the number of observations needed for each work element.

Work element 1:

$$n \geq \left[\left(\frac{1.65}{0.05}\right)\left(\frac{0.20}{2.40}\right) \right]^2 = 7.56 \text{ or } 8 \text{ observations}$$

Work element 2:

$$n \geq \left[\left(\frac{1.65}{0.05}\right)\left(\frac{0.005}{0.08}\right) \right]^2 = 4.25 \text{ or } 5 \text{ observations}$$

Work element 3:

$$n \geq \left[\left(\frac{1.65}{0.05} \right) \left(\frac{0.55}{4.0} \right) \right]^2 = 20.59 \text{ or } 21 \text{ observations}$$

Work element 4:

$$n \geq \left[\left(\frac{1.65}{0.05} \right) \left(\frac{0.015}{0.25} \right) \right]^2 = 3.92 \text{ or } 4 \text{ observations}$$

Work element 5:

$$n \geq \left[\left(\frac{1.65}{0.05} \right) \left(\frac{0.01}{0.10} \right) \right]^2 = 10.89 \text{ or } 11 \text{ observations}$$

Work element 6:

$$n \geq \left[\left(\frac{1.65}{0.05} \right) \left(\frac{0.0125}{0.10} \right) \right]^2 = 17.02 \text{ or } 18 \text{ observations}$$

Work element 7:

$$n \geq \left[\left(\frac{1.65}{0.05} \right) \left(\frac{0.01}{0.15} \right) \right]^2 = 4.84 \text{ or } 5 \text{ observations}$$

Calculate the number of observations needed for each of the work elements. Then determine that we need a total of 21 observations to be 90 percent confident that we will be within 5 percent of the true mean. After you make the additional 11 observations, the following data are available.

Work Unit	Mean Observed Time (minutes)	Performance Rating Factor	Frequency
1	2.20	1.10	0.083
2	0.10	0.90	1
3	4.25	0.95	0.125
4	0.20	1.25	1
5	0.10	1.00	1
6	0.12	0.90	1
7	0.12	1.25	1

The following spreadsheet shows how this data could be used in a spreadsheet:

	A	B	C	D	E	F	G	H	I	J	K
1											
2	**Frank's BBQ Delight (all times in minutes)**										
3											
4		**Problem Parameters**									
5		Allowance	10%								
6		Accuracy/Precision (a)	0.05								
7		Confidence Level	90%			G11: =ROUNDUP(F11,0)			K11: =J11*(1+C$5)		
8		Z-value (z)	1.650						J11: =H11*E11*I11		
9						F11: =((C$8/C$6)*(C11/D11))^2					
10		**Work Element**	Standard Deviation	Mean Observed Time	Frequency	Observations Needed	Observations (Rounded)	Revised Mean Observed Time	Performance Rating Factor	Normal Time	Standard Time
11	1	Get bulkie rolls (box of 12).	0.200	2.40	0.083	7.56	8	2.20	1.10	0.2017	0.2218
12	2	Prepare bulkie roll, move to prep area, open up roll.	0.005	0.08	1.000	4.25	5	0.10	0.90	0.0900	0.0990
13	3	Get barbecued chicken (4 lb. box).	0.550	4.00	0.125	20.59	21	4.25	0.95	0.5047	0.5552
14	4	Place 8 oz. of chicken on roll.	0.015	0.25	1.000	3.92	4	0.20	1.25	0.2500	0.2750
15	5	Spread on special BBQ sauce.	0.010	0.10	1.000	10.89	11	0.10	1.00	0.1000	0.1100
16	6	Close bulkie roll, slice in half.	0.0125	0.10	1.000	17.02	18	0.12	0.90	0.1080	0.1188
17	7	Wrap sandwich, place in pickup area.	0.010	0.15	1.000	4.84	5	0.12	1.25	0.1500	0.1650
18											
19						Observations Needed	21	Total Cycle Time (minutes)		1.4044	1.5448
20											
21						G19: =MAX(G11:G17)			K19: =SUM(K11:K17)		

• Before You Begin:

To calculate normal time for an element, you multiply the mean observed time by the performance rating factor and then by the frequency. In this case, use the revised mean observed time, which includes all of the observations.

• Solution b

The normal times are shown in the spreadsheet. To calculate the normal times, multiply the mean observed time by the performance factor and the frequency factor.

To determine standard time, we multiply the normal time by the allowance factor. Since the allowance is based on job time, we use the formula 1 + allowances. The company has decided on a 10 percent allowance.

The standard times are shown in the far right column in the spreadsheet.

• *Before You Begin:*
As long as the employee is working at the standard rate, you can determine how many sandwiches the employee can prepare per hour, by dividing the 60 minutes in an hour by the standard time per sandwich (1.5448 minutes).

• *Solution c*
Since the standard time is 1.5448 minutes per cycle, a worker performing at the standard should be able to produce 38.84 sandwiches per hour (60 minutes/1.5448 minutes per sandwich).

• *Before You Begin:*
When you know how many sandwiches need to be made each hour and you know how many can be made by an employee working at standard, you determine the number of employees needed by dividing the quantity needed (100 per hour) by the number an employee working at standard can produce in one hour (38.84).

• *Solution d*
If the owner plans to have staffing to prepare 100 Super Chicken sandwiches, he will need 3 employees (100 sandwiches per hour divided by 38.84 sandwiches per employee per hour).

• **Problem 2**
You make twenty observations of a business professor at State University. The results of the observations are as follows:

Activity	Times Observed
Professor at class	5
Professor grading	2
Meeting with students	1
Preparing for class	3
Working on research	3
Idle	2
Speaking on phone	1
Not available	3

Based on this information, how many observations do you need to estimate the proportion of the professor's time spent on classroom preparations? Assume a 95 percent confidence ($z = 1.96$) that the resulting estimate will be within 5 percent of the true value.

• *Before You Begin:*
To determine the number of observations needed to estimate the proportion of the professor's time spent on classroom preparations, you use the formula $n = (z/e)^2 \hat{p}(1 - \hat{p})$. Calculate the initial proportion estimate using the results of the initial observations.

• *Solution*
Based on the preliminary observations, the estimate of the proportion of time the professor spends preparing for class is 0.15 (3 observed times/20 observations taken).

$$n = \left(\frac{1.96}{0.05}\right)^2 [0.15(1 - 0.15)] = 195.92 \text{ observations}$$

We need to take a total of 196 observations to satisfy our confidence and error constraints.

• **Problem 3**
You need to develop a cost estimate for a customer order of twelve custom commercial printing presses. It is estimated that the first press will require 750 labor-hours; a learning curve of 80 percent is expected.

(a) How many labor-hours are required for the sixth printing press?

(b) How many labor-hours are required for the twelfth printing press?

(c) How many labor-hours are required to complete all twelve printing presses?

(d) If the average labor-hour cost is $24, what is the total labor cost for building the twelve printing presses?

(e) If your company typically prices products at $2\frac{1}{2}$ times the labor cost, what is the price quoted to the customer?

• *Solution*
(a) Using Table 11-9, the coefficient for the sixth unit with an 80 percent learning curve is 0.562. The time for the sixth unit is 421.50 hours (or 750 hours × 0.562).

(b) The coefficient for the twelfth unit is 0.449, so the time to build the twelfth unit is 336.75 hours.

(c) The total time to build all twelve printing presses is 5420.25 hours (or 750 hours × 7.227).

(d) Total labor cost is $130,086 (or $24 per hour × 5420.25 hours).

(e) The price quoted to the customer is $325,215 (or $130,086 × 2.5).

Discussion Questions

1. Describe the major components of work system design.

2. Visit a local business and describe the jobs to be done, the workers needed for the jobs, and how the workers help achieve the objectives of the business.

3. Describe the objectives of job design.

4. Explain why it is hard to design jobs in a business setting.

5. Explain what we mean by technical feasibility, economic feasibility, and behavioral feasibility.

6. Describe cases in which people are preferable to machines.

7. Describe cases in which machines are preferable to people.

8. Describe the advantages and disadvantages of using a high level of job specialization.

9. Describe factors affecting the work environment that must be considered in work systems design.

10. Describe the alternative workplace approach.

11. Create a process flowchart for an activity that you do daily—for example, getting ready for school each day.

12. Analyze a daily activity to see whether you can improve the process.

13. Compare and contrast the four work measurement techniques.

14. Explain the difference between time-based and output-based compensation plans.

15. Explain why it makes sense to use time-based compensation systems.

16. Explain why it makes sense to use an output-based compensation system.

Problems

1. Given the following information, determine the sample size needed if the standard time estimate is to be within 5 percent of the true mean 97 percent of the time.

Work Element	Standard Deviation (minutes)	Mean Observed Time (minutes)
1	0.20	1.10
2	0.10	0.80
3	0.15	0.90
4	0.10	1.00

2. Using the information in Problem 1, determine the sample size needed if the standard time estimate is to be within 5 percent of the true mean 99 percent of the time.

3. Using the following information, determine the sample size needed if the standard time estimate is to be within 5 percent of the true mean 95 percent of the time.

Work Element	Standard Deviation (minutes)	Mean Observed Time (minutes)
1	0.60	2.40
2	0.20	1.50
3	1.10	3.85
4	0.85	2.55
5	0.40	1.60
6	0.50	2.50

4. Using the information in Problem 3, calculate the sample size needed if the standard time estimate is to be within 5 percent of the true mean 99 percent of the time. Calculate the percentage increase in sample size for the higher precision.

Use the following information from the Arkade Company for Problems 5–10.

Work Element	Mean Observed Time (minutes)	Performance Rating Factor
1	1.20	0.95
2	1.00	0.85
3	0.80	1.10
4	0.90	1.10

5. Calculate the normal time for each of the work elements.

6. The Arkade Company has decided to use a 15 percent allowance factor based on job time. Calculate the standard time for each work element and for the total job.

7. Based on the standard time calculated in Problem 6, how many units should an employee operating at 100 percent of standard complete during an eight-hour workday?

8. The Arkade Company is considering switching to a 15 percent allowance based on time worked. Calculate the new standard time for each work element and for the total job.

9. Based on the standard time calculated in Problem 8, how many units should an employee operating at 100 percent of standard complete during an eight-hour workday?

10. Compare the two standards calculated in Problems 6 and 8. What other factors should be considered in selecting the method for determining the allowance factor?

11. Jake's Jumbo Jacks has collected the following information to develop a standard time for building jumbo jacks.

Observations	Element (in minutes)				
	1	2	3	4	5
Cycle 1	2.18	1.25	1.70	2.74	1.57
Cycle 2	2.22	1.23	1.75	2.66	1.55
Cycle 3	2.20	1.29	1.72	2.60	1.57
Cycle 4	2.18	1.30	1.80	2.56	1.57
Cycle 5	2.21	1.26	1.84	2.58	1.59
Cycle 6	2.22	1.22	1.79	2.58	1.61
Cycle 7	2.17	1.26	1.78	2.60	1.57
Cycle 8	2.21	1.26	1.75	2.58	1.61
Cycle 9	2.18	1.30	1.80	2.60	1.55
Cycle 10	2.17	1.28	1.78	2.58	1.57
Rating factor	0.90	0.80	1.10	1.05	0.95
Frequency	1	1	1	1	1

(a) Calculate the mean observed time for each element.
(b) Calculate the normal time for each element.
(c) Using an allowance factor of 20 percent of job time, calculate the standard time for each element and for the entire job.
(d) How many units should be completed each hour if the worker performs at 100 percent of the standard?
(e) How many units should be completed each hour if the worker performs at 90 percent of the standard?

12. Frank's Fabricators has collected the following information to develop a standard time for producing their high-volume Navigator III, a universal remote control. All of the times are in minutes.

Observations	Elements					
	1	2	3	4	5	6
Cycle 1	1.10	3.00	0.92	1.23	1.46	1.80
Cycle 2	1.08		0.88	1.30	1.64	1.78
Cycle 3	1.15	3.20	0.85	1.26	1.55	1.76
Cycle 4	1.16		0.88	1.33	1.52	1.80
Cycle 5	1.07	3.10	0.90	1.28	1.62	1.82
Cycle 6	1.10		0.94	1.30	1.60	1.82
Rating factor	0.95	0.90	1.05	1.0	0.85	1.10
Frequency	1.00	0.50	1.0	1.0	1.0	1.0

(a) Calculate the mean observed time for each element.
(b) Calculate the normal time for each element.
(c) Using an allowance factor of 15 percent of job time, calculate the standard time for each element.
(d) Calculate the standard time for completing one Navigator III.
(e) If an employee is able to produce at a rate equal to the standard (100 percent efficiency), how many units should she produce each hour?

(f) If an employee is working at 90 percent efficiency, how many units should she complete in one hour?
(g) If a process improvement has changed the mean observed time for element 6 to 1.50 minutes, what is the new standard time for the Navigator III?
(h) If the company builds 20,000 Navigator IIIs each month, how much less time does it require using the new process?

13. The following information is provided to you for each of five elements performed in building the Aviator model, a basic universal remote control.

Element	Mean Observed Time (minutes)	Performance Rating Factor	Frequency
1	0.96	0.96	1.0
2	1.45	1.10	1.0
3	3.33	1.00	0.33
4	1.24	0.90	1.0
5	1.18	1.05	1.0

(a) Calculate the normal time for each element.
(b) If the company uses a 15 percent allowance factor based on time worked, calculate the standard time for each element.
(c) Calculate the standard hourly output.
(d) Calculate the expected hourly output at 90 percent of standard.

14. You have twenty-five observations of university policeman Sgt. Jack B. Nimble during his normal workday. The results are shown here. Assume that the estimated proportion is to be within 5 percent of the true proportion 95 percent of the time.

Activity Observed	Number of Times Observed
Doing paperwork	9
On the phone	3
Eating doughnuts	3
Cleaning weapon	4
Idle	2
Not in sight	4

(a) Based on your preliminary observations, how many total observations do you need to estimate the proportion of time Sgt. Nimble spends doing paperwork?
(b) How many total observations do you need to estimate the proportion of time Sgt. Nimble spends on the phone?
(c) How many total observations do you need to estimate the proportion of time Sgt. Nimble seems to be unavailable?

15. You are given the following information.

Observations	Element (in minutes)				
	1	2	3	4	5
Cycle 1	0.58	1.50	0.79	0.30	
Cycle 2	0.61		0.75	0.35	
Cycle 3	0.59		0.73	0.33	
Cycle 4	0.54		0.72	0.35	
Cycle 5	0.60	1.40	0.72	0.30	2.00
Cycle 6	0.57		0.71	0.32	
Cycle 7	0.53		0.80	0.30	
Cycle 8	0.59		0.78	0.28	
Cycle 9	0.63	1.54	0.77	0.35	
Cycle 10	0.58		0.79	0.33	2.20
Cycle 11	0.56		0.72	0.32	
Cycle 12	0.55		0.79	0.34	
Cycle 13	0.58	1.62	0.77	0.29	
Cycle 14	0.60		0.80	0.33	
Cycle 15	0.62		0.74	0.30	2.10
Rating factor	0.95	0.90	1.00	1.10	0.90
Frequency	1	0.25	1	1	0.20

(a) Develop the mean observed time for each element.
(b) Calculate the normal time for each element.
(c) Using an allowance factor of 15 percent of job time, calculate the standard time for each element and for the entire job.
(d) How many units should be completed each hour if the worker performs at 100 percent of the standard?
(e) How many units should be completed each hour if the worker performs at 110 percent of the standard?

16. As a class project you have been asked to project the proportion of time a professor spends on various activities. You have decided to use the work sampling method. Your initial observations are shown.

Activity Observed	Number of Times Observed
Grading	4
Administrative paperwork	6
Preparing for class	5
Teaching class	5
Meeting with student(s)	8
On the phone	2
Working on research	6
Unavailable	4
Total	**40**

You are instructed that your estimates are to be within 5 percent of the true value with 97 percent confidence ($z = 2.17$).

(a) Based on your initial observations, how many total observations are needed to estimate the proportion of time the professor spends on each activity?

After taking additional observations, the following data are available.

Activity Observed	Number of Times Observed
Grading	30
Administrative paperwork	50
Preparing for class	30
Teaching class	30
Meeting with student(s)	66
On the phone	17
Working on research	45
Unavailable	34
Total	**299**

(b) Determine what proportion of time the professor spends teaching class.
(c) Determine what proportion of time the professor spends working on research.
(d) If the professor works approximately fifty-four hours per week, determine the amount of time that would normally be spent on each activity.

17. Your twenty observations of Dr. Knowitall reveal the following information. Assume that the estimate is to be within 5 percent of the true proportion 95 percent of the time.

Activity Observed	Number of Times Observed
With patient	6
Reviewing test results	3
On phone	2
Idle	1
Away on emergency	4
Not available	4

(a) Calculate the sample size needed to estimate the proportion of time Dr. Knowitall spends away on emergencies.
(b) Calculate the sample size needed to estimate the proportion of time Dr. Knowitall spends reviewing test results.
(c) Calculate the minimum number of observations that must be made to complete the work-sampling analysis.

18. You need to develop a labor time estimate for a customer order of twenty network installations. It is estimated that the first installation will require sixty hours of labor and a learning curve of 90 percent is expected.

(a) How many labor-hours are required for the fifteenth installation?
(b) How many labor-hours are required for the twentieth installation?
(c) How many labor-hours are required to complete all twenty installations?
(d) If the average labor cost is $32.00, what is the total labor cost for installing the networks?

19. Students in an operations management class have been assigned six similar computer homework problems. Alexis needed forty minutes to complete the first problem. Assuming an 80 percent learning curve, how much total time will Alexis need to complete the assignment?

20. Your company has received an order for twenty units of a product. The labor cost to produce the item is $9.50 per hour. The setup cost for the item is $60 and material costs are $25 per unit. The item is sold for $92. The learning rate is 80 percent. Overhead is assessed at a rate of 55 percent of unit labor cost.

(a) Determine the average unit cost for the twenty units if the first unit takes four hours.

(b) Determine the minimum number of units that need to be made before the selling price meets or exceeds the average unit cost.

CASE: The Navigator III

Frank Jones, the owner of Frank's Fabricators, has collected the following information to develop a standard time for producing the Navigator III, a universal remote control. All of the times are in minutes.

Observations	Elements					
	1	2	3	4	5	6
Cycle 1	1.10	3.00	0.92	1.23	1.46	1.80
Cycle 2	1.08		0.88	1.30	1.64	1.78
Cycle 3	1.15	3.20	0.85	1.26	1.55	1.76
Cycle 4	1.16		0.88	1.33	1.52	1.80
Cycle 5	1.07	3.10	0.90	1.28	1.62	1.82
Cycle 6	1.10		0.94	1.30	1.60	1.82
Rating Factor	0.95	0.90	1.05	1.0	0.85	1.10
Frequency	1.00	0.50	1.0	1.0	1.0	1.0

Frank has noticed that one of his senior operators, Sam, is able to consistently produce the Navigator III much quicker than other employees. However, Sam always produces exactly what the standard requires each day. Sam insists that he does everything according to the job directions. He offers no additional insight into how quickly he achieves the standard output levels.

During casual observations, Frank noticed that Sam appears to be doing element 6 much quicker than anyone else. Because of this, he asks Susan, a time-study analyst to observe how Sam is doing element 6. After observing Sam, she determined that his mean observed time for element 6 was 1.50 minutes and she rated his performance at 100 percent. This suggests that his output is not being accomplished by unusual effort on his part. Since Sam was significantly quicker than the standard but was only working at 100 percent, Susan suggested that he had developed a new method for doing element 6.

Questions

1. Based on Susan's observations, determine how long it actually takes Sam to produce a Navigator III.

2. If direct labor is assessed at $18 per hour, what would the labor savings per Navigator III be if all the employees used the same method that Sam uses?

3. If Frank's Fabricators produces 20,000 Navigator IIIs each month, what are the potential annual savings by using Sam's method for element 6?

4. Why do you think Sam is reluctant to share his method improvement for element 6 with the company?

5. Do standard times inhibit process improvement?

6. How can you ensure that employees will share time-saving improvements?

7. From an employee's perspective, why wouldn't you share a process improvement with the company?

CASE: Northeast State University

Dr. Woodrow Bay, chairperson of the Decision Sciences Department in the College of Business Administration, sat at his desk pondering his latest predicament. For the last forty-five minutes at the faculty meeting, faculty members complained about poor administrative support. Numerous examples of unavailable administrative assistants were given. As the professors left, one muttered, "There are universities that provide plenty of administrative support, maybe it is time to update our resumes."

Dr. Bay knew this to be true and that these professors could easily leave for another university given the current job market. He needed to determine whether their perceptions regarding inadequate administrative support were justified.

Background

The Decision Sciences Department houses four functional areas: operations management, quantitative methods, statistics, and information systems. The faculty have national or international reputations based on their excellent scholarship. Higher student enrollments have resulted in the department increasing its faculty from twelve to twenty full-time professors during the past three years. Unfortunately, there was no increase in the administrative support for the department.

As professors were added, the strain on the administrative staff increased. There were more classes, so more course materials needed to be prepared (syllabi, handouts, and exams). In addition, since the faculty were expected to publish research, the administrative assistants spent more time working on manuscripts. New professors required significantly more interaction with the support staff to explain what was wanted and when. Administrative assistants often ran errands for faculty members (placing items on reserve at the library, dealing with the book store, making photocopies, distributing mail, doing correspondence, providing supplies, making travel arrangements, arranging meetings, and placing meal orders). The administrative assistants seemed unable to complete all of their work in a normal eight-hour day.

The faculty, on the other hand, believed the primary work activity of the administrative assistants was keyboard entry: keying in manuscripts, course outlines, correspondence, and grant proposals. When faculty did not see the administrative assistants keying in information, the impression was that the staff was not doing its job. It seemed that too much time was wasted talking with faculty, students, or each other, and work was not being done. Dr. Bay did not believe this was the case. He needed to gather information about how the administrative assistants spent their time and compare that with data from the faculty concerning the administrative assistants. Both the faculty and the administrative assistants believed that the solution was hiring an additional administrative assistant. For Dr. Bay this was next to impossible, given the proposed budget cuts at the university, so he decided to collect data to gain insight into the problem.

For two weeks data were collected. From the faculty, Dr. Bay received estimates as to what percentage of the administrative assistants' time the faculty perceived was spent on different activities. He also did a work sample of the administrative assistants. The results are shown here.

Estimates of Administrative Assistants' Use of Time

Activity	Faculty Estimate (%)	Work Sample (%)
Working on computer	20	40
Talking on phone	25	7
Away from office	20	10
Talking with faculty	2	8
Talking with others	15	10
Filing	3	5
Photocopying	5	15
Other	10	5

Case Questions

Your assignment is to analyze the data collected by Dr. Bay. In particular, you should

1. Describe how Dr. Bay can use the data.

2. Suggest ways in which the administrative assistants' jobs can be changed to make better use of their time and be more supportive to the faculty.

3. Suggest ways the faculty can change work habits to reduce the burden on the administrative assistants.

4. Consider other alternatives to reduce the strain on the administrative assistants.

INTERACTIVE CASE ▶ **Virtual Company** www.wiley.com/college/reid

On-line Case: Work System Design at Valley Memorial Hospital

Assignment: *Work System Design at Valley Memorial Hospital* You have been asked to work with Lee Jordan, director of the Medical/Surgical Nursing Unit. Lee is concerned about nursing services in the obstetrics area. Recently, patients have been complaining about the timeliness of the response to their nursing needs. Recognizing that nursing is extremely important to the success of VMH, Lee has always tried to make sure that these areas are adequately staffed. Her staffing decisions have been based on a conservative assumption that nurses should be able to devote about 60 percent of their time to actual patient nursing, with the remainder used for other nonnursing activities. These include (a) paperwork or documentation pertaining to record keeping and insurance, (b) answering queries from doctors and patients either in person or on the telephone, and (c) other activities such as breaks and personal needs. Lee wants you to design a study to estimate the percentage of the nurses' time spent on actual nursing and nonnursing activities and prepare a concise report addressing a few specific questions. This assignment will enable you to enhance your knowledge of the material in this chapter.

To complete this assignment, go to **www.wiley.com/college/reid** to get the details needed. Assignment questions are given at the site.

To access the Web site:

- Go to **www.wiley.com/college/reid**
- Click **Student Companion Site**
- Click **Virtual Company**
- Click **Kaizen Consulting, Inc.**
- Click **Consulting Assignments**
- Click **Work System Design at Valley Memorial Hospital**

INTERNET CHALLENGE E-commerce Job Design

You have been chosen to head up the development of an e-commerce direct retail site for your company. Since this is new to both you and your company, you need to gather some initial information. You will use this information to develop standard times for measuring your company Web site's performance. Your company is planning to start by offering between 100 and 200 popular products on-line. Of particular concern to your company is the customer's ease in using your site.

Begin by visiting at least three different Web sites and documenting your experience at the site with a process flowchart.

Show the sequential steps you as the customer must follow when visiting the site to gain product information, to place an order, to arrange payment, and to track the order. For one of the sites you visit, collect data on how long it takes a customer to complete a visit to the site. Break the visit into distinct elements such as finding product information, placing an order, choosing the shipping method, making payment, and confirming your order. For one of the three sites you visit, analyze the procedures used and propose changes that you think would improve the customer effectiveness of the site.

On-line Resources

Companion Website www.wiley.com/college/reid:
- Take interactive *practice quizzes* to assess your knowledge and help you study in a dynamic way
- Review *PowerPoint slides* or print slides for notetaking
- Download *Excel Templates* to use for problem solving
- Access the *Virtual Company: Valley Memorial Hospital*
- Find links to *Company Tours* for this chapter
  SuperbServ, Inc.
  3M-AiT, Ltd.
- Find links for *Additional Web Resources* for this chapter
  The AES Corporation, _www.aesc.org_
  Southwest Airlines, _www.southwest.org_

Irving Paper Mill, Irving Forest Discovery Network, _www.ifdn.com/paper/paper.htm_

Additional Resources Available Only in WileyPLUS:
- Use the *e-Book* and launch directly to all interactive resources
- Take the interactive *Quick Test* to check your understanding of the chapter material and get immediate feedback on your responses.
- Check your understanding of the key vocabulary in the chapter with *Interactive Flash Cards*
- Use the *Animated Demo Problems* to review key problem types.
- Practice for your tests with *additional problem sets*
- *And more!*

Selected Bibliography

Barnes, Ralph M. *Motion and Time Study: Design and Measurement of Work*, Eighth Edition. New York: Wiley, 1980.

Hatcher, Larry, and Timothy L. Ross. "From Individual Incentives to an Organization-Wide Gainsharing Plan: Effects on Teamwork and Product Quality," *Journal of Organizational Behavior*, May 1991, 169.

Ledford, Gerald E., Jr., Edward E. Lawlet III, and Susan A. Mohrman, "Reward Innovations in Fortune 1000 Companies," *Compensation and Benefits Review*, April 1995, 76.

Marwell, Gerald. "Altruism and the Problem of Collective Action." In *Cooperation and Helping Behavior: Theories and Research*. New York: Academic Press, 1982.

Niebel, Benjamin, and Andris Freivalds. *Methods, Standards, and Work Design*, Eleventh Edition. New York: McGraw-Hill

Higher Education, 2003. "The 100 Best Companies to Work for 2006." *Fortune*, 153, 1, January 2006.

Pace, Randy. "Santa Cruz Operation's Self Managing Work Groups, A Team Member's Story," *Target*, 8, 6, November/December 1992, 7.

Patterson, Gregory A. "Distressed Shoppers, Disaffected Workers Prompt Stores to Alter Sales Commissions," *Wall Street Journal*, July 1, 1992, B1.

Pearce, Jone L., William B. Stevenson, and James L. Perry. "Managerial Compensation Based on Organizational Performance: A Time Series Analysis of the Effects of Merit Pay," *Academy of Management Journal*, June 1985, 261.

Pfeffer, Jeffrey. "Six Dangerous Myths About Pay," *Harvard Business Review*, 76, 3, May/June 1998, 109.

CHAPTER 12

Independent Demand Inventory Management

Before studying this chapter, you should know or, if necessary, review

1. Competitive priorities, Chapter 2, pages 35–38.
2. Internal and external customers, Chapter 4, page 101.
3. Advantages of small lot sizes, Chapter 7, pages 231–232.
4. Forecast error, Chapter 8, pages 279–281.

LEARNING OBJECTIVES

After studying this chapter, you should be able to

1. Describe the different types and uses of inventory.
2. Describe the objectives of inventory management.
3. Calculate inventory performance measures.
4. Understand the relevant costs associated with inventory.
5. Calculate order quantities.
6. Evaluate the total relevant costs of different inventory policies.
7. Why companies don't always use the optimal order quantity.
8. Understand how to justify smaller order sizes.
9. Calculate appropriate safety stock inventory policies.
10. Calculate order quantities for single-period inventory.
11. Perform ABC inventory control and analysis.
12. Understand the role of cycle counting in inventory record accuracy.

CHAPTER OUTLINE

WHAT'S IN OM FOR ME?

ACC

FIN

MKT

OM

HRM

MIS

Have you ever been in a rush to get through the grocery checkout only to be stuck in line behind a person buying numerous varieties of the same general item? Perhaps a person buying twenty-four cans of pet food, with each can being a different flavor. You watch in dismay as the cashier scans each individual can, wondering why the cashier doesn't just scan one can and enter a quantity of twenty-four. Although it would be much easier to let the cash register do the work, it is critical that the cashier scan each individual can.

Many retailers, like Wal-Mart, Sears, Victoria's Secret, Home Depot, and Kroger, use point-of-sale cash registers to collect data on each item sold. This information is then used to update their inventory records to determine when a replenishment order should be placed.

When the cashier scans only a single flavor and enters a quantity of twenty-four, the register reports that twenty-four cans of that specific flavor have been bought by this customer and adjusts the inventory record for that item. In reality, the customer bought one can each of twenty-four different varieties. Failure to scan each item results in all twenty-four inventory records becoming inaccurate. These inaccurate inventory records cause companies to replenish the wrong items and result in shortages on the shelves.

Jeff Zaruba/Stone/Getty Images, Inc.

Information collected with point-of-sale registers is the basis for generating automatic replenishment orders. When making replenishment decisions, a business decides what, when, and how much should be purchased. When a company replenishes the wrong item because of inaccurate inventory records, the customer is often not satisfied. If a company replenishes items too soon because of inaccurate records, it has invested money in unnecessary inventory and risks item spoiling or deteriorating. It is also possible that the company might not have the necessary storage space because of ordering the wrong item.

Companies make replenishment decisions when managing inventory. In this chapter we look at different types of inventory and how companies use those inventories, the costs of different inventory policies, inventory management objectives and performance measures, and techniques for determining how much of an item to replenish.

TYPES OF INVENTORY

Inventory comes in many shapes and sizes, as shown in Figure 12-1. Most manufacturing firms have the following types of inventory. **Raw materials** are the purchased items or extracted materials that are transformed into components or products. For example, gold is a raw material that is transformed into jewelry. **Components** are parts or subassemblies used in building the final product. For example, a transformer is a component in an electronic product. **Work-in-process (WIP)** refers to all items in process throughout the plant. Since products are not manufactured instantaneously, there is

▶ **Raw materials**
Purchased items or extracted materials transformed into components or products.

▶ **Components**
Parts or subassemblies used in final product.

FIGURE 12-1

Types of inventory

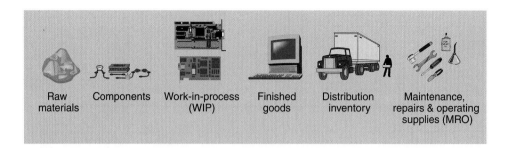

Raw materials | Components | Work-in-process (WIP) | Finished goods | Distribution inventory | Maintenance, repairs & operating supplies (MRO)

► **Work-in-process (WIP)**
Items in process throughout the plant.

► **Finished goods**
Products sold to customers.

► **Distribution inventory**
Finished goods in the distribution system.

always some WIP inventory flowing through the plant. After the product is completed, it becomes **finished goods**—the bicycles, stereos, CDs, and automobiles that the company sells to its customers. **Distribution inventory** consists of finished goods and spare parts at various points in the distribution system—for example, stored in warehouses or in transit between warehouses and consumers. *Maintenance, repair, and operational (MRO) inventory* are supplies that are used in manufacturing but do not become part of the finished product. Examples of MRO are hand tools, lubricants, and cleaning supplies.

HOW COMPANIES USE THEIR INVENTORY

Companies have different kinds of inventory. They also use inventory for different purposes. Let's look at six ways of using inventory.

► **Anticipation inventory**
Inventory built in anticipation of future demand.

1. Anticipation Inventory or Seasonal Inventory is built in anticipation of future demand, planned promotional programs, seasonal fluctuations, plant shutdowns, and vacations. Companies build **anticipation inventory** to maintain level production throughout the year. For example, the toy industry builds toys throughout the year in anticipation of high seasonal sales in December.

► **Fluctuation inventory**
Provides a cushion against unexpected demand.

2. Fluctuation Inventory or Safety Stock is carried as a cushion to protect against possible demand variation, "just in case" of unexpected demand. For example, you might keep extra food in the freezer just in case unexpected company drops in. **Fluctuation inventory** or safety stock is also called *buffer stock* or *reserve stock*.

► **Lot-size inventory**
A result of the quantity ordered or produced.

3. Lot-size Inventory or Cycle Stock results when a company buys or produces more than is immediately needed. The extra units of **lot-size inventory** are carried in inventory and depleted as customers place orders. Consider what happens when you buy a 24-can case of soda. You do not normally drink all 24 cans at once. Instead, what you do not need right away, you store for future consumption. You may buy more of an item than you need to take advantage of lower unit costs or quantity discounts. Cycle stock also occurs when making products and the process has a minimum greater than is needed.

► **Transportation inventory**
Inventory in movement between locations.

4. Transportation or Pipeline Inventory is in transit between the manufacturing plant and the distribution warehouse. **Transportation inventory** are items that are not available for satisfying customer demand until they reach the distribution warehouse, so the company needs to decide between using slower, inexpensive transportation or faster, more expensive transportation. To calculate the average amount of inventory in transit, we use the formula

$$ATI = \frac{tD}{365}$$

where ATI = average transportation inventory (in units)
t = transit time (in days)
D = annual demand (in units)

EXAMPLE 12.1

Calculating Average Transportation Inventory

Suppose the Nadan Company, a producer of brass sculptures, needs to ship finished goods from its manufacturing facility to its distribution warehouse. Annual demand at Nadan is 1460 units. The company has a choice of sending the finished goods regular parcel service (three days transit time) or via public carrier, which takes eight days transit time. Calculate the average annual transportation inventory for each of the alternatives. Note that the average transportation inventory does not consider shipment quantity but only transit time and annual demand. To reduce transit inventory, you reduce transit time.

• **Solution:**
When using the regular parcel service,

$$ATI = \frac{3 \times 1460}{365} = 12 \text{ units}$$

When using the public carrier,

$$ATI = \frac{8 \times 1460}{365} = 32 \text{ units}$$

---

5. Speculative or Hedge Inventory is a buildup to protect against some future event such as a strike at your supplier, a price increase, or the scarcity of a product that may or may not happen. A company typically builds **speculative inventory** to ensure a continuous supply of necessary items. Think about booking an airline flight three months in advance so you can take advantage of a reduced fare. You assume that the airfare will not be reduced further and that you will still need the ticket three months from now. It is a gamble.

▶ **Speculative inventory**
Used to protect against some future event.

6. Maintenance, Repair, and Operating (MRO) Inventory includes maintenance supplies, spare parts, lubricants, cleaning compounds, and daily operating supplies such as pens, pencils, and note pads. **MRO** items support general operations and maintenance but are not part of the product the company builds.

Inventory plays multiple roles in a company's operations. For this reason, companies develop inventory management objectives and performance measures to evaluate how well they are handling their inventory investment. The six functions of inventory are summarized in Table 12-1.

▶ **MRO**
Items used in support of manufacturing and maintenance.

TABLE 12-1

Functions of Inventory

Anticipation inventory	Items built in anticipation of future demand. Allows company to maintain a level production strategy.
Fluctuation inventory	Protects against unexpected demand variations. Assures customer service levels.
Lot-size inventory	Results from the actual quantity purchased. Allows for lower unit costs.
Transportation inventory	Items in movement between locations. Inventory moves from manufacturer to distribution facilities.
Speculative inventory	Extra inventory built up or purchased to protect against some future event. Allows for continuous supply.
MRO	Includes maintenance supplies, spare parts, lubricants, cleaning agents, and daily operating supplies. Facilitates day-to-day operations.

OBJECTIVES OF INVENTORY MANAGEMENT

 The objectives of inventory management are to provide the desired level of customer service, to allow cost-efficient operations, and to minimize the inventory investment.

Customer Service

▶ **Customer service**
The ability to satisfy customer requirements.

▶ **Percentage of orders shipped on schedule**
A customer service measure appropriate for use when orders have similar value.

What is customer service? **Customer service** is a company's ability to satisfy the needs of its customers. When we talk about customer service in inventory management, we mean whether or not a product is available for the customer when the customer wants it. In this sense, customer service measures the effectiveness of the company's inventory management. Customers can be either external or internal: any entity in the supply chain is considered a customer.

Suppose your company, Kayaks!Incorporated, offers a line of kayaks and kayaking equipment through catalog sales and an accompanying Web site. As product manager, you need to know whether the inventory management system you introduced is effective. One way to measure its effectiveness would be to measure the level of customer service: are customers getting the kayaking equipment they request and are their orders shipped on time? To answer your questions, you can measure the percentage of orders shipped on schedule, the percentage of line items shipped on schedule, the percentage of dollar volume shipped on schedule, or manufacturing idle time due to inventory shortages.

Percentage of Orders Shipped on Schedule is a good measure for finished goods customer service, such as your kayaking equipment company, if all orders and customers have similar value and late deliveries are not excessively late. For a different kind of company, such as one that designs computer networks, some customers have much greater value. Obviously, this method does not adequately capture the value of those customers' orders.

For example, if the book publishing company John Wiley & Sons, Inc. represents 50 percent of your demand but is only one out of twenty orders on the schedule, delivering late to Wiley is certainly more harmful to your company than shipping a smaller order late. With this measure, however, all late orders are treated equally. If you have

Good inventory management results in satisfied customers.

only one late shipment, the customer service level is 95 percent (nineteen of twenty shipped on schedule). But if the late order is to Wiley, you have met only 50 percent of your demand.

Percentage of Line Items Shipped on Schedule

Percentage of Line Items Shipped on Schedule recognizes that not all orders are equal but fails to take into account dollar value of orders. This measure needs more information—the number of line items instead of the number of orders—than the previous measure. Therefore, this measure is more expensive to use and is most appropriate for finished goods inventory.

As an example of the percentage of line items shipped on schedule consider the following. Your sister company, White Water Rafts Inc., determines that from the twenty orders scheduled for delivery this month, customers requested 250 different line items. White Water can ship 225 of these line items on schedule. Their customer service level is 90 percent (225 items shipped on time divided by 250 line items requested).

> ▶ **Percentage of line items shipped on schedule**
> A customer service measure appropriate when customer orders vary in number of line items ordered.

Percentage of Dollar Volume Shipped on Schedule

Percentage of Dollar Volume Shipped on Schedule recognizes the differences in orders in terms of both line items and dollar value. Instead of measuring line items to determine the customer service level, a company totals the value of the orders. For example, if the twenty orders to the Palm Pilot™ handheld-computer manufacturing company had a total value of $400,000 and the company shipped on schedule handheld computers valued at $380,000, the customer service level is 95 percent ($380,000 shipped, divided by $400,000 ordered).

> ▶ **Percentage of dollar volume shipped on schedule**
> A customer service measure appropriate when customer orders vary in value.

Idle Time Due to Material and Component Shortages

Idle Time Due to Material and Component Shortages applies to internal customer service. This is an absolute measure of the manufacturing or service time lost because material or parts are not available to the workforce. Absolute measures make sense when a company has historical data to use in comparisons. For example, Kayaks!Incorporated's supplier historically has lost no more than two manufacturing days per year because of material and component shortages. This year, however, it has lost four manufacturing days for this reason. Obviously, this year's case is worse and needs management's attention.

These are only a few of the measures companies use to evaluate customer service. The desired level of customer service should be consistent with the company's overall strategy. If customer service is your company's competitive advantage, the company must achieve a very high level of customer service. Even when customer service isn't the primary focus, your company must still maintain an acceptable level of customer service.

Now let's look at how inventory helps manufacturers operate efficiently.

Customer service of Palm hand-held computers can be measured as a percentage of dollar volume shipped on schedule.

Cost-Efficient Operations

Companies can achieve *cost-efficient operations* by using inventory in the following ways. First, companies use work-in-process (WIP) inventory to buffer operations. Suppose one of the Hewlett-Packard (HP) printed circuit board (PCB) manufacturing facilities runs two or more operations in a sequence at different rates of output. In this case, buffer inventories build up between the workstations to ensure that each of the operations runs efficiently. For example, PCBs flow from Ken's workstation (tasks take 120 seconds) to Barbara's workstation (tasks take only 90 seconds). If there are no PCBs between the two workstations, Barbara will be idle for 30 seconds out of every 120 seconds because she finishes her tasks 30 seconds before Ken finishes his.

If the floor supervisor, Maria, ensures that there is buffer stock between the workstations, Barbara's idle time will be eliminated so she can produce more PCBs.

Second, inventories allow manufacturing organizations to maintain a level workforce throughout the year despite seasonal demand for production. (Level production plans are discussed in Chapter 13.) A company can do this by building inventory in advance of seasonal demands. This in turn allows the company to maintain a level workforce throughout the year and to reduce the costs of overtime, hiring and firing, training, subcontracting, and additional capacity.

▶ **Setup cost**
Costs such as scrap costs, calibration costs, and downtime costs associated with preparing the equipment for the next product being produced.

Third, by building inventory in long production runs, the **setup cost** is spread over a larger number of units, decreasing the per unit setup cost. Setup costs include the cost of scrap (wasted material and labor), calibration, and downtime to prepare the equipment and materials for the next product to be manufactured. Longer runs mean that the equipment does not need as many setups, so less machine time is lost preparing for production.

Fourth, a company that is willing to acquire inventory can buy in larger quantities at a discount. These larger purchases decrease the ordering cost per unit. For example, the Rustic Garden Furniture Company needs 50,000 pieces of wrought iron annually. Rustic's supplier has offered a unit price of $1.10 if Rustic buys the wrought iron in orders of 10,000 or more pieces at a time. If Rustic chooses to buy in smaller quantities, the unit price is $1.29.

Now let's look at ways to measure inventory investment.

Minimum Inventory Investment

▶ **Inventory turnover**
A measure of inventory policy effectiveness.

A company can measure its *minimum inventory investment* by its **inventory turnover**—that is, by the level of customer demand satisfied by the supply on hand. We calculate the inventory turnover measure as

$$\text{Inventory turnover} = \frac{\text{annual cost of goods sold}}{\text{average inventory in dollars}}$$

EXAMPLE 12.2

Computing Inventory Turns

If the annual cost of goods sold at the Nadan Company is $5,200,000 and the average inventory in dollars is $1,040,000, what is the inventory turnover?

• **Solution:**

$$\text{Inventory turnover} = \frac{\$5,200,000}{\$1,040,000} = 5 \text{ inventory turns}$$

The ratio at the Nadan Company should be compared with that achieved by other companies within the industry. Although there is no magic number for inventory turnover, the higher the number, the more effectively the company is using its inventory. One measure of the level of demand that can be satisfied by on-hand inventory is **weeks of supply**. Weeks of supply is calculated by dividing the average on-hand inventory by the average weekly demand.

▶ **Weeks of supply**
A measure of inventory policy effectiveness.

$$\text{Weeks of supply} = \frac{\text{average inventory on hand in dollars}}{\text{average weekly usage in dollars}}$$

EXAMPLE 12.3

**Calculating
Weeks of Supply**

Suppose that the Nadan Company wants to calculate its weeks of supply. From the previous example, we know that annual cost of goods sold is $5,200,000.

• **Solution:**

To determine the weekly cost of goods sold, we divide the annual cost of goods sold by fifty-two weeks ($5,200,000/52 = $100,000). Given that Nadan maintains an average inventory of $1,040,000, we calculate the weeks of supply as follows:

$$\text{Weeks of supply} = \frac{\$1,040,000}{\$100,000} = 10.4 \text{ weeks of supply}$$

Note that there is a relationship between inventory turnover and weeks of supply. If you divide total weeks per year (52) by the weeks of supply (10.4), you see that the answer is the same as when you calculated inventory turnover. If you divide total number of weeks (52) by the inventory turnover rate (5), the answer is 10.4 weeks of supply. In some companies, inventory performance is measured in either days or hours of supply. To calculate days of supply, we use the formula

$$\text{Days of supply} = \frac{\text{average inventory on hand in dollars}}{\text{average daily usage in dollars}}$$

and hours of supply is calculated as

$$\text{Hours of supply} = \frac{\text{average inventory on hand in dollars}}{\text{average hourly usage in dollars}}$$

Let's look at an example using both of these measures.

EXAMPLE 12.4

**Calculating
Inventory Supply
at the Jenny
Company**

Suppose that the Jenny Company, a specialty gift organization, wants to calculate its days of supply. The annual cot of goods sold is $1,300,000, the average inventory is $15,600, and the company operates 250 days per year.

• **Solution:**

First, we calculate the average daily usage. We divide the annual cost of goods sold by the number of days the company operates ($1,300,000 divided by 250 days equals $5200). Second, using the formula, we divide the average inventory on hand by the average daily usage.

$$\text{Days of supply} = \frac{\$15,600}{\$5200} = 3 \text{ days of supply}$$

Suppose the Jenny Company uses a new process that reduces the average inventory held to $3250. To calculate its current hours of supply, we first calculate the average hourly usage. Using the data provided and assuming an eight-hour day, we divide the average daily usage ($5200) by eight hours. The average hourly usage is $650. Therefore, the hours of supply are

$$\text{Hours of supply} = \frac{\$3250}{\$650} = 5 \text{ hours of supply}$$

TABLE 12-2

Inventory Objectives

	Inventory Objectives
Customer service	Measured by any of the following: • Percentage of orders shipped on schedule • Percentage of line items shipped on schedule • Percentage of dollar volume shipped on schedule • Idle time due to component and material shortages
Cost-efficient operations	Inventories help achieve cost-effective operations by • Using buffer stock to assure smooth production flow • Maintaining a level workforce • Allowing longer production runs, which spreads the cost of setups • Taking advantage of quantity discounts
Minimum inventory investment	Measured by any of the following: • Inventory turnover • Weeks of supply • Days of supply

Table 12-2 summarizes the inventory objectives we just discussed.

RELEVANT INVENTORY COSTS

Inventory management policies have cost implications. Decisions about how much inventory to hold affect item costs, holding costs, ordering costs, and stockout (shortage) costs.

Item Costs

▶ **Item cost**
Includes price paid for the item plus other direct costs associated with the purchase.

The **item costs** of a purchased item include the price paid for the item and any other direct costs for getting the item to the plant, such as inbound transportation, insurance, duty, or taxes. For an item built by the manufacturing company, the item costs include direct labor, direct materials, and factory overhead.

Holding Costs

▶ **Holding costs**
Include the variable expenses incurred by the plant related to the volume of inventory held.

▶ **Capital cost**
The higher of the cost of capital or the opportunity cost for the company.

Holding costs include the variable expenses incurred by the firm for the volume of inventory held. As inventory increases, so do the holding costs. We can determine unit holding costs by examining three cost components: capital costs, storage costs, and risk costs. Annual holding costs are typically stated in either dollars per unit ($3.50 per unit per year) or as a percentage of the item value (25 percent of the unit value).

Capital costs are the higher of either the cost of the capital or the opportunity cost for the company. The cost of the capital is the interest rate the company pays to borrow money to invest in inventory. The opportunity cost is the rate of return the company could have earned on the money if it were used for something other than investing in inventory. The opportunity cost is at least as much as the interest the company could get at the prevailing interest rate. It may be higher if more lucrative opportunities are available. Suppose you have a startup company and need to finance your inventory with a bank loan at 8 percent. Or the company can invest its capital in the stock market and generate a 20 percent return on the investment. For its capital cost, the company would use the 20 percent opportunity cost rather than the 8 percent cost of the loan. The capital cost is typically expressed as an annual interest rate.

Storage costs usually include the cost of space, workers, and equipment. For our purposes, however, we are concerned only with the additional out-of-pocket expenses resulting from the size of the inventory. For example, we include the cost of storage space if it is public warehousing and varies based on the amount of inventory held. If the company already owns the storage space and incurs no additional expense for storing the inventory, we do not include it in the holding cost. The same is true for employees. If an employee works overtime because of the level of inventory, this is an out-of-pocket expense and needs to be included. However, if the employee's workload is merely higher during the normal day, the cost of the employee is not included.

Risk costs include obsolescence, damage or deterioration, theft, insurance, and taxes. These costs vary based on industry. Companies operating in a high-tech environment typically experience much greater obsolescence and theft. Companies that manufacture consumer products may find higher levels of theft.

In general, risk costs are associated with higher levels of inventory. The more inventory you have, the longer it lasts—therefore, the greater the chance of it becoming obsolete. The more inventory you have sitting around, the more likely it is to be damaged. Think of walking through an overloaded basement: you bump into something, it falls and breaks. Theft also typically increases as inventory increases. When a company has few items in inventory, it is more noticeable when an item disappears. However, if the company has a lot of inventory, it is harder to notice when only one item disappears. Insurance costs are typically based on the value of the inventory, so larger inventories have higher insurance premiums. The same is true for taxes: the more valuable the inventory, the higher the tax.

Although many textbooks use an annual holding cost of between 20 percent and 30 percent, in real life it depends on the type of business. The risk costs can vary significantly. Let's look at how annual holding costs are calculated.

▶ **Storage costs**
Include the variable expenses for space, workers, and equipment related to the volume of inventory held.

▶ **Risk costs**
Include obsolescence, damage or deterioration, theft, insurance, and taxes associated with the volume of inventory held.

The Nadan Company currently maintains an average inventory of $1,040,000. The company estimates its capital cost at 12 percent, its storage costs at 5 percent, and its risk costs at 8 percent. Calculate the annual holding costs for the Nadan Company.

EXAMPLE 12.5

Calculating Annual Holding Costs

• **Solution:**
Annual holding cost per unit of inventory equals 25 percent (capital cost + storage costs + risk costs).

$$\text{Annual cost of holding inventory} = \$1,040,000 \times 0.25 = \$260,000$$

Ordering Costs

▶ **Ordering costs**
The fixed costs associated with either placing an order with a supplier or setup costs incurred for in-house production.

Ordering costs are fixed costs for either placing an order with a supplier for a purchased component or raw material or for placing an order to the manufacturing organization for a product built in-house. When you buy an item, the ordering costs include the cost of the clerical work to prepare, release, monitor, and receive orders and the physical handling of the goods. The ordering costs are considered constant regardless of the number of items or the quantities ordered. For example, if the cost to place an order is estimated at $100, every time you place an order with a supplier, the ordering cost is constant ($100).

When an order is released for manufacturing in-house, the ordering or setup costs are the clerical work to prepare the manufacturing order and the list of materials to be picked and delivered to the manufacturing location, plus the cost to prepare the equipment for the job (calibration, appropriate jigs and fixtures, etc.). Like the ordering costs for purchased items, the ordering or setup costs for jobs done in-house are constant.

Shortage Costs

▶ **Shortage costs**
Incurred when demand exceeds supply.

▶ **Back order**
Delaying delivery to the customer until the item becomes available.

▶ **Lost sale**
Occurs when the customer is not willing to wait for delivery.

Companies incur **shortage costs** when customer demand exceeds the available inventory for an item. Suppose a customer, Tom Martin, places an order through your kayaking equipment Web site for a high-end kayak, but that kayak is out of stock. One of two things happens. Either Tom allows you to **back-order** the kayak—that is, Tom is willing to wait until the kayak is available—or Tom decides to buy the kayak from another company and the result for your company is a **lost sale**.

In both cases, your company incurs shortage costs. In the case of the back order, shortage costs result from the additional paperwork to track the order and the possible added expense of overnight shipping rather than normal delivery. There is also the lost customer goodwill, an intangible cost. Although Tom accepted the delay this time, you have no guarantee that he will buy from your company again. In the case of the lost sale, the shortage costs typically include loss of the possible profit, plus loss of the contribution to overhead costs. Your company also faces the risk that Tom will not return with future orders. Shortage costs can also result from internal parts shortages, including the cost of downtime due to lack of materials, additional setups, premium transportation costs, and so forth.

Before You Go On

Before you continue further into the chapter, you need to be sure that you understand the relevant inventory costs. Item cost, holding cost, ordering cost, and shortage cost are summarized in Table 12-3. The next section of this chapter focuses on determining order quantities and uses inventory cost information.

TABLE 12-3   Relevant Inventory Costs

Item cost	Price paid per item plus any other direct costs associated with getting the item to the plant
Holding costs	Capital, storage, and risk costs
Ordering costs	Fixed, constant dollar amount incurred for each order placed
Shortage costs	Loss of customer goodwill, back-order handling, and lost sales

DETERMINING ORDER QUANTITIES

The objectives of inventory management are to provide the desired level of customer service, enable cost-efficient operations, and minimize the inventory investment. To achieve these objectives, a company must first determine how much of an item to order at a time.

Inventory management and control are done at the level of the individual item or **stock-keeping unit (SKU)**. An SKU is a specific item at a particular geographic location. For example, a pair of jeans, size 32 × 32, in inventory at the plant and also eight different warehouses, represents nine different SKUs. A pair of the same jeans held at the same locations but a different size (32 × 34) represents nine additional SKUs. The same style of jeans in a different color represents additional SKUs.

▶ **Stock-keeping unit (SKU)**
An item in a particular geographic location.

Let's look at how a company determines how much of an SKU to order. We will consider some common approaches in this section, summarized in Table 12-4. In the next section we will look at mathematical models for determining order quantity.

Lot-for-lot is ordering exactly what you need. You adjust the ordering quantity to your ordering needs, which ensures that you will not have leftover inventory. You use lot-for-lot when demand is not constant and you have information about expected needs. Ordering sandwiches for a business lunch meeting is a good example of when to use lot-for-lot. The number of persons attending the meeting can vary based on the meeting topic. Since sandwiches are perishable, you do not want to have leftover inventory. This system is also commonly used in material requirements planning (MRP) systems, which we discuss in Chapter 14.

▶ **Lot-for-lot**
The company orders exactly what is needed.

Fixed-order quantity specifies the number of units to order each time you place an order for a certain SKU or item. The quantity may be arbitrary (perhaps 100 units at a time) or it may be the result of how the item is packaged or prepared (such as 144 per box or a loaf of bread). The advantage of this system is that it is easily understood; the disadvantage is that it does not minimize inventory costs.

▶ **Fixed-order quantity**
Specifies the number of units to order whenever an order is placed.

The **min-max system** is to place an order when the on-hand inventory falls below a predetermined minimum level. The quantity ordered is the difference between the quantity available and the predetermined maximum inventory level. For example, if the minimum is set at 50 units, the maximum is set at 250 units, and the quantity available at the time of the order is 40 units, the order quantity is 210 units (250 − 40). With this system, both the time between orders and the quantity ordered can vary.

▶ **Min-max system**
Places a replenishment order when the on-hand inventory falls below the predetermined minimum level. An order is placed to bring the inventory back up to the maximum inventory level.

Lot-for-lot	Order exactly what is needed.
Fixed-order quantity	Order a predetermined amount each time an order is placed.
Min-max system	When on-hand inventory falls below a predetermined minimum level, order a quantity that will take the inventory back up to its predetermined maximum level.
Order *n* periods	Order enough to satisfy demand for the next *n* periods.

TABLE 12-4

Common Ordering Approaches

SKUs at a retail store

©AP/Wide World Photos

▶ **Order *n* periods**
The order quantity is determined by total demand for the item for the next *n* periods.

Order *n* periods means that you determine the order quantity by summing your company's requirements for the next *n* periods. Suppose you have to order enough each time you place an order to satisfy your company's requirements for the next three periods. If these requirements for the next three weeks are 60, 45, and 100, your order is for 205 units. A concern with this system is determining the number of periods to include in the order.

MATHEMATICAL MODELS FOR DETERMINING ORDER QUANTITY

Now let's look at some mathematical models that determine order quantity and minimize inventory costs, beginning with the economic order quantity (EOQ) model.

Economic Order Quantity (EOQ)

▶ **Economic order quantity model (EOQ)**
An optimizing method used for determining order quantity and reorder points.

▶ **Continuous review systems**
Update inventory balances after each inventory transaction.

The **economic order quantity model (EOQ)** has been around since the early 1900s and remains useful for determining order quantities. EOQ is a **continuous review system**, used to keep track of the inventory on hand each time stock is added or withdrawn. If the withdrawal reduces the inventory level to the reorder point or below, you make a replenishment order.

Thus, EOQ tells you when to place a replenishment order and determines the order quantity that minimizes annual inventory cost. Suppose you decide that your kayaking equipment company needs to place a replenishment order whenever the inventory level of item K310 reaches 100 units. Right now you have 105 units of item K310 in inventory. You withdraw 5 K310s to satisfy a customer order, resulting in an updated inventory level of 100 units. Since the inventory level has reached the reorder point, it is time to place a replenishment order for K310. A key characteristic of the continuous review system is that it keeps track of inventory as it is withdrawn.

In the following section we look at some assumptions made by the basic EOQ model.

EOQ Assumptions The basic EOQ model makes these assumptions:

- Demand for the product is known and constant. This means that we know how much the demand is for every time period and that this amount never changes. For example, demand is fifty units per week every week or ten units per day every day. This assumption is indicated by the straight line that shows the depletion of our inventory in Figure 12-2.

- **Lead time** is known and constant. Lead time is the amount of time it takes from order placement until it arrives at the manufacturing company (for example, ten working days between order placement and receipt of merchandise).

  Because you know how long it takes for the replenishment order to arrive, you can determine when you need to place the order. By finding the reorder point (shown in Figure 12-2), you schedule the arrival of the replenishment quantity just as your company's inventory level reaches zero. The minimum inventory level with the basic EOQ should be zero.

- Quantity discounts are not considered: the cost of all units is the same, regardless of the quantity ordered. (We discuss this in more detail later in the chapter.)

- Ordering and setup costs are fixed and constant: the dollar amount to place an order is always the same, regardless of the size of the order.

- Since the company knows demand with certainty, the assumption is that all demand is met. The basic model does not permit back orders, but more advanced models are less rigid.

- The quantity ordered arrives at once, as shown in Figure 12-2. Since the order is scheduled to arrive just as the company runs out of inventory, the maximum inventory level equals the economic order quantity.

▶ **Lead time**
The amount of time it takes from order placement until the item is received.

Figure 12-2 shows the basic workings of the EOQ model. The inventory replenishment process begins when the inventory reaches the reorder point. This is the point at which you place an order for Q units, which are timed to arrive just as your

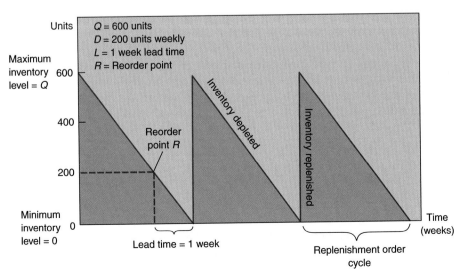

FIGURE 12-2

The EOQ model

company's inventory level reaches zero. The inventory goes from zero to Q and then is depleted at a constant rate. Once the inventory reaches the reorder point, the process begins again.

Since the basic model assumes certainty about demand and lead time, the reorder point is set equal to demand during lead time, or

$$R = dL$$

where R = reorder point
d = average daily demand
L = lead time in days

Problem-Solving Tip   When solving for R, it is possible to use other than daily demand and lead time in days. Use whatever is convenient. If lead time is given in weeks, then use average weekly demand. If lead time is given in months, then use average monthly demand.

For example, if average daily demand is 40 units and lead time is five days, then the reorder point is 200 (40 units times five days). When the inventory reaches 200, it is time to place an order.

Calculating Inventory Policy Costs   Since companies are interested in the costs associated with inventory policies, let's calculate the annual ordering or setup costs and the annual holding costs associated with the basic EOQ model. We do not include shortage costs since all demand is satisfied with the basic EOQ model. We do not include the annual item cost either: no quantity discounts are considered in the basic EOQ model, so the annual item cost remains constant regardless of the quantity ordered each time. Given that, our total costs are

Total annual cost = annual ordering costs + annual holding costs

---

Problem-Solving Tip   When calculating total annual costs, do not round off the number of orders to whole numbers. Although it is true that a partial order cannot be placed, for purposes of comparison we leave the number of orders as a mixed number.

We calculate annual ordering costs by multiplying the number of orders placed per year by the cost to place an order. To find the number of orders placed per year, we divide the annual demand by the quantity ordered.

Suppose annual demand for motherboards at Palm Pilot, the handheld-computer company, is 10,000 units and it currently orders 500 motherboards each time. The number of orders placed per year is twenty (10,000/500). If the cost to place an order is $75, then the annual ordering cost is $1500 (20 orders × $75 ordering cost).

Problem-Solving Tip   When solving for Q, it is not necessary to always use annual demand and annual holding costs. If you have demand given in a different time frame (days, weeks, or months), you can use that as long as the holding costs are expressed in the same time frame, that is, daily demand and daily holding costs, or weekly demand and weekly holding costs.

We calculate annual holding costs by multiplying the average inventory level by the annual holding cost per unit. The average inventory is equal to the maximum inventory plus the minimum inventory divided by 2. In the EOQ model, the maximum inventory is Q and the minimum is zero. Therefore, the average inventory level is $Q/2$. For example, if the order quantity is 500 units, the holding cost is $6 per unit per year, and the annual holding cost is $1500 (500 units/2 × $6 per unit). Sometimes the holding cost is given as a percentage, such as 20 percent of the item price. In this case, we multiply the item price by the percentage to determine the annual unit holding costs. For example, if the holding cost is 20 percent of the item price and the item price is $30, then the annual holding cost is $6 per unit ($30 item price × 20 percent holding cost).

The formula for calculating the total relevant annual costs for the basic EOQ model is

$$TC = \left(\frac{D}{Q}S\right) + \left(\frac{Q}{2}H\right)$$

where TC = total annual cost
$\quad\quad\quad D$ = annual demand
$\quad\quad\quad Q$ = quantity to be ordered
$\quad\quad\quad H$ = annual holding cost
$\quad\quad\quad S$ = ordering or setup cost

For our example, the total cost is

$$TC = \left(\frac{10{,}000}{500}\,\$75\right) + \left(\frac{500}{2}\,\$6\right)$$

or

$$TC = \$1500 + \$1500 = \$3000$$

Note that the annual ordering costs equal the annual holding costs. This is true when we use the EOQ model without rounding. In addition, with the EOQ model, the minimum total cost always results when the annual ordering costs equal the annual holding costs, as shown in Figure 12-3. Note, too, in Figure 12-3 that as order quantity increases so do holding costs and, at the same time, ordering costs decrease since fewer orders are placed. The total costs, however, are always higher when we use an order quantity other than the EOQ.

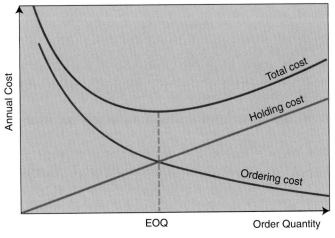

Economic order quantity

FIGURE 12-3

Holding costs equal ordering costs

Calculating the EOQ

We calculate the economic order quantity (Q) using the following formula:

$$Q = \sqrt{\frac{2DS}{H}}$$

where Q = optimal order quantity
D = annual demand
S = ordering or setup cost
H = holding cost

EXAMPLE 12.6

Calculating the Economic Order Quantity

Find the economic order quantity and the reorder point, given the following information:

Annual demand (D) = 10,000 units
Ordering cost (S) = $75 per order
Annual holding cost (H) = $6 per unit
Lead time (L) = 5 days
The company operates 250 days per year.

• **Before You Begin:** Identify the appropriate formula to use for calculating the economic order quantity (EOQ) and the reorder point. The formula for the EOQ is

$$Q = \sqrt{\frac{2DS}{H}}$$

and the formula for finding the reorder point is $R = dL$. Remember to make sure that the holding cost is for the same time period as your demand. For example, if demand is annual, then the holding cost must be an annual holding cost per unit. If demand is monthly, then use a monthly holding cost per unit. You also need to convert annual demand into daily demand to use the reorder point formula. Do this by dividing annual demand by the number of days the company operates per year.

• **Solution:**

$$Q = \sqrt{\frac{2 \times 10,000 \times \$75}{\$6}} = 500 \text{ units}$$

Daily demand is 40 units per day (10,000 units demanded annually, divided by 250 days of operation).

$$R = 40 \text{ units} \times 5 \text{ days} = 200 \text{ units}$$

The inventory policy for this item is to place a replenishment order for 500 units (Q) when the inventory reaches 200 units (R). The replenishment order will arrive just as the current inventory reaches zero. On the previous page, we calculated total annual cost for this policy ($3000). *The EOQ model always minimizes total annual costs.*

What Happens When a Non-EOQ Order Quantity Is Used? To illustrate what happens to annual inventory costs when we use an order quantity other than the EOQ, let's look at an example with a non-EOQ quantity. Determine the total annual costs for your company if you choose to order 1000 units each time a replenishment order is placed.

$$TC = \left(\frac{10,000}{1000} \$75\right) + \left(\frac{1000}{2} \$6\right) = \$3750$$

The total annual cost for this non-EOQ inventory policy is $3750 compared to $3000 for the EOQ policy. Thus we can say that the *difference* between the EOQ policy and any other policy is a penalty cost incurred by your company for *not* using the EOQ policy.

Economic Production Quantity (EPQ)

The basic EOQ model assumes that the entire replenishment order arrives at one time, but this is not always the case. For example, if we bake four batches each of one-dozen chocolate-chip cookies, our inventory will probably never reach four-dozen cookies. Why? Because we or our friends are sure to eat some of the cookies as soon as we bake them! This means that the maximum inventory level will always be less than the total quantity we produce. If out of every batch of one-dozen cookies, we eat four cookies immediately, we will end up with thirty-two cookies in inventory after baking the four one-dozen batches ((12 baked − 4 used) × 4 batches).

Figure 12-4 shows the **economic production quantity (EPQ)** model. The cycle begins when we start making the product. Each day, we use some of what we make to satisfy immediate demand; we put the remainder in inventory. We make the product until we have completed Q units. At that point, the inventory has reached its maximum level. From this point on, we satisfy demand from the on-hand inventory, depleting it daily. When we reach the reorder point, we order another batch. Our company starts producing the new batch just as we run out of the current inventory.

The EPQ model is appropriate when some of the product we make is used as soon as we make it. In manufacturing, this is typical when a single manufacturing facility produces the parts to build the end product. For example, HP builds deskjet printers using printed circuit boards (PCBs). HP's manufacturing facility builds PCBs in batches; some of these PCBs are assembled into the end product immediately, and the rest are put into inventory.

The total cost formula for the EPQ model is

$$TC = \left(\frac{D}{Q} S\right) + \left(\frac{I_{Max}}{2} H\right)$$

▶ **Economic production quantity (EPQ)**
A model that allows for incremental product delivery.

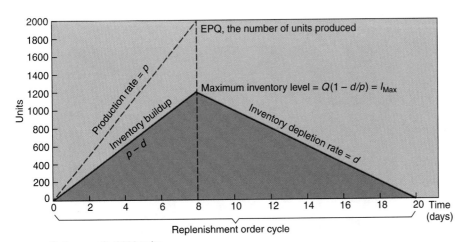

FIGURE 12-4

The EPQ model

Order quantity 2000 units
Daily demand (d) = 100 units
Daily production (p) = 250 units

where TC = total annual cost
D = annual demand
Q = quantity to be ordered
H = annual holding cost
S = ordering or setup cost

$$I_{Max} = Q\left(1 - \frac{d}{p}\right)$$

where d = average daily demand rate
p = daily production rate

EXAMPLE 12.7

Calculating the Maximum Inventory Level

If HP uses 6 PCBs per day, can produce 20 PCBs, and produces PCBs in batches of 200 units, determine the maximum inventory level.

• **Before You Begin:** Remember that when calculating I_{Max}, your answer will always be less than the economic production quantity (EPQ) since you are using some items as soon as they are completed. You really don't need a formula to compute I_{Max}. In the following example, you are producing a total of 200 PCBs, which takes a total of ten days to complete (200 units required/20 units produced daily). Each of the ten days you produce this PCB, you use 6 of the just completed units to satisfy immediate demand and the remaining 14 units go into inventory. Since we do this for ten straight days, our maximum inventory is 140 units (14 units per day times 10 days). As shown here, you can also use the equation.

• **Solution:**

$$I_{Max} = 200\left(1 - \frac{6}{20}\right) = 140 \text{ units}$$

The production rate must always be greater than the demand rate. Otherwise, a company could never produce enough to satisfy demand and no inventory would be generated. Using the chocolate-chip cookie scenario as an example: it is impossible to eat more than twelve cookies after the batch is baked, because no matter how much we might *want* to eat more than twelve, we must wait for the next batch to be completed.

Making cookies!

Will & Deni McIntyre/Stone/Getty Images, Inc.

Although the formula identifies *d* as daily demand and *p* as daily production, we can use other time frames for these variables. We can use hourly demand and hourly production, weekly demand and weekly production, monthly demand and monthly production, quarterly demand and quarterly production, or even annual demand and annual production. The important thing to remember is that the time frame must be the same for both demand and production. That way, the ratio always remains the same.

EXAMPLE 12.8

Calculating Ratios

Calculate the ratio of *d/p* using daily, weekly, and annual demand. Annual demand is 10,000 units and annual production is 25,000 units. The company operates fifty weeks per year, five days per week.

• **Before You Begin:** This example is to show you that the most important issue in calculating ratios of demand/production is to use the same time frame. The ratio remains constant whether we use daily demand/daily production, weekly demand/weekly production, or annual demand/annual production. Just make sure that both the demand and production rates are for the same time period

• **Solution:**

When using daily figures,

Average daily demand: *d* = 10,000 units/250 days = 40 units per day
Daily production: *p* = 25,000 units/250 = 100 units per day
Therefore, the ratio *d/p* = 40/100 or 0.4.

When using weekly figures,

Average weekly demand: *d* = 10,000 units/50 weeks = 200 units per week
Weekly production: *p* = 25,000 units/50 weeks = 500 units per week
Therefore, the ratio *d/p* = 200/500 or 0.4.

When using annual figures,

Average annual demand: *d* = 10,000 units
Annual production: *p* = 25,000 units
Therefore, the ratio *d/p* = 10,000/25,000 or 0.4.

Calculating EPQ The formula to calculate the economic production quantity is

$$Q = \sqrt{\frac{2DS}{H\left(1 - \frac{d}{p}\right)}}$$

where *D* = annual demand in units
S = setup or ordering cost
H = annual holding costs per unit
d = average daily demand rate
p = daily production rate

EXAMPLE 12.9

Calculating EPQ at Ashlee's Beach Chairs

Ashlee's Beach Chairs company produces upscale beach chairs. Annual demand for the chairs is estimated at 18,000 units. The frames are made in batches before the final assembly process. Ashlee's final assembly department needs frames at a rate of 1500 per month. Ashlee's frame department can produce 2500 frames per month. The setup cost is $800, and the annual holding cost is $18 per unit. The company operates twenty days per month. Lead time is five days. Determine the optimal order quantity, the total annual costs, and the reorder point.

- **Before You Begin:** To determine the optimal EPQ, use the formula

$$Q = \sqrt{\frac{2DS}{H\left(1 - \frac{d}{p}\right)}}$$

Remember that the demand and production rates used to calculate the ratio must be in the same time frame (daily, weekly, monthly, quarterly, or annually). To calculate the reorder point, use the formula $R = dL$. Don't forget to transform monthly demand into daily demand to find the reorder point. Reorder points should be found using the easiest numbers possible. For example, if lead time is given as three weeks, then you should find average weekly demand and multiply by the three weeks. If lead time is given in months, use average monthly demand.

- **Solution:**
To determine the total cost, you must calculate the maximum inventory level. To do this you must first calculate the economic production quantity:

$$Q = \sqrt{\frac{2 \times 18,000 \times \$800}{\$18\left(1 - \frac{1500}{2500}\right)}} = 2000 \text{ units}$$

Therefore, I_{Max} is

$$I_{\text{Max}} = 2000\left(1 - \frac{1500}{2500}\right) = 800 \text{ units}$$

and the total annual cost is

$$TC = \left(\frac{18,000}{2000}\$800\right) + \left(\frac{800}{2}\$18\right)$$

$$= \$7200 + \$7200$$

$$= \$14,400$$

Note that the ordering cost equals the annual holding cost. The reorder point is calculated as $R = 75 \text{ units} \times 5 \text{ days} = 375 \text{ units}$. Therefore, the inventory policy is to order a quantity of 2000 frames when the inventory reaches 375 units. The total annual cost (excluding item cost) associated with this policy is $14,400.

Compare this policy to Ashlee's current inventory policy of producing in quantities of 1500 units. First, determine the maximum inventory level.

$$I_{\text{Max}} = 1500\left(1 - \frac{1500}{2500}\right) = 600 \text{ units}$$

Therefore, total cost is

$$TC = \left(\frac{18,000}{1500}\$800\right) + \left(\frac{600}{2}\$18\right) = \$15,000$$

The extra cost or penalty cost associated with Ashlee's current policy is $600 ($15,000 − $14,400).

When you use the EOQ and/or the EPQ model, you need to know when the inventory level reaches the reorder point. A **perpetual inventory record** provides an up-to-date inventory balance by recording all inventory transactions—items received into inventory or items disbursed from inventory—as they happen.

An alternative to using perpetual inventory records is the **two-bin system**. In a two-bin system, a quantity equal to demand during replenishment time is held back, often in a second bin. When stock available is depleted, the held-back quantity is made available for use and a replenishment order is placed. Deciding on the right quantity replenishment order is complicated when quantity discounts are available. Let's extend the basic EOQ model to consider quantity discounts.

▶ **Perpetual inventory record**
Provides an up-to-date inventory balance.

▶ **Two-bin system**
Splits replenishment orders into two bins, placing one bin in reserve. When the initial bin is empty, the contents of the second bin are used and a replenishment order is placed.

Quantity Discount Model

The basic EOQ model assumes that no quantity discounts are available. In real life, however, **quantity discounts** are often available, so we need to modify the basic model for these situations. Quantity discounts are price incentives to encourage a company to buy in larger quantities. For example, a supplier charges your company $7.50 per pound if your company's order is less than 500 pounds. If your order is for 500 to 999 pounds, the price per pound is $6.90. On orders of 1000 pounds or more, the supplier charges $6.20 per pound.

▶ **Quantity discount model**
Modifies the EOQ process to consider cases where quantity discounts are available.

Whenever the price per unit is not fixed but varies based on the size of your order, the total annual cost formula for any inventory policy used must include the cost of material, as shown next.

$$TC = \left(\frac{D}{Q}S\right) + \left(\frac{Q}{2}H\right) + CD$$

where D = annual demand in units
Q = order quantity in units
S = ordering or setup cost
H = annual holding cost
C = unit price

EXAMPLE 12.10

Annual Total Costs at Jeannette's Steak House

Jeannette's Steak House currently orders 200 pounds of single-portion filet mignons at a time (a two-week supply). The annual demand for the filets is 5200 pounds. The ordering cost is estimated at $50. The annual holding cost is 30 percent of the unit price. Jeannette pays $7.50 per pound for the steaks. Therefore, the annual holding cost rate is $2.25 ($7.50 × 0.30). What are the annual total costs?

• **Before You Begin:** In this problem we must include the cost of the steaks as we consider quantity discounts. It is never wrong to include the material costs in the total cost calculation, but we usually omit the material cost unless different replenishment policies result in different material costs. If the material cost is not affected by the policy, then it is a constant and does not need to be included.

• **Solution:**

$$TC = \left(\frac{5200}{200}\$50\right) + \left(\frac{200}{2}\$2.25\right) + (\$7.50 \times 5200) = \$40,525$$

FIGURE 12-5

Quality discount total cost
curves

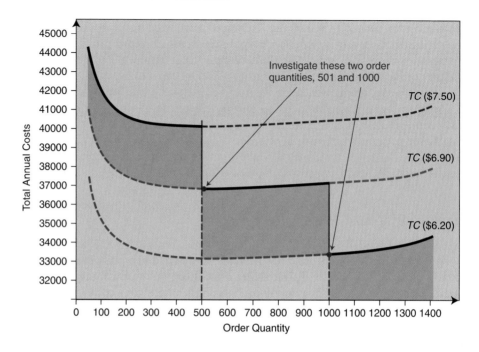

Jeannette's supplier has offered the following price incentives. If Jeannette places an order for 500 or more pounds, the cost per pound is $6.90. For orders of 1000 pounds or more, the supplier will charge Jeannette $6.20 per pound. For orders of less than 500 pounds, Jeannette would continue to pay $7.50 per pound. Now there are three possible prices based on the size of the order. Let's look at how Jeannette can determine the best policy for her business.

Figure 12-5 shows the total annual cost curves for each of the three prices. You can see that the $7.50 price is only valid when the order quantity falls between 1 and 499 pounds; the $6.90 price per pound is only valid when the order quantity falls between 500 and 999 pounds; and the $6.20 price is valid for orders of 1000 or more pounds.

The Quantity Discount Procedure The first step is to calculate the order quantity using the basic EOQ model and the cheapest price available. In our example, Jeannette's cheapest price is $6.20 per pound. Therefore, the annual holding cost is $1.86 (that is, $6.20 × 0.30), and the EOQ is

$$Q = \sqrt{\frac{2 \times 5200 \times \$50}{\$1.86}} = 528.74 \text{ pounds}$$

Now determine whether the order quantity is feasible. If Jeannette orders this quantity, will she be charged the price used to calculate the EOQ? If Jeannette orders 528.74 pounds, the supplier will charge her $6.90 per pound rather than the $6.20 she used in calculating the order quantity. Therefore, this is an infeasible quantity. If it were feasible, we would be done calculating Jeannette's optimal inventory policy. Since the order quantity is infeasible, we calculate the order quantity using the next higher price, $6.90 per pound.

$$Q = \sqrt{\frac{2 \times 5200 \times \$50}{\$2.07}} = 501.20 \text{ pounds}$$

If Jeannette orders 501 pounds, the supplier charges her $6.90 per pound, which is the same as the price we used in calculating the order quantity. Therefore, this is a feasible order quantity. Once Jeannette finds the feasible quantity, she calculates the total annual costs for this order quantity.

$$TC = \left(\frac{5200}{501}\ \$50\right) + \left(\frac{501}{2}\ \$2.07\right) + (\$6.90 \times 5200) = \$36{,}917.50$$

Jeannette compares the total annual cost of this feasible order quantity with the total annual cost of the minimum order quantities necessary to qualify for any prices lower than the price at which she found the feasible solution. For example, to qualify for a price of $6.20 per pound, Jeannette must order a minimum of 1000 pounds at a time. The total annual cost of ordering 1000 pounds at a time is

$$TC = \left(\frac{5200}{1000}\ \$50\right) + \left(\frac{1000}{2}\ \$1.86\right) + (\$6.20 \times 5200) = \$33{,}430.00$$

In this case, Jeannette's annual cost is less if she orders 1000 pounds at a time rather than the EOQ quantity of 501 pounds at a time. The optimal inventory policy for Jeannette is to order 1000 pounds at a time.

Note that this assumes Jeannette has adequate storage capacity and can accommodate 1000 pounds at a time. The quantity discount procedure when holding costs are given as a percentage of the unit price is summarized in Table 12-5.

At times, the holding cost can remain constant regardless of the price paid for an item. When the holding cost is a constant dollar amount, there is a common Q. The Q calculated will only be feasible in one of the price ranges. If the Q is in the least expensive price range, that is the optimal order quantity. If the Q is in a higher price range, total costs must be calculated and compared to the total costs of all lower price breaks.

TABLE 12-5

Quantity Discount Procedure

1. Calculate the order quantity using the basic EOQ model and the cheapest price possible.
2. Determine whether the order quantity is feasible. That is, if we order this quantity will the supplier charge us the price we used to determine our order quantity? If this is a feasible order quantity, you are done. Otherwise, go to Step 3.
3. If the EOQ quantity found in Step 1 was infeasible, calculate the EOQ for the next higher price.
4. Check again to determine if this quantity is feasible. If it is not feasible, repeat Step 3. If it is feasible, move on to Step 5.
5. Calculate the total annual costs associated with your feasible order quantity. You must include ordering, holding, and material costs.
6. Calculate the total annual costs associated with buying the minimum quantity required to qualify for any prices that are lower than the price at which the feasible solution was found.
7. Compare the total annual costs of buying these minimum quantities to receive the cheaper price against the cost of the feasible Q.
8. Recommend whichever order policy has the lowest total annual cost.

EXAMPLE 12.11

Quantity Discounts with Constant Holding Costs at Valley Grand Health Clinic (VGHC)

VGHC operates its own laboratory on-site. The lab maintains an inventory of test kits for a variety of procedures. VGHC uses 780 A1C kits each year. Ordering costs are $15 and holding costs are $3 per kit per year. The new price list indicates that orders of fewer than 73 kits will cost $60 per kit, 73 through 144 kits will cost $56 per kit, and orders of more than 144 kits will cost $53 per kit. Determine the optimal order quantity and the total cost.

- **Before You Begin:** When you have constant holding costs, you only need to calculate a single Q value using the basic EOQ formula:

$$Q = \sqrt{\frac{2DS}{H}}$$

Check to see what price you must pay per unit if this order quantity is used. If it is the cheapest possible price, this is your optimal replenishment order quantity. If cheaper prices are available, calculate the total annual cost if you buy just enough to qualify for the cheaper price. Do this for all prices cheaper than the price you qualified for with the EOQ. Select the policy that has the lowest total costs, making sure that material costs were included.

- **Solution:**

The first step is to calculate the common Q.

$$Q = \sqrt{\frac{2 \times 780 \times \$15}{\$3}} = 88.3, \text{ or } 89 \text{ kits}$$

This quantity qualifies for a price of $56 per kit. Since it is not the lowest possible price, we calculate the total cost at this price and compare it to the total cost at any lower price breaks. The total cost when ordering 89 kits is

$$TC = \left(\frac{780}{89}\$15\right) + \left(\frac{89}{2}\$3\right) + (\$56 \times 780) = \$43,944.96$$

Total cost when ordering 145 kits is

$$TC = \left(\frac{780}{145}\$15\right) + \left(\frac{145}{2}\$3\right) + (\$53 \times 780) = \$41,638.19$$

Therefore, the VGHC should order 145 kits at a time since it will save $2306.77 each year ($43,944.96 − $41,638.19). The total annual cost curves are shown in Figure 12-6.

FIGURE 12-6

Quantity discount total annual cost with constant holding cost

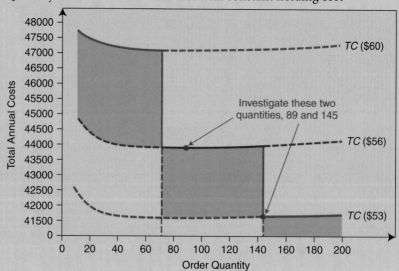

WHY COMPANIES DON'T ALWAYS USE THE OPTIMAL ORDER QUANTITY

Even though it can be shown mathematically that not using the optimal EOQ quantity results in additional costs for a company, it is not unusual for companies to order a quantity other than the EOQ.

Some companies do not have known uniform demand. In some cases, companies experience lumpy demand (that is, some periods with significant demand and other periods with no demand). This violates one of the underlying assumptions of the EOQ model. In such cases, it is better to use a period-order quantity (discussed later in this chapter).

Some suppliers have a minimum order quantity that they will sell to a company. This minimum order quantity can be based on how the item is packaged. If the item comes in boxes of 1000, the minimum order for the item becomes 1000 pieces. If you need more than one box, you must order additional boxes. To obtain 4000 pieces, you would order four boxes. Some suppliers are willing to break boxes, but many are not. At other times, the minimum order quantity can be based on how the material is shipped. The minimum order quantity may be what is needed to qualify for a full truckload or full railcar load rate. There are also times when a company may not have sufficient storage capacity to accommodate a large order quantity. When that is the case, companies must order less than the EOQ.

Remember that the EOQ must be checked when quantity discounts are available. The basic model did not allow for discounts, so you must confirm what the optimal order policy should be.

The EOQ policy always provides a benchmark to compare against other policies. It is not wrong not to use the EOQ, but it should be more expensive. You need to justify the additional expenses incurred.

DETERMINING SAFETY STOCK LEVELS

Companies are vulnerable to shortages during replenishment lead times, so one function of inventory is to provide safety stock as a cushion for satisfying unexpected customer demand. Remember that you typically place the replenishment order when the inventory level reaches the reorder point. Remember, too, that your company may experience a shortage between the time you place the replenishment order and the time you receive the items you ordered.

When we have no demand uncertainty, we set the reorder point to equal-to-average demand during lead time, or

$$R = dL$$

where R = reorder point in units
d = daily demand in units
L = lead time in days

Therefore, if $d = 20$ units and $L = 10$ days, the reorder point is 200 units. Since we know demand and lead time with certainty, the replenishment order arrives just as the on-hand inventory is depleted.

Suppose your kayak suppliers cannot always keep a firm delivery date because of fluctuation in materials availability at their end. As a result, uncertainty is a condition of your kayaking equipment operation. To support your company's customer service objectives, your policy is to carry safety stock. You add the amount of safety stock carried to the reorder point, and the reorder point becomes

$$R = dL + SS$$

where SS = safety stock in units

FIGURE 12-7

How safety stock changes the reorder point

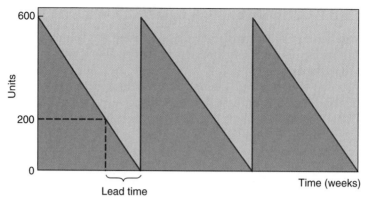

$Q = 600$ units, $R = 200$ units, no safety stock

If demand during lead time equals average demand, then replenishment arrives as on-hand inventory reaches safety stock level.

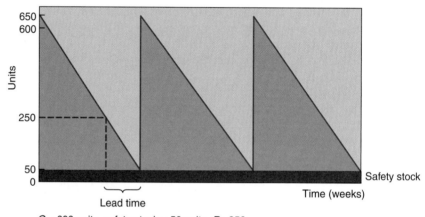

$Q = 600$ units, safety stock = 50 units, $R = 250$

For example, if $d = 20$ units, $L = 10$ days, and $SS = 50$ units, the reorder point is 250 units. When your company carries safety stock, it increases the reorder point, as shown in Figure 12-7. The replenishment order is now expected to arrive when the inventory on hand equals the safety stock level rather than zero. If demand is greater than expected, then your customers are satisfied from the safety stock. If demand is less than expected, the replacement inventory arrives before the on-hand inventory reaches the safety stock level. Figure 12-8 shows when the replenishment order will arrive.

How Much Safety Stock?

As safety stock increases, so does the customer service level, thus decreasing the chance of shortage. At the same time, however, holding safety stock requires additional inventory investment. Thus it is important to limit the amount of safety stock your company holds.

▶ **Order-cycle service level**
The probability that demand during lead time will not exceed on-hand inventory.

Order-cycle service level is the probability that demand during lead time does not exceed on-hand inventory—that on-hand stock is adequate to meet demand. A service level of 95 percent implies that demand does not exceed supply 95 percent of the time. If your company places twenty orders annually, a 95 percent service level implies that demand will not exceed the on-hand quantity in nineteen of the twenty replenishment lead times. We calculate the stockout risk as (1 − the order-cycle service level), or 5 percent in the preceding example.

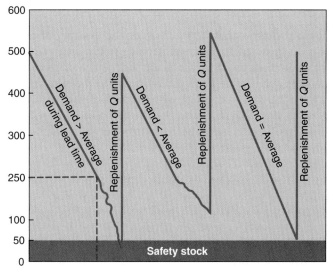

FIGURE 12-8

Demand uncertainty

$Q = 400$ units, $SS = 50$ units, $R = 250$ units

The amount of safety stock to hold depends on the variability of demand and lead time and the desired order-cycle service level. The safety stock needed to achieve a particular order-cycle service level increases as demand and lead time variability increases. The greater the uncertainty, the more safety stock is needed.

Let's look at a case in which an estimate of demand during lead time and its standard deviation are known. In this case, the formula for calculating safety stock is

$$SS = z\sigma_{dL}$$

where SS = safety stock in units
  z = number of standard deviations
  σ_{dL} = standard deviation of demand during lead time in units

Suppose that the owner of the campus bar, Nick's, has determined that demand for beer during lead time averages 5000 bottles. Nick, the owner, believes the demand during lead time can be described by a normal distribution with a mean of 5000 bottles and a standard deviation of 300 bottles. Nick is willing to accept a stockout risk of approximately 4 percent. Determine the appropriate z value to use. Calculate how much safety stock Nick should hold. Also determine the reorder point.

EXAMPLE 12.12

Nick's Safety Stock

• **Before You Begin:** To determine how much safety stock, use the formula $SS = z\sigma_{dL}$. You also need to use Appendix B to determine the appropriate z value. To determine the reorder point, use the formula $R = dL + SS$. Note that safety stock always results in a higher reorder point.

• **Solution:**
Go to Appendix B. To find the appropriate z value associated with the order-cycle service level $(1 - 0.04 = 0.9600)$, you must understand that the appendix shows only positive z values. A z value of 0 represents 0.5000. You need to find the z value that is the difference between the desired service level and a z value of 0 $(0.9600 - 0.5000 = 0.4600)$. Look for the entry closest to 0.4600. If you look at the entry associated with a z value of 1.75, you should see 0.4599, which is as close to 0.4600 as we can get. Therefore, the appropriate z value is 1.75. To determine the appropriate amount of safety stock, do the following calculation:

$$SS = 1.75 \times 300 \text{ bottles} = 525 \text{ bottles of safety stock}$$

The reorder point would now be

$$R = 5000 + 525 = 5525 \text{ bottles}$$

PERIODIC REVIEW SYSTEM

▶ **Periodic review system**
Requires periodic reviews of the on-hand quantity to determine the size of the replenishment order.

▶ **Target inventory level (*TI*)**
Used in determining order quantity in the periodic review system. Target inventory less on-hand inventory equals order quantity.

With the **periodic review system**, you determine the quantity of an item your company has on hand at specified, fixed-time intervals (such as every Friday or the last day of every month). You place an order for an amount (*Q*) equal to the **target inventory level (*TI*)**, minus the quantity on hand (OH), similar to the min-max system. The difference is that with the periodic review system, the time between orders is constant (such as every hour, every day, every week, or every month) with varying quantities ordered. The min-max system varies both the time between orders and the quantities ordered.

An advantage of the periodic review system is that inventory is counted only at specific time intervals. You do not need to monitor the inventory level between review periods. This system also makes sense when you order several different items from a supplier. For example, if your company buys ten different items from the same supplier, you can place one order for all ten items rather than ten individual orders, one for each item.

Potential disadvantages include the varying replenishment levels. First, since you must have sufficient space to store the largest possible order quantity, often you will have excess space when the replenishment orders are smaller. Second, because of varying quantities, you may not be able to qualify for specific quantity discounts.

One result from using the periodic review system is a larger average inventory level. Your company must carry enough inventory to protect against stockout for the replenishment lead time plus the review period. The two major decisions to be made when using the periodic review system concern the time between orders and the target inventory level.

The time between orders (TBO) may be selected for convenience reasons. That is, it may be easier for you to review your inventory at the end of each week and prepare your replenishment order then. An alternative is to base your TBO on the economic order quantity calculation. For example, if you determine that the EOQ = 75 units and that weekly demand is 25 units, it makes sense to place orders every three weeks. You simply divide the EOQ by the average weekly demand.

The target inventory (*TI*) level is calculated as:

$$TI = d(RP + L) + SS$$

where TI = target inventory level in units
d = average period demand in units (period can be day, week, month, etc.)
RP = review period (in days, weeks, or months)
L = lead time (in days, weeks, or months)
SS = safety stock in units

The safety stock is calculated as

$$SS = z\sigma_{RP+L}$$

where z = number of standard deviations
σ_{RP+L} = standard deviation of demand during review period and lead time and is calculated as

$$\sigma_{RP+L} = \sigma_t \sqrt{RP + L}$$

where σ_t = standard deviation of demand during interval t
RP = review period
L = lead time

To calculate the replenishment order quantity, use the following formula:

$$Q = TI - OH$$

where Q = replenishment order quantity
TI = target inventory level
OH = on-hand quantity

Note that when the lead time is greater than the review period, the on-hand quantity must include any on-order amounts.

Gray's Pharmacy uses a periodic review inventory system. Every Friday, the pharmacist reviews her inventory and determines the size of the replenishment order. For example, she knows that demand for 500 mg metformin tablets, a drug for diabetics, is normally distributed with a mean of 6000 tablets each week with a standard deviation of 500 tablets per week. Lead time is three weeks. The desired cycle-service level is 95 percent. There are currently no outstanding orders.

(a) Calculate the required safety stock.
(b) Calculate the target inventory level.
(c) If, when she reviews her inventory of metformin, the pharmacist finds that she currently has 19,000 tablets, calculate the appropriate replenishment order quantity.

EXAMPLE 12.13

Using the Periodic Review System

• **Before You Begin:** For this problem, you must determine the target inventory level and make a decision as to the replenishment quantity to order. To calculate the target inventory, find the appropriate safety stock level. Use the formula $SS = z\sigma_{RP+L}$. Calculate the target inventory as $TI = d(RP + L + SS)$. After determining the target inventory, calculate the appropriate order size as $Q = TI - OH$.

• **Solution:**
(a) Go to Appendix B, the area under the standardized normal curve, and look for the z value that equates to 95 percent of the area under the curve. Since the appendix only uses positive z values, and they start at 0.50, we need to look for a z value that matches the difference between the desired cycle-service level (0.95) and the starting point of 0.50. So we are looking for a value close to 0.4500. In the appendix we can see that $z = 1.64$ has a value of 0.4495 while $z = 1.65$ has a value of 0.4505. By interpolation, a $z = 1.645$ has a value of exactly 0.4500. Therefore, our desired z value is 1.645.

$$SS = 1.645(\sigma_t \sqrt{RP + L})$$
$$SS = 1.645(500\sqrt{1 + 3}) = 1645 \text{ tablets}$$

(b) The target inventory level is

$$TI = 6000(1 + 3) + 1645 = 25,645 \text{ units}$$

(c) If the current inventory of metformin is 19,000 tablets, the pharmacist should order 6645 tablets, or $Q = 25,645 - 19,000$ tablets.

Comparison of Continuous Review Systems and Periodic Review Systems

The advantages of continuous review systems (CRS) are the disadvantages of periodic review systems (PRS). For instance, a CRS has no set review periods. This lack of specified review periods means that less inventory is needed to protect against stockouts.

With a PRS, enough inventory must be carried to cover both the lead time and the review period. Since a CRS has no review period, it has a smaller average inventory investment. On the other hand, a CRS means significantly more work because the inventory balances are updated after each transaction rather than periodically. A PRS means less work because inventory balances are only reviewed and updated periodically. So a PRS makes it easier to consolidate orders from a single supplier because you can review all of those items at the same time interval, whereas the CRS is designed to handle items individually.

In general, companies use CRS for items that are expensive and/or critical to the company because CRS more closely monitors these items and reduces inventory investment. Companies typically use both systems depending on the value and criticality of the items to be monitored.

THE SINGLE-PERIOD INVENTORY MODEL

Some finished goods inventories have very short selling seasons. Items such as holiday decorations, Christmas trees, long-stemmed red roses, newspapers, and magazines are good examples. These products typically have a high value for a relatively short period; then the value diminishes dramatically to either zero or some minimum salvage value. For example, week-old newspapers are inexpensive compared to newspapers offering fresh news. The question is how many of these products you should order to maximize your expected profit.

▶ **Single-period model**
Designed for use with products that are highly perishable.

The **single-period model** is designed for products that share the following characteristics:

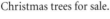

- They are sold at their regular price only during a single time period.
- Demand for these products is highly variable but follows a known probability distribution.
- Salvage value of these products is less than its original cost, so you lose money when they are sold for their salvage value.

The objective is to balance the gross profit generated by the sale of a unit with the cost incurred for each unit that is not sold until after the primary selling period has elapsed. When demand follows a discrete probability distribution, we can solve the problem using an expected value matrix.

Christmas trees for sale.

©AP/Wide World Photos

EXAMPLE 12.14

**Walk for
Diabetes**

Rick Jones is chairman of this year's Walk for Diabetes event. Each year, the organizers of the event typically have commemorative T-shirts available for purchase by the entrants in the walk. Rick needs to order the shirts well in advance of the actual event. He must place his order in multiples of 10 (60, 70, 80, etc.). Based on past walks, the organizers have determined that the probability of selling different quantities of T-shirts in a given year is as follows:

Demand (shirts)	Probability
80	.20
90	.25
100	.30
110	.15
120	.10

Rick plans to sell the T-shirts for $20 each. He pays his supplier $8 for each shirt and can sell any unsold shirts for rags at $2 each. Determine how many T-shirts Rick should order to maximize his expected profits.

• **Before You Begin:** In this problem, you need to determine how many T-shirts to order for the event. If you order too many, you will have leftover shirts with little value. If you don't order enough, you forgo achieving the profit associated with each shirt plus creating some customers ill will. The easiest way to approach this decision is to develop a payoff table to calculate expected profit with each possible order quantity.

• **Solution:**
Based on the information provided, develop a payoff table to determine expected profit with each possible order quantity. Calculate net profit for each combination of order quantity and demand as shown next.

Payoff Table

Probability of occurrence	.20	.25	.30	.15	.10	
Customer demand (shirts)	80	90	100	110	120	
Number of Shirts Ordered						**Expected Profit**
80	$960	$ 960	$ 960	$ 960	$ 960	$ 960
90	$900	$1080	$1080	$1080	$1080	$1044
100	$840	$1020	$1200	$1200	$1200	$1083
110	$780	$ 960	$1140	$1320	$1320	$1068
120	$720	$ 900	$1080	$1260	$1440	$1026

The numbers in the payoff table are calculated based on what happened. The three possible outcomes are: (1) the number of shirts ordered equals the number of shirts demanded, (2) the number of shirts ordered is greater than the number of shirts demanded, and (3) the number of shirts ordered is less than the number of shirts demanded. To find the payoff when supply equals demand,

$$Payoff = demand(selling\ price - unit\ cost)$$

In our example, look at what happens when 100 T-shirts are bought and 100 T-shirts are sold.

$$Payoff = 100(\$20 - \$8) = \$1200$$

When the number of shirts ordered exceeds demand, the payoff is calculated as

Payoff = (number of items demanded) × (selling price − item cost)
− ((items ordered − items demanded) × (item cost − item salvage value))

If 100 T-shirts are ordered and demand is for only 80 shirts, the payoff is

Payoff = 80($20 − $8) − ((100 − 80) × ($8 − $2)) = $840

When the number of shirts ordered is less than demand, the payoff is calculated as

Payoff = number of items ordered × (selling price − item cost)

Returning to the example, determine the payoff when 100 T-shirts are ordered but 120 shirts are demanded.

Payoff = 100($20 − $8) = $1200

After we calculate the payoffs for each combination, we can determine the expected profit for each order quantity. We do this by multiplying the payoff for an order quantity by the probability for each level of demand. For example, we calculate the payoff for ordering 100 shirts, $1083, as

($840 × .20) + ($1020 × .25) + ($1200 × .30) + ($1200 × .15) + ($1200 × .10)

Once we generate the expected profit for each of the possible order quantities, we select the order quantity with the highest expected profit. In our case, Rick should order 100 shirts since doing so has an expected profit of $1083.

ABC INVENTORY CLASSIFICATION

▶ **Pareto's law**
Implies that about 20 percent of the inventory items will account for about 80 percent of the inventory value.

All items in a company's inventory are not equal and do not need the same level of control. Fortunately, we can apply **Pareto's law** to determine the level of control needed for individual items. Pareto's law implies that roughly 10 percent to 20 percent of a company's inventory items accounts for approximately 60 to 80 percent of its inventory costs. These relatively few high-dollar-volume items are classified as A items. Moderate-dollar-volume items, roughly 30 percent of the items, account for about 25 to 35 percent of the company's inventory investment. These are classified as B items. Low-dollar-volume items, about 50 to 60 percent of the items, represent only 5 to 15 percent of the company's inventory investment and are classified as C items. These percentages are not absolute and are used only as guidelines to determine an item's **ABC classification**.

▶ **ABC classification**
A method for determining level of control and frequency of review of inventory items.

Procedure for an ABC Inventory Analysis

The first step for an ABC inventory analysis is to determine the annual usage for each item. We calculate the total annual dollar volume by multiplying the annual usage by the item cost. We then rank items in descending order based on total dollar volume and calculate the total inventory investment.

1. Calculate the annual dollar usage for each item.
2. List the items in descending order based on annual dollar usage.
3. Calculate the cumulative annual dollar volume.
4. Classify the items into groups.

AAU is considering doing an ABC analysis of its entire inventory but has decided to test the technique on a small sample of fifteen of its SKUs. The annual usage and unit cost for these items are shown in the table.

EXAMPLE 12.15

ABC Analysis at Auto Accessories Unlimited (AAU)

(a) Calculate the annual dollar volume for each item.
(b) List the items in descending order based on annual dollar usage.
(c) Calculate the cumulative annual dollar volume.
(d) Group the items into classes.

ABC Problem Data

Item	Unit $ Value	Annual Usage (in units)
101	12.00	80
102	50.00	10
103	15.00	50
104	50.00	40
105	40.00	80
106	75.00	220
107	4.00	250
108	1.50	400
109	2.00	250
110	25.00	500
111	5.00	450
112	7.50	80
113	3.50	250
114	1.00	1200
115	15.00	300

• **Before You Begin:** To do an ABC analysis, you need to know the annual usage and the value of each item. That information is provided for you in the problem data. Multiply the unit value by the annual usage of the item to determine the annual dollar volume for each item. Now list the items in descending order based on annual dollar usage. You can now calculate the percentage of the total inventory value each part represents. This allows you to classify the items into groups.

• **Solution:**

(a)

ABC Annual Usage Values

Item	Unit $ Value	Annual Usage (in units)	Annual Usage ($)
101	12.00	80	960
102	50.00	10	500
103	15.00	50	750
104	50.00	40	2000
105	40.00	80	3200
106	75.00	220	16,500
107	4.00	250	1000
108	1.50	400	600
109	2.00	250	500
110	25.00	500	12,500
111	5.00	450	2250
112	7.50	80	600
113	3.50	250	875
114	1.00	1200	1200
115	15.00	300	4500
		Total	$47,935

(b, c, and d)

		ABC Solution		
Item	Annual Usage ($)	Percentage of Total Dollars	Cumulative Percentage of Total Dollars	Item Classification
106	16,500	34.4	34.4	A
110	12,500	26.1	60.5	A
115	4,500	9.4	69.9	B
105	3,200	6.7	76.6	B
111	2,250	4.7	81.3	B
104	2,000	4.2	85.5	B
114	1,200	2.5	88.0	C
107	1,000	2.1	90.1	C
101	960	2.0	92.1	C
113	875	1.8	93.9	C
103	750	1.6	95.5	C
108	600	1.3	96.8	C
112	600	1.3	98.1	C
102	500	1.0	99.1	C
109	500	1.0	100.1*	C
Total	**$47,935**			

*Total exceeds 100% due to rounding.

Remember that these are not absolute rules for classifying items. Your company wants to group their more valuable items together to make sure that they get the most control.

Figure 12-9 graphically depicts the results of the ABC classification. The A items, 106 and 110, combine for 60.5 percent of the total dollar value in inventory and approximately 13.3 percent of the items in inventory. The B items, 115, 105, 111, and 104, account for 25 percent of the total dollar value and 26.7 percent of the items. The C items make up the last 14.5 percent of the total dollar value and 60 percent of the items.

FIGURE 12-9

ABC classification of materials

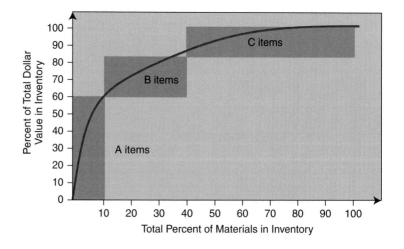

Inventory Control Using ABC Classification

By classifying items into A, B, and C categories, we can determine the level of inventory control. For example, A items need tight control, accurate inventory records, and frequent review. B items need normal control, good inventory records, and normal review. C items need the simplest control—possibly a two-bin system or a periodic review system with infrequent reviews. For C items, companies should order large quantities and carry safety stock.

JUSTIFYING SMALLER ORDER QUANTITIES

One of the principles of the just-in-time philosophy, discussed in Chapter 7, is to reduce order quantities ideally down to an order size of one unit. Smaller orders improve customer responsiveness, reduce cycle inventory, reduce work-in-process (WIP) inventory, and reduce inventories of raw materials and purchased components. Since many good things happen with smaller order quantities, we need to understand how companies economically reduce their order quantities.

LINKS TO PRACTICE

Kenworth Trucks
www.kenworth.com

Kenworth Trucks, a manufacturer of elite custom-built trucks, leads the industry in operations due largely to the just-in-time effect. Turning out over thirty-five trucks a day, Kenworth has been able to cut production time from the industry norm of six to eight weeks down to a mere three weeks. Such an outstanding feat is the result of the implementation of several cutting-edge ideas. Most importantly, there is the use of electronic transmission, which allows the plant to receive specifications as soon as a buyer has placed an order and which immediately involves parts suppliers in the details of the order. This synchronization results in supplies going almost directly to the assembly line. With such a fine-tuned operation, it is no wonder Kenworth Trucks is known as the premier of its industry!

Let's use the economic production quantity model to illustrate how companies justify smaller lot sizes.

Understanding the EPQ Factors

Looking at the EPQ formulation, we can see that there are three variables that influence the size of the optimal order quantity. The demand, the setup cost, and holding cost are the variables used.

$$Q = \sqrt{\frac{2DS}{H\left(1 - \dfrac{d}{p}\right)}}$$

where, D = annual demand
S = setup cost
H = annual holding cost per unit
d = average daily demand
p = average daily production

To decrease the optimal order quantity, we must reduce the product of the terms under the square root. We can reduce the numerator or increase the denominator. It doesn't make sense for a company to want to increase its holding costs, so we eliminate the idea of increasing the denominator. To reduce the numerator, we can reduce either the annual demand or the setup cost. Most companies are not trying to reduce their annual demand, so we have only one variable left to use: setup cost.

Let's look at an example to see what happens when setup cost is reduced. The Gamma Toy Company has an annual demand of 10,000 units for one of its toys. The daily demand is 50 units. The daily production rate is 75 units. Annual holding cost per unit per period is $6. Setup cost is estimated to be $100. Using these values, the economic production quantity is 1000 units, as shown.

$$Q = \sqrt{\frac{2(10,000)100}{6\left(1 - \frac{50}{75}\right)}} = 1000 \text{ units}$$

Now let's look at what happens if we reduce the setup cost from $100 down to $25. Using the new setup cost, the economic production quantity is 500 units, as shown.

$$Q = \sqrt{\frac{2(10,000)25}{H\left(1 - \frac{50}{75}\right)}} = 500 \text{ units}$$

Let's compare the total annual costs of these two different lot sizes. When $Q = 1000$ units, the total annual cost is

$$TC = \frac{10,000}{1000} \times 100 + \left(\frac{(1000)\left(1 - \frac{50}{75}\right)(6)}{2}\right) = \$2000$$

as opposed to a total cost of $1000 when using $Q = 500$ units.

$$TC = \frac{10,000}{500} \times 25 + \left(\frac{(500)\left(1 - \frac{50}{75}\right)(6)}{2}\right) = \$1000$$

You can see that reducing the setup cost allows us to economically decrease order quantity. If a company fails to reduce its setup costs and just starts producing in smaller order quantities, it will face higher total annual inventory costs.

INVENTORY RECORD ACCURACY

For effective inventory use, the inventory records must accurately reflect the quantity of materials available. Inaccurate inventory records can result in lost sales (finished good not available at time of sale), disrupted operations (not enough of a component or raw material to complete a job), poor customer service (late deliveries to customers), lower productivity (additional setups to complete a job), poor material planning (the inventory records are critical in determining MRP quantities), and excessive expediting (trying to obtain necessary items in less than normal lead time).

One exceptionally productive approach to inventory management is the automated inventory tracking system used by the very successful Cisco Systems—a world leader in providing networking solutions for all types of businesses. This tracking system forms an intricate network of suppliers, manufacturers, and customers and provides for real-time transactions. When a customer places an order via the Internet, suppliers can instantaneously see what parts are needed and can quickly respond by shipping the needed parts and then restocking. Such a system provides accurate, timely information, which helps both Cisco and suppliers to schedule, budget, and forecast. Since most of Cisco's orders are transacted over the Web, Cisco is able to save millions of dollars annually.

©AP/Wide World Photos

Inventory record errors occur because of unauthorized withdrawals of material, unsecured stockrooms, inaccurate paperwork, and/or human errors. Since an accurate database is needed to successfully use the information systems, it is important to detect errors in the inventory records. Two methods are available for checking inventory record accuracy: periodically counting all of the items (typically annually) and cyclically counting specified items (typically daily).

Periodic counting satisfies auditors that the inventory records accurately reflect the value of the inventory on hand. For material planners, the physical inventory is an opportunity to correct errors. The four steps in taking a physical inventory are

▶ **Periodic counting**
A physical inventory is taken periodically, usually annually.

1. Count the quantity of the item and record the count on a ticket attached to the item.
2. Verify by recounting.
3. After verification, collect the tickets.
4. Reconcile inventory records with actual counts. For major discrepancies, investigate further. For minor discrepancies, adjust the inventory records.

Taking physical inventories does not always improve inventory record accuracy. In many cases, companies close down manufacturing to take the physical inventory; the job is often rushed and is typically done by employees not trained for checking inventory. In some cases, inventory record errors are increased rather than reduced. The other alternative method is cycle counting.

Cycle counting is a method of counting inventory throughout the year. This is a series of mini-physical inventories done daily of some prespecified items. The frequency of counting a particular item depends on the importance and value of the item. Typically, A items are counted most frequently.

▶ **Cycle counting**
Prespecified items are counted daily.

The advantages of cycle counting are

- Timely detection and correction of inventory record problems;
- Elimination of lost production time since the company does not need to shut down operations;
- The use of employees dedicated to cycle counting.

Scheduling individual item counts can be done in several ways. An item can be counted just before a replenishment order is placed. At this time, the planner has an accurate count of the item on hand and can determine whether a replenishment order is needed. The quantity to be counted also is relatively low. A planner also can choose to count when new orders arrive. This way, the inventory is at its lowest level. Remember that most replenishment orders arrive just as the on-hand inventory is running out. Another possibility is to schedule a count after a certain number of transactions have occurred. For example, a planner can request a physical count after every twenty transactions involving a particular item. Since errors typically occur during transactions, the greater the number of transactions, the more likely an error will be introduced. One other possibility is to do a count whenever an error is detected. This allows for corrective action to be taken immediately. Regardless of the method, the intent is to improve inventory record accuracy.

▶ **Vendor-managed inventory**
The supplier maintains an inventory at the customer's facility.

In some cases, companies have shifted the burden of inventory accuracy and replenishment decisions to their vendor. **Vendor-managed inventory (VMI)** requires the vendor to maintain an inventory of certain items at the customer's facility. The supplier still owns the inventory until the customer actually withdraws it for use. At that time, the customer pays for the items. The customer does not have to order any of the inventory, as the supplier is responsible for maintaining an adequate supply. Companies use this approach most frequently with lower-level C items that have a relatively standard design.

INVENTORY MANAGEMENT WITHIN OM: HOW IT ALL FITS TOGETHER

Inventory management provides the materials and supplies needed to support actual manufacturing or service operations. A product cannot be built unless the required material is available. Inventory replenishment policies guide the master production scheduler when determining which jobs and what quantity should be scheduled (Chapter 13). The master production schedule inserted into the material requirements planning (MRP) system generates the replenishment orders. This output is used to guide purchasing in terms of the frequency and size of orders. Too much inventory is costly to the organization, yet too little can create major inefficiencies.

Inventory record accuracy is especially critical for MRP users. MRP relies on inventory records to process material requirements, so inaccurate records make the MRP output worthless. This, in turn, can cause manufacturing to shut down and/or miss a deadline.

Inventory management policies also affect the layout of the facility. A policy of small lot sizes and frequent shipments reduces the space needed to store materials (Chapter 7). Point-of-delivery placement of inventory affects the size of work centers. Inventory management also affects throughput time. As a facility increases its work-in-process, throughput times increase. Longer throughput times reduce an organization's ability to respond quickly to changing customer demands (Chapter 4).

Good inventory management assures continuous supply and minimizes inventory investment while achieving customer service objectives.

INVENTORY MANAGEMENT ACROSS THE ORGANIZATION

Inventory management policies affect functional areas throughout a company. Let's consider why individual functional areas are concerned with inventory management policies.

Accounting is concerned because of the cost implications of inventory, such as the holding costs incurred, the capital needed to invest in inventory, and projected cash flow budgets. Accounting is concerned with all types of inventory.

Marketing is concerned because stocking decisions affect the level of customer service provided. Marketing's primary focus is finished goods inventory, where the goods are held within the distribution system, the response time to satisfy customers, and safety stock levels.

Information systems is involved because a system to track and control inventories is needed, especially when perpetual inventory records are used. Given the large number of SKUs and a high volume of inventory transactions, manual processing is impractical for most companies, so a computerized information system is essential.

Purchasing's workload is directly affected by inventory policies. Policies regarding order frequency, order volume, acceptable suppliers, and inventory investment determine the number of purchases made. Purchasing is concerned primarily with buying raw materials, components, and subassemblies.

Manufacturing's cost efficiency can be affected by inventory decisions. If insufficient material is available, either because items are not ordered on time or not ordered in the right quantities, manufacturing efficiency decreases and unit costs increase. Unit costs can also increase when too much material is ordered or when it is ordered too soon.

As you can see, inventory decisions affect many functional areas in a company and may involve input from management in these areas. In addition, inventory decisions have a significant impact on the company's profitability.

Who makes aggregate inventory decisions? Typically, it is the materials manager. This person is evaluated based on customer service levels achieved and inventory turnover. For individual finished goods products, the master scheduler makes decisions about how much of a particular item to produce and how much to keep in inventory. A master scheduler is evaluated based on customer service levels and manufacturing efficiency.

For raw materials, components, and subassemblies, inventory planners, material planners, or controllers make decisions about when to place replenishment orders, either for in-house manufacturing or for external purchasing. Planners and controllers are typically evaluated according to customer service levels and inventory investment.

THE SUPPLY CHAIN LINK

Inventory management deals with economically based item-replenishment policies, safety stock levels, and the appropriate review system for use within a supply chain. Inventory flows from the suppliers to the manufacturers to the distributors. Inventory management provides an understanding of the total costs of inventory as well as the customer service ramifications of specific policies. By themselves, uncoordinated replenishment policies can cause the bullwhip effect (discussed in Chapter 4) in the supply chain. Vendor-managed inventory is one approach committed to improving service levels while reducing inventory investment in the supply chain. A policy of making demand information available (point-of-sales information) to all members of the supply chain reduces demand uncertainty and allows a company to achieve its desired customer service levels with a smaller inventory investment. Inventory management is a key component of effective supply chain performance.

Chapter Highlights

1 Raw materials, purchased components, work-in-process (WIP), finished goods, distribution inventory and maintenance, repair and operating supplies are all types of inventory. Inventories have several uses: anticipation inventory is built before it is needed; fluctuation stock provides a cushion against uncertain demand; cycle stock is a result of the company's ordering quantity; transportation inventory includes items in transit; speculative inventory is a buildup to protect against some future event; and MRO inventory supports daily operations.

2 The objectives of inventory management are to provide the desired level of customer service, to allow cost-efficient operations, and to minimize inventory investment. Customer service can be measured in several ways, including as a percentage of orders shipped on schedule, a percentage of line items shipped on schedule, a percentage of dollar volume shipped on schedule, or idle time due to material and component shortages. Cost-efficient operations are achieved by using inventory as buffer stocks, allowing a stable year-round workforce, and spreading the setup cost over a larger number of units.

3 Inventory investment is measured in inventory turnover and/or level of supply. Inventory performance is calculated as inventory turnover or weeks, days, or hours of supply.

4 Relevant inventory costs include item costs, holding costs, ordering costs, and shortage costs. Holding costs include capital costs, storage costs, and risk costs. Ordering costs are fixed costs for placing an order or performing a setup. Shortage costs include costs related to additional paperwork, additional shipping expense, and the intangible cost of lost customer goodwill.

5 Lot-for-lot, fixed-order quantity, min-max systems, order n periods, periodic review systems, EOQ models, quantity discount models, and single-period models can be used to determine order quantities.

6 Ordering decisions can be improved by analyzing total costs of an inventory policy. Total costs include ordering cost, holding cost, and material cost.

7 Practical considerations can cause a company to not use the optimal order quantity, that is, minimum order requirements.

8 Smaller lot sizes give a company flexibility and shorter response times. The key to reducing order quantities is to reduce ordering or setup costs.

9 Calculating the appropriate safety stock policy enables companies to satisfy their customer service objectives at minimum cost. The desired customer service level determines the appropriate z value.

10 Inventory decisions about perishable products (like newspapers) can be made using the single-period inventory model. The expected payoff is calculated to assist the quantity decision.

11 The ABC classification system allows a company to assign the appropriate level of control and frequency of review of an item based on its annual dollar volume.

12 Cycle counting is a method for maintaining accurate inventory records. Determining what and when to count are the major decisions.

Key Terms

raw materials 417
components 417
work-in-process (WIP) 418
finished goods 418
distribution inventory 418
anticipation inventory 418
fluctuation inventory 418
lot-size inventory 418
transportation inventory 418
speculative inventory 419
maintenance, repair, and operating
  inventory (MRO) 419
customer service 420
percentage of orders shipped
  on schedule 420
percentage of line items shipped
  on schedule 421
percentage of dollar volume shipped
  on schedule 421

setup cost 422
inventory turnover 422
weeks of supply 422
item cost 424
holding costs 424
capital cost 424
storage costs 425
risk costs 425
ordering costs 426
shortage costs 426
back order 426
lost sale 426
stock-keeping unit (SKU) 427
lot-for-lot 427
fixed-order quantity 427
min-max system 427
order n periods 428
economic order quantity model
  (EOQ) 428

continuous review systems 428
lead time 429
economic production quantity
  (EPQ) 433
perpetual inventory record 437
two-bin system 437
quantity discount model 437
order-cycle service level 442
periodic review system 444
target inventory level (TI) 444
single-period model 446
Pareto's law 448
ABC classification 448
periodic counting 453
cycle counting 453
vendor-managed inventory 454

Formula Review

Calculating average transportation inventory (*ATI*):

$$ATI = \frac{tD}{365}$$

where t = transit time in days and D = annual demand in units.

Calculating inventory turnover and periods of supply:

$$\text{Inventory turnover} = \frac{\text{annual cost of goods sold}}{\text{average inventory in dollars}}$$

$$\text{Weeks of supply} = \frac{\text{average inventory on hand in dollars}}{\text{average weekly usage in dollars}}$$

$$\text{Days of supply} = \frac{\text{average inventory on hand in dollars}}{\text{average daily usage in dollars}}$$

Calculating target inventory (*TI*):

$$TI = d(RP + L) + SS$$

where d = average daily demand, RP = review period in days, and SS = safety stock.

Calculating safety stock in a periodic review model:

$$SS = z\sigma_{RP+L}$$

Standard deviation of demand during review period and lead time:

$$\sigma_{RP+L} = \sigma_t\sqrt{RP + L}$$

Calculating reorder point without safety stock:

$$R = dL$$

where d = average daily demand and L = lead time in days.

Calculating the economic order quantity (EOQ):

$$Q = \sqrt{\frac{2DS}{H}}$$

where D = annual demand, S = ordering cost, and H = holding cost.

Calculating total costs:

$$TC = \left(\frac{D}{Q}S\right) + \left(\frac{Q}{2}H\right)$$

Calculating the economic production quantity (EPQ):

$$Q = \sqrt{\frac{2DS}{H\left(1 - \dfrac{d}{p}\right)}}$$

Calculating total costs:

$$TC = \left(\frac{D}{Q}S\right) + \left(\frac{I_{Max}}{2}H\right)$$

where I_{Max} is the maximum inventory level.

Calculating I_{Max}:

$$I_{Max} = Q\left(1 - \frac{d}{p}\right)$$

where d = daily demand and p = daily production rate.

Calculating total costs for quantity discount comparisons:

$$TC = \left(\frac{D}{Q}S\right) + \left(\frac{Q}{2}H\right) + CD$$

where C = price per unit.

Calculating amount of safety stock:

$$SS = z\sigma_{dL}$$

where SS = safety stock, z = number of standard deviations, and σ_{dL} = standard deviation of demand during lead time in units.

Solved Problems

 (See student companion site for Excel template.)

• Problem 1

Tacky Souvenirs sells lovely handmade tablecloths at its island store. These tablecloths cost Tacky $15 each. Customers want to buy the tablecloths at a rate of 240 per week. The company operates fifty-two weeks per year. Tacky, the owner, estimates his ordering cost at $50. Annual holding costs are 20 percent of the unit cost. Lead time is two weeks. Using the information given,

(a) Calculate the economic order quantity.
(b) Calculate the total annual costs using the EOQ.
(c) Determine the reorder point.

• *Before You Begin:*

To calculate the economic order quantity, you use the formula

$$Q = \sqrt{\frac{2DS}{H}}$$

Remember that the demand information and the holding cost must be for the same time frame. That is, if you use annual demand, you must use an annual holding cost. Once you have calculated the EOQ, you calculate total annual costs with the formula

$$TC = \left(\frac{D}{Q}S\right) + \left(\frac{Q}{2}H\right)$$

458 • CHAPTER 12   INDEPENDENT DEMAND INVENTORY MANAGEMENT

To find the reorder point, use the formula: $R = dL$. Remember that demand must be in the same time frame as is given for lead time. For example, if lead time is given as three weeks, then use weekly demand. If lead time is given in days, use daily demand.

• Solution

(a) First, calculate the annual demand and the annual holding cost.

$$\text{Annual demand} = (52 \text{ weeks} \times 240 \text{ units per week})$$
$$= 12{,}480 \text{ units}$$

$$\text{Annual holding cost} = (0.20 \times \$15)$$
$$= \$3.00 \text{ per unit per year}$$

Now calculate the economic order quantity as shown in the spreadsheet.

$$Q = \sqrt{\frac{2 \times 12480 \times \$50}{\$3}} = 644.98, \text{ or } 645 \text{ tablecloths}$$

Examine the spreadsheet to see how you can solve EOQ problems using a spreadsheet. Note that you can use weekly demand since the lead time is given in weekly increments. Just make sure that the average demand time frame matches the time frame used with lead time.

(b) The total costs are

$$TC = \left(\frac{12480}{645}\$50\right) + \left(\frac{645}{2}\$3\right) = \$1934.94$$

(c) The reorder point is

$$R = 240 \text{ units} \times 2 \text{ weeks} = 480 \text{ units}$$

	A	B	C
1			
2	**Tacky Souvenirs**		
3			
4	**Problem Inputs**		
5	Weekly Demand	240	
6	Operating Weeks per year	52	B7: =B5*B6
7	Annual Demand (units)	12480	
8			
9	Ordering Cost	$50.00	
10			
11	Annual Holding Cost (%)	20.0%	
12	Unit Cost	$15.00	B13: =B12*B11
13	Annual Holding Cost ($/unit)	$3.00	
14			
15	Lead Time (weeks)	2	
16			
17	**Calculations and Solution**		B18: =SQRT((2*B7*B9)/B13)
18	EOQ (exact calculation)	644.98062	B19: =ROUND(B18,0)
19	EOQ (rounded to nearest integer)	**645**	B20: =(B7/B19)*B9
20	Annual Ordering Costs	$967.44	B21: =(B19/2)*B13
21	Annual Holding Costs	$967.50	B22: =B20+B21
22	Total Annual Costs	**$1,934.94**	B23: =B5*B15
23	Reorder Point (units)	**480**	

• Problem 2

Jack's Packs manufactures backpacks made from microfabrics. The cutting department prepares the material for use by the backpack stitching department. The cutting department can cut enough material to make 200 backpacks per day. The backpack stitching department produces 90 backpacks per day. Annual demand for the product is 22,500 units. The company operates 250 days per year. Estimated setup cost is $60. Annual holding cost is $6 per backpack.

(a) Calculate the economic production quantity for the cutting department.

(b) Calculate the total annual costs for the EPQ.

• Before You Begin:

For this problem, calculate the EPQ. We use a modified version of the EOQ formula since we have relaxed the assumption regarding all of the items being delivered at one time. With the EPQ model, units are produced daily. Some are used immediately to satisfy demand while the other units are put into inventory. The appropriate formula is

$$Q = \sqrt{\frac{2DS}{H\left(1 - \frac{d}{p}\right)}}$$

Remember that the ratio d/p does not have to be daily demand divided by daily production. You need only use figures for the same time frame. The ratio of annual demand divided by annual production is equivalent to the daily demand divided by daily production. You also should check to be sure that the demand rate is smaller than the production rate. Otherwise, you can never produce enough to satisfy demand. When calculating total costs, make sure that you determine the maximum inventory level when assessing holding costs.

• Solution

(a) First, calculate the EPQ as follows:

$$Q = \sqrt{\frac{2 \times 22{,}500 \times \$60}{\$6\left(1 - \frac{90}{200}\right)}} = 904.53, \text{ or } 905 \text{ backpacks}$$

(b) To calculate total costs, determine the maximum inventory level as follows:

$$I_{\text{Max}} = 905\left(1 - \frac{90}{200}\right) = 497.75, \text{ or } 498 \text{ backpacks}$$

Now that you have determined the maximum inventory level, calculate total costs:

$$TC = \left(\frac{22{,}500}{905}\$60\right) + \left(\frac{498}{2}\$6\right) = \$2985.71$$

• Problem 3

Ye Olde Shoe Repaire has customers requesting leather soles throughout the year. The owner, Warren, buys these soles from The Leather Company (TLC) at a price of $8 per pair. In an effort to improve profitability by selling in greater quantities, the sales rep for TLC has made the following offer to Ye Olde Shoe Repaire: If Warren orders from 1 to 50 pairs at a time, the cost per pair is $8.00. If the order is between 51 and 100 pairs at a time, the cost is $7.60. On orders for more than 100 pairs at a time, the cost per pair is $7.40. The owner estimates annual demand to be 625 pairs of soles. Holding costs are 20 percent of unit price. The cost to place an order is $10. Determine the most cost-effective ordering policy for Ye Olde Shoe Repaire.

• Before You Begin:

This is a quantity discount problem with proportional holding costs. You begin by calculating the EOQ for the least expensive unit price. Check to see if this quantity is feasible. Feasibility occurs when you can order the EOQ quantity and pay the unit price that was used in your calculation. For example, if the EOQ turns out to be 92 pairs of leather soles and you used a unit price of $7.40 per pair, you need to check to see whether or not you will be charged $7.40 per pair if you place an order for 92 pairs. If the initial price assumption does not match what you would actually pay, then the quantity is infeasible. Once you find a feasible quantity, calculate the total annual costs for that policy, including the annual material costs. You must also calculate the total costs associated with ordering just enough units to qualify for any cheaper prices available. For example, if the feasible quantity occurs with a cost of $7.60 per pair and you know that if you buy 100 pairs at a time you qualify for a unit price of $7.40, you calculate the total annual cost assuming that you

would order just enough (100 pairs) to qualify for the lower unit price. You must do this for all prices lower than the price of the feasible EOQ. Your best policy is based on the total annual costs.

• Solution

(a) First, we need to calculate the EOQ at the lowest price offered. The annual holding cost is 20 percent of the unit cost, or $1.48—that is, $7.40 times 20 percent.

$$Q = \sqrt{\frac{2 \times 625 \times \$10}{\$1.48}} = 91.9, \text{ or } 92 \text{ pairs}$$

Since this order quantity does not match the unit price used to calculate the EOQ, this answer is infeasible. This means if we place an order for 92 pairs, we are charged $7.60 per pair rather than the $7.40 we used in calculating the EOQ.

(b) Since the first Q is infeasible, we calculate the EOQ for the next higher price. Make sure to calculate the new annual holding cost, 20 percent of $7.60, or $1.52.

$$Q = \sqrt{\frac{2 \times 625 \times \$10}{\$1.52}} = 90.68, \text{ or } 91 \text{ pairs}$$

If we place an order for 91 pairs, we will be charged $7.60 per pair, which is the price we used to calculate this EOQ. Therefore, this is a feasible order quantity. We are ready to calculate the total annual cost for this policy:

$$TC = \left(\frac{625}{91}\$10\right) + \left(\frac{91}{2}\$1.52\right) + (\$7.60 \times 625)$$

$$= \$4887.84$$

Since the feasible solution was not at the lowest price, we must now compute the total cost of any cheaper price, assuming that we order just enough to qualify for the cheaper price. This means we need to order 101 pairs to qualify for the $7.40 price. The total cost of this policy is

$$TC = \left(\frac{625}{101}\,\$10\right) + \left(\frac{101}{2}\,\$1.48\right) + (\$7.40 \times 625)$$

$$= \$4761.62$$

Since the total annual cost of ordering 101 pairs at a time is less expensive, Ye Olde Shoe Repair should order 101 pairs each time leather soles are needed.

• Problem 4

Frank's Ribs knows that the demand during lead time for his world-famous ribs is described by a normal distribution with a mean of 1000 pounds and a standard deviation of 100 pounds. Frank is willing to accept a stockout risk of approximately 2 percent.
(a) Determine the appropriate z value.
(b) Calculate how much safety stock Frank should hold.

• Before You Begin:

In this problem, you need to find out how much safety stock should be held. First, use Appendix B to determine the z value for the desired safety stock level. Then, using the formula $SS = z\sigma_{dL}$, calculate the required safety stock.

• Solution

(a) Go to Appendix B. You need to find the z value associated with 0.4800, which is the difference between the desired service level, 0.9800, and the z value of 0, 0.5000. Looking at the entry for $z = 2.05$, you should see 0.4798, which is as close to 0.4800 as we can get. Therefore, the appropriate z value is 2.05.

(b) To determine the amount of safety stock Frank should hold, multiply the z value by the standard deviation:

$$SS = 2.05 \times 100 \text{ pounds} = 205 \text{ pounds}$$

Frank should hold 205 pounds of ribs in safety stock.

• Problem 5

Peter sells programs at State University's home football games. Peter must buy the programs before the game in multiples of 100 (2000, 2100, 2200, etc.). Peter has determined that the probability of selling different quantities of programs at a given game is as follows:

Demand for Programs	Probability of Demand
2000	.10
2100	.20
2200	.40
2300	.20
2400	.10

Peter plans to sell the programs for $4 each. He pays $2.50 for each program and there is no salvage value. Determine how many programs Peter should buy to maximize his profit.

• Before You Begin:

For this problem, we are only able to make a single purchase. Determine which order quantity has the highest expected payoff. Develop a payoff table to show the expected value from each order quantity.

• Solution

Based on the information given, we developed a payoff table to determine the expected profit for each possible order quantity. Net profit for each combination or order quantity and demand are calculated as shown. The order quantity with the highest expected profit is 2200 programs. Peter should order 2200 programs.

Number of Programs Ordered	Probability of Occurrence					Expected Profit
	.10	.20	.40	.20	.10	
Actual customer demand (programs)	2000	2100	2200	2300	2400	
2000	$3000	$3000	$3000	$3000	$3000	$3000
2100	$2750	$3150	$3150	$3150	$3150	$3110
2200	$2500	$2900	$3300	$3300	$3300	$3140
2300	$2250	$2650	$3050	$3450	$3450	$3010
2400	$2000	$2400	$2800	$3200	$3600	$2800

Discussion Questions

1. Visit a local business and identify the different types of inventory used.

2. After visiting a local business, explain the different functions of its inventory.

3. Explain the objectives of inventory management at the local business.

4. Describe how the objectives of inventory management can be measured.

5. Explain the different methods for measuring customer service.

6. Compare the two techniques, inventory turnover and weeks of supply.

7. Describe the relevant costs associated with inventory policies.

8. Explain what is included in the annual holding cost.

9. Describe what is included in ordering or setup costs.

10. Describe what is included in shortage costs.

11. Explain the assumptions of the EOQ model.

12. Describe techniques for determining order quantities other than the EOQ or EPQ.

13. Describe how changes in the demand, ordering cost, or holding cost affect the EOQ.

14. Explain how a company can justify smaller order quantities.

15. Explain what safety stock is for.

16. Explain how safety stock affects the reorder point.

17. Describe the type of products that require a single-period model.

18. Explain the basic concept of ABC analysis.

19. Explain the concept of perpetual review.

20. Explain how two-bin systems work.

Problems

1. Elyssa's Elegant Eveningwear (EEE) needs to ship finished goods from its manufacturing facility to its distribution warehouse. Annual demand for EEE is 2400 gowns. EEE can ship the gowns via regular parcel service (three days transit time), premium parcel service (one day transit time), or via public carrier (seven days transit time). Calculate the average annual transportation inventory for each alternative.

2. Yasuko's Art Emporium (YAE) ships art from its studio located in the Far East to its distribution center located on the West Coast of the United States. YAE can send the art either via transoceanic ship freight service (fifteen days transit) or by air freight (two days transit time). YAE ships 18,000 pieces of art annually.

(a) Calculate the average annual transportation inventory when sending the art via transoceanic ship freight service.

(b) Calculate the average annual transportation inventory when sending the art via air freight.

(c) What additional information is needed to compare the two alternatives?

3. Joe, the owner of Genuine Reproductions (GR), a company that manufactures reproduction furniture, is interested in measuring inventory effectiveness. Last year the cost of goods sold at GR was $3,000,000. The average inventory in dollars was $250,000.

(a) Calculate the inventory turnover for GR.

(b) Calculate the weeks of supply. Assume fifty-two weeks per year.

(c) Calculate the days of supply. Assume that GR operates five days per week.

4. Genuine Reproductions (GR) from Problem 3, plans on increasing next year's sales by 20 percent while maintaining its same average inventory in dollars of $250,000.

(a) Calculate the expected inventory turnover for next year.

(b) Calculate the expected weeks of supply.

5. What is the inventory turnover for Genuine Reproductions from Problems 3 and 4 if sales actually increase 20 percent but the average inventory rises to $325,000?

6. Frederick's Farm Factory (FFF) currently maintains an average inventory valued at $3,400,000. The company estimates its capital cost at 10 percent, its storage cost at 4.5 percent, and its risk cost at 6 percent.

(a) Calculate the annual holding cost rate for FFF.

(b) Calculate the total annual holding costs for FFF.

7. The Federal Reserve Board has just increased the interest rate. FFF in Problem 6 now has to pay 12 percent for its capital. Calculate the impact on total annual holding costs for FFF.

8. A technology problem has rendered some of the inventory at FFF (Problem 6) obsolete. FFF estimates that the risk cost of its inventory is now 10 percent.

(a) Calculate the new annual holding cost rate.

(b) Calculate the new total annual holding costs for FFF.

9. Custom Computers, Inc. assembles custom home computer systems. The heat sinks needed are bought for $12 each and are ordered in quantities of 1300 units. Annual demand is 5200 heat sinks, the annual inventory holding cost rate is $3 per unit, and the cost to place an order is estimated to be $50. Calculate the following:

(a) Average inventory level

(b) The number of orders placed per year

(c) The total annual inventory holding cost

(d) The total annual ordering cost

(e) The total annual cost

10. Custom Computers, Inc. from Problem 9 is considering a new ordering policy. The new order quantity would be 650 heat sinks. Recalculate Problem 9, parts (a) through (e), and compare results.

11. Bill Maze, recently hired by Custom Computers, Inc. has suggested using the economic order quantity for the heat sinks. Using the information in Problem 9, calculate the following:

(a) Economic order quantity

(b) Average inventory level

(c) The number of orders placed per year

(d) The total annual ordering cost

(e) The total annual holding cost

(f) The total annual cost

Compare these results with the costs calculated in Problems 9 and 10.

12. A local nursery, Greens, uses 1560 bags of plant food annually. Greens works fifty-two weeks per year. It costs $10 to

place an order for plant food. The annual holding cost rate is $5 per bag. Lead time is one week.

(a) Calculate the economic order quantity.
(b) Calculate the total annual costs.
(c) Determine the reorder point.

13. Rapid Grower, the supplier of plant food for Greens in Problem 12, has offered the following quantity discounts. If the nursery places orders of 50 bags or less, the cost per bag is $20. For orders greater than 50 bags but less than 100 bags, the cost per bag is $19. For orders of 100 bags or more, the cost is $18 per bag. Greens estimates its holding cost to be 25 percent of the unit price. Determine the most cost-effective ordering policy for Greens.

14. In an effort to reduce its inventory, Rapid Grower is offering Greens, a local nursery (Problems 12 and 13), two additional price breaks to consider. If the nursery orders a three-month supply, the cost per bag is $16. If Greens orders a six-month supply, the cost per bag is $14.50. Should Greens change its order quantity calculated in Problem 13?

15. In a further attempt to liquidate its inventory, Rapid Grower has offered Greens, the local nursery, an option to buy the entire year's supply at one time. The cost per bag would be $12. Should Greens take advantage of this offer?

16. Sam's Auto Shop services and repairs a particular brand of foreign automobile. Sam uses oil filters throughout the year. The shop operates fifty-two weeks per year and weekly demand is 150 filters. Sam estimates that it costs $20 to place an order and his annual holding cost rate is $3 per oil filter. Currently, Sam orders in quantities of 650 filters. Calculate the total annual costs associated with Sam's current ordering policy.

17. Using the information in Problem 16, calculate the following:

(a) The economic order quantity
(b) The total annual costs using the EOQ ordering policy
(c) The penalty costs Sam is incurring by using his current policy

18. The local Office of Tourism sells souvenir calendars. Sue, the head of the office, needs to order these calendars in advance of the main tourist season. Based on past seasons, Sue has determined the probability of selling different quantities of the calendars for a particular tourist season.

Demand for Calendars	Probability of Demand
75,000	0.15
80,000	0.25
85,000	0.30
90,000	0.20
95,000	0.10

The Office of Tourism sells the calendars for $12.95 each. The calendars cost Sue $5 each. The salvage value is estimated to be $0.50 per unsold calendar. Determine how many calendars Sue should order to maximize expected profits.

19. The Office of Tourism (Problem 18) has decided to heavily promote local events this year and anticipates more tourists this season. Sue has changed the probability of selling different quantities of calendars as shown. Given the new probabilities, determine

how many calendars Sue should order to maximize expected profits.

Demand for Calendars	Probability of Demand
75,000	.05
80,000	.20
85,000	.25
90,000	.30
95,000	.20

20. Given the following list of items,

(a) Calculate the annual usage cost of each item.
(b) Classify the items as A, B, or C.

Item	Annual Demand	Ordering Cost ($)	Holding Cost (%)	Unit Price ($)
101	500	10	20	0.50
102	1500	10	30	0.20
103	5000	25	30	1.00
104	250	15	25	4.50
105	1500	35	35	1.20
201	10000	25	15	0.75
202	1000	10	20	1.35
203	1500	20	25	0.20
204	500	40	25	0.80
205	100	10	15	2.50

21. Using the information provided in Problem 20,

(a) Calculate the economic order quantity for each item. (Round to the nearest whole number.)
(b) Calculate the company's maximum inventory investment throughout the year.
(c) Calculate the company's average inventory level.

22. Tax Preparers Inc. works 250 days per year. The company uses adding machine tape at a rate of eight rolls per day. Usage is believed to be normally distributed with a standard deviation of three rolls during lead time. The cost of ordering the tape is $10 and holding costs are $0.30 per roll per year. Lead time is two days.

(a) Calculate the economic order quantity.
(b) What reorder point will provide an order cycle service level of 97 percent?
(c) How much safety stock must the company hold to have a 97 percent order-cycle service level?
(d) What reorder point is needed to provide an order-cycle service level of 99 percent?
(e) How much safety stock must the company hold to have a 99 percent order-cycle service level?

23. Healthy Plants Ltd. (HP) produces its premium plant food in 50-pound bags. Demand for the product is 100,000 pounds per week. HP operates fifty weeks per year and can produce 250,000 pounds per week. The setup cost is $200 and the annual holding cost rate is $0.55 per bag. Currently, HP produces its premium plant food in batches of 1,000,000 pounds.

(a) Calculate the maximum inventory level for HP.
(b) Calculate the total annual costs of this operating policy.

24. Using the data provided in Problem 23, determine what will happen if HP uses the economic production quantity model to establish the quantity produced each cycle.
    (a) Calculate the economic production quantity (EPQ).
    (b) Calculate the maximum inventory level using the EPQ.
    (c) Calculate the total annual cost of using the EPQ.
    (d) Calculate the penalty cost HP is incurring with its current policy.

25. Greener Pastures Incorporated (GPI) produces a high-quality organic lawn food and weed eliminator called Super Green (SG). Super Green is sold in 50-pound bags. Monthly demand for Super Green is 75,000 pounds. Greener Pastures has capacity to produce 24,000 50-pound bags per year. The setup cost to produce Super Green is $300. Annual holding cost is estimated to be $3 per 50-pound bag. Currently, GP is producing in batches of 2500 bags.
    (a) Calculate the total annual costs of the current operating policy at GPI.
    (b) Calculate the economic production quantity (EPQ).
    (c) Calculate the total annual costs of using the EPQ.
    (d) Calculate the penalty cost incurred with the present policy.

26. Lissette Jones, the materials manager for an upscale retailer, wants to measure her customer service level. She has collected the following representative data.

Order Number	Number of Line Items	Dollar Value of Order
1	4	1000
2	8	1440
3	2	1600
4	6	920
5	10	1800
6	8	1200
7	8	2700
8	4	1560
9	5	1780
10	5	1000
Totals	**60**	**$15,000**

Assuming that orders 1–6 and 8–10 shipped on schedule:
    (a) Calculate the customer service level using the percentage of orders that shipped on schedule.
    (b) Calculate the customer service level using the percentage of line orders shipped on schedule.
    (c) Calculate the customer service level using the percentage of dollar volume that shipped on schedule.
    (d) Which of these measures would you recommend to Lissette?

27. Your new company has decided to use a periodic review system. You have learned that average weekly demand is forty-eight units per week with a standard deviation of eight units. You believe that your cycle-service level should be 94 percent. Lead time is two weeks. Initially, you believe that you should do a review every Friday. Determine the required safety stock and the target inventory level.

    (a) How would this procedure change if the cycle-service level needed to be 98 percent?
    (b) What is the impact of changing the review period from every Friday to every other Friday, assuming that the cycle-service level is 94 percent?

28. Michael's Office Supply (MOS) sells office furniture, equipment, and supplies. This week the company has received fifty customer orders. Each order has an average of five line items. The average dollar amount of each order is $1200. MOS was able to ship forty-seven of the fifty orders on schedule.
    (a) Using the percentage of orders shipped on time, calculate the customer service level.
    (b) If Michael's calculates customer service level by using the percentage of line items shipped on schedule, how many line items must be shipped to achieve the same customer service level calculated in part (a)?
    (c) If Michael's calculates customer service level by the percentage of dollar volume shipped, how many dollars of product must be shipped to achieve the same customer service level calculated in part (a)?
    (d) What factors determine the customer service level measure that MOS should use?

29. My Kitchen Delights (MKD), a regional producer of gourmet jams and jellies, uses approximately 24,000 glass jars each month during its production. Because of space limitations, MKD orders 5000 jars at a time. Monthly holding cost is $0.08 per jar, and the ordering cost is $60 per order. The company operates twenty days per month.
    (a) What penalty cost is the company incurring by its present replenishment policy?
    (b) MKD would prefer to order 8 times each month but needs to justify any change in order size. How much would ordering cost need to be reduced to justify a lot size of 3000 jars?
    (c) If MKD can reduce its ordering cost to $30, what is the optimal replenishment order quantity?

30. My Kitchen Delights (MKD) is considering two new suppliers for the jars used in the production process. The quality at both suppliers is equal. Assume that the annual holding cost is 30 percent of the unit price. Monthly demand averages 20,000 jars. Ordering cost with these two suppliers is $30 per order. The price lists for the suppliers are as follows:

Supplier A		Supplier B	
Quantity	**Unit Price**	**Quantity**	**Unit Price**
1–2499	$3.00	1–1999	$3.50
2500–3499	2.90	2000–2999	3.15
3500–4999	2.80	3000–3999	2.85
5000 or more	2.70	4000–4999	2.75
		5000 or more	2.60

    (a) Determine the optimal order quantity when using Supplier A.
    (b) Determine the optimal order quantity when using Supplier B.
    (c) Given MKD's lack of space, which supplier do you recommend be used? Justify your answer.

CASE: FabQual Ltd.

FabQual Ltd. manufactures parts and subassemblies for a number of small-volume manufacturers of specialized construction equipment, including bulldozers, graders, and cement mixers. FabQual also manufactures and distributes spare parts. The company has made a specialty of providing spare parts for equipment no longer in production; this includes wear parts that are no longer in production for any OEM.

The Materials Management Group (MMG) orders parts—both for delivery to a customer's production line and for spares—from the Fabrication Department. Spares are stocked in a Finished Goods Store. FabQual's part number 650810/ss/R9/o is a wear part made only for spares demand. It has had demand averaging 300 units per week for more than a year, and this level of demand is expected to persist for at least four more years. The standard deviation of weekly demand is 50 units.

The MMG has been ordering 1300 units monthly of part number 650810/ss/R9/o from the Fabrication Department to meet the forecast annual demand of 15,600 units. The order is placed in the first week of each month. In order to provide Fabrication with scheduling flexibility, as well as to help with planning raw material requirements, a three-week manufacturing lead time is allowed for parts.

In the Fabrication Department, two hours is now allowed for each setup for a run of part number 650810/ss/R9/o. This time includes strip-down of the previous setup; delivery of raw materials, drawings, tools and fixtures, etc.; and buildup of the new setup. The two-hour setup time is a recent improvement over the previous four hours, as the result of setup reduction activities in the Fabrication Department. The Fabrication Department charges £20 per hour for setups. (If you prefer to work in

dollars, you can find the current exchange rate in the *Wall Street Journal*.) Part number 650810/ss/R9/o enters the Finished Goods Stores at a full manufacturing cost of £55. The Financial Office requires a 25 percent per item per year cost for inventory planning and control. (This is your annual holding cost rate.)

Case Questions

1. What is the total annual cost of the present ordering policy for part number 650810/ss/R9/o?

2. What would be the lot size for part number 650810/ss/R9/o if FabQual were to use an economic order quantity (EOQ)?

3. What would be the total annual cost of using an economic order quantity for part number 650810/ss/R9/o?

4. What would be the reorder point for part number 650810/ss/R9/o if FabQual wanted a delivery performance of 95 percent? What would it be if the company wanted a delivery performance of 99 percent?

5. Under the present scheme—ordering 1300 units each month in the first week of each month—there are typically 700 to 800 units on hand when the new batch of 1300 units arrives toward the end of each month. What would be the impact on the overall inventory level of part number 650810/ss/R9/o of a change from the present order policy to an EOQ-based policy?

6. What are other implications of a change from the present scheme to one based on the economic order quantity? If this part is representative of a great many spare parts, what would be the overall impact?

Source: Copyright © by Professor L.G. Sprague, 1999. Reprinted with permission.

CASE: Kayaks!Incorporated

Kayaks!Incorporated manufactures a line of sea kayaks and accessories in a make-to-stock environment. These products are sold to boat dealers and major department stores throughout North America, which then sell these products to the final customer. Customers expect immediate receipt of the goods, so it is critical to have sufficient inventory held by the dealers and department stores. Aeesha Grant, the materials manager at Kayaks! wants to make sure that the customer service level is being correctly calculated before she considers any changes to manufacturing. She has collected the following information for you to analyze and prepare a report on the customer service level being provided by Kayaks!Incorporated to the boat dealers and department stores.

Case Questions

1. Kayaks!Incorporated has always measured customer service as the number of complete orders that ship on schedule. Using this measure, calculate the customer service level provided by Kayaks!Incorporated.

2. Does this method of calculating the customer service level make sense for Kayaks!Incorporated?

3. What other methods might be useful in measuring Kayaks! customer service level? How would these affect your analysis of customer service?

4. What is your report to Aeesha Grant with regard to the customer service being provided by Kayaks!Incorporated?

Customer	Line Items	Dollar Value	Line Items Shipped on Schedule	Dollar Value on Schedule	Customer	Line Items	Dollar Value	Line Items Shipped on Schedule	Dollar Value on Schedule
1	2	2,000	2	2,000	14	5	8,000	5	8,000
2	17	40,000	16	37,500	15	5	6,000	5	6,000
3	9	16,000	9	16,000	16	7	12,000	6	11,500
4	7	9,500	6	9,000	17	16	28,000	15	24,500
5	24	68,000	22	64,000	18	11	12,000	11	12,000
6	4	6,000	4	6,000	19	9	17,500	9	17,500
7	7	14,000	7	14,000	20	3	7,500	3	7,500
8	3	14,000	3	14,000	21	4	11,000	4	11,000
9	9	6,000	7	4,800	22	8	12,000	8	12,000
10	12	18,500	11	18,000	23	20	48,000	19	44,000
11	7	16,000	7	16,000	24	1	2,500	1	2,500
12	12	14,000	11	11,000	25	12	9,000	12	9,000
13	11	19,500	9	15,000	**Totals**	**225**	**417,000**	**212**	**392,800**

INTERACTIVE CASE ▶ Virtual Company

www.wiley.com/college/reid

On-line Case: Inventory Management at Valley Memorial Hospital

Assignment: *Independent Demand Inventory Management*
"This assignment just came up yesterday," says Meg Willoughby, head of Materials Management at VMH. "We've been purchasing 600 cholesterol-testing kits for the lab here every three months. Yesterday, our supplier called and offered us a discount on the price per kit if we purchase in greater bulk. One complication is that Peggy Dundee in the lab says that a new cholesterol kit being tested by the Food and Drug Administration might make the current kits obsolete. So I'm not sure whether to take the deal or not and could use your help. Of course, you'll want precise information about costs and such, so let's sit down in the conference room and I'll show you everything you need to know."

To complete this assignment, go to **www.wiley.com/college/reid** to get the details needed. Assignment questions are given at the site.

To access the Web site:

- Go to **www.wiley.com/college/reid**
- Click **Student Companion Site**
- Click **Virtual Company**
- Click **Kaizen Consulting, Inc.**
- Click **Consulting Assignments**
- Click **Independent Demand Inventory Management**

INTERNET CHALLENGE ▶ Community Fund Raiser (A)

Your nonprofit club holds a major fund-raiser for two weeks each year to support community improvement projects. The club sells packages of cookies throughout the community and donates the proceeds. The goal of the event is to raise at least $40,000 for the community. This year you are in charge of the fund-raising event. Your first step is to search the Internet and identify at least three potential suppliers of the cookies to be sold this year. At least one of the suppliers should be in the immediate vicinity of your town or city.

From past fund-raisers, the club believes that an acceptable price of the cookies to the customers does not allow for more than a $1 markup over the regular cost per package. However, if quantity discounts can be obtained, then the profit per package can exceed $1. It is believed that regardless of the cookies sold, demand will be 40,000 packages. If you decide to buy more than 40,000 packages, any leftover cookies will be donated to local shelters. Since you are a nonprofit organization, no tax advantage is gained.

For each of the potential suppliers, you need to identify the total cost associated with buying the packages of cookies. Be sure to consider transportation costs as well as any quantity discounts. Remember that your objective is to raise at least $40,000 for the community. It is also important to consider the logistics of your plan. Will all of the cookies arrive at one time or will deliveries be spread over the two-week fund-raiser? Find out how far in advance you need to place your order and when payment for the cookies is due. Explain how you can be sure the cookies will arrive on time. You need to put together a report for your next meeting comparing your three suppliers and make a recommendation as to which supplier should be used, the quantity of cookies to purchase, the expected profit to be donated, and the logistics for the fund-raiser.

On-line Resources

Companion Website www.wiley.com/college/reid:
- Take interactive *practice quizzes* to assess your knowledge and help you study in a dynamic way
- Review *PowerPoint slides* or print slides for notetaking
- Download *Excel Templates* to use for problem solving
- Access the *Virtual Company: Valley Memorial Hospital*
- Find links to *Company Tours* for this chapter
    Coffman Stairs—Division of Visador Company
    Canadian Springs Water Company
- Find links for *Additional Web Resources* for this chapter
    Coffman Stairs, www.coffmanstairs.com/about.htm
    Folbot, www.folbot.com/plant.tour.html
    Universal Screenprinting, www.simon.ca/simonfr.htm

Additional Resources Available Only in WileyPLUS:
- Use the *e-Book* and launch directly to all interactive resources
- Take the interactive *Quick Test* to check your understanding of the chapter material and get immediate feedback on your responses.
- Check your understanding of the key vocabulary in the chapter with *Interactive Flash Cards*
- Use the *Animated Demo Problems* to review key problem types.
- Practice for your tests with *additional problem sets*
- *And more!*

Selected Bibliography

Arnold, J.R. Tony, and Stephen N. Chapman. *Introduction to Materials Management*, Fifth Edition. Upper Saddle River, N.J.: Pearson Prentice-Hall, 2004.

Buffa, Elwood S., and Jeffrey G. Miller. *Production-Inventory Systems: Planning and Control*, Third Edition. Homewood, Ill.: Irwin, 1979.

Cox, James F., III, John H. Blackstone, and Michael S. Spencer, eds. *APICS Dictionary*, Eleventh Edition. Falls Church, Va.: American Production and Inventory Control Society, Inc., 2005.

Fogarty, Donald W., John H. Blackstone, and Thomas R. Hoffman. *Production and Inventory Management*. Second Edition. Cincinnati, Ohio: South-Western Publishing, 1991.

Inventory Management Reprints. Falls Church, Va.: American Production and Inventory Control Society, 1993.

Love, Stephen F. *Inventory Control*. New York: McGraw-Hill, 1979.

Vollmann, Thomas E., William L. Berry, D. Clay Whybark, and F. Robert Jacobs. *Manufacturing Planning and Control Systems*, Fifth Edition. Burr Ridge, Ill.: McGraw-Hill/Irwin, 2005.

CHAPTER **13**

Aggregate Planning

Before studying this chapter, you should know or, if necessary, review

1. Competitive priorities, Chapter 2, pages 35–38.
2. Capacity management concepts, Chapter 9, pages 304–310.
3. Work standards, Chapter 11, pages 389–395.
4. Relevant inventory costs, Chapter 12, pages 424–426.
5. Order quantity models, Chapter 12, pages 427–440.

LEARNING OBJECTIVES

After studying this chapter, you should be able to

1 Explain business planning.

2 Explain sales and operations planning.

3 Identify different aggregate planning strategies and options for changing demand and/or capacity in aggregate plans.

4 Develop aggregate plans, calculate associated costs, and evaluate the plan in terms of operations, marketing, finance, and human resources.

5 Describe the differences between aggregate plans for service organizations and manufacturing companies.

6 Explain the role of the master production schedule and describe the objectives of master production scheduling.

7 Develop a master production schedule and project the capacity needed using rough-cut capacity planning.

8 Calculate available-to-promise quantities.

9 Describe time fence policies.

CHAPTER OUTLINE

WHAT'S IN **OM** FOR ME?

 ACC

 FIN

 MKT

 OM

 HRM

 MIS

Superstock

As a student, you have a limited amount of hours available for you to study. You probably prepare for an exam in one of two ways. You wait until the night before the exam to cram three to five weeks of studying into one night. Or you regularly review your notes, maybe two or three times a week, and just do your normal review the night before the exam. While cramming might work if you have only a single exam to prepare for, sometimes that is not the case. Changing demands on your fixed amount of time (capacity) can create problems in achieving your objectives.

Companies also often have limited capacity to handle changing demands and typically take one of these two approaches or a combination of the two approaches to satisfy demand fluctuations. Companies providing perishable products or services are often forced to wait until the very last possible minute in order to assure fresh products or timely services. For example, consider how G's Naturally Fresh, a salad and vegetable-growing company based in the United Kingdom, must handle both seasonal demand and seasonal production.

Lettuce is a perishable item and must be kept refrigerated prior to shipment and during transport. Even then the product stays fresh for only one week. In northern Europe, demand for lettuce occurs year-round, decreasing during the winter to about half the summer demand. However, lettuce cannot be grown outdoors during the winter months and greenhouse cultivation is considered to be too expensive.

G's Naturally Fresh responded to the problem by buying a farm and packaging facility located in southeastern Spain to provide the lettuce needed during the winter. The lettuce is transported daily to the United Kingdom by a fleet of refrigerated trucks. When demand is higher than expected, the picking rigs and their crews pick into the middle of the night using floodlights. Staffing is a problem for G's Naturally Fresh. The UK operation maintains a permanent full-time staff while the Spanish workforce is primarily temporary, with very few employees working through the summer season.

Companies typically use a planning approach that tries to level the workload, or they try to change capacity to meet demand fluctuations. Companies trying to level the workload carry inventory, use back orders, and try to level demand. Companies changing capacity to meet demand fluctuations use overtime, undertime, hiring and firing, and/or subcontracting.

The level and timing of resources for production are detailed in a company's aggregate plan. The master production schedule determines how those resources are to be used. Let's look at the role of aggregate planning in your company's strategic business plan.

THE ROLE OF AGGREGATE PLANNING

▶ **Strategic business plan**
A statement of long-range strategy and revenue, cost, and profit objectives.

Aggregate planning is an integral part of the business planning process. This process begins when your company's top management gathers input from finance, marketing, operations, and engineering to develop a strategic business plan. The **strategic business plan**, with its long-term focus, provides your company's direction and objectives for the next two to ten years. The strategic business plan is normally updated and reevaluated annually. The strategic business plan is also the starting point for sales and operations planning. It states the company's objectives for profitability, growth rate, and return on investment.

Sales and operations planning integrates the medium-range functional plans developed by marketing, operations, engineering, and finance. Sales and operations planning begins with the **marketing plan** developed by the marketing group based on information shared with operations, finance, and engineering.

▶ **Sales and operations planning**
The process that brings together all the functional business plans (marketing, operations, engineering, and finance) into one integrated plan.

▶ **Marketing plan**
Identifies the markets to be served, desired levels of customer service, product competitive advantage, profit margins, and the market share needed to achieve the objectives of the strategic business plan.

Marketing Plan

The marketing plan is intended to meet the objectives of the strategic business plan. The marketing plan identifies the sales needed to achieve the profitability level, the growth rate, and the return on investment stated in the strategic business plan. Detailed in the marketing plan are the targeted market segments; necessary market share; competitive focus such as price, quality, flexibility, or time; expected profit margins; and any new products needed.

If the marketing plan does not meet the strategic business objectives, top management and marketing management revise either the objectives or the marketing plan itself until it fully supports the strategic objectives.

Aggregate or Production Plan

▶ **Aggregate plan**
Includes the budgeted levels of finished products, inventory, backlogs, workforce size, and aggregate production rate needed to support the marketing plan.

The aggregate plan, also called the *production plan*, identifies the resources needed by the operations group during the next six to eighteen months to support the marketing plan. The **aggregate plan** details the aggregate production rate and the size of the workforce, which enables planners to determine the amount of inventory to be held; the amount of overtime or undertime authorized; any authorized subcontracting, hiring, or firing of employees; and back-ordering of customer orders. The aggregate plan is usually updated and reevaluated monthly by the operations group.

Your company normally develops the aggregate plan based on a *composite* product that represents the expected product mix (to minimize the level of detail, individual products are not represented in the aggregate plan). Companies may group products into major product families to facilitate aggregate planning. For example, if your company produces several varieties of stereo equipment, you might have product families based on kinds of stereos. Product families could include home theater stereos, portable stereos, or automobile stereo systems. Each family can include different items as long as each item has similar processing needs.

Regardless of the method, the goal is to reduce the number of calculations to develop the aggregate plan. Using a composite product, or product families, reduces the level of detail but still provides the information needed for decision making at this stage. Common terms of output used in the aggregate plan are units, gallons, pounds, standard hours, and dollars.

To summarize, the purpose of the aggregate plan is to develop production rates and authorize resources that accommodate the marketing plan and allow your company to

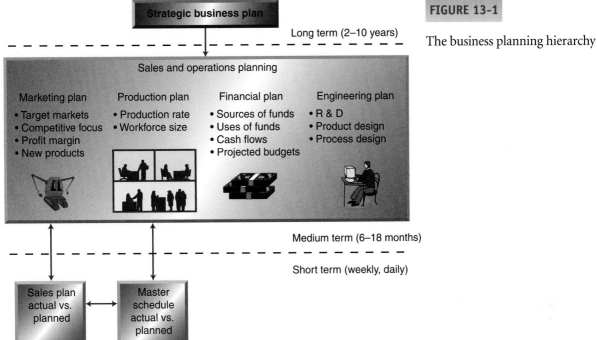

FIGURE 13-1

The business planning hierarchy

meet the objectives of the strategic business plan. Figure 13-1 summarizes the business planning flow.

Financial and Engineering Plans

The **financial plan** indicates the sources and uses of funds, expected cash flows, anticipated profits, and projected budgets. The **engineering plan** supports the research and development of new products introduced in the marketing plan and subsequently planned for in the aggregate plan.

The sales and operations planning process evaluates the company's performance regularly throughout the year. The process begins in sales and marketing with comparisons of real demand against forecasted demand. The forecast is updated and the market reevaluated. Based on the updated forecast, marketing communicates to the operations, finance, and engineering groups the proposed changes to the marketing plan and makes the changes all three groups agree on. The other groups adjust their plans accordingly. If operations, finance, or engineering cannot support the proposed changes to the marketing plan, marketing again revises the marketing plan.

▶ **Financial plan**
Identifies the sources and uses of funds; projects cash flows, profits, return on investment; and provides budgets in support of the strategic business plan.

▶ **Engineering plan**
Identifies new products or modifications to existing products that are needed to support the marketing plan.

Master Production Schedule

The sales and operations plan is evaluated and updated monthly. The master production schedule and the detailed sales plan are reviewed weekly or even daily. The **master production schedule** is an anticipated production schedule and is typically stated as specific finished goods. It details how operations will use available resources and which units or models will be built in each time frame. This allows marketing to make informed commitments to customers. Master production scheduling and customer commitments are discussed later in this chapter.

▶ **Master production schedule**
The anticipated production schedule for the company expressed in specific configurations, quantities, and dates.

Courtesy Apple Computers

Aggregate planning has been important for Apple Computer, Inc. The company's strategic plan focused on revolutionizing its products by making them more stylish and feature-specific. In turn, sales and operational planning streamlined operations by (1) slashing expenses over $2 billion; (2) reducing the lineup of fifteen product families to just a few that share common components; (3) outsourcing manufacturing to more efficient contractors; (4) substantially trimming the amount of inventory, the number of key suppliers, and the number of distributors; and (5) devising its own system to handle on-line purchases and shifting sales to an on-line store. Finally, the marketing plan targeted a specific audience of consumers, schools, and imaginative individuals using catchy ad campaigns (including the "Think different" slogan and iMovie ads). For Apple, as for any company, strong aggregate planning has been extremely important.

Now let's look at different kinds of aggregate plans so we can see how the aggregate plan fits into the business planning hierarchy. We use the terms *aggregate plan* and *production plan* interchangeably.

TYPES OF AGGREGATE PLANS

Level Aggregate Plan

▶ **Level aggregate plan**
A planning approach that produces the same quantity each time period. Inventory and back orders are used to absorb demand fluctuations.

We categorize aggregate plans as level, chase, or hybrid plans. A **level aggregate plan** maintains a constant workforce and produces the same amount of product in each time period of the plan. Example 13.1 shows how to calculate the number of employees needed to produce a specified output.

EXAMPLE 13.1 **Calculating the Number of Employees**	Wavetop Inc. currently has ten employees, each producing 5 complete units per day, for a total of 50 units every workday. Calculate the number of employees needed in the company's level aggregate plan if the company has an average weekly demand of 500 units, and plans on satisfying all of its demand. **• Solution:** If average weekly demand is 500 units and employees work five days per week, we need to produce 100 units per day. Thus, the workforce should be twenty employees (100 units needed each day divided by 5 units completed per employee per day). If we use this method, inventory accumulates when demand is below average and depletes when demand exceeds the average level. If we do not have enough inventory on hand to satisfy demand, then back orders result.

One advantage of a level production plan is workforce stability. Your company sets labor and equipment capacity equal to average demand, rather than hire excess labor or buy additional tools and equipment just to meet peak demand. In addition, the labor force is not subjected to varying work levels during the year, such as periods of layoff or undertime followed by periods of hiring and/or overtime.

The disadvantages of the level plan are the buildup of inventory and/or possible poor customer service from extensive use of back orders. The level plan is often used with make-to-stock products such as stereos, kitchen appliances, and hardware. Example 13.2 calculates the level workforce needed when demand varies throughout the planning horizon.

Calculating Average Monthly Net Demand for Wavetop Inc.

EXAMPLE 13.2

Wavetop Inc., a producer of water ski equipment, anticipates the following demand for its water skis. Demand for January is 12,000 units; for February, 9000; March, 12,000; April, 15,000; May, 18,000; and June, 24,000. The company has 6000 units in beginning inventory. Calculate the average monthly net demand for the company.

• Solution

Summing the monthly demands, the company needs a total of 90,000 units during the next six months. Since Wavetop Inc. already has 6000 units in inventory, net demand is 84,000 units. The company has six months to satisfy demand, so it must build 14,000 units monthly (84,000 units divided by six months = 14,000 units needed per month).

By calculating the amount of production needed each month, the company can plan the appropriately sized workforce. If each employee can build 25 units per normal workday and the company operates twenty days per month, then each employee builds 500 units per month. To calculate the number of employees needed, divide the number of units needed per month by the monthly output per employee (14,000 units divided by 500 units per employee = 28 employees needed).

Tom King/The Image Bank/Getty Images, Inc.

Chase Aggregate Plan

A **chase aggregate plan** produces exactly what is needed to satisfy demand during each period. The production rate changes in response to demand fluctuations. Whereas the level aggregate plan sets capacity to accommodate average demand, the chase aggregate plan sets labor and equipment capacity to satisfy demand each period.

The advantage of the chase plan is that it minimizes finished goods holding costs. This may be a better option when a company produces make-to-order products such as custom cabinets, special-purpose equipment, one-of-a-kind items, or highly perishable products. The disadvantages are constantly changing capacity needs and the need for enough equipment to meet peak demand. The additional equipment needed to meet peak demand creates excess capacity in nonpeak demand periods. Many options for short-term capacity changes are expensive. Example 13.3 shows how the workforce size fluctuates for Wavetop when a chase plan is used.

▶ **Chase aggregate plan**
A planning approach that varies production to meet demand each period.

Let's look at what would happen if Wavetop Inc. decides to adjust its capacity by hiring and firing employees each month. We calculate the number of employees needed during each period based on the net demand.

• Solution:

For example, January demand is 12,000 units, but since we have 6000 units in inventory, the net demand is only 6000 units. Each employee builds 500 units per month, so Wavetop Inc. needs twelve employees (6000 units divided by 500 units per employee per month) in January. The company needs eighteen employees in February, twenty-four employees in March, thirty employees in April, thirty-six employees in May, and forty-eight employees in June. How does this affect the space needed, the number of workstations, the sets of tools, and so forth?

When Wavetop Inc. used a level aggregate plan, it needed space and equipment to accommodate twenty-eight employees. With the chase aggregate plan, however, the company needs space and equipment for forty-eight people.

EXAMPLE 13.3

Chase Aggregate Plan at Wavetop Inc.

Hybrid Aggregate Plan

► **Hybrid aggregate plan**
A planning approach that uses a combination of level and chase approaches while developing the aggregate plan.

A **hybrid aggregate plan** typically uses a combination of options. With this plan, your company might maintain a stable workforce supplemented by an inventory buildup and some overtime production to meet demand. Or the company may back-order a portion of its demand. Any combination of options is possible. Because of the number of options you can combine in a hybrid plan, you need to evaluate your company's current situation and limit the options you choose from.

Next, let's look at the demand-based and capacity-based options used in aggregate plans.

AGGREGATE PLANNING OPTIONS
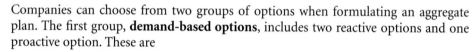

► **Demand-based options**
A group of options that respond to demand fluctuations through the use of inventory or back orders, or by shifting the demand pattern.

Companies can choose from two groups of options when formulating an aggregate plan. The first group, **demand-based options**, includes two reactive options and one proactive option. These are

- Reactive options, in which the operations department uses inventories and back orders to react to demand fluctuations.
- The proactive option, in which marketing tries to shift the demand patterns to minimize demand fluctuations.

An example for the proactive option is the early-bird dinners offered by some restaurants. The reduced price for a specific time period encourages customers to dine earlier and spreads the demand out over a longer period of time.

The second group, **capacity-based options**, changes output capacity to meet demand through the use of overtime, undertime, subcontracting, hires, fires, and part-timers or temps. These options are required when current capacity isn't equal to current demand. Each of these offers relief for fluctuating demand, but each has cost and operational implications for the company. Let's look at each option individually.

► **Capacity-based options**
A group of options that allow the firm to change its current operating capacity.

Demand-Based Options

► **Finished goods inventory**
Products available for shipment to the customer.

Using **finished goods inventory** to absorb demand fluctuations allows your company to develop a stable work environment. The company produces at average demand levels throughout the year rather than change capacity from one period to the next. When demand is less than average, the extra units go into inventory. When demand exceeds production, the extra units come out of inventory. Producing at average demand levels allows your company to invest less in capacity.

As we saw earlier, when Wavetop Inc. used a level aggregate plan using inventory, the company needed space and equipment for only twenty-eight employees. With the chase aggregate plan using hires and fires, the company needed space and equipment for forty-eight employees. However, the stable working environment isn't free. The company does have increased inventory holding costs because inventory is built and warehoused in anticipation of future demand. Inventory holding costs range from 15 to 35 percent of the cost of the inventory. Unfortunately, some companies with highly seasonal sales may have no choice but to use this option. For example, companies that make holiday products often experience 60 to 90 percent of their demand over a short period of time (one or two months out of the year). Producing the majority of its annual demand at the last minute could mean enormous machine and labor capacity, which would be underused or even idle the rest of the year.

Back orders result when your company does not have enough production and/or inventory on hand to cover current demand, so it promises to deliver the product to the customer at a later date. Customers may wait or they may take their business elsewhere. When a customer is unwilling to wait, the back order turns into a lost sale. Your company must understand its customers and its marketplace to judge whether or not back orders are a viable option. If alternative products or sources are readily available, customers probably will not wait. They are more likely to wait for unique products.

Unique has different meanings. Perhaps your company is the sole producer of a certain product, the reputation of your company merits waiting, or the price is much lower than for any substitute product. Whatever your reason for choosing back orders as an option, it must be a good one if you expect a customer to wait for your product.

In addition to possible lost sales, your company may have extra administrative costs because of the back order, such as higher shipping costs for overnight delivery. (These costs are discussed in Chapter 12.) In general, the back order should be used sparingly.

Shifting demand is a proactive marketing approach to leveling demand in which your company tries to change consumer buying patterns by offering incentives. Prime examples of this are movie matinees, early-bird dinners, and preseason or off-season discounts. In most cases, there is no out-of-pocket cost to the company—the profit is simply less per sale. This strategy makes sense when the company has high fixed costs and low variable costs. For example, a movie theater has a high fixed cost (the building and the projection equipment) but is empty during most of a 24-hour day. The variable cost for showing the movie is quite low. A matinee allows the theater to make better use of its capital investment.

Another way to level demand is offering preseason or off-season discounts. Shifting some of the company's demand means that less inventory is needed to satisfy demand during the prime season. Thus the inventory investment is lower, less floor space is needed, and some customers are pleased by the discount.

Capacity-Based Options

Overtime is the most common method for increasing output capacity. It is an expensive option, however, and should only be used short-term. Using overtime to increase output typically means your company pays a 50 percent wage premium to its workers. Unfortunately, when people work overtime, their productivity does not increase proportionately, so the cost of labor per unit increases. Workers typically do not produce more during overtime.

Worker productivity—and the quality of the work—may even decrease. In fact, the more overtime a company uses, the more likely it will experience reduced productivity and quality. Reduced productivity and quality tend to increase costs even more. Therefore, overtime is at best a short-term option for increasing production capacity.

Undertime results when a company does not need an employee to produce at 100 percent of his or her capability. Undertime is normally the result of reduced demand and a desire not to build up inventory levels. Undertime does not cost a company a wage premium, but it does increase the labor cost per unit, because fewer units are built but regular-time wages stay the same.

Why would a company keep employees around if they are not needed? The answer is straightforward: economics. It may be cost-effective to carry valuable workers for a short period of time if the company expects demand to return to previous levels.

▶ **Back orders**
Unfilled customer orders

▶ **Shifting demand**
A marketing strategy that attempts to shift demand from peak periods to nonpeak periods to smooth out the demand pattern.

▶ **Overtime**
Work beyond normal established operation hours that usually requires a premium be paid to the workers.

▶ **Undertime**
A condition occurring when there are more people on the payroll than are needed to produce the planned output.

If the company releases employees immediately, it may incur high replacement costs when it eventually hires new employees. The problem with undertime is that employee morale may suffer when people realize that there is not enough work to keep everyone busy. Thus undertime is also a short-term option.

▶ **Subcontracting**
Sending production work outside to another manufacturer or service provider.

Subcontracting means letting another company do some of the work for you. Subcontracting provides additional output capacity during periods of high demand. Unlike strategic outsourcing decisions that have components, subassemblies, or final products previously done in-house instead produced by another company, subcontracting is a tactical decision as to how to increase output in periods of high demand. For example, a publishing company may choose to outsource technical information development (a task requiring technical writing expertise) and have no in-house capability. Or a publishing company may need to subcontract additional technical information development because the in-house group has more work than it can handle. Outsourcing decisions identify the core business that the company is in. Subcontracting decisions provide extra capacity for the company.

The advantages of subcontracting are additional output without investing in additional tools, equipment, and labor. The disadvantage of subcontracting is the cost, which is substantial. The first step is to find a qualified subcontractor for the job. Then you have the additional cost of shipping parts to the subcontractor and having finished subassemblies or products shipped back to you. In addition, subcontracting means your company loses some degree of control. By contrast, work done in-house is always under your control: you know exactly where it is and how it is progressing. Since finding a good subcontractor takes time, subcontracting is a medium- to long-term option.

▶ **Hiring and firing**
Long-term option for increasing or decreasing capacity.

Hiring and firing changes the size of the workforce. Both hiring and firing can mean high costs for your company. Hiring requires the administrative work of identifying the position, communicating with potential applicants, evaluating the materials submitted by applicants, interviewing, verifying employment and references, running background checks, making decisions, verifying physical condition, making offers, and completing negotiations. After the employee is hired, your company sets up payroll, health insurance, security ID and badge, computer log-in, phone extension, and so forth. During employee training, output is normally lower and mistakes are typically higher. Thus hiring a permanent employee is a long-term option.

Firing employees is also expensive. Excessive firing can lead to increased unemployment compensation premiums. (Unemployment compensation is like any insurance policy: when you have a lot of claims, your rates increase.) Add to that the severance pay that companies typically pay to permanently laid-off employees, and the cost mounts. Significant, too, is the expense in lost knowledge when you terminate employees. Employees may leave with individual know-how that the remaining workforce will have to learn for themselves. For example, your employee may not have documented a minor change to the job instructions that increases productivity or improves product quality. The next employee on the job will have to learn this secret of improved output.

Finally, you have the cost in morale, which may affect productivity. Deciding who will stay and who will go is not a pleasant exercise. Some companies base the decision on seniority rather than what makes sense from an operational standpoint. When senior employees remain and junior employees are forced out, the remaining employees may return to jobs that have experienced major technological change. Thus respect for seniority rewards company loyalty but often at the expense of lost productivity.

For all of these reasons, hiring and firing employees is in the category of long-term options. Table 13-1 summarizes aggregate planning options.

Demand-Based Options	Capacity-Based Options	**TABLE 13-1**
• Inventory • Back orders • Shifting demand	• Overtime/undertime • Subcontracting • Hiring and firing	Summary of Aggregate Planning Options

Before You Go On

Make sure you understand the two kinds of options used in aggregate planning: demand-based options and capacity-based options.

Demand-based options stabilize capacity and react to demand fluctuations through the use of inventories and back orders, which may enable you to shift some demand to make the demand pattern smoother. Still, the longer you use either inventories or back orders, the riskier they become. Consumer preferences change over time and demand for your product may erode. Demand-based options are used primarily with level aggregate plans.

Capacity-based options are used to change capacity levels. Some capacity-based options are short-term, such as overtime and undertime; some are medium-term, such as subcontracting or using temporaries; and some are long-term, such as hiring or firing employees.

Your company should choose the option that satisfies the time frame needed (short, medium, or long) for the capacity change. Capacity-based options are used primarily with chase aggregate plans; all options can be used with hybrid aggregate plans.

Now that you understand the options and the kinds of aggregate plans, let's consider some additional factors in developing aggregate plans.

EVALUATING THE CURRENT SITUATION

When you are considering the different options, it is important to evaluate your company's current situation in terms of point of departure, magnitude of the change, and duration of the change.

The **point of departure** is the percentage of normal capacity your company is currently operating at. For example, if you are operating at 100 percent of normal capacity and need to increase capacity by 10 percent, you might use a relatively simple option such as overtime to achieve that 10 percent extra capacity. If you are already using overtime—say, you are operating at 125 percent of normal capacity—you might look for a different way to increase capacity. At this point, subcontracting or hiring temporary workers might be more economical. If you need to increase capacity even more, maybe it is time to hire some new permanent workers. The same is true when you need to reduce capacity. If you are making a small reduction—perhaps down to 90 percent of normal capacity—you might decided to use undertime. For even greater reduction, you might cut back hours or furlough employees. If the need to reduce is still greater, you might choose permanent layoffs. Thus point of departure affords your company perspective on the best options.

Magnitude of the change is the size of change needed. Smaller changes may be easier to implement—as we saw when Wavetop Inc. used the chase aggregate plan and increased its workforce from twelve to forty-eight employees in a six-month period. Larger capacity changes need more drastic measures, such as hiring or firing a shift, and the effects on productivity are greater.

Duration of the change is the length of time you expect to need the different level of capacity. If the duration is a brief seasonal surge, then hiring temporary or seasonal

▶ **Point of departure**
The percentage of normal capacity the company is currently using.

▶ **Magnitude of the change**
The relative size of the change needed.

▶ **Duration of the change**
The expected length of time the different capacity level is needed.

workers makes sense. For example, many retail stores hire additional clerks during holiday seasons. Some of these employees work for several years at the same store. When you expect the increased need for capacity to be permanent, a long-term solution like subcontracting or hiring new employees is more appropriate.

Evaluating the point of departure, magnitude of change, and duration of change allows your company to reduce the number of viable options for its aggregate plan.

Alex Farnsworth/The Image Works

When companies face highly seasonal demand, an alternative to hiring full-time permanent employees is the use of seasonal employees. UPS experiences highly seasonal demand each year, delivering approximately 300 million packages globally during the four weeks between Thanksgiving and Christmas. To meet this high demand, UPS hires around 90,000 part-time seasonal employees. That number includes 50,000 package handlers, who load and unload packages; 34,000 driver helpers; 2400 seasonal drivers for the delivery vans; and 850 tractor-trailer drivers. UPS hires and trains these employees each year. These trained, seasonal employees are often considered for permanent part-time jobs with UPS after the holidays. UPS has successfully implemented the use of seasonal workers to achieve its corporate strategy. As a result, UPS was recognized by *Your Money* magazine as providing the best part-time jobs in the nation.

DEVELOPING THE AGGREGATE PLAN

Here are the steps in developing an aggregate plan:

Step 1 Identify the aggregate plan that matches your company's objectives: level, chase, or hybrid.

Step 2 Based on the aggregate plan, determine the aggregate production rate.

- If you use the level plan with inventories and back orders, the aggregate production rate is set equal to average demand. In addition, if you allow no back orders, the size of the workforce is changed initially so that all demand is met on time.

- If you use the chase aggregate plan, calculate how much output capacity you need each period. Calculate how many units will be produced on regular time and overtime and how many units will be subcontracted.

Step 3 Calculate the size of the workforce.

- If you use the level aggregate plan, calculate how many workers you need to achieve the average production rate needed.

- If you change capacity each period with hires and fires, calculate how many workers you need each period and make the necessary change in the workforce.

- If you change capacity through a variety of options, calculate how much of a particular option you need each period.

Step 4   Test the aggregate plan.

- Using the production rate and initial workforce size, calculate your inventory levels (excesses and shortages), any shortages you face, expected number of employees hired and fired, and when you will need overtime.

- Calculate the total costs for your plan.

Step 5   Evaluate the plan's performance in terms of cost, customer service, human resources, and operations.

After you develop a plan, it is critical to evaluate it in terms of cost, customer service, operations, and human resources. Cost comparisons are simple if you are comparing similar ending positions—that is, plans with the same ending inventory level or producing the same number of units.

The comparisons are less clear when plans produce different quantities and leave different ending inventories. In this case, you can use a per unit cost comparison. To do this for customer service, measure how many back orders were placed during each period and throughout the duration of the plan. Decide whether this is an acceptable level of customer service to satisfy marketing's objectives. Assess the plan first in terms of operations, then in terms of human resources. Are the workers putting in excessive overtime one month and doing little the next? How does this plan affect the workforce? Does it lower morale or does it provide stability for the workers?

When you evaluate the plan from several perspectives, you can decide how it can best satisfy your company's objectives. Table 13-2 shows you how to do this. Table 13-3 summarizes the steps to develop an aggregate plan.

Perspective	Measurements
Cost	Total cost
	Unit cost
	Inventory levels
Customer service level	Number of back orders
Operations	Stability of schedule
	Equipment utilization
	Labor use
Human resources	Effect on workforce
	Employment stability

TABLE 13-2

Evaluation Perspectives and Measurements

Before You Go On

Review the five steps to develop an aggregate plan:

TABLE 13-3   Steps to Develop an Aggregate Plan

Step 1: Identify the type of aggregate plan: level, chase, or hybrid.
Step 2: Calculate the aggregate production rate.
Step 3: Calculate the size of the workforce.
Step 4: Test the plan and calculate costs.
Step 5: Evaluate the plan in terms of cost, customer service, operations, and human resources.

AGGREGATE PLANS FOR COMPANIES WITH TANGIBLE PRODUCTS

Now let's develop a couple of aggregate plans so we can evaluate their effectiveness. We use the problem data in Table 13-4.

TABLE 13-4

Data for Sophisticated Skates

	A	B
4	**Cost Data**	
5	Regular time labor cost per hour	$15.00
6	Overtime labor cost per hour	$22.00
7	Hiring cost per employee	$500.00
8	Firing cost per employee	$750.00
9	Inventory holding cost per unit per period	$5.00
10	Shortage cost per unit per period	$7.50
11	Material Cost per unit	$30.00
12		
13	**Capacity Data**	
14	Beginning workforce (employees)	18
15	Beginning inventory (units)	2500
16	Production standard per unit (hours)	0.64
17	Regular time available per period (hours)	160
18	Overtime available per period (hours)	20
19		
20	**Demand Data (units)**	
21	Nov	3000
22	Dec	6000
23	Jan	2000
24	Feb	8500
25	Mar	4000
26	Apr	5500
27	May	1500
28		
29	**Total Number of Periods**	7

EXAMPLE 13.4   **Plan A: Level Aggregate Plan Using Inventories and Back Orders**

Sophisticated Skates produces a variety of inline roller skates. Management wants you to develop an aggregate plan that covers the next seven months. Develop an aggregate plan using a level production strategy (stable workforce throughout the plan, inventories, and back orders).

• **Before You Begin:** Be sure that you understand the data provided in Table 13-4. The labor costs are given as the hourly wage cost of one employee. If you are working regular time, you are paid $15.00 per hour. For overtime, you receive $22.50 per hour. Employees are hired or fired at the beginning of the plan. For level plans you can adjust your workforce at the beginning of the plan and then it remains constant throughout the plan. The hiring and firing costs are per person. The inventory holding cost is assessed to the ending inventory for each period. In this case, there is a $5 holding cost per unit per period. The shortage or back-order cost is given as $7.50 per unit per period. The material cost used to build each unit is $30.00. In terms of capacity, the company currently has eighteen employees. There is a beginning inventory of 2500 units. Every unit produced takes 0.64 labor hours, and each period of the plan has 160 regular-time hours available for production from each employee. Each employee can work up to 20 hours of overtime each period. The demand data, given in units, indicates total demand for the plan of 30,500 units. We are concerned with the net cumulative demand so we subtract the beginning inventory of 2500 units, leaving us with a net cumulative demand of 28,000 units.

　　Since the type of aggregate plan has been identified (level), you need to understand how that affects your options. A level plan has the same output every period, whether you define your period as a month, quarter, week, or day. You must first determine what the aggregate production rate must be for each period. Then you will check to see how many employees are required to produce that number of units each period. At this point you are ready to try out your plan. Then you show what happens each period. Next you calculate the costs of your plan. And finally, you evaluate your plan in terms of customer service, costs, operations, and human resources.

• Solution:

Step 1 *Identify the type of aggregate plan.* This is given as a level production strategy, using a constant workforce, inventories, and back orders to satisfy demand.

Step 2 *Calculate the aggregate production rate.* You calculate the aggregate production rate by dividing the net cumulative demand by the number of periods in the plan. Net cumulative demand is the total demand for the plan less any beginning inventory. In this case, the aggregate production rate is 4000 units (28,000 units demanded divided by 7 periods).

Step 3 *Calculate the workforce.* The workforce is the aggregate production rate (4000 units) divided by the number of units per employee per period produced on regular time. Each employee works 160 regular-time hours per period; each unit requires 0.64 hours of labor time. Therefore, each employee produces 250 units per period on regular time. You need sixteen employees (4000 units divided by 250 units per employee). Since the current workforce has eighteen employees, you need to fire two employees.

Step 4 *Test and cost the plan.* The completed plan is shown in a spreadsheet in Table 13-5. Note that demand for November has been reduced from 3000 units to 500 units. This is because the beginning inventory is netted out in the first period of the plan. In the spreadsheet, notice the "Cum. Demand Minus Cum. Prod." row. This is shown merely to illustrate whether or not there is excess inventory or if there is a shortage (back order). For example, in November, net demand is 500 units and the company produced 4000 units, leaving −3500 units in cell F24. A negative number here means that you have produced more than is currently demanded, or you have excess inventory (as shown in cell F25). If the number in row 24 is positive (cell I24), it means that you do not have enough inventory to meet demand and you must back-order units.

The bottom section of the spreadsheet calculates the costs of your plan. In this case, the regular-time labor cost is regular-time hourly rate times number of regular hours per period times number of periods in plan times number of employees ($15.00 × 160 hours × 7 periods × 16 employees). Alternatively, since all of the regular-time hours were used productively, you could multiply the number of units built (28,000) times the cost to build 1 unit ($15.00 × 0.64 hours required to build 1 unit), or 28,000 × $15.00 × 0.64 hours. The total material cost is calculated by multiplying the 28,000 units built by the material cost per unit. Inventory cost is calculated by multiplying the ending inventory in units for each period by the period holding cost. The same is true for any back orders.

TABLE 13-5

	E	F	G	H	I	J	K	L	M
1									
2									
3	Solution for Level Aggregate Plan Using Inventories and Back Orders								
4									
5	Compute Level Production Rate								
6	Total Demand	30500							
7	Less: Beginning Inventory	2500							
8	Total Net Demand	28000							
9	Average Demand per Period	4000							
10									
11	Compute Workforce Needed								
12	Units per Worker per Period	250							
13	Worker Needed	16							
14	Number to Hire	0							
15	Number to Fire	2							
16									
17									
18	Detailed Plan Computations				Period				
19		Nov	Dec	Jan	Feb	Mar	Apr	May	
20	Demand (units) net of beginning inventory	500	6000	2000	8500	4000	5500	1500	
21	Cumulative demand (units)	500	6500	8500	17000	21000	26500	28000	
22	Production per period (units)	4000	4000	4000	4000	4000	4000	4000	28000
23	Cumulative production (units)	4000	8000	12000	16000	20000	24000	28000	
24	Cum. Dem. Minus Cum. Prod. (units)	-3500	-1500	-3500	1000	1000	2500	0	
25	Ending inventory (units)	3500	1500	3500	0	0	0	0	8500
26	Back orders (units)	0	0	0	1000	1000	2500	0	4500
27									
28	Cost Calculations for Plan								
29	Regular time labor cost	$268,800							
30	Materials cost	$840,000							
31	Inventory holding cost	$42,500							
32	Back order cost	$33,750							
33	Hiring cost	$0							
34	Firing cost	$1,500							
35	Total cost	$1,186,550							
36									

Step 5 *Evaluate the plan in terms of customer service, costs, operations, and human resources.* We won't compare costs yet since this is the only plan. We can look at customer service, noting that we experience back orders in February, March, and April. The fill rate (the number of customers satisfied out of the total demand) for this plan is 83.9 percent (23,500 units satisfied when demanded divided by a total demand of 28,000 units). This is likely too low a fill rate. Other than that, the inventory levels seem to be okay, assuming there is room to store up to 3500 units. From a human resources perspective, we fired two employees initially but the number remained stable for the rest of the plan.

A chase strategy is illustrated in Example 13.5

EXAMPLE 13.5   **Plan B: Chase Aggregate Plan Using Hiring and Firing**

Using the same problem data as Example 13-4, develop a chase aggregate plan using hires and fires, but no overtime production.

• **Before You Begin:** Since we are using a chase strategy that only allows hiring and firing, we need to determine how many employees are needed to satisfy the net demand for each period. We can do that by dividing net period demand by the number of units one employee can make per period on regular time. Once we determine the number of employees needed, we either hire or fire based on our requirements.

• **Solution:**

Step 1 *Identify the type of aggregate plan.* This is given as a chase aggregate plan. Remember that a chase plan has no ending inventory for any period. This problem limits you to hiring and firing employees as a means of adjusting your production output.

Step 2 *Calculate the aggregate production rate.* In a chase plan, the aggregate production rate is equal to each period's net requirements. Remember that a pure chase plan allows no ending inventory. However, in this example there is some beginning inventory that must be netted out. After netting out the initial inventory, no other period will have a beginning inventory. The production rate for each period is shown in Table 13-6.

TABLE 13-6

	E	F	G	H	I	J	K	L	M
37									
38	Solution for Chase Aggregate Plan Using Hiring and Firing (no overtime)								
39									
40	Beginning number of employees	18							
41	Units per Worker per Period	250							
42									
43	**Detailed Plan Computations**				Period				
44		Nov	Dec	Jan	Feb	Mar	Apr	May	
45	Demand (units) net of beginning inventory	500	6000	2000	8500	4000	5500	1500	
46	Production per period (units)	500	6000	2000	8500	4000	5500	1500	28000
47	Employees Needed in period	2	24	8	34	16	22	6	112
48	Number to hire	0	22	0	26	0	6	0	54
49	Number to fire	16	0	16	0	18	0	16	66
50									
51	**Cost Calculations for Plan**								
52	Regular time labor cost	$268,800							
53	Materials cost	$840,000							
54	Hiring cost	$27,000							
55	Firing cost	$49,500							
56	Total Cost	$1,185,300							

Step 3 *Calculate the workforce needed each period.* The number of workers needed equals the period production rate divided by the number of units produced per employee per period. Confirm the calculations shown in Table 13-6.

Step 4 *Test and cost the plan.* The completed plan and costs are shown in Table 13-6.

Step 5 *Evaluate the plan.* On the basis of cost, this plan is slightly less expensive than the level plan. However you should be concerned about whether you have captured all the costs associated with the chase plan. For example, in the chase plan, the number of employees required per period ranges from two in November up to thirty-four in February, which means you need space and equipment for thirty-four employees. However, space and equipment are underutilized in every other month of the plan. Even in December, the next busiest period, you need only roughly 70.6 percent of capacity (24/34). In other months, utilization is even lower. Chase plans with extreme ranges of output often waste capacity. The impact of this chase plan on morale would be significant. Employees would never be certain of their job. And this plan could not be used if the employees needed any significant level of skills.

Additional aggregate plans for companies with tangible products can be found in the Solved Problems at the end of the chapter. These plans provide a chance to consider additional aggregate planning alternatives.

AGGREGATE PLANS FOR SERVICE COMPANIES WITH NONTANGIBLE PRODUCTS

In the previous examples, your company used inventory buildup as a way of leveling the aggregate plan. When your company's product is nontangible—for example, if your company offers a service as do banks, healthcare providers, and hair stylists—inventory is no longer a viable option. We use the problem data shown in Table 13-7 to develop a level aggregate plan.

	A	B
4	**Cost Data**	
5	Regular time labor cost per hour	$8.00
6	Overtime labor cost per hour	$12.00
7	Subcontracting cost per unit (labor only)	$60.00
8	Hiring cost per employee	$250.00
9	Firing cost per employee	$150.00
10		
11	**Capacity Data**	
12	Beginning workforce (employees)	60
13	Service standard per call (hours)	4
14	Regular time available per period (hours)	160
15	Overtime available per period (hours)	24
16		
17	**Demand Data (calls)**	
18	Period 1	2400
19	Period 2	1560
20	Period 3	1200
21	Period 4	2040
22	Period 5	2760
23	Period 6	1680
24	Period 7	1320
25	Period 8	2400
26		
27	Total Number of Periods	8

TABLE 13-7

Data for Plans C, D, and E

EXAMPLE 13.6   **Plan C: Level Aggregate Plan with No Back Orders, No Tangible Product**

With this plan, your company maintains a level workforce with no backorders. Any demand not satisfied is lost to a competing service provider, so the company must meet all demand.

- **Before You Begin:** Remember that level aggregate plans use inventories and back orders to handle demand fluctuations. In this problem, you do not have a tangible product, so you cannot use inventories. The problem also stipulates that no back orders are allowed to occur. You need to determine the workforce size needed to satisfy demand during the peak period. Since this is a level plan, you must maintain this size workforce throughout the entire plan. Level aggregate plans for companies without a tangible product that require 100 percent customer service will always set the staff level to meet peak demand.

- **Solution:**

   Step 1   *Choose the kind of aggregate plan.* In this example, we use a level plan.

   Step 2   *Calculate the production rate.* Since the company is not going to back-order, you staff to accommodate peak demand. The aggregate production rate is set equal to the highest demand in any period during the plan. Period 5 has 2760 service calls, which means 11,040 hours of regular-time labor must be available.

   Step 3   *Calculate the size of the workforce.* You need sixty-nine employees (11,040 hours divided by 160 hours per employee per period). Each period, you have 11,040 hours of regular-time labor available.

   Step 4   *Test and cost the plan.* Table 13-8 shows Plan C using sixty-nine employees and meeting demand each period. As you can see, this plan creates excess labor: only period 5 uses the total workforce. Period 3 uses a little over 43 percent of capacity (4,800/11,040). Over the life of the plan, your company uses just under 70 percent of its available regular-time workforce (61,440/88,320). Table 13-8 shows the costs of the plan. An additional calculation not shown in the table is the cost per service call, which is $46.15 ($708,810 divided by 15,360 service calls).

HRM

   Step 5   *Evaluate the plan.* We have no other plans for nontangible products for comparison yet, but it is likely that underuse of the regular-time workforce will make Plan C cost-prohibitive. It is also likely that the high undertime will lower employee morale. From an operational perspective, it might be better to keep the present workforce and supplement with overtime. When we use overtime, we reduce undertime. In fact, when we use the maximum amount of overtime permitted, we minimize undertime.

TABLE 13-8

	D	E	F	G	H	I	J	K	L	M	N	O	P
3	**Plan C: Level Aggregate Plan with No Backorders, No Tangible Product**												
4													
5	**Compute Workforce Needed**											**Key Formulas (some are copied)**	
6	Maximum Demand	2760	<-- Need to staff to meet the maximum number of calls									$E$6	=MAX($B$18:$B$25)
7	Calls per Worker per Period	40										$E$7	=$B$14/$B$13
8	Workers Needed	69										$E$8	=E6/E7
9	Number to Hire	9										$E$9	=MAX(E8-$B$12,0)
10	Number to Fire	0										$E$10	=MAX(B12-$E$8,0)
11													
12	**Detailed Plan Computations**					Period							
13		1	2	3	4	5	6	7	8	Total			
14	Demand (calls)	2400	1560	1200	2040	2760	1680	1320	2400	15360		$E$14	=TRANSPOSE($B$18:$B$25)
15	Service hours needed	9600	6240	4800	8160	11040	6720	5280	9600	61440		$E$15	=E14*$B$13
16	Regular time hours available	11040	11040	11040	11040	11040	11040	11040	11040			$E$16	=$E$8*$B$14
17	Undertime hours	1440	4800	6240	2880	0	4320	5760	1440	26880		$E$17	=E16-E15
18													
19	**Cost Calculations for Plan E**												
20	Regular time labor cost	$706,560										$E$20	=E8*$B$14*$B$5*$B$27
21	Hiring cost	$2,250										$E$21	=E9*$B$8
22	Firing cost	$0										$E$22	=E10*$B$9
23	Total Cost	**$708,810**										$E$23	=SUM(E20:E22)

Let's look at a plan that uses some overtime.

Plan D: Hybrid Aggregate Plan Using Initial Workforce and Overtime as Needed EXAMPLE 13.7

Now we will develop a hybrid aggregate plan using a workforce of sixty employees working 160 regular-time hours per period. We use overtime when regular-time capacity is inadequate.

• **Before You Begin:** We have a workforce of sixty employees that provide 9600 regular-time hours each period. Calculate when overtime is needed and how much overtime should be authorized. Any period that requires less than 9600 hours to satisfy demand will not need overtime. In this case, the only time you need any overtime hours is in period 5. The amount of overtime is the difference between the total time needed less the regular time available. When such a plan is used, you might expect to see considerable amounts of undertime.

• **Solution:**

Step 1   *Choose the kind of aggregate plan.* We use a hybrid plan.

Step 2   *Calculate the production rate.* In this plan, our regular-time aggregate production rate is the same as for Plan C because we are keeping the initial workforce of sixty employees. Thus we have 9600 regular-time hours available each period (60 employees × 160 hours per employee per period). The overtime needed in a period depends on the number of service calls expected. For each period, we calculate the number of hours needed to satisfy the service calls. For example, in period 4, we need 8160 hours to meet demand (2040 calls × 4 hours per call).

Step 3   *Calculate the size of the workforce.* We know that the workforce is sixty employees working 160 hours of regular time each period.

Step 4   *Test and cost the plan.* Table 13-9 shows the completed plan. We need overtime only in period 5; the initial workforce has more than enough capacity during the other periods. We calculate the overtime by subtracting the available regular-time hours (9600 hours) from the service hours needed in period 5 (11,040), which yields 1440 hours of overtime. Table 13-9 shows the total costs of regular-time labor and overtime labor.

Step 5   *Evaluate the plan.* This plan reduces regular-time capacity from 88,320 hours in Plan C to 76,800 hours. Thus we increase regular-time labor use to 80 percent (61,440/76,800). In addition, the cost per call drops to $41.15. This is a major improvement over Plan C in terms of cost and customer service. However, it is still problematic in terms of the amount of undertime.

TABLE 13-9

	D	E	F	G	H	I	J	K	L	M	N	O	P
26	Plan D: Hybrid Aggregate Plan Using Initial Workforce and Overtime as Needed												
27													
28	Detailed Plan Computations					Period							
29		1	2	3	4	5	6	7	8	Total			
30	Demand (calls)	2400	1560	1200	2040	2760	1680	1320	2400	15360		$E$30	=TRANSPOSE($B$18:$B$25)
31	Service hours needed	9600	6240	4800	8160	11040	6720	5280	9600	61440		$E$31	=E30*$B$13
32	Regular time hours of capacity	9600	9600	9600	9600	9600	9600	9600	9600	76800		$E$32	=$B$12*$B$14
33	Overtime hours needed	0	0	0	0	1440	0	0	0	1440		$E$33	=MAX(E31-E32,0)
34	Undertime hours	0	3360	4800	1440	0	2880	4320	0	16800		$E$34	=MAX(E32-E31,0)
35													
36	Cost Calculations for Plan F												
37	Regular time labor cost	$614,400										$E$37	=$B$12*$B$14*$B$5*$B$27
38	Overtime labor cost	$17,280										$E$38	=M33*B6
39	Total Cost	$631,680										$E$39	=SUM(E37:E38)

Next, let's see what happens when we develop a plan that eliminates undertime.

EXAMPLE 13.8   **Plan E: Chase Aggregate Plan for Nontangible Products Using Hiring and Firing**

With this plan, your company reduces its undertime costs using hiring and firing.

- **Before You Begin:** This is a pure chase aggregate plan. Calculate exactly how many workers you need to satisfy demand each period. Once you have calculated the number of employees needed, either hire or fire as required.

- **Solution:**

Step 1   *Choose the kind of aggregate plan.* In this example, we use a chase plan.

Step 2   *Calculate the production rate.* We calculate the production rate based on the number of service calls each period, multiplied by the productivity rate of four hours per service call. Table 13-10 shows the production hours needed for each period.

Step 3   *Calculate the number of employees needed for each period.* To do this, we multiply the number of service calls for each period by the time per service call (for example, in period 2, 1560 calls × 4 hours each call = 6240 hours needed). Divide the number of hours needed by the number of hours per employee per period (160 hours per employee) and determine that thirty-nine employees are needed in period 2. Table 13-10 shows the appropriate workforce for each period.

Step 4   *Test and cost the plan.* Table 13-10 shows the completed plan. We calculate the number of hires or fires by comparing the number of employees needed in the current period with the number of employees used in the previous period. For example, in period 1, we used sixty employees and in period 2 we need thirty-nine employees. Thus we need to fire twenty-one employees at the start of period 2. In period 3, we need only thirty employees, so we must fire an additional nine employees.

In this plan, your company experiences fluctuations in the workforce with a low of thirty employees and a high of sixty-nine. The minimum change in workforce for any given period is nine workers, which represents a substantial portion of the workforce. We can easily calculate the regular-time wage costs and the cost of hiring and firing, but we cannot capture the intangible cost for such a widely fluctuating workforce. Table 13-10 evaluates the plan costs.

Step 5   *Evaluate the plan.* At $33.72, the cost per call is a good deal lower and regular-time labor utilization is 100 percent. Still, this plan has potential problems. Since employees interface with the customer, it is important to maintain performance level. Your company will have to train and retrain the changing workforce. This plan also needs an investment in enough space and equipment for up to sixty-nine employees. In periods of less than high demand, this extra capacity will be severely underused.

When we compare Plans C, D, and E, it is obvious that we have not yet found the best solution. Try working with the problem data further: maybe a smaller permanent workforce and additional overtime would be a better alternative.

TABLE 13-10

D	E	F	G	H	I	J	K	L	M	N	O	P
42	**Plan E: Chase Aggregate Plan Using Hiring and Firing**											
43												
44	Beginning Number of Employees	60										
45												
46	**Detailed Plan Computations**				Period							
47		1	2	3	4	5	6	7	8	Total		
48	Demand (calls)	2400	1560	1200	2040	2760	1680	1320	2400	15360	$F$48	=TRANSPOSE($B$18:$B$25)
49	Service hours needed	9600	6240	4800	8160	11040	6720	5280	9600	61440	$F$49	=F48*$B$13
50	Number of employees needed	60	39	30	51	69	42	33	60	384	$F$50	=F49/$B$14
51	Number of hires	0	0	0	21	18	0	0	27	66	$F$51	=MAX(F50-E50,0)
52	Number of fires	0	21	9	0	0	27	9	0	66	$F$52	=MAX(E50-F50,0)
53												
54	**Cost Calculations for Plan G**											
55	Regular time labor cost	$491,520										
56	Hiring cost	$16,500										
57	Firing cost	$9,900										
58	Total Cost	$517,920										

As you can see, the key is to look at a plan from different perspectives. Cost is important but so are customer service, operational effectiveness, and workforce morale. A successful aggregate plan considers each of these factors.

MASTER PRODUCTION SCHEDULING

Your company's aggregate plan specifies the resources authorized for use by the company's operations group. These resources include the size of the workforce, level of inventory held, number of planned shortages, authorized level of overtime and undertime, aggregate number of units or services to be produced in-house, and number of units or services to be subcontracted.

The **master production schedule (MPS)** is often stated in produce or service specifications rather than dollars. It shows how many products or services are planned for each time period, based on the resources authorized in the aggregate plan. In manufacturing, the **master scheduler** develops the schedule based on the available capacity. In service companies, the office manager, department manager, or assistant manager might develop the schedule.

The MPS is the anticipated build schedule for manufacturing specific end products or providing specific services. The key distinction here is that the MPS is a statement of production or services and is not a statement of demand—a plan to satisfy customer demand while considering operational effectiveness and cost. Because of this, individual products can be finished ahead of time and held in inventory rather than finished as needed. The master scheduler or office manager balances customer service and capacity usage.

The aggregate plan shows how many products or services are planned for each time period. The MPS identifies the specific products or services planned for a given time period. Let's look at an example of how an aggregate plan is linked to the MPS.

▶ **Master production schedule (MPS)**
The anticipated build schedule.

▶ **Master scheduler**
The person responsible for managing, developing, reviewing, and maintaining the master schedule.

Developing the MPS at Amber's Backpack Company   EXAMPLE 13.9

Amber's Backpack Company (ABC) produces three models of backpacks: the basic backpack, the urban backpack, and the evening backpack. Each model needs the same amount of production time. ABC's aggregate production rate is 400 backpacks per week. A possible MPS for ABC is shown here.

Week	1	2	3	4	5	6	7	8
Basic backpack	400		400	400		400	400	
Urban backpack		250			250			250
Evening backpack		150			150			150
Total	**400**	**400**	**400**	**400**	**400**	**400**	**400**	**400**

The aggregate plan states that ABC should produce 400 units each week. The MPS shows the models and quantities that constitute the 400 units to be produced each week of the schedule.

Ross Whitaker/The Image Bank/Getty Images, Inc.

Although this example involves manufacturing, think about how an MPS might look in a service operation such as a law firm. The firm knows how many hours of staff time are available (resources) and its current case load (demands). It must now decide how best to use the attorneys and law clerks each period to satisfy the corporate objectives.

MPS AS A BASIS OF COMMUNICATION

The MPS is a basis for communication between operations and other functional areas. It is stated in product or service specifications rather than dollars. Your company uses an effective MPS in making customer delivery promises, using company capacity wisely, achieving the company's objectives, and making trade-off decisions between marketing and operations. Figure 13-2 shows the connections between the master scheduling role and other parts of the planning process. Let's examine these connections, beginning with demand management.

Demand management includes a company's forecasting, order-entry, order-promising, and physical distribution activities. Demand management captures all activities that use capacity. These demands can be customer orders for products or services, a forecast of demand for products and services, interplant requirements, service parts requirements, and/or distribution requirements. If a demand is excluded, it will not be scheduled for completion. Communications between the master scheduler and demand management are ongoing.

The *production or aggregate plan* supports the marketing plan. The master scheduler must work within the authorized resources of the plan. The process for developing an MPS is as follows:

▶ **Demand management**
The function of recognizing all demands for goods and services to support the marketplace.

1. The master scheduler develops a proposed MPS.
2. The master scheduler uses a rough-cut capacity planning technique to calculate whether the company has the capacity to meet the proposed MPS. This is done using a rough-cut capacity planning technique.
3. If the proposed MPS is feasible, it is evaluated by the master scheduler in terms of customer service, effective use of resources, and inventory investment.
4. If the proposed MPS is accepted, it becomes the authorized MPS. If capacity is insufficient, either the MPS is modified or capacity is expanded.

▶ **Material requirements planning (MRP)**
A technique using the master production schedule, bill of material data, and inventory records to calculate requirements for materials.

The authorized MPS is a critical input into the **material requirements planning (MRP)** system. The MPS tells the MRP system what the company plans to build and when. The MRP system then calculates the materials needed to build the products in the schedule and plans for the necessary materials. (MRP systems are discussed in depth in Chapter 14.)

FIGURE 13-2

Master production schedule linkages

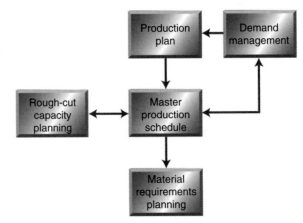

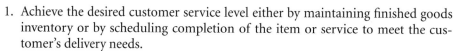

OBJECTIVES OF MASTER SCHEDULING

The master scheduler considers the following objectives when developing the MPS:

1. Achieve the desired customer service level either by maintaining finished goods inventory or by scheduling completion of the item or service to meet the customer's delivery needs.

2. Make the best use of the company's resources: material, labor, and equipment.

3. Ensure that the inventory investment is at the appropriate level.

To meet these objectives, the master schedule must satisfy customer demand, not exceed operation's capacity, and work within the constraints of the aggregate plan. Let's look at how to develop an MPS.

DEVELOPING AN MPS

The master scheduler develops a proposed MPS, checks the schedule for feasibility in terms of available capacity, modifies as needed, and authorizes the MPS. The master scheduler starts by creating, revising, and finishing an MPS record for each product. The master scheduler uses the finished MPS records to develop a proposed master production schedule, which he or she then checks for feasibility with a rough-cut capacity planning technique.

Consider the following examples of an MPS record for a product built in a make-to-stock environment with inventory held. The product is built in a fixed-order quantity of 125 units and there are *110 units in beginning inventory*. Table 13-11 is an initial MPS record showing the demand forecasts for the next twelve weeks.

The top row of the record shows the time periods (weeks, in our example); the forecast row shows the forecasted demand for the product. The projected available quantity row keeps track of how many units are available at the *end of each time period*. The MPS row shows when replenishment shipments need to arrive. MPS shipments arrive at the *beginning of the time period*. To calculate the projected available quantity, we use the following formula:

Projected available = beginning inventory + MPS shipment − forecasted demand

Period 1 To calculate the projected available quantity at the end of period 1, we take the beginning inventory (110 units), add any MPS shipments arriving that period (0 units), and subtract the forecasted demand for the period (50 units). This leaves the projected available quantity at the end of period 1, or (110 + 0) − 50 = 60 units projected available quantity.

Week	1	2	3	4	5	6	7	8	9	10	11	12
Forecast	50	50	50	50	75	75	75	75	50	50	50	50
Projected available	60	10	−40									
MPS	0	0	0	0	0	0	0	0	0	0	0	0

TABLE 13-11

First MPS Record

Week	1	2	3	4	5	6	7	8	9	10	11	12
Forecast	50	50	50	50	75	75	75	75	50	50	50	50
Projected available	60	10	85	35	−40							
MPS	0	0	125	0	0	0	0	0	0	0	0	0

Week	1	2	3	4	5	6	7	8	9	10	11	12
Forecast	50	50	50	50	75	75	75	75	50	50	50	50
Projected available	60	10	85	35	85	10	60	110	60	10	85	35
MPS	0	0	125	0	125	0	125	125	0	0	125	0

Period 2   The beginning inventory in period 2 is 60 units, no MPS shipment is scheduled, and the forecast is 50 units. Therefore, the projected available quantity at the end of period 2 is 10 units.

Period 3   In period 3, we have 10 units beginning inventory, no MPS quantity, a forecast of 50 units, and a projected available quantity of −40 units; that is, we do not have enough of this product available to satisfy the forecasted demand in period 3. Thus we need to plan an MPS shipment to arrive at the beginning of period 3. We calculate the size of the replenishment order by the order quantity rule—in our case, a fixed-order quantity of 125 units. Table 13-12 shows the revised MPS record with an MPS quantity of 125 units scheduled to arrive in period 3.

▶ **Rough-cut capacity planning (RCCP)**
The process of converting the master production schedule into requirements for key resources such as direct labor and machine time.

We continue to calculate the projected available quantity until we find the next period in which the projected available quantity is negative, which is period 5. Therefore, we need to schedule another MPS replenishment for delivery at the start of period 5. At that point, we add another MPS shipment and continue forward. Table 13-13 shows the completed MPS record, which shows replenishment orders needed in periods 3, 5, 7, 8, and 11. Each MPS quantity is determined using the given order quantity rule (125 units).

ROUGH-CUT CAPACITY PLANNING

▶ **Demonstrated capacity**
Proven capacity calculated from actual performance data.

▶ **Capacity planning using overall planning factors (CPOPF)**
A rough-cut capacity planning technique. MPS items are multiplied by historically determined planning factors for key resources.

Rough-cut capacity planning (RCCP) calculates a rough estimate of the workload placed on critical resources by the proposed MPS. This workload is compared against **demonstrated capacity** for each critical resource. This comparison enables the master scheduler to develop a feasible MPS. Among the several approaches to rough-cut capacity planning is capacity planning using overall planning factors (CPOPF).

Capacity planning using overall planning factors (CPOPF) is a simple, rough-cut capacity planning technique. CPOPF develops a planning factor for each critical resource based on historical data. A planning factor shows how much of a resource is needed for one completed unit. Table 13-14 shows the procedure for using CPOPF. Next, we will work through an example using the procedure.

1. Determine the appropriate planning factors using historical data.
2. Multiply the MPS quantities by the appropriate planning factor.
3. Sum capacity requirements for each resource by time period.
4. Allocate capacity requirements to individual work centers based on historical percentages.
5. Evaluate the workload at each resource to validate MPS feasibility.

TABLE 13-14

Procedure for CPOPF

EXAMPLE 13.10

CPOPF at Heavenly Ballroom Shoes

Heavenly Ballroom Shoes, Inc. (HBS) produces two models of ballroom dance shoes. One model is for men (Model M) and the other is for women (Model W). Charles, the master scheduler, has accumulated the following historical data. During the past three years, HBS has produced 72,000 pairs of Model M, using 21,600 hours of direct labor and 5760 machine hours. During that same period, HBS produced 108,000 pairs of Model W, using 43,200 hours of direct labor and 12,960 hours of machine time.

Jeremy Walker/The Image Bank/ Getty Images, Inc.

• **Before You Begin:** To implement capacity planning using overall planning factors (CPOPF), planning factors are needed. In this case, we have two products, Model M and Model W. Each product requires both direct labor and machine time. We have historical data to determine, on average, how much of each resource has been used in the past to build these products. After developing the planning factors, determine how much capacity is needed to satisfy a specific proposed master production schedule. That is, if you know how many Model M's you plan to produce and you know how much direct labor each Model M takes on average, you can calculate the total amount of direct labor needed to build the Model M's for a particular period. You do the same thing for Model W's. Then do this for all periods in your plan. Summing these requirements will give you the total amount of direct labor and machine hours you need to build the units in the proposed master production schedule. These data can be further broken down by individual work centers based on historical data.

Step 1   Determine the planning factors. Charles uses two resources, direct labor and machine time, for each of the products. He needs four planning factors: direct labor for Model M, machine time for Model M, direct labor for Model W, and machine time for Model W. Using the historical data, Charles computes the planning factors as follows:

$$\text{Planning factor for direct labor} = \frac{\text{total direct labor spent building model}}{\text{number of units of model built}}$$

For Model M, this translates to

$$\text{Planning factor for direct labor} = \frac{21{,}600 \text{ hours of direct labor}}{72{,}000 \text{ pairs}}$$

The planning factor for direct labor for Model M is 0.30 hours. That means he allows for 0.30 hours of direct labor for each pair of Model M shoes. To calculate the planning factor for machine time for Model M, Charles substitutes total machine hours spent building Model M into the numerator as shown.

$$\text{Planning factor for machine time} = \frac{\text{total machine hours spent building model}}{\text{number of units of model built}}$$

TABLE 13-15

Planning Factors

	A	B	C
3	**Planning Factors (hours per pair)**		
4		Direct	Machine
5		Labor	Time
6	Model M	0.30	0.08
7	Model W	0.40	0.12

TABLE 13-16

Proposed MPS

	A	B	C	D	E	F
9	**Quarterly Master Production Schedule (MPS) (pairs)**					
10		Q1	Q2	Q3	Q4	Totals
11	Model M	6000	5500	9500	6500	27500
12	Model W	10000	12000	7500	10100	39600

The planning factor for the Model M machine time is 0.08 hours (5760 hours of machine time divided by 72,000 pairs of Model M). Charles continues the process to calculate the planning factors for Model W. The direct labor planning factor for Model W is 0.40 hours and the machine time planning factor is 0.12 hours. Table 13-15 shows the four planning factors.

Given a proposed MPS, how would Charles calculate the workload for the proposed MPS? Table 13-16 shows the proposed quarterly MPS for HBS.

Step 2   Calculate the workload generated by this schedule. Charles multiplies the MPS quantity times the appropriate planning factor. For example, Charles begins in Quarter 1 and calculates how much labor is needed to build 6000 pairs of Model M and 10,000 pairs of Model W. He multiplies 6000 pairs of Model M by its labor planning factor of 0.30 hours to arrive at 1800 hours of direct labor needed. He continues for Model W, multiplying 10,000 pairs by its labor planning factor of 0.40 hours to arrive at 4000 hours of direct labor needed. The total number of direct hours needed in Quarter 1 is 5800 hours (1800 for Model M and 4000 for Model W). Charles continues to do this for each time period. Table 13-17 shows all the labor needs.

To calculate the machine needs, Charles continues the process. He multiplies the Quarter 1 needs for Model M by its machine time planning factor (6000 Model M's × 0.08 hours machine time = 480 hours needed). For Model W, 1680 hours of machine time are needed (10,000 Model W's × 0.12 hours machine time = 1200 hours needed). Table 13-18 shows the machine needs for each product in each quarter.

Step 3   Calculate the total capacity needs for each resource for each time period. Charles does this by summing up the individual capacity needs for each of the products. Table 13-17 shows the total labor hours needed for each quarter. Table 13-18 shows the same information for machine hours needed.

Step 4   Calculate individual work center capacity needs based on historical percentage allocation. Charles calculates that 60 percent of HBS's direct labor is used in work center 101 and 40 percent is used in work center 102. The same is true for its machine time. How would

TABLE 13-17

Direct Labor
Hours Required

	A	B	C	D	E	F
13				B16: =B11*$B6 (copied to B16:E17)		
14	**Direct Labor Hours Required**					
15		Q1	Q2	Q3	Q4	Totals
16	Model M	1800	1650	2850	1950	8250
17	Model W	4000	4800	3000	4040	15840
18	Totals	5800	6450	5850	5990	24090
19	B18: =SUM(B16:B17)				F16: =SUM(B16:E16)	
20						

	A	B	C	D	E	F
21						
22	**Machine Time (Hours) Required**			B24: =B11*$C6 (copied to B24:E25)		
23		Q1	Q2	Q3	Q4	Totals
24	Model M	480	440	760	520	2200
25	Model W	1200	1440	900	1212	4752
26	Totals	1680	1880	1660	1732	6952
27	B26: =SUM(B24:B25)				F24: =SUM(B24:E24)	
28						

TABLE 13-18

Machine Time
(Hours) Required

Charles calculate by quarters how much direct labor and machine time is needed at work centers 101 and 102? Table 13-19 shows direct labor needs by workcenter. To calculate the labor hours needed in work center 101 in Quarter 1, Charles multiplies the total Quarter 1 labor needs by 60 percent (5800 hours of total labor needed by 60 percent equals 3480 hours of labor needed in work center 101 in Quarter 1). The labor in work center 102 in Quarter 1 is 2320 hours (5800 hours × 40 percent). Charles now has an estimate of the direct labor needs by quarter for each of the work centers. He can compare the direct labor hours needed with the available direct labor hours and make adjustments either to the available capacity or to the MPS.

Charles calculates machine hour needs in each department for each quarter in the same way as he calculates labor needs. Table 13-20 shows the machine hours needed by each of the work centers for each quarter. Given this information, Charles can decide whether HBS needs additional equipment or whether it has adequate machine capacity in each of the work centers. Remember that a company can increase its capacity with overtime, temporary workers, subcontracting, or by using alternative manufacturing processes. When Charles is certain that the proposed MPS is feasible, he evaluates the MPS in terms of customer service, effectiveness of resource usage, and cost.

TABLE 13-19

Direct Labor Needs by Work Center

	A	B	C	D	E	F	G
30	**Direct Labor Hours Required by Work Center**						
31		Historical Allocation	Q1	Q2	Q3	Q4	Totals
				C32: =B18*$B32 (copied to C32:F33)			
32	Center 101	60%	3480	3870	3510	3594	14454
33	Center 102	40%	2320	2580	2340	2396	9636
34	Totals		5800	6450	5850	5990	24090
35		C34: =SUM(C32:C33)				G32: =SUM(C32:F32)	
36							

TABLE 13-20

Machine Hour Needs by Work Center

	A	B	C	D	E	F	G
38	**Machine Time Hours Required by Work Center**						
39		Historical Allocation	Q1	Q2	Q3	Q4	Totals
				C40: =B$26*$B40 (copied to C40:F41)			
40	Center 101	60%	1008	1128	996	1039.2	4171.2
41	Center 102	40%	672	752	664	692.8	2780.8
42	Totals		1680	1880	1660	1732	6952
43		C42: =SUM(C40:C41)				G40: =SUM(C40:F40)	
44							

EVALUATING AND ACCEPTING THE MPS

To evaluate the MPS in terms of customer service, the master scheduler checks that promised customer delivery dates are met. He or she also makes sure that the MPS provides enough flexibility to respond to new customer orders.

To evaluate the MPS for effective use of resources, the master scheduler checks that enough capacity is available to meet the schedule in each time period. This capacity includes short-term changes such as overtime, subcontracting, and temporary employees.

To evaluate the MPS in terms of cost, the master scheduler compares the MPS to the aggregate plan, which specifies available resources. If the MPS needs additional resources, the company may not achieve the objectives of the marketing plan and, consequently, the business plan.

When the master scheduler has evaluated and accepted the MPS, this authorized MPS is input into the MRP system, which we discuss further in Chapter 14.

Before You Go On

Be sure that you understand the sequential process of master scheduling:

1. The master scheduler uses a rough-cut capacity planning technique to calculate whether the company has the capacity to meet the proposed MPS.
2. If the proposed MPS is feasible, it is evaluated in terms of customer service, effective use of resources, and inventory investment.
3. If the proposed MPS is accepted, it becomes the authorized MPS. If capacity is insufficient, either the MPS is modified or capacity is expanded.

USING THE MPS

▶ **Order promising**
The process of making order-delivery commitments.

One use of the authorized MPS is order promising. When a customer places an order for a product but does not expect immediate delivery, the delivery date is negotiated. The customer typically requests delivery at a future date and the company decides whether it can promise delivery on that date. This is called **order promising**. For example, your parents order a new car custom-built for you at the factory for delivery on graduation day. The company is order promising when it decides whether it can produce the car and deliver it on that date. By extending the MPS records we began using in Table 13-11, we can do order promising. Let's look at an extended MPS record in Table 13-21.

The table now has two additional rows, one for customer orders and the other for available-to-promise quantity. The customer orders row has orders promised to customers for delivery in that time period. For example, the company has promised thirty-five units to be delivered in period 1, 25 units for delivery in period 2, and so forth.

▶ **Available-to-promise (ATP)**
The uncommitted portion of a company's inventory and planned production, maintained in the MPS to support order promising.

The **available-to-promise (ATP)** row shows how many uncommitted units the company has available for delivery at a given time. Next, we look at an example of how to calculate the ATP quantity and the projected available balances.

Period	1	2	3	4	5	6	7	8	9	10	11	12
Forecast	50	50	50	50	75	75	75	75	50	50	50	50
Customer orders	35	25	25	20	0	15	0	0	10	0	0	10
Projected available												
ATP												
MPS	0	0	125	0	125	0	125	125	0	0	125	0

TABLE 13-21

Extended MPS Record

EXAMPLE 13.11

Filling in the MPS Record

Using the data shown in Table 13-21, let's look at how we get the numbers. In this case, both the forecast numbers and the customer orders are already filled in. The first calculations we need to do are in the projected available row: we take the beginning inventory, add to it any MPS shipment, and subtract the greater of the forecast quantity or the customer orders. For example, in period 1, the beginning inventory is 110 units, there is no MPS shipment, and since the forecast of 50 is greater than the customer orders (35), we have 110 units + 0 units − 50 units = 60 units projected available at the end of period 1.

We calculate the projected available quantity as

Projected available = beginning inventory + MPS shipment − the greater of the period's forecast or the actual customer orders promised for delivery that period

Table 13-22 shows the appropriate projected available quantities.

Table 13-22 Completed ATP MPS Record

Period		1	2	3	4	5	6	7	8	9	10	11	12
Forecast		50	50	50	50	75	75	75	75	50	50	50	50
Customer orders		35	25	25	20	0	15	0	0	10	0	0	10
Projected available	110	60	10	85	35	85	10	60	110	60	10	85	35
Available-to-promise		50		80		110		125	115			115	
MPS				125		125		125	125			125	

We calculate the ATP quantity for the current period or, as it is called, the **action bucket**, and each time an MPS replenishment order is scheduled. In our example, that means we compute the ATP quantity in periods 1, 3, 5, 7, 8, and 11.

We calculate the ATP quantity in the current period differently from how we calculate it in the future replenishment periods. In the current period (the action bucket), the ATP quantity equals the beginning inventory, plus any MPS quantity. These two represent the available inventory we have to work with. In period 1, this is 110 units plus 0, or 110 total units available. From this amount, we subtract the customer orders promised for delivery between now and the next replenishment order (period 3 in our case). The number of units already promised is 60 (35 units for delivery in period 1 and 25 units for delivery in period 2). After subtracting the 60 units promised from the 110 units available, we still have 50 ATP units for delivery either in period 1, period 2, or at some future date. We calculate ATP in the action bucket as

$$\text{ATP}_{\text{Action Bucket}} = \text{beginning inventory} + \text{MPS shipment}$$
$$- \text{customer orders before next replenishment}$$

As we said, we calculate the ATP differently at future replenishment periods. In these cases, the ATP equals the MPS replenishment quantity less any customer orders promised for delivery between the date of the replenishment received and the next replenishment scheduled. For example, a replenishment order of 125 units is arriving in period 3. The customer orders already promised for delivery

► **Action bucket**
The current period.

before the next replenishment order (period 5) total 45 units (25 units in period 3 and 20 units in period 4). Of those 125 units arriving, we have already committed 45, leaving 80 units still available to promise. We calculate the ATP at periods other than the action bucket as

ATP = MPS shipment − customer orders between current MPS shipment and next scheduled replenishment

In periods other than the action bucket, we do not include the beginning inventory since it is not clear what the available amount will be. Remember that we subtracted the greater of the forecast or customer orders promised for delivery each period. Thus, if the forecast is greater than the customer orders, we end up with more units in inventory than are reflected on the MPS record. Table 13-22 shows the completed ATP quantities.

USING THE ATP RECORDS

The ATP records show how much inventory is available to satisfy customer demand, so your company bases its delivery promises to customers on these records. Using the completed ATP record in Table 13-22, let's look at whether or not your company can promise delivery of a new order.

Suppose that marketing has a customer willing to purchase 200 units if your company can deliver the units in period 5. Using the ATP record, we need to see whether that delivery is possible. One way to do this is to adjust the ATP record as if the order had already been accepted. Table 13-23 shows a revised ATP record including the new order.

In the customer orders row, 200 units are now scheduled for customer delivery in period 5. This changes the projected available quantities from period 5 onward and changes the ATP quantity in period 5. The two rules to remember here are the following.

"Would you like that delivered soon, pretty soon, or sometime-or-other?"

© 1996 Ted Goff Cartoons

1. *A negative number in the projected available row is **sometimes** a problem.* We calculate the projected available quantity by subtracting the greater of the forecast or the customer orders promised for delivery each period. If the forecast is subtracted because it is larger as in period 1 (50 units forecast compared to 35 units of customer orders), the company may not sell any more units for delivery in period 1. In that case, the ending inventory for period 1 would be 75 units (110 units to start with, less 35 units delivered).

TABLE 13-23

Revised ATP MPS Record

Period	1	2	3	4	5	6	7	8	9	10	11	12
Forecast	50	50	50	50	75	75	75	75	50	50	50	50
Customer orders	35	25	25	20	200	15	0	0	10	0	0	10
Projected available 110	60	10	85	35	−40	−115	−65	−15	−65	−115	−40	−90
Available-to-promise	50		80		−90		125	115			115	
MPS			125		125		125	125			125	

Period	1	2	3	4	5	6	7	8	9	10	11	12
Forecast	50	50	50	50	75	75	75	75	50	50	50	50
Customer orders	45[1]	25	105[1]	20	110[1]	15	0	0	10	0	0	10
Projected available 110	60	10	30	−20	−5	−80	−30	20	−30	−80	−5	−55
Available-to-promise	40		0		0		125	115			115	
MPS			125		125		125	125			125	

TABLE 13-24

Second Revised ATP Record

[1]These quantities have changed in order to account for the additional 90 units needed to satisfy the order of 200 units for delivery in period 5. We commit 80 units from the period 3 replenishment order and 10 units from the ATP quantity in period 1.

2. *A negative number in the available-to-promise row is **always** a problem.* This means your company does not have enough inventory to cover the delivery. In our example, the company needs an additional 90 units to cover the new order scheduled for delivery in period 5.

One way to handle this problem is to look at earlier ATP quantities to see whether any inventory is available from earlier shipments. Period 1 has 50 uncommitted units and period 3 has an additional 80 available units. If we set 90 of these units aside for the period 5 order, we can agree to the new customer order. Look at the revised ATP record in Table 13-24.

Think of it this way: We set 10 units aside in period 1 and put the customer's name on the boxes for delivery in period 5. In period 3, we put names on an additional 80 boxes of units. Then in period 5, we use the 90 boxes of units already set aside plus 110 of the new units to total the 200 units needed. In this way, we can promise delivery of 200 units in period 5.

After we agree to the order for 200 units for delivery in period 5, the next order arrives requesting an additional 50 units for period 4 delivery. We put this order into the record and see the results in Table 13-25.

Period	1	2	3	4	5	6	7	8	9	10	11	12
Forecast	50	50	50	50	75	75	75	75	50	50	50	50
Customer orders	45[1]	25	105[1]	70	110[1]	15	0	0	10	0	0	10
Projected available 110	60	10	30	−40	−25	−100	−50	0	−50	−100	−25	−75
Available-to-promise	40		−50		0		125	115			115	
MPS			125		125		125	125			125	

TABLE 13-25

Third Revised ATP Record

[1]These quantities have changed to account for the additional 90 units needed to satisfy the order of 200 units for delivery in period 5. We commit 80 units from the period 3 replenishment order and 10 units from the ATP quantity in period 1.

TABLE 13-26	Period	1	2	3	4	5	6	7	8	9	10	11	12
Final Revised ATP Record	Forecast	50	50	50	50	75	75	75	75	50	50	50	50
	Customer orders	45[1]	25	105[1]	20	110[1]	15	0	50	10	0	0	40
	Projected available 110	60	10	30	−20	−5	−80	−30	20	−30	−80	−5	−55
	Available-to-promise	40		0		0		125	65			85	
	MPS			125		125		125	125			125	

[1]These quantities have changed to account for the additional 90 units needed to satisfy the order of 200 units for delivery in period 5. We commit 80 units from the period 3 replenishment order and 10 units from the ATP quantity in period 1.

The ATP quantity in period 3 is now −50. Since a negative number in the ATP row is always a problem, we must check to see whether there is a way we can change that quantity to zero and accept the order. The only available inventory before delivery is requested is the 40 units available in period 1. Everything else has been promised. Therefore, we cannot accept this order for delivery in period 4. The earliest we can promise delivery is in period 7. Unless the customer is willing to agree with this delivery date, we cannot accept the order. We delete the 50 units from the period 4 customer orders and recalculate the other quantities. The ATP record reverts back to the numbers previously shown in Table 13-24.

Let's look at a couple of additional orders and calculate whether they can be accepted for delivery at the requested time. The first new order is for an additional 50 units to be delivered in period 8; the second order is for 30 additional units in period 12. When we put these orders into the customer order row, the ATP record is updated, as shown in Table 13-26. Since there are no negative values in the ATP row, we can promise both of these orders for delivery.

▶ **Time fence policies**
Partition the MPS into areas requiring different operating procedures.

The key requirement for using ATP is that manufacturing delivers the MPS replenishment on the scheduled date. For your company to meet these critical dates, operations must have the capacity specified in the MPS, and therefore the MPS itself must be feasible.

STABILIZING THE MPS

▶ **Demand time fence**
Establishes that point of time in the future inside of which changes to the MPS must be approved by a higher authority.

▶ **Planning time fence**
Establishes a point of time in the future inside of which changes must be made by the master scheduler and changes outside of which can be changed by system planning logic.

The master scheduler tries to minimize the number of changes made to an authorized MPS because each proposed change can affect the feasibility of the MPS. To deal with MPS changes, companies sometimes use **time fence policies**. Figure 13-3 illustrates the MPS and time fences. The figure shows the **demand time fence** and the **planning time fence**, which split the MPS into three parts. The portion of the master schedule from the current time up to the demand time fence is frozen and any changes are kept to a minimum.

Companies typically require these changes to be authorized by a person other than the master scheduler because they may need additional resources. This portion of the MPS normally uses all available capacity to produce customer orders. Adding any orders without adding resources results in a delay of the currently scheduled jobs.

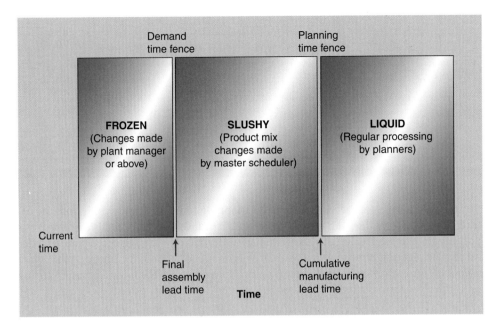

FIGURE 13-3

Time fences

Heavenly Ballroom Shoes (HBS) has frozen the first month of its MPS. Quarter 1 is shown in monthly time periods. The HBS marketing director, Marilee, has gotten an endorsement from this year's national ballroom champions for HBS shoes. Because of this endorsement, marketing needs two new, more upscale shoe models (Model WC and Model MC) for use in major competitions. The new models must be available by the end of January or HBS will lose market share. Marilee has asked Charles, the master scheduler, to schedule production of 500 pairs of each of these new models in January. The endorsement represents a major business opportunity for HBS, but HBS does not have the capacity to accept the order for the new shoes. HBS can accept the order only by authorizing more resources for manufacturing or by delaying the shoes that are currently scheduled.

EXAMPLE 13.12

Time Fences at HBS

Model	January (pairs)	February (pairs)	March (pairs)	Total Q-1 (pairs)
Model M		666	5,334	6,000
Model W	5,333	4,667		10,000
Total	5,333	5,333	5,334	16,000
Planned capacity available (pairs)	5,335	5,335	5,335	16,005

HBS has set up its MPS so that a decision to change the frozen portion has to be authorized by a manager who is also authorized to provide resources. In this way, HBS protects against jeopardizing existing orders to satisfy new ones.

The second portion of the MPS is the time between the demand time fence and the planning time fence. This is called the slushy portion of the MPS, during which it is the master scheduler's responsibility to negotiate changes in the MPS. For example, if Marilee in HBS marketing needs a product other than what is scheduled, Charles, the HBS master scheduler, first calculates whether the materials are available to make the other product. Then Charles asks Marilee which items marketing would be willing to do without. This is necessary to free up capacity so that the other product can be made.

In this portion of the MPS, changes in the product mix are possible, but changes needing additional resources are not. Thus, HBS will produce 5333 pairs of shoes during a month, but the mix of

MKT

the shoe models may vary. A revised MPS for February might look like the following. The product mix has changed but the total number of pairs produced remains constant.

Model	Quantity
Model M	166
Model MC	500
Model W	3667
Model WC	1000
Total pairs	5333

The third portion of the MPS starts at the planning time fence and extends into the future. This portion of the MPS is considered liquid because all orders requested during this portion are accepted as long as the resources authorized by the aggregate plan are adequate. The planning time fence is typically placed far enough into the future so that there is enough time to order any necessary materials and complete the normal manufacturing process. Production planners, discussed in Chapter 14, generally place these orders.

AGGREGATE PLANNING WITHIN OM: HOW IT ALL FITS TOGETHER

Aggregate planning determines the resources available to operations to support the overall business plan. It is critical that accurate demand forecasts be available (Chapter 8) so that a reasonable production plan can be developed. A company needs to know the aggregate production rate output required to determine the appropriate workforce size. If the plan requires seven-day-a-week operations, appropriate staff schedules need to be developed (Chapter 15).

The master production schedule (MPS) indicates how the resources are to be used period by period. Production quantities for different items can be established using inventory models (Chapter 12). The authorized MPS is one of the primary inputs in a material requirements planning (MRP) system (Chapter 14). The MRP system determines the timing and quantity of each component, subassembly, and final assembly. This subsequently can be used to do short-term capacity requirements planning (Chapter 14) to ensure that adequate capacity exists at critical work centers.

The aggregate plan specifies the number of employees needed. This allows a company to determine how much equipment and space is needed, as well as to provide the input needed for developing a layout (Chapter 9) for the operations area.

Aggregate planning determines the resources needed by operations to achieve the company's strategic objective. Master scheduling then allocates how those resources are to be used.

AGGREGATE PLANNING ACROSS THE ORGANIZATION

Aggregate planning, master production scheduling, and rough-cut capacity affect functional areas throughout an organization. The MPS is a basis for communication among those functional areas. Let's look at how each area is affected.

Accounting is affected because the aggregate plan details the resources needed by operations during the next twelve to eighteen months. Accounting uses this information to project cash flows, calculate the capital needed to support operations, and to project earnings. It also sets a benchmark for measuring the effectiveness of operations. From the MPS, accounting learns how and when resources will be consumed. The MPS enables revenue and cash flow management projections based on schedule completion dates. It is also a means for comparing planned performance versus real performance.

Marketing is involved because the aggregate plan supports the marketing plan. Marketing must know whether operations can provide the necessary output at a price that allows marketing to achieve its targeted profit margins. Further, the aggregate plan gives marketing insight into operations' goals and activities for the year. Marketing can use the MPS to make viable promises to customers because the MPS provides insight into planned production; for example, time fence policies show whether the MPS can be modified to accept orders. The MPS is also a basis for negotiation between marketing and operations.

Information systems (IS) maintains the databases that support demand forecasts and other such information used to develop the aggregate plan. IS also provides and supports the databases for MPS development and rough-cut capacity planning.

Purchasing calculates long-term needs based on the aggregate plan. The aggregate plan gives purchasing information about the future that facilitates long-term relationships and contracts with suppliers. This information also allows purchasing to evaluate quantity discounts. Purchasing is affected by the MPS because the MRP system uses the MPS to generate the timing and quantity of material requirements.

Manufacturing learns from the aggregate plan what resources are available to achieve its goals: how many workers, how much work can be subcontracted, how much inventory can be held, and so forth. Manufacturing is guided by the MPS in using the resources authorized by the aggregate plan. The time fence policies allow manufacturing to maintain stability in daily operations. Rough-cut capacity planning ensures the resources needed to meet the schedule.

In most companies, the operations manager develops the aggregate plan. The operations manager submits an annual operations budget request based on the resources identified in the aggregate plan, which justifies new hiring or expected firing during the year and planned or budgeted levels of overtime, subcontracting, and inventory.

When the plan is implemented, the operations manager measures operations' performance against the plan, checking progress at least monthly. The operations manager also evaluates performance against the authorized operations budget. Variances need to be explained at all levels and the plan updated. At that point, the past month is dropped from the aggregate plan and replaced by an additional month at the end of the aggregate plan. The monthly review and update allows the company to monitor its performance, maintain its medium-term plan, and correct for changes since the plan was developed.

The MPS is developed by the master scheduler. To develop the MPS, the master scheduler interacts with marketing, operations, demand management, and customers. The master scheduler's job is to develop an MPS that achieves the company's desired customer service level, uses capacity effectively, and minimizes inventory investment.

THE SUPPLY CHAIN LINK

Aggregate planning assures the necessary resources to satisfy an organization's objectives (profit, customer service, inventory investment, etc.). It determines both the output rate and the workforce size. These resources are based on product demand and reflect the customer service objectives of the company. The master production schedule is shared with all members of the supply chain so that everyone knows expected completion dates and availability of different products. Members of the chain also know when demand differs from the plan as well as any problems encountered by operations that affect the availability quantity or date for different products. This allows members of the chain to respond to potential problems and not make unsustainable delivery commitments. The master production schedule is the primary means of communication within the supply chain.

Chapter Highlights

1 Planning begins with the development of the strategic business plan that provides your company's direction and objectives for the next two to ten years. Marketing develops a plan that enables the company to satisfy the goals of the strategic business plan. The aggregate plan identifies the resources needed by operations to support the marketing plan.

2 Sales and operations planning integrates plans from the other functional areas and regularly evaluates the company's performance. The process begins with a comparison of actual demand and sales against planned demand. Forecasts are updated and the market reevaluated, and any changes in the marketing plan are reviewed by operations, engineering, and finance.

3 The level aggregate plan maintains the same size workforce and produces the same output each period. Inventories and back orders absorb fluctuations in demand. The chase aggregate plan changes the capacity each period to match demand.

4 Demand patterns can be smoothed through pricing incentives, reduced prices for out-of-season purchases, or nonprime service times. Capacity can be changed by using overtime or undertime, hiring or firing employees, subcontracting, using temporary employees, and so forth. You develop the aggregate plan by identifying the options you want to use; calculating the production rate; calculating the size of the workforce needed to reach the production rate; calculating the cost of the plan; and evaluating the plan in terms of cost, customer service, operations, and human resources.

5 The difference in aggregate planning for companies that do not provide a tangible product is that the option to use inventories is not available.

6 The MPS shows how the resources authorized by the aggregate plan will be used to satisfy the objectives of the organization. The MPS specifies the products and quantities to be built in each time period. The MPS is a common organizational document used to facilitate communication between different functional areas. The master scheduler develops a proposed MPS based on input received from the aggregate plan and demand management. This MPS is checked for feasibility using a rough-cut capacity planning technique.

7 The objectives of master scheduling are to satisfy customer service objectives, use resources effectively, and minimize costs. An MPS is developed by looking at individual MPS records and calculating when replenishment quantities are needed. The individual MPS records are summed together to show the total proposed workload.

8 Available-to-promise logic is used when promising order delivery dates to customers. ATP logic allows the company to make viable delivery promises.

9 Time fence policies stabilize the MPS. The demand time fence and the planning time fence divide the MPS into three portions: frozen, slushy, and liquid. Changes in the frozen portion are infrequent and must be authorized by a manager with authority to release additional resources to operations. Changes to the slushy portion are negotiated between the master scheduler and marketing. Changes in the product mix can occur but not changes in total volume. Changes in the liquid portion are made by planners since adequate lead time is available.

Key Terms

strategic business plan 470
sales and operations planning 470
marketing plan 470
aggregate plan 470
financial plan 471
engineering plan 471
master production schedule 471
level aggregate plan 472
chase aggregate plan 473
hybrid aggregate plan 474
demand-based options 474
capacity-based options 474
finished goods inventory 474

back orders 475
shifting demand 475
overtime 475
undertime 475
subcontracting 476
hiring and firing 476
point of departure 477
magnitude of the change 477
duration of the change 477
master production schedule (MPS) 487
master scheduler 487
demand management 488

material requirements planning (MRP) 488
rough-cut capacity planning (RCCP) 490
demonstrated capacity 490
capacity planning using overall planning factors (CPOPF) 490
order promising 494
available-to-promise (ATP) 494
action bucket 495
time fence policies 498
demand time fence 498
planning time fence 498

Formula Review

Calculating the projected available quantity:

Projected available = beginning inventory + MPS shipment − forecasted demand

Calculating a planning factor for direct labor:

Planning factor for direct labor

$$= \frac{\text{total direct labor spent building model}}{\text{number of units of model built}}$$

Calculating a planning factor for machine time:

Planning factor for machine time

$$= \frac{\text{total machine time spent building model}}{\text{number of units of model built}}$$

Calculating projected available quantity when using ATP MPS records:

Projected available = beginning inventory + MPS shipment − the greater of the period's forecast or the actual customer orders promised for delivery that period

Calculating ATP quantity in the action bucket:

$\text{ATP}_{\text{Action Bucket}}$ = beginning inventory + MPS shipment − customer orders before next replenishment

Calculating ATP quantity at future replenishment periods:

ATP = MPS shipment − customer orders between current MPS shipment and next scheduled replenishment

---

Solved Problems   (See student companion site for Excel template.)

Use the problem data in Table 13-27 for Solved Problems 1–4.

TABLE 13-27

Data for Solved Problems 1–4

	A	B
4	**Cost Data**	
5	Regular time labor cost per hour	$12.50
6	Overtime labor cost per hour	$18.75
7	Subcontracting cost per unit (labor only)	$125.00
8	Back order cost per unit per period	$25.00
9	Inventory holding cost per unit per period	$10.00
10	Hiring cost per employee	$800.00
11	Firing cost per employee	$500.00
12		
13	**Capacity Data**	
14	Beginning workforce (employees)	90
15	Beginning inventory (units)	0
16	Production standard per unit (hours)	8
17	Regular time available per period (hours)	160
18	Overtime available per period (hours)	40
19		
20	**Demand Data (units)**	
21	Period 1	1920
22	Period 2	2160
23	Period 3	1440
24	Period 4	1200
25	Period 5	2040
26	Period 6	2400
27	Period 7	1740
28	Period 8	1500
29		
30	**Total Number of Periods**	8

• Problem 1: Plan 1: Level Aggregate Plan Using Inventories and Back Orders

Develop a level aggregate plan using inventories and back orders. Test and evaluate the plan.

• *Before You Begin:*

Remember that a level strategy can use inventories and back orders to satisfy fluctuations in demand. You need to determine the aggregate production rate needed and then the size of workforce needed to produce that rate. Follow the steps below.

• *Solution*

Step 1 *Choose the kind of aggregate plan.* In this case we use a level aggregate plan.

Step 2 *Calculate the aggregate production rate.* We use the level option to calculate the average period demand rate. First, we add up the period demands and divide by the number of periods (14,400 units/8 = 1800 units per period), then we find the average production rate needed. If we have a beginning inventory, we subtract it from the total demand figure. If we have a desired ending inventory, we add that to the total demand figure. Otherwise, the 1800 units we calculated earlier is our average demand and subsequently our aggregate production rate.

Step 3 *Calculate the number of workers to produce 1800 units per period.* Since each employee works 160 hours per period and each unit takes eight hours of labor to produce, each employee can produce 20 units per period. We need 1800 units produced, so 1800 units divided by 20 units per employee means that we need a workforce of 90. Since we have 90 workers, we do not need to hire or fire any workers.

Now let's look at a level aggregate plan that would improve customer service with inventories but not allow back orders. All demand must be met each period.

• Problem 2: Plan 2: Level Aggregate Plan Using Inventories but No Back Orders

Develop a level aggregate plan using inventories but no back orders. Test and evaluate the plan. Compare to Plan 1.

• Before You Begin:

In this problem, you are constrained to a level strategy and are not allowed to have any back orders. Determine a production rate that does not allow for any back orders. To do this, use the cumulative demand divided by the number of periods up to that point. An example is shown in Step 2. Do this calculation for each period. The largest value represents the aggregate production rate needed to avoid back orders. Once the rate is determined, calculate the size of the workforce needed.

• Solution

Step 1   *Choose the kind of aggregate plan. In this case we use a level plan.*

Step 2   *Calculate the aggregate production rate.* When we do not allow back orders, we do not use the average demand rate to calculate the workforce, as shown in Table 13-28. A new row (row 44), labeled "cumulative demand/number of periods," divides the cumulative demand to each point by the number of periods in which to produce that quantity. For example, by the end of period 2, we need a total of 4080 units. Thus we plan to build 2040 units each month to sat-

isfy all demand for the first two periods with the level aggregate plan. We calculate this value for each period. The period with the highest needed production rate determines the aggregate production rate we use in the plan. For our plan, 2040 units is the highest production rate needed, so it becomes our planned aggregate production rate.

Step 3   *Calculate how many employees we need to produce 2040 units per period.* Since each employee can produce 20 units per period during regular time, we need 102 employees for this plan. We must hire 12 employees.

Step 4   *Test and cost the plan using a production rate per period of 2040 units and a workforce of 102 employees.* Table 13-28 shows the results of the plan.

This plan creates high inventory, especially after period 2. The inventory ranges from 0 to 1920 units, or from 0 weeks of supply to more than 4 weeks of supply.

We can calculate most of the costs of the plan. However, we cannot capture the true holding costs because we do not know when the ending inventory of 1920 units will be consumed. We need to remember this when we compare our plans. Table 13-28 shows the costs for this plan.

Step 5   *Evaluate the plan.* Compared with Plan 1, Plan 2 costs at least an additional $239,700 and possibly more given the ending inventory level. This is more than a 16 percent increase in total cost. However, we need to make sure our comparisons are fair. In Plan 1, we build 14,400 units, whereas in Plan 2, we build 16,320 units. We should expect total costs of Plan 2 to be higher since we need more labor

TABLE 13-28

	D	E	F	G	H	I	J	K	L	M	N	O	P
38	Plan 2: Level Aggregate Plan, Using Inventories but No Back Orders												
39													
40	Detailed Plan Computations					Period							
41		1	2	3	4	5	6	7	8	Total			
42	Demand (units) (net of beg. Inventory)	1920	2160	1440	1200	2040	2400	1740	1500			$E$42	=$B$21-$B$15
43	Cumulative demand (units)	1920	4080	5520	6720	8760	11160	12900	14400			$E$43	=SUM($E42:E42)
44	Cumulative demand/periods	1920	2040	1840	1680	1752	1860	1843	1800			$E$44	=E43/E$41
45	Period production (units)	2040	2040	2040	2040	2040	2040	2040	2040	16320		$E$45	=$E$52
46	Cumulative production (units)	2040	4080	6120	8160	10200	12240	14280	16320			$E$46	=SUM($E45:E45)
47	Cum.Dem. Minus Cum.Prod.	-120	0	-600	-1440	-1440	-1080	-1380	-1920			$E$47	=E43-E46
48	Ending Inventory (units)	120	0	600	1440	1440	1080	1380	1920	7980		$E$48	=IF(E47<0,-E47,0)
49	Backorders (units)	0	0	0	0	0	0	0	0	0		$E$49	=IF(E47>0,E47,0)
50													
51	Compute Level Production Rate and Workforce Needed												
52	Production Rate (units)	2040										$E$52	=MAX(E44:L44)
53	Units per Employee per Period	20										$E$53	=B$17/B$16
54	Employees Needed	102										$E$54	=E52/E53
55	Number to Hire	12										$E$55	=MAX(E54-B$14,0)
56	Number to Fire	0										$E$56	=MAX(B$14-E54,0)
57													
58	Cost Calculations for Plan B												
59	Regular time labor cost	$1,632,000										$E$59	=E54*B$17*B$5*B$30
60	Overtime labor cost	$0										$E$60	0
61	Inventory holding cost	$79,800										$E$61	=M48*B$9
62	Back order cost	$0										$E$62	=M49*B$8
63	Hiring cost	$9,600										$E$63	=E55*B$10
64	Firing cost	$0										$E$64	=E56*B$11
65	Total Cost	$1,721,400										$E$65	=SUM(E59:E64)

to build the additional units. Note that when plans require building different quantities, it may be easier to use the unit cost per plan for our comparisons. The unit cost for Plan 1 is $102.90 ($1,481,700 divided by 14,400 units). The unit cost for Plan 2 is $105.48 ($1,721,400 divided by 16,320 units). Plan 2 costs $2.58 more per unit, or roughly 2.5% more ($2.58 divided by $102.90).

What are we getting for this extra cost? Improved customer service. Plan 2 provides 100 percent customer service because no products are back-ordered. Now your company must decide whether 100 percent customer service is worth

at least an additional 2.5 percent in cost or if another approach might be more cost-effective.

Remember, we have understated our holding costs. From an operations standpoint, this is a relatively easy plan to implement. We increase our workforce by 12 employees, or just over 13 percent. Our output is still level and we do not need overtime or undertime. Morale should be fine.

• Problem 3: Plan 3: Chase Aggregate Plan Using Hiring and Firing

Develop a chase aggregate plan using hiring and firing. Test and evaluate the plan. Compare with Plans 1 and 2.

• Before You Begin:

When using a pure chase strategy with hires and fires, calculate the number of employees needed to satisfy each period's demand. Once you have established the number of employees needed, either hire or fire as required.

• Solution

Step 1 *Choose the kind of aggregate plan.* In this example we use a chase plan.

Step 2 *Calculate the production rate.* For example, in period 1, we need to build 1920 units. Since the company builds exactly what is needed to satisfy each period's demand, the production rate for each period is set equal to the

demand rate. Table 13-29 shows the level of output needed in each period.

Step 3 *Calculate the size of the workforce.* The initial workforce is 90, so we hire 6 employees for period 1. The number of employees we need to hire or fire depends on our ending workforce level in the previous period. We can see from Table 13-29 that we need 96 employees in period 1. We calculate this by dividing the number of units needed by the number of units produced by each employee per period (1920 units divided by 20 units per employee). Since we need 108 employees in period 2 and we ended period 1 with 96 employees, we must hire an additional 12 employees for period 2. We will have no ending inventories or back orders.

Step 4 *Test and cost the plan.* Table 13-29 shows the period-to-period testing of the plan. Note that this plan creates fluctuation in the size of the workforce, ranging from a high of 120 employees to a low of 60 employees. This means that the company must have enough space, tools, and equipment for up to 120 employees working simultaneously during a given time. It also means that half that space can be

TABLE 13-29

	D	E	F	G	H	I	J	K	L	M	N	O	P
68	**Plan 3: Chase Aggregate Plan, Using Hiring and Firing (no overtime)**												
69													
70	Beginning Number of Employees	90										$E$70	=$B$14
71	Units per Worker per Period	20	(used to compute workforce size requirement each period)									$E$71	=B17/B16
72													
73	**Detailed Plan Computations**				Period								
74			1	2	3	4	5	6	7	8	Total		
75	Demand (units) (net of beg. Inventory)	1920	2160	1440	1200	2040	2400	1740	1500			$E$75	=$B$21-$B$15
76	Production per period (units)	1920	2160	1440	1200	2040	2400	1740	1500	**14400**		$E$76	=E75
77	Employees needed in period	96	108	72	60	102	120	87	75	720		$E$77	=E76/$E$71
78	Number to hire	6	12	0	0	42	18	0	0	**78**		$E$78	=MAX(E77-E70,0)
79	Number to fire	0	0	36	12	0	0	33	12	**93**		$E$79	=MAX(E70-E77,0)
80													
81	**Cost Calculations for Plan C**												
82	Regular time labor cost	$1,440,000										$E$82	=M77*B$17*B$5
83	Overtime labor cost	$0										$E$83	0
84	Inventory holding cost	$0										$E$84	0
85	Back order cost	$0										$E$85	0
86	Hiring cost	$62,400										$E$86	=M78*B$10
87	Firing cost	$46,500										$E$87	=M79*B$11
88	Total Cost	**$1,548,900**										$E$88	=SUM(E82:E87)

idle during other periods. The number of changes in the size of the workforce and the magnitude of some of these changes could cause problems. Suppose we fire a total of 48 workers during periods 3 and 4, only to hire 42 new employees in period 5. Your workforce has increased by 70 percent (42 divided by 60). Imagine the mass confusion and the loss of productivity at the beginning!

Step 5   *Evaluate Plan 3.* The costs of Plan 3 are the highest of the three plans. The unit cost for Plan 3 is $107.56 ($1,548,900 divided by 14,400 units), an increase of more than $2 per unit from Plan 2, which also provided excellent customer service.

From a customer service standpoint, Plan 3 is fine because no products are back-ordered. From an operations standpoint, however, this plan is not easy to implement. We need space, tools, and equipment for up to 120 individuals in period 6, whereas we will have only 60 employees in period 4. We need to consider the feasibility of major changes like these. Employee morale might be low because of the lack of job security. How many employees can afford to take a month or two off?

• Problem 4: Plan 4: Hybrid Aggregate Plan Using Initial Workforce and Overtime as Needed

Develop a hybrid aggregate plan using the initial workforce of 90 employees supplemented with overtime when demand exceeds regular-time production. Test and evaluate the plan. Compare with Plans 1, 2, and 3.

• Before You Begin:

In this problem, the size of the workforce is given. You are to supplement the regular-time output of this workforce with overtime when needed. Determine when overtime is needed. The key to remember is that in periods when the demand is lower than the production rate, inventory is generated. The effect of ending inventory in any period is that it reduces the amount of production needed the following period. Be sure to carefully read Step 2 as you look at the results in Table 13-30.

• Solution

Step 1   *Choose the kind of aggregate plan.* In this example we use a hybrid plan.

Step 2   *Calculate the production rate.* We already know the regular-time production rate of 1800 units per period because we are using the initial workforce. This plan increases capacity when period demand exceeds the product available through that period's production and the beginning inven-

TABLE 13-30

	D	E	F	G	H	I	J	K	L	M
91	**Plan 4: Hybrid Aggregate Plan Using Initial Workforce and Overtime as Needed**									
92										
93	**Compute Regular Time Production Rate**									
94	Number of Employees	90								
95	Units per Employee per Period	20								
96	Regular Time Production per Period	1800								
97										
98	**Detailed Plan Computations**				Period					
99		**1**	**2**	**3**	**4**	**5**	**6**	**7**	**8**	**Total**
100	Total Demand in Period	1920	2160	1440	1200	2040	2400	1740	1500	
101	Net Demand After Inventory Considered	1920	2160	1440	840	1080	1680	1620	1320	
102	Regular Time Production	1800	1800	1800	1800	1800	1800	1800	1800	**14400**
103	Overtime Production Needed	120	360	0	0	0	0	0	0	**480**
104	Ending Inventory	0	0	360	960	720	120	180	480	**2820**
105										
106	**Cost Calculations for Plan D**									
107	Regular time labor cost	$1,440,000								
108	Overtime labor cost	$72,000								
109	Inventory holding cost	$28,200								
110	Back order cost	$0								
111	Hiring cost	$0								
112	Firing cost	$0								
113	**Total Cost**	**$1,540,200**								

tory for that period. For example, in period 1, we need 1920 units to satisfy demand. The hybrid aggregate plan in Table 13-30 shows that we build 1800 units during regular-time production and produce the remaining 120 units using overtime. We do not need overtime after period 2 because we can build up enough inventory to handle demand fluctuations.

We can see that the demand figures for periods 4, 5, 6, 7, and 8 have changed. These changes reflect the net demand for the period after subtracting the ending inventory of the previous period. For example, in period 4, demand is 1200 units. However, since we have 360 units in ending inventory in period 3, we subtract those out of period 4's demand to arrive at a net demand of 840 units.

Step 3 *Calculate the workforce size.* We know that the workforce size for this plan is 90 employees.

Step 4 *Test and cost the plan.* We test the plan using 90 employees producing 1800 units per period during regular time and using overtime for production when regular-time production is not adequate to satisfy demand. Table 13-30 shows the plan.

Plan 4 uses a stable workforce of 90 employees and uses overtime in periods 1 and 2. All other demand fluctuations

are handled through inventory. Total production for this plan is 14,880 units (14,400 during regular time and 480 during overtime). Ending inventories range from 0 to 960 units. Table 13-30 shows the total costs for Plan 4.

Step 5 *Evaluate Plan 4.* The per unit cost in Plan 4 is $103.51, which is only 61 cents higher than for our Plan 1 level aggregate plan using inventories and back orders. However, Plan 4 provides 100 percent customer service and the per unit cost differential is only about 0.6 percent. Plan 4 achieves excellent customer service at the lowest cost so far, which should satisfy both finance and marketing. In terms of operations and human resources, we are using overtime in the short term for periods 1 and 2. We do not ask workers to put in more than 20 percent overtime in period 2 (360 units on overtime in period 2, while producing 1,800 units on regular time). Overtime in period 1 is limited to 7 percent of the regular-time production. Thus we are not overusing the workers, and we keep overtime to a minimum. In addition, Plan 4 should not be hard to implement from an operations standpoint.

• Problem 5

Psychics of the World, Inc. wants an aggregate plan for its organization. Given the nature of the business, Psychics has decided that back orders are not acceptable. If a caller cannot be handled immediately, the call is a lost sale.

Psychics has predicted the following number of calls: May—8000 calls, June—5000 calls, July—6000 calls, August—7000 calls, September—6000 calls, October—8000 calls, November—10,000 calls, and December—12,000 calls.

Psychics of the World pays each of its forty-eight employees $4000 per month. Each psychic works 160 regular-time hours per month or 40 regular-time hours per week. The regular-time labor cost of a call is $20, the overtime labor cost per call is $30. Each psychic is expected to serve 200 callers per month. The management has limited overtime to 50 calls per month per psychic. It costs $3000 to hire a new psychic and $2000 to fire a psychic.

(a) Using the data in Table 13-31, develop a level aggregate without inventory, without back orders, and without overtime.

(b) Using the same problem data, develop an aggregate plan using a level workforce supplemented by overtime. Minimize the wasted capacity. No back orders are permitted.

• Before You Begin:

This requires an aggregate plan for a company without a tangible product, so inventory is not an option. The plan also does not allow for back orders or overtime. Therefore, you need to staff for peak demand and maintain that workforce throughout the plan.

TABLE 13-31

Data for Psychics of the World

	A	B
4	**Cost Data**	
5	Regular time labor cost per month	$4,000.00
6	Regular time labor cost per hour	$25.00
7	Overtime labor cost per hour	$37.50
8	Hiring cost per employee	$3,000.00
9	Firing cost per employee	$2,000.00
10		
11	**Capacity Data**	
12	Beginning workforce (employees)	48
13	Service standard per call (hours)	0.8
14	Regular time available per period (hours)	160
15	Overtime available per period (hours)	40
16		
17	**Demand Data (calls)**	
18	May	8000
19	June	5000
20	July	6000
21	Aug	7000
22	Sept	6000
23	Oct	8000
24	Nov	10000
25	Dec	12000
26		
27	Total Number of Periods	8

• Solution a

Step 1: *Choose the kind of aggregate plan.* We are using a level plan.

Step 2: *Calculate the aggregate production rate.* Since inventory and back orders are not permitted, find the period with the highest demand (December has demand of 12,000 calls). This is the aggregate production rate.

Step 3: *Calculate the workforce size given the aggregate production rate.* (12,000 calls divided by 200 calls per psychic per month.) The workforce should have sixty psychics, so we need to hire twelve more psychics.

Step 4: *Test and cost the plan.* The plan is shown in Table 13-32.

We calculate wasted capacity by subtracting the capacity used (calls to be serviced) from the available regular-time capacity. We calculate the costs in Step 5.

Step 5: *Evaluate the plan.* We have no other plan to compare the cost with but this plan appears to waste substantial capacity (34,000 more calls could have been handled). Total calls demanded were 62,000, whereas we had capacity for 96,000. Since management is concerned with wasting valuable psychic time, let's develop a plan that minimizes the amount of wasted capacity (minimizes undertime).

• Before You Begin:

In this scenario, you want to use a level workforce supplemented by overtime. No back orders are permitted and you are to minimize wasted capacity. To minimize wasted capacity, calculate how large a workforce is needed if each worker not only works the 160 regular-time hours per period but also works the available 40 hours of overtime. Therefore, when calculating how many employees are needed, divide by 200 total hours per employee per period (the sum of regular time and overtime). This reduces the size of your workforce, thus minimizing wasted capacity.

• Solution b

Step 1: *Choose the kind of aggregate plan.* Here, we use a level workforce.

Step 2: *Calculate the aggregate production rate.* This is the same as for the previous plan (12,000 calls).

Step 3: *Calculate the appropriate workforce.* This time we divide the aggregate production rate by the maximum number of calls per psychic per period (regular time plus overtime). Each psychic can provide up to 250 calls per period. This reduces the workforce from sixty psychics in the previous plan to forty-eight psychics in this plan (12,000 calls divided by 250 calls per psychic). No hires or fires are needed.

Step 4: *Test and cost the plan.* The plan is shown in Table 13-33.

Step 5: *Evaluate the plan.* This plan reduces the wasted regular-time capacity by 16,400 calls (34,000 − 17,600). The total cost is $336,000 less than the previous plan. Overtime is needed only in two periods so it should not create morale problems. This plan is an improvement, but better plans are possible.

TABLE 13-32

Solution for Psychics, Part a

	E	F	G	H	I	J	K	L	M	N	O	P	Q
3	Solution a: Level Aggregate Plan, No Inventory, No Back Orders, No Overtime												
4													
5	Compute Workforce Needed											Key Formulas (some are copied)	
6	Maximum Demand	12000	<-- Need to staff to meet the maximum number of calls									$F$6	=MAX($B$18:$B$25)
7	Calls per Worker per Period (Reg Time)	200										$F$7	=$B$14/$B$13
8	Workers Needed	60										$F$8	=F6/F7
9	Number to Hire	12										$F$9	=MAX(F8-$B$12,0)
10	Number to Fire	0										$F$10	=MAX(B12-$F$8,0)
11													
12	Detailed Plan Computations					Period							
13		May	June	July	Aug	Sept	Oct	Nov	Dec	Total			
14	Demand (calls)	8000	5000	6000	7000	6000	8000	10000	12000	62000		$F$14	=TRANSPOSE($B$18:$B$25)
15	Service hours needed	6400	4000	4800	5600	4800	6400	8000	9600	49600		$F$15	=F14*$B$13
16	Employees Needed	32	20	24	28	24	32	40	48			$F$16	=F15/$F$7
17	Regular time hours of capacity	9600	9600	9600	9600	9600	9600	9600	9600			$F$17	=$F$8*$B$14
18	Wasted Capacity Hours	3200	5600	4800	4000	4800	3200	1600	0	27200		$F$18	=F17-F15
19													
20	Cost Calculations for Part a												
21	Regular time labor cost	$1,920,000										$F$21	=F8*$B$14*$B$6*$B$27
22	Hiring cost	$36,000										$F$22	=F9*$B$8
23	Firing cost	$0										$F$23	=F10*$B$9
24	Total Cost	$1,956,000										$F$24	=SUM(F21:F23)

TABLE 13-33

Solution for Psychics, Part b

	E	F	G	H	I	J	K	L	M	N	O	P	Q
38	**Solution b: Level Aggregate Plan with Overtime, No Inventory, No Back Orders**												
39													
40	**Compute Workforce Needed**											**Key Formulas (some are copied)**	
41	Maximum Demand	12000	<-- Need to staff to meet the maximum number of calls									$F$41	=MAX($B$18:$B$25)
42	Calls per Worker per Period (Reg Time)	200										$F$42	=$B$14/$B$13
43	Calls per Worker per Period (Overtime)	50										$F$44	=F41/(F42+F43)
44	Workers Needed	48										$F$45	=MAX(F44-$B$12,0)
45	Number to Hire	0										$F$46	=MAX(B47-$F$8,0)
46	Number to Fire	0											
47													
48	**Detailed Plan Computations**					Period							
49		**May**	**June**	**July**	**Aug**	**Sept**	**Oct**	**Nov**	**Dec**	**Total**		$F$50	=TRANSPOSE($B$18:$B$25)
50	Demand (calls)	8000	5000	6000	7000	6000	8000	10000	12000	62000		$F$51	=F50*$B$13
51	Service hours needed	6400	4000	4800	5600	4800	6400	8000	9600	49600		$F$52	=$F$44*$B$14
52	Regular time hours of capacity	7680	7680	7680	7680	7680	7680	7680	7680	61440		$F$53	=MAX(F51-F52,0)
53	Overtime hours needed	0	0	0	0	0	0	320	1920	2240		$F$54	=MAX(F52-F51,0)
54	Wasted regular time capacity hours	1280	3680	2880	2080	2880	1280	0	0	14080			
55													
56	**Cost Calculations for Part b**												
57	Regular time labor cost	$1,536,000										$F$57	=F44*$B$14*$B$6*$B$27
58	Overtime labor cost	$84,000										$F$58	=N53*B7
59	Hiring cost	$0										$F$59	=F45*$B8
60	Firing cost	$0										$F$60	=F46*$B9
61	Total Cost	$1,620,000										$F$61	=SUM(F57:F60)

• Problem 6

Complete the following MPS records. The beginning inventory is 20 units and the order quantity is an FOQ = 50 units in part (a) and a POQ = two periods in part (b).

• Before You Begin:

This problem compares two different replenishment policies, an FOQ = 50 units with a POQ = two periods. Calculate the projected available quantity to determine when a replenishment order is needed. When the projected available quantity is negative, a replenishment order is needed in that period. Note that different policies can have orders due in different periods. The number of orders and the inventory levels can vary based on replenishment policy.

Period	1	2	3	4	5	6	7
Forecast	20	20	20	20	10	10	10
Projected available							
MPS							

Period	8	9	10	11	12	13
Forecast	10	10	10	20	20	20
Projected available						
MPS						

Period	1	2	3	4	5	6	7
Forecast	20	20	20	20	10	10	10
Projected available	0	30	10				
MPS		50					

Period	8	9	10	11	12	13
Forecast	10	10	10	20	20	20
Projected available						
MPS						

• Solution a

Begin by calculating the projected available quantities. At the end of period 1, the projected available should be 0 (20 units of beginning inventory less 20 units forecasted demand). If no order is received, the projected available row is negative at the end of period 2. When this row turns negative, we need a replenishment order for that period. The replenishment order in this case is 50 units. The updated MPS record is shown in Table 13-34.

When spreadsheeting this problem, you can include a conditional statement to check whether the projected available quantity is negative. When the projected available is negative, an MPS quantity is then entered into the appropriate cell. The program then recalculates the projected available quantity and continues on to the next negative result.

TABLE 13-34

Solution to Solved Problem 6a

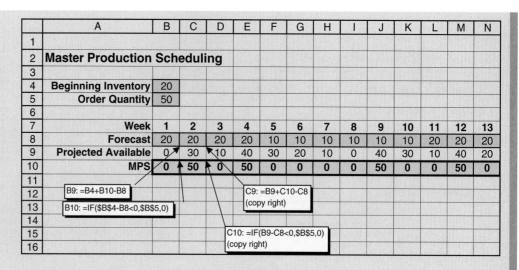

When you are solving the problem manually, continue calculating the projected available quantities until the next negative. At that point, we need another replenishment order. The completed MPS is shown here.

Period	1	2	3	4	5	6	7
Forecast	20	20	20	20	10	10	10
Projected available	0	30	10	40	30	20	10
MPS		50		50			

Period	8	9	10	11	12	13
Forecast	10	10	10	20	20	20
Projected available	0	40	30	10	40	20
MPS		50			50	

• Solution b

Period	1	2	3	4	5	6	7
Forecast	20	20	20	20	10	10	10
Projected available	0	20					
MPS		40					

Period	8	9	10	11	12	13
Forecast	10	10	10	20	20	20
Projected available						
MPS						

Once again, we need an MPS replenishment in period 2. To calculate the quantity, we sum the forecasted demand for the next two periods and subtract any beginning inventory. We need 20 units in both periods 2 and 3 for a total of 40 units; we have no beginning inventory, so we order 40 units. Look at the final MPS record that follows.

Period	1	2	3	4	5	6	7
Forecast	20	20	20	20	10	10	10
Projected available	0	20	0	10	0	10	0
MPS		40		30		20	

Period	8	9	10	11	12	13
Forecast	10	10	10	20	20	20
Projected available	10	0	20	0	20	0
MPS	20		30		40	

We need the next replenishment order in period 4, which should be for 30 units (20 demanded in period 4 and 10 units for period 5). The completed MPS record is shown above.

Note that replenishment orders are now scheduled for periods 2, 4, 6, 8, 10, and 12.

• Problem 7

Tim's Wire Shop builds two different, complicated wiring assemblies. Production of the WA-1001 model has averaged 50,000 units annually. Historically, Tim's Wire Shop has used 12,000 direct labor hours and 5000 hours of machine time annually to build the WA-1001 wiring harness. The other wiring assembly, WA-5005, has an average annual production of 40,000 units. Annual direct labor used on the WA-5005 is 26,000 hours and 2000 hours of machine time.

Develop the following four planning factors:

Planning factor for direct labor for WA-1001
Planning factor for direct labor for WA-5005
Planning factor for machine time for WA-1001
Planning factor for machine time for WA-5005

• Before You Begin:

In this problem, you need to calculate planning factors. Use the historical data to determine on average how much direct labor was used to make a model WA-1001 and a model WA-5005. Do the same for machine time.

• Solution

To calculate the planning factor for direct labor for WA-1001, divide the annual direct labor hours by the annual number of units produced.

Planning factor for direct labor for WA-1001 = 12,000 direct labor hours/50,000 units, or 0.24 hour per unit

Planning factor for direct labor for WA-5005 = 26,000 direct labor hours/40,000 units, or 0.65 hour per unit

Planning factor for machine time for WA-1001 = 5000 hours of machine time/50,000 units, or 0.10 hour per unit

Planning factor for machine time for WA-5005 = 2000 hours of machine time/40,000 units, or 0.05 hour per unit

• Problem 8

Given the proposed MPS shown here and the planning factors from Solved Problem 7, calculate the needed capacity for each period for direct labor and machine time.

• Before You Begin:

Use the planning factors developed in Solved Problem 7. Calculate the amount of capacity needed to satisfy the master production schedule shown. Determine the quarterly requirements for both direct labor and machine time.

Item	Quarter 1	Quarter 2	Quarter 3	Quarter 4
WA-1001	10,000	15,000	15,000	13,000
WA-5005	15,000	10,000	9,000	8,000
Total	25,000	25,000	24,000	21,000

Model	Direct Labor Factor	Q-1 MPS Qty	Q-1 Hours Req'd	Q-2 MPS Qty	Q-2 Hours Req'd	Q-3 MPS Qty	Q-3 Hours Req'd	Q-4 MPS Qty	Q-4 Hours Req'd	Total MPS Qty	Total Hours Req'd
WA-1001	0.24	10,000	2,400	15,000	3,600	15,000	3,600	13,000	3,120	53,000	12,720
WA-5005	0.65	15,000	9,750	10,000	6,500	9,000	5,850	8,000	5,200	42,000	27,300
Total		25,000	12,150	25,500	10,100	24,000	9,450	21,000	8,320	95,000	40,020

Use the same approach to calculate machine time needs.

Model	Machine Time Factor	Q-1 MPS Qty	Q-1 Hours Req'd	Q-2 MPS Qty	Q-2 Hours Req'd	Q-3 MPS Qty	Q-3 Hours Req'd	Q-4 MPS Qty	Q-4 Hours Req'd	Total MPS Qty	Total Hours Req'd
WA-1001	0.10	10,000	1,000	15,000	1,500	15,000	1,500	13,000	1,300	53,000	5,300
WA-5005	0.05	15,000	750	10,000	500	9,000	450	8,000	400	42,000	2,100
Total		25,000	1,750	25,000	2,000	24,000	1,950	21,000	1,700	95,000	7,400

• Solution

To find the direct labor hours needed, multiply the MPS quantity for each item by its planning factor. Do this for each period.

• Problem 9

Tim's Wire Shop uses three different departments to produce these wire assemblies. Each of these departments uses direct labor and machine time. Historically, Department 101 uses 25 percent of the direct labor time and machine time for these products, Department 102 uses 35 percent and Department 103 uses 40 percent. Calculate the direct labor and machine time needs for each department for each quarter.

• Before You Begin:

In this problem, allocate the capacity requirements calculated in Problem 8 among three different departments. Use the given historical averages to allocate the direct labor and machine hours needed each period by each department.

• Solution

To calculate the direct labor hours needed for each department, take the total direct labor needed for the quarter and multiply it by the appropriate percentage for each work center. For example, in Quarter 1, the total direct labor needed is 12,150 hours. Multiply that by 25 percent to allocate the appropriate amount of labor to Department 101. The same approach is used for allocating machine time among departments. The completed allocations are shown here.

Labor Allocations

Department	Historical Percentage Allocation	Labor Hours Required Q-1	Labor Hours Required Q-2	Labor Hours Required Q-3	Labor Hours Required Q-4	Total Labor Required
Department 101	25%	3,037.5	2,525	2,362.5	2,080	10,005
Department 102	35%	4,252.5	3,535	3,307.5	2,912	14,007
Department 103	40%	4,860	4,040	3,780	3,328	16,008
Total		12,150	10,100	9,450	8,320	40,020

Machine Allocations

Department	Historical Percentage Allocation	Machine Hours Required Q-1	Machine Hours Required Q-2	Machine Hours Required Q-3	Machine Hours Required Q-4	Total Machine Labor Required
Department 101	25%	437.5	500	487.5	425	1,850
Department 102	35%	612.5	700	682.5	595	2,590
Department 103	40%	700	800	780	680	2,960
Total		1,750	2,000	1,950	1,700	7,400

• Problem 10

Jeannette's Cashmere Sweaters has authorized the following MPS for her exclusive line of cashmere sweaters. She wants to use the MPS record for promising future orders. Current order promises are included. The MPS order quantity is 60 units. Beginning inventory is 0. Complete the following MPS record.

Period	1	2	3	4	5	6
Forecast	15	15	15	15	20	20
Customer orders	12	10	8	5	0	0
Projected available						
Available-to-promise						
MPS	60				60	

Period	7	8	9	10	11	12
Forecast	20	20	25	25	25	25
Customer orders	15	0	30	0	0	0
Projected available						
Available-to-promise						
MPS		60		60		60

• Before You Begin:

Complete the MPS record. Calculate the projected available quantity by subtracting the greater of the forecast or the actual customer orders from the sum of the previous period's projected available quantity plus any MPS order being received this period. Remember that a negative value in this row does not necessarily mean that you have a shortage. Calculate the available-to-promise quantity in the action bucket (period 1) and each period where an MPS shipment is due to arrive. Remem-

ber that only in the action bucket calculation is the beginning inventory included. In other periods, do not consider the beginning inventory since it is not clear what that quantity will be. A negative number in this row is always a problem.

• Solution

Projected available quantity is calculated as

Projected Available = beginning inventory + MPS shipment
  − the greater of the period's forecast or the
  customer orders promised for delivery

Therefore, the projected available quantity at the end of period 1 is 45 units (the beginning inventory of 0 plus the MPS shipment of 60, less the forecast of 15). The correct projected available quantities are shown here.

Period	1	2	3	4	5	6
Forecast	15	15	15	15	20	20
Customer orders	12	10	8	5	0	0
Projected available	45	30	15	0	40	20
Available-to-promise	25				45	
MPS	60				60	

Period	7	8	9	10	11	12
Forecast	20	20	25	25	25	25
Customer orders	15	0	30	0	0	0
Projected available	0	40	10	45	20	55
Available-to-promise		30		60		60
MPS		60		60		60

The ATP quantity in the action bucket is 25 units: a beginning inventory of 0 plus an MPS shipment of 60 units, less the customer orders of 35 units before the next replenishment (12 in period 1, 10 in period 2, 8 in period 3, and 5 in period 4). Use the formula for ATP at MPS replenishments to calculate the other ATP quantities.

$$ATP = MPS \text{ shipment} - \text{customer orders between current MPS shipment and next scheduled replenishment}$$

Compare your answers with those shown.

• Problem 11

Jeannette has received several additional orders to consider. Using the ATP record calculated in Problem 10, calculate which of the new orders Jeannette should accept. The new orders are (1) 20 units for delivery in period 4, (2) 50 units for delivery in period 8, (3) 40 units for delivery in period 12.

• *Before You Begin:*

In this problem, determine which orders can be promised for delivery. The key is to understand which units are not yet committed and might be used to satisfy a future delivery. Place the new orders into your MPS record and see what problems occur. Then try to determine how to solve these problems.

• *Solution*

The first step is to put the new orders into the MPS record and consider the implications. The updated MPS record is shown here.

Period	1	2	3	4	5	6
Forecast	15	15	15	15	20	20
Customer orders	12	10	8	25	20	0
Projected available	45	30	15	−10	30	10
Available-to-promise	5				25	
MPS	60				60	

Period	7	8	9	10	11	12
Forecast	20	20	25	25	25	25
Customer orders	15	50	30	0	0	40
Projected available	−10	0	−30	5	−20	0
Available-to-promise		−20		60		20
MPS		60		60		60

Note that Jeannette can accept order 1 for delivery of 20 additional sweaters in period 4. She can also accept order 3 for 40 units delivered in period 12. However, Jeannette has a problem accepting order 2. The ATP quantity in period 8 is −20, which means Jeannette must ensure that enough sweaters are available to satisfy that order. Since the ATP quantity in period 5 is 25 sweaters, Jeannette can set aside 20 of these sweaters so that she has enough to satisfy order 2. Therefore, she can accept all three orders.

On the revised MPS record, we see that the customer order in period 8 is reduced 20 units, which are transferred to period 5. The 20 units transferred to period 5 are the 20 units that were not available in period 8. Look at the changes in the updated MPS record.

Period	1	2	3	4	5	6
Forecast	15	15	15	15	20	20
Customer orders	12	10	8	25	40	0
Projected available	45	30	15	−10	10	−10
Available-to-promise	4				4	
MPS	60				60	

Period	7	8	9	10	11	12
Forecast	20	20	25	25	25	25
Customer orders	15	30	30	0	0	40
Projected available	−30	0	−30	5	−20	0
Available-to-promise		0		60		20
MPS		60		60		60

Discussion Questions

1. Explain the importance of the strategic business plan.
2. Describe sales and operations planning in terms of its purpose, components, and frequency.
3. Define the aggregate plan.
4. Explain why we use an aggregate or composite product when developing the aggregate plan.
5. Compare and contrast the level and the chase aggregate plans.
6. Describe the different demand-based options used in aggregate planning and their implications for a company.

7. Describe the different capacity-based options used in aggregate planning and their implications for a company.
8. Explain what the hybrid aggregate plan is and why it is used.
9. Explain the procedure for developing an aggregate plan.
10. Describe the factors to consider before developing an aggregate plan.
11. Explain how aggregate planning is different when the company does not provide a tangible product.

12. Visit a local manufacturer and determine how it uses aggregate planning.

13. Visit a local service provider and determine how it uses aggregate planning.

14. What two items must you calculate first when developing an aggregate plan?

15. Visit a local business and learn how it calculates its resources.

16. Describe the inputs needed to do master production scheduling.

17. Describe the different sources of demand.

18. Discuss the objectives of the master scheduler and how they influence master scheduling decisions.

19. Explain the process of developing an authorized MPS.

20. Explain the importance of rough-cut capacity planning in the MPS process.

21. Describe the role of time fence policies.

22. Explain the changes you can make in the frozen portion of the MPS and who must authorize such changes.

23. Explain the changes you can make in the slushy portion of the MPS and who authorizes such changes.

24. Discuss how the MPS might be used in a service organization.

Problems

Use the following data to solve the first seven problems.

Problem Data

Cost data	
Regular-time labor cost per hour	$10.00
Overtime labor cost per hour	$15.00
Subcontracting cost per unit (labor only)	$84.00
Holding cost per unit per period	$10.00
Back-order cost per unit per period	$20.00
Hiring cost per employee	$600.00
Firing cost per employee	$450.00
Capacity data	
Beginning workforce	210 employees
Beginning inventory	400 units
Labor standard per unit	6 hours
Regular time available per period	160 hours
Overtime available per period	32 hours
Subcontracting maximum per period	1000 units
Subcontracting minimum per period	500 units
Demand data	
Period 1	6000 units
Period 2	4800 units
Period 3	7840 units
Period 4	5200 units
Period 5	6560 units
Period 6	3600 units

1. The BackPack Company produces a line of backpacks. The manager, Jill Nicholas, is interested in using a level aggregate plan. Inventories and back orders will be used to handle demand fluctuations. She has asked you to develop such a plan.
   (a) Calculate the aggregate production rate.
   (b) Calculate the appropriate workforce given the aggregate production rate.
   (c) Show what would happen if this plan were implemented.
   (d) Calculate the costs of this plan.
   (e) Evaluate the plan in terms of cost, customer service, operations, and human resources.

2. Jill has decided that the BackPack Company must have very good customer service. She has asked you to develop a level aggregate plan using inventories but not back orders. All demand must be met each period. You must:
   (a) Calculate the aggregate production rate.
   (b) Calculate the appropriate workforce given the aggregate production rate.
   (c) Show what would happen if this plan were implemented.
   (d) Calculate the costs of this plan.
   (e) Evaluate the plan in terms of cost, customer service, operations, and human resources.

3. Although the BackPack Company has always used a level aggregate plan, Jill is interested in evaluating chase aggregate plans also. She has asked you to calculate how many hires and fires would be necessary to adjust capacity to meet demand exactly each period. If necessary, incur some undertime. Calculate the number of workers needed each period.

4. Now that you have calculated the number of workers needed each period in Problem 3, Jill wants to see how the plan would actually work. You need to:
   (a) Show what would happen if this plan were implemented.
   (b) Calculate the costs associated with this plan.
   (c) Evaluate the plan in terms of cost, customer service, operations, and human resources.

5. Jill Nicholas is concerned about BackPack's corporate image and has decided against using hires and fires. Instead, she has asked you to consider a chase aggregate plan using the current workforce supplemented by either overtime or undertime to change capacity to match demand exactly. She has asked for the following information from you:
   (a) How many production hours would be required each period to produce the exact quantity needed?
   (b) How many regular-time production hours are available each period?
   (c) How many overtime production hours would be needed each period?
   (d) Show what would happen if this plan were implemented.
   (e) Calculate the costs associated with this plan.
   (f) Evaluate the plan in terms of cost, customer service, operations, and human resources.

6. Jill Nicholas believes there must be a better aggregate plan. She has suggested a hybrid plan, using a permanent workforce of

195 employees and subcontracting as needed. Once again, Jill has requested you provide the following information:

(a) Calculate the regular-time production possible each period given a workforce of 195.

(b) Show what would happen if this plan were implemented.

(c) Calculate the costs associated with this plan.

(d) Evaluate the plan in terms of cost, customer service, operations, and human resources.

7. Jill wants you to consider a hybrid aggregate plan, using up to the maximum overtime per employee for any period where demand cannot be satisfied with the current regular-time production and the available inventory. Back orders can occur.

(a) Show what would happen if this plan were implemented.

(b) Calculate the costs associated with this plan.

(c) Evaluate the plan in terms of cost, customer service, operations, and human resources.

Use the information shown here for Problems 8 through 13. The Draper Tax Company provides tax services to local businesses. Draper chooses to meet all demand as it occurs because customers are unwilling to accept back orders. The company has provided the following cost, capacity, and demand information.

Draper Tax Company Problem Data

Cost data	
Regular-time labor cost per hour	$25.00
Overtime labor cost per hour	$37.50
Temporary worker cost per hour	$40.00
Hiring cost per permanent worker	$2000.00
Firing cost per permanent worker	$1200.00
Backorder cost	$500.00

Capacity data	
Beginning workforce	12 employees
Labor standard per service	12 hours
Regular-time hours per period	40 hours
Overtime hours per period	8 hours

Demand Data			
Week 1	48 clients	Week 4	40 clients
Week 2	36 clients	Week 5	38 clients
Week 3	50 clients	Week 6	48 clients

8. Calculate the size of the workforce needed for the company to meet average weekly demand.

9. Develop a level aggregate plan for the Draper Tax Company if back orders are permitted.

(a) Show what would happen if this plan were implemented.

(b) Calculate the costs associated with this plan.

(c) Evaluate the plan in terms of cost, customer service, operations, and human resources.

10. Develop a level aggregate plan for the Draper Company if no back orders are permitted.

(a) Show what would happen if this plan were implemented.

(b) Calculate the costs associated with this plan.

(c) Evaluate the plan in terms of cost, customer service, operations, and human resources.

11. Develop a chase aggregate plan using hires and fires to adjust the capacity for Draper. All demand must be met each period.

(a) Show what would happen if this plan were implemented.

(b) Calculate the costs associated with this plan.

(c) Evaluate the plan in terms of cost, customer service, operations, and human resources.

12. Develop a chase aggregate plan for Draper using a permanent workforce of twelve employees supplemented by overtime. All demand must be met each period.

(a) Show what would happen if this plan were implemented.

(b) Calculate the costs associated with this plan.

(c) Evaluate the plan in terms of cost, customer service, operations, and human resources.

13. Concerned about the welfare of its workers, Draper has decided to try a strategy without any overtime. Instead of overtime, Draper has decided to supplement the permanent workforce of twelve employees with temporary workers. Any temporary worker must work the entire week. There is no hiring or firing cost associated with temporary workers. Develop this aggregate plan for Draper.

(a) Show what would happen if this plan were implemented.

(b) Calculate the costs associated with this plan.

(c) Evaluate the plan in terms of cost, customer service, operations, and human resources.

14. W. C. Sanders, owner of Fort Engines, a producer of heavy-duty snow blower engines, needs to develop an aggregate plan for the coming year. The company currently uses twenty individuals working 160 regular-time hours each month. Each worker is capable of producing ten heavy-duty snow blowers per month. Employees are paid $12 per hour. Overtime is limited to a maximum of 40 hours per month per employee. Holding costs are $5 per unit per period. Back-order cost is $10 per unit per period. The beginning inventory is 40 units. Monthly demand projections are:

Month	Demand (units)	Month	Demand (units)
January	250	July	220
February	230	August	220
March	190	September	260
April	170	October	260
May	200	November	240
June	220	December	220

(a) Develop a hybrid aggregate plan using the initial workforce supplemented by overtime. If demand in any period exceeds regular-time production plus overtime production plus any beginning inventory, the company will use back orders. Calculate the cost of this plan.

(b) Another alternative is to try a level plan that uses inventory and back orders to absorb fluctuation. Calculate the cost of this plan.

(c) A third alternative being considered is to use a hybrid plan but also to close down the facility for the entire month of July. Overtime, inventory, and back orders can be used. Calculate the cost of this plan.

(d) Compare the three plans in terms of cost, customer service, operations, and human resources.

15. David's Delightful Kites Company (DDKC) manufactures kites. The most popular is David's Daredevil model. Demand management has prepared forecast estimates for the next six weeks. Beginning inventory is 15 David's Daredevils. As the master scheduler for DDKC, you must prepare an MPS. Your MPS order quantity is 72 kites.

Week	1	2	3	4	5	6
Forecast	20	35	50	50	45	40
Proj. Available 15						
MPS						

(a) Prepare the MPS using an order quantity of 72 kites.
(b) Calculate the ending inventory for each period.
(c) What is the maximum number of units held in inventory?
(d) How many MPS orders are needed?

16. In an effort to reduce setup frequency, DDKC has decided to use an MPS order quantity of 120 kites. (See Problem 15 for data.)

(a) Prepare the MPS using the new order quantity.
(b) Calculate the ending inventory for each period.
(c) Compare this MPS with the MPS developed in Problem 15.

17. DDKC has decided to change its replenishment policy. Instead of producing 72 or 120 kites each order, DDKC has reduced its MPS order quantity to 48 kites.

(a) Develop an MPS using 48 kites as the order quantity.
(b) Calculate the ending inventory for each period.
(c) Compare this MPS with the schedules developed in Problems 15 and 16.

18. Wine Accessories Inc. (WAI) produces two models of corkscrews, the standard model and a deluxe model. WAI follows a level aggregate plan, producing 20,000 corkscrews per month, or 5000 corkscrews per week. The MPS is developed in weekly time periods. The forecasts for each model and the projected available are shown in the next two tables. The replenishment order quantity is 2000 units for the standard model and 1000 units for the deluxe model. Note that you can place multiple orders if a single order is insufficient to cover the forecast (you can produce 4000 units of the standard model if necessary, or 2000 or 3000 units of the deluxe model). Remember that total weekly production is limited to 5000 corkscrews. Develop an MPS for each of the products.

Standard Corkscrew	1	2	3	4
Forecast	3000	3500	5000	4000
Proj. Available 2000				
MPS				

Deluxe Corkscrew	1	2	3	4
Forecast	2000	1500	1000	3000
Proj. Available 2000				
MPS				

19. WAI uses two resources for each product that it builds: direct labor and machine time. From historical records, WAI calculates the following planning factors:

Direct labor for standard corkscrew is 0.20 hour.
Direct labor for deluxe corkscrew is 0.50 hour.

Machine time for standard corkscrew is 0.10 hour.
Machine time for deluxe corkscrew is 0.30 hour.
Calculate the capacity needed for the MPS developed in Problem 18.

20. WAI is evaluating a new machine that reduces the machine time needed for the standard corkscrew to 0.08 hour, but increases the machine time for the deluxe corkscrew to 0.40 hour.

(a) Calculate the machine capacity needed for each period if WAI uses the new machine.
(b) Will the new machine prove beneficial to WAI?

21. WAI knows from historical records that approximately 40 percent of its labor is used in Department 101 and 60 percent is used in Department 102. The reverse is true of machine time; 60 percent is used in Department 101 and 40 percent is used in Department 102.

(a) Calculate the labor and machine hours needed in Department 101 for each period of the MPS developed in Problem 18.
(b) Calculate the labor and machine hours needed in Department 102 for each period of the MPS developed in Problem 18.

22. WAI has developed the following MPS. Calculate the projected available and the available-to-promise quantities for WAI.

	1	2	3	4	5	6	7	8
Forecast	30	30	30	40	40	40	45	45
Customer Orders	35	15	20	18	12	0	15	0
Proj. Available 50								
Available-to-promise								
MPS		100			100		100	

23. WAI, the company in Problem 22, has received the following additional customer orders shown here. You must determine which of the orders the company can accept. If the company must reject any orders, you must explain why.

Order Number	Order Quantity	Desired Week
1	10	3
2	25	1
3	40	5
4	20	6

24. Josh Randall, a sales representative for WAI, has convinced his customer (order #2 in Problem 23) to reschedule. Order #2 has agreed to accept delivery of 25 units in week 2 as long as WAI can also guarantee delivery of an additional 25 units in week 5. If WAI cannot meet both delivery requirements, the customer has threatened to withdraw its entire order. You have already promised orders 1, 3, and 4. Can you assure Josh that WAI will deliver on time? Show your calculations.

25. The Sno-More Company (SMC), a producer of snowmobiles, wants you to develop an aggregate plan for the coming year. Being a producer of a winter recreational product, SMC experiences highly seasonal demand for its product, with peaks during the fall and winter quarters and valleys during the spring and summer quarters. Use the following information in developing your aggregate plan.

Cost Data

Inventory holding cost	$100 per snowmobile per quarter
Production output per employee	50 snowmobiles per quarter
Regular-time (RT) production hours	500 hours per quarter
Beginning workforce	150 employees
Overtime (OT) constraint	20% of quarter's RT capacity

Cost Data

Subcontracting constraint	3500 snowmobiles per year
RT labor cost per unit	$400 per snowmobile
OT labor cost per unit	$600 per snowmobile
Cost of subcontracting per unit	$650 per snowmobile
Hiring cost per worker	$500 per worker
Firing cost per worker	$750 per worker
Beginning inventory	3000 snowmobiles

Demand Data

Quarter 1	14,000 snowmobiles
Quarter 2	6,000
Quarter 3	3,000
Quarter 4	16,000

(a) SMC wants to determine the cost of using a level production strategy. No back orders are allowed. Develop such an aggregate plan, determining the aggregate production rate, the number of workers needed, and the total cost of the plan.

(b) Evaluate the plan in terms of customer service, operations, finance, and human resources.

26. Using the information provided in Problem 25, develop an aggregate plan for SMC using a pure chase strategy. No ending inventory is allowed. Your beginning inventory is a result of last year's level strategy. SMC wants no finished goods inventory left at the end of any quarter in the coming year.

(a) Develop an aggregate plan using a pure chase strategy.

(b) Calculate the total cost of your aggregate plan.

(c) Evaluate the plan in terms of customer service, operations, finance, and human resources.

27. Using the information provided in Problem 25, develop a hybrid plan for SMC. All demand must be met each quarter.

(a) Calculate the cost of your hybrid aggregate plan.

(b) Evaluate your plan in terms of customer service, operations, finance, and human resources.

(c) Compare your plan with the plans developed in Problems 25 and 26.

CASE: Newmarket International Manufacturing Company (A)

Marcia Blakely, plant manager at the Newmarket International Manufacturing Company (NIMCO), was preparing for a meeting with her management team. Joining her would be Jack Novak, the company controller; Amy Granger, regional marketing manager; and Joe Barnes, the production manager. The goal of the meeting was to develop a staffing plan for the second quarter. A quick performance review covering the past two quarters proved disappointing. Customer service was poor in spite of higher component inventory levels. Stockouts of some components were a problem and caused production inefficiencies. Nothing seemed to be working smoothly.

Company History

NIMCO was founded by Marcia Blakely when she was only two years out of graduate school. Marcia's knowledge of mass customization has been the driving force behind NIMCO. The company produces three major custom products. Volume on the products is quite high even though each item is customized specifically for the customer. Each of the products is processed though up to four different work centers. Although each item is unique, the processing time at each work center is constant due to the sophisticated equipment used.

NIMCO currently has seventy-five full-time employees working in manufacturing. Each employee is scheduled to work 40 hours per week. Because mass customization is used, NIMCO carries no finished goods inventory. The company policy is to meet all demand each period; no back orders or stockouts are permitted.

Joe Barnes, the production manager, received the following information in advance of the meeting: demand forecasts for products A, B, and C for each week of the second quarter as shown in the table, and standard labor time estimates for each product. The standard labor times are: product A—0.24 hour, product B—0.38 hour, and product C—0.29 hour.

Joe knew that it would be useful to have you, his assistant, generate additional information for this meeting. You are to convert the individual product forecasts into the total number of labor hours needed each week. For example, in week 14, there are 3600 product A's multiplied by 0.24 hour, 4000 product B's times 0.38 hour, and 2000 product C's times 0.29 hour. The total standard labor time associated with products demanded in period 14 is 2964 hours. After determining the required labor hours each period, Joe wants you to develop three possible staffing plans. The first plan uses a level workforce and does not allow back orders in any period. The second plan uses the original full-time workforce (seventy-five employees) supplemented by the use of overtime to avoid back orders. The third plan adjusts the workforce each period to satisfy all demand by hiring and firing employees. To develop these plans and calculate their associated costs, you need to know that the regular-time wage rate is $14 per hour, overtime is $21 per hour, hiring costs are $500 per employee, and firing costs are $750 per employee.

Your job is to provide analyses of these three plans for Joe to use at the meeting. Make sure to include your recommendation after considering cost, customer service, and operations.

			Quarter 2 Demand Forecasts			
Week	Demand for Product A	Demand for Product B	Demand for Product C	Week	Demand for Product A	Demand for Product B	Demand for Product C
14	3600	4000	2000	21	4300	3600	3000
15	4000	4000	2500	22	4000	3600	3000
16	4300	4000	2800	23	4000	3800	2800
17	4400	3800	3100	24	3600	3800	2800
18	4500	3800	3200	25	3200	3800	2600
19	4500	3800	3200	26	3000	4000	2600
20	4400	3600	3200				

CASE: Newmarket International Manufacturing Company (B)

Newmarket International Manufacturing Company (NIMCO) was founded by Marcia Blakely only two years after leaving graduate school. Her knowledge of mass customization has been the driving force behind starting NIMCO. The company produces three major custom products. Volume on the products is high even though each item is customized specifically for the customer. The products are processed through up to four different work centers. Even though each item is unique, the processing time at each work center is constant due to the sophisticated equipment used.

Today's Opportunity

Joe Barnes had just left the staffing meeting. The information you provided was quite helpful and he believes he has ade-

quate resources to accomplish the required manufacturing for the second quarter. Effective capacity levels (including regular time and planned overtime) for each work center are shown here, as is the amount of time required for each product at each work center. The demand forecasts for each product are also shown.

Effective Weekly Capacity Levels			
Work Center 1	Work Center 2	Work Center 3	Work Center 4
920 hours	740 hours	920 hours	725 hours

			Product Standard Time by Work Center		
Product	Standard Hours at Work Center 1	Standard Hours at Work Center 2	Standard Hours at Work Center 3	Standard Hours at Work Center 4	Total Standard Time (Hours)
A	0.06		0.14	0.04	0.24
B	0.15	0.13		0.10	0.38
C	0.03	0.08	0.12	0.06	0.29

			Quarter 2 Demand Forecasts			
Week	Demand for Product A	Demand for Product B	Demand for Product C	Week	Demand for Product A	Demand for Product B	Demand for Product C
14	3600	4000	2000	21	4300	3600	3000
15	4000	4000	2500	22	4000	3600	3000
16	4300	4000	2800	23	4000	3800	2800
17	4400	3800	3100	24	3600	3800	2800
18	4500	3800	3200	25	3200	3800	2600
19	4500	3800	3200	26	3000	4000	2600
20	4400	3600	3200				

1. Joe now needs a rough-cut capacity check to determine whether the capacity at each work center is adequate to support the expected demand. Using the forecasted demand as your proposed master schedule, calculate the load profile for each work center for each week of the second quarter. Highlight any weeks in which problems might occur.

2. Joe knows from past experience that he has some flexibility in his workforce. Therefore, as long as the total capacity needed does not exceed the total available, the master schedule should be feasible. He also knows that he can increase his capacity total an additional 2.5 percent through extra overtime and still be within his budget. Given this new information, what recommendations do you have for Joe? What weeks are likely to be problems, and how should he use the capacity in those weeks? How important to NIMCO is it to have a flexible workforce?

INTERACTIVE CASE ► **Virtual Company** www.wiley.com/college/reid

On-line Case: Aggregate Planning at Valley Memorial Hospital

You're meeting today with Carol Gardner, assistant to the chief administrator at VMH. She tells you she's been saving a big project for you: "My job is scheduling all hospital staff for every shift, but I want you to focus on the nursing staff, so I can plan the nursing schedule for next year. After you finish, I've also got a smaller job for you. Let's go back in my office and I'll tell you what you need to know."

To complete this assignment, go to **www.wiley.com/college/reid** to get the details needed. Assignment questions are given at the site.

To access the Web site:

- Go to **www.wiley.com/college/reid**
- Click **Student Companion Site**
- Click **Virtual Company**
- Click **Kaizen Consulting, Inc.**
- Click **Consulting Assignments**
- Click **Capacity Planning**

INTERNET CHALLENGE ► **Cruising**

Aggregate planning identifies the resources needed by operations during a specified time period. Once these resources have been authorized, operations must make do or justify any deviations from the plan. With this in mind, identify the resources if you and three of your peers take a cruise of 10 to 14 days during a period when school is not in session.

On the Internet, investigate at least three different cruise lines. Develop a set of criteria for selecting which cruise line you will use. Select a cruise that you would like to take. The destination of the cruise is up to you. In preparation of the cruise, calculate how much and what kinds of clothing you'll take, as well as what accessories (cameras, binoculars, snorkeling gear, golf clubs, etc.) and how much cash. Then check to see which items you own and which items you need to buy.

Remember to check the site to see how many formal nights, informal nights, casual nights, and theme nights there will be during your cruise. Also check the shore excursions so you can calculate adequate funding. Don't forget to check your itinerary so you have proper clothes for any ports you'll be visiting (some countries frown on tank tops and shorts). Your professor should indicate any budgetary restrictions that you have.

You can put many of your expenses on a credit card but you'll also need cash for gratuities, incidental expenses at the different ports, and money for the casinos or bingo. You need to plan for transportation to and from the airport or for parking at the airport if one of you drive. You also need to be sure to take care of stopping your mail and taking care of any other responsibilities while you are away.

Develop an aggregate plan detailing the resources you will need for this cruise. Then disaggregate your aggregate plan by detailing what resources will be spent each day of your trip. Be ready to justify your expenditures.

On-line Resources

Companion Website www.wiley.com/college/reid:
- Take interactive *practice quizzes* to assess your knowledge and help you study in a dynamic way
- Review *PowerPoint slides* or print slides for notetaking
- Download *Excel Templates* to use for problem solving
- Access the *Virtual Company: Valley Memorial Hospital*
- Find links to *Company Tours* for this chapter
  Motorola, Inc.
  Ferrara Fire Apparatus, Inc.
- Find links for *Additional Web Resources* for this chapter
  H&R Block, *www.hrblock.com*
  United Parcel Service of America, Inc., *www.ups.com*
  APICS—Educational Society for Resource Management, *www.apics.org*

Additional Resources Available Only in WileyPLUS:
- Use the *e-Book* and launch directly to all interactive resources
- Take the interactive *Quick Test* to check your understanding of the chapter material and get immediate feedback on your responses.
- Check your understanding of the key vocabulary in the chapter with *Interactive Flash Cards*
- Use the *Animated Demo Problems* to review key problem types.
- Practice for your tests with *additional problem sets*
- *And more!*

Selected Bibliography

Arnold, J.R. Tony, and Stephen N. Chapman. *Introduction to Materials Management*, Fifth Edition. Upper Saddle River, N.J.: Pearson Education Limited, 2004.

Blackstone, John H. Jr., *Capacity Management*. Cincinnati, Ohio: South-Western, 1989.

Cox, James F., III, John H. Blackstone, and Michael S. Spencer, eds. *APICS Dictionary*, Eleventh Edition. Falls Church, Va.: American Production and Inventory Control Society, Inc., 2005.

Gessner, Robert A. *Master Production Schedule Planning*. New York: John Wiley & Sons, 1986.

Narasimhan, Sim, Dennis W. McLeavey, and Peter Billington. *Production Planning and Inventory Control*, Second Edition. Englewood Cliffs, N.J.: Prentice-Hall, 1995.

Plossl, George W. *Production and Inventory Control: Principles and Techniques*, Second Edition. Englewood Cliffs, N.J.: Prentice-Hall, 1985.

Slack, Nigel, Stuart Chambers, and Robert Johnston. *Operations Management*, Third Edition. Upper Saddle River, N.J.: Pearson Education Limited, 2001.

Vollmann, Thomas E., William L. Berry, D. Clay Whybark, and F. Robert Jacobs. *Manufacturing Planning and Control Systems*, Fifth Edition. Burr Ridge, Ill.: McGraw-Hill/Irwin, 2005.

Resource Planning

OM

Before studying this chapter you should know or, if necessary review

1. E-commerce, Chapter 4, pages 104–111.
2. Calculating available capacity, Chapter 9, pages 305–310.
3. Calculating order quantities, Chapter 12, pages 427–440.
4. Inventory record accuracy, Chapter 12, pages 452–454.
5. Developing the MPS, Chapter 13, pages 489–490.

LEARNING OBJECTIVES

After studying this chapter, you should be able to

1. Describe enterprise resource management.
2. Describe the evolution of ERP systems.
3. Describe the benefits and costs of ERP systems.
4. Provide an overview of MRP.
5. Explain the different types of demand.
6. Describe the objectives of MRP.
7. Describe the inputs needed for MRP.
8. Explain MRP operating logic.
9. Describe action notices.
10. Use different lot size rules with MRP.
11. Describe the role of capacity requirements planning (CRP).
12. Calculate the workloads at critical work centers using CRP.

CHAPTER OUTLINE

WHAT'S IN OM FOR ME?

ACC

FIN

MKT

OM

HRM

MIS

Do you remember the first time you invited your fiancée and parents for a very special dinner at your place? You decided to serve salad, grilled steaks, corn-on-the-cob, baked potatoes, and apple pie à la mode. You decided to special order the steaks two days ahead of time. You needed to make the pie the night before, so you made a special trip to get fresh apples and the other necessary ingredients. You bought the ice cream, corn, salad mix, some tomatoes, cucumbers, croutons, and salad dressing the day of the dinner as well as picked up the steaks. You also managed to pick up a special bottle of wine to go with dinner.

The night before the dinner, you baked the apple pie. The day of the dinner, you started the baked potatoes about an hour before dinnertime. You then mixed your salad. You seasoned the steaks and started the grill about thirty minutes before dinner. At the same time, you put a pot of water on to boil to cook the corn. You put the steaks on the grill to cook and the corn in the boiling water. You set the table while you were waiting. Just as you had planned, the dinner was ready on time. The steaks were done just right, the baked potatoes perfect, and the corn hot and juicy.

Your dinner was a huge success because you had used the basic concepts of material requirements planning: a master production schedule, bills of material, inventory records, and backward scheduling. The master production schedule was your planned menu for the dinner. To determine the materials needed, you had to know what you wanted to prepare. After setting the menu, the next step was to look at the bill of material (recipe) for each item. This allowed you to determine how much of each component or material was needed. Once you had the list assembled as to what was needed to make the dinner, you checked your inventory to see what you already had and what still had to be purchased.

▶ **Backward scheduling**
Starts with the due date for an order and works backward to determine the start date for each activity.

To use **backward scheduling**, we take a desired completion time or due date, consider all the activities that must be completed, and schedule the activities so that everything is ready at the appropriate time. Not all activities need the same amount of time to be completed, so we schedule when different activities must begin.

Your dinner didn't take too long to prepare, but building products typically takes some time. Consider a company like Dell Computer, well known for its rapidly built-to-order computers. Dell begins assembly of a customer's order almost immediately after receiving the order. To do this, Dell must carefully manage its component inventories, knowing the availability of needed components to complete the assembly. Information regarding the order is sent to members of its supply chain to assure on-time delivery of the finished computer. Dell uses this approach to support the concept of mass customization.

In this chapter, we will examine enterprise resource planning (ERP), as well as learn the basic mechanics of material requirements planning (MRP) and the role of capacity requirements planning (CRP).

ENTERPRISE RESOURCE PLANNING

Enterprise resource planning (ERP) is software designed for organizing and managing business processes (core and administrative) by sharing information across functional areas. Core processes include production planning and control, inventory management, purchasing, and distribution; administrative processes include accounting (cost control, accounts payable and receivable, etc.) and human resource management. Figure 14-1 shows an overview of enterprise resource planning.

The number of finished goods sold to final customers is a good example of the type of useful information shared throughout the supply chain. Knowing actual sales figures allows improved decision making by members of the supply chain and can help eliminate the bullwhip effect (discussed later in this chapter). For example, using the information about actual sales to the customer, manufacturing can determine more accurately the quantity and timing for product replenishments. Warehouse management then can plan for the receipt and subsequent distribution of the replenishments. Suppliers can determine the materials and components needed by manufacturing to meet the manufacturing schedule. All members of the supply chain are aware of what is happening and can plan accordingly. The primary objective of ERP is to integrate all departments and functions, internal and external, into a single computer system to serve the enterprise's needs.

The availability of information can increase productivity as well as customer satisfaction. For example, after Master Product Company began using ERP, sales increased by 20 percent while inventory investment decreased 30 percent. Owens Corning reported saving $65 million by using ERP to coordinate customer orders, financial reporting, and global procurement. Currently, ERP systems are used in thousands of medium and large companies globally. These systems typically consist of modules that can be used either alone or in various configurations. Let's look at the typical ERP modules.

▶ **Enterprise resource planning (ERP)**
An information system designed to integrate internal and external members of the supply chain.

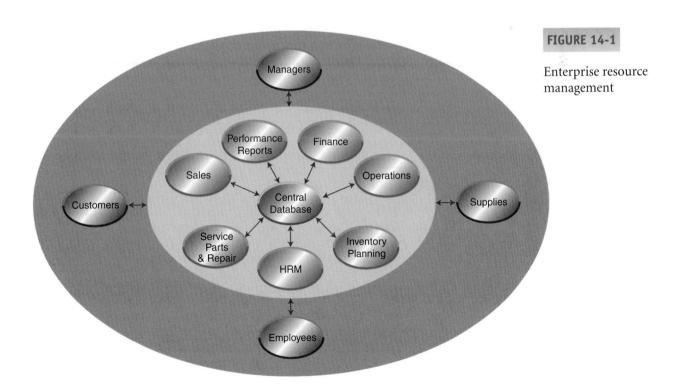

FIGURE 14-1

Enterprise resource management

ERP Modules

All modules are fully integrated, using a common database, and support processes that go across functional areas. A transaction in any module is immediately available to all other modules and to all relevant parties. There are four basic categories of ERP modules: finance and accounting, sales and marketing, production and materials management, and human resources.

The finance and accounting module can include the following capabilities: financial report generation, investment management, cost control analysis, asset management, capital management, debt management, and so on. It defines cost and profit centers, uses activity-based costing, facilitates capital budgeting, and profitability analysis, and tracks enterprise performance measures. A company can see the financial implication of every transaction.

The sales and marketing function handles customer-related activities. A customer can check for pricing, availability, and shipping options, as well as special promotions. The sales module can do a profitability analysis using different pricing options, discount structures, and rebates. The module also allows more accurate delivery date projections by providing insight into a company's finished goods and work-in-process inventories, as well as access to master scheduling information. Distribution requirements (documentation, packaging, etc.), transportation management (mode of transport), and shipping schedules are included. This module also handles billing, invoicing, rebate processing, product registrations, and customer complaints.

The production and materials module processes planning, bill of material generation, and product costing. The module implements engineer change orders, plans material requirements (MRP), allocates resources, and schedules and monitors production. It links manufacturing, sales, and finance together in real time. In terms of materials, it generates purchasing needs, manages inventory and warehouse functions, and supports supplier evaluations and invoice verification.

The human resources module includes workforce planning, employee scheduling, training and development, payroll and benefits, expense reimbursement, job descriptions, organizational charts, and workflow analysis.

These four modules can be implemented either individually or as a fully integrated system. ERP uses a common database to ensure the same information is used throughout the company to improve decision making across functional areas. Let's look at the evolution of ERP systems.

THE EVOLUTION OF ERP

First-Generation ERP

An ERP system provides a single interface for managing all routine activities performed in manufacturing—from order entry to after-sales customer service. In the later 1990s, ERP systems were extended to external members of the supply chain (suppliers and customers). These extensions provide customer interaction and supplier management modules. Using a single interface can provide significant savings. Large companies—for example ExxonMobil—consolidated 300 different information systems into one ERP system by implementing SAP R/3 (a leading ERP system) in its U.S. petrochemical operations. Initially, ERP was designed to handle business transactions and not to support supply chains. The second generation of ERP was designed to overcome this deficiency.

Second-Generation ERP

First-generation ERP was designed to automate routine business transactions and did it very well. Merrill Lynch reported that almost 40 percent of U.S. companies with greater than $1 billion in annual revenues had implemented ERP. Most companies had received the major benefits of ERP systems by the late 1990s. The development of second-generation ERP systems has begun. Its objectives are to leverage existing systems to increase efficiency in handling transactions, improve decision making, and to support e-commerce.

While first-generation ERP systems gave planners plenty of statistics about what happened in the company, in terms of costs and financial performance, the reports were merely snapshots of the business at a single point in time. These reports did not support the continuous planning needed in supply chain management. This deficiency led to the development of planning systems focused on decision making. These new systems are referred to as SCM (supply chain management) software.

SCM software is designed to improve decision making in the supply chain. It helps answer such questions as: (1) What is the best way to ship a product to a specific customer? (2) What is the optimal production plan? (3) How much product should ship to specific intermediaries? (4) How can outbound and inbound transportation costs be minimized? SCM software typically includes decision support modules, such as linear programming and simulation, to help answer these questions.

▶ **SCM software**
Designed to improve decision making in the supply chain.

Let's consider how ERP and SCM software can work together. Think about the task of order processing. With SCM software, the question is, "Should I take your order?" while the ERP approach is, "How can I best take or fulfill your order?" Both are merely information systems. SCM systems complement ERP systems, providing intelligent decision support. The SCM system is designed to overlay existing systems and extract data from every part of the supply chain. This way, the company has a clear picture of where it is heading rather than simply having automated processes. **Supply chain intelligence (SCI)** is the capability of collecting business intelligence along the supply chain. This intelligence enables strategic decision making by analyzing data along the entire supply chain.

▶ **Supply chain intelligence (SCI)**
Enables strategic decision making along the supply chain.

An example of a successful SCM system implementation is IBM. IBM restructured its global supply chain to achieve quick responsiveness to customers while holding minimal inventory. To do this, IBM developed an extended-enterprise supply chain analysis tool called the Asset Management Tool (AMT). AMT allows for quantitative analysis of interenterprise supply chains. IBM used AMT to analyze inventory budgets, inventory turnover objectives, customer service target levels, and new product introductions. AMT benefits have included the saving of over $750 million in material costs and price-protection expenses each year.

Another example of an ERP application with an SCM module is Colgate-Palmolive (C-P). C-P produces oral-care products (mouthwashes, toothpaste, and toothbrushes), personal-care products (baby care, deodorants, shampoos, and soaps), and pet food. Foreign sales account for about 70 percent of C-P's total revenues. An important factor for C-P was whether it could use ERP software across the entire spectrum of its business. The company needed the ability to coordinate globally, yet act locally. C-P's U.S. division opted to use SAP R/3 for this effort.

Another option for businesses wanting ERP functions is to lease applications rather than to build systems. In leased applications, the ERP vendor takes care of the functionalities and internal integration problems. The ERP vendor is typically referred to as an **application service provider (ASP)**. The ASP sets up the system and runs it for

▶ **Application service provider (ASP)**
Sets up and runs ERP systems.

the company. This approach often works well for small to medium companies. The software is usually delivered via the Internet.

Since many companies involved in e-commerce have ERP systems, and since e-commerce needs to interface with the ERP systems, integration is necessary, primarily for order fulfillment and collaboration with business partners. Cybex International, a producer of fitness machines, illustrates how e-commerce and ERP can be integrated.

LINKS TO PRACTICE

Cybex International, Inc.

David Sacks/The Image Bank/Getty Images, Inc.

Cybex International was not able to meet increased demand for its fitness machines. To maintain market share, the company paid premium prices for "rush" orders from close to 1000 suppliers. The rush orders were due to poor demand forecasts of the finished products and resulted in the wrong quantities of materials being ordered and supplemental orders being needed. Cybex installed an ERP system for its supply chain planning and manufacturing applications from PeopleSoft, Inc. In reviewing its business processes, Cybex reduced the number of suppliers to 550. The new system works with customer orders accepted at the corporate web site. These orders are instantly forwarded to the appropriate manufacturing facility. ERP uses its material requirements planning module (MRP) to calculate the materials and components needed; then the product configurator constructs a component list and a bill of materials for the item. At that time, suppliers are notified of components and materials needed. After implementing the ERP system, Cybex was able to reduce its number of bills of material from 15,200 to 200, the number of suppliers from 1000 to 550, paperwork by two-thirds, and build-to-order time from four to two weeks.

The logic behind integrating e-commerce and ERP is that organizations leverage their investment in ERP and speed up the development of e-commerce applications. You should understand that ERP systems deal more with back-office applications (accounting, inventory, scheduling) while e-commerce applications deal more with front-office applications such as sales, order entry, customer service, and customer relationship management. You should also understand that e-commerce supply chains can have order fulfillment problems.

E-commerce supply chains deliver small quantities to a very large number of customers. When companies sell on-line, they must find the products to be shipped, package them, arrange for delivery to the customer, collect money from customers, and handle the return of unwanted or defective products.

THE BENEFITS OF ERP

One benefit of ERP is that it integrates the complete range of an organization's operations in order to present a holistic view of the business functions from a single information and IT architecture. This single information source improves the organizational information flow. Because of improved information flow, an organization increases its ability to incorporate best practices that facilitate better managerial control, speedier decision making, and cost reductions throughout the organization. The basic architecture of an ERP system builds upon a single database, one application, and a unified interface across the entire enterprise, thus allowing an integrated approach.

A study by Benchmarking Partners for the Deloitte & Touche consulting corporation classifies companies' motivations for implementing ERP systems into two groups: technological and operational. Technological motivation relates to the replacement of disparate systems, improved quality and visibility of information, integration of business processes and systems, replacement of older, obsolete systems, and the acquisition of systems that can support future business growth. For example, ExxonMobil used ERP to replace 300 different systems.

Operational motivation is related to improving inadequate business performance, reducing high cost structures, improving customer responsiveness, simplifying complex processes, supporting global expansion, and standardizing best practices throughout the enterprise. Cybex International is a good example of an organization using ERP to improve customer responsiveness.

ERP provides both tangible and intangible benefits. Tangible benefits refer to reductions in inventory and staffing, increased productivity, improved order management, quicker closing of financial cycles, reduced IT and purchasing costs, improved cash flow management, increased revenue and profits, reduced transportation and logistics costs, and improved on-time delivery performance. Intangible benefits refer to the improved visibility of corporate data, improved customer responsiveness, better integration between systems, standardization of computing platforms, improved flexibility, global sharing of information, and better visibility into the supply chain management process.

A study of ERP implementations reported that it took companies eight months until after the new system was established to see any benefits. The median annual savings from a new ERP system was $1.6 million.

LINKS TO PRACTICE

i2 Technologies
www.i2.com

Ed Horowitz/Stone/ Getty Images, Inc.

One company that has developed various ERP software packages to enhance manufacturers' overall productivity is i2 Technologies. By using this software, manufacturers can now improve supply chain activities by monitoring, managing, and optimizing their internal and external activities. For example, manufacturers can connect immediately with suppliers and shippers in real time and can examine the supply chain. In addition, manufacturers can obtain reports that discuss efficiency and forecast potential problems. i2 Technologies' Transportation Solutions helps manufacturers optimize delivery schedules. Also, i2 Technologies' Softgoods Matrix.com helps softgoods retailers, manufacturers, and suppliers coordinate on-line business, improve response to changes in consumer trends, and attract potential customers. Some of the world's largest manufacturing firms have adopted software developed by i2 Technologies.

SAP AG, one of the leading developers of enterprise solutions software, provides companies with mySAP.com, a software platform for open systems. Open systems allow users to communicate with another user without being constrained by a particular organization's solution. This software includes functionality for material requirements planning, including manufacturing and financial applications, materials management, product design management, sales and distribution, human resources, production planning, quality assurance, and plant maintenance. SAP also provides functionality that promotes the ability to do collaborative planning on the web via collaborative exchanges and public marketplaces.

Although enterprise software (formerly known as ERP) is often associated with manufacturing operations, it also has applications in the service sector. SAP Public Sector and Education SAP Public Services, Inc. has announced a plan to offer an offender management system that may revolutionize the corrections industry. The initial implementation will modernize the Commonwealth of Virginia's Department of Corrections. The SAP offender management system will provide web-based case management. The new system will enable the Virginia Department of Corrections to enter into the e-government world.

THE COST OF ERP SYSTEMS

SAP AG, Peoplesoft, Oracle, and Baan are major suppliers of ERP systems. The cost of an ERP system ranges from hundreds of thousands of dollars to several million dollars. In addition to the software cost is the cost of outside consultants used in the selection, configuration, and implementation of the ERP system. An IT research firm, Gartner Group, reports that companies can expect to spend up to three times as much money for consultants as they do for the ERP system. Additional costs include the human resources needed to work on the implementation of the system, new hardware to run the program, and the development of a new, integrated database.

A review of successful ERP implementations indicates that the most critical factors are leadership and top management commitment. Top management must clearly set the vision and direction for the business, as well as establish a culture that enables the business to benefit by using the technological capabilities of an ERP system. Champions are needed to effectively implement change programs and promote best practices. Let's look at how some companies have used ERP.

©AP/Wide World Photos

In July 1999, Hershey Foods Corporation switched to a new $112 million computer system designed to automate and modernize its information flows—from taking new candy orders to loading the trucks.

Some $3\frac{1}{2}$ months later, Hershey was still working out the bugs in the new system. Hershey had plenty of candy to fill orders, but the new system was not releasing candy from the warehouses. As a result, Hershey was unable to satisfy some of its major customers. Poor delivery prior to major candy seasons has strained Hershey's relationships with several major customers.

Now that you have a basic understanding of ERP systems, let's examine the manufacturing planning systems that were the basis for today's production and materials modules.

MATERIAL PLANNING SYSTEMS

In the 1960s, manufacturing planning systems focused primarily on traditional inventory control issues (when to order, how much to order, etc.). This led to the development of material requirements planning systems (MRP). These systems translated the approved master production schedule of final products into time-phased net requirements for subassemblies and final assemblies for manufacturing and components and raw materials for purchasing. The initial MRP systems evolved into closed-loop MRP.

Closed-loop MRP is an MRP system that includes sales and operations planning, master production scheduling, and capacity requirements planning (discussed in Chapter 13). After realistic and attainable plans are developed, manufacturing executes the plan. This involves input–output capacity measurement, detailed scheduling and dispatching (we will discuss these in Chapter 15), anticipated delay reports from the manufacturing facility and the suppliers, as well as scheduling deliveries from suppliers. Closed-loop means that each function is included in the overall system and that feedback mechanisms are in place to make sure that the plan remains valid.

In the mid-1970s, **manufacturing resource planning (MRP II)**, the next generation of manufacturing planning systems, was developed. MRP II has three major components: management planning, operations planning, and operations execution. The company's strategy is translated into business objectives for the current year. These objectives drive the development of the marketing plan that in turn drives the development of the production plan. The production plan identifies the resources available to manufacturing to achieve the output needed by marketing. Then the master production schedule shows how the resources from the production plan are to be used. Operations planning is the MRP function. One of the primary inputs to the MRP system is the master production schedule. The output from the system is the order release schedule. Operations execution brings the plan to life. Raw materials and components are purchased, subassemblies and final assemblies scheduled, quality assured, labor managed, and production completed. Problems encountered in production are fed back to the MRP component. Ongoing performance evaluation provides feedback—that is, additional resource requirements, changing market demands, and so on—to business planning for any necessary corrective actions. Shortcomings in MRP II in managing a production facility's orders, production plans, and inventories, along with the need to integrate external functions, led to the development of ERP systems.

▶ **Closed-loop MRP**
An MRP system that includes production planning, master production scheduling, and capacity requirements planning

▶ **Manufacturing resource planning (MRP II)**
A method for the effective planning and integration of all internal resources.

▶ **Material requirements planning (MRP)**
A system that uses the MRP, inventory record data, and BOM to calculate material requirements.

AN OVERVIEW OF MRP

Material requirements planning (MRP) is an information system that uses the concept of backward scheduling. MRP enables companies that produce items in batches to have the right materials in the right amounts available at the right time. While having the material is critical, the company also needs the capacity to process the materials on time. Companies use **capacity requirements planning (CRP)** to check

▶ **Capacity requirements planning (CRP)**
Determines the labor and machine resources needed to fill the open and planned orders generated by the MRP.

that enough work is scheduled for operations and that the amount of work is feasible. CRP reveals potential problems, which gives operations a chance to prevent problems from occurring. For example, if you know that you need 250 hours of test equipment time four weeks from now and you only have 200 hours of test equipment time available during that week, you can do something about it now. You can change the master schedule so that some of the items needing testing are scheduled for a different time period, or you can authorize additional workers in the test area, or authorize overtime for that work center. You don't wait until four weeks from now and then figure out what to do.

When having your dinner party we described at the beginning of this chapter, you had to do several activities before you served the dinner. First, you planned the menu. Second, you determined the number of servings needed. Third, you reviewed the recipes for each item on the menu to determine the materials needed. Fourth, you checked your cupboards, refrigerator, and freezer to see if you had any of the materials on hand. Fifth, you purchased any materials that you still needed. Sixth, you prepared the dinner.

▶ **Bill of material (BOM)**
Lists all the subassemblies, component parts, and raw materials that go into an end item and shows the usage quantity of each required.

Planning the menu and calculating the number of servings is equivalent to creating an authorized master production schedule (MPS). Reviewing the recipes to determine the materials needed is equivalent to checking the **bill of material (BOM)** file to determine the materials needed to build a product. The BOM file lists all the subassemblies, component parts, and raw materials that go into the end item and shows the usage quantity of each. Using the list of components and materials needed, MRP checks the inventory records to determine if sufficient quantities of those materials are available or if the purchasing department needs to procure these materials. MRP systems are designed to handle dependent demand. Let's look at different types of demand.

TYPES OF DEMAND

▶ **Independent demand**
The demand for an item is unrelated to the demand for other items.

The two types of demand are independent and dependent. **Independent demand** is the demand for finished products; it does not depend on the demand for other products. Finished products include any item sold directly to a consumer. For example, if a company builds and sells CD cabinets, the demand for the CD cabinet is not dependent on anything else. The company could also sell decorative replacement hinges or handles as independent products. Figure 14-2 is a drawing of the CD cabinet. Although you can't see inside the cabinet, it does have four shelves.

▶ **Dependent demand**
Demand for component parts is based on the number of end items being produced.

Dependent demand is derived from finished products. For example, when a company makes CD cabinets (see Figure 14-2), it needs tops, bottoms, feet, doors, door magnets, door hinges, door handle, screws, left sides, right sides, door catch, cabinet shelves, and shelf holders. The company can determine how many of each of these items is needed based on how many CD cabinets the company plans to build. If the company builds 100 CD cabinets, operations needs 100 tops, 100 bottoms, 100 doors, 100 left sides, 100 right sides, 200 door hinges (two are needed to build one finished product), 400 feet and 400 cabinet shelves (4 are needed to build one finished product), 1000 screws (8 are needed for the door to attach the hinges, magnet, and handle; and 2 are needed for the right side to attach the door catch), and 1600 shelf holders (16 for each finished product). The company does not forecast dependent demand but, rather, calculates the material needs based on the final products to be produced. MRP, computerized information systems, are designed to manage dependent

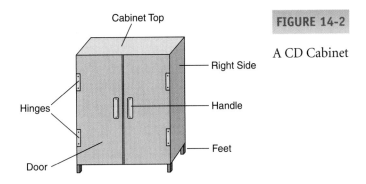

FIGURE 14-2

A CD Cabinet

demand inventory and to schedule necessary replenishment orders. Let's look at a typical MRP system.

Figure 14-3 is an overview of an MRP system. The authorized MPS is the primary input to the MRP system. The MPS details the company's planned products, quantity, and the schedule used by marketing when promising deliveries. The product due dates are critical to the MRP system since they set the completion dates used to backward-schedule production. Part of the MRP system is developing a **time-phased** schedule that shows future demand, supply, and inventories by time period. The time-phased schedule shows the production planner when in the production process parts and materials must be available. Not all parts and materials have to be available at the start of production, but they must be available at the stage of production in which they are needed. For example, when you are building a furniture cabinet, you do not need the stain before you start building the cabinet; you need it when you are ready to apply the finish. On the other hand, you must have the wood before you can begin building the cabinet.

The MRP system checks the BOM file to determine the materials needed, how much, and when. The system generates the **gross requirements** of each part and material needed to accomplish the MPS. The system inserts the gross requirements into the individual inventory records and computes the projected available quantity for

▶ **Time-phased**
Expressing future demand, supply, and inventories by time period.

▶ **Gross requirements**
The total-period demand for an item.

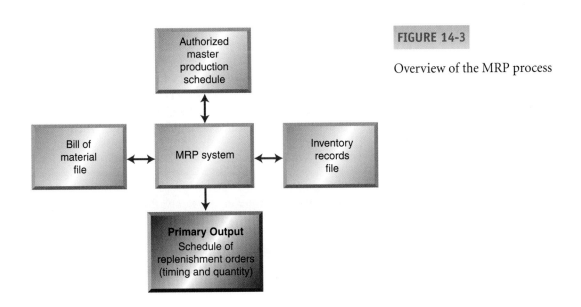

FIGURE 14-3

Overview of the MRP process

each item, so that you know if there's enough inventory or if you need a replenishment order. If you need a replenishment order, the MRP system tells you when to place the order, either to a supplier or to the manufacturing floor, to ensure that the parts or material are available when needed. The MRP system generates planned replenishment order release schedules and can generate additional reports, which we discuss later in the chapter. Now let's consider the objectives of an MRP system.

OBJECTIVES OF MRP

The objectives of an MRP system are to determine the quantity and timing of material requirements and to keep priorities updated and valid.

- *Determine the quantity and timing of material requirements.* Your company uses MRP to determine what to order (it checks the BOM), how much to order (it uses the lot size rule for the specific item), when to place the order (it looks at when the material is needed and backward-schedules to account for lead time), and when to schedule delivery (it schedules the material to arrive just as it is needed).

- *Maintain priorities.* Your company also uses MRP to keep priorities updated and valid. Requirements change. Customers change order quantities and/or timing. Suppliers deliver late and/or the wrong quantities. Unexpected scrap results from manufacturing. Equipment breaks down and production is delayed. In an ever-changing environment, you use an MRP system to respond to changes in the daily environment, to reorganize priorities, and to keep plans current and viable.

Next, we discuss the inputs needed to run an MRP system.

MRP INPUTS

The three inputs to an MRP system are the authorized MPS, the BOM, and the individual item inventory records. Using the CD cabinet from Figure 14-2 as our end item, let's look at each of these inputs.

Authorized MPS

The authorized MPS is a statement of what and when your company expects to build. Table 14-1 shows the first MPS record for the CD cabinet. From the MPS record, we calculate when we need to have replenishment orders of CD cabinets. We calculate the timing of MPS orders by the projected available quantity. When we do not have

TABLE 14-1

Initial MPS Record for CD Cabinet

Item: CD Cabinet				Lead time: 1 week								
Lot size rule: FOQ = 100				Beginning inventory: 80								
	1	2	3	4	5	6	7	8	9	10	11	12
Gross Requirements:	25	25	25	25	30	30	30	30	35	35	35	35
Projected Available:	55	30	5	−20								
MPS												

TABLE 14-2

Updated MPS Record
for CD Cabinet

Item: CD Cabinet Lot size rule: FOQ = 100				Lead time: 1 week Beginning inventory: 80								
	1	2	3	4	5	6	7	8	9	10	11	12
Gross Requirements:	25	25	25	25	30	30	30	30	35	35	35	35
Projected Available:	55	30	5	80	50	20	90	60	25	90	55	20
MPS				100			100			100		

enough inventory to satisfy the forecast for a particular period, we need an MPS order. The quantity of the replenishment order is based on the lot sizing rule used. Table 14-2 shows the completed MPS record.

Inventory Records

To determine whether enough inventory is available or whether a replenishment order is needed, the MRP system checks the inventory records of all items listed in the BOM. Table 14-3 shows the CD cabinet's inventory record. Let's look at the information in the record.

The top part of the record contains product or part identification information—typically either a part number, part name, or description. In our example, the part name is CD cabinet. The top portion also contains **planning factors**. These can include the lot size rule, **lead time**, safety stock requirements, and so forth.

In our example, the lot size rule is lot-for-lot (L4L), and the planned lead time is one week. This information remains relatively constant and is needed by the system to determine how much to order and when to place the replenishment order. Additional information in the records changes with each inventory transaction. These transactions include releasing new orders, receiving previously ordered materials, withdrawing inventory, canceling orders, correcting inventory record errors, and adjusting for rejected shipments. The record shows how much inventory of an item is available, projects future needs, and shows the projected inventory level in different time periods.

One problem with an MRP system is inventory record accuracy. Because the system checks the inventory record to see whether it has to generate a replenishment order, an inaccuracy in the record can cause an error in replenishment ordering. Cycle counting, discussed in Chapter 12, is a technique for improving inventory record accuracy. Let's look at the inventory record shown in Table 14-3.

▶ **Planning factors**
Factors include the lot size rule, replenishment lead times, and safety stock requirements.

▶ **Lead time**
The span of time needed to perform an activity or series of activities.

TABLE 14-3

First Inventory Record
for CD Cabinet

Item: CD Cabinet Lot size rule: L4L				Lead time: 1 week Beginning inventory: 0								
	1	2	3	4	5	6	7	8	9	10	11	12
Gross Requirements:	0	0	0	100	0	0	100	0	0	100	0	0
Scheduled Receipts:												
Projected Available:	0	0	0	−100								
Planned Orders												

The item is a CD cabinet and the lot size rule is lot-for-lot. The lead time is one week. Thus if we want 100 CD cabinets to be available in week 4, we have to begin the final assembly of the CD cabinets in week 3. For our purposes, gross requirements are due at the beginning of the period (Monday morning) and planned orders are started at the beginning of a time period. Final assembly is done during week 3 so we can have 100 CD cabinets at the beginning of week 4.

Gross requirements for finished products are taken from the authorized MPS. **Scheduled receipts** are replenishment orders that have been placed but not yet received. For example, if we placed an order last week and we know it will arrive in period 1, it would be in the scheduled receipts row.

The **projected available** quantity is a period-by-period projection of how much inventory should be available. The projected available quantity equals the beginning inventory, plus any replenishment order due, less the gross requirements for that period. For example, in period 4, we have no beginning inventory and we have 0 units scheduled to arrive, less our gross requirements of 100 units in period 4. Thus our projected available at the end of period 4 is −100, as shown in Table 14-3. The beginning inventory for any time period is equal to the projected available quantity at the end of the previous period.

Planned orders result when we do not have enough inventory to cover the gross requirements for a period. For example, unless we plan an order to arrive in period 4, we will be short 100 CD cabinets. When we need a replenishment order, we calculate the quantity by the lot size rule and we calculate the timing by the lead time. For example, we need an order to arrive in period 4, the lot size rule L4L dictates that we order just enough to cover our requirement (100 units), and the lead time of one week means that we must place the order one week before we need it (so we have a planned order of 100 units in period 3). Table 14-4 shows the updated inventory record for the CD cabinet.

Bills of Material

A *bill of material* (BOM) lists the subassemblies, intermediate assemblies, component parts, raw materials, and the quantities of each needed to produce one final product. It is exactly like a recipe for baking a cake. As we would follow the recipe for the cake, the manufacturer is expected to follow the BOM precisely. No extra parts are added. No substitutions are made without appropriate paperwork. Companies that use MRP systems must have a disciplined workforce that uses only the materials authorized by the BOM. The BOMs used as input to the MRP system are **indented bills of materials**. Table 14-5 shows an indented bill of material for the CD cabinet. In an indented

▶ **Scheduled receipt**
An open order that has an assigned due date.

▶ **Projected available**
The inventory balance projected into the future.

▶ **Planned orders**
Suggested order quantities, release dates, and due dates created by an MRP system.

▶ **Indented bill of material**
Shows the highest-level "parents" closest to the left margin and the "children" indented toward the right. Subsequent levels are indented farther to the right.

TABLE 14-4

Updated Inventory Record for CD Cabinet

Item: CD Cabinet		Lead time: 1 week										
Lot size rule: L4L		Beginning inventory: 0										
	1	2	3	4	5	6	7	8	9	10	11	12
Gross Requirements:	0	0	0	100	0	0	100	0	0	100	0	0
Scheduled Receipts:												
Projected Available:	0	0	0	0	0	0	0	0	0	0	0	0
Planned Orders			100			100			100			

Part Number	Description	Quantity Required
CD1001-01	CD Cabinet	1
CD1001T-01	Cabinet top	1
CD1001B-01	Cabinet bottom	1
CD1001F-01	Feet	4
CD1001D-01	Cabinet door	2
CD1001DM-01	Door magnet	1
CD1001DH-01	Door hinges	2
CD1001DK-01	Door handle	1
CD1001DS-01	Screws	8
CD1001S-01	Cabinet sides	2
CD1001SC-01	Door catch	1
CD1001DS-01	Screws	2
CD1001SH-01	Cabinet shelf	4
CD1001SS-01	Shelf holder	16

TABLE 14-5

Indented BOM

BOM, the highest-level item ("parent") is closest to the left margin, with components ("children") going into that item indented to the right. In our example, the CD cabinet is the highest-level item and all the components are indented. The components for the cabinet door are indented even further to the right since these components go directly into the door assembly rather than the CD cabinet.

A **product structure tree** visually represents the BOM for a product. Although product trees are seldom used in the workplace, for our purposes they make it easier to explain the MRP process. Figure 14-4 is a product structure tree for the CD cabinet with the name of the item, the usage quantity per parent item, and the replenishment lead time.

▶ **Product structure tree**
The visual representation of the BOM, clearly defining the parent–child

FIGURE 14-4

Product structure tree

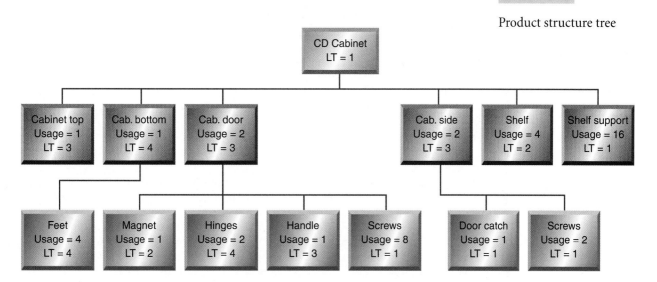

TABLE 14-6

Updated Inventory
Record for CD Cabinet

Item: CD Cabinet		Parent: none									
Lot size rule: L4L		Children: Top, bottom, doors, sides,									
Lead time: 1 week		shelves, shelf supports									
Beginning inventory: 0											

	1	2	3	4	5	6	7	8	9	10	11	12
Gross Requirements:	0	0	0	100	0	0	100	0	0	100	0	0
Scheduled Receipts:												
Projected Available:	0	0	0	0	0	0	0	0	0	0	0	0
Planned Orders			100			100			100			

▶ **End item**
A product sold as a completed item or repair part.

▶ **Parent item**
An item produced from one or more children (components).

▶ **Components**
Raw materials, purchased items, or subassemblies that are part of a larger assembly.

At the top of the product structure tree is the **end item**, the product sold to the customer. In this case, the end item is the CD cabinet, but the end item could also be a repair part such as decorative hinges or door handle.

In the MRP system, a **parent item** is any end item made from one or more **components**. In our example, the CD cabinet is made from these components: a cabinet top, a cabinet bottom, cabinet door, cabinet left side, cabinet right side, four cabinet shelves, and sixteen shelf holders. To simplify MRP processing logic, we call the end item the "parent" and its components the "children," and we show each item's parents or children in each of the inventory records. Table 14-6 shows the updated inventory record for the CD cabinet with this additional information. Since the CD cabinet is the end item, it has no parents. The immediate components of the CD cabinet are its children.

EXAMPLE 14.1

Calculating Cumulative Lead Time for a CD Cabinet

We need to calculate the cumulative lead time for the end item, a CD cabinet.

• **Before You Begin:** Determine how long it takes to build a CD cabinet if none of the activities has been completed. You need to order every component part, build every subassembly, and complete the final assembly. Start by looking at the product structure tree. Determine the total time required for each connected pathway or route from the bottom to the top. For example, look at the component hinges in Figure 14-4. The lead time for the hinges is four weeks. The parent of the hinges is the cabinet door. Lead time for the cabinet door is three weeks. Continue on to the parent for the cabinet door, the final assembly of the CD cabinet. Its lead time is one week. The total lead time for this connected pathway or route is eight weeks (4 + 3 + 1). Cumulative lead time for this product is the largest value associated with any individual connected path from the lowest level to the final assembly level. Beginning inventories can reduce the amount of time it takes to complete an order. For example, if sufficient hinges were already available, four weeks of lead time is subtracted from the lead time of this connected path.

• **Solution:**
We can use the product structure tree to calculate the cumulative lead time for the end item, a CD cabinet. We do this by summing the individual lead times for each route from the lowest level to the end item. The first possible route includes only the cabinet top and final assembly of the CD cabinet. Thus the total lead time for this route is four weeks (three weeks for the cabinet top and one week for the CD cabinet final assembly). The next path includes the feet, the cabinet bottom, and the final assembly of the CD cabinet for a total of nine weeks, which is the longest path through the product structure tree. Table 14-7 shows all the paths through the product structure tree.

Table 14-7   Paths through the Product Structure Tree

Path from Bottom to Top	Cumulative Lead Time (weeks)
Cabinet top to CD cabinet	4
Feet to cabinet bottom to CD cabinet	9
Magnet to cabinet door to CD cabinet	6
Hinge to cabinet door to CD cabinet	8
Handle to cabinet door to CD cabinet	7
Screws to cabinet door to CD cabinet	5
Cabinet side to CD cabinet	4
Door catch to side to CD cabinet	5
Screws to side to CD cabinet	5
Shelf to CD cabinet	3
Shelf holder to CD cabinet	2

When your company has inventory on hand, the lead time can be less than the cumulative lead time. Suppose all the feet were already in inventory. The lead time of the CD cabinet is reduced to eight weeks, the next-longest path through the product structure tree since the feet to cabinet bottom to CD cabinet path would only need five weeks now, since the feet are already in stock. Thus, having inventory on hand allows you to respond more quickly because you can reduce lead times.

Before You Go On

Be sure that you understand the logic behind MRP. The system checks the gross requirements for each period, compares that with the inventory available (the beginning inventory for that period, plus any replenishment orders due). If the gross requirements exceed the inventory available, an order must be scheduled to arrive in that period. The system calculates the timing of the replenishment order by subtracting the lead time (in weeks) from the period the material is needed to satisfy the gross requirements. The system calculates the quantity of the replenishment order by the lot size rule for that item.

THE MRP EXPLOSION PROCESS

Complete the MRP records for each of the items in the bill of material for the CD cabinet.

• **Before You Begin:** In this problem, determine the timing of planned orders for each item used in the construction of the CD cabinet. Using input from the master production schedule, determine the timing of the finished CD cabinet (shown in Table 14-6). Process the MRP records, level by level. Complete all of the level-one items before beginning the level-two items, and so on. The end result of this problem should be completed MRP records for every item used in the CD cabinet.

• **Solution:**
This example illustrates the MRP explosion process. Using Table 14-6, we begin the MRP **explosion process**. MRP calculates the materials needed to meet the authorized MPS. *The gross requirements for end items are **always** dictated by the authorized MPS.* When we input these quantities into the proper time frame, MRP calculates the gross requirements for components. The MRP program begins by processing the inventory records of each component of the end item.

EXAMPLE 14.2

The MRP System at Storage Solutions by Elyssa, Inc.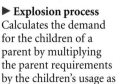

▶ **Explosion process** Calculates the demand for the children of a parent by multiplying the parent requirements by the children's usage as specified in the BOM.

We will work through this example starting with the cabinet top. Table 14-8a shows the appropriate inventory record. Let's look at the differences in the inventory record. First, the lot size rule is a fixed-order quantity of 144 units, which means the order quantity is always 144 units. If an order of 144 units is not enough to cover the gross requirements, we can place a double order (288 units) or triple order (432 units). The lead time is three weeks, so we must place the replenishment order three weeks before it is needed. *Gross requirements for a component, or child, are determined by the planned orders of its parent or parents.*

The planned orders of the parent item determine the timing of the gross requirements of the child. In our case, the parent item (the CD cabinet) has planned orders in periods 3, 6, and 9 and its children (the top, bottom, door, the sides, shelves, and shelf supports) will all have gross requirements in periods 3, 6, and 9. The quantity of the gross requirement for the child is determined by the usage quantity. Since each CD cabinet needs one cabinet top, the gross requirement for the cabinet top is 100 pieces. This is the planned order quantity of the parent multiplied by the usage rate of the child (100 × 1). The beginning inventory of the cabinet tops is 120 units.

We can see from the inventory record in Table 14-8a that we need replenishment orders (each for a quantity of 144 units) in periods 3 and 6. If no replenishment order is placed in period 3, we will not have enough cabinet tops to satisfy our gross requirement in period 6.

Table 14-8 (a–g) has the inventory records for all the children of the CD cabinet. Note that all of the CD cabinet children have gross requirements in periods 3, 6, and 9. This is because the timing of gross requirements for a child are derived from the planned orders of its parent or parents. After the system sets the gross requirements, it projects the available inventory and back-schedules replenishment orders using the lead time needed for the order to arrive in the appropriate period. For example, the 144 cabinet tops ordered in period 3 will arrive in period 6 to help satisfy the gross requirement in that period. The next order for cabinet tops will be placed in period 6 to arrive in period 9. Quantities shown as scheduled receipts have already been ordered. See Table 14-8b, period 3.

Table 14-8   Inventory Records for CD Cabinet Components

Table 14-8a   Inventory Record for Cabinet Top

Item: Cabinet Top	Parent: CD Cabinet
Lot size rule: FOQ = 144	Children: none
Lead time: 3 weeks	Beginning inventory: 120

	1	2	3	4	5	6	7	8	9	10	11	12
Gross Requirements:	0	0	100	0	0	100	0	0	100	0	0	0
Scheduled Receipts:												
Projected Available:	120	120	20	20	20	64	64	64	108	108	108	108
Planned Orders:			144			144						

Table 14-8b   Inventory Record for Cabinet Bottom

Item: Cabinet Bottom	Parent: CD Cabinet
Lot size rule: FOQ = 144	Children: Feet
Lead time: 3 weeks	Beginning inventory: 20

	1	2	3	4	5	6	7	8	9	10	11	12
Gross Requirements:	0	0	100	0	0	100	0	0	100	0	0	0
Scheduled Receipts:			144									
Projected Available:	20	20	64	64	64	108	108	108	8	8	8	8
Planned Orders:			144									

Table 14-8c   Inventory Record for Cabinet Door

Item: Cabinet Door	Parent: CD Cabinet
Lot size rule: FOQ = 216	Children: Magnet, hinge, handle, screws
Lead time: 4 weeks	Beginning inventory: 120

	1	2	3	4	5	6	7	8	9	10	11	12
Gross Requirements:	0	0	200	0	0	200	0	0	200	0	0	0
Scheduled Receipts:			216									
Projected Available:	120	120	136	136	136	152	152	152	168	168	168	168
Planned Orders:			216			216						

Table 14-8d   Inventory Record for Cabinet Sides

Item: Side   Parent: CD Cabinet
Lot size rule: FOQ = 216   Children: none
Lead time: 3 weeks   Beginning inventory: 0

	1	2	3	4	5	6	7	8	9	10	11	12
Gross Requirements:	0	0	200	0	0	200	0	0	200	0	0	0
Scheduled Receipts:			216									
Projected Available:	0	0	16	16	16	32	32	32	48	48	48	48
Planned Orders:			216			216						

Table 14-8e   Inventory Record for Cabinet Shelves

Item: Shelf   Parent: CD Cabinet
Lot size rule: L4L   Children: none
Lead time: 2 weeks   Beginning inventory: 0

	1	2	3	4	5	6	7	8	9	10	11	12
Gross Requirements:	0	0	400	0	0	400	0	0	400	0	0	0
Scheduled Receipts:												
Projected Available:	0	0	0	0	0	0	0	0	0	0	0	0
Planned Orders:	400			400			400					

Table 14-8f   Inventory Record for Shelf Supports

Item: Shelf Supports   Parent: CD Cabinet
Lot size rule: FOQ = 2500   Children: none
Lead time: 1 week   Beginning inventory: 0

	1	2	3	4	5	6	7	8	9	10	11	12
Gross Requirements:	0	0	1600	0	0	1600	0	0	1600	0	0	0
Scheduled Receipts:												
Projected Available:	0	0	900	900	900	1800	1800	1800	200	200	200	200
Planned Orders:		2500			2500							

After MRP reviews and updates the children of the CD cabinet, it drops to the next lower level in the BOM and processes the inventory records at that level. In our example, those records are for the door magnet, door hinge, handle, screws, door catch, and feet. The cabinet door is the parent item for the magnet, hinge, handle, and screws. The cabinet right side is the parent of the door catch as well as a second parent for the screws. The cabinet bottom is the parent of the feet. Table 14-9 shows the inventory records for these remaining components. The process is the same as for the children of the CD cabinet. You look to the planned order releases of the parent item to determine the gross requirements of the components. For example, look at Table 14-9c (the inventory record for the handle); its parent (cabinet door) has planned orders in periods 3 and 6. Therefore, the handle must have gross requirements in periods 3 and 6. Next, let's look at how MRP provides information to the production and inventory control planners.

Table 14-9   Inventory Records for Remaining Components

Table 14-9a   Inventory Record for Door Magnet

Item: Door Magnet   Parent: Cabinet Door
Lot size rule: FOQ = 250   Children: none
Lead time: 2 weeks   Beginning inventory: 12

	1	2	3	4	5	6	7	8	9	10	11	12
Gross Requirements:	0	0	216	0	0	216	0	0	0	0	0	0
Scheduled Receipts:												
Projected Available:	12	12	46	46	46	80	80	80	80	80	80	80
Planned Orders:	250			250								

Table 14-9b   Inventory Record for Door Hinge

Item: Door Hinge   Parent: Cabinet Door
Lot size rule: FOQ = 932 Children: none
Lead time: 4 weeks   Beginning inventory: 0

	1	2	3	4	5	6	7	8	9	10	11	12
Gross Requirements:	0	0	432	0	0	432	0	0	0	0	0	0
Scheduled Receipts:			932									
Projected Available:	0	0	500	500	500	68	68	68	68	68	68	68
Planned Orders:												

Table 14-9c   Inventory Record for Door Handle

Item: Handle   Parent: Cabinet Door
Lot size rule: FOQ = 200 Children: none
Lead time: 3 weeks   Beginning inventory: 50

	1	2	3	4	5	6	7	8	9	10	11	12
Gross Requirements:	0	0	216	0	0	216	0	0	0	0	0	0
Scheduled Receipts:			200									
Projected Available:	50	50	34	34	34	18	18	18	18	18	18	18
Planned Orders:			200									

Table 14-9d   Inventory Record for Door Screws

Item: Screw   Parent: Cabinet Door, Cabinet Side
Lot size rule: FOQ = 2000 Children: none
Lead time: 1 week   Beginning inventory: 500

	1	2	3	4	5	6	7	8	9	10	11	12
Gross Requirements:	0	0	2160	0	0	2160	0	0	0	0	0	0
Scheduled Receipts:												
Projected Available:	500	500	340	340	340	180	180	180	180	180	180	180
Planned Orders:		2000			2000							

Table 14-9e   Inventory Record for Door Catches

Item: Door Catch   Parent: Cabinet Sides
Lot size rule: FOQ = 252 Children: none
Lead time: 1 week   Beginning inventory: 0

	1	2	3	4	5	6	7	8	9	10	11	12
Gross Requirements:	0	0	216	0	0	216	0	0	0	0	0	0
Scheduled Receipts:												
Projected Available:	0	0	36	36	36	72	72	72	72	72	72	72
Planned Orders:		252			252							

Table 14-9f   Inventory Record for Feet

Item: Foot   Parent: Cabinet Bottom
Lot size rule: L4L Children: none
Lead time: 4 weeks Beginning inventory: 0

	1	2	3	4	5	6	7	8	9	10	11	12
Gross Requirements:	0	0	576	0	0	0	0	0	0	0	0	0
Scheduled Receipts:			576									
Projected Available:	0	0	0	0	0	0	0	0	0	0	0	0
Planned Orders:												

MRP systems typically provide inventory planners with **action notices**, which indicate the items that need the planner's attention. An action notice is created when a planned order needs to be released, when dues dates of orders need to be adjusted, or when there is insufficient lead time for a planned replenishment order. Let's look at the different kinds of action notices.

▶ **Action notices**
Output from an MRP system that identifies the need for an action to be taken.

A positive quantity in the current period's planned order row means that an order must be released. We call the current period the **action bucket** because that is the period in which we take actions such as releasing, rescheduling, or canceling orders.

▶ **Action bucket**
The current time period.

Production and inventory control planners release orders to either an external supplier or to the shop floor. An order released to a supplier authorizes the shipment of the material so that it arrives as needed. An order released to the shop authorizes withdrawal of the needed materials and the start of production. Action notices are generated only for actions taken in the current period. Production and inventory control planners adjust the due dates of orders (both opened and planned) to make sure the material does not arrive too soon or too late but just as it is needed. If an order is scheduled to arrive before it is needed (for example, because the gross requirements changed), the planner delays receipt of the replenishment order until it is needed. If the order is not scheduled to arrive in time, the planner tries to rush or **expedite** the order. Action notices indicate that a decision must be made or an action taken. The production and inventory control planner uses the available information and makes the decision.

▶ **Expedite**
To rush orders that are needed in less than the normal lead time.

COMPARISON OF LOT SIZE RULES

Different lot size rules can be used with MRP systems, such as least unit cost, least total costs, and parts period balancing. In this book, we cover the fixed-order quantity (FOQ), lot-for-lot (L4L), and period order quantity (POQ). These lot size rules are discussed in Chapter 12. Different lot size rules change the frequency of replenishment orders and determine the quantity of the order. Let's look at an example comparing FOQ, L4L, and POQ.

Given the following gross requirements, let's calculate the planned replenishment orders needed, then calculate the inventory and ordering costs for the next thirteen weeks. The CD cabinet has gross requirements of 25 in periods 2 and 3; 40 in periods 4 and 5; and 60 in periods 7, 8, 9, 11, 12, and 13. The first lot size to try is FOQ = 144, then use L4L, and finally use a POQ = 4 periods. The cost to place an order is $25, and the holding cost per unit per period is $0.10.

EXAMPLE 14.3

Comparing Different Lot Size Rules at Storage Solutions by Elyssa, Inc.

• **Before You Begin:** Companies using MRP often use different lot-sizing techniques. Different techniques determine the timing of replenishment orders, the amount of inventory carried, and the frequency of setups. In this problem, you compare three different lot size rules. Calculate the costs associated with each ordering policy and determine which lot size rule makes the most sense. Remember that the fixed order quantity (FOQ) rule requires you to order the same quantity each time, while lot-for-lot (L4) means you order just enough for the next period, and period order quantity (POQ) means that you order enough to satisfy your requirements for the next *n* periods.

• Solution:

Table 14-10a–c shows the completed inventory records. As you can see, the planned replenishment orders vary in frequency and in quantity. Note the different levels of inventory held because of the lot size rule. Lot-for-lot always minimizes a company's inventory investment because it orders only what is needed for one period. However, L4L also maximizes a company's ordering costs.

Table 14-10   Inventory Records Comparing Lot Size Rules

Table 14-10a   Inventory Record Using Fixed-Order Quantity

Item: CD Cabinet   Lead Time: 1 week
Lot size rule: FOQ = 144   Beginning inventory: 0

	1	2	3	4	5	6	7	8	9	10	11	12	13
Gross Requirements:	0	25	25	40	40	0	60	60	60	0	60	60	60
Scheduled Receipts:													
Projected Available:	0	119	94	54	14	14	98	38	122	122	62	2	86
Planned Orders:	144					144		144				144	

Table 14-10b   Inventory Record Using Lot-for-Lot

Item: CD Cabinet   Lead Time: 1 week
Lot size rule: L4L   Beginning inventory: 0

	1	2	3	4	5	6	7	8	9	10	11	12	13
Gross Requirements:	0	25	25	40	40	0	60	60	60	0	60	60	60
Scheduled Receipts:													
Projected Available:	0	0	0	0	0	0	0	0	0	0	0	0	0
Planned Orders:	25	25	40	40			60	60	60		60	60	60

Table 14-10c   Inventory Record Using Period Order Quantity

Item: CD Cabinet   Lead Time: 1 week
Lot size rule: POQ = 4 periods   Beginning inventory: 0

	1	2	3	4	5	6	7	8	9	10	11	12	13
Gross Requirements:	0	25	25	40	40	0	60	60	60	0	60	60	60
Scheduled Receipts:													
Projected Available:	0	105	80	40	0	0	120	60	0	0	120	60	0
Planned Orders:	130					180				180			

Let's calculate the costs for each of these different lot size rules for this thirteen-week situation. The FOQ lot size rule has ending inventory in all but the first period. In total, 825 units are held for a holding cost of $82.50 (825 units × $0.10 per unit per period). The ordering cost is $100 (4 orders × $25 per order). Total holding and ordering cost using the FOQ is $182.50. The L4L lot size rule has no ending inventory during the thirteen weeks. However, it does need a total of ten replenishment orders. The total holding and ordering cost for L4L is $250. The POQ = 4 periods lot size rule has ending inventory in periods 2, 3, 4, 7, 8, 11, and 12. Total units held are 585, for holding costs of $58.50. POQ requires three replenishment orders (ordering cost equals $75). Total costs for POQ are $133.50. In this case, the POQ lot size rule has the lowest total holding and ordering costs. To ensure that costs are minimized, we have to do the cost comparisons.

THE ROLE OF CAPACITY REQUIREMENTS PLANNING (CRP)

A company uses a rough-cut capacity planning technique to determine whether a proposed MPS is feasible. In Chapter 13, we saw how to evaluate the feasibility of a proposed MPS with capacity planning using overall planning factors (CPOPF). Rough-cut capacity planning techniques use data from the proposed MPS. Capacity requirements planning (CRP) uses data from MRP. We calculate workloads for critical work centers based on **open shop orders** and planned shop orders. Work begins on open shop orders while planned shop orders are scheduled to be done. We translate these orders into hours of work by work center and by time period.

▶ **Open shop orders**
Released manufacturing orders.

Table 14-11 shows items scheduled for Work Center 101. These items are either taken directly from MRP's planned orders or they are already open shop orders. We want to calculate workloads for Work Center 101.

EXAMPLE 14.4

Calculating Workloads

• **Before You Begin:** Capacity requirements planning (CRP) uses the planned order releases from the MRP output to calculate the workload for specific work centers. The workload associated with a planned order has two parts, the setup to do the job and the processing time for the job. The primary difference between rough-cut capacity planning (RCCP) and CRP is that CRP uses the actual planned orders instead of the quantity needed just to complete the final product assembly. For example, using RCCP, if we want to estimate the time needed to build 100 CD cabinets, we assume that we make just enough pieces of everything to build 100 units. We don't take into account beginning inventories. However, with CRP, we take into account only the items that have a planned order scheduled. This also indicates the quantity to be built of the item. If a lot size rule other than L4L (lot-for-lot) is used, more capacity must be used to complete the planned order for the item. CRP provides a better estimate of the total capacity needed.

Table 14-11   Workload for Work Center 101

Period	Item Number	Quantity	Setup Time (hours)	Run Time per Unit in Standard Hours	Total Item Time (hours)	Weekly Workload (hours)
4	DN100	250	3.0	0.20	53.0	
	DP100	250	5.0	0.18	50.0	
	DS119	150	2.5	0.30	47.5	
	DT136	400	3.5	0.27	111.5	262.0
5	EQ555	1000	8.0	0.08	88.0	
	ER616	500	4.0	0.22	114.0	
	ES871	100	2.0	0.35	37.0	239.0
6	FA314	250	3.0	0.30	78.0	
	FF369	100	1.5	0.12	13.5	
	FR766	50	0.5	0.15	8.0	
	FS119	200	3.0	0.35	73.0	
	FY486	500	6.0	0.27	141.0	313.5

• **Solution:**
We calculate the total item time by summing the setup time and the total run time for the item.

$$\text{Total item time} = \text{setup time} + (\text{quantity} \times \text{run time per unit})$$

The setup time is incurred each time the machine is prepared to produce the desired quantity of an item. We calculate the total run time by multiplying the quantity to be produced by the run time per unit. In our example, for item DN100, we plan to produce 250 units, with each unit needing 0.20 hour of run time. The total run time is 50.0 hours (250 units × 0.20 hour per unit). Total workload placed on the work center by item DN100 is 53 hours: 3 hours to set up the machine and 50 hours to run the quantity. We make similar calculations for each of the other items. When we have calculated the workloads, we compare it to the available capacity for the work center in those time period.

We calculate available capacity (discussed in Chapter 9) by multiplying the number of machines available × number of shifts used × number of hours per shift × number of days per week × usage × efficiency.

$$\text{Available capacity} = \frac{\text{number of}}{\text{machines available}} \times \frac{\text{number of}}{\text{shifts used}} \times \frac{\text{number of}}{\text{hours per shift}} \times \frac{\text{number of}}{\text{days per week}} \times \text{utilization} \times \text{efficiency}$$

In our case, we have four machines and we use two ten-hour shifts for five days per week, so our usage is 85 percent and our efficiency is 95 percent.

$$\frac{\text{Available}}{\text{capacity}} = 4\text{ machines} \times 2\text{ shifts} \times \frac{10\text{ hours}}{\text{per shift}} \times \frac{5\text{ days}}{\text{per week}} \times 0.85\text{ utilization} \times 0.95\text{ efficiency}$$

The available capacity per week is 323 standard hours. Figure 14-5 shows the workload compared to available capacity.

If the available capacity is not adequate, the company has a number of options. The easiest and quickest way to increase available capacity may be to authorize overtime at the work center. Another approach is to reduce the capacity needed by doing some of the work at an alternate work center. If the gap between available and needed capacity is significant, the company can hire a subcontractor for temporary extra capacity.

FIGURE 14-5

Workload for Work Center 101

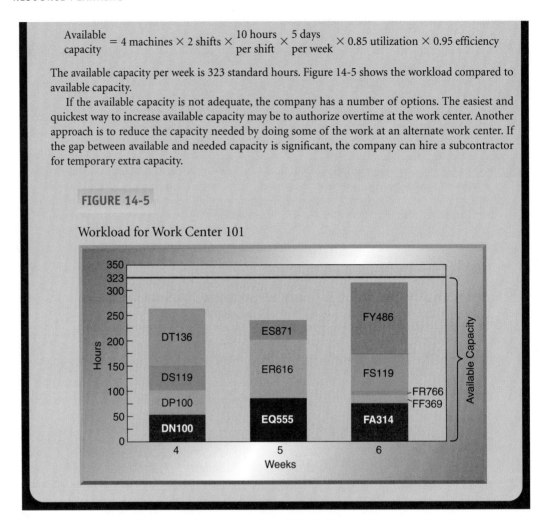

CRP enables a company to evaluate both the feasibility of the MRP system and how well the company is using its critical work centers.

RESOURCE PLANNING WITHIN OM: HOW IT ALL FITS TOGETHER

Enterprise resource planning provides a common database for use by an organization, its suppliers, and its customers. Second-generation ERP systems are designed to support supply chain management and e-commerce. These systems automate routine transactions and provide real-time information to all members of the enterprise. ERP systems typically have a production and materials module (MRP) to determine what is needed, how much is needed, and when it is needed.

MRP reports are used by the production and inventory planners to (1) generate purchasing requisitions and (2) develop schedules of different activities to be done on the manufacturing floor. Techniques for sequencing activities are discussed in Chapter 15. The authorized MPS, the bill of material (BOM) file, and the inventory records are inputs to the MRP system. It is critical that the MPS be feasible and that the BOM file and the inventory records be accurate. This implies that the time standards (Chapter 11) are valid and that cycle counting (Chapter 12) be used to maintain inventory record accuracy. If not, material is not ordered at the appropriate time in the right quantity. The master scheduler is responsible for the feasibility of the MPS, and a manufacturing engineer is probably responsible for the BOM file. The production and inventory planners are often held accountable for the accuracy of the inventory records.

Even though rough-cut capacity planning (RCCP) using MPS data was done to check for feasibility, it is still important to do capacity requirements planning (CRP) for any critical work centers (bottlenecks or potential bottlenecks). CRP operates at a greater level of detail than does RCCP, using information generated by the MRP system. Production planners do this to make sure the detailed schedule of production is feasible.

Resource planning is designed to ensure that the right materials, in the right quantities, are available at the right time. And to ensure that the right job is being done on the right equipment.

RESOURCE PLANNING ACROSS THE ORGANIZATION

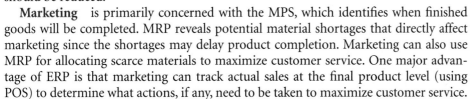

Since MRP determines the quantity and timing of materials needed, it affects several functional areas in the company. Let's first look at how each functional area is affected by MRP and then consider the effects of ERP.

Accounting calculates future material commitments based on MRP output. Accounting then develops cash flow budgets and the inventory investment to support the current MPS. With a common database, accounting should be able to determine the exact status of outstanding orders, including cost, quantity, and delivery date. Since there is a common database, discrepancies between supplier and manufacturer should be reduced.

Marketing is primarily concerned with the MPS, which identifies when finished goods will be completed. MRP reveals potential material shortages that directly affect marketing since the shortages may delay product completion. Marketing can also use MRP for allocating scarce materials to maximize customer service. One major advantage of ERP is that marketing can track actual sales at the final product level (using POS) to determine what actions, if any, need to be taken to maximize customer service.

Information systems maintains MRP, which is a large database that includes the BOM, the inventory records, and the MPS. Minimizing errors in the database is essential to producing useful reports. ERP will help IS by using a single integrated database for both internal and external members of the supply chain.

Purchasing uses the planned orders generated by MRP to evaluate the feasibility of long-term or blanket contracts and to determine delivery need. The lead times that are input into MRP often come directly from purchasing. ERP will facilitate supplier-managed inventory approaches and reduce transaction costs for purchasing.

Manufacturing uses the output generated by MRP to develop daily manufacturing schedules. MRP ensures that the right materials in the right quantity are available to support the MPS. Manufacturing also uses MRP to allocate scarce materials. ERP will provide manufacturing with improved insight into actual customer demand. It should increase the probability that manufacturing is working on products actually needed to satisfy customer demand.

In most manufacturing operations, production or inventory control planners are responsible for working with MRP. Planners are typically responsible for certain inventory items, including end items, subassemblies, and components. Planners check the MRP output for action notices related to the items for which they are responsible. Planners schedule, reschedule, and expedite materials to support the MPS. A planning position is often an entry-level job in the materials field.

As companies continue to move toward ERP, all functional areas will work from a central database. The database gives all areas in the company access to the same information simultaneously and improves organizational effectiveness.

THE SUPPLY CHAIN LINK

Enterprise resource planning provides the structure for common databases across the organization, its suppliers, and its customers. Suppliers can access the master production schedule (MPS) to see projected build dates for products that use materials supplied by them. The current trend is to integrate e-commerce and ERP systems. Tangible benefits of an ERP system include reduced inventory levels, reduced staffing, improved order launching, reduced IT and purchasing costs, improved cash flow, and increased profits. Intangible benefits include improved visibility of system demand, improved customer responsiveness, and improved flexibility. Enterprise resource planning systems provide the structure needed for effective supply chain management.

Chapter Highlights

1 Enterprise resource planning (ERP) is software designed for organizing and managing business processes by sharing information across functional areas using a common database and a single computer system. ERP systems typically have modules for finance and accounting, sales and marketing, production and materials management, and human resources.

2 First-generation ERP systems provide a single interface for managing routine activities performed in manufacturing. Second-generation ERP systems or SCM software is designed to improve decision making in the supply chain. The current trend is integrating e-commerce and ERP systems.

3 Tangible benefits from ERP systems include reductions in inventory and staffing, increased productivity, improved order management, quicker closing of financial cycles, reduced IT and purchasing costs, improved cash flow management, and increased revenue and profits. Intangible benefits include improved visibility of corporate data, improved customer responsiveness, and improved flexibility. The cost of ERP systems ranges from hundreds of thousands of dollars to several million dollars.

4 Material requirements planning (MRP) systems are designed to calculate material requirements for items with dependent demand. MRP systems use backward scheduling to determine when each activity starts so that the finished product or service is completed on time.

5 Independent demand is the demand for finished products, whereas dependent demand is demand that is derived from finished products. MRP systems use dependent demand.

6 The objectives of MRP are to determine the quantity and timing of material requirements and to keep schedule priorities updated and valid. MRP determines what to order, how much to order, when to place the order, and when to schedule the order's arrival. It maintains priorities by recognizing changes in the operations environment and making the necessary adjustments.

7 MRP needs three inputs: the authorized MPS, the BOM file, and the inventory records file. The MPS is the planned build schedule, the BOM file shows the materials needed to build an item, and the inventory records file shows the inventory on hand.

8 Once the MPS has been input, MRP checks the inventory records to determine if enough end-item inventory is available. If sufficient end-item inventory is not on hand, MRP checks the end-item's BOM file to determine what materials are needed and in what quantities. The MRP system then generates planned replenishment orders.

9 Action notices show when to release planned orders, reschedule orders, or adjust due dates. They allow the planner to use the MRP output information effectively.

10 Different lot size rules are used with MRP systems to generate different order quantities and order frequencies. The lot-for-lot (L4L) rule always minimizes inventory investment but maximizes ordering costs. A cost comparison shows the effect of using different lot sizing rules.

11 Planned orders generated by MRP, plus any open shop orders, are inputs to capacity requirements planning (CRP). CRP checks to see if available capacity is sufficient to complete the orders scheduled in a particular work center during a specific time period.

12 CRP calculates the workloads at critical work centers by using the planned orders generated by the MRP system. These planned orders are multiplied by the standard times to calculate individual work center loads.

Key Terms

Formula Review

To calculate total item time:

$$\text{Total item time} = \text{setup time} + (\text{quantity} \times \text{run time per unit})$$

To calculate available capacity:

$$\text{Available capacity} = \text{number of machines available} \times \text{number of shifts used} \times \text{number of hours per shift} \times \text{utilization} \times \text{efficiency}$$

Solved Problems

(See student companion site for Excel template.)

• Problem 1

Using the product tree shown in Figure 14-6, calculate the cumulative lead time for Item 100 if you have no inventory.

How long is the lead time if you have enough inventory for Parts 102, 104, 201, and 203?

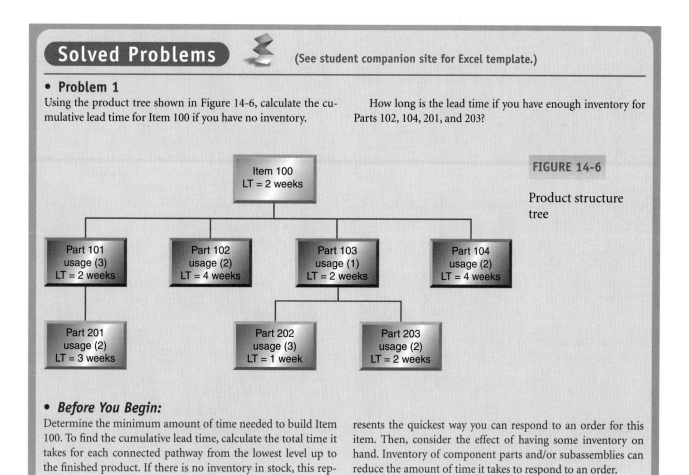

FIGURE 14-6

Product structure tree

• Before You Begin:

Determine the minimum amount of time needed to build Item 100. To find the cumulative lead time, calculate the total time it takes for each connected pathway from the lowest level up to the finished product. If there is no inventory in stock, this rep-

resents the quickest way you can respond to an order for this item. Then, consider the effect of having some inventory on hand. Inventory of component parts and/or subassemblies can reduce the amount of time it takes to respond to an order.

• Solution

Check all the paths through the product structure tree to find the longest path.

Path through the Product Structure	Total Lead Time (weeks)
Part 201 to Part 101 to Item 100	7
Part 102 to Item 100	6
Part 202 to Part 103 to Item 100	5
Part 203 to Part 103 to Item 100	6
Part 104 to Item 100	6

The path from Part 201 to Part 101 to Item 100 is the longest (7 weeks), so it is the cumulative lead time.

• Problem 2

Complete the inventory record for Item 500 and do an MRP explosion of its component parts. Figure 14-7 shows the product structure tree for Item 500.

• Before You Begin:

This problem requires an MRP explosion for Item 500. Begin the explosion process with the finished good, and then work downward level by level through the product structure tree. Remember that the timing and quantity of the gross requirements for children are determined by the planned orders of the parents. After the explosion, you will have the planned orders necessary to produce the units listed in the master production schedule.

Item: 500	Parent: none			
Lot Size Rule: L4L	Children: 501, 502, 503, 504			
Lead Time: 2 weeks	Beginning inventory: 0			
	1	2	3	4	5
Gross Requirements:	0	0	0	250	0
Scheduled Receipts:					
Projected Available:					
Planned Orders:					
	6	7	8	9	10
Gross Requirements:	250	0	250	0	250
Scheduled Receipts:					
Projected Available:					
Planned Orders:					

• Solution

Given the gross requirements, we will need planned orders for Item 500 in weeks 2, 4, 6, and 8. Each of the planned orders is for 250 units, exactly the quantity needed to satisfy the gross requirements. The completed record is shown here.

When we have enough inventory for some parts, we can eliminate that segment of the path and all levels below that inventory. For example, if we have enough of Part 101, we do not need any more of its component parts (201). The new paths when we have sufficient inventory for Parts 102, 104, 201, and 203 are shown here.

Path through the Product Structure	Total Lead Time (weeks)
Part 101 to Item 100	4
Part 202 to Part 103 to Item 100	5

Given that we have enough inventory, we are concerned with only two paths through the product tree. In this situation, the minimum time to produce this item is 5 weeks.

Item: 500	Parent: none			
Lot Size Rule: L4L	Children: 501, 502, 503, 504			
Lead Time: 2 weeks	Beginning inventory: 0			
	1	2	3	4	5
Gross Requirements:	0	0	0	250	0
Scheduled Receipts:					
Projected Available:	0	0	0	0	0
Planned Orders:	0	250	0	250	0
	6	7	8	9	10
Gross Requirements:	250	0	250	0	250
Scheduled Receipts:					
Projected Available:	0	0	0	0	0
Planned Orders:	250	0	250	0	0

Now that we have a completed inventory record for the end item, we can do the MRP explosions for its children. Remember that each of the children will have gross requirements in the periods that the parent has a planned order (weeks 2, 4, 6, and 8). The completed records for the four children follow.

Since the usage rate for Item 501 is (2) per parent item, the gross requirement is double the planned order quantity of the parent, or $250 \times 2 = 500$ units. The lot size rule is a fixed order quantity of 1000 pieces. Each time an order is placed, it is for 1000 pieces. Thus, Item 501 has two planned orders, one in period 2 and one in period 6.

Item: 501	Parent: 500	Usage: 2		
Lot Size Rule: FOQ = 1000	Children: none			
Lead Time: 2 weeks	Beginning inventory: 600			
	1	2	3	4	5
Gross Requirements:	0	500	0	500	0
Scheduled Receipts:					
Projected Available:	600	100	100	600	600
Planned Orders:	0	1000	0	0	0
	6	7	8	9	10
Gross Requirements:	500	0	500	0	0
Scheduled Receipts:					
Projected Available:	100	100	600	600	600
Planned Orders:	1000	0	0	0	0

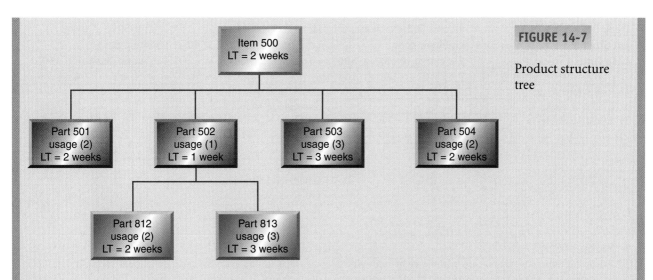

FIGURE 14-7

Product structure tree

Using lot-for-lot as our lot size rule, we need to place four orders for Item 502. We have planned orders in periods 1, 3, 5, and 7.

Item: 502   **Parent:**   **Usage: 1**
Lot Size Rule: L4L   **Children: 812, 813**
Lead Time: 1 week   **Beginning inventory: 0**

	1	2	3	4	5
Gross Requirements:	0	250	0	250	0
Scheduled Receipts:					
Projected Available:	0	0	0	0	0
Planned Orders:	250	0	250	0	250
	6	7	8	9	10
Gross Requirements:	250	0	250	0	0
Scheduled Receipts:					
Projected Available:	0	0	0	0	0
Planned Orders:	0	250	0	0	0

Once again, we calculate the gross requirements by multiplying the parent's planned order quantity by the usage factor (3) shown in the product structure tree. This results in the gross requirement for Item 503, which is triple the order quantity of the parent's planned order.

Item: 503   **Parent: 500**   **Usage: 3**
Lot Size Rule: FOQ = 1500   **Children: 812, 813**
Lead Time: 3 weeks   **Beginning inventory: 800**

	1	2	3	4	5
Gross Requirements:	0	750	0	750	0
Scheduled Receipts:					
Projected Available:	800	50	50	800	800
Planned Orders:	1500	0	0	0	1500
	6	7	8	9	10
Gross Requirements:	750	0	750	0	0
Scheduled Receipts:					
Projected Available:	50	50	800	800	800
Planned Orders:	0	0	0	0	0

Given the lot size rule for this item, we need only one planned order.

Item: 504   **Parent: 500**   **Usage: 2**
Lot Size Rule: FOQ = 2000   **Children: none**
Lead Time: 2 weeks   **Beginning inventory: 600**

	1	2	3	4	5
Gross Requirements:	0	500	0	500	0
Scheduled Receipts:					
Projected Available:	600	100	100	1600	1600
Planned Orders:	0	2000	0	0	0
	6	7	8	9	10
Gross Requirements:	500	0	500	0	0
Scheduled Receipts:					
Projected Available:	1100	1100	600	600	600
Planned Orders:	0	0	0	0	0

Now let's look at the children of Item 502. The gross requirements for Item 812 are double the quantity of its parent's planned orders. The lot size rule, POQ = 4 periods, means that the planned order quantity should be enough to cover the requirements in the period it is scheduled to arrive plus the next three periods. For example, we need an order to arrive in period 3. This planned order must be large enough to cover the gross requirements in periods 3, 4, 5, and 6. The inventory records for both 812 and 813 follow.

Item: 812   **Parent: 502**   **Usage: 2**
Lot Size Rule: POQ = 4 periods   **Children: none**
Lead Time: 2 weeks   **Beginning inventory: 500**

	1	2	3	4	5
Gross Requirements:	500	0	500	0	500
Scheduled Receipts:					
Projected Available:	0	0	500	500	0
Planned Orders:	1000	0	0	0	500

Item: 812			Parent: 502		Usage: 2
Lot Size Rule: POQ = 4 periods			Children: none		
Lead Time: 2 weeks			Beginning inventory: 500		
	6	7	8	9	10
Gross Requirements:	0	500	0	0	0
Scheduled Receipts:					
Projected Available:	0	0	0	0	0
Planned Orders:	0	0	0	0	0

Item: 813			Parent: 502		Usage: 3
Lot Size Rule: FOQ = 1500			Children: none		
Lead Time: 3 weeks			Beginning inventory: 1500		
	1	2	3	4	5
Gross Requirements:	750	0	750	0	750
Scheduled Receipts:					
Projected Available:	750	750	0	0	750
Planned Orders:	0	1500	0	0	0
	6	7	8	9	10
Gross Requirements:	0	750	0	0	0
Scheduled Receipts:					
Projected Available:	750	0	0	0	0
Planned Orders:	0	0	0	0	0

• Problem 3

EJ Fabricators operates six machines, three eight-hour shifts, five days per week. EJ's usage rate is 82 percent and its efficiency rate is 90 percent. Calculate the available capacity. Calculate EJ's workload in periods 7 and 8 and determine whether there is a capacity problem.

• Before You Begin:

In this problem, determine if adequate capacity is available. Calculate available capacity by multiplying the number of machines available for use by the number of shifts operated by the number of days per week by the utilization level by the efficiency level. This, in effect, reduces the output expected by factoring in utilization and efficiency. This allows more realistic expectations from manufacturing.

• Solution

We calculate the available capacity by multiplying the number of machines by the number of shifts by the number of hours per shift by the number of days per week by the utilization rate by the efficiency rate:

6 machines × 3 shifts × 8 hours per shift × 5 days per week
× 0.82 utilization × 0.90 efficiency

which equals 531.36 hours of available capacity. To calculate the workload, we need information about the jobs scheduled in each period. We have shown you how to calculate the capacity available. Now go to Spreadsheet 14.3 on your CD to calculate the workload for each period.

Discussion Questions

1. Describe enterprise resource planning and its role in an organization.

2. Describe the basic modules of an ERP system.

3. Describe the evolution of ERP systems.

4. Describe the role of SCM software and give examples of how it differs from generation-1 ERP.

5. Explain what independent demand is and give examples of products with independent demand.

6. Explain what dependent demand is and give examples of how you can use dependent demand in your personal life.

7. Explain the concept of backward scheduling and give examples of how you use backward scheduling in your personal life.

8. What are the objectives of MRP?

9. Describe how MRP works.

10. Describe the inputs needed for MRP.

11. For each input needed, describe problems that might arise when you run MRP.

12. Explain what happens when you use different lot size rules in MRP.

13. Explain why companies do capacity requirements planning.

14. Describe the inputs needed for capacity requirements planning.

15. Describe how MRP II differs from MRP.

16. Describe enterprise resource planning.

Problems

Use the information given here for the next five problems.

Item	Usage per Parent	Lead Time (weeks)
Q	—	2
R	2	3
S	1	4
T	3	2
X	2	3
Y	1	2
V	1	3
Z	3	2

1. Will's Welded Widgets (WWW) makes its Q Model from components R, S, and T. Component R is made from two units of component X and one unit of component Y. Component T is made from one unit of component V and three units of component Z. Draw the product structure tree for the Q Model.

2. Using the given information, calculate the replenishment lead time for the Q Model assuming that you have no beginning inventories.

3. Using the given information, calculate the gross requirements for each of the components if the company plans to build 100 of its Q Model. Assume that there are no beginning inventories.

4. Using the given information, calculate the gross requirements for each of the components when the company plans to build 100 of its Q Model if you have these inventories: 150 units of component T and 200 units of component R.

5. Using the given information and the beginning inventories from Problem 4, calculate the minimum replenishment time for the 100 Q Models.

Use the following information for Problems 6 through 10.

Component	Immediate Parent	Usage per Parent	Lead Time (weeks)	Beginning Inventory
A	none	—	1	0
B	A	2	2	250
C	A	1	6	500
D	A	3	3	750
E	A	2	2	750
F	B	4	2	3000
G	B	2	4	1000
H	D	3	2	5000
I	D	2	4	5000
J	E	1	8	1000
K	E	5	1	5000
L	E	2	4	2500
M	F	3	3	250
N	F	6	3	2560
O	H	2	4	0
P	K	1	2	500
Q	K	2	3	1000

6. Flora's Fabulous Fountains' (FFF) top product is its Model A. Using the information given, draw the product structure tree for the Model A.

7. Using the information given, calculate the replenishment time when no beginning inventory exists.

8. Flora is preparing for her busy season and is building 2500 Model A fountains. Calculate the gross requirements for each component assuming that there is no beginning inventory.

9. Using the information given and assuming that 2500 Model A fountains are scheduled for completion, calculate the gross requirements of each component. Use the beginning inventories given.

10. Calculate the minimum replenishment time for the Model A fountains given the beginning inventories.

11. Fill in the partially completed inventory record shown here.

Item: AB500   **Parent: None**
Lot Size Rule: L4L   **Children: AB501, AB511, AB521**
Lead Time: 2 weeks

	1	2	3	4	5
Gross Requirements:			150	250	150
Scheduled Receipts:					
Projected Available:					
Planned Orders:					
	6	7	8	9	10
Gross Requirements:	250	150	250	150	250
Scheduled Receipts:					
Projected Available:					
Planned Orders:					

12. Using the planned orders generated in Problem 11, complete inventory records for components AB501, AB511, and AB521. The lot size rule, lead time, and usage information are shown here.

Component	Lot Size Rule	Lead Time (weeks)	Usage Factor	Beginning Inventory
AB501	L4L	2	2	1100
AB511	FOQ = 350	3	1	650
AB521	POQ = 3	2	3	1650

13. Using the inventory records completed in Problem 12, calculate the average inventory level of AB501, AB511, AB521.

14. Use the planned orders generated in Problem 11. Calculate the average inventory records if the company decides to switch the lot size rule for AB511 and AB521 to lot-for-lot. Compare the number of replenishment orders using the new lot size rules.

15. Using the information given, fill in the partially completed inventory record shown here.

Item: AB500
Lot Size Rule: FOQ = 200
Lead Time: 2 weeks

Parent: None
Children: AB501, AB511, AB521

	1	2	3	4	5
Gross Requirements:			150	250	150
Scheduled Receipts:					
Projected Available:					
Planned Orders:					

	6	7	8	9	10
Gross Requirements:	250	150	250	150	250
Scheduled Receipts:					
Projected Available:					
Planned Orders:					

16. Using the planned orders generated in Problem 15, complete the inventory record for components AB501, AB511, and AB521. Use the lot size rule, lead time, and usage information given in Problem 12. Indicate any problems that occur.

17. Fill in the partially completed inventory record shown here.

Item: AB500
Lot Size Rule: POQ = 3
Lead Time: 2 weeks

Parent: None
Children: AB501, AB511, AB521

	1	2	3	4	5
Gross Requirements:			150	250	150
Scheduled Receipts:					
Projected Available:					
Planned Orders:					

	6	7	8	9	10
Gross Requirements:	250	150	250	150	250
Scheduled Receipts:					
Projected Available:					
Planned Orders:					

18. Using the planned orders generated in Problem 17, complete inventory records for components AB501, AB511, and AB521. Use the lot size rule, lead time, and usage information given in Problem 12.

19. The Yankee Machine Shop has the following orders scheduled in Workcenter 111 for week 12. Calculate the capacity needed.

Orders	Quantity	Setup Time (hours)	Run Time per Piece (hours)
LL110	10	2.0	1.2
LL118	25	4.0	0.4
LL131	100	6.0	0.6
LL140	50	4.0	0.2

20. The Yankee Machine Shop currently has three machines working in Work Center 111, eight hours per day, five days per week, a utilization rate of 90 percent and an efficiency rate of 90 pecent.

(a) Calculate the available capacity.

(b) Is the available capacity enough to complete the orders given in Problem 19 that are already scheduled in Work Center 111? If not, how much additional capacity is needed?

21. The Yankee Machine Shop has decided to schedule its workforce to work ten hours per day, five days per week. Does this new policy provide enough capacity to complete the orders shown in Problem 19?

22. Unfortunately, after extending the work day from eight hours to ten hours, the Yankee Machine Shop has noted that efficiency has decreased to 80 percent. Given this new piece of information, is there enough capacity to complete the orders given in Problem 19?

23. In week 13, the Yankee Machine Shop, has the following orders scheduled for Work Center 111. Calculate the capacity needed.

Orders	Quantity	Setup Time (hours)	Run Time per Piece (hours)
MM078	100	4.0	0.3
MM118	250	6.0	0.1
MM213	100	3.0	0.3
MM240	500	8.0	0.1

24. In an effort to increase capacity in Work Center 111 for week 13, Yankee Machine Shop has authorized overtime. The work center will be staffed twelve hours per day for six days. Because of the additional stress on the three machines, it is expected that the utilization rate will drop to 85 percent. The efficiency rate is expected to fall to 80 percent.

(a) Calculate the capacity available in Work Center 111 for week 13.

(b) Will this plan provide sufficient capacity to complete the orders given in Problem 23? If not, what do you recommend be done?

25. The Gamma Ray Company produces two products, the Gamma Blaster (GB) and the Gamma Disaster (GD). Each product is made from three components: A, B, and C. The Gamma Blaster is made from the following components: A (2), B (3), and C (4). The Gamma Disaster is made from A (3), B (2), and C (1). All other relevant information is provided. Complete the appropriate inventory records.

Item	On Hand	Scheduled Receipts	Lot Size Rule	MPS	Lead time
GB	0	0	L4L	150, period 8	1
GD	0	0	L4L	100, period 6	2
A	250	200, period 4	FOQ = 200		4
B	25	0	FOQ = 300		2
C	0	0	L4L		3

26. Using the information in Problem 25, determine the minimum lead time to satisfy a new order for the Gamma Blaster. Determine the minimum lead time required to satisfy a new order for the Gamma Disaster.

The Newmarket International Manufacturing Company (NIMCO) was started by Marcia Blakely just two years after she finished graduate school. Her knowledge of mass customization has been the driving force behind NIMCO. The company produces three major custom products. Volume on the products is high even though each item is customized specifically for the customer. The products are processed through up to four different work centers. Even though each item is unique, the processing time at each work center is constant due to the sophisticated equipment used.

Developing a Material Requirements Plan

Joe Barnes, the production manager, reviewed your rough-cut capacity planning report and developed a new MPS that better uses capacity at each work center. Joe has given you an authorized MPS and has asked you to generate the schedule of material requirements. The authorized master production schedule is shown in Table 14-12.

TABLE 14-12   Authorized MPS

Period	14	15	16	17	18	19	20
A	7600		8700		9000		8700
B	4000	4000	4000	3800	3800	3800	3600
C		5300		6300		6400	

Period	21	22	23	24	25	26
A		8000		6800		3000
B	3600	3600	3800	3800	3800	4000
C	6000		5600		5200	

(a) Generate the material requirements. You need a BOM for each of the three products (A, B, and C), beginning inventory levels, and scheduled receipts. The BOMs are shown in Figure 14-8. All items use lot-for-lot as the lot size rule. No beginning inventories exist. Lead time is two weeks for all items except items D and F which have

FIGURE 14-8

Product structure tree

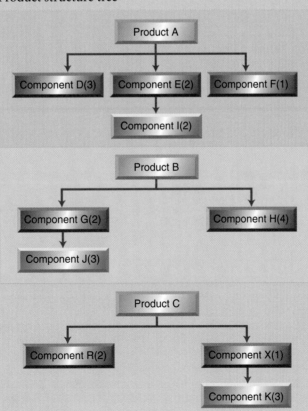

a lead time of three weeks. All other information is provided for you in Table 14-13.

(b) After completing the material requirements plan, develop a load profile for each work center for each week of the second quarter. Use the planned order releases and calculate the workload at each work center for weeks 14 through 26. The standard times are shown in the table. Use the load profiles to identify potential problems. The effective capacity at each work center is 960 hours each period.

TABLE 14-13   Additional Information

Item	Scheduled Receipts	Work Done at Work Center	Standard Hours per Piece
A	0	4	0.04
B	0	4	0.10
C	0	4	0.06
D	22,800 in Period 12 26,100 in Period 14	1	0.02
E	15,200 in Period 12	3	0.02
F	7,600 in Period 12 8,700 in Period 14	3	0.02
G	8,000 in Period 12	2	0.02
H	16,000 in Period 12	1	0.0375
I	34,800 in Period 12	3	0.02
J	48,000 in Period 12 22,800 in Period 13	2	0.015
K	15,900 in Period 12 18,900 in Period 13	3	0.03
R	none scheduled	2	0.04
X	none scheduled	3	0.04

CASE: Desserts by J.B.

Jay Brown (J.B. to his friends) is a student at the Northwest Culinary Institute and specializes in preparing elaborate desserts. After graduation, J.B. wants to open up a bakery. The bakery, Desserts by J.B., would offer elaborate, European-style desserts. As J.B. prepares his business plan, the issues of material and capacity planning arise. At the Institute, J.B. never worried about such issues. Someone else was responsible for assuring material was available and for scheduling the equipment.

Since J.B. knows that you are studying business, he has asked for your help. He needs some guidance on material planning and capacity management. In order to assist your analysis, J.B. has asked you to compile a list of necessary information. Once you have adequate information, J.B. needs to know how to determine his material requirements and how to determine his capacity needs.

(a) Develop a list of the information you will need before you can help J.B.

(b) Using at least five recipes for elaborate European-styled desserts, demonstrate how you would plan for materials.

(c) Discuss the factors J.B. needs to consider when determining his capacity needs.

(d) Explain to J.B. how he will be able to use an MRP approach in his bakery. Be sure to explain issues such as planned orders, projected available quantities, lot sizing rules, BOMs, and inventory records.

INTERACTIVE CASE Virtual Company

www.wiley.com/college/reid

On-line Case: An ERP System for Valley Memorial Hospital

Bob Reilly, head of Kaizen, just called you to say that he was impressed with your work on the various consulting assignments for VMH. As you are approaching the completion of your internship, he recognizes that you have a thorough understanding of the operations at VMH and wants you to examine a broader issue, which has implications across the entire organization. He tells you that, with the current buzz about applications of information technology, administrators and managers at VMH have heard a great deal about enterprise resource planning (ERP) systems. Although they are not sure if ERP would work well for VMH, they are interested in exploring whether an ERP system could be beneficial. Clearly, effective management (i.e., planning and coordination) of a wide range of resources is critical to VMH. Bob wants you to prepare a concise research report for the top management at VMH addressing relevant ERP issues. He

has provided a few specific questions for you to consider. This assignment will enable you to enhance your knowledge of the material in this chapter.

To complete this assignment, go to **www.wiley.com/college/ reid** to get more details. Assignment questions are given at the site.

To access the Web site:

- Go to **www.wiley.com/college/reid**
- Click **Student Companion Site**
- Click **Virtual Company**
- Click **Kaizen Consulting, Inc.**
- Click **Consulting Assignments**
- Click **ERP System for Valley Memorial Hospital**

INTERNET CHALLENGE The Gourmet Dinner

Your university's Department of Hospitality Management hosts several gourmet dinners throughout the year. To show how OM concepts are useful in the service industry, the department has asked you to help manage the next gourmet dinner from the standpoint of materials planning.

The dinner is typically a five-course meal: appetizer, soup, salad, entrée, and dessert. Your Internet challenge is to develop the menu using the many cooking Web sites available and then to calculate the kinds and quantities of raw material you will need. Assume that the facility where the dinner is hosted will take care of the beverages and that the kitchen and staff have enough capacity for your menu selections. The gourmet dinner

will have 300 attendees. If any menu items need more than 12 hours of preparation (remember you are planning for 300 guests), be sure the items arrive in time. Based on your menu, make a list of the raw materials you will need. Specify delivery dates for each item. Calculate how long each item on the menu will take to prepare for 300 guests. Decide what time the staff needs to start preparation for the dinner to be served beginning at 8:00 P.M. Calculate the time the staff needs to start preparing each item, assuming that the appetizers will be served at 8:00, the soup at 8:20, the salad at 8:35, the entrée at 8:50, and the dessert at 9:15. Bon appetit!

On-line Resources

Companion Website www.wiley.com/college/reid:
- Take interactive *practice quizzes* to assess your knowledge and help you study in a dynamic way
- Review *PowerPoint slides* or print slides for notetaking
- Download *Excel Templates* to use for problem solving
- Access the *Virtual Company: Valley Memorial Hospital*

- Find links to *Company Tours* for this chapter
   The Ashford Group
   Marrs Printing, Inc
- Find links for *Additional Web Resources* for this chapter
   IBM, *http://houns54.clearlake.ibm.com*
   Hershey Foods Corporation, *www.hersheys.com/tour/index.html*
   Mars, Inc., *www.m-ms.com/factory/tour*

Additional Resources Available Only in WileyPLUS:
- Use the *e-Book* and launch directly to all interactive resources
- Take the interactive *Quick Test* to check your understanding of the chapter material and get immediate feedback on your responses.
- Check your understanding of the key vocabulary in the chapter with *Interactive Flash Cards*
- Use the *Animated Demo Problems* to review key problem types.
- Practice for your tests with *additional problem sets*
- *And more!*

Selected Bibliography

Al-Mashari, Majed, Abdullah Al-Mudimigh, and Mohamed Zairi. "Enterprise Resource Planning: A Taxonomy of Critical Factors," *European Journal of Operational Research*, 146 (2003), 352–364.

Arnold, J.R. Tony, and Stephen N. Chapman. *Introduction to Materials Management*, Fifth Edition. Upper Saddle River, N.J.: Pearson Education Limited, 2004.

Blackstone, John H. *Capacity Management*. Cincinnati, Ohio: South-Western, 1989.

Cox, James F., III, John H. Blackstone, and Michael S. Spencer, eds. *APICS Dictionary*, Eleventh Edition. Falls Church, Va.: American Production and Inventory Control Society, Inc., 2005.

Nelson, Emily, and Evan Ramstad. "Hershey's Biggest Dud Has Turned Out to Be New Computer System," *Wall Street Journal* October 29, 1999, 1.

Orlicky, J. *Material Requirements Planning*. New York: McGraw-Hill, 1975.

"SAP Offers Supply Chain Optimization to Help Industry Meet Global Challenge," *Chemical Market Reporter*, 254, 15, October 12, 1998.

Stefanac, Rosalind. "As the Picture Gets Bigger, the Focus Becomes Sharper," *Computing Canada*, 24, 45, November 30, 1998.

Stein, Tom. "ERP's Future Linked to E-Supply Chain," *Information Week*, October 19, 1998.

Turban, Efraim, Ephraim McLean, and James Wetherbe. *Information Technology for Management*, Fourth Edition. Hoboken, N.J.: John Wiley & Sons, 2004.

Vollmann, Thomas E., William L. Berry, D. Clay Whybark, and F. Robert Jacobs. *Manufacturing Planning and Control Systems*, Fifth Edition. Burr Ridge, Ill.: McGraw-Hill/Irwin, 2005.

Wight, Oliver W. *Manufacturing Resource Planning: MRP II*. Essex Junction, Vt.: Oliver Wight, 1984.

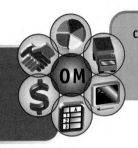

Scheduling

Before studying this chapter you should know or, if necessary, review

1. Operational impact of competitive priorities, Chapter 2, pages 35–38.
2. The differences between high-volume and low-volume operations, Chapter 10, pages 345–350.
3. Line balancing, Chapter 10, page 359.
4. Techniques for reducing employee boredom, Chapter 11, pages 383–385.
5. Order promising, Chapter 13, pages 494–498.
6. Order planning, Chapter 14, pages 532–536.

LEARNING OBJECTIVES

After studying this chapter, you should be able to

1. Explain the different kinds of scheduling operations.
2. Describe different shop loading methods.
3. Develop a schedule using priority rules.
4. Calculate scheduling performance measures.
5. Develop a schedule for multiple workstations.
6. Describe the theory of constraints.
7. Describe scheduling techniques for service applications.
8. Develop a workforce schedule in which each employee has two consecutive days off.

CHAPTER OUTLINE

WHAT'S IN OM FOR ME?

 ACC
 FIN
 MKT
 OM
 HRM
 MIS

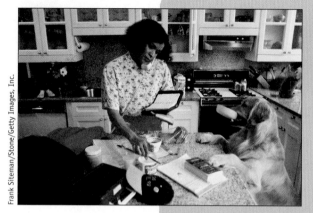

Frank Siteman/Stone/Getty Images, Inc.

Are you a list maker? Many of us are. For some people, the To Do list is a way of life. In fact, many people create electronic lists on their PDAs. We often make lists of errands, business meetings, and social events. The list might include picking up the dry cleaning, washing the dog, buying a new remote for the TV at the mall, going to the bank, paying bills, cleaning out the garage, meeting a friend for lunch, calling Mom, preparing dinner, and so forth. Organizing the list effectively into an operational schedule is more difficult.

Suppose that you needed to schedule all the activities listed above. Some of the tasks are errands, some are household chores, and some are social/family obligations. You could get the dry cleaning first since it is right near your home, but you need money to pay for the cleaning and the bank is in the other direction. So you head to the bank first. Then you pick up the dry cleaning and head home. You wash the dog, getting completely soaked in the process. You change clothes and go to the mall to pick up a new TV remote. You return home and clean the garage and your clothes get dirty. You shower and change clothes in time to meet your friend for lunch. Then it is back home to do the laundry. You still need to call Mom, pay your bills, and prepare dinner before your guests arrive. There must be a better way to do these tasks!

When developing an operational schedule, there are numerous things to consider. For example, are there some activities that can be done in parallel (simultaneously)? That is, can you pay your bills on-line while dinner is baking in the oven and a load of clothes is being washed? Can you arrange your schedule to avoid bottlenecks? For example, go to the bank early in the morning before lines develop. Can you let someone else do some of the tasks for you? Maybe a neighbor can pick up the dry cleaning, or maybe you can pay one of the neighborhood teens to clean out the garage. Are there some activities that can be postponed to another time? Put the garage cleaning off for a few days. Do you create additional tasks because of the sequence you choose to follow? For example, do you need to look nice when shopping at the mall or going to the bank? Will you look nice if you have just finished cleaning the garage or washing the dog? Sometimes the length of time needed to complete your scheduled jobs depends on whether certain jobs require more time because of the preceding task. For example, since you washed the dog before going to the mall, now you need to change clothes before your next task.

To schedule effectively, you must know what has to be done, how long it should take to do, who must do it, and what is its priority. Planning your schedule is the last step before actually completing the tasks on the schedule.

Businesses also make schedules to show how labor, materials, and equipment should be used. Consider an automobile maintenance and repair facility. The schedule can identify the start and finish time for each activity, and the resources to be used—

such as auto mechanic Alex using repair bay number two will do a tune-up on a PT Cruiser, starting at 9:00 and finishing by 9:45. Then Alex will be scheduled to do a brake job on a Lincoln Navigator (starting at 9:45 and finishing at 11:00, once again in repair bay number two). Well-defined schedules allow a company to make promises to customers concerning the completion time of the service provided.

In this chapter, we learn how the schedule affects on-time delivery to customers. We examine high-volume and low-volume scheduling operations. We look at different ways of scheduling jobs as well as ways to measure schedule effectiveness. We also consider the theory of constraints and scheduling for service operations. Let's begin with scheduling operations.

SCHEDULING OPERATIONS

A company's overall strategy provides the framework for making decisions in many operational areas. Companies differentiate themselves based on product volume and product variety. This differentiation affects how the company organizes its operations. A company providing a high-volume, standardized, consistent-quality, lower-margin product or service such as a commercial bakery or a fast-food restaurant focuses on product and layout. This type of operation needs dedicated equipment, less-skilled employees, and a continuous or repetitive process flow. Companies providing low-volume, customized, higher-margin products or services, such as a custom furniture maker or an upscale restaurant, focus on process. They need general-purpose equipment, more highly skilled employees, and flexible process flows. Each kind of operation needs a different scheduling technique. Let's look at high-volume operations first.

HIGH-VOLUME OPERATIONS

High-volume operations, also called **flow operations**, can be repetitive operations for discrete products like automobiles, appliances, or bread, or services like license renewals at the Division of Motor Vehicles. Or they can be continuous operations for goods produced in a continuous flow as in a product like gasoline or a service like waste treatment. High-volume standard items, either discrete or continuous, have smaller profit margins, so cost efficiency is important. Companies achieve cost efficiency in a high-volume operation through high levels of labor and equipment utilization. Design of the work environment ensures a smooth flow of products or customers through the system. One design is line balancing, which we covered in Chapter 10. Flow operations have the following characteristics.

Characteristics of Flow Operations

Flow operations use fixed **routings**—the product or service is always done the same way in the same sequence with the same workstations. The workstations are arranged sequentially according to the routing. Similar processing times are needed at each workstation to achieve a balanced line. Workstations are dedicated to a single product or a limited family of products. They use special-purpose equipment and tooling. In a service operation, individuals performing a specific but limited activity are the

▶ **Flow operations**
Processes designed to handle high-volume, standard products.

©AP/Wide World Photos

A high-volume operation at the DMV.

▶ **Routing**
Provides information about the operations to be performed, their sequence, the work centers, and the time standards.

equivalent of special-purpose equipment. For example, when you attend the theater, you go through a number of processing points. First you buy the tickets at the box office. Then you hand the ticket to the ticket taker. Next you are escorted to your seat by an usher. Each person attending the performance goes through these same processing points.

Material flows between workstations may be automated. A well-designed system minimizes work-in-process inventory and reduces the throughput time for the product or service. The design of the production line dictates the capacity of the flow system. The workstation or processing point that needs the greatest amount of time is the system's **bottleneck**, which determines how many products or services the system can complete. Thus the goal is to sequence the operations so they need the least control possible.

A major concern with flow operations is employee boredom with repetitive tasks. Companies use techniques like job enrichment, job enlargement, and job rotation (discussed in Chapter 11) to reduce boredom and maximize line output. At the other extreme in scheduling environments is the low-volume operation, discussed next.

▶ **Bottleneck**
A facility, department, or resource whose capacity is less than the demand placed on it.

LOW-VOLUME OPERATIONS

Kathy Tarantola/Index Stock

Personal trainer looks on.

▶ **Gantt chart**
Planning and control chart designed to graphically show workloads or to monitor job progress.

▶ **Load chart**
A chart that visually shows the workload relative to the capacity at a resource.

Low-volume or job-shop operations are used for high-quality, customized products such as custom stereo systems or custom automobile paint jobs, or for services such as personal fitness, with higher profit margins. Companies with low-volume operations use highly skilled employees, general-purpose equipment, and a process layout. The objective is flexibility, both in product variation and product volume. Equipment is not dedicated to particular jobs but is available for all jobs. In low-volume operations, products are made to order. Each product or service can have its own routing through a unique sequence of workstations, processes, materials, or setups. As a result, scheduling is complex. The workload must be distributed among the work centers or service personnel. A useful tool for viewing the schedule and workload is a Gantt chart. Let's look at how a Gantt chart is used.

Gantt Chart

Gantt charts are named after Henry Gantt, who developed these charts in the early 1900s. A Gantt chart is a visual representation of a schedule over time. Two kinds of Gantt charts are the **load chart** and the **progress chart**.

Load Chart   The load chart shows the planned workload and idle times for a group of machines or individual employees or for a department. Figure 15-1 is an example of a load chart showing the jobs assigned to each mechanic and each mechanic's lunch break. In this example, Bob and J.J. are at lunch from 12:00 to 1:00, and Alex and Sam are at lunch from 12:30 to 1:30 PM. All employees work from 8:00 AM to 5:00 PM.

FIGURE 15-1

Sample load chart

Mechanic	8–9	9–10	10–11	11–12	12–1	1–2	2–3	3–4	4–5
Bob	JOB A	JOB A	JOB A	JOB G	✕	JOB I	JOB I	JOB I	JOB I
Sam	JOB B	JOB B	JOB H	JOB H	✕	JOB J	JOB J	JOB N	JOB N
Alex	JOB C	JOB C	JOB E	JOB E	✕	✕	JOB K	JOB K	JOB O
J.J.	JOB D	JOB D	JOB F	JOB F	✕	JOB L	JOB M	JOB M	JOB M

Activity	Jan	Feb	Mar	April	May	June	July
Complete design specs	[ ]						
Source materials		[ ]					
Design process		[	]				
Pilot run				[ ]			
Feedback				[ ]			
Transition to manufacturing						[ ]	

[ ] = planned activity progress
▨ = actual activity progress

Current date

FIGURE 15-2

Sample progress chart

Progress Chart The progress chart monitors job progress by showing the relationship between planned performance and actual performance. In the progress chart in Figure 15-2, the brackets indicate when the activity is scheduled to be finished and the shaded area shows the progress of the activity. Note that the first activity, "Complete design specs," begins on time and is finished as scheduled. The second and third operations start on time. Materials sourcing is finished on time, but process design is not finished until late April. Because of the delay in the process design, the pilot run does not start as scheduled and the feedback activity has not yet begun. Both of these operations are behind schedule. The transition to manufacturing will probably also be behind schedule. Gantt charts provide a visual image of the progress of jobs through the system. Now we need to learn how to schedule work.

▶ **Progress chart**
A chart that visually shows the planned schedule compared to actual performance.

SCHEDULING WORK

Two kinds of work scheduling or work loading are **infinite loading and finite loading**. Infinite loading schedules work without regard to capacity limits. It lets you know how much capacity you need to meet a schedule.

Infinite Loading

Manufacturing companies can use infinite loading according to a proposed master production schedule (MPS). A service organization like a law firm can use infinite loading to identify the resources needed to complete the proposed case load. Infinite loading identifies uneven workloads and bottlenecks. Figure 15-3 is an example of infinite loading. We can see from the chart that the shop has enough capacity in periods

▶ **Infinite loading**
Scheduling that calculates the capacity needed at work centers in the time period needed without regard to the capacity available to do the work.

▶ **Finite loading**
Scheduling that loads work centers up to a predetermined amount of capacity.

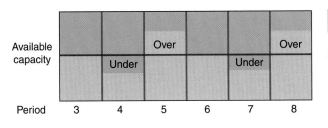

FIGURE 15-3

Infinite loading

4 and 7 but not enough capacity in periods 5 and 8. In this way, we identify time periods when capacity is either poorly used or inadequate and change the schedule to level the resource requirements.

Finite Loading

Finite loading is an operational schedule with start and finish times for each activity. It does not allow you to load more work than can be done with the available capacity. The finite loading schedule shows how a company plans to use available capacity at each work center. In a manufacturing company, the schedule shows the jobs to be done at a particular work center if the work center uses a set number of production hours each day. For example, if the work center can build 50 wire assemblies per hour and the company needs 1000 wire assemblies, the job will take 20 hours of capacity at that work center. In a service organization, a doctor's office is a good example. To spend ten minutes with each patient, the doctor can have six patients scheduled per hour.

Figure 15-4 is an example of finite loading. Note that no work center is assigned more work than it is able to handle. The disadvantage of finite loading is that it tends to break down over the long term: problems arise and the schedule slips, causing jobs to be rescheduled. Finite loading is why you may have to wait at the doctor's office.

Companies benefit from both infinite and finite loading. Infinite loading identifies resource bottlenecks for a proposed schedule so that planners can find solutions proactively, such as changing the schedule and increasing the resource capacity. Finite loading develops the operational schedule that uses the available capacity. Finite and infinite loading assign work to specific work centers based on a proposed schedule. Both techniques use either a schedule (infinite loading) or a prioritized list of jobs to be done (finite loading). Two additional techniques are forward scheduling and backward scheduling.

Forward Scheduling

▶ **Forward scheduling**
Schedule that determines the earliest possible completion date for a job.

▶ **Due date**
Time when the job is supposed to be finished.

With **forward scheduling**, processing starts immediately when a job is received, regardless of its **due date**. Each job activity is scheduled for completion as soon as possible, which allows you to determine the job's earliest possible completion date. Figure 15-5 shows an example of forward scheduling. The job is due at the end of week 10 but it can be finished as early as the end of week 7. With forward scheduling, it is not unusual for jobs to be finished before their due date. The disadvantage to finishing a job early is that it causes an inventory buildup if items are not delivered before the due date.

FIGURE 15-4

Finite loading

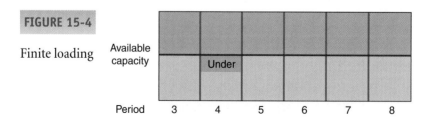

| Available capacity | | Under | | | |
| Period | 3 | 4 | 5 | 6 | 7 | 8 |

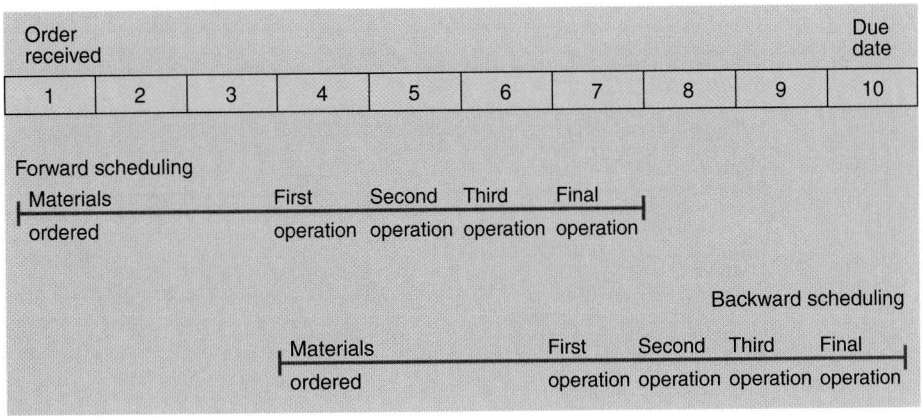

FIGURE 15-5

Forward and backward scheduling

Backward Scheduling

With **backward scheduling**, you begin scheduling the job's last activity so that the job is finished right on the due date. To do this, you start with the due date and work backward, calculating when to start the last activity, when to start the next-to-last activity, and so forth. Figure 15-5 gives an example of backward scheduling. Backward scheduling shows you how late the job can be started and still be finished on time. When you are using backward scheduling and forward scheduling together, a difference between the start time of the first activity indicates **slack** in the schedule. Slack means that you can start a job immediately but you do not have to do so. You can start it any time up to the start time in your backward schedule and still meet the due date.

▶ **Backward scheduling**
Scheduling method that determines when the job must be started to be done on the due date.

▶ **Slack**
The amount of time a job can be delayed and still be finished by its due date.

Monitoring Workflow

Input/output control is a capacity-control technique used to monitor workflow at individual work centers. Input/output control monitors the planned inputs and outputs at a work center against the actual inputs and outputs. Planned inputs are based on the operational schedule, whereas planned outputs use capacity-planning techniques. Actual input is compared with planned input to ensure that enough work enters the measured work center. A work center cannot process items that have not yet arrived. Actual output is used to identify possible problems in the work center, such as an equipment problem or unexpected absences.

▶ **Input/output control**
A technique for monitoring the flow of jobs between work centers.

JT's produces custom wine storage units. JT is very concerned about the performance of Work Center 101, the bottleneck in the manufacturing process. He has given you the input/output report shown in Figure 15-6 and asks you to explain the numbers.

• **Before You Begin:** Explain the numbers in the input/output report. The purpose of this report is to monitor the flow of work between work centers and backlog size. First, examine the input report to determine if the supplying work center is actually supplying the amount of work expected. Then examine the output report to see how Work Center 101 is performing. A key indicator is the size of its backlog. If the backlog is increasing, then Work Center 101 is unable to keep up with its input. If the backlog is decreasing, then Work Center 101 is outputting more product than is being inputted. If this continues, the backlog will disappear entirely.

EXAMPLE 15.1

Input/Output Control at JT's Custom Storage Units

FIGURE 15-6	Input information	Period				
		4	5	6	7	8
Input/output report for Work Center 101	Planned input	800 hours	750 hours	800 hours	820 hours	800 hours
	Actual input	750 hours	780 hours	780 hours	810 hours	810 hours
	Deviation	−50 hours	+30 hours	−20 hours	−10 hours	+10 hours
	Cumulative deviation	−50 hours	−20 hours	−40 hours	−50 hours	−40 hours

Output Information	Period				
	4	5	6	7	8
Planned output	800 hours	800 hours	800 hours	800 hours	800 hours
Actual output	800 hours	750 hours	780 hours	850 hours	825 hours
Deviation	0 hours	−50 hours	−20 hours	+50 hours	+25 hours
Cumulative deviation	0 hours	−50 hours	−70 hours	−20 hours	+5 hours

Backlog 100 hours	50 hours	80 hours	80 hours	40 hours	25 hours

• Solution:

The input/output report for Work Center 101 shows any deviations in input or output at the work center. The input deviation is calculated by subtracting the planned input from the actual input. The output deviation is calculated as planned output subtracted from actual output. For example, based on the input information in period 4, the planned input was 800 standard hours of work, but the actual input was only 750 standard hours. Remember that standard hours of work are the amount of time needed to complete the work if the employee works at 100 percent efficiency. Subtracting the planned input from the actual input (750 standard hours minus 800 standard hours) results in a deviation of 50 standard hours. In period 5, the actual input exceeded the planned input, resulting in a positive deviation (780 standard hours minus 750 standard hours = 30 standard hours deviation).

The cumulative deviation is a running sum of the deviations. For example, in period 4, the deviation is −50 hours; the cumulative deviation is equal to this period's deviation plus the previous cumulative deviation total. In our case, the previous cumulative deviation is zero, so the cumulative deviation at the end of period 4 is −50 hours. After period 5, the cumulative deviation is −20 hours [a +30 hour deviation in period 5 plus the previous cumulative deviation (−50 hours)]. We calculate the deviations and cumulative deviations in the same way for both input and output. Management uses cumulative deviation values to indicate possible input or output problems. If planned input is consistently below actual input, the feeding work center may not have enough capacity to meet the planned input. The same is true when the work center's actual output is consistently less than the planned output. The work center is not producing with the efficiency expected.

The backlog row is the amount of work waiting to be finished at the work center. In our example, Work Center 101 has 100 standard hours of work waiting. *The only time the size of the backlog changes is when actual input does not equal actual output.* When a work center receives more work than it finishes, the backlog increases. When a work center produces more output than the input received, the backlog decreases. In period 4, Work Center 101 receives 750 standard hours of new work. Work Center 101 finishes 800 standard hours of work during period 4; this is possible only if Work Center 101 finishes some of the 100 hours of backlog from the beginning of period 4. The new input plus the backlog equals the maximum amount of work that can be finished at Work Center 101 (850 standard hours). Since the work center finishes 800 standard hours of work, the backlog decreases to 50 standard hours of work. In period 5, the backlog increases because Work Center 101 receives 780 standard hours of work but only produces 750 standard hours of work. The difference between the actual input and the actual output is 30 standard hours; therefore, the backlog increases by 30 standard hours. The input/output report allows a planner to monitor how well the available capacity is used at individual work centers and provides insight into process problems.

HOW TO SEQUENCE JOBS

When several jobs need to be done, how do you decide which one to do first? Do you work on the job that you have to finish first? The job you enjoy doing? The job you can finish the fastest? The job that has the biggest payoff? When you decide which job to do first, you are sequencing them.

The eleventh edition of the *APICS Dictionary* defines **operation sequencing** or job sequencing as a technique for short-term planning of actual jobs to be run in each work center based on capacity and priorities. We expect a work center to have several jobs waiting to be processed, so we decide on the sequence for processing the jobs. Operation sequencing sets projected start and finish times and expected **queues**. A job's priority is its position in the sequence.

▶ **Operation sequencing**
A short-term plan of actual jobs to be run in each work center based on available capacity and priorities.

▶ **Queue**
Waiting line.

▶ **Priority rule**
Determines the priority of jobs at a work center.

▶ **Local priority rule**
Makes a priority decision based on jobs currently at that work center.

▶ **Global priority rule**
Makes a priority decision based on information that includes the remaining work centers a job must pass through.

Priority Rules

Job priority is often set by a **priority rule**. (See Table 15-1 for explanations of some commonly used priority rules.) Priority rules are typically classified as local or global. A **local priority rule** sets priority based only on the jobs waiting at that individual work center. For example, the highest priority might be given to the job that arrives first or the job that can be done the fastest. **Global priority rules**, like critical ratio or slack over remaining operations, set priority according to factors such as the scheduled workload at the remaining workstations that the job must be processed through.

TABLE 15-1

Commonly Used Priority Rules

> **First come, first served (FCFS):** Jobs are processed in the order in which they arrive at a machine or work center.
>
> **Last come, first served (LCFS):** The last job in to the work center or at the top of the stack is processed first.
>
> **Earliest due date (EDD):** The job due the earliest has the highest priority.
>
> **Shortest processing time (SPT):** The job that requires the least processing time has the highest priority.
>
> **Longest processing time (LPT):** The job that requires the longest processing time has the highest priority.
>
> **Critical ratio (CR):** The job with the smallest ratio of time remaining until due date to its processing time remaining has the highest priority.
>
> **Slack per remaining operations (S/RO):** The job with the least slack per remaining operations is given the highest priority. Calculate by dividing slack by remaining operations.

"They say the computer is down."

Lines are everywhere!

James Stevenson/The Cartoon Bank, Inc.

A work center needs priority rules when multiple jobs await processing (but not if only a single job needs processing). Priority rules assume that there is no variability in either the setup time or the run time of the job. Let's look at how to use priority rules.

How to Use Priority Rules

Using priority rules is straightforward. Just follow these steps.

Step 1   Decide Which Priority Rule to Use. Different priority rules achieve different results. We will discuss this when we look at performance measurements.

Step 2   List All the Jobs Waiting to Be Processed at the Work Center and Their Job Time. Job time includes setup and processing time.

Step 3   Using Your Priority Rule, Determine Which Job Has the Highest Priority and Should Be Worked on First, Second, Third, and So On. To illustrate the use of priority rules, let's use SPT to sequence a group of jobs waiting at Work Center 102, Jill's Machine Shop.

EXAMPLE 15.2

Using SPT at Jill's Machine Shop

Using SPT as a priority rule, determine the sequence for the following jobs waiting at Work Center 102 at Jill's Machine Shop. The job information follows.

• Before You Begin: In this problem, the objective is to develop a sequence to perform the batch of jobs. The priority rule is used when one or more jobs are available to be put in the sequence. SPT means that the job with the shortest processing time is put first in the sequence, and the job with the second shortest time is placed second. When there is a tie between available jobs, it does not matter which job is placed first in the sequence.

Job Number	Job Time at Work Center 102 (includes setup and run time)
AZK111	3 days
BRU872	2 days
CUF373	5 days
DBR664	4 days
EZE101	1 day
FID448	4 days

Step 1   Choose the priority rule. You must use SPT.

Step 2   List the jobs waiting for processing at Work Center 102 and their job times. This information is given in the table.

Step 3   Using the priority rule, determine the sequence of jobs.

The highest priority goes to job EZE101 (one day) since it takes the least amount of time. The second job is BRU872 (two days). The third job is AZK111 (three days). Job DBR664 and job FID448 are tied for fourth place because both take four days. Since we have no additional information, it does not matter which of these is done fourth and which one is done fifth. We will do DBR664 fourth and FID448 fifth. The last job is CUF373. Our completed sequence is

Position in Sequence	Job Number
First	EZE101
Second	BRU872
Third	AZK111
Fourth	DBR664
Fifth	FID448
Sixth	CUF373

How well a priority rule works depends on the performance measurement the company uses. In the next section, we will cover commonly used performance measurements.

MEASURING PERFORMANCE

Companies measure scheduling effectiveness according to their competitive priorities. For example, if your company is concerned with customer response time, you measure scheduling effectiveness in terms of response time. Mean job flow time and the mean number of jobs in the system each measure a company's responsiveness. On the other hand, if your company competes on cost, it is concerned with efficiency. If on-time delivery is of primary concern, the company measures on-time delivery performance. Makespan measures efficiency; mean job lateness and mean job tardiness measure due-date performance. After looking at airline scheduling, we discuss different performance measures.

LINKS TO PRACTICE

Airline Scheduling

Consider scheduling in the airline industry. Cheaper fares, competition factors, weather patterns, equipment and expansion difficulties, and poor scheduling are only some of the reasons why scheduling problems occur. However, various remedies can help alleviate these scheduling problems, including charging peak travel fares, requiring the FAA and weather service to work more closely for more accurate and frequent weather forecasts, "technologizing" (i.e., utilizing scheduling technology, modernizing the air traffic control system, and automating ticketing and boarding), building new runways and using abandoned military airfields, and, most important, designing realistic schedules (i.e., cutting back the number of flights, moving leisure flights to off-peak times, extending the operation day, and spreading out arrival and departure times). As long as the number of air travelers continues to boom, optimal scheduling will be an important issue to the airline industry.

©AP/Wide World Photos

Job Flow Time

Job flow time measures response time—the time a job spends in the shop, from the time it is ready to be worked on until it is finished. It includes waiting time, setup time, process time, and possible delays. We calculate job flow time as

▶ **Job flow time**
Measurement of the time a job spends in the shop before it is finished.

Job flow time = time of completion − time job was first available for processing

---

EXAMPLE 15.3

Calculating Mean Flow Time

Calculate the mean flow time for the following sequence of jobs.

- **Before You Begin:** In this problem, sum the individual job flow times and divide by the number of jobs in the sequence to calculate the mean job flow time. Flow time is the amount of time a job spends in the shop before being completed.

- **Solution:**
  To calculate mean job flow time, we sum the individual job flow times for each job and divide by the number of jobs. Viewing Figure 15-7, we can see that the job flow time for job A is 10 days, 13 days for job B, 17 days for job C, and 20 days for job D. Adding these job flow times together (10 + 13 + 17 + 20) gives us a total job flow time of 60 days. We divide this by the number of jobs to determine mean job flow time—that is, 60 days divided by 4 jobs equals a mean job flow time of 15 days.

Job A finishes on day 10	Job B finishes on day 13	Job C finishes on day 17	Job D ends on day 20

FIGURE 15-7

Job schedule

Average Number of Jobs in the System

▶ **Average number of jobs in the system**
Measures work-in-process inventory.

The **average number of jobs in the system** measures the work-in-process inventory and also affects response time. The greater the number of jobs in the system, the longer the queues and subsequently the longer the job flow times. If quick customer response is critical to your company, the number of jobs waiting in the system should be relatively low.

EXAMPLE 15.4

Calculating the Average Number of Jobs in the System

Calculate the average number of jobs in the system.

- **Before You Begin:** To calculate the average number of jobs in the system, sum the individual job flow times and divide that by the makespan (the amount of time it takes to finish the entire batch of jobs). This is the average number of jobs in the shop. If this number is too low, it is likely that some work centers will be starved for work. If the number is too high, it means that work-in-process inventories will be higher.

- **Solution:**
To calculate the average number of jobs in the system, we need to know the individual job flow times for each job. Once again, look at Figure 15-7 to determine job flow times. The total job flow time (10 + 13 + 17 + 20 + 60 days) is divided by the total number of days it takes to complete the whole batch of jobs (20 days). Therefore, the average number of jobs in the system is 3. The higher the average number of jobs in the system, the longer the waiting time.

Makespan

▶ **Makespan**
The amount of time it takes to finish a batch of jobs.

Makespan measures efficiency by telling us how long it takes to finish a batch of jobs. To calculate makespan, we subtract the starting time of the first job from the completion time of the last job in the group. Using the data from Example 15.4, a calendar showing the progress of the jobs would look like Figure 15-7. In this case, the makespan for this group of jobs is 20 days. Note that makespan has no link to customer due dates: you can have an efficient schedule in terms of finishing a batch of jobs but still have relatively poor customer service.

Job Lateness and Tardiness

▶ **Job lateness**
Measures whether the job is done ahead of, on, or behind schedule.

Job lateness, a measure of customer service, is the difference between the time a job is finished and the time it is supposed to be finished (its due date). When a job is finished ahead of schedule, it has negative lateness. For example, if job X is due on day 15 and it is finished on day 12, it has a lateness value of negative 3 days. If job X is finished on day 15, its lateness value is zero. If job X is done on day 17, its lateness value is a positive 2 days. Positive job lateness values are typically described as **job tardiness**. Tardiness indicates how many days pass after the due date before the job is completed.

▶ **Job tardiness**
Measures how long after the due date the job is completed.

Calculate mean job lateness using the following data.

EXAMPLE 15.5

Calculating Job Lateness

• **Before You Begin:** Lateness measures how closely to the due date different jobs are completed. A negative lateness value means that the job is completed before it is due. A positive lateness value means the job is completed after it was due. A value of zero means that the job was completed on its due date. Tardiness is used when companies do not include jobs completed early in their calculation.

Job	Completion Date	Due Date	Lateness
A	10	15	−5
B	13	15	−2
C	17	10	7
D	20	20	0

• **Solution:**

Job A is finished 5 days ahead of its due date, and job B is finished two days earlier than its due date. Job C is finished seven days tardy, and job D is finished on its due date. The performance measure we use to evaluate the schedule is mean job lateness, which sums all the individual lateness values and divides by the number of jobs processed. In our case, it is 0 divided by 4 jobs equals 0 days job lateness. On average, the jobs are finished on their due dates.

Some companies do not include negative values of lateness in the calculation because there is no perceived benefit to finishing the job early. In this case, we substitute zeroes for the negative numbers, and we sum the lateness values and then divide by the number of jobs to get the *average tardiness* of the jobs. The updated information using zeroes instead of negative lateness values is as shown in the table.

Job	Completion Date	Due Date	Tardiness
A	10	15	0
B	13	15	0
C	17	10	7
D	20	20	0

In this case, average tardiness is 1.75 days ((0 + 0 + 7 + 0)/4 jobs). If customer service is important to your company, average tardiness is probably a more relevant measurement than job lateness.

Before You Go On

Be sure you know how to use priority rules and how to measure a schedule's effectiveness. Different priority rules measure different aspects of performance, depending on your company's competitive priorities. SPT (shortest processing time) always minimizes mean job flow time, mean job lateness, and average number of jobs in the system. FCFS (first comes first served) is considered a fair rule because everyone is treated equally. EDD (earliest due date) and S/RO (slack per remaining operations) tend to perform well in terms of minimizing mean job tardiness.

Let's compare two priority rules.

COMPARING PRIORITY RULES

Now that you know how to use priority rules and how to measure schedule effectiveness, compare the effectiveness of different priority rules.

EXAMPLE 15.6

Using SPT

Using the job information shown in Table 15-2, compare the shortest processing time priority rule (SPT) to the slack per remaining operations priority rule (S/RO). Determine the job sequence and calculate mean job flow time, the average number of jobs in the system, mean job lateness, and mean job tardiness.

• **Before You Begin:** First, develop the sequence of jobs using the appropriate priority rule. Begin with SPT and calculate the performance measurements. Repeat using S/RO.

Table 15-2   Job Data

Job	Job Time at Work Center 301 (days)	Due Date (days from now)	Remaining Job Time at Other Work Centers (days)	Remaining Number of Operations
A	3	15	6	2
B	7	20	8	4
C	6	30	5	3
D	4	20	3	2
E	2	22	7	3
F	5	20	5	3

The first priority rule is SPT and the available jobs are listed, so we need to calculate only the sequence. Using SPT, we base the sequence on doing the job that needs the least amount of time at the work center first (in our case, job E). We do job E first and then we look for the next shortest job time (job A takes three days) to be second in our sequence. The complete sequence for SPT is job E, A, D, F, C, and then B, shown graphically here.

E done at end of day 2	A done at end of day 5	D done at end of day 9	F done at end of day 14	C done at end of day 20	D done at end of day 27

Using this information, we calculate the mean job flow time. The flow time for job E is 2 days; for job A it is 5 days; for job D it is 9 days; for job F it is 14 days; for job C it is 20 days; and for job B it is 27 days. To find the mean job flow time, we add up these individual job flow times and divide by the number of jobs: (2 + 5 + 9 + 14 + 20 + 27)/6 jobs = 12.83 days. We calculate the average number of jobs in the system by dividing total job flow time by the makespan, which is 27 days. Total job flow time is 77 days (2 + 5 + 9 + 14 + 20 + 27). The average number of jobs in the system is 2.85 jobs. To calculate the mean lateness and mean tardiness of the jobs processed, we need to know when each job leaves Work Center 301. Table 15-3 shows those results.

Problem-Solving Tip   Remember that job flow time is the amount of time the job is in the system (its completion date minus when the job was first available). Since all the jobs were available at the same time, their flow time is the same as their completion time.

To find mean job lateness, we add up the individual lateness values (−10 + 7 − 10 − 11 − 20 − 6), which equals −50 days. Dividing by the number of jobs (6), the mean job lateness is −8.33 days. On average, jobs take 8.33 fewer days to get through the shop than we expected. How is this information useful? Your company can correlate job flow time with lead times quoted to customers. If the job flow time is less than expected, marketing can consider using reduced lead times as a competitive advantage.

MKT

Table 15-3   Work Center 301 Completion Data Using SPT

Job	Completion Date	Due Date	Lateness (days)	Tardiness (days)
A	5	15	−10	0
B	27	20	7	7
C	20	30	−10	0
D	9	20	−11	0
E	2	22	−20	0
F	14	20	−6	0

Problem-Solving Tip   Negative lateness means the job is finished ahead of its due date. Zero lateness means the job finished on its due date. Positive lateness means the job finished after its due date.

Tardiness applies only to jobs finished after the due date. We treat all negative lateness values as zeroes. To find mean job tardiness, we sum the individual job tardiness values and divide by the number of jobs. In this example, only one job is tardy and the sum of the tardiness values is 7. The mean job tardiness is 1.17 days, or 7/6 jobs. The maximum tardiness is 7 days. This information is also important for marketing because it implies the level of customer service provided. Now let's look at what happens when we use the S/RO priority rule to develop our sequence.

• Solution:

We calculate the S/RO by finding the amount of slack each job has and then dividing that slack by the remaining number of operations (including the current operation). We calculate slack by subtracting the total work remaining (current operation plus all other undone operations times) from the amount of time left until the due date. We calculate the values in the slack time column by adding the job time at Work Center 301 plus the remaining job time at other work centers (for job A, $3 + 6 = 9$ days of remaining work) and subtracting that total from the number of days till the due date (for job A, 15 days). The difference is the slack (for job A, 6 days) as shown in Table 15-4.

Table 15-4   Job Data with Slack Calculations

Job	Job Time at Work Center 301 (days)	Remaining Job Time at Other Work Center (days)	Due Date (days from now)	Slack Time (days)	Remaining Number of Operations after Work Center 301	S/RO
A	3	6	15	6	2	2
B	7	8	20	5	4	1
C	6	5	30	19	3	4.75
D	4	3	20	13	2	4.33
E	2	7	22	13	3	3.25
F	5	5	20	10	3	2.5

We calculate the S/RO values by dividing the slack for the job (6 days for job A) by the number of remaining operations, including the current operation (two plus the current one, or three remaining operations), which equals an S/RO of 2 for job A. Table 15-4 shows the S/RO value for each job. The lower the value of the S/RO, the higher is its priority. For our problem, job B should be done first, followed by A, F, E, D, and then C. Graphically, the sequence appears as follows.

B done at end of day 7	A done at end of day 10	F done at end of day 15	E done at end of day 17	D done at end of day 21	C done at end of day 27

Table 15-5 shows the completion dates of the jobs when we use S/RO.

Table 15-5   Work Center 301 Completion Data Using S/RO

Job	Completion Date	Due Date	Lateness (days)	Tardiness (days)
A	10	15	−5	0
B	7	20	−13	0
C	27	30	−3	0
D	21	20	1	1
E	17	22	−5	0
F	15	20	−5	0

Comparing SPT and S/RO

Mean job lateness using S/RO is -5 days, compared to -8.33 days using SPT. The SPT rule always minimizes mean job lateness. The mean tardiness using S/RO is 0.167 days, compared to 1.17 days using SPT. The maximum tardiness is less using S/RO (3 days), compared to SPT (7 days). Priority rules based on due date are better at reducing the maximum tardiness. Mean job flow time using S/RO is 16.17 days, compared to only 12.83 days with SPT. Note that the SPT priority rule always minimizes mean job flow time. Average number of jobs in the system using S/RO is 3.59 jobs, compared to 2.85 jobs using SPT. Since SPT sets priority on getting several jobs done as quickly as possible, we can expect less work-in-process or fewer average jobs in the system.

Now that we have used two different priority rules to develop a sequence for a single machine or work center, let's look at a technique for developing the sequence when two different work centers are involved.

SEQUENCING JOBS THROUGH TWO WORK CENTERS

▶ **Johnson's rule**
A technique for minimizing makespan in a two-stage, unidirectional process.

At times, all jobs must be processed through the same two work centers sequentially. For example, when you do laundry, clothes go through the washer before the dryer. Different kinds of clothing need different wash cycles and different drying times, but the sequence is the same. To shorten the time it takes to do your laundry, you can use Johnson's rule. **Johnson's rule** is a scheduling technique for developing a sequence when jobs are processed through two successive operations. The operations can be at machine centers, departments, or different geographical locations. The job flow must be unidirectional: the first activity for every job is the same, and you must finish it before you can begin the second activity (wash the clothes before you dry the clothes). Johnson's rule is an optimizing technique and always minimizes makespan. To use Johnson's rule, follow this procedure.

Step 1 List the jobs and the processing time for each activity.

Step 2 Find the shortest activity processing time among all the jobs not yet scheduled. If the shortest activity processing time is a first activity, put the job needing that activity in the earliest available position in the job sequence. If the shortest activity processing time is a second activity, put the job needing that activity in the last available position in the job sequence. When you schedule a job, eliminate it from further consideration.

Step 3 Repeat Step 2 until you have put all the activities for the job in the schedule.

EXAMPLE 15.7
Vicki's Office Cleaners

Vicki's Office Cleaners does the annual major cleaning of university buildings. The job requires mopping and waxing the floors in five buildings at Mideast University. Each building must have the floors mopped and stripped (first activity), and then waxed and buffed (second activity). Vicki wants to minimize the time it takes her crews to finish cleaning the five buildings. Use Johnson's method to develop the sequence Vicki should follow.

• **Before You Begin:** In this problem, find the best sequence for mopping and waxing the different university buildings. Whenever the scheduling problem has a unidirectional flow and two different activities to be done, use Johnson's rule. This sequence, to be followed by the mopping and waxing crews, minimizes makespan.

• Solution:

Step 1   List the Jobs and the Processing Time.

	Activity 1 Mopping (days)	Activity 2 Waxing (days)
Adams Hall	1	2
Bryce Building	3	5
Chemistry Building	2	4
Drake Union	5	4
Evans Center	4	2

Step 2   Find the Shortest Activity Processing Time among the Jobs. The shortest activity processing time is one day for mopping Adams Hall. Since the shortest activity time is a first activity, we put mopping Adams Hall in the top available position in the sequence. The first job in our sequence is mopping Adams Hall. We eliminate Adams Hall since it has a spot in our sequence. We also eliminate the first position in our sequence. Let's look at the remaining jobs and repeat Step 2.

	Activity 1 Mopping (days)	Activity 2 Waxing (days)
Bryce Building	3	5
Chemistry Building	2	4
Drake Union	5	4
Evans Center	4	2

Step 2   Find the Shortest Activity Processing Time among the Remaining Jobs. There are two activities tied this time: waxing the Evans Center and mopping the Chemistry Building—each take two days. When a tie occurs and the shortest processing time is for the same activity, either building can be selected. In a case like this where the shortest processing times are for different activities, we schedule both. Since the shortest time for the Evans Center is the second activity, it takes the lowest available spot in our sequence. The Evans Center will be done fifth. The shortest processing time for the Chemistry Building is for its first activity, so it takes the highest available spot in our sequence. The Chemistry Building will be mopped second. We update our remaining jobs, removing the Evans Center and the Chemistry Building and the fifth and second positions. Now repeat Step 2 again.

	Activity 1 Mopping (days)	Activity 2 Waxing (days)
Bryce Building	3	5
Drake Union	5	4

Step 2   Find the Shortest Activity Processing Time among the Remaining Jobs. The shortest activity processing time is three days for mopping the Bryce Building. Since this is the first activity, we put mopping the Bryce Building in the earliest available spot in the sequence, which is third. Since only one job is left, Drake Union, we put it in the only remaining spot in the sequence, fourth.

The sequence Vicki should use is shown here. When we have a tie for the shortest activity, it does not matter which job we put first.

Sequence Position	Job
First	Adams Hall (A)
Second	Chemistry Bldg (C)
Third	Bryce Building (B)
Fourth	Drake Union (D)
Fifth	Evans Center (E)

Now let's look at the sequence graphically.

	1	2	3	4	5	6	7	8	9	10	11	12	13	14	15	16	17	18
Mopping	A	C	C	B	B	B	D	D	D	D	D	E	E	E	E			
Waxing		A	A	C	C	C	C	B	B	B	B	B	D	D	D	D	E	E

Vicki's Cleaners begins mopping Adams Hall on day 1. No waxing is done because none of the floors has been mopped yet. At the end of day 1, Vicki's Cleaners has finished mopping Adams Hall. On day 2, the mopping crew starts mopping the Chemistry Building while the waxing crew begins at Adams Hall. At the end of day 3, the mopping crew finishes the Chemistry Building and moves on to the Bryce Building to start day 4. The waxing crew finishes Adams Hall and starts the Chemistry Building on day 4. Note that this sequence has a makespan of eighteen days. We can find no other sequence for these jobs that can take less time because Johnson's rule always minimizes makespan.

SCHEDULING BOTTLENECKS

When companies schedule a job shop, bottlenecks are common. A bottleneck is any resource whose capacity is less than the demand placed on it. For example, let's consider Akito's Flowers, a retail florist. When a customer orders flowers, three steps follow. First, the clerk takes the order and processes payment. Second, the clerk gives the order to the flower arrangers, who gather the appropriate materials and do the flower arrangement. Third, the drivers deliver the flowers. At Akito's Flowers, the clerk can process thirty telephone orders per hour. Each of the three flower arrangers can make seven arrangements per hour and each of the three drivers can make ten deliveries per hour. The flower arrangers are the bottleneck in this process. Regardless of the number of orders processed by the clerk, the arrangers can do a maximum of twenty-one arrangements per hour, and Akito's can deliver no more than twenty-one floral arrangements per hour. Thus the output of the process is reduced to the capacity of the bottleneck. Bottlenecks typically result when one operation in a job takes longer than the other operations.

Techniques for scheduling bottleneck systems emerged in the late 1970s with the introduction of **optimized production technology (OPT)** by Eli Goldratt. OPT classifies resources as either bottlenecks or **nonbottlenecks**, and makes bottlenecks the basis for scheduling and capacity planning. According to OPT, companies should schedule bottleneck resources to full capacity and schedule nonbottleneck resources to support the bottleneck resources. In our example, the bottleneck resource is the flower arrangers; the nonbottleneck resources are the clerks processing orders and the delivery drivers. Nonbottleneck resources can be idle and still not affect the output of the system because output is determined by the bottleneck resource, not by capacity at the nonbottleneck resources. OPT also introduces the concept of **capacity-constrained resources**, which are resources that have become bottlenecks because of inefficient usage. In our florist shop example, the delivery drivers could become a capacity-constrained resource if Akito's does not attend to consolidating shipments and using the drivers efficiently. Table 15-6 lists OPT principles.

▶ **Optimized production technology (OPT)**
A technique used to schedule bottleneck systems.

▶ **Nonbottleneck**
A work center with more capacity than demand.

▶ **Capacity-constrained resource**
Bottleneck caused by inefficient usage.

- Balance the process rather than the flow.
- Use of a nonbottleneck resource is determined by some other constraint within the system.
- Use and activation of a resource are not the same.
- An hour lost at a bottleneck resource is an hour lost forever.
- An hour lost at a nonbottleneck resource is just a mirage.
- Bottlenecks determine throughput and inventory in the system.
- The transfer batch does not need to be equal to the process batch.
- The process batch should be variable.
- Schedules should be established by considering all constraints simultaneously. Lead times are the result of the schedule and are not predetermined.

TABLE 15-6

OPT Principles

Let's look at each of these principles.

Balance the process rather than the flow. Traditionally, managers try to make the same amount of capacity available in each department or work center. This means every resource is a bottleneck. At Akito's Flowers, balanced capacity means processing 21 orders per hour or needing only 0.7 order clerks and 2.1 drivers. Although in theory this approach provides capacity for 21 floral arrangements per hour, in real life we cannot use partial employees or machines, so we have some excess capacity. If we have no excess capacity, we guarantee that fewer than 21 orders will be processed each hour, because real life has statistical fluctuations and dependent events. At Akito's Flowers, processing does not begin until the clerk receives an order. What happens when no orders are received for the first twenty minutes of the day? That twenty minutes is lost capacity not only for the clerk but also for the floral arrangers and the delivery drivers. If we have some excess capacity at the nonbottleneck resources, we can operate the bottleneck at full capacity.

Nonbottleneck usage is determined by some other constraint in the system. At the floral shop, the order processing and the delivery service are nonbottlenecks. Their level of usage is determined by the flower arrangers (the bottleneck resource).

Usage and activation of a resource are not the same. Activation of a resource means the resource is used to process materials or products. Usage means that the resource activated is contributing positively to the company's performance. Thus usage means the resource is performing a needed activity.

An hour lost at a bottleneck resource is an hour lost forever. If an organization's goal is to maximize **throughput**, the bottleneck must be fully used. Suppose our floral arrangers cannot produce arrangements for an hour because the delivery of flowers to the shop is delayed. Thus the shop can only produce a maximum of 147 arrangements that day instead of 168 arrangements (7 hours × 3 arrangers × 7 arrangements per hour instead of 8 hours × 3 arrangers × 7 arrangements per hour).

An hour lost at a nonbottleneck is a mirage. Time lost at a nonbottleneck resource is critical only if the lost time causes the resource to become a bottleneck. For example, if one of the florist's drivers leaves work an hour early, it may or may

▶ **Throughput**
The quantity of finished goods that can be sold.

not affect the output for the day. It affects the output only if more than 14 deliveries must be made during that last hour. Otherwise, there is no decrease in output. If more than 14 deliveries are needed, the delivery service has become a bottleneck resource.

Bottlenecks determine throughput and system inventory. A bottleneck resource determines the throughput for the system. It also determines how much inventory is needed in the system to ensure the continuous operation of the bottleneck resource. For example, the florist can process 168 orders per day. Therefore, the flower inventory must be sufficient to produce 168 arrangements.

The transfer batch does not have to equal the process batch. The **transfer batch** is the quantity of items moved at the same time from one resource to the next. At Akito's Flowers, that is the number of orders the clerk processes before forwarding the orders to the floral arrangers. If the clerk forwards orders only once per hour, the floral arrangers' output is directly affected. If the clerk forwards each order as it arrives, the number of orders the clerk can process per hour is probably affected.

▶ **Transfer batch**
The quantity of items moved at the same time from one resource to the next.

The **process batch** is the quantity of an item processed at a resource before that resource is changed to produce a different product. If one of the floral arrangers specializes in preparing business floral arrangements and typically produces these arrangements in batches of 14, the process batch is 14 units. The arranger could transfer these arrangements immediately to the delivery area after each one is produced. In this case, the transfer batch quantity is 1. The delivery service could begin immediately to prepare the arrangement for delivery rather than waiting until all 14 arrangements are ready.

▶ **Process batch**
The quantity produced at a resource before the resource is switched over to produce another product.

The process batch should be variable. We do not always have to produce the same quantity, but instead we should produce what is needed. At Akito's Flowers, one of the floral arrangers produced a batch of 14 business floral arrangements at a time, but this does not mean that the arrangers always have to produce 14. Maybe two of the business customers close for summer vacation. In this case, the arranger should make only 12 arrangements and not 14, because the additional 2 will not be sold. Thus, the process batch quantity should be linked to demand.

Schedules should be established by considering all constraints simultaneously. Lead times are the result of the schedule and are not predetermined. You should develop the schedule considering all your constraints. If you do not know what your workload is, you cannot tell a customer how long it will take to do a job. Once you know how much work you need to do, you can determine how long it should take.

Instead of losing capacity because of order-processing delays, a florist can improve the order entry procedure. An approach by 1-800-FLOWERS.com, a nationwide network of 1500 independent florists, allows customers to enter a Web site and private chat room to discuss their order with a customer service representative in real time. With its on-line proprietary order processing system designed to handle a high volume of transactions, 1-800-FLOWERS.com is positioned to provide highly personalized real-time customer service. The company has been operating on the web since 1992.

THEORY OF CONSTRAINTS

The **theory of constraints (TOC)** is an extension of OPT. According to the TOC, a system's output is determined by three kinds of constraints: internal resource constraint, market constraint, and policy constraint. An **internal resource constraint** is the classic bottleneck discussed in the previous section. A **market constraint** results when market demand is less than production capacity. Since companies do not want excess inventory buildup, the market determines the rate of production. **Policy constraint** means that a specific policy dictates the rate of production (for example, a policy of no overtime).

TOC tries to improve system performance by focusing on constraints. Improvement is measured financially and operationally. Financial measurements are net profit, return on investment, and cash flow. Operational measurements include throughput, inventory, and operating expenses. Throughput is the rate at which money is generated by the system through sales. Unsold product is not throughput. Inventory is the money the system has invested in buying materials to produce items it intends to sell and does not include labor or overhead. Operating expense is the money spent to convert inventory into throughput, including all labor, overhead, and other expenses.

The procedure for using TOC consists of the following steps.

Step 1   Identify the System's Bottleneck(s). At Akito's Flowers, identify the floral arrangers as the bottleneck.

Step 2   Exploit the Bottleneck(s). For the floral shop, take orders ahead of time to make sure there is always a buffer of orders for the arrangers to work on. This prevents idle time at the bottleneck resource.

Step 3   Subordinate All Other Decisions to Step 2. Schedule nonbottleneck resources to support the maximum use of the bottleneck. For Akito's Flowers, have the clerk transfer orders to the arrangers every ten minutes at the start of the day to make sure the bottleneck is fully used. You may have to arrive early or stay late to be sure the orders are processed and waiting for the arrangers to arrive first thing each day.

Step 4   Elevate the Bottleneck(s). If after Steps 1 through 3 the bottleneck is still a constraint, then consider increasing the capacity of the bottleneck. At Akito's Flowers, add another floral arranger.

Step 5   Do Not Let Inertia Set In. Although the floral arrangers may improve their throughput, check to see whether new constraints have developed. If so, work on increasing throughput.

▶ **Theory of constraints (TOC)**
A management philosophy that extends the concepts of OPT.

▶ **Internal resource constraint**
A regular bottleneck.

▶ **Market constraint**
The condition that results when market demand is less than production capacity.

▶ **Policy constraint**
The condition that results when a specific policy dictates the rate of production.

SCHEDULING FOR SERVICE ORGANIZATIONS

In many service organizations, scheduling is complicated because service demand—quantity, type of service, and timing—is often variable and hard to forecast. In addition, inventories may not be possible and capacity is limited. For example, a movie theater cannot show the movie before the customers arrive and hope to satisfy demand. The theater is also limited as to how many people can occupy the theater at any given time. Because of these constraints, some additional techniques are available for scheduling services. These include scheduling the services demanded and scheduling the workforce.

Scheduling Services Demanded

Techniques for scheduling services demanded range from setting appointments, requiring reservations, using a public schedule, and delaying or back-ordering the service. Let's look at each of these individually.

Appointments   Appointment systems set a time for the customer to use the service. For example, students make appointments with professors to discuss class work. Appointments minimize customer waiting time and make good use of the service provider's capacity. Appointment systems are used by physicians, lawyers, auto repair or service shops, and hair salons. The shared component of each of these services is that no tangible inventory is usually possible. Disadvantages of an appointment system include the problem of "no-shows"—people who miss appointments—and insufficient time scheduled for customers. In the case of "no-shows," the service provider may be idle until the next scheduled appointment and incur a loss of revenue. In the case of insufficient time, the service provider often falls behind schedule and keeps customers waiting.

Research is being done on scheduling outpatients in a dynamic, multiperiod environment. The objectives are to minimize the delay between the time a patient requests an appointment and when the patient is actually seen and to determine where unscheduled appointment slots should be maintained during the day. These unscheduled slots are for urgent-care patients needing to be seen as soon as possible by the physician. For complete details of the study, see Klassen and Rohleder (2004).

Reservations   A reservation system enables the customer to take control or temporary possession of an item—for example, a hotel room, an automobile, or a banquet hall. A reservation system provides advance notice of when the item is needed and for how long. Deposits usually reduce the problem of last-minute cancellations or "no-shows."

Posted Schedules   Many service providers post a schedule indicating when a service is available. Movie theaters, universities, airlines, trains, buses, retail stores, museums, concerts, and sporting events are all examples of services that post schedules. The posted schedule tells the customer the event's date and time.

When demand occurs, service must be available.

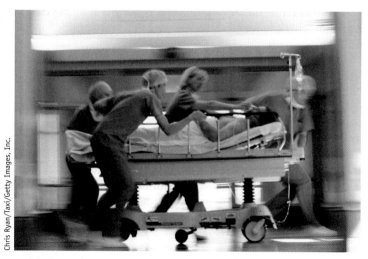

Chris Ryan/Taxi/Getty Images, Inc.

Delayed Services or Backlogs Another method used to schedule customer demand is delayed services or backlogs. Restaurants that do not take reservations are one example. The restaurant puts customers on a waiting list until a table becomes available. Other examples are banks, grocery stores, retail stores, repair services, and barber shops. In most of these organizations, customers are served in the order in which they arrive. These methods are aimed at better managing the service organization's capacity. An alternative method for managing capacity involves the way the workforce is scheduled.

Scheduling Employees

Since organizations may not always be able to schedule demand, the alternative is to manage capacity in the way they schedule employees. Organizations can staff for peak demand, use floating personnel, have employees on call, or use temporary employees, seasonal employees, part-time employees, or any combination of the above.

Staffing for Peak Demand With this procedure, the organization has enough service providers to accommodate the maximum level of customer demand. The obvious problem with this is cost. The workforce is fully used only during peak demand. Otherwise, a portion of the workforce is idle. Organizations typically staff for peak demand when the service providers have significant skills and the size of the workforce cannot be changed quickly. An example is your local fire or police department.

Floating Employees When customer demand for services can change daily, organizations use floating employees to their advantage. Floating employees perform a number of services and are assigned where they are needed each day. Hospitals use floating employees because the number of patients and degree of care needed can change daily. A disadvantage of this approach for some employees is the uncertainty of their work location and the transient nature of short-term assignments.

Employees on Call Some organization use on-call employees during specific periods of the week. Physicians at a hospital may be on call in case of emergencies, though not physically present unless needed. Maintenance employees may also be on call in case of emergencies. Although being on call restricts an employee's normal free time, it also means the employee does not have to be physically present in the workplace during the specified period.

Temporary Employees Using temporary employees is another way for an organization to adjust workforce level. An organization can hire temporary employees with almost any skill set through a temp agency. The agency provides the employees and bills the organization.

Seasonal Employees Service organizations such as retailers with seasonal customer demand hire seasonal employees. These are short-term hires who expect their job to be terminated at the end of the season. Growers, for example, use seasonal employees to process items as they ripen. These organizations need an expanded workforce for a short period of time and cannot justify hiring additional permanent employees.

Part-Time Employees For some organizations, customer demand is higher during certain times of the day and lower at other times. At a fast-food restaurant, for example, demand is high at meal times—breakfast, lunch, and dinner—and lower during the rest of the day. Instead of hiring employees for a full eight-hour shift, the organization uses its capacity more effectively by hiring part-time employees.

Organizations can combine any of these techniques to manage their service capacity effectively. Although these techniques provide the means for managing capacity, organizations still need to develop employee schedules that comply with legal requirements and contractual obligations. Legal requirements may dictate the minimum number of employees physically present and on duty at a fire station, for example. Contractual obligations are determined by labor agreements. These obligations may limit overtime and concern the number of consecutive days off each week.

Now let's look at a technique for developing a workforce schedule when each employee works full-time and needs to have two consecutive days off each week.

DEVELOPING A WORKFORCE SCHEDULE

  Tibrewala, Phillippe, and Brown developed a technique in 1972 that enables a company to operate seven days a week and give each of its full-time employees two consecutive days off. The purpose is to find the two consecutive days off for each employee, satisfy staffing needs, and minimize excess capacity. For example, a swimming pool or beach needs lifeguards seven days a week. This scheduling technique can develop the schedules to be used so that each lifeguard has two consecutive days off during the week. Since most companies define the starting day and ending day of their pay week, we will use Monday as the first day of the week. Thus an employee cannot be off on Sunday and Monday since those are not two consecutive days during the same pay week. We use Tibrewala, Phillippe, and Brown's technique for developing the schedule by following these steps:

Step 1   Find Out the Minimum Number of Employees Needed for Each Day of the Week.

Day of the Week	M	T	W	Th	F	Sa	Su
Number of staff needed	4	5	5	3	5	2	3

Step 2   Given the Minimum Number of Employees Needed Each Day, Calculate the Number of Employees Needed for Each Pair of Consecutive Days During the Pay Week. For example, a total of nine employees are needed on Monday and Tuesday. The sum for each pair of days is as shown in the table.

Pair of Consecutive Days	Total of Staff Needed
Monday and Tuesday	9 employees
Tuesday and Wednesday	10 employees
Wednesday and Thursday	8 employees
Thursday and Friday	8 employees
Friday and Saturday	7 employees
Saturday and Sunday	5 employees

Step 3   Find the Pair of Days with the Lowest Total Needed. These are the two consecutive days off for one employee, who will work the other five days of the week. In our case, the lowest total is for the Saturday and Sunday pair of days. Employee number 1 works Monday, Tuesday, Wednesday, Thursday, Friday, and is off on Saturday and Sunday. When there is a tie, we can choose any of the tied pairs. We base our decision on an existing labor contract or established company procedures, or we can break the tie arbitrarily.

Step 4   Update the Number of Employees You Still Need to Schedule for Each Day. We decrease our employee needs for Monday through Friday by 1 because employee number one is scheduled to work those days. The number of employees needed for Saturday and Sunday has not changed because no one has been scheduled yet to work those days. The updated staffing needs are shown here.

Day of the Week	M	T	W	Th	F	Sa	Su
Number of staff needed	3	4	4	2	4	2	3

Step 5   Using the Updated Staffing Needs, Repeat Steps 2 Through 4 Until You Have Satisfied All Needs.

Now we repeat Step 2.

Step 2   The New Total Number of Staff for Each Pair of Days Is as Follows:

Pair of Consecutive Days	Total of Staff Needed
Monday and Tuesday	7 employees
Tuesday and Wednesday	8 employees
Wednesday and Thursday	6 employees
Thursday and Friday	6 employees
Friday and Saturday	6 employees
Saturday and Sunday	5 employees

Step 3   The Days Off for Employee Number 2 Are Also Saturday and Sunday.

This employee will work Monday through Friday.

Step 4   Update the Staffing Needs.

Day of the Week	M	T	W	Th	F	Sa	Su
Number of staff needed	2	3	3	1	3	2	3

Since there are still unsatisfied needs, we return to Step 2. We continue doing this until there are no unsatisfied needs. The final schedule is shown next.

Employee	M	T	W	Th	F	Sa	Su
1	X	X	X	X	X	off	off
2	X	X	X	X	X	off	off
3	X	X	off	off	X	X	X
4	X	X	X	X	X	off	off
5	off	off	X	X	X	X	X
6	X	X	X	X	off	off	X

This technique gives the manager work schedules for each employee to satisfy minimum daily staffing requirements. Although it is not a unique solution, the schedule gives each full-time employee two consecutive days off. The next step is to replace employee numbers with employee names. The manager can give the senior employee first choice of schedules and proceed until all the employees have been assigned a schedule.

SCHEDULING WITHIN OM: PUTTING IT ALL TOGETHER

Scheduling is the final planning that occurs before the actual execution of the plan. A job's position in the schedule is determined by its priority status. Production planners track the performance of operations in meeting the planned schedule. This is critical because the master scheduler (Chapter 13) evaluates production planners on the level of customer service achieved for their product responsibilities.

Schedules are essential to shop floor supervisors. The schedule details when a job is to be worked on, what resources to use, and how much time the job should need. Schedules ensure that manufacturing is working on the right job, using the right equipment, at the right time. Dispatching with the use of priority rules allows floor supervisors to determine which job should be done next.

The amount of time to complete a job is often determined by a time standard (Chapter 11). If the time standards are inaccurate (either too stringent or too loose), the worker's morale may be affected. If standards are too stringent, it may be impossible to keep up with the schedule. If standards are too loose, there is no incentive to push and resources are often underutilized.

In service operations, the schedule is critical in terms of projecting when a job will be completed for the customer. Customers often need to know when the service will be provided (think of cable installers) so that the customer is available. Customers often link quality of service (Chapter 5) with adherence to the schedule (if the company delivers on time, everything is fine). If the company does not schedule adequate time for the service to be completed, the worker may either rush through the service or run late throughout the day. Think of the last time you waited in a doctor's office. In either case, the perceived quality of the service can be affected.

SCHEDULING ACROSS THE ORGANIZATION

Scheduling executes a company's strategic business plan, so it affects functional areas throughout the company.

Accounting   relies on schedule information and completion of customer orders to develop revenue projections, calculate actual job costs, and do cash flow analysis.

Marketing   uses schedule effectiveness measurements to determine whether the company is using lead times for competitive advantage, whether flow time is correlated to estimated lead times, and whether deliveries are made on time. Knowing lead times allows marketing to make realistic delivery promises to customers.

Information systems   maintains the scheduling database, which includes routings and processing times. Information systems also provides the software to monitor product movement through the scheduling process.

Purchasing follows items through the process to determine whether components and/or raw materials need to be expedited when the job is ahead of schedule or de-expedited when jobs are behind schedule to ensure the items are available when needed.

Operations   uses the schedule to maintain its priorities and to provide customer service by finishing jobs on time. The schedule reflects operations' workload and is used to measure performance.

In manufacturing companies, production planners typically schedule individual jobs; in service organizations, the office manager or shift supervisor does the scheduling. Both planners and managers are evaluated on the customer service levels they achieve. The production planner is concerned with the sequencing of jobs through the factory. The office manager or shift supervisor is concerned with adequate staffing. Scheduling jobs and developing work schedules should reflect the company's competitive strategy and serve as a tool to keep all the functional areas synchronized.

THE SUPPLY CHAIN LINK

Scheduling is the final planning step before a product is built or a service performed. The detailed schedule shows when work on a specific customer order is to begin and when it is to be completed. These two valuable pieces of information are shared with members of the supply chain, who can then track the progress of the order. Visibility into actual production performance can improve communications among the supply chain members and alert members when execution problems occur. Detailed scheduling often requires using the due-date information for the different jobs to be scheduled. These due dates should reflect the objectives of the supply chain. Different priority rules can be tested to see which rule provides the best schedule performance when considering supply chain objectives. The linkage of customer order priority and supply chain objectives should provide more effective operations.

Chapter Highlights

1 Different kinds of environments need different scheduling techniques. Scheduling in the high-volume environment is typically done through line design and balancing. Scheduling in a low-volume environment typically involves the use of priority rules. In this environment, Gantt charts are often used to view the workload and jobs in process.

2 Shop loading techniques include infinite and finite loading. Infinite loading schedules include jobs without capacity constraints. Finite loading loads jobs up to a predetermined capacity level. Loading can be done using forward or backward scheduling. Forward scheduling starts the job as soon as possible, whereas backward scheduling works back from the due date.

3 Priority rules are used to make scheduling decisions. SPT always minimizes mean job flow time, mean job lateness, and average number of jobs in system. FCFS is considered one of the fairest priority rules. Rules related to due dates tend to minimize the maximum tardiness of the jobs. Priority rules need to support organizational objectives.

4 Performance measurements reflect the priorities of the organization. Mean job flow time, mean job lateness, mean job tardiness, makespan, and the average number of jobs in the system measure the effectiveness of schedules.

5 Johnson's rule is an effective technique for minimizing makespan when two successive workstations are needed to complete the process.

6 When scheduling bottleneck systems, the basic principles of OPT apply. The theory of constraints expands OPT into a managerial philosophy of continuous improvement.

7 Service organizations use different scheduling techniques such as appointments, reservations, and posted schedules for effective use of service capacity.

8 A method developed by Tibrewala, Phillippe, and Brown constructs workforce schedules when a company uses full-time employees, operates seven days each week, and gives its employees two consecutive days off.

Key Terms

flow operations 559
routing 559
bottleneck 560
Gantt chart 560
load chart 560
progress chart 561
infinite loading 561
finite loading 561
forward scheduling 562
due date 562
backward scheduling 563
slack 563

input/output control 563
operation sequencing 565
queue 565
priority rule 565
local priority rule 565
global priority rule 565
job flow time 567
average number of jobs in the
 system 568
makespan 568
job lateness 568
job tardiness 568

Johnson's rule 572
optimized production technology
 (OPT) 574
nonbottleneck 574
capacity-constrained resource 574
throughput 575
transfer batch 576
process batch 576
theory of constraints (TOC) 577
internal resource constraint 577
market constraint 577
policy constraint 577

Formula Review

To calculate job flow time:

Job flow time = time of completion
        − time job was first available for processing

To calculate mean job flow time:

$$\text{Mean job flow time} = \frac{\text{sum of individual flow times}}{\text{number of jobs}}$$

To calculate average number of jobs in system:

$$\text{Average number of jobs in system} = \frac{\text{total flow time}}{\text{makespan}}$$

Solved Problems

• Problem 1

The Fargoe Forge Company has collected the following data regarding the input and output of work into Work Center 222. Complete the partially filled in input/output chart.

• Before You Begin:

This plan requires the completion of the input/output report. The planned input, actual input, planned output, and actual output are provided. Calculate the deviation by period, (actual minus planned). Do this for both input and output and calculate the cumulative deviation for both. Finally, calculate the backlog. The backlog only changes when actual input is different from actual output. If actual input is greater than actual output, the backlog increases. When actual output is greater, the backlog is reduced.

• Solution

Step 1   Calculate the period-by-period deviations. Subtract the planned input from the actual input. Subtract the planned output from the actual output. The results are shown in the spreadsheet.

Step 2   Calculate the cumulative deviation for input and output. Add the deviation for the current period to the cumulative deviation of the previous period. For example, in period 5, the cumulative deviation of the input is 75 hours of work (50 hours at the end of period 4, plus 25 hours in period 5). The cumulative deviations are shown in the spreadsheet.

Step 3   Calculate the backlog at Work Center 222. The backlog changes only when the actual input is different from the actual output in a period. The beginning backlog is 125 hours of work. The backlog at the end of period 4 changes to 95 hours because the actual input is only 650 hours of work, whereas the actual output is 680 hours of work. Since the work center completed 30 hours more than it actually received, the backlog has to be reduced by 30 hours, or a total of 95 hours. The backlog for period 5 remains at 95 hours. In period 6, the backlog drops to 45 hours. The backlog in period 7 is 20 hours and drops to 15 hours in period 8, as shown in the spreadsheet.

	A	B	C	D	E	F	G
1							
2	**Fargoe Forge Company**						
3							
4	**Input Information (hours)**				Period		
5			4	5	6	7	8
6	Planned Input		600	675	625	650	650
7	Actual Input		650	700	600	575	675
8	Deviation						
9	Cumulative Deviation						
10							
11	**Output Information (hours)**				Period		
12			4	5	6	7	8
13	Planned Output		680	680	680	680	680
14	Actual Output		680	700	650	600	680
15	Deviation						
16	Cumulative Deviation						
17			us 25				
18	Backlog	125					

	A	B	C	D	E	F	G
1			$C$8: =C7-C6 (copy right)	$C$9: =C8	$D$9: =C9+D8 (copy right)		
2	**Fargoe Forge Company**						
3							
4	Input Information (hours)				Period		
5			4	5	6	7	8
6	Planned Input		600	675	625	650	650
7	Actual Input		650	700	600	575	675
8	Deviation		50	25	–25	–75	25
9	Cumulative Deviation		50	75	50	–25	0
10							
11	Output Information (hours)				Period		
12			4	5	6	7	8
13	Planned Output		680	680	680	680	680
14	Actual Output		680	700	650	600	680
15	Deviation		0	20	–30	–80	0
16	Cumulative Deviation		0	20	–10	–90	–90
17							
18	Backlog	125	95	95	45	20	15
19			$C$18: =B18+C7-C14 (copy right)				
20							
21							
22	Key Formulas						
23	C8	=C7-C6	copy to right				
24	C9	=C8					
25	D9	=C9+D8	copy to right				
26	C15	=C14-C13	copy to right				
27	C16	=C15					
28	D16	=C16+D15	copy to right				
29	C18	=B18+C7-(	copy to right				

• Problem 2

Custom Glass, Inc. produces custom storm windows. The company has the following jobs waiting to be processed at its glass-cutting work center.

Job	Job Time (days)	Due Date (days from now)
A	8	20
B	4	15
C	6	30
D	7	24
E	9	10

(a) Using earliest due date as the priority rule, determine the sequence for these jobs.

(b) Using shortest processing time as the priority rule, determine the sequence for these jobs.

(c) Calculate the mean job flow time, average number of jobs in the system, mean job lateness, and mean job tardiness for the schedule using earliest due date.

(d) Calculate the mean job flow time, average number of jobs in the system, mean job lateness, and mean job tardiness for the schedule using the shortest processing time.

• Before You Begin:

This problem compares two different priority rules and evaluates their effectiveness when scheduling a batch of jobs. First,

develop the sequence for each rule. Then calculate the different performance measures. Compare the results.

• Solution

(a) The sequence generated using earliest due date as the priority rule is E, B, A, D, C. Job E has the highest priority since it is due in the least amount of time. The schedule is as follows:

- Job E is done after 9 days,
- Job B is done after 13 days,
- Job A is done after 21 days,
- Job D is done after 28 days,
- Job C is done after 34 days.

(b) The sequence generated using shortest processing time as the priority rule is B, C, D, A, E. Job B has the highest priority since it takes the least amount of time to complete. The SPT schedule is as follows:

- Job B is done after 4 days,
- Job C is done after 10 days,
- Job D is done after 17 days,
- Job A is done after 25 days,
- Job E is done after 34 days.

(c) Based on the schedule generated using the EDD rule, the results are as shown in the table.

EDD Results

Job	Job Flow Time (days)	Due Date (days from now)	Job Lateness (days)	Job Tardiness (days)
A	21	20	1	1
B	13	15	−2	0
C	34	30	4	4
D	28	24	4	4
E	9	10	−1	0
Totals	105		6	9

Mean job flow time is 21 days (105 days divided by 5 jobs). Remember that job flow time extends from the time the job is available to work on to its completion. Since all the jobs are available at the same time, the flow time for each job is equal to its completion time. The average number of jobs in the system is 3.1 jobs (105 days of total flow time divided by the makespan of 34 days). Total lateness is 6 days (1 − 2 + 4 + 4 − 1); therefore, mean job lateness is 1.2 days (6 days divided by 5 jobs). Total tardiness is 9 days; therefore, mean job tardiness is 1.8 days.

(d) Based on the schedule generated using the SPT rule, the results are as shown here.

SPT Results

Job	Job Flow Time (days)	Due Date (days from now)	Job Lateness (days)	Job Tardiness (days)
A	25	20	5	5
B	4	15	−11	0
C	10	30	−20	0
D	17	24	−7	0
E	34	10	24	24
Totals	90		−9	29

Mean job flow time is 18 days (90 days divided by 5 jobs). The average number of jobs in the system is 2.65 jobs (90 days of total flow time divided by the makespan of 34 days). Total lateness is negative 9 days (5 − 11 − 20 − 7 + 24); therefore, mean job lateness is 21.8 days (−9 days divided by 5 jobs). Total tardiness is 29 days; therefore, mean job tardiness is 5.8 days.

• Problem 3

Jack's Machine Shop has the following batch of jobs that need to be scheduled so that the makespan is minimized. Each job is processed first at Machine Center 1 and then at Machine Center 2. The job information is as follows.

Job	Machine Center 1 Processing Time (days)	Machine Center 2 Processing Time (days)
A	4	3
B	2	7
C	6	5
D	4	5
E	3	4
F	5	1

Using Johnson's rule, develop a sequence for Jack's Machine Shop that minimizes makespan.

• Before You Begin:

The objective is to minimize makespan. When the scheduling problem has a unidirectional flow and two different activities to be done, use Johnson's rule to minimize makespan.

• Solution

The jobs and the processing times are listed so we can begin at Step 2.

Step 2 The shortest individual activity processing time is one day for Job F at Machine Center 2. Since this time is on the second activity, Job F takes the last available spot in the sequence, which is sixth.

Step 3 Removing the job we just sequenced, we repeat Step 2 until we have sequenced all jobs. The remaining jobs are as follows.

Job	Machine Center 1 Processing Time (days)	Machine Center 2 Processing Time (days)
A	4	3
B	2	7
C	6	5
D	4	5
E	3	4

Step 2 The shortest individual activity processing time is from Job B at Machine Center 1. Therefore, we put Job B in the highest available spot in the sequence, which is first. Now we eliminate Job B from consideration and repeat Step 2.

Job	Machine Center 1 Processing Time (days)	Machine Center 2 Processing Time (days)
A	4	3
C	6	5
D	4	5
E	3	4

Step 2 The shortest activity processing time is now in two places, from Job A for three days at Machine Center 2 and from Job E for 3 days at Machine Center 1. We can put both of these jobs into our sequence. Job A goes into the last available spot, fifth, and Job A goes into the highest available spot, second. We can now eliminate both jobs from consideration. The updated list of remaining jobs is shown next.

Job	Machine Center 1 Processing Time (days)	Machine Center 2 Processing Time (days)
C	6	5
D	4	5

Step 2 The shortest activity processing time is four days for Job D at Machine Center 1. Job D should be placed in the highest available slot, third. We put the remaining job in the only available position in the sequence, fourth.

The final sequence is B, E, D, C, A, F.

• Problem 4

The Sports Injury Clinic operates seven days a week. Based on historical data, the manager, Joan, has determined the following daily minimum staffing requirements. She believes that she needs three employees on Monday and Thursday, four employees on Tuesday, two employees on Wednesday and Sunday, and five employees on Friday and Saturday. Joan wants a workforce schedule that allows each employee two consecutive days off each week and minimizes excess staffing. Develop a schedule.

• *Before You Begin:*

Many service operations conduct business seven days per week. When those companies schedule staff, they may do so with the objective of providing each staff member with two consecutive days off during the week. The technique developed by Tibrewala, Phillippe, and Brown determines how many employees are needed and what their schedules need to be.

• *Solution*

Step 1 Find out the minimum number of employees needed for each day of the week.

Day of the Week	M	T	W	Th	F	S	Su
Number of staff needed	3	4	2	3	5	5	2

Step 2 Given the minimum staff needed each day, calculate the number of employees needed for each pair of consecutive days.

Pair of Consecutive Days	Total of Staff Needed
Monday and Tuesday	7
Tuesday and Wednesday	6
Wednesday and Thursday	5
Thursday and Friday	8
Friday and Saturday	10
Saturday and Sunday	7

Step 3 Find the pair of days that has the lowest total need. Wednesday and Thursday have the lowest total need so they become the days off for the first employee.

Step 4 Update the number of staff still needed. Reduce the staff needed by one employee for Monday, Tuesday, Friday, Saturday, and Sunday since the first employee will work on those days.

Step 5 Using the updated requirements, repeat Steps 2 through 4 until all requirements have been met. If you continue to develop the workforce schedule, an alternative schedule is shown. Given the amount of slack, several other alternatives are also possible.

Employee	M	T	W	Th	F	S	Su
1	X	X	off	off	X	X	X
2	X	X	X	X	X	off	off
3	off	off	X	X	X	X	X
4	X	X	off	off	X	X	X
5	off	off	X	X	X	X	X
6	X	X	off	off	X	X	X

Discussion Questions

1. Compare and contrast high-volume and low-volume scheduling operations.

2. Describe a high-volume service operation and how scheduling should be done.

3. Describe a low-volume service operation and how scheduling should be done.

4. Visit a local service operation and describe its scheduling procedures.

5. Visit a local manufacturing operation and describe how it sequences jobs through the shop.

6. Describe infinite loading.

7. Explain how the output from infinite loading is used.

8. Explain how finite loading is done.

9. Explain the benefits of finite loading.

10. Describe forward scheduling.

11. Describe backward scheduling.

12. Visit a local service or manufacturing operation and learn how it measures schedule effectiveness.

13. Describe the principles of OPT.

14. Describe the theory of constraints.

15. Describe different methods that might be useful for scheduling service operations.

Problems

1. Jack, the owner and manager of Jack's Box Company, wants to monitor usage at Work Center 3, which is a bottleneck in the system. He has collected data on the planned and actual input and output.

Input Information
(in hours)

	4	5	6	7	8
Planned input	40	50	50	60	60
Actual input	45	45	45	55	60
Deviation					
Cumulative deviation					

Output Information
(in hours)

	4	5	6	7	8
Planned output	70	70	70	70	70
Actual output	60	60	60	60	60
Deviation					
Cumulative deviation					
Backlog 75 hours					

(a) Complete the input/output record.

(b) Describe your concerns based on the results of the input/output analysis.

2. Since Jack believes that Work Center 3 is his bottleneck, he has asked you to do the following:

(a) Calculate the percentage of planned output needed to complete the planned inputs (planned input + backlog/planned output) at Work Center 3.

(b) Calculate the percentage of planned input that actually happened (actual input + backlog/planned input + backlog).

(c) Calculate the percentage of available output that was actually accomplished (actual output/planned output) of Work Center 3.

(d) Given your results, do you believe that Jack is correct in assuming that Work Center 3 is his bottleneck? Justify your answer.

3. Based on your concerns, Jack has gathered the following information for Work Center 2, the work center that directly feeds Work Center 3. Complete the input/output analysis of Work Center 2.

Input Information (in hours)

	4	5	6	7	8
Planned input	40	50	50	60	60
Actual input	25	35	35	40	40
Deviation					
Cumulative deviation					

Output Information (in hours)

	4	5	6	7	8
Planned output	40	50	50	60	60
Actual output	45	45	45	55	60
Deviation					
Cumulative deviation					
Backlog 75 hours					

(a) Complete the input/output record.

(b) Describe your concerns based on the results of the input/output analysis.

4. Jack has asked you to calculate the following for Work Center 2.

(a) Calculate the percentage of planned output needed to complete the planned inputs (planned input + backlog/planned output) at Work Center 2.

(b) Calculate the percentage of planned input that actually happened (actual input + backlog/planned input + backlog) at Work Center 2.

(c) Calculate the percentage of available output that was actually accomplished (actual output/planned output) at Work Center 2.

(d) What insights can you offer Jack about Work Centers 2 and 3?

5. Henri's Custom Gowns has six jobs waiting to be processed. Each gown is at the beading work center. The job information is shown here.

Job	Job Time (in days)	Days Until Due	Job Time at Other Work Centers	Operations Remaining at Other Work Centers
A	9	30	10	3
B	5	10	2	1
C	8	24	8	2
D	10	40	18	3
E	7	26	12	1
F	6	15	6	2

(a) Determine the sequence Henri should follow if he uses the SPT (shortest processing time) priority rule.

(b) Based on the sequence developed in part (a), calculate the following performance measures: makespan, mean job flow time, average number of jobs in the system, mean job lateness, mean job tardiness, and maximum tardiness.

6. Henri has decided to try a different priority rule.

(a) Using the data in Problem 5, determine the sequence Henri should follow if he uses the EDD (earliest due date) priority rule.

(b) Based on the sequence developed in part (a), calculate the following performance measures: makespan, mean job flow time, average number of jobs in the system, mean job lateness, mean job tardiness, and maximum tardiness.

7. Henri has heard of the LPT (longest processing time) priority rule and wonders how that would change the sequence of the jobs listed in Problem 5.

(a) Determine the sequence Henri should follow if he uses the LPT priority rule.

(b) Based on the sequence developed in part (a), calculate the following performance measures: makespan, mean job flow time, average number of jobs in the system, mean job lateness, mean job tardiness, and maximum tardiness.

8. In an effort to be fair to his customers, Henri has decided to use the FCFS (first come, first served) priority rule. Using the job data from Problem 5, assume that the jobs arrive in order—that is, A first, then B, then C.

(a) Using the data in Problem 5, determine the sequence Henri should follow if he uses the FCFS (first come, first served) priority rule.

(b) Based on the sequence developed in part (a), calculate the following performance measures: makespan, mean job flow time, average number of jobs in the system, mean job lateness, mean job tardiness, and maximum tardiness.

9. Henri recently learned about global priority rules. He is interested in the slack over remaining operations (S/RO) rule.

(a) Using the data in Problem 5, determine the sequence Henri should follow if he uses the S/RO priority rule.

(b) Based on the sequence developed in part (a) calculate the following performance measures: makespan, mean job flow time, average number of jobs in the system, mean job lateness, mean job tardiness, and maximum tardiness.

10. Joe's Twenty-four Seven Laundromat has the following jobs waiting to be processed. The first step of the process includes washing and drying the clothes; the second step is pressing the clothing. Joe wants to minimize the amount of time it takes to do all the jobs. The five jobs waiting to be processed are shown here.

Job	Wash and Dry (hours)	Press (hours)
A	6	4
B	3	5
C	2	3
D	7	5
E	4	3

(a) Using FCFS, assume the jobs arrive in the order shown (A, then B, then C, etc.). Show the beginning and ending time for each job.

(b) Calculate the makespan, the mean job flow time, and the average number of jobs in the system.

11. Joe thinks that it is probably more efficient to use SPT (shortest processing time) as his priority rule.

(a) Develop a sequence using SPT based on processing time for the wash and dry operation.

(b) Calculate the makespan, the mean job flow time, and the average number of jobs in the system.

12. Joe has asked you to develop a sequence that minimizes makespan for the sequence of jobs given in Problem 10. Compare the makespan, mean job flow time, and the average number of jobs in the system to your results in Problems 10 and 11.

13. Raquel's Landscaping Company has contracted for several landscaping jobs. Each job requires preparing the areas (identifying the locations and types of plants, preparing the soil, etc.) and then planting the trees, bushes, and shrubs. The expected time for each of the jobs is shown next.

Job	Preparing the Area (days)	Planting (days)
R	3	2
S	1	3
T	4	5
U	8	5
V	6	4
W	4	3

(a) Using FCFS (first come, first served), assume the jobs arrive in the order shown (R, then S, then T, etc.). Show the beginning and ending time for each job.

(b) Calculate the makespan, the mean job flow time, and the average number of jobs in the system.

14. Raquel is concerned with efficiency. She believes it is probably more efficient to use SPT (shortest processing time) as her priority rule.

(a) Develop a sequence using SPT based on processing time for preparing the area.

(b) Calculate the makespan, the mean job flow time, and the average number of jobs in the system.

15. Raquel has asked you to develop a sequence that minimizes makespan for the sequence of jobs given in Problem 13. Compare the makespan, mean job flow time, and average number of jobs in the system to your results in Problems 13 and 14.

16. Barb's Beach Bar operates seven days per week. Barb uses only full-time employees and wants each employee to have two consecutive days off each week. She believes that she needs a minimum of three employees on Monday, Tuesday, Wednesday, Thursday, and Sunday. On Friday and Saturday, she believes that she needs six employees. Develop a workforce schedule for Barb.

17. Next week is a three-day weekend. Barb believes that she will need a minimum of six employees on Friday, Saturday, and Sunday. The other days will still need a minimum of three workers. Remember that Barb wants each employee to have two consecutive

days off each week. Develop a workforce schedule for the holiday weekend.

18. Marvin's Beach Cleaners is responsible for keeping the beach clean. Marvin estimates that he needs a minimum of two people on Monday; three people on Tuesday and Sunday; four people on Wednesday and Thursday, and five people on Friday and Saturday. Contractually, Marvin is required to give each employee two consecutive days off during the week. Develop a workforce schedule for Marvin to use.

19. Marvin is preparing for the upcoming three-day weekend. He estimates that he will need three additional workers on Sunday of that week. Using the requirements given in Problem 18 for the other days of the week, develop a workforce schedule for Marvin to use.

20. Cathy's Coney Islands operates seven days per week. Demand is relatively constant during the week and tails off on the weekend. She estimates that she needs five employees Monday through Friday, and two employees on Saturday and Sunday. She is committed to giving each employee two consecutive days off during the week. Develop a workforce schedule for Cathy.

21. Cathy's Coney Islands has just purchased new equipment. Cathy believes the improved efficiency will reduce the number of people needed Monday through Friday down to four. She does not believe she can ever have fewer than two persons working, so the weekend requirements remain the same. Develop a workforce schedule for Cathy.

22. Bill's Bar & Grill is open seven nights a week. Business is busiest on Thursday when there is a concert in the park across the street. Bill wants a workforce schedule that allows each employee two consecutive days off each week. He believes that he needs four employees every day except on Thursday, when he believes he needs six employees. Develop a workforce schedule for Bill.

23. During the winter, no concerts are given in the park. Bill believes that he needs a minimum of four employees every day of the week. Develop a workforce schedule for Bill that allows each employee two consecutive days off each week. Compare the number of workers he needs during the winter to the number of workers needed during the concert season.

24. Student Premier Painters (SPP) has six house painting jobs in a particular neighborhood. The houses vary in size, condition, and painting requirements, but each house must be prepped (cleaned, sanded, and primed) first, before it is painted. The relevant information is given.

| | Days | |
Houses	Prep	Paint
Arnold	4	3
Blake	3	6
Coffman	2	5
Downs	3	2
Eckels	6	4
Farber	5	7

(a) Sequence the painting jobs to minimize makespan.
(b) Calculate the mean job flow time associated with this sequence.
(c) Calculate the average number of jobs in the system with this sequence.

25. Using the job information in Problem 24, develop a sequence based on the shortest processing time priority rule. Prioritize based on prep time. In the case of ties, select the house that has the shortest paint time.
(a) Calculate the makespan.
(b) Calculate the mean job flow time associated with this sequence.
(c) Calculate the average number of jobs in the system with this sequence.

26. Using the information in Problem 24, develop a sequence based on the longest processing time priority rule. Prioritize based on prep time. In the case of ties, select the house that has the longest paint time.
(a) Calculate the makespan.
(b) Calculate the mean job flow time associated with this sequence.
(c) Calculate the average number of jobs in the system with this sequence.

CASE: Air Traffic Controller School (ATCS)

ATCS provides training for future air traffic controllers. One of the skills air traffic controllers need is the ability to sequence aircraft for landing purposes. The controller decides who lands immediately and who goes into a holding pattern. The following data are provided to you, the student, to develop an acceptable landing sequence. Any sequence that results in an aircraft not being scheduled to land before it runs out of remaining flying time is unacceptable. The following aircraft are currently awaiting your decision as to their landing sequence.

Flight Number	Minutes on Runway	Remaining Flying Time (minutes)	Cost per Minute of Flying Time ($)
101	2.00	10	100
118	3.00	15	150
217	2.75	8	125
8076	1.50	5	80
219	3.50	12	200
894	1.75	19	150
024	2.50	16	400
616	3.25	22	300

There are many ways to sequence this group of aircraft waiting to land. Since cost is an obvious factor, consider a sequence that minimizes total cost to land the aircraft. Multiply the cost per minute of flying time by the remaining number of minutes. This gives you the maximum cost associated with an airplane circling in a holding pattern until the last possible moment.

(a) Develop a landing sequence that gives priority to those aircraft with the highest cost of slack time (excess flying time multiplied by cost per minute of flying time). For example, Flight 616's 18.75 minutes of slack time $(22 - 3.25)$ times $300 per minute means that if Flight 616 does not land until its time is all used up, it incurs an extra flying cost of $5,625. Make a Gantt chart showing the landing sequence and evaluate the sequence in terms of performance. Calculate mean flow time, mean lateness, and average number of planes in the system.

(b) Develop a sequence using SPT as a priority rule. Make a Gantt chart showing the landing sequence and evaluate the sequence in terms of performance. Calculate mean flow time, mean lateness, and average number of planes in the system.

(c) Develop a third sequence using EDD (earliest due date) as a priority rule. The plane with the least amount of flying time remaining has the highest priority. Make a Gantt chart showing the landing sequence and evaluate the sequence in terms of performance. Calculate mean flow time, mean lateness, and average number of planes in the system. Calculate the total cost associated with this sequence (flow time multiplied by cost per minute of flying time for each flight).

(d) Try to develop an alternative sequence that lands all of the aircraft safely and reduces the total cost.

CASE: Scheduling at Red, White, and Blue Fireworks Company

Joan Bennett, the production manager at the Red, White, and Blue Fireworks Company (RWBFC), has decided to change the work schedule for her manufacturing employees. Because of high product demand and an inability to expand at the current facility, RWBFC needs to operate ten hours each day, seven days each week. In order to avoid the use of overtime and to keep her employees fresh, Joan decided to have employees work four ten-hour shifts each week. She insists that every employee must have three consecutive days off. The work week begins on Monday and ends on Sunday. The manufacturing process requires a minimum of twenty employees. Joan has asked you to develop a staffing plan that will determine the exact number of full-time employees needed, as well as the schedule each employee will need to work. Remember, each employee must have three consecutive days off.

Joan also has asked you to determine which other factors you consider relevant in making the transition to the new schedule. In particular, she is very interested in a method for determining which employees work which schedule and how to implement the new schedule with minimal dissatisfaction.

(a) Develop a staffing plan for RWBFC in accordance with the constraints stated above.

(b) Explain the method used in developing your plan.

(c) Explain how employees should be assigned to the different schedules.

(d) Discuss any concerns you have with the new staffing plan.

INTERACTIVE CASE Virtual Company

 www.wiley.com/college/reid

On-line Case: Scheduling at Valley Memorial Hospital

Today's assignment is with Carol Gardner, assistant to the chief administrator at Valley Memorial Hospital. "Actually," she says, "there are four different problems I'd like your help with. Two days ago, Tami Zarkin, the 2-East supervisor, called about a scheduling issue: how to assign the six nurses on the ward to the six patients there, given that some nurses are better than others with certain patients or at certain tasks. Then, Susie Berkman from the intensive care unit came by to ask for help scheduling the nurses on the 3 PM to 11 PM shift. Yesterday, Gail Johnson, our supervisor at the blood bank, said she needed help scheduling the volunteer staff there. And finally, this morning, Don Maltby, who manages the business office, asked me to help him figure out the most efficient way for his assistant, Naomi Engel, to process cost reports and for the data entry staff to get the processed reports into our database. Let's discuss how to get the information you'll need from each of these people."

To complete this assignment, go to **www.wiley.com/college/reid** to get more details. Assignment questions are given at the site.

To access the Web site:

- Go to **www.wiley.com/college/reid**
- Click **Student Companion Site**
- Click **Virtual Company**
- Click **Kaizen Consulting, Inc.**
- Click **Consulting Assignments**
- Click **Scheduling**

INTERNET CHALLENGE   Batter Up

As a world-class fan of major league baseball, you have always wanted to watch a game in person at each of the ballparks across the country. Now that you are about to graduate, you have decided it is time to achieve this goal. To do so, you must first know the location of each ballpark, when ball games are scheduled, and the driving distance between parks. The Internet can give you all this information.

Decide on a priority rule for building your schedule. You will drive between ballparks, so be sure to leave enough time to reach the next ballpark. You can average 60 miles per hour when traveling on the open road and cover up to 600 miles each day. You must visit each of the major league ballparks during the course of one season. Since you do not graduate until the end of May, you cannot start your adventure until June 1. Your objective is to minimize the total amount of time it takes to visit each ballpark and to minimize the number of miles you drive. You must include in any time it takes to return home. You are constrained to driving no more than 10 hours or 600 miles per day. Use the Internet to find the locations of each ballpark, the scheduled baseball games, and the mileage between cities. Batter up!

On-line Resources

Companion Website www.wiley.com/college/reid:
- Take interactive *practice quizzes* to assess your knowledge and help you study in a dynamic way
- Review *PowerPoint slides* or print slides for notetaking
- Access the *Virtual Company: Valley Memorial Hospital*
- Find links to *Company Tours* for this chapter
    Hershey Foods Corporation
    Northeast Knitting Mills
- Find links for *Additional Web Resources* for this chapter
    Herman Goelitz Candy Co., Inc.,
    www.jellybelly.com
    Merlin Metalworks,
    www.merlinbike.com/html/technology/technology/html
    Production-Scheduling.com,
    www.production-scheduling.com

Suzy Systems, Inc., www.suzy.com
Magi (Manufacturing Action Group, Inc.), www.magimfg.com
PeopleSoft, www.peoplesoft.com
SAP's R/3, www.sap.com
i2 Technologies, www.i2.com

Additional Resources Available Only in WileyPLUS:
- Use the *e-Book* and launch directly to all interactive resources
- Take the interactive *Quick Test* to check your understanding of the chapter material and get immediate feedback on your responses.
- Check your understanding of the key vocabulary in the chapter with *Interactive Flash Cards*
- Use the *Animated Demo Problems* to review key problem types.
- Practice for your tests with *additional problem sets*
- *And more!*

Selected Bibliography

Abernathy, W., N. Baloff, and J. Hershey. "The Nurse Staffing Problem: Issues and Prospects," *Sloan Management Review* 13, 1, Fall 1971.

Blackstone, John H., Jr. *Capacity Management.* Cincinnati, Ohio: South-Western, 1989.

Buffa, Elwood S., and Jeffrey G. Miller. *Production-Inventory Systems: Planning and Control,* Third Edition. Homewood, Ill.: Irwin, 1979.

Cox, James F., III, John H. Blackstone, and Michael S. Spencer, eds., *APICS Dictionary,* Eleventh Edition. Falls Church, Va.: American Production and Inventory Control Society, Inc., 2005.

Johnson, S.M. "Optimal Two Stage and Three Stage Production Schedules with Setup Times Included," *Naval Logistics Quarterly* 1, 1, March 1954.

Klassen, Kenneth J., and Thoms R. Rohleder. "Outpatient Appointment Scheduling with Urgent Clients in a Dynamic, Multi-period Environment," *International Journal of Service Industry Management,* 15, 2, 2004, 167–186.

Sipper, Daniel, and Robert L. Buffin, Jr. *Production: Planning, Control and Integration.* Burr Ridge, Ill.: McGraw-Hill, 1998.

Umble, M. Michael, and M.L. Srikanth. *Synchronous Manufacturing.* Cincinnati, Ohio: South-Western, 1990.

Vollmann, Thomas E., William L. Berry, and D. Clay Whybark, and F. Robert Jacobs. *Manufacturing Planning and Control,* Fifth Edition. Homewood, Ill.: McGraw-Hill/Irwin, 2005.

CHAPTER 16

Project Management

Before studying this chapter you should know or, if necessary, review

1. The implications of competitive priorities, Chapter 2, pages 35–38.
2. Time standards, Chapter 11, pages 390–395.
3. Gantt charts, Chapter 15, pages 560–561.

LEARNING OBJECTIVES

After studying this chapter, you should be able to

1. Describe project management applications.
2. Describe the project life cycle.
3. Diagram networks of project activities.
4. Estimate the completion time of a project.
5. Compute the probability of completing a project by a specific time.
6. Determine how to reduce the length of a project effectively.
7. Describe the critical chain approach to project management.

CHAPTER OUTLINE

WHAT'S IN OM FOR ME?

 ACC   FIN   MKT   OM   HRM   MIS

Think about life's major events and what it takes to make them successful. Consider what is involved in planning a surprise 50th wedding anniversary party for your grandparents. Such an event is a complex project with many simultaneous and sequential activities leading up to the day of the party. Consider the following partial list of activities to prepare the surprise.

1. Decide on the actual date for the celebration. (Sometimes the exact anniversary date doesn't work.)
2. Prepare a preliminary budget. (Most projects have some budgetary constraints.)
3. Develop the guest list of family and friends.
4. Determine the theme for the celebration (maybe a slide show of major events in the past fifty years).
5. Evaluate the possible facilities for the party. (Consider location, handicap accessibility, and size.)
6. Evaluate food options (full sit-down dinner, a buffet, or just appetizers?).
7. Book the facility.
8. Select and order invitations. (Consider lead time and quantities.)
9. Select and order decorations. (Consider the limitations of the facility that you booked.)
10. Evaluate party favors (maybe some personalized memento).
11. Select type of music (background or dance?).
11. Select type of music (background or dance?).
12. Evaluate music options (recorded, live, or DJ?).
13. Finalize the music.
14. Send invitations.
15. Collect RSVPs to determine final headcount.
16. Help out-of-area guests arrange local accommodations.
17. Finalize food options.
18. Finalize party favors.
19. Arrange seating chart.
20. Hire a limo service to pick up your grandparents.
21. Decorate the facility.

These activities need to be done before the surprise anniversary party. Many of these can be done simultaneously but you must do some activities sequentially. For example, you must know how many guests you are expecting before you can book the facility, order invitations, plan for food, or do a seating chart. Each activity in preparation for the surprise celebration is related to other activities, and the order of the activities is clearly defined.

David Bailey/SUPERSTOCK

While most of us dislike waiting in traffic due to road construction, think about all the activities that must be considered. Think about replacing a bridge on a country road. Once the local government begins to consider replacing the bridge, certain activities must occur. Engineers and architects need to develop a plan for the new bridge, to include materials needed, and a budget. After plan approval, the local government issues a request for bid to construction companies. Each company needs to submit a bid detailing the total cost of the project and the expected completion time. The local government then awards the contract. At that point the fun begins. The project manager coordinates the flow of equipment and materials to the site of the bridge and makes sure that the right workers are there at the right time (just imagine all the types of equipment and workers needed). The manager also maintains some flexibility in case of bad weather and makes sure that detours are set up or some type of traffic control is provided. Such projects easily take four to eight months for completion.

Project management techniques are useful when a project consists of several activities, some simultaneous and others sequential. A **project** is a unique, one-time set of activities that is intended to achieve an objective in a given time period. The project is of some length (weeks, months, or even years) and uses resources (human, capital, materials, and equipment).

▶ **Project**
Endeavor with a specific objective, multiple activities, and defined precedence relationships, to be completed in a specified time period.

For the surprise 50th anniversary party for your grandparents, it can easily take three to six months of planning and cost thousands of dollars. In the business world, projects can be designing new products, installing new systems, constructing new facilities, designing an advertising campaign, designing information systems, and developing company Web sites. In politics, a project can be designing a political campaign. Projects consist of several tasks and take place in a given time period. Every project has a life cycle.

PROJECT LIFE CYCLE

Projects vary in terms of objectives, but each project has a common life cycle or sequence of activities. The life cycle begins with an initial concept, followed by a feasibility study, the planning of the project, the execution of the plan, and finally the termination of the project. Let's look at each phase of a project life cycle.

Conception

Identify the need for the project. In our anniversary example, the concept is the recognition of two individuals' lifelong commitment to each other. In the business world, the concept might be the company's decision to launch a new product, implement a new information system, or become involved in e-commerce. In politics, the concept might be a candidate's decision to run for office.

Feasibility Analysis or Study

Evaluate expected costs, benefits, and risks of the project. For our anniversary example, a feasibility study might mean deciding whether the couple would be happier by being guests at the party or if they would rather take a getaway trip to visit some exotic part of the world. For the company launching a new product, a feasibility study means examining the potential market, the market share, and profits for the new product compared to the costs. In politics, a feasibility study is a candidate's assessment of the resources needed to run a successful political campaign and the benefits of elected office.

Presidential candidates debate

Planning

Analyze the work to be done and develop time estimates for completing each of the activities. In our wedding example, you plan what must be done, by whom, and when. When planning the party, a friend or another family member might do the initial screening of caterers, musicians, and so forth, allowing you to make the final decision. In business, planning consists of the activities needed to launch the new product. For example, the company must design the new product; source and order the materials, equipment, and tools; choose the process to use; design the layout; write the job instructions; do a pilot run; evaluate the process and the product design; and transition the product to manufacturing. In politics, planning might include deciding how to raise funds, schedule personal appearances and debates, handle public relations, and adopt policy positions.

Execution

Carry out the activities that make up the project. For our party, this means actually booking the facility, arranging the music, doing the seating arrangements, finalizing the menu, arranging the limo pickup, and so on. In business, the execution of the project entails completing the product design, obtaining the materials and equipment needed, setting up the process, writing job instructions, and making the product. For a political candidate, execution includes fund-raising, making public appearances, and showcasing the political message.

Termination

End the project. After this date, resources can be used for different activities. For you, termination occurs after the party is over. In business, termination means product design engineers work on new products, purchasing agents can return to routine activities or a new project, and manufacturing engineers work on new projects. For a political candidate, termination means serving in an elected office or looking for a new job. See Table 16-1 for a summary of these project life-cycle phases.

NETWORK PLANNING TECHNIQUES

LINKS TO PRACTICE

PERT and the Polaris Missile

Program evaluation and review technique (PERT) and **critical path method (CPM)** date back to the 1950s. PERT was originally developed to plan and monitor the Polaris missile, an extremely large project using over 3000 contractors and involving thousands of activities. PERT is credited with reducing the project duration by two years. Because of its success, most government contracts still require the use of PERT or a similar technique. CPM was initially developed to plan and coordinate maintenance projects in chemical plants.

Concept:	Identify the need for the project.	**TABLE 16-1**
Feasibility analysis or study:	Evaluate costs, benefits, and risks.	
Planning:	Decide who does what, how long it should take, and what you need to do it.	Project Life-Cycle Phases
Execution:	Do the project.	
Termination:	End the project.	

The benefits of network planning techniques include the following:

- Graphical display of the project, including the relationships and sequence of activities,
- Estimate of the expected project length,
- Method for determining which activities are critical to the timely completion of the project and are therefore included in the critical path,
- Method for determining the amount of slack associated with individual project activities.

Both PERT and CPM portray the project as a network diagram. The **project activities** and their **precedence relationships** are illustrated in the network diagram by nodes (circles) and arrows. Project activities are actions that consume resources and/or time. For example, making the drawings for a new product is an activity—it takes time and uses resources (human and equipment). Precedence relationships structure the sequencing of activities; that is, you have to finish one before you can start the next. These are like course prerequisites: before you can enroll in an operations management class, you have to take a basic statistics course. In business, before a company can source materials for a new product, the designers have to finish the product design. Project managers use these network planning techniques to

Identify project activities and precedent relationships. Project managers use this technique to create a document reflecting the activities, the responsible department, and the necessary resources (time, people, and equipment).

Calculate the expected completion time of the project. Project managers use this technique to plan additional projects and negotiate contracts with clients. For example, the customer may include a monetary penalty if the project is not completed by a certain date or a bonus if the project is completed ahead of schedule. The project manager can evaluate whether the probability risk of completing the project on schedule is acceptable or if additional resources are needed to assure timely completion.

Identify the activities critical to the timely completion of the project. Project managers use this technique to identify activities that can be delayed without affecting the project's completion, to provide some flexibility for the project manager.

Suppose you are a project manager using network planning techniques. You would typically describe the project, diagram the network, estimate the project's completion time, and monitor the project's progression. Let's look at these four steps in detail.

Step 1: Describe the Project

Describe the project in terms that everyone involved will understand. Include the project objective and the project end date. For example, the project may be the release of a

▶ **Program evaluation and review technique (PERT)** Network planning technique used to determine a project's planned completion date and identify the project's critical path.

▶ **Critical path method (CPM)** Network planning technique, with deterministic times, used to determine a project's planned completion date and identify the project's critical path.

▶ **Project activities** Specific tasks that must be completed and that require resources.

▶ **Precedence relationships** Establish the sequencing of activities to ensure that all necessary activities are completed before a subsequent activity is begun.

FIGURE 16-1

Network notation

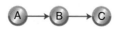

a. Activity A precedes activity B, which precedes activity C

b. Activity A must be completed before activities B and C can begin.

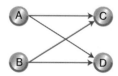
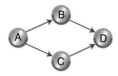

c. Activities A and B must both be completed before activity C or D can begin.

d. Activities B and C can begin once activity A has been completed; activity D cannot begin until both B and C are completed.

specific new product by September 15 or it may be ISO certification by the end of the calendar year. Given the project objective, define the project activities in terms of resource requirements (labor, equipment, and cash) and precedence relationships.

Step 2: Diagram the Network

Diagram the project as a network, visually displaying the interrelationships between the activities. There are two kinds of network diagrams: activity-on-arrow (AOA) and activity-on-node (AON). We will focus on activity-on-node diagrams.

▶ **Activity-on-node**
Network diagramming notation that places activities in the nodes and arrows to signify precedence relationships.

The **activity-on-nodes** (AON) diagram represents project activities by nodes and precedence relationships by arrows. Figure 16-1a shows the simple case in which we must do activity A before doing activity B, which we must do before activity C. In Figure 16-1b, the diagram indicates that we must finish activity A first before we can begin both activities B and C. In Figure 16-1c, we must finish both activities A and B before either activity C or D can begin. Figure 16-1d is an example in which we can begin two activities (B and C) when we finish activity A and we can begin activity D only after we finish both activities B and C.

▶ **Critical path**
The longest sequential path through the network diagram.

We can use the network diagram to determine the project's **critical path**. The critical path is the longest sequential path of interrelated activities in the network and shows the minimum completion time for the project. Any delay in an activity that is on the critical path will delay the whole project. Let's diagram a sample project.

EXAMPLE 16.1

Network Diagram of the New Product Project for Cables By Us

Two recent graduates, Michael and Elyssa, own Cables By Us, a company that produces cable assemblies. Business has been good so Michael and Elyssa have decided to expand their product line to include a new cable product. The new product will be manufactured in the current facility in an area not now in use. Michael and Elyssa have decided to use a project management approach to bring the new product on line and have identified eleven activities and their precedence relationships, as shown in Table 16-2. Develop an AON diagram of the project.

Table 16-2 Project Activities and Precedence Relationships

Activity	Description	Immediate Predecessors
A	Develop product specifications	none
B	Design manufacturing process	A
C	Source and purchase materials	A
D	Source and purchase tooling and equipment	B
E	Receive and install tooling and equipment	D
F	Receive materials	C
G	Pilot production run	E, F
H	Evaluate product design	G
I	Evaluate process performance	G
J	Write documentation report	H, I
K	Transition to manufacturing	J

• **Before You Begin:** A network diagram visually represents the different project activities and their precedence relationships. For Michael and Elyssa, the first activity (A) is developing product specifications. After activity A is completed, both activities B and C can begin. The diagram needs to reflect the connected pathways through the project.

• **Solution:**

In Figure 16-2, note that the project begins with activity A. Once activity A is completed, both activities B and C can begin. After completing activity B, activity D can be started. Following activity D's completion, activity E begins. When activity C is completed, we can start activity F. Activity G cannot be started until both activities E and F have been completed. Following the completion of activity G, we can begin working on both activities H and I. Activity J can begin once activities H and I are finished. The final activity, K, can be done after activity J is finished.

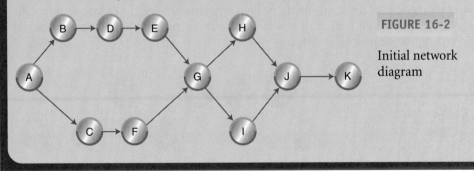

FIGURE 16-2

Initial network diagram

Step 3: Estimate the Project's Completion Time

To estimate the completion time of the project, the project manager evaluates the connected paths through the diagram to determine which of the routes takes the longest time. The longest connected route through the diagram is the critical path. The sum of the lengths of time of each of the activities on the critical path determines the minimum completion time for the project. If an activity on the critical path is delayed, the completion of the project is delayed.

We estimate the project completion time based on the time estimates for the project activities. Activity time estimates can be either **probabilistic** or **deterministic**. We use probabilistic time estimates when we are unsure about the duration of project activities—for example, because of technical problems, bad weather, delayed material delivery, and less-than-expected labor productivity. We use deterministic time estimates when we have done similar activities in the past and can make a reliable time estimate. Let's look first at estimating the project's completion date using deterministic time estimates.

▶ **Probabilistic time estimate**
Process that uses optimistic, most likely, and pessimistic time estimates.

▶ **Deterministic time estimate**
Assumption that the activity duration is known with certainty.

Activity	Description	Time Estimate (weeks)
A	Develop product specifications.	4
B	Design manufacturing process.	6
C	Source and purchase materials.	3
D	Source and purchase tooling and equipment.	6
E	Receive and install tooling and equipment.	14
F	Receive materials.	5
G	Pilot production run.	2
H	Evaluate product design.	2
I	Evaluate process performance.	3
J	Write documentation report.	4
K	Transition to manufacturing.	2

Step 3 (a): Deterministic Time Estimates

With the deterministic time estimate, we make a single time estimate for each project activity. Table 16-3 shows the time estimates for each of Michael and Elyssa's project activities.

Given this information, we need to transfer the activity time requirement to the network diagram, as shown in Figure 16-3. We include the time estimate with the activity designator in the appropriate node. For example, activity A should take four weeks. We determine project completion time by calculating how long each of the paths through the network will take.

FIGURE 16-3

Identifying paths

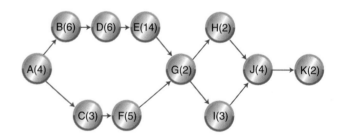

Connected paths
1. A, B, D, E, G, H, J, K
2. A, B, D, E, G, I, J, K
3. A, C, F, G, H, J, K
4. A, C, F, G, I, J, K

Identify the four connected paths in the project, running from the beginning to the end, and calculate how long it takes to complete each path.

- **Before You Begin:** First, identify the connected pathways through the network diagram. Sum the total time to complete all the activities on each pathway. Compare the results. The pathway that takes the greatest amont of time to finish determines the minimum completion time for this project.

- **Solution:**
  For example, the first path includes activities A, B, D, E, G, H, J, and K. Add the time estimates for each of these activities together to find the length of time it takes to complete the path. Verify the results shown in Table 16-4.

Table 16-4   Completion Times for Each Path

Activities on Path	Completion Time (weeks)
A, B, D, E, G, H, J, K	40
A, B, D, E, G, I, J, K	41
A, C, F, G, H, J, K	22
A, C, F, G, I, J, K	23

Since the critical path is the longest connected path through the network, the critical path includes activities A, B, D, E, G, I, J, and K. Activities C, F, and H are not included on the critical path.

When the project and number of pathways are larger, another technique can be used to determine the project's completion time and the project's critical path. In this case, ES (earliest start time), EF (earliest finish time), LS (latest start time), and LF (latest finish time) are used along with deterministic time estimates to identify any activity that has slack. **Slack** means that the start time for a specific activity can be delayed without delaying the project's planned completion date. Figure 16-4 shows the network diagram and the calculated ESs and EFs. By convention, the project starts at time 0, which is the earliest time any activity can start. Since activity A must be done first, it has $ES_A = 0$. The earliest that activity A can be finished is calculated as its earliest start time plus the time it takes to do the activity. The general formula is EF = ES + activity time estimate. For activity A, the formula is $EF_A = ES_A$ + the activity A time estimate. Or, $EF_A = 0 + 4$ weeks, or a total of 4 weeks. The earliest start time for both activities B or C is equal to the EF for activity A, the activity immediately preceding it.

▶ **Slack**
The amount of time an activity can be delayed without affecting the project's planned completion time.

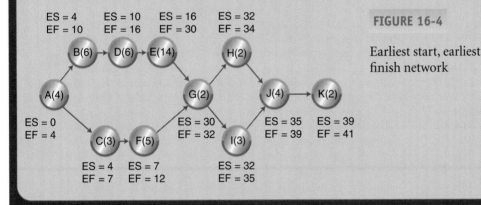

FIGURE 16-4

Earliest start, earliest finish network

EXAMPLE 16.3

Using ES, EF, LS, and LF to Find Slack

Confirm the calculations made in Figure 16-4 and Figure 16-5.

• **Before You Begin:** When confirming the ES and EF calculations, pay particular attention to activities G and J. In this situation, these activities have multiple immediate predecessors. Both activities E and F must be finished before activity G can begin. Both activities H and I must be completed before activity J can begin. Remember that since both immediate predecessors must be completed before the next activity can start, the immediate predecessor with the larger EF becomes the ES for the following activity.

• **Solution:**
By convention, the ES for activity A is 0. The earliest finish time is 4. Once activity A is completed, activities B and C can be started. The ES for each is equal to the EF of its immediate predecessor, activity A. Continue moving from left to right through the diagram. The ES for activity G is 30, since both activities E and F must be completed before activity G can begin. The larger EF time for these predecessors is the ES for activity G. The estimated project duration is 41 weeks, the EF for the final project activity.

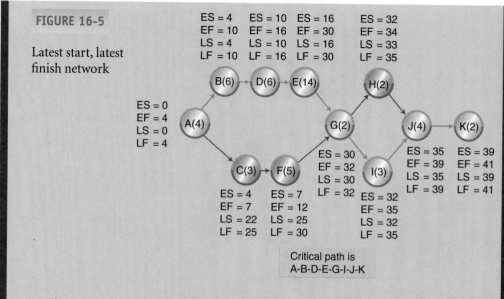

FIGURE 16-5

Latest start, latest finish network

ES = 4	ES = 10	ES = 16	ES = 32
EF = 10	EF = 16	EF = 30	EF = 34
LS = 4	LS = 10	LS = 16	LS = 33
LF = 10	LF = 16	LF = 30	LF = 35

ES = 0
EF = 4
LS = 0
LF = 4

ES = 30
EF = 32
LS = 30
LF = 32

ES = 35
EF = 39
LS = 35
LF = 39

ES = 39
EF = 41
LS = 39
LF = 41

ES = 4
EF = 7
LS = 22
LF = 25

ES = 7
EF = 12
LS = 25
LF = 30

ES = 32
EF = 35
LS = 32
LF = 35

Critical path is
A-B-D-E-G-I-J-K

After moving from left to right through the network computing the ESs and EFs, the LSs and LFs are calculated working from right to left. Since the project duration has been established as 41 weeks, the LF for the final project activity (K) is set to 41 weeks. Beginning with the LF for the final activity, move from right to left through the network diagram. If activity K must be finished by time 41, then it must be started no later than time 39 (the LF_K − the time to complete activity K). If activity K must be started no later than time 39, then its immediate predecessor (activity J) must be finished no later than time 39, so LF_J = 39. The latest activity J can be started and still be completed on schedule is time 35. At activity G, there are two activities that follow the completion of activity G. In this case when there are two or more activities (H and I) going back to a single activity (G), the smaller LS value (LS_I = 32) is the LF for activity G. Continue through the network.

After the LSs and LFs are completed, determine which activities are on the critical path. Any activity with slack is not on the critical path. To determine whether slack exists for an activity, compare its ES value with the LS value. If these two values are equal, then that activity has no slack. Look at activity I for an example with no slack. Look at activity H for an example with slack. In this example, activities A, B, D, E, G, I, J, and K are on the critical path. Activities C, F, and H have slack.

Step 3 (b): Probabilistic Time Estimates

▶ **Optimistic time estimate**
The shortest time period in which the activity can be completed.

▶ **Most likely time estimate**
The normal time that the activity is expected to take.

▶ **Pessimistic time estimate**
The longest time period in which the activity will be completed.

▶ **Beta probability distribution**
Typically represents project activities.

With probabilistic time estimates, we make three time estimates for each project activity: the **optimistic time**, the **most likely time**, and the **pessimistic time**. The optimistic time, denoted as (o), is the shortest time in which the activity can be completed. The most likely time, denoted as (m), is the most reasonable time estimate. The pessimistic time, denoted as (p), is the longest time in which the activity can be completed. Using Michael and Elyssa's plan for a new product, let's add some time estimates so we can determine the project's critical path. Table 16-5 shows the optimistic, most likely, and pessimistic time estimates for the project activities.

When we calculate the expected time for an activity, we treat each activity time estimate as a random variable derived from a **beta probability distribution**. The beta distribution can have various shapes typically found in project management activities and also has definite end points. These end points limit the possible completion times of the project between the optimistic and the pessimistic completion times. The most likely time completion date is the mode of the beta distribution. Figure 16-6 shows an example of a beta probability distribution.

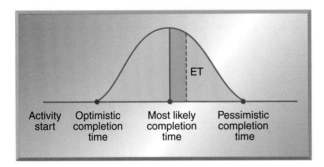

FIGURE 16-6

Beta distribution

We use three time estimates to compute an expected time for finishing each of the activities. The expected time for each activity is a weighted average, calculated using the formula

$$\text{Expected time} = \frac{\text{optimistic time} + 4(\text{most likely time}) + \text{the pessimistic time}}{6}$$

For activity A, the expected time is 4 weeks.

$$\text{Expected time}_A = \frac{2 + 4(4) + 6}{6} = \frac{24}{6} = 4 \text{ weeks}$$

Confirm the expected time for each of the activities in the Cables By Us project. Identify the different connected pathways through the network and calculate the expected completion time for each pathway.

EXAMPLE 16.4

Calculating the Expected Times

- **Before You Begin:** To calculate the expected time for each activity, use the following formula:

$$\text{Expected time} = \frac{\text{optimistic time} + 4(\text{most likely time}) + \text{pessimistic time}}{6}$$

Identify the connected pathways through the network and calculate the expected time for each. Remember that the pathway that takes the longest time to complete is the critical path for the project.

- **Solution:**
Table 16-5 shows the expected time for each of the activities. Note that in some cases, the optimistic, most likely, and pessimistic times can be identical, as they are for activities G and K. For those activities, no uncertainty exists; we know for sure how long those activities will take.

Table 16-5   **Probabilistic Time Estimates**

Activity	Description	Optimistic Time (o) (weeks)	Most Likely Time (m) (weeks)	Pessimistic Time (p) (weeks)	Expected Time (ET) (weeks)
A	Develop product specifications	2	4	6	4
B	Design manufacturing process	3	7	10	6.83
C	Source and purchase materials	2	3	5	3.17
D	Source and purchase tooling and equipment	4	7	9	6.83
E	Receive and install tooling and equipment	12	16	20	16

(*Continued*)

Table 16-5   (*Continued*)

Activity	Description	Optimistic Time (o) (weeks)	Most Likely Time (m) (weeks)	Pessimistic Time (p) (weeks)	Expected Time (ET) (weeks)
F	Receive materials	2	5	8	5
G	Pilot production run	2	2	2	2
H	Evaluate product design	2	3	4	3
I	Evaluate process performance	2	3	5	3.17
J	Write documentation report	2	4	6	4
K	Transition to manufacturing	2	2	2	2

The next step is to transfer the expected activity times to the network diagram, as shown in Figure 16-7. Now we determine the critical path through the project. We have two ways to find the critical path. The first, which is more practical for small network diagrams, is to calculate the expected time each path through the network takes to complete. In Figure 16-7, we can see four connected or sequential paths through the project. Table 16-6 shows these paths and the expected times to complete them.

FIGURE 16-7

Network diagram with expected activity times

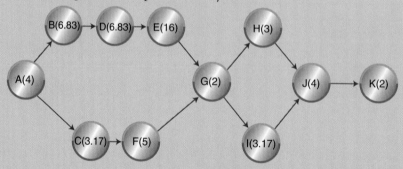

Connected paths
1. A, B, D, E, G, H, J, K
2. A, B, D, E, G, I, J, K
3. A, C, F, G, H, J, K
4. A, C, F, G, I, J, K

The first connected path includes activities A, B, D, E, G, H, J, and K. The second path includes activities A, B, D, E, G, I, J, and K. The third path includes activities A, C, F, G, H, J, and K. The fourth path includes activities A, C, F, G, I, J, and K. There are no other connected paths through the project. To calculate the expected time of each path, we sum the expected times for the activities on the path. For example, we expect the first path to take 44.66 weeks (4 weeks for activity A + 6.83 weeks for activity B + 6.83 weeks for activity D + 16 weeks for activity E + 2 weeks for activity G + 3 weeks for activity H + 4 weeks for activity J and 2 weeks for activity K). The critical path is the longest connected path through the network. Therefore, the second path—A, B, D, E, G, I, J, K—is the critical path and determines the expected completion time for the project.

Table 16-6   Paths through the Network

Path Number	Activities on Path	Expected Completion Time (weeks)
1	A, B, D, E, G, H, J, K	44.66
2	A, B, D, E, G, I, J, K	44.83
3	A, C, F, G, H, J, K	23.17
4	A, C, F, G, I, J, K	23.34

An alternative method for determining the expected project duration using probabilistic time estimates is to find which activities have slack time. These are the activities we can delay without affecting the project completion date.

Given Michael and Elyssa's project, determine which activities have slack by calculating the ES, EF, LS, and LF for each activity.

EXAMPLE 16.5

Calculating Earliest Start Times and Latest Start Times

- **Before You Begin:** The ES and LF calculations using probabilistic time estimates are done exactly as were the deterministic time estimates used in Example 16.3.

- **Solution:**

By convention, we set the timing at 0 to begin the project. Therefore, the earliest we can begin activity A is at time 0, which means that the earliest we can finish activity A is at time 4. Both activities B and C can begin as early as time 4. Activity B can be finished as early as time 10.83 (the earliest start time plus the expected activity time). Activity C can be finished as early as time 7.17.

When we have to finish two or more activities before another activity can begin, such as activities E and F being finished before beginning activity G, we calculate the earliest finish time for each activity. Figure 16-8 shows that the earliest we can finish activity E is time 33.66 whereas we can finish activity F as early as time 17.17. Since both activities must be finished before we can begin activity G, the earliest we can start activity G is time 33.66. Note that when two or more activities must be done before the next activity can begin, the earliest start time of that activity is the larger of the incoming earliest finish times.

FIGURE 16-8

Network diagram with early starts and early finishes

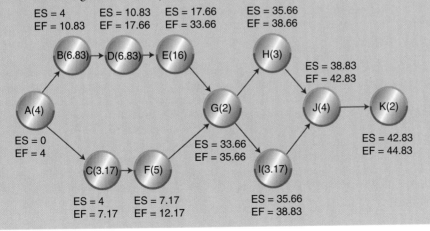

FIGURE 16-9

Earliest-start Gantt chart

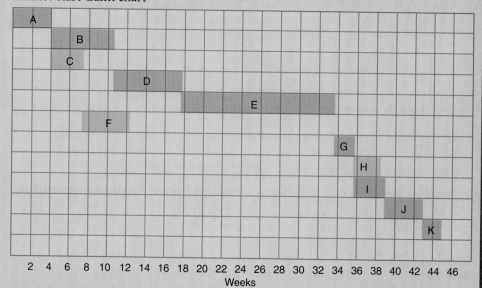

The Gantt chart in Figure 16-9 shows the project with each activity finished at the earliest possible start date. Note that we cannot begin activity D until we finish both activities B and C. We can begin activity F as soon as we finish activity C.

Using Michael and Elyssa's project, determine the latest start and latest finish times for each of the activities.

• Solution:

In Figure 16-10, we have added the latest start times (LS) and the latest finish times (LF) to the network diagram. LS is the latest time we start an activity without delaying the entire project. LF is the latest time we can finish an activity without delaying the entire project. By convention, we set the LF for the final activity equal to the EF for that activity (44.83 weeks in this case). To calculate the latest start time for activity K, we subtract the expected activity time (2 weeks) from the latest finish time ($44.83 - 2.0 = 42.83$). The latest finish time for activity J is the latest start time for activity K. When we have two activities going back to a common activity, such as activities B and C going back to activity A, we calculate the LS for each and then we use the smaller of the latest start times (for example, the LS for activity B is 4, the LS for activity C is 25.49, therefore the LF for activity A is 4). The Gantt chart in Figure 16-11 shows the project schedule using the latest possible start times for each of the activities if the project is to be completed in 44.83 weeks.

When we have computed the ES and EF for each activity, we can determine which activities are on the critical path. All activities that have equal ES and EF are on the critical path. From Figure 16-10 we can see that activities A, B, D, E, G, I, J, and K are on the critical path. Activities C, F, and H are not on the critical path. Any activity not on the critical path has slack time, so we can delay the completion of that activity. To illustrate this, let's look at our network diagram in Figure 16-10. We can see that activities C and F together need only an expected time of 8.17 weeks. The other activities that we must finish before activity G—activities B, D, and E—are expected to take 29.66 weeks. The difference (21.49 weeks) represents how long we can delay activities C and F and still not affect the project's completion date. As long as we finish C and F by time 33.66, we can finish the project as planned.

FIGURE 16-10

Network diagram with late starts and late finishes

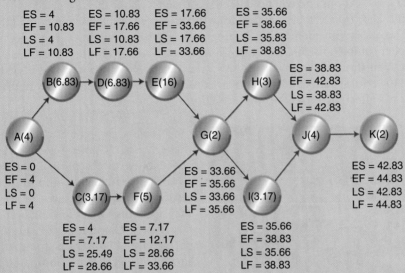

The Gantt chart in Figure 16-11 shows the project schedule using the latest possible start times for each of the activities if the project is to be completed in 44.83 weeks.

When we compare the earliest-start schedule with the latest-start schedule, we can see that three activities (C, F, and H) have different starting and finishing times. We can start activity C as early as week 4 or as late as week 25.49, so activity C has slack. The same is true for activity F: we can start it as early as week 7.17 and as late as week 28.66. Activity H has less slack. We can start it as early as week 35.66 and no later than week 35.83. Since each of these activities has slack, we do not include them in the project's critical path.

FIGURE 16-11

Latest-start Gantt chart

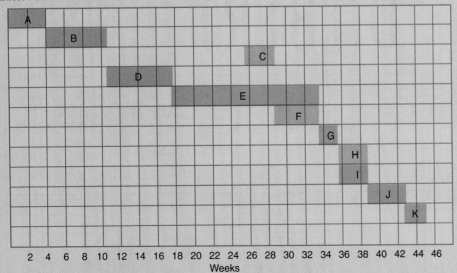

Step 4: Monitor the Project's Progression

Even though you have carefully planned the project, things happen that can affect its progress. Parts or equipment may arrive later than expected, materials may not meet quality specifications and will need to be replaced, less labor than expected may not be available, and bad weather—all can delay the project's completion. Planning the project is necessary, but monitoring its progress is even more important in meeting the scheduled completion date. You focus initially on activities in the critical path since any delay in these activities delays the whole project. You are also aware of activities not on the critical path that have little slack because a relatively short delay in these activities can affect the project's completion time.

LINKS TO PRACTICE

Managing the Olympic Games
www.olympics.com

©AP/Wide World Photos

One large-scale project to manage is the Olympic Games—a project that necessitates an exceptional amount of advance research and planning. The logistics and infrastructures of the city that hosts the Olympic Games and the Organizing Committee for the Games both have to oversee hundreds of smaller projects that culminate to ensure a successful run of the Olympics. From tasks such as shipping and receiving the tremendous amount of freight (for example, broadcast equipment) to facilitating the stay of the athletes, project managers must pay close attention to details. Of course, with such a large-scale event comes a myriad of problems, such as enough timely transportation, leadership changes, and security concerns. Only with extensive preparation can such a large-scale event be successful.

Dilbert's approach to project management

Before You Go On

Be sure that you understand how to use network planning techniques.

1. Describe the project in terms of your objective, the project activities, and the precedence relationships.
2. Estimate the project activities. For probabilistic time estimates, make an optimistic, most likely, and pessimistic estimate and compute the expected time for each project activity. For deterministic time estimates, make a single time estimate for each activity.
3. Diagram the project using either activity-on-arrow or activity-on-node notation to reflect the precedence relationships between activities.

ESTIMATING THE PROBABILITY OF COMPLETION DATES

An advantage of using probabilistic time estimates is the ability to predict the probability of project completion dates. We learned how to calculate the expected time for each activity with the three time estimates provided. Now we need to calculate the variance for each activity. The variance of the beta probability distribution for each activity is

$$\sigma^2 = \left(\frac{p - o}{6}\right)^2$$

where p = pessimistic activity time estimate
o = optimistic activity time estimate

EXAMPLE 16.6

Calculating the Variance of Activities

Calculate the variance of each activity in the Cables By Us project. Then calculate the variance associated with each connected pathway through the project.

• **Before You Begin:** The variance is calculated using the formula

$$\sigma^2 = \left(\frac{p - o}{6}\right)^2$$

• **Solution:**

Using activity A to illustrate the formula, the variance is 0.44:

$$\sigma_A^2 = \left(\frac{6 - 2}{6}\right)^2 = 0.44$$

Confirm the variances for the remaining activities as shown in Table 16-7. Then sum the total variances associated with each pathway. Confirm the values shown in Table 16-8.

Table 16-7 Project Activity Variance

Activity	Optimistic Time	Most Likely Time	Pessimistic Time	Variance
A	2	4	6	0.44
B	3	6	10	1.36
C	2	3	5	0.25
D	4	7	9	0.69
E	12	16	20	1.78
F	2	5	8	1.00
G	2	2	2	0.00
H	2	3	4	0.11
I	2	3	5	0.25
J	2	4	6	0.44
K	2	2	2	0.00

Using the variance for each activity, calculate the variance for paths through the network. To calculate the variance for a specific path through the network, add the variance for each of the activities on the path. For example, the variance for the critical path A, B, D, E, G, I, J, K is 4.96 weeks (0.44 + 1.36 + 0.69 + 1.78 + 0.00 + 0.25 + 0.44 + 0.00). The size of the variance reflects the degree of uncertainty for the path. The greater the variance, the greater is the uncertainty. The variance for the second-longest path through the network (A, B, D, E, G, H, J, K) is 4.82 weeks. Table 16-8 shows the four specific paths and their variances.

Table 16-8   Variances of Paths through the Network

Path Number	Activities on Path	Path Variance (weeks)
1	A, B, D, E, G, H, J, K	4.82
2	A, B, D, E, G, I, J, K	4.96
3	A, C, F, G, H, J, K	2.24
4	A, C, F, G, I, J, K	2.38

When you know the expected completion time of each path and its variance, you can determine the probability of specific completion dates. For example, you may want to know the probability of completing the project in 48 weeks. We can use the following formula to determine the probability of finishing each of the paths at a specified date:

$$z = \frac{\text{specified time} - \text{path expected completion time}}{\text{path standard deviation}}$$

or

$$z = \frac{D_T - EF_{Path}}{\sqrt{\sigma^2_{Path}}}$$

where D_T = the specified completion date
   EF_{Path} = the expected completion time of the path
   σ^2_{Path} = variance of path

For a particular path through the project, the *z-value* shows the path's number of standard deviations that the specified time is past the expected path completion time. A negative z-value shows that the specified time is earlier than the expected path completion time. After calculating the z-value, you can look it up in Appendix B to determine the probability of finishing the path by the specified time. Note that the probability of finishing the path by the specified time equals the area under the normal curve to the left of z, as shown in Figure 16-12.

FIGURE 16-12

Probability of path 1 finished in 48 days

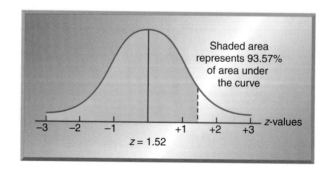

Shaded area represents 93.57% of area under the curve

z-values

z = 1.52

REDUCING PROJECT COMPLETION TIME • **611**

Calculate the probability of finishing the project in 48 weeks.

EXAMPLE 16.7

Calculating the Probability of Finishing the Project in 48 Weeks

• **Solution:**
We compute the probability of path number 1 as follows:

$$z = \frac{48 \text{ weeks} - 44.66 \text{ weeks}}{\sqrt{4.82}} = 1.52$$

The z-value of 1.52 in Appendix B shows that there is a .9357 probability of finishing the path in no longer than 48 weeks. Conversely, there is only a .0643 probability of not finishing this path by 48 weeks. Table 16-9 shows the z-value calculations and the probability of completion for the other three paths.

Table 16-9 z-Value Calculations and Path Probabilities of Finishing in 48 Weeks

Path Number	Activities on Path	Path Variance (weeks)	z-value	Probability of Completion
1	A, B, D, E, G, H, J, K	4.82	1.5216	.9357
2	A, B, D, E, G, I, J, K	4.96	1.4215	.9222
3	A, C, F, G, H, J, K	2.24	16.5898	1.000
4	A, C, F, G, I, J, K	2.38	15.9847	1.000

In general, we give any activity with a z-value of 2.50 or larger a 100 percent probability of completion by the specified time. You may be more concerned with the probability of the critical path's completion by the specified time. Still, it is a good idea to determine the probability of other paths with similar completion times. The probability of finishing the critical path for this project in 48 weeks is .9222. It is true that a delay in any activity in the critical path will delay the project's completion. This does not mean, however, that we ignore what happens in the other paths. These lengths of other paths through the project are sometimes almost the same as that of the critical path. Thus, an extended delay or delay in a combination of activities on an alternate path could ultimately delay the project's completion.

REDUCING PROJECT COMPLETION TIME

You may need to reduce the time you spend finishing a particular project because of deadlines, promised completion dates, penalty clauses for late completion, or the need to put resources on a new project. When you plan a project, you make time estimates based on normal procedures and resources. However, you may be able to speed up a project by making additional resources available. For example, your company could have materials shipped via premium rather than normal transportation to get the materials faster and the activity finished sooner. You could authorize overtime to speed up an activity. Another possibility, as is done in highway construction, is to bring in lights so workers can work through the night and minimize traffic disruptions. Whatever the method, you can often reduce the time needed to finish an activity.

Crashing Projects

At the same time that you shorten a project's duration, you also need to minimize the additional expense. We call shortening a project **crashing** the project. To crash the project and minimize expense, you need additional information about your project

▶ **Crashing**
Reducing the completion time of the project.

TABLE 16-10

Normal and Crash Cost Estimates

Activity	Normal Time (weeks)	Normal Cost ($)	Crash Time (weeks)	Crash Cost ($)	Maximum Weeks of Reduction	Cost per Week to Reduce ($)
A	4	8,000	3	11,000	1	3,000
B	6	30,000	5	35,000	1	5,000
C	3	6,000	3	6,000	0	0
D	6	24,000	4	28,000	2	2,000
E	14	60,000	12	72,000	2	6,000
F	5	5,000	4	6,500	1	1,500
G	2	6,000	2	6,000	0	0
H	2	4,000	2	4,000	0	0
I	3	4,000	2	5,000	1	1,000
J	4	4,000	2	6,400	2	1,200
K	2	5,000	2	5,000	0	0

activities. Let's use Michael and Elyssa's project with deterministic time estimates (shown in Figure 16-3). Table 16-10 shows the new crashing information.

In Table 16-10, normal time and normal cost refer to how long the activity typically takes to complete and the cost for completing the activity in that amount of time. Crash time is the least possible amount of time in which the activity can be done. The crash cost is the amount of money you must pay to complete the activity in the minimum amount of time. If you choose to only partially speed up an activity, the additional cost must be calculated. For example, if we choose to complete activity E in 13 weeks, the additional cost is $6,000. The difference between the crash cost and the normal cost ($72,000 − $60,000 = $12,000) is divided by the difference between normal time and crash time (14 weeks − 12 weeks = 2 weeks). The cost to crash activity E, then, is $12,000/2, which equals $6,000 per week.

FIGURE 16-13

Crashed project diagram

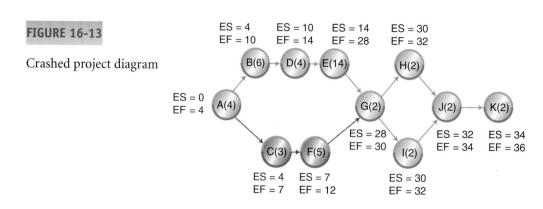

Critical paths: A, B, D, E, G, H, J, K
A, B, D, E, G, I, J, K

Note that we cannot reduce activities C, G, H, or K, so for those activities the maximum number of weeks of reduction is set to 0. Also note that reducing the lengths of different activities costs different amounts. We can reduce activity I by 1 week for a cost of $1,000, whereas we can reduce activity B by 1 week for a cost of $5,000. When you need to reduce the length of a project, you first consider reducing activities on the critical path. Activities not on the critical path have slack and typically do not need to be reduced. Figure 16-13 shows the revised network diagram.

Suppose you are the project manager for Cables By Us. Consider what activities you would crash if Michael and Elyssa want to finish their project in 36 weeks. A quick look at Table 16-4 shows you that the normal project completion time is 41 weeks and the critical path includes activities A, B, D, E, G, I, J, and K. You need to consider crashing these activities to reduce the overall project length from 41 to 36 weeks. Table 16-10 shows that activities G and K cannot be crashed so you eliminate them. Table 16-11 shows the remaining activities on the critical path.

Michael and Elyssa want their project completed in 36 weeks instead of the 41 weeks shown in Table 16-4. They also want to minimize the extra cost incurred for crashing the project. Recommend which activities should be crashed so that the project takes only 36 weeks.

• **Before You Begin:** Table 16-11 has additional information showing the costs of completing each of the activities on the critical path in the normal time allotted, as well as how quickly the activity can be completed, and the cost per week for reducing the activity time. For example activity A normally takes 4 weeks and costs $8,000 to complete. If needed, activity A can be done in only 3 weeks, but the cost of speeding up this activity raises the total cost of activity A up to $11,000. So to reduce activity A by 1 week costs an additional $3,000. Only activities on the critical path are considered initially. A reduction in time to complete an activity that already has slack does not reduce the time to complete the project. Be aware that it is possible to change the critical path of the network if an activity is crashed too much.

• **Solution:**
To minimize the cost to crash the project, look in the last column for the least expensive critical path activity to crash per week. Activity I costs $1,000 to crash per week and you can crash it by 1 week. If you crash activity I by 1 week, the project will take 40 weeks. You still need to cut the project by 4 more weeks. The next least expensive activity to crash is activity J. It costs $1,200 per week to crash and you can crash it for 2 weeks. This reduces the project's length to 38 weeks. The next least expensive activity to crash is activity D at a cost of $2,000 per week and you can crash it for 2 weeks. This reduces the total project duration to 36 weeks at a cost of $7,400, as shown in Figure 16-13.

Crash activity I from 3 weeks to 2 weeks	$1,000
Crash activity J from 4 weeks to 2 weeks	$2,400
Crash activity D from 6 weeks to 4 weeks	$4,000
Total Crash Cost	$7,400

Table 16-11   Normal and Crash Cost Estimates for Remaining Critical Path Activities

Activity	Normal Time (weeks)	Normal Cost ($)	Crash Time (weeks)	Crash Cost ($)	Maximum Weeks of Reduction	Cost per Week to Reduce ($)
A	4	8,000	3	11,000	1	3,000
B	6	30,000	5	35,000	1	5,000
D	6	24,000	4	28,000	2	2,000
E	14	60,000	12	72,000	2	6,000
I	3	4,000	2	5,000	1	1,000
J	4	4,000	2	6,400	2	1,200

Before You Go On

In summary, to reduce project length, you need this information:

1. Normal activity time estimate and normal activity cost;
2. Crash activity time estimate and crash activity cost;
3. The activities on the critical path.

When you have this information, you need to do the following:

1. Determine how much the project needs to be reduced;
2. Determine which activities on the critical path can be reduced;
3. Crash critical activities on the basis of increasing cost;
   - Crash the least expensive activity first, the next least expensive second, and so on, until you have shortened the project to the desired length;
   - Calculate the total costs associated with crashing the project and determine whether the cost is justified.

THE CRITICAL CHAIN APPROACH

▶ **Critical chain approach**
Focus on the final due date that is based on the theory of constraints.

The **critical chain approach** is to get projects done faster and more consistently at or before the project due date. The focus is on the final due date rather than on individual activities or project milestones. The idea of the critical chain is that project activities are uncertain. Because of this uncertainty, we add safety time to project time estimates. In some cases, the safety time added exceeds 200 percent of the work time estimate.

Adding Safety Time

We have three ways to add safety time. First, we base time estimates on a pessimistic experience. Most time estimates include enough safety time to ensure that the project activity is completed on time 80 to 90 percent of the time. From statistics, we know that to cover 80 to 90 percent of the area under the curve, we have to add a substantial safety factor. Second, the more management levels involved, the greater the safety factor. Since no manager wants to look bad, we add more safety factors (perhaps an extra 10 to 20 percent). When each management level adds this safety factor, the total safety is greatly increased. Third, top management may make global reductions in project length. If we know that the total project length is likely to be reduced by 20 to 25 percent, we inflate our time estimate by 20 to 25 percent.

Wasting Safety Time

Just as we have three ways to add safety time, we have three ways to waste safety time. One is the student syndrome. If we have six weeks allotted for an activity that should take only two weeks, we do not start it until two weeks before it is due. Then if anything unexpected happens, we miss the due date because we wasted the safety cushion. A second way is multitasking, which uses a person or resource for more than one project. Thus we have to decide which project to work on: assigning resources to a low-priority project wastes valuable safety time. On the other hand, the amount of safety time may be the reason for using it on a lower-priority project. Suppose we have two activities. Activity A is on schedule and has plenty of safety time, whereas activity B is behind schedule and has little safety time. Typically, we work on activity B first and waste activity A's safety time. The third way to waste safety time comes from depen-

FIGURE 16-14

Comparing critical paths

Comparing Critical Paths

Activity A	Activity B	Activity C	Activity D	Activity E

Original critical path

Activity A	Activity B	Activity C	Activity D	Activity E	**Project Buffer**

Critical path with project buffer

dencies between activities in which delays accumulate and advances are wasted. Let's look at an example. Activity A is scheduled to take ten days. Activity B is scheduled to start on day 10 after activity A is finished. Think about what happens if we finish activity A in eight days. Do we start activity B earlier? Typically, no: we start activity B on day 10 as originally planned and we waste the safety time. What happens if we do not finish activity A until day 12? When do we start activity B? Day 12. The delays accumulate and they are passed on.

How does the critical chain approach solve the problem of safety time? The critical chain removes safety time from the individual activities and puts the total safety time at the end of the critical path, which creates a **project buffer**. Let's compare the critical paths shown in Figure 16-14. The completion time is the same but the original critical path has safety time added to each activity. The critical path with the project buffer eliminates the individual safety times. Activities not finished on time eat into the project buffer instead of wasting activity safety time.

Since the theory of constraints (discussed in Chapter 15), which is the basis of the critical chain, focuses on keeping the bottleneck busy, we can put time buffers before bottlenecks in the critical path, as shown in Figure 16-15. The feeding buffer protects the critical path from delays in noncritical paths. When the delay exceeds the feeding buffer, the project completion date is still protected by the project buffer. (For more information, see *Critical Chain* by Eliyahu M. Goldratt.)

▶ **Project buffer**
Safety time placed at the end of the critical path.

Example with Feeder Buffers

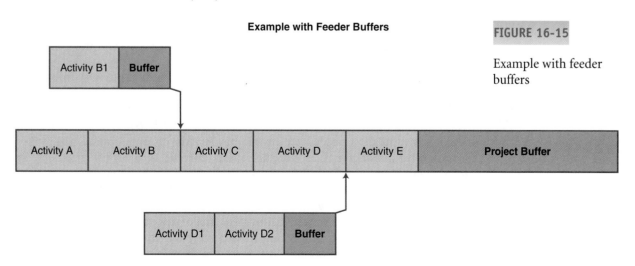

FIGURE 16-15

Example with feeder buffers

PROJECT MANAGEMENT WITHIN OM: HOW IT ALL FITS TOGETHER

Project management techniques provide a structure for the project manager to track the progress of different activities required to complete the project. Particular concern is given to critical path (the longest connected path through the project network) activities. Any delay to a critical path activity affects the project completion time. These techniques indicate the expected completion time and cost of a project. The project manager reviews this information to ensure that adequate resources exist and that the expected completion time is reasonable. If the expected completion date has a high probability of exceeding a contractual due date and incurring penalty costs, the project manager evaluates different methods for crashing the project (reducing project completion time). This evaluation is used to economically justify the application of more resources or to acknowledge a high probability of facing penalty costs. The project manager also looks at the resource load profile in an attempt to level resource requirements for the project.

After resolving the issue of resources, the project manager tracks the progress of the project. Once the earliest and latest start and finish times are determined, the production and material planners order materials and schedule required operations. The project manager interacts with the people responsible for different project activities and informs them of any proposed project schedule changes.

PROJECT MANAGEMENT OM ACROSS THE ORGANIZATION

Since projects tend to be long term and consume a company's resources, functional areas through the company work with expected completion dates, resource requirements, and the consequences of activity delays. Let's look at how the functional areas use project management information.

Accounting   uses project management information to provide a time line for major expenditures associated with the project. Accounting measures actual cost performance against planned costs to calculate profits. Accounting also calculates the cost benefit of crashing a particular project.

Marketing   uses project management information to monitor the progress of a project and to provide honest and realistic updates to the customer. The project schedule allows marketing to evaluate whether or not to crash a project.

Information systems   develop and maintain the software that supports project management. Choosing, installing, and training users in the appropriate software is vital to successful project management.

Purchasing uses project management information to deal with project delays by de-expediting items and rescheduling these items for later delivery. This allows the company to keep a lower inventory investment. Purchasing can also suggest when to avoid late deliveries to keep the project on schedule and how to reduce delivery time to help put a project back on schedule.

Operations   uses project management information to monitor the progress of activities on and off the critical path and to manage resource requirements in terms of the quantity and time needed for operations. Within an organization, the project manager or an assistant may develop the project schedule, typically using software for projects with many activities. Project managers can be product managers, manufacturing engineers, operations analysts, or office managers. Project management is a function not only of manufacturing companies but of service organizations too. Suppose you are planning the worldwide tour of a major art exhibit. Project scheduling techniques will help you effectively manage the many activities in this and other similar projects for your organization.

THE SUPPLY CHAIN LINK

Project management provides a structure to track the progress of a project. Any delays in an activity on the critical path delays the completion date for the entire project. Projects, such as introducing new products, can be undertaken by a supply chain. Communication among members of the chain to ensure a timely completion of the project is critical. Given that members of the supply chain share information, as well as a common database, all members should have real-time access to the project's progress. Any delays should be communicated throughout the chain. The project management approach indicates the timing and the quantity of resources needed. For manufacturing, this input is needed by the master production scheduler and is used to develop a valid MPS. Subsequently, this is input into the MRP system to develop the planned orders necessary to support the project.

Project tracking allows supply chain members to make changes as needed without surprising other members of the chain, thus increasing the chances of completing the project on schedule.

For service projects, the input is used by the project manager to develop the project structure. The project manager assures that members are aware of progress in the service project and the impact of any delays.

Chapter Highlights

1 A project is a unique, one-time event of some duration (weeks, months, or even years) that consumes resources (human, capital, materials, and equipment capacity) and is designed to achieve an objective in a given time period. In business, projects can be designing new products, installing new systems, constructing new facilities, mounting advertising campaigns, designing information systems, and developing company web pages. In politics, a project can be designing a political campaign.

2 Each project goes through a five-phase life cycle: concept, feasibility study, planning, execution, and termination. In the concept phase, we identify the need for the project. With the feasibility study, we evaluate expected costs, benefits, and risks. Planning consists of calculating the work and the time to do it; execution is doing the work; and termination is finishing the project.

3 Two network planning techniques are PERT and CPM. PERT uses probabilistic time estimates. CPM uses deterministic time estimates.

4 PERT and CPM determine the critical path of the project and the estimated completion time. On smaller projects, we determine completion time by evaluating each connected path through the network. On larger projects, software programs are available to identify the critical path.

5 PERT uses probabilistic time estimates to determine the probability that a project will be done by a specified time. We calculate a z-value and then determine the probability that the critical path and other near-critical paths will be completed by a given date.

6 To reduce the length of a project, we need to know the critical path and the cost of reducing individual activity times. Crashing activities that are not on the critical path typically does not reduce project completion time.

7 The critical chain approach removes excess safety time from individual activities and creates a project buffer at the end of the critical path. Feeder buffers are used on noncritical paths merged with the critical path.

Key Terms

Formula Review

Expected time for each activity:

$$\text{Expected time} = \frac{\text{optimistic time} + 4(\text{most likely time}) + \text{the pessimistic time}}{6}$$

Variance for each activity:

$$\sigma^2 = \left(\frac{p - o}{6}\right)^2$$

Calculating the z-value to estimate probability of completion:

$$z = \frac{\text{specified time} - \text{path expected completion time}}{\text{path standard deviation}} \quad \text{or} \quad z = \left(\frac{D_T - EF_{\text{Path}}}{\sqrt{\sigma^2_{\text{Path}}}}\right)$$

Solved Problems

Problem 1

Use the following information to diagram the project network.

Activity	Immediate Predecessors
A	none
B	A
C	A
D	B
E	C
F	D, E
G	F

Diagram the network using AON notation.

• Solution

The AON notation is straightforward for this project. Activity A is done first, then activities B and C can begin. When B is done,

activity D begins. When C is done, activity E begins. Activity F begins after both D and E are finished. Figure 16-16 shows the diagrammed network.

FIGURE 16-16

Project network diagram

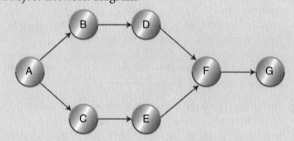

• Problem 2

Your boss gives you the following information about the new project you are leading. The information includes the activities, the three time estimates, and the precedence relationships.
(a) Calculate the expected time for each of the activities.
(b) Determine the expected completion time of the project.
(c) Calculate the variance of each of the project activities.
(d) Determine the probability that each of the connected paths through the project will be completed within 30 weeks.

Activity	Immediate Predecessors Time	Optimistic Time (weeks)	Most Likely Time (weeks)	Pessimistic Time (weeks)
A	none	6	10	14
B	A	3	6	10
C	A	4	8	10
D	B	5	6	7
E	C	4	6	12
F	D, E	3	3	3
G	F	3	4	5

• Before You Begin:

This project has three estimates for each activity. First, calculate the expected time for each project:

$$\text{Expected time of activity} = \frac{o + (4 \times m) + p}{6}$$

Determine the expected completion time by summing the total expected time for each pathway through the network. Then calculate the variance of each activity:

$$\text{Variance of activity} = \left(\frac{p - o}{6}\right)^2$$

Finally, determine the probability of completing each pathway in 30 weeks. To find the z-value, use the following formula:

$$z = \left(\frac{D_T - EF_{\text{Path}}}{\sqrt{\sigma_{\text{Path}}^2}}\right)$$

• Solution

(a) The formula for calculating the expected time for an activity is

$$\text{Expected time} = \frac{\text{optimistic time} + (4 \times \text{most likely time}) + \text{pessimistic time}}{6}$$

The expected times for each activity are shown in Table 16-12.

Table 16-12 Calculation of Activity Expected Times and Variances

Activity	Optimistic Time	Most Likely Time	Pessimistic Time	Expected Time	Variance
A	6	10	14	10.00	1.78
B	3	6	10	6.17	1.36
C	4	8	10	7.67	1.00
D	5	6	7	6.00	0.11
E	4	6	12	6.67	1.78
F	3	3	3	3.00	0.00
G	3	4	5	4.00	0.11

FIGURE 16-17

Project diagram

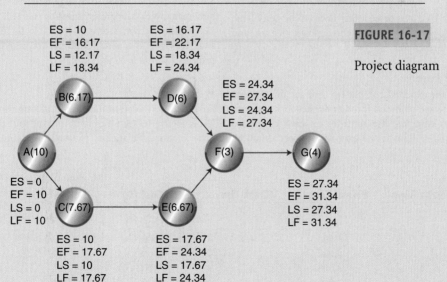

(b) Using Figure 16-17, we can identify the two connected paths running through the project. The first path includes activities A, B, C, F, and G and needs 29.17 weeks to complete. The second path includes activities A, C, E, F, and G and needs 31.34 weeks to complete. The early-start/early-finish and late-start/late-finish times are shown in Table 16-13.

Table 16-13   Calculation of Early-Start/Early-Finish Times and Late-Start/Late-Finish Times

Activity	Expected Time	First Immediate Predecessor	Second Immediate Predecessor	Early-Start Time	Early-Finish Time	Late-Start Time	Late-Finish Time	Slack
A	10.00	none		0.00	10.00	0.00	10.00	0.00
B	6.17	A		10.00	16.17	12.17	18.33	2.17
C	7.67	A		10.00	17.67	10.00	17.67	0.00
D	6.00	B		16.17	22.17	18.33	24.33	2.17
E	6.67	C		17.67	24.33	17.67	24.33	0.00
F	3.00	D	E	24.33	27.33	24.33	27.33	0.00
G	4.00	F		27.33	31.33	27.33	31.33	0.00

(c) We calculate the variance using the formula

$$\sigma^2 = \left(\frac{p - o}{6}\right)^2$$

The variance for each activity is shown in Table 16-12.

(d) To determine the probability of completing the project in 30 weeks, we need to calculate the variance for each path through the project. We do this by summing the individual variances of each activity included on the path. For the first path—A, B, D, F, and G—the variance is 3.36 weeks. The variance for the second path—A, C, E, F, and G—is 4.67 weeks. We use the following formula to determine the probability of completion by a specified time:

$$z = \left(\frac{D_T - EF_{Path}}{\sqrt{\sigma^2_{Path}}}\right)$$

The probability that the first path (A, B, D, F, G) will be completed within 30 weeks is

$$z = \left(\frac{30 - 29.17}{\sqrt{3.36}}\right) = .45$$

A z-value of .45 equates to a probability of .6736, or a 67.36 percent chance of this path being completed in 30 weeks. The probability that the second path (A, C, E, F, G) will be completed within 30 weeks is

$$z = \left(\frac{30 - 31.34}{\sqrt{4.67}}\right) = -.62$$

A z-value of −.62 equates to a probability of .2676, or a 26.76 percent chance that this path will be completed in 30 weeks.

• Problem 3

You are in charge of a new project that needs to be completed within 24 weeks. Figure 16-18 shows the network diagram and other relevant information.

• Before You Begin:

First, determine the expected completion time for this project. Identify the connected pathways through the network and sum the total time to complete the activities on each connected pathway. The longest time is the expected project duration.

Since the desired project completion date is 20 weeks, calculate how many weeks the project must be crashed. Crash the project by crashing activities on the critical path. Find the cheapest such activity and crash it. Continue crashing until the expected project duration is 20 weeks.

• Solution

First we need to determine the completion time for the project. Using Figure 16-18, we can identify the four paths through the project and calculate the project completion time. The first

Activity	Normal Time	Normal Cost ($)	Crash Time	Crash Cost ($)	Maximum Weeks Crashed	Crash Cost per Week ($)
A	4	4,000	3	4,500	1	500
B	6	9,000	6	9,000	0	0
C	5	1,500	3	2,000	2	250
D	3	6,000	2	9,000	1	3,000
E	4	8,000	2	16,000	2	4,000
F	6	3,000	5	3,500	1	500
G	8	4,000	6	6,000	2	1,000
H	3	3,600	2	4,800	1	1,200

FIGURE 16-18

Project diagram

B(6)
F(6)
A(4)
D(3) → E(4)
H(3)
C(5)
G(8)

Critical path: A, B, D, E, G, H

path (A, B, D, E, F, H) takes 26 weeks (4 + 6 + 3 + 4 + 6 + 3). Each of the paths and its completion time are shown here.

Path	Completion Time (weeks)
A, B, D, E, F, H	26
A, B, D, E, G, H	28
A, C, D, E, F, H	25
A, C, D, E, G, H	27

We determine the time to finish this project by the connected path that takes the longest time to complete. In this case, the completion time is 28 weeks. The critical path of this project includes activities A, B, D, E, G, and H.

Given the crash costs, we need to reduce the completion time from 28 weeks to 24 weeks. To do this, we consider the activities on the critical path and their associated crash cost. We do not need to consider crashing activities C or F because they are not part of the critical path and we cannot crash activity B because it cannot be reduced. Of the remaining activities, the least expensive activity to crash is A, which we can crash 1 week at a cost of $500. Since we want to reduce the project by 4 weeks, we have to find additional reductions. The next least expensive activity to crash is G, which we can crash 2 weeks at a total cost of $2,000. We need only one more week of reduction. Activity H is the next least expensive activity to crash, at $1,200 per week. By crashing these three activities, we can finish the project in 24 weeks. The additional cost for crashing the project is $3,700 ($500 for A, $2,000 for G, and $1,200 for H). Figure 16-19 shows the crashed project diagram.

FIGURE 16-19

Crashed project diagram

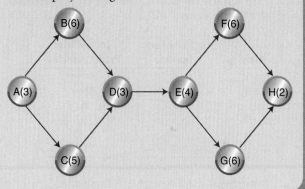

Discussion Questions

1. Identify some projects that are currently underway in your community. Is there a new hospital being built, a new retail store being opened, highway construction being done? For at least one project, try to identify the major activities.

2. Visit a local organization to learn about the kinds of projects it is working on and how it manages these projects.

3. Identify a personal project that you have recently completed or are in the process of completing—for example, a research paper or organizing a social event. Identify the major activities you had to complete.

4. Explain the advantage of using probabilistic time estimates.

5. Explain how we calculate the expected time value.

6. Explain the phases of a project's life cycle.

7. Describe the life cycle of a project you have done.

8. Provide an example of precedence relationships from your personal life.

9. Explain why determining the critical path is important in project management

Problems

Use the following project information for Problems 1 and 2.

Activity	Activity Time (weeks)	Immediate Predecessor(s)
A	3	none
B	4	A
C	2	B
D	5	B
E	4	C
F	3	D
G	2	E, F

1. Construct a network diagram using AON notation.
2. Using the network diagram constructed in Problem 1,
   (a) Calculate the completion time for the project.
   (b) Determine which activities are included on the critical path.
3. Jack's Floating Banana Party Company is planning to add a new party vessel for the upcoming season. Jack has identified several activities that must be finished before the start of the season. Using the following information,

Activity	Activity Time (weeks)	Immediate Predecessor(s)
A	6	none
B	5	none
C	3	A
D	3	B
E	6	C, D
F	9	D

(a) Draw the network diagram for this project.
(b) Identify the critical path.
(c) Calculate the expected project length.

Use the following project information for Problems 4 through 8.

Activity	Optimistic Time Estimate (weeks)	Most Likely Time Estimates (weeks)	Pessimistic Time Estimates (weeks)	Immediate Predecessor(s)
A	3	6	9	none
B	3	5	7	A
C	4	7	12	A
D	4	8	10	B
E	5	10	16	C
F	3	4	5	D, E
G	3	6	8	D, E
H	5	6	10	F
I	5	8	11	G
J	3	3	3	H, I

4. Using the information given, construct a network diagram using AON notation.
5. Using the information given, calculate the expected time for each of the project activities.
6. Using the information given, calculate the variance for each of the project activities.
7. Using your results from Problems 4 and 5,
   (a) Calculate the completion time for this project.
   (b) Identify the activities included on the critical path of this project.
8. Using your results from Problem 6,
   (a) Calculate the probability that the project will be completed in 38 weeks.
   (b) Calculate the probability that the project will be completed in 42 weeks.

Use the information provided in Table 16-14 and the network diagram in Figure 16-20 for the next four problems.

TABLE 16-14

Activity	Normal Time (weeks)	Normal Cost ($)	Crash Time (weeks)	Crash Cost ($)	Maximum Weeks Reduced	Crash Cost per Week($)
A	4	800	3	1,200	1	400
B	3	900	2	1,000	1	100
C	5	1,240	3	2,250	2	500
D	2	800	2	800	0	0
E	5	1,500	4	2,000	1	500
F	6	2,000	5	3,000	1	1,000
G	4	600	3	900	1	300
H	3	900	3	900	0	0

FIGURE 16-20

AON network diagram

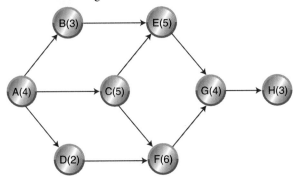

9. Using the information given,
   (a) Calculate the completion time of the project.
   (b) Identify the activities on the critical path.
   10. Using the information given and the project completion time calculated in Problem 9(a), reduce the completion time of the project by 3 weeks in the most economical way.
   11. Using the information given and the project completion time calculated in Problem 9(a), reduce the completion time of the project by 5 weeks in the most economical way.
   12. Using the information given and the project completion time calculated in Problem 9(a), calculate the minimum time for completing the project possible.
   Use Figure 16-21 and the following project data for the next two questions.
   13. Using the information given,
   (a) Calculate the expected time for each of the project activities.
   (b) Calculate the variance for each of the project activities.
   (c) Evaluate the connected paths through the diagram to determine the expected project completion time.

Activity	Optimistic Time (weeks)	Most Likely Time (weeks)	Pessimistic Time (weeks)
A	8	10	12
B	4	10	16
C	4	5	6
D	6	8	10
E	4	7	12
F	6	7	9
G	4	8	12
H	3	3	3

14. Using the information given and expected project completion time from Problem 13(c),
   (a) Calculate the probability of completing the project in 36 weeks.

   (b) Calculate the probability of completing the project in 40 weeks.
   15. The accounting department at Northeast University is offering a combined five-year B.S./M.S. in accounting. The senior accounting professor has identified the project activities and any precedence relationships, as shown in Table 16-15. Three time estimates for each activity are included.
   (a) Develop a network diagram for this project using AON notation.
   (b) Calculate the expected time for each of the project activities.
   (c) Identify the critical path for the project.
   (d) Calculate the expected project completion time.
   16. The dean of the business school wants to start offering this program starting 32 weeks from now. Using the information provided in Problem 15,
   (a) Calculate the probability of the program starting on time.
   (b) If the dean needs a 95 percent probability of being done on time, how long can the expected project duration be?

Use the following information for Problems 17 through 19.

Activity	Immediate Predecessor(s)	Normal Time (weeks)	Normal Cost	Crash Time (weeks)	Crash Cost
A	none	10	$16,000	8	$20,000
B	none	4	6,000	3	9,000
C	A, B	6	12,000	3	24,000
D	A	7	7,000	5	10,000
E	B	14	28,000	12	34,000
F	C, D, E	3	4,500	3	4,500
G	F	4	7,200	3	9,000
H	F	2	5,000	2	5,000
I	F	5	15,000	4	18,000
J	H, I	2	7,000	2	7,000
K	J	5	10,000	4	11,000
L	K	10	24,000	10	24,000

FIGURE 16-21

Network diagram

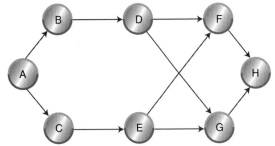

TABLE 16-15

Activity	Description of Activity	Immediate Predecessor(s)	Optimistic Time Estimates (weeks)	Most Likely Time Estimates (weeks)	Pessimistic Time Estimates (weeks)
A	Design general curriculum requirements	none	4	8	16
B	Develop program brochure	A	2	3	6
C	Identify prospective students	none	3	6	9
D	Develop advertising campaign	B, C	4	7	10
E	Design specific curriculum content	A	8	16	20
F	Send brochure and student application	D	2	3	4
G	Evaluate applications	F	2	4	6
H	Accept students, notify students	G	1	2	3
I	Schedule rooms for classes	H	1	1	7
J	Designate professors to teach courses	H	1	2	3
K	Select texts for courses	J	3	5	7
L	Order and receive texts	K	6	8	17

17. Draw the network diagram. Determine the normal time it will take to complete this project. Determine the critical path for the project. Calculate the cost of completing the project in normal time.

18. Determine the absolute minimum time it will take to complete the project if the project is crashed as far as possible. Calculate the cost associated with this approach to the project.

19. If the company wants to complete the project in 40 weeks, which activities should be crashed? Calculate the additional cost incurred to complete the project in 40 weeks.

CASE: The Research Office Moves

Jeannette, the senior administrative assistant, has just learned that she is in charge of the upcoming move of the research office at Southwest University. She has coordinated several such moves before and immediately begins organizing her thoughts. Determining what needs to be done, when it needs to be done, and who needs to do it are critical to a successful move. From past moves, Jeannette knows the first step is having the management team allocate the offices available to the different departments. She knows that each department manager fights for the best office space. Because of the politics, Jeannette expects this activity to take 3 weeks.

After the management team finalizes departmental allocations, each department manager allocates office space to individuals within the department. This is also quite political and typically takes 2 weeks. Individuals often take the office space allocations personally and each manager needs time to smooth

any ruffled feathers. The allocation decisions are returned to Jeannette so that she can develop an overall layout for the move. She normally does this in about 4 weeks. During the first week of this phase, Jeannette sends each individual a printout of the floor space they will have and requests that they determine how the furniture is to be arranged. Individuals inform her of any additional or replacement office furniture needs. They indicate where phone jacks and computer hookups should be. Each individual requests the packing supplies needed to pack up their office items. These requests are returned in 3 weeks.

When Jeannette receives the individual requests, she consolidates the requests to form lists of packing supplies and furniture. She orders the supplies from the university-approved supplier and the supplies arrive in 2 weeks. She chooses among three approved office furniture suppliers and selects and orders the office furniture, which is scheduled to arrive in 6 weeks.

When the packing supplies arrive, Jeannette distributes them to each individual so that packing can be done. This normally takes a week to sort and distribute supplies. Individuals pack their office items and tag their office furniture that is to be moved. They are expected to complete their packing in 2 weeks.

After ordering the furniture, Jeannette makes arrangements for the movers to move the items, the telecommunications office to move or install telephones, and computer services to provide Internet hookups. The movers require 3 weeks notice but move the items in a single day. The phone installers demand 2 weeks notice but complete the work in 1 day. The computer services technicians require 4 weeks notice and complete the hookups in 1 day. The final activity is moving day. All 3 of these groups—the movers, the phone installers, and the computer technicians—are there on the same date to minimize office disruption and minimize the time the office is unable to provide customer service.

In past moves, Jeannette has had trouble making sure that everything flows smoothly. She believes that there must be a method available to help her manage this office move.

(a) Why are office allocations so difficult? What factors must be considered when planning an office layout?

(b) Offer Jeannette a method for monitoring the office move. Explain why this method or approach would be reasonable.

(c) How long should it take from the day the decision is made to move until the move is completed? Employees only work Monday through Friday. All of Jeannette's activity time estimates assume a 5-day work week.

(d) What are the critical activities for the timely completion of this office move?

(e) What recommendations could you make to Jeannette to make this easier in the future?

CASE: Writing a Textbook

Two professors of operations management, Susan and Chris, have decided to write a new textbook for use in the undergraduate introductory operations management course. As they discuss the project, they put together the following list of activities that must be done

1. Write a prospectus. (This entails defining what is unique about the textbook and how it compares with other texts currently on the market.) Time estimate: 4 weeks.

2. Discuss the book concept with several publishers, provide publishers with prospectus. Time estimate: 1 week. (All major publishers attend annual professional academic meetings, so you can meet with all of them during that week.) This activity cannot be done before the prospectus is finished.

3. Conduct focus groups of faculty to test the concept of the text. Time estimate: 1 week. (This can be done at the same conference as activity 2.)

4. Select a publisher for the text from those expressing interest. Time estimate: 2 weeks. (This cannot be done until after completing activity 2.)

5. Update and submit prospectus and a sample chapter. Time estimate: 4 weeks. (This cannot be done until activities 3 and 4 are completed.)

6. Negotiate contract with publisher. Time estimate: 3 weeks. (This cannot be done until activity 5 is completed.)

7. Susan begins writing Chapters 1 through 8, at a rate of one per month. Susan works sequentially doing Chapter 1, then Chapter 2, etc. This activity begins after the contract has been signed.

8. Chris begins writing Chapters 9 through 16, at a rate of one per month. Chris also works sequentially. This activity begins after the contract has been signed.

9. Chapters are sent out for review. Each chapter undergoes external review after the publisher receives the chapter. Each review takes 4 weeks. Reviews can begin as soon as the publisher begins receiving chapters from the authors.

10. Susan reviews comments from external reviewers and revises chapters. Time estimate is 2 weeks per chapter. Susan can begin these as soon as the first reviews are received by the publisher. Susan will do these at the same time as she is writing new chapters.

11. Chris reviews comments from external reviewers and revises chapters. Time estimate is 2 weeks per chapter. Chris can begin these as soon as the first reviews are received by the publisher. Chris will do these at the same time as he is writing new chapters.

12. Develop list of photo and artwork requirements. Time estimate: 24 weeks. This can begin as soon as the revised first chapters are completed. Requirements for each chapter are needed.

13. Select persons to write instructor's manual, solutions manual, test bank, and PowerPoint presentation. Time estimate: 4 weeks. This can be done after activity 6 is completed.

14. Determine what will be placed on the student CD and determine a responsible individual to handle this process. Time estimate: 2 weeks. This activity can be done after activity 6 is completed.

15. Write instructor's manual. Time estimate: 12 weeks. This cannot be started until at least half of the revised chapters have been received by the publisher.

16. Write test bank. Time estimate: 12 weeks. This cannot be started until at least half of the revised chapters have been received by the publisher.

17. Write solutions manual. Time estimate: 12 weeks. This cannot be started until at least half of the revised chapters have been received by the publisher.

18. Write PowerPoint presentation. Time estimate: 12 weeks. This cannot be started until at least half of the revised chapters have been received by the publisher.

19. Design text cover. Time estimate: 8 weeks. This activity can be done after activity 6 is completed.

20. Design marketing campaign. Time estimate: 10 weeks. This activity can be done after activity 6 is completed.

21. Publisher produces galley proofs. Time estimate: 6 weeks following receipt of final revised chapters.

22. Proofreading galley proofs. Time estimate: 4 weeks after completion of galley proofs.

23. Produce student CD. Time estimate: 4 weeks. This activity can be done after activities 15, 17, and 18 have been finished.

24. Publisher prints text. Time estimate: 16 weeks. This activity can be done after activities 20 and 21 have been completed.

These activities represent a portion of the tasks involved in writing a textbook. The listed activities deal only with the actual production of the text and the ancillary materials. We have not considered the marketing activities or the logistics associated with a new text.

Susan and Chris are interested in establishing a project schedule for the new textbook.

(a) Add any additional activities that you think are necessary to the project.
(b) Draw the network diagram for this project.
(c) Determine how long it should take to complete the project.
(d) Consider what external issues might interfere with the timely completion of the project.

INTERACTIVE CASE Virtual Company

 www.wiley.com/college/reid

On-line Case: Project Management at Valley Memorial Hospital

For today's assignment you're meeting with Jim Hernandez from Valley Memorial Hospital's Marketing Department. "The project I have in mind for you," he says, "involves a new telemedicine procedure that we're ready to introduce at the clinic on the Native American reservation about 85 miles from here. The procedure requires the acquisition, installation, and marketing of a new telemedicine communications system. Dr. Henry Suver of our Emergency Department is responsible for implementing the system, and he can tell you all about it. Let's go over to Emergency, and I'll introduce you to him."

To complete this assignment, go to **www.wiley.com/college/reid** to get more details. Assignment questions are given at the site.

To access the Web site:

- Go to **www.wiley.com/college/reid**
- Click **Student Companion Site**
- Click **Virtual Company**
- Click **Kaizen Consulting, Inc.**
- Click **Consulting Assignments**
- Click **Project Management**

INTERNET CHALLENGE Creating Memories

Your Internet challenge is to help plan the 50th wedding anniversary party described at the beginning of this chapter. Use the list of activities that were identified for the party preparation and search the Internet for information on each activity. Complete the following:

1. Find time estimates for each activity. You can add to the list but you must include all the activities.

2. Develop a project schedule for the party. You can use either PERT or CPM. You can use PERT with single time estimates, but you will not be able to calculate the probability of on-time completion.

3. Determine the critical path for the party.

4. Based on the party date, determine when activities on the critical path must be started and finished.

On-line Resources

Companion Website www.wiley.com/college/reid:
- Take interactive *practice quizzes* to assess your knowledge and help you study in a dynamic way
- Review *PowerPoint slides* or print slides for notetaking
- Access the *Virtual Company: Valley Memorial Hospital*
- Find links to *Company Tours* for this chapter
    Thomson-Shore, Inc.
- Find links for *Additional Web Resources* for this chapter
    Project Management Institute, _www.pmi.org_
    The Project Management Site, _www.projectmanagement.com/main.htm_
    The PM Forum, _www.pmforum.org_

Additional Resources Available Only in WileyPLUS:
- Use the *e-Book* and launch directly to all interactive resources
- Take the interactive *Quick Test* to check your understanding of the chapter material and get immediate feedback on your responses.
- Check your understanding of the key vocabulary in the chapter with *Interactive Flash Cards*
- Use the *Animated Demo Problems* to review key problem types.
- Practice for your tests with *additional problem sets*
- *And more!*

Selected Bibliography

Denzler, David R. "A Review of CA-Super Project," *APICS—The Performance Advantage*, September 1991, 40–41.

Goldratt, Eliyahu M. *Critical Chain*. Great Barrington, Mass.: The North River Express, 1997.

Kerzner, Harold. *Advanced Project Management: Best Practices on Implementation*, Second Edition. New York: John Wiley & Sons, 2004.

Kerzner, Harold. *Project Management: A Systems Approach to Planning, Scheduling, and Controlling*, Sixth Edition. New York: John Wiley & Sons, 1999.

Kerzner, Harold, *Project Management for Executives*. New York: Van Nostrand Reinhold, 1984.

Mantel, Samuel J., Jr., Jack R. Meredith, Scott M. Shafer, and Margaret M. Sutton. *Project Management in Practice*, Second Edition. New York: John Wiley & Sons, 2005.

Meredith, Jack R., and Samuel J. Mantel, Jr. *Project Management, A Managerial Approach*, Fifth Edition. New York: John Wiley & Sons, 2003.

Moder, J.E., E.W. Davis, and C. Phillips. *Project Management with CPM and PERT*. New York: Van Nostrand Reinhold, 1983.

Smith-Daniels, Dwight E., and Nicholas J. Aquilano. "Constrained Resource Project Scheduling." *Journal of Operations Management*, 4, 4, 1984, 369–387.

Appendix A: Solutions to Odd-Numbered Problems

Solutions to selected problems are available on the Student web site. To access these solutions, go to www.wiley.com/college/reid. Select the second edition, then Student Resources; and then Selected Solutions.

Chapter 2

1. Productivity of worker 1 = 1000 labels/30 minutes = 33.3 labels per minute
   Productivity of worker 2 = 850 labels/20 minutes = 42.5 labels per minute
   Worker 2 is more productive.

3. Productivity of older model machine = 6 loaves/5 hours = 1.2 loaves per hour
   Productivity of newer model machine = 4 loaves/2 hours = 2.0 loaves per hour
   The newer machine is more productive.

5. Productivity using former method = 3 walls/45 minutes = .07 walls per minute
   Productivity using new method = 2 walls/20 minutes = .10 walls per minute
   The new method is more productive.

7. **a.** Using only the nondefective production, productivity went from $(20,000 \times 0.85) = 17,000$ units/month to $(25,000 \times 0.91) = 22,750$ units/month
   b. Change in productivity = $(22,750 - 17,000)/17,000 \times 100\% = 33.8\%$ increase

9. | Work crew | Productivity |
   |-----------|-------------|
   | Anna, Sue, and Tim | 10 homes/35 hours = 0.29 homes per hour |
   | Jim, Jose, and Andy | 15 homes/45 hours = 0.33 homes per hour |
   | Dan, Wendy, and Carry | 18 homes/56 hours = 0.32 homes per hour |
   | Rosie, Chandra, and Seth | 10 homes/30 hours = 0.33 homes per hour |
   | Sherry, Vicky, and Roger | 18 homes/42 hours = 0.43 homes per hour |

   Sherry, Vicky, and Roger are the most productive group.

Chapter 3

1. **a.** Total Cost = $\$40,000 + \$45Q$
   Total revenue = $\$100Q$

Break-even Quantity: Q = Fixed Cost/(Selling Price − Variable Cost) = $40,000/(100 - 45)$
$Q = 727.3$, so break even is exceeded at 728 units.

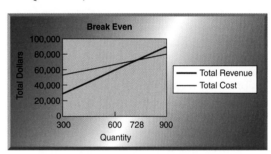

   b. Contribution to Profit = Total Revenue − Total Cost
   $= SP(Q) - [FC + VC(Q)]$
   $= 80(2000) - [40,000 + 45(2000)]$
   $= \$30,000$
   c. Contribution to Profit = Total Revenue − Total Cost
   $= SP(Q) - [FC + VC(Q)]$
   $= 100(1500) - [40,000 + 45(1500)]$
   $= \$42,500$

3. Break-even Quantity = Fixed Cost/(Selling Price − Variable Cost) = $200/(1 - 0.20) = 250$ hot chocolates

5. **a.**

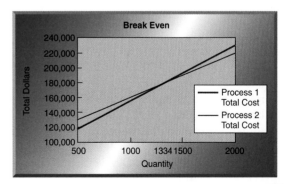

b. Process 1 is lower in total cost when the quantities are fewer than approximately 1300 tables. Process 2 becomes lower in total cost with quantities higher than 1300 tables. The actual break even may be calculated to be 1334.

7. a.

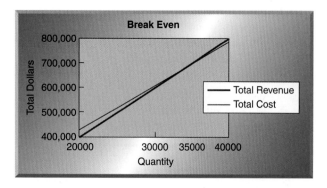

Break-even Quantity = Fixed Cost/(Selling Price − Variable Cost) = 70,000/(20 − 18) = 35,000 units of product

b. Increase Sales: 20,000(1.35) = 27,000 units
Contribution to Profit = Total Revenue − Total Cost = $SP(Q) − [FC + VC(Q)] =$
27,000(20) − [70,000 + 18(27,000)] = −$16,000
Reduce Variable Costs: 0.90(18) = $16.20
Contribution to Profit = Total Revenue − Total Cost = $SP(Q) − [FC + VC(Q)] =$
20,000(20) − [70,000 + 16.20(20,000)] = $6000
Reducing the variable costs contributes more to profits.

9. Break-even Quantity = Fixed Cost/(Selling Price − Variable Cost) = 9000/(80 − 50) = 300 units of service

11. Indifference Quantity between Process A and Process B
Total Cost A = Total Cost B = $[FC + VC(Q)]_A =$
$[FC + VC(Q)]_B$
The equation rearranges to: $Q = (FC_B − FC_A)/$
$(VC_A − VC_B) = (30,000 − 20,000)/(30 − 15) =$
666.7, or 667 chairs.
Process A is better than Process B when demand is below 667 chairs.
Indifference Quantity between Process A and Outsourcing
Total Cost A = Total Cost O = $[FC + VC(Q)]_A =$
$[FC + VC(Q)]_O$
$Q = 20,000/(50 − 30) = 1000$ chairs

Process A is better than outsourcing when demand is over 1000 chairs
Indifference Quantity between Process B and Outsourcing
Total Cost B = Total Cost O = $[FC + VC(Q)]_B =$
$[FC + VC(Q)]_O$
$Q = 30,000/(50 − 15) = 857.14$, or 858 chairs.
Process B is better than outsourcing when demand is over 857 chairs
In summation:

Demand Ranges	Cheapest Production
0 to 857	Outsource
858 and more	Process B

Process A is never the best alternative.

13. It is known from problem 12, money is lost if demand is under 8,000 units. Given they will proceed:
Breakeven Between Old and New Equipment: =
$FC_o + VC_o(Q) = FC_n + VC_n(Q)$
$Q = 2,000$
Use the old equipment if demand is at most 2,000 units. Use the new equipment if demand is over 2,000 units.

15. Arrive at Office → Wait in Reception Area → Brought to Examination Room → Wait for Doctor → Meet with Doctor → Return to Reception Desk → Depart
Bottlenecks occur during the waiting periods. Parallel activities such as lab results or x-rays may be analyzed during some of the waiting times.

17. *Utility = used/available =* (28/30) × 100% = 93.3%

Chapter 4

1. Indifference Point: Total Cost of Insourcing = Total Cost of Outsourcing
Total Cost = $FC + VC(Q)$
a. 300,000 + 1.5(Q) = 120,000 + 2.25(Q)
$Q = 240,000$ units
b. Since the demand is expected to be over the indifference point, insourcing is cheaper. The total cost for insourcing would be $750,000 and the total cost for outsourcing would be $795,000. The actual difference may be computed to be $45,000.

3. a. Total Cost = $FC + VC(Q)$ = 125,000 + 0.90(160,000) = $269,000
b. Total Cost from Durable = 170,000 + 0.65(160,000) = $274,000
c. Indifference point: Total Cost of Insourcing = Total Cost of Outsourcing
125,000 + 0.90(Q) = 170,000 + 0.65(Q)
$Q = 180,000$ snow boards

d. Annual demand must exceed 180,000 snow boards to justify outsourcing as the cheaper process. That increase is 12.5%, or 20,000 units over the current demand.

5. **a.** Total Cost Last Year $= FC + VC(Q) = 85,000 + 15(1450) = \$106,750$

b. Total Cost from VB $= 100,000 + 5(1450) = \$107,250$

c. Indifference point: Total Cost of Insourcing = Total Cost of Outsourcing
$85,000 + 15(Q) = 100,000 + 5(Q)$
$Q = 1500$ orders

d. Yes, VB is a cheaper alternative whenever demand exceeds 1500 orders.

e. Additional factors that should be considered include the economic stability of VB, the ability of VB to manage quality, the ability of VB to "partner," the ability of VB to deliver on time, and the impact of outsourcing on remaining employees.

Chapter 5

1. Reliability of CD player $= (0.90)^5 = 0.5905$

3. Reliability of copier $= (0.89)(0.95)(0.90)(0.90) = 0.6849$

5. Reliability of bank system $= (0.90)(0.89)(0.95) = 0.7610$

7. Probability of each component working $= P(A) + P(B) - P(A)P(B)$; or consider that either the original component or the backup must work, then one can compute 1-probability that both fail for that step and compute $P(1)P(2)$.
Reliability of LCD projector $= 1 - \{(1 - 0.90)(1 - 0.80)\} = 0.98$

9. Probability of developing vaccine $= 1 - \{(1 - 0.90)(1 - 0.85)(1 - 0.70)\} = 0.9955$

Chapter 6

1. **a.** Mean of sample 1 $= (5.8 + 5.9 + 6.0 + 6.1)/4 = 5.95$
Mean of sample 2 $= (6.2 + 6.0 + 5.9 + 5.9)/4 = 6.0$
Mean of sample 3 $= (6.1 + 5.9 + 6.0 + 5.8)/4 = 5.95$
Mean of sample 4 $= (6.0 + 5.9 + 5.8 + 6.1)/4 = 5.975$

b. The mean of the sampling distribution is the average of the sample means $\bar{\bar{x}} = $ Mean $= (5.95 + 6 + 5.95 + 5.975)/4 = 5.97$
The standard deviation of the sampling distribution is computed as $\dfrac{\sigma}{\sqrt{n}}$. The population

standard deviation σ can be estimated from the 4 samples using the equation: $\sqrt{\dfrac{\sum\limits_{i=1}^{n}(x_i - \bar{x})^2}{n-1}}$,

where $n = 16$, and $\bar{X} = 5.97$; therefore the estimate is 0.1138.
The standard deviation of the sampling distribution of the sample means is equal to 0.0569 which is

estimated using $\dfrac{\sigma}{\sqrt{n}}$, where $\sigma = 0.1138$, and $n = 4$

(i.e., the number of observations in each sample).

c. Center Line (CL) $= \bar{\bar{x}} = 5.97$

$$\text{UCL} = \bar{\bar{x}} + 3\dfrac{\sigma}{\sqrt{n}} = 5.97 + 3(0.0569) = 6.14$$

$$\text{LCL} = \bar{\bar{x}} - 3\dfrac{\sigma}{\sqrt{n}} = 5.97 - 3(0.0569) = 5.80$$

3. $\bar{\bar{x}} = 19.8$ ounces, $\bar{R} = 0.4$ ounces, $A_2 = 0.58$ for $n = 5$
$\text{CL} = \bar{\bar{x}} = 19.8$
$\text{UCL} = \bar{\bar{x}} + A_2\bar{R} = 19.8 + 0.58(0.4) = 20.03$
$\text{LCL} = \bar{\bar{x}} - A_2\bar{R} = 19.8 - 0.58(0.4) = 19.57$

5. $\bar{R} = 0.3$ ounces, $D_4 = 2.11$, $D_3 = 0$, $n = 5$
$\text{CL} = \bar{R} = 0.3$ ounces
$\text{UCL} = D_4\bar{R} = 2.11(0.3) = 0.633$
$\text{LCL} = D_3\bar{R} = 0(0.3) = 0$

7. $\text{CL} = \bar{P} = \dfrac{6}{100} = 0.06$

$$\text{UCL} = 0.06 + 3\sqrt{\dfrac{0.06(1 - 0.06)}{20}} = 0.22$$

$$\text{LCL} = 0.06 - 3\sqrt{\dfrac{0.06(1 - 0.06)}{20}} = 0$$

(rounded to zero since the LCL value is negative)

9. $\text{CL} = \bar{C} = \dfrac{12}{10} = 1.20$

$\text{UCL} = 1.20 + 3\sqrt{1.20} = 4.49$
$\text{LCL} = 1.20 - 3\sqrt{1.20} = 0$

(rounded to zero since the LCL value is negative)

11. $C_P(\text{Machine A}) = \dfrac{\text{USL} - \text{LSL}}{6\sigma} = \dfrac{16.2 - 15.8}{6(0.2)}$
$= 0.33$

$C_P(\text{Machine B}) = \dfrac{\text{USL} - \text{LSL}}{6\sigma} = \dfrac{16.2 - 15.8}{6(0.3)}$
$= 0.22$

$C_P(\text{Machine C}) = \dfrac{\text{USL} - \text{LSL}}{6\sigma} = \dfrac{16.2 - 15.8}{6(0.05)}$
$= 1.33$

Machine C is the only capable machine since its C_P value is greater than 1.

13.

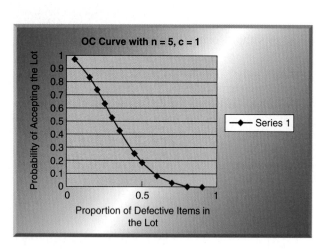

b.

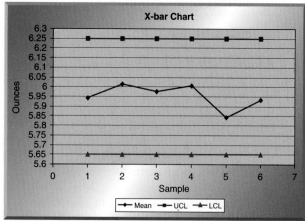

15.

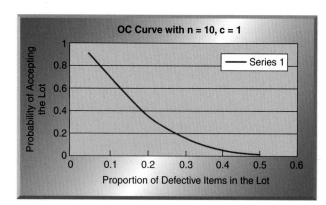

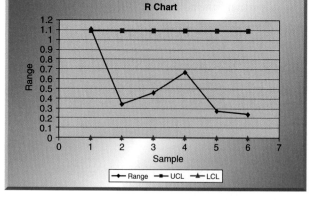

The mean is in control, but the range is not.
(Sample 1 is above the UCL)

21. $C_p = 1.39$, which appears the process is in control.
However, upon calculating the c_{pk};

$$C_{Pk} = \text{Min}\left\{\frac{10.50 - 9.80}{3(0.12)}, \frac{9.80 - 9.50}{3(0.12)}\right\}$$

$$= \text{Min}\{1.94, 0.833\} = 0.833$$

The process is not capable.

Percentage of Items Defective (p)				
0.05	0.1	0.15	0.2	0.25
0.9138	0.7361	0.5443	0.3758	0.244
0.3	0.35	0.4	0.45	0.5
0.1493	0.086	0.0464	0.0233	0.0107

17. Assuming the actual proportion of defect is 0.0022
(11 defects in the 5000) and using $n = 2000$, if
$c = 1$, the consumer's risk is 0.066. Using $c = 2$,
the consumer's risk is 0.1848.

19. a. Ranges in samples 1 through 6 are 1.11, 0.34,
0.46, 0.67, 0.27, 0.24, respectively. $\overline{R} = 0.515$.
x-bar chart: CL = 5.95
UCL = 5.95 + (0.58)(.515) = 6.25
LCL = 5.95 − (0.58)(0.515) = 5.65
R-chart: CL = 0.515
UCL = (2.11)(0.515) = 1.087
LCL = 0

Chapter 7

1. $D = 30$ packages per hour
$T = 20$ minutes = 1/3 hour
$C = 5$ packages per container
$$N = \frac{DT}{C} = \frac{(30)(1/3)}{5} = 2 \text{ Kanbans}$$

3. $D = (300 \text{ wicks/day})(1 \text{ day/5 hours})(1 \text{ hour/}$
$60 \text{ minutes}) = 1 \text{ wick/minute}$
Plus 10% safety stock = 1.1
$T = 20$ minutes
$C = 20$ per container
$N = DT/C = (1.1)(20)/20 = 1.1$ container

5. $D = (500 \text{ pounds/day})(1 \text{ day/8 hours}) =$
62.5 pounds/hour
Plus 10% safety stock $= 6.25$
$T = 1$ hour
$C = 10$ per container
$N = (62.5 + 6.25)(1)/10 = 6.875$ containers

7. $D = (300 \text{ units/hour})(1 \text{ hour/60 minutes}) =$
5 units/minute plus 10% safety stock $=$
5.5 units/minute
$T = 15$ minutes
$C = 30$ units/container
$N = \dfrac{(5.5)(15)}{30} = 2.75$ containers

9. **a.** $N = \dfrac{(5.5)(15)}{15} = 5.5$ containers

Number of containers increases. Inventory level is the same.

b. $N = \dfrac{(5.5)(15)}{40} = 2.06$

Number of containers decreases. Inventory level is the same.

c. $N = \dfrac{(6.0)15}{30} = 3.0$ containers

Both the number of containers and inventory level will increase.

Chapter 8

1. $F_4 = (A_1 + A_2 + A_3)/3 = (200 + 350 + 287)/3 = 279.0$
$F_5 = (A_2 + A_3 + A_4)/3 = (350 + 287 + 300)/3 = 312.33$

3. **a.** 3-Period Moving Average: $F_{June} = (A_{March} + A_{April} + A_{May})/3 = (38 + 39 + 43)/3 = 40$
5-Period Moving Average: $F_{June} = (A_{January} + A_{February} + A_{March} + A_{April} + A_{May})/5 = (32 + 41 + 38 + 39 + 43)/5 = 38.6$

b. Naïve: $F_{June} = A_{May} = 43$

c. 3-Period Moving Average: $F_{July} = (A_{April} + A_{May} + A_{June})/3 = (39 + 43 + 41)/3 = 41$
5-Period Moving Average: $F_{July} = (A_{February} + A_{March} + A_{April} + A_{May} + A_{June})/5 = (41 + 38 + 39 + 43 + 41)/5 = 40.4$
Naïve: $F_{July} = A_{June} = 41$

d. Assuming the June value is to be used as known:

Month	Actual	3-Period Moving Average	Absolute Error	5-Period Moving Average	Absolute Error	Naïve	Absolute Error
January	32						
February	41					32	9
March	38					41	3
April	39	37	2			38	1
May	43	39.33	3.67			39	4
June	41	40	1	38.6	2.4	43	2

$MAD \text{ (3-period moving average)} = \dfrac{\Sigma|\text{Actual} - \text{Forecast}|}{n}$
$= (2 + 3.67 + 1)/3 = 2.22$

$MAD \text{ (5-period moving average)} = \dfrac{\Sigma|\text{Actual} - \text{Forecast}|}{n}$
$= 2.4/1 = 2.4$

$MAD \text{ (Naive)} = \dfrac{\Sigma|\text{Actual} - \text{Forecast}|}{n}$
$= (9 + 3 + 1 + 4 + 2)/5$
$= 3.8$

The 3-period moving average provides the best historical fit using the *MAD* criterion and would be better to use.

e.

Month	Actual	3-Period Moving Average	Squared Error	5-Period Moving Average	Squared Error	Naïve	Squared Error
January	32						
February	41					32	81
March	38					41	9
April	39	37	4			38	1
May	43	39.33	13.47			39	16
June	41	40	1	38.6	5.76	43	4

$$MSE \text{ (3-period moving average)} = \frac{\Sigma(\text{Actual} - \text{Forecast})^2}{n}$$

$$= (4 + 13.47 + 1)/3 = 6.1567$$

$$MSE \text{ (5-period moving average)} = \frac{\Sigma(\text{Actual} - \text{Forecast})^2}{n} : 2.4.$$

$$MSE \text{ (Naive)} = \frac{\Sigma(\text{Actual} - \text{Forecast})^2}{n}$$

$$= (81 + 9 + 1 + 16 + 4)/5$$

$$= 111/5 = 22.20$$

The 5-period moving average provides the best historical fit using the *MSE* criterion, but it only measures one error term.

5. Forecasts using $\alpha = 0.1$:

Week	Demand	Exponential Smoothing	Absolute Error
1	330		
2	350	330	20
3	320	332	12
4	370	330.8	39.2
5	368	334.72	33.28
6	343	338.048	4.952
		MAD:	21.89

Forecasts using $\alpha = 0.7$:

Week	Demand	Exponential Smoothing	Absolute Error
1	330		
2	350	330	20
3	320	344	24
4	370	327.2	42.8
5	368	357.16	10.84
6	343	364.748	21.748
		MAD:	23.88

Using $\alpha = 0.1$ provides a better historical fit based on the *MAD* criterion.

7.

Week	Demand	3-Period Moving Average	Absolute Error
1	20		
2	31		
3	36		
4	38	29	9
5	42	35	7
6	40	38.67	1.33
		MAD:	5.77
		MSE:	43.92

Week	Demand	Exponential Smoothing	Absolute Error
1	20		
2	31	20	11
3	36	22.2	13.8

Week	Demand	Exponential Smoothing	Absolute Error
4	38	24.96	13.04
5	42	27.568	14.432
6	40	30.4544	9.545
		MAD:	12.36
		MSE:	156.17

Regression model: Demand = 21 + 3.857 Time

Time (X)	Demand (Y)	X^2	XY
1	20	1	20
2	31	4	62
3	36	9	108
4	38	16	152
5	42	25	210
6	40	36	240
Total: 21	207	91	792

$$\overline{X} = 21/6 = 3.5$$

$$\overline{Y} = 207/6 = 34.5$$

$$b = \frac{\Sigma XY - n\overline{X}\overline{Y}}{\Sigma X^2 - n\overline{X}^2} = \frac{792 - (6)(3.5)(34.5)}{91 - 6(3.5)^2} = 3.857$$

$$a = \overline{Y} - b\overline{X} = 34.5 - 3.857(3.5) = 21$$

Week	Demand	Regression Line	Absolute Error
1	20	24.857	4.857
2	31	28.714	2.286
3	36	32.571	3.429
4	38	36.428	1.572
5	42	40.285	1.715
6	40	44.142	4.142
		MAD:	3.00
		MSE:	10.52

The linear regression model provides the best historical fit using the *MAD* and the *MSE* criteria. The sales data has a reasonably good fit to a linear model.

9. **Step 1:** Average demand for each season:
Year 1: 2840/4 = 710
Year 2: 3241/4 = 810.25

Step 2: Seasonal index for each season:

Season	Year 1	Year 2
Fall	200/710 = 0.282	230/810.25 = 0.284
Winter	1400/710 = 1.972	1600/810.25 = 1.975
Spring	520/710 = 0.732	580/810.25 = 0.716
Summer	720/710 = 1.014	831/810.25 = 1.026

Step 3: Average seasonal index for each season:

Fall	0.283
Winter	1.973
Spring	0.724
Summer	1.020

Step 4: Average demand per season = 4000/4 = 1000.

Step 5: Multiply next year's average seasonal demand by each seasonal index.

Season	Forecast
Fall	283
Winter	1973
Spring	724
Summer	120

11. $\Sigma xy = 1978$ $\Sigma x^2 = 649$ $\Sigma y^2 = 6142$
$\Sigma x = 55$ $\Sigma y = 162$

a. The correlation coefficient is 0.9887. This high correlation indicated that there is a strong positive linear association between sales and training hours.

b. Using a regression model:
Sales = $-16.6 + 4.455$ training hours
If training hours = 18:
Sales = $-16.6 + 4.455 \times 18 = 63.59$
(in thousands)

13. $\Sigma xy = 6{,}021$ $\Sigma x^2 = 5{,}625$ $\Sigma y^2 = 7000$
$\Sigma x = 165$ $\Sigma y = 186$

a. Resort attendance = $a + b$ (average temperature)
Using regression analysis, the estimated model is:
Resort attendance = $58.65 - 0.65$ (average temperature)
Resort attendance forecast when the average temperature is 45 degrees:
= $58.65 - 0.65(45) = 29.4$ thousand attendees

b. The correlation coefficient is -0.97. Since this value is very close to negative 1, it indicates that the average temperature is a strong predictor of resort attendance. Note that since the sign is negative, it indicates that an inverse or negative relationship exists between the two variables.

15. Period 6 Forecasts:
Simple average: $F_6 = 348.8$
3-Period moving average: $F_6 = 348.33$
Exponential smoothing:
Using the fifth period forecast of 328, $F_6 = 336.40$
Looking at the error only in period 6,
MAD (simple average) = $|368 - 348.8| = 19.2$
MAD (3-Period moving average) = $|368 - 348.33| = 19.67$
MAD (exponential smoothing) = $|368 - 336.40| = 31.60$
Simple average provides the lowest MAD.

17. $\Sigma xy = 208.2$ $\Sigma x^2 = 204$ $\Sigma y^2 = 227.61$
$\Sigma x = 36$ $\Sigma y = 41.7$
Regression model:
Clinic attendance = $3.011 + 0.489$ month
$F_9 = 3.011 + 0.489(9) = 7.412$ attendees
(in thousands)

$F_{10} = 3.011 + 0.489(10) = 7.901$ attendees
(in thousands)

19. a. Forecast using a weighted moving average = $230(0.1) + 304(0.3) + 415(0.6) = 363.2$
b. Forecast using the naïve approach = 415
c. Absolute deviation using a weighted moving average = $|420 - 363.2| = 56.8$
Absolute deviation using naïve method = $|420 - 415| = 5$
The naïve approach is better.

21. $MAD_1 = (12 + 2 + 8 + 3 + 2 + 4)/6 = 31/6 = 5.17$
$MAD_2 = (3 + 1 + 2 + 2 + 4 + 3)/6 = 15/6 = 2.5$
Forecast 2 provides a better historical fit using the MAD criterion.

23. a. Sales = $243.07 + 7.424$ (month)
b. Correlation coefficient is 0.97.
It indicates a strong, positive linear relationship.
c. Forecast for month 25 = $243.07 + (7.424)25$ = 428.68 or 429 units.

Please see www.wiley.com/college/reid for solution to problem 25.

Chapter 9

1. $\text{Utilization}_{Effective} = \dfrac{\text{Actual Output}}{\text{Effective Capacity}} (100\%)$

$= \dfrac{300}{250} (100\%) = 120\%$

$\text{Utilization}_{Design} = \dfrac{\text{Actual Output}}{\text{Design Capacity}} (100\%)$

$= \dfrac{300}{400} (100\%) = 75\%$

The utilization rates show that the facility's current output is below its design capacity and considerably higher than its effective capacity. If the effective capacity is realistically set, it's expected the facility will operate over that level for a short time.

3. a. Effective capacity = 60 brownies
Design capacity = 100 brownies

b. $\text{Utilization}_{Effective} = \dfrac{\text{Actual Output}}{\text{Effective Capacity}} (100\%)$

$= \dfrac{64}{60} (100\%) = 106.67\%$

$\text{Utilization}_{Design} = \dfrac{\text{Actual Output}}{\text{Design Capacity}} (100\%)$

$= \dfrac{64}{100} (100\%) = 64\%$

The utilization rates show that the facility's current output is far below its design capacity and higher than its effective capacity. The design capacity occurs only with extra help.

5. $\text{Utilization}_{\text{Effective}} = \dfrac{\text{Actual Output}}{\text{Effective Capacity}}(100\%)$

$\qquad\qquad\quad = \dfrac{500}{600}(100\%) = 83.33\%$

$\text{Utilization}_{\text{Design}} = \dfrac{\text{Actual Output}}{\text{Design Capacity}}(100\%)$

$\qquad\qquad\quad = \dfrac{500}{1000}(100\%) = 50\%$

The computed utilization rates show that the facility's current output is below its design and effective capacities. This illustrates that the manufacturer is not using capacity to its fullest extent and there is room for improvement.

7. a.

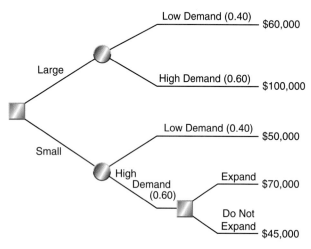

b. $\text{EV}_{\text{small expansion}} = 50{,}000(0.40) + 70{,}000(0.60)$
$\qquad\qquad\quad = \$62{,}000$
$\text{EV}_{\text{large expansion}} = 60{,}000(0.40) + 100{,}000(0.60)$
$\qquad\qquad\quad = \$84{,}000$
Company should opt for the large expansion.

9. a.

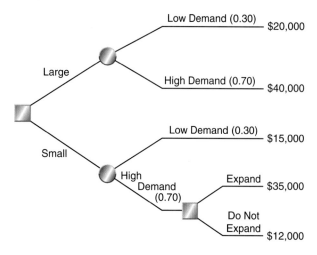

b. $\text{EV}_{\text{small expansion}} = 35{,}000(0.70) + 15{,}000(0.30)$
$\qquad\qquad\quad = \$29{,}000$
$\text{EV}_{\text{large expansion}} = 40{,}000(0.70) + 20{,}000(0.30)$
$\qquad\qquad\quad = \$34{,}000$
Company should opt for the large expansion.

11. a.

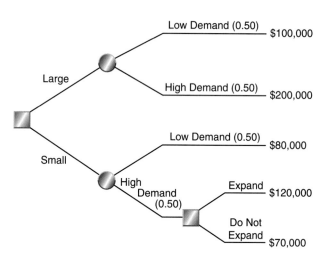

b. $\text{EV}_{\text{small expansion}} = 120{,}000(0.50) + 80{,}000(0.50)$
$\qquad\qquad\quad = \$100{,}000$
$\text{EV}_{\text{large expansion}} = 200{,}000(0.50) + 100{,}000(0.50)$
$\qquad\qquad\quad = \$150{,}000$
Company should opt for the large expansion.

13.

	Weighted Score	
	Location 1	**Location 2**
	50	20
	80	40
	60	150
	50	30
	90	150
Total:	330	390

Location 2 is the preferred one.

15. $\text{Load-Distance Score}_{\text{Jasper}} = \Sigma l_{ij}d_{ij} = (30)(15) + (6)(10) + (10.5)(12) + (4.5)(8) = 672$
$\text{Load-Distance Score}_{\text{Longboat}} = \Sigma l_{ij}d_{ij} = (12)(15) + (12)(10) + (30)(12) + (24)(8) = 852$
Warehouse should be located in Jasper.

17. $\text{Total Cost}_A = 70{,}000 + 1(2000) = \$72{,}000$
$\text{Total Cost}_B = 34{,}000 + 5(2000) = \$44{,}000$
$\text{Total Cost}_C = 20{,}000 + 8(2000) = \$36{,}000$
$\text{Total Cost}_D = 50{,}000 + 4(2000) = \$58{,}000$
Location C is best.

Chapter 10

1.

Departments	Number of Trips (l)	Current Layout Distance (d)	Current Layout Load-Distance Score (ld)	Proposed Layout Distance (d)	Proposed Layout Load-Distance Score (ld)
AB	15	1	15	2	30
AC	45	2	90	1	45
AD	25	1	25	2	50
AE	10	2	20	1	10
AF	50	3	150	3	150
BC	30	1	30	1	30
BD	16	2	32	2	32
BE	25	1	25	1	25
BF	25	2	50	1	25
CD	34	3	102	3	102
CE	15	2	30	2	30
CF	20	1	20	2	40
DE	40	1	40	1	40
DF	10	2	20	1	10
EF	20	1	20	2	40
		Total:	669		659

The proposed layout is the preferred one due to a slightly lower ld score.

3.

Departments	Number of Trips (l)	Current Layout Distance (d)	Current Layout Load-Distance Score (ld)	Proposed Layout Distance (d)	Proposed Layout Load-Distance Score (ld)
AB	5	1	5	1	5
AC	20	2	40	2	40
AD	5	1	5	1	5
AF	8	2	16	2	16
BD	30	2	60	2	60
BE	10	2	20	2	20
BF	10	3	30	1	10
CD	20	3	60	1	20
CE	15	1	15	1	15
CF	5	2	10	2	10
EF	17	1	17	1	17
		Total:	278		218

Proposed location is better based on the ld score.

5.

Departments	Number of Trips (l)	Current Layout Distance (d)	Current Layout Load-Distance Score (ld)	Proposed Layout Distance (d)	Proposed Layout Load-Distance Score (ld)
AB	30	3	90	3	90
AD	34	1	34	1	34
AE	50	1	50	2	100
AF	25	2	50	1	25
BD	55	2	110	2	110
BE	10	2	20	1	10
BF	10	1	10	2	20
CE	15	1	15	2	30
CF	5	2	10	3	15
EF	30	1	30	1	30
		Total:	419		464

The current location is better based on the ld score.

7. To assign departments to specific storage areas, we progressively assign departments with the highest number of trips closest to the dock. Using this logic, the following block plan is developed:

	2	4	5
Dock			
	6	1	3

---

9. It is reasonable to assume the layout can be improved. A starting point would have D directly next to F, B, and A.

Departments	Number of Trips (*l*)	Current Layout Distance (*d*)	Current Layout Load-Distance Score (*ld*)	Departments	Number of Trips (*l*)	Current Layout Distance (*d*)	Current Layout Load-Distance Score (*ld*)
AB	6	1	6	BF	0	2	0
AC	12	2	24	CD	5	3	15
AD	18	1	18	CE	0	2	0
AE	1	2	2	CF	0	1	0
AF	1	3	3	DE	7	1	7
BC	4	1	4	DF	19	2	38
BD	19	2	38	EF	0	1	0
BE	3	1	3			Total:	158

---

11. The following departments have the highest number of trips between them and should be located close to each other.

B and D, which have 19 trips between them
D and F, which have 19 trips between them
A and D, which have 18 trips between them
A and C, which have 12 trips between them

Proposed layout:

B	D	A
E	F	C

A slightly better layout exists.

	Proposed layout	
Departments	Distance (*d*)	Load-Distance Score (*ld*)
AB	2	12
AC	1	12
AD	1	18
AE	3	3
AF	2	2
BC	3	12
BD	1	19
BE	1	3
BF	2	0
CD	2	10
CE	2	0
CF	1	0
DE	2	14
DF	1	19
EF	1	0
Total:		124

13. a.

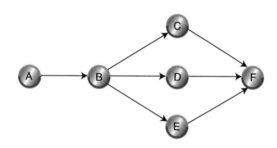

b. $C = (3600 \text{ seconds/hour})/(50 \text{ units/hour})$
$= 72$ seconds/unit

c. $\text{TM} = \dfrac{\Sigma t}{C} = \dfrac{225}{72} = 3.125$ or 4 stations

d.

Station	Task
1	A
2	B, E
3	D
4	C
5	F

e. Efficiency $= \dfrac{\Sigma t}{NC}(100\%) = \dfrac{225}{(5)(72)}(100\%)$
$= 62.5\%$
Balance delay (%) $= 37.5\%$

15. a. Task *A* is the bottleneck.
b. $C = (3600 \text{ seconds/hour})/(50 \text{ units/hour})$
$= 72$ seconds/unit

c.

Work Station	Task Selected	Task Time	Idle Time
1	A	55	17
2	B	30	42
	C	22	20
	F	15	5
3	D	35	37
4	E	50	22
	G	5	17
	H	10	7

d. $\text{TM} = \dfrac{\Sigma t}{C} = \dfrac{222}{72} = 3.08$ or 4 stations

Same number of stations as the theoretical minimum stations was used.

e. Efficiency $= \dfrac{\Sigma t}{NC}(100\%) = \dfrac{222}{(4)(72)}(100\%)$
$= 77.08\%$
Balance delay (%) $= 22.92\%$

17. a. $C = (3600 \text{ seconds/hour})/(30 \text{ units/hour})$
$= 120 \text{ seconds/unit}$

b. $\text{TM} = \dfrac{\Sigma t}{C} = \dfrac{270}{120} = 2.25$ or 3 stations

c.

Work Station	Task Selected
1	A
	B
	D
	F
	C
2	E
	G
	H
	I
3	J
	K

Work station 1 has no idle time, while work stations 2 and 3 have 20 seconds and 70 seconds, respectively.

d. Efficiency $= \dfrac{\Sigma t}{NC}(100\%)$

$= \dfrac{270}{(3)(120)}(100\%) = 75\%$

Balance delay $= 25\%$

19. a. $C = 480 \text{ doors}/8 \text{ hours} = 60 \text{ doors/hour}$;
$(3600 \text{ sec/hour}/60 \text{ doors/hour}) = 60 \text{ sec/door}$.

b. $\text{TM} = 175/60 = 2.9$ or 3 workstations

Work Station	Task Selected
1	A
2	B
3	C, D, E
4	F, G, H

Efficiency $= 175/240 = 72.9\%$

c. Maximum output would use the bottleneck task:
$(3600 \text{ seconds/hour})/(43 \text{ seconds/unit}) = 83.7 \text{ units per hour}$
Minimum output uses the total time in one workstation: $3600/175 = 20.57$ units per hour

Chapter 11

1. With $z = 2.17$ and $e = 0.05$, the number of observations needed for each work element is:

Work element 1: $n \geq \left[\dfrac{2.17}{0.05} \times \dfrac{0.20}{1.10}\right]^2 = 63$

Work element 2: $n \geq \left[\dfrac{2.17}{0.05} \times \dfrac{0.10}{0.80}\right]^2 = 30$

Work element 3: $n \geq \left[\dfrac{2.17}{0.05} \times \dfrac{0.15}{0.90}\right]^2 = 53$

Work element 4: $n \geq \left[\dfrac{2.17}{0.05} \times \dfrac{0.10}{1.00}\right]^2 = 19$

Sample size needed is 63.

3. Work element 1: $n \geq \left[\dfrac{1.96}{0.05} \times \dfrac{0.60}{2.40}\right]^2 = 97$

Work element 2: $n \geq \left[\dfrac{1.96}{0.05} \times \dfrac{0.20}{1.50}\right]^2 = 28$

Work element 3: $n \geq \left[\dfrac{1.96}{0.05} \times \dfrac{1.10}{3.85}\right]^2 = 126$

Work element 4: $n \geq \left[\dfrac{1.96}{0.05} \times \dfrac{0/85}{2.55}\right]^2 = 171$

Work element 5: $n \geq \left[\dfrac{1.96}{0.05} \times \dfrac{0.40}{1.60}\right]^2 = 97$

Work element 6: $n \geq \left[\dfrac{1.96}{0.05} \times \dfrac{0.50}{2.50}\right]^2 = 62$

Sample size needed is 171.

5.

Work Element	Normal Time (NT)
1	1.14
2	0.85
3	0.88
4	0.99

7. From Problem 6, the sum of the standard times is 4.439 minutes $(1.311 + 0.9775 + 1.012 + 1.1385)$. $(1 \text{ unit}/4.44 \text{ minutes}) \times (60 \text{ minutes/hour}) \times (8 \text{ hours/day}) = 108.1 \text{ units/day}$

9. From Problem 8, the sum of the standard times is 4.541 minutes $(1.341 + 1.000 + 1.035 + 1.165)$. $(1 \text{ unit}/4.541 \text{ minutes}) \times 60 \text{ minutes/hour} \times (8 \text{ hours/day}) = 105.7 \text{ units/day}$

11. a.

Element	Mean Observed Time
1	2.194
2	1.265
3	1.771
4	2.608
5	1.576

b. Normal time = (mean observed time) (performance rating factor)(frequency)
Normal time$_{\text{element 1}}$ = $(2.194)(0.90)(1)$ = 1.975 minutes
Normal time$_{\text{element 2}}$ = $(1.265)(0.80)(1)$ = 1.012 minutes
Normal time$_{\text{element 3}}$ = $(1.771)(1.10)(1)$ = 1.948 minutes
Normal time$_{\text{element 4}}$ = $(2.608)(1.05)(1)$ = 2.738 minutes
Normal time$_{\text{element 5}}$ = $(1.576)(0.95)(1)$ = 1.497 minutes

c. ST$_{\text{element 1}}$ = $(1.975)(1.20)$ = 2.370 minutes
ST$_{\text{element 2}}$ = $(1.012)(1.20)$ = 1.214 minutes
ST$_{\text{element 3}}$ = $(1.948)(1.20)$ = 2.338 minutes
ST$_{\text{element 4}}$ = $(2.738)(1.20)$ = 3.286 minutes
ST$_{\text{element 5}}$ = $(1.497)(1.20)$ = 1.796 minutes
Standard time for Job = $(2.37 + 1.214 + 2.338 + 3.286 + 1.796)$ = 11.004 minutes

d. $(60 \text{ minutes/hour})(1 \text{ unit}/11.004 \text{ minutes})$ = 5.45 units/hour

e. $(5.45 \text{ units/hour})(0.90)$ = 4.9 units/hour

13. a. b.

Element	Mean Time (minutes)	Normal Time	Standard Time
1	0.96	0.9216	1.084
2	1.45	1.595	1.876
3	3.33	1.110	1.306
4	1.24	1.116	1.313
5	1.18	1.239	1.458

Sum = 7.037 minutes

c. $60 \text{ minutes}/7.037$ = 8.526 units per hour

d. 8.526×0.90 = 7.6734 units per hour

15. a.

Element	Mean Observed Time (minutes)
1	0.582
2	1.515
3	0.759
4	0.319
5	2.1

b. Normal time$_{\text{element 1}}$ = $(0.582)(0.95)(1)$ = 0.553 minutes
Normal time$_{\text{element 2}}$ = $(1.515)(0.90)(0.25)$ = 0.341 minutes
Normal time$_{\text{element 3}}$ = $(0.759)(1)(1)$ = 0.759 minutes
Normal time$_{\text{element 4}}$ = $(0.319)(1.10)(1)$ = 0.351 minutes
Normal time$_{\text{element 5}}$ = $(2.10)(0.90)(0.20)$ = 0.378 minutes

c. ST$_{\text{element 1}}$ = $(0.553)(1.15)$ = 0.636 minutes
ST$_{\text{element 2}}$ = $(0.341)(1.15)$ = 0.392 minutes
ST$_{\text{element 3}}$ = $(0.759)(1.15)$ = 0.873 minutes
ST$_{\text{element 4}}$ = $(0.351)(1.15)$ = 0.404 minutes
ST$_{\text{element 5}}$ = $(0.378)(1.15)$ = 0.435 minutes
Standard time for job = $(0.636 + 0.392 + 0.873 + 0.404 + 0.435)$ = 2.740 minutes

d. $60/2.740$ = 21.898 units per hour

e. 21.898×1.1 = 24.088

17. a. $n = \left(\dfrac{1.96}{0.05}\right)^2 (0.2)(1 - 0.2) = 246$ observations

b. $n = \left(\dfrac{1.96}{0.05}\right)^2 (0.15)(1 - 0.15) = 196$ observations

c. The largest observed frequency was 6 (with patient)
$$n = \left(\dfrac{1.96}{0.05}\right)^2 (0.3)(1 - 0.3) = 323 \text{ observations}$$

19. T = 40 minutes, n = 6, total learning curve coefficient = 4.299. Total time = $40(4.299)$ = 171.96 minutes, or 2.87 hours.

Chapter 12

1. $\text{ATI}_{\text{regular service}} = \dfrac{(3)(2400)}{365} = 19.7 \text{ units}$

$\text{ATI}_{\text{premium service}} = \dfrac{(1)(2400)}{365} = 6.6 \text{ units}$

$\text{ATI}_{\text{public cararier}} = \dfrac{(7)(2400)}{365} = 46.0 \text{ units}$

3. a. Inventory Turnover $= \dfrac{\$3,000,000}{\$250,000} = 12$

b. Weeks of Supply $= \dfrac{\$250,000}{\dfrac{\$3,000,000}{52}} = 4.33$ weeks

c. Days of Supply $= \dfrac{\$250,000}{\dfrac{\$3,000,000}{260}} = 21.7$ days

5. Inventory Turnover $= \$3,600,000/\$325,000$
$= 11.1$ inventory turns

7. Annual holding cost $= (0.225)(\$3,400,00)$
$= \$765,000$
Annual holding cost increases $\$68,000$ or 9.76%

9. a. Average inventory level $= \dfrac{Q}{2} = \dfrac{1300}{2}$
$= 650$ units

b. Number of orders placed per year (N)
$= \dfrac{D}{Q} = \dfrac{5200}{1300}$
$= 4$ orders

c. Annual inventory holding cost
$= \dfrac{Q}{2}H = (650)(3)$
$= \$1950$

d. Total annual ordering cost $= (D/Q)(S)$
$= (4)(50) = \$200$

e. Total annual cost $= \$1950 + \$200 = \$2150$
(not counting the cost of the heat sinks, which is $\$62,400$)

11. a. EOQ $= \sqrt{\dfrac{2DS}{H}} = \sqrt{\dfrac{(2)(5200)(50)}{3}}$
$= 416.33$ units

b. Average inventory $= \dfrac{416.33}{2} = 208.2$ units

c. Number of orders placed per year $= \dfrac{D}{Q}$
$= \dfrac{5200}{416.33}$
$= 12.5$

d. Annual ordering cost $= (12.5)(50) = \$625$

e. Annual inventory holding cost
$= \dfrac{Q}{2}H = (208.2)(3)$
$= \$624.50$

f. Total annual cost $= \$624.50 + \$624 = \$1249.50$

g. The economic order quantity provides the lowest total annual costs.

13. EOQ at price of $\$18$/bag $= \sqrt{\dfrac{(2)(1560))(10)}{(18)(0.25)}} =$
83.3 bags (infeasible quantity)

EOQ at price of $\$19$/bag $= \sqrt{\dfrac{(2)(1560)(10)}{(19)(0.25)}} =$
81.0 bags (feasible quantity)
Total cost at feasible EOQ amount $= (81/2)(19 \times 0.25) + (1560/81)(10) + (19)(1560) = \$30024.97$
Total cost at $Q = 100$: $(100/2)(18 \times 0.25) + (1560/100)(10) + (18)(1560) = \$28461$
Optimal ordering policy is to order 100 bags at a time.

15. EOQ at price break of $\$12$/bag
$= \sqrt{\dfrac{(2)(1560)(10)}{(12.00)(0.25)}} = 101.98$
(not a feasible quantity at the given price break)
Total cost at $Q = 1560$ bags:
$= (1560/2)(12 \times 0.25) + (1560/1560)(10) + (12)(1560)$
$= \$21,070$
Greens should take advantage of this offer.

17. a. EOQ $= \sqrt{\dfrac{2\,DS}{H}}$
$= \sqrt{\dfrac{(2)(150 \times 52)(20)}{3}} = 322.5$ units

b. Total annual costs $= \dfrac{Q}{2}H + \dfrac{D}{Q}S$
$= \dfrac{(322.5)}{2}(3) + \dfrac{(150 \times 52)}{322.5}(20) = \$967.50$

c. Lost annual savings $= \$1215 - \$967.5$
$= \$247.50$

19.

		Demand (000's)					Expected
		75	80	85	90	95	Profit (000's)
	75	596.25	596.25	596.25	596.25	596.25	596.250
Order	80	573.75	636	636	636	636	632.888
Amount	85	551.25	613.5	675.75	675.75	675.75	657.075
(000's)	90	528.75	591	653.25	715.5	715.5	665.700
	95	506.25	568.5	630.75	693.00	755.25	655.650

Sue should order 90,000 calendars to maximize expected profits.

21. a.

Item	Annual Demand	Ordering Cost	Holding Cost (%)	Unit Price	EOQ
101	500	$ 10.00	20%	$ 0.50	316.228
102	1500	$ 10.00	30%	$ 0.20	707.1068
103	5000	$ 25.00	30%	$ 1.00	912.8709
104	250	$ 15.00	25%	$ 4.50	81.6497
105	1500	$ 35.00	35%	$ 1.20	500
201	10000	$ 25.00	15%	$ 0.75	2108.185
202	1000	$ 10.00	20%	$ 1.35	272.1655
203	1500	$ 20.00	25%	$ 0.20	1095.445
204	500	$ 40.00	25%	$ 0.80	447.2136
205	100	$ 10.00	15%	$ 2.50	73.0397

Rounded EOQ results.

Item	101	102	103	104	105	201	202	203	204	205
EOQ	316	707	913	82	500	2108	272	1095	447	73
Product Cost	158	141.48	913	369	600	1581	367.20	219	357.60	183.5

b. Using the EOQ number times the unit cost, the company's maximum inventory investment throughout the year occurs for item 201 with an inventory level of 2108 units and value of $1581.14.

c.

Item	EOQ	Average Inventory
101	316	158
102	707	353.5
103	913	456.5
104	82	41
105	500	250
201	2108	1054
202	272	136
203	1095	547.5
204	447	223.5
205	73	36.5

Average inventory in dollars = $2444.35

23. a. $I_{max} = Q(1 - d/p) = 1,000,000(1 - 100,000/250,000) = 600,000$ pounds

b. Total Cost $= \dfrac{(5,000,000)(200)}{1,000,000} +$
$\dfrac{(600,000)(0.55/50)}{2} = \$4300$

25. a. Setup Cost: Number of setups = Yearly demand/2500 bags per batch
$= (75,000 \times 12/50)/2500 = 7.2$ batches per year
$7.2 \times \$300 = \$2160$
$I_{max} = 2500(1 - .75) = 625$
Average inventory = 312.5 units
Total cost of existing policy is $3097.50

b. EPQ $= \sqrt{\dfrac{2 \times 18000 \times 300}{3\left(1 - \dfrac{18000}{24000}\right)}}$
$= 3794.73$, or 3795
$I_{max} = 3795(1 - .75) = 948.75$, or 949
Holding Cost $= (949/2) \times 3 = \$1423.50$
Setup Cost $= 18,000 \times 300/3795 = \$1422.92$
Total Cost $= \$2846.42$

c. Penalty Cost$= \$3097.50 - \$2846.42 = \$251.08$

27. a. The z for 94% is found to be approximately 1.55 (the area above it is the risk of stock outs).
Safety stock $= 1.55\,[\sigma\sqrt{RP + L}]$
$= 21.48$, or 22 units
$TI = d(RP + L) + SS = 48(3) + 22 = 166$ units

b. Z becomes 2.05, safety stock becomes 28.4 or 29, and the target inventory becomes 173.

c. Safety stock $= 1.55\,[\sigma\sqrt{RP + L}] = 24.8$, or 25
Target inventory becomes $192 + 25 = 217$ units

29. a. Current Total Cost at $Q = 5,000 = 4.8(60) + 2500(.08) = \$488$ per month
EOQ $= 6,000$ per month: Total Cost $= 4(60) + 3,000(.08) = \$480$
The penalty cost of the existing system is $8 per month.

b. With $Q = 3000$, holding costs are reduced to $120. To keep the total cost at $480, the order costs would be $360. Solving $8(S) = \$360$, order costs would have to be reduced to $45 to stay at the same expense as the EOQ.

c. If $S = \$30$, the EOQ becomes 4,242.6 jars

Chapter 13

1. a. Total aggregate production $= \sum_{i=1}^{6} demand_i = 34{,}000$ units

Production rate per period $= (34000 - 400)/6 = 5600$ units

b. (5600 units $\times$ 6 hours each)/160 hours per employee $= 210$ employees

c.

Period		1	2	3	4	5	6
Demand		6000	4800	7840	5200	6560	3600
Production		5600	5600	5600	5600	5600	5600
Ending Inventory	400		800				0
Back order		0		1440	1040	2000	0

d. Back order costs: 4480 units $\times$ \$20 $=$ \$89,600
Holding costs: 800 units $\times$ \$10 $=$ \$8000
Regular-time labor cost: \$2,016,000
Total cost $=$ \$2,113,600

e. The costs appear very high, considering the customer is served very poorly. However, the level aggregate plan is good for operations and human resources.

3.

Period	1	2	3	4	5	6	Total
Employees Needed	210	180	294	195	246	135	1260

5. a. The amount of production hours needed each period:

Period	1	2	3	4	5	6
Hours Needed	33,600	28,800	47,040	31,200	39,360	21,600

5. b. Amount of regular-time production using a workforce of 210 employees: (160 hours/employee/period)(210 employees) $=$ 33,600 hours/period

5. c. Using the hours required and the hours available from parts a and b:

Period	1	2	3	4	5	6	Total
Overtime Hours Needed	0	0	13,440	0	5,760	0	19,200
Undertime	0	4800		2400		12,000	19,200

5. d.

Period	1	2	3	4	5	6
Overtime hours per Employee			64		27.42	

The overtime available hours are exceeded by 100%.

5. e. Overtime cost: 19,200 $\times$ \$15 $=$ \$288,000
Regular labor cost: \$2,016,000
Total cost: \$2,304,000

5. f. The customer demand is being met, but costs are \$81,000 over the costs of the hiring and firing plan in problem 3. Once again, this chase plan is disruptive to operations and to human resources. Certainly, if this plan is implemented, arrangements must be made to increase available overtime.

7. a. Given the production rate i.e. 1/6 unit per hour (from 6 hours per unit), the production from the maximum of 32 hours of overtime for each of the 210 employees is computed to be 1120 units.

Period		1	2	3	4	5	6	Total
Demand		6000	4800	7840	5200	6560	3600	34,000
Production		5600	5600	5600	5600	5600	3600	
Overtime Units		0	0	1120	0	880	0	2000
Ending Inventory	400	0	800	0	80	0	0	880
Back Orders		0	0	320	0	0	0	320

b. Overtime cost: 12,000 hours $\times$ \$15 $=$ \$180,000
Back order costs: 320 $\times$ \$20 $=$ \$6400
Holding costs: 880 $\times$ \$10 $=$ \$8800
Regular labor cost: \$2,016,000
Total cost $=$ \$2,211,200

c. This hybrid aggregate plan provides some back orders, but only in period 3. Overtime costs are still a significant amount at \$180,000 but this expense is far less than using only overtime to meet demand. This plan fits the existing available overtime hours and should therefore not be too disruptive to operations.

9. a. Assuming no overtime and using 13 employees (from Problem 8):

Average weekly demand = 43.33 clients
Average hourly demand = 43.33 × 12 = 520 hours
Available time = 13 × 40 = 520

Period	1	2	3	4	5	6
Number of Clients	48	36	50	40	38	48
Hours Required	576	432	600	480	456	576
Backorders Carried Forward		56		80	40	
Total Hours Required	576	488	600	560	496	576
Regular Hours Available	520	520	520	520	520	520
Back Orders (hours)	56	0	80	40	0	56

b. Total cost = hiring cost (from Problem 8) + regular-time labor cost
Total cost = (1 employee)($2000/employee) + (3120 hours)($25/hour) = $80,000
Note that this total cost does not incorporate any consequences of the unmet hours.

c. This plan provides a uniform availability of weekly hours. However, in weeks 1, 3, 4, and 6 there are unmet client hours. If the clients are unwilling to wait for their services, this could result in potential revenue loss to the firm. Also, there are excess service hours in weeks 2 and 5, which cannot be inventoried.

11. a.

Period	1	2	3	4	5	6	Total
Number of Clients	48	36	50	40	38	48	260
Hours Required	576	432	600	480	456	576	
Number of Employees Required	12	9	12.5	10	9.5	12	
Actual Number of Employees	12	9	13	10	10	12	66
Number of Hires (beginning with 12)	0	0	4	0	0	2	6
Number of Fires	0	3	0	3	0	0	6
Overtime Hours Required	96	72	80	80	56	96	480

b. Hiring cost: 6 × $2000 = $12,000
Firing cost: 6 × $1200 = $7200
Regular hours: 66 × 40 × $25 = $66,000
Overtime hours: 480 × $37.50 = $18,000
Total cost: $103,200

c. Customer demand is met at a cost of $103,200. The hiring and firing would be very difficult for operations and for the employees.

13. a. Hours Available 12 × 40 = 480

Week	1	2	3	4	5	6	Total
Number of Clients	48	36	50	40	38	48	260
Hours Required	576	432	600	480	456	576	
Hours Available	480	480	480	480	480	480	
Unmet Hours	96	0	120	0	0	96	
Number of Temporary Employees	3	0	3	0	0	3	9

b. 9 employees = 360 hours @$40/hour
    = $14,400
12 permanent employees = 480 hours × 6 × $25 = $72,000
Total Cost = $86,400

c. Customer demand is met at a lower price than hiring and firing permanent employees. This plan is very good for the permanent employees with minimal operational issues if the temporary employees are readily available.

15. a. and b.

Week	1	2	3	4	5	6
Forecast	20	35	50	50	45	40
Proj Avail 15	67	32	54	4	31	63
MPS	72		72		72	72

c. 67 units in week 1.
d. 4 MPS orders are needed.

17. a. and b.

Week	1	2	3	4	5	6
Forecast	20	35	50	50	45	40
Proj Avail 15	43	8	6	4	7	15
MPS	48		48	48	48	48

c. This plan provides a high set up cost (5 of 6 periods) but a low average inventory per period (13.8 units)

19.

Standard Corkscrew	Week			
	1	2	3	4
MPS	4000	4000	4000	2000
Direct Labor (hours)	800	800	800	400
Machine Time (hours)	400	400	400	200

Deluxe Corkscrew	Week			
	1	2	3	4
MPS	1000	1000	1000	3000
Direct Labor (hours)	500	500	500	1500
Machine Time (hours)	300	300	300	900

Total capacity needed:

Period	Week			
	1	2	3	4
Direct Labor (hours)	1300	1300	1300	1900
Machine Time (hours)	700	700	700	1100

21. a. Department 101:

Period	1	2	3	4
Direct Labor (hours)	520	520	520	760
Machine Time (hours)	420	420	420	660

b. Department 102:

Period	1	2	3	4
Direct Labor (hours)	780	780	780	1140
Machine Time (hours)	280	280	280	440

23. From the answer to Problem 22, period 1 only has 15 units available so we reject order 2. Order 1 is accepted since we have 47 available to promise. The new ATP would be 37 units. Accept order 3, change ATP to 48. Accept order 4, reduce ATP in period 5 to 28.

25. a.

Period	1	2	3	4	Total
Demand (net) units	11000	6000	3000	16000	36000
Production (units)	9000	9000	9000	9000	36000
Subcontract (units)	2000	—	—	—	2000
Number of workers needed	180	180	180	180	720
Hires	30	—	—	—	30
Fires	—	—	—	—	—
Inventory (units)	—	3000	9000	2000	14000

Hiring cost: $30 \times 500 = \$15,000$
Regular production cost: $36000 \times 400 = \$14,400,000$
Subcontract cost: $2000 \times 650 = \$1,300,000$
Inventory holding cost: $14000 \times 100 = \$1,400,000$
Total cost: $17,115,000

b. Customer service is good because there are no backorders. This plan is good for operations and human services as well. But this cost may not be the minimum.

27. a.

Period	1	2	3	4	Total
Demand (net) units	11000	6000	3000	16000	36000
Production (RT) units	7500	7500	7500	7500	30000
Production (OT) units	1500	—	—	1500	3000
Subcontract units	2000	—	—	1000	3000
Number of workers	150	150	150	150	600
Number of Hires	0	0	0	0	0
Number of Fires	0	0	0	0	0
Inventory	0	1500	6000	0	7500

Regular production cost: $30,000 \times 400 = \$12,000,000$.
Overtime production cost: $3,000 \times 600 = 1,800,000$.
Subcontracting cost: $3,000 \times 650 = 1,950,000$.
Holding cost: $750,000
Total cost: $16,500,000

b. This plan is good for customer service because of no back-orders. It is also good for operations and human resources because of level workforce although overtime is planned in periods 1 and 4. It is great for finance because of the low cost.

c. While the total cost exceeds the pure chase strategy in problem 26, this hybrid plan is overall better for operations and human resources. This plan does have a lower total cost than the level production plan (by $615,000).

Chapter 14

1.

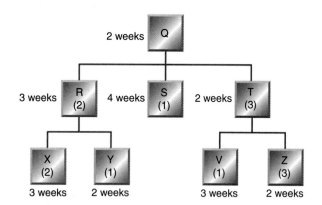

Note: numbers inside parentheses represent usage per parent while numbers outside the boxes indicate lead time in weeks.

3.

Product	Q	R	S	T	X	Y	V	Z
Gross Requirements	100	200	100	300	400	200	300	900

5. From Problem 4: The cumulative lead time is 7 weeks (VTQ).

7. From Problem 6: The cumulative lead time, the longest planned length of time to complete the end product is 11 weeks (i.e., path J, E, A).

9.

Component	Gross Requirement
A	2500
B	4750
C	2000
D	6750
E	4250
F	16,000
G	8500
H	15,250
I	8500
J	3250
K	16,250
L	6000
M	47,750
N	95,750
O	30,500
P	15,750
Q	31,500

11. Product: AB500

Week	1	2	3	4	5	6	7	8	9	10
Gross Requirements			150	250	150	250	150	250	150	250
Scheduled Receipts			150	250	150	250	150	250	150	250
Projected Available: 0	0	0	0	0	0	0	0	0	0	0
Planned Orders	150	250	150	250	150	250	150	250		

13. From the inventory records in Problem 12:
Average Inventory for AB501 = 1100/10 = 110 units
Average Inventory for AB511 = 1350/10 = 135 units (Assuming the remaining inventory after the gross requirements are satisfied, is used in the next production cycle.)
Average Inventory for AB521 = 4350/10 = 435 units

15.

Item: AB500	1	2	3	4	5	6	7	8	9	10
Gross Requirements			150	250	150	250	150	250	150	250
Scheduled Receipts			200	200	200	200	200	200	200	200
Projected Available	0	0	50	0	50	0	50	0	50	0
Planned Orders	200	200	200	200	200	200	200	200		

17.

Item: AB500	1	2	3	4	5	6	7	8	9	10
Gross Requirements			150	250	150	250	150	250	150	250
Scheduled Receipts			550			650			400	
Projected Available: 0	0	0	400	150	0	400	250	0	250	0
Planned Orders	550			650			400			

19.

Orders	Setup + Run Time (hours)
LL110	2.0 + 1.2(10) = 14
LL118	4.0 + .4(25) = 14
LL131	6.0 + .6(100) = 66
LL140	4.0 + .2(50) = 14

Total time: 108 hours
Capacity needed: 108 hours

21. From the capacity requirement of 108 hours in Problem 19 (and detail from Problem 20): Available weekly capacity = (3 machines)(10 hours/day)

(5 days/week)(0.90 utilization)(0.90 efficiency) = 121.5 hours
This new policy provides adequate capacity.

23.

Orders	Setup + Run Time (hours)
MM078	34
MM118	31
MM213	33
MM240	58

Total time: 156 hours
Capacity needed: 156 hours

25. The 150 Gamma Blasters need a planned order for period 7. The 100 Gamma Disasters need a planned order in period 4

Component A:

Period	1	2	3	4	5	6	7	8
Gross requirements				300			300	
Scheduled Receipts				200			200	
Projected Available 250	250	250	250	150	150	150	50	50
Planned Orders				200				

Component B:

Period	1	2	3	4	5	6	7	8
Gross requirements				200			450	
Scheduled Receipts				300			600	
Projected Available 25	25	25	25	125	125	125	275	275
Planned Orders			300		600			

Chapter 15

1. a. Workcenter 3

	4	5	6	7	8
Planned Input	40	50	50	60	60
Actual Input	45	45	45	55	60
Deviation	5	-5	-5	-5	0
Cumulative Deviation	5	0	-5	-10	-10

	4	5	6	7	8
Planned Output	70	70	70	70	70
Actual Output	60	60	60	60	60
Deviation	-10	-10	-10	-10	-10
Cumulative Deviation	-10	-20	-30	-40	-50
Backlog 75 hours	60	45	30	25	25

b. If actual output is consistently below planned output, Workcenter 3 may not have enough capacity to meet the planned input for Workcenter 4. However, the backlog is consistently decreasing in Workcenter 3, as their actual output exceeds the actual inputs in periods 4 through 7.

3. a. Workcenter 2

	4	5	6	7	8
Planned Input	40	50	50	60	60
Actual Input	25	35	35	40	40
Deviation	-15	-15	-15	-20	-20
Cumulative Deviation	-15	-30	-45	-65	-85

	4	5	6	7	8
Planned Output	40	50	50	60	60
Actual Output	45	45	45	55	60
Deviation	5	-5	-5	-5	0
Cumulative Deviation	5	0	-5	-10	-10
Backlog 75 hours	55	45	35	20	0

b. The workcenter nearly has the capacity to meet planned input if backlogs did not exist. Actual output is consistently less than the planned output especially in periods 5, 6, and 7, thus indicating that the workcenter is not producing with the efficiency expected. Workcenter 1 has to be studied regarding its output.

5. a. Job sequence: B, F, E, C, A, D

b.

B done at end of day 5	F done at end of day 11	E done at end of day 18	C done at end of day 26	A done at end of day 35	D done at end of day 45

Makespan = 45 days
Mean job flow time = (5 + 11 + 18 + 26 + 35 + 45)/6 = 23.33 days
Average number of jobs in the system = 140/45 = 3.11 jobs

Job	Completion Date	Due Date	Lateness (days)	Tardiness
B	5	10	−5	0
F	11	15	−4	0
E	18	26	−8	0
C	26	24	2	2
A	35	30	5	5
D	45	40	5	5
			Total = −5	Total = 12

Mean job lateness = −5/6 = −0.83 days
Mean job tardiness = 12/6 = 2.0 days
Maximum tardiness = 5 days

7. a.

D done at end of day 10	A done at end of day 19	C done at end of day 27	E done at end of day 34	F done at end of day 40	B done at end of day 45

b. Makespan = 45 days
Mean job flow time = (10 + 19 + 27 + 34 + 40 + 45)/6 = 29.17 days
Average number of jobs in the system = 175/45 = 3.89 jobs

Job	Completion Date	Due Date	Lateness (days)	Tardiness
D	10	40	−30	0
A	19	30	−11	0
C	27	24	3	3
E	34	26	8	8
F	40	15	25	25
B	45	10	35	35
			Total = 30	Total = 71

Mean job lateness = 30/6 = 5 days
Mean job tardiness = 71/6 = 11.83 days
Maximum tardiness = 35 days

9. a.

Job	Job Time	Remaining Job Time at Other w/c	Due Date	Slack Times	Remaining Number of Operations at Other w/c	S/RO
A	9	10	30	11	3	2.75
B	5	2	10	3	1	1.5
C	8	8	24	8	2	2.67
D	10	18	40	12	3	3
E	7	12	26	7	1	3.5
F	6	6	15	3	2	1

F done at end of day 6	B done at end of day 11	C done at end of day 19	A done at end of day 28	D done at end of day 38	E done at end of day 45

b. Makespan = 45 days
Mean job flow time = (6 + 11 + 19 + 28 +
38 + 45)/6 = 24.5 days
Average number of jobs in the system = 147/45 =
3.27 jobs

Job	Completion Date	Due Date	Lateness (days)	Tardiness
F	6	15	−9	0
B	11	10	1	1
C	19	24	−5	0
A	28	30	−2	0
D	38	40	−2	0
E	45	26	19	19
			Total = 2	Total = 20

Mean job lateness = 2/6 = 0.33 days
Mean job tardiness = 20/6 = 3.33 days
Maximum tardiness = 19 days

11. a.

b. Makespan = 27 hours
Mean job flow time = (5 + 10 + 13 + 19 +
27)/5 = 14.8 hours

Average number of jobs in the system = 74/27 =
2.74 jobs

13. a.

b. Makespan = 29 days
Mean job flow time = (5 + 8 + 13 + 21 + 26 +
29)/6 = 17 days

Average number of jobs in the system = 102/29 =
3.52 jobs

15. a.

b. Make span = 28 days
Mean job flow time = (4 + 10 + 18 + 23 + 26 +
28)/6 = 18.17 days
Average number of jobs in the system = 109/28 =
3.89 jobs

Johnson's Rule has produced the minimum
makespan. However, this has the highest mean
job flowtime and the highest average number
of jobs in the system.

17.

Employee	Monday	Tuesday	Wednesday	Thursday	Friday	Saturday	Sunday
1	OFF	OFF	X	X	X	X	X
2	X	X	OFF	OFF	X	X	X
3	OFF	OFF	X	X	X	X	X
4	X	X	OFF	OFF	X	X	X
5	OFF	OFF	X	X	X	X	X
6	X	X	OFF	OFF	X	X	X

Various answers may result given the ties that occur at the start of the exercise.

19.

Employee	Monday	Tuesday	Wednesday	Thursday	Friday	Saturday	Sunday
1	OFF	OFF	X	X	X	X	X
2	OFF	OFF	X	X	X	X	X
3	X	X	OFF	OFF	X	X	X
4	OFF	OFF	X	X	X	X	X
5	X	X	OFF	OFF	X	X	X
6	X	X	X	X	OFF	OFF	X

Various answers may result from ties that occur after the first four employees are assigned days off.

21.

Employee	Monday	Tuesday	Wednesday	Thursday	Friday	Saturday	Sunday
1	X	X	X	X	X	OFF	OFF
2	X	X	X	X	X	OFF	OFF
3	OFF	OFF	X	X	X	X	X
4	X	X	OFF	OFF	X	X	X
5	X	X	X	X	OFF	OFF	X

Various answers may result from ties that occur after the first two employees are assigned days off.

23.

Employee	Monday	Tuesday	Wednesday	Thursday	Friday	Saturday	Sunday
1	OFF	OFF	X	X	X	X	X
2	X	X	OFF	OFF	X	X	X
3	X	X	X	X	OFF	OFF	X
4	X	X	X	X	X	OFF	OFF
5	OFF	OFF	X	X	X	X	X
6	X	X	OFF	OFF	X	X	X

Various answers may result given the ties that occur at the start of the exercise. This winter schedule has one fewer employee, with 2 days out of 7 having 5 employees at work.

25. a.

Prepare

Paint

b. Makespan = 29 days

c. Mean job flow time = $(7 + 9 + 15 + 18 + 25 + 29)/6 = 17.17$ days

d. Average number of jobs in the system = $103/29 = 3.55$ jobs

Chapter 16

1.

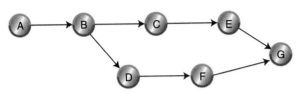

3. a.

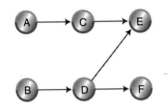

b. Critical path = BDF
c. Path completion times:
   A C E = 15 weeks
   B D E = 14 weeks
   B D F = 17 weeks
   Expected project length = 17 weeks

5.

Activity	A	B	C	D	E	F	G	H	I	J
Expected Time	6	5	7.33	7.67	10.17	4	5.83	6.33	8	3

7. a. Path completion times:
   ABDFHJ = 32 weeks
   ABDGIJ = 35.5 weeks
   ACEFHJ = 36.83 weeks
   ACEGIJ = 40.33
   Project completion time = 40.33 weeks
b. Critical activities: A C E G I J

9. a. Path completion times:
   ABEGH = 19 weeks
   ACEGH = 21 weeks
   ADFGH = 19 weeks
   ACFGH = 22 weeks
   Project completion time = 22 weeks
b. Critical activities: ACFGH

11. Reduce G by 1 week, then A by 1 week, then C by 2 weeks, and then F by 1 week. Total additional cost is $2700.

13. a.

Activity	A	B	C	D	E	F	G	H
Expected Time	10	10	5	8	7.33	7.17	8	3

b.

Activity	A	B	C	D	E	F	G	H
Variance	0.44	4	0.11	0.44	1.78	0.25	1.78	0

c. ABDFH = 38.17
   ABDGH = 39
   ACEFH = 32.5
   ACEGH = 33.33
   Expected project completion time = 39 weeks

15. a.

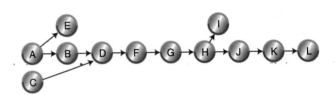

b.

Activity	A	B	C	D	E	F	G	H	I	J	K	L
Expected Time	8.67	3.33	6	7	15.33	3	4	2	2	2	5	9.17

c. Path completion times:
   AE = 24 weeks
   ABDFGHI = 30 weeks
   ABDFGHJKL = 44.17
   CDFGHI = 24 weeks
   CDFGHJKL = 38.17 weeks
   Critical path: ABDFGHJKL
d. Estimated project completion time = 44.17 weeks

17. a.

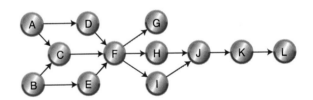

b. ADFIJKL = 42 weeks
   BEFIJKL = 43 weeks
   Normal time is 43 weeks (critical path).
c. The cost of the normal times for the project is $141,700.

19. a. Reduce K, I, and B by one week.
b. Total additional cost is $7000 = ($1000 + $3000 + $3000).

Appendix B:
The Standard Normal Distribution

This table gives the area under the standardized normal curve from 0 to z, as shown by the shaded portion of the following figure.

Examples: If z is the standard normal random variable, then
Prob $(0 \leq z \leq 1.32) = 0.4066$
Prob $(z \geq 1.32) = 0.5000 - 0.4066 = 0.0934$
Prob $(z \leq 1.32) = $ Prob $(z \leq 0) + $ Prob $(0 \leq z \leq 1.32)$
        $= 0.5000 + 0.4066 = 0.9066$
Prob $(z \leq -1.32) = $ Prob $(z \geq 1.32) = 0.0934$ (by symmetry)

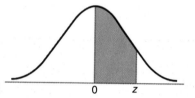

z	0.00	0.01	0.02	0.03	0.04	0.05	0.06	0.07	0.08	0.09
0.0	0.0000	0.0040	0.0080	0.0120	0.0160	0.0199	0.0239	0.0279	0.0319	0.0359
0.1	0.0398	0.0438	0.0478	0.0517	0.0557	0.0596	0.0636	0.0675	0.0714	0.0753
0.2	0.0793	0.0832	0.0871	0.0910	0.0948	0.0987	0.1026	0.1064	0.1103	0.1141
0.3	0.1179	0.1217	0.1255	0.1293	0.1331	0.1368	0.1406	0.1443	0.1480	0.1517
0.4	0.1554	0.1591	0.1628	0.1664	0.1700	0.1736	0.1772	0.1808	0.1844	0.1879
0.5	0.1915	0.1950	0.1985	0.2019	0.2054	0.2088	0.2123	0.2157	0.2190	0.2224
0.6	0.2257	0.2291	0.2324	0.2357	0.2389	0.2422	0.2454	0.2486	0.2518	0.2549
0.7	0.2580	0.2612	0.2642	0.2673	0.2704	0.2734	0.2764	0.2794	0.2823	0.2852
0.8	0.2881	0.2910	0.2939	0.2967	0.2995	0.3023	0.3051	0.3078	0.3106	0.3133
0.9	0.3159	0.3186	0.3212	0.3238	0.3264	0.3289	0.3315	0.3340	0.3365	0.3389
1.0	0.3413	0.3438	0.3461	0.3485	0.3508	0.3531	0.3554	0.3577	0.3599	0.3621
1.1	0.3643	0.3665	0.3686	0.3708	0.3729	0.3749	0.3770	0.3790	0.3810	0.3830
1.2	0.3849	0.3869	0.3888	0.3907	0.3925	0.3944	0.3962	0.3980	0.3997	0.4015
1.3	0.4032	0.4049	0.4066	0.4082	0.4099	0.4115	0.4131	0.4147	0.4162	0.4177
1.4	0.4192	0.4207	0.4222	0.4236	0.4251	0.4265	0.4279	0.4292	0.4306	0.4319
1.5	0.4332	0.4345	0.4357	0.4370	0.4382	0.4394	0.4406	0.4418	0.4429	0.4441
1.6	0.4452	0.4463	0.4474	0.4484	0.4495	0.4505	0.4515	0.4525	0.4535	0.4545
1.7	0.4554	0.4564	0.4573	0.4582	0.4591	0.4599	0.4608	0.4616	0.4625	0.4633
1.8	0.4641	0.4649	0.4656	0.4664	0.4671	0.4678	0.4686	0.4693	0.4699	0.4706
1.9	0.4713	0.4719	0.4726	0.4732	0.4738	0.4744	0.4750	0.4756	0.4761	0.4767
2.0	0.4772	0.4778	0.4783	0.4788	0.4793	0.4798	0.4803	0.4808	0.4812	0.4817
2.1	0.4821	0.4826	0.4830	0.4834	0.4838	0.4842	0.4846	0.4850	0.4854	0.4857
2.2	0.4861	0.4864	0.4868	0.4871	0.4875	0.4878	0.4881	0.4884	0.4887	0.4890
2.3	0.4893	0.4896	0.4898	0.4901	0.4904	0.4906	0.4909	0.4911	0.4913	0.4916
2.4	0.4918	0.4920	0.4922	0.4925	0.4927	0.4929	0.4931	0.4932	0.4934	0.4936
2.5	0.4938	0.4940	0.4941	0.4943	0.4945	0.4946	0.4948	0.4949	0.4951	0.4952
2.6	0.4953	0.4955	0.4956	0.4957	0.4959	0.4960	0.4961	0.4962	0.4963	0.4964
2.7	0.4965	0.4966	0.4967	0.4968	0.4969	0.4970	0.4971	0.4972	0.4973	0.4974
2.8	0.4974	0.4975	0.4976	0.4977	0.4977	0.4978	0.4979	0.4979	0.4980	0.4981
2.9	0.4981	0.4982	0.4982	0.4983	0.4984	0.4984	0.4985	0.4985	0.4986	0.4986
3.0	0.4986	0.4987	0.4987	0.4988	0.4988	0.4989	0.4989	0.4989	0.4990	0.4990
3.5	0.4998									

Source: Adapted from Robert Markland, *Topics in Management Science,* 3rd ed. New York: John Wiley & Sons, 1989.

Appendix C: P-Chart

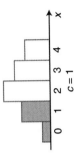

$$P(x \le c) = \sum_{x=0}^{c} \binom{n}{x} p^x (1-p)^{n-x}$$

n	x	.05	.10	.15	.20	.25	.30	.35	.40	.45	.50	.55	.60	.65	.70	.75	.80	.85	.90
1....	0	.9500	.9000	.8500	.8000	.7500	.7000	.6500	.6000	.5500	.5000	.4500	.4000	.3500	.3000	.2500	.2000	.1500	.1000
	1	1.0000	1.0000	1.0000	1.0000	1.0000	1.0000	1.0000	1.0000	1.0000	1.0000	1.0000	1.0000	1.0000	1.0000	1.0000	1.0000	1.0000	1.0000
2....	0	.9025	.8100	.7225	.6400	.5625	.4900	.4225	.3600	.3025	.2500	.2025	.1600	.1225	.0900	.0625	.0400	.0225	.0100
	1	.9975	.9900	.9775	.9600	.9375	.9100	.8775	.8400	.7975	.7500	.6975	.6400	.5775	.5100	.4375	.3600	.2775	.1900
	2	1.0000	1.0000	1.0000	1.0000	1.0000	1.0000	1.0000	1.0000	1.0000	1.0000	1.0000	1.0000	1.0000	1.0000	1.0000	1.0000	1.0000	1.0000
3....	0	.8574	.7290	.6141	.5120	.4219	.3430	.2746	.2160	.1664	.1250	.0911	.0640	.0429	.0270	.0156	.0080	.0034	.0010
	1	.9928	.9720	.9393	.8960	.8438	.7840	.7183	.6480	.5748	.5000	.4253	.3520	.2818	.2160	.1563	.1040	.0608	.0280
	2	.9999	.9990	.9966	.9920	.9844	.9730	.9571	.9360	.9089	.8750	.8336	.7840	.7254	.6570	.5781	.4880	.3859	.2710
	3	1.0000	1.0000	1.0000	1.0000	1.0000	1.0000	1.0000	1.0000	1.0000	1.0000	1.0000	1.0000	1.0000	1.0000	1.0000	1.0000	1.0000	1.0000
4....	0	.8145	.6561	.5220	.4096	.3164	.2401	.1785	.1296	.0915	.0625	.0410	.0256	.0150	.0081	.0039	.0016	.0005	.0001
	1	.9860	.9477	.8905	.8192	.7383	.6517	.5630	.4752	.3910	.3125	.2415	.1792	.1265	.0837	.0508	.0272	.0120	.0037
	2	.9995	.9963	.9880	.9728	.9492	.9163	.8735	.8208	.7585	.6875	.6090	.5248	.4370	.3483	.2617	.1808	.1095	.0523
	3	1.0000	.9999	.9995	.9984	.9961	.9919	.9850	.9744	.9590	.9375	.9085	.8704	.8215	.7599	.6836	.5904	.4780	.3439
	4	1.0000	1.0000	1.0000	1.0000	1.0000	1.0000	1.0000	1.0000	1.0000	1.0000	1.0000	1.0000	1.0000	1.0000	1.0000	1.0000	1.0000	1.0000
5....	0	.7738	.5905	.4437	.3277	.2373	.1681	.1160	.0778	.0503	.0313	.0185	.0102	.0053	.0024	.0010	.0003	.0001	.0000
	1	.9974	.9185	.8352	.7373	.6328	.5282	.4284	.3370	.2562	.1875	.1312	.0870	.0540	.0308	.0156	.0067	.0022	.0005
	2	.9988	.9914	.9734	.9421	.8965	.8369	.7648	.6826	.5931	.5000	.4069	.3174	.2352	.1631	.1035	.0579	.0266	.0086
	3	1.0000	.9995	.9978	.9933	.9844	.9692	.9460	.9130	.8688	.8125	.7438	.6630	.5716	.4718	.3672	.2627	.1648	.0815
	4	1.0000	1.0000	.9999	.9997	.9990	.9976	.9947	.9898	.9815	.9688	.9497	.9222	.8840	.8319	.7627	.6723	.5563	.4095
	5	1.0000	1.0000	1.0000	1.0000	1.0000	1.0000	1.0000	1.0000	1.0000	1.0000	1.0000	1.0000	1.0000	1.0000	1.0000	1.0000	1.0000	1.0000

P

653

n	x	.05	.10	.15	.20	.25	.30	.35	.40	.45	.50	.55	.60	.65	.70	.75	.80	.85	.90
6	0	.7351	.5314	.3771	.2621	.1780	.1176	.0754	.0467	.0277	.0156	.0083	.0041	.0018	.0007	.0002	.0001	.0000	.0000
	1	.9672	.8857	.7765	.6554	.5339	.4202	.3191	.2333	.1636	.1094	.0692	.0410	.0223	.0109	.0046	.0016	.0004	.0001
	2	.9978	.9842	.9527	.9011	.8306	.7443	.6471	.5443	.4415	.3438	.2553	.1792	.1174	.0705	.0376	.0170	.0059	.0013
	3	.9999	.9987	.9941	.9830	.9624	.9295	.8826	.8208	.7447	.6563	.5585	.4557	.3529	.2557	.1694	.0989	.0473	.0159
	4	1.0000	.9999	.9996	.9984	.9954	.9891	.9777	.9590	.9308	.8906	.8364	.7667	.6809	.5798	.4661	.3446	.2235	.1143
	5	1.0000	1.0000	1.0000	.9999	.9998	.9993	.9982	.9959	.9917	.9844	.9723	.9533	.9246	.8824	.8220	.7379	.6229	.4686
	6	1.0000	1.0000	1.0000	1.0000	1.0000	1.0000	1.0000	1.0000	1.0000	1.0000	1.0000	1.0000	1.0000	1.0000	1.0000	1.0000	1.0000	1.0000
7	0	.6983	.4783	.3206	.2097	.1335	.0824	.0490	.0280	.0152	.0078	.0037	.0016	.0006	.0002	.0001	.0000	.0000	.0000
	1	.9556	.8503	.7166	.5767	.4449	.3294	.2338	.1586	.1024	.0625	.0357	.0188	.0090	.0038	.0013	.0004	.0001	.0000
	2	.9962	.9743	.9262	.8520	.7564	.6471	.5323	.4199	.3164	.2266	.1529	.0963	.0556	.0288	.0129	.0047	.0012	.0002
	3	.9998	.9973	.9879	.9667	.9294	.8740	.8002	.7102	.6083	.5000	.3917	.2898	.1998	.1260	.0706	.0333	.0121	.0027
	4	1.0000	.9998	.9988	.9953	.9871	.9712	.9444	.9037	.8471	.7734	.6836	.5801	.4677	.3529	.2436	.1480	.0738	.0257
	5	1.0000	1.0000	.9999	.9996	.9987	.9962	.9910	.9812	.9643	.9375	.8976	.8414	.7662	.6706	.5551	.4233	.2834	.1497
	6	1.0000	1.0000	1.0000	1.0000	.9999	.9998	.9994	.9984	.9963	.9922	.9848	.9720	.9510	.9176	.8665	.7903	.6794	.5217
	7	1.0000	1.0000	1.0000	1.0000	1.0000	1.0000	1.0000	1.0000	1.0000	1.0000	1.0000	1.0000	1.0000	1.0000	1.0000	1.0000	1.0000	1.0000
8	0	.6634	.4305	.2725	.1678	.1001	.0576	.0319	.0168	.0084	.0039	.0017	.0007	.0002	.0001	.0000	.0000	.0000	.0000
	1	.9428	.8131	.6572	.5033	.3671	.2553	.1691	.1064	.0632	.0352	.0181	.0085	.0036	.0013	.0004	.0001	.0001	.0000
	2	.9942	.9619	.8948	.7969	.6785	.5518	.4278	.3154	.2201	.1445	.0885	.0498	.0253	.0113	.0042	.0012	.0002	.0000
	3	.9996	.9950	.9786	.9437	.8862	.8059	.7064	.5941	.4470	.3633	.2604	.1737	.1061	.0580	.0273	.0104	.0029	.0004
	4	1.0000	.9996	.9971	.9896	.9727	.9420	.8939	.8263	.7396	.6367	.5230	.4059	.2936	.1941	.1138	.0563	.0214	.0050
	5	1.0000	1.0000	.9998	.9988	.9958	.9887	.9747	.9502	.9115	.8555	.7799	.6846	.5722	.4482	.3215	.2031	.1052	.0381
	6	1.0000	1.0000	1.0000	.9999	.9996	.9987	.9964	.9915	.9819	.9648	.9368	.8936	.8309	.7447	.6329	.4967	.3428	.1869
	7	1.0000	1.0000	1.0000	1.0000	1.0000	.9999	.9998	.9993	.9983	.9961	.9916	.9832	.9681	.9424	.8999	.8322	.7275	.5695
	8	1.0000	1.0000	1.0000	1.0000	1.0000	1.0000	1.0000	1.0000	1.0000	1.0000	1.0000	1.0000	1.0000	1.0000	1.0000	1.0000	1.0000	1.0000
9	0	.6302	.3874	.2316	.1342	.0751	.0404	.0207	.0101	.0046	.0020	.0008	.0003	.0001	.0000	.0000	.0000	.0000	.0000
	1	.9288	.7748	.5995	.4362	.3003	.1960	.1211	.0705	.0385	.0195	.0091	.0038	.0014	.0004	.0001	.0000	.0000	.0000
	2	.9916	.9470	.8591	.7382	.6007	.4628	.3373	.2318	.1495	.0898	.0498	.0250	.0112	.0043	.0013	.0003	.0002	.0000
	3	.9994	.9917	.9661	.9144	.8343	.7297	.6089	.4826	.3614	.2539	.1658	.0994	.0536	.0253	.0100	.0031	.0006	.0001
	4	1.0000	.9991	.9944	.9804	.9511	.9012	.8283	.7334	.6214	.5000	.3786	.2666	.1717	.0988	.0489	.0196	.0056	.0009
	5	1.0000	.9999	.9994	.9969	.9900	.9747	.9496	.9006	.8342	.7461	.6386	.5174	.3911	.2703	.1657	.0856	.0339	.0083
	6	1.0000	1.0000	1.0000	.9997	.9987	.9957	.9888	.9750	.9502	.9102	.8505	.7682	.6627	.5372	.3993	.2618	.1409	.0530
	7	1.0000	1.0000	1.0000	1.0000	.9999	.9996	.9986	.9962	.9909	.9805	.9615	.9295	.8789	.8040	.6997	.5638	.4005	.2252
	8	1.0000	1.0000	1.0000	1.0000	1.0000	1.0000	.9999	.9997	.9992	.9980	.9954	.9899	.9793	.9596	.9249	.8658	.7684	.6126
	9	1.0000	1.0000	1.0000	1.0000	1.0000	1.0000	1.0000	1.0000	1.0000	1.0000	1.0000	1.0000	1.0000	1.0000	1.0000	1.0000	1.0000	1.0000
10	0	.5987	.3487	.1969	.1074	.0563	.0282	.0135	.0060	.0025	.0010	.0003	.0001	.0000	.0000	.0000	.0000	.0000	.0000
	1	.9139	.7361	.5443	.3758	.2440	.1493	.0860	.0464	.0233	.0107	.0045	.0017	.0005	.0001	.0000	.0000	.0000	.0000
	2	.9885	.9298	.8202	.6778	.5256	.3828	.2616	.1673	.0996	.0547	.0274	.0123	.0048	.0016	.0004	.0001	.0000	.0000
	3	.9990	.9872	.9500	.8791	.7759	.6496	.5138	.3823	.2660	.1719	.1020	.0548	.0260	.0106	.0035	.0009	.0001	.0000
	4	.9999	.9984	.9901	.9672	.9219	.8497	.7515	.6331	.5044	.3770	.2616	.1662	.0949	.0473	.0197	.0064	.0014	.0001
	5	1.0000	.9999	.9986	.9936	.9803	.9527	.9051	.8338	.7384	.6230	.4956	.3669	.2485	.1503	.0781	.0328	.0099	.0016
	6	1.0000	1.0000	.9999	.9991	.9965	.9894	.9740	.9452	.8980	.8281	.7340	.6177	.4862	.3504	.2241	.1209	.0500	.0128
	7	1.0000	1.0000	1.0000	.9999	.9996	.9984	.9952	.9877	.9726	.9453	.9004	.8327	.7384	.6172	.4744	.3222	.1798	.0702
	8	1.0000	1.0000	1.0000	1.0000	1.0000	.9999	.9995	.9983	.9955	.9893	.9767	.9536	.9140	.8507	.7560	.6242	.4557	.2639

									P										
n	x	.05	.10	.15	.20	.25	.30	.35	.40	.45	.50	.55	.60	.65	.70	.75	.80	.85	.90
	9	1.0000	1.0000	1.0000	1.0000	1.0000	1.0000	1.0000	.9999	.9997	.9990	.9975	.9940	.9865	.9718	.9437	.8926	.8031	.6513
	10	1.0000	1.0000	1.0000	1.0000	1.0000	1.0000	1.0000	1.0000	1.0000	1.0000	1.0000	1.0000	1.0000	1.0000	1.0000	1.0000	1.0000	1.0000
15	0	.4633	.2059	.0874	.0352	.0134	.0047	.0016	.0005	.0001	.0000	.0000	.0000	.0000	.0000	.0000	.0000	.0000	.0000
	1	.8290	.5490	.3186	.1671	.0802	.0353	.0142	.0052	.0017	.0005	.0001	.0000	.0000	.0000	.0000	.0000	.0000	.0000
	2	.9638	.8159	.6042	.3980	.2361	.1268	.0617	.0271	.0107	.0037	.0011	.0003	.0001	.0000	.0000	.0000	.0000	.0000
	3	.9945	.9444	.8227	.6482	.4613	.2969	.1727	.0905	.0424	.0176	.0063	.0019	.0005	.0001	.0000	.0000	.0000	.0000
	4	.9994	.9873	.9383	.8358	.6865	.5155	.3519	.2173	.1204	.0592	.0255	.0093	.0028	.0007	.0001	.0000	.0000	.0000
	5	.9999	.9978	.9832	.9389	.8516	.7216	.5643	.4032	.2608	.1509	.0769	.0338	.0124	.0037	.0008	.0001	.0000	.0000
	6	1.0000	.9997	.9964	.9819	.9434	.8689	.7548	.6098	.4522	.3036	.1818	.0950	.0422	.0152	.0042	.0008	.0001	.0000
	7	1.0000	1.0000	.9994	.9958	.9827	.9500	.8868	.7869	.6535	.5000	.3465	.2131	.1132	.0500	.0173	.0042	.0006	.0000
	8	1.0000	1.0000	.9999	.9992	.9958	.9848	.9578	.9050	.8182	.6964	.5478	.3902	.2452	.1311	.0566	.0181	.0036	.0003
	9	1.0000	1.0000	1.0000	.9999	.9992	.9963	.9876	.9662	.9231	.8491	.7392	.5968	.4357	.2784	.1484	.0611	.0168	.0022
	10	1.0000	1.0000	1.0000	1.0000	.9999	.9993	.9972	.9907	.9745	.9408	.8796	.7827	.6481	.4845	.3135	.1642	.0617	.0127
	11	1.0000	1.0000	1.0000	1.0000	1.0000	.9999	.9995	.9981	.9937	.9824	.9576	.9095	.8273	.7031	.5387	.3518	.1773	.0556
	12	1.0000	1.0000	1.0000	1.0000	1.0000	1.0000	.9999	.9997	.9989	.9963	.9893	.9729	.9383	.8732	.7639	.6020	.3958	.1841
	13	1.0000	1.0000	1.0000	1.0000	1.0000	1.0000	1.0000	1.0000	.9999	.9995	.9983	.9948	.9858	.9647	.9198	.8329	.6814	.4510
	14	1.0000	1.0000	1.0000	1.0000	1.0000	1.0000	1.0000	1.0000	1.0000	1.0000	.9999	.9995	.9984	.9953	.9866	.9648	.9126	.7941
	15	1.0000	1.0000	1.0000	1.0000	1.0000	1.0000	1.0000	1.0000	1.0000	1.0000	1.0000	1.0000	1.0000	1.0000	1.0000	1.0000	1.0000	1.0000
20	0	.3585	.1216	.0388	.0115	.0032	.0008	.0002	.0000	.0000	.0000	.0000	.0000	.0000	.0000	.0000	.0000	.0000	.0000
	1	.7358	.3917	.1756	.0692	.0243	.0076	.0021	.0005	.0001	.0000	.0000	.0000	.0000	.0000	.0000	.0000	.0000	.0000
	2	.9245	.6769	.4049	.2061	.0913	.0355	.0121	.0036	.0009	.0002	.0000	.0000	.0000	.0000	.0000	.0000	.0000	.0000
	3	.9841	.8670	.6477	.4114	.2252	.1071	.0444	.0160	.0049	.0013	.0003	.0000	.0000	.0000	.0000	.0000	.0000	.0000
	4	.9974	.9568	.8298	.6296	.4148	.2375	.1182	.0510	.0189	.0059	.0015	.0003	.0000	.0000	.0000	.0000	.0000	.0000
	5	.9997	.9887	.9327	.8042	.6172	.4164	.2454	.1256	.0553	.0207	.0064	.0016	.0003	.0000	.0000	.0000	.0000	.0000
	6	1.0000	.9976	.9781	.9133	.7858	.6080	.4166	.2500	.1299	.0577	.0214	.0065	.0015	.0003	.0000	.0000	.0000	.0000
	7	1.0000	.9996	.9941	.9679	.8982	.7723	.6010	.4159	.2520	.1316	.0580	.0210	.0060	.0013	.0002	.0000	.0000	.0000
	8	1.0000	.9999	.9987	.9900	.9591	.8867	.7624	.5956	.4143	.2517	.1308	.0565	.0196	.0051	.0009	.0001	.0000	.0000
	9	1.0000	1.0000	.9998	.9974	.9861	.9520	.8782	.7553	.5914	.4119	.2493	.1275	.0532	.0171	.0039	.0006	.0000	.0000
	10	1.0000	1.0000	1.0000	.9994	.9961	.9829	.9468	.8725	.7507	.5881	.4086	.2447	.1218	.0480	.0139	.0026	.0002	.0000
	11	1.0000	1.0000	1.0000	.9999	.9991	.9949	.9804	.9435	.8692	.7483	.5857	.4044	.2376	.1133	.0409	.0100	.0013	.0001
	12	1.0000	1.0000	1.0000	1.0000	.9998	.9987	.9940	.9790	.9420	.8684	.7480	.5841	.3990	.2277	.1018	.0321	.0059	.0004
	13	1.0000	1.0000	1.0000	1.0000	1.0000	.9997	.9985	.9935	.9786	.9423	.8701	.7500	.5834	.3920	.2142	.0867	.0219	.0024
	14	1.0000	1.0000	1.0000	1.0000	1.0000	1.0000	.9997	.9984	.9936	.9793	.9447	.8744	.7546	.5836	.3828	.1958	.0673	.0113
	15	1.0000	1.0000	1.0000	1.0000	1.0000	1.0000	1.0000	.9997	.9985	.9941	.9811	.9490	.8818	.7625	.5852	.3704	.1702	.0432
	16	1.0000	1.0000	1.0000	1.0000	1.0000	1.0000	1.0000	1.0000	.9997	.9987	.9951	.9840	.9556	.8929	.7748	.5886	.3523	.1330
	17	1.0000	1.0000	1.0000	1.0000	1.0000	1.0000	1.0000	1.0000	1.0000	.9998	.9991	.9964	.9879	.9645	.9087	.7939	.5951	.3231
	18	1.0000	1.0000	1.0000	1.0000	1.0000	1.0000	1.0000	1.0000	1.0000	1.0000	.9999	.9995	.9979	.9924	.9757	.9308	.8244	.6083
	19	1.0000	1.0000	1.0000	1.0000	1.0000	1.0000	1.0000	1.0000	1.0000	1.0000	1.0000	1.0000	.9998	.9992	.9968	.9885	.9612	.8784
	20	1.0000	1.0000	1.0000	1.0000	1.0000	1.0000	1.0000	1.0000	1.0000	1.0000	1.0000	1.0000	1.0000	1.0000	1.0000	1.0000	1.0000	1.0000

Source: William J. Stevenson, *Production/Operations Management*, 6th ed. Columbus, Ohio: McGraw-Hill/Irwin, 1999.

Company Index

Subject Index